BIBLIA SACRA

THE HOLY BIBLE IN LATIN AND ENGLISH

—

LIBRI NOVI TESTAMENTI ET PSALMORUM

THE BOOKS OF THE NEW TESTAMENT

AND THE PSALMS

THIRD EDITION

EX FONTIBUS COMPANY

MMIX, MXVII

English: *Douay-Rheims Bible*, Challoner (ed.).

Latin: *Biblia Sacra juxta Vulgatam Clementinam*, Tweedale (ed.).

Date of this revision: 9 June 2017.

EX FONTIBUS

COMPANY

http://www.exfontibus.com
http://www.facebook.com/exfont
contact@exfontibus.com
exfontibuscompany@gmail.com

BIBLIA SACRA

THE HOLY BIBLE IN LATIN AND ENGLISH

LIBRI NOVI TESTAMENTI ET PSALMORUM
THE BOOKS OF THE NEW TESTAMENT AND THE PSALMS

Series Bibliorum Sacrorum in Hoc Tomo
BOOKS OF THE HOLY BIBLE CONTAINED IN THIS VOLUME

✠

Sanctum Jesu Christi Evangelium
Secundum Matthæum

THE HOLY GOSPEL OF JESUS CHRIST ACCORDING TO MATTHEW

 IBER GENERATIONIS JESU CHRISTI filii David, filii Abraham.

1:2 Abraham genuit Isaac. Isaac autem genuit Jacob. Jacob autem genuit Judam, et fratres ejus.
1:3 Judas autem genuit Phares, et Zaram de Thamar. Phares autem genuit Esron. Esron autem genuit Aram.
1:4 Aram autem genuit Aminadab. Aminadab autem genuit Naasson. Naasson autem genuit Salmon.
1:5 Salmon autem genuit Booz de Rahab. Booz autem genuit Obed ex Ruth. Obed autem genuit Jesse. Jesse autem genuit David regem.
1:6 David autem rex genuit Salomonem ex ea quæ fuit Uriæ.

1:7 Salomon autem genuit Roboam. Roboam autem genuit Abiam. Abias autem genuit Asa.
1:8 Asa autem genuit Josophat. Josophat autem genuit Joram. Joram autem genuit Oziam.
1:9 Ozias autem genuit Joatham. Joatham autem genuit Achaz. Achaz autem genuit Ezechiam.
1:10 Ezechias autem genuit Manassen. Manasses autem genuit Amon. Amon autem genuit Josiam.
1:11 Josias autem genuit Jechoniam, et fratres ejus in transmigratione Babylonis.
1:12 Et post transmigrationem Babylonis : Jechonias genuit Salathiel. Salathiel autem genuit Zorobabel.
1:13 Zorobabel autem genuit Abiud. Abiud autem genuit Eliacim. Eliacim autem genuit

 HE BOOK OF THE GENERATION OF JESUS CHRIST, the son of David, the son of Abraham:

1:2 Abraham begot Isaac. And Isaac begot Jacob. And Jacob begot Judas and his brethren.
1:3 And Judas begot Phares and Zara of Thamar. And Phares begot Esron. And Esron begot Aram.
1:4 And Aram begot Aminadab. And Aminadab begot Naasson. And Naasson begot Salmon.

1:5 And Salmon begot Booz of Rahab. And Booz begot Obed of Ruth. And Obed begot Jesse.

1:6 And Jesse begot David the king. And David the king begot Solomon, of her that had been the wife of Urias.

1:7 And Solomon begot Roboam. And Roboam begot Abia. And Abia begot Asa.
1:8 And Asa begot Josaphat. And Josaphat begot Joram. And Joram begot Ozias.
1:9 And Ozias begot Joatham. And Joatham begot Achaz. And Achaz begot Ezechias.
1:10 And Ezechias begot Manasses. And Manesses begot Amon. And Amon begot Josias.
1:11 And Josias begot Jechonias and his brethren in the transmigration of Babylon.
1:12 And after the transmigration of Babylon, Jechonias begot Salathiel. And Salathiel begot Zorobabel.
1:13 And Zorobabel begot Abiud. And Abiud begot Eliacim. And Eliacim begot Azor.

Azor.

1:14 Azor autem genuit Sadoc. Sadoc autem genuit Achim. Achim autem genuit Eliud.

1:15 Eliud autem genuit Eleazar. Eleazar autem genuit Mathan. Mathan autem genuit Jacob.

1:16 Jacob autem genuit Joseph virum Mariæ, de qua natus est Jesus, qui vocatur Christus.

1:17 Omnes itaque generationes ab Abraham usque ad David, generationes quatuordecim : et a David usque ad transmigrationem Babylonis, generationes quatuordecim : et a transmigratione Babylonis usque ad Christum, generationes quatuordecim.

1:18 Christi autem generatio sic erat : cum esset desponsata mater ejus Maria Joseph, antequam convenirent inventa est in utero habens de Spiritu Sancto.

1:19 Joseph autem vir ejus cum esset justus, et nollet eam traducere, voluit occulte dimittere eam.

1:20 Hæc autem eo cogitante, ecce angelus Domini apparuit in somnis ei, dicens : Joseph, fili David, noli timere accipere Mariam conjugem tuam : quod enim in ea natum est, de Spiritu Sancto est.

1:21 Pariet autem filium : et vocabis nomen ejus Jesum : ipse enim salvum faciet populum suum a peccatis eorum.

1:22 Hoc autem totum factum est, ut adimpleretur quod dictum est a Domino per prophetam dicentem :

1:23 Ecce virgo in utero habebit, et pariet filium : et vocabunt nomen ejus Emmanuel, quod est interpretatum Nobiscum Deus.

1:24 Exsurgens autem Joseph a somno, fecit sicut præcepit ei angelus Domini, et accepit conjugem suam.

1:25 Et non cognoscebat eam donec peperit filium suum primogenitum : et vocavit nomen ejus Jesum.

2:1 Cum ergo natus esset Jesus in Bethlehem Juda in diebus Herodis regis, ecce magi ab oriente venerunt Jerosolymam,

2:2 dicentes : Ubi est qui natus est rex Judæorum ? vidimus enim stellam ejus in oriente, et venimus adorare eum.

2:3 Audiens autem Herodes rex, turbatus est, et omnis Jerosolyma cum illo.

2:4 Et congregans omnes principes sacerdotum,

1:14 And Azor begot Sadoc. And Sadoc begot Achim. And Achim begot Eliud.

1:15 And Eliud begot Eleazar. And Eleazar begot Mathan. And Mathan begot Jacob.

1:16 And Jacob begot Joseph the husband of Mary, of whom was born Jesus, who is called Christ.

1:17 So all the generations, from Abraham to David, are fourteen generations. And from David to the transmigration of Babylon, are fourteen generations: and from the transmigration of Babylon to Christ are fourteen generations.

1:18 Now the generation of Christ was in this wise. When as his mother Mary was espoused to Joseph, before they came together, she was found with child, of the Holy Ghost.

1:19 Whereupon Joseph her husband, being a just man, and not willing publicly to expose her, was minded to put her away privately.

1:20 But while he thought on these things, behold the angel of the Lord appeared to him in his sleep, saying: Joseph, son of David, fear not to take unto thee Mary thy wife, for that which is conceived in her, is of the Holy Ghost.

1:21 And she shall bring forth a son: and thou shalt call his name JESUS. For he shall save his people from their sins.

1:22 Now all this was done that it might be fulfilled which the Lord spoke by the prophet, saying:

1:23 Behold a virgin shall be with child, and bring forth a son, and they shall call his name Emmanuel, which being interpreted is, God with us.

1:24 And Joseph rising up from sleep, did as the angel of the Lord had commanded him, and took unto him his wife.

1:25 And he knew her not till she brought forth her firstborn son: and he called his name JESUS.

2:1 When Jesus therefore was born in Bethlehem of Juda, in the days of king Herod, behold, there came wise men from the east to Jerusalem.

2:2 Saying, Where is he that is born king of the Jews? For we have seen his star in the east, and are come to adore him.

2:3 And king Herod hearing this, was troubled, and all Jerusalem with him.

2:4 And assembling together all the chief priests

et scribas populi, sciscitabatur ab eis ubi Christus nasceretur.

2:5 At illi dixerunt : In Bethlehem Judæ : sic enim scriptum est per prophetam :

2:6 *Et tu Bethlehem terra Juda, nequaquam minima es in principibus Juda : ex te enim exiet dux, qui regat populum meum Israël.*

2:7 Tunc Herodes clam vocatis magis diligenter didicit ab eis tempus stellæ, quæ apparuit eis :

2:8 et mittens illos in Bethlehem, dixit : Ite, et interrogate diligenter de puero : et cum inveneritis, renuntiate mihi, ut et ego veniens adorem eum.

2:9 Qui cum audissent regem, abierunt, et ecce stella, quam viderant in oriente, antecedebat eos, usque dum veniens staret supra, ubi erat puer.

2:10 Videntes autem stellam gavisi sunt gaudio magno valde.

2:11 Et intrantes domum, invenerunt puerum cum Maria matre ejus, et procidentes adoraverunt eum : et apertis thesauris suis obtulerunt ei munera, aurum, thus, et myrrham.

2:12 Et responso accepto in somnis ne redirent ad Herodem, per aliam viam reversi sunt in regionem suam.

2:13 Qui cum recessissent, ecce angelus Domini apparuit in somnis Joseph, dicens : Surge, et accipe puerum, et matrem ejus, et fuge in Ægyptum, et esto ibi usque dum dicam tibi. Futurum est enim ut Herodes quærat puerum ad perdendum eum.

2:14 Qui consurgens accepit puerum et matrem ejus nocte, et secessit in Ægyptum :

2:15 et erat ibi usque ad obitum Herodis : ut adimpleretur quod dictum est a Domino per prophetam dicentem : Ex Ægypto vocavi filium meum.

2:16 Tunc Herodes videns quoniam illusus esset a magis, iratus est valde, et mittens occidit omnes pueros, qui erant in Bethlehem, et in omnibus finibus ejus, a bimatu et infra secundum tempus, quod exquisierat a magis.

2:17 Tunc adimpletum est quod dictum est per Jeremiam prophetam dicentem :

2:18 *Vox in Rama audita est ploratus, et ululatus mul-*

and the scribes of the people, he inquired of them where Christ should be born.

2:5 But they said to him: In Bethlehem of Juda. For so it is written by the prophet:

2:6 *And thou Bethlehem the land of Juda art not the least among the princes of Juda: for out of thee shall come forth the captain that shall rule my people Israel.*

2:7 Then Herod, privately calling the wise men, learned diligently of them the time of the star which appeared to them;

2:8 And sending them into Bethlehem, said: Go and diligently inquire after the child, and when you have found him, bring me word again, that I also may come to adore him.

2:9 Who having heard the king, went their way; and behold the star which they had seen in the east, went before them, until it came and stood over where the child was.

2:10 And seeing the star they rejoiced with exceeding great joy.

2:11 And entering into the house, they found the child with Mary his mother, and falling down they adored him; and opening their treasures, they offered him gifts; gold, frankincense, and myrrh.

2:12 And having received an answer in sleep that they should not return to Herod, they went back another way into their country.

2:13 And after they were departed, behold an angel of the Lord appeared in sleep to Joseph, saying: Arise, and take the child and his mother, and fly into Egypt: and be there until I shall tell thee. For it will come to pass that Herod will seek the child to destroy him.

2:14 Who arose, and took the child and his mother by night, and retired into Egypt: and he was there until the death of Herod:

2:15 That it might be fulfilled which the Lord spoke by the prophet, saying: Out of Egypt have I called my son.

2:16 Then Herod perceiving that he was deluded by the wise men, was exceeding angry; and sending killed all the men children that were in Bethlehem, and in all the borders thereof, from two years old and under, according to the time which he had diligently inquired of the wise men.

2:17 Then was fulfilled that which was spoken by Jeremias the prophet, saying:

2:18 *A voice in Rama was heard, lamentation and*

tus : *Rachel plorans filios suos, et noluit consolari, quia non sunt.*

2:19 Defuncto autem Herode, ecce angelus Domini apparuit in somnis Joseph in Ægypto,

2:20 dicens : Surge, et accipe puerum, et matrem ejus, et vade in terram Israël : defuncti sunt enim qui quærebant animam pueri.

2:21 Qui consurgens, accepit puerum, et matrem ejus, et venit in terram Israël.

2:22 Audiens autem quod Archelaus regnaret in Judæa pro Herode patre suo, timuit illo ire : et admonitus in somnis, secessit in partes Galilææ.

2:23 Et veniens habitavit in civitate quæ vocatur Nazareth : ut adimpleretur quod dictum est per prophetas : Quoniam Nazaræus vocabitur.

3:1 In diebus autem illis venit Joannes Baptista prædicans in deserto Judææ,

3:2 et dicens : Pœnitentiam agite : appropinquavit enim regnum cælorum.

3:3 Hic est enim, qui dictus est per Isaiam prophetam dicentem : *Vox clamantis in deserto : Parate viam Domini ; rectas facite semitas ejus.*

3:4 Ipse autem Joannes habebat vestimentum de pilis camelorum, et zonam pelliceam circa lumbos suos : esca autem ejus erat locustæ, et mel silvestre.

3:5 Tunc exibat ad eum Jerosolyma, et omnis Judæa, et omnis regio circa Jordanem ;

3:6 et baptizabantur ab eo in Jordane, confitentes peccata sua.

3:7 Videns autem multos pharisæorum, et sadducæorum, venientes ad baptismum suum, dixit eis : Progenies viperarum, quis demonstravit vobis fugere a ventura ira ?

3:8 Facite ergo fructum dignum pœnitentiæ.

3:9 Et ne velitis dicere intra vos : Patrem habemus Abraham. Dico enim vobis quoniam potens est Deus de lapidibus istis suscitare filios Abrahæ.

3:10 Jam enim securis ad radicem arborum posita est. Omnis ergo arbor, quæ non facit fructum bonum, excidetur, et in ignem mittetur.

3:11 Ego quidem baptizo vos in aqua in pœnitentiam : qui autem post me venturus est, fortior me est, cujus non sum dignus calceamenta portare : ipse vos baptizabit in Spiritu Sancto, et igni.

great mourning; Rachel bewailing her children, and would not be comforted, because they are not.

2:19 But when Herod was dead, behold an angel of the Lord appeared in sleep to Joseph in Egypt,

2:20 Saying: Arise, and take the child and his mother, and go into the land of Israel. For they are dead that sought the life of the child.

2:21 Who arose, and took the child and his mother, and came into the land of Israel.

2:22 But hearing that Archelaus reigned in Judea in the room of Herod his father, he was afraid to go thither: and being warned in sleep retired into the quarters of Galilee.

2:23 And coming he dwelt in a city called Nazareth: that it might be fulfilled which was said by prophets: That he shall be called a Nazarene.

3:1 And in those days cometh John the Baptist preaching in the desert of Judea.

3:2 And saying: Do penance: for the kingdom of heaven is at hand.

3:3 For this is he that was spoken of by Isaias the prophet, saying: *A voice of one crying in the desert, Prepare ye the way of the Lord, make straight his paths.*

3:4 And the same John had his garment of camels' hair, and a leathern girdle about his loins: and his meat was locusts and wild honey.

3:5 Then went out to him Jerusalem and all Judea, and all the country about Jordan:

3:6 And were baptized by him in the Jordan, confessing their sins.

3:7 And seeing many of the Pharisees and Sadducees coming to his baptism, he said to them: Ye brood of vipers, who hath shewed you to flee from the wrath to come?

3:8 Bring forth therefore fruit worthy of penance.

3:9 And think not to say within yourselves, We have Abraham for our father. For I tell you that God is able of these stones to raise up children to Abraham.

3:10 For now the axe is laid to the root of the trees. Every tree therefore that doth not yield good fruit, shall be cut down, and cast into the fire.

3:11 I indeed baptize you in the water unto penance, but he that shall come after me, is mightier than I, whose shoes I am not worthy to bear; he shall baptize you in the Holy Ghost and fire.

3:12 Cujus ventilabrum in manu sua : et permundabit aream suam : et congregabit triticum suum in horreum, paleas autem comburet igni inextinguibili.

3:13 Tunc venit Jesus a Galilæa in Jordanem ad Joannem, ut baptizaretur ab eo.

3:14 Joannes autem prohibebat eum, dicens : Ego a te debeo baptizari, et tu venis ad me ?

3:15 Respondens autem Jesus, dixit ei : Sine modo : sic enim decet nos implere omnem justitiam. Tunc dimisit eum.

3:16 Baptizatus autem Jesus, confestim ascendit de aqua, et ecce aperti sunt ei cæli : et vidit Spiritum Dei descendentem sicut columbam, et venientem super se.

3:17 Et ecce vox de cælis dicens : Hic est Filius meus dilectus, in quo mihi complacui.

4:1 Tunc Jesus ductus est in desertum a Spiritu, ut tentaretur a diabolo.

4:2 Et cum jejunasset quadraginta diebus, et quadraginta noctibus, postea esuriit.

4:3 Et accedens tentator dixit ei : Si Filius Dei es, dic ut lapides isti panes fiant.

4:4 Qui respondens dixit : Scriptum est : Non in solo pane vivit homo, sed in omni verbo, quod procedit de ore Dei.

4:5 Tunc assumpsit eum diabolus in sanctam civitatem, et statuit eum super pinnaculum templi,

4:6 et dixit ei : Si Filius Dei es, mitte te deorsum. Scriptum est enim : Quia angelis suis mandavit de te, et in manibus tollent te, ne forte offendas ad lapidem pedem tuum.

4:7 Ait illi Jesus : Rursum scriptum est : Non tentabis Dominum Deum tuum.

4:8 Iterum assumpsit eum diabolus in montem excelsum valde : et ostendit ei omnia regna mundi, et gloriam eorum,

4:9 et dixit ei : Hæc omnia tibi dabo, si cadens adoraveris me.

4:10 Tunc dicit ei Jesus : Vade Satana : Scriptum est enim : Dominum Deum tuum adorabis, et illi soli servies.

4:11 Tunc reliquit eum diabolus : et ecce angeli accesserunt, et ministrabant ei.

4:12 Cum autem audisset Jesus quod Joannes traditus esset, secessit in Galilæam :

4:13 et, relicta civitate Nazareth, venit, et habitavit in Capharnaum maritima, in finibus Zab-

3:12 Whose fan is in his hand, and he will thoroughly cleanse his floor and gather his wheat into the barn; but the chaff he will burn with unquenchable fire.

3:13 Then cometh Jesus from Galilee to the Jordan, unto John, to be baptized by him.

3:14 But John stayed him, saying: I ought to be baptized by thee, and comest thou to me?

3:15 And Jesus answering, said to him: Suffer it to be so now. For so it becometh us to fulfill all justice. Then he suffered him.

3:16 And Jesus being baptized, forthwith came out of the water: and lo, the heavens were opened to him: and he saw the Spirit of God descending as a dove, and coming upon him.

3:17 And behold a voice from heaven, saying: This is my beloved Son, in whom I am well pleased.

4:1 Then Jesus was led by the spirit into the desert, to be tempted by the devil.

4:2 And when he had fasted forty days and forty nights, afterwards he was hungry.

4:3 And the tempter coming said to him: If thou be the Son of God, command that these stones be made bread.

4:4 Who answered and said: It is written, Not in bread alone doth man live, but in every word that proceedeth from the mouth of God.

4:5 Then the devil took him up into the holy city, and set him upon the pinnacle of the temple,

4:6 And said to him: If thou be the Son of God, cast thyself down, for it is written: That he hath given his angels charge over thee, and in their hands shall they bear thee up, lest perhaps thou dash thy foot against a stone.

4:7 Jesus said to him: It is written again: Thou shalt not tempt the Lord thy God.

4:8 Again the devil took him up into a very high mountain, and shewed him all the kingdoms of the world, and the glory of them,

4:9 And said to him: All these will I give thee, if falling down thou wilt adore me.

4:10 Then Jesus saith to him: Begone, Satan: for it is written, The Lord thy God shalt thou adore, and him only shalt thou serve.

4:11 Then the devil left him; and behold angels came and ministered to him.

4:12 And when Jesus had heard that John was delivered up, he retired into Galilee:

4:13 And leaving the city Nazareth, he came and dwelt in Capharnaum on the sea coast, in the

ulon et Nephthalim :

4:14 ut adimpleretur quod dictum est per Isaiam prophetam :

4:15 *Terra Zabulon, et terra Nephthalim, via maris trans Jordanem, Galilæa gentium :*

4:16 *populus, qui sedebat in tenebris, vidit lucem magnam : et sedentibus in regione umbræ mortis, lux orta est eis.*

4:17 Exinde cœpit Jesus prædicare, et dicere : Pœnitentiam agite : appropinquavit enim regnum cælorum.

4:18 Ambulans autem Jesus juxta mare Galilææ, vidit duos fratres, Simonem, qui vocatur Petrus, et Andream fratrem ejus, mittentes rete in mare (erant enim piscatores),

4:19 et ait illis : Venite post me, et faciam vos fieri piscatores hominum.

4:20 At illi continuo relictis retibus secuti sunt eum.

4:21 Et procedens inde, vidit alios duos fratres, Jacobum Zebedæi, et Joannem fratrem ejus, in navi cum Zebedæo patre eorum, reficientes retia sua : et vocavit eos.

4:22 Illi autem statim relictis retibus et patre, secuti sunt eum.

4:23 Et circuibat Jesus totam Galilæam, docens in synagogis eorum, et prædicans Evangelium regni : et sanans omnem languorem, et omnem infirmitatem in populo.

4:24 Et abiit opinio ejus in totam Syriam, et obtulerunt ei omnes male habentes, variis languoribus, et tormentis comprehensos, et qui dæmonia habebant, et lunaticos, et paralyticos, et curavit eos :

4:25 et secutæ sunt eum turbæ multæ de Galilæa, et Decapoli, et de Jerosolymis, et de Judæa, et de trans Jordanem.

5:1 Videns autem Jesus turbas, ascendit in montem, et cum sedisset, accesserunt ad eum discipuli ejus,

5:2 et aperiens os suum docebat eos dicens :

5:3 Beati pauperes spiritu : quoniam ipsorum est regnum cælorum.

5:4 Beati mites : quoniam ipsi possidebunt terram.

5:5 Beati qui lugent : quoniam ipsi consolabuntur.

5:6 Beati qui esuriunt et sitiunt justitiam : quoniam ipsi saturabuntur.

borders of Zabulon and Nephthalim;

4:14 That it might be fulfilled which was said by Isaias the prophet:

4:15 *Land of Zabulon and land of Nephthalim, the way of the sea beyond the Jordan, Galilee of the Gentiles:*

4:16 *The people that sat in darkness, hath seen great light: and to them that sat in the region of the shadow of death, light is sprung up.*

4:17 From that time Jesus began to preach, and to say: Do penance, for the kingdom of heaven is at hand.

4:18 And Jesus walking by the sea of Galilee, saw two brethren, Simon who is called Peter, and Andrew his brother, casting a net into the sea (for they were fishers).

4:19 And he saith to them: Come ye after me, and I will make you to be fishers of men.

4:20 And they immediately leaving their nets, followed him.

4:21 And going on from thence, he saw other two brethren, James the son of Zebedee, and John his brother, in a ship with Zebedee their father, mending their nets: and he called them.

4:22 And they forthwith left their nets and father, and followed him.

4:23 And Jesus went about all Galilee, teaching in their synagogues, and preaching the gospel of the kingdom: and healing all manner of sickness and every infirmity, among the people.

4:24 And his fame went throughout all Syria, and they presented to him all sick people that were taken with divers diseases and torments, and such as were possessed by devils, and lunatics, and those that had palsy, and he cured them:

4:25 And much people followed him from Galilee, and from Decapolis, and from Jerusalem, and from Judea, and from beyond the Jordan.

5:1 And seeing the multitudes, he went up into a mountain, and when he was set down, his disciples came unto him.

5:2 And opening his mouth, he taught them, saying:

5:3 Blessed are the poor in spirit: for theirs is the kingdom of heaven.

5:4 Blessed are the meek: for they shall possess the land.

5:5 Blessed are they that mourn: for they shall be comforted.

5:6 Blessed are they that hunger and thirst after justice: for they shall have their fill.

5:7 Beati misericordes : quoniam ipsi misericordiam consequentur.

5:8 Beati mundo corde : quoniam ipsi Deum videbunt.

5:9 Beati pacifici : quoniam filii Dei vocabuntur.

5:10 Beati qui persecutionem patiuntur propter justitiam : quoniam ipsorum est regnum cælorum.

5:11 Beati estis cum maledixerint vobis, et persecuti vos fuerint, et dixerint omne malum adversum vos mentientes, propter me :

5:12 gaudete, et exsultate, quoniam merces vestra copiosa est in cælis. Sic enim persecuti sunt prophetas, qui fuerunt ante vos.

5:13 Vos estis sal terræ. Quod si sal evanuerit, in quo salietur ? ad nihilum valet ultra, nisi ut mittatur foras, et conculcetur ab hominibus.

5:14 Vos estis lux mundi. Non potest civitas abscondi supra montem posita,

5:15 neque accendunt lucernam, et ponunt eam sub modio, sed super candelabrum, ut luceat omnibus qui in domo sunt.

5:16 Sic luceat lux vestra coram hominibus : ut videant opera vestra bona, et glorificent Patrem vestrum, qui in cælis est.

5:17 Nolite putare quoniam veni solvere legem aut prophetas : non veni solvere, sed adimplere.

5:18 Amen quippe dico vobis, donec transeat cælum et terra, jota unum aut unus apex non præteribit a lege, donec omnia fiant.

5:19 Qui ergo solverit unum de mandatis istis minimis, et docuerit sic homines, minimus vocabitur in regno cælorum : qui autem fecerit et docuerit, hic magnus vocabitur in regno cælorum.

5:20 Dico enim vobis, quia nisi abundaverit justitia vestra plus quam scribarum et pharisæorum, non intrabitis in regnum cælorum.

5:21 Audistis quia dictum est antiquis : Non occides : qui autem occiderit, reus erit judicio.

5:22 Ego autem dico vobis : quia omnis qui irascitur fratri suo, reus erit judicio. Qui autem dixerit fratri suo, raca : reus erit concilio. Qui autem dixerit, fatue : reus erit gehennæ ignis.

5:23 Si ergo offers munus tuum ad altare, et ibi

5:7 Blessed are the merciful: for they shall obtain mercy.

5:8 Blessed are the clean of heart: for they shall see God.

5:9 Blessed are the peacemakers: for they shall be called children of God.

5:10 Blessed are they that suffer persecution for justice' sake: for theirs is the kingdom of heaven.

5:11 Blessed are ye when they shall revile you, and persecute you, and speak all that is evil against you, untruly, for my sake:

5:12 Be glad and rejoice, for your reward is very great in heaven. For so they persecuted the prophets that were before you.

5:13 You are the salt of the earth. But if the salt lose its savour, wherewith shall it be salted? It is good for nothing any more but to be cast out, and to be trodden on by men.

5:14 You are the light of the world. A city seated on a mountain cannot be hid.

5:15 Neither do men light a candle and put it under a bushel, but upon a candlestick, that it may shine to all that are in the house.

5:16 So let your light shine before men, that they may see your good works, and glorify your Father who is in heaven.

5:17 Do not think that I am come to destroy the law, or the prophets. I am not come to destroy, but to fulfill.

5:18 For amen I say unto you, till heaven and earth pass, one jot, or one tittle shall not pass of the law, till all be fulfilled.

5:19 He therefore that shall break one of these least commandments, and shall so teach men, shall be called the least in the kingdom of heaven. But he that shall do and teach, he shall be called great in the kingdom of heaven.

5:20 For I tell you, that unless your justice abound more than that of the scribes and Pharisees, you shall not enter into the kingdom of heaven.

5:21 You have heard that it was said to them of old: Thou shalt not kill. And whosoever shall kill shall be in danger of the judgment.

5:22 But I say to you, that whosoever is angry with his brother, shall be in danger of the judgment. And whosoever shall say to his brother, Raca, shall be in danger of the council. And whosoever shall say, Thou Fool, shall be in danger of hell fire.

5:23 If therefore thou offer thy gift at the altar,

recordatus fueris quia frater tuus habet aliquid adversum te :

5:24 relinque ibi munus tuum ante altare, et vade prius reconciliari fratri tuo : et tunc veniens offeres munus tuum.

5:25 Esto consentiens adversario tuo cito dum es in via cum eo : ne forte tradat te adversarius judici, et judex tradat te ministro : et in carcerem mittaris.

5:26 Amen dico tibi, non exies inde, donec reddas novissimum quadrantem.

5:27 Audistis quia dictum est antiquis : Non mœchaberis.

5:28 Ego autem dico vobis : quia omnis qui viderit mulierem ad concupiscendum eam, jam mœchatus est eam in corde suo.

5:29 Quod si oculus tuus dexter scandalizat te, erue eum, et projice abs te : expedit enim tibi ut pereat unum membrorum tuorum, quam totum corpus tuum mittatur in gehennam.

5:30 Et si dextra manus tua scandalizat te, abscide eam, et projice abs te : expedit enim tibi ut pereat unum membrorum tuorum, quam totum corpus tuum eat in gehennam.

5:31 Dictum est autem : Quicumque dimiserit uxorem suam, det ei libellum repudii.

5:32 Ego autem dico vobis : quia omnis qui dimiserit uxorem suam, excepta fornicationis causa, facit eam mœchari : et qui dimissam duxerit, adulterat.

5:33 Iterum audistis quia dictum est antiquis : Non perjurabis : reddes autem Domino juramenta tua.

5:34 Ego autem dico vobis, non jurare omnino, neque per cælum, quia thronus Dei est :

5:35 neque per terram, quia scabellum est pedum ejus : neque per Jerosolymam, quia civitas est magni regis :

5:36 neque per caput tuum juraveris, quia non potes unum capillum album facere, aut nigrum.

5:37 Sit autem sermo vester, est, est : non, non : quod autem his abundantius est, a malo est.

5:38 Audistis quia dictum est : Oculum pro oculo, et dentem pro dente.

5:39 Ego autem dico vobis, non resistere malo : sed si quis te percusserit in dexteram maxillam tuam, præbe illi et alteram :

and there thou remember that thy brother hath any thing against thee;

5:24 Leave there thy offering before the altar, and go first to be reconciled to thy brother: and then coming thou shalt offer thy gift.

5:25 Be at agreement with thy adversary betimes, whilst thou art in the way with him: lest perhaps the adversary deliver thee to the judge, and the judge deliver thee to the officer, and thou be cast into prison.

5:26 Amen I say to thee, thou shalt not go out from thence till thou repay the last farthing.

5:27 You have heard that it was said to them of old: Thou shalt not commit adultery.

5:28 But I say to you, that whosoever shall look on a woman to lust after her, hath already committed adultery with her in his heart.

5:29 And if thy right eye scandalize thee, pluck it out and cast it from thee. For it is expedient for thee that one of thy members should perish, rather than that thy whole body be cast into hell.

5:30 And if thy right hand scandalize thee, cut it off, and cast it from thee: for it is expedient for thee that one of thy members should perish, rather than that thy whole body be cast into hell.

5:31 And it hath been said, Whosoever shall put away his wife, let him give her a bill of divorce.

5:32 But I say to you, that whosoever shall put away his wife, excepting for the cause of fornication, maketh her to commit adultery: and he that shall marry her that is put away, committeth adultery.

5:33 Again you have heard that it was said to them of old, Thou shalt not forswear thyself: but thou shalt perform thy oaths to the Lord.

5:34 But I say to you not to swear at all, neither by heaven, for it is the throne of God:

5:35 Nor by the earth, for it is his footstool: nor by Jerusalem, for it is the city of the great king:

5:36 Neither shalt thou swear by thy head, because thou canst not make one hair white or black.

5:37 But let your speech be yea, yea: no, no: and that which is over and above these, is of evil.

5:38 You have heard that it hath been said, An eye for an eye, and a tooth for a tooth.

5:39 But I say to you not to resist evil: but if one strike thee on thy right cheek, turn to him also the other:

5:40 et ei, qui vult tecum judicio contendere, et tunicam tuam tollere, dimitte ei et pallium :

5:41 et quicumque te angariaverit mille passus, vade cum illo et alia duo.

5:42 Qui petit a te, da ei : et volenti mutuari a te, ne avertaris.

5:43 Audistis quia dictum est : Diliges proximum tuum, et odio habebis inimicum tuum.

5:44 Ego autem dico vobis : diligite inimicos vestros, benefacite his qui oderunt vos, et orate pro persequentibus et calumniantibus vos :

5:45 ut sitis filii Patris vestri, qui in cælis est : qui solem suum oriri facit super bonos et malos : et pluit super justos et injustos.

5:46 Si enim diligitis eos qui vos diligunt, quam mercedem habebitis ? nonne et publicani hoc faciunt ?

5:47 Et si salutaveritis fratres vestros tantum, quid amplius facitis ? nonne et ethnici hoc faciunt ?

5:48 Estote ergo vos perfecti, sicut et Pater vester cælestis perfectus est.

6:1 Attendite ne justitiam vestram faciatis coram hominibus, ut videamini ab eis : alioquin mercedem non habebitis apud Patrem vestrum qui in cælis est.

6:2 Cum ergo facis eleemosynam, noli tuba canere ante te, sicut hypocritæ faciunt in synagogis, et in vicis, ut honorificentur ab hominibus. Amen dico vobis, receperunt mercedem suam.

6:3 Te autem faciente eleemosynam, nesciat sinistra tua quid faciat dextera tua :

6:4 ut sit eleemosyna tua in abscondito, et Pater tuus, qui videt in abscondito, reddet tibi.

6:5 Et cum oratis, non eritis sicut hypocritæ qui amant in synagogis et in angulis platearum stantes orare, ut videantur ab hominibus : amen dico vobis, receperunt mercedem suam.

6:6 Tu autem cum oraveris, intra in cubiculum tuum, et clauso ostio, ora Patrem tuum in abscondito : et Pater tuus, qui videt in abscondito, reddet tibi.

6:7 Orantes autem, nolite multum loqui, sicut ethnici, putant enim quod in multiloquio suo exaudiantur.

6:8 Nolite ergo assimilari eis : scit enim Pater vester, quid opus sit vobis, antequam petatis eum.

5:40 And if a man will contend with thee in judgment, and take away thy coat, let go thy cloak also unto him.

5:41 And whosoever will force thee one mile, go with him other two,

5:42 Give to him that asketh of thee and from him that would borrow of thee turn not away.

5:43 You have heard that it hath been said, Thou shalt love thy neighbor, and hate thy enemy.

5:44 But I say to you, Love your enemies: do good to them that hate you: and pray for them that persecute and calumniate you:

5:45 That you may be the children of your Father who is in heaven, who maketh his sun to rise upon the good, and bad, and raineth upon the just and the unjust.

5:46 For if you love them that love you, what reward shall you have? do not even the publicans this?

5:47 And if you salute your brethren only, what do you more? do not also the heathens this?

5:48 Be you therefore perfect, as also your heavenly Father is perfect.

6:1 Take heed that you do not your justice before men, to be seen by them: otherwise you shall not have a reward of your Father who is in heaven.

6:2 Therefore when thou dost an almsdeed, sound not a trumpet before thee, as the hypocrites do in the synagogues and in the streets, that they may be honoured by men. Amen I say to you, they have received their reward.

6:3 But when thou dost alms, let not thy left hand know what thy right hand doth.

6:4 That thy alms may be in secret, and thy Father who seeth in secret will repay thee.

6:5 And when ye pray, you shall not be as the hypocrites, that love to stand and pray in the synagogues and corners of the streets, that they may be seen by men: Amen I say to you, they have received their reward.

6:6 But thou when thou shalt pray, enter into thy chamber, and having shut the door, pray to thy Father in secret: and thy Father who seeth in secret will repay thee.

6:7 And when you are praying, speak not much, as the heathens. For they think that in their much speaking they may be heard.

6:8 Be not you therefore like to them, for your Father knoweth what is needful for you, before you ask him.

6:9 Sic ergo vos orabitis : *Pater noster, qui es in cælis, sanctificetur nomen tuum.*

6:10 *Adveniat regnum tuum ; fiat voluntas tua, sicut in cælo et in terra.*

6:11 *Panem nostrum supersubstantialem da nobis hodie,*

6:12 *et dimitte nobis debita nostra, sicut et nos dimittimus debitoribus nostris.*

6:13 *Et ne nos inducas in tentationem, sed libera nos a malo. Amen.*

6:14 Si enim dimiseritis hominibus peccata eorum : dimittet et vobis Pater vester cælestis delicta vestra.

6:15 Si autem non dimiseritis hominibus : nec Pater vester dimittet vobis peccata vestra.

6:16 Cum autem jejunatis, nolite fieri sicut hypocritæ, tristes. Exterminant enim facies suas, ut appareant hominibus jejunantes. Amen dico vobis, quia receperunt mercedem suam.

6:17 Tu autem, cum jejunas, unge caput tuum, et faciem tuam lava,

6:18 ne videaris hominibus jejunans, sed Patri tuo, qui est in abscondito : et Pater tuus, qui videt in abscondito, reddet tibi.

6:19 Nolite thesaurizare vobis thesauros in terra : ubi ærugo, et tinea demolitur : et ubi fures effodiunt, et furantur.

6:20 Thesaurizate autem vobis thesauros in cælo, ubi neque ærugo, neque tinea demolitur, et ubi fures non effodiunt, nec furantur.

6:21 Ubi enim est thesaurus tuus, ibi est et cor tuum.

6:22 Lucerna corporis tui est oculus tuus. Si oculus tuus fuerit simplex, totum corpus tuum lucidum erit.

6:23 Si autem oculus tuus fuerit nequam, totum corpus tuum tenebrosum erit. Si ergo lumen, quod in te est, tenebræ sunt : ipsæ tenebræ quantæ erunt ?

6:24 Nemo potest duobus dominis servire : aut enim unum odio habebit, et alterum diliget : aut unum sustinebit, et alterum contemnet. Non potestis Deo servire et mammonæ.

6:25 Ideo dico vobis, ne solliciti sitis animæ vestræ quid manducetis, neque corpori vestro quid induamini. Nonne anima plus est quam esca, et corpus plus quam vestimentum ?

6:26 Respicite volatilia cæli, quoniam non serunt, neque metunt, neque congregant in horrea : et Pater vester cælestis pascit illa. Nonne vos magis pluris estis illis ?

6:9 Thus therefore shall you pray: *Our Father who art in heaven, hallowed be thy name.*

6:10 *Thy kingdom come. Thy will be done on earth as it is in heaven.*

6:11 *Give us this day our supersubstantial bread.*

6:12 *And forgive us our debts, as we also forgive our debtors.*

6:13 *And lead us not into temptation. But deliver us from evil. Amen.*

6:14 For if you will forgive men their offences, your heavenly Father will forgive you also your offences.

6:15 But if you will not forgive men, neither will your Father forgive you your offences.

6:16 And when you fast, be not as the hypocrites, sad. For they disfigure their faces, that they may appear unto men to fast. Amen I say to you, they have received their reward.

6:17 But thou, when thou fastest anoint thy head, and wash thy face;

6:18 That thou appear not to men to fast, but to thy Father who is in secret: and thy Father who seeth in secret, will repay thee.

6:19 Lay not up to yourselves treasures on earth: where the rust, and moth consume, and where thieves break through and steal.

6:20 But lay up to yourselves treasures in heaven: where neither the rust nor moth doth consume, and where thieves do not break through, nor steal.

6:21 For where thy treasure is, there is thy heart also.

6:22 The light of thy body is thy eye. If thy eye be single, thy whole body shall be lightsome.

6:23 But if thy eye be evil thy whole body shall be darksome. If then the light that is in thee, be darkness: the darkness itself how great shall it be!

6:24 No man can serve two masters. For either he will hate the one, and love the other: or he will sustain the one, and despise the other. You cannot serve God and mammon.

6:25 Therefore I say to you, be not solicitous for your life, what you shall eat, nor for your body, what you shall put on. Is not the life more than the meat: and the body more than the raiment?

6:26 Behold the birds of the air, for they neither sow, nor do they reap, nor gather into barns: and your heavenly Father feedeth them. Are not you of much more value than they?

6:27 Quis autem vestrum cogitans potest adjicere ad staturam suam cubitum unum ?

6:28 Et de vestimento quid solliciti estis ? Considerate lilia agri quomodo crescunt : non laborant, neque nent.

6:29 Dico autem vobis, quoniam nec Salomon in omni gloria sua coopertus est sicut unum ex istis.

6:30 Si autem fœnum agri, quod hodie est, et cras in clibanum mittitur, Deus sic vestit, quanto magis vos modicæ fidei ?

6:31 Nolite ergo solliciti esse, dicentes : Quid manducabimus, aut quid bibemus, aut quo operiemur ?

6:32 hæc enim omnia gentes inquirunt. Scit enim Pater vester, quia his omnibus indigetis.

6:33 Quærite ergo primum regnum Dei, et justitiam ejus : et hæc omnia adjicientur vobis.

6:34 Nolite ergo solliciti esse in crastinum. Crastinus enim dies sollicitus erit sibi ipsi : sufficit diei malitia sua.

7:1 Nolite judicare, ut non judicemini.

7:2 In quo enim judicio judicaveritis, judicabimini : et in qua mensura mensi fueritis, remetietur vobis.

7:3 Quid autem vides festucam in oculo fratris tui, et trabem in oculo tuo non vides ?

7:4 aut quomodo dicis fratri tuo : Sine ejiciam festucam de oculo tuo, et ecce trabs est in oculo tuo ?

7:5 Hypocrita, ejice primum trabem de oculo tuo, et tunc videbis ejicere festucam de oculo fratris tui.

7:6 Nolite dare sanctum canibus : neque mittatis margaritas vestras ante porcos, ne forte conculcent eas pedibus suis, et conversi dirumpant vos.

7:7 Petite, et dabitur vobis : quærite, et invenietis : pulsate, et aperietur vobis.

7:8 Omnis enim qui petit, accipit : et qui quærit, invenit : et pulsanti aperietur.

7:9 Aut quis est ex vobis homo, quem si petierit filius suus panem, numquid lapidem porriget ei ?

7:10 aut si piscem petierit, numquid serpentem porriget ei ?

7:11 Si ergo vos, cum sitis mali, nostis bona data

6:27 And which of you by taking thought, can add to his stature one cubit?

6:28 And for raiment why are you solicitous? Consider the lilies of the field, how they grow: they labour not, neither do they spin.

6:29 But I say to you, that not even Solomon in all his glory was arrayed as one of these.

6:30 And if the grass of the field, which is to day, and to morrow is cast into the oven, God doth so clothe: how much more you, O ye of little faith?

6:31 Be not solicitous therefore, saying, What shall we eat: or what shall we drink, or wherewith shall we be clothed?

6:32 For after all these things do the heathens seek. For your Father knoweth that you have need of all these things.

6:33 Seek ye therefore first the kingdom of God, and his justice, and all these things shall be added unto you.

6:34 Be not therefore solicitous for to morrow; for the morrow will be solicitous for itself. Sufficient for the day is the evil thereof.

7:1 Judge not, that you may not be judged,

7:2 For with what judgment you judge, you shall be judged: and with what measure you mete, it shall be measured to you again.

7:3 And why seest thou the mote that is in thy brother's eye; and seest not the beam that is in thy own eye?

7:4 Or how sayest thou to thy brother: Let me cast the mote out of thy eye; and behold a beam is in thy own eye?

7:5 Thou hypocrite, cast out first the beam out of thy own eye, and then shalt thou see to cast out the mote out of thy brother's eye.

7:6 Give not that which is holy to dogs; neither cast ye your pearls before swine, lest perhaps they trample them under their feet, and turning upon you, they tear you.

7:7 Ask, and it shall be given you: seek, and you shall find: knock, and it shall be opened to you.

7:8 For every one that asketh, receiveth: and he that seeketh, findeth: and to him that knocketh, it shall be opened.

7:9 Or what man is there among you, of whom if his son shall ask bread, will he reach him a stone?

7:10 Or if he shall ask him a fish, will he reach him a serpent?

7:11 If you then being evil, know how to give

dare filiis vestris : quanto magis Pater vester, qui in cælis est, dabit bona petentibus se ?

7:12 Omnia ergo quæcumque vultis ut faciant vobis homines, et vos facite illis. Hæc est enim lex, et prophetæ.

7:13 Intrate per angustam portam : quia lata porta, et spatiosa via est, quæ ducit ad perditionem, et multi sunt qui intrant per eam.

7:14 Quam angusta porta, et arcta via est, quæ ducit ad vitam : et pauci sunt qui inveniunt eam !

7:15 Attendite a falsis prophetis, qui veniunt ad vos in vestimentis ovium, intrinsecus autem sunt lupi rapaces :

7:16 a fructibus eorum cognoscetis eos. Numquid colligunt de spinis uvas, aut de tribulis ficus ?

7:17 Sic omnis arbor bona fructus bonos facit : mala autem arbor malos fructus facit.

7:18 Non potest arbor bona malos fructus facere : neque arbor mala bonos fructus facere.

7:19 Omnis arbor, quæ non facit fructum bonum, excidetur, et in ignem mittetur.

7:20 Igitur ex fructibus eorum cognoscetis eos.

7:21 Non omnis qui dicit mihi, Domine, Domine, intrabit in regnum cælorum : sed qui facit voluntatem Patris mei, qui in cælis est, ipse intrabit in regnum cælorum.

7:22 Multi dicent mihi in illa die : Domine, Domine, nonne in nomine tuo prophetavimus, et in nomine tuo dæmonia ejecimus, et in nomine tuo virtutes multas fecimus ?

7:23 Et tunc confitebor illis : Quia numquam novi vos : discedite a me, qui operamini iniquitatem.

7:24 Omnis ergo qui audit verba mea hæc, et facit ea, assimilabitur viro sapienti, qui ædificavit domum suam supra petram,

7:25 et descendit pluvia, et venerunt flumina, et flaverunt venti, et irruerunt in domum illam, et non cecidit : fundata enim erat super petram.

7:26 Et omnis qui audit verba mea hæc, et non facit ea, similis erit viro stulto, qui ædificavit domum suam super arenam :

7:27 et descendit pluvia, et venerunt flumina, et flaverunt venti, et irruerunt in domum illam,

good gifts to your children: how much more will your Father who is in heaven, give good things to them that ask him?

7:12 All things therefore whatsoever you would that men should do to you, do you also to them. For this is the law and the prophets.

7:13 Enter ye in at the narrow gate: for wide is the gate, and broad is the way that leadeth to destruction, and many there are who go in thereat.

7:14 How narrow is the gate, and strait is the way that leadeth to life: and few there are that find it!

7:15 Beware of false prophets, who come to you in the clothing of sheep, but inwardly they are ravening wolves.

7:16 By their fruits you shall know them. Do men gather grapes of thorns, or figs of thistles?

7:17 Even so every good tree bringeth forth good fruit, and the evil tree bringeth forth evil fruit.

7:18 A good tree cannot bring forth evil fruit, neither can an evil tree bring forth good fruit.

7:19 Every tree that bringeth not forth good fruit, shall be cut down, and shall be cast into the fire.

7:20 Wherefore by their fruits you shall know them.

7:21 Not every one that saith to me, Lord, Lord, shall enter into the kingdom of heaven: but he that doth the will of my Father who is in heaven, he shall enter into the kingdom of heaven.

7:22 Many will say to me in that day: Lord, Lord, have not we prophesied in thy name, and cast out devils in thy name, and done many miracles in thy name?

7:23 And then will I profess unto them, I never knew you: depart from me, you that work iniquity.

7:24 Every one therefore that heareth these my words, and doth them, shall be likened to a wise man that built his house upon a rock,

7:25 And the rain fell, and the floods came, and the winds blew, and they beat upon that house, and it fell not, for it was founded on a rock.

7:26 And every one that heareth these my words, and doth them not, shall be like a foolish man that built his house upon the sand,

7:27 And the rain fell, and the floods came, and the winds blew, and they beat upon that house,

et cecidit, et fuit ruina illius magna.

7:28 Et factum est : cum consummasset Jesus verba hæc, admirabantur turbæ super doctrina ejus.

7:29 Erat enim docens eos sicut potestatem habens, et non sicut scribæ eorum, et pharisæi.

8:1 Cum autem descendisset de monte, secutæ sunt eum turbæ multæ :

8:2 et ecce leprosus veniens, adorabat eum, dicens : Domine, si vis, potes me mundare.

8:3 Et extendens Jesus manum, tetigit eum, dicens : Volo : mundare. Et confestim mundata est lepra ejus.

8:4 Et ait illi Jesus : Vide, nemini dixeris : sed vade, ostende te sacerdoti, et offer munus, quod præcepit Moyses, in testimonium illis.

8:5 Cum autem introisset Capharnaum, accessit ad eum centurio, rogans eum,

8:6 et dicens : Domine, puer meus jacet in domo paralyticus, et male torquetur.

8:7 Et ait illi Jesus : Ego veniam, et curabo eum.

8:8 Et respondens centurio, ait : Domine, non sum dignus ut intres sub tectum meum : sed tantum dic verbo, et sanabitur puer meus.

8:9 Nam et ego homo sum sub potestate constitutus, habens sub me milites, et dico huic : Vade, et vadit : et alii : Veni, et venit : et servo meo : Fac hoc, et facit.

8:10 Audiens autem Jesus miratus est, et sequentibus se dixit : Amen dico vobis, non inveni tantam fidem in Israël.

8:11 Dico autem vobis, quod multi ab oriente et occidente venient, et recumbent cum Abraham, et Isaac, et Jacob in regno cælorum :

8:12 filii autem regni ejicientur in tenebras exteriores : ibi erit fletus et stridor dentium.

8:13 Et dixit Jesus centurioni : Vade, et sicut credidisti, fiat tibi. Et sanatus est puer in illa hora.

8:14 Et cum venisset Jesus in domum Petri, vidit socrum ejus jacentem, et febricitantem :

8:15 et tetigit manum ejus, et dimisit eam febris, et surrexit, et ministrabat eis.

and it fell, and great was the fall thereof.

7:28 And it came to pass when Jesus had fully ended these words, the people were in admiration at his doctrine.

7:29 For he was teaching them as one having power, and not as the scribes and Pharisees.

8:1 And when he was come down from the mountain, great multitudes followed him:

8:2 And behold a leper came and adored him, saying: Lord, if thou wilt, thou canst make me clean.

8:3 And Jesus stretching forth his hand, touched him, saying: I will, be thou made clean. And forthwith his leprosy was cleansed.

8:4 And Jesus saith to him: See thou tell no man: but go, shew thyself to the priest, and offer the gift which Moses commanded for a testimony unto them.

8:5 And when he had entered into Capharnaum, there came to him a centurion, beseeching him,

8:6 And saying, Lord, my servant lieth at home sick of the palsy, and is grievously tormented.

8:7 And Jesus saith to him: I will come and heal him.

8:8 And the centurion making answer, said: Lord, I am not worthy that thou shouldst enter under my roof: but only say the word, and my servant shall be healed.

8:9 For I also am a man subject to authority, having under me soldiers; and I say to this, Go, and he goeth, and to another, Come, and he cometh, and to my servant, Do this, and he doeth it.

8:10 And Jesus hearing this, marvelled; and said to them that followed him: Amen I say to you, I have not found so great faith in Israel.

8:11 And I say to you that many shall come from the east and the west, and shall sit down with Abraham, and Isaac, and Jacob in the kingdom of heaven:

8:12 But the children of the kingdom shall be cast out into the exterior darkness: there shall be weeping and gnashing of teeth.

8:13 And Jesus said to the centurion: Go, and as thou hast believed, so be it done to thee. And the servant was healed at the same hour.

8:14 And when Jesus was come into Peter's house, he saw his wife's mother lying, and sick of a fever:

8:15 And he touched her hand, and the fever left her, and she arose and ministered to them.

8:16 Vespere autem facto, obtulerunt ei multos dæmonia habentes : et ejiciebat spiritus verbo, et omnes male habentes curavit :

8:17 ut adimpleretur quod dictum est per Isaiam prophetam, dicentem : *Ipse infirmitates nostras accepit : et ægrotationes nostras portavit.*

8:18 Videns autem Jesus turbas multas circum se, jussit ire trans fretum.

8:19 Et accedens unus scriba, ait illi : Magister, sequar te, quocumque ieris.

8:20 Et dicit ei Jesus : Vulpes foveas habent, et volucres cæli nidos ; Filius autem hominis non habet ubi caput reclinet.

8:21 Alius autem de discipulis ejus ait illi : Domine, permitte me primum ire, et sepelire patrem meum.

8:22 Jesus autem ait illi : Sequere me, et dimitte mortuos sepelire mortuos suos.

8:23 Et ascendente eo in naviculam, secuti sunt eum discipuli ejus :

8:24 et ecce motus magnus factus est in mari, ita ut navicula operiretur fluctibus : ipse vero dormiebat.

8:25 Et accesserunt ad eum discipuli ejus, et suscitaverunt eum, dicentes : Domine, salva nos : perimus.

8:26 Et dicit eis Jesus : Quid timidi estis, modicæ fidei ? Tunc surgens imperavit ventis, et mari, et facta est tranquillitas magna.

8:27 Porro homines mirati sunt, dicentes : Qualis est hic, quia venti et mare obediunt ei ?

8:28 Et cum venisset trans fretum in regionem Gerasenorum, occurrerunt ei duo habentes dæmonia, de monumentis exeuntes, sævi nimis, ita ut nemo posset transire per viam illam.

8:29 Et ecce clamaverunt, dicentes : Quid nobis et tibi, Jesu fili Dei ? Venisti huc ante tempus torquere nos ?

8:30 Erat autem non longe ab illis grex multorum porcorum pascens.

8:31 Dæmones autem rogabant eum, dicentes : Si ejicis nos hinc, mitte nos in gregem porcorum.

8:32 Et ait illis : Ite. At illi exeuntes abierunt in porcos, et ecce impetu abiit totus grex per præceps in mare : et mortui sunt in aquis.

8:16 And when evening was come, they brought to him many that were possessed with devils: and he cast out the spirits with his word: and all that were sick he healed:

8:17 That it might be fulfilled, which was spoken by the prophet Isaias, saying: *He took our infirmities, and bore our diseases.*

8:18 And Jesus seeing great multitudes about him, gave orders to pass over the water.

8:19 And a certain scribe came and said to him: Master, I will follow thee whithersoever thou shalt go.

8:20 And Jesus saith to him: The foxes have holes, and the birds of the air nests: but the son of man hath not where to lay his head.

8:21 And another of his disciples said to him: Lord, suffer me first to go and bury my father.

8:22 But Jesus said to him: Follow me, and let the dead bury their dead.

8:23 And when he entered into the boat, his disciples followed him:

8:24 And behold a great tempest arose in the sea, so that the boat was covered with waves, but he was asleep.

8:25 And they came to him, and awaked him, saying: Lord, save us, we perish.

8:26 And Jesus saith to them: Why are you fearful, O ye of little faith? Then rising up he commanded the winds, and the sea, and there came a great calm.

8:27 But the men wondered, saying: What manner of man is this, for the winds and the sea obey him?

8:28 And when he was come on the other side of the water, into the country of the Gerasens, there met him two that were possessed with devils, coming out of the sepulchres, exceeding fierce, so that none could pass by that way.

8:29 And behold they cried out, saying: What have we to do with thee, Jesus Son of God? art thou come hither to torment us before the time?

8:30 And there was, not far from them, an herd of many swine feeding.

8:31 And the devils besought him, saying: If thou cast us out hence, send us into the herd of swine.

8:32 And he said to them: Go. But they going out went into the swine, and behold the whole herd ran violently down a steep place into the

8:33 Pastores autem fugerunt : et venientes in civitatem, nuntiaverunt omnia, et de eis qui dæmonia habuerant.

8:34 Et ecce tota civitas exiit obviam Jesu : et viso eo, rogabant ut transiret a finibus eorum.

9:1 Et ascendens in naviculam, transfretavit, et venit in civitatem suam.

9:2 Et ecce offerebant ei paralyticum jacentem in lecto. Et videns Jesus fidem illorum, dixit paralytico : Confide fili, remittuntur tibi peccata tua.

9:3 Et ecce quidam de scribis dixerunt intra se : Hic blasphemat.

9:4 Et cum vidisset Jesus cogitationes eorum, dixit : Ut quid cogitatis mala in cordibus vestris ?

9:5 Quid est facilius dicere : Dimittuntur tibi peccata tua : an dicere : Surge, et ambula ?

9:6 Ut autem sciatis, quia Filius hominis habet potestatem in terra dimittendi peccata, tunc ait paralytico : Surge, tolle lectum tuum, et vade in domum tuam.

9:7 Et surrexit, et abiit in domum suam.

9:8 Videntes autem turbæ timuerunt, et glorificaverunt Deum, qui dedit potestatem talem hominibus.

9:9 Et, cum transiret inde Jesus, vidit hominem sedentem in telonio, Matthæum nomine. Et ait illi : Sequere me. Et surgens, secutus est eum.

9:10 Et factum est, discumbente eo in domo, ecce multi publicani et peccatores venientes, discumbebant cum Jesu, et discipulis ejus.

9:11 Et videntes pharisæi, dicebant discipulis ejus : Quare cum publicanis et peccatoribus manducat magister vester ?

9:12 At Jesus audiens, ait : Non est opus valentibus medicus, sed male habentibus.

9:13 Euntes autem discite quid est : Misericordiam volo, et non sacrificium. Non enim veni vocare justos, sed peccatores.

9:14 Tunc accesserunt ad eum discipuli Joannis, dicentes : Quare nos, et pharisæi, jejunamus frequenter : discipuli autem tui non jejunant ?

9:15 Et ait illis Jesus : Numquid possunt filii sponsi lugere, quamdiu cum illis est sponsus ? Venient autem dies cum auferetur ab eis spon-

sea: and they perished in the waters.

8:33 And they that kept them fled: and coming into the city, told every thing, and concerning them that had been possessed by the devils.

8:34 And behold the whole city went out to meet Jesus, and when they saw him, they besought him that he would depart from their coasts.

9:1 And entering into a boat, he passed over the water and came into his own city.

9:2 And behold they brought to him one sick of the palsy lying in a bed. And Jesus, seeing their faith, said to the man sick of the palsy: Be of good heart, son, thy sins are forgiven thee.

9:3 And behold some of the scribes said within themselves: He blasphemeth.

9:4 And Jesus seeing their thoughts, said: Why do you think evil in your hearts?

9:5 Whether is easier, to say, Thy sins are forgiven thee: or to say, Arise, and walk?

9:6 But that you may know that the Son of man hath power on earth to forgive sins, (then said he to the man sick of palsy,) Arise, take up thy bed, and go into thy house.

9:7 And he arose, and went into his house.

9:8 And the multitude seeing it, feared, and glorified God that gave such power to men.

9:9 And when Jesus passed on from thence, he saw a man sitting in the custom house, named Matthew; and he saith to him: Follow me. And he rose up and followed him.

9:10 And it came to pass as he was sitting at meat in the house, behold many publicans and sinners came, and sat down with Jesus and his disciples.

9:11 And the Pharisees seeing it, said to his disciples: Why doth your master eat with publicans and sinners?

9:12 But Jesus hearing it, said: They that are in health need not a physician, but they that are ill.

9:13 Go then and learn what this meaneth, I will have mercy and not sacrifice. For I am not come to call the just, but sinners.

9:14 Then came to him the disciples of John, saying: Why do we and the Pharisees fast often, but thy disciples do not fast?

9:15 And Jesus said to them: Can the children of the bridegroom mourn, as long as the bridegroom is with them? But the days will come,

sus : et tunc jejunabunt.

9:16 Nemo autem immittit commissuram panni rudis in vestimentum vetus : tollit enim plenitudinem ejus a vestimento, et pejor scissura fit.

9:17 Neque mittunt vinum novum in utres veteres : alioquin rumpuntur utres, et vinum effunditur, et utres pereunt. Sed vinum novum in utres novos mittunt : et ambo conservantur.

9:18 Hæc illo loquente ad eos, ecce princeps unus accessit, et adorabat eum, dicens : Domine, filia mea modo defuncta est : sed veni, impone manum tuam super eam, et vivet.

9:19 Et surgens Jesus, sequebatur eum, et discipuli ejus.

9:20 Et ecce mulier, quæ sanguinis fluxum patiebatur duodecim annis, accessit retro, et tetigit fimbriam vestimenti ejus.

9:21 Dicebat enim intra se : Si tetigero tantum vestimentum ejus, salva ero.

9:22 At Jesus conversus, et videns eam, dixit : Confide, filia, fides tua te salvam fecit. Et salva facta est mulier ex illa hora.

9:23 Et cum venisset Jesus in domum principis, et vidisset tibicines et turbam tumultuantem, dicebat :

9:24 Recedite : non est enim mortua puella, sed dormit. Et deridebant eum.

9:25 Et cum ejecta esset turba, intravit : et tenuit manum ejus, et surrexit puella.

9:26 Et exiit fama hæc in universam terram illam.

9:27 Et transeunte inde Jesu, secuti sunt eum duo cæci, clamantes, et dicentes : Miserere nostri, fili David.

9:28 Cum autem venisset domum, accesserunt ad eum cæci. Et dicit eis Jesus : Creditis quia hoc possum facere vobis ? Dicunt ei : Utique, Domine.

9:29 Tunc tetigit oculos eorum, dicens : Secundum fidem vestram, fiat vobis.

9:30 Et aperti sunt oculi eorum : et comminatus est illis Jesus, dicens : Videte ne quis sciat.

9:31 Illi autem exeuntes, diffamaverunt eum in tota terra illa.

9:32 Egressis autem illis, ecce obtulerunt ei

when the bridegroom shall be taken away from them, and then they shall fast.

9:16 And nobody putteth a piece of raw cloth unto an old garment. For it taketh away the fullness thereof from the garment, and there is made a greater rent.

9:17 Neither do they put new wine into old bottles. Otherwise the bottles break, and the wine runneth out, and the bottles perish. But new wine they put into new bottles: and both are preserved.

9:18 As he was speaking these things unto them, behold a certain ruler came up, and adored him, saying: Lord, my daughter is even now dead; but come, lay thy hand upon her, and she shall live.

9:19 And Jesus rising up followed him, with his disciples.

9:20 And behold a woman who was troubled with an issue of blood twelve years, came behind him, and touched the hem of his garment.

9:21 For she said within herself: If I shall touch only his garment, I shall be healed.

9:22 But Jesus turning and seeing her, said: Be of good heart, daughter, thy faith hath made thee whole. And the woman was made whole from that hour.

9:23 And when Jesus was come into the house of the ruler, and saw the minstrels and the multitude making a rout,

9:24 He said: Give place, for the girl is not dead, but sleepeth. And they laughed him to scorn.

9:25 And when the multitude was put forth, he went in, and took her by the hand. And the maid arose.

9:26 And the fame hereof went abroad into all that country.

9:27 And as Jesus passed from thence, there followed him two blind men crying out and saying, Have mercy on us, O Son of David.

9:28 And when he was come to the house, the blind men came to him. And Jesus saith to them, Do you believe, that I can do this unto you? They say to him, Yea, Lord.

9:29 Then he touched their eyes, saying, According to your faith, be it done unto you.

9:30 And their eyes were opened, and Jesus strictly charged them, saying, See that no man know this.

9:31 But they going out, spread his fame abroad in all that country.

9:32 And when they were gone out, behold they

hominem mutum, dæmonium habentem.

brought him a dumb man, possessed with a devil.

9:33 Et ejecto dæmonio, locutus est mutus, et miratæ sunt turbæ, dicentes : Numquam apparuit sic in Israël.

9:33 And after the devil was cast out, the dumb man spoke, and the multitudes wondered, saying, Never was the like seen in Israel.

9:34 Pharisæi autem dicebant : In principe dæmoniorum ejicit dæmones.

9:34 But the Pharisees said, By the prince of devils he casteth out devils.

9:35 Et circuibat Jesus omnes civitates, et castella, docens in synagogis eorum, et prædicans Evangelium regni, et curans omnem languorem, et omnem infirmitatem.

9:35 And Jesus went about all the cities, and towns, teaching in their synagogues, and preaching the gospel of the kingdom, and healing every disease, and every infirmity.

9:36 Videns autem turbas, misertus est eis : quia erant vexati, et jacentes sicut oves non habentes pastorem.

9:36 And seeing the multitudes, he had compassion on them: because they were distressed, and lying like sheep that have no shepherd.

9:37 Tunc dicit discipulis suis : Messis quidem multa, operarii autem pauci.

9:37 Then he saith to his disciples, The harvest indeed is great, but the labourers are few.

9:38 Rogate ergo Dominum messis, ut mittat operarios in messem suam.

9:38 Pray ye therefore the Lord of the harvest, that he send forth labourers into his harvest.

10:1 Et convocatis duodecim discipulis suis, dedit illis potestatem spirituum immundorum, ut ejicerent eos, et curarent omnem languorem, et omnem infirmitatem.

10:1 And having called his twelve disciples together, he gave them power over unclean spirits, to cast them out, and to heal all manner of diseases, and all manner of infirmities.

10:2 Duodecim autem Apostolorum nomina sunt hæc. Primus, Simon, qui dicitur Petrus : et Andreas frater ejus,

10:2 And the names of the twelve apostles are these: The first, Simon who is called Peter, and Andrew his brother,

10:3 Jacobus Zebedæi, et Joannes frater ejus, Philippus, et Bartholomæus, Thomas, et Matthæus publicanus, Jacobus Alphæi, et Thaddæus,

10:3 James the son of Zebedee, and John his brother, Philip and Bartholomew, Thomas and Matthew the publican, and James the son of Alpheus, and Thaddeus,

10:4 Simon Chananæus, et Judas Iscariotes, qui et tradidit eum.

10:4 Simon the Cananean, and Judas Iscariot, who also betrayed him.

10:5 Hos duodecim misit Jesus, præcipiens eis, dicens : In viam gentium ne abieritis, et in civitates Samaritanorum ne intraveritis :

10:5 These twelve Jesus sent: commanding them, saying: Go ye not into the way of the Gentiles, and into the city of the Samaritans enter ye not.

10:6 sed potius ite ad oves quæ perierunt domus Israël.

10:6 But go ye rather to the lost sheep of the house of Israel.

10:7 Euntes autem prædicate, dicentes : Quia appropinquavit regnum cælorum.

10:7 And going, preach, saying: The kingdom of heaven is at hand.

10:8 Infirmos curate, mortuos suscitate, leprosos mundate, dæmones ejicite : gratis accepistis, gratis date.

10:8 Heal the sick, raise the dead, cleanse the lepers, cast out devils: freely have you received, freely give.

10:9 Nolite possidere aurum, neque argentum, neque pecuniam in zonis vestris :

10:9 Do not possess gold, nor silver, nor money in your purses:

10:10 non peram in via, neque duas tunicas, neque calceamenta, neque virgam : dignus enim est operarius cibo suo.

10:10 Nor scrip for your journey, nor two coats, nor shoes, nor a staff; for the workman is worthy of his meat.

10:11 In quamcumque autem civitatem aut castellum intraveritis, interrogate, quis in ea dignus sit : et ibi manete donec exeatis.

10:11 And into whatsoever city or town you shall enter, inquire who in it is worthy, and there abide till you go thence.

10:12 Intrantes autem in domum, salutate eam, dicentes : Pax huic domui.

10:12 And when you come into the house, salute it, saying: Peace be to this house.

10:13 Et siquidem fuerit domus illa digna, veniet pax vestra super eam : si autem non fuerit digna, pax vestra revertetur ad vos.

10:14 Et quicumque non receperit vos, neque audierit sermones vestros : exeuntes foras de domo, vel civitate, excutite pulverem de pedibus vestris.

10:15 Amen dico vobis : Tolerabilius erit terræ Sodomorum et Gomorrhæorum in die judicii, quam illi civitati.

10:16 Ecce ego mitto vos sicut oves in medio luporum. Estote ergo prudentes sicut serpentes, et simplices sicut columbæ.

10:17 Cavete autem ab hominibus. Tradent enim vos in conciliis, et in synagogis suis flagellabunt vos :

10:18 et ad præsides, et ad reges ducemini propter me in testimonium illis, et gentibus.

10:19 Cum autem tradent vos, nolite cogitare quomodo, aut quid loquamini : dabitur enim vobis in illa hora, quid loquamini :

10:20 non enim vos estis qui loquimini, sed Spiritus Patris vestri, qui loquitur in vobis.

10:21 Tradet autem frater fratrem in mortem, et pater filium : et insurgent filii in parentes, et morte eos afficient :

10:22 et eritis odio omnibus propter nomen meum : qui autem perseveraverit usque in finem, hic salvus erit.

10:23 Cum autem persequentur vos in civitate ista, fugite in aliam. Amen dico vobis, non consummabitis civitates Israël, donec veniat Filius hominis.

10:24 Non est discipulus super magistrum, nec servus super dominum suum :

10:25 sufficit discipulo ut sit sicut magister ejus, et servo, sicut dominus ejus. Si patremfamilias Beelzebub vocaverunt, quanto magis domesticos ejus ?

10:26 Ne ergo timueritis eos. Nihil enim est opertum, quod non revelabitur : et occultum, quod non scietur.

10:27 Quod dico vobis in tenebris, dicite in lumine : et quod in aure auditis, prædicate super tecta.

10:28 Et nolite timere eos qui occidunt corpus, animam autem non possunt occidere : sed potius timete eum, qui potest et animam et corpus perdere in gehennam.

10:29 Nonne duo passeres asse veneunt ? et unus

10:13 And if that house be worthy, your peace shall come upon it; but if it be not worthy, your peace shall return to you.

10:14 And whosoever shall not receive you, nor hear your words: going forth out of that house or city shake off the dust from your feet.

10:15 Amen I say to you, it shall be more tolerable for the land of Sodom and Gomorrha in the day of judgment, than for that city.

10:16 Behold I send you as sheep in the midst of wolves. Be ye therefore wise as serpents and simple as doves.

10:17 But beware of men. For they will deliver you up in councils, and they will scourge you in their synagogues.

10:18 And you shall be brought before governors, and before kings for my sake, for a testimony to them and to the Gentiles:

10:19 But when they shall deliver you up, take no thought how or what to speak: for it shall be given you in that hour what to speak.

10:20 For it is not you that speak, but the Spirit of your Father that speaketh in you.

10:21 The brother also shall deliver up the brother to death, and the father the son: and the children shall rise up against their parents, and shall put them to death.

10:22 And you shall be hated by all men for my name's sake: but he that shall persevere unto the end, he shall be saved.

10:23 And when they shall persecute you in this city, flee into another. Amen I say to you, you shall not finish all the cities of Israel, till the Son of man come.

10:24 The disciple is not above the master, nor the servant above his lord.

10:25 It is enough for the disciple that he be as his master, and the servant as his lord. If they have called the goodman of the house Beelzebub, how much more them of his household?

10:26 Therefore fear them not. For nothing is covered that shall not be revealed: nor hid, that shall not be known.

10:27 That which I tell you in the dark, speak ye in the light: and that which you hear in the ear, preach ye upon the housetops.

10:28 And fear ye not them that kill the body, and are not able to kill the soul: but rather fear him that can destroy both soul and body in hell.

10:29 Are not two sparrows sold for a farthing?

ex illis non cadet super terram sine Patre vestro.

10:30 Vestri autem capilli capitis omnes numerati sunt.

10:31 Nolite ergo timere : multis passeribus meliores estis vos.

10:32 Omnis ergo qui confitebitur me coram hominibus, confitebor et ego eum coram Patre meo, qui in cælis est.

10:33 Qui autem negaverit me coram hominibus, negabo et ego eum coram Patre meo, qui in cælis est.

10:34 Nolite arbitrari quia pacem venerim mittere in terram : non veni pacem mittere, sed gladium :

10:35 veni enim separare hominem adversus patrem suum, et filiam adversus matrem suam, et nurum adversus socrum suam :

10:36 et inimici hominis, domestici ejus.

10:37 Qui amat patrem aut matrem plus quam me, non est me dignus : et qui amat filium aut filiam super me, non est me dignus.

10:38 Et qui non accipit crucem suam, et sequitur me, non est me dignus.

10:39 Qui invenit animam suam, perdet illam : et qui perdiderit animam suam propter me, inveniet eam.

10:40 Qui recipit vos, me recipit : et qui me recipit, recipit eum qui me misit.

10:41 Qui recipit prophetam in nomine prophetæ, mercedem prophetæ accipiet : et qui recipit justum in nomine justi, mercedem justi accipiet.

10:42 Et quicumque potum dederit uni ex minimis istis calicem aquæ frigidæ tantum in nomine discipuli : amen dico vobis, non perdet mercedem suam.

11:1 Et factum est, cum consummasset Jesus, præcipiens duodecim discipulis suis, transiit inde ut doceret, et prædicaret in civitatibus eorum.

11:2 Joannes autem cum audisset in vinculis opera Christi, mittens duos de discipulis suis,

11:3 ait illi : Tu es, qui venturus es, an alium exspectamus ?

11:4 Et respondens Jesus ait illis : Euntes renun-

and not one of them shall fall on the ground without your Father.

10:30 But the very hairs of your head are all numbered.

10:31 Fear not therefore: better are you than many sparrows.

10:32 Every one therefore that shall confess me before men, I will also confess him before my Father who is in heaven.

10:33 But he that shall deny me before men, I will also deny him before my Father who is in heaven.

10:34 Do not think that I came to send peace upon earth: I came not to send peace, but the sword.

10:35 For I came to set a man at variance against his father, and the daughter against her mother, and the daughter in law against her mother in law.

10:36 And a man's enemies shall be they of his own household.

10:37 He that loveth father or mother more than me, is not worthy of me; and he that loveth son or daughter more than me, is not worthy of me.

10:38 And he that taketh not up his cross, and followeth me, is not worthy of me.

10:39 He that findeth his life, shall lose it: and he that shall lose his life for me, shall find it.

10:40 He that receiveth you, receiveth me: and he that receiveth me, receiveth him that sent me.

10:41 He that receiveth a prophet in the name of a prophet, shall receive the reward of a prophet: and he that receiveth a just man in the name of a just man, shall receive the reward of a just man.

10:42 And whosoever shall give to drink to one of these little ones a cup of cold water only in the name of a disciple, amen I say to you, he shall not lose his reward.

11:1 And it came to pass, when Jesus had made an end of commanding his twelve disciples, he passed from thence, to teach and preach in their cities.

11:2 Now when John had heard in prison the works of Christ: sending two of his disciples he said to him:

11:3 Art thou he that art to come, or look we for another?

11:4 And Jesus making answer said to them: Go

tiate Joanni quæ audistis, et vidistis.

11:5 Cæci vident, claudi ambulant, leprosi mundantur, surdi audiunt, mortui resurgunt, pauperes evangelizantur :

11:6 et beatus est, qui non fuerit scandalizatus in me.

11:7 Illis autem abeuntibus, cœpit Jesus dicere ad turbas de Joanne : Quid existis in desertum videre ? arundinem vento agitatam ?

11:8 Sed quid existis videre ? hominem mollibus vestitum ? Ecce qui mollibus vestiuntur, in domibus regum sunt.

11:9 Sed quid existis videre ? prophetam ? Etiam dico vobis, et plus quam prophetam.

11:10 Hic est enim de quo scriptum est : Ecce ego mitto angelum meum ante faciem tuam, qui præparabit viam tuam ante te.

11:11 Amen dico vobis, non surrexit inter natos mulierum major Joanne Baptista : qui autem minor est in regno cælorum, major est illo.

11:12 A diebus autem Joannis Baptistæ usque nunc, regnum cælorum vim patitur, et violenti rapiunt illud.

11:13 Omnes enim prophetæ et lex usque ad Joannem prophetaverunt :

11:14 et si vultis recipere, ipse est Elias, qui venturus est.

11:15 Qui habet aures audiendi, audiat.

11:16 Cui autem similem æstimabo generationem istam ? Similis est pueris sedentibus in foro : qui clamantes coæqualibus

11:17 dicunt : Cecinimus vobis, et non saltastis : lamentavimus, et non planxistis.

11:18 Venit enim Joannes neque manducans, neque bibens, et dicunt : Dæmonium habet.

11:19 Venit Filius hominis manducans, et bibens, et dicunt : Ecce homo vorax, et potator vini, publicanorum et peccatorum amicus. Et justificata est sapientia a filiis suis.

11:20 Tunc cœpit exprobrare civitatibus, in quibus factæ sunt plurimæ virtutes ejus, quia non egissent pœnitentiam :

11:21 Væ tibi Corozain, væ tibi Bethsaida : quia, si in Tyro et Sidone factæ essent virtutes quæ factæ sunt in vobis, olim in cilicio et cinere pœnitentiam egissent.

and relate to John what you have heard and seen.

11:5 The blind see, the lame walk, the lepers are cleansed, the deaf hear, the dead rise again, the poor have the gospel preached to them.

11:6 And blessed is he that shall not be scandalized in me.

11:7 And when they went their way, Jesus began to say to the multitudes concerning John: What went you out into the desert to see? a reed shaken with the wind?

11:8 But what went you out to see? a man clothed in soft garments? Behold they that are clothed in soft garments, are in the houses of kings.

11:9 But what went you out to see? a prophet? yea I tell you, and more than a prophet.

11:10 For this is he of whom it is written: Behold I send my angel before thy face, who shall prepare thy way before thee.

11:11 Amen I say to you, there hath not risen among them that are born of women a greater than John the Baptist: yet he that is the lesser in the kingdom of heaven is greater than he.

11:12 And from the days of John the Baptist until now, the kingdom of heaven suffereth violence, and the violent bear it away.

11:13 For all the prophets and the law prophesied until John:

11:14 And if you will receive it, he is Elias that is to come.

11:15 He that hath ears to hear, let him hear.

11:16 But whereunto shall I esteem this generation to be like? It is like to children sitting in the market place.

11:17 Who crying to their companions say: We have piped to you, and you have not danced: we have lamented, and you have not mourned.

11:18 For John came neither eating nor drinking; and they say: He hath a devil.

11:19 The Son of man came eating and drinking, and they say: Behold a man that is a glutton and a wine drinker, a friend of publicans and sinners. And wisdom is justified by her children.

11:20 Then began he to upbraid the cities wherein were done the most of his miracles, for that they had not done penance.

11:21 Woe to thee, Corozain, woe to thee, Bethsaida: for if in Tyre and Sidon had been wrought the miracles that have been wrought in you, they had long ago done penance in sackcloth and ashes.

11:22 Verumtamen dico vobis : Tyro et Sidoni remissius erit in die judicii, quam vobis.

11:23 Et tu Capharnaum, numquid usque in cælum exaltaberis ? usque in infernum descendes, quia si in Sodomis factæ fuissent virtutes quæ factæ sunt in te, forte mansissent usque in hanc diem.

11:24 Verumtamen dico vobis, quia terræ Sodomorum remissius erit in die judicii, quam tibi.

11:25 In illo tempore respondens Jesus dixit : Confiteor tibi, Pater, Domine cæli et terræ, quia abscondisti hæc a sapientibus, et prudentibus, et revelasti ea parvulis.

11:26 Ita Pater : quoniam sic fuit placitum ante te.

11:27 Omnia mihi tradita sunt a Patre meo. Et nemo novit Filium, nisi Pater : neque Patrem quis novit, nisi Filius, et cui voluerit Filius revelare.

11:28 Venite ad me omnes qui laboratis, et onerati estis, et ego reficiam vos.

11:29 Tollite jugum meum super vos, et discite a me, quia mitis sum, et humilis corde : et invenietis requiem animabus vestris.

11:30 Jugum enim meum suave est, et onus meum leve.

12:1 In illo tempore abiit Jesus per sata sabbato : discipuli autem ejus esurientes cœperunt vellere spicas, et manducare.

12:2 Pharisæi autem videntes, dixerunt ei : Ecce discipuli tui faciunt quod non licet facere sabbatis.

12:3 At ille dixit eis : Non legistis quid fecerit David, quando esuriit, et qui cum eo erant :

12:4 quomodo intravit in domum Dei, et panes propositionis comedit, quos non licebat ei edere, neque his qui cum eo erant, nisi solis sacerdotibus ?

12:5 aut non legistis in lege quia sabbatis sacerdotes in templo sabbatum violant, et sine crimine sunt ?

12:6 Dico autem vobis, quia templo major est hic.

12:7 Si autem sciretis, quid est : Misericordiam volo, et non sacrificium : numquam condemnassetis innocentes :

12:8 dominus enim est Filius hominis etiam sab-

11:22 But I say unto you, it shall be more tolerable for Tyre and Sidon in the day of judgment, than for you.

11:23 And thou Capharnaum, shalt thou be exalted up to heaven? thou shalt go down even unto hell. For if in Sodom had been wrought the miracles that have been wrought in thee, perhaps it had remained unto this day.

11:24 But I say unto you, that it shall be more tolerable for the land of Sodom in the day of judgment, than for thee.

11:25 At that time Jesus answered and said: I confess to thee, O Father, Lord of heaven and earth, because thou hast hid these things from the wise and prudent, and hast revealed them to the little ones.

11:26 Yea, Father; for so hath it seemed good in thy sight.

11:27 All things are delivered to me by my Father. And no one knoweth the Son, but the Father: neither doth any one know the Father, but the Son, and he to whom it shall please the Son to reveal him.

11:28 Come to me, all you that labour, and are burdened, and I will refresh you.

11:29 Take up my yoke upon you, and learn of me, because I am meek, and humble of heart: and you shall find rest to your souls.

11:30 For my yoke is sweet and my burden light.

12:1 At that time Jesus went through the corn on the sabbath: and his disciples being hungry, began to pluck the ears, and to eat.

12:2 And the Pharisees seeing them, said to him: Behold thy disciples do that which is not lawful to do on the sabbath days.

12:3 But he said to them: Have you not read what David did when he was hungry, and they that were with him:

12:4 How he entered into the house of God, and did eat the loaves of proposition, which it was not lawful for him to eat, nor for them that were with him, but for the priests only?

12:5 Or have ye not read in the law, that on the sabbath days the priests in the temple break the sabbath, and are without blame?

12:6 But I tell you that there is here a greater than the temple.

12:7 And if you knew what this meaneth: I will have mercy, and not sacrifice: you would never have condemned the innocent.

12:8 For the Son of man is Lord even of the sab-

bati.

12:9 Et cum inde transisset, venit in synagogam eorum.

12:10 Et ecce homo manum habens aridam, et interrogabant eum, dicentes : Si licet sabbatis curare ? ut accusarent eum.

12:11 Ipse autem dixit illis : Quis erit ex vobis homo, qui habeat ovem unam, et si ceciderit hæc sabbatis in foveam, nonne tenebit et levabit eam ?

12:12 Quanto magis melior est homo ove ? itaque licet sabbatis benefacere.

12:13 Tunc ait homini : Extende manum tuam. Et extendit, et restituta est sanitati sicut altera.

12:14 Exeuntes autem pharisæi, consilium faciebant adversus eum, quomodo perderent eum.

12:15 Jesus autem sciens recessit inde : et secuti sunt eum multi, et curavit eos omnes :

12:16 et præcepit eis ne manifestum eum facerent.

12:17 Ut adimpleretur quod dictum est per Isaiam prophetam, dicentem :

12:18 *Ecce puer meus, quem elegi, dilectus meus, in quo bene complacuit animæ meæ. Ponam spiritum meum super eum, et judicium gentibus nuntiabit.*

12:19 *Non contendet, neque clamabit, neque audiet aliquis in plateis vocem ejus :*

12:20 *arundinem quassatam non confringet, et linum fumigans non extinguet, donec ejiciat ad victoriam judicium :*

12:21 *et in nomine ejus gentes sperabunt.*

12:22 Tunc oblatus est ei dæmonium habens, cæcus, et mutus, et curavit eum ita ut loqueretur, et videret.

12:23 Et stupebant omnes turbæ, et dicebant : Numquid hic est filius David ?

12:24 Pharisæi autem audientes, dixerunt : Hic non ejicit dæmones nisi in Beelzebub principe dæmoniorum.

12:25 Jesus autem sciens cogitationes eorum, dixit eis : Omne regnum divisum contra se desolabitur : et omnis civitas vel domus divisa contra se, non stabit.

12:26 Et si Satanas Satanam ejicit, adversus se divisus est : quomodo ergo stabit regnum ejus ?

bath.

12:9 And when he had passed from thence, he came into their synagogues.

12:10 And behold there was a man who had a withered hand, and they asked him, saying: Is it lawful to heal on the sabbath days? that they might accuse him.

12:11 But he said to them: What man shall there be among you, that hath one sheep: and if the same fall into a pit on the sabbath day, will he not take hold on it and lift it up?

12:12 How much better is a man than a sheep? Therefore it it lawful to do a good deed on the sabbath days.

12:13 Then he saith to the man: Stretch forth thy hand; and he stretched it forth, and it was restored to health even as the other.

12:14 And the Pharisees going out made a consultation against him, how they might destroy him.

12:15 But Jesus knowing it, retired from thence: and many followed him, and he healed them all.

12:16 And he charged them that they should not make him known.

12:17 That it might be fulfilled which was spoken by Isaias the prophet, saying:

12:18 *Behold my servant whom I have chosen, my beloved in whom my soul hath been well pleased. I will put my spirit upon him, and he shall shew judgment to the Gentiles.*

12:19 *He shall not contend, nor cry out, neither shall any man hear his voice in the streets.*

12:20 *The bruised reed he shall not break: and smoking flax he shall not extinguish: till he send forth judgment unto victory.*

12:21 *And in his name the Gentiles shall hope.*

12:22 Then was offered to him one possessed with a devil, blind and dumb: and he healed him, so that he spoke and saw.

12:23 And all the multitudes were amazed, and said: Is not this the son of David?

12:24 But the Pharisees hearing it, said: This man casteth not out the devils but by Beelzebub the prince of the devils.

12:25 And Jesus knowing their thoughts, said to them: Every kingdom divided against itself shall be made desolate: and every city or house divided against itself shall not stand.

12:26 And if Satan cast out Satan, he is divided against himself: how then shall his kingdom stand?

12:27 Et si ego in Beelzebub ejicio dæmones, filii vestri in quo ejiciunt ? ideo ipsi judices vestri erunt.

12:28 Si autem ego in Spiritu Dei ejicio dæmones, igitur pervenit in vos regnum Dei.

12:29 Aut quomodo potest quisquam intrare in domum fortis, et vasa ejus diripere, nisi prius alligaverit fortem ? et tunc domum illius diripiet.

12:30 Qui non est mecum, contra me est ; et qui non congregat mecum, spargit.

12:31 Ideo dico vobis : Omne peccatum et blasphemia remittetur hominibus, Spiritus autem blasphemia non remittetur.

12:32 Et quicumque dixerit verbum contra Filium hominis, remittetur ei : qui autem dixerit contra Spiritum Sanctum, non remittetur ei, neque in hoc sæculo, neque in futuro.

12:33 Aut facite arborem bonam, et fructum ejus bonum : aut facite arborem malam, et fructum ejus malum : siquidem ex fructu arbor agnoscitur.

12:34 Progenies viperarum, quomodo potestis bona loqui, cum sitis mali ? ex abundantia enim cordis os loquitur.

12:35 Bonus homo de bono thesauro profert bona : et malus homo de malo thesauro profert mala.

12:36 Dico autem vobis quoniam omne verbum otiosum, quod locuti fuerint homines, reddent rationem de eo in die judicii.

12:37 Ex verbis enim tuis justificaberis et ex verbis tuis condemnaberis.

12:38 Tunc responderunt ei quidam de scribis et pharisæis, dicentes : Magister, volumus a te signum videre.

12:39 Qui respondens ait illis : Generatio mala et adultera signum quærit : et signum non dabitur ei, nisi signum Jonæ prophetæ.

12:40 Sicut enim fuit Jonas in ventre ceti tribus diebus, et tribus noctibus, sic erit Filius hominis in corde terræ tribus diebus et tribus noctibus.

12:41 Viri Ninivitæ surgent in judicio cum generatione ista, et condemnabunt eam : quia pœnitentiam egerunt in prædicatione Jonæ, et ecce plus quam Jonas hic.

12:42 Regina austri surget in judicio cum generatione ista, et condemnabit eam : quia venit a

12:27 And if I by Beelzebub cast out devils, by whom do your children cast them out? Therefore they shall be your judges.

12:28 But if I by the Spirit of God cast out devils, then is the kingdom of God come upon you.

12:29 Or how can any one enter into the house of the strong, and rifle his goods, unless he first bind the strong? and then he will rifle his house.

12:30 He that is not with me, is against me: and he that gathereth not with me, scattereth.

12:31 Therefore I say to you: Every sin and blasphemy shall be forgiven men, but the blasphemy of the Spirit shall not be forgiven.

12:32 And whosoever shall speak a word against the Son of man, it shall be forgiven him: but he that shall speak against the Holy Ghost, it shall not be forgiven him, neither in this world, nor in the world to come.

12:33 Either make the tree good and its fruit good: or make the tree evil, and its fruit evil. For by the fruit the tree is known.

12:34 O generation of vipers, how can you speak good things, whereas you are evil? for out of the abundance of the heart the mouth speaketh.

12:35 A good man out of a good treasure bringeth forth good things: and an evil man out of an evil treasure bringeth forth evil things.

12:36 But I say unto you, that every idle word that men shall speak, they shall render an account for it in the day of judgment.

12:37 For by thy words thou shalt be justified, and by thy words thou shalt be condemned.

12:38 Then some of the scribes and Pharisees answered him, saying: Master we would see a sign from thee.

12:39 Who answering said to them: An evil and adulterous generation seeketh a sign: and a sign shall not be given it, but the sign of Jonas the prophet.

12:40 For as Jonas was in the whale's belly three days and three nights: so shall the Son of man be in the heart of the earth three days and three nights.

12:41 The men of Ninive shall rise in judgment with this generation, and shall condemn it: because they did penance at the preaching of Jonas. And behold a greater than Jonas here.

12:42 The queen of the south shall rise in judgment with this generation, and shall condemn

finibus terræ audire sapientiam Salomonis, et ecce plus quam Salomon hic.

12:43 Cum autem immundus spiritus exierit ab homine, ambulat per loca arida, quærens requiem, et non invenit.

12:44 Tunc dicit : Revertar in domum meam, unde exivi. Et veniens invenit eam vacantem, scopis mundatam, et ornatam.

12:45 Tunc vadit, et assumit septem alios spiritus secum nequiores se, et intrantes habitant ibi : et fiunt novissima hominis illius pejora prioribus. Sic erit et generationi huic pessimæ.

12:46 Adhuc eo loquente ad turbas, ecce mater ejus et fratres stabant foris, quærentes loqui ei.

12:47 Dixit autem ei quidam : Ecce mater tua, et fratres tui foris stant quærentes te.

12:48 At ipse respondens dicenti sibi, ait : Quæ est mater mea, et qui sunt fratres mei ?

12:49 Et extendens manum in discipulos suos, dixit : Ecce mater mea, et fratres mei.

12:50 Quicumque enim fecerit voluntatem Patris mei, qui in cælis est, ipse meus frater, et soror, et mater est.

13:1 In illo die exiens Jesus de domo, sedebat secus mare.

13:2 Et congregatæ sunt ad eum turbæ multæ, ita ut naviculam ascendens sederet : et omnis turba stabat in littore,

13:3 et locutus est eis multa in parabolis, dicens : Ecce exiit qui seminat, seminare.

13:4 Et dum seminat, quædam ceciderunt secus viam, et venerunt volucres cæli, et comederunt ea.

13:5 Alia autem ceciderunt in petrosa, ubi non habebant terram multam : et continuo exorta sunt, quia non habebant altitudinem terræ :

13:6 sole autem orto æstuaverunt ; et quia non habebant radicem, aruerunt.

13:7 Alia autem ceciderunt in spinas : et creverunt spinæ, et suffocaverunt ea.

13:8 Alia autem ceciderunt in terram bonam : et dabant fructum, aliud centesimum, aliud sexagesimum, aliud trigesimum.

13:9 Qui habet aures audiendi, audiat.

it: because she came from the ends of the earth to hear the wisdom of Solomon, and behold a greater than Solomon here.

12:43 And when an unclean spirit is gone out of a man he walketh through dry places seeking rest, and findeth none.

12:44 Then he saith: I will return into my house from whence I came out. And coming he findeth it empty, swept, and garnished.

12:45 Then he goeth, and taketh with him seven other spirits more wicked than himself, and they enter in and dwell there: and the last state of that man in made worse than the first. So shall it be also to this wicked generation.

12:46 As he was yet speaking to the multitudes, behold his mother and his brethren stood without, seeking to speak to him.

12:47 And one said unto him: Behold thy mother and thy brethren stand without, seeking thee.

12:48 But he answering him that told him, said: Who is my mother, and who are my brethren?

12:49 And stretching forth his hand towards his disciples, he said: Behold my mother and my brethren.

12:50 For whosoever shall do the will of my Father, that is in heaven, he is my brother, and sister, and mother.

13:1 The same day Jesus going out of the house, sat by the sea side.

13:2 And great multitudes were gathered together unto him, so that he went up into a boat and sat: and all the multitude stood on the shore.

13:3 And he spoke to them many things in parables, saying: Behold the sower went forth to sow.

13:4 And whilst he soweth some fell by the way side, and the birds of the air came and ate them up.

13:5 And other some fell upon stony ground, where they had not much earth: and they sprung up immediately, because they had no deepness of earth.

13:6 And when the sun was up they were scorched: and because they had not root, they withered away.

13:7 And others fell among thorns: and the thorns grew up and choked them.

13:8 And others fell upon good ground: and they brought forth fruit, some an hundredfold, some sixtyfold, and some thirtyfold.

13:9 He that hath ears to hear, let him hear.

13:10 Et accedentes discipuli dixerunt ei : Quare in parabolis loqueris eis ?

13:11 Qui respondens, ait illis : Quia vobis datum est nosse mysteria regni cælorum : illis autem non est datum.

13:12 Qui enim habet, dabitur ei, et abundabit : qui autem non habet, et quod habet auferetur ab eo.

13:13 Ideo in parabolis loquor eis : quia videntes non vident, et audientes non audiunt, neque intelligunt.

13:14 Et adimpletur in eis prophetia Isaiæ, dicentis : *Auditu audietis, et non intelligetis : et videntes videbitis, et non videbitis.*

13:15 *Incrassatum est enim cor populi hujus, et auribus graviter audierunt, et oculos suos clauserunt : nequando videant oculis, et auribus audiant, et corde intelligant, et convertantur, et sanem eos.*

13:16 Vestri autem beati oculi quia vident, et aures vestræ quia audiunt.

13:17 Amen quippe dico vobis, quia multi prophetæ et justi cupierunt videre quæ videtis, et non viderunt : et audire quæ auditis, et non audierunt.

13:18 Vos ergo audite parabolam seminantis.

13:19 Omnis qui audit verbum regni, et non intelligit, venit malus, et rapit quod seminatum est in corde ejus : hic est qui secus viam seminatus est.

13:20 Qui autem super petrosa seminatus est, hic est qui verbum audit, et continuo cum gaudio accipit illud :

13:21 non habet autem in se radicem, sed est temporalis : facta autem tribulatione et persecutione propter verbum, continuo scandalizatur.

13:22 Qui autem seminatus est in spinis, hic est qui verbum audit, et sollicitudo sæculi istius, et fallacia divitiarum suffocat verbum, et sine fructu efficitur.

13:23 Qui vero in terram bonam seminatus est, hic est qui audit verbum, et intelligit, et fructum affert, et facit aliud quidem centesimum, aliud autem sexagesimum, aliud vero trigesimum.

13:24 Aliam parabolam proposuit illis, dicens :

13:10 And his disciples came and said to him: Why speakest thou to them in parables?

13:11 Who answered and said to them: Because to you it is given to know the mysteries of the kingdom of heaven: but to them it is not given.

13:12 For he that hath, to him shall be given, and he shall abound: but he that hath not, from him shall be taken away that also which he hath.

13:13 Therefore do I speak to them in parables: because seeing they see not, and hearing they hear not, neither do they understand.

13:14 And the prophecy of Isaias is fulfilled in them, who saith: *By hearing you shall hear, and shall not understand: and seeing you shall see, and shall not perceive.*

13:15 *For the heart of this people is grown gross, and with their ears they have been dull of hearing, and their eyes they have shut: lest at any time they should see with their eyes, and hear with their ears, and understand with their heart, and be converted, and I should heal them.*

13:16 But blessed are your eyes, because they see, and your ears, because they hear.

13:17 For, amen, I say to you, many prophets and just men have desired to see the things that you see, and have not seen them, and to hear the things that you hear and have not heard them.

13:18 Hear you therefore the parable of the sower.

13:19 When any one heareth the word of the kingdom, and understandeth it not, there cometh the wicked one, and catcheth away that which was sown in his heart: this is he that received the seed by the way side.

13:20 And he that received the seed upon stony ground, is he that heareth the word, and immediately receiveth it with joy.

13:21 Yet hath he not root in himself, but is only for a time: and when there ariseth tribulation and persecution because of the word, he is presently scandalized.

13:22 And he that received the seed among thorns, is he that heareth the word, and the care of this world and the deceitfulness of riches choketh up the word, and he becometh fruitless.

13:23 But he that received the seed upon good ground, is he that heareth the word, and understandeth, and beareth fruit, and yieldeth the one an hundredfold, and another sixty, and another thirty.

13:24 Another parable he proposed to them, say-

Simile factum est regnum cælorum homini, qui seminavit bonum semen in agro suo :

13:25 cum autem dormirent homines, venit inimicus ejus, et superseminavit zizania in medio tritici, et abiit.

13:26 Cum autem crevisset herba, et fructum fecisset, tunc apparuerunt et zizania.

13:27 Accedentes autem servi patrisfamilias, dixerunt ei : Domine, nonne bonum semen seminasti in agro tuo ? unde ergo habet zizania ?

13:28 Et ait illis : Inimicus homo hoc fecit. Servi autem dixerunt ei : Vis, imus, et colligimus ea ?

13:29 Et ait : Non : ne forte colligentes zizania, eradicetis simul cum eis et triticum.

13:30 Sinite utraque crescere usque ad messem, et in tempore messis dicam messoribus : Colligite primum zizania, et alligate ea in fasciculos ad comburendum : triticum autem congregate in horreum meum.

13:31 Aliam parabolam proposuit eis dicens : Simile est regnum cælorum grano sinapis, quod accipiens homo seminavit in agro suo :

13:32 quod minimum quidem est omnibus seminibus : cum autem creverit, majus est omnibus oleribus, et fit arbor, ita ut volucres cæli veniant, et habitent in ramis ejus.

13:33 Aliam parabolam locutus est eis : Simile est regnum cælorum fermento, quod acceptum mulier abscondit in farinæ satis tribus, donec fermentatum est totum.

13:34 Hæc omnia locutus est Jesus in parabolis ad turbas : et sine parabolis non loquebatur eis :

13:35 ut impleretur quod dictum erat per prophetam dicentem : Aperiam in parabolis os meum ; eructabo abscondita a constitutione mundi.

13:36 Tunc, dimissis turbis, venit in domum : et accesserunt ad eum discipuli ejus, dicentes : Edissere nobis parabolam zizaniorum agri.

13:37 Qui respondens ait illis : Qui seminat bonum semen, est Filius hominis.

13:38 Ager autem est mundus. Bonum vero semen, hi sunt filii regni. Zizania autem, filii sunt nequam.

13:39 Inimicus autem, qui seminavit ea, est di-

ing: The kingdom of heaven is likened to a man that sowed good seed in his field.

13:25 But while men were asleep, his enemy came and oversowed cockle among the wheat and went his way.

13:26 And when the blade was sprung up, and had brought forth fruit, then appeared also the cockle.

13:27 And the servants of the goodman of the house coming said to him: Sir, didst thou not sow good seed in thy field? whence then hath it cockle?

13:28 And he said to them: An enemy hath done this. And the servants said to him: Wilt thou that we go and gather it up?

13:29 And he said: No, lest perhaps gathering up the cockle, you root up the wheat also together with it.

13:30 Suffer both to grow until the harvest, and in the time of the harvest I will say to the reapers: Gather up first the cockle, and bind it into bundles to burn, but the wheat gather ye into my barn.

13:31 Another parable he proposed unto them, saying: The kingdom of heaven is like to a grain of mustard seed, which a man took and sowed in his field.

13:32 Which is the least indeed of all seeds; but when it is grown up, it is greater than all herbs, and becometh a tree, so that the birds of the air come, and dwell in the branches thereof.

13:33 Another parable he spoke to them: The kingdom of heaven is like to leaven, which a woman took and hid in three measures of meal, until the whole was leavened.

13:34 All these things Jesus spoke in parables to the multitudes: and without parables he did not speak to them.

13:35 That it might be fulfilled which was spoken by the prophet, saying: I will open my mouth in parables, I will utter things hidden from the foundation of the world.

13:36 Then having sent away the multitudes, he came into the house, and his disciples came to him, saying: Expound to us the parable of the cockle of the field.

13:37 Who made answer and said to them: He that soweth the good seed, is the Son of man.

13:38 And the field, is the world. And the good seed are the children of the kingdom. And the cockle, are the children of the wicked one.

13:39 And the enemy that sowed them, is the

abolus. Messis vero, consummatio sæculi est. Messores autem, angeli sunt.

¹³:⁴⁰ Sicut ergo colliguntur zizania, et igni comburuntur : sic erit in consummatione sæculi.

¹³:⁴¹ Mittet Filius hominis angelos suos, et colligent de regno ejus omnia scandala, et eos qui faciunt iniquitatem :
¹³:⁴² et mittent eos in caminum ignis. Ibi erit fletus et stridor dentium.

¹³:⁴³ Tunc justi fulgebunt sicut sol in regno Patris eorum. Qui habet aures audiendi, audiat.

¹³:⁴⁴ Simile est regnum cælorum thesauro abscondito in agro : quem qui invenit homo, abscondit, et præ gaudio illius vadit, et vendit universa quæ habet, et emit agrum illum.
¹³:⁴⁵ Iterum simile est regnum cælorum homini negotiatori, quærenti bonas margaritas.
¹³:⁴⁶ Inventa autem una pretiosa margarita, abiit, et vendidit omnia quæ habuit, et emit eam.
¹³:⁴⁷ Iterum simile est regnum cælorum sagenæ missæ in mare, et ex omni genere piscium congreganti.
¹³:⁴⁸ Quam, cum impleta esset, educentes, et secus littus sedentes, elegerunt bonos in vasa, malos autem foras miserunt.
¹³:⁴⁹ Sic erit in consummatione sæculi : exibunt angeli, et separabunt malos de medio justorum,
¹³:⁵⁰ et mittent eos in caminum ignis : ibi erit fletus, et stridor dentium.

¹³:⁵¹ Intellexistis hæc omnia ? Dicunt ei : Etiam.

¹³:⁵² Ait illis : Ideo omnis scriba doctus in regno cælorum, similis est homini patrifamilias, qui profert de thesauro suo nova et vetera.

¹³:⁵³ Et factum est, cum consummasset Jesus parabolas istas, transiit inde.
¹³:⁵⁴ Et veniens in patriam suam, docebat eos in synagogis eorum, ita ut mirarentur, et dicerent : Unde huic sapientia hæc, et virtutes ?

¹³:⁵⁵ Nonne hic est fabri filius ? nonne mater ejus dicitur Maria, et fratres ejus, Jacobus, et Joseph, et Simon, et Judas ?
¹³:⁵⁶ et sorores ejus, nonne omnes apud nos sunt ? unde ergo huic omnia ista ?

devil. But the harvest is the end of the world. And the reapers are the angels.

¹³:⁴⁰ Even as cockle therefore is gathered up, and burnt with fire: so shall it be at the end of the world.

¹³:⁴¹ The Son of man shall send his angels, and they shall gather out of his kingdom all scandals, and them that work iniquity.
¹³:⁴² And shall cast them into the furnace of fire: there shall be weeping and gnashing of teeth.

¹³:⁴³ Then shall the just shine as the sun, in the kingdom of their Father. He that hath ears to hear, let him hear.

¹³:⁴⁴ The kingdom of heaven is like unto a treasure hidden in a field. Which a man having found, hid it, and for joy thereof goeth, and selleth all that he hath, and buyeth that field.
¹³:⁴⁵ Again the kingdom of heaven is like to a merchant seeking good pearls.
¹³:⁴⁶ Who when he had found one pearl of great price, went his way, and sold all that he had, and bought it.
¹³:⁴⁷ Again the kingdom of heaven is like to a net cast into the sea, and gathering together of all kind of fishes.
¹³:⁴⁸ Which, when it was filled, they drew out, and sitting by the shore, they chose out the good into vessels, but the bad they cast forth.
¹³:⁴⁹ So shall it be at the end of the world. The angels shall go out, and shall separate the wicked from among the just.
¹³:⁵⁰ And shall cast them into the furnace of fire: there shall be weeping and gnashing of teeth.

¹³:⁵¹ Have ye understood all these things? They say to him: Yes.

¹³:⁵² He said unto them: Therefore every scribe instructed in the kingdom of heaven, is like to a man that is a householder, who bringeth forth out of his treasure new things and old.

¹³:⁵³ And it came to pass: when Jesus had finished these parables, he passed from thence.
¹³:⁵⁴ And coming into his own country, he taught them in their synagogues, so that they wondered and said: How came this man by this wisdom and miracles?

¹³:⁵⁵ Is not this the carpenter's son? Is not his mother called Mary, and his brethren James, and Joseph, and Simon, and Jude:
¹³:⁵⁶ And his sisters, are they not all with us? Whence therefore hath he all these things?

13:57 Et scandalizabantur in eo. Jesus autem dixit eis : Non est propheta sine honore, nisi in patria sua, et in domo sua.

13:58 Et non fecit ibi virtutes multas propter incredulitatem illorum.

14:1 In illo tempore audivit Herodes tetrarcha famam Jesu :

14:2 et ait pueris suis : Hic est Joannes Baptista : ipse surrexit a mortuis, et ideo virtutes operantur in eo.

14:3 Herodes enim tenuit Joannem, et alligavit eum : et posuit in carcerem propter Herodiadem uxorem fratris sui.

14:4 Dicebat enim illi Joannes : Non licet tibi habere eam.

14:5 Et volens illum occidere, timuit populum : quia sicut prophetam eum habebant.

14:6 Die autem natalis Herodis saltavit filia Herodiadis in medio, et placuit Herodi :

14:7 unde cum juramento pollicitus est ei dare quodcumque postulasset ab eo.

14:8 At illa præmonita a matre sua : Da mihi, inquit, hic in disco caput Joannis Baptistæ.

14:9 Et contristatus est rex : propter juramentum autem, et eos qui pariter recumbebant, jussit dari.

14:10 Misitque et decollavit Joannem in carcere.

14:11 Et allatum est caput ejus in disco, et datum est puellæ, et attulit matri suæ.

14:12 Et accedentes discipuli ejus, tulerunt corpus ejus, et sepelierunt illud : et venientes nuntiaverunt Jesu.

14:13 Quod cum audisset Jesus, secessit inde in navicula, in locum desertum seorsum : et cum audissent turbæ, secutæ sunt eum pedestres de civitatibus.

14:14 Et exiens vidit turbam multam, et misertus est eis, et curavit languidos eorum.

14:15 Vespere autem facto, accesserunt ad eum discipuli ejus, dicentes : Desertus est locus, et hora jam præteriit : dimitte turbas, ut euntes in castella, emant sibi escas.

14:16 Jesus autem dixit eis : Non habent necesse

13:57 And they were scandalized in his regard. But Jesus said to them: A prophet is not without honour, save in his own country, and in his own house.

13:58 And he wrought not many miracles there, because of their unbelief.

14:1 At that time Herod the Tetrarch heard the fame of Jesus.

14:2 And he said to his servants: This is John the Baptist: he is risen from the dead, and therefore mighty works shew forth themselves in him.

14:3 For Herod had apprehended John and bound him, and put him into prison, because of Herodias, his brother's wife.

14:4 For John said to him: It is not lawful for thee to have her.

14:5 And having a mind to put him to death, he feared the people: because they esteemed him as a prophet.

14:6 But on Herod's birthday, the daughter of Herodias danced before them: and pleased Herod.

14:7 Whereupon he promised with an oath, to give her whatsoever she would ask of him.

14:8 But she being instructed before by her mother, said: Give me here in a dish the head of John the Baptist.

14:9 And the king was struck sad: yet because of his oath, and for them that sat with him at table, he commanded it to be given.

14:10 And he sent, and beheaded John in the prison.

14:11 And his head was brought in a dish: and it was given to the damsel, and she brought it to her mother.

14:12 And his disciples came and took the body, and buried it, and came and told Jesus.

14:13 Which when Jesus had heard, he retired from thence by boat, into a desert place apart, and the multitudes having heard of it, followed him on foot out of the cities.

14:14 And he coming forth saw a great multitude, and had compassion on them, and healed their sick.

14:15 And when it was evening, his disciples came to him, saying: This is a desert place, and the hour is now past: send away the multitudes, that going into the towns, they may buy themselves victuals.

14:16 But Jesus said to them, They have no need

ire : date illis vos manducare.

14:17 Responderunt ei : Non habemus hic nisi quinque panes et duos pisces.

14:18 Qui ait eis : Afferte mihi illos huc.

14:19 Et cum jussisset turbam discumbere super fœnum, acceptis quinque panibus et duobus piscibus, aspiciens in cælum benedixit, et fregit, et dedit discipulis panes, discipuli autem turbis.

14:20 Et manducaverunt omnes, et saturati sunt. Et tulerunt reliquias, duodecim cophinos fragmentorum plenos.

14:21 Manducantium autem fuit numerus quinque millia virorum, exceptis mulieribus et parvulis.

14:22 Et statim compulit Jesus discipulos ascendere in naviculam, et præcedere eum trans fretum, donec dimitteret turbas.

14:23 Et dimissa turba, ascendit in montem solus orare. Vespere autem facto solus erat ibi :

14:24 navicula autem in medio mari jactabatur fluctibus : erat enim contrarius ventus.

14:25 Quarta enim vigilia noctis, venit ad eos ambulans super mare.

14:26 Et videntes eum super mare ambulantem, turbati sunt, dicentes : Quia phantasma est. Et præ timore clamaverunt.

14:27 Statimque Jesus locutus est eis, dicens : Habete fiduciam : ego sum, nolite timere.

14:28 Respondens autem Petrus, dixit : Domine, si tu es, jube me ad te venire super aquas.

14:29 At ipse ait : Veni. Et descendens Petrus de navicula, ambulabat super aquam ut veniret ad Jesum.

14:30 Videns vero ventum validum, timuit : et cum cœpisset mergi, clamavit dicens : Domine, salvum me fac.

14:31 Et continuo Jesus extendens manum, apprehendit eum : et ait illi : Modicæ fidei, quare dubitasti ?

14:32 Et cum ascendissent in naviculam, cessavit ventus.

14:33 Qui autem in navicula erant, venerunt, et adoraverunt eum, dicentes : Vere Filius Dei es.

14:34 Et cum transfretassent, venerunt in terram Genesar.

14:35 Et cum cognovissent eum viri loci illius, miserunt in universam regionem illam, et ob-

to go: give you them to eat.

14:17 They answered him: We have not here, but five loaves, and two fishes.

14:18 He said to them: Bring them hither to me.

14:19 And when he had commanded the multitudes to sit down upon the grass, he took the five loaves and the two fishes, and looking up to heaven, he blessed, and brake, and gave the loaves to his disciples, and the disciples to the multitudes.

14:20 And they did all eat, and were filled. And they took up what remained, twelve full baskets of fragments.

14:21 And the number of them that did eat, was five thousand men, besides women and children.

14:22 And forthwith Jesus obliged his disciples to go up into the boat, and to go before him over the water, till he dismissed the people.

14:23 And having dismissed the multitude, he went into a mountain alone to pray. And when it was evening, he was there alone.

14:24 But the boat in the midst of the sea was tossed with the waves: for the wind was contrary.

14:25 And in the fourth watch of the night, he came to them walking upon the sea.

14:26 And they seeing him walking upon the sea, were troubled, saying: It is an apparition. And they cried out for fear.

14:27 And immediately Jesus spoke to them, saying: Be of good heart: it is I, fear ye not.

14:28 And Peter making answer, said: Lord, if it be thou, bid me come to thee upon the waters.

14:29 And he said: Come. And Peter going down out of the boat, walked upon the water to come to Jesus.

14:30 But seeing the wind strong, he was afraid: and when he began to sink, he cried out, saying: Lord, save me.

14:31 And immediately Jesus stretching forth his hand took hold of him, and said to him: O thou of little faith, why didst thou doubt?

14:32 And when they were come up into the boat, the wind ceased.

14:33 And they that were in the boat came and adored him, saying: Indeed thou art the Son of God.

14:34 And having passed the water, they came into the country of Genesar.

14:35 And when the men of that place had knowledge of him, they sent into all that coun-

tulerunt ei omnes male habentes :

14:36 et rogabant eum ut vel fimbriam vestimenti ejus tangerent. Et quicumque tetigerunt, salvi facti sunt.

15:1 Tunc accesserunt ad eum ab Jerosolymis scribæ et pharisæi, dicentes :

15:2 Quare discipuli tui transgrediuntur traditionem seniorum ? non enim lavant manus suas cum panem manducant.

15:3 Ipse autem respondens ait illis : Quare et vos transgredimini mandatum Dei propter traditionem vestram ? Nam Deus dixit :

15:4 Honora patrem, et matrem : et, Qui maledixerit patri, vel matri, morte moriatur.

15:5 Vos autem dicitis : Quicumque dixerit patri, vel matri : Munus, quodcumque est ex me, tibi proderit :

15:6 et non honorificabit patrem suum, aut matrem suam : et irritum fecistis mandatum Dei propter traditionem vestram.

15:7 Hypocritæ, bene prophetavit de vobis Isaias, dicens :

15:8 *Populus hic labiis me honorat : cor autem eorum longe est a me.*

15:9 *Sine causa autem colunt me, docentes doctrinas et mandata hominum.*

15:10 Et convocatis ad se turbis, dixit eis : Audite, et intelligite.

15:11 Non quod intrat in os, coinquinat hominem : sed quod procedit ex ore, hoc coinquinat hominem.

15:12 Tunc accedentes discipuli ejus, dixerunt ei : Scis quia pharisæi audito verbo hoc, scandalizati sunt ?

15:13 At ille respondens ait : Omnis plantatio, quam non plantavit Pater meus cælestis, eradicabitur.

15:14 Sinite illos : cæci sunt, et duces cæcorum ; cæcus autem si cæco ducatum præstet, ambo in foveam cadunt.

15:15 Respondens autem Petrus dixit ei : Edissere nobis parabolam istam.

15:16 At ille dixit : Adhuc et vos sine intellectu estis ?

15:17 Non intelligitis quia omne quod in os intrat, in ventrem vadit, et in secessum emittitur ?

15:18 Quæ autem procedunt de ore, de corde exeunt, et ea coinquinant hominem :

try, and brought to him all that were diseased.

14:36 And they besought him that they might touch but the hem of his garment. And as many as touched, were made whole.

15:1 Then came to him from Jerusalem scribes and Pharisees, saying:

15:2 Why do thy disciples trangress the tradition of the ancients? For they wash not their hands when they eat bread.

15:3 But he answering, said to them: Why do you also transgress the commandment of God for your tradition? For God said:

15:4 Honour thy father and mother: And: He that shall curse father or mother, let him die the death.

15:5 But you say: Whosoever shall say to father or mother, The gift whatsoever proceedeth from me, shall profit thee.

15:6 And he shall not honour his father or his mother: and you have made void the commandment of God for your tradition.

15:7 Hypocrites, well hath Isaias prophesied of you, saying:

15:8 *This people honoureth me with their lips: but their heart is far from me.*

15:9 *And in vain do they worship me, teaching doctrines and commandments of men.*

15:10 And having called together the multitudes unto him, he said to them: Hear ye and understand.

15:11 Not that which goeth into the mouth defileth a man: but what cometh out of the mouth, this defileth a man.

15:12 Then came his disciples, and said to him: Dost thou know that the Pharisees, when they heard this word, were scandalized?

15:13 But he answering, said: Every plant which my heavenly Father hath not planted, shall be rooted up.

15:14 Let them alone: they are blind, and leaders of the blind. And if the blind lead the blind, both will fall into the pit.

15:15 And Peter answering, said to him: Expound to us this parable.

15:16 But he said: Are you also yet without understanding?

15:17 Do you not understand, that whatsoever entereth into the mouth, goeth into the belly, and is cast out into the privy?

15:18 But the things which proceed out of the mouth, come forth from the heart, and those things defile a man.

15:19 de corde enim exeunt cogitationes malæ, homicidia, adulteria, fornicationes, furta, falsa testimonia, blasphemiæ :

15:20 hæc sunt, quæ coinquinant hominem. Non lotis autem manibus manducare, non coinquinat hominem.

15:21 Et egressus inde Jesus secessit in partes Tyri et Sidonis.

15:22 Et ecce mulier chananæa a finibus illis egressa clamavit, dicens ei : Miserere mei, Domine fili David : filia mea male a dæmonio vexatur.

15:23 Qui non respondit ei verbum. Et accedentes discipuli ejus rogabant eum dicentes : Dimitte eam : quia clamat post nos.

15:24 Ipse autem respondens ait : Non sum missus nisi ad oves, quæ perierunt domus Israël.

15:25 At illa venit, et adoravit eum, dicens : Domine, adjuva me.

15:26 Qui respondens ait : Non est bonum sumere panem filiorum, et mittere canibus.

15:27 At illa dixit : Etiam Domine : nam et catelli edunt de micis quæ cadunt de mensa dominorum suorum.

15:28 Tunc respondens Jesus, ait illi : O mulier, magna est fides tua : fiat tibi sicut vis. Et sanata est filia ejus ex illa hora.

15:29 Et cum transisset inde Jesus, venit secus mare Galilææ : et ascendens in montem, sedebat ibi.

15:30 Et accesserunt ad eum turbæ multæ, habentes secum mutos, cæcos, claudos, debiles, et alios multos : et projecerunt eos ad pedes ejus, et curavit eos,

15:31 ita ut turbæ mirarentur, videntes mutos loquentes, claudos ambulantes, cæcos videntes : et magnificabant Deum Israël.

15:32 Jesus autem, convocatis discipulis suis, dixit : Misereor turbæ, quia triduo jam perseverant mecum, et non habent quod manducent : et dimittere eos jejunos nolo, ne deficiant in via.

15:33 Et dicunt ei discipuli : Unde ergo nobis in deserto panes tantos, ut saturemus turbam tantam ?

15:34 Et ait illis Jesus : Quot habetis panes ? At illi dixerunt : Septem, et paucos pisciculos.

15:19 For from the heart come forth evil thoughts, murders, adulteries, fornications, thefts, false testimonies, blasphemies.

15:20 These are the things that defile a man. But to eat with unwashed hands doth not defile a man.

15:21 And Jesus went from thence, and retired into the coasts of Tyre and Sidon.

15:22 And behold a woman of Canaan who came out of those coasts, crying out, said to him: Have mercy on me, O Lord, thou son of David: my daughter is grievously troubled by a devil.

15:23 Who answered her not a word. And his disciples came and besought him, saying: Send her away, for she crieth after us:

15:24 And he answering, said: I was not sent but to the sheep that are lost of the house of Israel.

15:25 But she came and adored him, saying: Lord, help me.

15:26 Who answering, said: It is not good to take the bread of the children, and to cast it to the dogs.

15:27 But she said: Yea, Lord; for the whelps also eat of the crumbs that fall from the table of their masters.

15:28 Then Jesus answering, said to her: O woman, great is thy faith: be it done to thee as thou wilt: and her daughter was cured from that hour.

15:29 And when Jesus had passed away from thence, he came nigh the sea of Galilee. And going up into a mountain, he sat there.

15:30 And there came to him great multitudes, having with them the dumb, the blind, the lame, the maimed, and many others: and they cast them down at his feet, and he healed them:

15:31 So that the multitudes marvelled seeing the dumb speak, the lame walk, and the blind see: and they glorified the God of Israel.

15:32 And Jesus called together his disciples, and said: I have compassion on the multitudes, because they continue with me now three days, and have not what to eat, and I will not send them away fasting, lest they faint in the way.

15:33 And the disciples say unto him: Whence then should we have so many loaves in the desert, as to fill so great a multitude?

15:34 And Jesus said to them: How many loaves have you? But they said: Seven, and a few little fishes.

15:35 Et præcepit turbæ ut discumberent super terram.

15:36 Et accipiens septem panes, et pisces, et gratias agens, fregit, et dedit discipulis suis, et discipuli dederunt populo.

15:37 Et comederunt omnes, et saturati sunt. Et quod superfuit de fragmentis, tulerunt septem sportas plenas.

15:38 Erant autem qui manducaverunt quatuor millia hominum, extra parvulos et mulieres.

15:39 Et, dimissa turba, ascendit in naviculam : et venit in fines Magedan.

16:1 Et accesserunt ad eum pharisæi et sadducæi tentantes : et rogaverunt eum ut signum de cælo ostenderet eis.

16:2 At ille respondens, ait illis : Facto vespere dicitis : Serenum erit, rubicundum est enim cælum.

16:3 Et mane : Hodie tempestas, rutilat enim triste cælum.

16:4 Faciem ergo cæli dijudicare nostis : signa autem temporum non potestis scire ? Generatio mala et adultera signum quærit : et signum non dabitur ei, nisi signum Jonæ prophetæ. Et relictis illis, abiit.

16:5 Et cum venissent discipuli ejus trans fretum, obliti sunt panes accipere.

16:6 Qui dixit illis : Intuemini, et cavete a fermento pharisæorum et sadducæorum.

16:7 At illi cogitabant intra se dicentes : Quia panes non accepimus.

16:8 Sciens autem Jesus, dixit : Quid cogitatis intra vos modicæ fidei, quia panes non habetis ?

16:9 Nondum intelligitis, neque recordamini quinque panum in quinque millia hominum, et quot cophinos sumpsistis ?

16:10 neque septem panum in quatuor millia hominum, et quot sportas sumpsistis ?

16:11 Quare non intelligitis, quia non de pane dixi vobis : Cavete a fermento pharisæorum et sadducæorum ?

16:12 Tunc intellexerunt quia non dixerit cavendum a fermento panum, sed a doctrina pharisæorum et sadducæorum.

16:13 Venit autem Jesus in partes Cæsareæ Philippi : et interrogabat discipulos suos, dicens : Quem dicunt homines esse Filium hominis ?

15:35 And he commanded the multitude to sit down upon the ground.

15:36 And taking the seven loaves and the fishes, and giving thanks, he brake, and gave to his disciples, and the disciples gave to the people.

15:37 And they did all eat, and had their fill. And they took up seven baskets full, of what remained of the fragments.

15:38 And they that did eat, were four thousand men, beside children and women.

15:39 And having dismissed the multitude, he went up into a boat, and came into the coasts of Magedan.

16:1 And there came to him the Pharisees and Sadduccees tempting: and they asked him to shew them a sign from heaven.

16:2 But he answered and said to them: When it is evening, you say, It will be fair weather, for the sky is red.

16:3 And in the morning: To day there will be a storm, for the sky is red and lowering. You know then how to discern the face of the sky: and can you not know the signs of the times?

16:4 A wicked and adulterous generation seeketh after a sign: and a sign shall not be given it, but the sign of Jonas the prophet. And he left them, and went away.

16:5 And when his disciples were come over the water, they had forgotten to take bread.

16:6 Who said to them: Take heed and beware of the leaven of the Pharisees and Sadducees.

16:7 But they thought within themselves, saying: Because we have taken no bread.

16:8 And Jesus knowing it, said: Why do you think within yourselves, O ye of little faith, for that you have no bread?

16:9 Do you not yet understand, neither do you remember the five loaves among five thousand men, and how many baskets you took up?

16:10 Nor the seven loaves among four thousand men, and how many baskets you took up?

16:11 Why do you not understand that it was not concerning bread I said to you: Beware of the leaven of the Pharisees and Sadducees?

16:12 Then they understood that he said not that they should beware of the leaven of bread, but of the doctrine of the Pharisees and Sadducees.

16:13 And Jesus came into the quarters of Cesarea Philippi: and he asked his disciples, saying: Whom do men say that the Son of man is?

16:14 At illi dixerunt : Alii Joannem Baptistam, alii autem Eliam, alii vero Jeremiam, aut unum ex prophetis.

16:15 Dicit illis Jesus : Vos autem, quem me esse dicitis ?

16:16 Respondens Simon Petrus dixit : Tu es Christus, Filius Dei vivi.

16:17 Respondens autem Jesus, dixit ei : Beatus es Simon Bar Jona : quia caro et sanguis non revelavit tibi, sed Pater meus, qui in cælis est.

16:18 Et ego dico tibi, quia tu es Petrus, et super hanc petram ædificabo Ecclesiam meam, et portæ inferi non prævalebunt adversus eam.

16:19 Et tibi dabo claves regni cælorum. Et quodcumque ligaveris super terram, erit ligatum et in cælis : et quodcumque solveris super terram, erit solutum et in cælis.

16:20 Tunc præcepit discipulis suis ut nemini dicerent quia ipse esset Jesus Christus.

16:21 Exinde cœpit Jesus ostendere discipulis suis, quia oporteret eum ire Jerosolymam, et multa pati a senioribus, et scribis, et principibus sacerdotum, et occidi, et tertia die resurgere.

16:22 Et assumens eum Petrus, cœpit increpare illum dicens : Absit a te, Domine : non erit tibi hoc.

16:23 Qui conversus, dixit Petro : Vade post me Satana, scandalum es mihi : quia non sapis ea quæ Dei sunt, sed ea quæ hominum.

16:24 Tunc Jesus dixit discipulis suis : Si quis vult post me venire, abneget semetipsum, et tollat crucem suam, et sequatur me.

16:25 Qui enim voluerit animam suam salvam facere, perdet eam : qui autem perdiderit animam suam propter me, inveniet eam.

16:26 Quid enim prodest homini, si mundum universum lucretur, animæ vero suæ detrimentum patiatur ? aut quam dabit homo commutationem pro anima sua ?

16:27 Filius enim hominis venturus est in gloria Patris sui cum angelis suis : et tunc reddet unicuique secundum opera ejus.

16:28 Amen dico vobis, sunt quidam de hic stantibus, qui non gustabunt mortem, donec videant Filium hominis venientem in regno suo.

16:14 But they said: Some John the Baptist, and other some Elias, and others Jeremias, or one of the prophets.

16:15 Jesus saith to them: But whom do you say that I am?

16:16 Simon Peter answered and said: Thou art Christ, the Son of the living God.

16:17 And Jesus answering, said to him: Blessed art thou, Simon Bar-Jona: because flesh and blood hath not revealed it to thee, but my Father who is in heaven.

16:18 And I say to thee: That thou art Peter; and upon this rock I will build my church, and the gates of hell shall not prevail against it.

16:19 And I will give to thee the keys of the kingdom of heaven. And whatsoever thou shalt bind upon earth, it shall be bound also in heaven: and whatsoever thou shalt loose on earth, it shall be loosed also in heaven.

16:20 Then he commanded his disciples, that they should tell no one that he was Jesus the Christ.

16:21 From that time Jesus began to shew to his disciples, that he must go to Jerusalem, and suffer many things from the ancients and scribes and chief priests, and be put to death, and the third day rise again.

16:22 And Peter taking him, began to rebuke him, saying: Lord, be it far from thee, this shall not be unto thee.

16:23 Who turning, said to Peter: Go behind me, Satan, thou art a scandal unto me: because thou savourest not the things that are of God, but the things that are of men.

16:24 Then Jesus said to his disciples: If any man will come after me, let him deny himself, and take up his cross, and follow me.

16:25 For he that will save his life, shall lose it: and he that shall lose his life for my sake, shall find it.

16:26 For what doth it profit a man, if he gain the whole world, and suffer the loss of his own soul? Or what exchange shall a man give for his soul?

16:27 For the Son of man shall come in the glory of his Father with his angels: and then will he render to every man according to his works.

16:28 Amen I say to you, there are some of them that stand here, that shall not taste death, till they see the Son of man coming in his kingdom.

17:1 Et post dies sex assumit Jesus Petrum, et Jacobum, et Joannem fratrem ejus, et ducit illos in montem excelsum seorsum :

17:2 et transfiguratus est ante eos. Et resplenduit facies ejus sicut sol : vestimenta autem ejus facta sunt alba sicut nix.

17:3 Et ecce apparuerunt illis Moyses et Elias cum eo loquentes.

17:4 Respondens autem Petrus, dixit ad Jesum : Domine, bonum est nos hic esse : si vis, faciamus tria tabernacula, tibi unum, Moysi unum, et Eliæ unum.

17:5 Adhuc eo loquente, ecce nubes lucida obumbravit eos. Et ecce vox de nube, dicens : Hic est Filius meus dilectus, in quo mihi bene complacui : ipsum audite.

17:6 Et audientes discipuli ceciderunt in faciem suam, et timuerunt valde.

17:7 Et accessit Jesus, et tetigit eos : dixitque eis : Surgite, et nolite timere.

17:8 Levantes autem oculos suos, neminem viderunt, nisi solum Jesum.

17:9 Et descendentibus illis de monte, præcepit eis Jesus, dicens : Nemini dixeritis visionem, donec Filius hominis a mortuis resurgat.

17:10 Et interrogaverunt eum discipuli, dicentes : Quid ergo scribæ dicunt, quod Eliam oporteat primum venire ?

17:11 At ille respondens, ait eis : Elias quidem venturus est, et restituet omnia.

17:12 Dico autem vobis, quia Elias jam venit, et non cognoverunt eum, sed fecerunt in eo quæcumque voluerunt. Sic et Filius hominis passurus est ab eis.

17:13 Tunc intellexerunt discipuli, quia de Joanne Baptista dixisset eis.

17:14 Et cum venisset ad turbam, accessit ad eum homo genibus provolutus ante eum, dicens : Domine, miserere filio meo, quia lunaticus est, et male patitur : nam sæpe cadit in ignem, et crebro in aquam.

17:15 Et obtuli eum discipulis tuis, et non potuerunt curare eum.

17:16 Respondens autem Jesus, ait : O generatio incredula, et perversa, quousque ero vobiscum ? usquequo patiar vos ? Afferte huc illum ad me.

17:17 Et increpavit illum Jesus, et exiit ab eo dæmonium, et curatus est puer ex illa hora.

17:1 And after six days Jesus taketh unto him Peter and James, and John his brother, and bringeth them up into a high mountain apart:

17:2 And he was transfigured before them. And his face did shine as the sun: and his garments became white as snow.

17:3 And behold there appeared to them Moses and Elias talking with him.

17:4 And Peter answering, said to Jesus: Lord, it is good for us to be here: if thou wilt, let us make here three tabernacles, one for thee, and one for Moses, and one for Elias.

17:5 And as he was yet speaking, behold a bright cloud overshadowed them. And lo, a voice out of the cloud, saying: This is my beloved Son, in whom I am well pleased: hear ye him.

17:6 And the disciples hearing, fell upon their face, and were very much afraid.

17:7 And Jesus came and touched them: and said to them, Arise, and fear not.

17:8 And they lifting up their eyes saw no one but only Jesus.

17:9 And as they came down from the mountain, Jesus charged them, saying: Tell the vision to no man, till the Son of man be risen from the dead.

17:10 And his disciples asked him, saying: Why then do the scribes say that Elias must come first?

17:11 But he answering, said to them: Elias indeed shall come, and restore all things.

17:12 But I say to you, that Elias is already come, and they knew him not, but have done unto him whatsoever they had a mind. So also the Son of man shall suffer from them.

17:13 Then the disciples understood, that he had spoken to them of John the Baptist.

17:14 And when he was come to the multitude, there came to him a man falling down on his knees before him, saying: Lord, have pity on my son, for he is a lunatic, and suffereth much: for he falleth often into the fire, and often into the water.

17:15 And I brought him to thy disciples, and they could not cure him.

17:16 Then Jesus answered and said: O unbelieving and perverse generation, how long shall I be with you? How long shall I suffer you? bring him hither to me.

17:17 And Jesus rebuked him, and the devil went out of him, and the child was cured from that hour.

17:18 Tunc accesserunt discipuli ad Jesum secreto, et dixerunt : Quare nos non potuimus ejicere illum ?

17:19 Dixit illis Jesus : Propter incredulitatem vestram. Amen quippe dico vobis, si habueritis fidem sicut granum sinapis, dicetis monti huic : Transi hinc illuc, et transibit, et nihil impossibile erit vobis.

17:20 Hoc autem genus non ejicitur nisi per orationem et jejunium.

17:21 Conversantibus autem eis in Galilæa, dixit illis Jesus : Filius hominis tradendus est in manus hominum :

17:22 et occident eum, et tertia die resurget. Et contristati sunt vehementer.

17:23 Et cum venissent Capharnaum, accesserunt qui didrachma accipiebant ad Petrum, et dixerunt ei : Magister vester non solvit didrachma ?

17:24 Ait : Etiam. Et cum intrasset in domum, prævenit eum Jesus, dicens : Quid tibi videtur Simon ? reges terræ a quibus accipiunt tributum vel censum ? a filiis suis, an ab alienis ?

17:25 Et ille dixit : Ab alienis. Dixit illi Jesus : Ergo liberi sunt filii.

17:26 Ut autem non scandalizemus eos, vade ad mare, et mitte hamum : et eum piscem, qui primus ascenderit, tolle : et aperto ore ejus, invenies staterem : illum sumens, da eis pro me et te.

18:1 In illa hora accesserunt discipuli ad Jesum, dicentes : Quis, putas, major est in regno cælorum ?

18:2 Et advocans Jesus parvulum, statuit eum in medio eorum,

18:3 et dixit : Amen dico vobis, nisi conversi fueritis, et efficiamini sicut parvuli, non intrabitis in regnum cælorum.

18:4 Quicumque ergo humiliaverit se sicut parvulus iste, hic est major in regno cælorum.

18:5 Et qui susceperit unum parvulum talem in nomine meo, me suscipit :

18:6 qui autem scandalizaverit unum de pusillis istis, qui in me credunt, expedit ei ut suspendatur mola asinaria in collo ejus, et demergatur in profundum maris.

18:7 Væ mundo a scandalis ! Necesse est enim ut

17:18 Then came the disciples to Jesus secretly, and said: Why could not we cast him out?

17:19 Jesus said to them: Because of your unbelief. For, amen I say to you, if you have faith as a grain of mustard seed, you shall say to this mountain, Remove from hence hither, and it shall remove; and nothing shall be impossible to you.

17:20 But this kind is not cast out but by prayer and fasting.

17:21 And when they abode together in Galilee, Jesus said to them: The Son of man shall be betrayed into the hands of men:

17:22 And they shall kill him, and the third day he shall rise again. And they were troubled exceedingly.

17:23 And when they were come to Capharnaum, they that recieved the didrachmas, came to Peter and said to him: Doth not your master pay the didrachmas?

17:24 He said: Yes. And when he was come into the house, Jesus prevented him, saying: What is thy opinion, Simon? The kings of the earth, of whom do they receive tribute or custom? of their own children, or of strangers?

17:25 And he said: Of strangers. Jesus said to him: Then the children are free.

17:26 But that we may not scandalize them, go to the sea, and cast in a hook: and that fish which shall first come up, take: and when thou hast opened its mouth, thou shalt find a stater: take that, and give it to them for me and thee.

18:1 At that hour the disciples came to Jesus, saying: Who thinkest thou is the greater in the kingdom of heaven?

18:2 And Jesus calling unto him a little child, set him in the midst of them,

18:3 And said: Amen I say to you, unless you be converted, and become as little children, you shall not enter into the kingdom of heaven.

18:4 Whosoever therefore shall humble himself as this little child, he is the greater in the kingdom of heaven.

18:5 And he that shall receive one such little child in my name, receiveth me.

18:6 But he that shall scandalize one of these little ones that believe in me, it were better for him that a millstone should be hanged about his neck, and that he should be drowned in the depth of the sea.

18:7 Woe to the world because of scandals. For

veniant scandala : verumtamen væ homini illi, per quem scandalum venit.

18:8 Si autem manus tua, vel pes tuus scandalizat te, abscide eum, et projice abs te : bonum tibi est ad vitam ingredi debilem, vel claudum, quam duas manus vel duos pedes habentem mitti in ignem æternum.

18:9 Et si oculus tuus scandalizat te, erue eum, et projice abs te : bonum tibi est cum uno oculo in vitam intrare, quam duos oculos habentem mitti in gehennam ignis.

18:10 Videte ne contemnatis unum ex his pusillis : dico enim vobis, quia angeli eorum in cælis semper vident faciem Patris mei, qui in cælis est.

18:11 Venit enim Filius hominis salvare quod perierat.

18:12 Quid vobis videtur ? si fuerit alicui centum oves, et erravit una ex eis : nonne relinquit nonaginta novem in montibus, et vadit quærere eam quæ erravit ?

18:13 Et si contigerit ut inveniat eam : amen dico vobis, quia gaudet super eam magis quam super nonaginta novem, quæ non erraverunt.

18:14 Sic non est voluntas ante Patrem vestrum, qui in cælis est, ut pereat unus de pusillis istis.

18:15 Si autem peccaverit in te frater tuus, vade, et corripe eum inter te, et ipsum solum : si te audierit, lucratus eris fratrem tuum.

18:16 Si autem te non audierit, adhibe tecum adhuc unum, vel duos, ut in ore duorum, vel trium testium stet omne verbum.

18:17 Quod si non audierit eos : dic ecclesiæ. Si autem ecclesiam non audierit, sit tibi sicut ethnicus et publicanus.

18:18 Amen dico vobis, quæcumque alligaveritis super terram, erunt ligata et in cælo : et quæcumque solveritis super terram, erunt soluta et in cælo.

18:19 Iterum dico vobis, quia si duo ex vobis consenserint super terram, de omni re quamcumque petierint, fiet illis a Patre meo, qui in cælis est.

18:20 Ubi enim sunt duo vel tres congregati in nomine meo, ibi sum in medio eorum.

18:21 Tunc accedens Petrus ad eum, dixit : Domine, quoties peccabit in me frater meus, et dimittam ei ? usque septies ?

it must needs be that scandals come: but nevertheless woe to that man by whom the scandal cometh.

18:8 And if thy hand, or thy foot scandalize thee, cut it off, and cast it from thee. It is better for thee to go into life maimed or lame, than having two hands or two feet, to be cast into everlasting fire.

18:9 And if thy eye scandalize thee, pluck it out, and cast it from thee. It is better for thee having one eye to enter into life, than having two eyes to be cast into hell fire.

18:10 See that you despise not one of these little ones: for I say to you, that their angels in heaven always see the face of my Father who is in heaven.

18:11 For the Son of man is come to save that which was lost.

18:12 What think you? If a man have an hundred sheep, and one of them should go astray: doth he not leave the ninety-nine in the mountains, and go to seek that which is gone astray?

18:13 And if it so be that he find it: Amen I say to you, he rejoiceth more for that, than for the ninety-nine that went not astray.

18:14 Even so it is not the will of your Father, who is in heaven, that one of these little ones should perish.

18:15 But if thy brother shall offend against thee, go, and rebuke him between thee and him alone. If he shall hear thee, thou shalt gain thy brother.

18:16 And if he will not hear thee, take with thee one or two more: that in the mouth of two or three witnesses every word may stand.

18:17 And if he will not hear them: tell the church. And if he will not hear the church, let him be to thee as the heathen and publican.

18:18 Amen I say to you, whatsoever you shall bind upon earth, shall be bound also in heaven; and whatsoever you shall loose upon earth, shall be loosed also in heaven.

18:19 Again I say to you, that if two of you shall consent upon earth, concerning any thing whatsoever they shall ask, it shall be done to them by my Father who is in heaven.

18:20 For where there are two or three gathered together in my name, there am I in the midst of them.

18:21 Then came Peter unto him and said: Lord, how often shall my brother offend against me, and I forgive him? till seven times?

18:22 Dicit illi Jesus : Non dico tibi usque septies : sed usque septuagies septies.

18:23 Ideo assimilatum est regnum cælorum homini regi, qui voluit rationem ponere cum servis suis.

18:24 Et cum cœpisset rationem ponere, oblatus est ei unus, qui debebat ei decem millia talenta.

18:25 Cum autem non haberet unde redderet, jussit eum dominus ejus venundari, et uxorem ejus, et filios, et omnia quæ habebat, et reddi.

18:26 Procidens autem servus ille, orabat eum, dicens : Patientiam habe in me, et omnia reddam tibi.

18:27 Misertus autem dominus servi illius, dimisit eum, et debitum dimisit ei.

18:28 Egressus autem servus ille invenit unum de conservis suis, qui debebat ei centum denarios : et tenens suffocavit eum, dicens : Redde quod debes.

18:29 Et procidens conservus ejus, rogabat eum, dicens : Patientiam habe in me, et omnia reddam tibi.

18:30 Ille autem noluit : sed abiit, et misit eum in carcerem donec redderet debitum.

18:31 Videntes autem conservi ejus quæ fiebant, contristati sunt valde : et venerunt, et narraverunt domino suo omnia quæ facta fuerant.

18:32 Tunc vocavit illum dominus suus : et ait illi : Serve nequam, omne debitum dimisi tibi quoniam rogasti me :

18:33 nonne ergo oportuit et te misereri conservi tui, sicut et ego tui misertus sum ?

18:34 Et iratus dominus ejus tradidit eum tortoribus, quoadusque redderet universum debitum.

18:35 Sic et Pater meus cælestis faciet vobis, si non remiseritis unusquisque fratri suo de cordibus vestris.

19:1 Et factum est, cum consummasset Jesus sermones istos, migravit a Galilæa, et venit in fines Judææ trans Jordanem,

19:2 et secutæ sunt eum turbæ multæ, et curavit eos ibi.

19:3 Et accesserunt ad eum pharisæi tentantes eum, et dicentes : Si licet homini dimittere uxorem suam, quacumque ex causa ?

19:4 Qui respondens, ait eis : Non legistis, quia qui fecit hominem ab initio, masculum et feminam fecit eos ? Et dixit :

18:22 Jesus saith to him: I say not to thee, till seven times; but till seventy times seven times.

18:23 Therefore is the kingdom of heaven likened to a king, who would take an account of his servants.

18:24 And when he had begun to take the account, one was brought to him, that owed him ten thousand talents.

18:25 And as he had not wherewith to pay it, his lord commanded that he should be sold, and his wife and children and all that he had, and payment to be made.

18:26 But that servant falling down, besought him, saying: Have patience with me, and I will pay thee all.

18:27 And the lord of that servant being moved with pity, let him go and forgave him the debt.

18:28 But when that servant was gone out, he found one of his fellow servants that owed him an hundred pence: and laying hold of him, throttled him, saying: Pay what thou owest.

18:29 And his fellow servant falling down, besought him, saying: Have patience with me, and I will pay thee all.

18:30 And he would not: but went and cast him into prison, till he paid the debt.

18:31 Now his fellow servants seeing what was done, were very much grieved, and they came and told their lord all that was done.

18:32 Then his lord called him; and said to him: Thou wicked servant, I forgave thee all the debt, because thou besoughtest me:

18:33 Shouldst not thou then have had compassion also on thy fellow servant, even as I had compassion on thee?

18:34 And his lord being angry, delivered him to the torturers until he paid all the debt.

18:35 So also shall my heavenly Father do to you, if you forgive not every one his brother from your hearts.

19:1 And it came to pass when Jesus had ended these words, he departed from Galilee, and came into the coasts of Judea, beyond Jordan.

19:2 And great multitudes followed him: and he healed them there.

19:3 And there came to him the Pharisees tempting him, and saying: Is it lawful for a man to put away his wife for every cause?

19:4 Who answering, said to them: Have ye not read, that he who made man from the beginning, Made them male and female? And he

19:5 Propter hoc dimittet homo patrem, et matrem, et adhærebit uxori suæ, et erunt duo in carne una.

19:6 Itaque jam non sunt duo, sed una caro. Quod ergo Deus conjunxit, homo non separet.

19:7 Dicunt illi : Quid ergo Moyses mandavit dare libellum repudii, et dimittere ?

19:8 Ait illis : Quoniam Moyses ad duritiam cordis vestri permisit vobis dimittere uxores vestras : ab initio autem non fuit sic.

19:9 Dico autem vobis, quia quicumque dimiserit uxorem suam, nisi ob fornicationem, et aliam duxerit, mœchatur : et qui dimissam duxerit, mœchatur.

19:10 Dicunt ei discipuli ejus : Si ita est causa hominis cum uxore, non expedit nubere.

19:11 Qui dixit illis : Non omnes capiunt verbum istud, sed quibus datum est.

19:12 Sunt enim eunuchi, qui de matris utero sic nati sunt : et sunt eunuchi, qui facti sunt ab hominibus : et sunt eunuchi, qui seipsos castraverunt propter regnum cælorum. Qui potest capere capiat.

19:13 Tunc oblati sunt ei parvuli, ut manus eis imponeret, et oraret. Discipuli autem increpabant eos.

19:14 Jesus vero ait eis : Sinite parvulos, et nolite eos prohibere ad me venire : talium est enim regnum cælorum.

19:15 Et cum imposuisset eis manus, abiit inde.

19:16 Et ecce unus accedens, ait illi : Magister bone, quid boni faciam ut habeam vitam æternam ?

19:17 Qui dixit ei : Quid me interrogas de bono ? Unus est bonus, Deus. Si autem vis ad vitam ingredi, serva mandata.

19:18 Dicit illi : Quæ ? Jesus autem dixit : Non homicidium facies ; non adulterabis ; non facies furtum ; non falsum testimonium dices ;

19:19 honora patrem tuum, et matrem tuam, et diliges proximum tuum sicut teipsum.

19:20 Dicit illi adolescens : Omnia hæc custodivi

said:

19:5 For this cause shall a man leave father and mother, and shall cleave to his wife, and they two shall be in one flesh.

19:6 Therefore now they are not two, but one flesh. What therefore God hath joined together, let no man put asunder.

19:7 They say to him: Why then did Moses command to give a bill of divorce, and to put away?

19:8 He saith to them: Because Moses by reason of the hardness of your heart permitted you to put away your wives: but from the beginning it was not so.

19:9 And I say to you, that whosoever shall put away his wife, except it be for fornication, and shall marry another, committeth adultery: and he that shall marry her that is put away, committeth adultery.

19:10 His disciples say unto him: If the case of a man with his wife be so, it is not expedient to marry.

19:11 Who said to them: All men take not this word, but they to whom it is given.

19:12 For there are eunuchs, who were born so from their mother's womb: and there are eunuchs, who were made so by men: and there are eunuchs, who have made themselves eunuchs for the kingdom of heaven. He that can take, let him take it.

19:13 Then were little children presented to him, that he should impose hands upon them and pray. And the disciples rebuked them.

19:14 But Jesus said to them: Suffer the little children, and forbid them not to come to me: for the kingdom of heaven is for such.

19:15 And when he had imposed hands upon them, he departed from thence.

19:16 And behold one came and said to him: Good master, what good shall I do that I may have life everlasting?

19:17 Who said to him: Why asketh thou me concerning good? One is good, God. But if thou wilt enter into life, keep the commandments.

19:18 He said to him: Which? And Jesus said: Thou shalt do no murder, Thou shalt not commit adultery, Thou shalt not steal, Thou shalt not bear false witness.

19:19 Honour thy father and thy mother: and, Thou shalt love thy neighbor as thyself.

19:20 The young man saith to him: All these I

a juventute mea : quid adhuc mihi deest ?

19:21 Ait illi Jesus : Si vis perfectus esse, vade, vende quæ habes, et da pauperibus, et habebis thesaurum in cælo : et veni, sequere me.

19:22 Cum audisset autem adolescens verbum, abiit tristis : erat enim habens multas possessiones.

19:23 Jesus autem dixit discipulis suis : Amen dico vobis, quia dives difficile intrabit in regnum cælorum.

19:24 Et iterum dico vobis : Facilius est camelum per foramen acus transire, quam divitem intrare in regnum cælorum.

19:25 Auditis autem his, discipuli mirabantur valde, dicentes : Quis ergo poterit salvus esse ?

19:26 Aspiciens autem Jesus, dixit illis : Apud homines hoc impossibile est : apud Deum autem omnia possibilia sunt.

19:27 Tunc respondens Petrus, dixit ei : Ecce nos reliquimus omnia, et secuti sumus te : quid ergo erit nobis ?

19:28 Jesus autem dixit illis : Amen dico vobis, quod vos, qui secuti estis me, in regeneratione cum sederit Filius hominis in sede majestatis suæ, sedebitis et vos super sedes duodecim, judicantes duodecim tribus Israël.

19:29 Et omnis qui reliquerit domum, vel fratres, aut sorores, aut patrem, aut matrem, aut uxorem, aut filios, aut agros propter nomen meum, centuplum accipiet, et vitam æternam possidebit.

19:30 Multi autem erunt primi novissimi, et novissimi primi.

20:1 Simile est regnum cælorum homini patrifamilias, qui exiit primo mane conducere operarios in vineam suam.

20:2 Conventione autem facta cum operariis ex denario diurno, misit eos in vineam suam.

20:3 Et egressus circa horam tertiam, vidit alios stantes in foro otiosos,

20:4 et dixit illis : Ite et vos in vineam meam, et quod justum fuerit dabo vobis.

20:5 Illi autem abierunt. Iterum autem exiit circa sextam et nonam horam : et fecit similiter.

20:6 Circa undecimam vero exiit, et invenit alios stantes, et dicit illis : Quid hic statis tota die otiosi ?

have kept from my youth, what is yet wanting to me?

19:21 Jesus saith to him: If thou wilt be perfect, go sell what thou hast, and give to the poor, and thou shalt have treasure in heaven: and come follow me.

19:22 And when the young man had heard this word, he went away sad: for he had great possessions.

19:23 Then Jesus said to his disciples: Amen, I say to you, that a rich man shall hardly enter into the kingdom of heaven.

19:24 And again I say to you: It is easier for a camel to pass through the eye of a needle, than for a rich man to enter into the kingdom of heaven.

19:25 And when they had heard this, the disciples wondered very much, saying: Who then can be saved?

19:26 And Jesus beholding, said to them: With men this is impossible: but with God all things are possible.

19:27 Then Peter answering, said to him: Behold we have left all things, and have followed thee: what therefore shall we have?

19:28 And Jesus said to them: Amen, I say to you, that you, who have followed me, in the regeneration, when the Son of man shall sit on the seat of his majesty, you also shall sit on twelve seats judging the twelve tribes of Israel.

19:29 And every one that hath left house, or brethren, or sisters, or father, or mother, or wife, or children, or lands for my name's sake, shall receive an hundredfold, and shall possess life everlasting.

19:30 And many that are first, shall be last: and the last shall be first.

20:1 The kingdom of heaven is like to an householder, who went out early in the morning to hire labourers into his vineyard.

20:2 And having agreed with the labourers for a penny a day, he sent them into his vineyard.

20:3 And going about the third hour, he saw others standing in the market place idle.

20:4 And he said to them: Go you also into my vineyard, and I will give you what shall be just.

20:5 And they went their way. And again he went out about the sixth and the ninth hour, and did in like manner.

20:6 But about the eleventh hour he went out and found others standing, and he saith to them: Why stand you here all the day idle?

20:7 Dicunt ei : Quia nemo nos conduxit. Dicit illis : Ite et vos in vineam meam.

20:8 Cum sero autem factum esset, dicit dominus vineæ procuratori suo : Voca operarios, et redde illis mercedem incipiens a novissimis usque ad primos.

20:9 Cum venissent ergo qui circa undecimam horam venerant, acceperunt singulos denarios.

20:10 Venientes autem et primi, arbitrati sunt quod plus essent accepturi : acceperunt autem et ipsi singulos denarios.

20:11 Et accipientes murmurabant adversus patremfamilias,

20:12 dicentes : Hi novissimi una hora fecerunt, et pares illos nobis fecisti, qui portavimus pondus diei, et æstus.

20:13 At ille respondens uni eorum, dixit : Amice, non facio tibi injuriam : nonne ex denario convenisti mecum ?

20:14 Tolle quod tuum est, et vade : volo autem et huic novissimo dare sicut et tibi.

20:15 Aut non licet mihi quod volo, facere ? an oculus tuus nequam est, quia ego bonus sum ?

20:16 Sic erunt novissimi primi, et primi novissimi. Multi enim sunt vocati, pauci vero electi.

20:17 Et ascendens Jesus Jerosolymam, assumpsit duodecim discipulos secreto, et ait illis :

20:18 Ecce ascendimus Jerosolymam, et Filius hominis tradetur principibus sacerdotum, et scribis, et condemnabunt eum morte,

20:19 et tradent eum gentibus ad illudendum, et flagellandum, et crucifigendum, et tertia die resurget.

20:20 Tunc accessit ad eum mater filiorum Zebedæi cum filiis suis, adorans et petens aliquid ab eo.

20:21 Qui dixit ei : Quid vis ? Ait illi : Dic ut sedeant hi duo filii mei, unus ad dexteram tuam, et unus ad sinistram in regno tuo.

20:22 Respondens autem Jesus, dixit : Nescitis quid petatis. Potestis bibere calicem, quem ego bibiturus sum ? Dicunt ei : Possumus.

20:23 Ait illis : Calicem quidem meum bibetis : sedere autem ad dexteram meam vel sinistram non est meum dare vobis, sed quibus paratum est a Patre meo.

20:24 Et audientes decem, indignati sunt de duo-

20:7 They say to him: Because no man hath hired us. He saith to them: Go you also into my vineyard.

20:8 And when evening was come, the lord of the vineyard saith to his steward: Call the labourers and pay them their hire, beginning from the last even to the first.

20:9 When therefore they were come, that came about the eleventh hour, they received every man a penny.

20:10 But when the first also came, they thought that they should receive more: and they also received every man a penny.

20:11 And receiving it they murmured against the master of the house,

20:12 Saying: These last have worked but one hour, and thou hast made them equal to us, that have borne the burden of the day and the heats.

20:13 But he answering said to one of them: Friend, I do thee no wrong: didst thou not agree with me for a penny?

20:14 Take what is thine, and go thy way: I will also give to this last even as to thee.

20:15 Or, is it not lawful for me to do what I will? is thy eye evil, because I am good?

20:16 So shall the last be first, and the first last. For many are called, but few chosen.

20:17 And Jesus going up to Jerusalem, took the twelve disciples apart, and said to them:

20:18 Behold we go up to Jerusalem, and the Son of man shall be betrayed to the chief priests and the scribes, and they shall condemn him to death.

20:19 And shall deliver him to the Gentiles to be mocked, and scourged, and crucified, and the third day he shall rise again.

20:20 Then came to him the mother of the sons of Zebedee with her sons, adoring and asking something of him.

20:21 Who said to her: What wilt thou? She saith to him: Say that these my two sons may sit, the one on thy right hand, and the other on thy left, in thy kingdom.

20:22 And Jesus answering, said: You know not what you ask. Can you drink the chalice that I shall drink? They say to him: We can.

20:23 He saith to them: My chalice indeed you shall drink; but to sit on my right or left hand, is not mine to give to you, but to them for whom it is prepared by my Father.

20:24 And the ten hearing it, were moved with

bus fratribus.

20:25 Jesus autem vocavit eos ad se, et ait : Scitis quia principes gentium dominantur eorum : et qui majores sunt, potestatem exercent in eos.

20:26 Non ita erit inter vos : sed quicumque voluerit inter vos major fieri, sit vester minister :

20:27 et qui voluerit inter vos primus esse, erit vester servus.

20:28 Sicut Filius hominis non venit ministrari, sed ministrare, et dare animam suam redemptionem pro multis.

20:29 Et egredientibus illis ab Jericho, secuta est eum turba multa,

20:30 et ecce duo cæci sedentes secus viam audierunt quia Jesus transiret : et clamaverunt, dicentes : Domine, miserere nostri, fili David.

20:31 Turba autem increpabat eos ut tacerent. At illi magis clamabant, dicentes : Domine, miserere nostri, fili David.

20:32 Et stetit Jesus, et vocavit eos, et ait : Quid vultis ut faciam vobis ?

20:33 Dicunt illi : Domine, ut aperiantur oculi nostri.

20:34 Misertus autem eorum Jesus, tetigit oculos eorum. Et confestim viderunt, et secuti sunt eum.

21:1 Et cum appropinquassent Jerosolymis, et venissent Bethphage ad montem Oliveti : tunc Jesus misit duos discipulos,

21:2 dicens eis : Ite in castellum, quod contra vos est, et statim invenietis asinam alligatam, et pullum cum ea : solvite, et adducite mihi :

21:3 et si quis vobis aliquid dixerit, dicite quia Dominus his opus habet : et confestim dimittet eos.

21:4 Hoc autem totum factum est, ut adimpleretur quod dictum est per prophetam dicentem :

21:5 *Dicite filiæ Sion : Ecce rex tuus venit tibi mansuetus, sedens super asinam, et pullum filium subjugalis.*

21:6 Euntes autem discipuli fecerunt sicut præcepit illis Jesus.

21:7 Et adduxerunt asinam, et pullum : et imposuerunt super eos vestimenta sua, et eum desuper sedere fecerunt.

21:8 Plurima autem turba straverunt vestimenta

indignation against the two brethren.

20:25 But Jesus called them to him, and said: You know that the princes of the Gentiles lord it over them; and they that are the greater, exercise power upon them.

20:26 It shall not be so among you: but whosoever will be the greater among you, let him be your minister:

20:27 And he that will be first among you, shall be your servant.

20:28 Even as the Son of man is not come to be ministered unto, but to minister, and to give his life a redemption for many.

20:29 And when they went out from Jericho, a great multitude followed him.

20:30 And behold two blind men sitting by the way side, heard that Jesus passed by, and they cried out, saying: O Lord, thou son of David, have mercy on us.

20:31 And the multitude rebuked them that they should hold their peace. But they cried out the more, saying: O Lord, thou son of David, have mercy on us.

20:32 And Jesus stood, and called them, and said: What will ye that I do to you?

20:33 They say to him: Lord, that our eyes be opened.

20:34 And Jesus having compassion on them, touched their eyes. And immediately they saw, and followed him.

21:1 And when they drew nigh to Jerusalem, and were come to Bethphage, unto mount Olivet, then Jesus sent two disciples,

21:2 Saying to them: Go ye into the village that is over against you, and immediately you shall find an ass tied, and a colt with her: loose them and bring them to me.

21:3 And if any man shall say anything to you, say ye, that the Lord hath need of them: and forthwith he will let them go.

21:4 Now all this was done that it might be fulfilled which was spoken by the prophet, saying:

21:5 *Tell ye the daughter of Sion: Behold thy king cometh to thee, meek, and sitting upon an ass, and a colt the foal of her that is used to the yoke.*

21:6 And the disciples going, did as Jesus commanded them.

21:7 And they brought the ass and the colt, and laid their garments upon them, and made him sit thereon.

21:8 And a very great multitude spread their

sua in via : alii autem cædebant ramos de arboribus, et sternebant in via :

21:9 turbæ autem, quæ præcedebant, et quæ sequebantur, clamabant, dicentes : Hosanna filio
David : benedictus, qui venit in nomine Domini : hosanna in altissimis.

21:10 Et cum intrasset Jerosolymam, commota
est universa civitas, dicens : Quis est hic ?

21:11 Populi autem dicebant : Hic est Jesus
propheta a Nazareth Galilææ.

21:12 Et intravit Jesus in templum Dei, et ejiciebat omnes vendentes et ementes in templo, et
mensas numulariorum, et cathedras vendentium columbas evertit :

21:13 et dicit eis : Scriptum est : Domus mea
domus orationis vocabitur : vos autem fecistis
illam speluncam latronum.

21:14 Et accesserunt ad eum cæci, et claudi in
templo : et sanavit eos.

21:15 Videntes autem principes sacerdotum et
scribæ mirabilia quæ fecit, et pueros clamantes
in templo, et dicentes : Hosanna filio David :
indignati sunt,

21:16 et dixerunt ei : Audis quid isti dicunt ? Jesus autem dixit eis : Utique. Numquam legistis : Quia ex ore infantium et lactentium
perfecisti laudem ?

21:17 Et relictis illis, abiit foras extra civitatem in
Bethaniam : ibique mansit.

21:18 Mane autem revertens in civitatem,
esuriit.

21:19 Et videns fici arborem unam secus viam,
venit ad eam : et nihil invenit in ea nisi folia
tantum, et ait illi : Numquam ex te fructus
nascatur in sempiternum. Et arefacta est continuo ficulnea.

21:20 Et videntes discipuli, mirati sunt, dicentes :
Quomodo continuo aruit ?

21:21 Respondens autem Jesus, ait eis : Amen dico vobis, si habueritis fidem, et non hæsitaveri-
tis, non solum de ficulnea facietis, sed et si
monti huic dixeritis : Tolle, et jacta te in mare,
fiet.

21:22 Et omnia quæcumque petieritis in oratione
credentes, accipietis.

21:23 Et cum venisset in templum, accesserunt
ad eum docentem principes sacerdotum, et
seniores populi, dicentes : In qua potestate hæc
facis ? et quis tibi dedit hanc potestatem ?

garments in the way: and others cut boughs
from the trees, and strewed them in the way:

21:9 And the multitudes that went before and
that followed, cried, saying: Hosanna to the son
of David: Blessed is he that cometh in the name
of the Lord: Hosanna in the highest.

21:10 And when he was come into Jerusalem,
the whole city was moved, saying: Who is this?

21:11 And the people said: This is Jesus the
prophet, from Nazareth of Galilee.

21:12 And Jesus went into the temple of God,
and cast out all them that sold and bought in
the temple, and overthrew the tables of the
money changers, and the chairs of them that
sold doves:

21:13 And he saith to them: It is written, My
house shall be called the house of prayer; but
you have made it a den of thieves.

21:14 And there came to him the blind and the
lame in the temple; and he healed them.

21:15 And the chief priests and scribes, seeing
the wonderful things that he did, and the children crying in the temple, and saying: Hosanna
to the son of David; were moved with indignation.

21:16 And said to him: Hearest thou what these
say? And Jesus said to them: Yea, have you never
read: Out of the mouth of infants and of sucklings thou hast perfected praise?

21:17 And leaving them, he went out of the city
into Bethania, and remained there.

21:18 And in the morning, returning into the
city, he was hungry.

21:19 And seeing a certain fig tree by the way
side, he came to it, and found nothing on it but
leaves only, and he saith to it: May no fruit
grow on thee henceforward for ever. And immediately the fig tree withered away.

21:20 And the disciples seeing it wondered, saying: How is it presently withered away?

21:21 And Jesus answering, said to them: Amen,
I say to you, if you shall have faith, and stagger
not, not only this of the fig tree shall you do,
but also if you shall say to this mountain, Take
up and cast thyself into the sea, it shall be
done.

21:22 And all things whatsoever you shall ask in
prayer, believing, you shall receive.

21:23 And when he was come into the temple,
there came to him, as he was teaching, the
chief priests and ancients of the people, saying:
By what authority dost thou these things? and

21:24 Respondens Jesus dixit eis : Interrogabo vos et ego unum sermonem : quem si dixeritis mihi, et ego vobis dicam in qua potestate hæc facio.

21:25 Baptismus Joannis unde erat ? e cælo, an ex hominibus ? At illi cogitabant inter se, dicentes :

21:26 Si dixerimus, e cælo, dicet nobis : Quare ergo non credidistis illi ? Si autem dixerimus, ex hominibus, timemus turbam : omnes enim habebant Joannem sicut prophetam.

21:27 Et respondentes Jesu, dixerunt : Nescimus. Ait illis et ipse : Nec ego dico vobis in qua potestate hæc facio.

21:28 Quid autem vobis videtur ? Homo quidam habebat duos filios, et accedens ad primum, dixit : Fili, vade hodie, operare in vinea mea.

21:29 Ille autem respondens, ait : Nolo. Postea autem, pœnitentia motus, abiit.

21:30 Accedens autem ad alterum, dixit similiter. At ille respondens, ait : Eo, domine, et non ivit :

21:31 quis ex duobus fecit voluntatem patris ? Dicunt ei : Primus. Dicit illis Jesus : Amen dico vobis, quia publicani et meretrices præcedent vos in regnum Dei.

21:32 Venit enim ad vos Joannes in via justitiæ, et non credidistis ei : publicani autem et meretrices crediderunt ei : vos autem videntes nec pœnitentiam habuistis postea, ut crederetis ei.

21:33 Aliam parabolam audite : Homo erat paterfamilias, qui plantavit vineam, et sepem circumdedit ei, et fodit in ea torcular, et ædificavit turrim, et locavit eam agricolis, et peregre profectus est.

21:34 Cum autem tempus fructuum appropinquasset, misit servos suos ad agricolas, ut acciperent fructus ejus.

21:35 Et agricolæ, apprehensis servis ejus, alium ceciderunt, alium occiderunt, alium vero lapidaverunt.

21:36 Iterum misit alios servos plures prioribus, et fecerunt illis similiter.

21:37 Novissime autem misit ad eos filium suum, dicens : Verebuntur filium meum.

21:38 Agricolæ autem videntes filium dixerunt intra se : Hic est hæres, venite, occidamus eum, et habebimus hæreditatem ejus.

who hath given thee this authority?

21:24 Jesus answering, said to them: I also will ask you one word, which if you shall tell me, I will also tell you by what authority I do these things.

21:25 The baptism of John, whence was it? from heaven or from men? But they thought within themselves, saying:

21:26 If we shall say, from heaven, he will say to us: Why then did you not believe him? But if we shall say, from men, we are afraid of the multitude: for all held John as a prophet.

21:27 And answering Jesus, they said: We know not. He also said to them: Neither do I tell you by what authority I do these things.

21:28 But what think you? A certain man had two sons; and coming to the first, he said: Son, go work to day in my vineyard.

21:29 And he answering, said: I will not. But afterwards, being moved with repentance, he went.

21:30 And coming to the other, he said in like manner. And he answering, said: I go, Sir; and he went not.

21:31 Which of the two did the father's will? They say to him: The first. Jesus saith to them: Amen I say to you, that the publicans and the harlots shall go into the kingdom of God before you.

21:32 For John came to you in the way of justice, and you did not believe him. But the publicans and the harlots believed him: but you, seeing it, did not even afterwards repent, that you might believe him.

21:33 Hear ye another parable. There was a man an householder, who planted a vineyard, and made a hedge round about it, and dug in it a press, and built a tower, and let it out to husbandmen; and went into a strange country.

21:34 And when the time of the fruits drew nigh, he sent his servants to the husbandmen that they might receive the fruits thereof.

21:35 And the husbandmen laying hands on his servants, beat one, and killed another, and stoned another.

21:36 Again he sent other servants more than the former; and they did to them in like manner.

21:37 And last of all he sent to them his son, saying: They will reverence my son.

21:38 But the husbandmen seeing the son, said among themselves: This is the heir: come, let us kill him, and we shall have his inheritance.

21:39 Et apprehensum eum ejecerunt extra vineam, et occiderunt.

21:40 Cum ergo venerit dominus vineæ, quid faciet agricolis illis ?

21:41 Aiunt illi : Malos male perdet : et vineam suam locabit aliis agricolis, qui reddant ei fructum temporibus suis.

21:42 Dicit illis Jesus : Numquam legistis in Scripturis : *Lapidem quem reprobaverunt ædificantes, hic factus est in caput anguli : a Domino factum est istud, et est mirabile in oculis nostris ?*

21:43 Ideo dico vobis, quia auferetur a vobis regnum Dei, et dabitur genti facienti fructus ejus.

21:44 Et qui ceciderit super lapidem istum, confringetur : super quem vero ceciderit, conteret eum.

21:45 Et cum audissent principes sacerdotum et pharisæi parabolas ejus, cognoverunt quod de ipsis diceret.

21:46 Et quærentes eum tenere, timuerunt turbas : quoniam sicut prophetam eum habebant.

22:1 Et respondens Jesus, dixit iterum in parabolis eis, dicens :

22:2 Simile factum est regnum cælorum homini regi, qui fecit nuptias filio suo.

22:3 Et misit servos suos vocare invitatos ad nuptias, et nolebant venire.

22:4 Iterum misit alios servos, dicens : Dicite invitatis : Ecce prandium meum paravi, tauri mei et altilia occisa sunt, et omnia parata : venite ad nuptias.

22:5 Illi autem neglexerunt : et abierunt, alius in villam suam, alius vero ad negotiationem suam :

22:6 reliqui vero tenuerunt servos ejus, et contumeliis affectos occiderunt.

22:7 Rex autem cum audisset, iratus est : et missis exercitibus suis, perdidit homicidas illos, et civitatem illorum succendit.

22:8 Tunc ait servis suis : Nuptiæ quidem paratæ sunt, sed qui invitati erant, non fuerunt digni :

22:9 ite ergo ad exitus viarum, et quoscumque inveneritis, vocate ad nuptias.

21:39 And taking him, they cast him forth out of the vineyard, and killed him.

21:40 When therefore the lord of the vineyard shall come, what will he do to those husbandmen?

21:41 They say to him: He will bring those evil men to an evil end; and will let out his vineyard to other husbandmen, that shall render him the fruit in due season.

21:42 Jesus saith to them: Have you never read in the Scriptures: *The stone which the builders rejected, the same is become the head of the corner? By the Lord this has been done; and it is wonderful in our eyes.*

21:43 Therefore I say to you, that the kingdom of God shall be taken from you, and shall be given to a nation yielding the fruits thereof.

21:44 And whosoever shall fall on this stone, shall be broken: but on whomsoever it shall fall, it shall grind him to powder.

21:45 And when the chief priests and Pharisees had heard his parables, they knew that he spoke of them.

21:46 And seeking to lay hands on him, they feared the multitudes: because they held him as a prophet.

22:1 And Jesus answering, spoke again in parables to them, saying:

22:2 The kingdom of heaven is likened to a king, who made a marriage for his son.

22:3 And he sent his servants, to call them that were invited to the marriage; and they would not come.

22:4 Again he sent other servants, saying: Tell them that were invited, Behold, I have prepared my dinner; my beeves and fatlings are killed, and all things are ready: come ye to the marriage.

22:5 But they neglected, and went their ways, one to his farm, and another to his merchandise.

22:6 And the rest laid hands on his servants, and having treated them contumeliously, put them to death.

22:7 But when the king had heard of it, he was angry, and sending his armies, he destroyed those murderers, and burnt their city.

22:8 Then he saith to his servants: The marriage indeed is ready; but they that were invited were not worthy.

22:9 Go ye therefore into the highways; and as many as you shall find, call to the marriage.

22:10 Et egressi servi ejus in vias, congregaverunt omnes quos invenerunt, malos et bonos : et impletæ sunt nuptiæ discumbentium.

22:11 Intravit autem rex ut videret discumbentes, et vidit ibi hominem non vestitum veste nuptiali.

22:12 Et ait illi : Amice, quomodo huc intrasti non habens vestem nuptialem ? At ille obmutuit.

22:13 Tunc dicit rex ministris : Ligatis manibus et pedibus ejus, mittite eum in tenebras exteriores : ibi erit fletus et stridor dentium.

22:14 Multi enim sunt vocati, pauci vero electi.

22:15 Tunc abeuntes pharisæi, consilium inierunt ut caperent eum in sermone.

22:16 Et mittunt ei discipulos suos cum Herodianis, dicentes : Magister, scimus quia verax es, et viam Dei in veritate doces, et non est tibi cura de aliquo : non enim respicis personam hominum :

22:17 dic ergo nobis quid tibi videtur, licet censum dare Cæsari, an non ?

22:18 Cognita autem Jesus nequitia eorum, ait : Quid me tentatis, hypocritæ ?

22:19 ostendite mihi numisma census. At illi obtulerunt ei denarium.

22:20 Et ait illis Jesus : Cujus est imago hæc, et superscriptio ?

22:21 Dicunt ei : Cæsaris. Tunc ait illis : Reddite ergo quæ sunt Cæsaris, Cæsari : et quæ sunt Dei, Deo.

22:22 Et audientes mirati sunt, et relicto eo abierunt.

22:23 In illo die accesserunt ad eum sadducæi, qui dicunt non esse resurrectionem : et interrogaverunt eum,

22:24 dicentes : Magister, Moyses dixit : Si quis mortuus fuerit non habens filium, ut ducat frater ejus uxorem illius, et suscitet semen fratri suo.

22:25 Erant autem apud nos septem fratres : et primus, uxore ducta, defunctus est : et non habens semen, reliquit uxorem suam fratri suo.

22:26 Similiter secundus, et tertius usque ad septimum.

22:27 Novissime autem omnium et mulier defuncta est.

22:28 In resurrectione ergo cujus erit de septem uxor ? omnes enim habuerunt eam.

22:10 And his servants going forth into the ways, gathered together all that they found, both bad and good: and the marriage was filled with guests.

22:11 And the king went in to see the guests: and he saw there a man who had not on a wedding garment.

22:12 And he saith to him: Friend, how camest thou in hither not having on a wedding garment? But he was silent.

22:13 Then the king said to the waiters: Bind his hands and feet, and cast him into the exterior darkness: there shall be weeping and gnashing of teeth.

22:14 For many are called, but few are chosen.

22:15 Then the Pharisees going, consulted among themselves how to insnare him in his speech.

22:16 And they sent to him their disciples with the Herodians, saying: Master, we know that thou art a true speaker, and teachest the way of God in truth, neither carest thou for any man: for thou dost not regard the person of men.

22:17 Tell us therefore what dost thou think, is it lawful to give tribute to Caesar, or not?

22:18 But Jesus knowing their wickedness, said: Why do you tempt me, ye hypocrites?

22:19 Shew me the coin of the tribute. And they offered him a penny.

22:20 And Jesus saith to them: Whose image and inscription is this?

22:21 They say to him: Caesar's. Then he saith to them: Render therefore to Caesar the things that are Caesar's; and to God, the things that are God's.

22:22 And hearing this they wondered, and leaving him, went their ways.

22:23 That day there came to him the Sadducees, who say there is no resurrection; and asked him,

22:24 Saying: Master, Moses said: If a man die having no son, his brother shall marry his wife, and raise up issue to his brother.

22:25 Now there were with us seven brethren: and the first having married a wife, died; and not having issue, left his wife to his brother.

22:26 In like manner the second, and the third, and so on to the seventh.

22:27 And last of all the woman died also.

22:28 At the resurrection therefore whose wife of the seven shall she be? for they all had her.

22:29 Respondens autem Jesus, ait illis : Erratis nescientes Scripturas, neque virtutem Dei.

22:30 In resurrectione enim neque nubent, neque nubentur : sed erunt sicut angeli Dei in cælo.

22:31 De resurrectione autem mortuorum non legistis quod dictum est a Deo dicente vobis :

22:32 Ego sum Deus Abraham, et Deus Isaac, et Deus Jacob ? Non est Deus mortuorum, sed viventium.

22:33 Et audientes turbæ, mirabantur in doctrina ejus.

22:34 Pharisæi autem audientes quod silentium imposuisset sadducæis, convenerunt in unum :

22:35 et interrogavit eum unus ex eis legis doctor, tentans eum :

22:36 Magister, quod est mandatum magnum in lege ?

22:37 Ait illi Jesus : Diliges Dominum Deum tuum ex toto corde tuo, et in tota anima tua, et in tota mente tua.

22:38 Hoc est maximum, et primum mandatum.

22:39 Secundum autem simile est huic : Diliges proximum tuum, sicut teipsum.

22:40 In his duobus mandatis universa lex pendet, et prophetæ.

22:41 Congregatis autem pharisæis, interrogavit eos Jesus,

22:42 dicens : Quid vobis videtur de Christo ? cujus filius est ? Dicunt ei : David.

22:43 Ait illis : Quomodo ergo David in spiritu vocat eum Dominum, dicens :

22:44 Dixit Dominus Domino meo : Sede a dextris meis, donec ponam inimicos tuos scabellum pedum tuorum ?

22:45 Si ergo David vocat eum Dominum, quomodo filius ejus est ?

22:46 Et nemo poterat ei respondere verbum : neque ausus fuit quisquam ex illa die eum amplius interrogare.

23:1 Tunc Jesus locutus est ad turbas, et ad discipulos suos,

23:2 dicens : Super cathedram Moysi sederunt scribæ et pharisæi.

23:3 Omnia ergo quæcumque dixerint vobis, servate, et facite : secundum opera vero eorum nolite facere : dicunt enim, et non faciunt.

23:4 Alligant enim onera gravia, et importabilia, et imponunt in humeros hominum : digito

22:29 And Jesus answering, said to them: You err, not knowing the Scriptures, nor the power of God.

22:30 For in the resurrection they shall neither marry nor be married; but shall be as the angels of God in heaven.

22:31 And concerning the resurrection of the dead, have you not read that which was spoken by God, saying to you:

22:32 I am the God of Abraham, and the God of Isaac, and the God of Jacob? He is not the God of the dead, but of the living.

22:33 And the multitudes hearing it, were in admiration at his doctrine.

22:34 But the Pharisees hearing that he had silenced the Sadducees, came together:

22:35 And one of them, a doctor of the law, asking him, tempting him:

22:36 Master, which is the greatest commandment in the law?

22:37 Jesus said to him: Thou shalt love the Lord thy God with thy whole heart, and with thy whole soul, and with thy whole mind.

22:38 This is the greatest and the first commandment.

22:39 And the second is like to this: Thou shalt love thy neighbor as thyself.

22:40 On these two commandments dependeth the whole law and the prophets.

22:41 And the Pharisees being gathered together, Jesus asked them,

22:42 Saying: What think you of Christ? whose son is he? They say to him: David's.

22:43 He saith to them: How then doth David in spirit call him Lord, saying:

22:44 The Lord said to my Lord, Sit on my right hand, until I make thy enemies thy footstool?

22:45 If David then call him Lord, how is he his son?

22:46 And no man was able to answer him a word; neither durst any man from that day forth ask him any more questions.

23:1 Then Jesus spoke to the multitudes and to his disciples,

23:2 Saying: The scribes and the Pharisees have sitten on the chair of Moses.

23:3 All things therefore whatsoever they shall say to you, observe and do: but according to their works do ye not; for they say, and do not.

23:4 For they bind heavy and insupportable burdens, and lay them on men's shoulders; but

autem suo nolunt ea movere.

23:5 Omnia vero opera sua faciunt ut videantur ab hominibus : dilatant enim phylacteria sua, et magnificant fimbrias.

23:6 Amant autem primos recubitus in cœnis, et primas cathedras in synagogis,

23:7 et salutationes in foro, et vocari ab hominibus Rabbi.

23:8 Vos autem nolite vocari Rabbi : unus est enim magister vester, omnes autem vos fratres estis.

23:9 Et patrem nolite vocare vobis super terram : unus est enim pater vester qui in cælis est.

23:10 Nec vocemini magistri : quia magister vester unus est, Christus.

23:11 Qui major est vestrum, erit minister vester.

23:12 Qui autem se exaltaverit, humiliabitur : et qui se humiliaverit, exaltabitur.

23:13 Væ autem vobis scribæ et pharisæi hypocritæ, quia clauditis regnum cælorum ante homines ! vos enim non intratis, nec introëuntes sinitis intrare.

23:14 Væ vobis scribæ et pharisæi hypocritæ, quia comeditis domos viduarum, orationes longas orantes ! propter hoc amplius accipietis judicium.

23:15 Væ vobis scribæ et pharisæi hypocritæ, quia circuitis mare, et aridam, ut faciatis unum proselytum, et cum fuerit factus, facitis eum filium gehennæ duplo quam vos.

23:16 Væ vobis duces cæci, qui dicitis : Quicumque juraverit per templum, nihil est : qui autem juraverit in auro templi, debet.

23:17 Stulti et cæci : quid enim majus est ? aurum, an templum, quod sanctificat aurum ?

23:18 Et quicumque juraverit in altari, nihil est : quicumque autem juraverit in dono, quod est super illud, debet.

23:19 Cæci : quid enim majus est, donum, an altare, quod sanctificat donum ?

23:20 Qui ergo jurat in altari, jurat in eo, et in omnibus quæ super illud sunt.

23:21 Et quicumque juraverit in templo, jurat in

with a finger of their own they will not move them.

23:5 And all their works they do for to be seen of men. For they make their phylacteries broad, and enlarge their fringes.

23:6 And they love the first places at feasts, and the first chairs in the synagogues,

23:7 And salutations in the market place, and to be called by men, Rabbi.

23:8 But be not you called Rabbi. For one is your master; and all you are brethren.

23:9 And call none your father upon earth; for one is your father, who is in heaven.

23:10 Neither be ye called masters; for one is your master, Christ.

23:11 He that is the greatest among you shall be your servant.

23:12 And whosoever shall exalt himself shall be humbled: and he that shall humble himself shall be exalted.

23:13 But woe to you scribes and Pharisees, hypocrites; because you shut the kingdom of heaven against men, for you yourselves do not enter in; and those that are going in, you suffer not to enter.

23:14 Woe to you scribes and Pharisees, hypocrites: because you devour the houses of widows, praying long prayers. For this you shall receive the greater judgment.

23:15 Woe to you scribes and Pharisees, hypocrites; because you go round about the sea and the land to make one proselyte; and when he is made, you make him the child of hell twofold more than yourselves.

23:16 Woe to you blind guides, that say, Whosoever shall swear by the temple, it is nothing; but he that shall swear by the gold of the temple, is a debtor.

23:17 Ye foolish and blind; for whether is greater, the gold, or the temple that sanctifieth the gold?

23:18 And whosoever shall swear by the altar, it is nothing; but whosoever shall swear by the gift that is upon it, is a debtor.

23:19 Ye blind: for whether is greater, the gift, or the altar that sanctifieth the gift?

23:20 He therefore that sweareth by the altar, sweareth by it, and by all things that are upon it:

23:21 And whosoever shall swear by temple,

illo, et in eo qui habitat in ipso :

23:22 et qui jurat in cælo, jurat in throno Dei, et in eo qui sedet super eum.

23:23 Væ vobis scribæ et pharisæi hypocritæ, qui decimatis mentham, et anethum, et cyminum, et reliquistis quæ graviora sunt legis, judicium, et misericordiam, et fidem ! hæc oportuit facere, et illa non omittere.

23:24 Duces cæci, excolantes culicem, camelum autem glutientes.

23:25 Væ vobis scribæ et pharisæi hypocritæ, quia mundatis quod deforis est calicis et paropsidis ; intus autem pleni estis rapina et immunditia !

23:26 Pharisæe cæce, munda prius quod intus est calicis, et paropsidis, ut fiat id, quod deforis est, mundum.

23:27 Væ vobis scribæ et pharisæi hypocritæ, quia similes estis sepulchris dealbatis, quæ a foris parent hominibus speciosa, intus vero pleni sunt ossibus mortuorum, et omni spurcitia !

23:28 Sic et vos a foris quidem paretis hominibus justi : intus autem pleni estis hypocrisi et iniquitate.

23:29 Væ vobis scribæ et pharisæi hypocritæ, qui ædificatis sepulchra prophetarum, et ornatis monumenta justorum,

23:30 et dicitis : Si fuissemus in diebus patrum nostrorum, non essemus socii eorum in sanguine prophetarum !

23:31 itaque testimonio estis vobismetipsis, quia filii estis eorum, qui prophetas occiderunt.

23:32 Et vos implete mensuram patrum vestrorum.

23:33 Serpentes, genimina viperarum, quomodo fugietis a judicio gehennæ ?

23:34 Ideo ecce ego mitto ad vos prophetas, et sapientes, et scribas, et ex illis occidetis, et crucifigetis, et ex eis flagellabitis in synagogis vestris, et persequemini de civitate in civitatem :

23:35 ut veniat super vos omnis sanguis justus, qui effusus est super terram, a sanguine Abel justi usque ad sanguinem Zachariæ, filii Barachiæ, quem occidistis inter templum et altare.

23:36 Amen dico vobis, venient hæc omnia super generationem istam.

swveareth by it, and by him that dwelleth in it:

23:22 And he that sweareth by heaven, sweareth by the throne of God, and by him that sitteth thereon.

23:23 Woe to you scribes and Pharisees, hypocrites; because you tithe mint, and anise, and cummin, and have left the weightier things of the law; judgment, and mercy, and faith. These things you ought to have done, and not to leave those undone.

23:24 Blind guides, who strain out a gnat, and swallow a camel.

23:25 Woe to you scribes and Pharisees, hypocrites; because you make clean the outside of the cup and of the dish, but within you are full of rapine and uncleanness.

23:26 Thou blind Pharisee, first make clean the inside of the cup and of the dish, that the outside may become clean.

23:27 Woe to you scribes and Pharisees, hypocrites; because you are like to whited sepulchres, which outwardly appear to men beautiful, but within are full of dead men's bones, and of all filthiness.

23:28 So you also outwardly indeed appear to men just; but inwardly you are full of hypocrisy and iniquity.

23:29 Woe to you scribes and Pharisees, hypocrites; that build the sepulchres of the prophets, and adorn the monuments of the just,

23:30 And say: If we had been in the days of our Fathers, we would not have been partakers with them in the blood of the prophets.

23:31 Wherefore you are witnesses against yourselves, that you are the sons of them that killed the prophets.

23:32 Fill ye up then the measure of your fathers.

23:33 You serpents, generation of vipers, how will you flee from the judgment of hell?

23:34 Therefore behold I send to you prophets, and wise men, and scribes: and some of them you will put to death and crucify, and some you will scourge in your synagogues, and persecute from city to city:

23:35 That upon you may come all the just blood that hath been shed upon the earth, from the blood of Abel the just, even unto the blood of Zacharias the son of Barachias, whom you killed between the temple and the altar.

23:36 Amen I say to you, all these things shall come upon this generation.

23:37 Jerusalem, Jerusalem, quæ occidis prophetas, et lapidas eos, qui ad te missi sunt, quoties volui congregare filios tuos, quemadmodum gallina congregat pullos suos sub alas, et noluisti ?

23:38 Ecce relinquetur vobis domus vestra deserta.

23:39 Dico enim vobis, non me videbitis amodo, donec dicatis : Benedictus, qui venit in nomine Domini.

24:1 Et egressus Jesus de templo, ibat. Et accesserunt discipuli ejus, ut ostenderent ei ædificationes templi.

24:2 Ipse autem respondens dixit illis : Videtis hæc omnia ? amen dico vobis, non relinquetur hic lapis super lapidem, qui non destruatur.

24:3 Sedente autem eo super montem Oliveti, accesserunt ad eum discipuli secreto, dicentes : Dic nobis, quando hæc erunt ? et quod signum adventus tui, et consummationis sæculi ?

24:4 Et respondens Jesus, dixit eis : Videte ne quis vos seducat :

24:5 multi enim venient in nomine meo, dicentes : Ego sum Christus : et multos seducent.

24:6 Audituri enim estis prælia, et opiniones præliorum. Videte ne turbemini : oportet enim hæc fieri, sed nondum est finis :

24:7 consurget enim gens in gentem, et regnum in regnum, et erunt pestilentiæ, et fames, et terræmotus per loca :

24:8 hæc autem omnia initia sunt dolorum.

24:9 Tunc tradent vos in tribulationem, et occident vos : et eritis odio omnibus gentibus propter nomen meum.

24:10 Et tunc scandalizabuntur multi, et invicem tradent, et odio habebunt invicem.

24:11 Et multi pseudoprophetæ surgent, et seducent multos.

24:12 Et quoniam abundavit iniquitas, refrigescet caritas multorum :

24:13 qui autem perseveraverit usque in finem, hic salvus erit.

24:14 Et prædicabitur hoc Evangelium regni in universo orbe, in testimonium omnibus gentibus : et tunc veniet consummatio.

23:37 Jerusalem, Jerusalem, thou that killest the prophets, and stonest them that are sent unto thee, how often would I have gathered together thy children, as the hen doth gather her chickens under her wings, and thou wouldest not?

23:38 Behold, your house shall be left to you, desolate.

23:39 For I say to you, you shall not see me henceforth till you say: Blessed is he that cometh in the name of the Lord.

24:1 And Jesus being come out of the temple, went away. And his disciples came to shew him the buildings of the temple.

24:2 And he answering, said to them: Do you see all these things? Amen I say to you there shall not be left here a stone upon a stone that shall not be destroyed.

24:3 And when he was sitting on mount Olivet, the disciples came to him privately, saying: Tell us when shall these things be? and what shall be the sign of thy coming, and of the consummation of the world?

24:4 And Jesus answering, said to them: Take heed that no man seduce you:

24:5 For many will come in my name saying, I am Christ: and they will seduce many.

24:6 And you shall hear of wars and rumours of wars. See that ye be not troubled. For these things must come to pass, but the end is not yet.

24:7 For nation shall rise against nation, and kingdom against kingdom; and there shall be pestilences, and famines, and earthquakes in places:

24:8 Now all these are the beginnings of sorrows.

24:9 Then shall they deliver you up to be afflicted, and shall put you to death: and you shall be hated by all nations for my name's sake.

24:10 And then shall many be scandalized: and shall betray one another: and shall hate one another.

24:11 And many false prophets shall rise, and shall seduce many.

24:12 And because iniquity hath abounded, the charity of many shall grow cold.

24:13 But he that shall persevere to the end, he shall be saved.

24:14 And this gospel of the kingdom, shall be preached in the whole world, for a testimony to all nations, and then shall the consummation come.

24:15 Cum ergo videritis abominationem desolationis, quæ dicta est a Daniele propheta, stantem in loco sancto, qui legit, intelligat :

24:16 tunc qui in Judæa sunt, fugiant ad montes :

24:17 et qui in tecto, non descendat tollere aliquid de domo sua :

24:18 et qui in agro, non revertatur tollere tunicam suam.

24:19 Væ autem prægnantibus et nutrientibus in illis diebus !

24:20 Orate autem ut non fiat fuga vestra in hieme, vel sabbato :

24:21 erit enim tunc tribulatio magna, qualis non fuit ab initio mundi usque modo, neque fiet.

24:22 Et nisi breviati fuissent dies illi, non fieret salva omnis caro : sed propter electos breviabuntur dies illi.

24:23 Tunc si quis vobis dixerit : Ecce hic est Christus, aut illic : nolite credere.

24:24 Surgent enim pseudochristi, et pseudoprophetæ : et dabunt signa magna, et prodigia, ita ut in errorem inducantur (si fieri potest) etiam electi.

24:25 Ecce prædixi vobis.

24:26 Si ergo dixerint vobis : Ecce in deserto est, nolite exire ; Ecce in penetralibus, nolite credere.

24:27 Sicut enim fulgur exit ab oriente, et paret usque in occidentem : ita erit et adventus Filii hominis.

24:28 Ubicumque fuerit corpus, illic congregabuntur et aquilæ.

24:29 Statim autem post tribulationem dierum illorum sol obscurabitur, et luna non dabit lumen suum, et stellæ cadent de cælo, et virtutes cælorum commovebuntur :

24:30 et tunc parebit signum Filii hominis in cælo : et tunc plangent omnes tribus terræ : et videbunt Filium hominis venientem in nubibus cæli cum virtute multa et majestate.

24:31 Et mittet angelos suos cum tuba, et voce magna : et congregabunt electos ejus a quatuor ventis, a summis cælorum usque ad terminos eorum.

24:32 Ab arbore autem fici discite parabolam : cum jam ramus ejus tener fuerit, et folia nata,

24:15 When therefore you shall see the abomination of desolation, which was spoken of by Daniel the prophet, standing in the holy place: he that readeth let him understand.

24:16 Then they that are in Judea, let them flee to the mountains:

24:17 And he that is on the housetop, let him not come down to take any thing out of his house:

24:18 And he that is in the field, let him not go back to take his coat.

24:19 And woe to them that are with child, and that give suck in those days.

24:20 But pray that your flight be not in the winter, or on the sabbath.

24:21 For there shall be then great tribulation, such as hath not been from the beginning of the world until now, neither shall be.

24:22 And unless those days had been shortened, no flesh should be saved: but for the sake of the elect those days shall be shortened.

24:23 Then if any man shall say to you: Lo here is Christ, or there, do not believe him.

24:24 For there shall arise false Christs and false prophets, and shall show great signs and wonders, insomuch as to deceive (if possible) even the elect.

24:25 Behold I have told it to you, beforehand.

24:26 If therefore they shall say to you: Behold he is in the desert, go ye not out: Behold he is in the closets, believe it not.

24:27 For as lightning cometh out of the east, and appeareth even into the west: so shall the coming of the Son of man be.

24:28 Wheresoever the body shall be, there shall the eagles also be gathered together.

24:29 And immediately after the tribulation of those days, the sun shall be darkened and the moon shall not give her light, and the stars shall fall from heaven, and the powers of heaven shall be moved:

24:30 And then shall appear the sign of the Son of man in heaven: and then shall all tribes of the earth mourn: and they shall see the Son of man coming in the clouds of heaven with much power and majesty.

24:31 And he shall send his angels with a trumpet, and a great voice: and they shall gather together his elect from the four winds, from the farthest parts of the heavens to the utmost bounds of them.

24:32 And from the fig tree learn a parable: When the branch thereof is now tender, and

scitis quia prope est æstas :

the leaves come forth, you know that summer is nigh.

24:33 ita et vos cum videritis hæc omnia, scitote quia prope est, in januis.

24:33 So you also, when you shall see all these things, know ye that it is nigh, even at the doors.

24:34 Amen dico vobis, quia non præteribit generatio hæc, donec omnia hæc fiant.

24:34 Amen I say to you, that this generation shall not pass, till all these things be done.

24:35 Cælum et terra transibunt, verba autem mea non præteribunt.

24:35 Heaven and earth shall pass, but my words shall not pass.

24:36 De die autem illa et hora nemo scit, neque angeli cælorum, nisi solus Pater.

24:36 But of that day and hour no one knoweth, not the angels of heaven, but the Father alone.

24:37 Sicut autem in diebus Noë, ita erit et adventus Filii hominis :

24:37 And as in the days of Noe, so shall also the coming of the Son of man be.

24:38 sicut enim erant in diebus ante diluvium comedentes et bibentes, nubentes et nuptum tradentes, usque ad eum diem, quo intravit Noë in arcam,

24:38 For as in the days before the flood, they were eating and drinking, marrying and giving in marriage, even till that day in which Noe entered into the ark,

24:39 et non cognoverunt donec venit diluvium, et tulit omnes : ita erit et adventus Filii hominis.

24:39 And they knew not till the flood came, and took them all away; so also shall the coming of the Son of man be.

24:40 Tunc duo erunt in agro : unus assumetur, et unus relinquetur.

24:40 Then two shall be in the field: one shall be taken, and one shall be left.

24:41 Duæ molentes in mola : una assumetur, et una relinquetur.

24:41 Two women shall be grinding at the mill: one shall be taken, and one shall be left.

24:42 Vigilate ergo, quia nescitis qua hora Dominus vester venturus sit.

24:42 Watch ye therefore, because ye know not what hour your Lord will come.

24:43 Illud autem scitote, quoniam si sciret paterfamilias qua hora fur venturus esset, vigilaret utique, et non sineret perfodi domum suam.

24:43 But know this ye, that if the goodman of the house knew at what hour the thief would come, he would certainly watch, and would not suffer his house to be broken open.

24:44 Ideo et vos estote parati : quia qua nescitis hora Filius hominis venturus est.

24:44 Wherefore be you also ready, because at what hour you know not the Son of man will come.

24:45 Quis, putas, est fidelis servus, et prudens, quem constituit dominus suus super familiam suam ut det illis cibum in tempore ?

24:45 Who, thinkest thou, is a faithful and wise servant, whom his lord hath appointed over his family, to give them meat in season.

24:46 Beatus ille servus, quem cum venerit dominus ejus, invenerit sic facientem.

24:46 Blessed is that servant, whom when his lord shall come he shall find so doing.

24:47 Amen dico vobis, quoniam super omnia bona sua constituet eum.

24:47 Amen I say to you, he shall place him over all his goods.

24:48 Si autem dixerit malus servus ille in corde suo : Moram fecit dominus meus venire :

24:48 But if that evil servant shall say in his heart: My lord is long a coming:

24:49 et cœperit percutere conservos suos, manducet autem et bibat cum ebriosis :

24:49 And shall begin to strike his fellow servants, and shall eat and drink with drunkards:

24:50 veniet dominus servi illius in die qua non sperat, et hora qua ignorat :

24:50 The lord of that servant shall come in a day that he hopeth not, and at an hour that he knoweth not:

24:51 et dividet eum, partemque ejus ponet cum hypocritis : illic erit fletus et stridor dentium.

24:51 And shall separate him, and appoint his portion with the hypocrites. There shall be weeping and gnashing of teeth.

25:1 Tunc simile erit regnum cælorum decem virginibus : quæ accipientes lampades suas exierunt obviam sponso et sponsæ.

25:2 Quinque autem ex eis erant fatuæ, et quinque prudentes :

25:3 sed quinque fatuæ, acceptis lampadibus, non sumpserunt oleum secum :

25:4 prudentes vero acceperunt oleum in vasis suis cum lampadibus.

25:5 Moram autem faciente sponso, dormitaverunt omnes et dormierunt.

25:6 Media autem nocte clamor factus est : Ecce sponsus venit, exite obviam ei.

25:7 Tunc surrexerunt omnes virgines illæ, et ornaverunt lampades suas.

25:8 Fatuæ autem sapientibus dixerunt : Date nobis de oleo vestro, quia lampades nostræ extinguuntur.

25:9 Responderunt prudentes, dicentes : Ne forte non sufficiat nobis, et vobis, ite potius ad vendentes, et emite vobis.

25:10 Dum autem irent emere, venit sponsus : et quæ paratæ erant, intraverunt cum eo ad nuptias, et clausa est janua.

25:11 Novissime vero veniunt et reliquæ virgines, dicentes : Domine, domine, aperi nobis.

25:12 At ille respondens, ait : Amen dico vobis, nescio vos.

25:13 Vigilate itaque, quia nescitis diem, neque horam.

25:14 Sicut enim homo peregre proficiscens, vocavit servos suos, et tradidit illis bona sua.

25:15 Et uni dedit quinque talenta, alii autem duo, alii vero unum, unicuique secundum propriam virtutem : et profectus est statim.

25:16 Abiit autem qui quinque talenta acceperat, et operatus est in eis, et lucratus est alia quinque.

25:17 Similiter et qui duo acceperat, lucratus est alia duo.

25:18 Qui autem unum acceperat, abiens fodit in terram, et abscondit pecuniam domini sui.

25:19 Post multum vero temporis venit dominus servorum illorum, et posuit rationem cum eis.

25:20 Et accedens qui quinque talenta acceperat, obtulit alia quinque talenta, dicens : Domine,

25:1 Then shall the kingdom of heaven be like to ten virgins, who taking their lamps went out to meet the bridegroom and the bride.

25:2 And five of them were foolish, and five wise.

25:3 But the five foolish, having taken their lamps, did not take oil with them:

25:4 But the wise took oil in their vessels with the lamps.

25:5 And the bridegroom tarrying, they all slumbered and slept.

25:6 And at midnight there was a cry made: Behold the bridegroom cometh, go ye forth to meet him.

25:7 Then all those virgins arose and trimmed their lamps.

25:8 And the foolish said to the wise: Give us of your oil, for our lamps are gone out.

25:9 The wise answered, saying: Lest perhaps there be not enough for us and for you, go ye rather to them that sell, and buy for yourselves.

25:10 Now whilst they went to buy, the bridegroom came: and they that were ready, went in with him to the marriage, and the door was shut.

25:11 But at last come also the other virgins, saying: Lord, Lord, open to us.

25:12 But he answering said: Amen I say to you, I know you not.

25:13 Watch ye therefore, because you know not the day nor the hour.

25:14 For even as a man going into a far country, called his servants, and delivered to them his goods;

25:15 And to one he gave five talents, and to another two, and to another one, to every one according to his proper ability: and immediately he took his journey.

25:16 And he that had received the five talents, went his way, and traded with the same, and gained other five.

25:17 And in like manner he that had received the two, gained other two.

25:18 But he that had received the one, going his way digged into the earth, and hid his lord's money.

25:19 But after a long time the lord of those servants came, and reckoned with them.

25:20 And he that had received the five talents coming, brought other five talents, saying:

quinque talenta tradidisti mihi, ecce alia quinque superlucratus sum.

25:21 Ait illi dominus ejus : Euge serve bone, et fidelis : quia super pauca fuisti fidelis, super multa te constituam ; intra in gaudium domini tui.

25:22 Accessit autem et qui duo talenta acceperat, et ait : Domine, duo talenta tradidisti mihi, ecce alia duo lucratus sum.

25:23 Ait illi dominus ejus : Euge serve bone, et fidelis : quia super pauca fuisti fidelis, super multa te constituam ; intra in gaudium domini tui.

25:24 Accedens autem et qui unum talentum acceperat, ait : Domine, scio quia homo durus es ; metis ubi non seminasti, et congregas ubi non sparsisti :

25:25 et timens abii, et abscondi talentum tuum in terra : ecce habes quod tuum est.

25:26 Respondens autem dominus ejus, dixit ei : Serve male, et piger, sciebas quia meto ubi non semino, et congrego ubi non sparsi :

25:27 oportuit ergo te committere pecuniam meam numulariis, et veniens ego recepissem utique quod meum est cum usura.

25:28 Tollite itaque ab eo talentum, et date ei qui habet decem talenta :

25:29 omni enim habenti dabitur, et abundabit : ei autem qui non habet, et quod videtur habere, auferetur ab eo.

25:30 Et inutilem servum ejicite in tenebras exteriores : illic erit fletus, et stridor dentium.

25:31 Cum autem venerit Filius hominis in majestate sua, et omnes angeli cum eo, tunc sedebit super sedem majestatis suæ :

25:32 et congregabuntur ante eum omnes gentes, et separabit eos ab invicem, sicut pastor segregat oves ab hædis :

25:33 et statuet oves quidem a dextris suis, hædos autem a sinistris.

25:34 Tunc dicet rex his qui a dextris ejus erunt : Venite benedicti Patris mei, possidete paratum vobis regnum a constitutione mundi :

25:35 esurivi enim, et dedistis mihi manducare : sitivi, et dedistis mihi bibere : hospes eram, et

Lord, thou didst deliver to me five talents, behold I have gained other five over and above.

25:21 His lord said to him: Well done, good and faithful servant, because thou hast been faithful over a few things, I will place thee over many things: enter thou into the joy of thy lord.

25:22 And he also that had received the two talents came and said: Lord, thou deliveredst two talents to me: behold I have gained other two.

25:23 His lord said to him: Well done, good and faithful servant: because thou hast been faithful over a few things, I will place thee over many things: enter thou into the joy of thy lord.

25:24 But he that had received the one talent, came and said: Lord, I know that thou art a hard man; thou reapest where thou hast not sown, and gatherest where thou hast not strewed.

25:25 And being afraid I went and hid thy talent in the earth: behold here thou hast that which is thine.

25:26 And his lord answering, said to him: Wicked and slothful servant, thou knewest that I reap where I sow not, and gather where I have not strewed:

25:27 Thou oughtest therefore to have committed my money to the bankers, and at my coming I should have received my own with usury.

25:28 Take ye away therefore the talent from him, and give it to him that hath ten talents.

25:29 For to every one that hath shall be given, and he shall abound: but from him that hath not, that also which he seemeth to have shall be taken away.

25:30 And the unprofitable servant cast ye out into the exterior darkness. There shall be weeping and gnashing of teeth.

25:31 And when the Son of man shall come in his majesty, and all the angels with him, then shall he sit upon the seat of his majesty.

25:32 And all nations shall be gathered together before him, and he shall separate them one from another, as the shepherd separateth the sheep from the goats:

25:33 And he shall set the sheep on his right hand, but the goats on his left.

25:34 Then shall the king say to them that shall be on his right hand: Come, ye blessed of my Father, possess you the kingdom prepared for you from the foundation of the world.

25:35 For I was hungry, and you gave me to eat; I was thirsty, and you gave me to drink; I was a

collegistis me :

25:36 nudus, et cooperuistis me : infirmus, et visitastis me : in carcere eram, et venistis ad me.

25:37 Tunc respondebunt ei justi, dicentes : Domine, quando te vidimus esurientem, et pavimus te : sitientem, et dedimus tibi potum ?

25:38 quando autem te vidimus hospitem, et collegimus te : aut nudum, et cooperuimus te ?

25:39 aut quando te vidimus infirmum, aut in carcere, et venimus ad te ?

25:40 Et respondens rex, dicet illis : Amen dico vobis, quamdiu fecistis uni ex his fratribus meis minimis, mihi fecistis.

25:41 Tunc dicet et his qui a sinistris erunt : Discedite a me maledicti in ignem æternum, qui paratus est diabolo, et angelis ejus :

25:42 esurivi enim, et non dedistis mihi manducare : sitivi, et non dedistis mihi potum :

25:43 hospes eram, et non collegistis me : nudus, et non cooperuistis me : infirmus, et in carcere, et non visitastis me.

25:44 Tunc respondebunt ei et ipsi, dicentes : Domine, quando te vidimus esurientem, aut sitientem, aut hospitem, aut nudum, aut infirmum, aut in carcere, et non ministravimus tibi ?

25:45 Tunc respondebit illis, dicens : Amen dico vobis : Quamdiu non fecistis uni de minoribus his, nec mihi fecistis.

25:46 Et ibunt hi in supplicium æternum : justi autem in vitam æternam.

26:1 Et factum est : cum consummasset Jesus sermones hos omnes, dixit discipulis suis :

26:2 Scitis quia post biduum Pascha fiet, et Filius hominis tradetur ut crucifigatur.

26:3 Tunc congregati sunt principes sacerdotum, et seniores populi, in atrium principis sacerdotum, qui dicebatur Caiphas :

26:4 et consilium fecerunt ut Jesum dolo tenerent, et occiderent.

26:5 Dicebant autem : Non in die festo, ne forte tumultus fieret in populo.

26:6 Cum autem Jesus esset in Bethania in domo Simonis leprosi,

26:7 accessit ad eum mulier habens alabastrum

stranger, and you took me in:

25:36 Naked, and you covered me: sick, and you visited me: I was in prison, and you came to me.

25:37 Then shall the just answer him, saying: Lord, when did we see thee hungry, and fed thee; thirsty, and gave thee drink?

25:38 And when did we see thee a stranger, and took thee in? or naked, and covered thee?

25:39 Or when did we see thee sick or in prison, and came to thee?

25:40 And the king answering, shall say to them: Amen I say to you, as long as you did it to one of these my least brethren, you did it to me.

25:41 Then he shall say to them also that shall be on his left hand: Depart from me, you cursed, into everlasting fire which was prepared for the devil and his angels.

25:42 For I was hungry, and you gave me not to eat: I was thirsty, and you gave me not to drink.

25:43 I was a stranger, and you took me not in: naked, and you covered me not: sick and in prison, and you did not visit me.

25:44 Then they also shall answer him, saying: Lord, when did we see thee hungry, or thirsty, or a stranger, or naked, or sick, or in prison, and did not minister to thee?

25:45 Then he shall answer them, saying: Amen I say to you, as long as you did it not to one of these least, neither did you do it to me.

25:46 And these shall go into everlasting punishment: but the just, into life everlasting.

26:1 And it came to pass, when Jesus had ended all these words, he said to his disciples:

26:2 You know that after two days shall be the pasch, and the son of man shall be delivered up to be crucified:

26:3 Then were gathered together the chief priests and ancients of the people into the court of the high priest, who was called Caiphas:

26:4 And they consulted together, that by subtilty they might apprehend Jesus, and put him to death.

26:5 But they said: Not on the festival day, lest perhaps there should be a tumult among the people.

26:6 And when Jesus was in Bethania, in the house of Simon the leper,

26:7 There came to him a woman having an ala-

unguenti pretiosi, et effudit super caput ipsius recumbentis.

^{26:8} Videntes autem discipuli, indignati sunt, dicentes : Ut quid perditio hæc ?

^{26:9} potuit enim istud venundari multo, et dari pauperibus.

^{26:10} Sciens autem Jesus, ait illis : Quid molesti estis huic mulieri ? opus enim bonum operata est in me.

^{26:11} Nam semper pauperes habetis vobiscum : me autem non semper habetis.

^{26:12} Mittens enim hæc unguentum hoc in corpus meum, ad sepeliendum me fecit.

^{26:13} Amen dico vobis, ubicumque prædicatum fuerit hoc Evangelium in toto mundo, dicetur et quod hæc fecit in memoriam ejus.

^{26:14} Tunc abiit unus de duodecim, qui dicebatur Judas Iscariotes, ad principes sacerdotum :

^{26:15} et ait illis : Quid vultis mihi dare, et ego vobis eum tradam ? At illi constituerunt ei triginta argenteos.

^{26:16} Et exinde quærebat opportunitatem ut eum traderet.

^{26:17} Prima autem die azymorum accesserunt discipuli ad Jesum, dicentes : Ubi vis paremus tibi comedere Pascha ?

^{26:18} At Jesus dixit : Ite in civitatem ad quemdam, et dicite ei : Magister dicit : Tempus meum prope est, apud te facio Pascha cum discipulis meis.

^{26:19} Et fecerunt discipuli sicut constituit illis Jesus, et paraverunt Pascha.

^{26:20} Vespere autem facto, discumbebat cum duodecim discipulis suis.

^{26:21} Et edentibus illis, dixit : Amen dico vobis, quia unus vestrum me traditurus est.

^{26:22} Et contristati valde, cœperunt singuli dicere : Numquid ego sum Domine ?

^{26:23} At ipse respondens, ait : Qui intingit mecum manum in paropside, hic me tradet.

^{26:24} Filius quidem hominis vadit, sicut scriptum est de illo : væ autem homini illi, per quem Filius hominis tradetur ! bonum erat ei, si natus non fuisset homo ille.

^{26:25} Respondens autem Judas, qui tradidit eum, dixit : Numquid ego sum Rabbi ? Ait illi : Tu dixisti.

^{26:26} Cœnantibus autem eis, accepit Jesus panem, et benedixit, ac fregit, deditque discipulis suis, et ait : Accipite, et comedite : hoc est

baster box of precious ointment, and poured it on his head as he was at table.

^{26:8} And the disciples seeing it, had indignation, saying: To what purpose is this waste?

^{26:9} For this might have been sold for much, and given to the poor.

^{26:10} And Jesus knowing it, said to them: Why do you trouble this woman? for she hath wrought a good work upon me.

^{26:11} For the poor you have always with you: but me you have not always.

^{26:12} For she in pouring this ointment upon my body, hath done it for my burial.

^{26:13} Amen I say to you, wheresoever this gospel shall be preached in the whole world, that also which she hath done, shall be told for a memory of her.

^{26:14} Then went one of the twelve, who was called Judas Iscariot, to the chief priests,

^{26:15} And said to them: What will you give me, and I will deliver him unto you? But they appointed him thirty pieces of silver.

^{26:16} And from thenceforth he sought opportunity to betray him.

^{26:17} And on the first day of the Azymes, the disciples came to Jesus, saying: Where wilt thou that we prepare for thee to eat the pasch?

^{26:18} But Jesus said: Go ye into the city to a certain man, and say to him: the master saith, My time is near at hand, with thee I make the pasch with my disciples.

^{26:19} And the disciples did as Jesus appointed to them, and they prepared the pasch.

^{26:20} But when it was evening, he sat down with his twelve disciples.

^{26:21} And whilst they were eating, he said: Amen I say to you, that one of you is about to betray me.

^{26:22} And they being very much troubled, began every one to say: Is it I, Lord?

^{26:23} But he answering, said: He that dippeth his hand with me in the dish, he shall betray me.

^{26:24} The Son of man indeed goeth, as it is written of him: but woe to that man by whom the Son of man shall be betrayed: it were better for him, if that man had not been born.

^{26:25} And Judas that betrayed him, answering, said: Is it I, Rabbi? He saith to him: Thou hast said it.

^{26:26} And whilst they were at supper, Jesus took bread, and blessed, and broke: and gave to his disciples, and said: Take ye, and eat. This is my

corpus meum.

26:27 Et accipiens calicem, gratias egit : et dedit illis, dicens : Bibite ex hoc omnes.

26:28 Hic est enim sanguis meus novi testamenti, qui pro multis effundetur in remissionem peccatorum.

26:29 Dico autem vobis : non bibam amodo de hoc genimine vitis usque in diem illum, cum illud bibam vobiscum novum in regno Patris mei.

26:30 Et hymno dicto, exierunt in montem Oliveti.

26:31 Tunc dicit illis Jesus : Omnes vos scandalum patiemini in me in ista nocte. Scriptum est enim : Percutiam pastorem, et dispergentur oves gregis.

26:32 Postquam autem resurrexero, præcedam vos in Galilæam.

26:33 Respondens autem Petrus, ait illi : Et si omnes scandalizati fuerint in te, ego numquam scandalizabor.

26:34 Ait illi Jesus : Amen dico tibi, quia in hac nocte, antequam gallus cantet, ter me negabis.

26:35 Ait illi Petrus : Etiamsi oportuerit me mori tecum, non te negabo. Similiter et omnes discipuli dixerunt.

26:36 Tunc venit Jesus cum illis in villam, quæ dicitur Gethsemani, et dixit discipulis suis : Sedete hic donec vadam illuc, et orem.

26:37 Et assumpto Petro, et duobus filiis Zebedæi, cœpit contristari et mœstus esse.

26:38 Tunc ait illis : Tristis est anima mea usque ad mortem : sustinete hic, et vigilate mecum.

26:39 Et progressus pusillum, procidit in faciem suam, orans, et dicens : Pater mi, si possibile est, transeat a me calix iste : verumtamen non sicut ego volo, sed sicut tu.

26:40 Et venit ad discipulos suos, et invenit eos dormientes, et dicit Petro : Sic non potuistis una hora vigilare mecum ?

26:41 Vigilate, et orate ut non intretis in tentationem. Spiritus quidem promptus est, caro autem infirma.

26:42 Iterum secundo abiit, et oravit, dicens : Pater mi, si non potest hic calix transire nisi bibam illum, fiat voluntas tua.

26:43 Et venit iterum, et invenit eos dormien-

body.

26:27 And taking the chalice, he gave thanks, and gave to them, saying: Drink ye all of this.

26:28 For this is my blood of the new testament, which shall be shed for many unto remission of sins.

26:29 And I say to you, I will not drink from henceforth of this fruit of the vine, until that day when I shall drink it with you new in the kingdom of my Father.

26:30 And a hymn being said, they went out unto mount Olivet.

26:31 Then Jesus said to them: All you shall be scandalized in me this night. For it is written: I will strike the shepherd, and the sheep of the flock shall be dispersed.

26:32 But after I shall be risen again, I will go before you into Galilee.

26:33 And Peter answering, said to him: Although all shall be scandalized in thee, I will never be scandalized.

26:34 Jesus said to him: Amen I say to thee, that in this night before the cock crow, thou wilt deny me thrice.

26:35 Peter saith to him: Yea, though I should die with thee, I will not deny thee. And in like manner said all the disciples.

26:36 Then Jesus came with them into a country place which is called Gethsemani; and he said to his disciples: Sit you here, till I go yonder and pray.

26:37 And taking with him Peter and the two sons of Zebedee, he began to grow sorrowful and to be sad.

26:38 Then he saith to them: My soul is sorrowful even unto death: stay you here, and watch with me.

26:39 And going a little further, he fell upon his face, praying, and saying: My Father, if it be possible, let this chalice pass from me. Nevertheless not as I will, but as thou wilt.

26:40 And he cometh to his disciples, and findeth them asleep, and he saith to Peter: What? Could you not watch one hour with me?

26:41 Watch ye, and pray that ye enter not into temptation. The spirit indeed is willing, but the flesh weak.

26:42 Again the second time, he went and prayed, saying: My Father, if this chalice may not pass away, but I must drink it, thy will be done.

26:43 And he cometh again and findeth them

tes : erant enim oculi eorum gravati.

26:44 Et relictis illis, iterum abiit, et oravit tertio, eumdem sermonem dicens.

26:45 Tunc venit ad discipulos suos, et dicit illis : Dormite jam, et requiescite : ecce appropinquavit hora, et Filius hominis tradetur in manus peccatorum.

26:46 Surgite, eamus : ecce appropinquavit qui me tradet.

26:47 Adhuc eo loquente, ecce Judas unus de duodecim venit, et cum eo turba multa cum gladiis et fustibus, missi a principibus sacerdotum, et senioribus populi.

26:48 Qui autem tradidit eum, dedit illis signum, dicens : Quemcumque osculatus fuero, ipse est, tenete eum.

26:49 Et confestim accedens ad Jesum, dixit : Ave Rabbi. Et osculatus est eum.

26:50 Dixitque illi Jesus : Amice, ad quid venisti ? Tunc accesserunt, et manus injecerunt in Jesum, et tenuerunt eum.

26:51 Et ecce unus ex his qui erant cum Jesu, extendens manum, exemit gladium suum, et percutiens servum principis sacerdotum amputavit auriculam ejus.

26:52 Tunc ait illi Jesus : Converte gladium tuum in locum suum : omnes enim, qui acceperint gladium, gladio peribunt.

26:53 An putas, quia non possum rogare patrem meum, et exhibebit mihi modo plusquam duodecim legiones angelorum ?

26:54 Quomodo ergo implebuntur Scripturæ, quia sic oportet fieri ?

26:55 In illa hora dixit Jesus turbis : Tamquam ad latronem existis cum gladiis et fustibus comprehendere me : quotidie apud vos sedebam docens in templo, et non me tenuistis.

26:56 Hoc autem totum factum est, ut adimplerentur Scripturæ prophetarum. Tunc discipuli omnes, relicto eo, fugerunt.

26:57 At illi tenentes Jesum, duxerunt ad Caipham principem sacerdotum, ubi scribæ et seniores convenerant.

26:58 Petrus autem sequebatur eum a longe, usque in atrium principis sacerdotum. Et ingressus intro, sedebat cum ministris, ut videret finem.

26:59 Principes autem sacerdotum, et omne concilium, quærebant falsum testimonium contra Jesum, ut eum morti traderent :

sleeping: for their eyes were heavy.

26:44 And leaving them, he went again: and he prayed the third time, saying the selfsame word.

26:45 Then he cometh to his disciples, and saith to them: Sleep ye now and take your rest; behold the hour is at hand, and the Son of man shall be betrayed into the hands of sinners.

26:46 Rise, let us go: behold he is at hand that will betray me.

26:47 As he yet spoke, behold Judas, one of the twelve, came, and with him a great multitude with swords and clubs, sent from the chief priests and the ancients of the people.

26:48 And he that betrayed him, gave them a sign, saying: Whomsoever I shall kiss, that is he, hold him fast.

26:49 And forthwith coming to Jesus, he said: Hail, Rabbi. And he kissed him.

26:50 And Jesus said to him: Friend, whereto art thou come? Then they came up, and laid hands on Jesus, and held him.

26:51 And behold one of them that were with Jesus, stretching forth his hand, drew out his sword: and striking the servant of the high priest, cut off his ear.

26:52 Then Jesus saith to him: Put up again thy sword into its place: for all that take the sword shall perish with the sword.

26:53 Thinkest thou that I cannot ask my Father, and he will give me presently more than twelve legions of angels?

26:54 How then shall the scriptures be fulfilled, that so it must be done?

26:55 In that same hour Jesus said to the multitudes: You are come out as it were to a robber with swords and clubs to apprehend me. I sat daily with you, teaching in the temple, and you laid not hands on me.

26:56 Now all this was done, that the scriptures of the prophets might be fulfilled. Then the disciples all leaving him, fled.

26:57 But they holding Jesus led him to Caiphas the high priest, where the scribes and the ancients were assembled.

26:58 And Peter followed him afar off, even to the court of the high priest. And going in, he sat with the servants, that he might see the end.

26:59 And the chief priests and the whole council sought false witness against Jesus, that they might put him to death:

26:60 et non invenerunt, cum multi falsi testes accessissent. Novissime autem venerunt duo falsi testes,

26:61 et dixerunt : Hic dixit : Possum destruere templum Dei, et post triduum reædificare illud.

26:62 Et surgens princeps sacerdotum, ait illi : Nihil respondes ad ea, quæ isti adversum te testificantur ?

26:63 Jesus autem tacebat. Et princeps sacerdotum ait illi : Adjuro te per Deum vivum, ut dicas nobis si tu es Christus Filius Dei.

26:64 Dicit illi Jesus : Tu dixisti. Verumtamen dico vobis, amodo videbitis Filium hominis sedentem a dextris virtutis Dei, et venientem in nubibus cæli.

26:65 Tunc princeps sacerdotum scidit vestimenta sua, dicens : Blasphemavit : quid adhuc egemus testibus ? ecce nunc audistis blasphemiam :

26:66 quid vobis videtur ? At illi respondentes dixerunt : Reus est mortis.

26:67 Tunc exspuerunt in faciem ejus, et colaphis eum ceciderunt, alii autem palmas in faciem ejus dederunt,

26:68 dicentes : Prophetiza nobis Christe, quis est qui te percussit ?

26:69 Petrus vero sedebat foris in atrio : et accessit ad eum una ancilla, dicens : Et tu cum Jesu Galilæo eras.

26:70 At ille negavit coram omnibus, dicens : Nescio quid dicis.

26:71 Exeunte autem illo januam, vidit eum alia ancilla, et ait his qui erant ibi : Et hic erat cum Jesu Nazareno.

26:72 Et iterum negavit cum juramento : Quia non novi hominem.

26:73 Et post pusillum accesserunt qui stabant, et dixerunt Petro : Vere et tu ex illis es : nam et loquela tua manifestum te facit.

26:74 Tunc cœpit detestari et jurare quia non novisset hominem. Et continuo gallus cantavit.

26:75 Et recordatus est Petrus verbi Jesu, quod dixerat : Priusquam gallus cantet, ter me negabis. Et egressus foras, flevit amare.

26:60 And they found not, whereas many false witnesses had come in. And last of all there came two false witnesses:

26:61 And they said: This man said, I am able to destroy the temple of God, and after three days to rebuild it.

26:62 And the high priest rising up, said to him: Answerest thou nothing to the things which these witness against thee?

26:63 But Jesus held his peace. And the high priest said to him: I adjure thee by the living God, that thou tell us if thou be the Christ the Son of God.

26:64 Jesus saith to him: Thou hast said it. Nevertheless I say to you, hereafter you shall see the Son of man sitting on the right hand of the power of God, and coming in the clouds of heaven.

26:65 Then the high priest rent his garments, saying: He hath blasphemed; what further need have we of witnesses? Behold, now you have heard the blasphemy:

26:66 What think you? But they answering, said: He is guilty of death.

26:67 Then did they spit in his face, and buffeted him: and others struck his face with the palms of their hands,

26:68 Saying: Prophesy unto us, O Christ, who is he that struck thee?

26:69 But Peter sat without in the court: and there came to him a servant maid, saying: Thou also wast with Jesus the Galilean.

26:70 But he denied before them all, saying: I know not what thou sayest.

26:71 And as he went out of the gate, another maid saw him, and she saith to them that were there: This man also was with Jesus of Nazareth.

26:72 And again he denied with an oath, I know not the man.

26:73 And after a little while they came that stood by, and said to Peter: Surely thou also art one of them; for even thy speech doth discover thee.

26:74 Then he began to curse and to swear that he knew not the man. And immediately the cock crew.

26:75 And Peter remembered the word of Jesus which he had said: Before the cock crow, thou wilt deny me thrice. And going forth, he wept bitterly.

27:1 Mane autem facto, consilium inierunt omnes principes sacerdotum et seniores populi adversus Jesum, ut eum morti traderent.

27:2 Et vinctum adduxerunt eum, et tradiderunt Pontio Pilato præsidi.

27:3 Tunc videns Judas, qui eum tradidit, quod damnatus esset, pœnitentia ductus, retulit triginta argenteos principibus sacerdotum, et senioribus,

27:4 dicens : Peccavi, tradens sanguinem justum. At illi dixerunt : Quid ad nos ? tu videris.

27:5 Et projectis argenteis in templo, recessit : et abiens laqueo se suspendit.

27:6 Principes autem sacerdotum, acceptis argenteis, dixerunt : Non licet eos mittere in corbonam : quia pretium sanguinis est.

27:7 Consilio autem inito, emerunt ex illis agrum figuli, in sepulturam peregrinorum.

27:8 Propter hoc vocatus est ager ille, Haceldama, hoc est, Ager sanguinis, usque in hodiernum diem.

27:9 Tunc impletum est quod dictum est per Jeremiam prophetam, dicentem : Et acceperunt triginta argenteos pretium appretiati, quem appretiaverunt a filiis Israël :

27:10 et dederunt eos in agrum figuli, sicut constituit mihi Dominus.

27:11 Jesus autem stetit ante præsidem, et interrogavit eum præses, dicens : Tu es rex Judæorum ? Dicit illi Jesus : Tu dicis.

27:12 Et cum accusaretur a principibus sacerdotum et senioribus, nihil respondit.

27:13 Tunc dicit illi Pilatus : Non audis quanta adversum te dicunt testimonia ?

27:14 Et non respondit ei ad ullum verbum, ita ut miraretur præses vehementer.

27:15 Per diem autem solemnem consueverat præses populo dimittere unum vinctum, quem voluissent :

27:16 habebat autem tunc vinctum insignem, qui dicebatur Barabbas.

27:17 Congregatis ergo illis, dixit Pilatus : Quem vultis dimittam vobis : Barabbam, an Jesum, qui dicitur Christus ?

27:18 Sciebat enim quod per invidiam tradidissent eum.

27:1 And when morning was come, all the chief priests and ancients of the people took counsel against Jesus, that they might put him to death.

27:2 And they brought him bound, and delivered him to Pontius Pilate the governor.

27:3 Then Judas, who betrayed him, seeing that he was condemned, repenting himself, brought back the thirty pieces of silver to the chief priests and ancients,

27:4 Saying: I have sinned in betraying innocent blood. But they said: What is that to us? look thou to it.

27:5 And casting down the pieces of silver in the temple, he departed: and went and hanged himself with an halter.

27:6 But the chief priests having taken the pieces of silver, said: It is not lawful to put them into the corbona, because it is the price of blood.

27:7 And after they had consulted together, they bought with them the potter's field, to be a burying place for strangers.

27:8 For this cause the field was called Haceldama, that is, The field of blood, even to this day.

27:9 Then was fulfilled that which was spoken by Jeremias the prophet, saying: And they took the thirty pieces of silver, the price of him that was prized, whom they prized of the children of Israel.

27:10 And they gave them unto the potter's field, as the Lord appointed to me.

27:11 And Jesus stood before the governor, and the governor asked him, saying: Art thou the king of the Jews? Jesus saith to him: Thou sayest it.

27:12 And when he was accused by the chief priests and ancients, he answered nothing.

27:13 Then Pilate saith to him: Dost not thou hear how great testimonies they allege against thee?

27:14 And he answered him to never a word; so that the governor wondered exceedingly.

27:15 Now upon the solemn day the governor was accustomed to release to the people one prisoner, whom they would.

27:16 And he had then a notorious prisoner, that was called Barabbas.

27:17 They therefore being gathered together, Pilate said: Whom will you that I release to you, Barabbas, or Jesus that is called Christ?

27:18 For he knew that for envy they had delivered him.

27:19 Sedente autem illo pro tribunali, misit ad eum uxor ejus, dicens : Nihil tibi, et justo illi : multa enim passa sum hodie per visum propter eum.

27:20 Principes autem sacerdotum et seniores persuaserunt populis ut peterent Barabbam, Jesum vero perderent.

27:21 Respondens autem præses, ait illis : Quem vultis vobis de duobus dimitti ? At illi dixerunt : Barabbam.

27:22 Dicit illis Pilatus : Quid igitur faciam de Jesu, qui dicitur Christus ?

27:23 Dicunt omnes : Crucifigatur. Ait illis præses : Quid enim mali fecit ? At illi magis clamabant dicentes : Crucifigatur.

27:24 Videns autem Pilatus quia nihil proficeret, sed magis tumultus fieret : accepta aqua, lavit manus coram populo, dicens : Innocens ego sum a sanguine justi hujus : vos videritis.

27:25 Et respondens universus populus, dixit : Sanguis ejus super nos, et super filios nostros.

27:26 Tunc dimisit illis Barabbam : Jesum autem flagellatum tradidit eis ut crucifigeretur.

27:27 Tunc milites præsidis suscipientes Jesum in prætorium, congregaverunt ad eum universam cohortem :

27:28 et exuentes eum, chlamydem coccineam circumdederunt ei,

27:29 et plectentes coronam de spinis, posuerunt super caput ejus, et arundinem in dextera ejus. Et genu flexo ante eum, illudebant ei, dicentes : Ave rex Judæorum.

27:30 Et exspuentes in eum, acceperunt arundinem, et percutiebant caput ejus.

27:31 Et postquam illuserunt ei, exuerunt eum chlamyde, et induerunt eum vestimentis ejus, et duxerunt eum ut crucifigerent.

27:32 Exeuntes autem invenerunt hominem Cyrenæum, nomine Simonem : hunc angariaverunt ut tolleret crucem ejus.

27:33 Et venerunt in locum qui dicitur Golgotha, quod est Calvariæ locus.

27:34 Et dederunt ei vinum bibere cum felle mistum. Et cum gustasset, noluit bibere.

27:35 Postquam autem crucifixerunt eum, diviserunt vestimenta ejus, sortem mittentes : ut impleretur quod dictum est per prophetam di-

27:19 And as he was sitting in the place of judgment, his wife sent to him, saying: Have thou nothing to do with that just man; for I have suffered many things this day in a dream because of him.

27:20 But the chief priests and ancients persuaded the people, that they should ask Barabbas, and make Jesus away.

27:21 And the governor answering, said to them: Whether will you of the two to be released unto you? But they said, Barabbas.

27:22 Pilate saith to them: What shall I do then with Jesus that is called Christ? They say all: Let him be crucified.

27:23 The governor said to them: Why, what evil hath he done? But they cried out the more, saying: Let him be crucified.

27:24 And Pilate seeing that he prevailed nothing, but that rather a tumult was made; taking water washed his hands before the people, saying: I am innocent of the blood of this just man; look you to it.

27:25 And the whole people answering, said: His blood be upon us and our children.

27:26 Then he released to them Barabbas, and having scourged Jesus, delivered him unto them to be crucified.

27:27 Then the soldiers of the governor taking Jesus into the hall, gathered together unto him the whole band;

27:28 And stripping him, they put a scarlet cloak about him.

27:29 And platting a crown of thorns, they put it upon his head, and a reed in his right hand. And bowing the knee before him, they mocked him, saying: Hail, king of the Jews.

27:30 And spitting upon him, they took the reed, and struck his head.

27:31 And after they had mocked him, they took off the cloak from him, and put on him his own garments, and led him away to crucify him.

27:32 And going out, they found a man of Cyrene, named Simon: him they forced to take up his cross.

27:33 And they came to the place that is called Golgotha, which is the place of Calvary.

27:34 And they gave him wine to drink mingled with gall. And when he had tasted, he would not drink.

27:35 And after they had crucified him, they divided his garments, casting lots; that it might be fulfilled which was spoken by the prophet,

centem : Diviserunt sibi vestimenta mea, et super vestem meam miserunt sortem.

27:36 Et sedentes servabant eum.

27:37 Et imposuerunt super caput ejus causam ipsius scriptam : Hic est Jesus rex Judæorum.

27:38 Tunc crucifixi sunt cum eo duo latrones : unus a dextris, et unus a sinistris.

27:39 Prætereuntes autem blasphemabant eum moventes capita sua,

27:40 et dicentes : Vah ! qui destruis templum Dei, et in triduo illud reædificas : salva temetipsum : si Filius Dei es, descende de cruce.

27:41 Similiter et principes sacerdotum illudentes cum scribis et senioribus dicebant :

27:42 Alios salvos fecit, seipsum non potest salvum facere : si rex Israël est, descendat nunc de cruce, et credimus ei :

27:43 confidit in Deo : liberet nunc, si vult eum : dixit enim : Quia Filius Dei sum.

27:44 Idipsum autem et latrones, qui crucifixi erant cum eo, improperabant ei.

27:45 A sexta autem hora tenebræ factæ sunt super universam terram usque ad horam nonam.

27:46 Et circa horam nonam clamavit Jesus voce magna, dicens : Eli, Eli, lamma sabacthani ? hoc est : Deus meus, Deus meus, ut quid dereliquisti me ?

27:47 Quidam autem illic stantes, et audientes, dicebant : Eliam vocat iste.

27:48 Et continuo currens unus ex eis, acceptam spongiam implevit aceto, et imposuit arundini, et dabat ei bibere.

27:49 Ceteri vero dicebant : Sine, videamus an veniat Elias liberans eum.

27:50 Jesus autem iterum clamans voce magna, emisit spiritum.

27:51 Et ecce velum templi scissum est in duas partes a summo usque deorsum : et terra mota est, et petræ scissæ sunt,

27:52 et monumenta aperta sunt : et multa corpora sanctorum, qui dormierant, surrexerunt.

27:53 Et exeuntes de monumentis post resurrectionem ejus, venerunt in sanctam civitatem, et apparuerunt multis.

27:54 Centurio autem, et qui cum eo erant, custodientes Jesum, viso terræmotu, et his quæ fiebant, timuerunt valde, dicentes : Vere Filius Dei erat iste.

saying: They divided my garments among them; and upon my vesture they cast lots.

27:36 And they sat and watched him.

27:37 And they put over his head his cause written: THIS IS JESUS THE KING OF THE JEWS.

27:38 Then were crucified with him two thieves: one on the right hand, and one on the left.

27:39 And they that passed by, blasphemed him, wagging their heads,

27:40 And saying: Vah, thou that destroyest the temple of God, and in three days dost rebuild it: save thy own self: if thou be the Son of God, come down from the cross.

27:41 In like manner also the chief priests, with the scribes and ancients, mocking, said:

27:42 He saved others; himself he cannot save. If he be the king of Israel, let him now come down from the cross, and we will believe him.

27:43 He trusted in God; let him now deliver him if he will have him; for he said: I am the Son of God.

27:44 And the selfsame thing the thieves also, that were crucified with him, reproached him with.

27:45 Now from the sixth hour there was darkness over the whole earth, until the ninth hour.

27:46 And about the ninth hour Jesus cried with a loud voice, saying: Eli, Eli, lamma sabacthani? that is, My God, my God, why hast thou forsaken me?

27:47 And some that stood there and heard, said: This man calleth Elias.

27:48 And immediately one of them running took a sponge, and filled it with vinegar; and put it on a reed, and gave him to drink.

27:49 And the others said: Let be, let us see whether Elias will come to deliver him.

27:50 And Jesus again crying with a loud voice, yielded up the ghost.

27:51 And behold the veil of the temple was rent in two from the top even to the bottom, and the earth quaked, and the rocks were rent.

27:52 And the graves were opened: and many bodies of the saints that had slept arose,

27:53 And coming out of the tombs after his resurrection, came into the holy city, and appeared to many.

27:54 Now the centurion and they that were with him watching Jesus, having seen the earthquake, and the things that were done, were sore afraid, saying: Indeed this was the

Son of God.

27:55 Erant autem ibi mulieres multæ a longe, quæ secutæ erant Jesum a Galilæa, ministrantes ei :

27:56 inter quas erat Maria Magdalene, et Maria Jacobi, et Joseph mater, et mater filiorum Zebedæi.

27:57 Cum autem sero factum esset, venit quidam homo dives ab Arimathæa, nomine Joseph, qui et ipse discipulus erat Jesu :

27:58 hic accessit ad Pilatum, et petiit corpus Jesu. Tunc Pilatus jussit reddi corpus.

27:59 Et accepto corpore, Joseph involvit illud in sindone munda,

27:60 et posuit illud in monumento suo novo, quod exciderat in petra. Et advolvit saxum magnum ad ostium monumenti, et abiit.

27:61 Erant autem ibi Maria Magdalene, et altera Maria, sedentes contra sepulchrum.

27:62 Altera autem die, quæ est post Parasceven, convenerunt principes sacerdotum et pharisæi ad Pilatum,

27:63 dicentes : Domine, recordati sumus, quia seductor ille dixit adhuc vivens : Post tres dies resurgam.

27:64 Jube ergo custodiri sepulchrum usque in diem tertium : ne forte veniant discipuli ejus, et furentur eum, et dicant plebi : Surrexit a mortuis : et erit novissimus error pejor priore.

27:65 Ait illis Pilatus : Habetis custodiam, ite, custodite sicut scitis.

27:66 Illi autem abeuntes, munierunt sepulchrum, signantes lapidem, cum custodibus.

28:1 Vespere autem sabbati, quæ lucescit in prima sabbati, venit Maria Magdalene, et altera Maria, videre sepulchrum.

28:2 Et ecce terræmotus factus est magnus. Angelus enim Domini descendit de cælo : et accedens revolvit lapidem, et sedebat super eum :

28:3 erat autem aspectus ejus sicut fulgur : et vestimentum ejus sicut nix.

28:4 Præ timore autem ejus exterriti sunt custodes, et facti sunt velut mortui.

28:5 Respondens autem angelus dixit mulieribus : Nolite timere vos : scio enim, quod Jesum, qui crucifixus est, quæritis.

27:55 And there were there many women afar off, who had followed Jesus from Galilee, ministering unto him:

27:56 Among whom was Mary Magdalen, and Mary the mother of James and Joseph, and the mother of the sons of Zebedee.

27:57 And when it was evening, there came a certain rich man of Arimathea, named Joseph, who also himself was a disciple of Jesus.

27:58 He went to Pilate, and asked the body of Jesus. Then Pilate commanded that the body should be delivered.

27:59 And Joseph taking the body, wrapped it up in a clean linen cloth.

27:60 And laid it in his own new monument, which he had hewed out in a rock. And he rolled a great stone to the door of the monument, and went his way.

27:61 And there was there Mary Magdalen, and the other Mary sitting over against the sepulchre.

27:62 And the next day, which followed the day of preparation, the chief priests and the Pharisees came together to Pilate,

27:63 Saying: Sir, we have remembered, that that seducer said, while he was yet alive: After three days I will rise again.

27:64 Command therefore the sepulchre to be guarded until the third day: lest perhaps his disciples come and steal him away, and say to the people: He is risen from the dead; and the last error shall be worse than the first.

27:65 Pilate saith to them: You have a guard; go, guard it as you know.

27:66 And they departing, made the sepulchre sure, sealing the stone, and setting guards.

28:1 And in the end of the sabbath, when it began to dawn towards the first day of the week, came Mary Magdalen and the other Mary, to see the sepulchre.

28:2 And behold there was a great earthquake. For an angel of the Lord descended from heaven, and coming, rolled back the stone, and sat upon it.

28:3 And his countenance was as lightning, and his raiment as snow.

28:4 And for fear of him, the guards were struck with terror, and became as dead men.

28:5 And the angel answering, said to the women: Fear not you; for I know that you seek Jesus who was crucified.

28:6 Non est hic : surrexit enim, sicut dixit : venite, et videte locum ubi positus erat Dominus.

28:7 Et cito euntes, dicite discipulis ejus quia surrexit : et ecce præcedit vos in Galilæam : ibi eum videbitis : ecce prædixi vobis.

28:8 Et exierunt cito de monumento cum timore et gaudio magno, currentes nuntiare discipulis ejus.

28:9 Et ecce Jesus occurrit illis, dicens : Avete. Illæ autem accesserunt, et tenuerunt pedes ejus, et adoraverunt eum.

28:10 Tunc ait illis Jesus : Nolite timere : ite, nuntiate fratribus meis ut eant in Galilæam ; ibi me videbunt.

28:11 Quæ cum abiissent, ecce quidam de custodibus venerunt in civitatem, et nuntiaverunt principibus sacerdotum omnia quæ facta fuerant.

28:12 Et congregati cum senioribus consilio accepto, pecuniam copiosam dederunt militibus,

28:13 dicentes : Dicite quia discipuli ejus nocte venerunt, et furati sunt eum, nobis dormientibus.

28:14 Et si hoc auditum fuerit a præside, nos suadebimus ei, et securos vos faciemus.

28:15 At illi, accepta pecunia, fecerunt sicut erant edocti. Et divulgatum est verbum istud apud Judæos, usque in hodiernum diem.

28:16 Undecim autem discipuli abierunt in Galilæam in montem ubi constituerat illis Jesus.

28:17 Et videntes eum adoraverunt : quidam autem dubitaverunt.

28:18 Et accedens Jesus locutus est eis, dicens : Data est mihi omnis potestas in cælo et in terra :

28:19 euntes ergo docete omnes gentes : baptizantes eos in nomine Patris, et Filii, et Spiritus Sancti :

28:20 docentes eos servare omnia quæcumque mandavi vobis : et ecce ego vobiscum sum omnibus diebus, usque ad consummationem sæculi.

28:6 He is not here, for he is risen, as he said. Come, and see the place where the Lord was laid.

28:7 And going quickly, tell ye his disciples that he is risen: and behold he will go before you into Galilee; there you shall see him. Lo, I have foretold it to you.

28:8 And they went out quickly from the sepulchre with fear and great joy, running to tell his disciples.

28:9 And behold Jesus met them, saying: All hail. But they came up and took hold of his feet, and adored him.

28:10 Then Jesus said to them: Fear not. Go, tell my brethren that they go into Galilee, there they shall see me.

28:11 Who when they were departed, behold some of the guards came into the city, and told the chief priests all things that had been done.

28:12 And they being assembled together with the ancients, taking counsel, gave a great sum of money to the soldiers,

28:13 Saying: Say you, His disciples came by night, and stole him away when we were asleep.

28:14 And if the governor shall hear this, we will persuade him, and secure you.

28:15 So they taking the money, did as they were taught: and this word was spread abroad among the Jews even unto this day.

28:16 And the eleven disciples went into Galilee, unto the mountain where Jesus had appointed them.

28:17 And seeing him they adored: but some doubted.

28:18 And Jesus coming, spoke to them, saying: All power is given to me in heaven and in earth.

28:19 Going therefore, teach ye all nations; baptizing them in the name of the Father, and of the Son, and of the Holy Ghost.

28:20 Teaching them to observe all things whatsoever I have commanded you: and behold I am with you all days, even to the consummation of the world.

Sanctum Jesu Christi Evangelium Secundum Marcum

THE HOLY GOSPEL OF JESUS CHRIST ACCORDING TO MARK

NITIUM EVANGELII Jesu Christi, Filii Dei.

1:2 Sicut scriptum est in Isaia propheta : *Ecce ego mitto angelum meum ante faciem tuam, qui præparabit viam tuam ante te.*
1:3 *Vox clamantis in deserto : Parate viam Domini, rectas facite semitas ejus.*
1:4 Fuit Joannes in deserto baptizans, et prædicans baptismum pœnitentiæ in remissionem peccatorum.
1:5 Et egrediebatur ad eum omnis Judææ regio, et Jerosolymitæ universi, et baptizabantur ab illo in Jordanis flumine, confitentes peccata sua.
1:6 Et erat Joannes vestitus pilis cameli, et zona pellicea circa lumbos ejus, et locustas et mel silvestre edebat.
1:7 Et prædicabat dicens : Venit fortior post me, cujus non sum dignus procumbens solvere corrigiam calceamentorum ejus.

1:8 Ego baptizavi vos aqua, ille vero baptizabit vos Spiritu Sancto.
1:9 Et factum est : in diebus illis venit Jesus a Nazareth Galilææ : et baptizatus est a Joanne in Jordane.
1:10 Et statim ascendens de aqua, vidit cælos apertos, et Spiritum tamquam columbam descendentem, et manentem in ipso.
1:11 Et vox facta est de cælis : Tu es Filius meus dilectus, in te complacui.
1:12 Et statim Spiritus expulit eum in desertum.

HE BEGINNING OF THE GOSPEL of Jesus Christ, the Son of God.

1:2 As it is written in Isaias the prophet: *Behold I send my angel before thy face, who shall prepare the way before thee.*
1:3 *A voice of one crying in the desert: Prepare ye the way of the Lord, make straight his paths.*
1:4 John was in the desert baptizing, and preaching the baptism of penance, unto remission of sins.
1:5 And there went out to him all the country of Judea, and all they of Jerusalem, and were baptized by him in the river of Jordan, confessing their sins.
1:6 And John was clothed with camel's hair, and a leathern girdle about his loins; and he ate locusts and wild honey.
1:7 And he preached, saying: There cometh after me one mightier than I, the latchet of whose shoes I am not worthy to stoop down and loose.
1:8 I have baptized you with water; but he shall baptize you with the Holy Ghost.
1:9 And it came to pass, in those days, Jesus came from Nazareth of Galilee, and was baptized by John in the Jordan.
1:10 And forthwith coming up out of the water, he saw the heavens opened, and the Spirit as a dove descending, and remaining on him.
1:11 And there came a voice from heaven: Thou art my beloved Son; in thee I am well pleased.
1:12 And immediately the Spirit drove him out

1:13 Et erat in deserto quadraginta diebus, et quadraginta noctibus : et tentabatur a Satana : eratque cum bestiis, et angeli ministrabant illi.

1:14 Postquam autem traditus est Joannes, venit Jesus in Galilæam, prædicans Evangelium regni Dei,

1:15 et dicens : Quoniam impletum est tempus, et appropinquavit regnum Dei : pœnitemini, et credite Evangelio.

1:16 Et præteriens secus mare Galilææ, vidit Simonem, et Andream fratrem ejus, mittentes retia in mare (erant enim piscatores),

1:17 et dixit eis Jesus : Venite post me, et faciam vos fieri piscatores hominum.

1:18 Et protinus relictis retibus, secuti sunt eum.

1:19 Et progressus inde pusillum, vidit Jacobum Zebedæi, et Joannem fratrem ejus, et ipsos componentes retia in navi :

1:20 et statim vocavit illos. Et relicto patre suo Zebedæo in navi cum mercenariis, secuti sunt eum.

1:21 Et ingrediuntur Capharnaum : et statim sabbatis ingressus in synagogam, docebat eos.

1:22 Et stupebant super doctrina ejus : erat enim docens eos quasi potestatem habens, et non sicut scribæ.

1:23 Et erat in synagoga eorum homo in spiritu immundo : et exclamavit,

1:24 dicens : Quid nobis et tibi, Jesu Nazarene ? venisti perdere nos ? scio qui sis, Sanctus Dei.

1:25 Et comminatus est ei Jesus, dicens : Obmutesce, et exi de homine.

1:26 Et discerpens eum spiritus immundus, et exclamans voce magna, exiit ab eo.

1:27 Et mirati sunt omnes, ita ut conquirerent inter se dicentes : Quidnam est hoc ? quænam doctrina hæc nova ? quia in potestate etiam spiritibus immundis imperat, et obediunt ei.

1:28 Et processit rumor ejus statim in omnem regionem Galilææ.

1:29 Et protinus egredientes de synagoga, venerunt in domum Simonis et Andreæ, cum Jacobo et Joanne.

1:30 Decumbebat autem socrus Simonis febricitans : et statim dicunt ei de illa.

into the desert.

1:13 And he was in the desert forty days and forty nights, and was tempted by Satan; and he was with beasts, and the angels ministered to him.

1:14 And after that John was delivered up, Jesus came into Galilee, preaching the gospel of the kingdom of God,

1:15 And saying: The time is accomplished, and the kingdom of God is at hand: repent, and believe the gospel.

1:16 And passing by the sea of Galilee, he saw Simon and Andrew his brother, casting nets into the sea (for they were fishermen).

1:17 And Jesus said to them: Come after me, and I will make you to become fishers of men.

1:18 And immediately leaving their nets, they followed him.

1:19 And going on from thence a little farther, he saw James the son of Zebedee, and John his brother, who also were mending their nets in the ship:

1:20 And forthwith he called them. And leaving their father Zebedee in the ship with his hired men, they followed him.

1:21 And they entered into Capharnaum, and forthwith upon the sabbath days going into the synagogue, he taught them.

1:22 And they were astonished at his doctrine. For he was teaching them as one having power, and not as the scribes.

1:23 And there was in their synagogue a man with an unclean spirit; and he cried out,

1:24 Saying: What have we to do with thee, Jesus of Nazareth? art thou come to destroy us? I know who thou art, the Holy One of God.

1:25 And Jesus threatened him, saying: Speak no more, and go out of the man.

1:26 And the unclean spirit tearing him, and crying out with a loud voice, went out of him.

1:27 And they were all amazed, insomuch that they questioned among themselves, saying: What thing is this? what is this new doctrine? for with power he commandeth even the unclean spirits, and they obey him.

1:28 And the fame of him was spread forthwith into all the country of Galilee.

1:29 And immediately going out of the synagogue they came into the house of Simon and Andrew, with James and John.

1:30 And Simon's wife's mother lay in a fit of a fever: and forthwith they tell him of her.

1:31 Et accedens elevavit eam, apprehensa manu ejus : et continuo dimisit eam febris, et ministrabat eis.

1:32 Vespere autem facto cum occidisset sol, afferebant ad eum omnes male habentes, et dæmonia habentes :

1:33 et erat omnis civitas congregata ad januam.

1:34 Et curavit multos, qui vexabantur variis languoribus, et dæmonia multa ejiciebat, et non sinebat ea loqui, quoniam sciebant eum.

1:35 Et diluculo valde surgens, egressus abiit in desertum locum, ibique orabat.

1:36 Et prosecutus est eum Simon, et qui cum illo erant.

1:37 Et cum invenissent eum, dixerunt ei : Quia omnes quærunt te.

1:38 Et ait illis : Eamus in proximos vicos, et civitates, ut et ibi prædicem : ad hoc enim veni.

1:39 Et erat prædicans in synagogis eorum, et in omni Galilæa, et dæmonia ejiciens.

1:40 Et venit ad eum leprosus deprecans eum : et genu flexo dixit ei : Si vis, potes me mundare.

1:41 Jesus autem misertus ejus, extendit manum suam : et tangens eum, ait illi : Volo : mundare.

1:42 Et cum dixisset, statim discessit ab eo lepra, et mundatus est.

1:43 Et comminatus est ei, statimque ejecit illum,

1:44 et dicit ei : Vide nemini dixeris : sed vade, ostende te principi sacerdotum, et offer pro emundatione tua, quæ præcepit Moyses in testimonium illis.

1:45 At ille egressus cœpit prædicare, et diffamare sermonem, ita ut jam non posset manifeste introire in civitatem, sed foris in desertis locis esset, et conveniebant ad eum undique.

2:1 Et iterum intravit Capharnaum post dies,

2:2 et auditum est quod in domo esset, et convenerunt multi, ita ut non caperet neque ad januam, et loquebatur eis verbum.

2:3 Et venerunt ad eum ferentes paralyticum, qui a quatuor portabatur.

1:31 And coming to her, he lifted her up, taking her by the hand; and immediately the fever left her, and she ministered unto them.

1:32 And when it was evening, after sunset, they brought to him all that were ill and that were possessed with devils.

1:33 And all the city was gathered together at the door.

1:34 And he healed many that were troubled with divers diseases; and he cast out many devils, and he suffered them not to speak, because they knew him.

1:35 And rising very early, going out, he went into a desert place: and there he prayed.

1:36 And Simon, and they that were with him, followed after him.

1:37 And when they had found him, they said to him: All seek for thee.

1:38 And he saith to them: Let us go into the neighbouring towns and cities, that I may preach there also; for to this purpose am I come.

1:39 And he was preaching in their synagogues, and in all Galilee, and casting out devils.

1:40 And there came a leper to him, beseeching him, and kneeling down said to him: If thou wilt, thou canst make me clean.

1:41 And Jesus having compassion on him, stretched forth his hand; and touching him, saith to him: I will. Be thou made clean.

1:42 And when he had spoken, immediately the leprosy departed from him, and he was made clean.

1:43 And he strictly charged him, and forthwith sent him away.

1:44 And he saith to him: See thou tell no one; but go, shew thyself to the high priest, and offer for thy cleansing the things that Moses commanded, for a testimony to them.

1:45 But he being gone out, began to publish and to blaze abroad the word: so that he could not openly go into the city, but was without in desert places: and they flocked to him from all sides.

2:1 And again he entered into Capharnaum after some days.

2:2 And it was heard that he was in the house, and many came together, so that there was no room; no, not even at the door; and he spoke to them the word.

2:3 And they came to him, bringing one sick of the palsy, who was carried by four.

2:4 Et cum non possent offerre eum illi præ turba, nudaverunt tectum ubi erat : et patefacientes submiserunt grabatum in quo paralyticus jacebat.

2:5 Cum autem vidisset Jesus fidem illorum, ait paralytico : Fili, dimittuntur tibi peccata tua.

2:6 Erant autem illic quidam de scribis sedentes, et cogitantes in cordibus suis :

2:7 Quid hic sic loquitur ? blasphemat. Quis potest dimittere peccata, nisi solus Deus ?

2:8 Quo statim cognito Jesus spiritu suo, quia sic cogitarent intra se, dicit illis : Quid ista cogitatis in cordibus vestris ?

2:9 Quid est facilius dicere paralytico : Dimittuntur tibi peccata : an dicere : Surge, tolle grabatum tuum, et ambula ?

2:10 Ut autem sciatis quia Filius hominis habet potestatem in terra dimittendi peccata (ait paralytico),

2:11 tibi dico : Surge, tolle grabatum tuum, et vade in domum tuam.

2:12 Et statim surrexit ille : et, sublato grabato, abiit coram omnibus, ita ut mirarentur omnes, et honorificent Deum, dicentes : Quia numquam sic vidimus.

2:13 Et egressus est rursus ad mare, omnisque turba veniebat ad eum, et docebat eos.

2:14 Et cum præteriret, vidit Levi Alphæi sedentem ad telonium, et ait illi : Sequere me. Et surgens secutus est eum.

2:15 Et factum est, cum accumberet in domo illius, multi publicani et peccatores simul discumbebant cum Jesu et discipulis ejus : erant enim multi, qui et sequebantur eum.

2:16 Et scribæ et pharisæi videntes quia manducaret cum publicanis et peccatoribus, dicebant discipulis ejus : Quare cum publicanis et peccatoribus manducat et bibit Magister vester ?

2:17 Hoc audito Jesus ait illis : Non necesse habent sani medico, sed qui male habent : non enim veni vocare justos, sed peccatores.

2:18 Et erant discipuli Joannis et pharisæi jejunantes : et veniunt, et dicunt illi : Quare discipuli Joannis et pharisæorum jejunant, tui autem discipuli non jejunant ?

2:19 Et ait illis Jesus : Numquid possunt filii nuptiarum, quamdiu sponsus cum illis est, jejunare

2:4 And when they could not offer him unto him for the multitude, they uncovered the roof where he was; and opening it, they let down the bed wherein the man sick of the palsy lay.

2:5 And when Jesus had seen their faith, he saith to the sick of the palsy: Son, thy sins are forgiven thee.

2:6 And there were some of the scribes sitting there, and thinking in their hearts:

2:7 Why doth this man speak thus? he blasphemeth. Who can forgive sins, but God only?

2:8 Which Jesus presently knowing in his spirit, that they so thought within themselves, saith to them: Why think you these things in your hearts?

2:9 Which is easier, to say to the sick of the palsy: Thy sins are forgiven thee; or to say: Arise, take up thy bed, and walk?

2:10 But that you may know that the Son of man hath power on earth to forgive sins, (he saith to the sick of the palsy,)

2:11 I say to thee: Arise, take up thy bed, and go into thy house.

2:12 And immediately he arose; and taking up his bed, went his way in the sight of all; so that all wondered and glorified God, saying: We never saw the like.

2:13 And he went forth again to the sea side; and all the multitude came to him, and he taught them.

2:14 And when he was passing by, he saw Levi the son of Alpheus sitting at the receipt of custom; and he saith to him: Follow me. And rising up, he followed him.

2:15 And it came to pass, that as he sat at meat in his house, many publicans and sinners sat down together with Jesus and his disciples. For they were many, who also followed him.

2:16 And the scribes and the Pharisees, seeing that he ate with publicans and sinners, said to his disiples: Why doth your master eat and drink with publicans and sinners?

2:17 Jesus hearing this, saith to them: They that are well have no need of a physician, but they that are sick. For I came not to call the just, but sinners.

2:18 And the disciples of John and the Pharisees used to fast; and they come and say to him: Why do the disciples of John and of the Pharisees fast; but thy disciples do not fast?

2:19 And Jesus saith to them: Can the children of the marriage fast, as long as the bridegroom

? Quanto tempore habent secum sponsum, non possunt jejunare.

2:20 Venient autem dies cum auferetur ab eis sponsus : et tunc jejunabunt in illis diebus.

2:21 Nemo assumentum panni rudis assuit vestimento veteri : alioquin aufert supplementum novum a veteri, et major scissura fit.

2:22 Et nemo mittit vinum novum in utres veteres : alioquin dirumpet vinum utres, et vinum effundetur, et utres peribunt : sed vinum novum in utres novos mitti debet.

2:23 Et factum est iterum Dominus sabbatis ambularet per sata, et discipuli ejus cœperunt progredi, et vellere spicas.

2:24 Pharisæi autem dicebant ei : Ecce, quid faciunt sabbatis quod non licet ?

2:25 Et ait illis : Numquam legistis quid fecerit David, quando necessitatem habuit, et esuriit ipse, et qui cum eo erant ?

2:26 quomodo introivit in domum Dei sub Abiathar principe sacerdotum, et panes propositionis manducavit, quos non licebat manducare, nisi sacerdotibus, et dedit eis qui cum eo erant ?

2:27 Et dicebat eis : Sabbatum propter hominem factum est, et non homo propter sabbatum.

2:28 Itaque Dominus est Filius hominis, etiam sabbati.

3:1 Et introivit iterum in synagogam : et erat ibi homo habens manum aridam.

3:2 Et observabant eum, si sabbatis curaret, ut accusarent illum.

3:3 Et ait homini habenti manum aridam : Surge in medium.

3:4 Et dicit eis : Licet sabbatis benefacere, an male ? animam salvam facere, an perdere ? At illi tacebant.

3:5 Et circumspiciens eos cum ira, contristatus super cæcitate cordis eorum, dicit homini : Extende manum tuam. Et extendit, et restituta est manus illi.

3:6 Exeuntes autem pharisæi, statim cum Herodianis consilium faciebant adversus eum quomodo eum perderent.

is with them? As long as they have the bridegroom with them, they cannot fast.

2:20 But the days will come when the bridegroom shall be taken away from them; and then they shall fast in those days.

2:21 No man seweth a piece of raw cloth to an old garment: otherwise the new piecing taketh away from the old, and there is made a greater rent.

2:22 And no man putteth new wine into old bottles: otherwise the wine will burst the bottles, and both the wine will be spilled, and the bottles will be lost. But new wine must be put into new bottles.

2:23 And it came to pass again, as the Lord walked through the corn fields on the sabbath, that his disciples began to go forward, and to pluck the ears of corn.

2:24 And the Pharisees said to him: Behold, why do they on the sabbath day that which is not lawful?

2:25 And he said to them: Have you never read what David did when he had need, and was hungry himself, and they that were with him?

2:26 How he went into the house of God, under Abiathar the high priest, and did eat the loaves of proposition, which was not lawful to eat but for the priests, and gave to them who were with him?

2:27 And he said to them: The sabbath was made for man, and not man for the sabbath.

2:28 Therefore the Son of man is Lord of the sabbath also.

3:1 And he entered again into the synagogue, and there was a man there who had a withered hand.

3:2 And they watched him whether he would heal on the sabbath days; that they might accuse him.

3:3 And he said to the man who had the withered hand: Stand up in the midst.

3:4 And he saith to them: Is it lawful to do good on the sabbath days, or to do evil? to save life, or to destroy? But they held their peace.

3:5 And looking round about on them with anger, being grieved for the blindness of their hearts, he saith to the man: Stretch forth thy hand. And he stretched it forth: and his hand was restored unto him.

3:6 And the Pharisees going out, immediately made a consultation with the Herodians against him, how they might destroy him.

3:7 Jesus autem cum discipulis suis secessit ad mare : et multa turba a Galilæa et Judæa secuta est eum,

3:8 et ab Jerosolymis, et ab Idumæa, et trans Jordanem : et qui circa Tyrum et Sidonem multitudo magna, audientes quæ faciebat, venerunt ad eum.

3:9 Et dicit discipulis suis ut navicula sibi deserviret propter turbam, ne comprimerent eum :

3:10 multos enim sanabat, ita ut irruerent in eum ut illum tangerent, quotquot habebant plagas.

3:11 Et spiritus immundi, cum illum videbant, procidebant ei : et clamabant, dicentes :

3:12 Tu es Filius Dei. Et vehementer comminabatur eis ne manifestarent illum.

3:13 Et ascendens in montem vocavit ad se quos voluit ipse : et venerunt ad eum.

3:14 Et fecit ut essent duodecim cum illo : et ut mitteret eos prædicare.

3:15 Et dedit illis potestatem curandi infirmitates et ejiciendi dæmonia.

3:16 Et imposuit Simoni nomen Petrus :

3:17 et Jacobum Zebedæi, et Joannem fratrem Jacobi, et imposuit eis nomina Boanerges, quod est, Filii tonitrui :

3:18 et Andræam, et Philippum, et Bartholomæum, et Matthæum, et Thomam, et Jacobum Alphæi, et Thaddæum, et Simonem Cananæum,

3:19 et Judam Iscariotem, qui et tradidit illum.

3:20 Et veniunt ad domum : et convenit iterum turba, ita ut non possent neque panem manducare.

3:21 Et cum audissent sui, exierunt tenere eum : dicebant enim : Quoniam in furorem versus est.

3:22 Et scribæ, qui ab Jerosolymis descenderant, dicebant : Quoniam Beelzebub habet, et quia in principe dæmoniorum ejicit dæmonia.

3:23 Et convocatis eis in parabolis dicebat illis : Quomodo potest Satanas Satanam ejicere ?

3:24 Et si regnum in se dividatur, non potest regnum illud stare.

3:25 Et si domus super semetipsam dispertiatur, non potest domus illa stare.

3:26 Et si Satanas consurrexerit in semetipsum,

3:7 But Jesus retired with his disciples to the sea; and a great multitude followed him from Galilee and Judea,

3:8 And from Jerusalem, and from Idumea, and from beyond the Jordan. And they about Tyre and Sidon, a great multitude, hearing the things which he did, came to him.

3:9 And he spoke to his disciples that a small ship should wait on him because of the multitude, lest they should throng him.

3:10 For he healed many, so that they pressed upon him for to touch him, as many as had evils.

3:11 And the unclean spirits, when they saw him, fell down before him: and they cried, saying:

3:12 Thou art the Son of God. And he strictly charged them that they should not make him known.

3:13 And going up into a mountain, he called unto him whom he would himself: and they came to him.

3:14 And he made that twelve should be with him, and that he might send them to preach.

3:15 And he gave them power to heal sicknesses, and to cast out devils.

3:16 And to Simon he gave the name Peter:

3:17 And James the son of Zebedee, and John the brother of James; and he named them Boanerges, which is, The sons of thunder:

3:18 And Andrew and Philip, and Bartholomew and Matthew, and Thomas and James of Alpheus, and Thaddeus, and Simon the Cananean:

3:19 And Judas Iscariot, who also betrayed him.

3:20 And they come to a house, and the multitude cometh together again, so that they could not so much as eat bread.

3:21 And when his friends had heard of it, they went out to lay hold on him. For they said: He is become mad.

3:22 And the scribes who were come down from Jerusalem, said: He hath Beelzebub, and by the prince of devils he casteth out devils.

3:23 And after he had called them together, he said to them in parables: How can Satan cast out Satan?

3:24 And if a kingdom be divided against itself, that kingdom cannot stand.

3:25 And if a house be divided against itself, that house cannot stand.

3:26 And if Satan be risen up against himself, he

dispertitus est, et non poterit stare, sed finem habet.

3:27 Nemo potest vasa fortis ingressus in domum diripere, nisi prius fortem alliget, et tunc domum ejus diripiet.

3:28 Amen dico vobis, quoniam omnia dimittentur filiis hominum peccata, et blasphemiæ quibus blasphemaverint :

3:29 qui autem blasphemaverit in Spiritum Sanctum, non habebit remissionem in æternum, sed reus erit æterni delicti.

3:30 Quoniam dicebant : Spiritum immundum habet.

3:31 Et veniunt mater ejus et fratres : et foris stantes miserunt ad eum vocantes eum,

3:32 et sedebat circa eum turba : et dicunt ei : Ecce mater tua et fratres tui foris quærunt te.

3:33 Et respondens eis, ait : Quæ est mater mea et fratres mei ?

3:34 Et circumspiciens eos, qui in circuitu ejus sedebant, ait : Ecce mater mea et fratres mei.

3:35 Qui enim fecerit voluntatem Dei, hic frater meus, et soror mea, et mater est.

4:1 Et iterum cœpit docere ad mare : et congregata est ad eum turba multa, ita ut navim ascendens sederet in mari, et omnis turba circa mare super terram erat :

4:2 et docebat eos in parabolis multa, et dicebat illis in doctrina sua :

4:3 Audite : ecce exiit seminans ad seminandum.

4:4 Et dum seminat, aliud cecidit circa viam, et venerunt volucres cæli, et comederunt illud.

4:5 Aliud vero cecidit super petrosa, ubi non habuit terram multam : et statim exortum est, quoniam non habebat altitudinem terræ :

4:6 et quando exortus est sol, exæstuavit : et eo quod non habebat radicem, exaruit.

4:7 Et aliud cecidit in spinas : et ascenderunt spinæ, et suffocaverunt illud, et fructum non dedit.

4:8 Et aliud cecidit in terram bonam : et dabat fructum ascendentem et crescentem, et afferebat unum triginta, unum sexaginta, et unum centum.

4:9 Et dicebat : Qui habet aures audiendi, audi-

is divided, and cannot stand, but hath an end.

3:27 No man can enter into the house of a strong man and rob him of his goods, unless he first bind the strong man, and then shall he plunder his house.

3:28 Amen I say to you, that all sins shall be forgiven unto the sons of men, and the blasphemies wherewith they shall blaspheme:

3:29 But he that shall blaspheme against the Holy Ghost, shall never have forgiveness, but shall be guilty of an everlasting sin.

3:30 Because they said: He hath an unclean spirit.

3:31 And his mother and his bretheren came; and standing without, sent unto him, calling him.

3:32 And the multitude sat about him; and they say to him: Behold thy mother and thy brethren without seek for thee.

3:33 And answering them, he said: Who is my mother and my brethren?

3:34 And looking round about on them who sat about him, he saith: Behold my mother and my brethren.

3:35 For whosoever shall do the will of God, he is my brother, and my sister, and mother.

4:1 And again he began to teach by the sea side; and a great multitude was gathered together unto him, so that he went up into a ship, and sat in the sea; and all the multitude was upon the land by the sea side.

4:2 And he taught them many things in parables, and said unto them in his doctrine:

4:3 Hear ye: Behold, the sower went out to sow.

4:4 And whilst he sowed, some fell by the way side, and the birds of the air came and ate it up.

4:5 And other some fell upon stony ground, where it had not much earth; and it shot up immediately, because it had no depth of earth.

4:6 And when the sun was risen, it was scorched; and because it had no root, it withered away.

4:7 And some fell among thorns; and the thorns grew up, and choked it, and it yielded no fruit.

4:8 And some fell upon good ground; and brought forth fruit that grew up, and increased and yielded, one thirty, another sixty, and another a hundred.

4:9 And he said: He that hath ears to hear, let

at.

4:10 Et cum esset singularis, interrogaverunt eum hi qui cum eo erant duodecim, parabolam.

4:11 Et dicebat eis : Vobis datum est nosse mysterium regni Dei : illis autem, qui foris sunt, in parabolis omnia fiunt :

4:12 ut videntes videant, et non videant : et audientes audiant, et non intelligant : nequando convertantur, et dimittantur eis peccata.

4:13 Et ait illis : Nescitis parabolam hanc ? Et quomodo omnes parabolas cognoscetis ?

4:14 Qui seminat, verbum seminat.

4:15 Hi autem sunt, qui circa viam, ubi seminatur verbum, et cum audierint, confestim venit Satanas, et aufert verbum, quod seminatum est in cordibus eorum.

4:16 Et hi sunt similiter, qui super petrosa seminantur : qui cum audierint verbum, statim cum gaudio accipiunt illud :

4:17 et non habent radicem in se, sed temporales sunt : deinde orta tribulatione et persecutione propter verbum, confestim scandalizantur.

4:18 Et alii sunt qui in spinas seminantur : hi sunt qui verbum audiunt,

4:19 et ærumnæ sæculi, et deceptio divitiarum, et circa reliqua concupiscentiæ introëuntes suffocant verbum, et sine fructu efficitur.

4:20 Et hi sunt qui super terram bonam seminati sunt, qui audiunt verbum, et suscipiunt, et fructificant, unum triginta, unum sexaginta, et unum centum.

4:21 Et dicebat illis : Numquid venit lucerna ut sub modo ponatur, aut sub lecto ? nonne ut super candelabrum ponatur ?

4:22 Non est enim aliquid absconditum, quod non manifestetur : nec factum est occultum, sed ut in palam veniat.

4:23 Si quis habet aures audiendi, audiat.

4:24 Et dicebat illis : Videte quid audiatis. In qua mensura mensi fueritis, remetietur vobis, et adjicietur vobis.

4:25 Qui enim habet, dabitur illi : et qui non habet, etiam quod habet auferetur ab eo.

him hear.

4:10 And when he was alone, the twelve that were with him asked him the parable.

4:11 And he said to them: To you it is given to know the mystery of the kingdom of God: but to them that are without, all things are done in parables:

4:12 That seeing they may see, and not perceive; and hearing they may hear, and not understand: lest at any time they should be converted, and their sins should be forgiven them.

4:13 And he saith to them: Are you ignorant of this parable? and how shall you know all parables?

4:14 He that soweth, soweth the word.

4:15 And these are they by the way side, where the word is sown, and as soon as they have heard, immediately Satan cometh and taketh away the word that was sown in their hearts.

4:16 And these likewise are they that are sown on the stony ground: who when they have heard the word, immediately recieve it with joy.

4:17 And they have no root in themselves, but are only for a time: and then when tribulation and persecution ariseth for the word they are presently scandalized.

4:18 And others there are who are sown among thorns: these are they that hear the word,

4:19 And the cares of the world, and the deceitfulness of riches, and the lusts after other things entering in choke the word, and it is made fruitless.

4:20 And these are they who are sown upon the good ground, who hear the word, and receive it, and yield fruit, the one thirty, another sixty, and another a hundred.

4:21 And he said to them: Doth a candle come in to be put under a bushel, or under a bed? and not to be set on a candlestick?

4:22 For there is nothing hid, which shall not be made manifest: neither was it made secret, but that it may come abroad.

4:23 If any man have ears to hear, let him hear.

4:24 And he said to them: Take heed what you hear. In what measure you shall mete, it shall be measured to you again, and more shall be given to you.

4:25 For he that hath, to him shall be given: and he that hath not, that also which he hath shall be taken away from him.

4:26 Et dicebat : Sic est regnum Dei, quemadmodum si homo jaciat sementem in terram,

4:27 et dormiat, et exsurgat nocte et die, et semen germinet, et increscat dum nescit ille.

4:28 Ultro enim terra fructificat, primum herbam, deinde spicam, deinde plenum frumentum in spica.

4:29 Et cum produxerit fructus, statim mittit falcem, quoniam adest messis.

4:30 Et dicebat : Cui assimilabimus regnum Dei ? aut cui parabolæ comparabimus illud ?

4:31 Sicut granum sinapis, quod cum seminatum fuerit in terra, minus est omnibus seminibus, quæ sunt in terra :

4:32 et cum seminatum fuerit, ascendit, et fit majus omnibus oleribus, et facit ramos magnos, ita ut possint sub umbra ejus aves cæli habitare.

4:33 Et talibus multis parabolis loquebatur eis verbum, prout poterant audire :

4:34 sine parabola autem non loquebatur eis : seorsum autem discipulis suis disserebat omnia.

4:35 Et ait illis in illa die, cum sero esset factum : Transeamus contra.

4:36 Et dimittentes turbam, assumunt eum ita ut erat in navi : et aliæ naves erant cum illo.

4:37 Et facta est procella magna venti, et fluctus mittebat in navim, ita ut impleretur navis.

4:38 Et erat ipse in puppi super cervical dormiens : et excitant eum, et dicunt illi : Magister, non ad te pertinet, quia perimus ?

4:39 Et exsurgens comminatus est vento, et dixit mari : Tace, obmutesce. Et cessavit ventus : et facta est tranquillitas magna.

4:40 Et ait illis : Quid timidi estis ? necdum habetis fidem ? et timuerunt timore magno, et dicebant ad alterutrum : Quis, putas, est iste, quia et ventus et mare obediunt ei ?

5:1 Et venerunt trans fretum maris in regionem Gerasenorum.

5:2 Et exeunti ei de navi, statim occurrit de monumentis homo in spiritu immundo,

4:26 And he said: So is the kingdom of God, as if a man should cast seed into the earth,

4:27 And should sleep, and rise, night and day, and the seed should spring, and grow up whilst he knoweth not.

4:28 For the earth of itself bringeth forth fruit, first the blade, then the ear, afterwards the full corn in the ear.

4:29 And when the fruit is brought forth, immediately he putteth in the sickle, because the harvest is come.

4:30 And he said: To what shall we liken the kingdom of God? or to what parable shall we compare it?

4:31 It is as a grain of mustard seed: which when it is sown in the earth, is less than all the seeds that are in the earth:

4:32 And when it is sown, it groweth up, and becometh greater than all herbs, and shooteth out great branches, so that the birds of the air may dwell under the shadow thereof.

4:33 And with many such parables, he spoke to them the word, according as they were able to hear.

4:34 And without parable he did not speak unto them; but apart, he explained all things to his disciples.

4:35 And he saith to them that day, when evening was come: Let us pass over to the other side.

4:36 And sending away the multitude, they take him even as he was in the ship: and there were other ships with him.

4:37 And there arose a great storm of wind, and the waves beat into the ship, so that the ship was filled.

4:38 And he was in the hinder part of the ship, sleeping upon a pillow; and they awake him, and say to him: Master, doth it not concern thee that we perish?

4:39 And rising up, he rebuked the wind, and said to the sea: Peace, be still. And the wind ceased: and there was made a great calm.

4:40 And he said to them: Why are you fearful? have you not faith yet? And they feared exceedingly: and they said one to another: Who is this (thinkest thou) that both wind and sea obey him?

5:1 And they came over the strait of the sea into the country of the Gerasens.

5:2 And as he went out of the ship, immediately there met him out of the monuments a man with an unclean spirit,

5:3 qui domicilium habebat in monumentis, et neque catenis jam quisquam poterat eum ligare :

5:4 quoniam sæpe compedibus et catenis vinctus, dirupisset catenas, et compedes comminuisset, et nemo poterat eum domare :

5:5 et semper die ac nocte in monumentis, et in montibus erat, clamans, et concidens se lapidibus.

5:6 Videns autem Jesum a longe, cucurrit, et adoravit eum :

5:7 et clamans voce magna dixit : Quid mihi et tibi, Jesu Fili Dei altissimi ? adjuro te per Deum, ne me torqueas.

5:8 Dicebat enim illi : Exi spiritus immunde ab homine.

5:9 Et interrogabat eum : Quod tibi nomen est ? Et dicit ei : Legio mihi nomen est, quia multi sumus.

5:10 Et deprecabatur eum multum, ne se expelleret extra regionem.

5:11 Erat autem ibi circa montem grex porcorum magnus, pascens.

5:12 Et deprecabantur eum spiritus, dicentes : Mitte nos in porcos ut in eos introëamus.

5:13 Et concessit eis statim Jesus. Et exeuntes spiritus immundi introierunt in porcos : et magno impetu grex præcipitatus est in mare ad duo millia, et suffocati sunt in mari.

5:14 Qui autem pascebant eos, fugerunt, et nuntiaverunt in civitatem et in agros. Et egressi sunt videre quid esset factum :

5:15 et veniunt ad Jesum : et vident illum qui a dæmonio vexabatur, sedentem, vestitum, et sanæ mentis, et timuerunt.

5:16 Et narraverunt illis, qui viderant, qualiter factum esset ei qui dæmonium habuerat, et de porcis.

5:17 Et rogare cœperunt eum ut discederet de finibus eorum.

5:18 Cumque ascenderet navim, cœpit illum deprecari, qui a dæmonio vexatus fuerat, ut esset cum illo,

5:19 et non admisit eum, sed ait illi : Vade in domum tuam ad tuos, et annuntia illis quanta tibi Dominus fecerit, et misertus sit tui.

5:20 Et abiit, et cœpit prædicare in Decapoli,

5:3 Who had his dwelling in the tombs, and no man now could bind him, not even with chains.

5:4 For having been often bound with fetters and chains, he had burst the chains, and broken the fetters in pieces, and no one could tame him.

5:5 And he was always day and night in the monuments and in the mountains, crying and cutting himself with stones.

5:6 And seeing Jesus afar off, he ran and adored him.

5:7 And crying with a loud voice, he said: What have I to do with thee, Jesus the Son of the most high God? I adjure thee by God that thou torment me not.

5:8 For he said unto him: Go out of the man, thou unclean spirit.

5:9 And he asked him: What is thy name? And he saith to him: My name is Legion, for we are many.

5:10 And he besought him much, that he would not drive him away out of the country.

5:11 And there was there near the mountain a great herd of swine, feeding.

5:12 And the spirits besought him, saying: Send us into the swine, that we may enter into them.

5:13 And Jesus immediately gave them leave. And the unclean spirits going out, entered into the swine: and the herd with great violence was carried headlong into the sea, being about two thousand, and were stifled in the sea.

5:14 And they that fed them fled, and told it in the city and in the fields. And they went out to see what was done:

5:15 And they came to Jesus, and they see him that was troubled with the devil, sitting, clothed, and well in his wits, and they were afraid.

5:16 And they that had seen it, told them, in what manner he had been dealt with who had the devil; and concerning the swine.

5:17 And they began to pray him that he would depart from their coasts.

5:18 And when he went up into the ship, he that had been troubled with the devil, began to beseech him that he might be with him.

5:19 And he admitted him not, but saith to him: Go into thy house to thy friends, and tell them how great things the Lord hath done for thee, and hath had mercy on thee.

5:20 And he went his way, and began to publish

quanta sibi fecisset Jesus : et omnes mirabantur.

5:21 Et cum transcendisset Jesus in navi rursum trans fretum, convenit turba multa ad eum, et erat circa mare.

5:22 Et venit quidam de archisynagogis nomine Jairus, et videns eum procidit ad pedes ejus,

5:23 et deprecabatur eum multum, dicens : Quoniam filia mea in extremis est, veni, impone manum super eam, ut salva sit, et vivat.

5:24 Et abiit cum illo, et sequebatur eum turba multa, et comprimebant eum.

5:25 Et mulier, quæ erat in profluvio sanguinis annis duodecim,

5:26 et fuerat multa perpessa a compluribus medicis : et erogaverat omnia sua, nec quidquam profecerat, sed magis deterius habebat :

5:27 cum audisset de Jesu, venit in turba retro, et tetigit vestimentum ejus :

5:28 dicebat enim : Quia si vel vestimentum ejus tetigero, salva ero.

5:29 Et confestim siccatus est fons sanguinis ejus : et sensit corpore quia sanata esset a plaga.

5:30 Et statim Jesus in semetipso cognoscens virtutem quæ exierat de illo, conversus ad turbam, aiebat : Quis tetigit vestimenta mea ?

5:31 Et dicebant ei discipuli sui : Vides turbam comprimentem te, et dicis : Quis me tetigit ?

5:32 Et circumspiciebat videre eam, quæ hoc fecerat.

5:33 Mulier vero timens et tremens, sciens quod factum esset in se, venit et procidit ante eum, et dixit ei omnem veritatem.

5:34 Ille autem dixit ei : Filia, fides tua te salvam fecit : vade in pace, et esto sana a plaga tua.

5:35 Adhuc eo loquente, veniunt ab archisynagogo, dicentes : Quia filia tua mortua est : quid ultra vexas magistrum ?

5:36 Jesus autem audito verbo quod dicebatur, ait archisynagogo : Noli timere : tantummodo crede.

5:37 Et non admisit quemquam se sequi nisi Petrum, et Jacobum, et Joannem fratrem Jacobi.

5:38 Et veniunt in domum archisynagogi, et vi-

in Decapolis how great things Jesus had done for him: and all men wondered.

5:21 And when Jesus had passed again in the ship over the strait, a great multitude assembled together unto him, and he was nigh unto the sea.

5:22 And there cometh one of the rulers of the synagogue named Jairus: and seeing him, falleth down at his feet.

5:23 And he besought him much, saying: My daughter is at the point of death, come, lay thy hand upon her, that she may be safe, and may live.

5:24 And he went with him, and a great multitude followed him, and they thronged him.

5:25 And a woman who was under an issue of blood twelve years,

5:26 And had suffered many things from many physicians; and had spent all that she had, and was nothing the better, but rather worse,

5:27 When she had heard of Jesus, came in the crowd behind him, and touched his garment.

5:28 For she said: If I shall touch but his garment, I shall be whole.

5:29 And forthwith the fountain of her blood was dried up, and she felt in her body that she was healed of the evil.

5:30 And immediately Jesus knowing in himself the virtue that had proceeded from him, turning to the multitude, said: Who hath touched my garments?

5:31 And his disciples said to him: Thou seest the multitude thronging thee, and sayest thou who hath touched me?

5:32 And he looked about to see her who had done this.

5:33 But the woman fearing and trembling, knowing what was done in her, came and fell down before him, and told him all the truth.

5:34 And he said to her: Daughter, thy faith hath made thee whole: go in peace, and be thou whole of thy disease.

5:35 While he was yet speaking, some come from the ruler of the synagogue's house, saying: Thy daughter is dead: why dost thou trouble the master any further?

5:36 But Jesus having heard the word that was spoken, saith to the ruler of the synagogue: Fear not, only believe.

5:37 And he admitted not any man to follow him, but Peter, and James, and John the brother of James.

5:38 And they come to the house of the ruler of

det tumultum, et flentes, et ejulantes multum.

5:39 Et ingressus, ait illis : Quid turbamini, et ploratis ? puella non est mortua, sed dormit.

5:40 Et irridebant eum. Ipse vero ejectis omnibus assumit patrem, et matrem puellæ, et qui secum erant, et ingreditur ubi puella erat jacens.

5:41 Et tenens manum puellæ, ait illi : Talitha cumi, quod est interpretatum : Puella (tibi dico), surge.
5:42 Et confestim surrexit puella, et ambulabat : erat autem annorum duodecim : et obstupuerunt stupore magno.
5:43 Et præcepit illis vehementer ut nemo id sciret : et dixit dari illi manducare.

6:1 Et egressus inde, abiit in patriam suam : et sequebantur eum discipuli sui :
6:2 et facto sabbato cœpit in synagoga docere : et multi audientes admirabantur in doctrina ejus, dicentes : Unde huic hæc omnia ? et quæ est sapientia, quæ data est illi, et virtutes tales, quæ per manus ejus efficiuntur ?

6:3 Nonne hic est faber, filius Mariæ, frater Jacobi, et Joseph, et Judæ, et Simonis ? nonne et sorores ejus hic nobiscum sunt ? Et scandalizabantur in illo.
6:4 Et dicebat illis Jesus : Quia non est propheta sine honore nisi in patria sua, et in domo sua, et in cognatione sua.
6:5 Et non poterat ibi virtutem ullam facere, nisi paucos infirmos impositis manibus curavit :

6:6 et mirabatur propter incredulitatem eorum, et circuibat castella in circuitu docens.

6:7 Et vocavit duodecim : et cœpit eos mittere binos, et dabat illis potestatem spirituum immundorum.
6:8 Et præcepit eis ne quid tollerent in via, nisi virgam tantum : non peram, non panem, neque in zona æs,
6:9 sed calceatos sandaliis, et ne induerentur duabus tunicis.
6:10 Et dicebat eis : Quocumque introieritis in domum, illic manete donec exeatis inde :

the synagogue; and he seeth a tumult, and people weeping and wailing much.

5:39 And going in, he saith to them: Why make you this ado, and weep? the damsel is not dead, but sleepeth.

5:40 And they laughed him to scorn. But he having put them all out, taketh the father and the mother of the damsel, and them that were with him, and entereth in where the damsel was lying.

5:41 And taking the damsel by the hand, he saith to her: Talitha cumi, which is, being interpreted: Damsel (I say to thee) arise.
5:42 And immediately the damsel rose up, and walked: and she was twelve years old: and they were astonished with a great astonishment.
5:43 And he charged them strictly that no man should know it: and commanded that something should be given her to eat.

6:1 And going out from thence, he went into his own country; and his disciples followed him.
6:2 And when the sabbath was come, he began to teach in the synagogue: and many hearing him were in admiration at his doctrine, saying: How came this man by all these things? and what wisdom is this that is given to him, and such mighty works as are wrought by his hands?

6:3 Is not this the carpenter, the son of Mary, the brother of James, and Joseph, and Jude, and Simon? are not also his sisters here with us? And they were scandalized in regard of him.
6:4 And Jesus said to them: A prophet is not without honor, but in his own country, and in his own house, and among his own kindred.
6:5 And he could not do any miracles there, only that he cured a few that were sick, laying his hands upon them.

6:6 And he wondered because of their unbelief, and he went through the villages round about teaching.

6:7 And he called the twelve; and began to send them two and two, and gave them power over unclean spirits.
6:8 And he commanded them that they should take nothing for the way, but a staff only: no scrip, no bread, nor money in their purse,
6:9 But to be shod with sandals, and that they should not put on two coats.
6:10 And he said to them: Wheresoever you shall enter into an house, there abide till you depart from that place.

6:11 et quicumque non receperint vos, nec audierint vos, exeuntes inde, excutite pulverem de pedibus vestris in testimonium illis.

6:12 Et exeuntes prædicabant ut pœnitentiam agerent :

6:13 et dæmonia multa ejiciebant, et ungebant oleo multos ægros, et sanabant.

6:14 Et audivit rex Herodes (manifestum enim factum est nomen ejus), et dicebat : Quia Joannes Baptista resurrexit a mortuis : et propterea virtutes operantur in illo.

6:15 Alii autem dicebant : Quia Elias est ; alii vero dicebant : Quia propheta est, quasi unus ex prophetis.

6:16 Quo audito Herodes ait : Quem ego decollavi Joannem, hic a mortuis resurrexit.

6:17 Ipse enim Herodes misit, ac tenuit Joannem, et vinxit eum in carcere propter Herodiadem uxorem Philippi fratris sui, quia duxerat eam.

6:18 Dicebat enim Joannes Herodi : Non licet tibi habere uxorem fratris tui.

6:19 Herodias autem insidiabatur illi : et volebat occidere eum, nec poterat.

6:20 Herodes enim metuebat Joannem, sciens eum virum justum et sanctum : et custodiebat eum, et audito eo multa faciebat, et libenter eum audiebat.

6:21 Et cum dies opportunus accidisset, Herodes natalis sui cœnam fecit principibus, et tribunis, et primis Galilææ :

6:22 cumque introisset filia ipsius Herodiadis, et saltasset, et placuisset Herodi, simulque recumbentibus, rex ait puellæ : Pete a me quod vis, et dabo tibi :

6:23 et juravit illi : Quia quidquid petieris dabo tibi, licet dimidium regni mei.

6:24 Quæ cum exisset, dixit matri suæ : Quid petam ? At illa dixit : Caput Joannis Baptistæ.

6:25 Cumque introisset statim cum festinatione ad regem, petivit dicens : Volo ut protinus des mihi in disco caput Joannis Baptistæ.

6:26 Et contristatus est rex : propter jusjurandum, et propter simul discumbentes, noluit eam contristare :

6:27 sed misso spiculatore præcepit afferri caput

6:11 And whosoever shall not receive you, nor hear you; going forth from thence, shake off the dust from your feet for a testimony to them.

6:12 And going forth they preached that men should do penance:

6:13 And they cast out many devils, and anointed with oil many that were sick, and healed them.

6:14 And king Herod heard, (for his name was made manifest,) and he said: John the Baptist is risen again from the dead, and therefore mighty works shew forth themselves in him.

6:15 And others said: It is Elias. But others said: It is a prophet, as one of the prophets.

6:16 Which Herod hearing, said: John whom I beheaded, he is risen again from the dead.

6:17 For Herod himself had sent and apprehended John, and bound him in prison for the sake of Herodias the wife of Philip his brother, because he had married her.

6:18 For John said to Herod: It is not lawful for thee to have thy brother's wife.

6:19 Now Herodias laid snares for him: and was desirous to put him to death, and could not.

6:20 For Herod feared John, knowing him to be a just and holy man: and kept him, and when he heard him, did many things: and he heard him willingly.

6:21 And when a convenient day was come, Herod made a supper for his birthday, for the princes, and tribunes, and chief men of Galilee.

6:22 And when the daughter of the same Herodias had come in, and had danced, and pleased Herod, and them that were at table with him, the king said to the damsel: Ask of me what thou wilt, and I will give it thee.

6:23 And he swore to her: Whatsoever thou shalt ask I will give thee, though it be the half of my kingdom.

6:24 Who when she was gone out, said to her mother, What shall I ask? But she said: The head of John the Baptist.

6:25 And when she was come in immediately with haste to the king, she asked, saying: I will that forthwith thou give me in a dish, the head of John the Baptist.

6:26 And the king was struck sad. Yet because of his oath, and because of them that were with him at table, he would not displease her:

6:27 But sending an executioner, he commanded

ejus in disco. Et decollavit eum in carcere, 6:28 et attulit caput ejus in disco : et dedit illud puellæ, et puella dedit matri suæ.

6:29 Quo audito, discipuli ejus venerunt, et tulerunt corpus ejus : et posuerunt illud in monumento.

6:30 Et convenientes Apostoli ad Jesum, renuntiaverunt ei omnia quæ egerant, et docuerant.

6:31 Et ait illis : Venite seorsum in desertum locum, et requiescite pusillum. Erant enim qui veniebant et redibant multi : et nec spatium manducandi habebant.

6:32 Et ascendentes in navim, abierunt in desertum locum seorsum.

6:33 Et viderunt eos abeuntes, et cognoverunt multi : et pedestres de omnibus civitatibus concurrerunt illuc, et prævenerunt eos.

6:34 Et exiens vidit turbam multam Jesus : et misertus est super eos, quia erant sicut oves non habentes pastorem, et cœpit docere multa.

6:35 Et cum jam hora multa fieret, accesserunt discipuli ejus, dicentes : Desertus est locus hic, et jam hora præteriit :

6:36 dimitte illos, ut euntes in proximas villas et vicos, emant sibi cibos, quos manducent.

6:37 Et respondens ait illis : Date illis vos manducare. Et dixerunt ei : Euntes emamus ducentis denariis panes, et dabimus illis manducare.

6:38 Et dicit eis : Quot panes habetis ? ite, et videte. Et cum cognovissent, dicunt : Quinque, et duos pisces.

6:39 Et præcepit illis ut accumbere facerent omnes secundum contubernia super viride fœnum.

6:40 Et discubuerunt in partes per centenos et quinquagenos.

6:41 Et acceptis quinque panibus et duobus pisces, intuens in cælum, benedixit, et fregit panes, et dedit discipulis suis, ut ponerent ante eos : et duos pisces divisit omnibus.

6:42 Et manducaverunt omnes, et saturati sunt.

6:43 Et sustulerunt reliquias, fragmentorum duodecim cophinos plenos, et de piscibus.

6:44 Erant autem qui manducaverunt quinque millia virorum.

that his head should be brought in a dish.

6:28 And he beheaded him in the prison, and brought his head in a dish: and gave it to the damsel, and the damsel gave it to her mother.

6:29 Which his disciples hearing came, and took his body, and laid it in a tomb.

6:30 And the apostles coming together unto Jesus, related to him all things that they had done and taught.

6:31 And he said to them: Come apart into a desert place, and rest a little. For there were many coming and going: and they had not so much as time to eat.

6:32 And going up into a ship, they went into a desert place apart.

6:33 And they saw them going away, and many knew: and they ran flocking thither on foot from all the cities, and were there before them.

6:34 And Jesus going out saw a great multitude: and he had compassion on them, because they were as sheep not having a shepherd, and he began to teach them many things.

6:35 And when the day was now far spent, his disciples came to him, saying: This is a desert place, and the hour is now past:

6:36 Send them away, that going into the next villages and towns, they may buy themselves meat to eat.

6:37 And he answering said to them: Give you them to eat. And they said to him: Let us go and buy bread for two hundred pence, and we will give them to eat.

6:38 And he saith to them: How many loaves have you? go and see. And when they knew, they say: Five, and two fishes

6:39 And he commanded them that they should make them all sit down by companies upon the green grass.

6:40 And they sat down in ranks, by hundreds and by fifties.

6:41 And when he had taken the five loaves, and the two fishes: looking up to heaven, he blessed, and broke the loaves, and gave to his disciples to set before them: and the two fishes he divided among them all.

6:42 And they all did eat, and had their fill.

6:43 And they took up the leavings, twelve full baskets of fragments, and of the fishes.

6:44 And they that did eat, were five thousand men.

6:45 Et statim coëgit discipulos suos ascendere navim, ut præcederent eum trans fretum ad Bethsaidam, dum ipse dimitteret populum.

6:46 Et cum dimisisset eos, abiit in montem orare.

6:47 Et cum sero esset, erat navis in medio mari et ipse solus in terra.

6:48 Et videns eos laborantes in remigando (erat enim ventus contrarius eis) et circa quartam vigiliam noctis venit ad eos ambulans supra mare : et volebat præterire eos.

6:49 At illi ut viderunt eum ambulantem supra mare, putaverunt phantasma esse, et exclamaverunt.

6:50 Omnes enim viderunt eum, et conturbati sunt. Et statim locutus est cum eis, et dixit eis : Confidite, ego sum : nolite timere.

6:51 Et ascendit ad illos in navim, et cessavit ventus. Et plus magis intra se stupebant :

6:52 non enim intellexerunt de panibus : erat enim cor eorum obcæcatum.

6:53 Et cum transfretassent, venerunt in terram Genesareth, et applicuerunt.

6:54 Cumque egressi essent de navi, continuo cognoverunt eum :

6:55 et percurrentes universam regionem illam, cœperunt in grabatis eos, qui se male habebant, circumferre, ubi audiebant eum esse.

6:56 Et quocumque introibat, in vicos, vel in villas aut civitates, in plateis ponebant infirmos, et deprecabantur eum, ut vel fimbriam vestimenti ejus tangerent, et quotquot tangebant eum, salvi fiebant.

7:1 Et conveniunt ad eum pharisæi, et quidam de scribis, venientes ab Jerosolymis.

7:2 Et cum vidissent quosdam ex discipulis ejus communibus manibus, id est non lotis, manducare panes, vituperaverunt.

7:3 Pharisæi enim, et omnes Judæi, nisi crebro laverint manus, non manducant, tenentes traditionem seniorum :

7:4 et a foro nisi baptizentur, non comedunt : et alia multa sunt, quæ tradita sunt illis servare, baptismata calicum, et urceorum, et æramentorum, et lectorum :

7:5 et interrogabant eum pharisæi et scribæ :

6:45 And immediately he obliged his disciples to go up into the ship, that they might go before him over the water to Bethsaida, whilst he dismissed the people.

6:46 And when he had dismissed them, he went up to the mountain to pray.

6:47 And when it was late, the ship was in the midst of the sea, and himself alone on the land.

6:48 And seeing them labouring in rowing, (for the wind was against them,) and about the fourth watch of the night, he cometh to them walking upon the sea, and he would have passed by them.

6:49 But they seeing him walking upon the sea, thought it was an apparition, and they cried out.

6:50 For they all saw him, and were troubled. And immediately he spoke with them, and said to them: Have a good heart, it is I, fear ye not.

6:51 And he went up to them into the ship, and the wind ceased: and they were far more astonished within themselves:

6:52 For they understood not concerning the loaves; for their heart was blinded.

6:53 And when they had passed over, they came into the land of Genezareth, and set to the shore.

6:54 And when they were gone out of the ship, immediately they knew him:

6:55 And running through that whole country, they began to carry about in beds those that were sick, where they heard he was.

6:56 And whithersoever he entered, into towns or into villages or cities, they laid the sick in the streets, and besought him that they might touch but the hem of his garment: and as many as touched him were made whole.

7:1 And there assembled together unto him the Pharisees and some of the scribes, coming from Jerusalem.

7:2 And when they had seen some of his disciples eat bread with common, that is, with unwashed hands, they found fault.

7:3 For the Pharisees, and all the Jews eat not without often washing their hands, holding the tradition of the ancients:

7:4 And when they come from the market, unless they be washed, they eat not: and many other things there are that have been delivered to them to observe, the washings of cups and of pots, and of brazen vessels, and of beds.

7:5 And the Pharisees and scribes asked him:

Quare discipuli tui non ambulant juxta traditionem seniorum, sed communibus manibus manducant panem ?

7:6 At ille respondens, dixit eis : Bene prophetavit Isaias de vobis hypocritis, sicut scriptum est : *Populus hic labiis me honorat, cor autem eorum longe est a me :*

7:7 *in vanum autem me colunt, docentes doctrinas, et præcepta hominum.*

7:8 Relinquentes enim mandatum Dei, tenetis traditionem hominum, baptismata urceorum et calicum : et alia similia his facitis multa.

7:9 Et dicebat illis : Bene irritum facitis præceptum Dei, ut traditionem vestram servetis.

7:10 Moyses enim dixit : Honora patrem tuum, et matrem tuam. Et : Qui maledixerit patri, vel matri, morte moriatur.

7:11 Vos autem dicitis : Si dixerit homo patri, aut matri, Corban (quod est donum) quodcumque ex me, tibi profuerit :

7:12 et ultra non dimittitis eum quidquam facere patri suo, aut matri,

7:13 rescindentes verbum Dei per traditionem vestram, quam tradidistis : et similia hujusmodi multa facitis.

7:14 Et advocans iterum turbam, dicebat illis : Audite me omnes, et intelligite.

7:15 Nihil est extra hominem introiens in eum, quod possit eum coinquinare, sed quæ de homine procedunt illa sunt quæ communicant hominem.

7:16 Si quis habet aures audiendi, audiat.

7:17 Et cum introisset in domum a turba, interrogabant eum discipuli ejus parabolam.

7:18 Et ait illis : Sic et vos imprudentes estis ? Non intelligitis quia omne extrinsecus introiens in hominem, non potest eum communicare :

7:19 quia non intrat in cor ejus, sed in ventrum vadit, et in secessum exit, purgans omnes escas ?

7:20 Dicebat autem, quoniam quæ de homine exeunt, illa communicant hominem.

7:21 Ab intus enim de corde hominum malæ cogitationes procedunt, adulteria, fornicationes, homicidia,

7:22 furta, avaritiæ, nequitiæ, dolus, impudicitiæ, oculus malus, blasphemia, superbia, stulti-

Why do not thy disciples walk according to the tradition of the ancients, but they eat bread with common hands?

7:6 But he answering, said to them: Well did Isaias prophesy of you hypocrites, as it is written: *This people honoureth me with their lips, but their heart is far from me.*

7:7 *And in vain to they worship me, teaching doctrines and precepts of men.*

7:8 For leaving the commandment of God, you hold the tradition of men, the washing of pots and of cups: and many other things you do like to these.

7:9 And he said to them: Well do you make void the commandment of God, that you may keep your own tradition.

7:10 For Moses said: Honor thy father and thy mother; and He that shall curse father or mother, dying let him die.

7:11 But you say: If a man shall say to his father or mother, Corban, (which is a gift,) whatsoever is from me, shall profit thee.

7:12 And further you suffer him not to do any thing for his father or mother,

7:13 Making void the word of God by your own tradition, which you have given forth. And many other such like things you do.

7:14 And calling again the multitude unto him, he said to them: Hear ye me all, and understand.

7:15 There is nothing from without a man that entering into him, can defile him. But the things which come from a man, those are they that defile a man.

7:16 If any man have ears to hear, let him hear.

7:17 And when he was come into the house from the multitude, his disciples asked him the parable.

7:18 And he saith to them: So are you also without knowledge? understand you not that every thing from without, entering into a man cannot defile him:

7:19 Because it entereth not into his heart, but goeth into the belly, and goeth out into the privy, purging all meats?

7:20 But he said that the things which come out from a man, they defile a man.

7:21 For from within out of the heart of men proceed evil thoughts, adulteries, fornications, murders,

7:22 Thefts, covetousness, wickedness, deceit, lasciviousness, an evil eye, blasphemy, pride,

tia.

7:23 Omnia hæc mala ab intus procedunt, et communicant hominem.

7:24 Et inde surgens abiit in fines Tyri et Sidonis : et ingressus domum, neminem voluit scire, et non potuit latere.

7:25 Mulier enim statim ut audivit de eo, cujus filia habebat spiritum immundum, intravit, et procidit ad pedes ejus.

7:26 Erat enim mulier gentilis, Syrophœnissa genere. Et rogabat eum ut dæmonium ejiceret de filia ejus.

7:27 Qui dixit illi : Sine prius saturari filios : non est enim bonum sumere panem filiorum, et mittere canibus.

7:28 At illa respondit, et dixit illi : Utique Domine, nam et catelli comedunt sub mensa de micis puerorum.

7:29 Et ait illi : Propter hunc sermonem vade : exiit dæmonium a filia tua.

7:30 Et cum abiisset domum suam, invenit puellam jacentem supra lectum, et dæmonium exiisse.

7:31 Et iterum exiens de finibus Tyri, venit per Sidonem ad mare Galilææ inter medios fines Decapoleos.

7:32 Et adducunt ei surdum, et mutum, et deprecabantur eum, ut imponat illi manum.

7:33 Et apprehendens eum de turba seorsum, misit digitos suos in auriculas ejus : et exspuens, tetigit linguam ejus :

7:34 et suscipiens in cælum, ingemuit, et ait illi : Ephphetha, quod est, Adaperire.

7:35 Et statim apertæ sunt aures ejus, et solutum est vinculum linguæ ejus, et loquebatur recte.

7:36 Et præcepit illis ne cui dicerent. Quanto autem eis præcipiebat, tanto magis plus prædicabant :

7:37 et eo amplius admirabantur, dicentes : Bene omnia fecit : et surdos fecit audire, et mutos loqui.

8:1 In diebus illis iterum cum turba multa esset, nec haberent quod manducarent, convocatis discipulis, ait illis :

8:2 Misereor super turbam : quia ecce jam triduo sustinent me, nec habent quod manducent :

foolishness.

7:23 All these evil things come from within, and defile a man.

7:24 And rising from thence he went into the coasts of Tyre and Sidon: and entering into a house, he would that no man should know it, and he could not be hid.

7:25 For a woman as soon as she heard of him, whose daughter had an unclean spirit, came in and fell down at his feet.

7:26 For the woman was a Gentile, a Syrophenician born. And she besought him that he would cast forth the devil out of her daughter.

7:27 Who said to her: Suffer first the children to be filled: for it is not good to take the bread of the children, and cast it to the dogs.

7:28 But she answered and said to him: Yea, Lord; for the whelps also eat under the table of the crumbs of the children.

7:29 And he said to her: For this saying go thy way, the devil is gone out of thy daughter.

7:30 And when she was come into her house, she found the girl lying upon the bed, and that the devil was gone out.

7:31 And again going out of the coasts of Tyre, he came by Sidon to the sea of Galilee, through the midst of the coasts of Decapolis.

7:32 And they bring to him one deaf and dumb; and they besought him that he would lay his hand upon him.

7:33 And taking him from the multitude apart, he put his fingers into his ears, and spitting, he touched his tongue:

7:34 And looking up to heaven, he groaned, and said to him: Ephpheta, which is, Be thou opened.

7:35 And immediately his ears were opened, and the string of his tongue was loosed, and he spoke right.

7:36 And he charged them that they should tell no man. But the more he charged them, so much the more a great deal did they publish it.

7:37 And so much the more did they wonder, saying: He hath done all things well; he hath made both the deaf to hear, and the dumb to speak.

8:1 In those days again, when there was a great multitude, and had nothing to eat; calling his disciples together, he saith to them:

8:2 I have compassion on the multitude, for behold they have now been with me three days, and have nothing to eat.

8:3 et si dimisero eos jejunos in domum suam, deficient in via : quidam enim ex eis de longe venerunt.

8:4 Et responderunt ei discipuli sui : Unde illos quis poterit saturare panibus in solitudine ?

8:5 Et interrogavit eos : Quot panes habetis ? Qui dixerunt : Septem.

8:6 Et præcepit turbæ discumbere super terram. Et accipiens septem panes, gratias agens fregit, et dabat discipulis suis ut apponerent, et apposuerunt turbæ.

8:7 Et habebant pisciculos paucos : et ipsos benedixit, et jussit apponi.

8:8 Et manducaverunt, et saturati sunt, et sustulerunt quod superaverat de fragmentis, septem sportas.

8:9 Erant autem qui manducaverunt, quasi quatuor millia : et dimisit eos.

8:10 Et statim ascendens navim cum discipulis suis, venit in partes Dalmanutha.

8:11 Et exierunt pharisæi, et cœperunt conquirere cum eo, quærentes ab illo signum de cælo, tentantes eum.

8:12 Et ingemiscens spiritu, ait : Quid generatio ista signum quærit ? Amen dico vobis, si dabitur generationi isti signum.

8:13 Et dimittens eos, ascendit iterum navim et abiit trans fretum.

8:14 Et obliti sunt panes sumere : et nisi unum panem non habebant secum in navi.

8:15 Et præcipiebat eis, dicens : Videte, et cavete a fermento pharisæorum, et fermento Herodis.

8:16 Et cogitabant ad alterutrum, dicentes : quia panes non habemus.

8:17 Quo cognito, ait illis Jesus : Quid cogitatis, quia panes non habetis ? nondum cognoscetis nec intelligitis ? adhuc cæcatum habetis cor vestrum ?

8:18 oculos habentes non videtis ? et aures habentes non auditis ? nec recordamini,

8:19 quando quinque panes fregi in quinque millia : quot cophinos fragmentorum plenos sustulistis ? Dicunt ei : Duodecim.

8:20 Quando et septem panes in quatuor millia : quot sportas fragmentorum tulistis ? Et dicunt ei : Septem.

8:3 And if I shall send them away fasting to their home, they will faint in the way; for some of them came from afar off.

8:4 And his disciples answered him: From whence can any one fill them here with bread in the wilderness?

8:5 And he asked them: How many loaves have ye? Who said: Seven.

8:6 And taking the seven loaves, giving thanks, he broke, and gave to his disciples for to set before them; and they set them before the people.

8:7 And they had a few little fishes; and he blessed them, and commanded them to be set before them.

8:8 And they did eat and were filled; and they took up that which was left of the fragments, seven baskets.

8:9 And they that had eaten were about four thousand; and he sent them away.

8:10 And immediately going up into a ship with his disciples, he came into the parts of Dalmanutha.

8:11 And the Pharisees came forth, and began to question with him, asking him a sign from heaven, tempting him.

8:12 And sighing deeply in spirit, he saith: Why doth this generation seek a sign? Amen, I say to you, a sign shall not be given to this generation.

8:13 And leaving them, he went up again into the ship, and passed to the other side of the water.

8:14 And they forgot to take bread; and they had but one loaf with them in the ship.

8:15 And he charged them, saying: Take heed and beware of the leaven of the Pharisees, and of the leaven of Herod.

8:16 And they reasoned among themselves, saying: Because we have no bread.

8:17 Which Jesus knowing, saith to them: Why do you reason, because you have no bread? do you not yet know nor understand? have you still your heart blinded?

8:18 Having eyes, see you not? and having ears, hear you not? neither do you remember.

8:19 When I broke the five loaves among five thousand, how many baskets full of fragments took you up? They say to him, Twelve.

8:20 When also the seven loaves among four thousand, how many baskets of fragments took you up? And they say to him, Seven.

8:21 Et dicebat eis : Quomodo nondum intelligitis ?

8:22 Et veniunt Bethsaidam, et adducunt ei cæcum, et rogabant eum ut illum tangeret.

8:23 Et apprehensa manu cæci, eduxit eum extra vicum : et exspuens in oculos ejus impositis manibus suis, interrogavit eum si quid videret.

8:24 Et aspiciens, ait : Video homines velut arbores ambulantes.

8:25 Deinde iterum imposuit manus super oculos ejus : et cœpit videre : et restitutus est ita ut clare videret omnia.

8:26 Et misit illum in domum suam, dicens : Vade in domum tuam : et si in vicum introieris, nemini dixeris.

8:27 Et egressus est Jesus, et discipuli ejus in castella Cæsareæ Philippi : et in via interrogabat discipulos suos, dicens eis : Quem me dicunt esse homines ?

8:28 Qui responderunt illi, dicentes : Joannem Baptistam, alii Eliam, alii vero quasi unum de prophetis.

8:29 Tunc dicit illis : Vos vero quem me esse dicitis ? Respondens Petrus, ait ei : Tu es Christus.

8:30 Et comminatus est eis, ne cui dicerent de illo.

8:31 Et cœpit docere eos quoniam oportet Filium hominis pati multa, et reprobari a senioribus, et a summis sacerdotibus et scribis, et occidi : et post tres dies resurgere.

8:32 Et palam verbum loquebatur. Et apprehendens eum Petrus, cœpit increpare eum.

8:33 Qui conversus, et videns discipulos suos, comminatus est Petro, dicens : Vade retro me Satana, quoniam non sapis quæ Dei sunt, sed quæ sunt hominum.

8:34 Et convocata turba cum discipulis suis, dixit eis : Si quis vult me sequi, deneget semetipsum : et tollat crucem suam, et sequatur me.

8:35 Qui enim voluerit animam suam salvam facere, perdet eam : qui autem perdiderit animam suam propter me, et Evangelium, salvam faciet eam.

8:36 Quid enim proderit homini, si lucretur mundum totum et detrimentum animæ suæ faciat ?

8:37 Aut quid dabit homo commutationis pro

8:21 And he said to them: How do you not yet understand?

8:22 And they came to Bethsaida; and they bring to him a blind man, and they besought him that he would touch him.

8:23 And taking the blind man by the hand, he led him out of the town; and spitting upon his eyes, laying his hands on him, he asked him if he saw any thing.

8:24 And looking up, he said: I see men as it were trees, walking.

8:25 After that again he laid his hands upon his eyes, and he began to see, and was restored, so that he saw all things clearly.

8:26 And he sent him into his house, saying: Go into thy house, and if thou enter into the town, tell nobody.

8:27 And Jesus went out, and his disciples, into the towns of Caesarea Philippi. And in the way, he asked his disciples, saying to them: Whom do men say that I am?

8:28 Who answered him, saying: John the Baptist; but some Elias, and others as one of the prophets.

8:29 Then he saith to them: But whom do you say that I am? Peter answering said to him: Thou art the Christ.

8:30 And he strictly charged them that they should not tell any man of him.

8:31 And he began to teach them, that the Son of man must suffer many things, and be rejected by the ancients and by the high priests, and the scribes, and be killed: and after three days rise again.

8:32 And he spoke the word openly. And Peter taking him, began to rebuke him.

8:33 Who turning about and seeing his disciples, threatened Peter, saying: Go behind me, Satan, because thou savorest not the things that are of God, but that are of men.

8:34 And calling the multitude together with his disciples, he said to them: If any man will follow me, let him deny himself, and take up his cross, and follow me.

8:35 For whosoever will save his life, shall lose it: and whosoever shall lose his life for my sake and the gospel, shall save it.

8:36 For what shall it profit a man, if he gain the whole world, and suffer the loss of his soul?

8:37 Or what shall a man give in exchange for

anima sua ?

8:38 Qui enim me confusus fuerit, et verba mea in generatione ista adultera et peccatrice, et Filius hominis confundetur eum, cum venerit in gloria Patris sui cum angelis sanctis.

8:39 Et dicebat illis : Amen dico vobis, quia sunt quidam de hic stantibus, qui non gustabunt mortem donec videant regnum Dei veniens in virtute.

9:1 Et post dies sex assumit Jesus Petrum, et Jacobum, et Joannem, et ducit illos in montem excelsum seorsum solos, et transfiguratus est coram ipsis.

9:2 Et vestimenta ejus facta sunt splendentia, et candida nimis velut nix, qualia fullo non potest super terram candida facere.

9:3 Et apparuit illis Elias cum Moyse : et erant loquentes cum Jesu.

9:4 Et respondens Petrus, ait Jesu : Rabbi, bonum est nos hic esse : et faciamus tria tabernacula, tibi unum, et Moysi unum, et Eliæ unum.

9:5 Non enim sciebat quid diceret : erant enim timore exterriti.

9:6 Et facta est nubes obumbrans eos : et venit vox de nube, dicens : Hic est Filius meus carissimus : audite illum.

9:7 Et statim circumspicientes, neminem amplius viderunt, nisi Jesum tantum secum.

9:8 Et descendentibus illis de monte, præcepit illis ne cuiquam quæ vidissent, narrarent : nisi cum Filius hominis a mortuis resurrexerit.

9:9 Et verbum continuerunt apud se : conquirentes quid esset, cum a mortuis resurrexerit.

9:10 Et interrogabant eum, dicentes : Quid ergo dicunt pharisæi et scribæ, quia Eliam oportet venire primum ?

9:11 Qui respondens, ait illis : Elias cum venerit primo, restituet omnia : et quomodo scriptum est in Filium hominis, ut multa patiatur et contemnatur.

9:12 Sed dico vobis quia et Elias venit (et fecerunt illi quæcumque voluerunt) sicut scriptum est de eo.

9:13 Et veniens ad discipulos suos, vidit turbam magnam circa eos, et scribas conquirentes cum illis.

9:14 Et confestim omnis populus videns Jesum, stupefactus est, et expaverunt, et accurrentes

his soul?

8:38 For he that shall be ashamed of me, and of my words, in this adulterous and sinful generation: the Son of man also will be ashamed of him, when he shall come in the glory of his Father with the holy angels.

8:39 And he said to them: Amen I say to you, that there are some of them that stand here, who shall not taste death, till they see the kingdom of God coming in power.

9:1 And after six days Jesus taketh with him Peter and James and John, and leadeth them up into an high mountain apart by themselves, and was transfigured before them.

9:2 And his garments became shining and exceeding white as snow, so as no fuller upon earth can make white.

9:3 And there appeared to them Elias with Moses; and they were talking with Jesus.

9:4 And Peter answering, said to Jesus: Rabbi, it is good for us to be here: and let us make three tabernacles, one for thee, and one for Moses, and one for Elias.

9:5 For he knew not what he said: for they were struck with fear.

9:6 And there was a cloud overshadowing them: and a voice came out of the cloud, saying: This is my most beloved son; hear ye him.

9:7 And immediately looking about, they saw no man any more, but Jesus only with them.

9:8 And as they came down from the mountain, he charged them not to tell any man what things they had seen, till the Son of man shall be risen again from the dead.

9:9 And they kept the word to themselves; questioning together what that should mean, when he shall be risen from the dead.

9:10 And they asked him, saying: Why then do the Pharisees and scribes say that Elias must come first?

9:11 Who answering, said to them: Elias, when he shall come first, shall restore all things; and as it is written of the Son of man, that he must suffer many things and be despised.

9:12 But I say to you, that Elias also is come, (and they have done to him whatsoever they would,) as it is written of him.

9:13 And coming to his disciples, he saw a great multitude about them, and the scribes disputing with them.

9:14 And presently all the people seeing Jesus, were astonished and struck with fear; and run-

salutabant eum.

9:15 Et interrogavit eos : Quid inter vos conquiritis ?

9:16 Et respondens unus de turba, dixit : Magister, attuli filium meum ad te habentem spiritum mutum :

9:17 qui ubicumque eum apprehenderit, allidit illum, et spumat, et stridet dentibus, et arescit : et dixi discipulis tuis ut ejicerent illum, et non potuerunt.

9:18 Qui respondens eis, dixit : O generatio incredula, quamdiu apud vos ero ? quamdiu vos patiar ? afferte illum ad me.

9:19 Et attulerunt eum. Et cum vidisset eum, statim spiritus conturbavit illum : et elisus in terram, volutabatur spumans.

9:20 Et interrogavit patrem ejus : Quantum temporis est ex quo ei hoc accidit ? At ille ait : Ab infantia :

9:21 et frequenter eum in ignem, et in aquas misit ut eum perderet : sed si quid potes, adjuva nos, misertus nostri.

9:22 Jesus autem ait illi : Si potes credere, omnia possibilia sunt credenti.

9:23 Et continuo exclamans pater pueri, cum lacrimis aiebat : Credo, Domine ; adjuva incredulitatem meam.

9:24 Et cum videret Jesus concurrentem turbam, comminatus est spiritui immundo, dicens illi : Surde et mute spiritus, ego præcipio tibi, exi ab eo : et amplius ne introëas in eum.

9:25 Et exclamans, et multum discerpens eum, exiit ab eo, et factus est sicut mortuus, ita ut multi dicerent : Quia mortuus est.

9:26 Jesus autem tenens manum ejus elevavit eum, et surrexit.

9:27 Et cum introisset in domum, discipuli ejus secreto interrogabant eum : Quare nos non potuimus ejicere eum ?

9:28 Et dixit illis : Hoc genus in nullo potest exire, nisi in oratione et jejunio.

9:29 Et inde profecti prætergrediebantur Galilæam : nec volebat quemquam scire.

9:30 Docebat autem discipulos suos, et dicebat illis : Quoniam Filius hominis tradetur in manus hominum, et occident eum, et occisus tertia die resurget.

9:15 And he asked them: What do you question about among you?

9:16 And one of the multitude, answering, said: Master, I have brought my son to thee, having a dumb spirit.

9:17 Who, wheresoever he taketh him, dasheth him, and he foameth, and gnasheth with the teeth, and pineth away; and I spoke to thy disciples to cast him out, and they could not.

9:18 Who answering them, said: O incredulous generation, how long shall I be with you? how long shall I suffer you? bring him unto me.

9:19 And they brought him. And when he had seen him, immediately the spirit troubled him; and being thrown down upon the ground, he rolled about foaming.

9:20 And he asked his father: How long time is it since this hath happened unto him? But he said: From his infancy:

9:21 And oftentimes hath he cast him into the fire and into waters to destroy him. But if thou canst do any thing, help us, having compassion on us.

9:22 And Jesus saith to him: If thou canst believe, all things are possible to him that believeth.

9:23 And immediately the father of the boy crying out, with tears said: I do believe, Lord: help my unbelief.

9:24 And when Jesus saw the multitude running together, he threatened the unclean spirit, saying to him: Deaf and dumb spirit, I command thee, go out of him; and enter not any more into him.

9:25 And crying out, and greatly tearing him, he went out of him, and he became as dead, so that many said: He is dead.

9:26 But Jesus taking him by the hand, lifted him up; and he arose.

9:27 And when he was come into the house, his disciples secretly asked him: Why could not we cast him out?

9:28 And he said to them: This kind can go out by nothing, but by prayer and fasting.

9:29 And departing from thence, they passed through Galilee, and he would not that any man should know it.

9:30 And he taught his disciples, and said to them: The Son of man shall be betrayed into the hands of men, and they shall kill him; and after that he is killed, he shall rise again the third day.

9:31 At illi ignorabant verbum : et timebant interrogare eum.

9:32 Et venerunt Capharnaum. Qui cum domi essent, interrogabat eos : Quid in via tractabatis ?

9:33 At illi tacebant : siquidem in via inter se disputaverunt : quis eorum major esset.

9:34 Et residens vocavit duodecim, et ait illis : Si quis vult primus esse, erit omnium novissimus, et omnium minister.

9:35 Et accipiens puerum, statuit eum in medio eorum : quem cum complexus esset, ait illis :

9:36 Quisquis unum ex hujusmodi pueris receperit in nomine meo, me recipit : et quicumque me susceperit, non me suscipit, sed eum qui misit me.

9:37 Respondit illi Joannes, dicens : Magister, vidimus quemdam in nomine tuo ejicientem dæmonia, qui non sequitur nos, et prohibuimus eum.

9:38 Jesus autem ait : Nolite prohibere eum : nemo est enim qui faciat virtutem in nomine meo, et possit cito male loqui de me :

9:39 qui enim non est adversum vos, pro vobis est.

9:40 Quisquis enim potum dederit vobis calicem aquæ in nomine meo, quia Christi estis : amen dico vobis, non perdet mercedem suam.

9:41 Et quisquis scandalizaverit unum ex his pusillis credentibus in me : bonum est ei magis si circumdaretur mola asinaria collo ejus, et in mare mitteretur.

9:42 Et si scandalizaverit te manus tua, abscide illam : bonum est tibi debilem introire in vitam, quam duas manus habentem ire in gehennam, in ignem inextinguibilem,

9:43 ubi vermis eorum non moritur, et ignis non extinguitur.

9:44 Et si pes tuus te scandalizat, amputa illum : bonum est tibi claudum introire in vitam æternam, quam duos pedes habentem mitti in gehennam ignis inextinguibilis,

9:45 ubi vermis eorum non moritur, et ignis non extinguitur.

9:46 Quod si oculus tuus scandalizat te, ejice eum : bonum est tibi luscum introire in regnum Dei, quam duos oculos habentem mitti in gehennam ignis,

9:47 ubi vermis eorum non moritur, et ignis non

9:31 But they understood not the word, and they were afraid to ask him.

9:32 And they came to Capharnaum. And when they were in the house, he asked them: What did you treat of in the way?

9:33 But they held their peace, for in the way they had disputed among themselves, which of them should be the greatest.

9:34 And sitting down, he called the twelve, and saith to them: If any man desire to be first, he shall be the last of all, and the minister of all.

9:35 And taking a child, he set him in the midst of them. Whom when he had embraced, he saith to them:

9:36 Whosoever shall receive one such child as this in my name, receiveth me. And whosoever shall receive me, receiveth not me, but him that sent me.

9:37 John answered him, saying: Master, we saw one casting out devils in thy name, who followeth not us, and we forbade him.

9:38 But Jesus said: Do not forbid him. For there is no man that doth a miracle in my name, and can soon speak ill of me.

9:39 For he that is not against you, is for you.

9:40 For whosoever shall give you to drink a cup of water in my name, because you belong to Christ: amen I say to you, he shall not lose his reward.

9:41 And whosoever shall scandalize one of these little ones that believe in me; it were better for him that a millstone were hanged around his neck, and he were cast into the sea.

9:42 And if thy hand scandalize thee, cut it off: it is better for thee to enter into life, maimed, than having two hands to go into hell, into unquenchable fire:

9:43 Where their worm dieth not, and the fire is not extinguished.

9:44 And if thy foot scandalize thee, cut it off. It is better for thee to enter lame into life everlasting, than having two feet, to be cast into the hell of unquenchable fire:

9:45 Where their worm dieth not, and the fire is not extinguished.

9:46 And if thy eye scandalize thee, pluck it out. It is better for thee with one eye to enter into the kingdom of God, than having two eyes to be cast into the hell of fire:

9:47 Where their worm dieth not, and the fire is

extinguitur.

9:48 Omnis enim igne salietur, et omnis victima sale salietur.

9:49 Bonum est sal : quod si sal insulsum fuerit, in quo illud condietis ? Habete in vobis sal, et pacem habete inter vos.

10:1 Et inde exsurgens venit in fines Judææ ultra Jordanem : et conveniunt iterum turbæ ad eum : et sicut consueverat, iterum docebat illos.

10:2 Et accedentes pharisæi interrogabant eum : Si licet viro uxorem dimittere : tentantes eum.

10:3 At ille respondens, dixit eis : Quid vobis præcepit Moyses ?

10:4 Qui dixerunt : Moyses permisit libellum repudii scribere, et dimittere.

10:5 Quibus respondens Jesus, ait : Ad duritiam cordis vestri scripsit vobis præceptum istud :

10:6 ab initio autem creaturæ masculum et feminam fecit eos Deus.

10:7 Propter hoc relinquet homo patrem suum et matrem, et adhærebit ad uxorem suam :

10:8 et erunt duo in carne una. Itaque jam non sunt duo, sed una caro.

10:9 Quod ergo Deus conjunxit, homo non separet.

10:10 Et in domo iterum discipuli ejus de eodem interrogaverunt eum.

10:11 Et ait illis : Quicumque dimiserit uxorem suam, et aliam duxerit, adulterium committit super eam.

10:12 Et si uxor dimiserit virum suum, et alii nupserit, mœchatur.

10:13 Et offerebant illi parvulos ut tangeret illos. Discipuli autem comminabantur offerentibus.

10:14 Quos cum videret Jesus, indigne tulit, et ait illis : Sinite parvulos venire ad me, et ne prohibueritis eos : talium enim est regnum Dei.

10:15 Amen dico vobis : Quisquis non receperit regnum Dei velut parvulus, non intrabit in illud.

10:16 Et complexans eos, et imponens manus super illos, benedicebat eos.

10:17 Et cum egressus esset in viam, procurrens quidam genu flexo ante eum, rogabat eum : Magister bone, quid faciam ut vitam æternam percipiam ?

not extinguished.

9:48 For every one shall be salted with fire: and every victim shall be salted with salt.

9:49 Salt is good. But if the salt became unsavory; wherewith will you season it? Have salt in you, and have peace among you.

10:1 And rising up from thence, he cometh into the coasts of Judea beyond the Jordan: and the multitudes flock to him again. And as he was accustomed, he taught them again.

10:2 And the Pharisees coming to him asked him: Is it lawful for a man to put away his wife? tempting him.

10:3 But he answering, saith to them: What did Moses command you?

10:4 Who said: Moses permitted to write a bill of divorce, and to put her away.

10:5 To whom Jesus answering, said: Because of the hardness of your heart he wrote you that precept.

10:6 But from the beginning of the creation, God made them male and female.

10:7 For this cause a man shall leave his father and mother; and shall cleave to his wife.

10:8 And they two shall be in one flesh. Therefore now they are not two, but one flesh.

10:9 What therefore God hath joined together, let not man put asunder.

10:10 And in the house again his disciples asked him concerning the same thing.

10:11 And he saith to them: Whosoever shall put away his wife and marry another, committeth adultery against her.

10:12 And if the wife shall put away her husband, and be married to another, she committeth adultery.

10:13 And they brought to him young children, that he might touch them. And the disciples rebuked them that brought them.

10:14 Whom when Jesus saw, he was much displeased, and saith to them: Suffer the little children to come unto me, and forbid them not; for of such is the kingdom of God.

10:15 Amen I say to you, whosoever shall not receive the kingdom of God as a little child, shall not enter into it.

10:16 And embracing them, and laying his hands upon them, he blessed them.

10:17 And when he was gone forth into the way, a certain man running up and kneeling before him, asked him, Good Master, what shall I do that I may receive life everlasting?

10:18 Jesus autem dixit ei : Quid me dicis bonum ? nemo bonus, nisi unus Deus.

10:19 Præcepta nosti : ne adulteres, ne occidas, ne fureris, ne falsum testimonium dixeris, ne fraudum feceris, honora patrem tuum et matrem.

10:20 At ille respondens, ait illi : Magister, hæc omnia observavi a juventute mea.

10:21 Jesus autem intuitus eum, dilexit eum, et dixit ei : Unum tibi deest : vade, quæcumque habes vende, et da pauperibus, et habebis thesaurum in cælo : et veni, sequere me.

10:22 Qui contristatus in verbo, abiit mœrens : erat enim habens multas possessiones.

10:23 Et circumspiciens Jesus, ait discipulis suis : Quam difficile qui pecunias habent, in regnum Dei introibunt !

10:24 Discipuli autem obstupescebant in verbis ejus. At Jesus rursus respondens ait illis : Filioli, quam difficile est, confidentes in pecuniis, in regnum Dei introire !

10:25 Facilius est camelum per foramen acus transire, quam divitem intrare in regnum Dei.

10:26 Qui magis admirabantur, dicentes ad semetipsos : Et quis potest salvus fieri ?

10:27 Et intuens illos Jesus, ait : Apud homines impossibile est, sed non apud Deum : omnia enim possibilia sunt apud Deum.

10:28 Et cœpit ei Petrus dicere : Ecce nos dimisimus omnia, et secuti sumus te.

10:29 Respondens Jesus, ait : Amen dico vobis : Nemo est qui reliquerit domum, aut fratres, aut sorores, aut patrem, aut matrem, aut filios, aut agros propter me et propter Evangelium,

10:30 qui non accipiat centies tantum, nunc in tempore hoc : domos, et fratres, et sorores, et matres, et filios, et agros, cum persecutionibus, et in sæculo futuro vitam æternam.

10:31 Multi autem erunt primi novissimi, et novissimi primi.

10:32 Erant autem in via ascendentes Jerosolymam : et præcedebat illos Jesus, et stupebant : et sequentes timebant. Et assumens iterum duodecim, cœpit illis dicere quæ essent ei eventura.

10:33 Quia ecce ascendimus Jerosolymam, et Filius hominis tradetur principibus sacerdotum, et scribis, et senioribus, et damnabunt eum

10:18 And Jesus said to him, Why callest thou me good? None is good but one, that is God.

10:19 Thou knowest the commandments: Do not commit adultery, do not kill, do not steal, bear not false witness, do no fraud, honour thy father and mother.

10:20 But he answering, said to him: Master, all these things I have observed from my youth.

10:21 And Jesus looking on him, loved him, and said to him: One thing is wanting unto thee: go, sell whatsoever thou hast, and give to the poor, and thou shalt have treasure in heaven; and come, follow me.

10:22 Who being struck sad at that saying, went away sorrowful: for he had great possessions.

10:23 And Jesus looking round about, saith to his disciples: How hardly shall they that have riches, enter into the kingdom of God!

10:24 And the disciples were astonished at his words. But Jesus again answering, saith to them: Children, how hard is it for them that trust in riches, to enter into the kingdom of God?

10:25 It is easier for a camel to pass through the eye of a needle, than for a rich man to enter into the kingdom of God.

10:26 Who wondered the more, saying among themselves: Who then can be saved?

10:27 And Jesus looking on them, saith: With men it is impossible; but not with God: for all things are possible with God.

10:28 And Peter began to say unto him: Behold, we have left all things, and have followed thee.

10:29 Jesus answering, said: Amen I say to you, there is no man who hath left house or brethren, or sisters, or father, or mother, or children, or lands, for my sake and for the gospel,

10:30 Who shall not receive an hundred times as much, now in this time; houses, and brethren, and sisters, and mothers, and children, and lands, with persecutions: and in the world to come life everlasting.

10:31 But many that are first, shall be last: and the last, first.

10:32 And they were in the way going up to Jerusalem: and Jesus went before them, and they were astonished; and following were afraid. And taking again the twelve, he began to tell them the things that should befall him.

10:33 Saying: Behold we go up to Jerusalem, and the Son of man shall be betrayed to the chief priests, and to the scribes and ancients, and

morte, et tradent eum gentibus :

10:34 et illudent ei, et conspuent eum, et flagellabunt eum, et interficient eum : et tertia die resurget.

10:35 Et accedunt ad eum Jacobus et Joannes filii Zebedæi, dicentes : Magister, volumus ut quodcumque petierimus, facias nobis.

10:36 At ille dixit eis : Quid vultis ut faciam vobis ?

10:37 Et dixerunt : Da nobis ut unus ad dexteram tuam, et alius ad sinistram tuam sedeamus in gloria tua.

10:38 Jesus autem ait eis : Nescitis quid petatis : potestis bibere calicem, quem ego bibo, aut baptismo, quo ego baptizor, baptizari ?

10:39 At illi dixerunt ei : Possumus. Jesus autem ait eis : Calicem quidem, quem ego bibo, bibetis ; et baptismo, quo ego baptizor, baptizabimini :

10:40 sedere autem ad dexteram meam, vel ad sinistram, non est meum dare vobis, sed quibus paratum est.

10:41 Et audientes decem, cœperunt indignari de Jacobo et Joanne.

10:42 Jesus autem vocans eos, ait illis : Scitis quia hi, qui videntur principari gentibus, dominantur eis : et principes eorum potestatem habent ipsorum.

10:43 Non ita est autem in vobis, sed quicumque voluerit fieri major, erit vester minister :

10:44 et quicumque voluerit in vobis primus esse, erit omnium servus.

10:45 Nam et Filius hominis non venit ut ministraretur ei, sed ut ministraret, et daret animam suam redemptionem pro multis.

10:46 Et veniunt Jericho : et proficiscente eo de Jericho, et discipulis ejus, et plurima multitudine, filius Timæi Bartimæus cæcus, sedebat juxta viam mendicans.

10:47 Qui cum audisset quia Jesus Nazarenus est, cœpit clamare, et dicere : Jesu fili David, miserere mei.

10:48 Et comminabantur ei multi ut taceret. At ille multo magis clamabat : Fili David, miserere mei.

10:49 Et stans Jesus præcepit illum vocari. Et vocant cæcum, dicentes ei : Animæquior esto : surge, vocat te.

they shall condemn him to death, and shall deliver him to the Gentiles.

10:34 And they shall mock him, and spit on him, and scourge him, and kill him: and the third day he shall rise again.

10:35 And James and John the sons of Zebedee, come to him, saying: Master, we desire that whatsoever we shall ask, thou wouldst do it for us:

10:36 But he said to them: What would you that I should do for you?

10:37 And they said: Grant to us, that we may sit, one on thy right hand, and the other on thy left hand, in thy glory.

10:38 And Jesus said to them: You know not what you ask. Can you drink of the chalice that I drink of: or be baptized with the baptism wherewith I am baptized?

10:39 But they said to him: We can. And Jesus saith to them: You shall indeed drink of the chalice that I drink of: and with the baptism wherewith I am baptized, you shall be baptized:

10:40 But to sit on my right hand, or on my left, is not mine to give to you, but to them for whom it is prepared.

10:41 And the ten hearing it, began to be much displeased at James and John.

10:42 But Jesus calling them, saith to them: You know that they who seem to rule over the Gentiles, lord it over them: and their princes have power over them.

10:43 But it is not so among you: but whosoever will be greater, shall be your minister.

10:44 And whosoever will be first among you, shall be the servant of all.

10:45 For the Son of man also is not come to be ministered unto, but to minister, and to give his life a redemption for many.

10:46 And they came to Jericho: and as he went out of Jericho, with his disciples, and a very great multitude, Bartimeus the blind man, the son of Timeus, sat by the way side begging.

10:47 Who when he had heard, that it was Jesus of Nazareth, began to cry out, and to say: Jesus son of David, have mercy on me.

10:48 And many rebuked him, that he might hold his peace; but he cried a great deal the more: Son of David, have mercy on me.

10:49 And Jesus, standing still, commanded him to be called. And they call the blind man, saying to him: Be of better comfort: arise, he

10:50 Qui projecto vestimento suo exiliens, venit ad eum.

10:51 Et respondens Jesus dixit illi : Quid tibi vis faciam ? Cæcus autem dixit ei : Rabboni, ut videam.

10:52 Jesus autem ait illi : Vade, fides tua te salvum fecit. Et confestim vidit, et sequebatur eum in via.

11:1 Et cum appropinquarent Jerosolymæ et Bethaniæ ad montem Olivarum, mittit duos ex discipulis suis,

11:2 et ait illis : Ite in castellum, quod contra vos est, et statim introëuntes illuc, invenietis pullum ligatum, super quem nemo adhuc hominum sedit : solvite illum, et adducite.

11:3 Et si quis vobis dixerit : Quid facitis ? dicite, quia Domino necessarius est : et continuo illum dimittet huc.

11:4 Et abeuntes invenerunt pullum ligatum ante januam foris in bivio : et solvunt eum.

11:5 Et quidam de illic stantibus dicebant illis : Quid facitis solventes pullum ?

11:6 Qui dixerunt eis sicut præceperat illis Jesus, et dimiserunt eis.

11:7 Et duxerunt pullum ad Jesum : et imponunt illi vestimenta sua, et sedit super eum.

11:8 Multi autem vestimenta sua straverunt in via : alii autem frondes cædebant de arboribus, et sternebant in via.

11:9 Et qui præibant, et qui sequebantur, clamabant, dicentes : Hosanna : benedictus qui venit in nomine Domini :

11:10 benedictum quod venit regnum patris nostri David : hosanna in excelsis.

11:11 Et introivit Jerosolymam in templum : et circumspectis omnibus, cum jam vespera esset hora, exiit in Bethaniam cum duodecim.

11:12 Et alia die cum exirent a Bethania, esuriit.

11:13 Cumque vidisset a longe ficum habentem folia, venit si quid forte inveniret in ea : et cum venisset ad eam, nihil invenit præter folia : non enim erat tempus ficorum.

11:14 Et respondens dixit ei : Jam non amplius in æternum ex te fructum quisquam manducet.

calleth thee.

10:50 Who casting off his garment leaped up, and came to him.

10:51 And Jesus answering, said to him: What wilt thou that I should do to thee? And the blind man said to him: Rabboni, that I may see.

10:52 And Jesus saith to him: Go thy way, thy faith hath made thee whole. And immediately he saw, and followed him in the way.

11:1 And when they were drawing near to Jerusalem and to Bethania at the mount of Olives, he sendeth two of his disciples,

11:2 And saith to them: Go into the village that is over against you, and immediately at your coming in thither, you shall find a colt tied, upon which no man yet hath sat: loose him, and bring him.

11:3 And if any man shall say to you, What are you doing? say ye that the Lord hath need of him: and immediately he will let him come hither.

11:4 And going their way, they found the colt tied before the gate without, in the meeting of two ways: and they loose him.

11:5 And some of them that stood there, said to them: What do you loosing the colt?

11:6 Who said to them as Jesus had commanded them; and they let him go with them.

11:7 And they brought the colt to Jesus; and they lay their garments on him, and he sat upon him.

11:8 And many spread their garments in the way: and others cut down boughs from the trees, and strewed them in the way.

11:9 And they that went before and they that followed, cried, saying: Hosanna, blessed is he that cometh in the name of the Lord.

11:10 Blessed be the kingdom of our father David that cometh: Hosanna in the highest.

11:11 And he entered into Jerusalem, into the temple: and having viewed all things round about, when now the eventide was come, he went out to Bethania with the twelve.

11:12 And the next day when they came out from Bethania, he was hungry.

11:13 And when he had seen afar off a fig tree having leaves, he came if perhaps he might find any thing on it. And when he was come to it, he found nothing but leaves. For it was not the time for figs.

11:14 And answering he said to it: May no man hereafter eat fruit of thee any more for ever.

Et audiebant discipuli ejus.

11:15 Et veniunt in Jerosolymam. Et cum introisset in templum, cœpit ejicere vendentes et ementes in templo : et mensas numulariorum, et cathedras vendentium columbas evertit :

11:16 et non sinebat ut quisquam transferret vas per templum :

11:17 et docebat, dicens eis : Nonne scriptum est : Quia domus mea, domus orationis vocabitur omnibus gentibus ? vos autem fecistis eam speluncam latronum.

11:18 Quo audito principes sacerdotum et scribæ, quærebant quomodo eum perderent : timebant enim eum, quoniam universa turba admirabatur super doctrina ejus.

11:19 Et cum vespera facta esset, egrediebatur de civitate.

11:20 Et cum mane transirent, viderunt ficum aridam factam a radicibus.

11:21 Et recordatus Petrus, dixit ei : Rabbi, ecce ficus, cui maledixisti, aruit.

11:22 Et respondens Jesus ait illis : Habete fidem Dei.

11:23 Amen dico vobis, quia quicumque dixerit huic monti : Tollere, et mittere in mare, et non hæsitaverit in corde suo, sed crediderit, quia quodcumque dixerit fiat, fiet ei.

11:24 Propterea dico vobis, omnia quæcumque orantes petitis, credite quia accipietis, et evenient vobis.

11:25 Et cum stabitis ad orandum, dimittite si quis habetis adversus aliquem : ut et Pater vester, qui in cælis est, dimittat vobis peccata vestra.

11:26 Quod si vos non dimiseritis : nec Pater vester, qui in cælis est, dimittet vobis peccata vestra.

11:27 Et veniunt rursus Jerosolymam. Et cum ambularet in templo, accedunt ad eum summi sacerdotes, et scribæ, et seniores :

11:28 et dicunt ei : In qua potestate hæc facis ? et quis dedit tibi hanc potestatem ut ista facias ?

11:29 Jesus autem respondens, ait illis : Interrogabo vos et ego unum verbum, et respondete mihi : et dicam vobis in qua potestate hæc faci-

And his disciples heard it.

11:15 And they came to Jerusalem. And when he was entered into the temple, he began to cast out them that sold and bought in the temple, and overthrew the tables of the moneychangers, and the chairs of them that sold doves.

11:16 And he suffered not that any man should carry a vessel through the temple;

11:17 And he taught, saying to them: Is it not written, My house shall be called the house of prayer to all nations? But you have made it a den of thieves.

11:18 Which when the chief priests and the scribes had heard, they sought how they might destroy him. For they feared him, because the whole multitude was in admiration at his doctrine.

11:19 And when evening was come, he went forth out of the city.

11:20 And when they passed by in the morning they saw the fig tree dried up from the roots.

11:21 And Peter remembering, said to him: Rabbi, behold the fig tree, which thou didst curse, is withered away.

11:22 And Jesus answering, saith to them: Have the faith of God.

11:23 Amen I say to you, that whosoever shall say to this mountain, Be thou removed and be cast into the sea, and shall not stagger in his heart, but believe, that whatsoever he saith shall be done; it shall be done unto him.

11:24 Therefore I say unto you, all things, whatsoever you ask when ye pray, believe that you shall receive; and they shall come unto you.

11:25 And when you shall stand to pray, forgive, if you have aught against any man; that your Father also, who is in heaven, may forgive you your sins.

11:26 But if you will not forgive, neither will your Father that is in heaven, forgive you your sins.

11:27 And they come again to Jerusalem. And when he was walking in the temple, there come to him the chief priests and the scribes and the ancients,

11:28 And they say to him: By what authority dost thou these things? and who hath given thee this authority that thou shouldst do these things?

11:29 And Jesus answering, said to them: I will also ask you one word, and answer you me, and I will tell you by what authority I do these

am.

11:30 Baptismus Joannis, de cælo erat, an ex hominibus ? Respondete mihi.

11:31 At illi cogitabant secum, dicentes : Si dixerimus : De cælo, dicet : Quare ergo non credidistis ei ?

11:32 Si dixerimus : Ex hominibus, timemus populum : omnes enim habebant Joannem quia vere propheta esset.

11:33 Et respondentes dicunt Jesu : Nescimus. Et respondens Jesus ait illis : Neque ego dico vobis in qua potestate hæc faciam.

12:1 Et cœpit illis in parabolis loqui : Vineam pastinavit homo, et circumdedit sepem, et fodit lacum, et ædificavit turrim, et locavit eam agricolis, et peregre profectus est.

12:2 Et misit ad agricolas in tempore servum ut ab agricolis acciperet de fructu vineæ.

12:3 Qui apprehensum eum ceciderunt, et dimiserunt vacuum.

12:4 Et iterum misit ad illos alium servum : et illum in capite vulneraverunt, et contumeliis affecerunt.

12:5 Et rursum alium misit, et illum occiderunt : et plures alios : quosdam cædentes, alios vero occidentes.

12:6 Adhuc ergo unum habens filium carissimum, et illum misit ad eos novissimum, dicens : Quia reverebuntur filium meum.

12:7 Coloni autem dixerunt ad invicem : Hic est hæres : venite, occidamus eum : et nostra erit hæreditas.

12:8 Et apprehendentes eum, occiderunt : et ejecerunt extra vineam.

12:9 Quid ergo faciet dominus vineæ ? Veniet, et perdet colonos, et dabit vineam aliis.

12:10 Nec scripturam hanc legistis : Lapidem quem reprobaverunt ædificantes, hic factus est in caput anguli :

12:11 a Domino factum est istud, et est mirabile in oculis nostris ?

12:12 Et quærebant eum tenere : et timuerunt turbam : cognoverunt enim quoniam ad eos parabolam hanc dixerit. Et relicto eo abierunt.

12:13 Et mittunt ad eum quosdam ex pharisæis, et herodianis, ut eum caperent in verbo.

things.

11:30 The baptism of John, was it from heaven, or from men? Answer me.

11:31 But they thought with themselves, saying: If we say, From heaven; he will say, Why then did you not believe him?

11:32 If we say, From men, we fear the people. For all men counted John that he was a prophet indeed.

11:33 And they answering, say to Jesus: We know not. And Jesus answering, saith to them: Neither do I tell you by what authority I do these things.

12:1 And he began to speak to them in parables: A certain man planted a vineyard and made a hedge about it, and dug a place for the winefat, and built a tower, and let it to husbandmen; and went into a far country.

12:2 And at the season he sent to the husbandmen a servant to receive of the husbandmen of the fruit of the vineyard.

12:3 Who having laid hands on him, beat him, and sent him away empty.

12:4 And again he sent to them another servant; and him they wounded in the head, and used him reproachfully.

12:5 And again he sent another, and him they killed: and many others, of whom some they beat, and others they killed.

12:6 Therefore having yet one son, most dear to him; he also sent him unto them last of all, saying: They will reverence my son.

12:7 But the husbandmen said one to another: This is the heir; come let us kill him; and the inheritance shall be ours.

12:8 And laying hold on him, they killed him, and cast him out of the vineyard.

12:9 What therefore will the lord of the vineyard do? He will come and destroy those husbandmen; and will give the vineyard to others.

12:10 And have you not read this scripture, The stone which the builders rejected, the same is made the head of the corner:

12:11 By the Lord has this been done, and it is wonderful in our eyes.

12:12 And they sought to lay hands on him, but they feared the people. For they knew that he spoke this parable to them. And leaving him, they went their way.

12:13 And they sent to him some of the Pharisees and of the Herodians; that they should catch him in his words.

12:14 Qui venientes dicunt ei : Magister, scimus quia verax es, et non curas quemquam : nec enim vides in faciem hominum, sed in veritate viam Dei doces. Licet dari tributum Cæsari, an non dabimus ?

12:15 Qui sciens versutiam illorum, ait illos : Quid me tentatis ? afferte mihi denarium ut videam.

12:16 At illi attulerunt ei. Et ait illis : Cujus est imago hæc, et inscriptio ? Dicunt ei : Cæsaris.

12:17 Respondens autem Jesus dixit illis : Reddite igitur quæ sunt Cæsaris, Cæsari : et quæ sunt Dei, Deo. Et mirabantur super eo.

12:18 Et venerunt ad eum sadducæi, qui dicunt resurrectionem non esse : et interrogabant eum, dicentes :

12:19 Magister, Moyses nobis scripsit, ut si cujus frater mortuus fuerit, et dimiserit uxorem, et filios non reliquerit, accipiat frater ejus uxorem ipsius, et resuscitet semen fratri suo.

12:20 Septem ergo fratres erant : et primus accepit uxorem, et mortuus est non relicto semine.

12:21 Et secundus accepit eam, et mortuus est : et nec iste reliquit semen. Et tertius similiter.

12:22 Et acceperunt eam similiter septem : et non reliquerunt semen. Novissima omnium defuncta est et mulier.

12:23 In resurrectione ergo cum resurrexerint, cujus de his erit uxor ? septem enim habuerunt eam uxorem.

12:24 Et respondens Jesus, ait illis : Nonne ideo erratis, non scientes Scripturas, neque virtutem Dei ?

12:25 Cum enim a mortuis resurrexerint, neque nubent, neque nubentur, sed sunt sicut angeli in cælis.

12:26 De mortuis autem quod resurgant, non legistis in libro Moysi, super rubum, quomodo dixerit illi Deus, inquiens : Ego sum Deus Abraham, et Deus Isaac, et Deus Jacob ?

12:27 Non est Deus mortuorum, sed vivorum. Vos ergo multum erratis.

12:28 Et accessit unus de scribis, qui audierat illos conquirentes, et videns quoniam bene illis responderit, interrogavit eum quod esset primum omnium mandatum.

12:14 Who coming, say to him: Master, we know that thou art a true speaker, and carest not for any man; for thou regardest not the person of men, but teachest the way of God in truth. Is it lawful to give tribute to Caesar; or shall we not give it?

12:15 Who knowing their wiliness, saith to them: Why tempt you me? bring me a penny that I may see it.

12:16 And they brought it him. And he saith to them: Whose is this image and inscription? They say to him, Caesar's.

12:17 And Jesus answering, said to them: Render therefore to Caesar the things that are Caesar's, and to God the things that are God's. And they marvelled at him.

12:18 And there came to him the Sadducees, who say there is no resurrection; and they asked him, saying:

12:19 Master, Moses wrote unto us, that if any man's brother die, and leave his wife behind him, and leave no children, his brother should take his wife, and raise up seed to his brother.

12:20 Now there were seven brethren; and the first took a wife, and died leaving no issue.

12:21 And the second took her, and died: and neither did he leave any issue. And the third in like manner.

12:22 And the seven all took her in like manner; and did not leave issue. Last of all the woman also died.

12:23 In the resurrection therefore, when they shall rise again, whose wife shall she be of them? for the seven had her to wife.

12:24 And Jesus answering, saith to them: Do ye not therefore err, because you know not the scriptures, nor the power of God?

12:25 For when they shall rise again from the dead, they shall neither marry, nor be married, but are as the angels in heaven.

12:26 And as concerning the dead that they rise again, have you not read in the book of Moses, how in the bush God spoke to him, saying: I am the God of Abraham, and the God of Isaac, and the God of Jacob?

12:27 He is not the God of the dead, but of the living. You therefore do greatly err.

12:28 And there came one of the scribes that had heard them reasoning together, and seeing that he had answered them well, asked him which was the first commandment of all.

12:29 Jesus autem respondit ei : Quia primum omnium mandatum est : Audi Israël, Dominus Deus tuus, Deus unus est :

12:30 et diliges Dominum Deum tuum ex toto corde tuo, et ex tota anima tua, et ex tota mente tua, et ex tota virtute tua. Hoc est primum mandatum.

12:31 Secundum autem simile est illi : Diliges proximum tuum tamquam teipsum. Majus horum aliud mandatum non est.

12:32 Et ait illi scriba : Bene, Magister, in veritate dixisti, quia unus est Deus, et non est alius præter eum.

12:33 Et ut diligatur ex toto corde, et ex toto intellectu, et ex tota anima, et ex tota fortitudine, et diligere proximum tamquam seipsum, majus est omnibus holocautomatibus, et sacrificiis.

12:34 Jesus autem videns quod sapienter respondisset, dixit illi : Non es longe a regno Dei. Et nemo jam audebat eum interrogare.

12:35 Et respondens Jesus dicebat, docens in templo : Quomodo dicunt scribæ Christum filium esse David ?

12:36 Ipse enim David dicit in Spiritu Sancto : Dixit Dominus Domino meo : Sede a dextris meis, donec ponam inimicos tuos scabellum pedum tuorum.

12:37 Ipse ergo David dicit eum Dominum, et unde est filius ejus ? Et multa turba eum libenter audivit.

12:38 Et dicebat eis in doctrina sua : Cavete a scribis, qui volunt in stolis ambulare, et salutari in foro,

12:39 et in primis cathedris sedere in synagogis, et primos discubitus in cœnis :

12:40 qui devorant domos viduarum sub obtentu prolixæ orationis : hi accipient prolixius judicium.

12:41 Et sedens Jesus contra gazophylacium, aspiciebat quomodo turba jactaret æs in gazophylacium, et multi divites jactabant multa.

12:42 Cum venisset autem vidua una pauper, misit duo minuta, quod est quadrans,

12:43 et convocans discipulos suos, ait illis : Amen dico vobis, quoniam vidua hæc pauper plus omnibus misit, qui miserunt in gazophylacium.

12:44 Omnes enim ex eo, quod abundabat illis,

12:29 And Jesus answered him: The first commandment of all is, Hear, O Israel: the Lord thy God is one God.

12:30 And thou shalt love the Lord thy God, with thy whole heart, and with thy whole soul, and with thy whole mind, and with thy whole strength. This is the first commandment.

12:31 And the second is like to it: Thou shalt love thy neighbour as thyself. There is no other commandment greater than these.

12:32 And the scribe said to him: Well, Master, thou hast said in truth, that there is one God, and there is no other besides him.

12:33 And that he should be loved with the whole heart, and with the whole understanding, and with the whole soul, and with the whole strength; and to love one's neighbour as one's self, is a greater thing than all holocausts and sacrifices.

12:34 And Jesus seeing that he had answered wisely, said to him: Thou art not far from the kingdom of God. And no man after that durst ask him any question.

12:35 And Jesus answering, said, teaching in the temple: How do the scribes say, that Christ is the son of David?

12:36 For David himself saith by the Holy Ghost: The Lord said to my Lord, Sit on my right hand, until I make thy enemies thy footstool.

12:37 David therefore himself calleth him Lord, and whence is he then his son? And a great multitude heard him gladly.

12:38 And he said to them in his doctrine: Beware of the scribes, who love to walk in long robes, and to be saluted in the marketplace,

12:39 And to sit in the first chairs, in the synagogues, and to have the highest places at suppers:

12:40 Who devour the houses of widows under the pretence of long prayer: these shall receive greater judgment.

12:41 And Jesus sitting over against the treasury, beheld how the people cast money into the treasury, and many that were rich cast in much.

12:42 And there came a certain poor widow, and she cast in two mites, which make a farthing.

12:43 And calling his disciples together, he saith to them: Amen I say to you, this poor widow hath cast in more than all they who have cast into the treasury.

12:44 For all they did cast in of their abundance;

miserunt : hæc vero de penuria sua omnia quæ habuit misit totum victum suum.

13:1 Et cum egrederetur de templo, ait illi unus ex discipulis suis : Magister, aspice quales lapides, et quales structuræ.

13:2 Et respondens Jesus, ait illi : Vides has omnes magnas ædificationes ? Non relinquetur lapis super lapidem, qui non destruatur.

13:3 Et cum sederet in monte Olivarum contra templum, interrogabant eum separatim Petrus, et Jacobus, et Joannes, et Andreas :

13:4 Dic nobis, quando ista fient ? et quod signum erit, quando hæc omnia incipient consummari ?

13:5 Et respondens Jesus cœpit dicere illis : Videte ne quid vos seducat :

13:6 multi enim venient in nomine meo, dicentes quia ego sum : et multos seducent.

13:7 Cum audieritis autem bella, et opiniones bellorum, ne timueritis : oportet enim hæc fieri : sed nondum finis.

13:8 Exsurget enim gens contra gentem, et regnum super regnum, et erunt terræmotus per loca, et fames. Initium dolorum hæc.

13:9 Videte autem vosmetipsos. Tradent enim vos in consiliis, et in synagogis vapulabitis, et ante præsides et reges stabitis propter me, in testimonium illis.

13:10 Et in omnes gentes primum oportet prædicari Evangelium.

13:11 Et cum duxerint vos tradentes, nolite præcogitare quid loquamini : sed quod datum vobis fuerit in illa hora, id loquimini : non enim vos estis loquentes, sed Spiritus Sanctus.

13:12 Tradet autem frater fratrem in mortem, et pater filium : et consurgent filii in parentes, et morte afficient eos.

13:13 Et eritis odio omnibus propter nomen meum. Qui autem sustinuerit in finem, hic salvus erit.

13:14 Cum autem videritis abominationem desolationis stantem, ubi non debet, qui legit, intelligat : tunc qui in Judæa sunt, fugiant in montes :

13:15 et qui super tectum, ne descendat in domum, nec introëat ut tollat quid de domo

but she of her want cast in all she had, even her whole living.

13:1 And as he was going out of the temple, one of his disciples said to him: Master, behold what manner of stones and what buildings are here.

13:2 And Jesus answering, said to him: Seest thou all these great buildings? There shall not be left a stone upon a stone, that shall not be thrown down.

13:3 And as he sat on the mount of Olivet over against the temple, Peter and James and John and Andrew asked him apart:

13:4 Tell us, when shall these things be? and what shall be the sign when all these things shall begin to be fulfilled?

13:5 And Jesus answering, began to say to them, Take heed lest any man deceive you.

13:6 For many shall come in my name, saying, I am he; and they shall deceive many.

13:7 And when you shall hear of wars and rumours of wars, fear ye not. For such things must needs be, but the end is not yet.

13:8 For nation shall rise against nation and kingdom against kingdom, and there shall be earthquakes in divers places, and famines. These things are the beginning of sorrows.

13:9 But look to yourselves. For they shall deliver you up to councils, and in the synagogues you shall be beaten, and you shall stand before governors and kings for my sake, for a testimony unto them.

13:10 And unto all nations the gospel must first be preached.

13:11 And when they shall lead you and deliver you up, be not thoughtful beforehand what you shall speak; but whatsoever shall be given you in that hour, that speak ye. For it is not you that speak, but the Holy Ghost.

13:12 And the brother shall betray his brother unto death, and the father his son; and children shall rise up against the parents, and shall work their death.

13:13 And you shall be hated by all men for my name's sake. But he that shall endure unto the end, he shall be saved.

13:14 And when you shall see the abomination of desolation, standing where it ought not: he that readeth let him understand: then let them that are in Judea, flee unto the mountains:

13:15 And let him that is on the housetop, not go down into the house, nor enter therein to take

sua :

13:16 et qui in agro erit, non revertatur retro tollere vestimentum suum.

13:17 Væ autem prægnantibus et nutrientibus in illis diebus.

13:18 Orate vero ut hieme non fiant.

13:19 Erunt enim dies illi tribulationes tales quales non fuerunt ab initio creaturæ, quam condidit Deus usque nunc, neque fient.

13:20 Et nisi breviasset Dominus dies, non fuisset salva omnis caro : sed propter electos, quos elegit, breviavit dies.

13:21 Et tunc si quis vobis dixerit : Ecce hic est Christus, ecce illic, ne credideritis.

13:22 Exsurgent enim pseudochristi et pseudoprophetæ, et dabunt signa et portenta ad seducendos, si fieri potest, etiam electos.

13:23 Vos ergo videte : ecce prædixi vobis omnia.

13:24 Sed in illis diebus, post tribulationem illam, sol contenebrabitur, et luna non dabit splendorem suum :

13:25 et stellæ cæli erunt decidentes, et virtutes, quæ in cælis sunt, movebuntur.

13:26 Et tunc videbunt Filium hominis venientem in nubibus cum virtute multa et gloria.

13:27 Et tunc mittet angelos suos, et congregabit electos suos a quatuor ventis, a summo terræ usque ad summum cæli.

13:28 A ficu autem discite parabolam. Cum jam ramus ejus tener fuerit, et nata fuerint folia, cognoscitis quia in proximo sit æstas :

13:29 sic et vos cum videritis hæc fieri, scitote quod in proximo sit, in ostiis.

13:30 Amen dico vobis, quoniam non transibit generatio hæc, donec omnia ista fiant.

13:31 Cælum et terra transibunt, verba autem mea non transibunt.

13:32 De die autem illo vel hora nemo scit, neque angeli in cælo, neque Filius, nisi Pater.

13:33 Videte, vigilate, et orate : nescitis enim quando tempus sit.

13:34 Sicut homo qui peregrę profectus reliquit

any thing out of the house:

13:16 And let him that shall be in the field, not turn back to take up his garment.

13:17 And woe to them that are with child, and that give suck in those days.

13:18 But pray ye, that these things happen not in winter.

13:19 For in those days shall be such tribulations, as were not from the beginning of the creation which God created until now, neither shall be.

13:20 And unless the Lord had shortened the days, no flesh should be saved: but for the sake of the elect which he hath chosen, he hath shortened the days.

13:21 And then if any man shall say to you, Lo, here is Christ; lo, he is here: do not believe.

13:22 For there will rise up false Christs and false prophets, and they shall shew signs and wonders, to seduce (if it were possible) even the elect.

13:23 Take you heed therefore; behold I have foretold you all things.

13:24 But in those days, after that tribulation, the sun shall be darkened, and the moon shall not give her light.

13:25 And the stars of heaven shall be falling down, and the powers that are in heaven, shall be moved.

13:26 And then shall they see the Son of man coming in the clouds, with great power and glory.

13:27 And then shall he send his angels, and shall gather together his elect from the four winds, from the uttermost part of the earth to the uttermost part of heaven.

13:28 Now of the fig tree learn ye a parable. When the branch thereof is now tender, and the leaves are come forth, you know that summer is very near.

13:29 So you also when you shall see these things come to pass, know ye that it is very nigh, even at the doors.

13:30 Amen I say to you, that this generation shall not pass, until all these things be done.

13:31 Heaven and earth shall pass away, but my word shall not pass away.

13:32 But of that day or hour no man knoweth, neither the angels in heaven, nor the Son, but the Father.

13:33 Take ye heed, watch and pray. For ye know not when the time is.

13:34 Even as a man who going into a far coun-

domum suam, et dedit servis suis potestatem cujusque operis, et janitori præcepit ut vigilet,

^{13:35} vigilate ergo (nescitis enim quando dominus domus veniat : sero, an media nocte, an galli cantu, an mane),

^{13:36} ne, cum venerit repente, inveniat vos dormientes.

^{13:37} Quod autem vobis dico, omnibus dico : Vigilate.

^{14:1} Erat autem Pascha et azyma post biduum : et quærebant summi sacerdotes et scribæ quomodo eum dolo tenerent, et occiderent.

^{14:2} Dicebant autem : Non in die festo, ne forte tumultus fieret in populo.

^{14:3} Et cum esset Bethaniæ in domo Simonis leprosi, et recumberet, venit mulier habens alabastrum unguenti nardi spicati pretiosi : et fracto alabastro, effudit super caput ejus.

^{14:4} Erant autem quidam indigne ferentes intra semetipsos, et dicentes : Ut quid perditio ista unguenti facta est ?

^{14:5} poterat enim unguentum istud venundari plus quam trecentis denariis, et dari pauperibus. Et fremebant in eam.

^{14:6} Jesus autem dixit : Sinite eam, quid illi molesti estis ? Bonum opus operata est in me :

^{14:7} semper enim pauperes habetis vobiscum : et cum volueritis, potestis illis benefacere : me autem non semper habetis.

^{14:8} Quod habuit hæc, fecit : prævenit ungere corpus meum in sepulturam.

^{14:9} Amen dico vobis : Ubicumque prædicatum fuerit Evangelium istud in universo mundo, et quod fecit hæc, narrabitur in memoriam ejus.

^{14:10} Et Judas Iscariotes, unus de duodecim, abiit ad summos sacerdotes, ut proderet eum illis.

^{14:11} Qui audientes gavisi sunt : et promiserunt ei pecuniam se daturos. Et quærebat quomodo illum opportune traderet.

^{14:12} Et primo die azymorum quando Pascha immolabant, dicunt ei discipuli : Quo vis eamus, et paremus tibi ut manduces Pascha ?

^{14:13} Et mittit duos ex discipulis suis, et dicit

try, left his house; and gave authority to his servants over every work, and commanded the porter to watch.

^{13:35} Watch ye therefor, (for you know not when the lord of the house cometh: at even, or at midnight, or at the cockcrowing, or in the morning,)

^{13:36} Lest coming on a sudden, he find you sleeping.

^{13:37} And what I say to you, I say to all: Watch.

^{14:1} Now the feast of the pasch, and of the Azymes was after two days; and the chief priests and the scribes sought how they might by some wile lay hold on him, and kill him.

^{14:2} But they said: Not on the festival day, lest there should be a tumult among the people.

^{14:3} And when he was in Bethania, in the house of Simon the leper, and was at meat, there came a woman having an alabaster box of ointment of precious spikenard: and breaking the alabaster box, she poured it out upon his head.

^{14:4} Now there were some that had indignation within themselves, and said: Why was this waste of the ointment made?

^{14:5} For this ointment might have been sold for more than three hundred pence, and given to the poor. And they murmured against her.

^{14:6} But Jesus said: Let her alone, why do you molest her? She hath wrought a good work upon me.

^{14:7} For the poor you have always with you: and whensoever you will, you may do them good: but me you have not always.

^{14:8} She hath done what she could: she is come beforehand to anoint my body for burial.

^{14:9} Amen, I say to you, wheresoever this gospel shall be preached in the whole world, that also which she hath done, shall be told for a memorial of her.

^{14:10} And Judas Iscariot, one of the twelve, went to the chief priests, to betray him to them.

^{14:11} Who hearing it were glad; and they promised him they would give him money. And he sought how he might conveniently betray him.

^{14:12} Now on the first day of the unleavened bread, when they sacrificed the pasch, the disciples say to him: Whither wilt thou that we go, and prepare for thee to eat the pasch?

^{14:13} And he sendeth two of his disciples, and

eis : Ite in civitatem, et occurret vobis homo lagenam aquæ bajulans : sequimini eum,

14:14 et quocumque introierit, dicite domino domus, quia magister dicit : Ubi est refectio mea, ubi Pascha cum discipulis meis manducem ?

14:15 Et ipse vobis demonstrabit cœnaculum grande, stratum : et illic parate nobis.

14:16 Et abierunt discipuli ejus, et venerunt in civitatem : et invenerunt sicut dixerat illis, et paraverunt Pascha.

14:17 Vespere autem facto, venit cum duodecim.

14:18 Et discumbentibus eis, et manducantibus, ait Jesus : Amen dico vobis, quia unus ex vobis tradet me, qui manducat mecum.

14:19 At illi cœperunt contristari, et dicere ei singulatim : Numquid ego ?

14:20 Qui ait illis : Unus ex duodecim, qui intingit mecum manum in catino.

14:21 Et Filius quidem hominis vadit sicut scriptum est de eo : væ autem homini illi per quem Filius hominis tradetur ! bonum erat ei, si non esset natus homo ille.

14:22 Et manducantibus illis, accepit Jesus panem : et benedicens fregit, et dedit eis, et ait : Sumite, hoc est corpus meum.

14:23 Et accepto calice, gratias agens dedit eis : et biberunt ex illo omnes.

14:24 Et ait illis : Hic est sanguis meus novi testamenti, qui pro multis effundetur.

14:25 Amen dico vobis, quia jam non bibam de hoc genimine vitis usque in diem illum, cum illud bibam novum in regno Dei.

14:26 Et hymno dicto exierunt in montem Olivarum.

14:27 Et ait eis Jesus : Omnes scandalizabimini in me in nocte ista : quia scriptum est : Percutiam pastorem, et dispergentur oves.

14:28 Sed postquam resurrexero, præcedam vos in Galilæam.

14:29 Petrus autem ait illi : Et si omnes scandalizati fuerint in te, sed non ego.

14:30 Et ait illi Jesus : Amen dico tibi, quia tu hodie in nocte hac, priusquam gallus vocem bis dederit, ter me es negaturus.

14:31 At ille amplius loquebatur : Et si opor-

saith to them: Go ye into the city; and there shall meet you a man carrying a pitcher of water, follow him;

14:14 And whithersoever he shall go in, say to the master of the house, The master saith, Where is my refectory, where I may eat the pasch with my disciples?

14:15 And he will shew you a large dining room furnished; and there prepare ye for us.

14:16 And his disciples went their way, and came into the city; and they found as he had told them, and they prepared the pasch.

14:17 And when evening was come, he cometh with the twelve.

14:18 And when they were at table and eating, Jesus saith: Amen I say to you, one of you that eateth with me shall betray me.

14:19 But they began to be sorrowful, and to say to him one by one: Is it I?

14:20 Who saith to them: One of the twelve, who dippeth with me his hand in the dish.

14:21 And the Son of man indeed goeth, as it is written of him: but woe to that man by whom the Son of man shall be betrayed. It were better for him, if that man had not been born.

14:22 And whilst they were eating, Jesus took bread; and blessing, broke, and gave to them, and said: Take ye. This is my body.

14:23 And having taken the chalice, giving thanks, he gave it to them. And they all drank of it.

14:24 And he said to them: This is my blood of the new testament, which shall be shed for many.

14:25 Amen I say to you, that I will drink no more of the fruit of the vine, until that day when I shall drink it new in the kingdom of God.

14:26 And when they had said an hymn, they went forth to the mount of Olives.

14:27 And Jesus saith to them: You will all be scandalized in my regard this night; for it is written, I will strike the shepherd, and the sheep shall be dispersed.

14:28 But after I shall be risen again, I will go before you into Galilee.

14:29 But Peter saith to him: Although all shall be scandalized in thee, yet not I.

14:30 And Jesus saith to him: Amen I say to thee, to day, even in this night, before the cock crow twice, thou shall deny me thrice.

14:31 But he spoke the more vehemently: Alt-

tuerit me simul commori tibi, non te negabo. Similiter autem et omnes dicebant.

¹⁴:³² Et veniunt in prædium, cui nomen Gethsemani. Et ait discipulis suis : Sedete hic donec orem.

¹⁴:³³ Et assumit Petrum, et Jacobum, et Joannem secum : et cœpit pavere et tædere.

¹⁴:³⁴ Et ait illis : Tristis est anima mea usque ad mortem : sustinete hic, et vigilate.

¹⁴:³⁵ Et cum processisset paululum, procidit super terram, et orabat ut, si fieri posset, transiret ab eo hora.

¹⁴:³⁶ Et dixit : Abba pater, omnia tibi possibilia sunt : transfer calicem hunc a me : sed non quod ego volo, sed quod tu.

¹⁴:³⁷ Et venit, et invenit eos dormientes. Et ait Petro : Simon, dormis ? non potuisti una hora vigilare ?

¹⁴:³⁸ vigilate et orate, ut non intretis in tentationem. Spiritus quidem promptus est, caro vero infirma.

¹⁴:³⁹ Et iterum abiens oravit, eumdem sermonem dicens.

¹⁴:⁴⁰ Et reversus, denuo invenit eos dormientes (erant enim oculi eorum gravati), et ignorabant quid responderent ei.

¹⁴:⁴¹ Et venit tertio, et ait illis : Dormite jam, et requiescite. Sufficit : venit hora : ecce Filius hominis tradetur in manus peccatorum.

¹⁴:⁴² Surgite, eamus : ecce qui me tradet, prope est.

¹⁴:⁴³ Et, adhuc eo loquente, venit Judas Iscariotes unus de duodecim, et cum eo turba multa cum gladiis et lignis, a summis sacerdotibus, et scribis, et senioribus.

¹⁴:⁴⁴ Dederat autem traditor ejus signum eis, dicens : Quemcumque osculatus fuero, ipse est, tenete eum, et ducite caute.

¹⁴:⁴⁵ Et cum venisset, statim accedens ad eum, ait : Ave Rabbi : et osculatus est eum.

¹⁴:⁴⁶ At illi manus injecerunt in eum, et tenuerunt eum.

¹⁴:⁴⁷ Unus autem quidam de circumstantibus educens gladium, percussit servum summi sacerdotis, et amputavit illi auriculam.

¹⁴:⁴⁸ Et respondens Jesus, ait illis : Tamquam ad latronem existis cum gladiis et lignis compre-

hough I should die together with thee, I will not deny thee. And in like manner also said they all.

¹⁴:³² And they came to a farm called Gethsemani. And he saith to his disciples: Sit you here, while I pray.

¹⁴:³³ And he taketh Peter and James and John with him; and he began to fear and to be heavy.

¹⁴:³⁴ And he saith to them: My soul is sorrowful even unto death; stay you here, and watch.

¹⁴:³⁵ And when he was gone forward a little, he fell flat on the ground; and he prayed, that if it might be, the hour might pass from him.

¹⁴:³⁶ And he saith: Abba, Father, all things are possible to thee: remove this chalice from me; but not what I will, but what thou wilt.

¹⁴:³⁷ And he cometh, and findeth them sleeping. And he saith to Peter: Simon, sleepest thou? couldst thou not watch one hour?

¹⁴:³⁸ Watch ye, and pray that you enter not into temptation. The spirit indeed is willing, but the flesh is weak.

¹⁴:³⁹ And going away again, he prayed, saying the same words.

¹⁴:⁴⁰ And when he returned, he found them again asleep, (for their eyes were heavy,) and they knew not what to answer him.

¹⁴:⁴¹ And he cometh the third time, and saith to them: Sleep ye now, and take your rest. It is enough: the hour is come: behold the Son of man shall be betrayed into the hands of sinners.

¹⁴:⁴² Rise up, let us go. Behold, he that will betray me is at hand.

¹⁴:⁴³ And while he was yet speaking, cometh Judas Iscariot, one of the twelve: and with him a great multitude with swords and staves, from the chief priests and the scribes and the ancients.

¹⁴:⁴⁴ And he that betrayed him, had given them a sign, saying: Whomsoever I shall kiss, that is he; lay hold on him, and lead him away carefully.

¹⁴:⁴⁵ And when he was come, immediately going up to him, he saith: Hail, Rabbi; and he kissed him.

¹⁴:⁴⁶ But they laid hands on him, and held him.

¹⁴:⁴⁷ An one of them that stood by, drawing a sword, struck a servant of the chief priest, and cut off his ear.

¹⁴:⁴⁸ And Jesus answering, said to them: Are you come out as to a robber, with swords and staves

hendere me ?

14:49 quotidie eram apud vos in templo docens, et non me tenuistis. Sed ut impleantur Scripturæ.

14:50 Tunc discipuli ejus relinquentes eum, omnes fugerunt.

14:51 Adolescens autem quidam sequebatur eum amictus sindone super nudo : et tenuerunt eum.

14:52 At ille rejecta sindone, nudus profugit ab eis.

14:53 Et adduxerunt Jesum ad summum sacerdotem : et convenerunt omnes sacerdotes, et scribæ, et seniores.

14:54 Petrus autem a longe secutus est eum usque intro in atrium summi sacerdotis : et sedebat cum ministris ad ignem, et calefaciebat se.

14:55 Summi vero sacerdotes et omne concilium quærebant adversus Jesum testimonium ut eum morti traderent : nec inveniebant.

14:56 Multi enim testimonium falsum dicebant adversus eum : et convenientia testimonia non erant.

14:57 Et quidam surgentes, falsum testimonium ferebant adversus eum, dicentes :

14:58 Quoniam nos audivimus eum dicentem : Ego dissolvam templum hoc manu factum, et per triduum aliud non manu factum ædificabo.

14:59 Et non erat conveniens testimonium illorum.

14:60 Et exsurgens summus sacerdos in medium, interrogavit Jesum, dicens : Non respondes quidquam ad ea quæ tibi objiciuntur ab his ?

14:61 Ille autem tacebat, et nihil respondit. Rursum summus sacerdos interrogabat eum, et dixit ei : Tu es Christus Filius Dei benedicti ?

14:62 Jesus autem dixit illi : Ego sum : et videbitis Filium hominis sedentem a dextris virtutis Dei, et venientem cum nubibus cæli.

14:63 Summus autem sacerdos scindens vestimenta sua, ait : Quid adhuc desideramus testes ?

14:64 Audistis blasphemiam : quid vobis videtur ? Qui omnes condemnaverunt eum esse reum mortis.

14:65 Et cœperunt quidam conspuere eum, et velare faciem ejus, et colaphis eum cædere, et dicere ei : Prophetiza : et ministri alapis eum

to apprehend me?

14:49 I was daily with you in the temple teaching, and you did not lay hands on me. But that the scriptures may be fulfilled.

14:50 Then his disciples leaving him, all fled away.

14:51 And a certain young man followed him, having a linen cloth cast about his naked body; and they laid hold on him.

14:52 But he, casting off the linen cloth, fled from them naked.

14:53 And they brought Jesus to the high priest; and all the priests and the scribes and the ancients assembled together.

14:54 And Peter followed him from afar off, even into the court of the high priest; and he sat with the servants at the fire, and warmed himself.

14:55 And the chief priests and all the council sought for evidence against Jesus, that they might put him to death, and found none.

14:56 For many bore false witness against him, and their evidences were not agreeing.

14:57 And some rising up, bore false witness against him, saying:

14:58 We heard him say, I will destroy this temple made with hands, and within three days I will build another not made with hands.

14:59 And their witness did not agree.

14:60 And the high priest rising up in the midst, asked Jesus, saying: Answerest thou nothing to the things that are laid to thy charge by these men?

14:61 But he held his peace, and answered nothing. Again the high priest asked him, and said to him: Art thou the Christ the Son of the blessed God?

14:62 And Jesus said to him: I am. And you shall see the Son of man sitting on the right hand of the power of God, and coming with the clouds of heaven.

14:63 Then the high priest rending his garments, saith: What need we any further witnesses?

14:64 You have heard the blasphemy. What think you? Who all condemned him to be guilty of death.

14:65 And some began to spit on him, and to cover his face, and to buffet him, and to say unto him: Prophesy: and the servants struck him

cædebant.

14:66 Et cum esset Petrus in atrio deorsum, venit una ex ancillis summi sacerdotis :

14:67 et cum vidisset Petrum calefacientem se, aspiciens illum, ait : Et tu cum Jesu Nazareno eras.

14:68 At ille negavit, dicens : Neque scio, neque novi quid dicas. Et exiit foras ante atrium, et gallus cantavit.

14:69 Rursus autem cum vidisset illum ancilla, cœpit dicere circumstantibus : Quia hic ex illis est.

14:70 At ille iterum negavit. Et post pusillum rursus qui astabant, dicebant Petro : Vere ex illis es : nam et Galilæus es.

14:71 Ille autem cœpit anathematizare et jurare : Quia nescio hominem istum, quem dicitis.

14:72 Et statim gallus iterum cantavit. Et recordatus est Petrus verbi quod dixerat ei Jesus : Priusquam gallus cantet bis, ter me negabis. Et cœpit flere.

15:1 Et confestim mane consilium facientes summi sacerdotes cum senioribus, et scribis, et universo concilio, vincientes Jesum, duxerunt, et tradiderunt Pilato.

15:2 Et interrogavit eum Pilatus : Tu es rex Judæorum ? At ille respondens, ait illi : Tu dicis.

15:3 Et accusabant eum summi sacerdotes in multis.

15:4 Pilatus autem rursum interrogavit eum, dicens : Non respondes quidquam ? vide in quantis te accusant.

15:5 Jesus autem amplius nihil respondit, ita ut miraretur Pilatus.

15:6 Per diem autem festum solebat dimittere illis unum ex vinctis, quemcumque petissent.

15:7 Erat autem qui dicebatur Barrabas, qui cum seditiosis erat vinctus, qui in seditione fecerat homicidium.

15:8 Et cum ascendisset turba, cœpit rogare, sicut semper faciebat illis.

15:9 Pilatus autem respondit eis, et dixit : Vultis dimittam vobis regem Judæorum ?

15:10 Sciebat enim quod per invidiam tradidissent eum summi sacerdotes.

15:11 Pontifices autem concitaverunt turbam, ut magis Barabbam dimitteret eis.

with the palms of their hands.

14:66 Now when Peter was in the court below, there cometh one of the maidservants of the high priest.

14:67 And when she had seen Peter warming himself, looking on him she saith: Thou also wast with Jesus of Nazareth.

14:68 But he denied, saying: I neither know nor understand what thou sayest. And he went forth before the court; and the cock crew.

14:69 And again a maidservant seeing him, began to say to the standers by: This is one of them.

14:70 But he denied again. And after a while they that stood by said again to Peter: Surely thou art one of them; for thou art also a Galilean.

14:71 But he began to curse and to swear, saying; I know not this man of whom you speak.

14:72 And immediately the cock crew again. And Peter remembered the word that Jesus had said unto him: Before the cock crow twice, thou shalt thrice deny me. And he began to weep.

15:1 And straightway in the morning, the chief priests holding a consultation with the ancients and the scribes and the whole council, binding Jesus, led him away, and delivered him to Pilate.

15:2 And Pilate asked him: Art thou the king of the Jews? But he answering, saith to him: Thou sayest it.

15:3 And the chief priests accused him in many things.

15:4 And Pilate again asked him, saying: Answerest thou nothing? behold in how many things they accuse thee.

15:5 But Jesus still answered nothing; so that Pilate wondered.

15:6 Now on the festival day he was wont to release unto them one of the prisoners, whomsoever they demanded.

15:7 And there was one called Barabbas, who was put in prison with some seditious men, who in the sedition had committed murder.

15:8 And when the multitude was come up, they began to desire that he would do, as he had ever done unto them.

15:9 And Pilate answered them, and said: Will you that I release to you the king of the Jews?

15:10 For he knew that the chief priests had delivered him up out of envy.

15:11 But the chief priests moved the people, that he should rather release Barabbas to them.

15:12 Pilatus autem iterum respondens, ait illis : Quid ergo vultis faciam regi Judæorum ?

15:13 At illi iterum clamaverunt : Crucifige eum.
15:14 Pilatus vero dicebat illis : Quid enim mali fecit ? At illi magis clamabant : Crucifige eum.

15:15 Pilatus autem volens populo satisfacere, dimisit illis Barabbam, et tradidit Jesum flagellis cæsum, ut crucifigeretur.

15:16 Milites autem duxerunt eum in atrium prætorii, et convocant totam cohortem,

15:17 et induunt eum purpura, et imponunt ei plectentes spineam coronam.
15:18 Et cœperunt salutare eum : Ave rex Judæorum.
15:19 Et percutiebant caput ejus arundine : et conspuebant eum, et ponentes genua, adorabant eum.
15:20 Et postquam illuserunt ei, exuerunt illum purpura, et induerunt eum vestimentis suis : et educunt illum ut crucifigerent eum.

15:21 Et angariaverunt prætereuntem quempiam, Simonem Cyrenæum venientem de villa, patrem Alexandri et Rufi, ut tolleret crucem ejus.
15:22 Et perducunt illum in Golgotha locum : quod est interpretatum Calvariæ locus.

15:23 Et dabant ei bibere myrrhatum vinum : et non accepit.
15:24 Et crucifigentes eum, diviserunt vestimenta ejus, mittentes sortem super eis, quis quid tolleret.
15:25 Erat autem hora tertia : et crucifixerunt eum.
15:26 Et erat titulus causæ ejus inscriptus : Rex Judæorum.
15:27 Et cum eo crucifigunt duos latrones : unum a dextris, et alium a sinistris ejus.
15:28 Et impleta est Scriptura, quæ dicit : Et cum iniquis reputatus est.
15:29 Et prætereuntes blasphemabant eum, moventes capita sua, et dicentes : Vah ! qui destruis templum Dei, et in tribus diebus reædificas,
15:30 salvum fac temetipsum descendens de cruce.
15:31 Similiter et summi sacerdotes illudentes,

15:12 And Pilate again answering, saith to them: What will you then that I do to the king of the Jews?
15:13 But they again cried out: Crucify him.
15:14 And Pilate saith to them: Why, what evil hath he done? But they cried out the more: Crucify him.
15:15 And so Pilate being willing to satisfy the people, released to them Barabbas, and delivered up Jesus, when he had scourged him, to be crucified.
15:16 And the soldiers led him away into the court of the palace, and they called together the whole band:
15:17 And they clothe him with purple, and platting a crown of thorns, they put it upon him.
15:18 And they began to salute him: Hail, king of the Jews.
15:19 And they struck his head with a reed: and they did spit on him. And bowing their knees, they adored him.
15:20 And after they had mocked him, they took off the purple from him, and put his own garments on him, and they led him out to crucify him.
15:21 And they forced one Simon a Cyrenian who passed by, coming out of the country, the father of Alexander and of Rufus, to take up his cross.
15:22 And they bring him into the place called Golgotha, which being interpreted is, The place of Calvary.
15:23 And they gave him to drink wine mingled with myrrh; but he took it not.
15:24 And crucifying him, they divided his garments, casting lots upon them, what every man should take.
15:25 And it was the third hour, and they crucified him.
15:26 And the inscription of his cause was written over: THE KING OF THE JEWS.
15:27 And with him they crucify two thieves; the one on his right hand, and the other on his left.
15:28 And the scripture was fulfilled, which saith: And with the wicked he was reputed.
15:29 And they that passed by blasphemed him, wagging their heads, and saying: Vah, thou that destroyest the temple of God, and in three days buildest it up again;
15:30 Save thyself, coming down from the cross.
15:31 In like manner also the chief priests mock-

ad alterutrum cum scribis dicebant : Alios salvos fecit ; seipsum non potest salvum facere.

15:32 Christus rex Israël descendat nunc de cruce, ut videamus, et credamus. Et qui cum eo crucifixi erant, convitiabantur ei.

15:33 Et facta hora sexta, tenebræ factæ sunt per totam terram usque in horam nonam.

15:34 Et hora nona exclamavit Jesus voce magna, dicens : Eloi, eloi, lamma sabacthani ? quod est interpretatum : Deus meus, Deus meus, ut quid dereliquisti me ?

15:35 Et quidam de circumstantibus audientes, dicebant : Ecce Eliam vocat.

15:36 Currens autem unus, et implens spongiam aceto, circumponensque calamo, potum dabat ei, dicens : Sinite, videamus si veniat Elias ad deponendum eum.

15:37 Jesus autem emissa voce magna expiravit.

15:38 Et velum templi scissum est in duo, a summo usque deorsum.

15:39 Videns autem centurio, qui ex adverso stabat, quia sic clamans expirasset, ait : Vere hic homo Filius Dei erat.

15:40 Erant autem et mulieres de longe aspicientes : inter quas erat Maria Magdalene, et Maria Jacobi minoris, et Joseph mater, et Salome :

15:41 et cum esset in Galilæa, sequebantur eum, et ministrabant ei, et aliæ multæ, quæ simul cum eo ascenderant Jerosolymam.

15:42 Et cum jam sero esset factum (quia erat parasceve, quod est ante sabbatum),

15:43 venit Joseph ab Arimathæa nobilis decurio, qui et ipse erat exspectans regnum Dei, et audacter introivit ad Pilatum, et petiit corpus Jesu.

15:44 Pilatus autem mirabatur si jam obiisset. Et accersito centurione, interrogavit eum si jam mortuus esset.

15:45 Et cum cognovisset a centurione, donavit corpus Joseph.

15:46 Joseph autem mercatus sindonem, et deponens eum involvit sindone, et posuit eum in monumento quod erat excisum de petra, et advolvit lapidem ad ostium monumenti.

15:47 Maria autem Magdalene et Maria Joseph

ing, said with the scribes one to another: He saved others; himself he cannot save.

15:32 Let Christ the king of Israel come down now from the cross, that we may see and believe. And they that were crucified with him reviled him.

15:33 And when the sixth hour was come, there was darkness over the whole earth until the ninth hour.

15:34 And at the ninth hour, Jesus cried out with a loud voice, saying: Eloi, Eloi, lamma sabacthani? Which is, being interpreted, My God, my God, why hast thou forsaken me?

15:35 And some of the standers by hearing, said: Behold he calleth Elias.

15:36 And one running and filling a sponge with vinegar, and putting it upon a reed, gave him to drink, saying: Stay, let us see if Elias come to take him down.

15:37 And Jesus having cried out with a loud voice, gave up the ghost.

15:38 And the veil of the temple was rent in two, from the top to the bottom.

15:39 And the centurion who stood over against him, seeing that crying out in this manner he had given up the ghost, said: Indeed this man was the son of God.

15:40 And there were also women looking on afar off: among whom was Mary Magdalen, and Mary the mother of James the less and of Joseph, and Salome:

15:41 Who also when he was in Galilee followed him, and ministered to him, and many other women that came up with him to Jerusalem.

15:42 And when evening was now come, (because it was the Parasceve, that is, the day before the sabbath,)

15:43 Joseph of Arimathea, a noble counsellor, who was also himself looking for the kingdom of God, came and went in boldly to Pilate, and begged the body of Jesus.

15:44 But Pilate wondered that he should be already dead. And sending for the centurion, he asked him if he were already dead.

15:45 And when he had understood it by the centurion, he gave the body to Joseph.

15:46 And Joseph buying fine linen, and taking him down, wrapped him up in the fine linen, and laid him in a sepulchre which was hewed out of a rock. And he rolled a stone to the door of the sepulchre.

15:47 And Mary Magdalen, and Mary the mother

aspiciebant ubi poneretur.

16:1 Et cum transisset sabbatum, Maria Magdalene, et Maria Jacobi, et Salome emerunt aromata ut venientes ungerent Jesum.

16:2 Et valde mane una sabbatorum, veniunt ad monumentum, orto jam sole.

16:3 Et dicebant ad invicem : Quis revolvet nobis lapidem ab ostio monumenti ?

16:4 Et respicientes viderunt revolutum lapidem. Erat quippe magnus valde.

16:5 Et introëuntes in monumentum viderunt juvenem sedentem in dextris, coopertum stola candida, et obstupuerunt.

16:6 Qui dicit illis : Nolite expavescere : Jesum quæritis Nazarenum, crucifixum : surrexit, non est hic, ecce locus ubi posuerunt eum.

16:7 Sed ite, dicite discipulis ejus, et Petro, quia præcedit vos in Galilæam : ibi eum videbitis, sicut dixit vobis.

16:8 At illæ exeuntes, fugerunt de monumento : invaserat enim eas tremor et pavor : et nemini quidquam dixerunt : timebant enim.

16:9 Surgens autem mane prima sabbati, apparuit primo Mariæ Magdalene, de qua ejecerat septem dæmonia.

16:10 Illa vadens nuntiavit his, qui cum eo fuerant, lugentibus et flentibus.

16:11 Et illi audientes quia viveret, et visus esset ab ea, non crediderunt.

16:12 Post hæc autem duobus ex his ambulantibus ostensus est in alia effigie, euntibus in villam :

16:13 et illi euntes nuntiaverunt ceteris : nec illis crediderunt.

16:14 Novissime recumbentibus illis undecim apparuit : et exprobravit incredulitatem eorum et duritiam cordis : quia iis, qui viderant eum resurrexisse, non crediderunt.

16:15 Et dixit eis : Euntes in mundum universum prædicate Evangelium omni creaturæ.

16:16 Qui crediderit, et baptizatus fuerit, salvus erit : qui vero non crediderit, condemnabitur.

16:17 Signa autem eos qui crediderint, hæc sequentur : in nomine meo dæmonia ejicient : linguis loquentur novis :

of Joseph, beheld where he was laid.

16:1 And when the sabbath was past, Mary Magdalen, and Mary the mother of James, and Salome, bought sweet spices, that coming, they might anoint Jesus.

16:2 And very early in the morning, the first day of the week, they come to the sepulchre, the sun being now risen.

16:3 And they said one to another: Who shall roll us back the stone from the door of the sepulchre?

16:4 And looking, they saw the stone rolled back. For it was very great.

16:5 And entering into the sepulchre, they saw a young man sitting on the right side, clothed with a white robe: and they were astonished.

16:6 Who saith to them: Be not affrighted; you seek Jesus of Nazareth, who was crucified: he is risen, he is not here, behold the place where they laid him.

16:7 But go, tell his disciples and Peter that he goeth before you into Galilee; there you shall see him, as he told you.

16:8 But they going out, fled from the sepulchre. For a trembling and fear had seized them: and they said nothing to any man; for they were afraid.

16:9 But he rising early the first day of the week, appeared first to Mary Magdalen, out of whom he had cast seven devils.

16:10 She went and told them that had been with him, who were mourning and weeping.

16:11 And they hearing that he was alive, and had been seen by her, did not believe.

16:12 And after that he appeared in another shape to two of them walking, as they were going into the country.

16:13 And they going told it to the rest: neither did they believe them.

16:14 At length he appeared to the eleven as they were at table: and he upbraided them with their incredulity and hardness of heart, because they did not believe them who had seen him after he was risen again.

16:15 And he said to them: Go ye into the whole world, and preach the gospel to every creature.

16:16 He that believeth and is baptized, shall be saved: but he that believeth not shall be condemned.

16:17 And these signs shall follow them that believe: In my name they shall cast out devils: they shall speak with new tongues.

16:18 serpentes tollent : et si mortiferum quid biberint, non eis nocebit : super ægros manus imponent, et bene habebunt.

16:19 Et Dominus quidem Jesus postquam locutus est eis, assumptus est in cælum, et sedet a dextris Dei.

16:20 Illi autem profecti prædicaverunt ubique, Domino cooperante, et sermonem confirmante, sequentibus signis.

16:18 They shall take up serpents; and if they shall drink any deadly thing, it shall not hurt them: they shall lay their hands upon the sick, and they shall recover.

16:19 And the Lord Jesus, after he had spoken to them, was taken up into heaven, and sitteth on the right hand of God.

16:20 But they going forth preached every where: the Lord working withal, and confirming the word with signs that followed.

Sanctum Jesu Christi Evangelium
Secundum Lucam

THE HOLY GOSPEL OF JESUS CHRIST ACCORDING TO LUKE

 UONIAM QUIDEM MULTI conati sunt ordinare narrationem, quæ in nobis completæ sunt, rerum :

1:2 sicut tradiderunt nobis, qui ab initio ipsi viderunt, et ministri fuerunt sermonis :

1:3 visum est et mihi, assecuto omnia a principio diligenter, ex ordine tibi scribere, optime Theophile,

1:4 ut cognoscas eorum verborum, de quibus eruditus es, veritatem.

1:5 Fuit in diebus Herodis, regis Judææ, sacerdos quidam nomine Zacharias de vice Abia, et uxor illius de filiabus Aaron, et nomen ejus Elisabeth.

1:6 Erant autem justi ambo ante Deum, incedentes in omnibus mandatis et justificationibus Domini sine querela.

1:7 Et non erat illis filius, eo quod esset Elisabeth sterilis, et ambo processissent in diebus suis.

1:8 Factum est autem, cum sacerdotio fungeretur in ordine vicis suæ ante Deum,

1:9 secundum consuetudinem sacerdotii, sorte exiit ut incensum poneret, ingressus in templum Domini :

1:10 et omnis multitudo populi erat orans foris hora incensi.

1:11 Apparuit autem illi angelus Domini, stans a dextris altaris incensi.

ORASMUCH AS MANY have taken in hand to set forth in order a narration of the things that have been accomplished among us;

1:2 According as they have delivered them unto us, who from the beginning were eyewitnesses and ministers of the word:

1:3 It seemed good to me also, having diligently attained to all things from the beginning, to write to thee in order, most excellent Theophilus,

1:4 That thou mayest know the verity of those words in which thou hast been instructed.

1:5 There was in the days of Herod, the king of Judea, a certain priest named Zachary, of the course of Abia; and his wife was of the daughters of Aaron, and her name Elizabeth.

1:6 And they were both just before God, walking in all the commandments and justifications of the Lord without blame.

1:7 And they had no son, for that Elizabeth was barren, and they both were well advanced in years.

1:8 And it came to pass, when he executed the priestly function in the order of his course before God,

1:9 According to the custom of the priestly office, it was his lot to offer incense, going into the temple of the Lord.

1:10 And all the multitude of the people was praying without, at the hour of incense.

1:11 And there appeared to him an angel of the Lord, standing on the right side of the alter of

1:12 Et Zacharias turbatus est videns, et timor irruit super eum.

1:13 Ait autem ad illum angelus : Ne timeas, Zacharia, quoniam exaudita est deprecatio tua : et uxor tua Elisabeth pariet tibi filium, et vocabis nomen ejus Joannem :

1:14 et erit gaudium tibi, et exsultatio, et multi in nativitate ejus gaudebunt :

1:15 erit enim magnus coram Domino : et vinum et siceram non bibet, et Spiritu Sancto replebitur adhuc ex utero matris suæ :

1:16 et multos filiorum Israël convertet ad Dominum Deum ipsorum :

1:17 et ipse præcedet ante illum in spiritu et virtute Eliæ : ut convertat corda patrum in filios, et incredulos ad prudentiam justorum, parare Domino plebem perfectam.

1:18 Et dixit Zacharias ad angelum : Unde hoc sciam ? ego enim sum senex, et uxor mea processit in diebus suis.

1:19 Et respondens angelus dixit ei : Ego sum Gabriel, qui asto ante Deum : et missus sum loqui ad te, et hæc tibi evangelizare.

1:20 Et ecce eris tacens, et non poteris loqui usque in diem quo hæc fiant, pro eo quod non credidisti verbis meis, quæ implebuntur in tempore suo.

1:21 Et erat plebs exspectans Zachariam : et mirabantur quod tardaret ipse in templo.

1:22 Egressus autem non poterat loqui ad illos, et cognoverunt quod visionem vidisset in templo. Et ipse erat innuens illis, et permansit mutus.

1:23 Et factum est, ut impleti sunt dies officii ejus, abiit in domum suam :

1:24 post hos autem dies concepit Elisabeth uxor ejus, et occultabat se mensibus quinque, dicens :

1:25 Quia sic fecit mihi Dominus in diebus, quibus respexit auferre opprobrium meum inter homines.

1:26 In mense autem sexto, missus est angelus Gabriel a Deo in civitatem Galilææ, cui nomen Nazareth,

1:27 ad virginem desponsatam viro, cui nomen

incense.

1:12 And Zachary seeing him, was troubled, and fear fell upon him.

1:13 But the angel said to him: Fear not, Zachary, for thy prayer is heard; and thy wife Elizabeth shall bear thee a son, and thou shalt call his name John:

1:14 And thou shalt have joy and gladness, and many shall rejoice in his nativity.

1:15 For he shall be great before the Lord; and shall drink no wine nor strong drink: and he shall be filled with the Holy Ghost, even from his mother's womb.

1:16 And he shall convert many of the children of Israel to the Lord their God.

1:17 And he shall go before him in the spirit and power of Elias; that he may turn the hearts of the fathers unto the children, and the incredulous to the wisdom of the just, to prepare unto the Lord a perfect people.

1:18 And Zachary said to the angel: Whereby shall I know this? for I am an old man, and my wife is advanced in years.

1:19 And the angel answering, said to him: I am Gabriel, who stand before God: and am sent to speak to thee, and to bring thee these good tidings.

1:20 And behold, thou shalt be dumb, and shalt not be able to speak until the day wherein these things shall come to pass, because thou hast not believed my words, which shall be fulfilled in their time.

1:21 And the people were waiting for Zachary; and they wondered that he tarried so long in the temple.

1:22 And when he came out, he could not speak to them: and they understood that he had seen a vision in the temple. And he made signs to them, and remained dumb.

1:23 And it came to pass, after the days of his office were accomplished, he departed to his own house.

1:24 And after those days, Elizabeth his wife conceived, and hid herself five months, saying:

1:25 Thus hath the Lord dealt with me in the days wherein he hath had regard to take away my reproach among men.

1:26 And in the sixth month, the angel Gabriel was sent from God into a city of Galilee, called Nazareth,

1:27 To a virgin espoused to a man whose name

erat Joseph, de domo David : et nomen virginis Maria.

1:28 Et ingressus angelus ad eam dixit : Ave gratia plena : Dominus tecum : benedicta tu in mulieribus.

1:29 Quæ cum audisset, turbata est in sermone ejus, et cogitabat qualis esset ista salutatio.

1:30 Et ait angelus ei : Ne timeas, Maria : invenisti enim gratiam apud Deum.

1:31 Ecce concipies in utero, et paries filium, et vocabis nomen ejus Jesum :

1:32 hic erit magnus, et Filius Altissimi vocabitur, et dabit illi Dominus Deus sedem David patris ejus : et regnabit in domo Jacob in æternum,

1:33 et regni ejus non erit finis.

1:34 Dixit autem Maria ad angelum : Quomodo fiet istud, quoniam virum non cognosco ?

1:35 Et respondens angelus dixit ei : Spiritus Sanctus superveniet in te, et virtus Altissimi obumbrabit tibi. Ideoque et quod nascetur ex te sanctum, vocabitur Filius Dei.

1:36 Et ecce Elisabeth cognata tua, et ipsa concepit filium in senectute sua : et hic mensis sextus est illi, quæ vocatur sterilis :

1:37 quia non erit impossibile apud Deum omne verbum.

1:38 Dixit autem Maria : Ecce ancilla Domini : fiat mihi secundum verbum tuum. Et discessit ab illa angelus.

1:39 Exsurgens autem Maria in diebus illis, abiit in montana cum festinatione, in civitatem Juda :

1:40 et intravit in domum Zachariæ, et salutavit Elisabeth.

1:41 Et factum est, ut audivit salutationem Mariæ Elisabeth, exsultavit infans in utero ejus : et repleta est Spiritu Sancto Elisabeth :

1:42 et exclamavit voce magna, et dixit : Benedicta tu inter mulieres, et benedictus fructus ventris tui.

1:43 Et unde hoc mihi, ut veniat mater Domini mei ad me ?

1:44 Ecce enim ut facta est vox salutationis tuæ in auribus meis, exsultavit in gaudio infans in utero meo.

1:45 Et beata, quæ credidisti, quoniam perficien-

was Joseph, of the house of David; and the virgin's name was Mary.

1:28 And the angel being come in, said unto her: Hail, full of grace, the Lord is with thee: blessed art thou among women.

1:29 Who having heard, was troubled at his saying, and thought with herself what manner of salutation this should be.

1:30 And the angel said to her: Fear not, Mary, for thou hast found grace with God.

1:31 Behold thou shalt conceive in thy womb, and shalt bring forth a son; and thou shalt call his name Jesus.

1:32 He shall be great, and shall be called the Son of the most High; and the Lord God shall give unto him the throne of David his father; and he shall reign in the house of Jacob for ever.

1:33 And of his kingdom there shall be no end.

1:34 And Mary said to the angel: How shall this be done, because I know not man?

1:35 And the angel answering, said to her: The Holy Ghost shall come upon thee, and the power of the most High shall overshadow thee. And therefore also the Holy which shall be born of thee shall be called the Son of God.

1:36 And behold thy cousin Elizabeth, she also hath conceived a son in her old age; and this is the sixth month with her that is called barren:

1:37 Because no word shall be impossible with God.

1:38 And Mary said: Behold the handmaid of the Lord; be it done to me according to thy word. And the angel departed from her.

1:39 And Mary rising up in those days, went into the hill country with haste into a city of Juda.

1:40 And she entered into the house of Zachary, and saluted Elizabeth.

1:41 And it came to pass, that when Elizabeth heard the salutation of Mary, the infant leaped in her womb. And Elizabeth was filled with the Holy Ghost:

1:42 And she cried out with a loud voice, and said: Blessed art thou among women, and blessed is the fruit of thy womb.

1:43 And whence is this to me, that the mother of my Lord should come to me?

1:44 For behold as soon as the voice of thy salutation sounded in my ears, the infant in my womb leaped for joy.

1:45 And blessed art thou that hast believed, be-

tur ea, quæ dicta sunt tibi a Domino.

1:46 Et ait Maria : *Magnificat anima mea Dominum :*

1:47 *et exsultavit spiritus meus in Deo salutari meo.*

1:48 *Quia respexit humilitatem ancillæ suæ : ecce enim ex hoc beatam me dicent omnes generationes,*

1:49 *quia fecit mihi magna qui potens est : et sanctum nomen ejus,*

1:50 *et misericordia ejus a progenie in progenies timentibus eum.*

1:51 *Fecit potentiam in brachio suo : dispersit superbos mente cordis sui.*

1:52 *Deposuit potentes de sede, et exaltavit humiles.*

1:53 *Esurientes implevit bonis : et divites dimisit inanes.*

1:54 *Suscepit Israël puerum suum, recordatus misericordiæ suæ :*

1:55 *sicut locutus est ad patres nostros, Abraham et semini ejus in sæcula.*

1:56 Mansit autem Maria cum illa quasi mensibus tribus : et reversa est in domum suam.

1:57 Elisabeth autem impletum est tempus pariendi, et peperit filium.

1:58 Et audierunt vicini et cognati ejus quia magnificavit Dominus misericordiam suam cum illa, et congratulabantur ei.

1:59 Et factum est in die octavo, venerunt circumcidere puerum, et vocabant eum nomine patris sui Zachariam.

1:60 Et respondens mater ejus, dixit : Nequaquam, sed vocabitur Joannes.

1:61 Et dixerunt ad illam : Quia nemo est in cognatione tua, qui vocetur hoc nomine.

1:62 Innuebant autem patri ejus, quem vellet vocari eum.

1:63 Et postulans pugillarem scripsit, dicens : Joannes est nomen ejus. Et mirati sunt universi.

1:64 Apertum est autem illico os ejus, et lingua ejus, et loquebatur benedicens Deum.

1:65 Et factus est timor super omnes vicinos eorum : et super omnia montana Judææ divulgabantur omnia verba hæc :

1:66 et posuerunt omnes qui audierant in corde suo, dicentes : Quis, putas, puer iste erit ? etenim manus Domini erat cum illo.

1:67 Et Zacharias pater ejus repletus est Spiritu

cause those things shall be accomplished that were spoken to thee by the Lord.

1:46 And Mary said: *My soul doth magnify the Lord.*

1:47 *And my spirit hath rejoiced in God my Saviour.*

1:48 *Because he hath regarded the humility of his handmaid; for behold from henceforth all generations shall call me blessed.*

1:49 *Because he that is mighty, hath done great things to me; and holy is his name.*

1:50 *And his mercy is from generation unto generations, to them that fear him.*

1:51 *He hath shewed might in his arm: he hath scattered the proud in the conceit of their heart.*

1:52 *He hath put down the mighty from their seat, and hath exalted the humble.*

1:53 *He hath filled the hungry with good things; and the rich he hath sent empty away.*

1:54 *He hath received Israel his servant, being mindful of his mercy:*

1:55 *As he spoke to our fathers, to Abraham and to his seed for ever.*

1:56 And Mary abode with her about three months; and she returned to her own house.

1:57 Now Elizabeth's full time of being delivered was come, and she brought forth a son.

1:58 And her neighbours and kinsfolks heard that the Lord had shewed his great mercy towards her, and they congratulated with her.

1:59 And it came to pass, that on the eighth day they came to circumcise the child, and they called him by his father's name Zachary.

1:60 And his mother answering, said: Not so; but he shall be called John.

1:61 And they said to her: There is none of thy kindred that is called by this name.

1:62 And they made signs to his father, how he would have him called.

1:63 And demanding a writing table, he wrote, saying: John is his name. And they all wondered.

1:64 And immediately his mouth was opened, and his tongue loosed, and he spoke, blessing God.

1:65 And fear came upon all their neighbours; and all these things were noised abroad over all the hill country of Judea.

1:66 And all they that had heard them laid them up in their heart, saying: What an one, think ye, shall this child be? For the hand of the Lord was with him.

1:67 And Zachary his father was filled with the

Sancto : et prophetavit, dicens :

1:68 *Benedictus Dominus Deus Israël, quia visitavit, et fecit redemptionem plebis suæ :*

1:69 *et erexit cornu salutis nobis in domo David pueri sui,*

1:70 *sicut locutus est per os sanctorum, qui a sæculo sunt, prophetarum ejus :*

1:71 *salutem ex inimicis nostris, et de manu omnium qui oderunt nos :*

1:72 *ad faciendam misericordiam cum patribus nostris : et memorari testamenti sui sancti :*

1:73 *jusjurandum, quod juravit ad Abraham patrem nostrum, daturum se nobis*

1:74 *ut sine timore, de manu inimicorum nostrorum liberati, serviamus illi*

1:75 *in sanctitate et justitia coram ipso, omnibus diebus nostris.*

1:76 *Et tu puer, propheta Altissimi vocaberis : præibis enim ante faciem Domini parare vias ejus,*

1:77 *ad dandam scientiam salutis plebi ejus in remissionem peccatorum eorum*

1:78 *per viscera misericordiæ Dei nostri, in quibus visitavit nos, oriens ex alto :*

1:79 *illuminare his qui in tenebris et in umbra mortis sedent : ad dirigendos pedes nostros in viam pacis.*

1:80 Puer autem crescebat, et confortabatur spiritu : et erat in desertis usque in diem ostensionis suæ ad Israël.

2:1 Factum est autem in diebus illis, exiit edictum a Cæsare Augusto ut describeretur universus orbis.

2:2 Hæc descriptio prima facta est a præside Syriæ Cyrino :

2:3 et ibant omnes ut profiterentur singuli in suam civitatem.

2:4 Ascendit autem et Joseph a Galilæa de civitate Nazareth in Judæam, in civitatem David, quæ vocatur Bethlehem : eo quod esset de domo et familia David,

2:5 ut profiteretur cum Maria desponsata sibi uxore prægnante.

2:6 Factum est autem, cum essent ibi, impleti sunt dies ut pareret.

2:7 Et peperit filium suum primogenitum, et pannis eum involvit, et reclinavit eum in præsepio : quia non erat eis locus in diversorio.

2:8 Et pastores erant in regione eadem vigilantes, et custodientes vigilias noctis super

Holy Ghost; and he prophesied, saying:

1:68 *Blessed be the Lord God of Israel; because he hath visited and wrought the redemption of his people:*

1:69 *And hath raised up an horn of salvation to us, in the house of David his servant:*

1:70 *As he spoke by the mouth of his holy prophets, who are from the beginning:*

1:71 *Salvation from our enemies, and from the hand of all that hate us:*

1:72 *To perform mercy to our fathers, and to remember his holy testament,*

1:73 *The oath, which he swore to Abraham our father, that he would grant to us,*

1:74 *That being delivered from the hand of our enemies, we may serve him without fear,*

1:75 *In holiness and justice before him, all our days.*

1:76 *And thou, child, shalt be called the prophet of the Highest: for thou shalt go before the face of the Lord to prepare his ways:*

1:77 *To give knowledge of salvation to his people, unto the remission of their sins:*

1:78 *Through the bowels of the mercy of our God, in which the Orient from on high hath visited us:*

1:79 *To enlighten them that sit in darkness, and in the shadow of death: to direct our feet into the way of peace.*

1:80 And the child grew, and was strengthened in spirit; and was in the deserts until the day of his manifestation to Israel.

2:1 And it came to pass, that in those days there went out a decree from Caesar Augustus, that the whole world should be enrolled.

2:2 This enrolling was first made by Cyrinus, the governor of Syria.

2:3 And all went to be enrolled, every one into his own city.

2:4 And Joseph also went up from Galilee, out of the city of Nazareth into Judea, to the city of David, which is called Bethlehem: because he was of the house and family of David,

2:5 To be enrolled with Mary his espoused wife, who was with child.

2:6 And it came to pass, that when they were there, her days were accomplished, that she should be delivered.

2:7 And she brought forth her firstborn son, and wrapped him up in swaddling clothes, and laid him in a manger; because there was no room for them in the inn.

2:8 And there were in the same country shepherds watching, and keeping the night watches

gregem suum.

2:9 Et ecce angelus Domini stetit juxta illos, et claritas Dei circumfulsit illos, et timuerunt timore magno.

2:10 Et dixit illis angelus : Nolite timere : ecce enim evangelizo vobis gaudium magnum, quod erit omni populo :

2:11 quia natus est vobis hodie Salvator, qui est Christus Dominus, in civitate David.

2:12 Et hoc vobis signum : invenietis infantem pannis involutum, et positum in præsepio.

2:13 Et subito facta est cum angelo multitudo militiæ cælestis laudantium Deum, et dicentium :

2:14 *Gloria in altissimis Deo, et in terra pax hominibus bonæ voluntatis.*

2:15 Et factum est, ut discesserunt ab eis angeli in cælum : pastores loquebantur ad invicem : Transeamus usque Bethlehem, et videamus hoc verbum, quod factum est, quod Dominus ostendit nobis.

2:16 Et venerunt festinantes : et invenerunt Mariam, et Joseph, et infantem positum in præsepio.

2:17 Videntes autem cognoverunt de verbo, quod dictum erat illis de puero hoc.

2:18 Et omnes qui audierunt, mirati sunt : et de his quæ dicta erant a pastoribus ad ipsos.

2:19 Maria autem conservabat omnia verba hæc, conferens in corde suo.

2:20 Et reversi sunt pastores glorificantes et laudantes Deum in omnibus quæ audierant et viderant, sicut dictum est ad illos.

2:21 Et postquam consummati sunt dies octo, ut circumcideretur puer, vocatum est nomen ejus Jesus, quod vocatum est ab angelo priusquam in utero conciperetur.

2:22 Et postquam impleti sunt dies purgationis ejus secundum legem Moysi, tulerunt illum in Jerusalem, ut sisterent eum Domino,

2:23 sicut scriptum est in lege Domini : Quia omne masculinum adaperiens vulvam, sanctum Domino vocabitur :

2:24 et ut darent hostiam secundum quod dictum est in lege Domini, par turturum, aut duos pullos columbarum.

2:25 Et ecce homo erat in Jerusalem, cui nomen Simeon, et homo iste justus, et timoratus, exspectans consolationem Israël : et Spiritus

over their flock.

2:9 And behold an angel of the Lord stood by them, and the brightness of God shone round about them; and they feared with a great fear.

2:10 And the angel said to them: Fear not; for, behold, I bring you good tidings of great joy, that shall be to all the people:

2:11 For, this day, is born to you a Saviour, who is Christ the Lord, in the city of David.

2:12 And this shall be a sign unto you. You shall find the infant wrapped in swaddling clothes, and laid in a manger.

2:13 And suddenly there was with the angel a multitude of the heavenly army, praising God, and saying:

2:14 *Glory to God in the highest; and on earth peace to men of good will.*

2:15 And it came to pass, after the angels departed from them into heaven, the shepherds said one to another: Let us go over to Bethlehem, and let us see this word that is come to pass, which the Lord hath shewed to us.

2:16 And they came with haste; and they found Mary and Joseph, and the infant lying in the manger.

2:17 And seeing, they understood of the word that had been spoken to them concerning this child.

2:18 And all that heard, wondered; and at those things that were told them by the shepherds.

2:19 But Mary kept all these words, pondering them in her heart.

2:20 And the shepherds returned, glorifying and praising God, for all the things they had heard and seen, as it was told unto them.

2:21 And after eight days were accomplished, that the child should be circumcised, his name was called JESUS, which was called by the angel, before he was conceived in the womb.

2:22 And after the days of her purification, according to the law of Moses, were accomplished, they carried him to Jerusalem, to present him to the Lord:

2:23 As it is written in the law of the Lord: Every male opening the womb shall be called holy to the Lord:

2:24 And to offer a sacrifice, according as it is written in the law of the Lord, a pair of turtledoves, or two young pigeons:

2:25 And behold there was a man in Jerusalem named Simeon, and this man was just and devout, waiting for the consolation of Israel; and

Sanctus erat in eo.

2:26 Et responsum acceperat a Spiritu Sancto, non visurum se mortem, nisi prius videret Christum Domini.

2:27 Et venit in spiritu in templum. Et cum inducerent puerum Jesum parentes ejus, ut facerent secundum consuetudinem legis pro eo,

2:28 et ipse accepit eum in ulnas suas : et benedixit Deum, et dixit :

2:29 *Nunc dimittis servum tuum Domine, secundum verbum tuum in pace :*

2:30 *quia viderunt oculi mei salutare tuum,*

2:31 *quod parasti ante faciem omnium populorum :*

2:32 *lumen ad revelationem gentium, et gloriam plebis tuæ Israël.*

2:33 Et erat pater ejus et mater mirantes super his quæ dicebantur de illo.

2:34 Et benedixit illis Simeon, et dixit ad Mariam matrem ejus : Ecce positus est hic in ruinam et in resurrectionem multorum in Israël, et in signum cui contradicetur :

2:35 et tuam ipsius animam pertransibit gladius ut revelentur ex multis cordibus cogitationes.

2:36 Et erat Anna prophetissa, filia Phanuel, de tribu Aser : hæc processerat in diebus multis, et vixerat cum viro suo annis septem a virginitate sua.

2:37 Et hæc vidua usque ad annos octoginta quatuor : quæ non discedebat de templo, jejuniis et obsecrationibus serviens nocte ac die.

2:38 Et hæc, ipsa hora superveniens, confitebatur Domino : et loquebatur de illo omnibus, qui exspectabant redemptionem Israël.

2:39 Et ut perfecerunt omnia secundum legem Domini, reversi sunt in Galilæam in civitatem suam Nazareth.

2:40 Puer autem crescebat, et confortabatur plenus sapientia : et gratia Dei erat in illo.

2:41 Et ibant parentes ejus per omnes annos in Jerusalem, in die solemni Paschæ.

2:42 Et cum factus esset annorum duodecim, ascendentibus illis Jerosolymam secundum consuetudinem diei festi,

2:43 consummatisque diebus, cum redirent, remansit puer Jesus in Jerusalem, et non cognoverunt parentes ejus.

2:44 Existimantes autem illum esse in comitatu, venerunt iter diei, et requirebant eum inter cognatos et notos.

the Holy Ghost was in him.

2:26 And he had received an answer from the Holy Ghost, that he should not see death, before he had seen the Christ of the Lord.

2:27 And he came by the Spirit into the temple. And when his parents brought in the child Jesus, to do for him according to the custom of the law,

2:28 He also took him into his arms, and blessed God, and said:

2:29 *Now thou dost dismiss thy servant, O Lord, according to thy word in peace;*

2:30 *Because my eyes have seen thy salvation,*

2:31 *Which thou hast prepared before the face of all peoples:*

2:32 *A light to the revelation of the Gentiles, and the glory of thy people Israel.*

2:33 And his father and mother were wondering at those things which were spoken concerning him.

2:34 And Simeon blessed them, and said to Mary his mother: Behold this child is set for the fall, and for the resurrection of many in Israel, and for a sign which shall be contradicted;

2:35 And thy own soul a sword shall pierce, that, out of many hearts, thoughts may be revealed.

2:36 And there was one Anna, a prophetess, the daughter of Phanuel, of the tribe of Aser; she was far advanced in years, and had lived with her husband seven years from her virginity.

2:37 And she was a widow until fourscore and four years; who departed not from the temple, by fastings and prayers serving night and day.

2:38 Now she, at the same hour, coming in, confessed to the Lord; and spoke of him to all that looked for the redemption of Israel.

2:39 And after they had performed all things according to the law of the Lord, they returned into Galilee, to their city Nazareth.

2:40 And the child grew, and waxed strong, full of wisdom; and the grace of God was in him.

2:41 And his parents went every year to Jerusalem, at the solemn day of the pasch,

2:42 And when he was twelve years old, they going up into Jerusalem, according to the custom of the feast,

2:43 And having fulfilled the days, when they returned, the child Jesus remained in Jerusalem; and his parents knew it not.

2:44 And thinking that he was in the company, they came a day's journey, and sought him among their kinsfolks and acquaintance.

2:45 Et non invenientes, regressi sunt in Jerusalem, requirentes eum.

2:46 Et factum est, post triduum invenerunt illum in templo sedentem in medio doctorum, audientem illos, et interrogantem eos.

2:47 Stupebant autem omnes qui eum audiebant, super prudentia et responsis ejus.

2:48 Et videntes admirati sunt. Et dixit mater ejus ad illum : Fili, quid fecisti nobis sic ? ecce pater tuus et ego dolentes quærebamus te.

2:49 Et ait ad illos : Quid est quod me quærebatis ? nesciebatis quia in his quæ Patris mei sunt, oportet me esse ?

2:50 Et ipsi non intellexerunt verbum quod locutus est ad eos.

2:51 Et descendit cum eis, et venit Nazareth : et erat subditus illis. Et mater ejus conservabat omnia verba hæc in corde suo.

2:52 Et Jesus proficiebat sapientia, et ætate, et gratia apud Deum et homines.

3:1 Anno autem quintodecimo imperii Tiberii Cæsaris, procurante Pontio Pilato Judæam, tetrarcha autem Galilææ Herode, Philippo autem fratre ejus tetrarcha Ituræae, et Trachonitidis regionis, et Lysania Abilinæ tetrarcha,

3:2 sub principibus sacerdotum Anna et Caipha : factum est verbum Domini super Joannem, Zachariæ filium, in deserto.

3:3 Et venit in omnem regionem Jordanis, prædicans baptismum pœnitentiæ in remissionem peccatorum,

3:4 sicut scriptum est in libro sermonum Isaiæ prophetæ : *Vox clamantis in deserto : Parate viam Domini ; rectas facite semitas ejus :*

3:5 *omnis vallis implebitur, et omnis mons, et collis humiliabitur : et erunt prava in directa, et aspera in vias planas :*

3:6 *et videbit omnis caro salutare Dei.*

3:7 Dicebat ergo ad turbas quæ exibant ut baptizarentur ab ipso : Genimina viperarum, quis ostendit vobis fugere a ventura ira ?

3:8 Facite ergo fructus dignos pœnitentiæ, et ne cœperitis dicere : Patrem habemus Abraham. Dico enim vobis quia potens est Deus de lapidibus istis suscitare filios Abrahæ.

3:9 Jam enim securis ad radicem arborum posita

2:45 And not finding him, they returned into Jerusalem, seeking him.

2:46 And it came to pass, that, after three days, they found him in the temple, sitting in the midst of the doctors, hearing them, and asking them questions.

2:47 And all that heard him were astonished at his wisdom and his answers.

2:48 And seeing him, they wondered. And his mother said to him: Son, why hast thou done so to us? behold thy father and I have sought thee sorrowing.

2:49 And he said to them: How is it that you sought me? did you not know, that I must be about my father's business?

2:50 And they understood not the word that he spoke unto them.

2:51 And he went down with them, and came to Nazareth, and was subject to them. And his mother kept all these words in her heart.

2:52 And Jesus advanced in wisdom, and age, and grace with God and men.

3:1 Now in the fifteenth year of the reign of Tiberius Caesar, Pontius Pilate being governor of Judea, and Herod being tetrarch of Galilee, and Philip his brother tetrarch of Iturea, and the country of Trachonitis, and Lysanias tetrarch of Abilina;

3:2 Under the high priests Annas and Caiphas; the word of the Lord was made unto John, the son of Zachary, in the desert.

3:3 And he came into all the country about the Jordan, preaching the baptism of penance for the remission of sins;

3:4 As it was written in the book of the sayings of Isaias the prophet: *A voice of one crying in the wilderness: Prepare ye the way of the Lord, make straight his paths.*

3:5 *Every valley shall be filled; and every mountain and hill shall be brought low; and the crooked shall be made straight; and the rough ways plain;*

3:6 *And all flesh shall see the salvation of God.*

3:7 He said therefore to the multitudes that went forth to be baptized by him: Ye offspring of vipers, who hath shewed you to flee from the wrath to come?

3:8 Bring forth therefore fruits worthy of penance; and do not begin to say, We have Abraham for our father. For I say unto you, that God is able of these stones to raise up children to Abraham.

3:9 For now the axe is laid to the root of the

est. Omnis ergo arbor non faciens fructum bonum, excidetur, et in ignem mittetur.

3:10 Et interrogabant eum turbæ, dicentes : Quid ergo faciemus ?

3:11 Respondens autem dicebat illis : Qui habet duas tunicas, det non habenti : et qui habet escas, similiter faciat.

3:12 Venerunt autem et publicani ut baptizarentur, et dixerunt ad illum : Magister, quid faciemus ?

3:13 At ille dixit ad eos : Nihil amplius, quam quod constitutum est vobis, faciatis.

3:14 Interrogabant autem eum et milites, dicentes : Quid faciemus et nos ? Et ait illis : Neminem concutiatis, neque calumniam faciatis : et contenti estote stipendiis vestris.

3:15 Existimante autem populo, et cogitantibus omnibus in cordibus suis de Joanne, ne forte ipse esset Christus,

3:16 respondit Joannes, dicens omnibus : Ego quidem aqua baptizo vos : veniet autem fortior me, cujus non sum dignus solvere corrigiam calceamentorum ejus : ipse vos baptizabit in Spiritu Sancto et igni :

3:17 cujus ventilabrum in manu ejus, et purgabit aream suam, et congregabit triticum in horreum suum, paleas autem comburet igni inextinguibili.

3:18 Multa quidem et alia exhortans evangelizabat populo.

3:19 Herodes autem tetrarcha cum corriperetur ab illo de Herodiade uxore fratris sui, et de omnibus malis quæ fecit Herodes,

3:20 adjecit et hoc super omnia, et inclusit Joannem in carcere.

3:21 Factum est autem cum baptizaretur omnis populus, et Jesu baptizato, et orante, apertum est cælum :

3:22 et descendit Spiritus Sanctus corporali specie sicut columba in ipsum : et vox de cælo facta est : Tu es filius meus dilectus, in te complacui mihi.

3:23 Et ipse Jesus erat incipiens quasi annorum triginta, ut putabatur, filius Joseph, qui fuit Heli, qui fuit Mathat,

3:24 qui fuit Levi, qui fuit Melchi, qui fuit Janne, qui fuit Joseph,

3:25 qui fuit Mathathiæ, qui fuit Amos, qui fuit Nahum, qui fuit Hesli, qui fuit Nagge,

trees. Every tree therefore that bringeth not forth good fruit, shall be cut down and cast into the fire.

3:10 And the people asked him, saying: What then shall we do?

3:11 And he answering, said to them: He that hath two coats, let him give to him that hath none; and he that hath meat, let him do in like manner.

3:12 And the publicans also came to be baptized, and said to him: Master, what shall we do?

3:13 But he said to them: Do nothing more than that which is appointed you.

3:14 And the soldiers also asked him, saying: And what shall we do? And he said to them: Do violence to no man; neither calumniate any man; and be content with your pay.

3:15 And as the people were of opinion, and all were thinking in their hearts of John, that perhaps he might be the Christ;

3:16 John answered, saying unto all: I indeed baptize you with water; but there shall come one mightier than I, the latchet of whose shoes I am not worthy to loose: he shall baptize you with the Holy Ghost, and with fire:

3:17 Whose fan is in his hand, and he will purge his floor, and will gather the wheat into his barn; but the chaff he will burn with unquenchable fire.

3:18 And many other things exhorting, did he preach to the people.

3:19 But Herod the tetrarch, when he was reproved by him for Herodias, his brother's wife, and for all the evils which Herod had done;

3:20 He added this also above all, and shut up John in prison.

3:21 Now it came to pass, when all the people were baptized, that Jesus also being baptized and praying, heaven was opened;

3:22 And the Holy Ghost descended in a bodily shape, as a dove upon him; and a voice came from heaven: Thou art my beloved Son; in thee I am well pleased.

3:23 And Jesus himself was beginning about the age of thirty years; being (as it was supposed) the son of Joseph, who was of Heli, who was of Mathat,

3:24 Who was of Levi, who was of Melchi, who was of Janne, who was of Joseph,

3:25 Who was of Mathathias, who was of Amos, who was of Nahum, who was of Hesli, who

3:26 qui fuit Mahath, qui fuit Mathathiæ, qui fuit Semei, qui fuit Joseph, qui fuit Juda,

3:27 qui fuit Joanna, qui fuit Resa, qui fuit Zorobabel, qui fuit Salathiel, qui fuit Neri,

3:28 qui fuit Melchi, qui fuit Addi, qui fuit Cosan, qui fuit Elmadan, qui fuit Her,

3:29 qui fuit Jesu, qui fuit Eliezer, qui fuit Jorim, qui fuit Mathat, qui fuit Levi,

3:30 qui fuit Simeon, qui fuit Juda, qui fuit Joseph, qui fuit Jona, qui fuit Eliakim,

3:31 qui fuit Melea, qui fuit Menna, qui fuit Mathatha, qui fuit Natham, qui fuit David,

3:32 qui fuit Jesse, qui fuit Obed, qui fuit Booz, qui fuit Salmon, qui fuit Naasson,

3:33 qui fuit Aminadab, qui fuit Aram, qui fuit Esron, qui fuit Phares, qui fuit Judæ,

3:34 qui fuit Jacob, qui fuit Isaac, qui fuit Abrahæ, qui fuit Thare, qui fuit Nachor,

3:35 qui fuit Sarug, qui fuit Ragau, qui fuit Phaleg, qui fuit Heber, qui fuit Sale,

3:36 qui fuit Cainan, qui fuit Arphaxad, qui fuit Sem, qui fuit Noë, qui fuit Lamech,

3:37 qui fuit Methusale, qui fuit Henoch, qui fuit Jared, qui fuit Malaleel, qui fuit Cainan,

3:38 qui fuit Henos, qui fuit Seth, qui fuit Adam, qui fuit Dei.

4:1 Jesus autem plenus Spiritu Sancto regressus est a Jordane : et agebatur a Spiritu in desertum

4:2 diebus quadraginta, et tentabatur a diabolo. Et nihil manducavit in diebus illis : et consummatis illis esuriit.

4:3 Dixit autem illi diabolus : Si Filius Dei es, dic lapidi huic ut panis fiat.

4:4 Et respondit ad illum Jesus : Scriptum est : Quia non in solo pane vivit homo, sed in omni verbo Dei.

4:5 Et duxit illum diabolus in montem excelsum, et ostendit illi omnia regna orbis terræ in

was of Nagge,

3:26 Who was of Mahath, who was of Mathathias, who was of Semei, who was of Joseph, who was of Juda,

3:27 Who was of Joanna, who was of Reza, who was of Zorobabel, who was of Salathiel, who was of Neri,

3:28 Who was of Melchi, who was of Addi, who was of Cosan, who was of Helmadan, who was of Her,

3:29 Who was of Jesus, who was of Eliezer, who was of Jorim, who was of Mathat, who was of Levi,

3:30 Who was of Simeon, who was of Judas, who was of Joseph, who was of Jona, who was of Eliakim,

3:31 Who was of Melea, who was of Menna, who was of Mathatha, who was of Nathan, who was of David,

3:32 Who was of Jesse, who was of Obed, who was of Booz, who was of Salmon, who was of Naasson,

3:33 Who was of Aminadab, who was of Aram, who was of Esron, who was of Phares, who was of Judas,

3:34 Who was of Jacob, who was of Isaac, who was of Abraham, who was of Thare, who was of Nachor,

3:35 Who was of Sarug, who was of Ragau, who was of Phaleg, who was of Heber, who was of Sale,

3:36 Who was of Cainan, who was of Arphaxad, who was of Sem, who was of Noe, who was of Lamech,

3:37 Who was of Mathusale, who was of Henoch, who was of Jared, who was of Malaleel, who was of Cainan,

3:38 Who was of Henos, who was of Seth, who was of Adam, who was of God.

4:1 And Jesus being full of the Holy Ghost, returned from the Jordan, and was led by the Spirit into the desert,

4:2 For the space of forty days; and was tempted by the devil. And he ate nothing in those days; and when they were ended, he was hungry.

4:3 And the devil said to him: If thou be the Son of God, say to this stone that it be made bread.

4:4 And Jesus answered him: It is written, that Man liveth not by bread alone, but by every word of God.

4:5 And the devil led him into a high mountain, and shewed him all the kingdoms of the world

momento temporis,

4:6 et ait illi : Tibi dabo potestatem hanc universam, et gloriam illorum : quia mihi tradita sunt, et cui volo do illa.

4:7 Tu ergo si adoraveris coram me, erunt tua omnia.

4:8 Et respondens Jesus, dixit illi : Scriptum est : Dominum Deum tuum adorabis, et illi soli servies.

4:9 Et duxit illum in Jerusalem, et statuit eum super pinnam templi, et dixit illi : Si Filius Dei es, mitte te hinc deorsum.

4:10 Scriptum est enim quod angelis suis mandavit de te, ut conservent te :

4:11 et quia in manibus tollent te, ne forte offendas ad lapidem pedem tuum.

4:12 Et respondens Jesus, ait illi : Dictum est : Non tentabis Dominum Deum tuum.

4:13 Et consummata omni tentatione, diabolus recessit ab illo, usque ad tempus.

4:14 Et regressus est Jesus in virtute Spiritus in Galilæam, et fama exiit per universam regionem de illo.

4:15 Et ipse docebat in synagogis eorum, et magnificabatur ab omnibus.

4:16 Et venit Nazareth, ubi erat nutritus, et intravit secundum consuetudinem suam die sabbati in synagogam, et surrexit legere.

4:17 Et traditus est illi liber Isaiæ prophetæ. Et ut revolvit librum, invenit locum ubi scriptum erat :

4:18 Spiritus Domini super me : propter quod unxit me, evangelizare pauperibus misit me, sanare contritos corde,

4:19 prædicare captivis remissionem, et cæcis visum, dimittere confractos in remissionem, prædicare annum Domini acceptum et diem retributionis.

4:20 Et cum plicuisset librum, reddit ministro, et sedit. Et omnium in synagoga oculi erant intendentes in eum.

4:21 Cœpit autem dicere ad illos : Quia hodie impleta est hæc scriptura in auribus vestris.

4:22 Et omnes testimonium illi dabant : et mirabantur in verbis gratiæ, quæ procedebant de ore ipsius, et dicebant : Nonne hic est filius Joseph ?

4:23 Et ait illis : Utique dicetis mihi hanc simili-

in a moment of time;

4:6 And he said to him: To thee will I give all this power, and the glory of them; for to me they are delivered, and to whom I will, I give them.

4:7 If thou therefore wilt adore before me, all shall be thine.

4:8 And Jesus answering said to him: It is written: Thou shalt adore the Lord thy God, and him only shalt thou serve.

4:9 And he brought him to Jerusalem, and set him on a pinnacle of the temple, and he said to him: If thou be the Son of God, cast thyself from hence.

4:10 For it is written, that He hath given his angels charge over thee, that they keep thee.

4:11 And that in their hands they shall bear thee up, lest perhaps thou dash thy foot against a stone.

4:12 And Jesus answering, said to him: It is said: Thou shalt not tempt the Lord thy God.

4:13 And all the temptation being ended, the devil departed from him for a time.

4:14 And Jesus returned in the power of the spirit, into Galilee, and the fame of him went out through the whole country.

4:15 And he taught in their synagogues, and was magnified by all.

4:16 And he came to Nazareth, where he was brought up: and he went into the synagogue, according to his custom, on the sabbath day; and he rose up to read.

4:17 And the book of Isaias the prophet was delivered unto him. And as he unfolded the book, he found the place where it was written:

4:18 The Spirit of the Lord is upon me. Wherefore he hath anointed me to preach the gospel to the poor, he hath sent me to heal the contrite of heart,

4:19 To preach deliverance to the captives, and sight to the blind, to set at liberty them that are bruised, to preach the acceptable year of the Lord, and the day of reward.

4:20 And when he had folded the book, he restored it to the minister, and sat down. And the eyes of all in the synagogue were fixed on him.

4:21 And he began to say to them: This day is fulfilled this scripture in your ears.

4:22 And all gave testimony to him: and they wondered at the words of grace that proceeded from his mouth, and they said: Is not this the son of Joseph?

4:23 And he said to them: Doubtless you will say

tudinem : Medice cura teipsum : quanta audivimus facta in Capharnaum, fac et hic in patria tua.

4:24 Ait autem : Amen dico vobis, quia nemo propheta acceptus est in patria sua.

4:25 In veritate dico vobis, multæ viduæ erant in diebus Eliæ in Israël, quando clausum est cælum annis tribus et mensibus sex, cum facta esset fames magna in omni terra :

4:26 et ad nullam illarum missus est Elias, nisi in Sarepta Sidoniæ, ad mulierem viduam.

4:27 Et multi leprosi erant in Israël sub Eliseo propheta : et nemo eorum mundatus est nisi Naaman Syrus.

4:28 Et repleti sunt omnes in synagoga ira, hæc audientes.

4:29 Et surrexerunt, et ejecerunt illum extra civitatem : et duxerunt illum usque ad supercilium montis, super quem civitas illorum erat ædificata, ut præcipitarent eum.

4:30 Ipse autem transiens per medium illorum, ibat.

4:31 Et descendit in Capharnaum civitatem Galilææ, ibique docebat illos sabbatis.

4:32 Et stupebant in doctrina ejus, quia in potestate erat sermo ipsius.

4:33 Et in synagoga erat homo habens dæmonium immundum, et exclamavit voce magna,

4:34 dicens : Sine, quid nobis et tibi, Jesu Nazarene ? venisti perdere nos ? scio te quis sis, Sanctus Dei.

4:35 Et increpavit illum Jesus, dicens : Obmutesce, et exi ab eo. Et cum projecisset illum dæmonium in medium, exiit ab illo, nihilque illum nocuit.

4:36 Et factus est pavor in omnibus, et colloquebantur ad invicem, dicentes : Quod est hoc verbum, quia in potestate et virtute imperat immundis spiritibus, et exeunt ?

4:37 Et divulgabatur fama de illo in omnem locum regionis.

4:38 Surgens autem Jesus de synagoga, introivit in domum Simonis. Socrus autem Simonis tenebatur magnis febribus : et rogaverunt illum pro ea.

4:39 Et stans super illam imperavit febri : et dimisit illam. Et continuo surgens, ministrabat illis.

to me this similitude: Physician, heal thyself: as great things as we have heard done in Capharnaum, do also here in thy own country.

4:24 And he said: Amen I say to you, that no prophet is accepted in his own country.

4:25 In truth I say to you, there were many widows in the days of Elias in Israel, when heaven was shut up three years and six months, when there was a great famine throughout all the earth.

4:26 And to none of them was Elias sent, but to Sarepta of Sidon, to a widow woman.

4:27 And there were many lepers in Israel in the time of Eliseus the prophet: and none of them was cleansed but Naaman the Syrian.

4:28 And all they in the synagogue, hearing these things, were filled with anger.

4:29 And they rose up and thrust him out of the city; and they brought him to the brow of the hill, whereon their city was built, that they might cast him down headlong.

4:30 But he passing through the midst of them, went his way.

4:31 And he went down into Capharnaum, a city of Galilee, and there he taught them on the sabbath days.

4:32 And they were astonished at his doctrine: for his speech was with power.

4:33 And in the synagogue there was a man who had an unclean devil, and he cried out with a loud voice,

4:34 Saying: Let us alone, what have we to do with thee, Jesus of Nazareth? art thou come to destroy us? I know thee who thou art, the holy one of God.

4:35 And Jesus rebuked him, saying: Hold thy peace, and go out of him. And when the devil had thrown him into the midst, he went out of him, and hurt him not at all.

4:36 And there came fear upon all, and they talked among themselves, saying: What word is this, for with authority and power he commandeth the unclean spirits, and they go out?

4:37 And the fame of him was published into every place of the country.

4:38 And Jesus rising up out of the synagogue, went into Simon's house. And Simon's wife's mother was taken with a great fever, and they besought him for her.

4:39 And standing over her, he commanded the fever, and it left her. And immediately rising, she ministered to them.

4:40 Cum autem sol occidisset, omnes qui habebant infirmos variis languoribus, ducebant illos ad eum. At ille singulis manus imponens, curabat eos.

4:41 Exibant autem dæmonia a multis clamantia, et dicentia : Quia tu es Filius Dei : et increpans non sinebat ea loqui : quia sciebant ipsum esse Christum.

4:42 Facta autem die egressus ibat in desertum locum, et turbæ requirebant eum, et venerunt usque ad ipsum : et detinebant illum ne discederet ab eis.

4:43 Quibus ille ait : Quia et aliis civitatibus oportet me evangelizare regnum Dei : quia ideo missus sum.

4:44 Et erat prædicans in synagogis Galilææ.

5:1 Factum est autem, cum turbæ irruerunt in eum ut audirent verbum Dei, et ipse stabat secus stagnum Genesareth.

5:2 Et vidit duas naves stantes secus stagnum : piscatores autem descenderant, et lavabant retia.

5:3 Ascendens autem in unam navim, quæ erat Simonis, rogavit eum a terra reducere pusillum. Et sedens docebat de navicula turbas.

5:4 Ut cessavit autem loqui, dixit ad Simonem : Duc in altum, et laxate retia vestra in capturam.

5:5 Et respondens Simon, dixit illi : Præceptor, per totam noctem laborantes nihil cepimus : in verbo autem tuo laxabo rete.

5:6 Et cum hoc fecissent, concluserunt piscium multitudinem copiosam : rumpebatur autem rete eorum.

5:7 Et annuerunt sociis, qui erant in alia navi, ut venirent, et adjuvarent eos. Et venerunt, et impleverunt ambas naviculas, ita ut pene mergerentur.

5:8 Quod cum videret Simon Petrus, procidit ad genua Jesu, dicens : Exi a me, quia homo peccator sum, Domine.

5:9 Stupor enim circumdederat eum, et omnes qui cum illo erant, in captura piscium, quam ceperant :

5:10 similiter autem Jacobum et Joannem, filios Zebedæi, qui erant socii Simonis. Et ait ad Simonem Jesus : Noli timere : ex hoc jam homines eris capiens.

5:11 Et subductis ad terram navibus, relictis om-

4:40 And when the sun was down, all they that had any sick with divers diseases, brought them to him. But he laying his hands on every one of them, healed them.

4:41 And devils went out from many, crying out and saying: Thou art the Son of God. And rebuking them he suffered them not to speak, for they knew that he was Christ.

4:42 And when it was day, going out he went into a desert place, and the multitudes sought him, and came unto him: and they stayed him that he should not depart from them.

4:43 To whom he said: To other cities also I must preach the kingdom of God: for therefore am I sent.

4:44 And he was preaching in the synagogues of Galilee.

5:1 And it came to pass, that when the multitudes pressed upon him to hear the word of God, he stood by the lake of Genesareth,

5:2 And saw two ships standing by the lake: but the fishermen were gone out of them, and were washing their nets.

5:3 And going into one of the ships that was Simon's, he desired him to draw back a little from the land. And sitting he taught the multitudes out of the ship.

5:4 Now when he had ceased to speak, he said to Simon: Launch out into the deep, and let down your nets for a draught.

5:5 And Simon answering said to him: Master, we have labored all the night, and have taken nothing: but at thy word I will let down the net.

5:6 And when they had done this, they enclosed a very great multitude of fishes, and their net broke.

5:7 And they beckoned to their partners that were in the other ship, that they should come and help them. And they came, and filled both the ships, so that they were almost sinking.

5:8 Which when Simon Peter saw, he fell down at Jesus' knees, saying: Depart from me, for I am a sinful man, O Lord.

5:9 For he was wholly astonished, and all that were with him, at the draught of the fishes which they had taken.

5:10 And so were also James and John the sons of Zebedee, who were Simon's partners. And Jesus saith to Simon: Fear not: from henceforth thou shalt catch men.

5:11 And having brought their ships to land,

nibus, secuti sunt eum.

5:12 Et factum est, cum esset in una civitatum, et ecce vir plenus lepra, et videns Jesum, et procidens in faciem, rogavit eum, dicens : Domine, si vis, potes me mundare.

5:13 Et extendens manum, tetigit eum dicens : Volo : mundare. Et confestim lepra discessit ab illo.

5:14 Et ipse præcepit illi ut nemini diceret : sed, Vade, ostende te sacerdoti, et offer pro emundatione tua, sicut præcepit Moyses, in testimonium illis.

5:15 Perambulabat autem magis sermo de illo : et conveniebant turbæ multæ ut audirent, et curarentur ab infirmitatibus suis.

5:16 Ipse autem secedebat in desertum, et orabat.

5:17 Et factum est in una dierum, et ipse sedebat docens. Et erant pharisæi sedentes, et legis doctores, qui venerant ex omni castello Galilææ, et Judææ, et Jerusalem : et virtus Domini erat ad sanandum eos.

5:18 Et ecce viri portantes in lecto hominem, qui erat paralyticus : et quærebant eum inferre, et ponere ante eum.

5:19 Et non invenientes qua parte illum inferrent præ turba, ascenderunt supra tectum, et per tegulas summiserunt eum cum lecto in medium ante Jesum.

5:20 Quorum fidem ut vidit, dixit : Homo, remittuntur tibi peccata tua.

5:21 Et cœperunt cogitare scribæ et pharisæi, dicentes : Quis est hic, qui loquitur blasphemias ? quis potest dimittere peccata, nisi solus Deus ?

5:22 Ut cognovit autem Jesus cogitationes eorum, respondens, dixit ad illos : Quid cogitatis in cordibus vestris ?

5:23 Quid est facilius dicere : Dimittuntur tibi peccata : an dicere : Surge, et ambula ?

5:24 Ut autem sciatis quia Filius hominis habet potestatem in terra dimittendi peccata, (ait paralytico) tibi dico, surge, tolle lectum tuum, et vade in domum tuam.

5:25 Et confestim consurgens coram illis, tulit lectum in quo jacebat : et abiit in domum suam, magnificans Deum.

5:26 Et stupor apprehendit omnes, et magnificabant Deum. Et repleti sunt timore, dicentes :

leaving all things, they followed him.

5:12 And it came to pass, when he was in a certain city, behold a man full of leprosy, who seeing Jesus, and falling on his face, besought him, saying: Lord, if thou wilt, thou canst make me clean.

5:13 And stretching forth his hand, he touched him, saying: I will. Be thou cleansed. And immediately the leprosy departed from him.

5:14 And he charged him that he should tell no man, but, Go, shew thyself to the priest, and offer for thy cleansing according as Moses commanded, for a testimony to them.

5:15 But the fame of him went abroad the more, and great multitudes came together to hear, and to be healed by him of their infirmities.

5:16 And he retired into the desert, and prayed.

5:17 And it came to pass on a certain day, as he sat teaching, that there were also Pharisees and doctors of the law sitting by, that were come out of every town of Galilee, and Judea and Jerusalem: and the power of the Lord was to heal them.

5:18 And behold, men brought in a bed a man, who had the palsy: and they sought means to bring him in, and to lay him before him.

5:19 And when they could not find by what way they might bring him in, because of the multitude, they went up upon the roof, and let him down through the tiles with his bed into the midst before Jesus.

5:20 Whose faith when he saw, he said: Man, thy sins are forgiven thee.

5:21 And the scribes and Pharisees began to think, saying: Who is this who speaketh blasphemies? Who can forgive sins, but God alone?

5:22 And when Jesus knew their thoughts, answering, he said to them: What is it you think in your hearts?

5:23 Which is easier to say, Thy sins are forgiven thee; or to say, Arise and walk?

5:24 But that you may know that the Son of man hath power on earth to forgive sins, (he saith to the sick of the palsy,) I say to thee, Arise, take up thy bed, and go into thy house.

5:25 And immediately rising up before them, he took up the bed on which he lay; and he went away to his own house, glorifying God.

5:26 And all were astonished; and they glorified God. And they were filled with fear, saying: We

Quia vidimus mirabilia hodie.

5:27 Et post hæc exiit, et vidit publicanum nomine Levi, sedentem ad telonium, et ait illi : Sequere me.

5:28 Et relictis omnibus, surgens secutus est eum.

5:29 Et fecit ei convivium magnum Levi in domo sua : et erat turba multa publicanorum, et aliorum qui cum illis erant discumbentes.

5:30 Et murmurabant pharisæi et scribæ eorum, dicentes ad discipulos ejus : Quare cum publicanis et peccatoribus manducatis et bibitis ?

5:31 Et respondens Jesus, dixit ad illos : Non egent qui sani sunt medico, sed qui male habent.

5:32 Non veni vocare justos, sed peccatores ad pœnitentiam.

5:33 At illi dixerunt ad eum : Quare discipuli Joannis jejunant frequenter, et obsecrationes faciunt, similiter et pharisæorum : tui autem edunt et bibunt ?

5:34 Quibus ipse ait : Numquid potestis filios sponsi, dum cum illis est sponsus, facere jejunare ?

5:35 Venient autem dies, cum ablatus fuerit ab illis sponsus : tunc jejunabunt in illis diebus.

5:36 Dicebat autem et similitudinem ad illos : Quia nemo commissuram a novo vestimento immittit in vestimentum vetus : alioquin et novum rumpit, et veteri non convenit commissura a novo.

5:37 Et nemo mittit vinum novum in utres veteres : alioquin rumpet vinum novum utres, et ipsum effundetur, et utres peribunt :

5:38 sed vinum novum in utres novos mittendum est, et utraque conservantur.

5:39 Et nemo bibens vetus, statim vult novum : dicit enim : Vetus melius est.

6:1 Factum est autem in sabbato secundo, primo, cum transiret per sata, vellebant discipuli ejus spicas, et manducabant confricantes manibus.

6:2 Quidam autem pharisæorum, dicebant illis : Quid facitis quod non licet in sabbatis ?

6:3 Et respondens Jesus ad eos, dixit : Nec hoc legistis quod fecit David, cum esurisset ipse, et qui cum illo erant ?

have seen wonderful things to day.

5:27 And after these things he went forth, and saw a publican named Levi, sitting at the receipt of custom, and he said to him: Follow me.

5:28 And leaving all things, he rose up and followed him.

5:29 And Levi made him a great feast in his own house; and there was a great company of publicans, and of others, that were at table with them.

5:30 But the Pharisees and scribes murmured, saying to his disciples: Why do you eat and drink with publicans and sinners?

5:31 And Jesus answering, said to them: They that are whole, need not the physician: but they that are sick.

5:32 I came not to call the just, but sinners to penance.

5:33 And they said to him: Why do the disciples of John fast often, and make prayers, and the disciples of the Pharisees in like manner; but thine eat and drink?

5:34 To whom he said: Can you make the children of the bridegroom fast, whilst the bridegroom is with them?

5:35 But the days will come, when the bridegroom shall be taken away from them, then shall they fast in those days.

5:36 And he spoke also a similitude to them: That no man putteth a piece from a new garment upon an old garment; otherwise he both rendeth the new, and the piece taken from the new agreeth not with the old.

5:37 And no man putteth new wine into old bottles: otherwise the new wine will break the bottles, and it will be spilled, and the bottles will be lost.

5:38 But new wine must be put into new bottles; and both are preserved.

5:39 And no man drinking old, hath presently a mind to new: for he saith, The old is better.

6:1 And it came to pass on the second first sabbath, that as he went through the corn fields, his disciples plucked the ears, and did eat, rubbing them in their hands.

6:2 And some of the Pharisees said to them: Why do you that which is not lawful on the sabbath days?

6:3 And Jesus answering them, said: Have you not read so much as this, what David did, when himself was hungry, and they that were with

6:4 quomodo intravit in domum Dei, et panes propositionis sumpsit, et manducavit, et dedit his qui cum ipso erant : quos non licet manducare nisi tantum sacerdotibus ?

6:5 Et dicebat illis : Quia dominus est Filius hominis etiam sabbati.

6:6 Factum est autem in alio sabbato, ut intraret in synagogam, et doceret. Et erat ibi homo, et manus ejus dextra erat arida.

6:7 Observabant autem scribæ et pharisæi si in sabbato curaret, ut invenirent unde accusarent eum.

6:8 Ipse vero sciebat cogitationes eorum : et ait homini qui habebat manum aridam : Surge, et sta in medium. Et surgens stetit.

6:9 Ait autem ad illos Jesus : Interrogo vos si licet sabbatis benefacere, an male : animam salvam facere, an perdere ?

6:10 Et circumspectis omnibus dixit homini : Extende manum tuam. Et extendit : et restituta est manus ejus.

6:11 Ipsi autem repleti sunt insipientia, et colloquebantur ad invicem, quidnam facerent Jesu.

6:12 Factum est autem in illis diebus, exiit in montem orare, et erat pernoctans in oratione Dei.

6:13 Et cum dies factus esset, vocavit discipulos suos : et elegit duodecim ex ipsis (quos et apostolos nominavit) :

6:14 Simonem, quem cognominavit Petrum, et Andream fratrem ejus, Jacobum, et Joannem, Philippum, et Bartholomæum,

6:15 Matthæum, et Thomam, Jacobum Alphæi, et Simonem, qui vocatur Zelotes,

6:16 et Judam Jacobi, et Judam Iscariotem, qui fuit proditor.

6:17 Et descendens cum illis, stetit in loco campestri, et turba discipulorum ejus, et multitudo copiosa plebis ab omni Judæa, et Jerusalem, et maritima, et Tyri, et Sidonis,

6:18 qui venerant ut audirent eum, et sanarentur a languoribus suis. Et qui vexabantur a spiritibus immundis, curabantur.

6:19 Et omnis turba quærebat eum tangere : quia virtus de illo exibat, et sanabat omnes.

6:20 Et ipse elevatis oculis in discipulis suis, dicebat : Beati pauperes, quia vestrum est reg-

him:

6:4 How he went into the house of God, and took and ate the bread of proposition, and gave to them that were with him, which is not lawful to eat but only for the priests?

6:5 And he said to them: The Son of man is Lord also of the sabbath.

6:6 And it came to pass also on another sabbath, that he entered into the synagogue, and taught. And there was a man, whose right hand was withered.

6:7 And the scribes and Pharisees watched if he would heal on the sabbath; that they might find an accusation against him.

6:8 But he knew their thoughts; and said to the man who had the withered hand: Arise, and stand forth in the midst. And rising he stood forth.

6:9 Then Jesus said to them: I ask you, if it be lawful on the sabbath days to do good, or to do evil; to save life, or to destroy?

6:10 And looking round about on them all, he said to the man: Stretch forth thy hand. And he stretched it forth: and his hand was restored.

6:11 And they were filled with madness; and they talked one with another, what they might do to Jesus.

6:12 And it came to pass in those days, that he went out into a mountain to pray, and he passed the whole night in the prayer of God.

6:13 And when day was come, he called unto him his disciples; and he chose twelve of them (whom also he named apostles):

6:14 Simon, whom he surnamed Peter, and Andrew his brother, James and John, Philip and Bartholomew,

6:15 Matthew and Thomas, James the son of Alpheus, and Simon who is called Zelotes,

6:16 And Jude, the brother of James, and Judas Iscariot, who was the traitor.

6:17 And coming down with them, he stood in a plain place, and the company of his disciples, and a very great multitude of people from all Judea and Jerusalem, and the sea coast both of Tyre and Sidon,

6:18 Who were come to hear him, and to be healed of their diseases. And they that were troubled with unclean spirits, were cured.

6:19 And all the multitude sought to touch him, for virtue went out from him, and healed all.

6:20 And he, lifting up his eyes on his disciples, said: Blessed are ye poor, for yours is the king-

num Dei.

6:21 Beati qui nunc esuritis, quia saturabimini. Beati qui nunc fletis, quia ridebitis.

6:22 Beati eritis cum vos oderint homines, et cum separaverint vos, et exprobraverint, et ejicerint nomen vestrum tamquam malum propter Filium hominis.

6:23 Gaudete in illa die, et exsultate : ecce enim merces vestra multa est in cælo : secundum hæc enim faciebant prophetis patres eorum.

6:24 Verumtamen væ vobis divitibus, quia habetis consolationem vestram.

6:25 Væ vobis, qui saturati estis : quia esurietis. Væ vobis, qui ridetis nunc : quia lugebitis et flebitis.

6:26 Væ cum benedixerint vobis homines : secundum hæc enim faciebant pseudoprophetis patres eorum.

6:27 Sed vobis dico, qui auditis : diligite inimicos vestros, benefacite his qui oderunt vos.

6:28 Benedicite maledicentibus vobis, et orate pro calumniantibus vos.

6:29 Et qui te percutit in maxillam, præbe et alteram. Et ab eo qui aufert tibi vestimentum, etiam tunicam noli prohibere.

6:30 Omni autem petenti te, tribue : et qui aufert quæ tua sunt, ne repetas.

6:31 Et prout vultis ut faciant vobis homines, et vos facite illis similiter.

6:32 Et si diligitis eos qui vos diligunt, quæ vobis est gratia ? nam et peccatores diligentes se diligunt.

6:33 Et si benefeceritis his qui vobis benefaciunt, quæ vobis est gratia ? siquidem et peccatores hoc faciunt.

6:34 Et si mutuum dederitis his a quibus speratis recipere, quæ gratia est vobis ? nam et peccatores peccatoribus fœnerantur, ut recipiant æqualia.

6:35 Verumtamen diligite inimicos vestros : benefacite, et mutuum date, nihil inde sperantes : et erit merces vestra multa, et eritis filii Altissimi, quia ipse benignus est super ingratos et malos.

6:36 Estote ergo misericordes sicut et Pater vester misericors est.

6:37 Nolite judicare, et non judicabimini : nolite condemnare, et non condemnabimini. Dimitte,

dom of God.

6:21 Blessed are ye that hunger now: for you shall be filled. Blessed are ye that weep now: for you shall laugh.

6:22 Blessed shall you be when men shall hate you, and when they shall separate you, and shall reproach you, and cast out your name as evil, for the Son of man's sake.

6:23 Be glad in that day and rejoice; for behold, your reward is great in heaven. For according to these things did their fathers to the prophets.

6:24 But woe to you that are rich: for you have your consolation.

6:25 Woe to you that are filled: for you shall hunger. Woe to you that now laugh: for you shall mourn and weep.

6:26 Woe to you when men shall bless you: for according to these things did their fathers to the false prophets.

6:27 But I say to you that hear: Love your enemies, do good to them that hate you.

6:28 Bless them that curse you, and pray for them that calumniate you.

6:29 And to him that striketh thee on the one cheek, offer also the other. And him that taketh away from thee thy cloak, forbid not to take thy coat also.

6:30 Give to every one that asketh thee, and of him that taketh away thy goods, ask them not again.

6:31 And as you would that men should do to you, do you also to them in like manner.

6:32 And if you love them that love you, what thanks are to you? for sinners also love those that love them.

6:33 And if you do good to them who do good to you, what thanks are to you? for sinners also do this.

6:34 And if you lend to them of whom you hope to receive, what thanks are to you? for sinners also lend to sinners, for to receive as much.

6:35 But love ye your enemies: do good, and lend, hoping for nothing thereby: and your reward shall be great, and you shall be the sons of the Highest; for he is kind to the unthankful, and to the evil.

6:36 Be ye therefore merciful, as your Father also is merciful.

6:37 Judge not, and you shall not be judged. Condemn not, and you shall not be con-

et dimittemini.

6:38 Date, et dabitur vobis : mensuram bonam, et confertam, et coagitatam, et supereffluentem dabunt in sinum vestrum. Eadem quippe mensura, qua mensi fueritis, remetietur vobis.

6:39 Dicebat autem illis et similitudinem : Numquid potest cæcus cæcum ducere ? nonne ambo in foveam cadunt ?

6:40 Non est discipulus super magistrum : perfectus autem omnis erit, si sit sicut magister ejus.

6:41 Quid autem vides festucam in oculo fratris tui, trabem autem, quæ in oculo tuo est, non consideras ?

6:42 aut quomodo potes dicere fratri tuo : Frater, sine ejiciam festucam de oculo tuo : ipse in oculo tuo trabem non videns ? Hypocrita, ejice primum trabem de oculo tuo : et tunc perspicies ut educas festucam de oculo fratris tui.

6:43 Non est enim arbor bona, quæ facit fructus malos : neque arbor mala, faciens fructum bonum.

6:44 Unaquæque enim arbor de fructu suo cognoscitur. Neque enim de spinis colligunt ficus : neque de rubo vindemiant uvam.

6:45 Bonus homo de bono thesauro cordis sui profert bonum : et malus homo de malo thesauro profert malum. Ex abundantia enim cordis os loquitur.

6:46 Quid autem vocatis me Domine, Domine : et non facitis quæ dico ?

6:47 Omnis qui venit ad me, et audit sermones meos, et facit eos, ostendam vobis cui similis sit :

6:48 similis est homini ædificanti domum, qui fodit in altum, et posuit fundamentum super petram : inundatione autem facta, illisum est flumen domui illi, et non potuit eam movere : fundata enim erat super petram.

6:49 Qui autem audit, et non facit, similis est homini ædificanti domum suam super terram sine fundamento : in quam illisus est fluvius, et continuo cecidit : et facta est ruina domus illius magna.

7:1 Cum autem implesset omnia verba sua in aures plebis, intravit Capharnaum.

7:2 Centurionis autem cujusdam servus male

demned. Forgive, and you shall be forgiven.

6:38 Give, and it shall be given to you: good measure and pressed down and shaken together and running over shall they give into your bosom. For with the same measure that you shall mete withal, it shall be measured to you again.

6:39 And he spoke also to them a similitude: Can the blind lead the blind? do they not both fall into the ditch?

6:40 The disciple is not above his master: but every one shall be perfect, if he be as his master.

6:41 And why seest thou the mote in thy brother's eye: but the beam that is in thy own eye thou considerest not?

6:42 Or how canst thou say to thy brother: Brother, let me pull the mote out of thy eye, when thou thyself seest not the beam in thy own eye? Hypocrite, cast first the beam out of thy own eye; and then shalt thou see clearly to take out the mote from thy brother's eye.

6:43 For there is no good tree that bringeth forth evil fruit; nor an evil tree that bringeth forth good fruit.

6:44 For every tree is known by its fruit. For men do not gather figs from thorns; nor from a bramble bush do they gather the grape.

6:45 A good man out of the good treasure of his heart bringeth forth that which is good: and an evil man out of the evil treasure bringeth forth that which is evil. For out of the abundance of the heart the mouth speaketh.

6:46 And why call you me, Lord, Lord; and do not the things which I say?

6:47 Every one that cometh to me, and heareth my words, and doth them, I will shew you to whom he is like.

6:48 He is like to a man building a house, who digged deep, and laid the foundation upon a rock. And when a flood came, the stream beat vehemently upon that house, and it could not shake it; for it was founded on a rock.

6:49 But he that heareth, and doth not, is like to a man building his house upon the earth without a foundation: against which the stream beat vehemently, and immediately it fell, and the ruin of that house was great.

7:1 And when he had finished all his words in the hearing of the people, he entered into Capharnaum.

7:2 And the servant of a certain centurion, who

habens, erat moriturus : qui illi erat pretiosus.

7:3 Et cum audisset de Jesu, misit ad eum seniores Judæorum, rogans eum ut veniret et salvaret servum ejus.

7:4 At illi cum venissent ad Jesum, rogabant eum sollicite, dicentes ei : Quia dignus est ut hoc illi præstes :

7:5 diligit enim gentem nostram, et synagogam ipse ædificavit nobis.

7:6 Jesus autem ibat cum illis. Et cum jam non longe esset a domo, misit ad eum centurio amicos, dicens : Domine, noli vexari : non enim sum dignus ut sub tectum meum intres :

7:7 propter quod et meipsum non sum dignum arbitratus ut venirem ad te : sed dic verbo, et sanabitur puer meus.

7:8 Nam et ego homo sum sub potestate constitutus, habens sub me milites : et dico huic, Vade, et vadit : et alii, Veni, et venit : et servo meo, Fac hoc, et facit.

7:9 Quo audito Jesus miratus est : et conversus sequentibus se turbis, dixit : Amen dico vobis, nec in Israël tantam fidem inveni.

7:10 Et reversi, qui missi fuerant, domum, invenerunt servum, qui languerat, sanum.

7:11 Et factum est : deinceps ibat in civitatem quæ vocatur Naim : et ibant cum eo discipuli ejus et turba copiosa.

7:12 Cum autem appropinquaret portæ civitatis, ecce defunctus efferebatur filius unicus matris suæ : et hæc vidua erat : et turba civitatis multa cum illa.

7:13 Quam cum vidisset Dominus, misericordia motus super eam, dixit illi : Noli flere.

7:14 Et accessit, et tetigit loculum. (Hi autem qui portabant, steterunt.) Et ait : Adolescens, tibi dico, surge.

7:15 Et resedit qui erat mortuus, et cœpit loqui. Et dedit illum matri suæ.

7:16 Accepit autem omnes timor : et magnificabant Deum, dicentes : Quia propheta magnus surrexit in nobis : et quia Deus visitavit plebem suam.

7:17 Et exiit hic sermo in universam Judæam de eo, et in omnem circa regionem.

was dear to him, being sick, was ready to die.

7:3 And when he had heard of Jesus, he sent unto him the ancients of the Jews, desiring him to come and heal his servant.

7:4 And when they came to Jesus, they besought him earnestly, saying to him: He is worthy that thou shouldest do this for him.

7:5 For he loveth our nation; and he hath built us a synagogue.

7:6 And Jesus went with them. And when he was now not far from the house, the centurion sent his friends to him, saying: Lord, trouble not thyself; for I am not worthy that thou shouldest enter under my roof.

7:7 For which cause neither did I think myself worthy to come to thee; but say the word, and my servant shall be healed.

7:8 For I also am a man subject to authority, having under me soldiers: and I say to one, Go, and he goeth; and to another, Come, and he cometh; and to my servant, Do this, and he doth it.

7:9 Which Jesus hearing, marvelled: and turning about to the multitude that followed him, he said: Amen I say to you, I have not found so great faith, not even in Israel.

7:10 And they who were sent, being returned to the house, found the servant whole who had been sick.

7:11 And it came to pass afterwards, that he went into a city that is called Naim; and there went with him his disciples, and a great multitude.

7:12 And when he came nigh to the gate of the city, behold a dead man was carried out, the only son of his mother; and she was a widow: and a great multitude of the city was with her.

7:13 Whom when the Lord had seen, being moved with mercy towards her, he said to her: Weep not.

7:14 And he came near and touched the bier. And they that carried it, stood still. And he said: Young man, I say to thee, arise.

7:15 And he that was dead, sat up, and began to speak. And he gave him to his mother.

7:16 And there came a fear on them all: and they glorified God, saying: A great prophet is risen up among us: and, God hath visited his people.

7:17 And this rumour of him went forth throughout all Judea, and throughout all the country round about.

7:18 Et nuntiaverunt Joanni discipuli ejus de omnibus his.

7:19 Et convocavit duos de discipulis suis Joannes, et misit ad Jesum, dicens : Tu es qui venturus es, an alium exspectamus ?

7:20 Cum autem venissent ad eum viri, dixerunt : Joannes Baptista misit nos ad te dicens : Tu es qui venturus es, an alium exspectamus ?

7:21 (In ipsa autem hora multos curavit a languoribus, et plagis, et spiritibus malis, et cæcis multis donavit visum.)

7:22 Et respondens, dixit illis : Euntes renuntiate Joanni quæ audistis et vidistis : quia cæci vident, claudi ambulant, leprosi mundantur, surdi audiunt, mortui resurgunt, pauperes evangelizantur :

7:23 et beatus est quicumque non fuerit scandalizatus in me.

7:24 Et cum discessissent nuntii Joannis, cœpit de Joanne dicere ad turbas : Quid existis in desertum videre ? arundinem vento agitatam ?

7:25 Sed quid existis videre ? hominem mollibus vestibus indutum ? Ecce qui in veste pretiosa sunt et deliciis, in domibus regum sunt.

7:26 Sed quid existis videre ? prophetam ? Utique dico vobis, et plus quam prophetam :

7:27 hic est, de quo scriptum est : Ecce mitto angelum meum ante faciem tuam, qui præparabit viam tuam ante te.

7:28 Dico enim vobis : major inter natos mulierum propheta Joanne Baptista nemo est : qui autem minor est in regno Dei, major est illo.

7:29 Et omnis populus audiens et publicani, justificaverunt Deum, baptizati baptismo Joannis.

7:30 Pharisæi autem et legisperiti consilium Dei spreverunt in semetipsos, non baptizati ab eo.

7:31 Ait autem Dominus : Cui ergo similes dicam homines generationis hujus ? et cui similes sunt ?

7:32 Similes sunt pueris sedentibus in foro, et loquentibus ad invicem, et dicentibus : Cantavimus vobis tibiis, et non saltastis : lamentavimus, et non plorastis.

7:33 Venit enim Joannes Baptista, neque manducans panem, neque bibens vinum, et dicitis :

7:18 And John's disciples told him of all these things.

7:19 And John called to him two of his disciples, and sent them to Jesus, saying: Art thou he that art to come; or look we for another?

7:20 And when the men were come unto him, they said: John the Baptist hath sent us to thee, saying: Art thou he that art to come; or look we for another?

7:21 (And in that same hour, he cured many of their diseases, and hurts, and evil spirits: and to many that were blind he gave sight.)

7:22 And answering, he said to them: Go and relate to John what you have heard and seen: the blind see, the lame walk, the lepers are made clean, the deaf hear, the dead rise again, to the poor the gospel is preached:

7:23 And blessed is he whosoever shall not be scandalized in me.

7:24 And when the messengers of John were departed, he began to speak to the multitudes concerning John. What went ye out into the desert to see? a reed shaken with the wind?

7:25 But what went you out to see? a man clothed in soft garments? Behold they that are in costly apparel and live delicately, are in the houses of kings.

7:26 But what went you out to see? a prophet? Yea, I say to you, and more than a prophet.

7:27 This is he of whom it is written: Behold I send my angel before thy face, who shall prepare thy way before thee.

7:28 For I say to you: Amongst those that are born of women, there is not a greater prophet that John the Baptist. But he that is the lesser in the kingdom of God, is greater than he.

7:29 And all the people hearing, and the publicans, justified God, being baptized with John's baptism.

7:30 But the Pharisees and the lawyers despised the counsel of God against themselves, being not baptized by him.

7:31 And the Lord said: Whereunto then shall I liken the men of this generation? and to what are they like?

7:32 They are like to children sitting in the marketplace, and speaking one to another, and saying: We have piped to you, and you have not danced: we have mourned, and you have not wept.

7:33 For John the Baptist came neither eating bread nor drinking wine; and you say: He hath

Dæmonium habet.

7:34 Venit Filius hominis manducans, et bibens, et dicitis : Ecce homo devorator, et bibens vinum, amicus publicanorum et peccatorum.

7:35 Et justificata est sapientia ab omnibus filiis suis.

7:36 Rogabat autem illum quidam de pharisæis ut manducaret cum illo. Et ingressus domum pharisæi discubuit.

7:37 Et ecce mulier, quæ erat in civitate peccatrix, ut cognovit quod accubuisset in domo pharisæi, attulit alabastrum unguenti :

7:38 et stans retro secus pedes ejus, lacrimis cœpit rigare pedes ejus, et capillis capitis sui tergebat, et osculabatur pedes ejus, et unguento ungebat.

7:39 Videns autem pharisæus, qui vocaverat eum, ait intra se dicens : Hic si esset propheta, sciret utique quæ et qualis est mulier, quæ tangit eum : quia peccatrix est.

7:40 Et respondens Jesus, dixit ad illum : Simon, habeo tibi aliquid dicere. At ille ait : Magister, dic.

7:41 Duo debitores erant cuidam fœneratori : unus debebat denarios quingentos, et alius quinquaginta.

7:42 Non habentibus illis unde redderent, donavit utrisque. Quis ergo eum plus diligit ?

7:43 Respondens Simon dixit : Æstimo quia is cui plus donavit. At ille dixit ei : Recte judicasti.

7:44 Et conversus ad mulierem, dixit Simoni : Vides hanc mulierem ? Intravi in domum tuam, aquam pedibus meis non dedisti : hæc autem lacrimis rigavit pedes meos, et capillis suis tersit.

7:45 Osculum mihi non dedisti : hæc autem ex quo intravit, non cessavit osculari pedes meos.

7:46 Oleo caput meum non unxisti : hæc autem unguento unxit pedes meos.

7:47 Propter quod dico tibi : remittuntur ei peccata multa, quoniam dilexit multum. Cui autem minus dimittitur, minus diligit.

7:48 Dixit autem ad illam : Remittuntur tibi peccata.

7:49 Et cœperunt qui simul accumbebant, dicere intra se : Quis est hic qui etiam peccata dimittit ?

a devil.

7:34 The Son of man is come eating and drinking: and you say: Behold a man that is a glutton and a drinker of wine, a friend of publicans and sinners.

7:35 And wisdom is justified by all her children.

7:36 And one of the Pharisees desired him to eat with him. And he went into the house of the Pharisee, and sat down to meat.

7:37 And behold a woman that was in the city, a sinner, when she knew that he sat at meat in the Pharisee's house, brought an alabaster box of ointment;

7:38 And standing behind at his feet, she began to wash his feet, with tears, and wiped them with the hairs of her head, and kissed his feet, and anointed them with the ointment.

7:39 And the Pharisee, who had invited him, seeing it, spoke within himself, saying: This man, if he were a prophet, would know surely who and what manner of woman this is that toucheth him, that she is a sinner.

7:40 And Jesus answering, said to him: Simon, I have somewhat to say to thee. But he said: Master, say it.

7:41 A certain creditor had two debtors, the one who owed five hundred pence, and the other fifty.

7:42 And whereas they had not wherewith to pay, he forgave them both. Which therefore of the two loveth him most?

7:43 Simon answering, said: I suppose that he to whom he forgave most. And he said to him: Thou hast judged rightly.

7:44 And turning to the woman, he said unto Simon: Dost thou see this woman? I entered into thy house, thou gavest me no water for my feet; but she with tears hath washed my feet, and with her hairs hath wiped them.

7:45 Thou gavest me no kiss; but she, since she came in, hath not ceased to kiss my feet.

7:46 My head with oil thou didst not anoint; but she with ointment hath anointed my feet.

7:47 Wherefore I say to thee: Many sins are forgiven her, because she hath loved much. But to whom less is forgiven, he loveth less.

7:48 And he said to her: Thy sins are forgiven thee.

7:49 And they that sat at meat with him began to say within themselves: Who is this that forgiveth sins also?

7:50 Dixit autem ad mulierem : Fides tua te salvam fecit : vade in pace.

8:1 Et factum est deinceps, et ipse iter faciebat per civitates, et castella prædicans, et evangelizans regnum Dei : et duodecim cum illo,

8:2 et mulieres aliquæ, quæ erant curatæ a spiritibus malignis et infirmantibus : Maria, quæ vocatur Magdalene, de qua septem dæmonia exierant,

8:3 et Joanna uxor Chusæ procuratoris Herodis, et Susanna, et aliæ multæ, quæ ministrabant ei de facultatibus suis.

8:4 Cum autem turba plurima convenirent, et de civitatibus properarent ad eum, dixit per similitudinem :

8:5 Exiit qui seminat, seminare semen suum. Et dum seminat, aliud cecidit secus viam, et conculcatum est, et volucres cæli comederunt illud.

8:6 Et aliud cecidit supra petram : et natum aruit, quia non habebat humorem.

8:7 Et aliud cecidit inter spinas, et simul exortæ spinæ suffocaverunt illud.

8:8 Et aliud cecidit in terram bonam : et ortum fecit fructum centuplum. Hæc dicens clamabat : Qui habet aures audiendi, audiat.

8:9 Interrogabant autem eum discipuli ejus, quæ esset hæc parabola.

8:10 Quibus ipse dixit : Vobis datum est nosse mysterium regni Dei, ceteris autem in parabolis : ut videntes non videant, et audientes non intelligant.

8:11 Est autem hæc parabola : Semen est verbum Dei.

8:12 Qui autem secus viam, hi sunt qui audiunt : deinde venit diabolus, et tollit verbum de corde eorum, ne credentes salvi fiant.

8:13 Nam qui supra petram, qui cum audierint, cum gaudio suscipiunt verbum : et hi radices non habent : qui ad tempus credunt, et in tempore tentationis recedunt.

8:14 Quod autem in spinas cecidit : hi sunt qui audierunt, et a sollicitudinibus, et divitiis, et voluptatibus vitæ euntes, suffocantur, et non referunt fructum.

8:15 Quod autem in bonam terram : hi sunt qui in corde bono et optimo audientes verbum ret-

7:50 And he said to the woman: Thy faith hath made thee safe, go in peace.

8:1 And it came to pass afterwards, that he travelled through the cities and towns, preaching and evangelizing the kingdom of God; and the twelve with him:

8:2 And certain women who had been healed of evil spirits and infirmities; Mary who is called Magdalen, out of whom seven devils were gone forth,

8:3 And Joanna the wife of Chusa, Herod's steward, and Susanna, and many others who ministered unto him of their substance.

8:4 And when a very great multitude was gathered together, and hastened out of the cities unto him, he spoke by a similitude.

8:5 The sower went out to sow his seed. And as he sowed, some fell by the way side, and it was trodden down, and the fowls of the air devoured it.

8:6 And other some fell upon a rock: and as soon as it was sprung up, it withered away, because it had no moisture.

8:7 And other some fell among thorns, and the thorns growing up with it, choked it.

8:8 And other some fell upon good ground; and being sprung up, yielded fruit a hundredfold. Saying these things, he cried out: He that hath ears to hear, let him hear.

8:9 And his disciples asked him what this parable might be.

8:10 To whom he said: To you it is given to know the mystery of the kingdom of God; but to the rest in parables, that seeing they may not see, and hearing may not understand.

8:11 Now the parable is this: The seed is the word of God.

8:12 And they by the way side are they that hear; then the devil cometh, and taketh the word out of their heart, lest believing they should be saved.

8:13 Now they upon the rock, are they who when they hear, receive the word with joy: and these have no roots; for they believe for a while, and in time of temptation, they fall away.

8:14 And that which fell among thorns, are they who have heard, and going their way, are choked with the cares and riches and pleasures of this life, and yield no fruit.

8:15 But that on the good ground, are they who in a good and perfect heart, hearing the word,

inent, et fructum afferunt in patientia.

8:16 Nemo autem lucernam accendens, operit eam vase, aut subtus lectum ponit : sed supra candelabrum ponit, ut intrantes videant lumen.

8:17 Non est enim occultum, quod non manifestetur : nec absconditum, quod non cognoscatur, et in palam veniat.

8:18 Videte ergo quomodo audiatis ? Qui enim habet, dabitur illi : et quicumque non habet, etiam quod putat se habere, auferetur ab illo.

8:19 Venerunt autem ad illum mater et fratres ejus, et non poterant adire eum præ turba.

8:20 Et nuntiatum est illi : Mater tua et fratres tui stant foris, volentes te videre.

8:21 Qui respondens, dixit ad eos : Mater mea et fratres mei hi sunt, qui verbum Dei audiunt et faciunt.

8:22 Factum est autem in una dierum : et ipse ascendit in naviculam, et discipuli ejus, et ait ad illos : Transfretemus trans stagnum. Et ascenderunt.

8:23 Et navigantibus illis, obdormivit, et descendit procella venti in stagnum, et complebantur, et periclitabantur.

8:24 Accedentes autem suscitaverunt eum, dicentes : Præceptor, perimus. At ille surgens, increpavit ventum, et tempestatem aquæ, et cessavit : et facta est tranquillitas.

8:25 Dixit autem illis : Ubi est fides vestra ? Qui timentes, mirati sunt ad invicem, dicentes : Quis putas hic est, quia et ventis, et mari imperat, et obediunt ei ?

8:26 Et navigaverunt ad regionem Gerasenorum, quæ est contra Galilæam.

8:27 Et cum egressus esset ad terram, occurrit illi vir quidam, qui habebat dæmonium jam temporibus multis, et vestimento non induebatur, neque in domo manebat, sed in monumentis.

8:28 Is, ut vidit Jesum, procidit ante illum : et exclamans voce magna, dixit : Quid mihi et tibi est, Jesu Fili Dei Altissimi ? obsecro te, ne me torqueas.

8:29 Præcipiebat enim spiritui immundo ut exiret ab homine. Multis enim temporibus arripiebat illum, et vinciebatur catenis, et compedibus custoditus. Et ruptis vinculis age-

keep it, and bring forth fruit in patience.

8:16 Now no man lighting a candle covereth it with a vessel, or putteth it under a bed; but setteth it upon a candlestick, that they who come in may see the light.

8:17 For there is not any thing secret that shall not be made manifest, nor hidden, that shall not be known and come abroad.

8:18 Take heed therefore how you hear. For whosoever hath, to him shall be given: and whosoever hath not, that also which he thinketh he hath, shall be taken away from him.

8:19 And his mother and brethren came unto him; and they could not come at him for the crowd.

8:20 And it was told him: Thy mother and thy brethren stand without, desiring to see thee.

8:21 Who answering, said to them: My mother and my brethren are they who hear the word of God, and do it.

8:22 And it came to pass on a certain day that he went into a little ship with his disciples, and he said to them: Let us go over to the other side of the lake. And they launched forth.

8:23 And when they were sailing, he slept; and there came down a storm of wind upon the lake, and they were filled, and were in danger.

8:24 And they came and awaked him, saying: Master, we perish. But he arising, rebuked the wind and the rage of the water; and it ceased, and there was a calm.

8:25 And he said to them: Where is your faith? Who being afraid, wondered, saying one to another: Who is this, (think you), that he commandeth both the winds and the sea, and they obey him?

8:26 And they sailed to the country of the Gerasens, which is over against Galilee.

8:27 And when he was come forth to the land, there met him a certain man who had a devil now a very long time, and he wore no clothes, neither did he abide in a house, but in the sepulchres.

8:28 And when he saw Jesus, he fell down before him; and crying out with a loud voice, he said: What have I to do with thee, Jesus, Son of the most high God? I beseech thee, do not torment me.

8:29 For he commanded the unclean spirit to go out of the man. For many times it seized him, and he was bound with chains, and kept in fetters; and breaking the bonds, he was driven by

batur a dæmonio in deserta.

8:30 Interrogavit autem illum Jesus, dicens : Quod tibi nomen est ? At ille dixit : Legio : quia intraverant dæmonia multa in eum.

8:31 Et rogabant illum ne imperaret illis ut in abyssum irent.

8:32 Erat autem ibi grex porcorum multorum pascentium in monte : et rogabant eum, ut permitteret eis in illos ingredi. Et permisit illis.

8:33 Exierunt ergo dæmonia ab homine, et intraverunt in porcos : et impetu abiit grex per præceps in stagnum, et suffocatus est.

8:34 Quod ut viderunt factum qui pascebant, fugerunt, et nuntiaverunt in civitatem et in villas.

8:35 Exierunt autem videre quod factum est, et venerunt ad Jesum, et invenerunt hominem sedentem, a quo dæmonia exierant, vestitum ac sana mente, ad pedes ejus, et timuerunt.

8:36 Nuntiaverunt autem illis et qui viderant, quomodo sanus factus esset a legione :

8:37 et rogaverunt illum omnis multitudo regionis Gerasenorum ut discederet ab ipsis : quia magno timore tenebantur. Ipse autem ascendens navim, reversus est.

8:38 Et rogabat illum vir, a quo dæmonia exierant, ut cum eo esset. Dimisit autem eum Jesus, dicens :

8:39 Redi in domum tuam, et narra quanta tibi fecit Deus. Et abiit per universam civitatem, prædicans quanta illi fecisset Jesus.

8:40 Factum est autem cum rediisset Jesus, excepit illum turba : erunt enim omnes exspectantes eum.

8:41 Et ecce venit vir, cui nomen Jairus, et ipse princeps synagogæ erat : et cecidit ad pedes Jesu, rogans eum ut intraret in domum ejus,

8:42 quia unica filia erat ei fere annorum duodecim, et hæc moriebatur. Et contigit, dum iret, a turba comprimebatur.

8:43 Et mulier quædam erat in fluxu sanguinis ab annis duodecim, quæ in medicos erogaverat omnem substantiam suam, nec ab ullo potuit curari :

8:44 accessit retro, et tetigit fimbriam vestimenti

the devil into the deserts.

8:30 And Jesus asked him, saying: What is thy name? But he said: Legion; because many devils were entered into him.

8:31 And they besought him that he would not command them to go into the abyss.

8:32 And there was there a herd of many swine feeding on the mountain; and they besought him that he would suffer them to enter into them. And he suffered them.

8:33 The devils therefore went out of the man, and entered into the swine; and the herd ran violently down a steep place into the lake, and were stifled.

8:34 Which when they that fed them saw done, they fled away, and told it in the city and in the villages.

8:35 And they went out to see what was done; and they came to Jesus, and found the man, out of whom the devils were departed, sitting at his feet, clothed, and in his right mind; and they were afraid.

8:36 And they also that had seen, told them how he had been healed from the legion.

8:37 And all the multitude of the country of the Gerasens besought him to depart from them; for they were taken with great fear. And he, going up into the ship, returned back again.

8:38 Now the man, out of whom the devils were departed, besought him that he might be with him. But Jesus sent him away, saying:

8:39 Return to thy house, and tell how great things God hath done to thee. And he went through the whole city, publishing how great things Jesus had done to him.

8:40 And it came to pass, that when Jesus was returned, the multitude received him: for they were all waiting for him.

8:41 And behold there came a man whose name was Jairus, and he was a ruler of the synagogue: and he fell down at the feet of Jesus, beseeching him that he would come into his house:

8:42 For he had an only daughter, almost twelve years old, and she was dying. And it happened as he went, that he was thronged by the multitudes.

8:43 And there was a certain woman having an issue of blood twelve years, who had bestowed all her substance on physicians, and could not be healed by any.

8:44 She came behind him, and touched the hem

ejus : et confestim stetit fluxus sanguinis ejus.

8:45 Et ait Jesus : Quis est, qui me tetigit ? Negantibus autem omnibus, dixit Petrus, et qui cum illo erant : Præceptor, turbæ te comprimunt, et affligunt, et dicis : Quis me tetigit ?

8:46 Et dicit Jesus : Tetigit me aliquis : nam ego novi virtutem de me exiisse.

8:47 Videns autem mulier, quia non latuit, tremens venit, et procidit ante pedes ejus : et ob quam causam tetigerit eum, indicavit coram omni populo : et quemadmodum confestim sanata sit.

8:48 At ipse dixit ei : Filia, fides tua salvam te fecit : vade in pace.

8:49 Adhuc illo loquente, venit quidam ad principem synagogæ, dicens ei : Quia mortua est filia tua, noli vexare illum.

8:50 Jesus autem, audito hoc verbo, respondit patri puellæ : Noli timere, crede tantum, et salva erit.

8:51 Et cum venisset domum, non permisit intrare secum quemquam, nisi Petrum, et Jacobum, et Joannem, et patrem, et matrem puellæ.

8:52 Flebant autem omnes, et plangebant illam. At ille dixit : Nolite flere : non est mortua puella, sed dormit.

8:53 Et deridebant eum, scientes quod mortua esset.

8:54 Ipse autem tenens manum ejus clamavit, dicens : Puella, surge.

8:55 Et reversus est spiritus ejus, et surrexit continuo. Et jussit illi dari manducare.

8:56 Et stupuerunt parentes ejus, quibus præcepit ne alicui dicerent quod factum erat.

9:1 Convocatis autem duodecim Apostolis, dedit illis virtutem et potestatem super omnia dæmonia, et ut languores curarent.

9:2 Et misit illos prædicare regnum Dei, et sanare infirmos.

9:3 Et ait ad illos : Nihil tuleritis in via, neque virgam, neque peram, neque panem, neque pecuniam, neque duas tunicas habeatis.

9:4 Et in quamcumque domum intraveritis, ibi manete, et inde ne exeatis.

9:5 Et quicumque non receperint vos : exeuntes de civitate illa, etiam pulverem pedum vestrorum excutite in testimonium supra illos.

9:6 Egressi autem circuibant per castella evangelizantes, et curantes ubique.

of his garment; and immediately the issue of her blood stopped.

8:45 And Jesus said: Who is it that touched me? And all denying, Peter and they that were with him said: Master, the multitudes throng and press thee, and dost thou say, Who touched me?

8:46 And Jesus said: Somebody hath touched me; for I know that virtue is gone out from me.

8:47 And the woman seeing that she was not hid, came trembling, and fell down before his feet, and declared before all the people for what cause she had touched him, and how she was immediately healed.

8:48 But he said to her: Daughter, thy faith hath made thee whole; go thy way in peace.

8:49 As he was yet speaking, there cometh one to the ruler of the synagogue, saying to him: Thy daughter is dead, trouble him not.

8:50 And Jesus hearing this word, answered the father of the maid: Fear not; believe only, and she shall be safe.

8:51 And when he was come to the house, he suffered not any man to go in with him, but Peter and James and John, and the father and mother of the maiden.

8:52 And all wept and mourned for her. But he said: Weep not; the maid is not dead, but sleepeth.

8:53 And they laughed him to scorn, knowing that she was dead.

8:54 But he taking her by the hand, cried out, saying: Maid, arise.

8:55 And her spirit returned, and she arose immediately. And he bid them give her to eat.

8:56 And her parents were astonished, whom he charged to tell no man what was done.

9:1 Then calling together the twelve apostles, he gave them power and authority over all devils, and to cure diseases.

9:2 And he sent them to preach the kingdom of God, and to heal the sick.

9:3 And he said to them: Take nothing for your journey; neither staff, nor scrip, nor bread, nor money; neither have two coats.

9:4 And whatsoever house you shall enter into, abide there, and depart not from thence.

9:5 And whosoever will not receive you, when ye go out of that city, shake off even the dust of your feet, for a testimony against them.

9:6 And going out, they went about through the towns, preaching the gospel, and healing every

9:7 Audivit autem Herodes tetrarcha omnia quæ fiebant ab eo, et hæsitabat eo quod diceretur

9:8 a quibusdam : Quia Joannes surrexit a mortuis : a quibusdam vero : Quia Elias apparuit : ab aliis autem : Quia propheta unus de antiquis surrexit.
9:9 Et ait Herodes : Joannem ego decollavi : quis est autem iste, de quo ego talia audio ? Et quærebat videre eum.
9:10 Et reversi Apostoli, narraverunt illi quæcumque fecerunt : et assumptis illis secessit seorsum in locum desertum, qui est Bethsaidæ.
9:11 Quod cum cognovissent turbæ, secutæ sunt illum : et excepit eos, et loquebatur illis de regno Dei, et eos, qui cura indigebant, sanabat.

9:12 Dies autem cœperat declinare, et accedentes duodecim dixerunt illi : Dimitte turbas, ut euntes in castella villasque quæ circa sunt, divertant, et inveniant escas : quia hic in loco deserto sumus.
9:13 Ait autem ad illos : Vos date illis manducare. At illi dixerunt : Non sunt nobis plus quam quinque panes et duo pisces : nisi forte nos eamus, et emamus in omnem hanc turbam escas.
9:14 Erant autem fere viri quinque millia. Ait autem ad discipulos suos : Facite illos discumbere per convivia quinquagenos.
9:15 Et ita fecerunt : et discumbere fecerunt omnes.
9:16 Acceptis autem quinque panibus et duobus piscibus, respexit in cælum, et benedixit illis : et fregit, et distribuit discipulis suis, ut ponerent ante turbas.
9:17 Et manducaverunt omnes, et saturati sunt. Et sublatum est quod superfuit illis, fragmentorum cophini duodecim.
9:18 Et factum est cum solus esset orans, erant cum illo et discipuli : et interrogavit illos, dicens : Quem me dicunt esse turbæ ?

9:19 At illi responderunt, et dixerunt : Joannem Baptistam, alii autem Eliam, alii vero quia unus propheta de prioribus surrexit.
9:20 Dixit autem illis : Vos autem quem me esse dicitis ? Respondens Simon Petrus, dixit : Christum Dei.
9:21 At ille increpans illos, præcepit ne cui dic-

where.
9:7 Now Herod, the tetrarch, heard of all things that were done by him; and he was in a doubt, because it was said
9:8 By some, that John was risen from the dead: but by other some, that Elias had appeared; and by others, that one of the old prophets was risen again.
9:9 And Herod said: John I have beheaded; but who is this of whom I hear such things? And he sought to see him.
9:10 And the apostles, when they were returned, told him all they had done. And taking them, he went aside into a desert place, apart, which belongeth to Bethsaida.
9:11 Which when the people knew, they followed him; and he received them, and spoke to them of the kingdom of God, and healed them who had need of healing.
9:12 Now the day began to decline. And the twelve came and said to him: Send away the multitude, that going into the towns and villages round about, they may lodge and get victuals; for we are here in a desert place.
9:13 But he said to them: Give you them to eat. And they said: We have no more than five loaves and two fishes; unless perhaps we should go and buy food for all this multitude.
9:14 Now there were about five thousand men. And he said to his disciples: Make them sit down by fifties in a company.
9:15 And they did so; and made them all sit down.
9:16 And taking the five loaves and the two fishes, he looked up to heaven, and blessed them; and he broke, and distributed to his disciples, to set before the multitude.
9:17 And they did all eat, and were filled. And there were taken up of fragments that remained to them, twelve baskets.
9:18 And it came to pass, as he was alone praying, his disciples also were with him: and he asked them, saying: Whom do the people say that I am?
9:19 But they answered, and said: John the Baptist; but some say Elias; and others say that one of the former prophets is risen again.
9:20 And he said to them: But whom do you say that I am? Simon Peter answering, said: The Christ of God.
9:21 But he strictly charging them, commanded

erent hoc,

9:22 dicens : Quia oportet Filium hominis multa pati, et reprobari a senioribus, et principibus sacerdotum, et scribis, et occidi, et tertia die resurgere.

9:23 Dicebat autem ad omnes : Si quis vult post me venire, abneget semetipsum, et tollat crucem suam quotidie, et sequatur me.

9:24 Qui enim voluerit animam suam salvam facere, perdet illam : nam qui perdiderit animam suam propter me, salvam faciet illam.

9:25 Quid enim proficit homo, si lucretur universum mundum, se autem ipsum perdat, et detrimentum sui faciat ?

9:26 Nam qui me erubuerit, et meos sermones : hunc Filius hominis erubescet cum venerit in majestate sua, et Patris, et sanctorum angelorum.

9:27 Dico autem vobis vere : sunt aliqui hic stantes, qui non gustabunt mortem donec videant regnum Dei.

9:28 Factum est autem post hæc verba fere dies octo, et assumpsit Petrum, et Jacobum, et Joannem, et ascendit in montem ut oraret.

9:29 Et facta est, dum oraret, species vultus ejus altera : et vestitus ejus albus et refulgens.

9:30 Et ecce duo viri loquebantur cum illo. Erant autem Moyses et Elias,

9:31 visi in majestate : et dicebant excessum ejus, quem completurus erat in Jerusalem.

9:32 Petrus vero, et qui cum illo erant, gravati erant somno. Et evigilantes viderunt majestatem ejus, et duos viros qui stabant cum illo.

9:33 Et factum est cum discederent ab illo, ait Petrus ad Jesum : Præceptor, bonum est nos hic esse : et faciamus tria tabernacula, unum tibi, et unum Moysi, et unum Eliæ : nesciens quid diceret.

9:34 Hæc autem illo loquente, facta est nubes, et obumbravit eos : et timuerunt, intrantibus illis in nubem.

9:35 Et vox facta est de nube, dicens : Hic est Filius meus dilectus, ipsum audite.

9:36 Et dum fieret vox, inventus est Jesus solus. Et ipsi tacuerunt, et nemini dixerunt in illis diebus quidquam ex his quæ viderant.

9:37 Factum est autem in sequenti die, descendentibus illis de monte, occurrit illis turba

they should tell this to no man.

9:22 Saying: The Son of man must suffer many things, and be rejected by the ancients and chief priests and scribes, and be killed, and the third day rise again.

9:23 And he said to all: If any man will come after me, let him deny himself, and take up his cross daily, and follow me.

9:24 For whosoever will save his life, shall lose it; for he that shall lose his life for my sake, shall save it.

9:25 For what is a man advantaged, if he gain the whole world, and lose himself, and cast away himself?

9:26 For he that shall be ashamed of me and of my words, of him the Son of man shall be ashamed, when he shall come in his majesty, and that of his Father, and of the holy angels.

9:27 But I tell you of a truth: There are some standing here that shall not taste death, till they see the kingdom of God.

9:28 And it came to pass about eight days after these words, that he took Peter, and James, and John, and went up into a mountain to pray.

9:29 And whilst he prayed, the shape of his countenance was altered, and his raiment became white and glittering.

9:30 And behold two men were talking with him. And they were Moses and Elias,

9:31 Appearing in majesty. And they spoke of his decease that he should accomplish in Jerusalem.

9:32 But Peter and they that were with him were heavy with sleep. And waking, they saw his glory, and the two men that stood with him.

9:33 And it came to pass, that as they were departing from him, Peter saith to Jesus: Master, it is good for us to be here; and let us make three tabernacles, one for thee, and one for Moses, and one for Elias; not knowing what he said.

9:34 And as he spoke these things, there came a cloud, and overshadowed them; and they were afraid, when they entered into the cloud.

9:35 And a voice came out of the cloud, saying: This is my beloved Son; hear him.

9:36 And whilst the voice was uttered, Jesus was found alone. And they held their peace, and told no man in those days any of these things which they had seen.

9:37 And it came to pass the day following, when they came down from the mountain, there met

multa.

9:38 Et ecce vir de turba exclamavit, dicens : Magister, obsecro te, respice in filium meum quia unicus est mihi :

9:39 et ecce spiritus apprehendit eum, et subito clamat, et elidit, et dissipat eum cum spuma, et vix discedit dilanians eum :

9:40 et rogavi discipulos tuos ut ejicerent illum, et non potuerunt.

9:41 Respondens autem Jesus, dixit : O generatio infidelis, et perversa, usquequo ero apud vos, et patiar vos ? adduc huc filium tuum.

9:42 Et cum accederet, elisit illum dæmonium, et dissipavit.

9:43 Et increpavit Jesus spiritum immundum, et sanavit puerum, et reddidit illum patri ejus.

9:44 Stupebant autem omnes in magnitudine Dei : omnibusque mirantibus in omnibus quæ faciebat, dixit ad discipulos suos : Ponite vos in cordibus vestris sermones istos : Filius enim hominis futurum est ut tradatur in manus hominum.

9:45 At illi ignorabant verbum istud, et erat velatum ante eos ut non sentirent illud : et timebant eum interrogare de hoc verbo.

9:46 Intravit autem cogitatio in eos quis eorum major esset.

9:47 At Jesus videns cogitationes cordis illorum, apprehendit puerum, et statuit illum secus se,

9:48 et ait illis : Quicumque susceperit puerum istum in nomine meo, me recipit : et quicumque me receperit, recipit eum qui me misit. Nam qui minor est inter vos omnes, hic major est.

9:49 Respondens autem Joannes dixit : Præceptor, vidimus quemdam in nomine tuo ejicientem dæmonia, et prohibuimus eum : quia non sequitur nobiscum.

9:50 Et ait ad illum Jesus : Nolite prohibere : qui enim non est adversum vos, pro vobis est.

9:51 Factum est autem dum complerentur dies assumptionis ejus, et ipse faciem suam firmavit ut iret in Jerusalem.

9:52 Et misit nuntios ante conspectum suum : et euntes intraverunt in civitatem Samaritanorum ut parerent illi.

9:53 Et non receperunt eum, quia facies ejus erat euntis in Jerusalem.

9:54 Cum vidissent autem discipuli ejus Jacobus et Joannes, dixerunt : Domine, vis dicimus ut

him a great multitude.

9:38 And behold a man among the crowd cried out, saying: Master, I beseech thee, look upon my son, because he is my only one.

9:39 And lo, a spirit seizeth him, and he suddenly crieth out, and he throweth him down and teareth him, so that he foameth; and bruising him, he hardly departeth from him.

9:40 And I desired thy disciples to cast him out, and they could not.

9:41 And Jesus answering, said: O faithless and perverse generation, how long shall I be with you, and suffer you? Bring hither thy son.

9:42 And as he was coming to him, the devil threw him down, and tore him.

9:43 And Jesus rebuked the unclean spirit, and cured the boy, and restored him to his father.

9:44 And all were astonished at the mighty power of God. But while all wondered at all the things he did, he said to his disciples: Lay you up in your hearts these words, for it shall come to pass, that the Son of man shall be delivered into the hands of men.

9:45 But they understood not this word; and it was hid from them, so that they perceived it not. And they were afraid to ask him concerning this word.

9:46 And there entered a thought into them, which of them should be greater.

9:47 But Jesus seeing the thoughts of their heart, took a child and set him by him,

9:48 And said to them: Whosoever shall receive this child in my name, receiveth me; and whosoever shall receive me, receiveth him that sent me. For he that is the lesser among you all, he is the greater.

9:49 And John, answering, said: Master, we saw a certain man casting out devils in thy name, and we forbade him, because he followeth not with us.

9:50 And Jesus said to him: Forbid him not; for he that is not against you, is for you.

9:51 And it came to pass, when the days of his assumption were accomplishing, that he steadfastly set his face to go to Jerusalem.

9:52 And he sent messengers before his face; and going, they entered into a city of the Samaritans, to prepare for him.

9:53 And they received him not, because his face was of one going to Jerusalem.

9:54 And when his disciples James and John had seen this, they said: Lord, wilt thou that we

ignis descendat de cælo, et consumat illos ?

9:55 Et conversus increpavit illos, dicens : Nescitis cujus spiritus estis.

9:56 Filius hominis non venit animas perdere, sed salvare. Et abierunt in aliud castellum.

9:57 Factum est autem : ambulantibus illis in via, dixit quidam ad illum : Sequar te quocumque ieris.

9:58 Dixit illi Jesus : Vulpes foveas habent, et volucres cæli nidos : Filius autem hominis non habet ubi caput reclinet.

9:59 Ait autem ad alterum : Sequere me : ille autem dixit : Domine, permitte mihi primum ire, et sepelire patrem meum.

9:60 Dixitque ei Jesus : Sine ut mortui sepeliant mortuos suos : tu autem vade, et annuntia regnum Dei.

9:61 Et ait alter : Sequar te Domine, sed permitte mihi primum renuntiare his quæ domi sunt.

9:62 Ait ad illum Jesus : Nemo mittens manum suam ad aratrum, et respiciens retro, aptus est regno Dei.

10:1 Post hæc autem designavit Dominus et alios septuaginta duos : et misit illos binos ante faciem suam in omnem civitatem et locum, quo erat ipse venturus.

10:2 Et dicebat illis : Messis quidem multa, operarii autem pauci. Rogate ergo dominum messis ut mittat operarios in messem suam.

10:3 Ite : ecce ego mitto vos sicut agnos inter lupos.

10:4 Nolite portare sacculum, neque peram, neque calceamenta, et neminem per viam salutaveritis.

10:5 In quamcumque domum intraveritis, primum dicite : Pax huic domui :

10:6 et si ibi fuerit filius pacis, requiescet super illum pax vestra : sin autem, ad vos revertetur.

10:7 In eadem autem domo manete, edentes et bibentes quæ apud illos sunt : dignus est enim operarius mercede sua. Nolite transire de domo in domum.

10:8 Et in quamcumque civitatem intraveritis, et susceperint vos, manducate quæ apponuntur vobis :

10:9 et curate infirmos, qui in illa sunt, et dicite illis : Appropinquavit in vos regnum Dei.

command fire to come down from heaven, and consume them?

9:55 And turning, he rebuked them, saying: You know not of what spirit you are.

9:56 The Son of man came not to destroy souls, but to save. And they went into another town.

9:57 And it came to pass, as they walked in the way, that a certain man said to him: I will follow thee withersoever thou goest.

9:58 Jesus said to him: The foxes have holes, and the birds of the air nests; but the Son of man hath not where to lay his head.

9:59 But he said to another: Follow me. And he said: Lord, suffer me first to go, and to bury my father.

9:60 And Jesus said to him: Let the dead bury their dead: but go thou, and preach the kingdom of God.

9:61 And another said: I will follow thee, Lord; but let me first take my leave of them that are at my house.

9:62 Jesus said to him: No man putting his hand to the plough, and looking back, is fit for the kingdom of God.

10:1 And after these things the Lord appointed also other seventy-two: and he sent them two and two before his face into every city and place whither he himself was to come.

10:2 And he said to them: The harvest indeed is great, but the labourers are few. Pray ye therefore the Lord of the harvest, that he send labourers into his harvest.

10:3 Go: Behold I send you as lambs among wolves.

10:4 Carry neither purse, nor scrip, nor shoes; and salute no man by the way.

10:5 Into whatsoever house you enter, first say: Peace be to this house.

10:6 And if the son of peace be there, your peace shall rest upon him; but if not, it shall return to you.

10:7 And in the same house, remain, eating and drinking such things as they have: for the labourer is worthy of his hire. Remove not from house to house.

10:8 And into what city soever you enter, and they receive you, eat such things as are set before you.

10:9 And heal the sick that are therein, and say to them: The kingdom of God is come nigh unto you.

10:10 In quamcumque autem civitatem intraveritis, et non susceperint vos, exeuntes in plateas ejus, dicite :

10:11 Etiam pulverem, qui adhæsit nobis de civitate vestra, extergimus in vos : tamen hoc scitote, quia appropinquavit regnum Dei.

10:12 Dico vobis, quia Sodomis in die illa remissius erit, quam illi civitati.

10:13 Væ tibi Corozain ! væ tibi Bethsaida ! quia si in Tyro et Sidone factæ fuissent virtutes quæ factæ sunt in vobis, olim in cilicio et cinere sedentes pœniterent.

10:14 Verumtamen Tyro et Sidoni remissius erit in judicio, quam vobis.

10:15 Et tu Capharnaum, usque ad cælum exaltata, usque ad infernum demergeris.

10:16 Qui vos audit, me audit : et qui vos spernit, me spernit. Qui autem me spernit, spernit eum qui misit me.

10:17 Reversi sunt autem septuaginta duo cum gaudio, dicentes : Domine, etiam dæmonia subjiciuntur nobis in nomine tuo.

10:18 Et ait illis : Videbam Satanam sicut fulgor de cælo cadentem.

10:19 Ecce dedi vobis potestatem calcandi supra serpentes, et scorpiones, et super omnem virtutem inimici : et nihil vobis nocebit.

10:20 Verumtamen in hoc nolite gaudere quia spiritus vobis subjiciuntur : gaudete autem, quod nomina vestra scripta sunt in cælis.

10:21 In ipsa hora exsultavit Spiritu Sancto, et dixit : Confiteor tibi Pater, Domine cæli et terræ, quod abscondisti hæc a sapientibus et prudentibus, et revelasti ea parvulis. Etiam Pater : quoniam sic placuit ante te.

10:22 Omnia mihi tradita sunt a Patre meo. Et nemo scit quis sit Filius, nisi Pater : et quis sit Pater, nisi Filius, et cui voluerit Filius revelare.

10:23 Et conversus ad discipulos suos, dixit : Beati oculi qui vident quæ vos videtis.

10:24 Dico enim vobis quod multi prophetæ et reges voluerunt videre quæ vos videtis, et non viderunt : et audire quæ auditis, et non audierunt.

10:25 Et ecce quidam legisperitus surrexit tentans illum, et dicens : Magister, quid faciendo vitam æternam possidebo ?

10:10 But into whatsoever city you enter, and they receive you not, going forth into the streets thereof, say:

10:11 Even the very dust of your city that cleaveth to us, we wipe off against you. Yet know this, that the kingdom of God is at hand.

10:12 I say to you, it shall be more tolerable at that day for Sodom, than for that city.

10:13 Woe to thee, Corozain, woe to thee, Bethsaida. For if in Tyre and Sidon had been wrought the mighty works that have been wrought in you, they would have done penance long ago, sitting in sackcloth and ashes.

10:14 But it shall be more tolerable for Tyre and Sidon at the judgement, than for you.

10:15 And thou, Capharnaum, which art exalted unto heaven, thou shalt be thrust down to hell.

10:16 He that heareth you, heareth me; and he that despiseth you, despiseth me; and he that despiseth me, despiseth him that sent me.

10:17 And the seventy-two returned with joy, saying: Lord, the devils also are subject to us in thy name.

10:18 And he said to them: I saw Satan like lightening falling from heaven.

10:19 Behold, I have given you power to tread upon serpents and scorpions, and upon all the power of the enemy: and nothing shall hurt you.

10:20 But yet rejoice not in this, that spirits are subject unto you; but rejoice in this, that your names are written in heaven.

10:21 In that same hour, he rejoiced in the Holy Ghost, and said: I confess to thee, O Father, Lord of heaven and earth, because thou hast hidden these things from the wise and prudent, and hast revealed them to little ones. Yea, Father, for so it hath seemed good in thy sight.

10:22 All things are delivered to me by my Father; and no one knoweth who the Son is, but the Father; and who the Father is, but the Son, and to whom the Son will reveal him.

10:23 And turning to his disciples, he said: Blessed are the eyes that see the things which you see.

10:24 For I say to you, that many prophets and kings have desired to see the things that you see, and have not seen them; and to hear the things that you hear, and have not heard them.

10:25 And behold a certain lawyer stood up, tempting him, and saying, Master, what must I do to possess eternal life?

10:26 At ille dixit ad eum : In lege quid scriptum est ? quomodo legis ?

10:27 Ille respondens dixit : Diliges Dominum Deum tuum ex toto corde tuo, et ex tota anima tua, et ex omnibus virtutibus tuis, et ex omni mente tua : et proximum tuum sicut teipsum.

10:28 Dixitque illi : Recte respondisti : hoc fac, et vives.

10:29 Ille autem volens justificare seipsum, dixit ad Jesum : Et quis est meus proximus ?

10:30 Suscipiens autem Jesus, dixit : Homo quidam descendebat ab Jerusalem in Jericho, et incidit in latrones, qui etiam despoliaverunt eum : et plagis impositis abierunt semivivo relicto.

10:31 Accidit autem ut sacerdos quidam descenderet eadem via : et viso illo præterivit.

10:32 Similiter et Levita, cum esset secus locum, et videret eum, pertransiit.

10:33 Samaritanus autem quidam iter faciens, venit secus eum : et videns eum, misericordia motus est.

10:34 Et appropians alligavit vulnera ejus, infundens oleum et vinum : et imponens illum in jumentum suum, duxit in stabulum, et curam ejus egit.

10:35 Et altera die protulit duos denarios, et dedit stabulario, et ait : Curam illius habe : et quodcumque supererogaveris, ego cum rediero reddam tibi.

10:36 Quis horum trium videtur tibi proximus fuisse illi, qui incidit in latrones ?

10:37 At ille dixit : Qui fecit misericordiam in illum. Et ait illi Jesus : Vade, et tu fac similiter.

10:38 Factum est autem, dum irent, et ipse intravit in quoddam castellum : et mulier quædam, Martha nomine, excepit illum in domum suam,

10:39 et huic erat soror nomine Maria, quæ etiam sedens secus pedes Domini, audiebat verbum illius.

10:40 Martha autem satagebat circa frequens ministerium : quæ stetit, et ait : Domine, non est tibi curæ quod soror mea reliquit me solam ministrare ? dic ergo illi ut me adjuvet.

10:41 Et respondens dixit illi Dominus : Martha, Martha, sollicita es, et turbaris erga plurima,

10:42 porro unum est necessarium. Maria optimam partem elegit, quæ non auferetur ab ea.

10:26 But he said to him: What is written in the law? how readest thou?

10:27 He answering, said: Thou shalt love the Lord thy God with thy whole heart, and with thy whole soul, and with all thy strength, and with all thy mind: and thy neighbour as thyself.

10:28 And he said to him: Thou hast answered right: this do, and thou shalt live.

10:29 But he willing to justify himself, said to Jesus: And who is my neighbour?

10:30 And Jesus answering, said: A certain man went down from Jerusalem to Jericho, and fell among robbers, who also stripped him, and having wounded him went away, leaving him half dead.

10:31 And it chanced, that a certain priest went down the same way: and seeing him, passed by.

10:32 In like manner also a Levite, when he was near the place and saw him, passed by.

10:33 But a certain Samaritan being on his journey, came near him; and seeing him, was moved with compassion.

10:34 And going up to him, bound up his wounds, pouring in oil and wine: and setting him upon his own beast, brought him to an inn, and took care of him.

10:35 And the next day he took out two pence, and gave to the host, and said: Take care of him; and whatsoever thou shalt spend over and above, I, at my return, will repay thee.

10:36 Which of these three, in thy opinion, was neighbour to him that fell among the robbers?

10:37 But he said: He that shewed mercy to him. And Jesus said to him: Go, and do thou in like manner.

10:38 Now it came to pass as they went, that he entered into a certain town: and a certain woman named Martha, received him into her house.

10:39 And she had a sister called Mary, who sitting also at the Lord's feet, heard his word.

10:40 But Martha was busy about much serving. Who stood and said: Lord, hast thou no care that my sister hath left me alone to serve? speak to her therefore, that she help me.

10:41 And the Lord answering, said to her: Martha, Martha, thou art careful, and art troubled about many things:

10:42 But one thing is necessary. Mary hath chosen the best part, which shall not be taken

11:1 Et factum est : cum esset in quodam loco orans, ut cessavit, dixit unus ex discipulis ejus ad eum : Domine, doce nos orare, sicut docuit et Joannes discipulos suos.

11:2 Et ait illis : Cum oratis, dicite : Pater, sanctificetur nomen tuum. Adveniat regnum tuum.

11:3 Panem nostrum quotidianum da nobis hodie.

11:4 Et dimitte nobis peccata nostra, siquidem et ipsi dimittimus omni debenti nobis. Et ne nos inducas in tentationem.

11:5 Et ait ad illos : Quis vestrum habebit amicum, et ibit ad illum media nocte, et dicet illi : Amice, commoda mihi tres panes,

11:6 quoniam amicus meus venit de via ad me, et non habeo quod ponam ante illum,

11:7 et ille de intus respondens dicat : Noli mihi molestus esse, jam ostium clausum est, et pueri mei mecum sunt in cubili : non possum surgere, et dare tibi.

11:8 Et si ille perseveraverit pulsans : dico vobis, etsi non dabit illi surgens eo quod amicus ejus sit, propter improbitatem tamen ejus surget, et dabit illi quotquot habet necessarios.

11:9 Et ego dico vobis : Petite, et dabitur vobis ; quærite, et invenietis ; pulsate, et aperietur vobis.

11:10 Omnis enim qui petit, accipit : et qui quærit, invenit : et pulsanti aperietur.

11:11 Quis autem ex vobis patrem petit panem, numquid lapidem dabit illi ? aut piscem, numquid pro pisce serpentem dabit illi ?

11:12 aut si petierit ovum, numquid porriget illi scorpionem ?

11:13 Si ergo vos, cum sitis mali, nostis bona data dare filiis vestris : quanto magis Pater vester de cælo dabit spiritum bonum petentibus se ?

11:14 Et erat ejiciens dæmonium, et illud erat mutum. Et cum ejecisset dæmonium, locutus est mutus, et admiratæ sunt turbæ.

11:15 Quidam autem ex eis dixerunt : In Beelzebub principe dæmoniorum ejicit dæmonia.

11:16 Et alii tentantes, signum de cælo quærebant ab eo.

away from her.

11:1 And it came to pass, that as he was in a certain place praying, when he ceased, one of his disciples said to him: Lord, teach us to pray, as John also taught his disciples.

11:2 And he said to them: When you pray, say: Father, hallowed be thy name. Thy kingdom come.

11:3 Give us this day our daily bread.

11:4 And forgive us our sins, for we also forgive every one that is indebted to us. And lead us not into temptation.

11:5 And he said to them: Which of you shall have a friend, and shall go to him at midnight, and shall say to him: Friend, lend me three loaves,

11:6 Because a friend of mine is come off his journey to me, and I have not what to set before him.

11:7 And he from within should answer, and say: Trouble me not, the door is now shut, and my children are with me in bed; I cannot rise and give thee.

11:8 Yet if he shall continue knocking, I say to you, although he will not rise and give him, because he is his friend; yet, because of his importunity, he will rise, and give him as many as he needeth.

11:9 And I say to you, Ask, and it shall be given you: seek, and you shall find: knock, and it shall be opened to you.

11:10 For every one that asketh, receiveth; and he that seeketh, findeth; and to him that knocketh, it shall be opened.

11:11 And which of you, if he ask his father bread, will he give him a stone? or a fish, will he for a fish give him a serpent?

11:12 Or if he shall ask an egg, will he reach him a scorpion?

11:13 If you then, being evil, know how to give good gifts to your children, how much more will your Father from heaven give the good Spirit to them that ask him?

11:14 And he was casting out a devil, and the same was dumb: and when he had cast out the devil, the dumb spoke: and the multitudes were in admiration at it:

11:15 But some of them said: He casteth out devils by Beelzebub, the prince of devils.

11:16 And others tempting, asked of him a sign from heaven.

11:17 Ipse autem ut vidit cogitationes eorum, dixit eis : Omne regnum in seipsum divisum desolabitur, et domus supra domum cadet.

11:18 Si autem et Satanas in seipsum divisus est, quomodo stabit regnum ejus ? quia dicitis in Beelzebub me ejicere dæmonia.

11:19 Si autem ego in Beelzebub ejicio dæmonia : filii vestri in quo ejiciunt ? ideo ipsi judices vestri erunt.

11:20 Porro si in digito Dei ejicio dæmonia : profecto pervenit in vos regnum Dei.

11:21 Cum fortis armatus custodit atrium suum, in pace sunt ea quæ possidet.

11:22 Si autem fortior eo superveniens vicerit eum, universa arma ejus auferet, in quibus confidebat, et spolia ejus distribuet.

11:23 Qui non est mecum, contra me est : et qui non colligit mecum, dispergit.

11:24 Cum immundus spiritus exierit de homine, ambulat per loca inaquosa, quærens requiem : et non inveniens dicit : Revertar in domum meam unde exivi.

11:25 Et cum venerit, invenit eam scopis mundatam, et ornatam.

11:26 Tunc vadit, et assumit septem alios spiritus secum, nequiores se, et ingressi habitant ibi. Et fiunt novissima hominis illius pejora prioribus.

11:27 Factum est autem, cum hæc diceret : extollens vocem quædam mulier de turba dixit illi : Beatus venter qui te portavit, et ubera quæ suxisti.

11:28 At ille dixit : Quinimmo beati, qui audiunt verbum Dei et custodiunt illud.

11:29 Turbis autem concurrentibus cœpit dicere : Generatio hæc, generatio nequam est : signum quærit, et signum non dabitur ei, nisi signum Jonæ prophetæ.

11:30 Nam sicut fuit Jonas signum Ninivitis, ita erit et Filius hominis generationi isti.

11:31 Regina austri surget in judicio cum viris generationis hujus, et condemnabit illos : quia venit a finibus terræ audire sapientiam Salomonis : et ecce plus quam Salomon hic.

11:32 Viri Ninivitæ surgent in judicio cum gen-

11:17 But he seeing their thoughts, said to them: Every kingdom divided against itself, shall be brought to desolation, and house upon house shall fall.

11:18 And if Satan also be divided against himself, how shall his kingdom stand? because you say, that through Beelzebub I cast out devils.

11:19 Now if I cast out devils by Beelzebub; by whom do your children cast them out? Therefore they shall be your judges.

11:20 But if I by the finger of God cast out devils; doubtless the kingdom of God is come upon you.

11:21 When a strong man armed keepeth his court, those things are in peace which he possesseth.

11:22 But if a stronger than he come upon him, and overcome him; he will take away all his armour wherein he trusted, and will distribute his spoils.

11:23 He that is not with me, is against me; and he that gathereth not with me, scattereth.

11:24 When the unclean spirit is gone out of a man, he walketh through places without water, seeking rest; and not finding, he saith: I will return into my house whence I came out.

11:25 And when he is come, he findeth it swept and garnished.

11:26 Then he goeth and taketh with him seven other spirits more wicked than himself, and entering in they dwell there. And the last state of that man becomes worse than the first.

11:27 And it came to pass, as he spoke these things, a certain woman from the crowd, lifting up her voice, said to him: Blessed is the womb that bore thee, and the paps that gave thee suck.

11:28 But he said: Yea rather, blessed are they who hear the word of God, and keep it.

11:29 And the multitudes running together, he began to say: This generation is a wicked generation: it asketh a sign, and a sign shall not be given it, but the sign of Jonas the prophet.

11:30 For as Jonas was a sign to the Ninivites; so shall the Son of man also be to this generation.

11:31 The queen of the south shall rise in the judgment with the men of this generation, and shall condemn them: because she came from the ends of the earth to hear the wisdom of Solomon; and behold more than Solomon here.

11:32 The men of Ninive shall rise in the judg-

eratione hac, et condemnabunt illam : quia pœnitentiam egerunt ad prædicationem Jonæ, et ecce plus quam Jonas hic.

11:33 Nemo lucernam accendit, et in abscondito ponit, neque sub modio : sed supra candelabrum, ut qui ingrediuntur, lumen videant.

11:34 Lucerna corporis tui est oculus tuus. Si oculus tuus fuerit simplex, totum corpus tuum lucidum erit : si autem nequam fuerit, etiam corpus tuum tenebrosum erit.

11:35 Vide ergo ne lumen quod in te est, tenebræ sint.

11:36 Si ergo corpus tuum totum lucidum fuerit, non habens aliquam partem tenebrarum, erit lucidum totum, et sicut lucerna fulgoris illuminabit te.

11:37 Et cum loqueretur, rogavit illum quidam pharisæus ut pranderet apud se. Et ingressus recubuit.

11:38 Pharisæus autem cœpit intra se reputans dicere, quare non baptizatus esset ante prandium.

11:39 Et ait Dominus ad illum : Nunc vos pharisæi, quod deforis est calicis et catini, mundatis : quod autem intus est vestrum, plenum est rapina et iniquitate.

11:40 Stulti ! nonne qui fecit quod deforis est, etiam id quod deintus est fecit ?

11:41 Verumtamen quod superest, date eleemosynam : et ecce omnia munda sunt vobis.

11:42 Sed væ vobis, pharisæis, quia decimatis mentham, et rutam, et omne olus, et præteritis judicium et caritatem Dei : hæc autem oportuit facere, et illa non omittere.

11:43 Væ vobis, pharisæis, quia diligitis primas cathedras in synagogis, et salutationes in foro.

11:44 Væ vobis, quia estis ut monumenta, quæ non apparent, et homines ambulantes supra, nesciunt.

11:45 Respondens autem quidam ex legisperitis, ait illi : Magister, hæc dicens etiam contumeliam nobis facis.

11:46 At ille ait : Et vobis legisperitis væ : quia oneratis homines oneribus, quæ portare non possunt, et ipsi uno digito vestro non tangitis sarcinas.

11:47 Væ vobis, qui ædificatis monumenta prophetarum : patres autem vestri occiderunt illos.

ment with this generation, and shall condemn it; because they did penance at the preaching of Jonas; and behold more than Jonas here.

11:33 No man lighteth a candle, and putteth it in a hidden place, nor under a bushel; but upon a candlestick, that they that come in, may see the light.

11:34 The light of thy body is thy eye. If thy eye be single, thy whole body will be lightsome: but if it be evil, thy body also will be darksome.

11:35 Take heed therefore, that the light which is in thee, be not darkness.

11:36 If then thy whole body be lightsome, having no part of darkness; the whole shall be lightsome; and as a bright lamp, shall enlighten thee.

11:37 And as he was speaking, a certain Pharisee prayed him, that he would dine with him. And he going in, sat down to eat.

11:38 And the Pharisee began to say, thinking within himself, why he was not washed before dinner.

11:39 And the Lord said to him: Now you Pharisees make clean the outside of the cup and of the platter; but your inside is full of rapine and iniquity.

11:40 Ye fools, did not he that made that which is without, make also that which is within?

11:41 But yet that which remaineth, give alms; and behold, all things are clean unto you.

11:42 But woe to you, Pharisees, because you tithe mint and rue and every herb; and pass over judgment, and the charity of God. Now these things you ought to have done, and not to leave the other undone.

11:43 Woe to you, Pharisees, because you love the uppermost seats in the synagogues, and salutations in the marketplace.

11:44 Woe to you, because you are as sepulchres that appear not, and men that walk over are not aware.

11:45 And one of the lawyers answering, saith to him: Master, in saying these things, thou reproachest us also.

11:46 But he said: Woe to you lawyers also, because you load men with burdens which they cannot bear, and you yourselves touch not the packs with one of your fingers.

11:47 Woe to you who build the monuments of the prophets: and your fathers killed them.

11:48 Profecto testificamini quod consentitis operibus patrum vestrorum : quoniam ipsi quidem eos occiderunt, vos autem ædificatis eorum sepulchra.

11:49 Propterea et sapientia Dei dixit : Mittam ad illos prophetas, et apostolos, et ex illis occident, et persequentur :

11:50 ut inquiratur sanguis omnium prophetarum, qui effusus est a constitutione mundi a generatione ista,

11:51 a sanguine Abel, usque ad sanguinem Zachariæ, qui periit inter altare et ædem. Ita dico vobis, requiretur ab hac generatione.

11:52 Væ vobis, legisperitis, quia tulistis clavem scientiæ : ipsi non introistis, et eos qui introibant, prohibuistis.

11:53 Cum autem hæc ad illos diceret, cœperunt pharisæi et legisperiti graviter insistere, et os ejus opprimere de multis,

11:54 insidiantes ei, et quærentes aliquid capere de ore ejus, ut accusarent eum.

12:1 Multis autem turbis circumstantibus, ita ut se invicem conculcarent, cœpit dicere ad discipulos suos : Attendite a fermento pharisæorum, quod est hypocrisis.

12:2 Nihil autem opertum est, quod non reveletur : neque absconditum, quod non sciatur.

12:3 Quoniam quæ in tenebris dixistis, in lumine dicentur : et quod in aurem locuti estis in cubiculis, prædicabitur in tectis.

12:4 Dico autem vobis amicis meis : Ne terreamini ab his qui occidunt corpus, et post hæc non habent amplius quid faciant.

12:5 Ostendam autem vobis quem timeatis : timete eum qui, postquam occiderit, habet potestatem mittere in gehennam : ita dico vobis, hunc timete.

12:6 Nonne quinque passeres veneunt dipondio, et unus ex illis non est in oblivione coram Deo ?

12:7 sed et capilli capitis vestri omnes numerati sunt. Nolite ergo timere : multis passeribus pluris estis vos.

12:8 Dico autem vobis : Omnis quicumque confessus fuerit me coram hominibus, et Filius hominis confitebitur illum coram angelis Dei :

11:48 Truly you bear witness that you consent to the doings of your fathers: for they indeed killed them, and you build their sepulchres.

11:49 For this cause also the wisdom of God said: I will send to them prophets and apostles; and some of them they will kill and persecute.

11:50 That the blood of all the prophets which was shed from the foundation of the world, may be required of this generation,

11:51 From the blood of Abel unto the blood of Zacharias, who was slain between the altar and the temple: Yea I say to you, It shall be required of this generation.

11:52 Woe to you lawyers, for you have taken away the key of knowledge: you yourselves have not entered in, and those that were entering in, you have hindered.

11:53 And as he was saying these things to them, the Pharisees and the lawyers began violently to urge him, and to oppress his mouth about many things,

11:54 Lying in wait for him, and seeking to catch something from his mouth, that they might accuse him.

12:1 And when great multitudes stood about him, so that they trod one upon another, he began to say to his disciples: Beware ye of the leaven of the Pharisees, which is hypocrisy.

12:2 For there is nothing covered, that shall not be revealed: nor hidden, that shall not be known.

12:3 For whatsoever things you have spoken in darkness, shall be published in the light: and that which you have spoken in the ear in the chambers, shall be preached on the housetops.

12:4 And I say to you, my friends: Be not afraid of them who kill the body, and after that have no more that they can do.

12:5 But I will shew you whom you shall fear: fear ye him, who after he hath killed, hath power to cast into hell. Yea, I say to you, fear him.

12:6 Are not five sparrows sold for two farthings, and not one of them is forgotten before God?

12:7 Yea, the very hairs of your head are all numbered. Fear not therefore: you are of more value than many sparrows.

12:8 And I say to you, Whosoever shall confess me before men, him shall the Son of man also confess before the angels of God.

12:9 qui autem negaverit me coram hominibus, negabitur coram angelis Dei.

12:10 Et omnis qui dicit verbum in Filium hominis, remittetur illi : ei autem qui in Spiritum Sanctum blasphemaverit, non remittetur.

12:11 Cum autem inducent vos in synagogas, et ad magistratus, et potestates, nolite solliciti esse qualiter, aut quid respondeatis, aut quid dicatis.

12:12 Spiritus enim Sanctus docebit vos in ipsa hora quid oporteat vos dicere.

12:13 Ait autem ei quidam de turba : Magister, dic fratri meo ut dividat mecum hæreditatem.

12:14 At ille dixit illi : Homo, quis me constituit judicem, aut divisorem super vos ?

12:15 Dixitque ad illos : Videte, et cavete ab omni avaritia : quia non in abundantia cujusquam vita ejus est ex his quæ possidet.

12:16 Dixit autem similitudinem ad illos, dicens : Hominis cujusdam divitis uberes fructus ager attulit :

12:17 et cogitabat intra se dicens : Quid faciam, quia non habeo quo congregem fructus meos ?

12:18 Et dixit : Hoc faciam : destruam horrea mea, et majora faciam : et illuc congregabo omnia quæ nata sunt mihi, et bona mea,

12:19 et dicam animæ meæ : Anima, habes multa bona posita in annos plurimos : requiesce, comede, bibe, epulare.

12:20 Dixit autem illi Deus : Stulte, hac nocte animam tuam repetunt a te : quæ autem parasti, cujus erunt ?

12:21 Sic est qui sibi thesaurizat, et non est in Deum dives.

12:22 Dixitque ad discipulos suos : Ideo dico vobis, nolite solliciti esse animæ vestræ quid manducetis, neque corpori quid induamini.

12:23 Anima plus est quam esca, et corpus plus quam vestimentum.

12:24 Considerate corvos, quia non seminant, neque metunt, quibus non est cellarium, neque horreum, et Deus pascit illos. Quanto magis vos pluris estis illis ?

12:25 Quis autem vestrum cogitando potest adjicere ad staturam suam cubitum unum ?

12:26 Si ergo neque quod minimum est potestis,

12:9 But he that shall deny me before men, shall be denied before the angels of God.

12:10 And whosoever speaketh a word against the Son of man, it shall be forgiven him: but to him that shall blaspheme against the Holy Ghost, it shall not be forgiven.

12:11 And when they shall bring you into the synagogues, and to magistrates and powers, be not solicitous how or what you shall answer, or what you shall say;

12:12 For the Holy Ghost shall teach you in the same hour what you must say.

12:13 And one of the multitude said to him: Master, speak to my brother that he divide the inheritance with me.

12:14 But he said to him: Man, who hath appointed me judge, or divider, over you?

12:15 And he said to them: Take heed and beware of all covetousness; for a man's life doth not consist in the abundance of things which he possesseth.

12:16 And he spoke a similitude to them, saying: The land of a certain rich man brought forth plenty of fruits.

12:17 And he thought within himself, saying: What shall I do, because I have no room where to bestow my fruits?

12:18 And he said: This will I do: I will pull down my barns, and will build greater; and into them will I gather all things that are grown to me, and my goods.

12:19 And I will say to my soul: Soul, thou hast much goods laid up for many years take thy rest; eat, drink, make good cheer.

12:20 But God said to him: Thou fool, this night do they require thy soul of thee: and whose shall those things be which thou hast provided?

12:21 So is he that layeth up treasure for himself, and is not rich towards God.

12:22 And he said to his disciples: Therefore I say to you, be not solicitous for your life, what you shall eat; nor for your body, what you shall put on.

12:23 The life is more than the meat, and the body is more than the raiment.

12:24 Consider the ravens, for they sow not, neither do they reap, neither have they storehouse nor barn, and God feedeth them. How much are you more valuable than they?

12:25 And which of you, by taking thought, can add to his stature one cubit?

12:26 If then ye be not able to do so much as the

quid de ceteris solliciti estis ?

12:27 Considerate lilia quomodo crescunt : non laborant, neque nent : dico autem vobis, nec Salomon in omni gloria sua vestiebatur sicut unum ex istis.

12:28 Si autem fœnum, quod hodie est in agro, et cras in clibanum mittitur, Deus sic vestit : quanto magis vos pusillæ fidei ?

12:29 Et vos nolite quærere quid manducetis, aut quid bibatis : et nolite in sublime tolli :

12:30 hæc enim omnia gentes mundi quærunt. Pater autem vester scit quoniam his indigetis.

12:31 Verumtamen quærite primum regnum Dei, et justitiam ejus : et hæc omnia adjicientur vobis.

12:32 Nolite timere pusillus grex, quia complacuit Patri vestro dare vobis regnum.

12:33 Vendite quæ possidetis, et date eleemosynam. Facite vobis sacculos, qui non veterascunt, thesaurum non deficientem in cælis : quo fur non appropriat, neque tinea corrumpit.

12:34 Ubi enim thesaurus vester est, ibi et cor vestrum erit.

12:35 Sint lumbi vestri præcincti, et lucernæ ardentes in manibus vestris,

12:36 et vos similes hominibus exspectantibus dominum suum quando revertatur a nuptiis : ut, cum venerit et pulsaverit, confestim aperiant ei.

12:37 Beati servi illi quos, cum venerit dominus, invenerit vigilantes : amen dico vobis, quod præcinget se, et faciet illos discumbere, et transiens ministrabit illis.

12:38 Et si venerit in secunda vigilia, et si in tertia vigilia venerit, et ita invenerit, beati sunt servi illi.

12:39 Hoc autem scitote, quoniam si sciret paterfamilias, qua hora fur veniret, vigilaret utique, et non sineret perfodi domum suam.

12:40 Et vos estote parati : quia qua hora non putatis, Filius hominis veniet.

12:41 Ait autem ei Petrus : Domine, ad nos dicis hanc parabolam, an et ad omnes ?

12:42 Dixit autem Dominus : Quis, putas, est fidelis dispensator, et prudens, quem constituit dominus supra familiam suam, ut det illis in tempore tritici mensuram ?

least thing, why are you solicitous for the rest?

12:27 Consider the lilies, how they grow: they labour not, neither do they spin. But I say to you, not even Solomon in all his glory was clothed like one of these.

12:28 Now if God clothe in this manner the grass that is to day in the field, and to morrow is cast into the oven; how much more you, O ye of little faith?

12:29 And seek not you what you shall eat, or what you shall drink: and be not lifted up on high.

12:30 For all these things do the nations of the world seek. But your Father knoweth that you have need of these things.

12:31 But seek ye first the kingdom of God and his justice, and all these things shall be added unto you.

12:32 Fear not, little flock, for it hath pleased your Father to give you a kingdom.

12:33 Sell what you possess and give alms. Make to yourselves bags which grow not old, a treasure in heaven which faileth not: where no thief approacheth, nor moth corrupteth.

12:34 For where your treasure is, there will your heart be also.

12:35 Let your loins be girt, and lamps burning in your hands.

12:36 And you yourselves like to men who wait for their lord, when he shall return from the wedding; that when he cometh and knocketh, they may open to him immediately.

12:37 Blessed are those servants, whom the Lord when he cometh, shall find watching. Amen I say to you, that he will gird himself, and make them sit down to meat, and passing will minister unto them.

12:38 And if he shall come in the second watch, or come in the third watch, and find them so, blessed are those servants.

12:39 But this know ye, that if the householder did know at what hour the thief would come, he would surely watch, and would not suffer his house to be broken open.

12:40 Be you then also ready: for at what hour you think not, the Son of man will come.

12:41 And Peter said to him: Lord, dost thou speak this parable to us, or likewise to all?

12:42 And the Lord said: Who (thinkest thou) is the faithful and wise steward, whom his lord setteth over his family, to give them their measure of wheat in due season?

12:43 Beatus ille servus quem, cum venerit dominus, invenerit ita facientem.

12:44 Vere dico vobis, quoniam supra omnia quæ possidet, constituet illum.

12:45 Quod si dixerit servus ille in corde suo : Moram facit dominus meus venire : et cœperit percutere servos, et ancillas, et edere, et bibere, et inebriari :

12:46 veniet dominus servi illius in die qua non sperat, et hora qua nescit, et dividet eum, partemque ejus cum infidelibus ponet.

12:47 Ille autem servus qui cognovit voluntatem domini sui, et non præparavit, et non facit secundum voluntatem ejus, vapulabit multis :

12:48 qui autem non cognovit, et fecit digna plagis, vapulabit paucis. Omni autem cui multum datum est, multum quæretur ab eo : et cui commendaverunt multum, plus petent ab eo.

12:49 Ignem veni mittere in terram, et quid volo nisi ut accendatur ?

12:50 Baptismo autem habeo baptizari : et quomodo coarctor usque dum perficiatur ?

12:51 Putatis quia pacem veni dare in terram ? non, dico vobis, sed separationem :

12:52 erunt enim ex hoc quinque in domo una divisi, tres in duos, et duo in tres

12:53 dividentur : pater in filium, et filius in patrem suum, mater in filiam, et filia in matrem, socrus in nurum suam, et nurus in socrum suam.

12:54 Dicebat autem et ad turbas : Cum videritis nubem orientem ab occasu, statim dicitis : Nimbus venit : et ita fit.

12:55 Et cum austrum flantem, dicitis : Quia æstus erit : et fit.

12:56 Hypocritæ ! faciem cæli et terræ nostis probare : hoc autem tempus quomodo non probatis ?

12:57 quid autem et a vobis ipsis non judicatis quod justum est ?

12:58 Cum autem vadis cum adversario tuo ad principem, in via da operam liberari ab illo, ne forte trahat te ad judicem, et judex tradat te

12:43 Blessed is that servant, whom when his lord shall come, he shall find so doing.

12:44 Verily I say to you, he will set him over all that he possesseth.

12:45 But if that servant shall say in his heart: My lord is long a coming; and shall begin to strike the menservants and maidservants, and to eat and to drink and be drunk:

12:46 The lord of that servant will come in the day that he hopeth not, and at the hour that he knoweth not, and shall separate him, and shall appoint him his portion with unbelievers.

12:47 And that servant who knew the will of his lord, and prepared not himself, and did not according to his will, shall be beaten with many stripes.

12:48 But he that knew not, and did things worthy of stripes, shall be beaten with few stripes. And unto whomsoever much is given, of him much shall be required: and to whom they have committed much, of him they will demand the more.

12:49 I am come to cast fire on the earth; and what will I, but that it be kindled?

12:50 And I have a baptism wherewith I am to be baptized: and how am I straitened until it be accomplished?

12:51 Think ye, that I am come to give peace on earth? I tell you, no; but separation.

12:52 For there shall be from henceforth five in one house divided: three against two, and two against three.

12:53 The father shall be divided against the son, and the son against his father, the mother against the daughter, and the daughter against the mother, the mother in law against her daughter in law, and the daughter in law against her mother in law.

12:54 And he said also to the multitudes: When you see a cloud rising from the west, presently you say: A shower is coming: and so it happeneth:

12:55 And when ye see the south wind blow, you say: There will be heat: and it cometh to pass.

12:56 You hypocrites, you know how to discern the face of the heaven and of the earth: but how is it that you do not discern this time?

12:57 And why even of yourselves, do you not judge that which is just?

12:58 And when thou goest with thy adversary to the prince, whilst thou art in the way, endeavour to be delivered from him: lest perhaps he

exactori, et exactor mittat te in carcerem.

12:59 Dico tibi, non exies inde, donec etiam novissimum minutum reddas.

13:1 Aderant autem quidam ipso in tempore, nuntiantes illi de Galilæis, quorum sanguinem Pilatus miscuit cum sacrificiis eorum.

13:2 Et respondens dixit illis : Putatis quod hi Galilæi præ omnibus Galilæis peccatores fuerint, quia talia passi sunt ?

13:3 Non, dico vobis : sed nisi pœnitentiam habueritis, omnes similiter peribitis.

13:4 Sicut illi decem et octo, supra quos cecidit turris in Siloë, et occidit eos : putatis quia et ipsi debitores fuerint præter omnes homines habitantes in Jerusalem ?

13:5 Non, dico vobis : sed si pœnitentiam non egeritis, omnes similiter peribitis.

13:6 Dicebat autem et hanc similitudinem : Arborem fici habebat quidam plantatam in vinea sua, et venit quærens fructum in illa, et non invenit.

13:7 Dixit autem ad cultorem vineæ : Ecce anni tres sunt ex quo venio quærens fructum in ficulnea hac, et non invenio : succide ergo illam : ut quid etiam terram occupat ?

13:8 At ille respondens, dicit illi : Domine dimitte illam et hoc anno, usque dum fodiam circa illam, et mittam stercora,

13:9 et siquidem fecerit fructum : sin autem, in futurum succides eam.

13:10 Erat autem docens in synagoga eorum sabbatis.

13:11 Et ecce mulier, quæ habebat spiritum infirmitatis annis decem et octo : et erat inclinata, nec omnino poterat sursum respicere.

13:12 Quam cum videret Jesus, vocavit eam ad se, et ait illi : Mulier, dimissa es ab infirmitate tua.

13:13 Et imposuit illi manus, et confestim erecta est, et glorificabat Deum.

13:14 Respondens autem archisynagogus, indignans quia sabbato curasset Jesus, dicebat turbæ : Sex dies sunt in quibus oportet operari : in his ergo venite, et curamini, et non in die sabbati.

13:15 Respondens autem ad illum Dominus, dix-

draw thee to the judge, and the judge deliver thee to the exacter, and the exacter cast thee into prison.

12:59 I say to thee, thou shalt not go out thence, until thou pay the very last mite.

13:1 And there were present, at that very time, some that told him of the Galileans, whose blood Pilate had mingled with their sacrifices.

13:2 And he answering, said to them: Think you that these Galileans were sinners above all the men of Galilee, because they suffered such things?

13:3 No, I say to you: but unless you shall do penance, you shall all likewise perish.

13:4 Or those eighteen upon whom the tower fell in Siloe, and slew them: think you, that they also were debtors above all the men that dwelt in Jerusalem?

13:5 No, I say to you; but except you do penance, you shall all likewise perish.

13:6 He spoke also this parable: A certain man had a fig tree planted in his vineyard, and he came seeking fruit on it, and found none.

13:7 And he said to the dresser of the vineyard: Behold, for these three years I come seeking fruit on this fig tree, and I find none. Cut it done therefore: why cumbereth it the ground?

13:8 But he answering, said to him: Lord, let it alone this year also, until I dig about it, and dung it.

13:9 And if happily it bear fruit: but if not, then after that thou shalt cut it down.

13:10 And he was teaching in their synagogue on their sabbath.

13:11 And behold there was a woman, who had a spirit of infirmity eighteen years: and she was bowed together, neither could she look upwards at all.

13:12 Whom when Jesus saw, he called her unto him, and said to her: Woman, thou art delivered from thy infirmity.

13:13 And he laid his hands upon her, and immediately she was made straight, and glorified God.

13:14 And the ruler of the synagogue (being angry that Jesus had healed on the sabbath) answering, said to the multitude: Six days there are wherein you ought to work. In them therefore come, and be healed; and not on the sabbath day.

13:15 And the Lord answering him, said: Ye hyp-

it : Hypocritæ, unusquisque vestrum sabbato non solvit bovem suum, aut asinum a præsepio, et ducit adaquare ?

13:16 Hanc autem filiam Abrahæ, quam alligavit Satanas, ecce decem et octo annis, non oportuit solvi a vinculo isto die sabbati ?

13:17 Et cum hæc diceret, erubescebant omnes adversarii ejus : et omnis populus gaudebat in universis, quæ gloriose fiebant ab eo.

13:18 Dicebat ergo : Cui simile est regnum Dei, et cui simile æstimabo illud ?

13:19 Simile est grano sinapis, quod acceptum homo misit in hortum suum, et crevit, et factum est in arborem magnam : et volucres cæli requieverunt in ramis ejus.

13:20 Et iterum dixit : Cui simile æstimabo regnum Dei ?

13:21 Simile est fermento, quod acceptum mulier abscondit in farinæ sata tria, donec fermentaretur totum.

13:22 Et ibat per civitates et castella, docens, et iter faciens in Jerusalem.

13:23 Ait autem illi quidam : Domine, si pauci sunt, qui salvantur ? Ipse autem dixit ad illos :

13:24 Contendite intrare per angustam portam : quia multi, dico vobis, quærent intrare, et non poterunt.

13:25 Cum autem intraverit paterfamilias, et clauserit ostium, incipietis foris stare, et pulsare ostium, dicentes : Domine, aperi nobis : et respondens dicet vobis : Nescio vos unde sitis :

13:26 tunc incipietis dicere : Manducavimus coram te, et bibimus, et in plateis nostris docuisti.

13:27 Et dicet vobis : Nescio vos unde sitis : discedite a me omnes operarii iniquitatis.

13:28 Ibi erit fletus et stridor dentium : cum videritis Abraham, et Isaac, et Jacob, et omnes prophetas in regno Dei, vos autem expelli foras.

13:29 Et venient ab oriente, et occidente, et aquilone, et austro, et accumbent in regno Dei.

13:30 Et ecce sunt novissimi qui erunt primi, et sunt primi qui erunt novissimi.

13:31 In ipsa die accesserunt quidam pharisæorum, dicentes illi : Exi, et vade hinc : quia Herodes vult te occidere.

ocrites, doth not every one of you, on the sabbath day, loose his ox or his ass from the manger, and lead them to water?

13:16 And ought not this daughter of Abraham, whom Satan hath bound, lo, these eighteen years, be loosed from this bond on the sabbath day?

13:17 And when he said these things, all his adversaries were ashamed: and all the people rejoiced for all the things that were gloriously done by him.

13:18 He said therefore: To what is the kingdom of God like, and whereunto shall I resemble it?

13:19 It is like to a grain of mustard seed, which a man took and cast into his garden, and it grew and became a great tree, and the birds of the air lodged in the branches thereof.

13:20 And again he said: Whereunto shall I esteem the kingdom of God to be like?

13:21 It is like to leaven, which a woman took and hid in three measures of meal, till the whole was leavened.

13:22 And he went through the cities and towns teaching, and making his journey to Jerusalem.

13:23 And a certain man said to him: Lord, are they few that are saved? But he said to them:

13:24 Strive to enter by the narrow gate; for many, I say to you, shall seek to enter, and shall not be able.

13:25 But when the master of the house shall be gone in, and shall shut the door, you shall begin to stand without, and knock at the door, saying: Lord, open to us. And he answering, shall say to you: I know you not, whence you are.

13:26 Then you shall begin to say: We have eaten and drunk in thy presence, and thou hast taught in our streets.

13:27 And he shall say to you: I know you not, whence you are: depart from me, all ye workers of iniquity.

13:28 There shall be weeping and gnashing of teeth, when you shall see Abraham and Isaac and Jacob, and all the prophets, in the kingdom of God, and you yourselves thrust out.

13:29 And there shall come from the east and the west, and the north and the south; and shall sit down in the kingdom of God.

13:30 And behold, they are last that shall be first; and they are first that shall be last.

13:31 The same day, there came some of the Pharisees, saying to him: Depart, and get thee hence, for Herod hath a mind to kill thee.

13:32 Et ait illis : Ite, et dicite vulpi illi : Ecce ejicio dæmonia, et sanitates perficio hodie, et cras, et tertia die consummor.

13:33 Verumtamen oportet me hodie et cras et sequenti die ambulare : quia non capit prophetam perire extra Jerusalem.

13:34 Jerusalem, Jerusalem, quæ occidis prophetas, et lapidas eos qui mittuntur ad te, quoties volui congregare filios tuos quemadmodum avis nidum suum sub pennis, et noluisti ?

13:35 Ecce relinquetur vobis domus vestra deserta. Dico autem vobis, quia non videbitis me donec veniat cum dicetis : Benedictus qui venit in nomine Domini.

14:1 Et factum est cum intraret Jesus in domum cujusdam principis pharisæorum sabbato manducare panem, et ipsi observabant eum.

14:2 Et ecce homo quidam hydropicus erat ante illum.

14:3 Et respondens Jesus dixit ad legisperitos et pharisæos, dicens : Si licet sabbato curare ?

14:4 At illi tacuerunt. Ipse vero apprehensum sanavit eum, ac dimisit.

14:5 Et respondens ad illos dixit : Cujus vestrum asinus, aut bos in puteum cadet, et non continuo extrahet illum die sabbati ?

14:6 Et non poterant ad hæc respondere illi.

14:7 Dicebat autem et ad invitatos parabolam, intendens quomodo primos accubitus eligerent, dicens ad illos :

14:8 Cum invitatus fueris ad nuptias, non discumbas in primo loco, ne forte honoratior te sit invitatus ab illo.

14:9 Et veniens is, qui te et illum vocavit, dicat tibi : Da huic locum : et tunc incipias cum rubore novissimum locum tenere.

14:10 Sed cum vocatus fueris, vade, recumbe in novissimo loco : ut, cum venerit qui te invitavit, dicat tibi : Amice, ascende superius. Tunc erit tibi gloria coram simul discumbentibus :

14:11 quia omnis, qui se exaltat, humiliabitur : et qui se humiliat, exaltabitur.

14:12 Dicebat autem et ei, qui invitaverat : Cum

13:32 And he said to them: Go and tell that fox, Behold, I cast out devils, and do cures to day and to morrow, and the third day I am consummated.

13:33 Nevertheless I must walk to day and to morrow, and the day following, because it cannot be that a prophet perish, out of Jerusalem.

13:34 Jerusalem, Jerusalem, that killest the prophets, and stonest them that are sent to thee, how often would I have gathered thy children as the bird doth her brood under her wings, and thou wouldest not?

13:35 Behold your house shall be left to you desolate. And I say to you, that you shall not see me till the time come, when you shall say: Blessed is he that cometh in the name of the Lord.

14:1 And it came to pass, when Jesus went into the house of one of the chief of the Pharisees, on the sabbath day, to eat bread, that they watched him.

14:2 And behold, there was a certain man before him that had the dropsy.

14:3 And Jesus answering, spoke to the lawyers and Pharisees, saying: Is it lawful to heal on the sabbath day?

14:4 But they held their peace. But he taking him, healed him, and sent him away.

14:5 And answering them, he said: Which of you shall have an ass or an ox fall into a pit, and will not immediately draw him out, on the sabbath day?

14:6 And they could not answer him to these things.

14:7 And he spoke a parable also to them that were invited, marking how they chose the first seats at the table, saying to them:

14:8 When thou art invited to a wedding, sit not down in the first place, lest perhaps one more honourable than thou be invited by him:

14:9 And he that invited thee and him, come and say to thee, Give this man place: and then thou begin with shame to take the lowest place.

14:10 But when thou art invited, go, sit down in the lowest place; that when he who invited thee, cometh, he may say to thee: Friend, go up higher. Then shalt thou have glory before them that sit at table with thee.

14:11 Because every one that exalteth himself, shall be humbled; and he that humbleth himself, shall be exalted.

14:12 And he said to him also that had invited

facis prandium, aut cœnam, noli vocare amicos tuos, neque fratres tuos, neque cognatos, neque vicinos divites : ne forte te et ipsi reinvitent, et fiat tibi retributio ;

14:13 sed cum facis convivium, voca pauperes, debiles, claudos, et cæcos :

14:14 et beatus eris, quia non habent retribuere tibi : retribuetur enim tibi in resurrectione justorum.

14:15 Hæc cum audisset quidam de simul discumbentibus, dixit illi : Beatus qui manducabit panem in regno Dei.

14:16 At ipse dixit ei : Homo quidam fecit cœnam magnam, et vocavit multos.

14:17 Et misit servum suum hora cœnæ dicere invitatis ut venirent, quia jam parata sunt omnia.

14:18 Et cœperunt simul omnes excusare. Primus dixit ei : Villam emi, et necesse habeo exire, et videre illam : rogo te, habe me excusatum.

14:19 Et alter dixit : Juga boum emi quinque, et eo probare illa : rogo te, habe me excusatum.

14:20 Et alius dixit : Uxorem duxi, et ideo non possum venire.

14:21 Et reversus servus nuntiavit hæc domino suo. Tunc iratus paterfamilias, dixit servo suo : Exi cito in plateas et vicos civitatis : et pauperes, ac debiles, et cæcos, et claudos introduc huc.

14:22 Et ait servus : Domine, factum est ut imperasti, et adhuc locus est.

14:23 Et ait dominus servo : Exi in vias, et sæpes : et compelle intrare, ut impleatur domus mea.

14:24 Dico autem vobis quod nemo virorum illorum qui vocati sunt, gustabit cœnam meam.

14:25 Ibant autem turbæ multæ cum eo : et conversus dixit ad illos :

14:26 Si quis venit ad me, et non odit patrem suum, et matrem, et uxorem, et filios, et fratres, et sorores, adhuc autem et animam suam, non potest meus esse discipulus.

14:27 Et qui non bajulat crucem suam, et venit post me, non potest meus esse discipulus.

14:28 Quis enim ex vobis volens turrim ædificare, non prius sedens computat sumptus, qui

him: When thou makest a dinner or a supper, call not thy friends, nor thy brethren, nor thy kinsmen, nor thy neighbours who are rich; lest perhaps they also invite thee again, and a recompense be made to thee.

14:13 But when thou makest a feast, call the poor, the maimed, the lame, and the blind;

14:14 And thou shalt be blessed, because they have not wherewith to make thee recompense: for recompense shall be made thee at the resurrection of the just.

14:15 When one of them that sat at table with him, had heard these things, he said to him: Blessed is he that shall eat bread in the kingdom of God.

14:16 But he said to him: A certain man made a great supper, and invited many.

14:17 And he sent his servant at the hour of supper to say to them that were invited, that they should come, for now all things are ready.

14:18 And they began all at once to make excuse. The first said to him: I have bought a farm, and I must needs go out and see it: I pray thee, hold me excused.

14:19 And another said: I have bought five yoke of oxen, and I go to try them: I pray thee, hold me excused.

14:20 And another said: I have married a wife, and therefore I cannot come.

14:21 And the servant returning, told these things to his lord. Then the master of the house, being angry, said to his servant: Go out quickly into the streets and lanes of the city, and bring in hither the poor, and the feeble, and the blind, and the lame.

14:22 And the servant said: Lord, it is done as thou hast commanded, and yet there is room.

14:23 And the Lord said to the servant: Go out into the highways and hedges, and compel them to come in, that my house may be filled.

14:24 But I say unto you, that none of those men that were invited, shall taste of my supper.

14:25 And there went great multitudes with him. And turning, he said to them:

14:26 If any man come to me, and hate not his father, and mother, and wife, and children, and brethren, and sisters, yea and his own life also, he cannot be my disciple.

14:27 And whosoever doth not carry his cross and come after me, cannot be my disciple.

14:28 For which of you having a mind to build a tower, doth not first sit down, and reckon the

necessarii sunt, si habeat ad perficiendum,

14:29 ne, posteaquam posuerit fundamentum, et non potuerit perficere, omnes qui vident, incipiant illudere ei,

14:30 dicentes : Quia hic homo cœpit ædificare, et non potuit consummare ?

14:31 Aut quis rex iturus committere bellum adversus alium regem, non sedens prius cogitat, si possit cum decem millibus occurrere ei, qui cum viginti millibus venit ad se ?

14:32 Alioquin adhuc illo longe agente, legationem mittens rogat ea quæ pacis sunt.

14:33 Sic ergo omnis ex vobis, qui non renuntiat omnibus quæ possidet, non potest meus esse discipulus.

14:34 Bonum est sal : si autem sal evanuerit, in quo condietur ?

14:35 Neque in terram, neque in sterquilinium utile est, sed foras mittetur. Qui habet aures audiendi, audiat.

15:1 Erant autem appropinquantes ei publicani, et peccatores ut audirent illum.

15:2 Et murmurabant pharisæi, et scribæ, dicentes : Quia hic peccatores recipit, et manducat cum illis.

15:3 Et ait ad illos parabolam istam dicens :

15:4 Quis ex vobis homo, qui habet centum oves, et si perdiderit unam ex illis, nonne dimittit nonaginta novem in deserto, et vadit ad illam quæ perierat, donec inveniat eam ?

15:5 Et cum invenerit eam, imponit in humeros suos gaudens :

15:6 et veniens domum convocat amicos et vicinos, dicens illis : Congratulamini mihi, quia inveni ovem meam, quæ perierat.

15:7 Dico vobis quod ita gaudium erit in cælo super uno peccatore pœnitentiam agente, quam super nonaginta novem justis, qui non indigent pœnitentia.

15:8 Aut quæ mulier habens drachmas decem, si perdiderit drachmam unam, nonne accendit lucernam, et everrit domum, et quærit diligenter, donec inveniat ?

15:9 Et cum invenerit convocat amicas et vicinas, dicens : Congratulamini mihi, quia inveni drachmam quam perdideram.

15:10 Ita, dico vobis, gaudium erit coram angelis

charges that are necessary, whether he have wherewithal to finish it:

14:29 Lest, after he hath laid the foundation, and is not able to finish it, all that see it begin to mock him,

14:30 Saying: This man began to build, and was not able to finish.

14:31 Or what king, about to go to make war against another king, doth not first sit down, and think whether he be able, with ten thousand, to meet him that, with twenty thousand, cometh against him?

14:32 Or else, whilst the other is yet afar off, sending an embassy, he desireth conditions of peace.

14:33 So likewise every one of you that doth not renounce all that he possesseth, cannot be my disciple.

14:34 Salt is good. But if the salt shall lose its savour, wherewith shall it be seasoned?

14:35 It is neither profitable for the land nor for the dunghill, but shall be cast out. He that hath ears to hear, let him hear.

15:1 Now the publicans and sinners drew near unto him to hear him.

15:2 And the Pharisees and the scribes murmured, saying: This man receiveth sinners, and eateth with them.

15:3 And he spoke to them this parable, saying:

15:4 What man of you that hath an hundred sheep: and if he shall lose one of them, doth he not leave the ninety-nine in the desert, and go after that which was lost, until he find it?

15:5 And when he hath found it, lay it upon his shoulders, rejoicing:

15:6 And coming home, call together his friends and neighbours, saying to them: Rejoice with me, because I have found my sheep that was lost?

15:7 I say to you, that even so there shall be joy in heaven upon one sinner that doth penance, more than upon ninety-nine just who need not penance.

15:8 Or what woman having ten groats; if she lose one groat, doth not light a candle, and sweep the house, and seek diligently until she find it?

15:9 And when she hath found it, call together her friends and neighbours, saying: Rejoice with me, because I have found the groat which I had lost.

15:10 So I say to you, there shall be joy before

Dei super uno peccatore pœnitentiam agente.

15:11 Ait autem : Homo quidam habuit duos filios :

15:12 et dixit adolescentior ex illis patri : Pater, da mihi portionem substantiæ, quæ me contingit. Et divisit illis substantiam.

15:13 Et non post multos dies, congregatis omnibus, adolescentior filius peregre profectus est in regionem longinquam, et ibi dissipavit substantiam suam vivendo luxuriose.

15:14 Et postquam omnia consummasset, facta est fames valida in regione illa, et ipse cœpit egere.

15:15 Et abiit, et adhæsit uni civium regionis illius : et misit illum in villam suam ut pasceret porcos.

15:16 Et cupiebat implere ventrem suum de siliquis, quas porci manducabant : et nemo illi dabat.

15:17 In se autem reversus, dixit : Quanti mercenarii in domo patris mei abundant panibus, ego autem hic fame pereo !

15:18 surgam, et ibo ad patrem meum, et dicam ei : Pater, peccavi in cælum, et coram te :

15:19 jam non sum dignus vocari filius tuus : fac me sicut unum de mercenariis tuis.

15:20 Et surgens venit ad patrem suum. Cum autem adhuc longe esset, vidit illum pater ipsius, et misericordia motus est, et accurrens cecidit super collum ejus, et osculatus est eum.

15:21 Dixitque ei filius : Pater, peccavi in cælum, et coram te : jam non sum dignus vocari filius tuus.

15:22 Dixit autem pater ad servos suos : Cito proferte stolam primam, et induite illum, et date annulum in manum ejus, et calceamenta in pedes ejus :

15:23 et adducite vitulum saginatum, et occidite, et manducemus, et epulemur :

15:24 quia hic filius meus mortuus erat, et revixit : perierat, et inventus est. Et cœperunt epulari.

15:25 Erat autem filius ejus senior in agro : et cum veniret, et appropinquaret domui, audivit symphoniam et chorum :

15:26 et vocavit unum de servis, et interrogavit quid hæc essent.

the angels of God upon one sinner doing penance.

15:11 And he said: A certain man had two sons:

15:12 And the younger of them said to his father: Father, give me the portion of substance that falleth to me. And he divided unto them his substance.

15:13 And not many days after, the younger son, gathering all together, went abroad into a far country: and there wasted his substance, living riotously.

15:14 And after he had spent all, there came a mighty famine in that country; and he began to be in want.

15:15 And he went and cleaved to one of the citizens of that country. And he sent him into his farm to feed swine.

15:16 And he would fain have filled his belly with the husks the swine did eat; and no man gave unto him.

15:17 And returning to himself, he said: How many hired servants in my father's house abound with bread, and I here perish with hunger?

15:18 I will arise, and will go to my father, and say to him: Father, I have sinned against heaven, and before thee:

15:19 I am not worthy to be called thy son: make me as one of thy hired servants.

15:20 And rising up he came to his father. And when he was yet a great way off, his father saw him, and was moved with compassion, and running to him fell upon his neck, and kissed him.

15:21 And the son said to him: Father, I have sinned against heaven, and before thee, I am not now worthy to be called thy son.

15:22 And the father said to his servants: Bring forth quickly the first robe, and put it on him, and put a ring on his hand, and shoes on his feet:

15:23 And bring hither the fatted calf, and kill it, and let us eat and make merry:

15:24 Because this my son was dead, and is come to life again: was lost, and is found. And they began to be merry.

15:25 Now his elder son was in the field, and when he came and drew nigh to the house, he heard music and dancing:

15:26 And he called one of the servants, and asked what these things meant.

15:27 Isque dixit illi : Frater tuus venit, et occidit pater tuus vitulum saginatum, quia salvum illum recepit.

15:28 Indignatus est autem, et nolebat introire. Pater ergo illius egressus, cœpit rogare illum.

15:29 At ille respondens, dixit patri suo : Ecce tot annis servio tibi, et numquam mandatum tuum præterivi : et numquam dedisti mihi hædum ut cum amicis meis epularer.

15:30 Sed postquam filius tuus hic, qui devoravit substantiam suam cum meretricibus, venit, occidisti illi vitulum saginatum.

15:31 At ipse dixit illi : Fili, tu semper mecum es, et omnia mea tua sunt :

15:32 epulari autem, et gaudere oportebat, quia frater tuus hic mortuus erat, et revixit ; perierat, et inventus est.

16:1 Dicebat autem et ad discipulos suos : Homo quidam erat dives, qui habebat villicum : et hic diffamatus est apud illum quasi dissipasset bona ipsius.

16:2 Et vocavit illum, et ait illi : Quid hoc audio de te ? redde rationem villicationis tuæ : jam enim non poteris villicare.

16:3 Ait autem villicus intra se : Quid faciam, quia dominus meus aufert a me villicationem ? Fodere non valeo, mendicare erubesco.

16:4 Scio quid faciam, ut, cum amotus fuero a villicatione, recipiant me in domos suas.

16:5 Convocatis itaque singulis debitoribus domini sui, dicebat primo : Quantum debes domino meo ?

16:6 At ille dixit : Centum cados olei. Dixitque illi : Accipe cautionem tuam : et sede cito, scribe quinquaginta.

16:7 Deinde alii dixit : Tu vero quantum debes ? Qui ait : Centum coros tritici. Ait illi : Accipe litteras tuas, et scribe octoginta.

16:8 Et laudavit dominus villicum iniquitatis, quia prudenter fecisset : quia filii hujus sæculi prudentiores filiis lucis in generatione sua sunt.

16:9 Et ego vobis dico : facite vobis amicos de mammona iniquitatis : ut, cum defeceritis, recipiant vos in æterna tabernacula.

15:27 And he said to him: Thy brother is come, and thy father hath killed the fatted calf, because he hath received him safe.

15:28 And he was angry, and would not go in. His father therefore coming out began to entreat him.

15:29 And he answering, said to his father: Behold, for so many years do I serve thee, and I have never transgressed thy commandment, and yet thou hast never given me a kid to make merry with my friends:

15:30 But as soon as this thy son is come, who hath devoured his substance with harlots, thou hast killed for him the fatted calf.

15:31 But he said to him: Son, thou art always with me, and all I have is thine.

15:32 But it was fit that we should make merry and be glad, for this thy brother was dead and is come to life again; he was lost, and is found.

16:1 And he said also to his disciples: There was a certain rich man who had a steward: and the same was accused unto him, that he had wasted his goods.

16:2 And he called him, and said to him: How is it that I hear this of thee? give an account of thy stewardship: for now thou canst be steward no longer.

16:3 And the steward said within himself: What shall I do, because my lord taketh away from me the stewardship? To dig I am not able; to beg I am ashamed.

16:4 I know what I will do, that when I shall be removed from the stewardship, they may receive me into their houses.

16:5 Therefore calling together every one of his lord's debtors, he said to the first: How much dost thou owe my lord?

16:6 But he said: An hundred barrels of oil. And he said to him: Take thy bill and sit down quickly, and write fifty.

16:7 Then he said to another: And how much dost thou owe? Who said: An hundred quarters of wheat. He said to him: Take thy bill, and write eighty.

16:8 And the lord commended the unjust steward, forasmuch as he had done wisely: for the children of this world are wiser in their generation than the children of light.

16:9 And I say to you: Make unto you friends of the mammon of iniquity; that when you shall fail, they may receive you into everlasting dwellings.

16:10 Qui fidelis est in minimo, et in majori fidelis est : et qui in modico iniquus est, et in majori iniquus est.

16:11 Si ergo in iniquo mammona fideles non fuistis quod verum est, quis credet vobis ?

16:12 Et si in alieno fideles non fuistis, quod vestrum est, quis dabit vobis ?

16:13 Nemo servus potest duobus dominis servire : aut enim unum odiet, et alterum diliget : aut uni adhærebit, et alterum contemnet. Non potestis Deo servire et mammonæ.

16:14 Audiebant autem omnia hæc pharisæi, qui erant avari : et deridebant illum.

16:15 Et ait illis : Vos estis qui justificatis vos coram hominibus : Deus autem novit corda vestra : quia quod hominibus altum est, abominatio est ante Deum.

16:16 Lex et prophetæ usque ad Joannem : ex eo regnum Dei evangelizatur, et omnis in illud vim facit.

16:17 Facilius est autem cælum et terram præterire, quam de lege unum apicem cadere.

16:18 Omnis qui dimittit uxorem suam et alteram ducit, mœchatur : et qui dimissam a viro ducit, mœchatur.

16:19 Homo quidam erat dives, qui induebatur purpura et bysso, et epulabatur quotidie splendide.

16:20 Et erat quidam mendicus, nomine Lazarus, qui jacebat ad januam ejus, ulceribus plenus,

16:21 cupiens saturari de micis quæ cadebant de mensa divitis, et nemo illi dabat : sed et canes veniebant, et lingebant ulcera ejus.

16:22 Factum est autem ut moreretur mendicus, et portaretur ab angelis in sinum Abrahæ. Mortuus est autem et dives, et sepultus est in inferno.

16:23 Elevans autem oculos suos, cum esset in tormentis, vidit Abraham a longe, et Lazarum in sinu ejus :

16:24 et ipse clamans dixit : Pater Abraham, miserere mei, et mitte Lazarum ut intingat extremum digiti sui in aquam, ut refrigeret linguam meam, quia crucior in hac flamma.

16:25 Et dixit illi Abraham : Fili, recordare quia recepisti bona in vita tua, et Lazarus similiter

16:10 He that is faithful in that which is least, is faithful also in that which is greater: and he that is unjust in that which is little, is unjust also in that which is greater.

16:11 If then you have not been faithful in the unjust mammon; who will trust you with that which is the true?

16:12 And if you have not been faithful in that which is another's; who will give you that which is your own?

16:13 No servant can serve two masters: for either he will hate the one, and love the other; or he will hold to the one, and despise the other. You cannot serve God and mammon.

16:14 Now the Pharisees, who were covetous, heard all these things: and they derided him.

16:15 And he said to them: You are they who justify yourselves before men, but God knoweth your hearts; for that which is high to men, is an abomination before God.

16:16 The law and the prophets were until John; from that time the kingdom of God is preached, and every one useth violence towards it.

16:17 And it is easier for heaven and earth to pass, than one tittle of the law to fall.

16:18 Every one that putteth away his wife, and marrieth another, committeth adultery: and he that marrieth her that is put away from her husband, commmitteth adultery.

16:19 There was a certain rich man, who was clothed in purple and fine linen; and feasted sumptuously every day.

16:20 And there was a certain beggar, named Lazarus, who lay at his gate, full of sores,

16:21 Desiring to be filled with the crumbs that fell from the rich man's table, and no one did give him; moreover the dogs came, and licked his sores.

16:22 And it came to pass, that the beggar died, and was carried by the angels into Abraham's bosom. And the rich man also died: and he was buried in hell.

16:23 And lifting up his eyes when he was in torments, he saw Abraham afar off, and Lazarus in his bosom:

16:24 And he cried, and said: Father Abraham, have mercy on me, and send Lazarus, that he may dip the tip of his finger in water, to cool my tongue: for I am tormented in this flame.

16:25 And Abraham said to him: Son, remember that thou didst receive good things in thy life-

mala : nunc autem hic consolatur, tu vero cruciaris :

16:26 et in his omnibus inter nos et vos chaos magnum firmatum est : ut hi qui volunt hinc transire ad vos, non possint, neque inde huc transmeare.

16:27 Et ait : Rogo ergo te, pater, ut mittas eum in domum patris mei :

16:28 habeo enim quinque fratres : ut testetur illis, ne et ipsi veniant in hunc locum tormentorum.

16:29 Et ait illi Abraham : Habent Moysen et prophetas : audiant illos.

16:30 At ille dixit : Non, pater Abraham : sed si quis ex mortuis ierit ad eos, pœnitentiam agent.

16:31 Ait autem illi : Si Moysen et prophetas non audiunt, neque si quis ex mortuis resurrexerit, credent.

17:1 Et ait ad discipulos suos : Impossibile est ut non veniant scandala : væ autem illi per quem veniunt.

17:2 Utilius est illi si lapis molaris imponatur circa collum ejus, et projiciatur in mare quam ut scandalizet unum de pusillis istis.

17:3 Attendite vobis : Si peccaverit in te frater tuus, increpa illum : et si pœnitentiam egerit, dimitte illi.

17:4 Et si septies in die peccaverit in te, et septies in die conversus fuerit ad te, dicens : Pœnitet me, dimitte illi.

17:5 Et dixerunt apostoli Domino : Adauge nobis fidem.

17:6 Dixit autem Dominus : Si habueritis fidem sicut granum sinapis, dicetis huic arbori moro : Eradicare, et transplantare in mare, et obediet vobis.

17:7 Quis autem vestrum habens servum arantem aut pascentem, qui regresso de agro dicat illi : Statim transi, recumbe :

17:8 et non dicat ei : Para quod cœnem, et præcinge te, et ministra mihi donec manducem, et bibam, et post hæc tu manducabis, et bibes ?

17:9 Numquid gratiam habet servo illi, quia fecit quæ ei imperaverat ?

17:10 non puto. Sic et vos cum feceritis omnia quæ præcepta sunt vobis, dicite : Servi inutiles

time, and likewise Lazareth evil things, but now he is comforted; and thou art tormented.

16:26 And besides all this, between us and you, there is fixed a great chaos: so that they who would pass from hence to you, cannot, nor from thence come hither.

16:27 And he said: Then, father, I beseech thee, that thou wouldst send him to my father's house, for I have five brethren,

16:28 That he may testify unto them, lest they also come into this place of torments.

16:29 And Abraham said to him: They have Moses and the prophets; let them hear them.

16:30 But he said: No, father Abraham: but if one went to them from the dead, they will do penance.

16:31 And he said to him: If they hear not Moses and the prophets, neither will they believe, if one rise again from the dead.

17:1 And he said to his disciples: It is impossible that scandals should not come: but woe to him through whom they come.

17:2 It were better for him, that a millstone were hanged about his neck, and he cast into the sea, than that he should scandalize one of these little ones.

17:3 Take heed to yourselves. If thy brother sin against thee, reprove him: and if he do penance, forgive him.

17:4 And if he sin against thee seven times in a day, and seven times in a day be converted unto thee, saying, I repent; forgive him.

17:5 And the apostles said to the Lord: Increase our faith.

17:6 And the Lord said: If you had faith like to a grain of mustard seed, you might say to this mulberry tree, Be thou rooted up, and be thou transplanted into the sea: and it would obey you.

17:7 But which of you having a servant ploughing, or feeding cattle, will say to him, when he is come from the field: Immediately go, sit down to meat:

17:8 And will not rather say to him: Make ready my supper, and gird thyself, and serve me, whilst I eat and drink, and afterwards thou shalt eat and drink?

17:9 Doth he thank that servant, for doing the things which he commanded him?

17:10 I think not. So you also, when you shall have done all these things that are commanded

sumus : quod debuimus facere, fecimus.

17:11 Et factum est, dum iret in Jerusalem, transibat per mediam Samariam et Galilæam.

17:12 Et cum ingrederetur quoddam castellum, occurrerunt ei decem viri leprosi, qui steterunt a longe :

17:13 et levaverunt vocem, dicentes : Jesu præceptor, miserere nostri.

17:14 Quos ut vidit, dixit : Ite, ostendite vos sacerdotibus. Et factum est, dum irent, mundati sunt.

17:15 Unus autem ex illis, ut vidit quia mundatus est, regressus est, cum magna voce magnificans Deum,

17:16 et cecidit in faciem ante pedes ejus, gratias agens : et hic erat Samaritanus.

17:17 Respondens autem Jesus, dixit : Nonne decem mundati sunt ? et novem ubi sunt ?

17:18 Non est inventus qui rediret, et daret gloriam Deo, nisi hic alienigena.

17:19 Et ait illi : Surge, vade : quia fides tua te salvum fecit.

17:20 Interrogatus autem a pharisæis : Quando venit regnum Dei ? respondens eis, dixit : Non venit regnum Dei cum observatione :

17:21 neque dicent : Ecce hic, aut ecce illic. Ecce enim regnum Dei intra vos est.

17:22 Et ait ad discipulos suos : Venient dies quando desideretis videre unum diem Filii hominis, et non videbitis.

17:23 Et dicent vobis : Ecce hic, et ecce illic. Nolite ire, neque sectemini :

17:24 nam, sicut fulgur coruscans de sub cælo in ea quæ sub cælo sunt, fulget : ita erit Filius hominis in die sua.

17:25 Primum autem oportet illum multa pati, et reprobari a generatione hac.

17:26 Et sicut factum est in diebus Noë, ita erit et in diebus Filii hominis :

17:27 edebant et bibebant : uxores ducebant et dabantur ad nuptias, usque in diem, qua intravit Noë in arcam : et venit diluvium, et perdidit omnes.

17:28 Similiter sicut factum est in diebus Lot : edebant et bibebant, emebant et vendebant, plantabant et ædificabant :

17:29 qua die autem exiit Lot a Sodomis, pluit

you, say: We are unprofitable servants; we have done that which we ought to do.

17:11 And it came to pass, as he was going to Jerusalem, he passed through the midst of Samaria and Galilee.

17:12 And as he entered into a certain town, there met him ten men that were lepers, who stood afar off;

17:13 And lifted up their voice, saying: Jesus, master, have mercy on us.

17:14 Whom when he saw, he said: Go, shew yourselves to the priests. And it came to pass, as they went, they were made clean.

17:15 And one of them, when he saw that he was made clean, went back, with a loud voice glorifying God.

17:16 And he fell on his face before his feet, giving thanks: and this was a Samaritan.

17:17 And Jesus answering, said, Were not ten made clean? and where are the nine?

17:18 There is no one found to return and give glory to God, but this stranger.

17:19 And he said to him: Arise, go thy way; for thy faith hath made thee whole.

17:20 And being asked by the Pharisees, when the kingdom of God should come? he answered them, and said: The kingdom of God cometh not with observation:

17:21 Neither shall they say: Behold here, or behold there. For lo, the kingdom of God is within you.

17:22 And he said to his disciples: The days will come, when you shall desire to see one day of the Son of man; and you shall not see it.

17:23 And they will say to you: See here, and see there. Go ye not after, nor follow them:

17:24 For as the lightening that lighteneth from under heaven, shineth unto the parts that are under heaven, so shall the Son of man be in his day.

17:25 But first he must suffer many things, and be rejected by this generation.

17:26 And as it came to pass in the days of Noe, so shall it be also in the days of the Son of man.

17:27 They did eat and drink, they married wives, and were given in marriage, until the day that Noe entered into the ark: and the flood came and destroyed them all.

17:28 Likewise as it came to pass, in the days of Lot: they did eat and drink, they bought and sold, they planted and built.

17:29 And in the day that Lot went out of Sod-

ignem et sulphur de cælo, et omnes perdidit :

17:30 secundum hæc erit qua die Filius hominis revelabitur.

17:31 In illa hora, qui fuerit in tecto, et vasa ejus in domo, ne descendat tollere illa : et qui in agro, similiter non redeat retro.

17:32 Memores estote uxoris Lot.

17:33 Quicumque quæsierit animam suam salvam facere, perdet illam : et quicumque perdiderit illam, vivificabit eam.

17:34 Dico vobis : In illa nocte erunt duo in lecto uno : unus assumetur, et alter relinquetur :

17:35 duæ erunt molentes in unum : una assumetur, et altera relinquetur : duo in agro : unus assumetur, et alter relinquetur.

17:36 Respondentes dicunt illi : Ubi Domine ?

17:37 Qui dixit illis : Ubicumque fuerit corpus, illuc congregabuntur et aquilæ.

18:1 Dicebat autem et parabolam ad illos, quoniam oportet semper orare et non deficere,

18:2 dicens : Judex quidam erat in quadam civitate, qui Deum non timebat, et hominem non reverebatur.

18:3 Vidua autem quædam erat in civitate illa, et veniebat ad eum, dicens : Vindica me de adversario meo.

18:4 Et nolebat per multum tempus. Post hæc autem dixit intra se : Etsi Deum non timeo, nec hominem revereor :

18:5 tamen quia molesta est mihi hæc vidua, vindicabo illam, ne in novissimo veniens sugillet me.

18:6 Ait autem Dominus : Audite quid judex iniquitatis dicit :

18:7 Deus autem non faciet vindictam electorum suorum clamantium ad se die ac nocte, et patientiam habebit in illis ?

18:8 Dico vobis quia cito faciet vindictam illorum. Verumtamen Filius hominis veniens, putas, inveniet fidem in terra ?

18:9 Dixit autem et ad quosdam qui in se confidebant tamquam justi, et aspernabantur ceteros, parabolam istam :

18:10 Duo homines ascenderunt in templum ut orarent : unus pharisæus et alter publicanus.

18:11 Pharisæus stans, hæc apud se orabat : De-

om, it rained fire and brimstone from heaven, and destroyed them all.

17:30 Even thus shall it be in the day when the Son of man shall be revealed.

17:31 In that hour, he that shall be on the housetop, and his goods in the house, let him not go down to take them away: and he that shall be in the field, in like manner, let him not return back.

17:32 Remember Lot's wife.

17:33 Whosoever shall seek to save his life, shall lose it: and whosoever shall lose it, shall preserve it.

17:34 I say to you: in that night there shall be two men in one bed; the one shall be taken, and the other shall be left.

17:35 Two women shall be grinding together: the one shall be taken, and the other shall be left: two men shall be in the field; the one shall be taken, and the other shall be left.

17:36 They answering, say to him: Where, Lord?

17:37 Who said to them: Wheresoever the body shall be, thither will the eagles also be gathered together.

18:1 And he spoke also a parable to them, that we ought always to pray, and not to faint,

18:2 Saying: There was a judge in a certain city, who feared not God, nor regarded man.

18:3 And there was a certain widow in that city, and she came to him, saying: Avenge me of my adversary.

18:4 And he would not for a long time. But afterwards he said within himself: Although I fear not God, nor regard man,

18:5 Yet because this widow is troublesome to me, I will avenge her, lest continually coming she weary me.

18:6 And the Lord said: Hear what the unjust judge saith.

18:7 And will not God revenge his elect who cry to him day and night: and will he have patience in their regard?

18:8 I say to you, that he will quickly revenge them. But yet the Son of man, when he cometh, shall he find, think you, faith on earth?

18:9 And to some who trusted in themselves as just, and despised others, he spoke also this parable:

18:10 Two men went up into the temple to pray: the one a Pharisee, and the other a publican.

18:11 The Pharisee standing, prayed thus with

us, gratias ago tibi, quia non sum sicut ceteri hominum : raptores, injusti, adulteri, velut etiam hic publicanus :

18:12 jejuno bis in sabbato, decimas do omnium quæ possideo.

18:13 Et publicanus a longe stans, nolebat nec oculos ad cælum levare : sed percutiebat pectus suum, dicens : Deus propitius esto mihi peccatori.

18:14 Dico vobis, descendit hic justificatus in domum suam ab illo : quia omnis qui se exaltat, humiliabitur, et qui se humiliat, exaltabitur.

18:15 Afferebant autem ad illum et infantes, ut eos tangeret. Quod cum viderent discipuli, increpabant illos.

18:16 Jesus autem convocans illos, dixit : Sinite pueros venire ad me, et nolite vetare eos : talium est enim regnum Dei.

18:17 Amen dico vobis, quicumque non acceperit regnum Dei sicut puer, non intrabit in illud.

18:18 Et interrogavit eum quidam princeps, dicens : Magister bone, quid faciens vitam æternam possidebo ?

18:19 Dixit autem ei Jesus : Quid me dicis bonum ? nemo bonus nisi solus Deus.

18:20 Mandata nosti : non occides ; non mœchaberis ; non furtum facies ; non falsum testimonium dices ; honora patrem tuum et matrem.

18:21 Qui ait : Hæc omnia custodivi a juventute mea.

18:22 Quo audito, Jesus ait ei : Adhuc unum tibi deest : omnia quæcumque habes vende, et da pauperibus, et habebis thesaurum in cælo : et veni, sequere me.

18:23 His ille auditis, contristatus est : quia dives erat valde.

18:24 Videns autem Jesus illum tristem factum, dixit : Quam difficile, qui pecunias habent, in regnum Dei intrabunt !

18:25 facilius est enim camelum per foramen acus transire quam divitem intrare in regnum Dei.

18:26 Et dixerunt qui audiebant : Et quis potest salvus fieri ?

18:27 Ait illis : Quæ impossibilia sunt apud homines, possibilia sunt apud Deum.

18:28 Ait autem Petrus : Ecce nos dimisimus

himself: O God, I give thee thanks that I am not as the rest of men, extortioners, unjust, adulterers, as also is this publican.

18:12 I fast twice in a week: I give tithes of all that I possess.

18:13 And the publican, standing afar off, would not so much as lift up his eyes towards heaven; but struck his breast, saying: O god, be merciful to me a sinner.

18:14 I say to you, this man went down into his house justified rather that the other: because every one that exalteth himself, shall be humbled: and he that humbleth himself, shall be exalted.

18:15 And they brought unto him also infants, that he might touch them. Which when the disciples saw, they rebuked them.

18:16 But Jesus, calling them together, said: Suffer children to come to me, and forbid them not: for of such is the kingdom of God.

18:17 Amen, I say to you: Whosoever shall not receive the kingdom of God as a child, shall not enter into it.

18:18 And a certain ruler asked him, saying: Good master, what shall I do to possess everlasting life?

18:19 And Jesus said to him: Why dost thou call me good? None is good but God alone.

18:20 Thou knowest the commandments: Thou shalt not kill: Thou shalt not commit adultery: Thou shalt not steal: Thou shalt not bear false witness: Honour thy father and mother.

18:21 Who said: All these things have I kept from my youth.

18:22 Which when Jesus had heard, he said to him: Yet one thing is wanting to thee: sell all whatever thou hast, and give to the poor, and thou shalt have treasure in heaven: and come, follow me.

18:23 He having heard these things, be came sorrowful; for he was very rich.

18:24 And Jesus seeing him become sorrowful, said: How hardly shall they that have riches enter into the kingdom of God.

18:25 For it is easier for a camel to pass through the eye of a needle, than for a rich man to enter into the kingdom of God.

18:26 And they that heard it, said: Who then can be saved?

18:27 He said to them: The things that are impossible with men, are possible with God.

18:28 Then Peter said: Behold, we have left all

omnia et secuti sumus te.

18:29 Qui dixit eis : Amen dico vobis, nemo est qui reliquit domum, aut parentes, aut fratres, aut uxorem, aut filios propter regnum Dei,

18:30 et non recipiat multo plura in hoc tempore, et in sæculo venturo vitam æternam.

18:31 Assumpsit autem Jesus duodecim, et ait illis : Ecce ascendimus Jerosolymam, et consummabuntur omnia quæ scripta sunt per prophetas de Filio hominis :

18:32 tradetur enim gentibus, et illudetur, et flagellabitur, et conspuetur :

18:33 et postquam flagellaverint, occident eum, et tertia die resurget.

18:34 Et ipsi nihil horum intellexerunt, et erat verbum istud absconditum ab eis, et non intelligebant quæ dicebantur.

18:35 Factum est autem, cum appropinquaret Jericho, cæcus quidam sedebat secus viam, mendicans.

18:36 Et cum audiret turbam prætereuntem, interrogabat quid hoc esset.

18:37 Dixerunt autem ei quod Jesus Nazarenus transiret.

18:38 Et clamavit, dicens : Jesu, fili David, miserere mei.

18:39 Et qui præibant, increpabant eum ut taceret. Ipse vero multo magis clamabat : Fili David, miserere mei.

18:40 Stans autem Jesus jussit illum adduci ad se. Et cum appropinquasset, interrogavit illum,

18:41 dicens : Quid tibi vis faciam ? At ille dixit : Domine, ut videam.

18:42 Et Jesus dixit illi : Respice, fides tua te salvum fecit.

18:43 Et confestim vidit, et sequebatur illum magnificans Deum. Et omnis plebs ut vidit, dedit laudem Deo.

19:1 Et ingressus perambulabat Jericho.

19:2 Et ecce vir nomine Zachæus : et hic princeps erat publicanorum, et ipse dives :

19:3 et quærebat videre Jesum, quis esset : et non poterat præ turba, quia statura pusillus erat.

things, and have followed thee.

18:29 Who said to them: Amen, I say to you, there is no man that hath left house, or parents, or brethren, or wife, or children, for the kingdom of God's sake,

18:30 Who shall not receive much more in this present time, and in the world to come life everlasting.

18:31 Then Jesus took unto him the twelve, and said to them: Behold, we go up to Jerusalem, and all things shall be accomplished which were written by the prophets concerning the Son of man.

18:32 For he shall be delivered to the Gentiles, and shall be mocked, and scourged, and spit upon:

18:33 And after they have scourged him, they will put him to death; and the third day he shall rise again.

18:34 And they understood none of these things, and this word was hid from them, and they understood not the things that were said.

18:35 Now it came to pass, when he drew nigh to Jericho, that a certain blind man sat by the way side, begging.

18:36 And when he heard the multitude passing by, he asked what this meant.

18:37 And they told him, that Jesus of Nazareth was passing by.

18:38 And he cried out, saying: Jesus, son of David, have mercy on me.

18:39 And they that went before, rebuked him, that he should hold his peace: but he cried out much more: Son of David, have mercy on me.

18:40 And Jesus standing, commanded him to be brought unto him. And when he was come near, he asked him,

18:41 Saying: What wilt thou that I do to thee? But he said: Lord, that I may see.

18:42 And Jesus said to him: Receive thy sight: thy faith hath made thee whole.

18:43 And immediately he saw, and followed him, glorifying God. And all the people, when they saw it, gave praise to God.

19:1 And entering in, he walked through Jericho.

19:2 And behold, there was a man named Zacheus, who was the chief of the publicans, and he was rich.

19:3 And he sought to see Jesus who he was, and he could not for the crowd, because he was low of stature.

19:4 Et præcurrens ascendit in arborem sycomorum ut videret eum : quia inde erat transiturus.

19:5 Et cum venisset ad locum, suspiciens Jesus vidit illum, et dixit ad eum : Zachæe, festinans descende : quia hodie in domo tua oportet me manere.

19:6 Et festinans descendit, et excepit illum gaudens.

19:7 Et cum viderent omnes, murmurabant, dicentes quod ad hominem peccatorem divertisset.

19:8 Stans autem Zachæus, dixit ad Dominum : Ecce dimidium bonorum meorum, Domine, do pauperibus : et si quid aliquem defraudavi, reddo quadruplum.

19:9 Ait Jesus ad eum : Quia hodie salus domui huic facta est : eo quod et ipse filius sit Abrahæ.

19:10 Venit enim Filius hominis quærere, et salvum facere quod perierat.

19:11 Hæc illis audientibus adjiciens, dixit parabolam, eo quod esset prope Jerusalem : et quia existimarent quod confestim regnum Dei manifestaretur.

19:12 Dixit ergo : Homo quidam nobilis abiit in regionem longinquam accipere sibi regnum, et reverti.

19:13 Vocatis autem decem servis suis, dedit eis decem mnas, et ait ad illos : Negotiamini dum venio.

19:14 Cives autem ejus oderant eum : et miserunt legationem post illum, dicentes : Nolumus hunc regnare super nos.

19:15 Et factum est ut rediret accepto regno : et jussit vocari servos, quibus dedit pecuniam, ut sciret quantum quisque negotiatus esset.

19:16 Venit autem primus dicens : Domine, mna tua decem mnas acquisivit.

19:17 Et ait illi : Euge bone serve, quia in modico fuisti fidelis, eris potestatem habens super decem civitates.

19:18 Et alter venit, dicens : Domine, mna tua fecit quinque mnas.

19:19 Et huic ait : Et tu esto super quinque civitates.

19:20 Et alter venit, dicens : Domine, ecce mna tua, quam habui repositam in sudario :

19:4 And running before, he climbed up into a sycamore tree, that he might see him; for he was to pass that way.

19:5 And when Jesus was come to the place, looking up, he saw him, and said to him: Zacheus, make haste and come down; for this day I must abide in thy house.

19:6 And he made haste and came down; and received him with joy.

19:7 And when all saw it, they murmured, saying, that he was gone to be a guest with a man that was a sinner.

19:8 But Zacheus standing, said to the Lord: Behold, Lord, the half of my goods I give to the poor; and if I have wronged any man of any thing, I restore him fourfold.

19:9 Jesus said to him: This day is salvation come to this house, because he also is a son of Abraham.

19:10 For the Son of man is come to seek and to save that which was lost.

19:11 As they were hearing these things, he added and spoke a parable, because he was nigh to Jerusalem, and because they thought that the kingdom of God should immediately be manifested.

19:12 He said therefore: A certain nobleman went into a far country, to receive for himself a kingdom, and to return.

19:13 And calling his ten servants, he gave them ten pounds, and said to them: Trade till I come.

19:14 But his citizens hated him: and they sent an embassage after him, saying: We will not have this man to reign over us.

19:15 And it came to pass, that he returned, having received the kingdom: and he commanded his servants to be called, to whom he had given the money, that he might know how much every man had gained by trading.

19:16 And the first came, saying: Lord, thy pound hath gained ten pounds.

19:17 And he said to him: Well done, thou good servant, because thou hast been faithful in a little, thou shalt have power over ten cities.

19:18 And the second came, saying: Lord, thy pound hath gained five pounds.

19:19 And he said to him: Be thou also over five cities.

19:20 And another came, saying: Lord, behold here is thy pound, which I have kept laid up in a napkin;

19:21 timui enim te, quia homo austerus es : tollis quod non posuisti, et metis quod non seminasti.

19:22 Dicit ei : De ore tuo te judico, serve nequam. Sciebas quod ego homo austerus sum, tollens quod non posui, et metens quod non seminavi :

19:23 et quare non dedisti pecuniam meam ad mensam, ut ego veniens cum usuris utique exegissem illam ?

19:24 Et astantibus dixit : Auferte ab illo mnam, et date illi qui decem mnas habet.

19:25 Et dixerunt ei : Domine, habet decem mnas.

19:26 Dico autem vobis, quia omni habenti dabitur, et abundabit : ab eo autem qui non habet, et quod habet auferetur ab eo.

19:27 Verumtamen inimicos meos illos, qui noluerunt me regnare super se, adducite huc : et interficite ante me.

19:28 Et his dictis, præcedebat ascendens Jerosolymam.

19:29 Et factum est, cum appropinquasset ad Bethphage et Bethaniam, ad montem qui vocatur Oliveti, misit duos discipulos suos,

19:30 dicens : Ite in castellum quod contra est : in quod introëuntes, invenietis pullum asinæ alligatum, cui nemo umquam hominum sedit : solvite illum, et adducite.

19:31 Et si quis vos interrogaverit : Quare solvitis ? sic dicetis ei : Quia Dominus operam ejus desiderat.

19:32 Abierunt autem qui missi erant : et invenerunt, sicut dixit illis, stantem pullum.

19:33 Solventibus autem illis pullum, dixerunt domini ejus ad illos : Quid solvitis pullum ?

19:34 At illi dixerunt : Quia Dominus eum necessarium habet.

19:35 Et duxerunt illum ad Jesum. Et jactantes vestimenta sua supra pullum, imposuerunt Jesum.

19:36 Eunte autem illo, substernebant vestimenta sua in via :

19:37 et cum appropinquaret jam ad descensum

19:21 For I feared thee, because thou art an austere man: thou takest up what thou didst not lay down, and thou reapest that which thou didst not sow.

19:22 He saith to him: Out of thy own mouth I judge thee, thou wicked servant. Thou knewest that I was an austere man, taking up what I laid not down, and reaping that which I did not sow:

19:23 And why then didst thou not give my money into the bank, that at my coming, I might have exacted it with usury?

19:24 And he said to them that stood by: Take the pound away from him, and give it to him that hath ten pounds.

19:25 And they said to him: Lord, he hath ten pounds.

19:26 But I say to you, that to every one that hath shall be given, and he shall abound: and from him that hath not, even that which he hath, shall be taken from him.

19:27 But as for those my enemies, who would not have me reign over them, bring them hither, and kill them before me.

19:28 And having said these things, he went before, going up to Jerusalem.

19:29 And it came to pass, when he was come nigh to Bethphage and Bethania, unto the mount called Olivet, he sent two of his disciples,

19:30 Saying: Go into the town which is over against you, at your entering into which you shall find the colt of an ass tied, on which no man ever hath sitten: loose him, and bring him hither.

19:31 And if any man shall ask you: Why do you loose him? you shall say thus unto him: Because the Lord hath need of his service.

19:32 And they that were sent, went their way, and found the colt standing, as he had said unto them.

19:33 And as they were loosing the colt, the owners thereof said to them: Why loose you the colt?

19:34 But they said: Because the Lord hath need of him.

19:35 And they brought him to Jesus. And casting their garments on the colt, they set Jesus thereon.

19:36 And as he went, they spread their clothes underneath in the way.

19:37 And when he was now coming near the de-

montis Oliveti, cœperunt omnes turbæ discipulorum gaudentes laudare Deum voce magna super omnibus, quas viderant, virtutibus,

19:38 dicentes : Benedictus, qui venit rex in nomine Domini : pax in cælo, et gloria in excelsis.

19:39 Et quidam pharisæorum de turbis dixerunt ad illum : Magister, increpa discipulos tuos.

19:40 Quibus ipse ait : Dico vobis, quia si hi tacuerint, lapides clamabunt.

19:41 Et ut appropinquavit, videns civitatem flevit super illam, dicens :

19:42 Quia si cognovisses et tu, et quidem in hac die tua, quæ ad pacem tibi : nunc autem abscondita sunt ab oculis tuis.

19:43 Quia venient dies in te : et circumdabunt te inimici tui vallo, et circumdabunt te : et coangustabunt te undique :

19:44 et ad terram prosternent te, et filios tuos, qui in te sunt, et non relinquent in te lapidem super lapidem : eo quod non cognoveris tempus visitationis tuæ.

19:45 Et ingressus in templum, cœpit ejicere vendentes in illo, et ementes,

19:46 dicens illis : Scriptum est : Quia domus mea domus orationis est : vos autem fecistis illam speluncam latronum.

19:47 Et erat docens quotidie in templo. Principes autem sacerdotum, et scribæ, et princeps plebis quærebant illum perdere :

19:48 et non inveniebant quid facerent illi. Omnis enim populus suspensus erat, audiens illum.

20:1 Et factum est in una dierum, docente illo populum in templo, et evangelizante, convenerunt principes sacerdotum, et scribæ cum senioribus,

20:2 et aiunt dicentes ad illum : Dic nobis in qua potestate hæc facis ? aut quis est qui dedit tibi hanc potestatem ?

20:3 Respondens autem Jesus, dixit ad illos : Interrogabo vos et ego unum verbum. Respondete mihi :

20:4 baptismus Joannis de cælo erat, an ex hominibus ?

20:5 At illi cogitabant intra se, dicentes : Quia si dixerimus : De cælo, dicet : Quare ergo non credidistis illi ?

20:6 Si autem dixerimus : Ex hominibus, plebs

scent of mount Olivet, the whole multitude of his disciples began with joy to praise God with a loud voice, for all the mighty works they had seen,

19:38 Saying: Blessed be the king who cometh in the name of the Lord, peace in heaven, and glory on high!

19:39 And some of the Pharisees, from amongst the multitude, said to him: Master, rebuke thy disciples.

19:40 To whom he said: I say to you, that if these shall hold their peace, the stones will cry out.

19:41 And when he drew near, seeing the city, he wept over it, saying:

19:42 If thou also hadst known, and that in this thy day, the things that are to thy peace; but now they are hidden from thy eyes.

19:43 For the days shall come upon thee, and thy enemies shall cast a trench about thee, and compass thee round, and straiten thee on every side,

19:44 And beat thee flat to the ground, and thy children who are in thee: and they shall not leave in thee a stone upon a stone: because thou hast not known the time of thy visitation.

19:45 And entering into the temple, he began to cast out them that sold therein, and them that bought.

19:46 Saying to them: It is written: My house is the house of prayer. But you have made it a den of thieves.

19:47 And he was teaching daily in the temple. And the chief priests and the scribes and the rulers of the people sought to destroy him:

19:48 And they found not what to do to him: for all the people were very attentive to hear him.

20:1 And it came to pass, that on one of the days, as he was teaching the people in the temple, and preaching the gospel, the chief priests and the scribes, with the ancients, met together,

20:2 And spoke to him, saying: Tell us, by what authority dost thou these things? or, Who is he that hath given thee this authority?

20:3 And Jesus answering, said to them: I will also ask you one thing. Answer me:

20:4 The baptism of John, was it from heaven, or of men?

20:5 But they thought within themselves, saying: If we shall say, From heaven: he will say: Why then did you not believe him?

20:6 But if we say, Of men, the whole people

universa lapidabit nos : certi sunt enim Joannem prophetam esse.

20:7 Et responderunt se nescire unde esset.

20:8 Et Jesus ait illis : Neque ego dico vobis in qua potestate hæc facio.

20:9 Cœpit autem dicere ad plebem parabolam hanc : Homo plantavit vineam, et locavit eam colonis : et ipse peregre fuit multis temporibus.

20:10 Et in tempore misit ad cultores servum, ut de fructu vineæ darent illi. Qui cæsum dimiserunt eum inanem.

20:11 Et addidit alterum servum mittere. Illi autem hunc quoque cædentes, et afficientes contumelia, dimiserunt inanem.

20:12 Et addidit tertium mittere : qui et illum vulnerantes ejecerunt.

20:13 Dixit autem dominus vineæ : Quid faciam ? Mittam filium meum dilectum : forsitan, cum hunc viderint, verebuntur.

20:14 Quem cum vidissent coloni, cogitaverunt intra se, dicentes : Hic est hæres, occidamus illum, ut nostra fiat hæreditas.

20:15 Et ejectum illum extra vineam, occiderunt. Quid ergo faciet illis dominus vineæ ?

20:16 veniet, et perdet colonos istos, et dabit vineam aliis. Quo audito, dixerunt illi : Absit.

20:17 Ille autem aspiciens eos, ait : Quid est ergo hoc quod scriptum est : Lapidem quem reprobaverunt ædificantes, hic factus est in caput anguli ?

20:18 Omnis qui ceciderit super illum lapidem, conquassabitur : super quem autem ceciderit, comminuet illum.

20:19 Et quærebant principes sacerdotum et scribæ mittere in illum manus illa hora, et timuerunt populum : cognoverunt enim quod ad ipsos dixerit similitudinem hanc.

20:20 Et observantes miserunt insidiatores, qui se justos simularent, ut caperent eum in sermone, ut traderent illum principatui, et potestati præsidis.

20:21 Et interrogaverunt eum, dicentes : Magister, scimus quia recte dicis et doces : et non accipis personam, sed viam Dei in veritate doces.

will stone us: for they are persuaded that John was a prophet.

20:7 And they answered, that they knew not whence it was.

20:8 And Jesus said to them: Neither do I tell thee by what authority I do these things.

20:9 And he began to speak to the people this parable: A certain man planted a vineyard, and let it out to husbandmen: and he was abroad for a long time.

20:10 And at the season he sent a servant to the husbandmen, that they should give him of the fruit of the vineyard. Who, beating him, sent him away empty.

20:11 And again he sent another servant. But they beat him also, and treating him reproachfully, sent him away empty.

20:12 And again he sent the third: and they wounded him also, and cast him out.

20:13 Then the lord of the vineyard said: What shall I do? I will send my beloved son: it may be, when they see him, they will reverence him.

20:14 Whom when the husbandmen saw, they thought within themselves, saying: This is the heir, let us kill him, that the inheritance may be ours.

20:15 So casting him out of the vineyard, they killed him. What therefore will the lord of the vineyard do to them?

20:16 He will come, and will destroy these husbandmen, and will give the vineyard to others. Which they hearing, said to him: God forbid.

20:17 But he looking on them, said: What is this then that is written, The stone, which the builders rejected, the same is become the head of the corner?

20:18 Whosoever shall fall upon that stone, shall be bruised: and upon whomsoever it shall fall, it will grind him to powder.

20:19 And the chief priests and the scribes sought to lay hands on him the same hour: but they feared the people, for they knew that he spoke this parable to them.

20:20 And being upon the watch, they sent spies, who should feign themselves just, that they might take hold of him in his words, that they might deliver him up to the authority and power of the governor.

20:21 And they asked him, saying: Master, we know that thou speakest and teachest rightly: and thou dost not respect any person, but

20:22 Licet nobis tributum dare Cæsari, an non ?

20:23 Considerans autem dolum illorum, dixit ad eos : Quid me tentatis ?

20:24 ostendite mihi denarium. Cujus habet imaginem et inscriptionem ? Respondentes dixerunt ei : Cæsaris.

20:25 Et ait illis : Reddite ergo quæ sunt Cæsaris, Cæsari : et quæ sunt Dei, Deo.

20:26 Et non potuerunt verbum ejus reprehendere coram plebe : et mirati in responso ejus, tacuerunt.

20:27 Accesserunt autem quidam sadducæorum, qui negant esse resurrectionem, et interrogaverunt eum,

20:28 dicentes : Magister, Moyses scripsit nobis : Si frater alicujus mortuus fuerit habens uxorem, et hic sine liberis fuerit, ut accipiat eam frater ejus uxorem, et suscitet semen fratri suo.

20:29 Septem ergo fratres erant : et primus accepit uxorem, et mortuus est sine filiis.

20:30 Et sequens accepit illam, et ipse mortuus est sine filio.

20:31 Et tertius accepit illam. Similiter et omnes septem, et non reliquerunt semen, et mortui sunt.

20:32 Novissime omnium mortua est et mulier.

20:33 In resurrectione ergo, cujus eorum erit uxor ? siquidem septem habuerunt eam uxorem.

20:34 Et ait illis Jesus : Filii hujus sæculi nubunt, et traduntur ad nuptias :

20:35 illi vero qui digni habebuntur sæculo illo, et resurrectione ex mortuis, neque nubent, neque ducent uxores :

20:36 neque enim ultra mori potuerunt : æquales enim angelis sunt, et filii sunt Dei, cum sint filii resurrectionis.

20:37 Quia vero resurgant mortui, et Moyses ostendit secus rubum, sicut dicit Dominum, Deum Abraham, et Deum Isaac, et Deum Jacob.

20:38 Deus autem non est mortuorum, sed vivorum : omnes enim vivunt ei.

20:39 Respondentes autem quidam scribarum, dixerunt ei : Magister, bene dixisti.

20:40 Et amplius non audebant eum quidquam interrogare.

teachest the way of God in truth.

20:22 Is it lawful for us to give tribute to Caesar, or no?

20:23 But he considering their guile, said to them: Why tempt you me?

20:24 Shew me a penny. Whose image and inscription hath it? They answering, said to him, Caesar's.

20:25 And he said to them: Render therefore to Caesar the things that are Caesar's: and to God the things that are God's.

20:26 And they could not reprehend his word before the people: and wondering at his answer, they held their peace.

20:27 And there came to him some of the Sadducees, who deny that there is any resurrection, and they asked him,

20:28 Saying: Master, Moses wrote unto us, If any man's brother die, having a wife, and he leave no children, that his brother should take her to wife, and raise up seed unto his brother.

20:29 There were therefore seven brethren: and the first took a wife, and died without children.

20:30 And the next took her to wife, and he also died childless.

20:31 And the third took her. And in like manner all the seven, and they left no children, and died.

20:32 Last of all the woman died also.

20:33 In the resurrection therefore, whose wife of them shall she be? For all the seven had her to wife.

20:34 And Jesus said to them: The children of this world marry, and are given in marriage:

20:35 But they that shall be accounted worthy of that world, and of the resurrection from the dead, shall neither be married, nor take wives.

20:36 Neither can they die any more: for they are equal to the angels, and are the children of God, being the children of the resurrection.

20:37 Now that the dead rise again, Moses also shewed, at the bush, when he called the Lord, The God of Abraham, and the God of Isaac, and the God of Jacob;

20:38 For he is not the God of the dead, but of the living: for all live to him.

20:39 And some of the scribes answering, said to him: Master, thou hast said well.

20:40 And after that they durst not ask him any more questions.

20:41 Dixit autem ad illos : Quomodo dicunt Christum filium esse David ?

20:42 et ipse David dicit in libro Psalmorum : Dixit Dominus Domino meo : sede a dextris meis,

20:43 donec ponam inimicos tuos scabellum pedum tuorum.

20:44 David ergo Dominum illum vocat : et quomodo filius ejus est ?

20:45 Audiente autem omni populo, dixit discipulis suis :

20:46 Attendite a scribis, qui volunt ambulare in stolis, et amant salutationes in foro, et primas cathedras in synagogis, et primos discubitus in conviviis,

20:47 qui devorant domos viduarum, simulantes longam orationem : hi accipient damnationem majorem.

21:1 Respiciens autem, vidit eos qui mittebant munera sua in gazophylacium, divites.

21:2 Vidit autem et quamdam viduam pauperculam mittentem æra minuta duo.

21:3 Et dixit : Vere dico vobis, quia vidua hæc pauper plus quam omnes misit.

21:4 Nam omnes hi ex abundanti sibi miserunt in munera Dei : hæc autem ex eo quod deest illi, omnem victum suum quem habuit, misit.

21:5 Et quibusdam dicentibus de templo quod bonis lapidibus et donis ornatum esset, dixit :

21:6 Hæc quæ videtis, venient dies in quibus non relinquetur lapis super lapidem, qui non destruatur.

21:7 Interrogaverunt autem illum, dicentes : Præceptor, quando hæc erunt, et quod signum cum fieri incipient ?

21:8 Qui dixit : Videte ne seducamini : multi enim venient in nomine meo, dicentes quia ego sum : et tempus appropinquavit : nolite ergo ire post eos.

21:9 Cum autem audieritis prælia et seditiones, nolite terreri : oportet primum hæc fieri, sed nondum statim finis.

21:10 Tunc dicebat illis : Surget gens contra gentem, et regnum adversus regnum.

21:11 Et terræmotus magni erunt per loca, et pestilentiæ, et fames, terroresque de cælo, et signa magna erunt.

21:12 Sed ante hæc omnia injicient vobis manus suas, et persequentur tradentes in synagogas et custodias, trahentes ad reges et præsides propter nomen meum :

20:41 But he said to them: How say they that Christ is the son of David?

20:42 And David himself saith in the book of Psalms: The Lord said to my Lord, sit thou on my right hand,

20:43 Till I make thy enemies thy footstool.

20:44 David then calleth him Lord: and how is he his son?

20:45 And in the hearing of all the people, he said to his disciples:

20:46 Beware of the scribes, who desire to walk in long robes, and love salutations in the marketplace, and the first chairs in the synagogues, and the chief rooms at feasts:

20:47 Who devour the houses of widows, feigning long prayer. These shall receive greater damnation.

21:1 And looking on, he saw the rich men cast their gifts into the treasury.

21:2 And he saw also a certain poor widow casting in two brass mites.

21:3 And he said: Verily I say to you, that this poor widow hath cast in more than they all:

21:4 For all these have of their abundance cast into the offerings of God: but she of her want, hath cast in all the living that she had.

21:5 And some saying of the temple, that it was adorned with goodly stones and gifts, he said:

21:6 These things which you see, the days will come in which there shall not be left a stone upon a stone that shall not be thrown down.

21:7 And they asked him, saying: Master, when shall these things be? and what shall be the sign when they shall begin to come to pass?

21:8 Who said: Take heed you be not seduced; for many will come in my name, saying, I am he; and the time is at hand: go ye not therefore after them.

21:9 And when you shall hear of wars and seditions, be not terrified: these things must first come to pass; but the end is not yet presently.

21:10 Then he said to them: Nation shall rise against nation, and kingdom against kingdom.

21:11 And there shall be great earthquakes in divers places, and pestilences, and famines, and terrors from heaven; and there shall be great signs.

21:12 But before all these things, they will lay their hands upon you, and persecute you, delivering you up to the synagogues and into prisons, dragging you before kings and gover-

21:13 continget autem vobis in testimonium.

21:14 Ponite ergo in cordibus vestris non præmeditari quemadmodum respondeatis :

21:15 ego enim dabo vobis os et sapientiam, cui non poterunt resistere et contradicere omnes adversarii vestri.

21:16 Trademini autem a parentibus, et fratribus, et cognatis, et amicis, et morte afficient ex vobis :

21:17 et eritis odio omnibus propter nomen meum :

21:18 et capillus de capite vestro non peribit.

21:19 In patientia vestra possidebitis animas vestras.

21:20 Cum autem videritis circumdari ab exercitu Jerusalem, tunc scitote quia appropinquavit desolatio ejus :

21:21 tunc qui in Judæa sunt, fugiant ad montes, et qui in medio ejus, discedant : et qui in regionibus, non intrent in eam,

21:22 quia dies ultionis hi sunt, ut impleantur omnia quæ scripta sunt.

21:23 Væ autem prægnantibus et nutrientibus in illis diebus ! erit enim pressura magna super terram, et ira populo huic.

21:24 Et cadent in ore gladii, et captivi ducentur in omnes gentes, et Jerusalem calcabitur a gentibus, donec impleantur tempora nationum.

21:25 Et erunt signa in sole, et luna, et stellis, et in terris pressura gentium præ confusione sonitus maris, et fluctuum :

21:26 arescentibus hominibus præ timore, et exspectatione, quæ supervenient universo orbi : nam virtutes cælorum movebuntur :

21:27 et tunc videbunt Filium hominis venientem in nube cum potestate magna et majestate.

21:28 His autem fieri incipientibus, respicite, et levate capita vestra : quoniam appropinquat redemptio vestra.

21:29 Et dixit illis similitudinem : Videte ficulneam, et omnes arbores :

21:30 cum producunt jam ex se fructum, scitis quoniam prope est æstas.

21:31 Ita et vos cum videritis hæc fieri, scitote

nors, for my name's sake.

21:13 And it shall happen unto you for a testimony.

21:14 Lay it up therefore into your hearts, not to meditate before how you shall answer:

21:15 For I will give you a mouth and wisdom, which all your adversaries shall not be able to resist and gainsay.

21:16 And you shall be betrayed by your parents and brethren, and kinsmen and friends; and some of you they will put to death.

21:17 And you shall be hated by all men for my name's sake.

21:18 But a hair of your head shall not perish.

21:19 In your patience you shall possess your souls.

21:20 And when you shall see Jerusalem compassed about with an army; then know that the desolation thereof is at hand.

21:21 Then let those who are in Judea, flee to the mountains; and those who are in the midst thereof, depart out: and those who are in the countries, not enter into it.

21:22 For these are the days of vengeance, that all things may be fulfilled, that are written.

21:23 But woe to them that are with child, and give suck in those days; for there shall be great distress in the land, and wrath upon this people.

21:24 And they shall fall by the edge of the sword; and shall be led away captives into all nations; and Jerusalem shall be trodden down by the Gentiles; till the times of the nations be fulfilled.

21:25 And there shall be signs in the sun, and in the moon, and in the stars; and upon the earth distress of nations, by reason of the confusion of the roaring of the sea and of the waves;

21:26 Men withering away for fear, and expectation of what shall come upon the whole world. For the powers of heaven shall be moved;

21:27 And then they shall see the Son of man coming in a cloud, with great power and majesty.

21:28 But when these things begin to come to pass, look up, and lift up your heads, because your redemption is at hand.

21:29 And he spoke to them in a similitude. See the fig tree, and all the trees:

21:30 When they now shoot forth their fruit, you know that summer is nigh;

21:31 So you also, when you shall see these

quoniam prope est regnum Dei.

21:32 Amen dico vobis, quia non præteribit generatio hæc, donec omnia fiant.

21:33 Cælum et terra transibunt : verba autem mea non transibunt.

21:34 Attendite autem vobis, ne forte graventur corda vestra in crapula, et ebrietate, et curis hujus vitæ, et superveniat in vos repentina dies illa :

21:35 tamquam laqueus enim superveniet in omnes qui sedent super faciem omnis terræ.

21:36 Vigilate itaque, omni tempore orantes, ut digni habeamini fugere ista omnia quæ futura sunt, et stare ante Filium hominis.

21:37 Erat autem diebus docens in templo : noctibus vero exiens, morabatur in monte qui vocatur Oliveti.

21:38 Et omnis populus manicabat ad eum in templo audire eum.

22:1 Appropinquabat autem dies festus azymorum, qui dicitur Pascha :

22:2 et quærebant principes sacerdotum, et scribæ, quomodo Jesum interficerent : timebant vero plebem.

22:3 Intravit autem Satanas in Judam, qui cognominabatur Iscariotes, unum de duodecim :

22:4 et abiit, et locutus est cum principibus sacerdotum, et magistratibus, quemadmodum illum traderet eis.

22:5 Et gavisi sunt, et pacti sunt pecuniam illi dare.

22:6 Et spopondit, et quærebat opportunitatem ut traderet illum sine turbis.

22:7 Venit autem dies azymorum, in qua necesse erat occidi pascha.

22:8 Et misit Petrum et Joannem, dicens : Euntes parate nobis pascha, ut manducemus.

22:9 At illi dixerunt : Ubi vis paremus ?

22:10 Et dixit ad eos : Ecce introëuntibus vobis in civitatem occurret vobis homo quidam amphoram aquæ portans : sequimini eum in domum, in quam intrat,

22:11 et dicetis patrifamilias domus : Dicit tibi Magister : Ubi est diversorium, ubi pascha cum discipulis meis manducem ?

22:12 Et ipse ostendet vobis cœnaculum mag-

things come to pass, know that the kingdom of God is at hand.

21:32 Amen, I say to you, this generation shall not pass away, till all things be fulfilled.

21:33 Heaven and earth shall pass away, but my words shall not pass away.

21:34 And take heed to yourselves, lest perhaps your hearts be overcharged with surfeiting and drunkenness, and the cares of this life, and that day come upon you suddenly.

21:35 For as a snare shall it come upon all that sit upon the face of the whole earth.

21:36 Watch ye, therefore, praying at all times, that you may be accounted worthy to escape all these things that are to come, and to stand before the Son of man.

21:37 And in the daytime, he was teaching in the temple; but at night, going out, he abode in the mount that is called Olivet.

21:38 And all the people came early in the morning to him in the temple, to hear him.

22:1 Now the feast of unleavened bread, which is called the pasch, was at hand.

22:2 And the chief priests and the scribes sought how they might put Jesus to death: but they feared the people.

22:3 And Satan entered into Judas, who was surnamed Iscariot, one of the twelve.

22:4 And he went, and discoursed with the chief priests and the magistrates, how he might betray him to them.

22:5 And they were glad, and covenanted to give him money.

22:6 And he promised. And he sought opportunity to betray him in the absence of the multitude.

22:7 And the day of the unleavened bread came, on which it was necessary that the pasch should be killed.

22:8 And he sent Peter and John, saying: Go, and prepare for us the pasch, that we may eat.

22:9 But they said: Where wilt thou that we prepare?

22:10 And he said to them: Behold, as you go into the city, there shall meet you a man carrying a pitcher of water: follow him into the house where he entereth in.

22:11 And you shall say to the goodman of the house: The master saith to thee, Where is the guest chamber, where I may eat the pasch with my disciples?

22:12 And he will shew you a large dining room,

num stratum, et ibi parate.

22:13 Euntes autem invenerunt sicut dixit illis, et paraverunt pascha.

22:14 Et cum facta esset hora, discubuit, et duodecim apostoli cum eo.

22:15 Et ait illis : Desiderio desideravi hoc pascha manducare vobiscum, antequam patiar.

22:16 Dico enim vobis, quia ex hoc non manducabo illud, donec impleatur in regno Dei.

22:17 Et accepto calice gratias egit, et dixit : Accipite, et dividite inter vos.

22:18 Dico enim vobis quod non bibam de generatione vitis donec regnum Dei veniat.

22:19 Et accepto pane gratias egit, et fregit, et dedit eis, dicens : Hoc est corpus meum, quod pro vobis datur : hoc facite in meam commemorationem.

22:20 Similiter et calicem, postquam cœnavit, dicens : Hic est calix novum testamentum in sanguine meo, qui pro vobis fundetur.

22:21 Verumtamen ecce manus tradentis me, mecum est in mensa.

22:22 Et quidem Filius hominis, secundum quod definitum est, vadit : verumtamen væ homini illi per quem tradetur.

22:23 Et ipsi cœperunt quærere inter se quis esset ex eis qui hoc facturus esset.

22:24 Facta est autem et contentio inter eos, quis eorum videretur esse major.

22:25 Dixit autem eis : Reges gentium dominantur eorum : et qui potestatem habent super eos, benefici vocantur.

22:26 Vos autem non sic : sed qui major est in vobis, fiat sicut minor : et qui præcessor est, sicut ministrator.

22:27 Nam quis major est, qui recumbit, an qui ministrat ? nonne qui recumbit ? Ego autem in medio vestrum sum, sicut qui ministrat :

22:28 vos autem estis, qui permansistis mecum in tentationibus meis.

22:29 Et ego dispono vobis sicut disposuit mihi Pater meus regnum,

22:30 ut edatis et bibatis super mensam meam in regno meo, et sedeatis super thronos judicantes duodecim tribus Israël.

22:31 Ait autem Dominus : Simon, Simon, ecce Satanas expetivit vos ut cribraret sicut triti-

furnished; and there prepare.

22:13 And they going, found as he had said to them, and made ready the pasch.

22:14 And when the hour was come, he sat down, and the twelve apostles with him.

22:15 And he said to them: With desire I have desired to eat this pasch with you, before I suffer.

22:16 For I say to you, that from this time I will not eat it, till it be fulfilled in the kingdom of God.

22:17 And having taken the chalice, he gave thanks, and said: Take, and divide it among you:

22:18 For I say to you, that I will not drink of the fruit of the vine, till the kingdom of God come.

22:19 And taking bread, he gave thanks, and brake; and gave to them, saying: This is my body, which is given for you. Do this for a commemoration of me.

22:20 In like manner the chalice also, after he had supped, saying: This is the chalice, the new testament in my blood, which shall be shed for you.

22:21 But yet behold, the hand of him that betrayeth me is with me on the table.

22:22 And the Son of man indeed goeth, according to that which is determined: but yet, woe to that man by whom he shall be betrayed.

22:23 And they began to inquire among themselves, which of them it was that should do this thing.

22:24 And there was also a strife amongst them, which of them should seem to be the greater.

22:25 And he said to them: The kings of the Gentiles lord it over them; and they that have power over them, are called beneficent.

22:26 But you not so: but he that is the greater among you, let him become as the younger; and he that is the leader, as he that serveth.

22:27 For which is greater, he that sitteth at table, or he that serveth? Is it not he that sitteth at table? But I am in the midst of you, as he that serveth:

22:28 And you are they who have continued with me in my temptations:

22:29 And I dispose to you, as my Father hath disposed to me, a kingdom;

22:30 That you may eat and drink at my table, in my kingdom: and may sit upon thrones, judging the twelve tribes of Israel.

22:31 And the Lord said: Simon, Simon, behold Satan hath desired to have you, that he may sift

cum :

²²:³² ego autem rogavi pro te ut non deficiat fides tua : et tu aliquando conversus, confirma fratres tuos.

²²:³³ Qui dixit ei : Domine, tecum paratus sum et in carcerem et in mortem ire.

²²:³⁴ At ille dixit : Dico tibi, Petre, non cantabit hodie gallus, donec ter abneges nosse me. Et dixit eis :

²²:³⁵ Quando misi vos sine sacculo, et pera, et calceamentis, numquid aliquid defuit vobis ?

²²:³⁶ At illi dixerunt : Nihil. Dixit ergo eis : Sed nunc qui habet sacculum, tollat ; similiter et peram : et qui non habet, vendat tunicam suam et emat gladium.

²²:³⁷ Dico enim vobis, quoniam adhuc hoc quod scriptum est, oportet impleri in me : Et cum iniquis deputatus est. Etenim ea quæ sunt de me finem habent.

²²:³⁸ At illi dixerunt : Domine, ecce duo gladii hic. At ille dixit eis : Satis est.

²²:³⁹ Et egressus ibat secundum consuetudinem in monte Olivarum. Secuti sunt autem illum et discipuli.

²²:⁴⁰ Et cum pervenisset ad locum, dixit illis : Orate ne intretis in tentationem.

²²:⁴¹ Et ipse avulsus est ab eis quantum jactus est lapidis : et positis genibus orabat,

²²:⁴² dicens : Pater, si vis, transfer calicem istum a me : verumtamen non mea voluntas, sed tua fiat.

²²:⁴³ Apparuit autem illi angelus de cælo, confortans eum. Et factus in agonia, prolixius orabat.

²²:⁴⁴ Et factus est sudor ejus sicut guttæ sanguinis decurrentis in terram.

²²:⁴⁵ Et cum surrexisset ab oratione et venisset ad discipulos suos, invenit eos dormientes præ tristitia.

²²:⁴⁶ Et ait illis : Quid dormitis ? surgite, orate, ne intretis in tentationem.

²²:⁴⁷ Adhuc eo loquente, ecce turba : et qui vocabatur Judas, unus de duodecim, antecedebat eos, et appropinquavit Jesu ut oscularetur eum.

²²:⁴⁸ Jesus autem dixit illi : Juda, osculo Filium hominis tradis ?

²²:⁴⁹ Videntes autem hi qui circa ipsum erant, quod futurum erat, dixerunt ei : Domine, si percutimus in gladio ?

²²:⁵⁰ Et percussit unus ex illis servum principis

you as wheat:

²²:³² But I have prayed for thee, that thy faith fail not: and thou, being once converted, confirm thy brethren.

²²:³³ Who said to him: Lord, I am ready to go with thee, both into prison, and to death.

²²:³⁴ And he said: I say to thee, Peter, the cock shall not crow this day, till thou thrice deniest that thou knowest me. And he said to them:

²²:³⁵ When I sent you without purse, and scrip, and shoes, did you want anything?

²²:³⁶ But they said: Nothing. Then said he unto them: But now he that hath a purse, let him take it, and likewise a scrip; and he that hath not, let him sell his coat, and buy a sword.

²²:³⁷ For I say to you, that this that is written must yet be fulfilled in me: And with the wicked was he reckoned. For the things concerning me have an end.

²²:³⁸ But they said: Lord, behold here are two swords. And he said to them, It is enough.

²²:³⁹ And going out, he went, according to his custom, to the mount of Olives. And his disciples also followed him.

²²:⁴⁰ And when he was come to the place, he said to them: Pray, lest ye enter into temptation.

²²:⁴¹ And he was withdrawn away from them a stone's cast; and kneeling down, he prayed,

²²:⁴² Saying: Father, if thou wilt, remove this chalice from me: but yet not my will, but thine be done.

²²:⁴³ And there appeared to him an angel from heaven, strengthening him. And being in an agony, he prayed the longer.

²²:⁴⁴ And his sweat became as drops of blood, trickling down upon the ground.

²²:⁴⁵ And when he rose up from prayer, and was come to his disciples, he found them sleeping for sorrow.

²²:⁴⁶ And he said to them: Why sleep you? arise, pray, lest you enter into temptation.

²²:⁴⁷ As he was yet speaking, behold a multitude; and he that was called Judas, one of the twelve, went before them, and drew near to Jesus, for to kiss him.

²²:⁴⁸ And Jesus said to him: Judas, dost thou betray the Son of man with a kiss?

²²:⁴⁹ And they that were about him, seeing what would follow, said to him: Lord, shall we strike with the sword?

²²:⁵⁰ And one of them struck the servant of the

sacerdotum, et amputavit auriculam ejus dexteram.

22:51 Respondens autem Jesus, ait : Sinite usque huc. Et cum tetigisset auriculam ejus, sanavit eum.

22:52 Dixit autem Jesus ad eos qui venerant ad se principes sacerdotum, et magistratus templi, et seniores : Quasi ad latronem existis cum gladiis et fustibus ?

22:53 Cum quotidie vobiscum fuerim in templo, non extendistis manus in me : sed hæc est hora vestra, et potestas tenebrarum.

22:54 Comprehendentes autem eum, duxerunt ad domum principis sacerdotum : Petrus vero sequebatur a longe.

22:55 Accenso autem igne in medio atrii et circumsedentibus illis, erat Petrus in medio eorum.

22:56 Quem cum vidisset ancilla quædam sedentem ad lumen, et eum fuisset intuita, dixit : Et hic cum illo erat.

22:57 At ille negavit eum, dicens : Mulier, non novi illum.

22:58 Et post pusillum alius videns eum, dixit : Et tu de illis es. Petrus vero ait : O homo, non sum.

22:59 Et intervallo facto quasi horæ unius, alius quidam affirmabat, dicens : Vere et hic cum illo erat : nam et Galilæus est.

22:60 Et ait Petrus : Homo, nescio quid dicis. Et continuo, adhuc illo loquente, cantavit gallus.

22:61 Et conversus Dominus respexit Petrum, et recordatus est Petrus verbi Domini, sicut dixerat : Quia priusquam gallus cantet, ter me negabis.

22:62 Et egressus foras Petrus flevit amare.

22:63 Et viri qui tenebant illum, illudebant ei, cædentes.

22:64 Et velaverunt eum, et percutiebant faciem ejus : et interrogabant eum, dicentes : Prophetiza, quis est, qui te percussit ?

22:65 Et alia multa blasphemantes dicebant in eum.

22:66 Et ut factus est dies, convenerunt seniores plebis, et principes sacerdotum, et scribæ, et duxerunt illum in concilium suum, dicentes : Si tu es Christus, dic nobis.

22:67 Et ait illis : Si vobis dixero, non credetis mihi :

high priest, and cut off his right ear.

22:51 But Jesus answering, said: Suffer ye thus far. And when he had touched his ear, he healed him.

22:52 And Jesus said to the chief priests, and magistrates of the temple, and the ancients, that were come unto him: Are ye come out, as it were against a thief, with swords and clubs?

22:53 When I was daily with you in the temple, you did not stretch forth your hands against me: but this is your hour, and the power of darkness.

22:54 And apprehending him, they led him to the high priest's house. But Peter followed afar off.

22:55 And when they had kindled a fire in the midst of the hall, and were sitting about it, Peter was in the midst of them.

22:56 Whom when a certain servant maid had seen sitting at the light, and had earnestly beheld him, she said: This man also was with him.

22:57 But he denied him, saying: Woman, I know him not.

22:58 And after a little while, another seeing him, said: Thou also art one of them. But Peter said: O man, I am not.

22:59 And after the space, as it were of one hour, another certain man affirmed, saying: Of a truth, this man was also with him; for he is also a Galilean.

22:60 And Peter said: Man, I know not what thou sayest. And immediately, as he was yet speaking, the cock crew.

22:61 And the Lord turning looked on Peter. And Peter remembered the word of the Lord, as he had said: Before the cock crow, thou shalt deny me thrice.

22:62 And Peter going out, wept bitterly.

22:63 And the men that held him, mocked him, and struck him.

22:64 And they blindfolded him, and smote his face. And they asked him, saying: Prophesy, who is it that struck thee?

22:65 And blaspheming, many other things they said against him.

22:66 And as soon as it was day, the ancients of the people, and the chief priests and scribes, came together; and they brought him into their council, saying: If thou be the Christ, tell us.

22:67 And he saith to them: If I shall tell you, you will not believe me.

22:68 si autem et interrogavero, non respondebitis mihi, neque dimittetis.

22:69 Ex hoc autem erit Filius hominis sedens a dextris virtutis Dei.

22:70 Dixerunt autem omnes : Tu ergo es Filius Dei ? Qui ait : Vos dicitis, quia ego sum.

22:71 At illi dixerunt : Quid adhuc desideramus testimonium ? ipsi enim audivimus de ore ejus.

23:1 Et surgens omnis multitudo eorum, duxerunt illum ad Pilatum.

23:2 Cœperunt autem illum accusare, dicentes : Hunc invenimus subvertentem gentem nostram, et prohibentem tributa dare Cæsari, et dicentem se Christum regem esse.

23:3 Pilatus autem interrogavit eum, dicens : Tu es rex Judæorum ? At ille respondens ait : Tu dicis.

23:4 Ait autem Pilatus ad principes sacerdotum et turbas : Nihil invenio causæ in hoc homine.

23:5 At illi invalescebant, dicentes : Commovet populum docens per universam Judæam, incipiens a Galilæa usque huc.

23:6 Pilatus autem audiens Galilæam, interrogavit si homo Galilæus esset.

23:7 Et ut cognovit quod de Herodis potestate esset, remisit eum ad Herodem, qui et ipse Jerosolymis erat illis diebus.

23:8 Herodes autem viso Jesu, gavisus est valde. Erat enim cupiens ex multo tempore videre eum, eo quod audierat multa de eo, et sperabat signum aliquod videre ab eo fieri.

23:9 Interrogabat autem eum multis sermonibus. At ipse nihil illi respondebat.

23:10 Stabant autem principes sacerdotum et scribæ constanter accusantes eum.

23:11 Sprevit autem illum Herodes cum exercitu suo : et illusit indutum veste alba, et remisit ad Pilatum.

23:12 Et facti sunt amici Herodes et Pilatus in ipsa die : nam antea inimici erant ad invicem.

23:13 Pilatus autem, convocatis principibus sacerdotum, et magistratibus, et plebe,

23:14 dixit ad illos : Obtulistis mihi hunc hominem, quasi avertentem populum, et ecce ego coram vobis interrogans, nullam causam inveni in homine isto ex his in quibus eum accusatis.

23:15 Sed neque Herodes : nam remisi vos ad illum, et ecce nihil dignum morte actum est ei.

22:68 And if I shall also ask you, you will not answer me, nor let me go.

22:69 But hereafter the Son of man shall be sitting on the right hand of the power of God.

22:70 Then said they all: Art thou then the Son of God? Who said: You say that I am.

22:71 And they said: What need we any further testimony? for we ourselves have heard it from his own mouth.

23:1 And the whole multitude of them rising up, led him to Pilate.

23:2 And they began to accuse him, saying: We have found this man perverting our nation, and forbidding to give tribute to Caesar, and saying that he is Christ the king.

23:3 And Pilate asked him, saying: Art thou the king of the Jews? But he answering, said: Thou sayest it.

23:4 And Pilate said to the chief priests and to the multitudes: I find no cause in this man.

23:5 But they were more earnest, saying: He stirreth up the people, teaching throughout all Judea, beginning from Galilee to this place.

23:6 But Pilate hearing Galilee, asked if the man were of Galilee?

23:7 And when he understood that he was of Herod's jurisdiction, he sent him away to Herod, who was also himself at Jerusalem, in those days.

23:8 And Herod, seeing Jesus, was very glad; for he was desirous of a long time to see him, because he had heard many things of him; and he hoped to see some sign wrought by him.

23:9 And he questioned him in many words. But he answered him nothing.

23:10 And the chief priests and the scribes stood by, earnestly accusing him.

23:11 And Herod with his army set him at nought, and mocked him, putting on him a white garment, and sent him back to Pilate.

23:12 And Herod and Pilate were made friends, that same day; for before they were enemies one to another.

23:13 And Pilate, calling together the chief priests, and the magistrates, and the people,

23:14 Said to them: You have presented unto me this man, as one that perverteth the people; and behold I, having examined him before you, find no cause in this man, in those things wherein you accuse him.

23:15 No, nor Herod neither. For I sent you to him, and behold, nothing worthy of death is

23:16 Emendatum ergo illum dimittam.

23:17 Necesse autem habebat dimittere eis per diem festum unum.

23:18 Exclamavit autem simul universa turba, dicens : Tolle hunc, et dimitte nobis Barabbam :

23:19 qui erat propter seditionem quamdam factam in civitate et homicidium missus in carcerem.

23:20 Iterum autem Pilatus locutus est ad eos, volens dimittere Jesum.

23:21 At illi succlamabant, dicentes : Crucifige, crucifige eum.

23:22 Ille autem tertio dixit ad illos : Quid enim mali fecit iste ? nullam causam mortis invenio in eo : corripiam ergo illum et dimittam.

23:23 At illi instabant vocibus magnis postulantes ut crucifigeretur : et invalescebant voces eorum.

23:24 Et Pilatus adjudicavit fieri petitionem eorum.

23:25 Dimisit autem illis eum qui propter homicidium et seditionem missus fuerat in carcerem, quem petebant : Jesum vero tradidit voluntati eorum.

23:26 Et cum ducerent eum, apprehenderunt Simonem quemdam Cyrenensem venientem de villa : et imposuerunt illi crucem portare post Jesum.

23:27 Sequebatur autem illum multa turba populi et mulierum, quæ plangebant et lamentabantur eum.

23:28 Conversus autem ad illas Jesus, dixit : Filiæ Jerusalem, nolite flere super me, sed super vos ipsas flete et super filios vestros.

23:29 Quoniam ecce venient dies in quibus dicent : Beatæ steriles, et ventres qui non genuerunt, et ubera quæ non lactaverunt.

23:30 Tunc incipient dicere montibus : Cadite super nos ; et collibus : Operite nos.

23:31 Quia si in viridi ligno hæc faciunt, in arido quid fiet ?

23:32 Ducebantur autem et alii duo nequam cum eo, ut interficerentur.

23:33 Et postquam venerunt in locum qui vocatur Calvariæ, ibi crucifixerunt eum : et latrones, unum a dextris, et alterum a sinistris.

23:16 done to him. I will chastise him therefore, and release him.

23:17 Now of necessity he was to release unto them one upon the feast day.

23:18 But the whole multitude together cried out, saying: Away with this man, and release unto us Barabbas:

23:19 Who, for a certain sedition made in the city, and for a murder, was cast into prison.

23:20 And Pilate again spoke to them, desiring to release Jesus.

23:21 But they cried again, saying: Crucify him, crucify him.

23:22 And he said to them the third time: Why, what evil hath this man done? I find no cause of death in him. I will chastise him therefore, and let him go.

23:23 But they were instant with loud voices, requiring that he might be crucified; and their voices prevailed.

23:24 And Pilate gave sentence that it should be as they required.

23:25 And he released unto them him who for murder and sedition, had been cast into prison, whom they had desired; but Jesus he delivered up to their will.

23:26 And as they led him away, they laid hold of one Simon of Cyrene, coming from the country; and they laid the cross on him to carry after Jesus.

23:27 And there followed him a great multitude of people, and of women, who bewailed and lamented him.

23:28 But Jesus turning to them, said: Daughters of Jerusalem, weep not over me; but weep for yourselves, and for your children.

23:29 For behold, the days shall come, wherein they will say: Blessed are the barren, and the wombs that have not borne, and the paps that have not given suck.

23:30 Then shall they begin to say to the mountains: Fall upon us; and to the hills: Cover us.

23:31 For if in the green wood they do these things, what shall be done in the dry?

23:32 And there were also two other malefactors led with him to be put to death.

23:33 And when they were come to the place which is called Calvary, they crucified him there; and the robbers, one on the right hand, and the other on the left.

23:34 Jesus autem dicebat : Pater, dimitte illis : non enim sciunt quid faciunt. Dividentes vero vestimenta ejus, miserunt sortes.

23:35 Et stabat populus spectans, et deridebant eum principes cum eis, dicentes : Alios salvos fecit, se salvum faciat, si hic est Christus Dei electus.

23:36 Illudebant autem ei et milites accedentes, et acetum offerentes ei,

23:37 et dicentes : Si tu es rex Judæorum, salvum te fac.

23:38 Erat autem et superscriptio scripta super eum litteris græcis, et latinis, et hebraicis : Hic est rex Judæorum.

23:39 Unus autem de his, qui pendebant, latronibus, blasphemabat eum, dicens : Si tu es Christus, salvum fac temetipsum et nos.

23:40 Respondens autem alter increpabat eum, dicens : Neque tu times Deum, quod in eadem damnatione es.

23:41 Et nos quidem juste, nam digna factis recipimus : hic vero nihil mali gessit.

23:42 Et dicebat ad Jesum : Domine, memento mei cum veneris in regnum tuum.

23:43 Et dixit illi Jesus : Amen dico tibi : hodie mecum eris in paradiso.

23:44 Erat autem fere hora sexta, et tenebræ factæ sunt in universam terram usque ad horam nonam.

23:45 Et obscuratus est sol, et velum templi scissum est medium.

23:46 Et clamans voce magna Jesus ait : Pater, in manus tuas commendo spiritum meum. Et hæc dicens, expiravit.

23:47 Videns autem centurio quod factum fuerat, glorificavit Deum, dicens : Vere hic homo justus erat.

23:48 Et omnis turba eorum, qui simul aderant ad spectaculum istud, et videbant quæ fiebant, percutientes pectora sua revertebantur.

23:49 Stabant autem omnes noti ejus a longe, et mulieres, quæ secutæ eum erant a Galilæa, hæc videntes.

23:50 Et ecce vir nomine Joseph, qui erat decurio, vir bonus et justus :

23:51 hic non consenserat consilio, et actibus eorum : ab Arimathæa civitate Judææ, qui exspectabat et ipse regnum Dei :

23:52 hic accessit ad Pilatum et petiit corpus Je-

23:34 And Jesus said: Father, forgive them, for they know not what they do. But they, dividing his garments, cast lots.

23:35 And the people stood beholding, and the rulers with them derided him, saying: He saved others; let him save himself, if he be Christ, the elect of God.

23:36 And the soldiers also mocked him, coming to him, and offering him vinegar,

23:37 And saying: If thou be the king of the Jews, save thyself.

23:38 And there was also a superscription written over him in letters of Greek, and Latin, and Hebrew: THIS IS THE KING OF THE JEWS.

23:39 And one of those robbers who were hanged, blasphemed him, saying: If thou be Christ, save thyself and us.

23:40 But the other answering, rebuked him, saying: Neither dost thou fear God, seeing thou art condemned under the same condemnation?

23:41 And we indeed justly, for we receive the due reward of our deeds; but this man hath done no evil.

23:42 And he said to Jesus: Lord, remember me when thou shalt come into thy kingdom.

23:43 And Jesus said to him: Amen I say to thee, this day thou shalt be with me in paradise.

23:44 And it was almost the sixth hour; and there was darkness over all the earth until the ninth hour.

23:45 And the sun was darkened, and the veil of the temple was rent in the midst.

23:46 And Jesus crying out with a loud voice, said: Father, into thy hands I commend my spirit. And saying this, he gave up the ghost.

23:47 Now the centurion, seeing what was done, glorified God, saying: Indeed this was a just man.

23:48 And all the multitude of them that were come together to that sight, and saw the things that were done, returned striking their breasts.

23:49 And all his acquaintance, and the women that had followed him from Galilee, stood afar off, beholding these things.

23:50 And behold there was a man named Joseph, who was a counsellor, a good and just man,

23:51 (The same had not consented to their counsel and doings;) of Arimathea, a city of Judea; who also himself looked for the kingdom of God.

23:52 This man went to Pilate, and begged the

su :

23:53 et depositum involvit sindone, et posuit eum in monumento exciso, in quo nondum quisquam positus fuerat.

23:54 Et dies erat parasceves, et sabbatum illucescebat.

23:55 Subsecutæ autem mulieres, quæ cum eo venerant de Galilæa, viderunt monumentum, et quemadmodum positum erat corpus ejus.

23:56 Et revertentes paraverunt aromata, et unguenta : et sabbato quidem siluerunt secundum mandatum.

24:1 Una autem sabbati valde diluculo venerunt ad monumentum, portantes quæ paraverant aromata :

24:2 et invenerunt lapidem revolutum a monumento.

24:3 Et ingressæ non invenerunt corpus Domini Jesu.

24:4 Et factum est, dum mente consternatæ essent de isto, ecce duo viri steterunt secus illas in veste fulgenti.

24:5 Cum timerent autem, et declinarent vultum in terram, dixerunt ad illas : Quid quæritis viventem cum mortuis ?

24:6 non est hic, sed surrexit : recordamini qualiter locutus est vobis, cum adhuc in Galilæa esset,

24:7 dicens : Quia oportet Filium hominis tradi in manus hominum peccatorum, et crucifigi, et die tertia resurgere.

24:8 Et recordatæ sunt verborum ejus.

24:9 Et regressæ a monumento nuntiaverunt hæc omnia illis undecim, et ceteris omnibus.

24:10 Erat autem Maria Magdalene, et Joanna, et Maria Jacobi, et ceteræ quæ cum eis erant, quæ dicebant ad apostolos hæc.

24:11 Et visa sunt ante illos sicut deliramentum verba ista, et non crediderunt illis.

24:12 Petrus autem surgens cucurrit ad monumentum : et procumbens vidit linteamina sola posita, et abiit secum mirans quod factum fuerat.

24:13 Et ecce duo ex illis ibant ipsa die in castellum, quod erat in spatio stadiorum sexaginta ab Jerusalem, nomine Emmaus.

24:14 Et ipsi loquebantur ad invicem de his omnibus quæ acciderant.

body of Jesus.

23:53 And taking him down, he wrapped him in fine linen, and laid him in a sepulchre that was hewed in stone, wherein never yet any man had been laid.

23:54 And it was the day of the Parasceve, and the sabbath drew on.

23:55 And the women that were come with him from Galilee, following after, saw the sepulchre, and how his body was laid.

23:56 And returning, they prepared spices and ointments; and on the sabbath day they rested, according to the commandment.

24:1 And on the first day of the week, very early in the morning, they came to the sepulchre, bringing the spices which they had prepared.

24:2 And they found the stone rolled back from the sepulchre.

24:3 And going in, they found not the body of the Lord Jesus.

24:4 And it came to pass, as they were astonished in their mind at this, behold, two men stood by them, in shining apparel.

24:5 And as they were afraid, and bowed down their countenance towards the ground, they said unto them: Why seek you the living with the dead?

24:6 He is not here, but is risen. Remember how he spoke unto you, when he was yet in Galilee,

24:7 Saying: The Son of man must be delivered into the hands of sinful men, and be crucified, and the third day rise again.

24:8 And they remembered his words.

24:9 And going back from the sepulchre, they told all these things to the eleven, and to all the rest.

24:10 And it was Mary Magdalen, and Joanna, and Mary of James, and the other women that were with them, who told these things to the apostles.

24:11 And these words seemed to them as idle tales; and they did not believe them.

24:12 But Peter rising up, ran to the sepulchre, and stooping down, he saw the linen cloths laid by themselves; and went away wondering in himself at that which was come to pass.

24:13 And behold, two of them went, the same day, to a town which was sixty furlongs from Jerusalem, named Emmaus.

24:14 And they talked together of all these things which had happened.

24:15 Et factum est, dum fabularentur, et secum quærerent : et ipse Jesus appropinquans ibat cum illis :

24:16 oculi autem illorum tenebantur ne eum agnoscerent.

24:17 Et ait ad illos : Qui sunt hi sermones, quos confertis ad invicem ambulantes, et estis tristes ?

24:18 Et respondens unus, cui nomen Cleophas, dixit ei : Tu solus peregrinus es in Jerusalem, et non cognovisti quæ facta sunt in illa his diebus ?

24:19 Quibus ille dixit : Quæ ? Et dixerunt : De Jesu Nazareno, qui fuit vir propheta, potens in opere et sermone coram Deo et omni populo :

24:20 et quomodo eum tradiderunt summi sacerdotes et principes nostri in damnationem mortis, et crucifixerunt eum :

24:21 nos autem sperabamus quia ipse esset redempturus Israël : et nunc super hæc omnia, tertia dies est hodie quod hæc facta sunt.

24:22 Sed et mulieres quædam ex nostris terruerunt nos, quæ ante lucem fuerunt ad monumentum,

24:23 et non invento corpore ejus, venerunt, dicentes se etiam visionem angelorum vidisse, qui dicunt eum vivere.

24:24 Et abierunt quidam ex nostris ad monumentum : et ita invenerunt sicut mulieres dixerunt, ipsum vero non invenerunt.

24:25 Et ipse dixit ad eos : O stulti, et tardi corde ad credendum in omnibus quæ locuti sunt prophetæ !

24:26 Nonne hæc oportuit pati Christum, et ita intrare in gloriam suam ?

24:27 Et incipiens a Moyse, et omnibus prophetis, interpretabatur illis in omnibus scripturis quæ de ipso erant.

24:28 Et appropinquaverunt castello quo ibant : et ipse se finxit longius ire.

24:29 Et coëgerunt illum, dicentes : Mane nobiscum, quoniam advesperascit, et inclinata est jam dies. Et intravit cum illis.

24:30 Et factum est, dum recumberet cum eis, accepit panem, et benedixit, ac fregit, et porrigebat illis.

24:31 Et aperti sunt oculi eorum, et cognoverunt eum : et ipse evanuit ex oculis eorum.

24:15 And it came to pass, that while they talked and reasoned with themselves, Jesus himself also drawing near, went with them.

24:16 But their eyes were held, that they should not know him.

24:17 And he said to them: What are these discourses that you hold one with another as you walk, and are sad?

24:18 And the one of them, whose name was Cleophas, answering, said to him: Art thou only a stranger in Jerusalem, and hast not known the things that have been done there in these days?

24:19 To whom he said: What things? And they said: Concerning Jesus of Nazareth, who was a prophet, mighty in work and word before God and all the people;

24:20 And how our chief priests and princes delivered him to be condemned to death, and crucified him.

24:21 But we hoped, that it was he that should have redeemed Israel: and now besides all this, to day is the third day since these things were done.

24:22 Yea and certain women also of our company affrighted us, who before it was light, were at the sepulchre,

24:23 And not finding his body, came, saying, that they had also seen a vision of angels, who say that he is alive.

24:24 And some of our people went to the sepulchre, and found it so as the women had said, but him they found not.

24:25 Then he said to them: O foolish, and slow of heart to believe in all things which the prophets have spoken.

24:26 Ought not Christ to have suffered these things, and so to enter into his glory?

24:27 And beginning at Moses and all the prophets, he expounded to them in all the scriptures, the things that were concerning him.

24:28 And they drew nigh to the town, whither they were going: and he made as though he would go farther.

24:29 But they constrained him; saying: Stay with us, because it is towards evening, and the day is now far spent. And he went in with them.

24:30 And it came to pass, whilst he was at table with them, he took bread, and blessed, and brake, and gave to them.

24:31 And their eyes were opened, and they knew him: and he vanished out of their sight.

24:32 Et dixerunt ad invicem : Nonne cor nostrum ardens erat in nobis dum loqueretur in via, et aperiret nobis Scripturas ?

24:33 Et surgentes eadem hora regressi sunt in Jerusalem : et invenerunt congregatos undecim, et eos qui cum illis erant,

24:34 dicentes : Quod surrexit Dominus vere, et apparuit Simoni.

24:35 Et ipsi narrabant quæ gesta erant in via, et quomodo cognoverunt eum in fractione panis.

24:36 Dum autem hæc loquuntur, stetit Jesus in medio eorum, et dicit eis : Pax vobis : ego sum, nolite timere.

24:37 Conturbati vero et conterriti, existimabant se spiritum videre.

24:38 Et dixit eis : Quid turbati estis, et cogitationes ascendunt in corda vestra ?

24:39 videte manus meas, et pedes, quia ego ipse sum ; palpate et videte, quia spiritus carnem et ossa non habet, sicut me videtis habere.

24:40 Et cum hoc dixisset, ostendit eis manus et pedes.

24:41 Adhuc autem illis non credentibus, et mirantibus præ gaudio, dixit : Habetis hic aliquid quod manducetur ?

24:42 At illi obtulerunt ei partem piscis assi et favum mellis.

24:43 Et cum manducasset coram eis, sumens reliquias dedit eis.

24:44 Et dixit ad eos : Hæc sunt verba quæ locutus sum ad vos cum adhuc essem vobiscum, quoniam necesse est impleri omnia quæ scripta sunt in lege Moysi, et prophetis, et Psalmis de me.

24:45 Tunc aperuit illis sensum ut intelligerent Scripturas,

24:46 et dixit eis : Quoniam sic scriptum est, et sic oportebat Christum pati, et resurgere a mortuis tertia die :

24:47 et prædicari in nomine ejus pœnitentiam, et remissionem peccatorum in omnes gentes, incipientibus ab Jerosolyma.

24:48 Vos autem testes estis horum.

24:49 Et ego mitto promissum Patris mei in vos ; vos autem sedete in civitate, quoadusque induamini virtute ex alto.

24:50 Eduxit autem eos foras in Bethaniam, et elevatis manibus suis benedixit eis.

24:51 Et factum est, dum benediceret illis, recessit ab eis, et ferebatur in cælum.

24:32 And they said one to the other: Was not our heart burning within us, whilst he spoke in this way, and opened to us the scriptures?

24:33 And rising up, the same hour, they went back to Jerusalem: and they found the eleven gathered together, and those that were with them,

24:34 Saying: The Lord is risen indeed, and hath appeared to Simon.

24:35 And they told what things were done in the way; and how they knew him in the breaking of the bread.

24:36 Now whilst they were speaking these things, Jesus stood in the midst of them, and saith to them: Peace be to you; it is I, fear not.

24:37 But they being troubled and frightened, supposed that they saw a spirit.

24:38 And he said to them: Why are you troubled, and why do thoughts arise in your hearts?

24:39 See my hands and feet, that it is I myself; handle, and see: for a spirit hath not flesh and bones, as you see me to have.

24:40 And when he had said this, he shewed them his hands and feet.

24:41 But while they yet believed not, and wondered for joy, he said: Have you any thing to eat?

24:42 And they offered him a piece of a broiled fish, and a honeycomb.

24:43 And when he had eaten before them, taking the remains, he gave to them.

24:44 And he said to them: These are the words which I spoke to you, while I was yet with you, that all things must needs be fulfilled, which are written in the law of Moses, and in the prophets, and in the psalms, concerning me.

24:45 Then he opened their understanding, that they might understand the scriptures.

24:46 And he said to them: Thus it is written, and thus it behoved Christ to suffer, and to rise again from the dead, the third day:

24:47 And that penance and remission of sins should be preached in his name, unto all nations, beginning at Jerusalem.

24:48 And you are witnesses of these things.

24:49 And I send the promise of my Father upon you: but stay you in the city till you be endued with power from on high.

24:50 And he led them out as far as Bethania: and lifting up his hands, he blessed them.

24:51 And it came to pass, whilst he blessed them, he departed from them, and was carried

up to heaven.

24:52 Et ipsi adorantes regressi sunt in Jerusalem cum gaudio magno :

24:52 And they adoring went back into Jerusalem with great joy.

24:53 et erant semper in templo, laudantes et benedicentes Deum. Amen.

24:53 And they were always in the temple, praising and blessing God. Amen.

Sanctum Jesu Christi Evangelium
Secundum Joannem

THE HOLY GOSPEL OF JESUS CHRIST ACCORDING TO JOHN

✠

N PRINCIPIO erat Verbum, et Verbum erat apud Deum, et Deus erat Verbum.

1:2 Hoc erat in principio apud Deum.

1:3 Omnia per ipsum facta sunt : et sine ipso factum est nihil, quod factum est.

1:4 In ipso vita erat, et vita erat lux hominum :

1:5 et lux in tenebris lucet, et tenebræ eam non comprehenderunt.

1:6 Fuit homo missus a Deo, cui nomen erat Joannes.

1:7 Hic venit in testimonium ut testimonium perhiberet de lumine, ut omnes crederent per illum.

1:8 Non erat ille lux, sed ut testimonium perhiberet de lumine.

1:9 Erat lux vera, quæ illuminat omnem hominem venientem in hunc mundum.

1:10 In mundo erat, et mundus per ipsum factus est, et mundus eum non cognovit.

1:11 In propria venit, et sui eum non receperunt.

1:12 Quotquot autem receperunt eum, dedit eis potestatem filios Dei fieri, his qui credunt in nomine ejus :

1:13 qui non ex sanguinibus, neque ex voluntate carnis, neque ex voluntate viri, sed ex Deo nati sunt.

1:14 Et Verbum caro factum est, et habitavit in nobis : et vidimus gloriam ejus, gloriam quasi unigeniti a Patre plenum gratiæ et veritatis.

N THE BEGINNING was the Word, and the Word was with God, and the Word was God.

1:2 The same was in the beginning with God.

1:3 All things were made by him: and without him was made nothing that was made.

1:4 In him was life, and the life was the light of men.

1:5 And the light shineth in darkness, and the darkness did not comprehend it.

1:6 There was a man sent from God, whose name was John.

1:7 This man came for a witness, to give testimony of the light, that all men might believe through him.

1:8 He was not the light, but was to give testimony of the light.

1:9 That was the true light, which enlighteneth every man that cometh into this world.

1:10 He was in the world, and the world was made by him, and the world knew him not.

1:11 He came unto his own, and his own received him not.

1:12 But as many as received him, he gave them power to be made the sons of God, to them that believe in his name.

1:13 Who are born, not of blood, nor of the will of the flesh, nor of the will of man, but of God.

1:14 And the Word was made flesh, and dwelt among us, (and we saw his glory, the glory as it were of the only begotten of the Father,) full of grace and truth.

1:15 Joannes testimonium perhibet de ipso, et clamat dicens : Hic erat quem dixi : Qui post me venturus est, ante me factus est : quia prior me erat.

1:16 Et de plenitudine ejus nos omnes accepimus, et gratiam pro gratia :

1:17 quia lex per Moysen data est, gratia et veritas per Jesum Christum facta est.

1:18 Deum nemo vidit umquam : unigenitus Filius, qui est in sinu Patris, ipse enarravit.

1:19 Et hoc est testimonium Joannis, quando miserunt Judæi ab Jerosolymis sacerdotes et Levitas ad eum ut interrogarent eum : Tu quis es ?

1:20 Et confessus est, et non negavit, et confessus est : Quia non sum ego Christus.

1:21 Et interrogaverunt eum : Quid ergo ? Elias es tu ? Et dixit : Non sum. Propheta es tu ? Et respondit : Non.

1:22 Dixerunt ergo ei : Quis es ut responsum demus his qui miserunt nos ? quid dicis de teipso ?

1:23 Ait : Ego vox clamantis in deserto : Dirigite viam Domini, sicut dixit Isaias propheta.

1:24 Et qui missi fuerant, erant ex pharisæis.

1:25 Et interrogaverunt eum, et dixerunt ei : Quid ergo baptizas, si tu non es Christus, neque Elias, neque propheta ?

1:26 Respondit eis Joannes, dicens : Ego baptizo in aqua : medius autem vestrum stetit, quem vos nescitis.

1:27 Ipse est qui post me venturus est, qui ante me factus est : cujus ego non sum dignus ut solvam ejus corrigiam calceamenti.

1:28 Hæc in Bethania facta sunt trans Jordanem, ubi erat Joannes baptizans.

1:29 Altera die vidit Joannes Jesum venientem ad se, et ait : Ecce agnus Dei, ecce qui tollit peccatum mundi.

1:30 Hic est de quo dixi : Post me venit vir qui ante me factus est : quia prior me erat :

1:31 et ego nesciebam eum, sed ut manifestetur in Israël, propterea veni ego in aqua baptizans.

1:32 Et testimonium perhibuit Joannes, dicens : Quia vidi Spiritum descendentem quasi columbam de cælo, et mansit super eum.

1:15 John beareth witness of him, and crieth out, saying: This was he of whom I spoke: He that shall come after me, is preferred before me: because he was before me.

1:16 And of his fulness we all have received, and grace for grace.

1:17 For the law was given by Moses; grace and truth came by Jesus Christ.

1:18 No man hath seen God at any time: the only begotten Son who is in the bosom of the Father, he hath declared him.

1:19 And this is the testimony of John, when the Jews sent from Jerusalem priests and Levites to him, to ask him: Who art thou?

1:20 And he confessed, and did not deny: and he confessed: I am not the Christ.

1:21 And they asked him: What then? Art thou Elias? And he said: I am not. Art thou the prophet? And he answered: No.

1:22 They said therefore unto him: Who art thou, that we may give an answer to them that sent us? What sayest thou of thyself?

1:23 He said: I am the voice of one crying out in the wilderness, make straight the way of the Lord, as said the prophet Isaias.

1:24 And they that were sent, were of the Pharisees.

1:25 And they asked him, and said to him: Why then dost thou baptize, if thou be not Christ, nor Elias, nor the prophet?

1:26 John answered them, saying: I baptize with water; but there hath stood one in the midst of you, whom you know not.

1:27 The same is he that shall come after me, who is preferred before me: the latchet of whose shoe I am not worthy to loose.

1:28 These things were done in Bethania, beyond the Jordan, where John was baptizing.

1:29 The next day, John saw Jesus coming to him, and he saith: Behold the Lamb of God, behold him who taketh away the sin of the world.

1:30 This is he, of whom I said: After me there cometh a man, who is preferred before me: because he was before me.

1:31 And I knew him not, but that he may be made manifest in Israel, therefore am I come baptizing with water.

1:32 And John gave testimony, saying: I saw the Spirit coming down, as a dove from heaven, and he remained upon him.

1:33 Et ego nesciebam eum : sed qui misit me baptizare in aqua, ille mihi dixit : Super quem videris Spiritum descendentem, et manentem super eum, hic est qui baptizat in Spiritu Sancto.
1:34 Et ego vidi : et testimonium perhibui quia hic est Filius Dei.
1:35 Altera die iterum stabat Joannes, et ex discipulis ejus duo.
1:36 Et respiciens Jesum ambulantem, dicit : Ecce agnus Dei.
1:37 Et audierunt eum duo discipuli loquentem, et secuti sunt Jesum.
1:38 Conversus autem Jesus, et videns eos sequentes se, dicit eis : Quid quæritis ? Qui dixerunt ei : Rabbi (quod dicitur interpretatum Magister), ubi habitas ?
1:39 Dicit eis : Venite et videte. Venerunt, et viderunt ubi maneret, et apud eum manserunt die illo : hora autem erat quasi decima.

1:40 Erat autem Andreas, frater Simonis Petri, unus ex duobus qui audierant a Joanne, et secuti fuerant eum.
1:41 Invenit hic primum fratrem suum Simonem, et dicit ei : Invenimus Messiam (quod est interpretatum Christus).
1:42 Et adduxit eum ad Jesum. Intuitus autem eum Jesus, dixit : Tu es Simon, filius Jona ; tu vocaberis Cephas, quod interpretatur Petrus.

1:43 In crastinum voluit exire in Galilæam, et invenit Philippum. Et dicit ei Jesus : Sequere me.
1:44 Erat autem Philippus a Bethsaida, civitate Andreæ et Petri.
1:45 Invenit Philippus Nathanaël, et dicit ei : Quem scripsit Moyses in lege, et prophetæ, invenimus Jesum filium Joseph a Nazareth.

1:46 Et dixit ei Nathanaël : A Nazareth potest aliquid boni esse ? Dicit ei Philippus : Veni et vide.
1:47 Vidit Jesus Nathanaël venientem ad se, et dicit de eo : Ecce vere Israëlita, in quo dolus non est.
1:48 Dicit ei Nathanaël : Unde me nosti ? Respondit Jesus, et dixit ei : Priusquam te Philippus vocavit, cum esses sub ficu, vidi te.

1:49 Respondit ei Nathanaël, et ait : Rabbi, tu es Filius Dei, tu es rex Israël.

1:33 And I knew him not; but he who sent me to baptize with water, said to me: He upon whom thou shalt see the Spirit descending, and remaining upon him, he it is that baptizeth with the Holy Ghost.
1:34 And I saw, and I gave testimony, that this is the Son of God.
1:35 The next day again John stood, and two of his disciples.
1:36 And beholding Jesus walking, he saith: Behold the Lamb of God.
1:37 And the two disciples heard him speak, and they followed Jesus.
1:38 And Jesus turning, and seeing them following him, saith to them: What seek you? Who said to him, Rabbi, (which is to say, being interpreted, Master,) where dwellest thou?
1:39 He saith to them: Come and see. They came, and saw where he abode, and they stayed with him that day: now it was about the tenth hour.

1:40 And Andrew, the brother of Simon Peter, was one of the two who had heard of John, and followed him.
1:41 He findeth first his brother Simon, and saith to him: We have found the Messias, which is, being interpreted, the Christ.
1:42 And he brought him to Jesus. And Jesus looking upon him, said: Thou art Simon the son of Jona: thou shalt be called Cephas, which is interpreted Peter.

1:43 On the following day, he would go forth into Galilee, and he findeth Philip. And Jesus saith to him: Follow me.
1:44 Now Philip was of Bethsaida, the city of Andrew and Peter.
1:45 Philip findeth Nathanael, and saith to him: We have found him of whom Moses in the law, and the prophets did write, Jesus the son of Joseph of Nazareth.

1:46 And Nathanael said to him: Can any thing of good come from Nazareth? Philip saith to him: Come and see.
1:47 Jesus saw Nathanael coming to him: and he saith of him: Behold an Israelite indeed, in whom there is no guile.
1:48 Nathanael saith to him: Whence knowest thou me? Jesus answered, and said to him: Before that Philip called thee, when thou wast under the fig tree, I saw thee.

1:49 Nathanael answered him, and said: Rabbi, thou art the Son of God, thou art the King of

1:50 Respondit Jesus, et dixit ei : Quia dixi tibi : Vidi te sub ficu, credis ; majus his videbis.

1:51 Et dicit ei : Amen, amen dico vobis, videbitis cælum apertum, et angelos Dei ascendentes, et descendentes supra Filium hominis.

2:1 Et die tertia nuptiæ factæ sunt in Cana Galilææ, et erat mater Jesu ibi.

2:2 Vocatus est autem et Jesus, et discipuli ejus, ad nuptias.

2:3 Et deficiente vino, dicit mater Jesu ad eum : Vinum non habent.

2:4 Et dicit ei Jesus : Quid mihi et tibi est, mulier ? nondum venit hora mea.

2:5 Dicit mater ejus ministris : Quodcumque dixerit vobis, facite.

2:6 Erant autem ibi lapideæ hydriæ sex positæ secundum purificationem Judæorum, capientes singulæ metretas binas vel ternas.

2:7 Dicit eis Jesus : Implete hydrias aqua. Et impleverunt eas usque ad summum.

2:8 Et dicit eis Jesus : Haurite nunc, et ferte architriclino. Et tulerunt.

2:9 Ut autem gustavit architriclinus aquam vinum factam, et non sciebat unde esset, ministri autem sciebant, qui hauserant aquam : vocat sponsum architriclinus,

2:10 et dicit ei : Omnis homo primum bonum vinum ponit et cum inebriati fuerint, tunc id, quod deterius est. Tu autem servasti bonum vinum usque adhuc.

2:11 Hoc fecit initium signorum Jesus in Cana Galilææ ; et manifestavit gloriam suam, et crediderunt in eum discipuli ejus.

2:12 Post hoc descendit Capharnaum ipse, et mater ejus, et fratres ejus, et discipuli ejus : et ibi manserunt non multis diebus.

2:13 Et prope erat Pascha Judæorum, et ascendit Jesus Jerosolymam :

2:14 et invenit in templo vendentes boves, et oves, et columbas, et numularios sedentes.

2:15 Et cum fecisset quasi flagellum de funiculis, omnes ejecit de templo, oves quoque, et boves, et numulariorum effudit æs, et mensas sub-

Israel.

1:50 Jesus answered, and said to him: Because I said unto thee, I saw thee under the fig tree, thou believest: greater things than these shalt thou see.

1:51 And he saith to him: Amen, amen I say to you, you shall see the heaven opened, and the angels of God ascending and descending upon the Son of man.

2:1 And the third day, there was a marriage in Cana of Galilee: and the mother of Jesus was there.

2:2 And Jesus also was invited, and his disciples, to the marriage.

2:3 And the wine failing, the mother of Jesus saith to him: They have no wine.

2:4 And Jesus saith to her: Woman, what is that to me and to thee? my hour is not yet come.

2:5 His mother saith to the waiters: Whatsoever he shall say to you, do ye.

2:6 Now there were set there six waterpots of stone, according to the manner of the purifying of the Jews, containing two or three measures apiece.

2:7 Jesus saith to them: Fill the waterpots with water. And they filled them up to the brim.

2:8 And Jesus saith to them: Draw out now, and carry to the chief steward of the feast. And they carried it.

2:9 And when the chief steward had tasted the water made wine, and knew not whence it was, but the waiters knew who had drawn the water; the chief steward calleth the bridegroom,

2:10 And saith to him: Every man at first setteth forth good wine, and when men have well drunk, then that which is worse. But thou hast kept the good wine until now.

2:11 This beginning of miracles did Jesus in Cana of Galilee; and manifested his glory, and his disciples believed in him.

2:12 After this he went down to Capharnaum, he and his mother, and his brethren, and his disciples: and they remained there not many days.

2:13 And the pasch of the Jews was at hand, and Jesus went up to Jerusalem.

2:14 And he found in the temple them that sold oxen and sheep and doves, and the changers of money sitting.

2:15 And when he had made, as it were, a scourge of little cords, he drove them all out of the temple, the sheep also and the oxen, and

vertit.

2:16 Et his qui columbas vendebant, dixit : Auferte ista hinc, et nolite facere domum patris mei, domum negotiationis.

2:17 Recordati sunt vero discipuli ejus quia scriptum est : Zelus domus tuæ comedit me.

2:18 Responderunt ergo Judæi, et dixerunt ei : Quod signum ostendis nobis, quia hæc facis ?

2:19 Respondit Jesus, et dixit eis : Solvite templum hoc, et in tribus diebus excitabo illud.

2:20 Dixerunt ergo Judæi : Quadraginta et sex annis ædificatum est templum hoc, et tu in tribus diebus excitabis illud ?

2:21 Ille autem dicebat de templo corporis sui.

2:22 Cum ergo resurrexisset a mortuis, recordati sunt discipuli ejus, quia hoc dicebat, et crediderunt scripturæ et sermoni quem dixit Jesus.

2:23 Cum autem esset Jerosolymis in Pascha in die festo, multi crediderunt in nomine ejus, videntes signa ejus, quæ faciebat.

2:24 Ipse autem Jesus non credebat semetipsum eis, eo quod ipse nosset omnes,

2:25 et quia opus ei non erat ut quis testimonium perhiberet de homine : ipse enim sciebat quid esset in homine.

3:1 Erat autem homo ex pharisæis, Nicodemus nomine, princeps Judæorum.

3:2 Hic venit ad Jesum nocte, et dixit ei : Rabbi, scimus quia a Deo venisti magister, nemo enim potest hæc signa facere, quæ tu facis, nisi fuerit Deus cum eo.

3:3 Respondit Jesus, et dixit ei : Amen, amen dico tibi, nisi quis renatus fuerit denuo, non potest videre regnum Dei.

3:4 Dicit ad eum Nicodemus : Quomodo potest homo nasci, cum sit senex ? numquid potest in ventrem matris suæ iterato introire et renasci ?

3:5 Respondit Jesus : Amen, amen dico tibi, nisi quis renatus fuerit ex aqua, et Spiritu Sancto, non potest introire in regnum Dei.

3:6 Quod natum est ex carne, caro est : et quod natum est ex spiritu, spiritus est.

3:7 Non mireris quia dixi tibi : oportet vos nasci denuo.

3:8 Spiritus ubi vult spirat, et vocem ejus audis, sed nescis unde veniat, aut quo vadat : sic est

the money of the changers he poured out, and the tables he overthrew.

2:16 And to them that sold doves he said: Take these things hence, and make not the house of my Father a house of traffic.

2:17 And his disciples remembered, that it was written: The zeal of thy house hath eaten me up.

2:18 The Jews, therefore, answered, and said to him: What sign dost thou shew unto us, seeing thou dost these things?

2:19 Jesus answered, and said to them: Destroy this temple, and in three days I will raise it up.

2:20 The Jews then said: Six and forty years was this temple in building; and wilt thou raise it up in three days?

2:21 But he spoke of the temple of his body.

2:22 When therefore he was risen again from the dead, his disciples remembered, that he had said this, and they believed the scripture, and the word that Jesus had said.

2:23 Now when he was at Jerusalem, at the pasch, upon the festival day, many believed in his name, seeing his signs which he did.

2:24 But Jesus did not trust himself unto them, for that he knew all men,

2:25 And because he needed not that any should give testimony of man: for he knew what was in man.

3:1 And there was a man of the Pharisees, named Nicodemus, a ruler of the Jews.

3:2 This man came to Jesus by night, and said to him: Rabbi, we know that thou art come a teacher from God; for no man can do these signs which thou dost, unless God be with him.

3:3 Jesus answered, and said to him: Amen, amen I say to thee, unless a man be born again, he cannot see the kingdom of God.

3:4 Nicodemus saith to him: How can a man be born when he is old? can he enter a second time into his mother's womb, and be born again?

3:5 Jesus answered: Amen, amen I say to thee, unless a man be born again of water and the Holy Ghost, he cannot enter into the kingdom of God.

3:6 That which is born of the flesh, is flesh; and that which is born of the Spirit, is spirit.

3:7 Wonder not, that I said to thee, you must be born again.

3:8 The Spirit breatheth where he will; and thou hearest his voice, but thou knowest not whence

omnis qui natus est ex spiritu.

3:9 Respondit Nicodemus, et dixit ei : Quomodo possunt hæc fieri ?

3:10 Respondit Jesus, et dixit ei : Tu es magister in Israël, et hæc ignoras ?

3:11 amen, amen dico tibi, quia quod scimus loquimur, et quod vidimus testamur, et testimonium nostrum non accipitis.

3:12 Si terrena dixi vobis, et non creditis : quomodo, si dixero vobis cælestia, credetis ?

3:13 Et nemo ascendit in cælum, nisi qui descendit de cælo, Filius hominis, qui est in cælo.

3:14 Et sicut Moyses exaltavit serpentem in deserto, ita exaltari oportet Filium hominis :

3:15 ut omnis qui credit in ipsum, non pereat, sed habeat vitam æternam.

3:16 Sic enim Deus dilexit mundum, ut Filium suum unigenitum daret : ut omnis qui credit in eum, non pereat, sed habeat vitam æternam.

3:17 Non enim misit Deus Filium suum in mundum, ut judicet mundum, sed ut salvetur mundus per ipsum.

3:18 Qui credit in eum, non judicatur ; qui autem non credit, jam judicatus est : quia non credit in nomine unigeniti Filii Dei.

3:19 Hoc est autem judicium : quia lux venit in mundum, et dilexerunt homines magis tenebras quam lucem : erant enim eorum mala opera.

3:20 Omnis enim qui male agit, odit lucem, et non venit ad lucem, ut non arguantur opera ejus :

3:21 qui autem facit veritatem, venit ad lucem, ut manifestentur opera ejus, quia in Deo sunt facta.

3:22 Post hæc venit Jesus et discipuli ejus in terram Judæam : et illic demorabatur cum eis, et baptizabat.

3:23 Erat autem et Joannes baptizans, in Ænnon, juxta Salim : quia aquæ multæ erant illic, et veniebant et baptizabantur.

3:24 Nondum enim missus fuerat Joannes in carcerem.

3:25 Facta est autem quæstio ex discipulis Joannis cum Judæis de purificatione.

3:26 Et venerunt ad Joannem, et dixerunt ei :

he cometh, and whither he goeth: so is every one that is born of the Spirit.

3:9 Nicodemus answered, and said to him: How can these things be done?

3:10 Jesus answered, and said to him: Art thou a master in Israel, and knowest not these things?

3:11 Amen, amen I say to thee, that we speak what we know, and we testify what we have seen, and you receive not our testimony.

3:12 If I have spoken to you earthly things, and you believe not; how will you believe, if I shall speak to you heavenly things?

3:13 And no man hath ascended into heaven, but he that descended from heaven, the Son of man who is in heaven.

3:14 And as Moses lifted up the serpent in the desert, so must the Son of man be lifted up:

3:15 That whosoever believeth in him, may not perish; but may have life everlasting.

3:16 For God so loved the world, as to give his only begotten Son; that whosoever believeth in him, may not perish, but may have life everlasting.

3:17 For God sent not his Son into the world, to judge the world, but that the world may be saved by him.

3:18 He that believeth in him is not judged. But he that doth not believe, is already judged: because he believeth not in the name of the only begotten Son of God.

3:19 And this is the judgment: because the light is come into the world, and men loved darkness rather than the light: for their works were evil.

3:20 For every one that doth evil hateth the light, and cometh not to the light, that his works may not be reproved.

3:21 But he that doth truth, cometh to the light, that his works may be made manifest, because they are done in God.

3:22 After these things Jesus and his disciples came into the land of Judea: and there he abode with them, and baptized.

3:23 And John also was baptizing in Ennon near Salim; because there was much water there; and they came and were baptized.

3:24 For John was not yet cast into prison.

3:25 And there arose a question between some of John's disciples and the Jews concerning purification:

3:26 And they came to John, and said to him:

Rabbi, qui erat tecum trans Jordanem, cui tu testimonium perhibuisti, ecce hic baptizat, et omnes veniunt ad eum.

3:27 Respondit Joannes, et dixit : Non potest homo accipere quidquam, nisi fuerit ei datum de cælo.

3:28 Ipsi vos mihi testimonium perhibetis, quod dixerim : Non sum ego Christus : sed quia missus sum ante illum.

3:29 Qui habet sponsam, sponsus est : amicus autem sponsi, qui stat, et audit eum, gaudio gaudet propter vocem sponsi. Hoc ergo gaudium meum impletum est.

3:30 Illum oportet crescere, me autem minui.

3:31 Qui desursum venit, super omnes est. Qui est de terra, de terra est, et de terra loquitur. Qui de cælo venit, super omnes est.

3:32 Et quod vidit, et audivit, hoc testatur : et testimonium ejus nemo accipit.

3:33 Qui accepit ejus testimonium signavit, quia Deus verax est.

3:34 Quem enim misit Deus, verba Dei loquitur : non enim ad mensuram dat Deus spiritum.

3:35 Pater diligit Filium et omnia dedit in manu ejus.

3:36 Qui credit in Filium, habet vitam æternam ; qui autem incredulus est Filio, non videbit vitam, sed ira Dei manet super eum.

4:1 Ut ergo cognovit Jesus quia audierunt pharisæi quod Jesus plures discipulos facit, et baptizat, quam Joannes

4:2 (quamquam Jesus non baptizaret, sed discipuli ejus),

4:3 reliquit Judæam, et abiit iterum in Galilæam.

4:4 Oportebat autem eum transire per Samariam.

4:5 Venit ergo in civitatem Samariæ, quæ dicitur Sichar, juxta prædium quod dedit Jacob Joseph filio suo.

4:6 Erat autem ibi fons Jacob. Jesus ergo fatigatus ex itinere, sedebat sic supra fontem. Hora erat quasi sexta.

4:7 Venit mulier de Samaria haurire aquam. Dicit ei Jesus : Da mihi bibere.

4:8 (Discipuli enim ejus abierant in civitatem ut cibos emerent.)

4:9 Dicit ergo ei mulier illa Samaritana : Quo-

Rabbi, he that was with thee beyond the Jordan, to whom thou gavest testimony, behold he baptizeth, and all men come to him.

3:27 John answered, and said: A man cannot receive any thing, unless it be given him from heaven.

3:28 You yourselves do bear me witness, that I said, I am not Christ, but that I am sent before him.

3:29 He that hath the bride, is the bridegroom: but the friend of the bridegroom, who standeth and heareth him, rejoiceth with joy because of the bridegroom's voice. This my joy therefore is fulfilled.

3:30 He must increase, but I must decrease.

3:31 He that cometh from above, is above all. He that is of the earth, of the earth he is, and of the earth he speaketh. He that cometh from heaven, is above all.

3:32 And what he hath seen and heard, that he testifieth: and no man receiveth his testimony.

3:33 He that hath received his testimony, hath set to his seal that God is true.

3:34 For he whom God hath sent, speaketh the words of God: for God doth not give the Spirit by measure.

3:35 The Father loveth the Son: and he hath given all things into his hand.

3:36 He that believeth in the Son, hath life everlasting; but he that believeth not the Son, shall not see life; but the wrath of God abideth on him.

4:1 When Jesus therefore understood that the Pharisees had heard that Jesus maketh more disciples, and baptizeth more than John,

4:2 (Though Jesus himself did not baptize, but his disciples,)

4:3 He left Judea, and went again into Galilee.

4:4 And he was of necessity to pass through Samaria.

4:5 He cometh therefore to a city of Samaria, which is called Sichar, near the land which Jacob gave to his son Joseph.

4:6 Now Jacob's well was there. Jesus therefore being wearied with his journey, sat thus on the well. It was about the sixth hour.

4:7 There cometh a woman of Samaria, to draw water. Jesus saith to her: Give me to drink.

4:8 For his disciples were gone into the city to buy meats.

4:9 Then that Samaritan woman saith to him:

modo tu, Judæus cum sis, bibere a me poscis, quæ sum mulier Samaritana ? non enim coutuntur Judæi Samaritanis.

4:10 Respondit Jesus, et dixit ei : Si scires donum Dei, et quis est qui dicit tibi : Da mihi bibere, tu forsitan petisses ab eo, et dedisset tibi aquam vivam.

4:11 Dicit ei mulier : Domine, neque in quo haurias habes, et puteus altus est : unde ergo habes aquam vivam ?

4:12 Numquid tu major es patre nostro Jacob, qui dedit nobis puteum, et ipse ex eo bibit, et filii ejus, et pecora ejus ?

4:13 Respondit Jesus, et dixit ei : Omnis qui bibit ex aqua hac, sitiet iterum ; qui autem biberit ex aqua quam ego dabo ei, non sitiet in æternum :

4:14 sed aqua quam ego dabo ei, fiet in eo fons aquæ salientis in vitam æternam.

4:15 Dicit ad eum mulier : Domine, da mihi hanc aquam, ut non sitiam, neque veniam huc haurire.

4:16 Dicit ei Jesus : Vade, voca virum tuum, et veni huc.

4:17 Respondit mulier, et dixit : Non habeo virum. Dicit ei Jesus : Bene dixisti, quia non habeo virum ;

4:18 quinque enim viros habuisti, et nunc, quem habes, non est tuus vir : hoc vere dixisti.

4:19 Dicit ei mulier : Domine, video quia propheta es tu.

4:20 Patres nostri in monte hoc adoraverunt, et vos dicitis, quia Jerosolymis est locus ubi adorare oportet.

4:21 Dicit ei Jesus : Mulier, crede mihi, quia venit hora, quando neque in monte hoc, neque in Jerosolymis adorabitis Patrem.

4:22 Vos adoratis quod nescitis : nos adoramus quod scimus, quia salus ex Judæis est.

4:23 Sed venit hora, et nunc est, quando veri adoratores adorabunt Patrem in spiritu et veritate. Nam et Pater tales quærit, qui adorent eum.

4:24 Spiritus est Deus : et eos qui adorant eum, in spiritu et veritate oportet adorare.

4:25 Dicit ei mulier : Scio quia Messias venit (qui dicitur Christus) : cum ergo venerit ille, nobis

How dost thou, being a Jew, ask of me to drink, who am a Samaritan woman? For the Jews do not communicate with the Samaritans.

4:10 Jesus answered, and said to her: If thou didst know the gift of God, and who he is that saith to thee, Give me to drink; thou perhaps wouldst have asked of him, and he would have given thee living water.

4:11 The woman saith to him: Sir, thou hast nothing wherein to draw, and the well is deep; from whence then hast thou living water?

4:12 Art thou greater than our father Jacob, who gave us the well, and drank thereof himself, and his children, and his cattle?

4:13 Jesus answered, and said to her: Whosoever drinketh of this water, shall thirst again; but he that shall drink of the water that I will give him, shall not thirst for ever:

4:14 But the water that I will give him, shall become in him a fountain of water, springing up into life everlasting.

4:15 The woman saith to him: Sir, give me this water, that I may not thirst, nor come hither to draw.

4:16 Jesus saith to her: Go, call thy husband, and come hither.

4:17 The woman answered, and said: I have no husband. Jesus said to her: Thou hast said well, I have no husband:

4:18 For thou hast had five husbands: and he whom thou now hast, is not thy husband. This thou hast said truly.

4:19 The woman saith to him: Sir, I perceive that thou art a prophet.

4:20 Our fathers adored on this mountain, and you say, that at Jerusalem is the place where men must adore.

4:21 Jesus saith to her: Woman, believe me, that the hour cometh, when you shall neither on this mountain, nor in Jerusalem, adore the Father.

4:22 You adore that which you know not: we adore that which we know; for salvation is of the Jews.

4:23 But the hour cometh, and now is, when the true adorers shall adore the Father in spirit and in truth. For the Father also seeketh such to adore him.

4:24 God is a spirit; and they that adore him, must adore him in spirit and in truth.

4:25 The woman saith to him: I know that the Messias cometh (who is called Christ); there-

annuntiabit omnia.

4:26 Dicit ei Jesus : Ego sum, qui loquor tecum.

4:27 Et continuo venerunt discipuli ejus, et mirabantur quia cum muliere loquebatur. Nemo tamen dixit : Quid quæris ? aut, Quid loqueris cum ea ?

4:28 Reliquit ergo hydriam suam mulier, et abiit in civitatem, et dicit illis hominibus :

4:29 Venite, et videte hominem qui dixit mihi omnia quæcumque feci : numquid ipse est Christus ?

4:30 Exierunt ergo de civitate et veniebant ad eum.

4:31 Interea rogabant eum discipuli, dicentes : Rabbi, manduca.

4:32 Ille autem dicit eis : Ego cibum habeo manducare, quem vos nescitis.

4:33 Dicebant ergo discipuli ad invicem : Numquid aliquis attulit ei manducare ?

4:34 Dicit eis Jesus : Meus cibus est ut faciam voluntatem ejus qui misit me, ut perficiam opus ejus.

4:35 Nonne vos dicitis quod adhuc quatuor menses sunt, et messis venit ? Ecce dico vobis : levate oculos vestros, et videte regiones, quia albæ sunt jam ad messem.

4:36 Et qui metit, mercedem accipit, et congregat fructum in vitam æternam : ut et qui seminat, simul gaudeat, et qui metit.

4:37 In hoc enim est verbum verum : quia alius est qui seminat, et alius est qui metit.

4:38 Ego misi vos metere quod vos non laborastis : alii laboraverunt, et vos in labores eorum introistis.

4:39 Ex civitate autem illa multi crediderunt in eum Samaritanorum, propter verbum mulieris testimonium perhibentis : Quia dixit mihi omnia quæcumque feci.

4:40 Cum venissent ergo ad illum Samaritani, rogaverunt eum ut ibi maneret. Et mansit ibi duos dies.

4:41 Et multo plures crediderunt in eum propter sermonem ejus.

4:42 Et mulieri dicebant : Quia jam non propter tuam loquelam credimus : ipsi enim audivimus, et scimus quia hic est vere Salvator mundi.

4:43 Post duos autem dies exiit inde, et abiit in Galilæam.

fore, when he is come, he will tell us all things.

4:26 Jesus saith to her: I am he, who am speaking with thee.

4:27 And immediately his disciples came; and they wondered that he talked with the woman. Yet no man said: What seekest thou? or, why talkest thou with her?

4:28 The woman therefore left her waterpot, and went her way into the city, and saith to the men there:

4:29 Come, and see a man who has told me all things whatsoever I have done. Is not he the Christ?

4:30 They went therefore out of the city, and came unto him.

4:31 In the mean time the disciples prayed him, saying: Rabbi, eat.

4:32 But he said to them: I have meat to eat, which you know not.

4:33 The disciples therefore said one to another: Hath any man brought him to eat?

4:34 Jesus saith to them: My meat is to do the will of him that sent me, that I may perfect his work.

4:35 Do you not say, There are yet four months, and then the harvest cometh? Behold, I say to you, lift up your eyes, and see the countries; for they are white already to harvest.

4:36 And he that reapeth receiveth wages, and gathereth fruit unto life everlasting: that both he that soweth, and he that reapeth, may rejoice together.

4:37 For in this is the saying true: That it is one man that soweth, and it is another that reapeth.

4:38 I have sent you to reap that in which you did not labour: others have laboured, and you have entered into their labours.

4:39 Now of that city many of the Samaritans believed in him, for the word of the woman giving testimony: He told me all things whatsoever I have done.

4:40 So when the Samaritans were come to him, they desired that he would tarry there. And he abode there two days.

4:41 And many more believed in him because of his own word.

4:42 And they said to the woman: We now believe, not for thy saying: for we ourselves have heard him, and know that this is indeed the Saviour of the world.

4:43 Now after two days, he departed thence, and went into Galilee.

4:44 Ipse enim Jesus testimonium perhibuit, quia propheta in sua patria honorem non habet.

4:45 Cum ergo venisset in Galilæam, exceperunt eum Galilæi, cum omnia vidissent quæ fecerat Jerosolymis in die festo : et ipsi enim venerant ad diem festum.

4:46 Venit ergo iterum in Cana Galilææ, ubi fecit aquam vinum. Et erat quidam regulus, cujus filius infirmabatur Capharnaum.

4:47 Hic cum audisset quia Jesus adveniret a Judæa in Galilæam, abiit ad eum, et rogabat eum ut descenderet, et sanaret filium ejus : incipiebat enim mori.

4:48 Dixit ergo Jesus ad eum : Nisi signa et prodigia videritis, non creditis.

4:49 Dicit ad eum regulus : Domine, descende priusquam moriatur filius meus.

4:50 Dicit ei Jesus : Vade, filius tuus vivit. Credidit homo sermoni quem dixit ei Jesus, et ibat.

4:51 Jam autem eo descendente, servi occurrerunt ei, et nuntiaverunt dicentes, quia filius ejus viveret.

4:52 Interrogabat ergo horam ab eis in qua melius habuerit. Et dixerunt ei : Quia heri hora septima reliquit eum febris.

4:53 Cognovit ergo pater, quia illa hora erat in qua dixit ei Jesus : Filius tuus vivit ; et credidit ipse et domus ejus tota.

4:54 Hoc iterum secundum signum fecit Jesus, cum venisset a Judæa in Galilæam.

5:1 Post hæc erat dies festus Judæorum, et ascendit Jesus Jerosolymam.

5:2 Est autem Jerosolymis probatica piscina, quæ cognominatur hebraice Bethsaida, quinque porticus habens.

5:3 In his jacebat multitudo magna languentium, cæcorum, claudorum, aridorum, exspectantium aquæ motum.

5:4 Angelus autem Domini descendebat secundum tempus in piscinam, et movebatur aqua. Et qui prior descendisset in piscinam post motionem aquæ, sanus fiebat a quacumque detinebatur infirmitate.

5:5 Erat autem quidam homo ibi triginta et octo annos habens in infirmitate sua.

5:6 Hunc autem cum vidisset Jesus jacentem, et cognovisset quia jam multum tempus haberet,

4:44 For Jesus himself gave testimony that a prophet hath no honour in his own country.

4:45 And when he was come into Galilee, the Galileans received him, having seen all the things he had done at Jerusalem on the festival day; for they also went to the festival day.

4:46 He came again therefore into Cana of Galilee, where he made the water wine. And there was a certain ruler, whose son was sick at Capharnaum.

4:47 He having heard that Jesus was come from Judea into Galilee, went to him, and prayed him to come down, and heal his son; for he was at the point of death.

4:48 Jesus therefore said to him: Unless you see signs and wonders, you believe not.

4:49 The ruler saith to him: Lord, come down before that my son die.

4:50 Jesus saith to him: Go thy way; thy son liveth. The man believed the word which Jesus said to him, and went his way.

4:51 And as he was going down, his servants met him; and they brought word, saying, that his son lived.

4:52 He asked therefore of them the hour wherein he grew better. And they said to him: Yesterday, at the seventh hour, the fever left him.

4:53 The father therefore knew, that it was at the same hour that Jesus said to him, Thy son liveth; and himself believed, and his whole house.

4:54 This is again the second miracle that Jesus did, when he was come out of Judea into Galilee.

5:1 After these things was a festival day of the Jews, and Jesus went up to Jerusalem.

5:2 Now there is at Jerusalem a pond, called Probatica, which in Hebrew is named Bethsaida, having five porches.

5:3 In these lay a great multitude of sick, of blind, of lame, of withered; waiting for the moving of the water.

5:4 And an angel of the Lord descended at certain times into the pond; and the water was moved. And he that went down first into the pond after the motion of the water, was made whole, of whatsoever infirmity he lay under.

5:5 And there was a certain man there, that had been eight and thirty years under his infirmity.

5:6 Him when Jesus had seen lying, and knew that he had been now a long time, he saith to

dicit ei : Vis sanus fieri ?

5:7 Respondit ei languidus : Domine, hominem non habeo, ut, cum turbata fuerit aqua, mittat me in piscinam : dum venio enim ego, alius ante me descendit.

5:8 Dicit ei Jesus : Surge, tolle grabatum tuum et ambula.

5:9 Et statim sanus factus est homo ille : et sustulit grabatum suum, et ambulabat. Erat autem sabbatum in die illo.

5:10 Dicebant ergo Judæi illi qui sanatus fuerat : Sabbatum est, non licet tibi tollere grabatum tuum.

5:11 Respondit eis : Qui me sanum fecit, ille mihi dixit : Tolle grabatum tuum et ambula.

5:12 Interrogaverunt ergo eum : Quis est ille homo qui dixit tibi : Tolle grabatum tuum et ambula ?

5:13 Is autem qui sanus fuerat effectus, nesciebat quis esset. Jesus enim declinavit a turba constituta in loco.

5:14 Postea invenit eum Jesus in templo, et dixit illi : Ecce sanus factus es ; jam noli peccare, ne deterius tibi aliquid contingat.

5:15 Abiit ille homo, et nuntiavit Judæis quia Jesus esset, qui fecit eum sanum.

5:16 Propterea persequebantur Judæi Jesum, quia hæc faciebat in sabbato.

5:17 Jesus autem respondit eis : Pater meus usque modo operatur, et ego operor.

5:18 Propterea ergo magis quærebant eum Judæi interficere : quia non solum solvebat sabbatum, sed et patrem suum dicebat Deum, æqualem se faciens Deo. Respondit itaque Jesus, et dixit eis :

5:19 Amen, amen dico vobis : non potest Filius a se facere quidquam, nisi quod viderit Patrem facientem : quæcumque enim ille fecerit, hæc et Filius similiter facit.

5:20 Pater enim diligit Filium, et omnia demonstrat ei quæ ipse facit : et majora his demonstrabit ei opera, ut vos miremini.

5:21 Sicut enim Pater suscitat mortuos, et vivificat, sic et Filius, quos vult, vivificat.

5:22 Neque enim Pater judicat quemquam : sed omne judicium dedit Filio,

5:23 ut omnes honorificent Filium, sicut honor-

him: Wilt thou be made whole?

5:7 The infirm man answered him: Sir, I have no man, when the water is troubled, to put me into the pond. For whilst I am coming, another goeth down before me.

5:8 Jesus saith to him: Arise, take up thy bed, and walk.

5:9 And immediately the man was made whole: and he took up his bed, and walked. And it was the sabbath that day.

5:10 The Jews therefore said to him that was healed: It is the sabbath; it is not lawful for thee to take up thy bed.

5:11 He answered them: He that made me whole, he said to me, Take up thy bed, and walk.

5:12 They asked him therefore: Who is that man who said to thee, Take up thy bed, and walk?

5:13 But he who was healed, knew not who it was; for Jesus went aside from the multitude standing in the place.

5:14 Afterwards, Jesus findeth him in the temple, and saith to him: Behold thou art made whole: sin no more, lest some worse thing happen to thee.

5:15 The man went his way, and told the Jews, that it was Jesus who had made him whole.

5:16 Therefore did the Jews persecute Jesus, because he did these things on the sabbath.

5:17 But Jesus answered them: My Father worketh until now; and I work.

5:18 Hereupon therefore the Jews sought the more to kill him, because he did not only break the sabbath, but also said God was his Father, making himself equal to God.

5:19 Then Jesus answered, and said to them: Amen, amen, I say unto you, the Son cannot do any thing of himself, but what he seeth the Father doing: for what things soever he doth, these the Son also doth in like manner.

5:20 For the Father loveth the Son, and sheweth him all things which himself doth: and greater works than these will he shew him, that you may wonder.

5:21 For as the Father raiseth up the dead, and giveth life: so the Son also giveth life to whom he will.

5:22 For neither doth the Father judge any man, but hath given all judgment to the Son.

5:23 That all men may honour the Son, as they

ificant Patrem ; qui non honorificat Filium, non honorificat Patrem, qui misit illum.

5:24 Amen, amen dico vobis, quia qui verbum meum audit, et credit ei qui misit me, habet vitam æternam, et in judicium non venit, sed transiit a morte in vitam.

5:25 Amen, amen dico vobis, quia venit hora, et nunc est, quando mortui audient vocem Filii Dei : et qui audierint, vivent.

5:26 Sicut enim Pater habet vitam in semetipso, sic dedit et Filio habere vitam in semetipso :

5:27 et potestatem dedit ei judicium facere, quia Filius hominis est.

5:28 Nolite mirari hoc, quia venit hora in qua omnes qui in monumentis sunt audient vocem Filii Dei :

5:29 et procedent qui bona fecerunt, in resurrectionem vitæ ; qui vero mala egerunt, in resurrectionem judicii.

5:30 Non possum ego a meipso facere quidquam. Sicut audio, judico : et judicium meum justum est, quia non quæro voluntatem meam, sed voluntatem ejus qui misit me.

5:31 Si ego testimonium perhibeo de meipso, testimonium meum non est verum.

5:32 Alius est qui testimonium perhibet de me : et scio quia verum est testimonium, quod perhibet de me.

5:33 Vos misistis ad Joannem, et testimonium perhibuit veritati.

5:34 Ego autem non ab homine testimonium accipio : sed hæc dico ut vos salvi sitis.

5:35 Ille erat lucerna ardens et lucens : vos autem voluistis ad horam exsultare in luce ejus.

5:36 Ego autem habeo testimonium majus Joanne. Opera enim quæ dedit mihi Pater ut perficiam ea : ipsa opera, quæ ego facio, testimonium perhibent de me, quia Pater misit me :

5:37 et qui misit me Pater, ipse testimonium perhibuit de me : neque vocem ejus umquam audistis, neque speciem ejus vidistis :

5:38 et verbum ejus non habetis in vobis manens : quia quem misit ille, huic vos non creditis.

5:39 Scrutamini Scripturas, quia vos putatis in ipsis vitam æternam habere : et illæ sunt quæ testimonium perhibent de me :

honour the Father. He who honoureth not the Son, honoureth not the Father, who hath sent him.

5:24 Amen, amen I say unto you, that he who heareth my word, and believeth him that sent me, hath life everlasting; and cometh not into judgment, but is passed from death to life.

5:25 Amen, amen I say unto you, that the hour cometh, and now is, when the dead shall hear the voice of the Son of God, and they that hear shall live.

5:26 For as the Father hath life in himself, so he hath given the Son also to have life in himself:

5:27 And he hath given him power to do judgment, because he is the Son of man.

5:28 Wonder not at this; for the hour cometh, wherein all that are in the graves shall hear the voice of the Son of God.

5:29 And they that have done good things, shall come forth unto the resurrection of life; but they that have done evil, unto the resurrection of judgment.

5:30 I cannot of myself do any thing. As I hear, so I judge: and my judgment is just; because I seek not my own will, but the will of him that sent me.

5:31 If I bear witness of myself, my witness is not true.

5:32 There is another that beareth witness of me; and I know that the witness which he witnesseth of me is true.

5:33 You sent to John, and he gave testimony to the truth.

5:34 But I receive not testimony from man: but I say these things, that you may be saved.

5:35 He was a burning and a shining light: and you were willing for a time to rejoice in his light.

5:36 But I have a greater testimony than that of John: for the works which the Father hath given me to perfect; the works themselves, which I do, give testimony of me, that the Father hath sent me.

5:37 And the Father himself who hath sent me, hath given testimony of me: neither have you heard his voice at any time, nor seen his shape.

5:38 And you have not his word abiding in you: for whom he hath sent, him you believe not.

5:39 Search the scriptures, for you think in them to have life everlasting; and the same are they that give testimony of me.

5:40 et non vultis venire ad me ut vitam habeatis.

5:41 Claritatem ab hominibus non accipio.

5:42 Sed cognovi vos, quia dilectionem Dei non habetis in vobis.

5:43 Ego veni in nomine Patris mei, et non accipitis me ; si alius venerit in nomine suo, illum accipietis.

5:44 Quomodo vos potestis credere, qui gloriam ab invicem accipitis, et gloriam quæ a solo Deo est, non quæritis ?

5:45 Nolite putare quia ego accusaturus sim vos apud Patrem : est qui accusat vos Moyses, in quo vos speratis.

5:46 Si enim crederetis Moysi, crederetis forsitan et mihi : de me enim ille scripsit.

5:47 Si autem illius litteris non creditis, quomodo verbis meis credetis ?

6:1 Post hæc abiit Jesus trans mare Galilææ, quod est Tiberiadis :

6:2 et sequebatur eum multitudo magna, quia videbant signa quæ faciebat super his qui infirmabantur.

6:3 Subiit ergo in montem Jesus et ibi sedebat cum discipulis suis.

6:4 Erat autem proximum Pascha dies festus Judæorum.

6:5 Cum sublevasset ergo oculos Jesus, et vidisset quia multitudo maxima venit ad eum, dixit ad Philippum : Unde ememus panes, ut manducent hi ?

6:6 Hoc autem dicebat tentans eum : ipse enim sciebat quid esset facturus.

6:7 Respondit ei Philippus : Ducentorum denariorum panes non sufficiunt eis, ut unusquisque modicum quid accipiat.

6:8 Dicit ei unus ex discipulis ejus, Andreas, frater Simonis Petri :

6:9 Est puer unus hic qui habet quinque panes hordeaceos et duos pisces : sed hæc quid sunt inter tantos ?

6:10 Dixit ergo Jesus : Facite homines discumbere. Erat autem fœnum multum in loco. Discubuerunt ergo viri, numero quasi quinque millia.

6:11 Accepit ergo Jesus panes : et cum gratias egisset, distribuit discumbentibus : similiter et ex piscibus quantum volebant.

6:12 Ut autem impleti sunt, dixit discipulis suis : Colligite quæ superaverunt fragmenta, ne pereant.

5:40 And you will not come to me that you may have life.

5:41 I receive glory not from men.

5:42 But I know you, that you have not the love of God in you.

5:43 I am come in the name of my Father, and you receive me not: if another shall come in his own name, him you will receive.

5:44 How can you believe, who receive glory one from another: and the glory which is from God alone, you do not seek?

5:45 Think not that I will accuse you to the Father. There is one that accuseth you, Moses, in whom you trust.

5:46 For if you did believe Moses, you would perhaps believe me also; for he wrote of me.

5:47 But if you do not believe his writings, how will you believe my words?

6:1 After these things Jesus went over the sea of Galilee, which is that of Tiberias.

6:2 And a great multitude followed him, because they saw the miracles which he did on them that were diseased.

6:3 Jesus therefore went up into a mountain, and there he sat with his disciples.

6:4 Now the pasch, the festival day of the Jews, was near at hand.

6:5 When Jesus therefore had lifted up his eyes, and seen that a very great multitude cometh to him, he said to Philip: Whence shall we buy bread, that these may eat?

6:6 And this he said to try him; for he himself knew what he would do.

6:7 Philip answered him: Two hundred pennyworth of bread is not sufficient for them, that every one may take a little.

6:8 One of his disciples, Andrew, the brother of Simon Peter, saith to him:

6:9 There is a boy here that hath five barley loaves, and two fishes; but what are these among so many?

6:10 Then Jesus said: Make the men sit down. Now there was much grass in the place. The men therefore sat down, in number about five thousand.

6:11 And Jesus took the loaves: and when he had given thanks, he distributed to them that were set down. In like manner also of the fishes, as much as they would.

6:12 And when they were filled, he said to his disciples: Gather up the fragments that remain, lest they be lost.

6:13 Collegerunt ergo, et impleverunt duodecim cophinos fragmentorum ex quinque panibus hordeaceis, quæ superfuerunt his qui manducaverant.

6:14 Illi ergo homines cum vidissent quod Jesus fecerat signum, dicebant : Quia hic est vere propheta, qui venturus est in mundum.

6:15 Jesus ergo cum cognovisset quia venturi essent ut raperent eum, et facerent eum regem, fugit iterum in montem ipse solus.

6:16 Ut autem sero factum est, descenderunt discipuli ejus ad mare.

6:17 Et cum ascendissent navim, venerunt trans mare in Capharnaum : et tenebræ jam factæ erant et non venerat ad eos Jesus.

6:18 Mare autem, vento magno flante, exsurgebat.

6:19 Cum remigassent ergo quasi stadia viginti quinque aut triginta, vident Jesum ambulantem supra mare, et proximum navi fieri, et timuerunt.

6:20 Ille autem dicit eis : Ego sum, nolite timere.

6:21 Voluerunt ergo accipere eum in navim et statim navis fuit ad terram, in quam ibant.

6:22 Altera die, turba, quæ stabat trans mare, vidit quia navicula alia non erat ibi nisi una, et quia non introisset cum discipulis suis Jesus in navim, sed soli discipuli ejus abiissent :

6:23 aliæ vero supervenerunt naves a Tiberiade juxta locum ubi manducaverant panem, gratias agente Domino.

6:24 Cum ergo vidisset turba quia Jesus non esset ibi, neque discipuli ejus, ascenderunt in naviculas, et venerunt Capharnaum quærentes Jesum.

6:25 Et cum invenissent eum trans mare, dixerunt ei : Rabbi, quando huc venisti ?

6:26 Respondit eis Jesus, et dixit : Amen, amen dico vobis : quæritis me non quia vidistis signa, sed quia manducastis ex panibus et saturati estis.

6:27 Operamini non cibum, qui perit, sed qui permanet in vitam æternam, quem Filius hominis dabit vobis. Hunc enim Pater signavit Deus.

6:28 Dixerunt ergo ad eum : Quid faciemus ut operemur opera Dei ?

6:13 They gathered up therefore, and filled twelve baskets with the fragments of the five barley loaves, which remained over and above to them that had eaten.

6:14 Now those men, when they had seen what a miracle Jesus had done, said: This is of a truth the prophet, that is to come into the world.

6:15 Jesus therefore, when he knew that they would come to take him by force, and make him king, fled again into the mountain himself alone.

6:16 And when evening was come, his disciples went down to the sea.

6:17 And when they had gone up into a ship, they went over the sea to Capharnaum; and it was now dark, and Jesus was not come unto them.

6:18 And the sea arose, by reason of a great wind that blew.

6:19 When they had rowed therefore about five and twenty or thirty furlongs, they see Jesus walking upon the sea, and drawing nigh to the ship, and they were afraid.

6:20 But he saith to them: It is I; be not afraid.

6:21 They were willing therefore to take him into the ship; and presently the ship was at the land to which they were going.

6:22 The next day, the multitude that stood on the other side of the sea, saw that there was no other ship there but one, and that Jesus had not entered into the ship with his disciples, but that his disciples were gone away alone.

6:23 But other ships came in from Tiberias; nigh unto the place where they had eaten the bread, the Lord giving thanks.

6:24 When therefore the multitude saw that Jesus was not there, nor his disciples, they took shipping, and came to Capharnaum, seeking for Jesus.

6:25 And when they had found him on the other side of the sea, they said to him: Rabbi, when camest thou hither?

6:26 Jesus answered them, and said: Amen, amen I say to you, you seek me, not because you have seen miracles, but because you did eat of the loaves, and were filled.

6:27 Labour not for the meat which perisheth, but for that which endureth unto life everlasting, which the Son of man will give you. For him hath God, the Father, sealed.

6:28 They said therefore unto him: What shall we do, that we may work the works of God?

6:29 Respondit Jesus, et dixit eis : Hoc est opus Dei, ut credatis in eum quem misit ille.

6:30 Dixerunt ergo ei : Quod ergo tu facis signum ut videamus et credamus tibi ? quid operaris ?

6:31 Patres nostri manducaverunt manna in deserto, sicut scriptum est : Panem de cælo dedit eis manducare.

6:32 Dixit ergo eis Jesus : Amen, amen dico vobis : non Moyses dedit vobis panem de cælo, sed Pater meus dat vobis panem de cælo verum.

6:33 Panis enim Dei est, qui de cælo descendit, et dat vitam mundo.

6:34 Dixerunt ergo ad eum : Domine, semper da nobis panem hunc.

6:35 Dixit autem eis Jesus : Ego sum panis vitæ : qui venit ad me, non esuriet, et qui credit in me, non sitiet umquam.

6:36 Sed dixi vobis quia et vidistis me, et non creditis.

6:37 Omne quod dat mihi Pater, ad me veniet : et eum qui venit ad me, non ejiciam foras :

6:38 quia descendi de cælo, non ut faciam voluntatem meam, sed voluntatem ejus qui misit me.

6:39 Hæc est autem voluntas ejus qui misit me, Patris : ut omne quod dedit mihi, non perdam ex eo, sed resuscitem illud in novissimo die.

6:40 Hæc est autem voluntas Patris mei, qui misit me : ut omnis qui videt Filium et credit in eum, habeat vitam æternam, et ego resuscitabo eum in novissimo die.

6:41 Murmurabant ergo Judæi de illo, quia dixisset : Ego sum panis vivus, qui de cælo descendi,

6:42 et dicebant : Nonne hic est Jesus filius Joseph, cujus nos novimus patrem et matrem ? quomodo ergo dicit hic : Quia de cælo descendi ?

6:43 Respondit ergo Jesus, et dixit eis : Nolite murmurare in invicem :

6:44 nemo potest venire ad me, nisi Pater, qui misit me, traxerit eum ; et ego resuscitabo eum in novissimo die.

6:45 Est scriptum in prophetis : Et erunt omnes docibiles Dei. Omnis qui audivit a Patre, et didicit, venit ad me.

6:29 Jesus answered, and said to them: This is the work of God, that you believe in him whom he hath sent.

6:30 They said therefore to him: What sign therefore dost thou shew, that we may see, and may believe thee? What dost thou work?

6:31 Our fathers did eat manna in the desert, as it is written: He gave them bread from heaven to eat.

6:32 Then Jesus said to them: Amen, amen I say to you; Moses gave you not bread from heaven, but my Father giveth you the true bread from heaven.

6:33 For the bread of God is that which cometh down from heaven, and giveth life to the world.

6:34 They said therefore unto him: Lord, give us always this bread.

6:35 And Jesus said to them: I am the bread of life: he that cometh to me shall not hunger: and he that believeth in me shall never thirst.

6:36 But I said unto you, that you also have seen me, and you believe not.

6:37 All that the Father giveth to me shall come to me; and him that cometh to me, I will not cast out.

6:38 Because I came down from heaven, not to do my own will, but the will of him that sent me.

6:39 Now this is the will of the Father who sent me: that of all that he hath given me, I should lose nothing; but should raise it up again in the last day.

6:40 And this is the will of my Father that sent me: that every one who seeth the Son, and believeth in him, may have life everlasting, and I will raise him up in the last day.

6:41 The Jews therefore murmured at him, because he had said: I am the living bread which came down from heaven.

6:42 And they said: Is not this Jesus, the son of Joseph, whose father and mother we know? How then saith he, I came down from heaven?

6:43 Jesus therefore answered, and said to them: Murmur not among yourselves.

6:44 No man can come to me, except the Father, who hath sent me, draw him; and I will raise him up in the last day.

6:45 It is written in the prophets: And they shall all be taught of God. Every one that hath heard of the Father, and hath learned, cometh to me.

6:46 Non quia Patrem vidit quisquam, nisi is, qui est a Deo, hic vidit Patrem.

6:47 Amen, amen dico vobis : qui credit in me, habet vitam æternam.

6:48 Ego sum panis vitæ.

6:49 Patres vestri manducaverunt manna in deserto, et mortui sunt.

6:50 Hic est panis de cælo descendens : ut si quis ex ipso manducaverit, non moriatur.

6:51 Ego sum panis vivus, qui de cælo descendi.

6:52 Si quis manducaverit ex hoc pane, vivet in æternum : et panis quem ego dabo, caro mea est pro mundi vita.

6:53 Litigabant ergo Judæi ad invicem, dicentes : Quomodo potest hic nobis carnem suam dare ad manducandum ?

6:54 Dixit ergo eis Jesus : Amen, amen dico vobis : nisi manducaveritis carnem Filii hominis, et biberitis ejus sanguinem, non habebitis vitam in vobis.

6:55 Qui manducat meam carnem, et bibit meum sanguinem, habet vitam æternam : et ego resuscitabo eum in novissimo die.

6:56 Caro enim mea vere est cibus : et sanguis meus, vere est potus ;

6:57 qui manducat meam carnem et bibit meum sanguinem, in me manet, et ego in illo.

6:58 Sicut misit me vivens Pater, et ego vivo propter Patrem : et qui manducat me, et ipse vivet propter me.

6:59 Hic est panis qui de cælo descendit. Non sicut manducaverunt patres vestri manna, et mortui sunt. Qui manducat hunc panem, vivet in æternum.

6:60 Hæc dixit in synagoga docens, in Capharnaum.

6:61 Multi ergo audientes ex discipulis ejus, dixerunt : Durus est hic sermo, et quis potest eum audire ?

6:62 Sciens autem Jesus apud semetipsum quia murmurarent de hoc discipuli ejus, dixit eis : Hoc vos scandalizat ?

6:63 si ergo videritis Filium hominis ascendentem ubi erat prius ?

6:64 Spiritus est qui vivificat : caro non prodest quidquam : verba quæ ego locutus sum vobis, spiritus et vita sunt.

6:65 Sed sunt quidam ex vobis qui non credunt. Sciebat enim ab initio Jesus qui essent non credentes, et quis traditurus esset eum.

6:46 Not that any man hath seen the Father; but he who is of God, he hath seen the Father.

6:47 Amen, amen I say unto you: He that believeth in me, hath everlasting life.

6:48 I am the bread of life.

6:49 Your fathers did eat manna in the desert, and are dead.

6:50 This is the bread which cometh down from heaven; that if any man eat of it, he may not die.

6:51 I am the living bread which came down from heaven.

6:52 If any man eat of this bread, he shall live for ever; and the bread that I will give, is my flesh, for the life of the world.

6:53 The Jews therefore strove among themselves, saying: How can this man give us his flesh to eat?

6:54 Then Jesus said to them: Amen, amen I say unto you: Except you eat the flesh of the Son of man, and drink his blood, you shall not have life in you.

6:55 He that eateth my flesh, and drinketh my blood, hath everlasting life: and I will raise him up in the last day.

6:56 For my flesh is meat indeed: and my blood is drink indeed.

6:57 He that eateth my flesh, and drinketh my blood, abideth in me, and I in him.

6:58 As the living Father hath sent me, and I live by the Father; so he that eateth me, the same also shall live by me.

6:59 This is the bread that came down from heaven. Not as your fathers did eat manna, and are dead. He that eateth this bread, shall live for ever.

6:60 These things he said, teaching in the synagogue, in Capharnaum.

6:61 Many therefore of his disciples, hearing it, said: This saying is hard, and who can hear it?

6:62 But Jesus, knowing in himself, that his disciples murmured at this, said to them: Doth this scandalize you?

6:63 If then you shall see the Son of man ascend up where he was before?

6:64 It is the spirit that quickeneth: the flesh profiteth nothing. The words that I have spoken to you, are spirit and life.

6:65 But there are some of you that believe not. For Jesus knew from the beginning, who they were that did not believe, and who he was, that

6:66 Et dicebat : Propterea dixi vobis, quia nemo potest venire ad me, nisi fuerit ei datum a Patre meo.

6:67 Ex hoc multi discipulorum ejus abierunt retro : et jam non cum illo ambulabant.

6:68 Dixit ergo Jesus ad duodecim : Numquid et vos vultis abire ?

6:69 Respondit ergo ei Simon Petrus : Domine, ad quem ibimus ? verba vitæ æternæ habes :

6:70 et nos credidimus, et cognovimus quia tu es Christus Filius Dei.

6:71 Respondit eis Jesus : Nonne ego vos duodecim elegi : et ex vobis unus diabolus est ?

6:72 Dicebat autem Judam Simonis Iscariotem : hic enim erat traditurus eum, cum esset unus ex duodecim.

7:1 Post hæc autem ambulabat Jesus in Galilæam : non enim volebat in Judæam ambulare, quia quærebant eum Judæi interficere.

7:2 Erat autem in proximo dies festus Judæorum, Scenopegia.

7:3 Dixerunt autem ad eum fratres ejus : Transi hinc, et vade in Judæam, ut et discipuli tui videant opera tua, quæ facis.

7:4 Nemo quippe in occulto quid facit, et quærit ipse in palam esse : si hæc facis, manifesta teipsum mundo.

7:5 Neque enim fratres ejus credebant in eum.

7:6 Dicit ergo eis Jesus : Tempus meum nondum advenit : tempus autem vestrum semper est paratum.

7:7 Non potest mundus odisse vos : me autem odit, quia ego testimonium perhibeo de illo quod opera ejus mala sunt.

7:8 Vos ascendite ad diem festum hunc, ego autem non ascendo ad diem festum istum : quia meum tempus nondum impletum est.

7:9 Hæc cum dixisset, ipse mansit in Galilæa.

7:10 Ut autem ascenderunt fratres ejus, tunc et ipse ascendit ad diem festum non manifeste, sed quasi in occulto.

7:11 Judæi ergo quærebant eum in die festo, et dicebant : Ubi est ille ?

7:12 Et murmur multum erat in turba de eo. Quidam enim dicebant : Quia bonus est. Alii autem dicebant : Non, sed seducit turbas.

7:13 Nemo tamen palam loquebatur de illo

would betray him.

6:66 And he said: Therefore did I say to you, that no man can come to me, unless it be given him by my Father.

6:67 After this many of his disciples went back; and walked no more with him.

6:68 Then Jesus said to the twelve: Will you also go away?

6:69 And Simon Peter answered him: Lord, to whom shall we go? thou hast the words of eternal life.

6:70 And we have believed and have known, that thou art the Christ, the Son of God.

6:71 Jesus answered them: Have not I chosen you twelve; and one of you is a devil?

6:72 Now he meant Judas Iscariot, the son of Simon: for this same was about to betray him, whereas he was one of the twelve.

7:1 After these things Jesus walked in Galilee; for he would not walk in Judea, because the Jews sought to kill him.

7:2 Now the Jews' feast of tabernacles was at hand.

7:3 And his brethren said to him: Pass from hence, and go into Judea; that thy disciples also may see thy works which thou dost.

7:4 For there is no man that doth any thing in secret, and he himself seeketh to be known openly. If thou do these things, manifest thyself to the world.

7:5 For neither did his brethren believe in him.

7:6 Then Jesus said to them: My time is not yet come; but your time is always ready.

7:7 The world cannot hate you; but me it hateth: because I give testimony of it, that the works thereof are evil.

7:8 Go you up to this festival day, but I go not up to this festival day: because my time is not accomplished.

7:9 When he had said these things, he himself stayed in Galilee.

7:10 But after his brethren were gone up, then he also went up to the feast, not openly, but, as it were, in secret.

7:11 The Jews therefore sought him on the festival day, and said: Where is he?

7:12 And there was much murmuring among the multitude concerning him. For some said: He is a good man. And others said: No, but he seduceth the people.

7:13 Yet no man spoke openly of him, for fear of

propter metum Judæorum.

7:14 Jam autem die festo mediante, ascendit Jesus in templum, et docebat.

7:15 Et mirabantur Judæi, dicentes : Quomodo hic litteras scit, cum non didicerit ?

7:16 Respondit eis Jesus, et dixit : Mea doctrina non est mea, sed ejus qui misit me.

7:17 Si quis voluerit voluntatem ejus facere, cognoscet de doctrina, utrum ex Deo sit, an ego a meipso loquar.

7:18 Qui a semetipso loquitur, gloriam propriam quærit ; qui autem quærit gloriam ejus qui misit eum, hic verax est, et injustitia in illo non est.

7:19 Nonne Moyses dedit vobis legem : et nemo ex vobis facit legem ?

7:20 Quid me quæritis interficere ? Respondit turba, et dixit : Dæmonium habes : quis te quærit interficere ?

7:21 Respondit Jesus et dixit eis : Unum opus feci, et omnes miramini :

7:22 propterea Moyses dedit vobis circumcisionem (non quia ex Moyse est, sed ex patribus), et in sabbato circumciditis hominem.

7:23 Si circumcisionem accipit homo in sabbato, ut non solvatur lex Moysi : mihi indignamini quia totum hominem sanum feci in sabbato ?

7:24 Nolite judicare secundum faciem, sed justum judicium judicate.

7:25 Dicebant ergo quidam ex Jerosolymis : Nonne hic est, quem quærunt interficere ?

7:26 et ecce palam loquitur, et nihil ei dicunt. Numquid vere cognoverunt principes quia hic est Christus ?

7:27 Sed hunc scimus unde sit : Christus autem cum venerit, nemo scit unde sit.

7:28 Clamabat ergo Jesus in templo docens, et dicens : Et me scitis, et unde sim scitis : et a meipso non veni, sed est verus qui misit me, quem vos nescitis.

7:29 Ego scio eum : quia ab ipso sum, et ipse me misit.

7:30 Quærebant ergo eum apprehendere : et nemo misit in illum manus, quia nondum venerat hora ejus.

7:31 De turba autem multi crediderunt in eum, et dicebant : Christus cum venerit, numquid plura signa faciet quam quæ hic facit ?

the Jews.

7:14 Now about the midst of the feast, Jesus went up into the temple, and taught.

7:15 And the Jews wondered, saying: How doth this man know letters, having never learned?

7:16 Jesus answered them, and said: My doctrine is not mine, but his that sent me.

7:17 If any man do the will of him; he shall know of the doctrine, whether it be of God, or whether I speak of myself.

7:18 He that speaketh of himself, seeketh his own glory: but he that seeketh the glory of him that sent him, he is true, and there is no injustice in him.

7:19 Did Moses not give you the law, and yet none of you keepeth the law?

7:20 Why seek you to kill me? The multitude answered, and said: Thou hast a devil; who seeketh to kill thee?

7:21 Jesus answered, and said to them: One work I have done; and you all wonder:

7:22 Therefore, Moses gave you circumcision, (not because it is of Moses, but of the fathers;) and on the sabbath day you circumcise a man.

7:23 If a man receive circumcision on the sabbath day, that the law of Moses may not be broken; are you angry at me because I have healed the whole man on the sabbath day?

7:24 Judge not according to the appearance, but judge just judgment.

7:25 Some therefore of Jerusalem said: Is not this he whom they seek to kill?

7:26 And behold, he speaketh openly, and they say nothing to him. Have the rulers known for a truth, that this is the Christ?

7:27 But we know this man, whence he is: but when the Christ cometh, no man knoweth whence he is.

7:28 Jesus therefore cried out in the temple, teaching, and saying: You both know me, and you know whence I am: and I am not come of myself; but he that sent me, is true, whom you know not.

7:29 I know him, because I am from him, and he hath sent me.

7:30 They sought therefore to apprehend him: and no man laid hands on him, because his hour was not yet come.

7:31 But of the people many believed in him, and said: When the Christ cometh, shall he do more miracles, than these which this man doth?

7:32 Audierunt pharisæi turbam murmurantem de illo hæc : et miserunt principes et pharisæi ministros ut apprehenderent eum.

7:33 Dixit ergo eis Jesus : Adhuc modicum tempus vobiscum sum : et vado ad eum qui me misit.

7:34 Quæretis me, et non invenietis : et ubi ego sum, vos non potestis venire.

7:35 Dixerunt ergo Judæi ad semetipsos : Quo hic iturus est, quia non inveniemus eum ? numquid in dispersionem gentium iturus est, et docturus gentes ?

7:36 quis est hic sermo, quem dixit : Quæretis me, et non invenietis : et ubi sum ego, vos non potestis venire ?

7:37 In novissimo autem die magno festivitatis stabat Jesus, et clamabat dicens : Si quis sitit, veniat ad me et bibat.

7:38 Qui credit in me, sicut dicit Scriptura, flumina de ventre ejus fluent aquæ vivæ.

7:39 Hoc autem dixit de Spiritu, quem accepturi erant credentes in eum : nondum enim erat Spiritus datus, quia Jesus nondum erat glorificatus.

7:40 Ex illa ergo turba cum audissent hos sermones ejus, dicebant : Hic est vere propheta.

7:41 Alii dicebant : Hic est Christus. Quidam autem dicebant : Numquid a Galilæa venit Christus ?

7:42 nonne Scriptura dicit : Quia ex semine David, et de Bethlehem castello, ubi erat David, venit Christus ?

7:43 Dissensio itaque facta est in turba propter eum.

7:44 Quidam autem ex ipsis volebant apprehendere eum : sed nemo misit super eum manus.

7:45 Venerunt ergo ministri ad pontifices et pharisæos. Et dixerunt eis illi : Quare non adduxistis illum ?

7:46 Responderunt ministri : Numquam sic locutus est homo, sicut hic homo.

7:47 Responderunt ergo eis pharisæi : Numquid et vos seducti estis ?

7:48 numquid ex principibus aliquis credidit in eum, aut ex pharisæis ?

7:49 sed turba hæc, quæ non novit legem, maledicti sunt.

7:50 Dixit Nicodemus ad eos, ille qui venit ad eum nocte, qui unus erat ex ipsis :

7:32 The Pharisees heard the people murmuring these things concerning him: and the rulers and Pharisees sent ministers to apprehend him.

7:33 Jesus therefore said to them: Yet a little while I am with you: and then I go to him that sent me.

7:34 You shall seek me, and shall not find me: and where I am, thither you cannot come.

7:35 The Jews therefore said among themselves: Whither will he go, that we shall not find him? will he go unto the dispersed among the Gentiles, and teach the Gentiles?

7:36 What is this saying that he hath said: You shall seek me, and shall not find me; and where I am, you cannot come?

7:37 And on the last, and great day of the festivity, Jesus stood and cried, saying: If any man thirst, let him come to me, and drink.

7:38 He that believeth in me, as the scripture saith, Out of his belly shall flow rivers of living water.

7:39 Now this he said of the Spirit which they should receive, who believed in him: for as yet the Spirit was not given, because Jesus was not yet glorified.

7:40 Of that multitude therefore, when they had heard these words of his, some said: This is the prophet indeed.

7:41 Others said: This is the Christ. But some said: Doth the Christ come out of Galilee?

7:42 Doth not the scripture say: That Christ cometh of the seed of David, and from Bethlehem the town where David was?

7:43 So there arose a dissension among the people because of him.

7:44 And some of them would have apprehended him: but no man laid hands on him.

7:45 The ministers therefore came to the chief priests and the Pharisees. And they said to them: Why have you not brought him?

7:46 The ministers answered: Never did man speak like this man.

7:47 The Pharisees therefore answered them: Are you also seduced?

7:48 Hath any one of the rulers believed in him, or of the Pharisees?

7:49 But this multitude, that knoweth not the law, are accursed.

7:50 Nicodemus said to them, (he that came to him by night, who was one of them:)

7:51 Numquid lex nostra judicat hominem, nisi prius audierit ab ipso, et cognoverit quid faciat ?

7:52 Responderunt, et dixerunt ei : Numquid et tu Galilæus es ? scrutare Scripturas, et vide quia a Galilæa propheta non surgit.

7:53 Et reversi sunt unusquisque in domum suam.

8:1 Jesus autem perrexit in montem Oliveti :

8:2 et diluculo iterum venit in templum, et omnis populus venit ad eum, et sedens docebat eos.

8:3 Adducunt autem scribæ et pharisæi mulierem in adulterio deprehensam : et statuerunt eam in medio,

8:4 et dixerunt ei : Magister, hæc mulier modo deprehensa est in adulterio.

8:5 In lege autem Moyses mandavit nobis hujusmodi lapidare. Tu ergo quid dicis ?

8:6 Hoc autem dicebant tentantes eum, ut possent accusare eum. Jesus autem inclinans se deorsum, digito scribebat in terra.

8:7 Cum ergo perseverarent interrogantes eum, erexit se, et dixit eis : Qui sine peccato est vestrum, primus in illam lapidem mittat.

8:8 Et iterum se inclinans, scribebat in terra.

8:9 Audientes autem unus post unum exibant, incipientes a senioribus : et remansit solus Jesus, et mulier in medio stans.

8:10 Erigens autem se Jesus, dixit ei : Mulier, ubi sunt qui te accusabant ? nemo te condemnavit ?

8:11 Quæ dixit : Nemo, Domine. Dixit autem Jesus : Nec ego te condemnabo : vade, et jam amplius noli peccare.

8:12 Iterum ergo locutus est eis Jesus, dicens : Ego sum lux mundi : qui sequitur me, non ambulat in tenebris, sed habebit lumen vitæ.

8:13 Dixerunt ergo ei pharisæi : Tu de teipso testimonium perhibes ; testimonium tuum non est verum.

8:14 Respondit Jesus, et dixit eis : Et si ego testimonium perhibeo de meipso, verum est testimonium meum : quia scio unde veni et quo vado ; vos autem nescitis unde venio aut quo vado.

8:15 Vos secundum carnem judicatis : ego non judico quemquam ;

8:16 et si judico ego, judicium meum verum est,

7:51 Doth our law judge any man, unless it first hear him, and know what he doth?

7:52 They answered, and said to him: Art thou also a Galilean? Search the scriptures, and see, that out of Galilee a prophet riseth not.

7:53 And every man returned to his own house.

8:1 And Jesus went unto mount Olivet.

8:2 And early in the morning he came again into the temple, and all the people came to him, and sitting down he taught them.

8:3 And the scribes and the Pharisees bring unto him a woman taken in adultery: and they set her in the midst,

8:4 And said to him: Master, this woman was even now taken in adultery.

8:5 Now Moses in the law commanded us to stone such a one. But what sayest thou?

8:6 And this they said tempting him, that they might accuse him. But Jesus bowing himself down, wrote with his finger on the ground.

8:7 When therefore they continued asking him, he lifted up himself, and said to them: He that is without sin among you, let him first cast a stone at her.

8:8 And again stooping down, he wrote on the ground.

8:9 But they hearing this, went out one by one, beginning at the eldest. And Jesus alone remained, and the woman standing in the midst.

8:10 Then Jesus lifting up himself, said to her: Woman, where are they that accused thee? Hath no man condemned thee?

8:11 Who said: No man, Lord. And Jesus said: Neither will I condemn thee. Go, and now sin no more.

8:12 Again therefore, Jesus spoke to them, saying: I am the light of the world: he that followeth me, walketh not in darkness, but shall have the light of life.

8:13 The Pharisees therefore said to him: Thou givest testimony of thyself: thy testimony is not true.

8:14 Jesus answered, and said to them: Although I give testimony of myself, my testimony is true: for I know whence I came, and whither I go: but you know not whence I come, or whither I go.

8:15 You judge according to the flesh: I judge not any man.

8:16 And if I do judge, my judgment is true: be-

quia solus non sum : sed ego et qui misit me, Pater.

8:17 Et in lege vestra scriptum est, quia duorum hominum testimonium verum est.

8:18 Ego sum qui testimonium perhibeo de meipso, et testimonium perhibet de me qui misit me, Pater.

8:19 Dicebant ergo ei : Ubi est Pater tuus ? Respondit Jesus : Neque me scitis, neque Patrem meum : si me sciretis, forsitan et Patrem meum sciretis.

8:20 Hæc verba locutus est Jesus in gazophylacio, docens in templo : et nemo apprehendit eum, quia necdum venerat hora ejus.

8:21 Dixit ergo iterum eis Jesus : Ego vado, et quæretis me, et in peccato vestro moriemini. Quo ego vado, vos non potestis venire.

8:22 Dicebant ergo Judæi : Numquid interficiet semetipsum, quia dixit : Quo ego vado, vos non potestis venire ?

8:23 Et dicebat eis : Vos de deorsum estis, ego de supernis sum. Vos de mundo hoc estis, ego non sum de hoc mundo.

8:24 Dixi ergo vobis quia moriemini in peccatis vestris : si enim non credideritis quia ego sum, moriemini in peccato vestro.

8:25 Dicebant ergo ei : Tu quis es ? Dixit eis Jesus : Principium, qui et loquor vobis.

8:26 Multa habeo de vobis loqui, et judicare ; sed qui me misit, verax est ; et ego quæ audivi ab eo, hæc loquor in mundo.

8:27 Et non cognoverunt quia Patrem ejus dicebat Deum.

8:28 Dixit ergo eis Jesus : Cum exaltaveritis Filium hominis, tunc cognoscetis quia ego sum, et a meipso facio nihil, sed sicut docuit me Pater, hæc loquor :

8:29 et qui me misit, mecum est, et non reliquit me solum : quia ego quæ placita sunt ei, facio semper.

8:30 Hæc illo loquente, multi crediderunt in eum.

8:31 Dicebat ergo Jesus ad eos, qui crediderunt ei, Judæos : Si vos manseritis in sermone meo, vere discipuli mei eritis,

8:32 et cognoscetis veritatem, et veritas liberabit vos.

8:33 Responderunt ei : Semen Abrahæ sumus, et nemini servivimus umquam : quomodo tu dic-

cause I am not alone, but I and the Father that sent me.

8:17 And in your law it is written, that the testimony of two men is true.

8:18 I am one that give testimony of myself: and the Father that sent me giveth testimony of me.

8:19 They said therefore to him: Where is thy Father? Jesus answered: Neither me do you know, nor my Father: if you did know me, perhaps you would know my Father also.

8:20 These words Jesus spoke in the treasury, teaching in the temple: and no man laid hands on him, because his hour was not yet come.

8:21 Again therefore Jesus said to them: I go, and you shall seek me, and you shall die in your sin. Whither I go, you cannot come.

8:22 The Jews therefore said: Will he kill himself, because he said: Whither I go, you cannot come?

8:23 And he said to them: You are from beneath, I am from above. You are of this world, I am not of this world.

8:24 Therefore I said to you, that you shall die in your sins. For if you believe not that I am he, you shall die in your sin.

8:25 They said therefore to him: Who art thou? Jesus said to them: The beginning, who also speak unto you.

8:26 Many things I have to speak and to judge of you. But he that sent me, is true: and the things I have heard of him, these same I speak in the world.

8:27 And they understood not, that he called God his Father.

8:28 Jesus therefore said to them: When you shall have lifted up the Son of man, then shall you know, that I am he, and that I do nothing of myself, but as the Father hath taught me, these things I speak:

8:29 And he that sent me, is with me, and he hath not left me alone: for I do always the things that please him.

8:30 When he spoke these things, many believed in him.

8:31 Then Jesus said to those Jews, who believed him: If you continue in my word, you shall be my disciples indeed.

8:32 And you shall know the truth, and the truth shall make you free.

8:33 They answered him: We are the seed of Abraham, and we have never been slaves to any

is : Liberi eritis ?

8:34 Respondit eis Jesus : Amen, amen dico vobis : quia omnis qui facit peccatum, servus est peccati.

8:35 Servus autem non manet in domo in æternum : filius autem manet in æternum.

8:36 Si ergo vos filius liberaverit, vere liberi eritis.

8:37 Scio quia filii Abrahæ estis : sed quæritis me interficere, quia sermo meus non capit in vobis.

8:38 Ego quod vidi apud Patrem meum, loquor : et vos quæ vidistis apud patrem vestrum, facitis.

8:39 Responderunt, et dixerunt ei : Pater noster Abraham est. Dicit eis Jesus : Si filii Abrahæ estis, opera Abrahæ facite.

8:40 Nunc autem quæritis me interficere, hominem, qui veritatem vobis locutus sum, quam audivi a Deo : hoc Abraham non fecit.

8:41 Vos facitis opera patris vestri. Dixerunt itaque ei : Nos ex fornicatione non sumus nati : unum patrem habemus Deum.

8:42 Dixit ergo eis Jesus : Si Deus pater vester esset, diligeretis utique et me ; ego enim ex Deo processi, et veni : neque enim a meipso veni, sed ille me misit.

8:43 Quare loquelam meam non cognoscitis ? Quia non potestis audire sermonem meum.

8:44 Vos ex patre diabolo estis : et desideria patris vestri vultis facere. Ille homicida erat ab initio, et in veritate non stetit : quia non est veritas in eo : cum loquitur mendacium, ex propriis loquitur, quia mendax est, et pater ejus.

8:45 Ego autem si veritatem dico, non creditis mihi.

8:46 Quis ex vobis arguet me de peccato ? si veritatem dico vobis, quare non creditis mihi ?

8:47 Qui ex Deo est, verba Dei audit. Propterea vos non auditis, quia ex Deo non estis.

8:48 Responderunt ergo Judæi, et dixerunt ei : Nonne bene dicimus nos quia Samaritanus es tu, et dæmonium habes ?

8:49 Respondit Jesus : Ego dæmonium non habeo : sed honorifico Patrem meum, et vos inhonorastis me.

8:50 Ego autem non quæro gloriam meam : est qui quærat, et judicet.

man: how sayest thou: you shall be free?

8:34 Jesus answered them: Amen, amen I say unto you: that whosoever committeth sin, is the servant of sin.

8:35 Now the servant abideth not in the house for ever; but the son abideth for ever.

8:36 If therefore the son shall make you free, you shall be free indeed.

8:37 I know that you are the children of Abraham: but you seek to kill me, because my word hath no place in you.

8:38 I speak that which I have seen with my Father: and you do the things that you have seen with your father.

8:39 They answered, and said to him: Abraham is our father. Jesus saith to them: If you be the children of Abraham, do the works of Abraham.

8:40 But now you seek to kill me, a man who have spoken the truth to you, which I have heard of God. This Abraham did not.

8:41 You do the works of your father. They said therefore to him: We are not born of fornication: we have one Father, even God.

8:42 Jesus therefore said to them: If God were your Father, you would indeed love me. For from God I proceeded, and came; for I came not of myself, but he sent me:

8:43 Why do you not know my speech? Because you cannot hear my word.

8:44 You are of your father the devil, and the desires of your father you will do. He was a murderer from the beginning, and he stood not in the truth; because truth is not in him. When he speaketh a lie, he speaketh of his own: for he is a liar, and the father thereof.

8:45 But if I say the truth, you believe me not.

8:46 Which of you shall convince me of sin? If I say the truth to you, why do you not believe me?

8:47 He that is of God, heareth the words of God. Therefore you hear them not, because you are not of God.

8:48 The Jews therefore answered, and said to him: Do not we say well that thou art a Samaritan, and hast a devil?

8:49 Jesus answered: I have not a devil: but I honour my Father, and you have dishonoured me.

8:50 But I seek not my own glory: there is one that seeketh and judgeth.

8:51 Amen, amen dico vobis : si quis sermonem meum servaverit, mortem non videbit in æternum.

8:52 Dixerunt ergo Judæi : Nunc cognovimus quia dæmonium habes. Abraham mortuus est, et prophetæ ; et tu dicis : Si quis sermonem meum servaverit, non gustabit mortem in æternum.

8:53 Numquid tu major es patre nostro Abraham, qui mortuus est ? et prophetæ mortui sunt. Quem teipsum facis ?

8:54 Respondit Jesus : Si ego glorifico meipsum, gloria mea nihil est : est Pater meus, qui glorificat me, quem vos dicitis quia Deus vester est,

8:55 et non cognovistis eum : ego autem novi eum. Et si dixero quia non scio eum, ero similis vobis, mendax. Sed scio eum, et sermonem ejus servo.

8:56 Abraham pater vester exsultavit ut videret diem meum : vidit, et gavisus est.

8:57 Dixerunt ergo Judæi ad eum : Quinquaginta annos nondum habes, et Abraham vidisti ?

8:58 Dixit eis Jesus : Amen, amen dico vobis, antequam Abraham fieret, ego sum.

8:59 Tulerunt ergo lapides, ut jacerent in eum : Jesus autem abscondit se, et exivit de templo.

9:1 Et præteriens Jesus vidit hominem cæcum a nativitate :

9:2 et interrogaverunt eum discipuli ejus : Rabbi, quis peccavit, hic, aut parentes ejus, ut cæcus nasceretur ?

9:3 Respondit Jesus : Neque hic peccavit, neque parentes ejus : sed ut manifestentur opera Dei in illo.

9:4 Me oportet operari opera ejus qui misit me, donec dies est : venit nox, quando nemo potest operari :

9:5 quamdiu sum in mundo, lux sum mundi.

9:6 Hæc cum dixisset, exspuit in terram, et fecit lutum ex sputo, et linivit lutum super oculos ejus,

9:7 et dixit ei : Vade, lava in natatoria Siloë (quod interpretatur Missus). Abiit ergo, et lavit, et venit videns.

9:8 Itaque vicini, et qui viderant eum prius quia mendicus erat, dicebant : Nonne hic est qui sedebat, et mendicabat ? Alii dicebant : Quia hic est.

9:9 Alii autem : Nequaquam, sed similis est ei.

8:51 Amen, amen I say to you: If any man keep my word, he shall not see death for ever.

8:52 The Jews therefore said: Now we know that thou hast a devil. Abraham is dead, and the prophets; and thou sayest: If any man keep my word, he shall not taste death for ever.

8:53 Art thou greater than our father Abraham, who is dead? and the prophets are dead. Whom dost thou make thyself?

8:54 Jesus answered: If I glorify myself, my glory is nothing. It is my Father that glorifieth me, of whom you say that he is your God.

8:55 And you have not known him, but I know him. And if I shall say that I know him not, I shall be like to you, a liar. But I do know him, and do keep his word.

8:56 Abraham your father rejoiced that he might see my day: he saw it, and was glad.

8:57 The Jews therefore said to him: Thou art not yet fifty years old, and hast thou seen Abraham?

8:58 Jesus said to them: Amen, amen I say to you, before Abraham was made, I am.

8:59 They took up stones therefore to cast at him. But Jesus hid himself, and went out of the temple.

9:1 And Jesus passing by, saw a man, who was blind from his birth:

9:2 And his disciples asked him: Rabbi, who hath sinned, this man, or his parents, that he should be born blind?

9:3 Jesus answered: Neither hath this man sinned, nor his parents; but that the works of God should be made manifest in him.

9:4 I must work the works of him that sent me, whilst it is day: the night cometh, when no man can work.

9:5 As long as I am in the world, I am the light of the world.

9:6 When he had said these things, he spat on the ground, and made clay of the spittle, and spread the clay on his eyes,

9:7 And said to him: Go, wash in the pool of Siloe, which is interpreted, Sent. He went therefore, and washed, and he came seeing.

9:8 The neighbours therefore, and they who had seen him before that he was a beggar, said: Is not this he that sat and begged? Some said: This is he.

9:9 But others said: No, but he is like him. But

Ille vero dicebat : Quia ego sum.

9:10 Dicebant ergo ei : Quomodo aperti sunt tibi oculi ?

9:11 Respondit : Ille homo qui dicitur Jesus, lutum fecit : et unxit oculos meos, et dixit mihi : Vade ad natatoria Siloë, et lava. Et abii, et lavi, et video.

9:12 Et dixerunt ei : Ubi est ille ? Ait : Nescio.

9:13 Adducunt eum ad pharisæos, qui cæcus fuerat.

9:14 Erat autem sabbatum quando lutum fecit Jesus, et aperuit oculos ejus.

9:15 Iterum ergo interrogabant eum pharisæi quomodo vidisset. Ille autem dixit eis : Lutum mihi posuit super oculos, et lavi, et video.

9:16 Dicebant ergo ex pharisæis quidam : Non est hic homo a Deo, qui sabbatum non custodit. Alii autem dicebant : Quomodo potest homo peccator hæc signa facere ? Et schisma erat inter eos.

9:17 Dicunt ergo cæco iterum : Tu quid dicis de illo qui aperuit oculos tuos ? Ille autem dixit : Quia propheta est.

9:18 Non crediderunt ergo Judæi de illo, quia cæcus fuisset et vidisset, donec vocaverunt parentes ejus, qui viderat :

9:19 et interrogaverunt eos, dicentes : Hic est filius vester, quem vos dicitis quia cæcus natus est ? quomodo ergo nunc videt ?

9:20 Responderunt eis parentes ejus, et dixerunt : Scimus quia hic est filius noster, et quia cæcus natus est :

9:21 quomodo autem nunc videat, nescimus : aut quis ejus aperuit oculos, nos nescimus ; ipsum interrogate : ætatem habet, ipse de se loquatur.

9:22 Hæc dixerunt parentes ejus, quoniam timebant Judæos : jam enim conspiraverunt Judæi, ut si quis eum confiteretur esse Christum, extra synagogam fieret.

9:23 Propterea parentes ejus dixerunt : Quia ætatem habet, ipsum interrogate.

9:24 Vocaverunt ergo rursum hominem qui fuerat cæcus, et dixerunt ei : Da gloriam Deo : nos scimus quia hic homo peccator est.

9:25 Dixit ergo eis ille : Si peccator est, nescio ; unum scio, quia cæcus cum essem, modo video.

9:26 Dixerunt ergo illi : Quid fecit tibi ? quo-

he said: I am he.

9:10 They said therefore to him: How were thy eyes opened?

9:11 He answered: That man that is called Jesus made clay, and anointed my eyes, and said to me: Go to the pool of Siloe, and wash. And I went, I washed, and I see.

9:12 And they said to him: Where is he? He saith: I know not.

9:13 They bring him that had been blind to the Pharisees.

9:14 Now it was the sabbath, when Jesus made the clay, and opened his eyes.

9:15 Again therefore the Pharisees asked him, how he had received his sight. But he said to them: He put clay upon my eyes, and I washed, and I see.

9:16 Some therefore of the Pharisees said: This man is not of God, who keepeth not the sabbath. But others said: How can a man that is a sinner do such miracles? And there was a division among them.

9:17 They say therefore to the blind man again: What sayest thou of him that hath opened they eyes? And he said: He is a prophet.

9:18 The Jews then did not believe concerning him, that he had been blind, and had received his sight, until they called the parents of him that had received his sight,

9:19 And asked them, saying: Is this your son, who you say was born blind? How then doth he now see?

9:20 His parents answered them, and said: We know that this is our son, and that he was born blind:

9:21 But how he now seeth, we know not; or who hath opened his eyes, we know not: ask himself: he is of age, let him speak for himself.

9:22 These things his parents said, because they feared the Jews: for the Jews had already agreed among themselves, that if any man should confess him to be Christ, he should be put out of the synagogue.

9:23 Therefore did his parents say: He is of age, ask himself.

9:24 They therefore called the man again that had been blind, and said to him: Give glory to God. We know that this man is a sinner.

9:25 He said therefore to them: If he be a sinner, I know not: one thing I know, that whereas I was blind, now I see.

9:26 They said then to him: What did he to thee?

modo aperuit tibi oculos ?

9:27 Respondit eis : Dixi vobis jam, et audistis : quod iterum vultis audire ? numquid et vos vultis discipuli ejus fieri ?

9:28 Maledixerunt ergo ei, et dixerunt : Tu discipulus illius sis : nos autem Moysi discipuli sumus.

9:29 Nos scimus quia Moysi locutus est Deus ; hunc autem nescimus unde sit.

9:30 Respondit ille homo, et dixit eis : In hoc enim mirabile est quia vos nescitis unde sit, et aperuit meos oculos :

9:31 scimus autem quia peccatores Deus non audit : sed si quis Dei cultor est, et voluntatem ejus facit, hunc exaudit.

9:32 A sæculo non est auditum quia quis aperuit oculos cæci nati.

9:33 Nisi esset hic a Deo, non poterat facere quidquam.

9:34 Responderunt, et dixerunt ei : In peccatis natus es totus, et tu doces nos ? Et ejecerunt eum foras.

9:35 Audivit Jesus quia ejecerunt eum foras : et cum invenisset eum, dixit ei : Tu credis in Filium Dei ?

9:36 Respondit ille, et dixit : Quis est, Domine, ut credam in eum ?

9:37 Et dixit ei Jesus : Et vidisti eum, et qui loquitur tecum, ipse est.

9:38 At ille ait : Credo, Domine. Et procidens adoravit eum.

9:39 Et dixit Jesus : In judicium ego in hunc mundum veni : ut qui non vident videant, et qui vident cæci fiant.

9:40 Et audierunt quidam ex pharisæis qui cum ipso erant, et dixerunt ei : Numquid et nos cæci sumus ?

9:41 Dixit eis Jesus : Si cæci essetis, non haberetis peccatum. Nunc vero dicitis, Quia videmus : peccatum vestrum manet.

10:1 Amen, amen dico vobis : qui non intrat per ostium in ovile ovium, sed ascendit aliunde, ille fur est et latro.

10:2 Qui autem intrat per ostium, pastor est ovium.

10:3 Huic ostiarius aperit, et oves vocem ejus audiunt, et proprias ovas vocat nominatim, et educit eas.

10:4 Et cum proprias oves emiserit, ante eas va-

How did he open thy eyes?

9:27 He answered them: I have told you already, and you have heard: why would you hear it again? will you also become his disciples?

9:28 They reviled him therefore, and said: Be thou his disciple; but we are the disciples of Moses.

9:29 We know that God spoke to Moses: but as to this man, we know not from whence he is.

9:30 The man answered, and said to them: Why, herein is a wonderful thing, that you know not from whence he is, and he hath opened my eyes.

9:31 Now we know that God doth not hear sinners: but if a man be a server of God, and doth his will, him he heareth.

9:32 From the beginning of the world it hath not been heard, that any man hath opened the eyes of one born blind.

9:33 Unless this man were of God, he could not do any thing.

9:34 They answered, and said to him: Thou wast wholly born in sins, and dost thou teach us? And they cast him out.

9:35 Jesus heard that they had cast him out: and when he had found him, he said to him: Dost thou believe in the Son of God?

9:36 He answered, and said: Who is he, Lord, that I may believe in him?

9:37 And Jesus said to him: Thou hast both seen him; and it is he that talketh with thee.

9:38 And he said: I believe, Lord. And falling down, he adored him.

9:39 And Jesus said: For judgment I am come into this world; that they who see not, may see; and they who see, may become blind.

9:40 And some of the Pharisees, who were with him, heard: and they said unto him: Are we also blind?

9:41 Jesus said to them: If you were blind, you should not have sin: but now you say: We see. Your sin remaineth.

10:1 Amen, amen I say to you: He that entereth not by the door into the sheepfold, but climbeth up another way, the same is a thief and a robber.

10:2 But he that entereth in by the door is the shepherd of the sheep.

10:3 To him the porter openeth; and the sheep hear his voice: and he calleth his own sheep by name, and leadeth them out.

10:4 And when he hath let out his own sheep, he

dit : et oves illum sequuntur, quia sciunt vocem ejus.

10:5 Alienum autem non sequuntur, sed fugiunt ab eo : quia non noverunt vocem alienorum.

10:6 Hoc proverbium dixit eis Jesus : illi autem non cognoverunt quid loqueretur eis.

10:7 Dixit ergo eis iterum Jesus : Amen, amen dico vobis, quia ego sum ostium ovium.

10:8 Omnes quotquot venerunt, fures sunt, et latrones, et non audierunt eos oves.

10:9 Ego sum ostium. Per me si quis introierit, salvabitur : et ingredietur, et egredietur, et pascua inveniet.

10:10 Fur non venit nisi ut furetur, et mactet, et perdat. Ego veni ut vitam habeant, et abundantius habeant.

10:11 Ego sum pastor bonus. Bonus pastor animam suam dat pro ovibus suis.

10:12 Mercenarius autem, et qui non est pastor, cujus non sunt oves propriæ, videt lupum venientem, et dimittit oves, et fugit : et lupus rapit, et dispergit oves ;

10:13 mercenarius autem fugit, quia mercenarius est, et non pertinet ad eum de ovibus.

10:14 Ego sum pastor bonus : et cognosco meas, et cognoscunt me meæ.

10:15 Sicut novit me Pater, et ego agnosco Patrem : et animam meam pono pro ovibus meis.

10:16 Et alias oves habeo, quæ non sunt ex hoc ovili : et illas oportet me adducere, et vocem meam audient, et fiet unum ovile et unus pastor.

10:17 Propterea me diligit Pater : quia ego pono animam meam, ut iterum sumam eam.

10:18 Nemo tollit eam a me : sed ego pono eam a meipso, et potestatem habeo ponendi eam, et potestatem habeo iterum sumendi eam. Hoc mandatum accepi a Patre meo.

10:19 Dissensio iterum facta est inter Judæos propter sermones hos.

10:20 Dicebant autem multi ex ipsis : Dæmonium habet, et insanit : quid eum auditis ?

10:21 Alii dicebant : Hæc verba non sunt dæmonium habentis : numquid dæmonium potest cæcorum oculos aperire ?

10:22 Facta sunt autem Encænia in Jerosolymis,

goeth before them: and the sheep follow him, because they know his voice.

10:5 But a stranger they follow not, but fly from him, because they know not the voice of strangers.

10:6 This proverb Jesus spoke to them. But they understood not what he spoke to them.

10:7 Jesus therefore said to them again: Amen, amen I say to you, I am the door of the sheep.

10:8 All others, as many as have come, are thieves and robbers: and the sheep heard them not.

10:9 I am the door. By me, if any man enter in, he shall be saved: and he shall go in, and go out, and shall find pastures.

10:10 The thief cometh not, but for to steal, and to kill, and to destroy. I am come that they may have life, and may have it more abundantly.

10:11 I am the good shepherd. The good shepherd giveth his life for his sheep.

10:12 But the hireling, and he that is not the shepherd, whose own the sheep are not, seeth the wolf coming, and leaveth the sheep, and flieth: and the wolf catcheth, and scattereth the sheep:

10:13 And the hireling flieth, because he is a hireling: and he hath no care for the sheep.

10:14 I am the good shepherd; and I know mine, and mine know me.

10:15 As the Father knoweth me, and I know the Father: and I lay down my life for my sheep.

10:16 And other sheep I have, that are not of this fold: them also I must bring, and they shall hear my voice, and there shall be one fold and one shepherd.

10:17 Therefore doth the Father love me: because I lay down my life, that I may take it again.

10:18 No man taketh it away from me: but I lay it down of myself, and I have power to lay it down: and I have power to take it up again. This commandment have I received of my Father.

10:19 A dissension rose again among the Jews for these words.

10:20 And many of them said: He hath a devil, and is mad: why hear you him?

10:21 Others said: These are not the words of one that hath a devil: Can a devil open the eyes of the blind?

10:22 And it was the feast of the dedication at Je-

et hiems erat.

10:23 Et ambulabat Jesus in templo, in porticu Salomonis.

10:24 Circumdederunt ergo eum Judæi, et dicebant ei : Quousque animam nostram tollis ? si tu es Christus, dic nobis palam.

10:25 Respondit eis Jesus : Loquor vobis, et non creditis : opera quæ ego facio in nomine Patris mei, hæc testimonium perhibent de me :

10:26 sed vos non creditis, quia non estis ex ovibus meis.

10:27 Oves meæ vocem meam audiunt, et ego cognosco eas, et sequuntur me :

10:28 et ego vitam æternam do eis, et non peribunt in æternum, et non rapiet eas quisquam de manu mea.

10:29 Pater meus quod dedit mihi, majus omnibus est : et nemo potest rapere de manu Patris mei.

10:30 Ego et Pater unum sumus.

10:31 Sustulerunt ergo lapides Judæi, ut lapidarent eum.

10:32 Respondit eis Jesus : Multa bona opera ostendi vobis ex Patre meo : propter quod eorum opus me lapidatis ?

10:33 Responderunt ei Judæi : De bono opere non lapidamus te, sed de blasphemia ; et quia tu homo cum sis, facis teipsum Deum.

10:34 Respondit eis Jesus : Nonne scriptum est in lege vestra, Quia ego dixi : Dii estis ?

10:35 Si illos dixit deos, ad quos sermo Dei factus est, et non potest solvi Scriptura :

10:36 quem Pater sanctificavit, et misit in mundum vos dicitis : Quia blasphemas, quia dixi : Filius Dei sum ?

10:37 Si non facio opera Patris mei, nolite credere mihi.

10:38 Si autem facio : etsi mihi non vultis credere, operibus credite, ut cognoscatis, et credatis quia Pater in me est, et ego in Patre.

10:39 Quærebant ergo eum apprehendere : et exivit de manibus eorum.

10:40 Et abiit iterum trans Jordanem, in eum locum ubi erat Joannes baptizans primum, et mansit illic ;

10:41 et multi venerunt ad eum, et dicebant : Quia Joannes quidem signum fecit nullum.

10:42 Omnia autem quæcumque dixit Joannes de

rusalem: and it was winter.

10:23 And Jesus walked in the temple, in Solomon's porch.

10:24 The Jews therefore came round about him, and said to him: How long dost thou hold our souls in suspense? If thou be the Christ, tell us plainly.

10:25 Jesus answered them: I speak to you, and you believe not: the works that I do in the name of my Father, they give testimony of me.

10:26 But you do not believe, because you are not of my sheep.

10:27 My sheep hear my voice: and I know them, and they follow me.

10:28 And I give them life everlasting; and they shall not perish for ever, and no man shall pluck them out of my hand.

10:29 That which my Father hath given me, is greater than all: and no one can snatch them out of the hand of my Father.

10:30 I and the Father are one.

10:31 The Jews then took up stones to stone him.

10:32 Jesus answered them: Many good works I have shewed you from my Father; for which of these works do you stone me?

10:33 The Jews answered him: For a good work we stone thee not, but for blasphemy; and because that thou, being a man, maketh thyself God.

10:34 Jesus answered them: Is it not written in your law: I said you are gods?

10:35 If he called them gods, to whom the word of God was spoken, and the scripture cannot be broken;

10:36 Do you say of him whom the Father hath sanctified and sent into the world: Thou blasphemest, because I said, I am the Son of God?

10:37 If I do not the works of my Father, believe me not.

10:38 But if I do, though you will not believe me, believe the works: that you may know and believe that the Father is in me, and I in the Father.

10:39 They sought therefore to take him; and he escaped out of their hands.

10:40 And he went again beyond the Jordan, into that place where John was baptizing first; and there he abode.

10:41 And many resorted to him, and they said: John indeed did no sign.

10:42 But all things whatsoever John said of this

hoc, vera erant. Et multi crediderunt in eum.

11:1 Erat autem quidam languens Lazarus a Bethania, de castello Mariæ et Marthæ sororis ejus.

11:2 (Maria autem erat quæ unxit Dominum unguento, et extersit pedes ejus capillis suis : cujus frater Lazarus infirmabatur.)

11:3 Miserunt ergo sorores ejus ad eum dicentes : Domine, ecce quem amas infirmatur.

11:4 Audiens autem Jesus dixit eis : Infirmitas hæc non est ad mortem, sed pro gloria Dei, ut glorificetur Filius Dei per eam.

11:5 Diligebat autem Jesus Martham, et sororem ejus Mariam, et Lazarum.

11:6 Ut ergo audivit quia infirmabatur, tunc quidem mansit in eodem loco duobus diebus ;

11:7 deinde post hæc dixit discipulis suis : Eamus in Judæam iterum.

11:8 Dicunt ei discipuli : Rabbi, nunc quærebant te Judæi lapidare, et iterum vadis illuc ?

11:9 Respondit Jesus : Nonne duodecim sunt horæ diei ? Si quis ambulaverit in die, non offendit, quia lucem hujus mundi videt :

11:10 si autem ambulaverit in nocte, offendit, quia lux non est in eo.

11:11 Hæc ait, et post hæc dixit eis : Lazarus amicus noster dormit : sed vado ut a somno excitem eum.

11:12 Dixerunt ergo discipuli ejus : Domine, si dormit, salvus erit.

11:13 Dixerat autem Jesus de morte ejus : illi autem putaverunt quia de dormitione somni diceret.

11:14 Tunc ergo Jesus dixit eis manifeste : Lazarus mortuus est :

11:15 et gaudeo propter vos, ut credatis, quoniam non eram ibi, sed eamus ad eum.

11:16 Dixit ergo Thomas, qui dicitur Didymus, ad condiscipulos : Eamus et nos, ut moriamur cum eo.

11:17 Venit itaque Jesus : et invenit eum quatuor dies jam in monumento habentem.

11:18 (Erat autem Bethania juxta Jerosolymam quasi stadiis quindecim.)

11:19 Multi autem ex Judæis venerant ad Martham et Mariam, ut consolarentur eas de fratre suo.

man, were true. And many believed in him.

11:1 Now there was a certain man sick, named Lazarus, of Bethania, of the town of Mary and Martha her sister.

11:2 (And Mary was she that anointed the Lord with ointment, and wiped his feet with her hair: whose brother Lazarus was sick.)

11:3 His sisters therefore sent to him, saying: Lord, behold, he whom thou lovest is sick.

11:4 And Jesus hearing it, said to them: This sickness is not unto death, but for the glory of God: that the Son of God may be glorified by it.

11:5 Now Jesus loved Martha, and her sister Mary, and Lazarus.

11:6 When he had heard therefore that he was sick, he still remained in the same place two days.

11:7 Then after that, he said to his disciples: Let us go into Judea again.

11:8 The disciples say to him: Rabbi, the Jews but now sought to stone thee: and goest thou thither again?

11:9 Jesus answered: Are there not twelve hours of the day? If a man walk in the day, he stumbleth not, because he seeth the light of this world:

11:10 But if he walk in the night, he stumbleth, because the light is not in him.

11:11 These things he said; and after that he said to them: Lazarus our friend sleepeth; but I go that I may awake him out of sleep.

11:12 His disciples therefore said: Lord, if he sleep, he shall do well.

11:13 But Jesus spoke of his death; and they thought that he spoke of the repose of sleep.

11:14 Then therefore Jesus said to them plainly: Lazarus is dead.

11:15 And I am glad, for your sakes, that I was not there, that you may believe: but let us go to him.

11:16 Thomas therefore, who is called Didymus, said to his fellow disciples: Let us also go, that we may die with him.

11:17 Jesus therefore came, and found that he had been four days already in the grave.

11:18 (Now Bethania was near Jerusalem, about fifteen furlongs off.)

11:19 And many of the Jews were come to Martha and Mary, to comfort them concerning their brother.

11:20 Martha ergo ut audivit quia Jesus venit, occurrit illi : Maria autem domi sedebat.

11:21 Dixit ergo Martha ad Jesum : Domine, si fuisses hic, frater meus non fuisset mortuus :
11:22 sed et nunc scio quia quæcumque poposceris a Deo, dabit tibi Deus.
11:23 Dicit illi Jesus : Resurget frater tuus.

11:24 Dicit ei Martha : Scio quia resurget in resurrectione in novissimo die.
11:25 Dixit ei Jesus : Ego sum resurrectio et vita : qui credit in me, etiam si mortuus fuerit, vivet :
11:26 et omnis qui vivit et credit in me, non morietur in æternum. Credis hoc ?
11:27 Ait illi : Utique Domine, ego credidi quia tu es Christus, Filius Dei vivi, qui in hunc mundum venisti.
11:28 Et cum hæc dixisset, abiit, et vocavit Mariam sororem suam silentio, dicens : Magister adest, et vocat te.
11:29 Illa ut audivit, surgit cito, et venit ad eum ;

11:30 nondum enim venerat Jesus in castellum : sed erat adhuc in illo loco, ubi occurrerat ei Martha.
11:31 Judæi ergo, qui erant cum ea in domo, et consolabantur eam, cum vidissent Mariam quia cito surrexit, et exiit, secuti sunt eam dicentes : Quia vadit ad monumentum, ut ploret ibi.

11:32 Maria ergo, cum venisset ubi erat Jesus, videns eum, cecidit ad pedes ejus, et dicit ei : Domine, si fuisses hic, non esset mortuus frater meus.
11:33 Jesus ergo, ut vidit eam plorantem, et Judæos, qui venerant cum ea, plorantes, infremuit spiritu, et turbavit seipsum,
11:34 et dixit : Ubi posuistis eum ? Dicunt ei : Domine, veni, et vide.
11:35 Et lacrimatus est Jesus.
11:36 Dixerunt ergo Judæi : Ecce quomodo amabat eum.
11:37 Quidam autem ex ipsis dixerunt : Non poterat hic, qui aperuit oculos cæci nati, facere ut hic non moreretur ?
11:38 Jesus ergo rursum fremens in semetipso, venit ad monumentum. Erat autem spelunca, et lapis superpositus erat ei.
11:39 Ait Jesus : Tollite lapidem. Dicit ei Martha, soror ejus qui mortuus fuerat : Domine, jam

11:20 Martha therefore, as soon as she heard that Jesus had come, went to meet him: but Mary sat at home.
11:21 Martha therefore said to Jesus: Lord, if thou hadst been here, my brother had not died.
11:22 But now also I know that whatsoever thou wilt ask of God, God will give it thee.
11:23 Jesus saith to her: Thy brother shall rise again.
11:24 Martha saith to him: I know that he shall rise again, in the resurrection at the last day.
11:25 Jesus said to her: I am the resurrection and the life: he that believeth in me, although he be dead, shall live:
11:26 And every one that liveth, and believeth in me, shall not die for ever. Believest thou this?
11:27 She saith to him: Yea, Lord, I have believed that thou art Christ the Son of the living God, who art come into this world.
11:28 And when she had said these things, she went, and called her sister Mary secretly, saying: The master is come, and calleth for thee.
11:29 She, as soon as she heard this, riseth quickly, and cometh to him.
11:30 For Jesus was not yet come into the town: but he was still in that place where Martha had met him.
11:31 The Jews therefore, who were with her in the house, and comforted her, when they saw Mary that she rose up speedily and went out, followed her, saying: She goeth to the grave to weep there.
11:32 When Mary therefore was come where Jesus was, seeing him, she fell down at his feet, and saith to him: Lord, if thou hadst been here, my brother had not died.
11:33 Jesus, therefore, when he saw her weeping, and the Jews that were come with her, weeping, groaned in the spirit, and troubled himself,
11:34 And said: Where have you laid him? They say to him: Lord, come and see.
11:35 And Jesus wept.
11:36 The Jews therefore said: Behold how he loved him.
11:37 But some of them said: Could not he that opened the eyes of the man born blind, have caused that this man should not die?
11:38 Jesus therefore again groaning in himself, cometh to the sepulchre. Now it was a cave; and a stone was laid over it.
11:39 Jesus saith: Take away the stone. Martha, the sister of him that was dead, saith to him:

fœtet, quatriduanus est enim.

11:40 Dicit ei Jesus : Nonne dixi tibi quoniam si credideris, videbis gloriam Dei ?

11:41 Tulerunt ergo lapidem : Jesus autem, elevatis sursum oculis, dixit : Pater, gratias ago tibi quoniam audisti me.

11:42 Ego autem sciebam quia semper me audis, sed propter populum qui circumstat, dixi : ut credant quia tu me misisti.

11:43 Hæc cum dixisset, voce magna clamavit : Lazare, veni foras.

11:44 Et statim prodiit qui fuerat mortuus, ligatus pedes, et manus institis, et facies illius sudario erat ligata. Dixit eis Jesus : Solvite eum et sinite abire.

11:45 Multi ergo ex Judæis, qui venerant ad Mariam, et Martham, et viderant quæ fecit Jesus, crediderunt in eum.

11:46 Quidam autem ex ipsis abierunt ad pharisæos, et dixerunt eis quæ fecit Jesus.

11:47 Collegerunt ergo pontifices et pharisæi concilium, et dicebant : Quid facimus, quia hic homo multa signa facit ?

11:48 Si dimittimus eum sic, omnes credent in eum, et venient Romani, et tollent nostrum locum, et gentem.

11:49 Unus autem ex ipsis, Caiphas nomine, cum esset pontifex anni illius, dixit eis : Vos nescitis quidquam,

11:50 nec cogitatis quia expedit vobis ut unus moriatur homo pro populo, et non tota gens pereat.

11:51 Hoc autem a semetipso non dixit : sed cum esset pontifex anni illius, prophetavit, quod Jesus moriturus erat pro gente,

11:52 et non tantum pro gente, sed ut filios Dei, qui erant dispersi, congregaret in unum.

11:53 Ab illo ergo die cogitaverunt ut interficerent eum.

11:54 Jesus ergo jam non in palam ambulabat apud Judæos, sed abiit in regionem juxta desertum, in civitatem quæ dicitur Ephrem, et ibi morabatur cum discipulis suis.

11:55 Proximum autem erat Pascha Judæorum, et ascenderunt multi Jerosolymam de regione ante Pascha, ut sanctificarent seipsos.

11:56 Quærebant ergo Jesum, et colloquebantur

Lord, by this time he stinketh, for he is now of four days.

11:40 Jesus saith to her: Did not I say to thee, that if thou believe, thou shalt see the glory of God?

11:41 They took therefore the stone away. And Jesus lifting up his eyes said: Father, I give thee thanks that thou hast heard me.

11:42 And I knew that thou hearest me always; but because of the people who stand about have I said it, that they may believe that thou hast sent me.

11:43 When he had said these things, he cried with a loud voice: Lazarus, come forth.

11:44 And presently he that had been dead came forth, bound feet and hands with winding bands; and his face was bound about with a napkin. Jesus said to them: Loose him, and let him go.

11:45 Many therefore of the Jews, who were come to Mary and Martha, and had seen the things that Jesus did, believed in him.

11:46 But some of them went to the Pharisees, and told them the things that Jesus had done.

11:47 The chief priests therefore, and the Pharisees, gathered a council, and said: What do we, for this man doth many miracles?

11:48 If we let him alone so, all will believe in him; and the Romans will come, and take away our place and nation.

11:49 But one of them, named Caiphas, being the high priest that year, said to them: You know nothing.

11:50 Neither do you consider that it is expedient for you that one man should die for the people, and that the whole nation perish not.

11:51 And this he spoke not of himself: but being the high priest of that year, he prophesied that Jesus should die for the nation.

11:52 And not only for the nation, but to gather together in one the children of God, that were dispersed.

11:53 From that day therefore they devised to put him to death.

11:54 Wherefore Jesus walked no more openly among the Jews; but he went into a country near the desert, unto a city that is called Ephrem, and there he abode with his disciples.

11:55 And the pasch of the Jews was at hand; and many from the country went up to Jerusalem, before the pasch to purify themselves.

11:56 They sought therefore for Jesus; and they

ad invicem, in templo stantes : Quid putatis, quia non venit ad diem festum ?

11:57 Dederant autem pontifices et pharisæi mandatum ut si quis cognoverit ubi sit, indicet, ut apprehendant eum.

12:1 Jesus ergo ante sex dies Paschæ venit Bethaniam, ubi Lazarus fuerat mortuus, quem suscitavit Jesus.

12:2 Fecerunt autem ei cœnam ibi, et Martha ministrabat, Lazarus vero unus erat ex discumbentibus cum eo.

12:3 Maria ergo accepit libram unguenti nardi pistici pretiosi, et unxit pedes Jesu, et extersit pedes ejus capillis suis : et domus impleta est ex odore unguenti.

12:4 Dixit ergo unus ex discipulis ejus, Judas Iscariotes, qui erat eum traditurus :

12:5 Quare hoc unguentum non veniit trecentis denariis, et datum est egenis ?

12:6 Dixit autem hoc, non quia de egenis pertinebat ad eum, sed quia fur erat, et loculos habens, ea quæ mittebantur, portabat.

12:7 Dixit ergo Jesus : Sinite illam ut in diem sepulturæ meæ servet illud.

12:8 Pauperes enim semper habetis vobiscum : me autem non semper habetis.

12:9 Cognovit ergo turba multa ex Judæis quia illic est, et venerunt, non propter Jesum tantum, sed ut Lazarum viderent, quem suscitavit a mortuis.

12:10 Cogitaverunt autem principes sacerdotum ut et Lazarum interficerent :

12:11 quia multi propter illum abibant ex Judæis, et credebant in Jesum.

12:12 In crastinum autem, turba multa quæ venerat ad diem festum, cum audissent quia venit Jesus Jerosolymam,

12:13 acceperunt ramos palmarum, et processerunt obviam ei, et clamabant : Hosanna, benedictus qui venit in nomine Domini, rex Israël.

12:14 Et invenit Jesus asellum, et sedit super eum, sicut scriptum est :

12:15 Noli timere, filia Sion : ecce rex tuus venit sedens super pullum asinæ.

12:16 Hæc non cognoverunt discipuli ejus primum : sed quando glorificatus est Jesus, tunc recordati sunt quia hæc erant scripta de eo, et

discoursed one with another, standing in the temple: What think you that he is not come to the festival day?

11:57 And the chief priests and Pharisees had given a commandment, that if any man knew where he was, he should tell, that they might apprehend him.

12:1 Jesus therefore, six days before the pasch, came to Bethania, where Lazarus had been dead, whom Jesus raised to life.

12:2 And they made him a supper there: and Martha served: but Lazarus was one of them that were at table with him.

12:3 Mary therefore took a pound of ointment of right spikenard, of great price, and anointed the feet of Jesus, and wiped his feet with her hair; and the house was filled with the odour of the ointment.

12:4 Then one of his disciples, Judas Iscariot, he that was about to betray him, said:

12:5 Why was not this ointment sold for three hundred pence, and given to the poor?

12:6 Now he said this, not because he cared for the poor; but because he was a thief, and having the purse, carried the things that were put therein.

12:7 Jesus therefore said: Let her alone, that she may keep it against the day of my burial.

12:8 For the poor you have always with you; but me you have not always.

12:9 A great multitude therefore of the Jews knew that he was there; and they came, not for Jesus' sake only, but that they might see Lazarus, whom he had raised from the dead.

12:10 But the chief priests thought to kill Lazarus also:

12:11 Because many of the Jews, by reason of him, went away, and believed in Jesus.

12:12 And on the next day, a great multitude that was to come to the festival day, when they had heard that Jesus was coming to Jerusalem,

12:13 Took branches of palm trees, and went forth to meet him, and cried: Hosanna, blessed is he that cometh in the name of the Lord, the king of Israel.

12:14 And Jesus found a young ass, and sat upon it, as it is written:

12:15 Fear not, daughter of Sion: behold, thy king cometh, sitting on an ass's colt.

12:16 These things his disciples did not know at the first; but when Jesus was glorified, then they remembered that these things were writ-

hæc fecerunt ei.

12:17 Testimonium ergo perhibebat turba, quæ erat cum eo quando Lazarum vocavit de monumento, et suscitavit eum a mortuis.

12:18 Propterea et obviam venit ei turba : quia audierunt fecisse hoc signum.

12:19 Pharisæi ergo dixerunt ad semetipsos : Videtis quia nihil proficimus ? ecce mundus totus post eum abiit.

12:20 Erant autem quidam gentiles, ex his qui ascenderant ut adorarent in die festo.

12:21 Hi ergo accesserunt ad Philippum, qui erat a Bethsaida Galilææ, et rogabant eum, dicentes : Domine, volumus Jesum videre.

12:22 Venit Philippus, et dicit Andreæ ; Andreas rursum et Philippus dixerunt Jesu.

12:23 Jesus autem respondit eis, dicens : Venit hora, ut clarificetur Filius hominis.

12:24 Amen, amen dico vobis, nisi granum frumenti cadens in terram, mortuum fuerit,

12:25 ipsum solum manet : si autem mortuum fuerit, multum fructum affert. Qui amat animam suam, perdet eam ; et qui odit animam suam in hoc mundo, in vitam æternam custodit eam.

12:26 Si quis mihi ministrat, me sequatur, et ubi sum ego, illic et minister meus erit. Si quis mihi ministraverit, honorificabit eum Pater meus.

12:27 Nunc anima mea turbata est. Et quid dicam ? Pater, salvifica me ex hac hora. Sed propterea veni in horam hanc :

12:28 Pater, clarifica nomen tuum. Venit ergo vox de cælo : Et clarificavi, et iterum clarificabo.

12:29 Turba ergo, quæ stabat, et audierat, dicebat tonitruum esse factum. Alii dicebant : Angelus ei locutus est.

12:30 Respondit Jesus, et dixit : Non propter me hæc vox venit, sed propter vos.

12:31 Nunc judicium est mundi : nunc princeps hujus mundi ejicietur foras.

12:32 Et ego, si exaltatus fuero a terra, omnia traham ad meipsum.

12:33 (Hoc autem dicebat, significans qua morte esset moriturus.)

12:34 Respondit ei turba : Nos audivimus ex lege, quia Christus manet in æternum : et

ten of him, and that they had done these things to him.

12:17 The multitude therefore gave testimony, which was with him, when he called Lazarus out of the grave, and raised him from the dead.

12:18 For which reason also the people came to meet him, because they heard that he had done this miracle.

12:19 The Pharisees therefore said among themselves: Do you see that we prevail nothing? behold, the whole world is gone after him.

12:20 Now there were certain Gentiles among them, who came up to adore on the festival day.

12:21 These therefore came to Philip, who was of Bethsaida of Galilee, and desired him, saying: Sir, we would see Jesus.

12:22 Philip cometh, and telleth Andrew. Again Andrew and Philip told Jesus.

12:23 But Jesus answered them, saying: The hour is come, that the Son of man should be glorified.

12:24 Amen, amen I say to you, unless the grain of wheat falling into the ground die,

12:25 Itself remaineth alone. But if it die, it bringeth forth much fruit. He that loveth his life shall lose it; and he that hateth his life in this world, keepeth it unto life eternal.

12:26 If any man minister to me, let him follow me; and where I am, there also shall my minister be. If any man minister to me, him will my Father honour.

12:27 Now is my soul troubled. And what shall I say? Father, save me from this hour. But for this cause I came unto this hour.

12:28 Father, glorify thy name. A voice therefore came from heaven: I have both glorified it, and will glorify it again.

12:29 The multitude therefore that stood and heard, said that it thundered. Others said: An angel spoke to him.

12:30 Jesus answered, and said: This voice came not because of me, but for your sakes.

12:31 Now is the judgment of the world: now shall the prince of this world be cast out.

12:32 And I, if I be lifted up from the earth, will draw all things to myself.

12:33 (Now this he said, signifying what death he should die.)

12:34 The multitude answered him: We have heard out of the law, that Christ abideth for ev-

quomodo tu dicis : Oportet exaltari Filium hominis ? quis est iste Filius hominis ?

12:35 Dixit ergo eis Jesus : Adhuc modicum, lumen in vobis est. Ambulate dum lucem habetis, ut non vos tenebræ comprehendant ; et qui ambulat in tenebris, nescit quo vadat.

12:36 Dum lucem habetis, credite in lucem, ut filii lucis sitis. Hæc locutus est Jesus, et abiit et abscondit se ab eis.

12:37 Cum autem tanta signa fecisset coram eis, non credebant in eum ;

12:38 ut sermo Isaiæ prophetæ impleretur, quem dixit : *Domine, quis credidit auditui nostro ? et brachium Domini cui revelatum est ?*

12:39 Propterea non poterant credere, quia iterum dixit Isaias :

12:40 *Excæcavit oculos eorum, et induravit cor eorum ut non videant oculis, et non intelligant corde, et convertantur, et sanem eos.*

12:41 Hæc dixit Isaias, quando vidit gloriam ejus, et locutus est de eo.

12:42 Verumtamen et ex principibus multi crediderunt in eum : sed propter pharisæos non confitebantur, ut e synagoga non ejicerentur.

12:43 Dilexerunt enim gloriam hominum magis quam gloriam Dei.

12:44 Jesus autem clamavit, et dixit : Qui credit in me, non credit in me, sed in eum qui misit me.

12:45 Et qui videt me, videt eum qui misit me.

12:46 Ego lux in mundum veni, ut omnis qui credit in me, in tenebris non maneat.

12:47 Et si quis audierit verba mea, et non custodierit, ego non judico eum ; non enim veni ut judicem mundum, sed ut salvificem mundum.

12:48 Qui spernit me et non accipit verba mea, habet qui judicet eum. Sermo quem locutus sum, ille judicabit eum in novissimo die.

12:49 Quia ego ex meipso non sum locutus, sed qui misit me, Pater, ipse mihi mandatum dedit quid dicam et quid loquar.

12:50 Et scio quia mandatum ejus vita æterna est : quæ ergo ego loquor, sicut dixit mihi Pa-

er; and how sayest thou: The Son of man must be lifted up? Who is this Son of man?

12:35 Jesus therefore said to them: Yet a little while, the light is among you. Walk whilst you have the light, that the darkness overtake you not. And he that walketh in darkness, knoweth not whither he goeth.

12:36 Whilst you have the light, believe in the light, that you may be the children of light. These things Jesus spoke; and he went away, and hid himself from them.

12:37 And whereas he had done so many miracles before them, they believed not in him:

12:38 That the saying of Isaias the prophet might be fulfilled, which he said: *Lord, who hath believed our hearing? and to whom hath the arm of the Lord been revealed?*

12:39 Therefore they could not believe, because Isaias said again:

12:40 *He hath blinded their eyes, and hardened their heart, that they should not see with their eyes, nor understand with their heart, and be converted, and I should heal them.*

12:41 These things said Isaias, when he saw his glory, and spoke of him.

12:42 However, many of the chief men also believed in him; but because of the Pharisees they did not confess him, that they might not be cast out of the synagogue.

12:43 For they loved the glory of men more than the glory of God.

12:44 But Jesus cried, and said: He that believeth in me, doth not believe in me, but in him that sent me.

12:45 And he that seeth me, seeth him that sent me.

12:46 I am come a light into the world; that whosoever believeth in me, may not remain in darkness.

12:47 And if any man hear my words, and keep them not, I do not judge him: for I came not to judge the world, but to save the world.

12:48 He that despiseth me, and receiveth not my words, hath one that judgeth him; the word that I have spoken, the same shall judge him in the last day.

12:49 For I have not spoken of myself; but the Father who sent me, he gave me commandment what I should say, and what I should speak.

12:50 And I know that his commandment is life everlasting. The things therefore that I speak,

ter, sic loquor.

13:1 Ante diem festum Paschæ, sciens Jesus quia venit hora ejus ut transeat ex hoc mundo ad Patrem : cum dilexisset suos, qui erant in mundo, in finem dilexit eos.

13:2 Et cœna facta, cum diabolus jam misisset in cor ut traderet eum Judas Simonis Iscariotæ :

13:3 sciens quia omnia dedit ei Pater in manus, et quia a Deo exivit, et ad Deum vadit :

13:4 surgit a cœna, et ponit vestimenta sua, et cum accepisset linteum, præcinxit se.

13:5 Deinde mittit aquam in pelvim, et cœpit lavare pedes discipulorum, et extergere linteo, quo erat præcinctus.

13:6 Venit ergo ad Simonem Petrum. Et dicit ei Petrus : Domine, tu mihi lavas pedes ?

13:7 Respondit Jesus, et dixit ei : Quod ego facio, tu nescis modo : scies autem postea.

13:8 Dicit ei Petrus : Non lavabis mihi pedes in æternum. Respondit ei Jesus : Si non lavero te, non habebis partem mecum.

13:9 Dicit ei Simon Petrus : Domine, non tantum pedes meos, sed et manus, et caput.

13:10 Dicit ei Jesus : Qui lotus est, non indiget nisi ut pedes lavet, sed est mundus totus. Et vos mundi estis, sed non omnes.

13:11 Sciebat enim quisnam esset qui traderet eum ; propterea dixit : Non estis mundi omnes.

13:12 Postquam ergo lavit pedes eorum, et accepit vestimenta sua, cum recubuisset iterum, dixit eis : Scitis quid fecerim vobis ?

13:13 Vos vocatis me Magister et Domine, et bene dicitis : sum etenim.

13:14 Si ergo ego lavi pedes vestros, Dominus et Magister, et vos debetis alter alterius lavare pedes.

13:15 Exemplum enim dedi vobis, ut quemadmodum ego feci vobis, ita et vos faciatis.

13:16 Amen, amen dico vobis : non est servus major domino suo : neque apostolus major est eo qui misit illum.

13:17 Si hæc scitis, beati eritis si feceritis ea.

even as the Father said unto me, so do I speak.

13:1 Before the festival day of the pasch, Jesus knowing that his hour was come, that he should pass out of this world to the Father: having loved his own who were in the world, he loved them unto the end.

13:2 And when supper was done, (the devil having now put into the heart of Judas Iscariot, the son of Simon, to betray him,)

13:3 Knowing that the Father had given him all things into his hands, and that he came from God, and goeth to God;

13:4 He riseth from supper, and layeth aside his garments, and having taken a towel, girded himself.

13:5 After that, he putteth water into a basin, and began to wash the feet of the disciples, and to wipe them with the towel wherewith he was girded.

13:6 He cometh therefore to Simon Peter. And Peter saith to him: Lord, dost thou wash my feet?

13:7 Jesus answered, and said to him: What I do thou knowest not now; but thou shalt know hereafter.

13:8 Peter saith to him: Thou shalt never wash my feet. Jesus answered him: If I wash thee not, thou shalt have no part with me.

13:9 Simon Peter saith to him: Lord, not only my feet, but also my hands and my head.

13:10 Jesus saith to him: He that is washed, needeth not but to wash his feet, but is clean wholly. And you are clean, but not all.

13:11 For he knew who he was that would betray him; therefore he said: You are not all clean.

13:12 Then after he had washed their feet, and taken his garments, being set down again, he said to them: Know you what I have done to you?

13:13 You call me Master, and Lord; and you say well, for so I am.

13:14 If then I being your Lord and Master, have washed your feet; you also ought to wash one another's feet.

13:15 For I have given you an example, that as I have done to you, so you do also.

13:16 Amen, amen I say to you: The servant is not greater than his lord; neither is the apostle greater than he that sent him.

13:17 If you know these things, you shall be blessed if you do them.

13:18 Non de omnibus vobis dico : ego scio quos elegerim ; sed ut adimpleatur Scriptura : Qui manducat mecum panem, levabit contra me calcaneum suum.

13:19 Amodo dico vobis, priusquam fiat : ut cum factum fuerit, credatis quia ego sum.

13:20 Amen, amen dico vobis : qui accipit si quem misero, me accipit ; qui autem me accipit, accipit eum qui me misit.

13:21 Cum hæc dixisset Jesus, turbatus est spiritu : et protestatus est, et dixit : Amen, amen dico vobis, quia unus ex vobis tradet me.

13:22 Aspiciebant ergo ad invicem discipuli, hæsitantes de quo diceret.

13:23 Erat ergo recumbens unus ex discipulis ejus in sinu Jesu, quem diligebat Jesus.

13:24 Innuit ergo huic Simon Petrus, et dixit ei : Quis est, de quo dicit ?

13:25 Itaque cum recubuisset ille supra pectus Jesu, dicit ei : Domine, quis est ?

13:26 Respondit Jesus : Ille est cui ego intinctum panem porrexero. Et cum intinxisset panem, dedit Judæ Simonis Iscariotæ.

13:27 Et post buccellam, introivit in eum Satanas. Et dixit ei Jesus : Quod facis, fac citius.

13:28 Hoc autem nemo scivit discumbentium ad quid dixerit ei.

13:29 Quidam enim putabant, quia loculos habebat Judas, quod dixisset ei Jesus : Eme ea quæ opus sunt nobis ad diem festum : aut egenis ut aliquid daret.

13:30 Cum ergo accepisset ille buccellam, exivit continuo. Erat autem nox.

13:31 Cum ergo exisset, dixit Jesus : Nunc clarificatus est Filius hominis, et Deus clarificatus est in eo.

13:32 Si Deus clarificatus est in eo, et Deus clarificabit eum in semetipso : et continuo clarificabit eum.

13:33 Filioli, adhuc modicum vobiscum sum. Quæretis me ; et sicut dixi Judæis, quo ego vado, vos non potestis venire : et vobis dico modo.

13:34 Mandatum novum do vobis : ut diligatis invicem : sicut dilexi vos, ut et vos diligatis invicem.

13:18 I speak not of you all: I know whom I have chosen. But that the scripture may be fulfilled: He that eateth bread with me, shall lift up his heel against me.

13:19 At present I tell you, before it come to pass: that when it shall come to pass, you may believe that I am he.

13:20 Amen, amen I say to you, he that receiveth whomsoever I send, receiveth me; and he that receiveth me, receiveth him that sent me.

13:21 When Jesus had said these things, he was troubled in spirit; and he testified, and said: Amen, amen I say to you, one of you shall betray me.

13:22 The disciples therefore looked one upon another, doubting of whom he spoke.

13:23 Now there was leaning on Jesus' bosom one of his disciples, whom Jesus loved.

13:24 Simon Peter therefore beckoned to him, and said to him: Who is it of whom he speaketh?

13:25 He therefore, leaning on the breast of Jesus, saith to him: Lord, who is it?

13:26 Jesus answered: He it is to whom I shall reach bread dipped. And when he had dipped the bread, he gave it to Judas Iscariot, the son of Simon.

13:27 And after the morsel, Satan entered into him. And Jesus said to him: That which thou dost, do quickly.

13:28 Now no man at the table knew to what purpose he said this unto him.

13:29 For some thought, because Judas had the purse, that Jesus had said to him: Buy those things which we have need of for the festival day: or that he should give something to the poor.

13:30 He therefore having received the morsel, went out immediately. And it was night.

13:31 When he therefore was gone out, Jesus said: Now is the Son of man glorified, and God is glorified in him.

13:32 If God be glorified in him, God also will glorify him in himself; and immediately will he glorify him.

13:33 Little children, yet a little while I am with you. You shall seek me; and as I said to the Jews: Whither I go you cannot come; so I say to you now.

13:34 A new commandment I give unto you: That you love one another, as I have loved you, that you also love one another.

13:35 In hoc cognoscent omnes quia discipuli mei estis, si dilectionem habueritis ad invicem.

13:36 Dicit ei Simon Petrus : Domine, quo vadis ? Respondit Jesus : Quo ego vado non potes me modo sequi : sequeris autem postea.

13:37 Dicit ei Petrus : Quare non possum te sequi modo ? animam meam pro te ponam.

13:38 Respondit ei Jesus : Animam tuam pro me pones ? amen, amen dico tibi : non cantabit gallus, donec ter me neges.

14:1 Non turbetur cor vestrum. Creditis in Deum, et in me credite.

14:2 In domo Patris mei mansiones multæ sunt ; si quominus dixissem vobis : quia vado parare vobis locum.

14:3 Et si abiero, et præparavero vobis locum, iterum venio, et accipiam vos ad meipsum : ut ubi sum ego, et vos sitis.

14:4 Et quo ego vado scitis, et viam scitis.

14:5 Dicit ei Thomas : Domine, nescimus quo vadis : et quomodo possumus viam scire ?

14:6 Dicit ei Jesus : Ego sum via, et veritas, et vita. Nemo venit ad Patrem, nisi per me.

14:7 Si cognovissetis me, et Patrem meum utique cognovissetis : et amodo cognoscetis eum, et vidistis eum.

14:8 Dicit ei Philippus : Domine, ostende nobis Patrem, et sufficit nobis.

14:9 Dicit ei Jesus : Tanto tempore vobiscum sum, et non cognovistis me ? Philippe, qui videt me, videt et Patrem. Quomodo tu dicis : Ostende nobis Patrem ?

14:10 Non creditis quia ego in Patre, et Pater in me est ? Verba quæ ego loquor vobis, a meipso non loquor. Pater autem in me manens, ipse fecit opera.

14:11 Non creditis quia ego in Patre, et Pater in me est ?

14:12 alioquin propter opera ipsa credite. Amen, amen dico vobis, qui credit in me, opera quæ ego facio, et ipse faciet, et majora horum faciet : quia ego ad Patrem vado.

14:13 Et quodcumque petieritis Patrem in nomine meo, hoc faciam : ut glorificetur Pater in Filio.

14:14 Si quid petieritis me in nomine meo, hoc faciam.

13:35 By this shall all men know that you are my disciples, if you have love one for another.

13:36 Simon Peter saith to him: Lord, whither goest thou? Jesus answered: Whither I go, thou canst not follow me now; but thou shalt follow hereafter.

13:37 Peter saith to him: Why cannot I follow thee now? I will lay down my life for thee.

13:38 Jesus answered him: Wilt thou lay down thy life for me? Amen, amen I say to thee, the cock shall not crow, till thou deny me thrice.

14:1 Let not your heart be troubled. You believe in God, believe also in me.

14:2 In my Father's house there are many mansions. If not, I would have told you: because I go to prepare a place for you.

14:3 And if I shall go, and prepare a place for you, I will come again, and will take you to myself; that where I am, you also may be.

14:4 And whither I go you know, and the way you know.

14:5 Thomas saith to him: Lord, we know not whither thou goest; and how can we know the way?

14:6 Jesus saith to him: I am the way, and the truth, and the life. No man cometh to the Father, but by me.

14:7 If you had known me, you would without doubt have known my Father also: and from henceforth you shall know him, and you have seen him.

14:8 Philip saith to him: Lord, shew us the Father, and it is enough for us.

14:9 Jesus saith to him: Have I been so long a time with you; and have you not known me? Philip, he that seeth me seeth the Father also. How sayest thou, Shew us the Father?

14:10 Do you not believe, that I am in the Father, and the Father in me? The words that I speak to you, I speak not of myself. But the Father who abideth in me, he doth the works.

14:11 Believe you not that I am in the Father, and the Father in me?

14:12 Otherwise believe for the very works' sake. Amen, amen I say to you, he that believeth in me, the works that I do, he also shall do; and greater than these shall he do.

14:13 Because I go to the Father: and whatsoever you shall ask the Father in my name, that will I do: that the Father may be glorified in the Son.

14:14 If you shall ask me any thing in my name, that I will do.

14:15 Si diligitis me, mandata mea servate :

14:16 et ego rogabo Patrem, et alium Paraclitum dabit vobis, ut maneat vobiscum in æternum,

14:17 Spiritum veritatis, quem mundus non potest accipere, quia non videt eum, nec scit eum : vos autem cognoscetis eum, quia apud vos manebit, et in vobis erit.

14:18 Non relinquam vos orphanos : veniam ad vos.

14:19 Adhuc modicum, et mundus me jam non videt. Vos autem videtis me : quia ego vivo, et vos vivetis.

14:20 In illo die vos cognoscetis quia ego sum in Patre meo, et vos in me, et ego in vobis.

14:21 Qui habet mandata mea, et servat ea : ille est qui diligit me. Qui autem diligit me, diligetur a Patre meo : et ego diligam eum, et manifestabo ei meipsum.

14:22 Dicit ei Judas, non ille Iscariotes : Domine, quid factum est, quia manifestaturus es nobis teipsum, et non mundo ?

14:23 Respondit Jesus, et dixit ei : Si quis diligit me, sermonem meum servabit, et Pater meus diliget eum, et ad eum veniemus, et mansionem apud eum faciemus ;

14:24 qui non diligit me, sermones meos non servat. Et sermonem, quem audistis, non est meus : sed ejus qui misit me, Patris.

14:25 Hæc locutus sum vobis apud vos manens.

14:26 Paraclitus autem Spiritus Sanctus, quem mittet Pater in nomine meo, ille vos docebit omnia, et suggeret vobis omnia quæcumque dixero vobis.

14:27 Pacem relinquo vobis, pacem meam do vobis : non quomodo mundus dat, ego do vobis. Non turbetur cor vestrum, neque formidet.

14:28 Audistis quia ego dixi vobis : Vado, et venio ad vos. Si diligeretis me, gauderetis utique, quia vado ad Patrem : quia Pater major me est.

14:29 Et nunc dixi vobis priusquam fiat : ut cum factum fuerit, credatis.

14:30 Jam non multa loquar vobiscum : venit enim princeps mundi hujus, et in me non habet quidquam.

14:31 Sed ut cognoscat mundus quia diligo Patrem, et sicut mandatum dedit mihi Pater, sic

14:15 If you love me, keep my commandments.

14:16 And I will ask the Father, and he shall give you another Paraclete, that he may abide with you for ever.

14:17 The spirit of truth, whom the world cannot receive, because it seeth him not, nor knoweth him: but you shall know him; because he shall abide with you, and shall be in you.

14:18 I will not leave you orphans, I will come to you.

14:19 Yet a little while: and the world seeth me no more. But you see me: because I live, and you shall live.

14:20 In that day you shall know, that I am in my Father, and you in me, and I in you.

14:21 He that hath my commandments, and keepeth them; he it is that loveth me. And he that loveth me, shall be loved of my Father: and I will love him, and will manifest myself to him.

14:22 Judas saith to him, not the Iscariot: Lord, how is it, that thou wilt manifest thyself to us, and not to the world?

14:23 Jesus answered, and said to him: If any one love me, he will keep my word, and my Father will love him, and we will come to him, and will make our abode with him.

14:24 He that loveth me not, keepeth not my words. And the word which you have heard, is not mine; but the Father's who sent me.

14:25 These things have I spoken to you, abiding with you.

14:26 But the Paraclete, the Holy Ghost, whom the Father will send in my name, he will teach you all things, and bring all things to your mind, whatsoever I shall have said to you.

14:27 Peace I leave with you, my peace I give unto you: not as the world giveth, do I give unto you. Let not your heart be troubled, nor let it be afraid.

14:28 You have heard that I said to you: I go away, and I come unto you. If you loved me, you would indeed be glad, because I go to the Father: for the Father is greater than I.

14:29 And now I have told you before it come to pass: that when it shall come to pass, you may believe.

14:30 I will not now speak many things with you. For the prince of this world cometh, and in me he hath not any thing.

14:31 But that the world may know, that I love the Father: and as the Father hath given me

facio. Surgite, eamus hinc.

15:1 Ego sum vitis vera, et Pater meus agricola est.

15:2 Omnem palmitem in me non ferentem fructum, tollet eum, et omnem qui fert fructum, purgabit eum, ut fructum plus afferat.

15:3 Jam vos mundi estis propter sermonem quem locutus sum vobis.

15:4 Manete in me, et ego in vobis. Sicut palmes non potest ferre fructum a semetipso, nisi manserit in vite, sic nec vos, nisi in me manseritis.

15:5 Ego sum vitis, vos palmites : qui manet in me, et ego in eo, hic fert fructum multum, quia sine me nihil potestis facere.

15:6 Si quis in me non manserit, mittetur foras sicut palmes, et arescet, et colligent eum, et in ignem mittent, et ardet.

15:7 Si manseritis in me, et verba mea in vobis manserint, quodcumque volueritis petetis, et fiet vobis.

15:8 In hoc clarificatus est Pater meus, ut fructum plurimum afferatis, et efficiamini mei discipuli.

15:9 Sicut dilexit me Pater, et ego dilexi vos. Manete in dilectione mea.

15:10 Si præcepta mea servaveritis, manebitis in dilectione mea, sicut et ego Patris mei præcepta servavi, et maneo in ejus dilectione.

15:11 Hæc locutus sum vobis : ut gaudium meum in vobis sit, et gaudium vestrum impleatur.

15:12 Hoc est præceptum meum, ut diligatis invicem, sicut dilexi vos.

15:13 Majorem hac dilectionem nemo habet, ut animam suam ponat quis pro amicis suis.

15:14 Vos amici mei estis, si feceritis quæ ego præcipio vobis.

15:15 Jam non dicam vos servos : quia servus nescit quid faciat dominus ejus. Vos autem dixi amicos : quia omnia quæcumque audivi a Patre meo, nota feci vobis.

15:16 Non vos me elegistis, sed ego elegi vos, et posui vos ut eatis, et fructum afferatis, et fructus vester maneat : ut quodcumque petieritis Patrem in nomine meo, det vobis.

15:17 Hæc mando vobis : ut diligatis invicem.

commandment, so do I: Arise, let us go hence.

15:1 I AM the true vine; and my Father is the husbandman.

15:2 Every branch in me, that beareth not fruit, he will take away: and every one that beareth fruit, he will purge it, that it may bring forth more fruit.

15:3 Now you are clean by reason of the word, which I have spoken to you.

15:4 Abide in me, and I in you. As the branch cannot bear fruit of itself, unless it abide in the vine, so neither can you, unless you abide in me.

15:5 I am the vine; you the branches: he that abideth in me, and I in him, the same beareth much fruit: for without me you can do nothing.

15:6 If any one abide not in me, he shall be cast forth as a branch, and shall wither, and they shall gather him up, and cast him into the fire, and he burneth.

15:7 If you abide in me, and my words abide in you, you shall ask whatever you will, and it shall be done unto you.

15:8 In this is my Father glorified; that you bring forth very much fruit, and become my disciples.

15:9 As the Father hath loved me, I also have loved you. Abide in my love.

15:10 If you keep my commandments, you shall abide in my love; as I also have kept my Father's commandments, and do abide in his love.

15:11 These things I have spoken to you, that my joy may be in you, and your joy may be filled.

15:12 This is my commandment, that you love one another, as I have loved you.

15:13 Greater love than this no man hath, that a man lay down his life for his friends.

15:14 You are my friends, if you do the things that I command you.

15:15 I will not now call you servants: for the servant knoweth not what his lord doth. But I have called you friends: because all things whatsoever I have heard of my Father, I have made known to you.

15:16 You have not chosen me: but I have chosen you; and have appointed you, that you should go, and should bring forth fruit; and your fruit should remain: that whatsoever you shall ask of the Father in my name, he may give it you.

15:17 These things I command you, that you love one another.

15:18 Si mundus vos odit, scitote quia me priorem vobis odio habuit.

15:19 Si de mundo fuissetis, mundus quod suum erat diligeret : quia vero de mundo non estis, sed ego elegi vos de mundo, propterea odit vos mundus.

15:20 Mementote sermonis mei, quem ego dixi vobis : non est servus major domino suo. Si me persecuti sunt, et vos persequentur ; si sermonem meum servaverunt, et vestrum servabunt.

15:21 Sed hæc omnia facient vobis propter nomen meum : quia nesciunt eum qui misit me.

15:22 Si non venissem, et locutus fuissem eis, peccatum non haberent : nunc autem excusationem non habent de peccato suo.

15:23 Qui me odit, et Patrem meum odit.

15:24 Si opera non fecissem in eis quæ nemo alius fecit, peccatum non haberent : nunc autem et viderunt, et oderunt et me, et Patrem meum.

15:25 Sed ut adimpleatur sermo, qui in lege eorum scriptus est : Quia odio habuerunt me gratis.

15:26 Cum autem venerit Paraclitus, quem ego mittam vobis a Patre, Spiritum veritatis, qui a Patre procedit, ille testimonium perhibebit de me ;

15:27 et vos testimonium perhibebitis, quia ab initio mecum estis.

16:1 Hæc locutus sum vobis, ut non scandalizemini.

16:2 Absque synagogis facient vos : sed venit hora, ut omnis qui interficit vos arbitretur obsequium se præstare Deo.

16:3 Et hæc facient vobis, quia non noverunt Patrem, neque me.

16:4 Sed hæc locutus sum vobis, ut cum venerit hora eorum, reminiscamini quia ego dixi vobis.

16:5 Hæc autem vobis ab initio non dixi, quia vobiscum eram. Et nunc vado ad eum qui misit me ; et nemo ex vobis interrogat me : Quo vadis ?

16:6 sed quia hæc locutus sum vobis, tristitia implevit cor vestrum.

16:7 Sed ego veritatem dico vobis : expedit vobis ut ego vadam : si enim non abiero, Paraclitus non veniet ad vos ; si autem abiero, mittam eum ad vos.

16:8 Et cum venerit ille, arguet mundum de

15:18 If the world hate you, know ye, that it hath hated me before you.

15:19 If you had been of the world, the world would love its own: but because you are not of the world, but I have chosen you out of the world, therefore the world hateth you.

15:20 Remember my word that I said to you: The servant is not greater than his master. If they have persecuted me, they will also persecute you: if they have kept my word, they will keep yours also.

15:21 But all these things they will do to you for my name's sake: because they know not him who sent me.

15:22 If I had not come, and spoken to them, they would not have sin; but now they have no excuse for their sin.

15:23 He that hateth me, hateth my Father also.

15:24 If I had not done among them the works that no other man hath done, they would not have sin; but now they have both seen and hated both me and my Father.

15:25 But that the word may be fulfilled which is written in their law: They hated me without cause.

15:26 But when the Paraclete cometh, whom I will send you from the Father, the Spirit of truth, who proceedeth from the Father, he shall give testimony of me.

15:27 And you shall give testimony, because you are with me from the beginning.

16:1 These things have I spoken to you, that you may not be scandalized.

16:2 They will put you out of the synagogues: yea, the hour cometh, that whosoever killeth you, will think that he doth a service to God.

16:3 And these things will they do to you; because they have not known the Father, nor me.

16:4 But these things I have told you, that when the hour shall come, you may remember that I told you of them.

16:5 But I told you not these things from the beginning, because I was with you. And now I go to him that sent me, and none of you asketh me: Whither goest thou?

16:6 But because I have spoken these things to you, sorrow hath filled your heart.

16:7 But I tell you the truth: it is expedient to you that I go: for if I go not, the Paraclete will not come to you; but if I go, I will send him to you.

16:8 And when he is come, he will convince the

peccato, et de justitia, et de judicio.

16:9 De peccato quidem, quia non crediderunt in me.

16:10 De justitia vero, quia ad Patrem vado, et jam non videbitis me.

16:11 De judicio autem, quia princeps hujus mundi jam judicatus est.

16:12 Adhuc multa habeo vobis dicere, sed non potestis portare modo.

16:13 Cum autem venerit ille Spiritus veritatis, docebit vos omnem veritatem : non enim loquetur a semetipso, sed quæcumque audiet loquetur, et quæ ventura sunt annuntiabit vobis.

16:14 Ille me clarificabit, quia de meo accipiet, et annuntiabit vobis.

16:15 Omnia quæcumque habet Pater, mea sunt. Propterea dixi : quia de meo accipiet, et annuntiabit vobis.

16:16 Modicum, et jam non videbitis me ; et iterum modicum, et videbitis me : quia vado ad Patrem.

16:17 Dixerunt ergo ex discipulis ejus ad invicem : Quid est hoc quod dicit nobis : Modicum, et non videbitis me ; et iterum modicum, et videbitis me, et quia vado ad Patrem ?

16:18 Dicebant ergo : Quid est hoc quod dicit : Modicum ? nescimus quid loquitur.

16:19 Cognovit autem Jesus, quia volebant eum interrogare, et dixit eis : De hoc quæritis inter vos quia dixi : Modicum, et non videbitis me ; et iterum modicum, et videbitis me.

16:20 Amen, amen dico vobis : quia plorabitis, et flebitis vos, mundus autem gaudebit ; vos autem contristabimini, sed tristitia vestra vertetur in gaudium.

16:21 Mulier cum parit, tristitiam habet, quia venit hora ejus ; cum autem pepererit puerum, jam non meminit pressuræ propter gaudium, quia natus est homo in mundum.

16:22 Et vos igitur nunc quidem tristitiam habetis, iterum autem videbo vos, et gaudebit cor vestrum : et gaudium vestrum nemo tollet a vobis.

16:23 Et in illo die me non rogabitis quidquam. Amen, amen dico vobis : si quid petieritis Patrem in nomine meo, dabit vobis.

world of sin, and of justice, and of judgment.

16:9 Of sin: because they believed not in me.

16:10 And of justice: because I go to the Father; and you shall see me no longer.

16:11 And of judgment: because the prince of this world is already judged.

16:12 I have yet many things to say to you: but you cannot bear them now.

16:13 But when he, the Spirit of truth, is come, he will teach you all truth. For he shall not speak of himself; but what things soever he shall hear, he shall speak; and the things that are to come, he shall shew you.

16:14 He shall glorify me; because he shall receive of mine, and shall shew it to you.

16:15 All things whatsoever the Father hath, are mine. Therefore I said, that he shall receive of mine, and shew it to you.

16:16 A little while, and now you shall not see me; and again a little while, and you shall see me: because I go to the Father.

16:17 Then some of the disciples said one to another: What is this that he saith to us: A little while, and you shall not see me; and again a little while, and you shall see me, and, because I go to the Father?

16:18 They said therefore: What is this that he saith, A little while? we know not what he speaketh.

16:19 And Jesus knew that they had a mind to ask him; and he said to them: Of this do you inquire among yourselves, because I said: A little while, and you shall not see me; and again a little while, and you shall see me?

16:20 Amen, amen I say to you, that you shall lament and weep, but the world shall rejoice; and you shall be made sorrowful, but your sorrow shall be turned into joy.

16:21 A woman, when she is in labour, hath sorrow, because her hour is come; but when she hath brought forth the child, she remembereth no more the anguish, for joy that a man is born into the world.

16:22 So also you now indeed have sorrow; but I will see you again, and your heart shall rejoice; and your joy no man shall take from you.

16:23 And in that day you shall not ask me any thing. Amen, amen I say to you: if you ask the Father any thing in my name, he will give it you.

16:24 Usque modo non petistis quidquam in nomine meo : petite, et accipietis, ut gaudium vestrum sit plenum.

16:25 Hæc in proverbiis locutus sum vobis. Venit hora cum jam non in proverbiis loquar vobis, sed palam de Patre annuntiabo vobis :

16:26 in illo die in nomine meo petetis : et non dico vobis quia ego rogabo Patrem de vobis :

16:27 ipse enim Pater amat vos, quia vos me amastis, et credidistis, quia ego a Deo exivi.

16:28 Exivi a Patre, et veni in mundum : iterum relinquo mundum, et vado ad Patrem.

16:29 Dicunt ei discipuli ejus : Ecce nunc palam loqueris, et proverbium nullum dicis :

16:30 nunc scimus quia scis omnia, et non opus est tibi ut quis te interroget : in hoc credimus quia a Deo existi.

16:31 Respondit eis Jesus : Modo creditis ?

16:32 ecce venit hora, et jam venit, ut dispergamini unusquisque in propria, et me solum relinquatis : et non sum solus, quia Pater mecum est.

16:33 Hæc locutus sum vobis, ut in me pacem habeatis. In mundo pressuram habebitis : sed confidite, ego vici mundum.

17:1 Hæc locutus est Jesus : et sublevatis oculis in cælum, dixit : Pater, venit hora : clarifica Filium tuum, ut Filius tuus clarificet te :

17:2 sicut dedisti ei potestatem omnis carnis, ut omne, quod dedisti ei, det eis vitam æternam.

17:3 Hæc est autem vita æterna : ut cognoscant te, solum Deum verum, et quem misisti Jesum Christum.

17:4 Ego te clarificavi super terram : opus consummavi, quod dedisti mihi ut faciam :

17:5 et nunc clarifica me tu, Pater, apud temetipsum, claritate quam habui, priusquam mundus esset, apud te.

17:6 Manifestavi nomen tuum hominibus, quos dedisti mihi de mundo : tui erant, et mihi eos dedisti : et sermonem tuum servaverunt.

17:7 Nunc cognoverunt quia omnia quæ dedisti mihi, abs te sunt :

16:24 Hitherto you have not asked any thing in my name. Ask, and you shall receive; that your joy may be full.

16:25 These things I have spoken to you in proverbs. The hour cometh, when I will no more speak to you in proverbs, but will shew you plainly of the Father.

16:26 In that day you shall ask in my name; and I say not to you, that I will ask the Father for you:

16:27 For the Father himself loveth you, because you have loved me, and have believed that I came out from God.

16:28 I came forth from the Father, and am come into the world: again I leave the world, and I go to the Father.

16:29 His disciples say to him: Behold, now thou speakest plainly, and speakest no proverb.

16:30 Now we know that thou knowest all things, and thou needest not that any man should ask thee. By this we believe that thou camest forth from God.

16:31 Jesus answered them: Do you now believe?

16:32 Behold, the hour cometh, and it is now come, that you shall be scattered every man to his own, and shall leave me alone; and yet I am not alone, because the Father is with me.

16:33 These things I have spoken to you, that in me you may have peace. In the world you shall have distress: but have confidence, I have overcome the world.

17:1 These things Jesus spoke, and lifting up his eyes to heaven, he said: Father, the hour is come, glorify thy Son, that thy Son may glorify thee.

17:2 As thou hast given him power over all flesh, that he may give eternal life to all whom thou hast given him.

17:3 Now this is eternal life: That they may know thee, the only true God, and Jesus Christ, whom thou hast sent.

17:4 I have glorified thee on the earth; I have finished the work which thou gavest me to do.

17:5 And now glorify thou me, O Father, with thyself, with the glory which I had, before the world was, with thee.

17:6 I have manifested thy name to the men whom thou hast given me out of the world. Thine they were, and to me thou gavest them; and they have kept thy word.

17:7 Now they have known, that all things which thou hast given me, are from thee:

17:8 quia verba quæ dedisti mihi, dedi eis : et ipsi acceperunt, et cognoverunt vere quia a te exivi, et crediderunt quia tu me misisti.

17:9 Ego pro eis rogo ; non pro mundo rogo, sed pro his quos dedisti mihi : quia tui sunt :

17:10 et mea omnia tua sunt, et tua mea sunt : et clarificatus sum in eis.

17:11 Et jam non sum in mundo, et hi in mundo sunt, et ego ad te venio. Pater sancte, serva eos in nomine tuo, quos dedisti mihi : ut sint unum, sicut et nos.

17:12 Cum essem cum eis, ego servabam eos in nomine tuo. Quos dedisti mihi, custodivi : et nemo ex eis periit, nisi filius perditionis, ut Scriptura impleatur.

17:13 Nunc autem ad te venio : et hæc loquor in mundo, ut habeant gaudium meum impletum in semetipsis.

17:14 Ego dedi eis sermonem tuum, et mundus eos odio habuit, quia non sunt de mundo, sicut et ego non sum de mundo.

17:15 Non rogo ut tollas eos de mundo, sed ut serves eos a malo.

17:16 De mundo non sunt, sicut et ego non sum de mundo.

17:17 Sanctifica eos in veritate. Sermo tuus veritas est.

17:18 Sicut tu me misisti in mundum, et ego misi eos in mundum :

17:19 et pro eis ego sanctifico meipsum : ut sint et ipsi sanctificati in veritate.

17:20 Non pro eis autem rogo tantum, sed et pro eis qui credituri sunt per verbum eorum in me :

17:21 ut omnes unum sint, sicut tu Pater in me, et ego in te, ut et ipsi in nobis unum sint : ut credat mundus, quia tu me misisti.

17:22 Et ego claritatem, quam dedisti mihi, dedi eis : ut sint unum, sicut et nos unum sumus.

17:23 Ego in eis, et tu in me : ut sint consummati in unum : et cognoscat mundus quia tu me misisti, et dilexisti eos, sicut et me dilexisti.

17:24 Pater, quos dedisti mihi, volo ut ubi sum ego, et illi sint mecum : ut videant claritatem meam, quam dedisti mihi : quia dilexisti me

17:8 Because the words which thou gavest me, I have given to them; and they have received them, and have known in very deed that I came out from thee, and they have believed that thou didst send me.

17:9 I pray for them: I pray not for the world, but for them whom thou hast given me: because they are thine:

17:10 And all my things are thine, and thine are mine; and I am glorified in them.

17:11 And now I am not in the world, and these are in the world, and I come to thee. Holy Father, keep them in thy name whom thou has given me; that they may be one, as we also are.

17:12 While I was with them, I kept them in thy name. Those whom thou gavest me have I kept; and none of them is lost, but the son of perdition, that the scripture may be fulfilled.

17:13 And now I come to thee; and these things I speak in the world, that they may have my joy filled in themselves.

17:14 I have given them thy word, and the world hath hated them, because they are not of the world; as I also am not of the world.

17:15 I pray not that thou shouldst take them out of the world, but that thou shouldst keep them from evil.

17:16 They are not of the world, as I also am not of the world.

17:17 Sanctify them in truth. Thy word is truth.

17:18 As thou hast sent me into the world, I also have sent them into the world.

17:19 And for them do I sanctify myself, that they also may be sanctified in truth.

17:20 And not for them only do I pray, but for them also who through their word shall believe in me;

17:21 That they all may be one, as thou, Father, in me, and I in thee; that they also may be one in us; that the world may believe that thou hast sent me.

17:22 And the glory which thou hast given me, I have given to them; that they may be one, as we also are one:

17:23 I in them, and thou in me; that they may be made perfect in one: and the world may know that thou hast sent me, and hast loved them, as thou hast also loved me.

17:24 Father, I will that where I am, they also whom thou hast given me may be with me; that they may see my glory which thou hast

ante constitutionem mundi.

17:25 Pater juste, mundus te non cognovit, ego autem te cognovi : et hi cognoverunt, quia tu me misisti.

17:26 Et notum feci eis nomen tuum, et notum faciam : ut dilectio, qua dilexisti me, in ipsis sit, et ego in ipsis.

18:1 Hæc cum dixisset Jesus, egressus est cum discipulis suis trans torrentem Cedron, ubi erat hortus, in quem introivit ipse, et discipuli ejus.

18:2 Sciebat autem et Judas, qui tradebat eum, locum : quia frequenter Jesus convenerat illuc cum discipulis suis.

18:3 Judas ergo cum accepisset cohortem, et a pontificibus et pharisæis ministros, venit illuc cum laternis, et facibus, et armis.

18:4 Jesus itaque sciens omnia quæ ventura erant super eum, processit, et dixit eis : Quem quæritis ?

18:5 Responderunt ei : Jesum Nazarenum. Dicit eis Jesus : Ego sum. Stabat autem et Judas, qui tradebat eum, cum ipsis.

18:6 Ut ergo dixit eis : Ego sum : abierunt retrorsum, et ceciderunt in terram.

18:7 Iterum ergo interrogavit eos : Quem quæritis ? Illi autem dixerunt : Jesum Nazarenum.

18:8 Respondit Jesus : Dixi vobis, quia ego sum : si ergo me quæritis, sinite hos abire.

18:9 Ut impleretur sermo, quem dixit : Quia quos dedisti mihi, non perdidi ex eis quemquam.

18:10 Simon ergo Petrus habens gladium eduxit eum : et percussit pontificis servum, et abscidit auriculam ejus dexteram. Erat autem nomen servo Malchus.

18:11 Dixit ergo Jesus Petro : Mitte gladium tuum in vaginam. Calicem, quem dedit mihi Pater, non bibam illum ?

18:12 Cohors ergo, et tribunus, et ministri Judæorum comprehenderunt Jesum, et ligaverunt eum.

18:13 Et adduxerunt eum ad Annam primum : erat enim socer Caiphæ, qui erat pontifex anni illius.

18:14 Erat autem Caiphas, qui consilium dederat

given me, because thou hast loved me before the creation of the world.

17:25 Just Father, the world hath not known thee; but I have known thee: and these have known that thou hast sent me.

17:26 And I have made known thy name to them, and will make it known; that the love wherewith thou hast loved me, may be in them, and I in them.

18:1 When Jesus had said these things, he went forth with his disciples over the brook Cedron, where there was a garden, into which he entered with his disciples.

18:2 And Judas also, who betrayed him, knew the place; because Jesus had often resorted thither together with his disciples.

18:3 Judas therefore having received a band of soldiers and servants from the chief priests and the Pharisees, cometh thither with lanterns and torches and weapons.

18:4 Jesus therefore, knowing all things that should come upon him, went forth, and said to them: Whom seek ye?

18:5 They answered him: Jesus of Nazareth. Jesus saith to them: I am he. And Judas also, who betrayed him, stood with them.

18:6 As soon therefore as he had said to them: I am he; they went backward, and fell to the ground.

18:7 Again therefore he asked them: Whom seek ye? And they said, Jesus of Nazareth.

18:8 Jesus answered, I have told you that I am he. If therefore you seek me, let these go their way.

18:9 That the word might be fulfilled which he said: Of them whom thou hast given me, I have not lost any one.

18:10 Then Simon Peter, having a sword, drew it, and struck the servant of the high priest, and cut off his right ear. And the name of the servant was Malchus.

18:11 Jesus therefore said to Peter: Put up thy sword into the scabbard. The chalice which my Father hath given me, shall I not drink it?

18:12 Then the band and the tribune, and the servants of the Jews, took Jesus, and bound him:

18:13 And they led him away to Annas first, for he was father in law to Caiphas, who was the high priest of that year.

18:14 Now Caiphas was he who had given the

Judæis : Quia expedit unum hominem mori pro populo.

18:15 Sequebatur autem Jesum Simon Petrus, et alius discipulus. Discipulus autem ille erat notus pontifici, et introivit cum Jesu in atrium pontificis.

18:16 Petrus autem stabat ad ostium foris. Exivit ergo discipulus alius, qui erat notus pontifici, et dixit ostiariæ : et introduxit Petrum.

18:17 Dicit ergo Petro ancilla ostiaria : Numquid et tu ex discipulis es hominis istius ? Dicit ille : Non sum.

18:18 Stabant autem servi et ministri ad prunas, quia frigus erat, et calefaciebant se : erat autem cum eis et Petrus stans, et calefaciens se.

18:19 Pontifex ergo interrogavit Jesum de discipulis suis, et de doctrina ejus.

18:20 Respondit ei Jesus : Ego palam locutus sum mundo : ego semper docui in synagoga, et in templo, quo omnes Judæi conveniunt, et in occulto locutus sum nihil.

18:21 Quid me interrogas ? interroga eos qui audierunt quid locutus sim ipsis : ecce hi sciunt quæ dixerim ego.

18:22 Hæc autem cum dixisset, unus assistens ministrorum dedit alapam Jesu, dicens : Sic respondes pontifici ?

18:23 Respondit ei Jesus : Si male locutus sum, testimonium perhibe de malo : si autem bene, quid me cædis ?

18:24 Et misit eum Annas ligatum ad Caipham pontificem.

18:25 Erat autem Simon Petrus stans, et calefaciens se. Dixerunt ergo ei : Numquid et tu ex discipulis ejus es ? Negavit ille, et dixit : Non sum.

18:26 Dicit ei unus ex servis pontificis, cognatus ejus, cujus abscidit Petrus auriculam : Nonne ego te vidi in horto cum illo ?

18:27 Iterum ergo negavit Petrus : et statim gallus cantavit.

18:28 Adducunt ergo Jesum a Caipha in prætorium. Erat autem mane : et ipsi non introierunt in prætorium, ut non contaminarentur, sed ut manducarent Pascha.

18:29 Exivit ergo Pilatus ad eos foras, et dixit : Quam accusationem affertis adversus hominem hunc ?

18:30 Responderunt, et dixerunt ei : Si non esset

counsel to the Jews: That it was expedient that one man should die for the people.

18:15 And Simon Peter followed Jesus, and so did another disciple. And that disciple was known to the high priest, and went in with Jesus into the court of the high priest.

18:16 But Peter stood at the door without. The other disciple therefore, who was known to the high priest, went out, and spoke to the portress, and brought in Peter.

18:17 The maid therefore that was portress, saith to Peter: Art not thou also one of this man's disciples? He saith: I am not.

18:18 Now the servants and ministers stood at a fire of coals, because it was cold, and warmed themselves. And with them was Peter also, standing, and warming himself.

18:19 The high priest therefore asked Jesus of his disciples, and of his doctrine.

18:20 Jesus answered him: I have spoken openly to the world: I have always taught in the synagogue, and in the temple, whither all the Jews resort; and in secret I have spoken nothing.

18:21 Why asketh thou me? ask them who have heard what I have spoken unto them: behold they know what things I have said.

18:22 And when he had said these things, one of the servants standing by, gave Jesus a blow, saying: Answerest thou the high priest so?

18:23 Jesus answered him: If I have spoken evil, give testimony of the evil; but if well, why strikest thou me?

18:24 And Annas sent him bound to Caiphas the high priest.

18:25 And Simon Peter was standing, and warming himself. They said therefore to him: Art not thou also one of his disciples? He denied it, and said: I am not.

18:26 One of the servants of the high priest (a kinsman to him whose ear Peter cut off) saith to him: Did I not see thee in the garden with him?

18:27 Again therefore Peter denied; and immediately the cock crew.

18:28 Then they led Jesus from Caiphas to the governor's hall. And it was morning; and they went not into the hall, that they might not be defiled, but that they might eat the pasch.

18:29 Pilate therefore went out to them, and said: What accusation bring you against this man?

18:30 They answered, and said to him: If he were

hic malefactor, non tibi tradidissemus eum.

18:31 Dixit ergo eis Pilatus : Accipite eum vos, et secundum legem vestram judicate eum. Dixerunt ergo ei Judæi : Nobis non licet interficere quemquam.

18:32 Ut sermo Jesu impleretur, quem dixit, significans qua morte esset moriturus.

18:33 Introivit ergo iterum in prætorium Pilatus : et vocavit Jesum, et dixit ei : Tu es rex Judæorum ?

18:34 Respondit Jesus : A temetipso hoc dicis, an alii dixerunt tibi de me ?

18:35 Respondit Pilatus : Numquid ego Judæus sum ? gens tua et pontifices tradiderunt te mihi : quid fecisti ?

18:36 Respondit Jesus : Regnum meum non est de hoc mundo. Si ex hoc mundo esset regnum meum, ministri mei utique decertarent ut non traderer Judæis : nunc autem regnum meum non est hinc.

18:37 Dixit itaque ei Pilatus : Ergo rex es tu ? Respondit Jesus : Tu dicis quia rex sum ego. Ego in hoc natus sum, et ad hoc veni in mundum, ut testimonium perhibeam veritati : omnis qui est ex veritate, audit vocem meam.

18:38 Dicit ei Pilatus : Quid est veritas ? Et cum hoc dixisset, iterum exivit ad Judæos, et dicit eis : Ego nullam invenio in eo causam.

18:39 Est autem consuetudo vobis ut unum dimittam vobis in Pascha : vultis ergo dimittam vobis regem Judæorum ?

18:40 Clamaverunt ergo rursum omnes, dicentes : Non hunc, sed Barabbam. Erat autem Barabbas latro.

19:1 Tunc ergo apprehendit Pilatus Jesum, et flagellavit.

19:2 Et milites plectentes coronam de spinis, imposuerunt capiti ejus : et veste purpurea circumdederunt eum.

19:3 Et veniebant ad eum, et dicebant : Ave, rex Judæorum : et dabant ei alapas.

19:4 Exivit ergo iterum Pilatus foras, et dicit eis : Ecce adduco vobis eum foras, ut cognoscatis quia nullam invenio in eo causam.

19:5 (Exivit ergo Jesus portans coronam spineam, et purpureum vestimentum.) Et dicit eis : Ecce homo.

19:6 Cum ergo vidissent eum pontifices et ministri, clamabant, dicentes : Crucifige, crucifige

not a malefactor, we would not have delivered him up to thee.

18:31 Pilate therefore said to them: Take him you, and judge him according to your law. The Jews therefore said to him: It is not lawful for us to put any man to death;

18:32 That the word of Jesus might be fulfilled, which he said, signifying what death he should die.

18:33 Pilate therefore went into the hall again, and called Jesus, and said to him: Art thou the king of the Jews?

18:34 Jesus answered: Sayest thou this thing of thyself, or have others told it thee of me?

18:35 Pilate answered: Am I a Jew? Thy own nation, and the chief priests, have delivered thee up to me: what hast thou done?

18:36 Jesus answered: My kingdom is not of this world. If my kingdom were of this world, my servants would certainly strive that I should not be delivered to the Jews: but now my kingdom is not from hence.

18:37 Pilate therefore said to him: Art thou a king then? Jesus answered: Thou sayest that I am a king. For this was I born, and for this came I into the world; that I should give testimony to the truth. Every one that is of the truth, heareth my voice.

18:38 Pilate saith to him: What is truth? And when he said this, he went out again to the Jews, and saith to them: I find no cause in him.

18:39 But you have a custom that I should release one unto you at the pasch: will you, therefore, that I release unto you the king of the Jews?

18:40 Then cried they all again, saying: Not this man, but Barabbas. Now Barabbas was a robber.

19:1 Then therefore, Pilate took Jesus, and scourged him.

19:2 And the soldiers platting a crown of thorns, put it upon his head; and they put on him a purple garment.

19:3 And they came to him, and said: Hail, king of the Jews; and they gave him blows.

19:4 Pilate therefore went forth again, and saith to them: Behold, I bring him forth unto you, that you may know that I find no cause in him.

19:5 (Jesus therefore came forth, bearing the crown of thorns and the purple garment.) And he saith to them: Behold the Man.

19:6 When the chief priests, therefore, and the servants, had seen him, they cried out, saying:

eum. Dicit eis Pilatus : Accipite eum vos, et crucifigite : ego enim non invenio in eo causam.

19:7 Responderunt ei Judæi : Nos legem habemus, et secundum legem debet mori, quia Filium Dei se fecit.

19:8 Cum ergo audisset Pilatus hunc sermonem, magis timuit.

19:9 Et ingressus est prætorium iterum : et dixit ad Jesum : Unde es tu ? Jesus autem responsum non dedit ei.

19:10 Dicit ergo ei Pilatus : Mihi non loqueris ? nescis quia potestatem habeo crucifigere te, et potestatem habeo dimittere te ?

19:11 Respondit Jesus : Non haberes potestatem adversum me ullam, nisi tibi datum esset desuper. Propterea qui me tradidit tibi, majus peccatum habet.

19:12 Et exinde quærebat Pilatus dimittere eum. Judæi autem clamabant dicentes : Si hunc dimittis, non es amicus Cæsaris. Omnis enim qui se regem facit, contradicit Cæsari.

19:13 Pilatus autem cum audisset hos sermones, adduxit foras Jesum : et sedit pro tribunali, in loco qui dicitur Lithostrotos, hebraice autem Gabbatha.

19:14 Erat autem parasceve Paschæ, hora quasi sexta, et dicit Judæis : Ecce rex vester.

19:15 Illi autem clamabant : Tolle, tolle, crucifige eum. Dicit eis Pilatus : Regem vestrum crucifigam ? Responderunt pontifices : Non habemus regem, nisi Cæsarem.

19:16 Tunc ergo tradidit eis illum ut crucifigeretur. Susceperunt autem Jesum, et eduxerunt.

19:17 Et bajulans sibi crucem exivit in eum, qui dicitur Calvariæ locum, hebraice autem Golgotha :

19:18 ubi crucifixerunt eum, et cum eo alios duos hinc et hinc, medium autem Jesum.

19:19 Scripsit autem et titulum Pilatus, et posuit super crucem. Erat autem scriptum : Jesus Nazarenus, Rex Judæorum.

19:20 Hunc ergo titulum multi Judæorum legerunt : quia prope civitatem erat locus, ubi crucifixus est Jesus, et erat scriptum hebraice, græce, et latine.

19:21 Dicebant ergo Pilato pontifices

Crucify him, crucify him. Pilate saith to them: Take him you, and crucify him: for I find no cause in him.

19:7 The Jews answered him: We have a law; and according to the law he ought to die, because he made himself the Son of God.

19:8 When Pilate therefore had heard this saying, he feared the more.

19:9 And he entered into the hall again, and he said to Jesus: Whence art thou? But Jesus gave him no answer.

19:10 Pilate therefore saith to him: Speakest thou not to me? knowest thou not that I have power to crucify thee, and I have power to release thee?

19:11 Jesus answered: Thou shouldst not have any power against me, unless it were given thee from above. Therefore, he that hath delivered me to thee, hath the greater sin.

19:12 And from henceforth Pilate sought to release him. But the Jews cried out, saying: If thou release this man, thou art not Caesar's friend. For whosoever maketh himself a king, speaketh against Caesar.

19:13 Now when Pilate had heard these words, he brought Jesus forth, and sat down in the judgment seat, in the place that is called Lithostrotos, and in Hebrew Gabbatha.

19:14 And it was the parasceve of the pasch, about the sixth hour, and he saith to the Jews: Behold your king.

19:15 But they cried out: Away with him; away with him; crucify him. Pilate saith to them: Shall I crucify your king? The chief priests answered: We have no king but Caesar.

19:16 Then therefore he delivered him to them to be crucified. And they took Jesus, and led him forth.

19:17 And bearing his own cross, he went forth to that place which is called Calvary, but in Hebrew Golgotha.

19:18 Where they crucified him, and with him two others, one on each side, and Jesus in the midst.

19:19 And Pilate wrote a title also, and he put it upon the cross. And the writing was: JESUS OF NAZARETH, THE KING OF THE JEWS.

19:20 This title therefore many of the Jews did read: because the place where Jesus was crucified was nigh to the city: and it was written in Hebrew, in Greek, and in Latin.

19:21 Then the chief priests of the Jews said to

Judæorum : Noli scribere : Rex Judæorum : sed quia ipse dixit : Rex sum Judæorum.

19:22 Respondit Pilatus : Quod scripsi, scripsi.

19:23 Milites ergo cum crucifixissent eum, acceperunt vestimenta ejus (et fecerunt quatuor partes, unicuique militi partem) et tunicam. Erat autem tunica inconsutilis, desuper contexta per totum.

19:24 Dixerunt ergo ad invicem : Non scindamus eam, sed sortiamur de illa cujus sit. Ut Scriptura impleretur, dicens : Partiti sunt vestimenta mea sibi : et in vestem meam miserunt sortem. Et milites quidem hæc fecerunt.

19:25 Stabant autem juxta crucem Jesu mater ejus, et soror matris ejus, Maria Cleophæ, et Maria Magdalene.

19:26 Cum vidisset ergo Jesus matrem, et discipulum stantem, quem diligebat, dicit matri suæ : Mulier, ecce filius tuus.

19:27 Deinde dicit discipulo : Ecce mater tua. Et ex illa hora accepit eam discipulus in sua.

19:28 Postea sciens Jesus quia omnia consummata sunt, ut consummaretur Scriptura, dixit : Sitio.

19:29 Vas ergo erat positum aceto plenum. Illi autem spongiam plenam aceto, hyssopo circumponentes, obtulerunt ori ejus.

19:30 Cum ergo accepisset Jesus acetum, dixit : Consummatum est. Et inclinato capite tradidit spiritum.

19:31 Judæi ergo (quoniam parasceve erat) ut non remanerent in cruce corpora sabbato (erat enim magnus dies ille sabbati), rogaverunt Pilatum ut frangerentur eorum crura, et tollerentur.

19:32 Venerunt ergo milites : et primi quidem fregerunt crura, et alterius, qui crucifixus est cum eo.

19:33 Ad Jesum autem cum venissent, ut viderunt eum jam mortuum, non fregerunt ejus crura,

19:34 sed unus militum lancea latus ejus aperuit, et continuo exivit sanguis et aqua.

19:35 Et qui vidit, testimonium perhibuit : et verum est testimonium ejus. Et ille scit quia vera dicit : ut et vos credatis.

19:36 Facta sunt enim hæc ut Scriptura im-

Pilate: Write not, The King of the Jews; but that he said, I am the King of the Jews.

19:22 Pilate answered: What I have written, I have written.

19:23 The soldiers therefore, when they had crucified him, took his garments, (and they made four parts, to every soldier a part,) and also his coat. Now the coat was without seam, woven from the top throughout.

19:24 They said then one to another: Let us not cut it, but let us cast lots for it, whose it shall be; that the scripture might be fulfilled, saying: They have parted my garments among them, and upon my vesture they have cast lot. And the soldiers indeed did these things.

19:25 Now there stood by the cross of Jesus, his mother, and his mother's sister, Mary of Cleophas, and Mary Magdalen.

19:26 When Jesus therefore had seen his mother and the disciple standing whom he loved, he saith to his mother: Woman, behold thy son.

19:27 After that, he saith to the disciple: Behold thy mother. And from that hour, the disciple took her to his own.

19:28 Afterwards, Jesus knowing that all things were now accomplished, that the scripture might be fulfilled, said: I thirst.

19:29 Now there was a vessel set there full of vinegar. And they, putting a sponge full of vinegar about hyssop, put it to his mouth.

19:30 Jesus therefore, when he had taken the vinegar, said: It is consummated. And bowing his head, he gave up the ghost.

19:31 Then the Jews, (because it was the parasceve,) that the bodies might not remain on the cross on the sabbath day, (for that was a great sabbath day,) besought Pilate that their legs might be broken, and that they might be taken away.

19:32 The soldiers therefore came; and they broke the legs of the first, and of the other that was crucified with him.

19:33 But after they were come to Jesus, when they saw that he was already dead, they did not break his legs.

19:34 But one of the soldiers with a spear opened his side, and immediately there came out blood and water.

19:35 And he that saw it, hath given testimony, and his testimony is true. And he knoweth that he saith true; that you also may believe.

19:36 For these things were done, that the scrip-

pleretur : Os non comminuetis ex eo.

19:37 Et iterum alia Scriptura dicit : Videbunt in quem transfixerunt.

19:38 Post hæc autem rogavit Pilatum Joseph ab Arimathæa (eo quod esset discipulus Jesu, occultus autem propter metum Judæorum), ut tolleret corpus Jesu. Et permisit Pilatus. Venit ergo, et tulit corpus Jesu.

19:39 Venit autem et Nicodemus, qui venerat ad Jesum nocte primum, ferens mixturam myrrhæ et aloës, quasi libras centum.

19:40 Acceperunt ergo corpus Jesu, et ligaverunt illud linteis cum aromatibus, sicut mos est Judæis sepelire.

19:41 Erat autem in loco, ubi crucifixus est, hortus : et in horto monumentum novum, in quo nondum quisquam positus erat.

19:42 Ibi ergo propter parasceven Judæorum, quia juxta erat monumentum, posuerunt Jesum.

20:1 Una autem sabbati, Maria Magdalene venit mane, cum adhuc tenebræ essent, ad monumentum : et vidit lapidem sublatum a monumento.

20:2 Cucurrit ergo, et venit ad Simonem Petrum, et ad alium discipulum, quem amabat Jesus, et dicit illis : Tulerunt Dominum de monumento, et nescimus ubi posuerunt eum.

20:3 Exiit ergo Petrus, et ille alius discipulus, et venerunt ad monumentum.

20:4 Currebant autem duo simul, et ille alius discipulus præcucurrit citius Petro, et venit primus ad monumentum.

20:5 Et cum se inclinasset, vidit posita linteamina : non tamen introivit.

20:6 Venit ergo Simon Petrus sequens eum, et introivit in monumentum, et vidit linteamina posita,

20:7 et sudarium, quod fuerat super caput ejus, non cum linteaminibus positum, sed separatim involutum in unum locum.

20:8 Tunc ergo introivit et ille discipulus qui venerat primus ad monumentum : et vidit, et credidit :

20:9 nondum enim sciebant Scripturam, quia oportebat eum a mortuis resurgere.

20:10 Abierunt ergo iterum discipuli ad semetipsos.

ture might be fulfilled: You shall not break a bone of him.

19:37 And again another scripture saith: They shall look on him whom they pierced.

19:38 And after these things, Joseph of Arimathea (because he was a disciple of Jesus, but secretly for fear of the Jews) besought Pilate that he might take away the body of Jesus. And Pilate gave leave. He came therefore, and took the body of Jesus.

19:39 And Nicodemus also came, (he who at the first came to Jesus by night,) bringing a mixture of myrrh and aloes, about an hundred pound weight.

19:40 They took therefore the body of Jesus, and bound it in linen cloths, with the spices, as the manner of the Jews is to bury.

19:41 Now there was in the place where he was crucified, a garden; and in the garden a new sepulchre, wherein no man yet had been laid.

19:42 There, therefore, because of the parasceve of the Jews, they laid Jesus, because the sepulchre was nigh at hand.

20:1 And on the first day of the week, Mary Magdalen cometh early, when it was yet dark, unto the sepulchre; and she saw the stone taken away from the sepulchre.

20:2 She ran, therefore, and cometh to Simon Peter, and to the other disciple whom Jesus loved, and saith to them: They have taken away the Lord out of the sepulchre, and we know not where they have laid him.

20:3 Peter therefore went out, and that other disciple, and they came to the sepulchre.

20:4 And they both ran together, and that other disciple did outrun Peter, and came first to the sepulchre.

20:5 And when he stooped down, he saw the linen cloths lying; but yet he went not in.

20:6 Then cometh Simon Peter, following him, and went into the sepulchre, and saw the linen cloths lying,

20:7 And the napkin that had been about his head, not lying with the linen cloths, but apart, wrapped up into one place.

20:8 Then that other disciple also went in, who came first to the sepulchre: and he saw, and believed.

20:9 For as yet they knew not the scripture, that he must rise again from the dead.

20:10 The disciples therefore departed again to their home.

20:11 Maria autem stabat ad monumentum foris, plorans. Dum ergo fleret, inclinavit se, et prospexit in monumentum :

20:12 et vidit duos angelos in albis sedentes, unum ad caput, et unum ad pedes, ubi positum fuerat corpus Jesu.

20:13 Dicunt ei illi : Mulier, quid ploras ? Dicit eis : Quia tulerunt Dominum meum : et nescio ubi posuerunt eum.

20:14 Hæc cum dixisset, conversa est retrorsum, et vidit Jesum stantem : et non sciebat quia Jesus est.

20:15 Dicit ei Jesus : Mulier, quid ploras ? quem quæris ? Illa existimans quia hortulanus esset, dicit ei : Domine, si tu sustulisti eum, dicito mihi ubi posuisti eum, et ego eum tollam.

20:16 Dicit ei Jesus : Maria. Conversa illa, dicit ei : Rabboni (quod dicitur Magister).

20:17 Dicit ei Jesus : Noli me tangere, nondum enim ascendi ad Patrem meum : vade autem ad fratres meos, et dic eis : Ascendo ad Patrem meum, et Patrem vestrum, Deum meum, et Deum vestrum.

20:18 Venit Maria Magdalene annuntians discipulis : Quia vidi Dominum, et hæc dixit mihi.

20:19 Cum ergo sero esset die illo, una sabbatorum, et fores essent clausæ, ubi erant discipuli congregati propter metum Judæorum : venit Jesus, et stetit in medio, et dixit eis : Pax vobis.

20:20 Et cum hoc dixisset, ostendit eis manus et latus. Gavisi sunt ergo discipuli, viso Domino.

20:21 Dixit ergo eis iterum : Pax vobis. Sicut misit me Pater, et ego mitto vos.

20:22 Hæc cum dixisset, insufflavit, et dixit eis : Accipite Spiritum Sanctum :

20:23 quorum remiseritis peccata, remittuntur eis : et quorum retinueritis, retenta sunt.

20:24 Thomas autem unus ex duodecim, qui dicitur Didymus, non erat cum eis quando venit Jesus.

20:25 Dixerunt ergo ei alii discipuli : Vidimus Dominum. Ille autem dixit eis : Nisi videro in manibus ejus fixuram clavorum, et mittam digitum meum in locum clavorum, et mittam

20:11 But Mary stood at the sepulchre without, weeping. Now as she was weeping, she stooped down, and looked into the sepulchre,

20:12 And she saw two angels in white, sitting, one at the head, and one at the feet, where the body of Jesus had been laid.

20:13 They say to her: Woman, why weepest thou? She saith to them: Because they have taken away my Lord; and I know not where they have laid him.

20:14 When she had thus said, she turned herself back, and saw Jesus standing; and she knew not that it was Jesus.

20:15 Jesus saith to her: Woman, why weepest thou? whom seekest thou? She, thinking it was the gardener, saith to him: Sir, if thou hast taken him hence, tell me where thou hast laid him, and I will take him away.

20:16 Jesus saith to her: Mary. She turning, saith to him: Rabboni (which is to say, Master).

20:17 Jesus saith to her: Do not touch me, for I am not yet ascended to my Father. But go to my brethren, and say to them: I ascend to my Father and to your Father, to my God and your God.

20:18 Mary Magdalen cometh, and telleth the disciples: I have seen the Lord, and these things he said to me.

20:19 Now when it was late that same day, the first of the week, and the doors were shut, where the disciples were gathered together, for fear of the Jews, Jesus came and stood in the midst, and said to them: Peace be to you.

20:20 And when he had said this, he shewed them his hands and his side. The disciples therefore were glad, when they saw the Lord.

20:21 He said therefore to them again: Peace be to you. As the Father hath sent me, I also send you.

20:22 When he had said this, he breathed on them; and he said to them: Receive ye the Holy Ghost.

20:23 Whose sins you shall forgive, they are forgiven them; and whose sins you shall retain, they are retained.

20:24 Now Thomas, one of the twelve, who is called Didymus, was not with them when Jesus came.

20:25 The other disciples therefore said to him: We have seen the Lord. But he said to them: Except I shall see in his hands the print of the nails, and put my finger into the place of the

manum meam in latus ejus, non credam.

20:26 Et post dies octo, iterum erant discipuli ejus intus, et Thomas cum eis. Venit Jesus januis clausis, et stetit in medio, et dixit : Pax vobis.

20:27 Deinde dicit Thomæ : Infer digitum tuum huc, et vide manus meas, et affer manum tuam, et mitte in latus meum : et noli esse incredulus, sed fidelis.

20:28 Respondit Thomas, et dixit ei : Dominus meus et Deus meus.

20:29 Dixit ei Jesus : Quia vidisti me, Thoma, credidisti : beati qui non viderunt, et crediderunt.

20:30 Multa quidem et alia signa fecit Jesus in conspectu discipulorum suorum, quæ non sunt scripta in libro hoc.

20:31 Hæc autem scripta sunt ut credatis, quia Jesus est Christus Filius Dei : et ut credentes, vitam habeatis in nomine ejus.

21:1 Postea manifestavit se iterum Jesus discipulis ad mare Tiberiadis. Manifestavit autem sic :

21:2 erant simul Simon Petrus, et Thomas, qui dicitur Didymus, et Nathanaël, qui erat a Cana Galilææ, et filii Zebedæi, et alii ex discipulis ejus duo.

21:3 Dicit eis Simon Petrus : Vado piscari. Dicunt ei : Venimus et nos tecum. Et exierunt, et ascenderunt in navim : et illa nocte nihil prendiderunt.

21:4 Mane autem facto stetit Jesus in littore : non tamen cognoverunt discipuli quia Jesus est.

21:5 Dixit ergo eis Jesus : Pueri, numquid pulmentarium habetis ? Responderunt ei : Non.

21:6 Dicit eis : Mittite in dexteram navigii rete, et invenietis. Miserunt ergo : et jam non valebant illud trahere præ multitudine piscium.

21:7 Dixit ergo discipulus ille, quem diligebat Jesus, Petro : Dominus est. Simon Petrus cum audisset quia Dominus est, tunica succinxit se (erat enim nudus) et misit se in mare.

21:8 Alii autem discipuli navigio venerunt (non enim longe erant a terra, sed quasi cubitis ducentis), trahentes rete piscium.

21:9 Ut ergo descenderunt in terram, viderunt prunas positas, et piscem superpositum, et

nails, and put my hand into his side, I will not believe.

20:26 And after eight days again his disciples were within, and Thomas with them. Jesus cometh, the doors being shut, and stood in the midst, and said: Peace be to you.

20:27 Then he saith to Thomas: Put in thy finger hither, and see my hands; and bring hither thy hand, and put it into my side; and be not faithless, but believing.

20:28 Thomas answered, and said to him: My Lord, and my God.

20:29 Jesus saith to him: Because thou hast seen me, Thomas, thou hast believed: blessed are they that have not seen, and have believed.

20:30 Many other signs also did Jesus in the sight of his disciples, which are not written in this book.

20:31 But these are written, that you may believe that Jesus is the Christ, the Son of God: and that believing, you may have life in his name.

21:1 After this, Jesus shewed himself again to the disciples at the sea of Tiberias. And he shewed himself after this manner.

21:2 There were together Simon Peter, and Thomas, who is called Didymus, and Nathanael, who was of Cana of Galilee, and the sons of Zebedee, and two others of his disciples.

21:3 Simon Peter saith to them: I go a fishing. They say to him: We also come with thee. And they went forth, and entered into the ship: and that night they caught nothing.

21:4 But when the morning was come, Jesus stood on the shore: yet the disciples knew not that it was Jesus.

21:5 Jesus therefore said to them: Children, have you any meat? They answered him: No.

21:6 He saith to them: Cast the net on the right side of the ship, and you shall find. They cast therefore; and now they were not able to draw it, for the multitude of fishes.

21:7 That disciple therefore whom Jesus loved, said to Peter: It is the Lord. Simon Peter, when he heard that it was the Lord, girt his coat about him, (for he was naked,) and cast himself into the sea.

21:8 But the other disciples came in the ship, (for they were not far from the land, but as it were two hundred cubits,) dragging the net with fishes.

21:9 As soon then as they came to land, they saw hot coals lying, and a fish laid thereon, and

panem.

21:10 Dicit eis Jesus : Afferte de piscibus, quos prendidistis nunc.

21:11 Ascendit Simon Petrus et traxit rete in terram, plenum magnis piscibus centum quinquaginta tribus. Et cum tanti essent, non est scissum rete.

21:12 Dicit eis Jesus : Venite, prandete. Et nemo audebat discumbentium interrogare eum : Tu quis es ? scientes, quia Dominus est.

21:13 Et venit Jesus, et accipit panem, et dat eis, et piscem similiter.

21:14 Hoc jam tertio manifestatus est Jesus discipulis suis cum resurrexisset a mortuis.

21:15 Cum ergo prandissent, dicit Simoni Petro Jesus : Simon Joannis, diligis me plus his ? Dicit ei : Etiam Domine, tu scis quia amo te. Dicit ei : Pasce agnos meos.

21:16 Dicit ei iterum : Simon Joannis, diligis me ? Ait illi : Etiam Domine, tu scis quia amo te. Dicit ei : Pasce agnos meos.

21:17 Dicit ei tertio : Simon Joannis, amas me ? Contristatus est Petrus, quia dixit ei tertio : Amas me ? et dixit ei : Domine, tu omnia nosti, tu scis quia amo te. Dixit ei : Pasce oves meas.

21:18 Amen, amen dico tibi : cum esses junior, cingebas te, et ambulabas ubi volebas : cum autem senueris, extendes manus tuas, et alius te cinget, et ducet quo tu non vis.

21:19 Hoc autem dixit significans qua morte clarificaturus esset Deum. Et cum hoc dixisset, dicit ei : Sequere me.

21:20 Conversus Petrus vidit illum discipulum, quem diligebat Jesus, sequentem, qui et recubuit in cœna super pectus ejus, et dixit : Domine, quis est qui tradet te ?

21:21 Hunc ergo cum vidisset Petrus, dixit Jesu : Domine, hic autem quid ?

21:22 Dicit ei Jesus : Sic eum volo manere donec veniam, quid ad te ? tu me sequere.

21:23 Exiit ergo sermo iste inter fratres quia discipulus ille non moritur. Et non dixit ei Jesus : Non moritur, sed : Sic eum volo manere donec

bread.

21:10 Jesus saith to them: Bring hither of the fishes which you have now caught.

21:11 Simon Peter went up, and drew the net to land, full of great fishes, one hundred and fifty-three. And although there were so many, the net was not broken.

21:12 Jesus saith to them: Come, and dine. And none of them who were at meat, durst ask him: Who art thou? knowing that it was the Lord.

21:13 And Jesus cometh and taketh bread, and giveth them, and fish in like manner.

21:14 This is now the third time that Jesus was manifested to his disciples, after he was risen from the dead.

21:15 When therefore they had dined, Jesus saith to Simon Peter: Simon son of John, lovest thou me more than these? He saith to him: Yea, Lord, thou knowest that I love thee. He saith to him: Feed my lambs.

21:16 He saith to him again: Simon, son of John, lovest thou me? He saith to him: Yea, Lord, thou knowest that I love thee. He saith to him: Feed my lambs.

21:17 He said to him the third time: Simon, son of John, lovest thou me? Peter was grieved, because he had said to him the third time: Lovest thou me? And he said to him: Lord, thou knowest all things: thou knowest that I love thee. He said to him: Feed my sheep.

21:18 Amen, amen I say to thee, when thou wast younger, thou didst gird thyself, and didst walk where thou wouldst. But when thou shalt be old, thou shalt stretch forth thy hands, and another shall gird thee, and lead thee whither thou wouldst not.

21:19 And this he said, signifying by what death he should glorify God. And when he had said this, he saith to him: Follow me.

21:20 Peter turning about, saw that disciple whom Jesus loved following, who also leaned on his breast at supper, and said: Lord, who is he that shall betray thee?

21:21 Him therefore when Peter had seen, he saith to Jesus: Lord, and what shall this man do?

21:22 Jesus saith to him: So I will have him to remain till I come, what is it to thee? follow thou me.

21:23 This saying therefore went abroad among the brethren, that that disciple should not die. And Jesus did not say to him: He should not

veniam, quid ad te ?

21:24 Hic est discipulus ille qui testimonium perhibet de his, et scripsit hæc : et scimus quia verum est testimonium ejus.

21:25 Sunt autem et alia multa quæ fecit Jesus : quæ si scribantur per singula, nec ipsum arbitror mundum capere posse eos, qui scribendi sunt, libros.

die; but, So I will have him to remain till I come, what is it to thee?

21:24 This is that disciple who giveth testimony of these things, and hath written these things; and we know that his testimony is true.

21:25 But there are also many other things which Jesus did; which, if they were written every one, the world itself, I think, would not be able to contain the books that should be written.

𝔄𝔠𝔱𝔲𝔰 𝔄𝔭𝔬𝔰𝔱𝔬𝔩𝔬𝔯𝔲𝔪

THE ACTS OF THE APOSTLES

1:1 PRIMUM QUIDEM SERMONEM feci de omnibus, o Theophile, quæ cœpit Jesus facere et docere

1:2 usque in diem qua præcipiens Apostolis per Spiritum Sanctum, quos elegit, assumptus est :

1:3 quibus et præbuit seipsum vivum post passionem suam in multis argumentis, per dies quadraginta apparens eis, et loquens de regno Dei.

1:4 Et convescens, præcepit eis ab Jerosolymis ne discederent, sed exspectarent promissionem Patris, quam audistis (inquit) per os meum :

1:5 quia Joannes quidem baptizavit aqua, vos autem baptizabimini Spiritu Sancto non post multos hos dies.

1:6 Igitur qui convenerant, interrogabant eum, dicentes : Domine, si in tempore hoc restitues regnum Israël ?

1:7 Dixit autem eis : Non est vestrum nosse tempora vel momenta quæ Pater posuit in sua potestate :

1:8 sed accipietis virtutem supervenientis Spiritus Sancti in vos, et eritis mihi testes in Jerusalem, et in omni Judæa, et Samaria, et usque ad ultimum terræ.

1:9 Et cum hæc dixisset, videntibus illis, elevatus est : et nubes suscepit eum ab oculis eorum.

1:10 Cumque intuerentur in cælum euntem illum, ecce duo viri astiterunt juxta illos in vestibus albis,

1:1 THE FORMER TREATISE I made, O Theophilus, of all things which Jesus began to do and to teach,

1:2 Until the day on which, giving commandments by the Holy Ghost to the apostles whom he had chosen, he was taken up.

1:3 To whom also he shewed himself alive after his passion, by many proofs, for forty days appearing to them, and speaking of the kingdom of God.

1:4 And eating together with them, he commanded them, that they should not depart from Jerusalem, but should wait for the promise of the Father, which you have heard (saith he) by my mouth.

1:5 For John indeed baptized with water, but you shall be baptized with the Holy Ghost, not many days hence.

1:6 They therefore who were come together, asked him, saying: Lord, wilt thou at this time restore again the kingdom to Israel?

1:7 But he said to them: It is not for you to know the times or moments, which the Father hath put in his own power:

1:8 But you shall receive the power of the Holy Ghost coming upon you, and you shall be witnesses unto me in Jerusalem, and in all Judea, and Samaria, and even to the uttermost part of the earth.

1:9 And when he had said these things, while they looked on, he was raised up: and a cloud received him out of their sight.

1:10 And while they were beholding him going up to heaven, behold two men stood by them in white garments.

1:11 qui et dixerunt : Viri Galilæi, quid statis aspicientes in cælum ? Hic Jesus, qui assumptus est a vobis in cælum, sic veniet quemadmodum vidistis eum euntem in cælum.

1:12 Tunc reversi sunt Jerosolymam a monte qui vocatur Oliveti, qui est juxta Jerusalem, sabbati habens iter.

1:13 Et cum introissent in cœnaculum, ascenderunt ubi manebant Petrus, et Joannes, Jacobus, et Andreas, Philippus, et Thomas, Bartholomæus, et Matthæus, Jacobus Alphæi, et Simon Zelotes, et Judas Jacobi.

1:14 Hi omnes erant perseverantes unanimiter in oratione cum mulieribus, et Maria matre Jesu, et fratribus ejus.

1:15 In diebus illis, exsurgens Petrus in medio fratrum, dixit (erat autem turba hominum simul, fere centum viginti) :

1:16 Viri fratres, oportet impleri Scripturam quam prædixit Spiritus Sanctus per os David de Juda, qui fuit dux eorum qui comprehenderunt Jesum :

1:17 qui connumeratus erat in nobis, et sortitus est sortem ministerii hujus.

1:18 Et hic quidem possedit agrum de mercede iniquitatis, et suspensus crepuit medius : et diffusa sunt omnia viscera ejus.

1:19 Et notum factum est omnibus habitantibus Jerusalem, ita ut appellaretur ager ille, lingua eorum, Haceldama, hoc est, ager sanguinis.

1:20 Scriptum est enim in libro Psalmorum : Fiat commoratio eorum deserta, et non sit qui inhabitet in ea : et episcopatum ejus accipiat alter.

1:21 Oportet ergo ex his viris qui nobiscum sunt congregati in omni tempore quo intravit et exivit inter nos Dominus Jesus,

1:22 incipiens a baptismate Joannis usque in diem qua assumptus est a nobis, testem resurrectionis ejus nobiscum fieri unum ex istis.

1:23 Et statuerunt duos, Joseph, qui vocabatur Barsabas, qui cognominatus est Justus, et Mathiam.

1:24 Et orantes dixerunt : Tu Domine, qui corda nosti omnium, ostende quem elegeris ex his duobus unum,

1:25 accipere locum ministerii hujus et apostolatus, de quo prævaricatus est Judas ut abiret in

1:11 Who also said: Ye men of Galilee, why stand you looking up to heaven? This Jesus who is taken up from you into heaven, shall so come, as you have seen him going into heaven.

1:12 Then they returned to Jerusalem from the mount that is called Olivet, which is nigh Jerusalem, within a sabbath day's journey.

1:13 And when they were come in, they went up into an upper room, where abode Peter and John, James and Andrew, Philip and Thomas, Bartholomew and Matthew, James of Alpheus, and Simon Zelotes, and Jude the brother of James.

1:14 All these were persevering with one mind in prayer with the women, and Mary the mother of Jesus, and with his brethren.

1:15 In those days Peter rising up in the midst of the brethren, said: (now the number of persons together was about an hundred and twenty:)

1:16 Men, brethren, the scripture must needs be fulfilled, which the Holy Ghost spoke before by the mouth of David concerning Judas, who was the leader of them that apprehended Jesus:

1:17 Who was numbered with us, and had obtained part of this ministry.

1:18 And he indeed hath possessed a field of the reward of iniquity, and being hanged, burst asunder in the midst: and all his bowels gushed out.

1:19 And it became known to all the inhabitants of Jerusalem: so that the same field was called in their tongue, Haceldama, that is to say, The field of blood.

1:20 For it is written in the book of Psalms: Let their habitation become desolate, and let there be none to dwell therein. And his bishopric let another take.

1:21 Wherefore of these men who have companied with us all the time that the Lord Jesus came in and went out among us,

1:22 Beginning from the baptism of John, until the day wherein he was taken up from us, one of these must be made a witness with us of his resurrection.

1:23 And they appointed two, Joseph, called Barsabas, who was surnamed Justus, and Matthias.

1:24 And praying, they said: Thou, Lord, who knowest the hearts of all men, shew whether of these two thou hast chosen,

1:25 To take the place of this ministry and apostleship, from which Judas hath by trans-

1:26 Et dederunt sortes eis, et cecidit sors super Mathiam : et annumeratus est cum undecim Apostolis.

2:1 Et cum complerentur dies Pentecostes, erant omnes pariter in eodem loco :

2:2 et factus est repente de cælo sonus, tamquam advenientis spiritus vehementis, et replevit totam domum ubi erant sedentes.

2:3 Et apparuerunt illis dispertitæ linguæ tamquam ignis, seditque supra singulos eorum :

2:4 et repleti sunt omnes Spiritu Sancto, et cœperunt loqui variis linguis, prout Spiritus Sanctus dabat eloqui illis.

2:5 Erant autem in Jerusalem habitantes Judæi, viri religiosi ex omni natione quæ sub cælo est.

2:6 Facta autem hac voce, convenit multitudo, et mente confusa est, quoniam audiebat unusquisque lingua sua illos loquentes.

2:7 Stupebant autem omnes, et mirabantur, dicentes : Nonne ecce omnes isti qui loquuntur, Galilæi sunt ?

2:8 et quomodo nos audivimus unusquisque linguam nostram in qua nati sumus ?

2:9 Parthi, et Medi, et Ælamitæ, et qui habitant Mesopotamiam, Judæam, et Cappadociam, Pontum, et Asiam,

2:10 Phrygiam, et Pamphyliam, Ægyptum, et partes Libyæ quæ est circa Cyrenen : et advenæ Romani,

2:11 Judæi quoque, et Proselyti, Cretes, et Arabes : audivimus eos loquentes nostris linguis magnalia Dei.

2:12 Stupebant autem omnes, et mirabantur ad invicem, dicentes : Quidnam vult hoc esse ?

2:13 Alii autem irridentes dicebant : Quia musto pleni sunt isti.

2:14 Stans autem Petrus cum undecim, levavit vocem suam, et locutus est eis : Viri Judæi, et qui habitatis Jerusalem universi, hoc vobis notum sit, et auribus percipite verba mea.

2:15 Non enim, sicut vos æstimatis, hi ebrii sunt, cum sit hora diei tertia :

2:16 sed hoc est quod dictum est per prophetam

gression fallen, that he might go to his own place.

1:26 And they gave them lots, and the lot fell upon Matthias, and he was numbered with the eleven apostles.

2:1 And when the days of the Pentecost were accomplished, they were all together in one place:

2:2 And suddenly there came a sound from heaven, as of a mighty wind coming, and it filled the whole house where they were sitting.

2:3 And there appeared to them parted tongues as it were of fire, and it sat upon every one of them:

2:4 And they were all filled with the Holy Ghost, and they began to speak with divers tongues, according as the Holy Ghost gave them to speak.

2:5 Now there were dwelling at Jerusalem, Jews, devout men, out of every nation under heaven.

2:6 And when this was noised abroad, the multitude came together, and were confounded in mind, because that every man heard them speak in his own tongue.

2:7 And they were all amazed, and wondered, saying: Behold, are not all these, that speak, Galileans?

2:8 And how have we heard, every man our own tongue wherein we were born?

2:9 Parthians, and Medes, and Elamites, and inhabitants of Mesopotamia, Judea, and Cappadocia, Pontus and Asia,

2:10 Phrygia, and Pamphylia, Egypt, and the parts of Libya about Cyrene, and strangers of Rome,

2:11 Jews also, and proselytes, Cretes, and Arabians: we have heard them speak in our own tongues the wonderful works of God.

2:12 And they were all astonished, and wondered, saying one to another: What meaneth this?

2:13 But others mocking, said: These men are full of new wine.

2:14 But Peter standing up with the eleven, lifted up his voice, and spoke to them: Ye men of Judea, and all you that dwell in Jerusalem, be this known to you, and with your ears receive my words.

2:15 For these are not drunk, as you suppose, seeing it is but the third hour of the day:

2:16 But this is that which was spoken of by the

Joël :

2:17 *Et erit in novissimis diebus, dicit Dominus, effundam de Spiritu meo super omnem carnem : et prophetabunt filii vestri et filiæ vestræ, et juvenes vestri visiones videbunt, et seniores vestri somnia somniabunt.*

2:18 *Et quidem super servos meos, et super ancillas meas, in diebus illis effundam de Spiritu meo, et prophetabunt :*

2:19 *et dabo prodigia in cælo sursum, et signa in terra deorsum, sanguinem, et ignem, et vaporem fumi :*

2:20 *sol convertetur in tenebras, et luna in sanguinem, antequam veniat dies Domini magnus et manifestus.*

2:21 *Et erit : omnis quicumque invocaverit nomen Domini, salvus erit.*

2:22 Viri Israëlitæ, audite verba hæc : Jesum Nazarenum, virum approbatum a Deo in vobis, virtutibus, et prodigiis, et signis, quæ fecit Deus per illum in medio vestri, sicut et vos scitis :

2:23 hunc, definito consilio et præscientia Dei traditum, per manus iniquorum affligentes interemistis :

2:24 quem Deus suscitavit, solutis doloribus inferni, juxta quod impossibile erat teneri illum ab eo.

2:25 David enim dicit in eum : *Providebam Dominum in conspectu meo semper : quoniam a dextris est mihi, ne commovear :*

2:26 *propter hoc lætatum est cor meum, et exsultavit lingua mea, insuper et caro mea requiescet in spe :*

2:27 *quoniam non derelinques animam meam in inferno, nec dabis sanctum tuum videre corruptionem.*

2:28 *Notas mihi fecisti vias vitæ : et replebis me jucunditate cum facie tua.*

2:29 Viri fratres, liceat audenter dicere ad vos de patriarcha David, quoniam defunctus est, et sepultus : et sepulchrum ejus est apud nos usque in hodiernum diem.

2:30 Propheta igitur cum esset, et sciret quia jurejurando jurasset illi Deus de fructu lumbi ejus sedere super sedem ejus :

2:31 providens locutus est de resurrectione Christi, quia neque derelictus est in inferno, neque caro ejus vidit corruptionem.

2:32 Hunc Jesum resuscitavit Deus, cujus omnes nos testes sumus.

prophet Joel:

2:17 *And it shall come to pass, in the last days, (saith the Lord,) I will pour out of my Spirit upon all flesh: and your sons and your daughters shall prophesy, and your young men shall see visions, and your old men shall dream dreams.*

2:18 *And upon my servants indeed, and upon my handmaids will I pour out in those days of my spirit, and they shall prophesy.*

2:19 *And I will shew wonders in the heaven above, and signs on the earth beneath: blood and fire, and vapour of smoke.*

2:20 *The sun shall be turned into darkness, and the moon into blood, before the great and manifest day of the Lord come.*

2:21 *And it shall come to pass, that whosoever shall call upon the name of the Lord, shall be saved.*

2:22 Ye men of Israel, hear these words: Jesus of Nazareth, a man approved of God among you, by miracles, and wonders, and signs, which God did by him, in the midst of you, as you also know:

2:23 This same being delivered up, by the determinate counsel and foreknowledge of God, you by the hands of wicked men have crucified and slain.

2:24 Whom God hath raised up, having loosed the sorrows of hell, as it was impossible that he should be holden by it.

2:25 For David saith concerning him: *I foresaw the Lord before my face: because he is at my right hand, that I may not be moved.*

2:26 *For this my heart hath been glad, and my tongue hath rejoiced: moreover my flesh also shall rest in hope.*

2:27 *Because thou wilt not leave my soul in hell, nor suffer thy Holy One to see corruption.*

2:28 *Thou hast made known to me the ways of life: thou shalt make me full of joy with thy countenance.*

2:29 Ye men, brethren, let me freely speak to you of the patriarch David; that he died, and was buried; and his sepulchre is with us to this present day.

2:30 Whereas therefore he was a prophet, and knew that God hath sworn to him with an oath, that of the fruit of his loins one should sit upon his throne.

2:31 Foreseeing this, he spoke of the resurrection of Christ. For neither was he left in hell, neither did his flesh see corruption.

2:32 This Jesus hath God raised again, whereof all we are witnesses.

2:33 Dextera igitur Dei exaltatus, et promissione Spiritus Sancti accepta a Patre, effudit hunc, quem vos videtis et auditis.

2:34 Non enim David ascendit in cælum : dixit autem ipse : *Dixit Dominus Domino meo : Sede a dextris meis,*
2:35 *donec ponam inimicos tuos scabellum pedum tuorum.*
2:36 Certissime sciat ergo omnis domus Israël, quia et Dominum eum et Christum fecit Deus hunc Jesum, quem vos crucifixistis.

2:37 His autem auditis, compuncti sunt corde, et dixerunt ad Petrum et ad reliquos Apostolos : Quid faciemus, viri fratres ?

2:38 Petrus vero ad illos : Pœnitentiam, inquit, agite, et baptizetur unusquisque vestrum in nomine Jesu Christi in remissionem peccatorum vestrorum : et accipietis donum Spiritus Sancti.
2:39 Vobis enim est repromissio, et filiis vestris, et omnibus qui longe sunt, quoscumque advocaverit Dominus Deus noster.
2:40 Aliis etiam verbis plurimis testificatus est, et exhortabatur eos, dicens : Salvamini a generatione ista prava.
2:41 Qui ergo receperunt sermonem ejus, baptizati sunt : et appositæ sunt in die illa animæ circiter tria millia.
2:42 Erant autem perseverantes in doctrina Apostolorum, et communicatione fractionis panis, et orationibus.
2:43 Fiebat autem omni animæ timor : multa quoque prodigia et signa per Apostolos in Jerusalem fiebant, et metus erat magnus in universis.
2:44 Omnes etiam qui credebant, erant pariter, et habebant omnia communia.
2:45 Possessiones et substantias vendebant, et dividebant illa omnibus, prout cuique opus erat.
2:46 Quotidie quoque perdurantes unanimiter in templo, et frangentes circa domos panem, sumebant cibum cum exsultatione et simplicitate cordis,
2:47 collaudantes Deum et habentes gratiam ad omnem plebem. Dominus autem augebat qui salvi fierent quotidie in idipsum.

2:33 Being exalted therefore by the right hand of God, and having received of the Father the promise of the Holy Ghost, he hath poured forth this which you see and hear.

2:34 For David ascended not into heaven; but he himself said: *The Lord said to my Lord, sit thou on my right hand,*
2:35 *Until I make thy enemies thy footstool.*

2:36 Therefore let all the house of Israel know most certainly, that God hath made both Lord and Christ, this same Jesus, whom you have crucified.

2:37 Now when they had heard these things, they had compunction in their heart, and said to Peter, and to the rest of the apostles: What shall we do, men and brethren?

2:38 But Peter said to them: Do penance, and be baptized every one of you in the name of Jesus Christ, for the remission of your sins: and you shall receive the gift of the Holy Ghost.

2:39 For the promise is to you, and to your children, and to all that are far off, whomsoever the Lord our God shall call.

2:40 And with very many other words did he testify and exhort them, saying: Save yourselves from this perverse generation.

2:41 They therefore that received his word, were baptized; and there were added in that day about three thousand souls.

2:42 And they were persevering in the doctrine of the apostles, and in the communication of the breaking of bread, and in prayers.

2:43 And fear came upon every soul: many wonders also and signs were done by the apostles in Jerusalem, and there was great fear in all.

2:44 And all they that believed, were together, and had all things common.

2:45 Their possessions and goods they sold, and divided them to all, according as every one had need.

2:46 And continuing daily with one accord in the temple, and breaking bread from house to house, they took their meat with gladness and simplicity of heart;

2:47 Praising God, and having favour with all the people. And the Lord increased daily together such as should be saved.

3:1 Petrus autem et Joannes ascendebant in templum ad horam orationis nonam.

3:2 Et quidam vir, qui erat claudus ex utero matris suæ, bajulabatur : quem ponebant quotidie ad portam templi, quæ dicitur Speciosa, ut peteret eleemosynam ab introëuntibus in templum.

3:3 Is cum vidisset Petrum et Joannem incipientes introire in templum, rogabat ut eleemosynam acciperet.

3:4 Intuens autem in eum Petrus cum Joanne, dixit : Respice in nos.

3:5 At ille intendebat in eos, sperans se aliquid accepturum ab eis.

3:6 Petrus autem dixit : Argentum et aurum non est mihi : quod autem habeo, hoc tibi do : in nomine Jesu Christi Nazareni surge, et ambula.

3:7 Et apprehensa manu ejus dextera, allevavit eum, et protinus consolidatæ sunt bases ejus et plantæ.

3:8 Et exiliens stetit, et ambulabat : et intravit cum illis in templum ambulans, et exiliens, et laudans Deum.

3:9 Et vidit omnis populus eum ambulantem et laudantem Deum.

3:10 Cognoscebant autem illum, quod ipse erat qui ad eleemosynam sedebat ad Speciosam portam templi : et impleti sunt stupore et extasi in eo quod contigerat illi.

3:11 Cum teneret autem Petrum et Joannem, cucurrit omnis populus ad eos ad porticum quæ appellatur Salomonis, stupentes.

3:12 Videns autem Petrus, respondit ad populum : Viri Israëlitæ, quid miramini in hoc, aut nos quid intuemini, quasi nostra virtute aut potestate fecerimus hunc ambulare ?

3:13 Deus Abraham, et Deus Isaac, et Deus Jacob, Deus patrum nostrorum glorificavit filium suum Jesum, quem vos quidem tradidistis, et negastis ante faciem Pilati, judicante illo dimitti.

3:14 Vos autem sanctum et justum negastis, et petistis virum homicidam donari vobis :

3:15 auctorem vero vitæ interfecistis, quem Deus suscitavit a mortuis, cujus nos testes sumus.

3:16 Et in fide nominis ejus, hunc quem vos vidistis et nostis, confirmavit nomen ejus : et fides, quæ per eum est, dedit integram sanitatem istam in conspectu omnium vestrum.

3:1 Now Peter and John went up into the temple at the ninth hour of prayer.

3:2 And a certain man who was lame from his mother's womb, was carried: whom they laid every day at the gate of the temple, which is called Beautiful, that he might ask alms of them that went into the temple.

3:3 He, when he had seen Peter and John about to go into the temple, asked to receive an alms.

3:4 But Peter with John fastening his eyes upon him, said: Look upon us.

3:5 But he looked earnestly upon them, hoping that he should receive something of them.

3:6 But Peter said: Silver and gold I have none; but what I have, I give thee: In the name of Jesus Christ of Nazareth, arise, and walk.

3:7 And taking him by the right hand, he lifted him up, and forthwith his feet and soles received strength.

3:8 And he leaping up, stood, and walked, and went in with them into the temple, walking, and leaping, and praising God.

3:9 And all the people saw him walking and praising God.

3:10 And they knew him, that it was he who sat begging alms at the Beartiful gate of the temple: and they were filled with wonder and amazement at that which had happened to him.

3:11 And as he held Peter and John, all the people ran to them to the porch which is called Solomon's, greatly wondering.

3:12 But Peter seeing, made answer to the people: Ye men of Israel, why wonder you at this? or why look you upon us, as if by our strength or power we had made this man to walk?

3:13 The God of Abraham, and the God of Isaac, and the God of Jacob, the God of our fathers, hath glorified his Son Jesus, whom you indeed delivered up and denied before the face of Pilate, when he judged he should be released.

3:14 But you denied the Holy One and the Just, and desired a murderer to be granted unto you.

3:15 But the author of life you killed, whom God hath raised from the dead, of which we are witnesses.

3:16 And in the faith of his name, this man, whom you have seen and known, hath his name strengthened; and the faith which is by him, hath given this perfect soundness in the sight of you all.

3:17 Et nunc, fratres, scio quia per ignorantiam fecistis, sicut et principes vestri.

3:18 Deus autem, quæ prænuntiavit per os omnium prophetarum, pati Christum suum, sic implevit.

3:19 Pœnitemini igitur et convertimini, ut deleantur peccata vestra :

3:20 ut cum venerint tempora refrigerii a conspectu Domini, et miserit eum qui prædicatus est vobis, Jesum Christum,

3:21 quem oportet quidem cælum suscipere usque in tempora restitutionis omnium quæ locutus est Deus per os sanctorum suorum a sæculo prophetarum.

3:22 Moyses quidem dixit : Quoniam prophetam suscitabit vobis Dominus Deus vester de fratribus vestris, tamquam me : ipsum audietis juxta omnia quæcumque locutus fuerit vobis.

3:23 Erit autem : omnis anima quæ non audierit prophetam illum, exterminabitur de plebe.

3:24 Et omnes prophetæ, a Samuel et deinceps, qui locuti sunt, annuntiaverunt dies istos.

3:25 Vos estis filii prophetarum, et testamenti quod disposuit Deus ad patres nostros, dicens ad Abraham : Et in semine tuo benedicentur omnes familiæ terræ.

3:26 Vobis primum Deus suscitans filium suum, misit eum benedicentem vobis : ut convertat se unusquisque a nequitia sua.

4:1 Loquentibus autem illis ad populum, supervenerunt sacerdotes, et magistratus templi, et sadducæi,

4:2 dolentes quod docerent populum, et annuntiarent in Jesu resurrectionem ex mortuis :

4:3 et injecerunt in eos manus, et posuerunt eos in custodiam in crastinum : erat enim jam vespera.

4:4 Multi autem eorum qui audierant verbum, crediderunt : et factus est numerus virorum quinque millia.

4:5 Factum est autem in crastinum, ut congregarentur principes eorum, et seniores, et scribæ, in Jerusalem :

4:6 et Annas princeps sacerdotum, et Caiphas, et Joannes, et Alexander, et quotquot erant de genere sacerdotali.

4:7 Et statuentes eos in medio, interrogabant : In qua virtute, aut in quo nomine fecistis hoc

3:17 And now, brethren, I know that you did it through ignorance, as did also your rulers.

3:18 But those things which God before had shewed by the mouth of all the prophets, that his Christ should suffer, he hath so fulfilled.

3:19 Be penitent, therefore, and be converted, that your sins may be blotted out.

3:20 That when the times of refreshment shall come from the presence of the Lord, and he shall send him who hath been preached unto you, Jesus Christ,

3:21 Whom heaven indeed must receive, until the times of the restitution of all things, which God hath spoken by the mouth of his holy prophets, from the beginning of the world.

3:22 For Moses said: A prophet shall the Lord your God raise up unto you of your brethren, like unto me: him you shall hear according to all things whatsoever he shall speak to you.

3:23 And it shall be, that every soul which will not hear that prophet, shall be destroyed from among the people.

3:24 And all the prophets, from Samuel and afterwards, who have spoken, have told of these days.

3:25 You are the children of the prophets, and of the testament which God made to our fathers, saying to Abraham: And in thy seed shall all the kindreds of the earth be blessed.

3:26 To you first God, raising up his Son, hath sent him to bless you; that every one may convert himself from his wickedness.

4:1 And as they were speaking to the people, the priests, and the officer of the temple, and the Sadducees, came upon them,

4:2 Being grieved that they taught the people, and preached in Jesus the resurrection from the dead:

4:3 And they laid hands upon them, and put them in hold till the next day; for it was now evening.

4:4 But many of them who had heard the word, believed; and the number of the men was made five thousand.

4:5 And it came to pass on the morrow, that their princes, and ancients, and scribes, were gathered together in Jerusalem;

4:6 And Annas the high priest, and Caiphas, and John, and Alexander, and as many as were of the kindred of the high priest.

4:7 And setting them in the midst, they asked: By what power, or by what name, have you

vos ?

4:8 Tunc repletus Spiritu Sancto Petrus, dixit ad eos : Principes populi, et seniores, audite :

4:9 si nos hodie dijudicamur in benefacto hominis infirmi, in quo iste salvus factus est,

4:10 notum sit omnibus vobis, et omni plebi Israël, quia in nomine Domini nostri Jesu Christi Nazareni, quem vos crucifixistis, quem Deus suscitavit a mortuis, in hoc iste astat coram vobis sanus.

4:11 Hic est lapis qui reprobatus est a vobis ædificantibus, qui factus est in caput anguli :

4:12 et non est in alio aliquo salus. Nec enim aliud nomen est sub cælo datum hominibus, in quo oporteat nos salvos fieri.

4:13 Videntes autem Petri constantiam, et Joannis, comperto quod homines essent sine litteris, et idiotæ, admirabantur, et cognoscebant eos quoniam cum Jesu fuerant :

4:14 hominem quoque videntes stantem cum eis, qui curatus fuerat, nihil poterant contradicere.

4:15 Jusserunt autem eos foras extra concilium secedere : et conferebant ad invicem,

4:16 dicentes : Quid faciemus hominibus istis ? quoniam quidem notum signum factum est per eos omnibus habitantibus Jerusalem : manifestum est, et non possumus negare.

4:17 Sed ne amplius divulgetur in populum, comminemur eis ne ultra loquantur in nomine hoc ulli hominum.

4:18 Et vocantes eos, denuntiaverunt ne omnino loquerentur neque docerent in nomine Jesu.

4:19 Petrus vero et Joannes respondentes, dixerunt ad eos : Si justum est in conspectu Dei vos potius audire quam Deum, judicate.

4:20 Non enim possumus quæ vidimus et audivimus non loqui.

4:21 At illi comminantes dimiserunt eos, non invenientes quomodo punirent eos propter populum : quia omnes clarificabant id quod factum fuerat in eo quod acciderat.

4:22 Annorum enim erat amplius quadraginta homo, in quo factum fuerat signum istud sanitatis.

4:23 Dimissi autem venerunt ad suos, et annuntiaverunt eis quanta ad eos principes sacerdotum et seniores dixissent.

done this?

4:8 Then Peter, filled with the Holy Ghost, said to them: Ye princes of the people, and ancients, hear:

4:9 If we this day are examined concerning the good deed done to the infirm man, by what means he hath been made whole:

4:10 Be it known to you all, and to all the people of Israel, that by the name of our Lord Jesus Christ of Nazareth, whom you crucified, whom God hath raised from the dead, even by him this man standeth here before you whole.

4:11 This is the stone which was rejected by you the builders, which is become the head of the corner.

4:12 Neither is there salvation in any other. For there is no other name under heaven given to men, whereby we must be saved.

4:13 Now seeing the constancy of Peter and of John, understanding that they were illiterate and ignorant men, they wondered; and they knew them that they had been with Jesus.

4:14 Seeing the man also who had been healed standing with them, they could say nothing against it.

4:15 But they commanded them to go aside out of the council; and they conferred among themselves,

4:16 Saying: What shall we do to these men? for indeed a known miracle hath been done by them, to all the inhabitants of Jerusalem: it is manifest, and we cannot deny it.

4:17 But that it may be no farther spread among the people, let us threaten them that they speak no more in this name to any man.

4:18 And calling them, they charged them not to speak at all, nor teach in the name of Jesus.

4:19 But Peter and John answering, said to them: If it be just in the sight of God, to hear you rather than God, judge ye.

4:20 For we cannot but speak the things which we have seen and heard.

4:21 But they threatening, sent them away, not finding how they might punish them, because of the people; for all men glorified what had been done, in that which had come to pass.

4:22 For the man was above forty years old, in whom that miraculous cure had been wrought.

4:23 And being let go, they came to their own company, and related all that the chief priests and ancients had said to them.

4:24 Qui cum audissent, unanimiter levaverunt vocem ad Deum, et dixerunt : Domine, tu es qui fecisti cælum et terram, mare et omnia quæ in eis sunt :

4:25 qui Spiritu Sancto per os patris nostri David pueri tui dixisti : *Quare fremuerunt gentes, et populi meditati sunt inania ?*

4:26 *Astiterunt reges terræ, et principes convenerunt in unum adversus Dominum, et adversus Christum ejus.*

4:27 Convenerunt enim vere in civitate ista adversus sanctum puerum tuum Jesum, quem unxisti, Herodes et Pontius Pilatus, cum gentibus et populis Israël,

4:28 facere quæ manus tua et consilium tuum decreverunt fieri.

4:29 Et nunc, Domine, respice in minas eorum, et da servis tuis cum omni fiducia loqui verbum tuum,

4:30 in eo quod manum tuam extendas ad sanitates, et signa, et prodigia fieri per nomen sancti filii tui Jesu.

4:31 Et cum orassent, motus est locus in quo erant congregati : et repleti sunt omnes Spiritu Sancto, et loquebantur verbum Dei cum fiducia.

4:32 Multitudinis autem credentium erat cor unum et anima una : nec quisquam eorum quæ possidebat, aliquid suum esse dicebat, sed erant illis omnia communia.

4:33 Et virtute magna reddebant Apostoli testimonium resurrectionis Jesu Christi Domini nostri : et gratia magna erat in omnibus illis.

4:34 Neque enim quisquam egens erat inter illos. Quotquot enim possessores agrorum aut domorum erant, vendentes afferebant pretia eorum quæ vendebant,

4:35 et ponebant ante pedes Apostolorum. Dividebatur autem singulis prout cuique opus erat.

4:36 Joseph autem, qui cognominatus est Barnabas ab Apostolis (quod est interpretatum, Filius consolationis), Levites, Cyprius genere,

4:37 cum haberet agrum, vendidit eum, et attulit pretium, et posuit ante pedes Apostolorum.

5:1 Vir autem quidam nomine Ananias, cum Saphira uxore suo vendidit agrum,

5:2 et fraudavit de pretio agri, conscia uxore sua : et afferens partem quamdam, ad pedes Apostolorum posuit.

4:24 Who having heard it, with one accord lifted up their voice to God, and said: Lord, thou art he that didst make heaven and earth, the sea, and all things that are in them.

4:25 Who, by the Holy Ghost, by the mouth of our father David, thy servant, hast said: *Why did the Gentiles rage, and the people meditate vain things?*

4:26 *The kings of the earth stood up, and the princes assembled together against the Lord and his Christ.*

4:27 For of a truth there assembled together in this city against thy holy child Jesus, whom thou hast anointed, Herod, and Pontius Pilate, with the Gentiles and the people of Israel,

4:28 To do what thy hand and thy counsel decreed to be done.

4:29 And now, Lord, behold their threatenings, and grant unto thy servants, that with all confidence they may speak thy word,

4:30 By stretching forth thy hand to cures, and signs, and wonders to be done by the name of thy holy Son Jesus.

4:31 And when they had prayed, the place was moved wherein they were assembled; and they were all filled with the Holy Ghost, and they spoke the word of God with confidence.

4:32 And the multitude of believers had but one heart and one soul: neither did any one say that aught of the things which he possessed, was his own; but all things were common unto them.

4:33 And with great power did the apostles give testimony of the resurrection of Jesus Christ our Lord; and great grace was in them all.

4:34 For neither was there any one needy among them. For as many as were owners of lands or houses, sold them, and brought the price of the things they sold,

4:35 And laid it down before the feet of the apostles. And distribution was made to every one, according as he had need.

4:36 And Joseph, who, by the apostles, was surnamed Barnabas, (which is, by interpretation, The son of consolation,) a Levite, a Cyprian born,

4:37 Having land, sold it, and brought the price, and laid it at the feet of the apostles.

5:1 But a certain man named Ananias, with Saphira his wife, sold a piece of land,

5:2 And by fraud kept back part of the price of the land, his wife being privy thereunto: and bringing a certain part of it, laid it at the feet of the apostles.

5:3 Dixit autem Petrus : Anania, cur tentavit Satanas cor tuum, mentiri te Spiritui Sancto, et fraudare de pretio agri ?

5:4 nonne manens tibi manebat, et venundatum in tua erat potestate ? quare posuisti in corde tuo hanc rem ? non es mentitus hominibus, sed Deo.

5:5 Audiens autem Ananias hæc verba, cecidit, et expiravit. Et factus est timor magnus super omnes qui audierunt.

5:6 Surgentes autem juvenes amoverunt eum, et efferentes sepelierunt.

5:7 Factum est autem quasi horarum trium spatium, et uxor ipsius, nesciens quod factum fuerat, introivit.

5:8 Dixit autem ei Petrus : Dic mihi mulier, si tanti agrum vendidistis ? At illa dixit : Etiam tanti.

5:9 Petrus autem ad eam : Quid utique convenit vobis tentare Spiritum Domini ? Ecce pedes eorum qui sepelierunt virum tuum ad ostium, et efferent te.

5:10 Confestim cecidit ante pedes ejus, et expiravit. Intrantes autem juvenes invenerunt illam mortuam : et extulerunt, et sepelierunt ad virum suum.

5:11 Et factus est timor magnus in universa ecclesia, et in omnes qui audierunt hæc.

5:12 Per manus autem Apostolorum fiebant signa et prodigia multa in plebe. Et erant unanimiter omnes in porticu Salomonis.

5:13 Ceterorum autem nemo audebat se conjungere illis : sed magnificabat eos populus.

5:14 Magis autem augebatur credentium in Domino multitudo virorum ac mulierum,

5:15 ita ut in plateas ejicerent infirmos, et ponerent in lectulis et grabatis, ut, veniente Petro, saltem umbra illius obumbraret quemquam illorum, et liberarentur ab infirmitatibus suis.

5:16 Concurrebat autem et multitudo vicinarum civitatum Jerusalem, afferentes ægros, et vexatos a spiritibus immundis : qui curabantur omnes.

5:17 Exsurgens autem princeps sacerdotum, et omnes qui cum illo erant (quæ est hæresis sadducæorum), repleti sunt zelo :

5:18 et injecerunt manus in Apostolos, et

5:3 But Peter said: Ananias, why hath Satan tempted thy heart, that thou shouldst lie to the Holy Ghost, and by fraud keep part of the price of the land?

5:4 Whilst it remained, did it not remain to thee? and after it was sold, was it not in thy power? Why hast thou conceived this thing in thy heart? Thou hast not lied to men, but to God.

5:5 And Ananias hearing these words, fell down, and gave up the ghost. And there came great fear upon all that heard it.

5:6 And the young men rising up, removed him, and carrying him out, buried him.

5:7 And it was about the space of three hours after, when his wife, not knowing what had happened, came in.

5:8 And Peter said to her: Tell me, woman, whether you sold the land for so much? And she said: Yea, for so much.

5:9 And Peter said unto her: Why have you agreed together to tempt the Spirit of the Lord? Behold the feet of them who have buried thy husband are at the door, and they shall carry thee out.

5:10 Immediately she fell down before his feet, and gave up the ghost. And the young men coming in, found her dead: and carried her out, and buried her by her husband.

5:11 And there came great fear upon the whole church, and upon all that heard these things.

5:12 And by the hands of the apostles were many signs and wonders wrought among the people. And they were all with one accord in Solomon's porch.

5:13 But of the rest no man durst join himself unto them; but the people magnified them.

5:14 And the multitude of men and women who believed in the Lord, was more increased:

5:15 Insomuch that they brought forth the sick into the streets, and laid them on beds and couches, that when Peter came, his shadow at the least, might overshadow any of them, and they might be delivered from their infirmities.

5:16 And there came also together to Jerusalem a multitude out of the neighboring cities, bringing sick persons, and such as were troubled with unclean spirits; who were all healed.

5:17 Then the high prist rising up, and all they that were with him, (which is the heresy of the Sadducees,) were filled with envy.

5:18 And they laid hands on the apostles, and put

posuerunt eos in custodia publica.

5:19 Angelus autem Domini per noctem aperiens januas carceris, et educens eos, dixit :

5:20 Ite, et stantes loquimini in templo plebi omnia verba vitæ hujus.

5:21 Qui cum audissent, intraverunt diluculo in templum, et docebant. Adveniens autem princeps sacerdotum, et qui cum eo erant, convocaverunt concilium, et omnes seniores filiorum Israël : et miserunt ad carcerem ut adducerentur.

5:22 Cum autem venissent ministri, et aperto carcere non invenissent illos, reversi nuntiaverunt,

5:23 dicentes : Carcerem quidem invenimus clausum cum omni diligentia, et custodes stantes ante januas : aperientes autem neminem intus invenimus.

5:24 Ut autem audierunt hos sermones magistratus templi et principes sacerdotum, ambigebant de illis quidnam fieret.

5:25 Adveniens autem quidam, nuntiavit eis : Quia ecce viri quos posuistis in carcerem, sunt in templo, stantes et docentes populum.

5:26 Tunc abiit magistratus cum ministris, et adduxit illos sine vi : timebant enim populum ne lapidarentur.

5:27 Et cum adduxissent illos, statuerunt in concilio : et interrogavit eos princeps sacerdotum,

5:28 dicens : Præcipiendo præcepimus vobis ne doceretis in nomine isto, et ecce replestis Jerusalem doctrina vestra : et vultis inducere super nos sanguinem hominis istius.

5:29 Respondens autem Petrus et Apostoli, dixerunt : Obedire oportet Deo magis quam hominibus.

5:30 Deus patrum nostrorum suscitavit Jesum, quem vos interemistis, suspendentes in ligno.

5:31 Hunc principem et salvatorem Deus exaltavit dextera sua ad dandam pœnitentiam Israëli, et remissionem peccatorum :

5:32 et nos sumus testes horum verborum, et Spiritus Sanctus, quem dedit Deus omnibus obedientibus sibi.

5:33 Hæc cum audissent, dissecabantur, et cogitabant interficere illos.

them in the common prison.

5:19 But an angel of the Lord by night opening the doors of the prison, and leading them out, said:

5:20 Go, and standing speak in the temple to the people all the words of this life.

5:21 Who having heard this, early in the morning, entered into the temple, and taught. And the high priest coming, and they that were with him, called together the council, and all the ancients of the children of Israel; and they sent to the prison to have them brought.

5:22 But when the ministers came, and opening the prison, found them not there, they returned and told,

5:23 Saying: The prison indeed we found shut with all diligence, and the keepers standing before the doors; but opening it, we found no man within.

5:24 Now when the officer of the temple and the chief priests heard these words, they were in doubt concerning them, what would come to pass.

5:25 But one came and told them: Behold, the men whom you put in prison are in the temple standing, and teaching the people.

5:26 Then went the officer with the ministers, and brought them without violence; for they feared the people, lest they should be stoned.

5:27 And when they had brought them, they set them before the council. And the high priest asked them,

5:28 Saying: Commanding we commanded you, that you should not teach in this name; and behold, you have filled Jerusalem with your doctrine, and you have a mind to bring the blood of this man upon us.

5:29 But Peter and the apostles answering, said: We ought to obey God, rather than men.

5:30 The God of our fathers hath raised up Jesus, whom you put to death, hanging him upon a tree.

5:31 Him hath God exalted with his right hand, to be Prince and Saviour, to give repentance to Israel, and remission of sins.

5:32 And we are witnesses of these things and the Holy Ghost, whom God hath given to all that obey him.

5:33 When they had heard these things, they were cut to the heart, and they thought to put them to death.

5:34 Surgens autem quidam in concilio pharisæus, nomine Gamaliel, legis doctor, honorabilis universæ plebi, jussit foras ad breve homines fieri,

5:35 dixitque ad illos : Viri Israëlitæ, attendite vobis super hominibus istis quid acturi sitis.

5:36 Ante hos enim dies extitit Theodas, dicens se esse aliquem, cui consensit numerus virorum circiter quadringentorum : qui occisus est, et omnes qui credebant ei, dissipati sunt, et redacti ad nihilum.

5:37 Post hunc extitit Judas Galilæus in diebus professionis, et avertit populum post se : et ipse periit, et omnes quotquot consenserunt ei, dispersi sunt.

5:38 Et nunc itaque dico vobis, discedite ab hominibus istis, et sinite illos : quoniam si est ex hominibus consilium hoc aut opus, dissolvetur :

5:39 si vero ex Deo est, non poteritis dissolvere illud, ne forte et Deo repugnare inveniamini. Consenserunt autem illi.

5:40 Et convocantes Apostolos, cæsis denuntiaverunt ne omnino loquerentur in nomine Jesu, et dimiserunt eos.

5:41 Et illi quidem ibant gaudentes a conspectu concilii, quoniam digni habiti sunt pro nomine Jesu contumeliam pati.

5:42 Omni autem die non cessabant in templo et circa domos, docentes et evangelizantes Christum Jesum.

6:1 In diebus illis, crescente numero discipulorum, factum est murmur Græcorum adversus Hebræos, eo quod despicerentur in ministerio quotidiano viduæ eorum.

6:2 Convocantes autem duodecim multitudinem discipulorum, dixerunt : Non est æquum nos derelinquere verbum Dei, et ministrare mensis.

6:3 Considerate ergo, fratres, viros ex vobis boni testimonii septem, plenos Spiritu Sancto et sapientia, quos constituamus super hoc opus.

6:4 Nos vero orationi et ministerio verbi instantes erimus.

6:5 Et placuit sermo coram omni multitudine. Et elegerunt Stephanum, virum plenum fide et

5:34 But one in the council rising up, a Pharisee, named Gamaliel, a doctor of the law, respected by all the people, commanded the men to be put forth a little while.

5:35 And he said to them: Ye men of Israel, take heed to yourselves what you intend to do, as touching these men.

5:36 For before these days rose up Theodas, affirming himself to be somebody, to whom a number of men, about four hundred, joined themselves: who was slain; and all that believed him were scattered, and brought to nothing.

5:37 After this man, rose up Judas of Galilee, in the days of the enrolling, and drew away the people after him: he also perished; and all, even as many as consented to him, were dispersed.

5:38 And now, therefore, I say to you, refrain from these men, and let them alone; for if this council or this work be of men, it will come to nought;

5:39 But if it be of God, you cannot overthrow it, lest perhaps you be found even to fight against God. And they consented to him.

5:40 And calling in the apostles, after they had scourged them, they charged them that they should not speak at all in the name of Jesus; and they dismissed them.

5:41 And they indeed went from the presence of the council, rejoicing that they were accounted worthy to suffer reproach for the name of Jesus.

5:42 And every day they ceased not in the temple, and from house to house, to teach and preach Christ Jesus.

6:1 And in those days, the number of the disciples increasing, there arose a murmuring of the Greeks against the Hebrews, for that their widows were neglected in the daily ministration.

6:2 Then the twelve calling together the multitude of the disciples, said: It is not reason that we should leave the word of God, and serve tables.

6:3 Wherefore, brethren, look ye out among you seven men of good reputation, full of the Holy Ghost and wisdom, whom we may appoint over this business.

6:4 But we will give ourselves continually to prayer, and to the ministry of the word.

6:5 And the saying was liked by all the multitude. And they chose Stephen, a man full of

Spiritu Sancto, et Philippum, et Prochorum, et Nicanorem, et Timonem, et Parmenam, et Nicolaum advenam Antiochenum.

6:6 Hos statuerunt ante conspectum Apostolorum : et orantes imposuerunt eis manus.

6:7 Et verbum Domini crescebat, et multiplicabatur numerus discipulorum in Jerusalem valde : multa etiam turba sacerdotum obediebat fidei.

6:8 Stephanus autem plenus gratia et fortitudine, faciebat prodigia et signa magna in populo.

6:9 Surrexerunt autem quidam de synagoga quæ appellatur Libertinorum, et Cyrenensium, et Alexandrinorum, et eorum qui erant a Cilicia, et Asia, disputantes cum Stephano :

6:10 et non poterant resistere sapientiæ, et Spiritui qui loquebatur.

6:11 Tunc summiserunt viros, qui dicerent se audivisse eum dicentem verba blasphemiæ in Moysen et in Deum.

6:12 Commoverunt itaque plebem, et seniores, et scribas : et concurrentes rapuerunt eum, et adduxerunt in concilium,

6:13 et statuerunt falsos testes, qui dicerent : Homo iste non cessat loqui verba adversus locum sanctum, et legem :

6:14 audivimus enim eum dicentem quoniam Jesus Nazarenus hic destruet locum istum, et mutabit traditiones quas tradidit nobis Moyses.

6:15 Et intuentes eum omnes qui sedebant in concilio, viderunt faciem ejus tamquam faciem angeli.

7:1 Dixit autem princeps sacerdotum : Si hæc ita se habent ?

7:2 Qui ait : Viri fratres et patres, audite : Deus gloriæ apparuit patri nostro Abrahæ cum esset in Mesopotamia, priusquam moraretur in Charan,

7:3 et dixit ad illum : Exi de terra tua, et de cognatione tua, et veni in terram quam monstravero tibi.

7:4 Tunc exiit de terra Chaldæorum, et habitavit in Charan. Et inde, postquam mortuus est pater ejus, transtulit illum in terram istam, in qua nunc vos habitatis.

7:5 Et non dedit illi hæreditatem in ea, nec passum pedis : sed repromisit dare illi eam in possessionem, et semini ejus post ipsum, cum non haberet filium.

7:6 Locutus est autem ei Deus : Quia erit semen

faith, and of the Holy Ghost, and Philip, and Prochorus, and Nicanor, and Timon, and Parmenas, and Nicolas, a proselyte of Antioch.

6:6 These they set before the apostles; and they praying, imposed hands upon them.

6:7 And the word of the Lord increased; and the number of the disciples was multiplied in Jerusalem exceedingly: a great multitude also of the priests obeyed the faith.

6:8 And Stephen, full of grace and fortitude, did great wonders and signs among the people.

6:9 Now there arose some of that which is called the synagogue of the Libertines, and of the Cyrenians, and of the Alexandrians, and of them that were of Cilicia and Asia, disputing with Stephen.

6:10 And they were not able to resist the wisdom and the spirit that spoke.

6:11 Then they suborned men to say, they had heard him speak words of blasphemy against Moses and against God.

6:12 And they stirred up the people, and the ancients, and the scribes; and running together, they took him, and brought him to the council.

6:13 And they set up false witnesses, who said: This man ceaseth not to speak words against the holy place and the law.

6:14 For we have heard him say, that this Jesus of Nazareth shall destroy this place, and shall change the traditions which Moses delivered unto us.

6:15 And all that sat in the council, looking on him, saw his face as if it had been the face of an angel.

7:1 Then the high priest said: Are these things so?

7:2 Who said: Ye men, brethren, and fathers, hear. The God of glory appeared to our father Abraham, when he was in Mesopotamia, before he dwelt in Charan.

7:3 And said to him: Go forth out of thy country, and from thy kindred, and come into the land which I shall shew thee.

7:4 Then he went out of the land of the Chaldeans, and dwelt in Charan. And from thence, after his father was dead, he removed him into this land, wherein you now dwell.

7:5 And he gave him no inheritance in it; no, not the pace of a foot: but he promised to give it him in possession, and to his seed after him, when as yet he had no child.

7:6 And God said to him: That his seed should

ejus accola in terra aliena, et servituti eos subjicient, et male tractabunt eos annis quadringentis :

7:7 et gentem cui servierint, judicabo ego, dixit Dominus : et post hæc exibunt, et servient mihi in loco isto.

7:8 Et dedit illi testamentum circumcisionis : et sic genuit Isaac, et circumcidit eum die octavo : et Isaac, Jacob : et Jacob, duodecim patriarchas.

7:9 Et patriarchæ æmulantes, Joseph vendiderunt in Ægyptum : et erat Deus cum eo,

7:10 et eripuit eum ex omnibus tribulationibus ejus, et dedit ei gratiam et sapientiam in conspectu pharaonis regis Ægypti : et constituit eum præpositum super Ægyptum, et super omnem domum suam.

7:11 Venit autem fames in universam Ægyptum et Chanaan, et tribulatio magna : et non inveniebant cibos patres nostri.

7:12 Cum audisset autem Jacob esse frumentum in Ægypto, misit patres nostros primum :

7:13 et in secundo cognitus est Joseph a fratribus suis, et manifestatum est Pharaoni genus ejus.

7:14 Mittens autem Joseph, accersivit Jacob patrem suum et omnem cognationem suam, in animabus septuaginta quinque.

7:15 Et descendit Jacob in Ægyptum : et defunctus est ipse, et patres nostri.

7:16 Et translati sunt in Sichem, et positi sunt in sepulchro, quod emit Abraham pretio argenti a filiis Hemor filii Sichem.

7:17 Cum autem appropinquaret tempus promissionis quam confessus erat Deus Abrahæ, crevit populus, et multiplicatus est in Ægypto,

7:18 quoadusque surrexit alius rex in Ægypto, qui non sciebat Joseph.

7:19 Hic circumveniens genus nostrum, afflixit patres nostros ut exponerent infantes suos, ne vivificarentur.

7:20 Eodem tempore natus est Moyses, et fuit gratus Deo : qui nutritus est tribus mensibus in domo patris sui.

7:21 Exposito autem illo, sustulit eum filia Pharaonis, et nutrivit eum sibi in filium.

7:22 Et eruditus est Moyses omni sapientia Ægyptiorum, et erat potens in verbis et in

sojourn in a strange country, and that they should bring them under bondage, and treat them evil four hundred years.

7:7 And the nation which they shall serve will I judge, said the Lord; and after these things they shall go out, and shall serve me in this place.

7:8 And he gave him the covenant of circumcision, and so he begot Isaac, and circumcised him the eighth day; and Isaac begot Jacob; and Jacob the twelve patriarchs.

7:9 And the patriarchs, through envy, sold Joseph into Egypt; and God was with him,

7:10 And delivered him out of all his tribulations: and he gave him favour and wisdom in the sight of Pharao, the king of Egypt; and he appointed him governor over Egypt, and over all his house.

7:11 Now there came a famine upon all Egypt and Chanaan, and great tribulation; and our fathers found no food.

7:12 But when Jacob had heard that there was corn in Egypt, he sent our fathers first:

7:13 And at the second time, Joseph was known by his brethren, and his kindred was made known to Pharao.

7:14 And Joseph sending, called thither Jacob, his father, and all his kindred, seventy-five souls.

7:15 So Jacob went down into Egypt; and he died, and our fathers.

7:16 And they were translated into Sichem, and were laid in the sepulchre, that Abraham bought for a sum of money of the sons of Hemor, the son of Sichem.

7:17 And when the time of the promise drew near, which God had promised to Abraham, the people increased, and were multiplied in Egypt,

7:18 Till another king arose in Egypt, who knew not Joseph.

7:19 This same dealing craftily with our race, afflicted our fathers, that they should expose their children, to the end they might not be kept alive.

7:20 At the same time was Moses born, and he was acceptable to God: who was nourished three months in his father's house.

7:21 And when he was exposed, Pharao's daughter took him up, and nourished him for her own son.

7:22 And Moses was instructed in all the wisdom of the Egyptians; and he was mighty in his

operibus suis.

7:23 Cum autem impleretur ei quadraginta annorum tempus, ascendit in cor ejus ut visitaret fratres suos filios Israël.

7:24 Et cum vidisset quemdam injuriam patientem, vindicavit illum, et fecit ultionem ei qui injuriam sustinebat, percusso Ægyptio.

7:25 Existimabat autem intelligere fratres, quoniam Deus per manum ipsius daret salutem illis : at illi non intellexerunt.

7:26 Sequenti vero die apparuit illis litigantibus : et reconciliabat eos in pace, dicens : Viri, fratres estis : ut quid nocetis alterutrum ?

7:27 Qui autem injuriam faciebat proximo, repulit eum, dicens : Quis te constituit principem et judicem super nos ?

7:28 Numquid interficere me tu vis, quemadmodum interfecisti heri Ægyptium ?

7:29 Fugit autem Moyses in verbo isto : et factus est advena in terra Madian, ubi generavit filios duos.

7:30 Et expletis annis quadraginta, apparuit illi in deserto montis Sina angelus in igne flammæ rubi.

7:31 Moyses autem videns, admiratus est visum. Et accedente illo ut consideraret, facta est ad eum vox Domini, dicens :

7:32 Ego sum Deus patrum tuorum, Deus Abraham, Deus Isaac, et Deus Jacob. Tremefactus autem Moyses, non audebat considerare.

7:33 Dixit autem illi Dominus : Solve calceamentum pedum tuorum : locus enim in quo stas, terra sancta est.

7:34 Videns vidi afflictionem populi mei qui est in Ægypto, et gemitum eorum audivi, et descendi liberare eos. Et nunc veni, et mittam te in Ægyptum.

7:35 Hunc Moysen, quem negaverunt, dicentes : Quis te constituit principem et judicem ? hunc Deus principem et redemptorem misit, cum manu angeli qui apparuit illi in rubo.

7:36 Hic eduxit illos faciens prodigia et signa in terra Ægypti, et in rubro mari, et in deserto annis quadraginta.

7:37 Hic est Moyses, qui dixit filiis Israël : Prophetam suscitabit vobis Deus de fratribus vestris, tamquam me : ipsum audietis.

words and in his deeds.

7:23 And when he was full forty years old, it came into his heart to visit his brethren, the children of Israel.

7:24 And when he had seen one of them suffer wrong, he defended him; and striking the Egyptian, he avenged him who suffered the injury.

7:25 And he thought that his brethren understood that God by his hand would save them; but they understood it not.

7:26 And the day following, he shewed himself to them when they were at strife; and would have reconciled them in peace, saying: Men, ye are brethren; why hurt you one another?

7:27 But he that did the injury to his neighbour thrust him away, saying: Who hath appointed thee prince and judge over us?

7:28 What, wilt thou kill me, as thou didst yesterday kill the Egyptian?

7:29 And Moses fled upon this word, and was a stranger in the land of Madian, where he begot two sons.

7:30 And when forty years were expired, there appeared to him in the desert of mount Sina, an angel in a flame of fire in a bush.

7:31 And Moses seeing it, wondered at the sight. And as he drew near to view it, the voice of the Lord came unto him, saying:

7:32 I am the God of thy fathers; the God of Abraham, the God of Isaac, and the God of Jacob. And Moses being terrified, durst not behold.

7:33 And the Lord said to him: Loose the shoes from thy feet, for the place wherein thou standest, is holy ground.

7:34 Seeing I have seen the affliction of my people which is in Egypt, and I have heard their groaning, and am come down to deliver them. And now come, and I will send thee into Egypt.

7:35 This Moses, whom they refused, saying: Who hath appointed thee prince and judge? him God sent to be prince and redeemer by the hand of the angel who appeared to him in the bush.

7:36 He brought them out, doing wonders and signs in the land of Egypt, and in the Red Sea, and in the desert forty years.

7:37 This is that Moses who said to the children of Israel: A prophet shall God raise up to you of your own brethren, as myself: him shall you

hear.

7:38 Hic est qui fuit in ecclesia in solitudine cum angelo, qui loquebatur ei in monte Sina, et cum patribus nostris : qui accepit verba vitæ dare nobis.

7:39 Cui noluerunt obedire patres nostri : sed repulerunt, et aversi sunt cordibus suis in Ægyptum,

7:40 dicentes ad Aaron : Fac nobis deos qui præcedant nos : Moyses enim hic, qui eduxit nos de terra Ægypti, nescimus quid factum sit ei.

7:41 Et vitulum fecerunt in diebus illis, et obtulerunt hostiam simulacro, et lætabantur in operibus manuum suarum.

7:42 Convertit autem Deus, et tradidit eos servire militiæ cæli, sicut scriptum est in libro prophetarum : *Numquid victimas et hostias obtulistis mihi annis quadraginta in deserto, domus Israël ?*

7:43 *Et suscepistis tabernaculum Moloch, et sidus dei vestri Rempham, figuras quas fecistis adorare eas : et transferam vos trans Babylonem.*

7:44 Tabernaculum testimonii fuit cum patribus nostris in deserto, sicut disposuit illis Deus loquens ad Moysen, ut faceret illud secundum formam quam viderat.

7:45 Quod et induxerunt, suscipientes patres nostri cum Jesu in possessionem gentium quas expulit Deus a facie patrum nostrorum, usque in diebus David,

7:46 qui invenit gratiam ante Deum, et petiit ut inveniret tabernaculum Deo Jacob.

7:47 Salomon autem ædificavit illi domum.

7:48 Sed non Excelsus in manufactis habitat, sicut propheta dicit :

7:49 *Cælum mihi sedes est : terra autem scabellum pedum meorum. Quam domum ædificabitis mihi ? dicit Dominus : aut quis locus requietionis meæ est ?*

7:50 *Nonne manus mea fecit hæc omnia ?*

7:51 Dura cervice, et incircumcisis cordibus et auribus, vos semper Spiritui Sancto resistitis : sicut patres vestri, ita et vos.

7:52 Quem prophetarum non sunt persecuti patres vestri ? et occiderunt eos qui prænuntiabant de adventu Justi, cujus vos nunc proditores et homicidæ fuistis :

7:53 qui accepistis legem in dispositione angelorum, et non custodistis.

7:54 Audientes autem hæc, dissecabantur cordi-

7:38 This is he that was in the church in the wilderness, with the angel who spoke to him on mount Sina, and with our fathers; who received the words of life to give unto us.

7:39 Whom our fathers would not obey; but thrust him away, and in their hearts turned back into Egypt,

7:40 Saying to Aaron: Make us gods to go before us. For as for this Moses, who brought us out of the land of Egypt, we know not what is become of him.

7:41 And they made a calf in those days, and offered sacrifices to the idol, and rejoiced in the works of their own hands.

7:42 And God turned, and gave them up to serve the host of heaven, as it is written in the books of the prophets: *Did you offer victims and sacrifices to me for forty years, in the desert, O house of Israel?*

7:43 *And you took unto you the tabernacle of Moloch, and the star of your god Rempham, figures which you made to adore them. And I will carry you away beyond Babylon.*

7:44 The tabernacle of the testimony was with our fathers in the desert, as God ordained for them, speaking to Moses, that he should make it according to the form which he had seen.

7:45 Which also our fathers receiving, brought in with Jesus, into the possession of the Gentiles, whom God drove out before the face of our fathers, unto the days of David.

7:46 Who found grace before God, and desired to find a tabernacle for the God of Jacob.

7:47 But Solomon built him a house.

7:48 Yet the most High dwelleth not in houses made by hands, as the prophet saith:

7:49 *Heaven is my throne, and the earth my footstool. What house will you build me? saith the Lord; or what is the place of my resting?*

7:50 *Hath not my hand made all these things?*

7:51 You stiffnecked and uncircumcised in heart and ears, you always resist the Holy Ghost: as your fathers did, so do you also.

7:52 Which of the prophets have not your fathers persecuted? And they have slain them who foretold of the coming of the Just One; of whom you have been now the betrayers and murderers:

7:53 Who have received the law by the disposition of angels, and have not kept it.

7:54 Now hearing these things, they were cut to

bus suis, et stridebant dentibus in eum.

7:55 Cum autem esset plenus Spiritu Sancto, intendens in cælum, vidit gloriam Dei, et Jesum stantem a dextris Dei. Et ait : Ecce video cælos apertos, et Filium hominis stantem a dextris Dei.

7:56 Exclamantes autem voce magna continuerunt aures suas, et impetum fecerunt unanimiter in eum.

7:57 Et ejicientes eum extra civitatem, lapidabant : et testes deposuerunt vestimenta sua secus pedes adolescentis qui vocabatur Saulus.

7:58 Et lapidabant Stephanum invocantem, et dicentem : Domine Jesu, suscipe spiritum meum.

7:59 Positis autem genibus, clamavit voce magna, dicens : Domine, ne statuas illis hoc peccatum. Et cum hoc dixisset, obdormivit in Domino. Saulus autem erat consentiens neci ejus.

8:1 Facta est autem in illa die persecutio magna in ecclesia quæ erat Jerosolymis, et omnes dispersi sunt per regiones Judææ et Samariæ præter Apostolos.

8:2 Curaverunt autem Stephanum viri timorati, et fecerunt planctum magnum super eum.

8:3 Saulus autem devastabat ecclesiam per domos intrans, et trahens viros ac mulieres, tradebat in custodiam.

8:4 Igitur qui dispersi erant pertransibant, evangelizantes verbum Dei.

8:5 Philippus autem descendens in civitatem Samariæ, prædicabant illis Christum.

8:6 Intendebant autem turbæ his quæ a Philippo dicebantur, unanimiter audientes, et videntes signa quæ faciebat.

8:7 Multi enim eorum qui habebant spiritus immundos, clamantes voce magna exibant. Multi autem paralytici et claudi curati sunt.

8:8 Factum est ergo gaudium magnum in illa civitate.

8:9 Vir autem quidam nomine Simon, qui ante fuerat in civitate magus, seducens gentem Samariæ, dicens se esse aliquem magnum :

8:10 cui auscultabant omnes a minimo usque ad maximum, dicentes : Hic est virtus Dei, quæ

the heart, and they gnashed with their teeth at him.

7:55 But he, being full of the Holy Ghost, looking up steadfastly to heaven, saw the glory of God, and Jesus standing on the right hand of God. And he said: Behold, I see the heavens opened, and the Son of man standing on the right hand of God.

7:56 And they crying out with a loud voice, stopped their ears, and with one accord ran violently upon him.

7:57 And casting him forth without the city, they stoned him; and the witnesses laid down their garments at the feet of a young man, whose name was Saul.

7:58 And they stoned Stephen, invoking, and saying: Lord Jesus, receive my spirit.

7:59 And falling on his knees, he cried with a loud voice, saying: Lord, lay not this sin to their charge. And when he had said this, he fell asleep in the Lord. And Saul was consenting to his death.

8:1 And at that time there was raised a great persecution against the church which was at Jerusalem; and they were all dispersed through the countries of Judea, and Samaria, except the apostles.

8:2 And devout men took order for Stephen's funeral, and made great mourning over him.

8:3 But Saul made havock of the church, entering in from house to house, and dragging away men and women, committed them to prison.

8:4 They therefore that were dispersed, went about preaching the word of God.

8:5 And Philip going down to the city of Samaria, preached Christ unto them.

8:6 And the people with one accord were attentive to those things which were said by Philip, hearing, and seeing the miracles which he did.

8:7 For many of them who had unclean spirits, crying with a loud voice, went out.

8:8 And many, taken with the palsy, and that were lame, were healed.

8:9 There was therefore great joy in that city. Now there was a certain man named Simon, who before had been a magician in that city, seducing the people of Samaria, giving out that he was some great one:

8:10 To whom they all gave ear, from the least to the greatest, saying: This man is the power of

vocatur magna.

8:11 Attendebant autem eum : propter quod multo tempore magiis suis dementasset eos.

8:12 Cum vero credidissent Philippo evangelizanti de regno Dei, in nomine Jesu Christi baptizabantur viri ac mulieres.

8:13 Tunc Simon et ipse credidit : et cum baptizatus esset, adhærebat Philippo. Videns etiam signa et virtutes maximas fieri, stupens admirabatur.

8:14 Cum autem audissent Apostoli qui erant Jerosolymis, quod recepisset Samaria verbum Dei, miserunt ad eos Petrum et Joannem.

8:15 Qui cum venissent, oraverunt pro ipsis ut acciperent Spiritum Sanctum :

8:16 nondum enim in quemquam illorum venerat, sed baptizati tantum erant in nomine Domini Jesu.

8:17 Tunc imponebant manus super illos, et accipiebant Spiritum Sanctum.

8:18 Cum vidisset autem Simon quia per impositionem manus Apostolorum daretur Spiritus Sanctus, obtulit eis pecuniam,

8:19 dicens : Date et mihi hanc potestatem, ut cuicumque imposuero manus, accipiat Spiritum Sanctum. Petrus autem dixit ad eum :

8:20 Pecunia tua tecum sit in perditionem : quoniam donum Dei existimasti pecunia possideri.

8:21 Non est tibi pars neque sors in sermone isto : cor enim tuum non est rectum coram Deo.

8:22 Pœnitentiam itaque age ab hac nequitia tua : et roga Deum, si forte remittatur tibi hæc cogitatio cordis tui.

8:23 In felle enim amaritudinis, et obligatione iniquitatis, video te esse.

8:24 Respondens autem Simon, dixit : Precamini vos pro me ad Dominum, ut nihil veniat super me horum quæ dixistis.

8:25 Et illi quidem testificati, et locuti verbum Domini, redibant Jerosolymam, et multis regionibus Samaritanorum evangelizabant.

8:26 Angelus autem Domini locutus est ad Philippum, dicens : Surge, et vade contra meridianum, ad viam quæ descendit ab Jerusalem in Gazam : hæc est deserta.

8:27 Et surgens abiit. Et ecce vir Æthiops, eunuchus, potens Candacis reginæ Æthiopum,

God, which is called great.

8:11 And they were attentive to him, because, for a long time, he had bewitched them with his magical practices.

8:12 But when they had believed Philip preaching of the kingdom of God, in the name of Jesus Christ, they were baptized, both men and women.

8:13 Then Simon himself believed also; and being baptized, he adhered to Philip. And being astonished, wondered to see the signs and exceeding great miracles which were done.

8:14 Now when the apostles, who were in Jerusalem, had heard that Samaria had received the word of God, they sent unto them Peter and John.

8:15 Who, when they were come, prayed for them, that they might receive the Holy Ghost.

8:16 For he was not as yet come upon any of them; but they were only baptized in the name of the Lord Jesus.

8:17 Then they laid their hands upon them, and they received the Holy Ghost.

8:18 And when Simon saw, that by the imposition of the hands of the apostles, the Holy Ghost was given, he offered them money,

8:19 Saying: Give me also this power, that on whomsoever I shall lay my hands, he may receive the Holy Ghost. But Peter said to him:

8:20 Keep thy money to thyself, to perish with thee, because thou hast thought that the gift of God may be purchased with money.

8:21 Thou hast no part nor lot in this matter. For thy heart is not right in the sight of God.

8:22 Do penance therefore for this thy wickedness; and pray to God, that perhaps this thought of thy heart may be forgiven thee.

8:23 For I see thou art in the gall of bitterness, and in the bonds of iniquity.

8:24 Then Simon answering, said: Pray you for me to the Lord, that none of these things which you have spoken may come upon me.

8:25 And they indeed having testified and preached the word of the Lord, returned to Jerusalem, and preached the gospel to many countries of the Samaritans.

8:26 Now an angel of the Lord spoke to Philip, saying: Arise, go towards the south, to the way that goeth down from Jerusalem into Gaza: this is desert.

8:27 And rising up, he went. And behold a man of Ethiopia, an eunuch, of great authority un-

qui erat super omnes gazas ejus, venerat adorare in Jerusalem :

^{8:28} et revertebatur sedens super currum suum, legensque Isaiam prophetam.

^{8:29} Dixit autem Spiritus Philippo : Accede, et adjunge te ad currum istum.

^{8:30} Accurrens autem Philippus, audivit eum legentem Isaiam prophetam, et dixit : Putasne intelligis quæ legis ?

^{8:31} Qui ait : Et quomodo possum, si non aliquis ostenderit mihi ? Rogavitque Philippum ut ascenderet, et sederet secum.

^{8:32} Locus autem Scripturæ quem legebat, erat hic : *Tamquam ovis ad occisionem ductus est : et sicut agnus coram tondente se, sine voce, sic non aperuit os suum.*

^{8:33} *In humilitate judicium ejus sublatum est. Generationem ejus quis enarrabit ? quoniam tolletur de terra vita ejus.*

^{8:34} Respondens autem eunuchus Philippo, dixit : Obsecro te, de quo propheta dicit hoc ? de se, an de alio aliquo ?

^{8:35} Aperiens autem Philippus os suum, et incipiens a Scriptura ista, evangelizavit illi Jesum.

^{8:36} Et dum irent per viam, venerunt ad quamdam aquam : et ait eunuchus : Ecce aqua : quid prohibet me baptizari ?

^{8:37} Dixit autem Philippus : Si credis ex toto corde, licet. Et respondens ait : Credo Filium Dei esse Jesum Christum.

^{8:38} Et jussit stare currum : et descenderunt uterque in aquam, Philippus et eunuchus, et baptizavit eum.

^{8:39} Cum autem ascendissent de aqua, Spiritus Domini rapuit Philippum, et amplius non vidit eum eunuchus. Ibat autem per viam suam gaudens.

^{8:40} Philippus autem inventus est in Azoto, et pertransiens evangelizabat civitatibus cunctis, donec veniret Cæsaream.

^{9:1} Saulus autem adhuc spirans minarum et cædis in discipulos Domini, accessit ad principem sacerdotum,

^{9:2} et petiit ab eo epistolas in Damascum ad synagogas : ut si quos invenisset hujus viæ viros ac mulieres, vinctos perduceret in Jerusalem.

^{9:3} Et cum iter faceret, contigit ut appropinquaret Damasco : et subito circumfulsit eum

der Candace the queen of the Ethiopians, who had charge over all her treasures, had come to Jerusalem to adore.

^{8:28} And he was returning, sitting in his chariot, and reading Isaias the prophet.

^{8:29} And the Spirit said to Philip: Go near, and join thyself to this chariot.

^{8:30} And Philip running thither, heard him reading the prophet Isaias. And he said: Thinkest thou that thou understandest what thou readest?

^{8:31} Who said: And how can I, unless some man shew me? And he desired Philip that he would come up and sit with him.

^{8:32} And the place of the scripture which he was reading was this: *He was led as a sheep to the slaughter; and like a lamb without voice before his shearer, so openeth he not his mouth.*

^{8:33} *In humility his judgment was taken away. His generation who shall declare, for his life shall be taken from the earth?*

^{8:34} And the eunuch answering Philip, said: I beseech thee, of whom doth the prophet speak this? of himself, or of some other man?

^{8:35} Then Philip, opening his mouth, and beginning at this scripture, preached unto him Jesus.

^{8:36} And as they went on their way, they came to a certain water; and the eunuch said: See, here is water: what doth hinder me from being baptized?

^{8:37} And Philip said: If thou believest with all thy heart, thou mayest. And he answering, said: I believe that Jesus Christ is the Son of God.

^{8:38} And he commanded the chariot to stand still; and they went down into the water, both Philip and the eunuch: and he baptized him.

^{8:39} And when they were come up out of the water, the Spirit of the Lord took away Philip; and the eunuch saw him no more. And he went on his way rejoicing.

^{8:40} But Philip was found in Azotus; and passing through, he preached the gospel to all the cities, till he came to Caesarea.

^{9:1} And Saul, as yet breathing out threatenings and slaughter against the disciples of the Lord, went to the high priest,

^{9:2} And asked of him letters to Damascus, to the synagogues: that if he found any men and women of this way, he might bring them bound to Jerusalem.

^{9:3} And as he went on his journey, it came to pass that he drew nigh to Damascus; and sud-

lux de cælo.

9:4 Et cadens in terram audivit vocem dicentem sibi : Saule, Saule, quid me persequeris ?

9:5 Qui dixit : Quis es, domine ? Et ille : Ego sum Jesus, quem tu persequeris : durum est tibi contra stimulum calcitrare.

9:6 Et tremens ac stupens dixit : Domine, quid me vis facere ?

9:7 Et Dominus ad eum : Surge, et ingredere civitatem, et ibi dicetur tibi quid te oporteat facere. Viri autem illi qui comitabantur cum eo, stabant stupefacti, audientes quidem vocem, neminem autem videntes.

9:8 Surrexit autem Saulus de terra, apertisque oculis nihil videbat. Ad manus autem illum trahentes, introduxerunt Damascum.

9:9 Et erat ibi tribus diebus non videns, et non manducavit, neque bibit.

9:10 Erat autem quidam discipulus Damasci, nomine Ananias : et dixit ad illum in visu Dominus : Anania. At ille ait : Ecce ego, Domine.

9:11 Et Dominus ad eum : Surge, et vade in vicum qui vocatur Rectus : et quære in domo Judæ Saulum nomine Tarsensem : ecce enim orat.

9:12 (Et vidit virum Ananiam nomine, introëuntem, et imponentem sibi manus ut visum recipiat.)

9:13 Respondit autem Ananias : Domine, audivi a multis de viro hoc, quanta mala fecerit sanctis tuis in Jerusalem :

9:14 et hic habet potestatem a principibus sacerdotum alligandi omnes qui invocant nomen tuum.

9:15 Dixit autem ad eum Dominus : Vade, quoniam vas electionis est mihi iste, ut portet nomen meum coram gentibus, et regibus, et filiis Israël.

9:16 Ego enim ostendam illi quanta oporteat eum pro nomine meo pati.

9:17 Et abiit Ananias, et introivit in domum : et imponens ei manus, dixit : Saule frater, Dominus misit me Jesus, qui apparuit tibi in via qua veniebas, ut videas, et implearis Spiritu Sancto.

9:18 Et confestim ceciderunt ab oculis ejus tamquam squamæ, et visum recepit : et sur-

denly a light from heaven shined round about him.

9:4 And falling on the ground, he heard a voice saying to him: Saul, Saul, why persecutest thou me?

9:5 Who said: Who art thou, Lord? And he: I am Jesus whom thou persecutest. It is hard for thee to kick against the goad.

9:6 And he trembling and astonished, said: Lord, what wilt thou have me to do?

9:7 And the Lord said to him: Arise, and go into the city, and there it shall be told thee what thou must do. Now the men who went in company with him, stood amazed, hearing indeed a voice, but seeing no man.

9:8 And Saul arose from the ground; and when his eyes were opened, he saw nothing. But they leading him by the hands, brought him to Damascus.

9:9 And he was there three days, without sight, and he did neither eat nor drink.

9:10 Now there was a certain disciple at Damascus, named Ananias. And the Lord said to him in a vision: Ananias. And he said: Behold I am here, Lord.

9:11 And the Lord said to him: Arise, and go into the street that is called Strait, and seek in the house of Judas, one named Saul of Tarsus. For behold he prayeth.

9:12 (And he saw a man named Ananias coming in, and putting his hands upon him, that he might receive his sight.)

9:13 But Ananias answered: Lord, I have heard by many of this man, how much evil he hath done to thy saints in Jerusalem.

9:14 And here he hath authority from the chief priests to bind all that invoke thy name.

9:15 And the Lord said to him: Go thy way; for this man is to me a vessel of election, to carry my name before the Gentiles, and kings, and the children of Israel.

9:16 For I will shew him how great things he must suffer for my name's sake.

9:17 And Ananias went his way, and entered into the house. And laying his hands upon him, he said: Brother Saul, the Lord Jesus hath sent me, he that appeared to thee in the way as thou camest; that thou mayest receive thy sight, and be filled with the Holy Ghost.

9:18 And immediately there fell from his eyes as it were scales, and he received his sight; and

gens baptizatus est.

9:19 Et cum accepisset cibum, confortatus est. Fuit autem cum discipulis qui erant Damasci per dies aliquot.

9:20 Et continuo in synagogis prædicabat Jesum, quoniam hic est Filius Dei.

9:21 Stupebant autem omnes qui audiebant, et dicebant : Nonne hic est qui expugnabat in Jerusalem eos qui invocabant nomen istud : et huc ad hoc venit, ut vinctos illos duceret ad principes sacerdotum ?

9:22 Saulus autem multo magis convalescebat, et confundebat Judæos qui habitabant Damasci, affirmans quoniam hic est Christus.

9:23 Cum autem implerentur dies multi, consilium fecerunt in unum Judæi ut eum interficerent.

9:24 Notæ autem factæ sunt Saulo insidiæ eorum. Custodiebant autem et portas die ac nocte, ut eum interficerent.

9:25 Accipientes autem eum discipuli nocte, per murum dimiserunt eum, submittentes in sporta.

9:26 Cum autem venisset in Jerusalem, tentabat se jungere discipulis, et omnes timebant eum, non credentes quod esset discipulus.

9:27 Barnabas autem apprehensum illum duxit ad Apostolos : et narravit illis quomodo in via vidisset Dominum, et quia locutus est ei, et quomodo in Damasco fiducialiter egerit in nomine Jesu.

9:28 Et erat cum illis intrans et exiens in Jerusalem, et fiducialiter agens in nomine Domini.

9:29 Loquebatur quoque gentibus, et disputabat cum Græcis : illi autem quærebant occidere eum.

9:30 Quod cum cognovissent fratres, deduxerunt eum Cæsaream, et dimiserunt Tarsum.

9:31 Ecclesia quidem per totam Judæam, et Galilæam, et Samariam habebat pacem, et ædificabatur ambulans in timore Domini, et consolatione Sancti Spiritus replebatur.

9:32 Factum est autem, ut Petrus dum pertransiret universos, deveniret ad sanctos qui habitabant Lyddæ.

9:33 Invenit autem ibi hominem quemdam, nomine Æneam, ab annis octo jacentem in grabato, qui erat paralyticus.

9:34 Et ait illi Petrus : Ænea, sanat te Dominus

rising up, he was baptized.

9:19 And when he had taken meat, he was strengthened. And he was with the disciples that were at Damascus, for some days.

9:20 And immediately he preached Jesus in the synagogues, that he is the Son of God.

9:21 And all that heard him, were astonished, and said: Is not this he who persecuted in Jerusalem those that called upon this name: and came hither for that intent, that he might carry them bound to the chief priests?

9:22 But Saul increased much more in strength, and confounded the Jews who dwelt at Damascus, affirming that this is the Christ.

9:23 And when many days were passed, the Jews consulted together to kill him.

9:24 But their laying in wait was made known to Saul. And they watched the gates also day and night, that they might kill him.

9:25 But the disciples taking him in the night, conveyed him away by the wall, letting him down in a basket.

9:26 And when he was come into Jerusalem, he essayed to join himself to the disciples; and they all were afraid of him, not believing that he was a disciple.

9:27 But Barnabas took him, and brought him to the apostles, and told them how he had seen the Lord, and that he had spoken to him; and how in Damascus he had dealt confidently in the name of Jesus.

9:28 And he was with them coming in and going out in Jerusalem, and dealing confidently in the name of the Lord.

9:29 He spoke also to the Gentiles, and disputed with the Greeks; but they sought to kill him.

9:30 Which when the brethren had known, they brought him down to Caesarea, and sent him away to Tarsus.

9:31 Now the church had peace throughout all Judea, and Galilee, and Samaria; and was edified, walking in the fear of the Lord, and was filled with the consolation of the Holy Ghost.

9:32 And it came to pass that Peter, as he passed through, visiting all, came to the saints who dwelt at Lydda.

9:33 And he found there a certain man named Eneas, who had kept his bed for eight years, who was ill of the palsy.

9:34 And Peter said to him: Eneas, the Lord Je-

Jesus Christus : surge, et sterne tibi. Et continuo surrexit.

9:35 Et viderunt eum omnes qui habitabant Lyddæ et Saronæ : qui conversi sunt ad Dominum.

9:36 In Joppe autem fuit quædam discipula, nomine Tabitha, quæ interpretata dicitur Dorcas. Hæc erat plena operibus bonis et eleemosynis quas faciebat.

9:37 Factum est autem in diebus illis ut infirmata moreretur. Quam cum lavissent, posuerunt eam in cœnaculo.

9:38 Cum autem prope esset Lydda ad Joppen, discipuli, audientes quia Petrus esset in ea, miserunt duos viros ad eum, rogantes : Ne pigriteris venire ad nos.

9:39 Exsurgens autem Petrus, venit cum illis. Et cum advenisset, duxerunt illum in cœnaculum : et circumsteterunt illum omnes viduæ flentes, et ostendentes ei tunicas et vestes quas faciebat illis Dorcas.

9:40 Ejectis autem omnibus foras, Petrus ponens genua oravit : et conversus ad corpus, dixit : Tabitha, surge. At illa aperuit oculos suos : et viso Petro, resedit.

9:41 Dans autem illi manum, erexit eam. Et cum vocasset sanctos et viduas, assignavit eam vivam.

9:42 Notum autem factum est per universam Joppen : et crediderunt multi in Domino.

9:43 Factum est autem ut dies multos moraretur in Joppe, apud Simonem quemdam coriarium.

10:1 Vir autem quidam erat in Cæsarea, nomine Cornelius, centurio cohortis quæ dicitur Italica,

10:2 religiosus, ac timens Deum cum omni domo sua, faciens eleemosynas multas plebi, et deprecans Deum semper.

10:3 Is vidit in visu manifeste, quasi hora diei nona, angelum Dei introëuntem ad se, et dicentem sibi : Corneli.

10:4 At ille intuens eum, timore correptus, dixit : Quid est, domine ? Dixit autem illi : Orationes tuæ et eleemosynæ tuæ ascenderunt in memoriam in conspectu Dei.

10:5 Et nunc mitte viros in Joppen, et accersi Simonem quemdam, qui cognominatur Petrus :

10:6 hic hospitatur apud Simonem quemdam coriarium, cujus est domus juxta mare : hic dicet tibi quid te oporteat facere.

10:7 Et cum discessisset angelus qui loquebatur illi, vocavit duos domesticos suos, et militem

sus Christ healeth thee: arise, and make thy bed. And immediately he arose.

9:35 And all that dwelt at Lydda and Saron, saw him: who were converted to the Lord.

9:36 And in Joppe there was a certain disciple named Tabitha, which by interpretation is called Dorcas. This woman was full of good works and almsdeeds which she did.

9:37 And it came to pass in those days that she was sick, and died. Whom when they had washed, they laid her in an upper chamber.

9:38 And forasmuch as Lydda was nigh to Joppe, the disciples hearing that Peter was there, sent unto him two men, desiring him that he would not be slack to come unto them.

9:39 And Peter rising up, went with them. And when he was come, they brought him into the upper chamber. And all the widows stood about him weeping, and shewing him the coats and garments which Dorcas made them.

9:40 And they all being put forth, Peter kneeling down prayed, and turning to the body, he said: Tabitha, arise. And she opened her eyes; and seeing Peter, she sat up.

9:41 And giving her his hand, he lifted her up. And when he had called the saints and the widows, he presented her alive.

9:42 And it was made known throughout all Joppe; and many believed in the Lord.

9:43 And it came to pass, that he abode many days in Joppe, with one Simon a tanner.

10:1 And there was a certain man in Caesarea, named Cornelius, a centurion of that which is called the Italian band;

10:2 A religious man, and fearing God with all his house, giving much alms to the people, and always praying to God.

10:3 This man saw in a vision manifestly, about the ninth hour of the day, an angel of God coming in unto him, and saying to him: Cornelius.

10:4 And he, beholding him, being seized with fear, said: What is it, Lord? And he said to him: Thy prayers and thy alms are ascended for a memorial in the sight of God.

10:5 And now send men to Joppe, and call hither one Simon, who is surnamed Peter:

10:6 He lodgeth with one Simon a tanner, whose house is by the sea side. He will tell thee what thou must do.

10:7 And when the angel who spoke to him was departed, he called two of his household serv-

metuentem Dominum ex his qui illi parebant.

10:8 Quibus cum narrasset omnia, misit illos in Joppen.

10:9 Postera autem die, iter illis facientibus, et appropinquantibus civitati, ascendit Petrus in superiora ut oraret circa horam sextam.

10:10 Et cum esuriret, voluit gustare. Parantibus autem illis, cecidit super eum mentis excessus :

10:11 et vidit cælum apertum, et descendens vas quoddam, velut linteum magnum, quatuor initiis submitti de cælo in terram,

10:12 in quo erant omnia quadrupedia, et serpentia terræ, et volatilia cæli.

10:13 Et facta est vox ad eum : Surge, Petre : occide, et manduca.

10:14 Ait autem Petrus : Absit Domine, quia numquam manducavi omne commune et immundum.

10:15 Et vox iterum secundo ad eum : Quod Deus purificavit, tu commune ne dixeris.

10:16 Hoc autem factum est per ter : et statim receptum est vas in cælum.

10:17 Et dum intra se hæsitaret Petrus quidnam esset visio quam vidisset, ecce viri qui missi erant a Cornelio, inquirentes domum Simonis astiterunt ad januam.

10:18 Et cum vocassent, interrogabant, si Simon qui cognominatur Petrus illic haberet hospitium.

10:19 Petro autem cogitante de visione, dixit Spiritus ei : Ecce viri tres quærunt te.

10:20 Surge itaque, descende, et vade cum eis nihil dubitans : quia ego misi illos.

10:21 Descendens autem Petrus ad viros, dixit : Ecce ego sum, quem quæritis : quæ causa est, propter quam venistis ?

10:22 Qui dixerunt : Cornelius centurio, vir justus et timens Deum, et testimonium habens ab universa gente Judæorum, responsum accepit ab angelo sancto accersire te in domum suam, et audire verba abs te.

10:23 Introducens ergo eos, recepit hospitio. Sequenti autem die, surgens profectus est cum illis, et quidam ex fratribus ab Joppe comitati

ants, and a soldier who feared the Lord, of them that were under him.

10:8 To whom when he had related all, he sent them to Joppe.

10:9 And on the next day, whilst they were going on their journey, and drawing nigh to the city, Peter went up to the higher parts of the house to pray, about the sixth hour.

10:10 And being hungry, he was desirous to taste somewhat. And as they were preparing, there came upon him an ecstasy of mind.

10:11 And he saw the heaven opened, and a certain vessel descending, as it were a great linen sheet let down by the four corners from heaven to the earth:

10:12 Wherein were all manner of fourfooted beasts, and creeping things of the earth, and fowls of the air.

10:13 And there came a voice to him: Arise, Peter; kill and eat.

10:14 But Peter said: Far be it from me; for I never did eat any thing that is common and unclean.

10:15 And the voice spoke to him again the second time: That which God hath cleansed, do not thou call common.

10:16 And this was done thrice; and presently the vessel was taken up into heaven.

10:17 Now, whilst Peter was doubting within himself, what the vision that he had seen should mean, behold the men who were sent from Cornelius, inquiring for Simon's house, stood at the gate.

10:18 And when they had called, they asked, if Simon, who is surnamed Peter, were lodged there.

10:19 And as Peter was thinking of the vision, the Spirit said to him: Behold three men seek thee.

10:20 Arise, therefore, get thee down and go with them, doubting nothing: for I have sent them.

10:21 Then Peter, going down to the men, said: Behold, I am he whom you seek; what is the cause for which you are come?

10:22 Who said: Cornelius, a centurion, a just man, and one that feareth God, and having good testimony from all the nation of the Jews, received an answer of an holy angel, to send for thee into his house, and to hear words of thee.

10:23 Then bringing them in, he lodged them. And the day following he arose, and went with them: and some of the brethren from Joppe ac-

sunt eum.

10:24 Altera autem die introivit Cæsaream. Cornelius vero exspectabat illos, convocatis cognatis suis et necessariis amicis.

10:25 Et factum est cum introisset Petrus, obvius venit ei Cornelius, et procidens ad pedes ejus adoravit.

10:26 Petrus vero elevavit eum, dicens : Surge : et ego ipse homo sum.

10:27 Et loquens cum illo intravit, et invenit multos qui convenerant :

10:28 dixitque ad illos : Vos scitis quomodo abominatum sit viro Judæo conjungi aut accedere ad alienigenam : sed mihi ostendit Deus neminem communem aut immundum dicere hominem.

10:29 Propter quod sine dubitatione veni accersitus. Interrogo ergo, quam ob causam accersistis me ?

10:30 Et Cornelius ait : A nudiusquarta die usque ad hanc horam, orans eram hora nona in domo mea, et ecce vir stetit ante me in veste candida, et ait :

10:31 Corneli, exaudita est oratio tua, et eleemosynæ tuæ commemoratæ sunt in conspectu Dei.

10:32 Mitte ergo in Joppen, et accersi Simonem qui cognominatur Petrus : hic hospitatur in domo Simonis coriarii juxta mare.

10:33 Confestim ergo misi ad te : et tu benefecisti veniendo. Nunc ergo omnes nos in conspectu tuo adsumus audire omnia quæcumque tibi præcepta sunt a Domino.

10:34 Aperiens autem Petrus os suum, dixit : In veritate comperi quia non est personarum acceptor Deus ;

10:35 sed in omni gente qui timet eum, et operatur justitiam, acceptus est illi.

10:36 Verbum misit Deus filiis Israël, annuntians pacem per Jesum Christum (hic est omnium Dominus).

10:37 Vos scitis quod factum est verbum per universam Judæam : incipiens enim a Galilæa post baptismum quod prædicavit Joannes,

10:38 Jesum a Nazareth : quomodo unxit eum Deus Spiritu Sancto, et virtute, qui pertransiit benefaciendo, et sanando omnes oppressos a diabolo, quoniam Deus erat cum illo.

10:39 Et nos testes sumus omnium quæ fecit in

companied him.

10:24 And the morrow after, he entered into Caesarea. And Cornelius waited for them, having called together his kinsmen and special friends.

10:25 And it came to pass, that when Peter was come in, Cornelius came to meet him, and falling at his feet adored.

10:26 But Peter lifted him up, saying: Arise, I myself also am a man.

10:27 And talking with him, he went in, and found many that were come together.

10:28 And he said to them: You know how abominable it is for a man that is a Jew, to keep company or to come unto one of another nation: but God hath shewed to me, to call no man common or unclean.

10:29 For which cause, making no doubt, I came when I was sent for. I ask, therefore, for what cause you have sent for me?

10:30 And Cornelius said: Four days ago, unto this hour, I was praying in my house, at the ninth hour, and behold a man stood before me in white apparel, and said:

10:31 Cornelius, thy prayer is heard, and thy alms are had in remembrance in the sight of God.

10:32 Send therefore to Joppe, and call hither Simon, who is surnamed Peter: he lodgeth in the house of Simon a tanner, by the sea side.

10:33 Immediately therefore I sent to thee: and thou hast done well in coming. Now therefore all we are present in thy sight, to hear all things whatsoever are commanded thee by the Lord.

10:34 And Peter opening his mouth, said: In very deed I perceive, that God is not a respecter of persons.

10:35 But in every nation, he that feareth him, and worketh justice, is acceptable to him.

10:36 God sent the word to the children of Israel, preaching peace by Jesus Christ: (he is Lord of all.)

10:37 You know the word which hath been published through all Judea: for it began from Galilee, after the baptism which John preached,

10:38 Jesus of Nazareth: how God anointed him with the Holy Ghost, and with power, who went about doing good, and healing all that were oppressed by the devil, for God was with him.

10:39 And we are witnesses of all things that he

regione Judæorum, et Jerusalem, quem occiderunt suspendentes in ligno.

10:40 Hunc Deus suscitavit tertia die, et dedit eum manifestum fieri,

10:41 non omni populo, sed testibus præordinatis a Deo : nobis, qui manducavimus et bibimus cum illo postquam resurrexit a mortuis.

10:42 Et præcepit nobis prædicare populo, et testificari, quia ipse est qui constitutus est a Deo judex vivorum et mortuorum.

10:43 Huic omnes prophetæ testimonium perhibent remissionem peccatorum accipere per nomen ejus omnes qui credunt in eum.

10:44 Adhuc loquente Petro verba hæc, cecidit Spiritus Sanctus super omnes qui audiebant verbum.

10:45 Et obstupuerunt ex circumcisione fideles qui venerant cum Petro, quia et in nationes gratia Spiritus Sancti effusa est.

10:46 Audiebant enim illos loquentes linguis, et magnificantes Deum.

10:47 Tunc respondit Petrus : Numquid aquam quis prohibere potest ut non baptizentur hi qui Spiritum Sanctum acceperunt sicut et nos ?

10:48 Et jussit eos baptizari in nomine Domini Jesu Christi. Tunc rogaverunt eum ut maneret apud eos aliquot diebus.

11:1 Audierunt autem Apostoli et fratres qui erant in Judæa, quoniam et gentes receperunt verbum Dei.

11:2 Cum autem ascendisset Petrus Jerosolymam, disceptabant adversus illum qui erant ex circumcisione,

11:3 dicentes : Quare introisti ad viros præputium habentes, et manducasti cum illis ?

11:4 Incipiens autem Petrus exponebat illis ordinem, dicens :

11:5 Ego eram in civitate Joppe orans, et vidi in excessu mentis visionem, descendens vas quoddam velut linteum magnum quatuor initiis summitti de cælo, et venit usque ad me.

11:6 In quod intuens considerabam, et vidi quadrupedia terræ, et bestias, et reptilia, et volatilia cæli.

11:7 Audivi autem et vocem dicentem mihi : Surge, Petre : occide, et manduca.

11:8 Dixi autem : Nequaquam Domine : quia commune aut immundum numquam introivit

did in the land of the Jews and in Jerusalem, whom they killed, hanging him upon a tree.

10:40 Him God raised up the third day, and gave him to be made manifest,

10:41 Not to all the people, but to witnesses preordained by God, even to us, who did eat and drink with him after he arose again from the dead;

10:42 And he commanded us to preach to the people, and to testify that it is he who was appointed by God, to be judge of the living and of the dead.

10:43 To him all the prophets give testimony, that by his name all receive remission of sins, who believe in him.

10:44 While Peter was yet speaking these words, the Holy Ghost fell on all them that heard the word.

10:45 And the faithful of the circumcision, who came with Peter, were astonished, for that the grace of the Holy Ghost was poured out upon the Gentiles also.

10:46 For they heard them speaking with tongues, and magnifying God.

10:47 Then Peter answered: Can any man forbid water, that these should not be baptized, who have received the Holy Ghost, as well as we?

10:48 And he commanded them to be baptized in the name of the Lord Jesus Christ. Then they desired him to tarry with them some days.

11:1 And the apostles and brethren, who were in Judea, heard that the Gentiles also had received the word of God.

11:2 And when Peter was come up to Jerusalem, they that were of the circumcision contended with him,

11:3 Saying: Why didst thou go in to men uncircumcised, and didst eat with them?

11:4 But Peter began and declared to them the matter in order, saying:

11:5 I was in the city of Joppe praying, and I saw in an ecstasy of mind a vision, a certain vessel descending, as it were a great sheet let down from heaven by four corners, and it came even unto me.

11:6 Into which looking, I considered, and saw fourfooted creatures of the earth, and beasts, and creeping things, and fowls of the air:

11:7 And I heard also a voice saying to me: Arise, Peter; kill and eat.

11:8 And I said: Not so, Lord; for nothing common or unclean hath ever entered into my

in os meum.

11:9 Respondit autem vox secundo de cælo : Quæ Deus mundavit, tu ne commune dixeris.

11:10 Hoc autem factum est per ter : et recepta sunt omnia rursum in cælum.

11:11 Et ecce viri tres confestim astiterunt in domo in qua eram, missi a Cæsarea ad me.

11:12 Dixit autem Spiritus mihi ut irem cum illis, nihil hæsitans. Venerunt autem mecum et sex fratres isti, et ingressi sumus in domum viri.

11:13 Narravit autem nobis quomodo vidisset angelum in domo sua, stantem et dicentem sibi : Mitte in Joppen, et accersi Simonem qui cognominatur Petrus,

11:14 qui loquetur tibi verba in quibus salvus eris tu, et universa domus tua.

11:15 Cum autem cœpissem loqui, cecidit Spiritus Sanctus super eos, sicut et in nos in initio.

11:16 Recordatus sum autem verbi Domini, sicut dicebat : Joannes quidem baptizavit aqua, vos autem baptizabimini Spiritu Sancto.

11:17 Si ergo eamdem gratiam dedit illis Deus, sicut et nobis qui credidimus in Dominum Jesum Christum : ego quis eram, qui possem prohibere Deum ?

11:18 His auditis, tacuerunt : et glorificaverunt Deum, dicentes : Ergo et gentibus pœnitentiam dedit Deus ad vitam.

11:19 Et illi quidem qui dispersi fuerant a tribulatione quæ facta fuerat sub Stephano, perambulaverunt usque Phœnicen, et Cyprum, et Antiochiam, nemini loquentes verbum, nisi solis Judæis.

11:20 Erant autem quidam ex eis viri Cyprii et Cyrenæi, qui cum introissent Antiochiam, loquebantur et ad Græcos, annuntiantes Dominum Jesum.

11:21 Et erat manus Domini cum eis : multusque numerus credentium conversus est ad Dominum.

11:22 Pervenit autem sermo ad aures ecclesiæ quæ erat Jerosolymis super istis : et miserunt Barnabam usque ad Antiochiam.

11:23 Qui cum pervenisset, et vidisset gratiam Dei, gavisus est : et hortabatur omnes in

mouth.

11:9 And the voice answered again from heaven: What God hath made clean, do not thou call common.

11:10 And this was done three times: and all were taken up again into heaven.

11:11 And behold, immediately there were three men come to the house wherein I was, sent to me from Caesarea.

11:12 And the Spirit said to me, that I should go with them, nothing doubting. And these six brethren went with me also: and we entered into the man's house.

11:13 And he told us how he had seen an angel in his house, standing, and saying to him: Send to Joppe, and call hither Simon, who is surnamed Peter,

11:14 Who shall speak to thee words, whereby thou shalt be saved, and all thy house.

11:15 And when I had begun to speak, the Holy Ghost fell upon them, as upon us also in the beginning.

11:16 And I remembered the word of the Lord, how that he said: John indeed baptized with water, but you shall be baptized with the Holy Ghost.

11:17 If then God gave them the same grace, as to us also who believed in the Lord Jesus Christ; who was I, that could withstand God?

11:18 Having heard these things, they held their peace, and glorified God, saying: God then hath also to the Gentiles given repentance unto life.

11:19 Now they who had been dispersed by the persecution that arose on occasion of Stephen, went about as far as Phenice and Cyprus and Antioch, speaking the word to none, but to the Jews only.

11:20 But some of them were men of Cyprus and Cyrene, who, when they were entered into Antioch, spoke also to the Greeks, preaching the Lord Jesus.

11:21 And the hand of the Lord was with them: and a great number believing, were converted to the Lord.

11:22 And the tidings came to the ears of the church that was at Jerusalem, touching these things: and they sent Barnabas as far as Antioch.

11:23 Who, when he was come, and had seen the grace of God, rejoiced: and he exhorted them

proposito cordis permanere in Domino :

11:24 quia erat vir bonus, et plenus Spiritu Sancto, et fide. Et apposita est multa turba Domino.

11:25 Profectus est autem Barnabas Tarsum, ut quæreret Saulum : quem cum invenisset, perduxit Antiochiam.

11:26 Et annum totum conversati sunt ibi in ecclesia : et docuerunt turbam multam, ita ut cognominarentur primum Antiochiæ discipuli, christiani.

11:27 In his autem diebus supervenerunt ab Jerosolymis prophetæ Antiochiam :

11:28 et surgens unus ex eis nomine Agabus, significabat per spiritum famem magnam futuram in universo orbe terrarum, quæ facta est sub Claudio.

11:29 Discipuli autem, prout quis habebat, proposuerunt singuli in ministerium mittere habitantibus in Judæa fratribus :

11:30 quod et fecerunt, mittentes ad seniores per manus Barnabæ et Sauli.

12:1 Eodem autem tempore misit Herodes rex manus, ut affligeret quosdam de ecclesia.

12:2 Occidit autem Jacobum fratrem Joannis gladio.

12:3 Videns autem quia placeret Judæis, apposuit ut apprehenderet et Petrum. Erant autem dies Azymorum.

12:4 Quem cum apprehendisset, misit in carcerem, tradens quatuor quaternionibus militum custodiendum, volens post Pascha producere eum populo.

12:5 Et Petrus quidem servabatur in carcere. Oratio autem fiebant sine intermissione ab ecclesia ad Deum pro eo.

12:6 Cum autem producturus eum esset Herodes, in ipsa nocte erat Petrus dormiens inter duos milites, vinctus catenis duabus : et custodes ante ostium custodiebant carcerem.

12:7 Et ecce angelus Domini astitit, et lumen refulsit in habitaculo : percussoque latere Petri, excitavit eum, dicens : Surge velociter. Et ceciderunt catenæ de manibus ejus.

12:8 Dixit autem angelus ad eum : Præcingere, et calcea te caligas tuas. Et fecit sic. Et dixit illi : Circumda tibi vestimentum tuum, et sequere me.

all with purpose of heart to continue in the Lord.

11:24 For he was a good man, and full of the Holy Ghost and of faith. And a great multitude was added to the Lord.

11:25 And Barnabas went to Tarsus to seek Saul: whom, when he had found, he brought to Antioch.

11:26 And they conversed there in the church a whole year; and they taught a great multitude, so that at Antioch the disciples were first named Christians.

11:27 And in these days there came prophets from Jerusalem to Antioch:

11:28 And one of them named Agabus, rising up, signified by the Spirit, that there should be a great famine over the whole world, which came to pass under Claudius.

11:29 And the disciples, every man according to his ability, purposed to send relief to the brethren who dwelt in Judea:

11:30 Which also they did, sending it to the ancients, by the hands of Barnabas and Saul.

12:1 And at the same time, Herod the king stretched forth his hands, to afflict some of the church.

12:2 And he killed James, the brother of John, with the sword.

12:3 And seeing that it pleased the Jews, he proceeded to take up Peter also. Now it was in the days of the Azymes.

12:4 And when he had apprehended him, he cast him into prison, delivering him to four files of soldiers to be kept, intending, after the pasch, to bring him forth to the people.

12:5 Peter therefore was kept in prison. But prayer was made without ceasing by the church unto God for him.

12:6 And when Herod would have brought him forth, the same night Peter was sleeping between two soldiers, bound with two chains: and the keepers before the door kept the prison.

12:7 And behold an angel of the Lord stood by him: and a light shined in the room: and he striking Peter on the side, raised him up, saying: Arise quickly. And the chains fell off from his hands.

12:8 And the angel said to him: Gird thyself, and put on thy sandals. And he did so. And he said to him: Cast thy garment about thee, and follow me.

12:9 Et exiens sequebatur eum, et nesciebat quia verum est, quod fiebat per angelum : existimabat autem se visum videre.

12:10 Transeuntes autem primam et secundam custodiam, venerunt ad portam ferream, quæ ducit ad civitatem : quæ ultro aperta est eis. Et exeuntes processerunt vicum unum : et continuo discessit angelus ab eo.

12:11 Et Petrus ad se reversus, dixit : Nunc scio vere quia misit Dominus angelum suum, et eripuit me de manu Herodis, et de omni exspectatione plebis Judæorum.

12:12 Consideransque venit ad domum Mariæ matris Joannis, qui cognominatus est Marcus, ubi erant multi congregati, et orantes.

12:13 Pulsante autem eo ostium januæ, processit puella ad audiendum, nomine Rhode.

12:14 Et ut cognovit vocem Petri, præ gaudio non aperuit januam, sed intro currens nuntiavit stare Petrum ante januam.

12:15 At illi dixerunt ad eam : Insanis. Illa autem affirmabat sic se habere. Illi autem dicebant : Angelus ejus est.

12:16 Petrus autem perseverabat pulsans. Cum autem aperuissent, viderunt eum, et obstupuerunt.

12:17 Annuens autem eis manu ut tacerent, narravit quomodo Dominus eduxisset eum de carcere, dixitque : Nuntiate Jacobo et fratribus hæc. Et egressus abiit in alium locum.

12:18 Facta autem die, erat non parva turbatio inter milites, quidnam factum esset de Petro.

12:19 Herodes autem cum requisisset eum et non invenisset, inquisitione facta de custodibus, jussit eos duci : descendensque a Judæa in Cæsaream, ibi commoratus est.

12:20 Erat autem iratus Tyriis et Sidoniis. At illi unanimes venerunt ad eum, et persuaso Blasto, qui erat super cubiculum regis, postulabant pacem, eo quod alerentur regiones eorum ab illo.

12:21 Statuto autem die Herodes vestitus veste regia sedit pro tribunali, et concionabatur ad eos.

12:22 Populus autem acclamabat : Dei voces, et

12:9 And going out, he followed him, and he knew not that it was true which was done by the angel: but thought he saw a vision.

12:10 And passing through the first and the second ward, they came to the iron gate that leadeth to the city, which of itself opened to them. And going out, they passed on through one street: and immediately the angel departed from him.

12:11 And Peter coming to himself, said: Now I know in very deed, that the Lord hath sent his angel, and hath delivered me out of the hand of Herod, and from all the expectation of the people of the Jews.

12:12 And considering, he came to the house of Mary the mother of John, who was surnamed Mark, where many were gathered together and praying.

12:13 And when he knocked at the door of the gate, a damsel came to hearken, whose name was Rhode.

12:14 And as soon as she knew Peter's voice, she opened not the gate for joy, but running in she told that Peter stood before the gate.

12:15 But they said to her: Thou art mad. But she affirmed that it was so. Then said they: It is his angel.

12:16 But Peter continued knocking. And when they had opened, they saw him, and were astonished.

12:17 But he beckoning to them with his hand to hold their peace, told how the Lord had brought him out of prison, and he said: Tell these things to James, and to the brethren. And going out, he went into another place.

12:18 Now when day was come, there was no small stir among the soldiers, what was become of Peter.

12:19 And when Herod had sought for him, and found him not; having examined the keepers, he commanded they should be put to death; and going down from Judea to Caesarea, he abode there.

12:20 And he was angry with the Tyrians and the Sidonians. But they with one accord came to him, and having gained Blastus, who was the king's chamberlain, they desired peace, because their countries were nourished by him.

12:21 And upon a day appointed, Herod being arrayed in kingly apparel, sat in the judgment seat, and made an oration to them.

12:22 And the people made acclamation, saying:

non hominis.

12:23 Confestim autem percussit eum angelus Domini, eo quod non dedisset honorem Deo : et consumptus a vermibus, expiravit.

12:24 Verbum autem Domini crescebat, et multiplicabatur.

12:25 Barnabas autem et Saulus reversi sunt ab Jerosolymis expleto ministerio assumpto Joanne, qui cognominatus est Marcus.

13:1 Erant autem in ecclesia quæ erat Antiochiæ, prophetæ et doctores, in quibus Barnabas, et Simon qui vocabatur Niger, et Lucius Cyrenensis, et Manahen, qui erat Herodis Tetrarchæ collactaneus, et Saulus.

13:2 Ministrantibus autem illis Domino, et jejunantibus, dixit illis Spiritus Sanctus : Segregate mihi Saulum et Barnabam in opus ad quod assumpsi eos.

13:3 Tunc jejunantes et orantes, imponentesque eis manus, dimiserunt illos.

13:4 Et ipsi quidem missi a Spiritu Sancto abierunt Seleuciam : et inde navigaverunt Cyprum.

13:5 Et cum venissent Salaminam, prædicabant verbum Dei in synagogis Judæorum. Habebant autem et Joannem in ministerio.

13:6 Et cum perambulassent universam insulam usque Paphum, invenerunt quemdam virum magum pseudoprophetam, Judæum, cui nomen erat Barjesu,

13:7 qui erat cum proconsule Sergio Paulo viro prudente. Hic, accersitis Barnaba et Saulo, desiderabat audire verbum Dei.

13:8 Resistebat autem illis Elymas magus (sic enim interpretatur nomen ejus), quærens avertere proconsulem a fide.

13:9 Saulus autem, qui et Paulus, repletus Spiritu Sancto, intuens in eum,

13:10 dixit : O plene omni dolo et omni fallacia, fili diaboli, inimice omnis justitiæ, non desinis subvertere vias Domini rectas.

13:11 Et nunc ecce manus Domini super te, et eris cæcus, non videns solem usque ad tempus. Et confestim cecidit in eum caligo et tenebræ : et circuiens quærebat qui ei manum daret.

13:12 Tunc proconsul cum vidisset factum, credidit admirans super doctrina Domini.

It is the voice of a god, and not of a man.

12:23 And forthwith an angel of the Lord struck him, because he had not given the honour to God: and being eaten up by worms, he gave up the ghost.

12:24 But the word of the Lord increased and multiplied.

12:25 And Barnabas and Saul returned from Jerusalem, having fulfilled their ministry, taking with them John, who was surnamed Mark.

13:1 Now there were in the church which was at Antioch, prophets and doctors, among whom was Barnabas, and Simon who was called Niger, and Lucius of Cyrene, and Manahen, who was the foster brother of Herod the tetrarch, and Saul.

13:2 And as they were ministering to the Lord, and fasting, the Holy Ghost said to them: Separate me Saul and Barnabas, for the work whereunto I have taken them.

13:3 Then they, fasting and praying, and imposing their hands upon them, sent them away.

13:4 So they being sent by the Holy Ghost, went to Seleucia: and from thence they sailed to Cyprus.

13:5 And when they were come to Salamina, they preached the word of God in the synagogues of the Jews. And they had John also in the ministry.

13:6 And when they had gone through the whole island, as far as Paphos, they found a certain man, a magician, a false prophet, a Jew, whose name was Bar-jesu:

13:7 Who was with the proconsul Sergius Paulus, a prudent man. He sending for Barnabas and Saul, desired to hear the word of God.

13:8 But Elymas the magician (for so his name is interpreted) withstood them, seeking to turn away the proconsul from the faith.

13:9 Then Saul, otherwise Paul, filled with the Holy Ghost, looking upon him,

13:10 Said: O full of all guile, and of all deceit, child of the devil, enemy of all justice, thou ceasest not to pervert the right ways of the Lord.

13:11 And now behold, the hand of the Lord is upon thee, and thou shalt be blind, not seeing the sun for a time. And immediately there fell a mist and darkness upon him, and going about, he sought some one to lead him by the hand.

13:12 Then the proconsul, when he had seen what was done, believed, admiring at the doc-

13:13 Et cum a Papho navigassent Paulus et qui cum eo erant, venerunt Pergen Pamphyliæ. Joannes autem discedens ab eis, reversus est Jerosolymam.

13:14 Illi vero pertranseuntes Pergen, venerunt Antiochiam Pisidiæ : et ingressi synagogam die sabbatorum, sederunt.

13:15 Post lectionem autem legis et prophetarum, miserunt principes synagogæ ad eos, dicentes : Viri fratres, si quis est in vobis sermo exhortationis ad plebem, dicite.

13:16 Surgens autem Paulus, et manu silentium indicens, ait : Viri Israëlitæ, et qui timetis Deum, audite :

13:17 Deus plebis Israël elegit patres nostros, et plebem exaltavit cum essent incolæ in terra Ægypti, et in brachio excelso eduxit eos ex ea,

13:18 et per quadraginta annorum tempus mores eorum sustinuit in deserto.

13:19 Et destruens gentes septem in terra Chanaan, sorte distribuit eis terram eorum,

13:20 quasi post quadringentos et quinquaginta annos : et post hæc dedit judices, usque ad Samuel prophetam.

13:21 Et exinde postulaverunt regem : et dedit illis Deus Saul filium Cis, virum de tribu Benjamin, annis quadraginta :

13:22 et amoto illo, suscitavit illis David regem : cui testimonium perhibens, dixit : Inveni David filium Jesse, virum secundum cor meum, qui faciet omnes voluntates meas.

13:23 Hujus Deus ex semine secundum promissionem eduxit Israël salvatorem Jesum,

13:24 prædicante Joanne ante faciem adventus ejus baptismum pœnitentiæ omni populo Israël.

13:25 Cum impleret autem Joannes cursum suum, dicebat : Quem me arbitramini esse, non sum ego : sed ecce venit post me, cujus non sum dignus calceamenta pedum solvere.

13:26 Viri fratres, filii generis Abraham, et qui in vobis timent Deum, vobis verbum salutis hujus missum est.

13:27 Qui enim habitabant Jerusalem, et principes ejus hunc ignorantes, et voces prophetarum quæ per omne sabbatum leguntur, judi-

trine of the Lord.

13:13 Now when Paul and they that were with him had sailed from Paphos, they came to Perge in Pamphylia. And John departing from them, returned to Jerusalem.

13:14 But they passing through Perge, came to Antioch in Pisidia: and entering into the synagogue on the sabbath day, they sat down.

13:15 And after the reading of the law and the prophets, the rulers of the synagogue sent to them, saying: Ye men, brethren, if you have any word of exhortation to make to the people, speak.

13:16 Then Paul rising up, and with his hand bespeaking silence, said: Ye men of Israel, and you that fear God, give ear.

13:17 The God of the people of Israel chose our fathers, and exalted the people when they were sojourners in the land of Egypt, and with an high arm brought them out from thence,

13:18 And for the space of forty years endured their manners in the desert.

13:19 And destroying seven nations in the land of Chanaan, divided their land among them, by lot,

13:20 As it were, after four hundred and fifty years: and after these things, he gave unto them judges, until Samuel the prophet.

13:21 And after that they desired a king: and God gave them Saul the son of Cis, a man of the tribe of Benjamin, forty years.

13:22 And when he had removed him, he raised them up David to be king: to whom giving testimony, he said: I have found David, the son of Jesse, a man according to my own heart, who shall do all my wills.

13:23 Of this man's seed God according to his promise, hath raised up to Israel a Saviour, Jesus:

13:24 John first preaching, before his coming, the baptism of penance to all the people of Israel.

13:25 And when John was fulfilling his course, he said: I am not he, whom you think me to be: but behold, there cometh one after me, whose shoes of his feet I am not worthy to loose.

13:26 Men, brethren, children of the stock of Abraham, and whosoever among you fear God, to you the word of this salvation is sent.

13:27 For they that inhabited Jerusalem, and the rulers thereof, not knowing him, nor the voices of the prophets, which are read every sab-

cantes impleverunt,

13:28 et nullam causam mortis invenientes in eo, petierunt a Pilato ut interficerent eum.

13:29 Cumque consummassent omnia quæ de eo scripta erant, deponentes eum de ligno, posuerunt eum in monumento.

13:30 Deus vero suscitavit eum a mortuis tertia die : qui visus est per dies multos his

13:31 qui simul ascenderant cum eo de Galilæa in Jerusalem : qui usque nunc sunt testes ejus ad plebem.

13:32 Et nos vobis annuntiamus eam, quæ ad patres nostros repromissio facta est :

13:33 quoniam hanc Deus adimplevit filiis nostris resuscitans Jesum, sicut et in psalmo secundo scriptum est : Filius meus es tu, ego hodie genui te.

13:34 Quod autem suscitavit eum a mortuis, amplius jam non reversurum in corruptionem, ita dixit : Quia dabo vobis sancta David fidelia.

13:35 Ideoque et alias dicit : Non dabis sanctum tuum videre corruptionem.

13:36 David enim in sua generatione cum administrasset, voluntati Dei dormivit : et appositus est ad patres suos, et vidit corruptionem.

13:37 Quem vero Deus suscitavit a mortuis, non vidit corruptionem.

13:38 Notum igitur sit vobis, viri fratres, quia per hunc vobis remissio peccatorum annuntiatur, et ab omnibus quibus non potuistis in lege Moysi justificari,

13:39 in hoc omnis qui credit, justificatur.

13:40 Videte ergo ne superveniat vobis quod dictum est in prophetis :

13:41 *Videte contemptores, et admiramini, et disperdimini : quia opus operor ego in diebus vestris, opus quod non credetis, si quis enarraverit vobis.*

13:42 Exeuntibus autem illis rogabant ut sequenti sabbato loquerentur sibi verba hæc.

13:43 Cumque dimissa esset synagoga, secuti sunt multi Judæorum, et colentium advenarum, Paulum et Barnabam : qui loquentes suadebant eis ut permanerent in gratia Dei.

13:44 Sequenti vero sabbato pene universa civitas convenit audire verbum Dei.

bath, judging him have fulfilled them.

13:28 And finding no cause of death in him, they desired of Pilate, that they might kill him.

13:29 And when they had fulfilled all things that were written of him, taking him down from the tree, they laid him in a sepulchre.

13:30 But God raised him up from the dead the third day:

13:31 Who was seen for many days, by them who came up with him from Galilee to Jerusalem, who to this present are his witnesses to the people.

13:32 And we declare unto you, that the promise which was made to our fathers,

13:33 This same God hath fulfilled to our children, raising up Jesus, as in the second psalm also is written: Thou art my Son, this day have I begotten thee.

13:34 And to shew that he raised him up from the dead, not to return now any more to corruption, he said thus: I will give you the holy things of David faithful.

13:35 And therefore, in another place also, he saith: Thou shalt not suffer thy holy one to see corruption.

13:36 For David, when he had served in his generation, according to the will of God, slept: and was laid unto his fathers, and saw corruption.

13:37 But he whom God hath raised from the dead, saw no corruption.

13:38 Be it known therefore to you, men, brethren, that through him forgiveness of sins is preached to you: and from all the things, from which you could not be justified by the law of Moses.

13:39 In him every one that believeth, is justified.

13:40 Beware, therefore, lest that come upon you which is spoken in the prophets:

13:41 *Behold, ye despisers, and wonder, and perish: for I work a work in your days, a work which you will not believe, if any man shall tell it you.*

13:42 And as they went out, they desired them, that on the next sabbath, they would speak unto them these words.

13:43 And when the synagogue was broken up, many of the Jews, and of the strangers who served God, followed Paul and Barnabas: who speaking to them, persuaded them to continue in the grace of God.

13:44 But the next sabbath day, the whole city almost came together, to hear the word of

13:45 Videntes autem turbas Judæi, repleti sunt zelo, et contradicebant his quæ a Paulo dicebantur, blasphemantes.

13:46 Tunc constanter Paulus et Barnabas dixerunt : Vobis oportebat primum loqui verbum Dei : sed quoniam repellitis illud, et indignos vos judicatis æternæ vitæ, ecce convertimur ad gentes.

13:47 Sic enim præcepit nobis Dominus : Posui te in lucem gentium, ut sis in salutem usque ad extremum terræ.

13:48 Audientes autem gentes, gavisæ sunt, et glorificabant verbum Domini : et crediderunt quotquot erant præordinati ad vitam æternam.

13:49 Disseminabatur autem verbum Domini per universam regionem.

13:50 Judæi autem concitaverunt mulieres religiosas et honestas, et primos civitatis, et excitaverunt persecutionem in Paulum et Barnabam : et ejecerunt eos de finibus suis.

13:51 At illi excusso pulvere pedum in eos, venerunt Iconium.

13:52 Discipuli quoque replebantur gaudio, et Spiritu Sancto.

14:1 Factum est autem Iconii, ut simul introirent in synagogam Judæorum, et loquerentur, ita ut crederet Judæorum et Græcorum copiosa multitudo.

14:2 Qui vero increduli fuerunt Judæi, suscitaverunt et ad iracundiam concitaverunt animas gentium adversus fratres.

14:3 Multo igitur tempore demorati sunt, fiducialiter agentes in Domino, testimonium perhibente verbo gratiæ suæ, dante signa et prodigia fieri per manus eorum.

14:4 Divisa est autem multitudo civitatis : et quidam quidem erant cum Judæis, quidam vero cum Apostolis.

14:5 Cum autem factus esset impetus gentilium et Judæorum cum principibus suis, ut contumeliis afficerent, et lapidarent eos,

14:6 intelligentes confugerunt ad civitates Lycaoniæ Lystram et Derben, et universam in circuitu regionem, et ibi evangelizantes erant.

14:7 Et quidam vir Lystris infirmus pedibus sedebat, claudus ex utero matris suæ, qui numquam ambulaverat.

14:8 Hic audivit Paulum loquentem. Qui intuitus eum, et videns quia fidem haberet ut salvus

God.

13:45 And the Jews seeing the multitudes, were filled with envy, and contradicted those things which were said by Paul, blaspheming.

13:46 Then Paul and Barnabas said boldly: To you it behoved us first to speak the word of God: but because you reject it, and judge yourselves unworthy of eternal life, behold we turn to the Gentiles.

13:47 For so the Lord hath commanded us: I have set thee to be the light of the Gentiles; that thou mayest be for salvation unto the utmost part of the earth.

13:48 And the Gentiles hearing it, were glad, and glorified the word of the Lord: and as many as were ordained to life everlasting, believed.

13:49 And the word of the Lord was published throughout the whole country.

13:50 But the Jews stirred up religious and honourable women, and the chief men of the city, and raised persecution against Paul and Barnabas: and cast them out of their coasts.

13:51 But they, shaking off the dust of their feet against them, came to Iconium.

13:52 And the disciples were filled with joy and with the Holy Ghost.

14:1 And it came to pass in Iconium, that they entered together into the synagogue of the Jews, and so spoke that a very great multitude both of the Jews and of the Greeks did believe.

14:2 But the unbelieving Jews stirred up and incensed the minds of the Gentiles against the brethren.

14:3 A long time therefore they abode there, dealing confidently in the Lord, who gave testimony to the word of his grace, granting signs and wonders to be done by their hands.

14:4 And the multitude of the city was divided; and some of them indeed held with the Jews, but some with the apostles.

14:5 And when there was an assault made by the Gentiles and the Jews with their rulers, to use them contumeliously, and to stone them:

14:6 They understanding it, fled to Lystra, and Derbe, cities of Lycaonia, and to the whole country round about, and were there preaching the gospel.

14:7 And there sat a certain man at Lystra, impotent in his feet, a cripple from his mother's womb, who never had walked.

14:8 This same heard Paul speaking. Who looking upon him, and seeing that he had faith to be

fieret,

14:9 dixit magna voce : Surge super pedes tuos rectus. Et exilivit, et ambulabat.

14:10 Turbæ autem cum vidissent quod fecerat Paulus, levaverunt vocem suam lycaonice, dicentes : Dii similes facti hominibus descenderunt ad nos.

14:11 Et vocabant Barnabam Jovem, Paulum vero Mercurium : quoniam ipse erat dux verbi.

14:12 Sacerdos quoque Jovis, qui erat ante civitatem, tauros et coronas ante januas afferens, cum populis volebat sacrificare.

14:13 Quod ubi audierunt Apostoli, Barnabas et Paulus, conscissis tunicis suis exilierunt in turbas, clamantes

14:14 et dicentes : Viri, quid hæc facitis ? et nos mortales sumus, similes vobis homines, annuntiantes vobis ab his vanis converti ad Deum vivum, qui fecit cælum, et terram, et mare, et omnia quæ in eis sunt :

14:15 qui in præteritis generationibus dimisit omnes gentes ingredi vias suas.

14:16 Et quidem non sine testimonio semetipsum reliquit benefaciens de cælo, dans pluvias et tempora fructifera, implens cibo et lætitia corda nostra.

14:17 Et hæc dicentes, vix sedaverunt turbas ne sibi immolarent.

14:18 Supervenerunt autem quidam ab Antiochia et Iconio Judæi : et persuasis turbis, lapidantesque Paulum, traxerunt extra civitatem, existimantes eum mortuum esse.

14:19 Circumdantibus autem eum discipulis, surgens intravit civitatem, et postera die profectus est cum Barnaba in Derben.

14:20 Cumque evangelizassent civitati illi, et docuissent multos, reversi sunt Lystram, et Iconium, et Antiochiam,

14:21 confirmantes animas discipulorum, exhortantesque ut permanerent in fide : et quoniam per multas tribulationes oportet nos intrare in regnum Dei.

14:22 Et cum constituissent illis per singulas ecclesias presbyteros, et orassent cum jejunationibus, commendaverunt eos Domino, in quem crediderunt.

14:23 Transeuntesque Pisidiam, venerunt in Pamphyliam,

14:24 et loquentes verbum Domini in Perge, de-

healed,

14:9 Said with a loud voice: Stand upright on thy feet. And he leaped up, and walked.

14:10 And when the multitudes had seen what Paul had done, they lifted up their voice in the Lycaonian tongue, saying: The gods are come down to us in the likeness of men;

14:11 And they called Barnabas, Jupiter: but Paul, Mercury; because he was chief speaker.

14:12 The priest also of Jupiter that was before the city, bringing oxen and garlands before the gate, would have offered sacrifice with the people.

14:13 Which, when the apostles Barnabas and Paul had heard, rending their clothes, they leaped out among the people, crying,

14:14 And saying: Ye men, why do ye these things? We also are mortals, men like unto you, preaching to you to be converted from these vain things, to the living God, who made the heaven, and the earth, and the sea, and all things that are in them:

14:15 Who in times past suffered all nations to walk in their own ways.

14:16 Nevertheless he left not himself without testimony, doing good from heaven, giving rains and fruitful seasons, filling our hearts with food and gladness.

14:17 And speaking these things, they scarce restrained the people from sacrificing to them.

14:18 Now there came thither certain Jews from Antioch, and Iconium: and persuading the multitude, and stoning Paul, drew him out of the city, thinking him to be dead.

14:19 But as the disciples stood round about him, he rose up and entered into the city, and the next day he departed with Barnabas to Derbe.

14:20 And when they had preached the gospel to that city, and had taught many, they returned again to Lystra, and to Iconium, and to Antioch:

14:21 Confirming the souls of the disciples, and exhorting them to continue in the faith: and that through many tribulations we must enter into the kingdom of God.

14:22 And when they had ordained to them priests in every church, and had prayed with fasting, they commended them to the Lord, in whom they believed.

14:23 And passing through Pisidia, they came into Pamphylia.

14:24 And having spoken the word of the Lord in

scenderunt in Attaliam :

14:25 et inde navigaverunt Antiochiam, unde erant traditi gratiæ Dei in opus quod compleverunt.

14:26 Cum autem venissent, et congregassent ecclesiam, retulerunt quanta fecisset Deus cum illis, et quia aperuisset gentibus ostium fidei.

14:27 Morati sunt autem tempus non modicum cum discipulis.

15:1 Et quidam descendentes de Judæa docebant fratres : Quia nisi circumcidamini secundum morem Moysi, non potestis salvari.

15:2 Facta ergo seditione non minima Paulo et Barnabæ adversus illos, statuerunt ut ascenderent Paulus et Barnabas, et quidam alii ex aliis ad Apostolos et presbyteros in Jerusalem super hac quæstione.

15:3 Illi ergo deducti ab ecclesia pertransibant Phœnicen et Samariam, narrantes conversionem gentium : et faciebant gaudium magnum omnibus fratribus.

15:4 Cum autem venissent Jerosolymam, suscepti sunt ab ecclesia, et ab Apostolis et senioribus, annuntiantes quanta Deus fecisset cum illis.

15:5 Surrexerunt autem quidam de hæresi pharisæorum, qui crediderunt, dicentes quia oportet circumcidi eos, præcipere quoque servare legem Moysi.

15:6 Conveneruntque Apostoli et seniores videre de verbo hoc.

15:7 Cum autem magna conquisitio fieret, surgens Petrus dixit ad eos : Viri fratres, vos scitis quoniam ab antiquis diebus Deus in nobis elegit, per os meum audire gentes verbum Evangelii et credere.

15:8 Et qui novit corda Deus, testimonium perhibuit, dans illis Spiritum Sanctum, sicut et nobis,

15:9 et nihil discrevit inter nos et illos, fide purificans corda eorum.

15:10 Nunc ergo quid tentatis Deum, imponere jugum super cervices discipulorum quod neque patres nostri, neque nos portare potuimus ?

15:11 sed per gratiam Domini Jesu Christi credimus salvari, quemadmodum et illi.

Perge, they went down into Attalia:

14:25 And thence they sailed to Antioch, from whence they had been delivered to the grace of God, unto the work which they accomplished.

14:26 And when they were come, and had assembled the church, they related what great things God had done with them, and how he had opened the door of faith to the Gentiles.

14:27 And they abode no small time with the disciples.

15:1 And some coming down from Judea, taught the brethren: That except you be circumcised after the manner of Moses, you cannot be saved.

15:2 And when Paul and Barnabas had no small contest with them, they determined that Paul and Barnabas, and certain others of the other side, should go up to the apostles and priests to Jerusalem about this question.

15:3 They therefore being brought on their way by the church, passed through Phenice, and Samaria, relating the conversion of the Gentiles; and they caused great joy to all the brethren.

15:4 And when they were come to Jerusalem, they were received by the church, and by the apostles and ancients, declaring how great things God had done with them.

15:5 But there arose some of the sect of the Pharisees that believed, saying: They must be circumcised, and be commanded to observe the law of Moses.

15:6 And the apostles and ancients assembled to consider of this matter.

15:7 And when there had been much disputing, Peter, rising up, said to them: Men, brethren, you know, that in former days God made choice among us, that by my mouth the Gentiles should hear the word of the gospel, and believe.

15:8 And God, who knoweth the hearts, gave testimony, giving unto them the Holy Ghost, as well as to us;

15:9 And put no difference between us and them, purifying their hearts by faith.

15:10 Now therefore, why tempt you God to put a yoke upon the necks of the disciples, which neither our fathers nor we have been able to bear?

15:11 But by the grace of the Lord Jesus Christ, we believe to be saved, in like manner as they also.

15:12 Tacuit autem omnis multitudo : et audiebant Barnabam et Paulum narrantes quanta Deus fecisset signa et prodigia in gentibus per eos.

15:13 Et postquam tacuerunt, respondit Jacobus, dicens : Viri fratres, audite me.

15:14 Simon narravit quemadmodum primum Deus visitavit sumere ex gentibus populum nomini suo.

15:15 Et huic concordant verba prophetarum : sicut scriptum est :

15:16 *Post hæc revertar, et reædificabo tabernaculum David quod decidit : et diruta ejus reædificabo, et erigam illud :*

15:17 *ut requirant ceteri hominum Dominum, et omnes gentes super quas invocatum est nomen meum, dicit Dominus faciens hæc.*

15:18 *Notum a sæculo est Domino opus suum.*

15:19 Propter quod ego judico non inquietari eos qui ex gentibus convertuntur ad Deum,

15:20 sed scribere ad eos ut abstineant se a contaminationibus simulacrorum, et fornicatione, et suffocatis, et sanguine.

15:21 Moyses enim a temporibus antiquis habet in singulis civitatibus qui eum prædicent in synagogis, ubi per omne sabbatum legitur.

15:22 Tunc placuit Apostolis et senioribus cum omni ecclesia eligere viros ex eis, et mittere Antiochiam cum Paulo et Barnaba : Judam, qui cognominabatur Barsabas, et Silam, viros primos in fratribus :

15:23 scribentes per manus eorum : Apostoli et seniores fratres, his qui sunt Antiochiæ, et Syriæ, et Ciliciæ, fratribus ex gentibus, salutem.

15:24 Quoniam audivimus quia quidam ex nobis exeuntes, turbaverunt vos verbis, evertentes animas vestras, quibus non mandavimus,

15:25 placuit nobis collectis in unum eligere viros, et mittere ad vos cum carissimis nostris Barnaba et Paulo,

15:26 hominibus qui tradiderunt animas suas pro nomine Domini nostri Jesu Christi.

15:27 Misimus ergo Judam et Silam, qui et ipsi vobis verbis referent eadem.

15:12 And all the multitude held their peace; and they heard Barnabas and Paul telling what great signs and wonders God had wrought among the Gentiles by them.

15:13 And after they had held their peace, James answered, saying: Men, brethren, hear me.

15:14 Simon hath related how God first visited to take of the Gentiles a people to his name.

15:15 And to this agree the words of the prophets, as it is written:

15:16 *After these things I will return, and will rebuild the tabernacle of David, which is fallen down; and the ruins thereof I will rebuild, and I will set it up:*

15:17 *That the residue of men may seek after the Lord, and all nations upon whom my name is invoked, saith the Lord, who doth these things.*

15:18 *To the Lord was his own work known from the beginning of the world.*

15:19 For which cause I judge that they, who from among the Gentiles are converted to God, are not to be disquieted.

15:20 But that we write unto them, that they refrain themselves from the pollutions of idols, and from fornication, and from things strangled, and from blood.

15:21 For Moses of old time hath in every city them that preach him in the synagogues, where he is read every sabbath.

15:22 Then it pleased the apostles and ancients, with the whole church, to choose men of their own company, and to send to Antioch, with Paul and Barnabas, namely, Judas, who was surnamed Barsabas, and Silas, chief men among the brethren.

15:23 Writing by their hands: The apostles and ancients, brethren, to the brethren of the Gentiles that are at Antioch, and in Syria and Cilicia, greeting.

15:24 Forasmuch as we have heard, that some going out from us have troubled you with words, subverting your souls; to whom we gave no commandment:

15:25 It hath seemed good to us, being assembled together, to choose out men, and to send them unto you, with our well beloved Barnabas and Paul:

15:26 Men that have given their lives for the name of our Lord Jesus Christ.

15:27 We have sent therefore Judas and Silas, who themselves also will, by word of mouth, tell you the same things.

15:28 Visum est enim Spiritui Sancto et nobis nihil ultra imponere vobis oneris quam hæc necessaria :

15:29 ut abstineatis vos ab immolatis simulacrorum, et sanguine, et suffocato, et fornicatione : a quibus custodientes vos, bene agetis. Valete.

15:30 Illi ergo dimissi, descenderunt Antiochiam : et congregata multitudine tradiderunt epistolam.

15:31 Quam cum legissent, gavisi sunt super consolatione.

15:32 Judas autem et Silas, et ipsi cum essent prophetæ, verbo plurimo consolati sunt fratres, et confirmaverunt.

15:33 Facto autem ibi aliquanto tempore, dimissi sunt cum pace a fratribus ad eos qui miserant illos.

15:34 Visum est autem Silæ ibi remanere : Judas autem solus abiit Jerusalem.

15:35 Paulus autem et Barnabas demorabantur Antiochiæ, docentes et evangelizantes cum aliis pluribus verbum Domini.

15:36 Post aliquot autem dies, dixit ad Barnabam Paulus : Revertentes visitemus fratres per universas civitates in quibus prædicavimus verbum Domini, quomodo se habeant.

15:37 Barnabas autem volebat secum assumere et Joannem, qui cognominabatur Marcus.

15:38 Paulus autem rogabat eum (ut qui discessisset ab eis de Pamphylia, et non isset cum eis in opus) non debere recipi.

15:39 Facta est autem dissensio, ita ut discederent ab invicem, et Barnabas quidem, assumpto Marco, navigaret Cyprum.

15:40 Paulus vero, electo Sila, profectus est, traditus gratiæ Dei a fratribus.

15:41 Perambulabat autem Syriam et Ciliciam, confirmans ecclesias : præcipiens custodire præcepta Apostolorum et seniorum.

16:1 Pervenit autem Derben et Lystram. Et ecce discipulus quidam erat ibi nomine Timotheus, filius mulieris Judææ fidelis, patre gentili.

16:2 Huic testimonium bonum reddebant qui in Lystris erant et Iconio fratres.

16:3 Hunc voluit Paulus secum proficisci : et assumens circumcidit eum propter Judæos qui erant in illis locis. Sciebant enim omnes quod pater ejus erat gentilis.

15:28 For it hath seemed good to the Holy Ghost and to us, to lay no further burden upon you than these necessary things:

15:29 That you abstain from things sacrificed to idols, and from blood, and from things strangled, and from fornication; from which things keeping yourselves, you shall do well. Fare ye well.

15:30 They therefore being dismissed, went down to Antioch; and gathering together the multitude, delivered the epistle.

15:31 Which when they had read, they rejoiced for the consolation.

15:32 But Judas and Silas, being prophets also themselves, with many words comforted the brethren, and confirmed them.

15:33 And after they had spent some time there, they were let go with peace by the brethren, unto them that had sent them.

15:34 But it seemed good unto Silas to remain there; and Judas alone departed to Jerusalem.

15:35 And Paul and Barnabas continued at Antioch, teaching and preaching, with many others, the word of the Lord.

15:36 And after some days, Paul said to Barnabas: Let us return and visit our brethren in all the cities wherein we have preached the word of the Lord, to see how they do.

15:37 And Barnabas would have taken with them John also, that was surnamed Mark;

15:38 But Paul desired that he (as having departed from them out of Pamphylia, and not gone with them to the work) might not be received.

15:39 And there arose a dissension, so that they departed one from another; and Barnabas indeed taking Mark, sailed to Cyprus.

15:40 But Paul choosing Silas, departed, being delivered by the brethren to the grace of God.

15:41 And he went through Syria and Cilicia, confirming the churches, commanding them to keep the precepts of the apostles and the ancients.

16:1 And he came to Derbe and Lystra. And behold, there was a certain disciple there named Timothy, the son of a Jewish woman that believed; but his father was a Gentile.

16:2 To this man the brethren that were in Lystra and Iconium, gave a good testimony.

16:3 Him Paul would have to go along with him: and taking him he circumcised him, because of the Jews who were in those places. For they all knew that his father was a Gentile.

16:4 Cum autem pertransirent civitates, tradebant eis custodiri dogmata quæ erant decreta ab Apostolis et senioribus qui erant Jerosolymis.

16:5 Et ecclesiæ quidem confirmabantur fide, et abundabunt numero quotidie.

16:6 Transeuntes autem Phrygiam et Galatiæ regionem, vetati sunt a Spiritu Sancto loqui verbum Dei in Asia.

16:7 Cum venissent autem in Mysiam, tentabant ire in Bithyniam : et non permisit eos Spiritus Jesu.

16:8 Cum autem pertransissent Mysiam, descenderunt Troadem :

16:9 et visio per noctem Paulo ostensa est : vir Macedo quidam erat stans et deprecans eum, et dicens : Transiens in Macedoniam, adjuva nos.

16:10 Ut autem visum vidit, statim quæsivimus proficisci in Macedoniam, certi facti quod vocasset nos Deus evangelizare eis.

16:11 Navigantes autem a Troade, recto cursu venimus Samothraciam, et sequenti die Neapolim :

16:12 et inde Philippos, quæ est prima partis Macedoniæ civitas, colonia. Eramus autem in hac urbe diebus aliquot, conferentes.

16:13 Die autem sabbatorum egressi sumus foras portam juxta flumen, ubi videbatur oratio esse : et sedentes loquebamur mulieribus quæ convenerant.

16:14 Et quædam mulier nomine Lydia, purpuraria civitatis Thyatirenorum, colens Deum, audivit : cujus Dominus aperuit cor intendere his quæ dicebantur a Paulo.

16:15 Cum autem baptizata esset, et domus ejus, deprecata est, dicens : Si judicastis me fidelem Domino esse, introite in domum meam, et manete. Et coëgit nos.

16:16 Factum est autem euntibus nobis ad orationem, puellam quamdam habentem spiritum pythonem obviare nobis, quæ quæstum magnum præstabat dominis suis divinando.

16:17 Hæc subsecuta Paulum et nos, clamabat dicens : Isti homines servi Dei excelsi sunt, qui annuntiant vobis viam salutis.

16:4 And as they passed through the cities, they delivered unto them the decrees for to keep, that were decreed by the apostles and ancients who were at Jerusalem.

16:5 And the churches were confirmed in faith, and increased in number daily.

16:6 And when they had passed through Phrygia, and the country of Galatia, they were forbidden by the Holy Ghost to preach the word in Asia.

16:7 And when they were come into Mysia, they attempted to go into Bithynia, and the Spirit of Jesus suffered them not.

16:8 And when they had passed through Mysia, they went down to Troas.

16:9 And a vision was shewed to Paul in the night, which was a man of Macedonia standing and beseeching him, and saying: Pass over into Macedonia, and help us.

16:10 And as soon as he had seen the vision, immediately we sought to go into Macedonia, being assured that God had called us to preach the gospel to them.

16:11 And sailing from Troas, we came with a straight course to Samothracia, and the day following to Neapolis;

16:12 And from thence to Philippi, which is the chief city of part of Macedonia, a colony. And we were in this city some days conferring together.

16:13 And upon the sabbath day, we went forth without the gate by a river side, where it seemed that there was prayer; and sitting down, we spoke to the women that were assembled.

16:14 And a certain woman named Lydia, a seller of purple, of the city of Thyatira, one that worshipped God, did hear: whose heart the Lord opened to attend to those things which were said by Paul.

16:15 And when she was baptized, and her household, she besought us, saying: If you have judged me to be faithful to the Lord, come into my house, and abide there. And she constrained us.

16:16 And it came to pass, as we went to prayer, a certain girl, having a pythonical spirit, met us, who brought to her masters much gain by divining.

16:17 This same following Paul and us, cried out, saying: These men are the servants of the most high God, who preach unto you the way of sal-

16:18 Hoc autem faciebat multis diebus. Dolens autem Paulus, et conversus, spiritui dixit : Præcipio tibi in nomine Jesu Christi exire ab ea. Et exiit eadem hora.

16:19 Videntes autem domini ejus quia exivit spes quæstus eorum, apprehendentes Paulum et Silam, perduxerunt in forum ad principes :

16:20 et offerentes eos magistratibus, dixerunt : Hi homines conturbant civitatem nostram, cum sint Judæi :

16:21 et annuntiant morem quem non licet nobis suscipere neque facere, cum simus Romani.

16:22 Et cucurrit plebs adversus eos : et magistratus, scissis tunicis eorum, jusserunt eos virgis cædi.

16:23 Et cum multas plagas eis imposuissent, miserunt eos in carcerem, præcipientes custodi ut diligenter custodiret eos.

16:24 Qui cum tale præceptum accepisset, misit eos in interiorem carcerem, et pedes eorum strinxit ligno.

16:25 Media autem nocte Paulus et Silas orantes, laudabant Deum : et audiebant eos qui in custodia erant.

16:26 Subito vero terræmotus factus est magnus, ita ut moverentur fundamenta carceris. Et statim aperta sunt omnia ostia : et universorum vincula soluta sunt.

16:27 Expergefactus autem custos carceris, et videns januas apertas carceris, evaginato gladio volebat se interficere, æstimans fugisse vinctos.

16:28 Clamavit autem Paulus voce magna, dicens : Nihil tibi mali feceris : universi enim hic sumus.

16:29 Petitoque lumine, introgressus est : et tremefactus procidit Paulo et Silæ ad pedes :

16:30 et producens eos foras, ait : Domini, quid me oportet facere, ut salvus fiam ?

16:31 At illi dixerunt : Crede in Dominum Jesum, et salvus eris tu, et domus tua.

16:32 Et locuti sunt ei verbum Domini cum omnibus qui erant in domo ejus.

16:33 Et tollens eos in illa hora noctis, lavit plagas eorum : et baptizatus est ipse, et omnis domus ejus continuo.

16:34 Cumque perduxisset eos in domum suam, apposuit eis mensam, et lætatus est cum omni

vation.

16:18 And this she did many days. But Paul being grieved, turned, and said to the spirit: I command thee, in the name of Jesus Christ, to go out from her. And he went out the same hour.

16:19 But her masters, seeing that the hope of their gain was gone, apprehending Paul and Silas, brought them into the marketplace to the rulers.

16:20 And presenting them to the magistrates, they said: These men disturb our city, being Jews;

16:21 And preach a fashion which it is not lawful for us to receive nor observe, being Romans.

16:22 And the people ran together against them; and the magistrates rending off their clothes, commanded them to be beaten with rods.

16:23 And when they had laid many stripes upon them, they cast them into prison, charging the gaoler to keep them diligently.

16:24 Who having received such a charge, thrust them into the inner prison, and made their feet fast in the stocks.

16:25 And at midnight, Paul and Silas praying, praised God. And they that were in prison, heard them.

16:26 And suddenly there was a great earthquake, so that the foundations of the prison were shaken. And immediately all the doors were opened, and the bands of all were loosed.

16:27 And the keeper of the prison, awaking out of his sleep, and seeing the doors of the prison open, drawing his sword, would have killed himself, supposing that the prisoners had been fled.

16:28 But Paul cried with a loud voice, saying: Do thyself no harm, for we all are here.

16:29 Then calling for a light, he went in, and trembling, fell down at the feet of Paul and Silas.

16:30 And bringing them out, he said: Masters, what must I do, that I may be saved?

16:31 But they said: Believe in the Lord Jesus, and thou shalt be saved, and thy house.

16:32 And they preached the word of the Lord to him and to all that were in his house.

16:33 And he, taking them the same hour of the night, washed their stripes, and himself was baptized, and all his house immediately.

16:34 And when he had brought them into his own house, he laid the table for them, and re-

domo sua credens Deo.

16:35 Et cum dies factus esset, miserunt magistratus lictores, dicentes : Dimitte homines illos.

16:36 Nuntiavit autem custos carceris verba hæc Paulo : Quia miserunt magistratus ut dimittamini : nunc igitur exeuntes, ite in pace.

16:37 Paulus autem dixit eis : Cæsos nos publice, indemnatos homines Romanos, miserunt in carcerem : et nunc occulte nos ejiciunt ? Non ita : sed veniant,

16:38 et ipsi nos ejiciant. Nuntiaverunt autem magistratibus lictores verba hæc. Timueruntque audito quod Romani essent :

16:39 et venientes deprecati sunt eos, et educentes rogabant ut egrederentur de urbe.

16:40 Exeuntes autem de carcere, introierunt ad Lydiam : et visis fratribus consolati sunt eos, et profecti sunt.

17:1 Cum autem perambulassent Amphipolim et Apolloniam, venerunt Thessalonicam, ubi erat synagoga Judæorum.

17:2 Secundum consuetudinem autem Paulus introivit ad eos, et per sabbata tria disserebat eis de Scripturis,

17:3 adaperiens et insinuans quia Christum oportuit pati, et resurgere a mortuis : et quia hic est Jesus Christus, quem ego annuntio vobis.

17:4 Et quidam ex eis crediderunt et adjuncti sunt Paulo et Silæ : et de colentibus gentilibusque multitudo magna, et mulieres nobiles non paucæ.

17:5 Zelantes autem Judæi, assumentesque de vulgo viros quosdam malos, et turba facta, concitaverunt civitatem : et assistentes domui Jasonis quærebant eos producere in populum.

17:6 Et cum non invenissent eos, trahebant Jasonem et quosdam fratres ad principes civitatis, clamantes : Quoniam hi qui urbem concitant, et huc venerunt,

17:7 quos suscepit Jason, et hi omnes contra decreta Cæsaris faciunt, regem alium dicentes esse, Jesum.

17:8 Concitaverunt autem plebem et principes civitatis audientes hæc.

17:9 Et accepta satisfactione a Jasone et a ceteris,

joiced with all his house, believing God.

16:35 And when the day was come, the magistrates sent the serjeants, saying, Let those men go.

16:36 And the keeper of the prison told these words to Paul: The magistrates have sent to let you go; now therefore depart, and go in peace.

16:37 But Paul said to them: They have beaten us publicly, uncondemned, men that are Romans, and have cast us into prison: and now do they thrust us out privately? Not so; but let them come,

16:38 And let us out themselves. And the serjeants told these words to the magistrates. And they were afraid, hearing that they were Romans.

16:39 And coming, they besought them; and bringing them out, they desired them to depart out of the city.

16:40 And they went out of the prison, and entered into the house of Lydia; and having seen the brethren, they comforted them, and departed.

17:1 And when they had passed through Amphipolis and Apollonia, they came to Thessalonica, where there was a synagogue of the Jews.

17:2 And Paul, according to his custom, went in unto them; and for three sabbath days he reasoned with them out of the scriptures:

17:3 Declaring and insinuating that the Christ was to suffer, and to rise again from the dead; and that this is Jesus Christ, whom I preach to you.

17:4 And some of them believed, and were associated to Paul and Silas; and of those that served God, and of the Gentiles a great multitude, and of noble women not a few.

17:5 But the Jews, moved with envy, and taking unto them some wicked men of the vulgar sort, and making a tumult, set the city in an uproar; and besetting Jason's house, sought to bring them out unto the people.

17:6 And not finding them, they drew Jason and certain brethren to the rulers of the city, crying: They that set the city in an uproar, are come hither also;

17:7 Whom Jason hath received; and these all do contrary to the decrees of Caesar, saying that there is another king, Jesus.

17:8 And they stirred up the people, and the rulers of the city hearing these things,

17:9 And having taken satisfaction of Jason and

dimiserunt eos.

17:10 Fratres vero confestim per noctem dimiserunt Paulum et Silam in Berœam. Qui cum venissent, in synagogam Judæorum introierunt.

17:11 Hi autem erant nobiliores eorum qui sunt Thessalonicæ, qui susceperunt verbum cum omni aviditate, quotidie scrutantes Scripturas, si hæc ita se haberent.

17:12 Et multi quidem crediderunt ex eis, et mulierum gentilium honestarum, et viri non pauci.

17:13 Cum autem cognovissent in Thessalonica Judæi quia et Berœæ prædicatum est a Paulo verbum Dei, venerunt et illuc commoventes, et turbantes multitudinem.

17:14 Statimque tunc Paulum dimiserunt fratres, ut iret usque ad mare : Silas autem et Timotheus remanserunt ibi.

17:15 Qui autem deducebant Paulum, perduxerunt eum usque Athenas, et accepto mandato ab eo ad Silam et Timotheum ut quam celeriter venirent ad illum, profecti sunt.

17:16 Paulus autem cum Athenis eos exspectaret, incitabatur spiritus ejus in ipso, videns idololatriæ deditam civitatem.

17:17 Disputabat igitur in synagoga cum Judæis et colentibus, et in foro, per omnes dies ad eos qui aderant.

17:18 Quidam autem epicurei et stoici philosophi disserebant cum eo, et quidam dicebant : Quid vult seminiverbius hic dicere ? Alii vero : Novorum dæmoniorum videtur annuntiator esse : quia Jesum et resurrectionem annuntiabat eis.

17:19 Et apprehensum eum ad Areopagum duxerunt, dicentes : Possumus scire quæ est hæc nova, quæ a te dicitur, doctrina ?

17:20 nova enim quædam infers auribus nostris : volumus ergo scire quidnam velint hæc esse.

17:21 (Athenienses autem omnes, et advenæ hospites, ad nihil aliud vacabant nisi aut dicere aut audire aliquid novi.)

17:22 Stans autem Paulus in medio Areopagi, ait : Viri Athenienses, per omnia quasi superstitiosiores vos video.

17:23 Præteriens enim, et videns simulacra vestra, inveni et aram in qua scriptum erat : Ignoto Deo. Quod ergo ignorantes colitis, hoc ego

of the rest, they let them go.

17:10 But the brethren immediately sent away Paul and Silas by night unto Berea. Who, when they were come thither, went into the synagogue of the Jews.

17:11 Now these were more noble than those in Thessalonica, who received the word with all eagerness, daily searching the scriptures, whether these things were so.

17:12 And many indeed of them believed, and of honourable women that were Gentiles, and of men not a few.

17:13 And when the Jews of Thessalonica had knowledge that the word of God was also preached by Paul at Berea, they came thither also, stirring up and troubling the multitude.

17:14 And then immediately the brethren sent away Paul, to go unto the sea; but Silas and Timothy remained there.

17:15 And they that conducted Paul, brought him as far as Athens; and receiving a commandment from him to Silas and Timothy, that they should come to him with all speed, they departed.

17:16 Now whilst Paul waited for them at Athens, his spirit was stirred within him, seeing the city wholly given to idolatry.

17:17 He disputed, therefore, in the synagogue with the Jews, and with them that served God, and in the marketplace, every day with them that were there.

17:18 And certain philosophers of the Epicureans and of the Stoics disputed with him; and some said: What is it, that this word sower would say? But others: He seemeth to be a setter forth of new gods; because he preached to them Jesus and the resurrection.

17:19 And taking him, they brought him to the Areopagus, saying: May we know what this new doctrine is, which thou speakest of?

17:20 For thou bringest in certain new things to our ears. We would know therefore what these things mean.

17:21 (Now all the Athenians, and strangers that were there, employed themselves in nothing else, but either in telling or in hearing some new thing.)

17:22 But Paul standing in the midst of the Areopagus, said: Ye men of Athens, I perceive that in all things you are too superstitious.

17:23 For passing by, and seeing your idols, I found an altar also, on which was written: To the unknown God. What therefore you wor-

annuntio vobis.

17:24 Deus, qui fecit mundum, et omnia quæ in eo sunt, hic cæli et terræ cum sit Dominus, non in manufactis templis habitat,

17:25 nec manibus humanis colitur indigens aliquo, cum ipse det omnibus vitam, et inspirationem, et omnia :

17:26 fecitque ex uno omne genus hominum inhabitare super universam faciem terræ, definiens statuta tempora, et terminos habitationis eorum,

17:27 quærere Deum si forte attrectent eum, aut inveniant, quamvis non longe sit ab unoquoque nostrum.

17:28 In ipso enim vivimus, et movemur, et sumus : sicut et quidam vestrorum poëtarum dixerunt : Ipsius enim et genus sumus.

17:29 Genus ergo cum simus Dei, non debemus æstimare auro, aut argento, aut lapidi, sculpturæ artis, et cogitationis hominis, divinum esse simile.

17:30 Et tempora quidem hujus ignorantiæ despiciens Deus, nunc annuntiat hominibus ut omnes ubique pœnitentiam agant,

17:31 eo quod statuit diem in quo judicaturus est orbem in æquitate, in viro in quo statuit, fidem præbens omnibus, suscitans eum a mortuis.

17:32 Cum audissent autem resurrectionem mortuorum, quidam quidem irridebant, quidam vero dixerunt : Audiemus te de hoc iterum.

17:33 Sic Paulus exivit de medio eorum.

17:34 Quidam vero viri adhærentes ei, crediderunt : in quibus et Dionysius Areopagita, et mulier nomine Damaris, et alii cum eis.

18:1 Post hæc egressus ab Athenis, venit Corinthum :

18:2 et inveniens quemdam Judæum nomine Aquilam, Ponticum genere, qui nuper venerat ab Italia, et Priscillam uxorem ejus (eo quod præcepisset Claudius discedere omnes Judæos a Roma), accessit ad eos.

18:3 Et quia ejusdem erat artis, manebat apud eos, et operabatur. (Erant autem scenofactoriæ artis.)

18:4 Et disputabat in synagoga per omne sabbatum, interponens nomen Domini Jesu : suadebatque Judæis et Græcis.

18:5 Cum venissent autem de Macedonia Silas et Timotheus, instabat verbo Paulus, testificans

ship, without knowing it, that I preach to you:

17:24 God, who made the world, and all things therein; he, being Lord of heaven and earth, dwelleth not in temples made with hands;

17:25 Neither is he served with men's hands, as though he needed any thing; seeing it is he who giveth to all life, and breath, and all things:

17:26 And hath made of one, all mankind, to dwell upon the whole face of the earth, determining appointed times, and the limits of their habitation.

17:27 That they should seek God, if happily they may feel after him or find him, although he be not far from every one of us:

17:28 For in him we live, and move, and are; as some also of your own poets said: For we are also his offspring.

17:29 Being therefore the offspring of God, we must not suppose the divinity to be like unto gold, or silver, or stone, the graving of art, and device of man.

17:30 And God indeed having winked at the times of this ignorance, now declareth unto men, that all should every where do penance.

17:31 Because he hath appointed a day wherein he will judge the world in equity, by the man whom he hath appointed; giving faith to all, by raising him up from the dead.

17:32 And when they had heard of the resurrection of the dead, some indeed mocked, but others said: We will hear thee again concerning this matter.

17:33 So Paul went out from among them.

17:34 But certain men adhering to him, did believe; among whom was also Dionysius, the Areopagite, and a woman named Damaris, and others with them.

18:1 After these things, departing from Athens, he came to Corinth.

18:2 And finding a certain Jew, named Aquila, born in Pontus, lately come from Italy, with Priscilla his wife, (because that Claudius had commanded all Jews to depart from Rome,) he came to them.

18:3 And because he was of the same trade, he remained with them, and wrought; (now they were tentmakers by trade.)

18:4 And he reasoned in the synagogue every sabbath, bringing in the name of the Lord Jesus; and he persuaded the Jews and the Greeks.

18:5 And when Silas and Timothy were come from Macedonia, Paul was earnest in preach-

Judæis esse Christum Jesum.

18:6 Contradicentibus autem eis, et blasphemantibus, excutiens vestimenta sua, dixit ad eos : Sanguis vester super caput vestrum : mundus ego : ex hoc ad gentes vadam.

18:7 Et migrans inde, intravit in domum cujusdam, nomine Titi Justi, colentis Deum, cujus domus erat conjuncta synagogæ.

18:8 Crispus autem archisynagogus credidit Domino cum omni domo sua : et multi Corinthiorum audientes credebant, et baptizabantur.

18:9 Dixit autem Dominus nocte per visionem Paulo : Noli timere, sed loquere, et ne taceas :

18:10 propter quod ego sum tecum, et nemo apponetur tibi ut noceat te : quoniam populus est mihi multus in hac civitate.

18:11 Sedit autem ibi annum et sex menses, docens apud eos verbum Dei.

18:12 Gallione autem proconsule Achaiæ, insurrexerunt uno animo Judæi in Paulum, et adduxerunt eum ad tribunal,

18:13 dicentes : Quia contra legem hic persuadet hominibus colere Deum.

18:14 Incipiente autem Paulo aperire os, dixit Gallio ad Judæos : Si quidem esset iniquum aliquid aut facinus pessimum, o viri Judæi, recte vos sustinerem.

18:15 Si vero quæstiones sunt de verbo, et nominibus, et lege vestra, vos ipsi videritis : judex ego horum nolo esse.

18:16 Et minavit eos a tribunali.

18:17 Apprehendentes autem omnes Sosthenem principem synagogæ, percutiebant eum ante tribunal : et nihil eorum Gallioni curæ erat.

18:18 Paulus vero cum adhuc sustinuisset dies multos fratribus valefaciens, navigavit in Syriam (et cum eo Priscilla et Aquila), qui sibi totonderat in Cenchris caput : habebat enim votum.

18:19 Devenitque Ephesum, et illos ibi reliquit. Ipse vero ingressus synagogam, disputabat cum Judæis.

18:20 Rogantibus autem eis ut ampliori tempore maneret, non consensit,

18:21 sed valefaciens, et dicens : Iterum revertar ad vos, Deo volente : profectus est ab Epheso.

ing, testifying to the Jews, that Jesus is the Christ.

18:6 But they gainsaying and blaspheming, he shook his garments, and said to them: Your blood be upon your own heads; I am clean: from henceforth I will go unto the Gentiles.

18:7 And departing thence, he entered into the house of a certain man, named Titus Justus, one that worshipped God, whose house was adjoining to the synagogue.

18:8 And Crispus, the ruler of the synagogue, believed in the Lord, with all his house; and many of the Corinthians hearing, believed, and were baptized.

18:9 And the Lord said to Paul in the night, by a vision: Do not fear, but speak; and hold not thy peace,

18:10 Because I am with thee: and no man shall set upon thee, to hurt thee; for I have much people in this city.

18:11 And he stayed there a year and six months, teaching among them the word of God.

18:12 But when Gallio was proconsul of Achaia, the Jews with one accord rose up against Paul, and brought him to the judgment seat,

18:13 Saying: This man persuadeth men to worship God contrary to the law.

18:14 And when Paul was beginning to open his mouth, Gallio said to the Jews: If it were some matter of injustice, or an heinous deed, O Jews, I should with reason bear with you.

18:15 But if they be questions of word and names, and of your law, look you to it: I will not be judge of such things.

18:16 And he drove them from the judgment seat.

18:17 And all laying hold on Sosthenes, the ruler of the synagogue, beat him before the judgment seat; and Gallio cared for none of those things.

18:18 But Paul, when he had stayed yet many days, taking his leave of the brethren, sailed thence into Syria (and with him Priscilla and Aquila), having shorn his head in Cenchrae: for he had a vow.

18:19 And he came to Ephesus, and left them there. But he himself entering into the synagogue, disputed with the Jews.

18:20 And when they desired him, that he would tarry a longer time, he consented not;

18:21 But taking his leave, and saying: I will return to you again, God willing, he departed

18:22 Et descendens Cæsaream, ascendit, et salutavit ecclesiam, et descendit Antiochiam.

18:23 Et facto ibi aliquanto tempore profectus est, perambulans ex ordine Galaticam regionem, et Phrygiam, confirmans omnes discipulos.

18:24 Judæus autem quidam, Apollo nomine, Alexandrinus genere, vir eloquens, devenit Ephesum, potens in scripturis.

18:25 Hic erat edoctus viam Domini : et fervens spiritu loquebatur, et docebat diligenter ea quæ sunt Jesu, sciens tantum baptisma Joannis.

18:26 Hic ergo cœpit fiducialiter agere in synagoga. Quem cum audissent Priscilla et Aquila, assumpserunt eum, et diligentius exposuerunt ei viam Domini.

18:27 Cum autem vellet ire Achaiam, exhortati fratres, scripserunt discipulis ut susciperent eum. Qui cum venisset, contulit multum his qui crediderant.

18:28 Vehementer enim Judæos revincebat publice, ostendens per Scripturas esse Christum Jesum.

19:1 Factum est autem cum Apollo esset Corinthi, ut Paulus peragratis superioribus partibus veniret Ephesum, et inveniret quosdam discipulos :

19:2 dixitque ad eos : Si Spiritum Sanctum accepistis credentes ? At illi dixerunt ad eum : Sed neque si Spiritus Sanctus est, audivimus.

19:3 Ille vero ait : In quo ergo baptizati estis ? Qui dixerunt : In Joannis baptismate.

19:4 Dixit autem Paulus : Joannes baptizavit baptismo pœnitentiæ populum, dicens in eum qui venturus esset post ipsum ut crederent, hoc est, in Jesum.

19:5 His auditis, baptizati sunt in nomine Domini Jesu.

19:6 Et cum imposuisset illis manus Paulus, venit Spiritus Sanctus super eos, et loquebantur linguis, et prophetabant.

19:7 Erant autem omnes viri fere duodecim.

19:8 Introgressus autem synagogam, cum fiducia loquebatur per tres menses, disputans et suadens de regno Dei.

19:9 Cum autem quidam indurarentur, et non

from Ephesus.

18:22 And going down to Caesarea, he went up to Jerusalem, and saluted the church, and so came down to Antioch.

18:23 And after he had spent some time there, he departed, and went through the country of Galatia and Phrygia, in order, confirming all the disciples.

18:24 Now a certain Jew, named Apollo, born at Alexandria, an eloquent man, came to Ephesus, one mighty in the scriptures.

18:25 This man was instructed in the way of the Lord; and being fervent in spirit, spoke, and taught diligently the things that are of Jesus, knowing only the baptism of John.

18:26 This man therefore began to speak boldly in the synagogue. Whom when Priscilla and Aquila had heard, they took him to them, and expounded to him the way of the Lord more diligently.

18:27 And whereas he was desirous to go to Achaia, the brethren exhorting, wrote to the disciples to receive him. Who, when he was come, helped them much who had believed.

18:28 For with much vigour he convinced the Jews openly, shewing by the scriptures, that Jesus is the Christ.

19:1 And it came to pass, while Apollo was at Corinth, that Paul having passed through the upper coasts, came to Ephesus, and found certain disciples.

19:2 And he said to them: Have you received the Holy Ghost since ye believed? But they said to him: We have not so much as heard whether there be a Holy Ghost.

19:3 And he said: In what then were you baptized? Who said: In John's baptism.

19:4 Then Paul said: John baptized the people with the baptism of penance, saying: That they should believe in him who was to come after him, that is to say, in Jesus.

19:5 Having heard these things, they were baptized in the name of the Lord Jesus.

19:6 And when Paul had imposed his hands on them, the Holy Ghost came upon them, and they spoke with tongues and prophesied.

19:7 And all the men were about twelve.

19:8 And entering into the synagogue, he spoke boldly for the space of three months, disputing and exhorting concerning the kingdom of God.

19:9 But when some were hardened, and be-

crederent, maledicentes viam Domini coram multitudine, discedens ab eis, segregavit discipulos, quotidie disputans in schola tyranni cujusdam.

19:10 Hoc autem factum est per biennium, ita ut omnes qui habitabant in Asia audirent verbum Domini, Judæi atque gentiles.

19:11 Virtutesque non quaslibet faciebat Deus per manum Pauli,

19:12 ita ut etiam super languidos deferrentur a corpore ejus sudaria et semicinctia, et recedebant ab eis languores, et spiritus nequam egrediebantur.

19:13 Tentaverunt autem quidam et de circumeuntibus Judæis exorcistis invocare super eos qui habebant spiritus malos nomen Domini Jesu, dicentes : Adjuro vos per Jesum, quem Paulus prædicat.

19:14 Erant autem quidam Judæi, Scevæ principis sacerdotum septem filii, qui hoc faciebant.

19:15 Respondens autem spiritus nequam dixit eis : Jesum novi, et Paulum scio : vos autem qui estis ?

19:16 Et insiliens in eos homo, in quo erat dæmonium pessimum, et dominatus amborum, invaluit contra eos, ita ut nudi et vulnerati effugerent de domo illa.

19:17 Hoc autem notum factum est omnibus Judæis, atque gentilibus qui habitabant Ephesi : et cecidit timor super omnes illos, et magnificabatur nomen Domini Jesu.

19:18 Multique credentium veniebant, confitentes et annuntiantes actus suos.

19:19 Multi autem ex eis, qui fuerant curiosa sectati, contulerunt libros, et combusserunt coram omnibus : et computatis pretiis illorum, invenerunt pecuniam denariorum quinquaginta millium.

19:20 Ita fortiter crescebat verbum Dei, et confirmabatur.

19:21 His autem expletis, proposuit Paulus in Spiritu, transita Macedonia et Achaia, ire Jerosolymam, dicens : Quoniam postquam fuero ibi, oportet me et Romam videre.

19:22 Mittens autem in Macedoniam duos ex ministrantibus sibi, Timotheum et Erastum, ipse remansit ad tempus in Asia.

19:23 Facta est autem illo tempore turbatio non minima de via Domini.

19:24 Demetrius enim quidam nomine, argentarius, faciens ædes argenteas Dianæ, præstabat

lieved not, speaking evil of the way of the Lord, before the multitude, departing from them, he separated the disciples, disputing daily in the school of one Tyrannus.

19:10 And this continued for the space of two years, so that all they who dwelt in Asia, heard the word of the Lord, both Jews and Gentiles.

19:11 And God wrought by the hand of Paul more than common miracles.

19:12 So that even there were brought from his body to the sick, handkerchiefs and aprons, and the diseases departed from them, and the wicked spirits went out of them.

19:13 Now some also of the Jewish exorcists who went about, attempted to invoke over them that had evil spirits, the name of the Lord Jesus, saying: I conjure you by Jesus, whom Paul preacheth.

19:14 And there were certain men, seven sons of Sceva, a Jew, a chief priest, that did this.

19:15 But the wicked spirit, answering, said to them: Jesus I know, and Paul I know; but who are you?

19:16 And the man in whom the wicked spirit was, leaping upon them, and mastering them both, prevailed against them, so that they fled out of that house naked and wounded.

19:17 And this became known to all the Jews and the Gentiles that dwelt at Ephesus; and fear fell on them all, and the name of the Lord Jesus was magnified.

19:18 And many of them that believed, came confessing and declaring their deeds.

19:19 And many of them who had followed curious arts, brought together their books, and burnt them before all; and counting the price of them, they found the money to be fifty thousand pieces of silver.

19:20 So mightily grew the word of God, and was confirmed.

19:21 And when these things were ended, Paul purposed in the spirit, when he had passed through Macedonia and Achaia, to go to Jerusalem, saying: After I have been there, I must see Rome also.

19:22 And sending into Macedonia two of them that ministered to him, Timothy and Erastus, he himself remained for a time in Asia.

19:23 Now at that time there arose no small disturbance about the way of the Lord.

19:24 For a certain man named Demetrius, a silversmith, who made silver temples for Diana,

artificibus non modicum quæstum :

19:25 quos convocans, et eos qui hujusmodi erant opifices, dixit : Viri, scitis quia de hoc artificio est nobis acquisitio :

19:26 et videtis et auditis quia non solum Ephesi, sed pene totius Asiæ, Paulus hic suadens avertit multam turbam, dicens : Quoniam non sunt dii, qui manibus fiunt.

19:27 Non solum autem hæc periclitabitur nobis pars in redargutionem venire, sed et magnæ Dianæ templum in nihilum reputabitur, sed et destrui incipiet majestas ejus, quam tota Asia et orbis colit.

19:28 His auditis, repleti sunt ira, et exclamaverunt dicentes : Magna Diana Ephesiorum.

19:29 Et impleta est civitas confusione, et impetum fecerunt uno animo in theatrum, rapto Gajo et Aristarcho Macedonibus, comitibus Pauli.

19:30 Paulo autem volente intrare in populum, non permiserunt discipuli.

19:31 Quidam autem et de Asiæ principibus, qui erant amici ejus, miserunt ad eum rogantes ne se daret in theatrum :

19:32 alii autem aliud clamabant. Erat enim ecclesia confusa : et plures nesciebant qua ex causa convenissent.

19:33 De turba autem detraxerunt Alexandrum, propellentibus eum Judæis. Alexander autem manu silentio postulato, volebat reddere rationem populo.

19:34 Quem ut cognoverunt Judæum esse, vox facta una est omnium, quasi per horas duas clamantium : Magna Diana Ephesiorum.

19:35 Et cum sedasset scriba turbas, dixit : Viri Ephesii, quis enim est hominum, qui nesciat Ephesiorum civitatem cultricem esse magnæ Dianæ, Jovisque prolis ?

19:36 Cum ergo his contradici non possit, oportet vos sedatos esse, et nihil temere agere.

19:37 Adduxistis enim homines istos, neque sacrilegos, neque blasphemantes deam vestram.

19:38 Quod si Demetrius et qui cum eo sunt artifices, habent adversus aliquem causam, conventus forenses aguntur, et proconsules sunt : accusent invicem.

brought no small gain to the craftsmen;

19:25 Whom he calling together, with the workmen of like occupation, said: Sirs, you know that our gain is by this trade;

19:26 And you see and hear, that this Paul by persuasion hath drawn away a great multitude, not only of Ephesus, but almost of all Asia, saying: They are not gods which are made by hands.

19:27 So that not only this our craft is in danger to be set at nought, but also the temple of great Diana shall be reputed for nothing; yea, and her majesty shall begin to be destroyed, whom all Asia and the world worshippeth.

19:28 Having heard these things, they were full of anger, and cried out, saying: Great is Diana of the Ephesians.

19:29 And the whole city was filled with confusion; and having caught Gaius and Aristarchus, men of Macedonia, Paul's companions, they rushed with one accord into the theatre.

19:30 And when Paul would have entered in unto the people, the disciples suffered him not.

19:31 And some also of the rulers of Asia, who were his friends, sent unto him, desiring that he would not venture himself into the theatre.

19:32 Now some cried one thing, some another. For the assembly was confused, and the greater part knew not for what cause they were come together.

19:33 And they drew forth Alexander out of the multitude, the Jews thrusting him forward. And Alexander beckoning with his hand for silence, would have given the people satisfaction.

19:34 But as soon as they perceived him to be a Jew, all with one voice, for the space of about two hours, cried out: Great is Diana of the Ephesians.

19:35 And when the town clerk had appeased the multitudes, he said: Ye men of Ephesus, what man is there that knoweth not that the city of the Ephesians is a worshipper of the great Diana, and of Jupiter's offspring.

19:36 For as much therefore as these things cannot be contradicted, you ought to be quiet, and to do nothing rashly.

19:37 For you have brought hither these men, who are neither guilty of sacrilege, nor of blasphemy against your goddess.

19:38 But if Demetrius and the craftsmen that are with him, have a matter against any man, the courts of justice are open, and there are proconsuls: let them accuse one another.

19:39 Si quid autem alterius rei quæritis, in legitima ecclesia poterit absolvi.

19:40 Nam et periclitamur argui seditionis hodiernæ, cum nullus obnoxius sit de quo possimus reddere rationem concursus istius. Et cum hæc dixisset, dimisit ecclesiam.

20:1 Postquam autem cessavit tumultus, vocatis Paulus discipulis, et exhortatus eos, valedixit, et profectus est ut iret in Macedoniam.

20:2 Cum autem perambulasset partes illas, et exhortatus eos fuisset multo sermone, venit ad Græciam :

20:3 ubi cum fecisset menses tres, factæ sunt illi insidiæ a Judæis navigaturo in Syriam : habuitque consilium ut reverteretur per Macedoniam.

20:4 Comitatus est autem eum Sopater Pyrrhi Berœensis, Thessalonicensium vero Aristarchus, et Secundus, et Gajus Derbeus, et Timotheus : Asiani vero Tychicus et Trophimus.

20:5 Hi cum præcessissent, sustinuerunt nos Troade :

20:6 nos vero navigavimus post dies azymorum a Philippis, et venimus ad eos Troadem in diebus quinque, ubi demorati sumus diebus septem.

20:7 Una autem sabbati cum convenissemus ad frangendum panem, Paulus disputabat cum eis profecturus in crastinum, protraxitque sermonem usque in mediam noctem.

20:8 Erant autem lampades copiosæ in cœnaculo, ubi eramus congregati.

20:9 Sedens autem quidam adolescens nomine Eutychus super fenestram, cum mergeretur somno gravi, disputante diu Paulo, ductus somno cecidit de tertio cœnaculo deorsum, et sublatus est mortuus.

20:10 Ad quem cum descendisset Paulus, incubuit super eum : et complexus dixit : Nolite turbari, anima enim ipsius in ipso est.

20:11 Ascendens autem, frangensque panem, et gustans, satisque allocutus usque in lucem, sic profectus est.

20:12 Adduxerunt autem puerum viventem, et consolati sunt non minime.

20:13 Nos autem ascendentes navem, navigavimus in Asson, inde suscepturi Paulum : sic enim disposuerat ipse per terram iter facturus.

20:14 Cum autem convenisset nos in Asson, as-

19:39 And if you inquire after any other matter, it may be decided in a lawful assembly.

19:40 For we are even in danger to be called in question for this day's uproar, there being no man guilty (of whom we may give account) of this concourse. And when he had said these things, he dismissed the assembly.

20:1 And after the tumult was ceased, Paul calling to him the disciples, and exhorting them, took his leave, and set forward to go into Macedonia.

20:2 And when he had gone over those parts, and had exhorted them with many words, he came into Greece;

20:3 Where, when he had spent three months, the Jews laid wait for him, as he was about to sail into Syria; so he took a resolution to return through Macedonia.

20:4 And there accompanied him Sopater the son of Pyrrhus, of Berea; and of the Thessalonians, Aristarchus, and Secundus, and Gaius of Derbe, and Timothy; and of Asia, Tychicus and Trophimus.

20:5 These going before, stayed for us at Troas.

20:6 But we sailed from Philippi after the days of the Azymes, and came to them to Troas in five days, where we abode seven days.

20:7 And on the first day of the week, when we were assembled to break bread, Paul discoursed with them, being to depart on the morrow: and he continued his speech until midnight.

20:8 And there were a great number of lamps in the upper chamber where we were assembled.

20:9 And a certain young man named Eutychus, sitting on the window, being oppressed with a deep sleep, (as Paul was long preaching,) by occasion of his sleep fell from the third loft down, and was taken up dead.

20:10 To whom, when Paul had gone down, he laid himself upon him, and embracing him, said: Be not troubled, for his soul is in him.

20:11 Then going up, and breaking bread and tasting, and having talked a long time to them, until daylight, so he departed.

20:12 And they brought the youth alive, and were not a little comforted.

20:13 But we, going aboard the ship, sailed to Assos, being there to take in Paul; for so he had appointed, himself purposing to travel by land.

20:14 And when he had met with us at Assos, we

sumpto eo, venimus Mitylenen.

20:15 Et inde navigantes, sequenti die venimus contra Chium, et alia applicuimus Samum, et sequenti die venimus Miletum.

20:16 Proposuerat enim Paulus transnavigare Ephesum, ne qua mora illi fieret in Asia. Festinabat enim, si possibile sibi esset, ut diem Pentecostes faceret Jerosolymis.

20:17 A Mileto autem mittens Ephesum, vocavit majores natu ecclesiæ.

20:18 Qui cum venissent ad eum, et simul essent, dixit eis : Vos scitis a prima die qua ingressus sum in Asiam, qualiter vobiscum per omne tempus fuerim,

20:19 serviens Domino cum omni humilitate, et lacrimis, et tentationibus, quæ mihi acciderunt ex insidiis Judæorum :

20:20 quomodo nihil subtraxerim utilium, quominus annuntiarem vobis et docerem vos, publice et per domos,

20:21 testificans Judæis atque gentilibus in Deum pœnitentiam, et fidem in Dominum nostrum Jesum Christum.

20:22 Et nunc ecce alligatus ego spiritu, vado in Jerusalem : quæ in ea ventura sint mihi, ignorans :

20:23 nisi quod Spiritus Sanctus per omnes civitates mihi protestatur, dicens quoniam vincula et tribulationes Jerosolymis me manent.

20:24 Sed nihil horum vereor : nec facio animam meam pretiosiorem quam me, dummodo consummem cursum meum, et ministerium verbi quod accepi a Domino Jesu, testificari Evangelium gratiæ Dei.

20:25 Et nunc ecce ego scio quia amplius non videbitis faciem meam vos omnes, per quos transivi prædicans regnum Dei.

20:26 Quapropter contestor vos hodierna die, quia mundus sum a sanguine omnium.

20:27 Non enim subterfugi, quominus annuntiarem omne consilium Dei vobis.

20:28 Attendite vobis, et universo gregi, in quo vos Spiritus Sanctus posuit episcopos regere ecclesiam Dei, quam acquisivit sanguine suo.

20:29 Ego scio quoniam intrabunt post discessionem meam lupi rapaces in vos, non parcentes gregi.

20:30 Et ex vobisipsis exsurgent viri loquentes

took him in, and came to Mitylene.

20:15 And sailing thence, the day following we came over against Chios; and the next day we arrived at Samos; and the day following we came to Miletus.

20:16 For Paul had determined to sail by Ephesus, lest he should be stayed any time in Asia. For he hasted, if it were possible for him, to keep the day of Pentecost at Jerusalem.

20:17 And sending from Miletus to Ephesus, he called the ancients of the church.

20:18 And when they were come to him, and were together, he said to them: You know from the first day that I came into Asia, in what manner I have been with you, for all the time,

20:19 Serving the Lord with all humility, and with tears, and temptations which befell me by the conspiracies of the Jews;

20:20 How I have kept back nothing that was profitable to you, but have preached it to you, and taught you publicly, and from house to house,

20:21 Testifying both to Jews and Gentiles penance towards God, and faith in our Lord Jesus Christ.

20:22 And now, behold, being bound in the spirit, I go to Jerusalem: not knowing the things which shall befall me there:

20:23 Save that the Holy Ghost in every city witnesseth to me, saying: That bands and afflictions wait for me at Jerusalem.

20:24 But I fear none of these things, neither do I count my life more precious than myself, so that I may consummate my course and the ministry of the word which I received from the Lord Jesus, to testify the gospel of the grace of God.

20:25 And now behold, I know that all you, among whom I have gone preaching the kingdom of God, shall see my face no more.

20:26 Wherefore I take you to witness this day, that I am clear from the blood of all men;

20:27 For I have not spared to declare unto you all the counsel of God.

20:28 Take heed to yourselves, and to the whole flock, wherein the Holy Ghost hath placed you bishops, to rule the church of God, which he hath purchased with his own blood.

20:29 I know that, after my departure, ravening wolves will enter in among you, not sparing the flock.

20:30 And of your own selves shall arise men

perversa, ut abducant discipulos post se.

20:31 Propter quod vigilate, memoria retinentes quoniam per triennium nocte et die non cessavi, cum lacrimis monens unumquemque vestrum.

20:32 Et nunc commendo vos Deo, et verbo gratiæ ipsius, qui potens est ædificare, et dare hæreditatem in sanctificatis omnibus.

20:33 Argentum, et aurum, aut vestem nullius concupivi, sicut

20:34 ipsi scitis : quoniam ad ea quæ mihi opus erant, et his qui mecum sunt, ministraverunt manus istæ.

20:35 Omnia ostendi vobis, quoniam sic laborantes, oportet suscipere infirmos ac meminisse verbi Domini Jesu : quoniam ipse dixit : Beatius est magis dare, quam accipere.

20:36 Et cum hæc dixisset, positis genibus suis oravit cum omnibus illis.

20:37 Magnus autem fletus factus est omnium : et procumbentes super collum Pauli, osculabantur eum,

20:38 dolentes maxime in verbo quod dixerat, quoniam amplius faciem ejus non essent visuri. Et deducebant eum ad navem.

21:1 Cum autem factum esset ut navigaremus abstracti ab eis, recto cursu venimus Coum, et sequenti die Rhodum, et inde Pataram.

21:2 Et cum invenissemus navem transfretantem in Phœnicen, ascendentes navigavimus.

21:3 Cum apparuissemus autem Cypro, relinquentes eam ad sinistram, navigavimus in Syriam, et venimus Tyrum : ibi enim navis expositura erat onus.

21:4 Inventis autem discipulis, mansimus ibi diebus septem : qui Paulo dicebant per Spiritum ne ascenderet Jerosolymam.

21:5 Et expletis diebus, profecti ibamus, deducentibus nos omnibus cum uxoribus et filiis usque foras civitatem : et positis genibus in littore, oravimus.

21:6 Et cum valefecissemus invicem, ascendimus navem : illi autem redierunt in sua.

21:7 Nos vero navigatione expleta a Tyro descendimus Ptolemaidam : et salutatis fratribus, mansimus die una apud illos.

speaking perverse things, to draw away disciples after them.

20:31 Therefore watch, keeping in memory, that for three years I ceased not, with tears to admonish every one of you night and day.

20:32 And now I commend you to God, and to the word of his grace, who is able to build up, and to give an inheritance among all the sanctified.

20:33 I have not coveted any man's silver, gold, or apparel, as

20:34 You yourselves know: for such things as were needful for me and them that are with me, these hands have furnished.

20:35 I have shewed you all things, how that so labouring you ought to support the weak, and to remember the word of the Lord Jesus, how he said: It is a more blessed thing to give, rather than to receive.

20:36 And when he had said these things, kneeling down, he prayed with them all.

20:37 And there was much weeping among them all; and falling on the neck of Paul, they kissed him,

20:38 Being grieved most of all for the word which he had said, that they should see his face no more. And they brought him on his way to the ship.

21:1 And when it came to pass that, being parted from them, we set sail, we came with a straight course to Coos, and the day following to Rhodes, and from thence to Patara.

21:2 And when we had found a ship sailing over to Phenice, we went aboard, and set forth.

21:3 And when we had discovered Cyprus, leaving it on the left hand, we sailed into Syria, and came to Tyre: for there the ship was to unlade her burden.

21:4 And finding disciples, we tarried there seven days: who said to Paul through the Spirit, that he should not go up to Jerusalem.

21:5 And the days being expired, departing we went forward, they all bringing us on our way, with their wives and children, till we were out of the city: and we kneeled down on the shore, and we prayed.

21:6 And when we had bid one another farewell, we took ship; and they returned home.

21:7 But we having finished the voyage by sea, from Tyre came down to Ptolemais: and saluting the brethren, we abode one day with them.

21:8 Alia autem die profecti, venimus Cæsaream. Et intrantes domum Philippi evangelistæ, qui erat unus de septem, mansimus apud eum.

21:9 Huic autem erant quatuor filiæ virgines prophetantes.

21:10 Et cum moraremur per dies aliquot, supervenit quidam a Judæa propheta, nomine Agabus.

21:11 Is cum venisset ad nos, tulit zonam Pauli : et alligans sibi pedes et manus, dixit : Hæc dicit Spiritus Sanctus : Virum, cujus est zona hæc, sic alligabunt in Jerusalem Judæi, et tradent in manus gentium.

21:12 Quod cum audissemus, rogabamus nos, et qui loci illius erant, ne ascenderet Jerosolymam.

21:13 Tunc respondit Paulus, et dixit : Quid facitis flentes, et affligentes cor meum ? Ego enim non solum alligari, sed et mori in Jerusalem paratus sum propter nomen Domini Jesu.

21:14 Et cum ei suadere non possemus, quievimus, dicentes : Domini voluntas fiat.

21:15 Post dies autem istos, præparati ascendebamus in Jerusalem.

21:16 Venerunt autem et ex discipulis a Cæsarea nobiscum, adducentes secum apud quem hospitaremur Mnasonem quemdam Cyprium, antiquum discipulum.

21:17 Et cum venissemus Jerosolymam, libenter exceperunt nos fratres.

21:18 Sequenti autem die introibat Paulus nobiscum ad Jacobum, omnesque collecti sunt seniores.

21:19 Quos cum salutasset, narrabat per singula quæ Deus fecisset in gentibus per ministerium ipsius.

21:20 At illi cum audissent, magnificabant Deum, dixeruntque ei : Vides, frater, quot millia sunt in Judæis qui crediderunt, et omnes æmulatores sunt legis.

21:21 Audierunt autem de te quia discessionem doceas a Moyse eorum qui per gentes sunt Judæorum, dicens non debere eos circumcidere filios suos, neque secundum consuetudinem ingredi.

21:22 Quid ergo est ? utique oportet convenire multitudinem : audient enim te supervenisse.

21:23 Hoc ergo fac quod tibi dicimus. Sunt nobis

21:8 And the next day departing, we came to Caesarea. And entering into the house of Philip the evangelist, who was one of the seven, we abode with him.

21:9 And he had four daughters, virgins, who did prophesy.

21:10 And as we tarried there for some days, there came from Judea a certain prophet, named Agabus.

21:11 Who, when he was come to us, took Paul's girdle: and binding his own feet and hands, he said: Thus saith the Holy Ghost: The man whose girdle this is, the Jews shall bind in this manner in Jerusalem, and shall deliver him into the hands of the Gentiles.

21:12 Which when we had heard, both we and they that were of that place, desired him that he would not go up to Jerusalem.

21:13 Then Paul answered, and said: What do you mean weeping and afflicting my heart? For I am ready not only to be bound, but to die also in Jerusalem, for the name of the Lord Jesus.

21:14 And when we could not persuade him, we ceased, saying: The will of the Lord be done.

21:15 And after those days, being prepared, we went up to Jerusalem.

21:16 And there went also with us some of the disciples from Caesarea, bringing with them one Mnason a Cyprian, an old disciple, with whom we should lodge.

21:17 And when we were come to Jerusalem, the brethren received us gladly.

21:18 And the day following, Paul went in with us unto James; and all the ancients were assembled.

21:19 Whom when he had saluted, he related particularly what things God had wrought among the Gentiles by his ministry.

21:20 But they hearing it, glorified God, and said to him: Thou seest, brother, how many thousands there are among the Jews that have believed: and they are all zealous for the law.

21:21 Now they have heard of thee that thou teachest those Jews, who are among the Gentiles, to depart from Moses: saying, that they ought not to circumcise their children, nor walk according to the custom.

21:22 What is it therefore? the multitude must needs come together: for they will hear that thou art come.

21:23 Do therefore this that we say to thee. We

viri quatuor, votum habentes super se.

21:24 His assumptis, sanctifica te cum illis, et impende in illis ut radant capita : et scient omnes quia quæ de te audierunt, falsa sunt, sed ambulas et ipse custodiens legem.

21:25 De his autem qui crediderunt ex gentibus, nos scripsimus judicantes ut abstineant se ab idolis immolato, et sanguine, et suffocato, et fornicatione.

21:26 Tunc Paulus, assumptis viris, postera die purificatus cum illis intravit in templum, annuntians expletionem dierum purificationis, donec offerretur pro unoquoque eorum oblatio.

21:27 Dum autem septem dies consummarentur, hi qui de Asia erant Judæi, cum vidissent eum in templo, concitaverunt omnem populum, et injecerunt ei manus, clamantes :

21:28 Viri Israëlitæ, adjuvate : hic est homo qui adversus populum, et legem, et locum hunc, omnes ubique docens, insuper et gentiles induxit in templum, et violavit sanctum locum istum.

21:29 Viderant enim Trophimum Ephesium in civitate cum ipso, quem æstimaverunt quoniam in templum introduxisset Paulus.

21:30 Commotaque est civitas tota, et facta est concursio populi. Et apprehendentes Paulum, trahebant eum extra templum : et statim clausæ sunt januæ.

21:31 Quærentibus autem eum occidere, nuntiatum est tribuno cohortis quia tota confunditur Jerusalem.

21:32 Qui statim, assumptis militibus et centurionibus, decurrit ad illos. Qui cum vidissent tribunum et milites, cessaverunt percutere Paulum.

21:33 Tunc accedens tribunus apprehendit eum, et jussit eum alligari catenis duabus : et interrogabat quis esset, et quid fecisset.

21:34 Alii autem aliud clamabant in turba. Et cum non posset certum cognoscere præ tumultu, jussit duci eum in castra.

21:35 Et cum venisset ad gradus, contigit ut portaretur a militibus propter vim populi.

21:36 Sequebatur enim multitudo populi, clamans : Tolle eum.

have four men, who have a vow on them.

21:24 Take these, and sanctify thyself with them: and bestow on them, that they may shave their heads: and all will know that the things which they have heard of thee, are false; but that thou thyself also walkest keeping the law.

21:25 But as touching the Gentiles that believe, we have written, decreeing that they should only refrain themselves from that which has been offered to idols, and from blood, and from things strangled, and from fornication.

21:26 Then Paul took the men, and the next day being purified with them, entered into the temple, giving notice of the accomplishment of the days of purification, until an oblation should be offered for every one of them.

21:27 But when the seven days were drawing to an end, those Jews that were of Asia, when they saw him in the temple, stirred up all the people, and laid hands upon him, crying out:

21:28 Men of Israel, help: This is the man that teacheth all men every where against the people, and the law, and this place; and moreover hath brought in Gentiles into the temple, and hath violated this holy place.

21:29 (For they had seen Trophimus the Ephesian in the city with him, whom they supposed that Paul had brought into the temple.)

21:30 And the whole city was in an uproar: and the people ran together. And taking Paul, they drew him out of the temple, and immediately the doors were shut.

21:31 And as they went about to kill him, it was told the tribune of the band, That all Jerusalem was in confusion.

21:32 Who, forthwith taking with him soldiers and centurions, ran down to them. And when they saw the tribune and the soldiers they left off beating Paul.

21:33 Then the tribune coming near, took him, and commanded him to be bound with two chains: and demanded who he was, and what he had done.

21:34 And some cried one thing, some another, among the multitude. And when he could not know the certainty for the tumult, he commanded him to be carried into the castle.

21:35 And when he was come to the stairs, it fell out that he was carried by the soldiers, because of the violence of the people.

21:36 For the multitude of the people followed after, crying: Away with him.

21:37 Et cum cœpisset induci in castra Paulus, dicit tribuno : Si licet mihi loqui aliquid ad te ? Qui dixit : Græce nosti ?

21:38 nonne tu es Ægyptius, qui ante hos dies tumultum concitasti, et eduxisti in desertum quatuor millia virorum sicariorum ?

21:39 Et dixit ad eum Paulus : Ego homo sum quidem Judæus a Tarso Ciliciæ, non ignotæ civitatis municeps. Rogo autem te, permitte mihi loqui ad populum.

21:40 Et cum ille permisisset, Paulus stans in gradibus annuit manu ad plebem, et magno silentio facto, allocutus est lingua hebræa, dicens :

22:1 Viri fratres, et patres, audite quam ad vos nunc reddo rationem.

22:2 Cum audissent autem quia hebræa lingua loqueretur ad illos, magis præstiterunt silentium.

22:3 Et dicit : Ego sum vir Judæus, natus in Tarso Ciliciæ, nutritus autem in ista civitate, secus pedes Gamaliel eruditus juxta veritatem paternæ legis, æmulator legis, sicut et vos omnes estis hodie :

22:4 qui hanc viam persecutus sum usque ad mortem, alligans et tradens in custodias viros ac mulieres,

22:5 sicut princeps sacerdotum mihi testimonium reddit, et omnes majores natu : a quibus et epistolas accipiens, ad fratres Damascum pergebam, ut adducerem inde vinctos in Jerusalem ut punirentur.

22:6 Factum est autem, eunte me, et appropinquante Damasco media die, subito de cælo circumfulsit me lux copiosa :

22:7 et decidens in terram, audivi vocem dicentem mihi : Saule, Saule, quid me persequeris ?

22:8 Ego autem respondi : Quis es, domine ? Dixitque ad me : Ego sum Jesus Nazarenus, quem tu persequeris.

22:9 Et qui mecum erant, lumen quidem viderunt, vocem autem non audierunt ejus qui loquebatur mecum.

22:10 Et dixi : Quid faciam, domine ? Dominus autem dixit ad me : Surgens vade Damascum : et ibi tibi dicetur de omnibus quæ te oporteat facere.

21:37 And as Paul was about to be brought into the castle, he saith to the tribune: May speak something to thee? Who said: Canst thou speak Greek?

21:38 Art not thou that Egyptian who before these days didst raise a tumult, and didst lead forth into the desert four thousand men that were murderers?

21:39 But Paul said to him: I am a Jew of Tarsus in Cilicia, a citizen of no mean city. And I beseech thee, suffer me to speak to the people.

21:40 And when he had given him leave, Paul standing on the stairs, beckoned with his hand to the people. And a great silence being made, he spoke unto them in the Hebrew tongue, saying:

22:1 Men, brethren, and fathers, hear ye the account which I now give unto you.

22:2 (And when they heard that he spoke to them in the Hebrew tongue, they kept the more silence.)

22:3 And he saith: I am a Jew, born at Tarsus in Cilicia, but brought up in this city, at the feet of Gamaliel, taught according to the truth of the law of the fathers, zealous for the law, as also all you are this day:

22:4 Who persecuted this way unto death, binding and delivering into prisons both men and women.

22:5 As the high priest doth bear me witness, and all the ancients: from whom also receiving letters to the brethren, I went to Damascus, that I might bring them bound from thence to Jerusalem to be punished.

22:6 And it came to pass, as I was going, and drawing nigh to Damascus at midday, that suddenly from heaven there shone round about me a great light:

22:7 And falling on the ground, I heard a voice saying to me: Saul, Saul, why persecutest thou me?

22:8 And I answered: Who art thou, Lord? And he said to me: I am Jesus of Nazareth, whom thou persecutest.

22:9 And they that were with me, saw indeed the light, but they heard not the voice of him that spoke with me.

22:10 And I said: What shall I do, Lord? And the Lord said to me: Arise, and go to Damascus; and there it shall be told thee of all things that thou must do.

22:11 Et cum non viderem præ claritate luminis illius, ad manum deductus a comitibus, veni Damascum.

22:12 Ananias autem quidam vir secundum legem, testimonium habens ab omnibus cohabitantibus Judæis,

22:13 veniens ad me et astans, dixit mihi : Saule frater, respice. Et ego eadem hora respexi in eum.

22:14 At ille dixit : Deus patrum nostrorum præordinavit te, ut cognosceres voluntatem ejus, et videres justum, et audires vocem ex ore ejus :

22:15 quia eris testis illius ad omnes homines eorum quæ vidisti et audisti.

22:16 Et nunc quid moraris ? Exsurge, et baptizare, et ablue peccata tua, invocato nomine ipsius.

22:17 Factum est autem revertenti mihi in Jerusalem, et oranti in templo, fieri me in stupore mentis,

22:18 et videre illum dicentem mihi : Festina, et exi velociter ex Jerusalem : quoniam non recipient testimonium tuum de me.

22:19 Et ego dixi : Domine, ipsi sciunt quia ego eram concludens in carcerem, et cædens per synagogas eos qui credebant in te :

22:20 et cum funderetur sanguis Stephani testis tui, ego astabam, et consentiebam, et custodiebam vestimenta interficientium illum.

22:21 Et dixit ad me : Vade, quoniam ego in nationes longe mittam te.

22:22 Audiebant autem eum usque ad hoc verbum, et levaverunt vocem suam, dicentes : Tolle de terra hujusmodi : non enim fas est eum vivere.

22:23 Vociferantibus autem eis, et projicientibus vestimenta sua, et pulverem jactantibus in aërem,

22:24 jussit tribunus induci eum in castra, et flagellis cædi, et torqueri eum, ut sciret propter quam causam sic acclamarent ei.

22:25 Et cum astrinxissent eum loris, dicit astanti sibi centurioni Paulus : Si hominem Romanum et indemnatum licet vobis flagellare ?

22:26 Quo audito, centurio accessit ad tribunum, et nuntiavit ei, dicens : Quid acturus es ? hic enim homo civis Romanus est.

22:27 Accedens autem tribunus, dixit illi : Dic

22:11 And whereas I did not see for the brightness of that light, being led by the hand by my companions, I came to Damascus.

22:12 And one Ananias, a man according to the law, having testimony of all the Jews who dwelt there,

22:13 Coming to me, and standing by me, said to me: Brother Saul, look up. And I the same hour looked upon him.

22:14 But he said: The God of our fathers hath preordained thee that thou shouldst know his will, and see the Just One, and shouldst hear the voice from his mouth.

22:15 For thou shalt be his witness to all men, of those things which thou hast seen and heard.

22:16 And now why tarriest thou? Rise up, and be baptized, and wash away thy sins, invoking his name.

22:17 And it came to pass, when I was come again to Jerusalem, and was praying in the temple, that I was in a trance,

22:18 And saw him saying unto me: Make haste, and get thee quickly out of Jerusalem; because they will not receive thy testimony concerning me.

22:19 And I said: Lord, they know that I cast into prison, and beat in every synagogue, them that believed in thee.

22:20 And when the blood of Stephen thy witness was shed, I stood by and consented, and kept the garments of them that killed him.

22:21 And he said to me: Go, for unto the Gentiles afar off, will I send thee.

22:22 And they heard him until this word, and then lifted up their voice, saying: Away with such an one from the earth; for it is not fit that he should live.

22:23 And as they cried out and threw off their garments, and cast dust into the air,

22:24 The tribune commanded him to be brought into the castle, and that he should be scourged and tortured: to know for what cause they did so cry out against him.

22:25 And when they had bound him with thongs, Paul saith to the centurion that stood by him: Is it lawful for you to scourge a man that is a Roman, and uncondemned?

22:26 Which the centurion hearing, went to the tribune, and told him, saying: What art thou about to do? For this man is a Roman citizen.

22:27 And the tribune coming, said to him: Tell

mihi si tu Romanus es ? At ille dixit : Etiam.

^{22:28} Et respondit tribunus : Ego multa summa civilitatem hanc consecutus sum. Et Paulus ait : Ego autem et natus sum.

^{22:29} Protinus ergo discesserunt ab illo qui eum torturi erant. Tribunus quoque timuit postquam rescivit, quia civis Romanus esset, et quia alligasset eum.

^{22:30} Postera autem die volens scire diligentius qua ex causa accusaretur a Judæis, solvit eum, et jussit sacerdotes convenire, et omne concilium : et producens Paulum, statuit inter illos.

^{23:1} Intendens autem in concilium Paulus, ait : Viri fratres, ego omni conscientia bona conversatus sum ante Deum usque in hodiernum diem.

^{23:2} Princeps autem sacerdotum Ananias præcepit astantibus sibi percutere os ejus.

^{23:3} Tunc Paulus dixit ad eum : Percutiet te Deus, paries dealbate. Et tu sedens judicas me secundum legem, et contra legem jubes me percuti ?

^{23:4} Et qui astabant dixerunt : Summum sacerdotem Dei maledicis.

^{23:5} Dixit autem Paulus : Nesciebam, fratres, quia princeps est sacerdotum. Scriptum est enim : Principem populi tui non maledices.

^{23:6} Sciens autem Paulus quia una pars esset sadducæorum, et altera pharisæorum, exclamavit in concilio : Viri fratres, ego pharisæus sum, filius pharisæorum : de spe et resurrectione mortuorum ego judicor.

^{23:7} Et cum hæc dixisset, facta est dissensio inter pharisæos et sadducæos, et soluta est multitudo.

^{23:8} Sadducæi enim dicunt non esse resurrectionem, neque angelum, neque spiritum : pharisæi autem utraque confitentur.

^{23:9} Factus est autem clamor magnus. Et surgentes quidam pharisæorum, pugnabant, dicentes : Nihil mali invenimus in homine isto : quid si spiritus locutus est ei, aut angelus ?

^{23:10} Et cum magna dissensio facta esset, timens tribunus ne discerperetur Paulus ab ipsis, jussit milites descendere, et rapere eum de medio eorum, ac deducere eum in castra.

me, art thou a Roman? But he said: Yea.

^{22:28} And the tribune answered: I obtained the being free of this city with a great sum. And Paul said: But I was born so.

^{22:29} Immediately therefore they departed from him that were about to torture him. The tribune also was afraid after he understood that he was a Roman citizen, and because he had bound him.

^{22:30} But on the next day, meaning to know more diligently for what cause he was accused by the Jews, he loosed him, and commanded the priests to come together, and all the council: and bringing forth Paul, he set him before them.

^{23:1} And Paul looking upon the council, said: Men, brethren, I have conversed with all good conscience before God until this present day.

^{23:2} And the high priest Ananias commanded them that stood by him to strike him on the mouth.

^{23:3} Then Paul said to him: God shall strike thee, thou whited wall. For sittest thou to judge me according to the law, and contrary to the law commandest me to be struck?

^{23:4} And they that stood by said: Dost thou revile the high priest of God?

^{23:5} And Paul said: I knew not, brethren, that he is the high priest. For it is written: Thou shalt not speak evil of the prince of thy people.

^{23:6} And Paul knowing that the one part were Sadducees, and the other Pharisees, cried out in the council: Men, brethren, I am a Pharisee, the son of Pharisees: concerning the hope and resurrection of the dead I am called in question.

^{23:7} And when he had so said, there arose a dissension between the Pharisees and the Sadducees; and the multitude was divided.

^{23:8} For the Sadducees say that there is no resurrection, neither angel, nor spirit: but the Pharisees confess both.

^{23:9} And there arose a great cry. And some of the Pharisees rising up, strove, saying: We find no evil in this man. What if a spirit hath spoken to him, or an angel?

^{23:10} And when there arose a great dissension, the tribune fearing lest Paul should be pulled in pieces by them, commanded the soldiers to go down, and to take him by force from among them, and to bring him into the castle.

23:11 Sequenti autem nocte assistens ei Dominus, ait : Constans esto : sicut enim testificatus es de me in Jerusalem, sic te oportet et Romæ testificari.

23:12 Facta autem die collegerunt se quidam ex Judæis, et devoverunt, se dicentes neque manducaturos, neque bibituros donec occiderent Paulum.

23:13 Erant autem plus quam quadraginta viri qui hanc conjurationem fecerant :

23:14 qui accesserunt ad principes sacerdotum et seniores, et dixerunt : Devotione devovimus nos nihil gustaturos, donec occidamus Paulum.

23:15 Nunc ergo vos notum facite tribuno cum concilio, ut producat illum ad vos, tamquam aliquid certius cognituri de eo. Nos vero priusquam appropiet, parati sumus interficere illum.

23:16 Quod cum audisset filius sororis Pauli insidias, venit, et intravit in castra, nuntiavitque Paulo.

23:17 Vocans autem Paulus ad se unum ex centurionibus, ait : Adolescentem hunc perduc ad tribunum, habet enim aliquid indicare illi.

23:18 Et ille quidem assumens eum duxit ad tribunum, et ait : Vinctus Paulus rogavit me hunc adolescentem perducere ad te, habentem aliquid loqui tibi.

23:19 Apprehendens autem tribunus manum illius, secessit cum eo seorsum, et interrogavit illum : Quid est quod habes indicare mihi ?

23:20 Ille autem dixit : Judæis convenit rogare te ut crastina die producas Paulum in concilium, quasi aliquid certius inquisituri sint de illo :

23:21 tu vero ne credideris illis : insidiantur enim ei ex eis viri amplius quam quadraginta, qui se devoverunt non manducare, neque bibere donec interficiant eum : et nunc parati sunt, exspectantes promissum tuum.

23:22 Tribunus igitur dimisit adolescentem, præcipiens ne cui loqueretur quoniam hæc nota sibi fecisset.

23:23 Et vocatis duobus centurionibus, dixit illis : Parate milites ducentos ut eant usque Cæsaream, et equites septuaginta, et lancearios ducentos a tertia hora noctis,

23:24 et jumenta præparate ut imponentes Paulum, salvum perducerent ad Felicem

23:11 And the night following the Lord standing by him, said: Be constant; for as thou hast testified of me in Jerusalem, so must thou bear witness also at Rome.

23:12 And when day was come, some of the Jews gathered together, and bound themselves under a curse, saying, that they would neither eat, nor drink, till they killed Paul.

23:13 And they were more than forty men that had made this conspiracy.

23:14 Who came to the chief priests and the ancients, and said: We have bound ourselves under a great curse that we will eat nothing till we have slain Paul.

23:15 Now therefore do you with the council signify to the tribune, that he bring him forth to you, as if you meant to know something more certain touching him. And we, before he come near, are ready to kill him.

23:16 Which when Paul's sister's son had heard, of their lying in wait, he came and entered into the castle and told Paul.

23:17 And Paul, calling to him one of the centurions, said: Bring this young man to the tribune, for he hath some thing to tell him.

23:18 And he taking him, brought him to the tribune, and said: Paul, the prisoner, desired me to bring this young man unto thee, who hath some thing to say to thee.

23:19 And the tribune taking him by the hand, went aside with him privately, and asked him: What is it that thou hast to tell me?

23:20 And he said: The Jews have agreed to desire thee, that thou wouldst bring forth Paul to morrow into the council, as if they meant to inquire some thing more certain touching him.

23:21 But do not thou give credit to them; for there lie in wait for him more than forty men of them, who have bound themselves by oath neither to eat, nor to drink, till they have killed him: and they are now ready, looking for a promise from thee.

23:22 The tribune therefore dismissed the young man, charging him that he should tell no man, that he had made known these things unto him.

23:23 Then having called two centurions, he said to them: Make ready two hundred soldiers to go as far as Caesarea, and seventy horsemen, and two hundred spearmen for the third hour of the night:

23:24 And provide beasts, that they may set Paul on, and bring him safe to Felix the governor.

præsidem.

23:25 (Timuit enim ne forte raperent eum Judæi, et occiderent, et ipse postea calumniam sustineret, tamquam accepturus pecuniam.)

23:26 Scribens epistolam continentem hæc : Claudius Lysias optimo præsidi Felici, salutem.

23:27 Virum hunc comprehensum a Judæis, et incipientem interfici ab eis, superveniens cum exercitu eripui, cognito quia Romanus est.

23:28 Volensque scire causam quam objiciebant illi, deduxi eum in concilium eorum.

23:29 Quem inveni accusari de quæstionibus legis ipsorum, nihil vero dignum morte aut vinculis habentem criminis.

23:30 Et cum mihi perlatum esset de insidiis quas paraverant illi, misi eum ad te, denuntians et accusatoribus ut dicant apud te. Vale.

23:31 Milites ergo secundum præceptum sibi assumentes Paulum, duxerunt per noctem in Antipatridem.

23:32 Et postera die dimissis equitibus ut cum eo irent, reversi sunt ad castra.

23:33 Qui cum venissent Cæsaream, et tradidissent epistolam præsidi, statuerunt ante illum et Paulum.

23:34 Cum legisset autem, et interrogasset de qua provincia esset, et cognoscens quia de Cilicia :

23:35 Audiam te, inquit, cum accusatores tui venerint. Jussitque in prætorio Herodis custodiri eum.

24:1 Post quinque autem dies descendit princeps sacerdotum Ananias, cum senioribus quibusdam, et Tertullo quodam oratore, qui adierunt præsidem adversus Paulum.

24:2 Et citato Paulo cœpit accusare Tertullus, dicens : Cum in multa pace agamus per te, et multa corrigantur per tuam providentiam,

24:3 semper et ubique suscipimus, optime Felix, cum omni gratiarum actione.

24:4 Ne diutius autem te protraham, oro, breviter audias nos pro tua clementia.

24:5 Invenimus hunc hominem pestiferum, et concitantem seditiones omnibus Judæis in universo orbe, et auctorem seditionis sectæ Naza-

23:25 (For he feared lest perhaps the Jews might take him away by force and kill him, and he should afterwards be slandered, as if he was to take money.) And he wrote a letter after this manner:

23:26 Claudius Lysias to the most excellent governor, Felix, greeting.

23:27 This man being taken by the Jews, and ready to be killed by them, I rescued coming in with an army, understanding that he is a Roman:

23:28 And meaning to know the cause which they objected unto him, I brought him forth into their council.

23:29 Whom I found to be accused concerning questions of their law; but having nothing laid to his charge worthy of death or of bands.

23:30 And when I was told of ambushes that they had prepared for him, I sent him to thee, signifying also to his accusers to plead before thee. Farewell.

23:31 Then the soldiers, according as it was commanded them, taking Paul, brought him by night to Antipatris.

23:32 And the next day, leaving the horsemen to go with him, they returned to the castle.

23:33 Who, when they were come to Caesarea, and had delivered the letter to the governor, did also present Paul before him.

23:34 And when he had read it, and had asked of what province he was, and understood that he was of Cilicia;

23:35 I will hear thee, said he, when thy accusers come. And he commanded him to be kept in Herod's judgment hall.

24:1 And after five days the high priest Ananias came down, with some of the ancients, and one Tertullus an orator, who went to the governor against Paul.

24:2 And Paul being called for, Tertullus began to accuse him, saying: Whereas through thee we live in much peace, and many things are rectified by thy providence,

24:3 We accept it always and in all places, most excellent Felix, with all thanksgiving.

24:4 But that I be no further tedious to thee, I desire thee of thy clemency to hear us in few words.

24:5 We have found this to be a pestilent man, and raising seditions among all the Jews throughout the world, and author of the sedi-

renorum :

24:6 qui etiam templum violare conatus est, quem et apprehensum voluimus secundum legem nostram judicare.

24:7 Superveniens autem tribunus Lysias, cum vi magna eripuit eum de manibus nostris,

24:8 jubens accusatores ejus ad te venire : a quo poteris ipse judicans, de omnibus istis cognoscere, de quibus nos accusamus eum.

24:9 Adjecerunt autem et Judæi, dicentes hæc ita se habere.

24:10 Respondit autem Paulus (annuente sibi præside dicere) : Ex multis annis te esse judicem genti huic sciens, bono animo pro me satisfaciam.

24:11 Potes enim cognoscere quia non plus sunt mihi dies quam duodecim, ex quo ascendi adorare in Jerusalem :

24:12 et neque in templo invenerunt me cum aliquo disputantem, aut concursum facientem turbæ, neque in synagogis, neque in civitate :

24:13 neque probare possunt tibi de quibus nunc me accusant.

24:14 Confiteor autem hoc tibi, quod secundum sectam quam dicunt hæresim, sic deservio Patri et Deo meo, credens omnibus quæ in lege et prophetis scripta sunt :

24:15 spem habens in Deum, quam et hi ipsi exspectant, resurrectionem futuram justorum et iniquorum.

24:16 In hoc et ipse studeo sine offendiculo conscientiam habere ad Deum et ad homines semper.

24:17 Post annos autem plures eleemosynas facturus in gentem meam, veni, et oblationes, et vota,

24:18 in quibus invenerunt me purificatum in templo : non cum turba, neque cum tumultu.

24:19 Quidam autem ex Asia Judæi, quos oportebat apud te præsto esse, et accusare si quid haberent adversum me :

24:20 aut hi ipsi dicant si quid invenerunt in me iniquitatis cum stem in concilio,

24:21 nisi de una hac solummodo voce qua clamavi inter eos stans : Quoniam de resurrectione mortuorum ego judicor hodie a vobis.

24:22 Distulit autem illos Felix, certissime sciens

tion of the sect of the Nazarenes.

24:6 Who also hath gone about to profane the temple: whom, we having apprehended, would also have judged according to our law.

24:7 But Lysias the tribune coming upon us, with great violence took him away out of our hands;

24:8 Commanding his accusers to come to thee: of whom thou mayest thyself, by examination, have knowledge of all these things, whereof we accuse him.

24:9 And the Jews also added, and said that these things were so.

24:10 Then Paul answered, (the governor making a sign to him to speak:) Knowing that for many years thou hast been judge over this nation, I will with good courage answer for myself.

24:11 For thou mayest understand, that there are yet but twelve days, since I went up to adore in Jerusalem:

24:12 And neither in the temple did they find me disputing with any man, or causing any concourse of the people, neither in the synagogues, nor in the city:

24:13 Neither can they prove unto thee the things whereof they now accuse me.

24:14 But this I confess to thee, that according to the way, which they call a heresy, so do I serve the Father and my God, believing all things which are written in the law and the prophets:

24:15 Having hope in God, which these also themselves look for, that there shall be a resurrection of the just and unjust.

24:16 And herein do I endeavour to have always a conscience without offence toward God, and towards men.

24:17 Now after many years, I came to bring alms to my nation, and offerings, and vows.

24:18 In which I was found purified in the temple: neither with multitude, nor with tumult.

24:19 But certain Jews of Asia, who ought to be present before thee, and to accuse, if they had any thing against me:

24:20 Or let these men themselves say, if they found in me any iniquity, when standing before the council,

24:21 Except it be for this one voice only that I cried, standing among them, Concerning the resurrection of the dead am I judged this day by you.

24:22 And Felix put them off, having most cer-

de via hac, dicens : Cum tribunus Lysias descenderit, audiam vos.

24:23 Jussitque centurioni custodire eum, et habere requiem, nec quemquam de suis prohibere ministrare ei.

24:24 Post aliquot autem dies veniens Felix cum Drusilla uxore sua, quæ erat Judæa, vocavit Paulum, et audivit ab eo fidem quæ est in Christum Jesum.

24:25 Disputante autem illo de justitia, et castitate, et de judicio futuro, tremefactus Felix, respondit : Quod nunc attinet, vade : tempore autem opportuno accersam te :

24:26 simul et sperans quod pecunia ei daretur a Paulo, propter quod et frequenter accersens eum, loquebatur cum eo.

24:27 Biennio autem expleto, accepit successorem Felix Portium Festum. Volens autem gratiam præstare Judæis Felix, reliquit Paulum vinctum.

25:1 Festus ergo cum venisset in provinciam, post triduum ascendit Jerosolymam a Cæsarea.

25:2 Adieruntque eum principes sacerdotum et primi Judæorum adversus Paulum : et rogabant eum,

25:3 postulantes gratiam adversus eum, ut juberet perduci eum in Jerusalem, insidias tendentes ut interficerent eum in via.

25:4 Festus autem respondit servari Paulum in Cæsarea : se autem maturius profecturum.

25:5 Qui ergo in vobis, ait, potentes sunt, descendentes simul, si quod est in viro crimen, accusent eum.

25:6 Demoratus autem inter eos dies non amplius quam octo aut decem, descendit Cæsaream, et altera die sedit pro tribunali, et jussit Paulum adduci.

25:7 Qui cum perductus esset, circumsteterunt eum, qui ab Jerosolyma descenderant Judæi, multas et graves causas objicientes, quas non poterant probare :

25:8 Paulo rationem reddente : Quoniam neque in legem Judæorum, neque in templum, neque in Cæsarem quidquam peccavi.

25:9 Festus autem volens gratiam præstare Judæis, respondens Paulo, dixit : Vis Jerosolymam ascendere, et ibi de his judicari

tain knowledge of this way, saying: When Lysias the tribune shall come down, I will hear you.

24:23 And he commanded a centurion to keep him, and that he should be easy, and that he should not prohibit any of his friends to minister unto him.

24:24 And after some days, Felix, coming with Drusilla his wife, who was a Jew, sent for Paul, and heard of him the faith, that is in Christ Jesus.

24:25 And as he treated of justice, and chastity, and of the judgment to come, Felix being terrified, answered: For this time, go thy way: but when I have a convenient time, I will send for thee.

24:26 Hoping also withal, that money should be given him by Paul; for which cause also oftentimes sending for him, he spoke with him.

24:27 But when two years were ended, Felix had for successor Portius Festus. And Felix being willing to shew the Jews a pleasure, left Paul bound.

25:1 Now when Festus was come into the province, after three days, he went up to Jerusalem from Caesarea.

25:2 And the chief priests, and principal men of the Jews, went unto him against Paul: and they besought him,

25:3 Requesting favour against him, that he would command him to be brought to Jerusalem, laying wait to kill him in the way.

25:4 But Festus answered: That Paul was kept in Caesarea, and that he himself would very shortly depart thither.

25:5 Let them, therefore, saith he, among you that are able, go down with me, and accuse him, if there be any crime in the man.

25:6 And having tarried among them no more than eight or ten days, he went down to Caesarea, and the next day he sat in the judgment seat; and commanded Paul to be brought.

25:7 Who being brought, the Jews stood about him, who were come down from Jerusalem, objecting many and grievous causes, which they could not prove;

25:8 Paul making answer for himself: Neither against the law of the Jews, nor against the temple, nor against Caesar, have I offended in any thing.

25:9 But Festus, willing to shew the Jews a pleasure, answering Paul, said: Wilt thou go up to Jerusalem, and there be judged of these

apud me ?

25:10 Dixit autem Paulus : Ad tribunal Cæsaris sto : ibi me oportet judicari : Judæis non nocui, sicut tu melius nosti.

25:11 Si enim nocui, aut dignum morte aliquid feci, non recuso mori : si vero nihil est eorum quæ hi accusant me, nemo potest me illis donare. Cæsarem appello.

25:12 Tunc Festus cum concilio locutus, respondit : Cæsarem appellasti ? ad Cæsarem ibis.

25:13 Et cum dies aliquot transacti essent, Agrippa rex et Bernice descenderunt Cæsaream ad salutandum Festum.

25:14 Et cum dies plures ibi demorarentur, Festus regi indicavit de Paulo, dicens : Vir quidam est derelictus a Felice vinctus,

25:15 de quo cum essem Jerosolymis, adierunt me principes sacerdotum et seniores Judæorum, postulantes adversus illum damnationem.

25:16 Ad quos respondi : Quia non est Romanis consuetudo damnare aliquem hominem priusquam is qui accusatur præsentes habeat accusatores, locumque defendendi accipiat ad abluenda crimina.

25:17 Cum ergo huc convenissent sine ulla dilatione, sequenti die sedens pro tribunali, jussi adduci virum.

25:18 De quo, cum stetissent accusatores, nullam causam deferebant, de quibus ego suspicabar malum.

25:19 Quæstiones vero quasdam de sua superstitione habebant adversus eum, et de quodam Jesu defuncto, quem affirmabat Paulus vivere.

25:20 Hæsitans autem ego de hujusmodi quæstione, dicebam si vellet ire Jerosolymam, et ibi judicari de istis.

25:21 Paulo autem appellante ut servaretur ad Augusti cognitionem, jussi servari eum, donec mittam eum ad Cæsarem.

25:22 Agrippa autem dixit ad Festum : Volebam et ipse hominem audire. Cras, inquit, audies eum.

25:23 Altera autem die cum venisset Agrippa et Bernice cum multa ambitione, et introissent in auditorium cum tribunis et viris principalibus civitatis, jubente Festo, adductus est Paulus.

things before me?

25:10 Then Paul said: I stand at Caesar's judgment seat, where I ought to be judged. To the Jews I have done no injury, as thou very well knowest.

25:11 For if I have injured them, or have committed any thing worthy of death, I refuse not to die. But if there be none of these things whereof they accuse me, no man may deliver me to them: I appeal to Caesar.

25:12 Then Festus having conferred with the council, answered: Hast thou appealed to Caesar? To Caesar shalt thou go.

25:13 And after some days, king Agrippa and Bernice came down to Caesarea to salute Festus.

25:14 And as they tarried there many days, Festus told the king of Paul, saying: A certain man was left prisoner by Felix.

25:15 About whom, when I was at Jerusalem, the chief priests, and the ancients of the Jews, came unto me, desiring condemnation against him.

25:16 To whom I answered: It is not the custom of the Romans to condemn any man, before that he who is accused have his accusers present, and have liberty to make his answer, to clear himself of the things laid to his charge.

25:17 When therefore they were come hither, without any delay, on the day following, sitting in the judgment seat, I commanded the man to be brought.

25:18 Against whom, when the accusers stood up, they brought no accusation of things which I thought ill of:

25:19 But had certain questions of their own superstition against him, and of one Jesus deceased, whom Paul affirmed to be alive.

25:20 I therefore being in a doubt of this manner of question, asked him whether he would go to Jerusalem, and there be judged of these things.

25:21 But Paul appealing to be reserved unto the hearing of Augustus, I commanded him to be kept, till I might send him to Caesar.

25:22 And Agrippa said to Festus: I would also hear the man, myself. To morrow, said he, thou shalt hear him.

25:23 And on the next day, when Agrippa and Bernice were come with great pomp, and had entered into the hall of audience, with the tribunes, and principal men of the city, at Festus' commandment, Paul was brought forth.

25:24 Et dicit Festus : Agrippa rex, et omnes qui simul adestis nobiscum viri, videtis hunc de quo omnis multitudo Judæorum interpellavit me Jerosolymis, petentes et acclamantes non oportere eum vivere amplius.

25:25 Ego vere comperi nihil dignum morte eum admisisse. Ipso autem hoc appellante ad Augustum, judicavi mittere.

25:26 De quo quid certum scribam domino, non habeo. Propter quod produxi eum ad vos, et maxime ad te, rex Agrippa, ut interrogatione facta habeam quid scribam.

25:27 Sine ratione enim mihi videtur mittere vinctum, et causas ejus non significare.

26:1 Agrippa vero ad Paulum ait : Permittitur tibi loqui pro temetipso. Tunc Paulus extenta manu cœpit rationem reddere :

26:2 De omnibus quibus accusor a Judæis, rex Agrippa, æstimo me beatum apud te cum sim defensurus me hodie,

26:3 maxime te sciente omnia, et quæ apud Judæos sunt consuetudines et quæstiones : propter quod obsecro patienter me audias.

26:4 Et quidem vitam meam a juventute, quæ ab initio fuit in gente mea in Jerosolymis, noverunt omnes Judæi :

26:5 præscientes me ab initio (si velint testimonium perhibere) quoniam secundum certissimam sectam nostræ religionis vixi pharisæus.

26:6 Et nunc, in spe quæ ad patres nostros repromissionis facta est a Deo, sto judicio subjectus :

26:7 in quam duodecim tribus nostræ nocte ac die deservientes, sperant devenire. De qua spe accusor a Judæis, rex.

26:8 Quid incredibile judicatur apud vos, si Deus mortuos suscitat ?

26:9 Et ego quidem existimaveram me adversus nomen Jesu Nazareni debere multa contraria agere,

26:10 quod et feci Jerosolymis, et multos sanctorum ego in carceribus inclusi, a principibus sacerdotum potestate accepta : et cum occiderentur, detuli sententiam.

26:11 Et per omnes synagogas frequenter puniens eos, compellebam blasphemare : et amplius insaniens in eos, persequebar usque in exteras

25:24 And Festus saith: King Agrippa, and all ye men who are here present with us, you see this man, about whom all the multitude of the Jews dealt with me at Jerusalem, requesting and crying out that he ought not to live any longer.

25:25 Yet have I found nothing that he hath committed worthy of death. But forasmuch as he himself hath appealed to Augustus, I have determined to send him.

25:26 Of whom I have nothing certain to write to my lord. For which cause I have brought him forth before you, and especially before thee, O king Agrippa, that examination being made, I may have what to write.

25:27 For it seemeth to me unreasonable to send a prisoner, and not to signify the things laid to his charge.

26:1 Then Agrippa said to Paul: Thou art permitted to speak for thyself. Then Paul stretching forth his hand, began to make his answer.

26:2 I think myself happy, O king Agrippa, that I am to answer for myself this day before thee, touching all the things whereof I am accused by the Jews.

26:3 Especially as thou knowest all, both customs and questions that are among the Jews: Wherefore I beseech thee to hear me patiently.

26:4 And my life indeed from my youth, which was from the beginning among my own nation in Jerusalem, all the Jews do know:

26:5 Having known me from the beginning (if they will give testimony) that according to the most sure sect of our religion I lived a Pharisee.

26:6 And now for the hope of the promise that was made by God to the fathers, do I stand subject to judgment:

26:7 Unto which, our twelve tribes, serving night and day, hope to come. For which hope, O king, I am accused by the Jews.

26:8 Why should it be thought a thing incredible, that God should raise the dead?

26:9 And I indeed did formerly think, that I ought to do many things contrary to the name of Jesus of Nazareth.

26:10 Which also I did at Jerusalem, and many of the saints did I shut up in prison, having received authority of the chief priests: and when they were put to death, I brought the sentence.

26:11 And oftentimes punishing them, in every synagogue, I compelled them to blaspheme: and being yet more mad against them, I perse-

civitates.

26:12 In quibus dum irem Damascum cum potestate et permissu principum sacerdotum,

26:13 die media in via vidi, rex, de cælo supra splendorem solis circumfulsisse me lumen, et eos qui mecum simul erant.

26:14 Omnesque nos cum decidissemus in terram, audivi vocem loquentem mihi hebraica lingua : Saule, Saule, quid me persequeris ? durum est tibi contra stimulum calcitrare.

26:15 Ego autem dixi : Quis es, domine ? Dominus autem dixit : Ego sum Jesus, quem tu persequeris.

26:16 Sed exsurge, et sta super pedes tuos : ad hoc enim apparui tibi, ut constituam te ministrum, et testem eorum quæ vidisti, et eorum quibus apparebo tibi,

26:17 eripiens te de populo et gentibus, in quas nunc ego mitto te,

26:18 aperire oculos eorum, ut convertantur a tenebris ad lucem, et de potestate Satanæ ad Deum, ut accipiant remissionem peccatorum, et sortem inter sanctos, per fidem quæ est in me.

26:19 Unde, rex Agrippa, non fui incredulus cælesti visioni :

26:20 sed his qui sunt Damasci primum, et Jerosolymis, et in omnem regionem Judææ, et gentibus, annuntiabam, ut pœnitentiam agerent, et converterentur ad Deum, digna pœnitentiæ opera facientes.

26:21 Hac ex causa me Judæi, cum essem in templo, comprehensum tentabant interficere.

26:22 Auxilio autem adjutus Dei usque in hodiernum diem, sto, testificans minori atque majori, nihil extra dicens quam ea quæ prophetæ locuti sunt futura esse, et Moyses,

26:23 si passibilis Christus, si primus ex resurrectione mortuorum, lumen annuntiaturus est populo et gentibus.

26:24 Hæc loquente eo, et rationem reddente, Festus magna voce dixit : Insanis, Paule : multæ te litteræ ad insaniam convertunt.

26:25 Et Paulus : Non insanio, inquit, optime

cuted them even unto foreign cities.

26:12 Whereupon when I was going to Damascus with authority and permission of the chief priest,

26:13 At midday, O king, I saw in the way a light from heaven above the brightness of the sun, shining round about me, and them that were in company with me.

26:14 And when we were all fallen down on the ground, I heard a voice speaking to me in the Hebrew tongue: Saul, Saul, why persecutest thou me? It is hard for thee to kick against the goad.

26:15 And I said: Who art thou, Lord? And the Lord answered: I am Jesus whom thou persecutest.

26:16 But rise up, and stand upon thy feet: for to this end have I appeared to thee, that I may make thee a minister, and a witness of those things which thou hast seen, and of those things wherein I will appear to thee,

26:17 Delivering thee from the people, and from the nations, unto which now I send thee:

26:18 To open their eyes, that they may be converted from darkness to light, and from the power of Satan to God, that they may receive forgiveness of sins, and a lot among the saints, by the faith that is in me.

26:19 Whereupon, O king Agrippa, I was not incredulous to the heavenly vision:

26:20 But to them first that are at Damascus, and at Jerusalem, and unto all the country of Judea, and to the Gentiles did I preach, that they should do penance, and turn to God, doing works worthy of penance.

26:21 For this cause the Jews, when I was in the temple, having apprehended me, went about to kill me.

26:22 But being aided by the help of God, I stand unto this day, witnessing both to small and great, saying no other thing than those which the prophets, and Moses did say should come to pass:

26:23 That Christ should suffer, and that he should be the first that should rise from the dead, and should shew light to the people, and to the Gentiles.

26:24 As he spoke these things, and made his answer, Festus said with a loud voice: Paul, thou art beside thyself: much learning doth make thee mad.

26:25 And Paul said: I am not mad, most excel-

Feste, sed veritatis et sobrietatis verba loquor.

26:26 Scit enim de his rex, ad quem et constanter loquor : latere enim eum nihil horum arbitror. Neque enim in angulo quidquam horum gestum est.

26:27 Credis, rex Agrippa, prophetis ? Scio quia credis.

26:28 Agrippa autem ad Paulum : In modico suades me christianum fieri.

26:29 Et Paulus : Opto apud Deum, et in modico et in magno, non tantum te, sed etiam omnes qui audiunt hodie fieri tales, qualis et ego sum, exceptis vinculis his.

26:30 Et exsurrexit rex, et præses, et Bernice, et qui assidebant eis.

26:31 Et cum secessissent, loquebantur ad invicem, dicentes : Quia nihil morte aut vinculis dignum quid fecit homo iste.

26:32 Agrippa autem Festo dixit : Dimitti poterat homo hic, si non appellasset Cæsarem.

27:1 Ut autem judicatum est navigare eum in Italiam, et tradi Paulum cum reliquis custodiis centurioni nomine Julio cohortis Augustæ,

27:2 ascendentes navem Adrumetinam, incipientes navigare circa Asiæ loca, sustulimus, perseverante nobiscum Aristarcho Macedone Thessalonicensi.

27:3 Sequenti autem die devenimus Sidonem. Humane autem tractans Julius Paulum, permisit ad amicos ire, et curam sui agere.

27:4 Et inde cum sustulissemus, subnavigavimus Cyprum, propterea quod essent venti contrarii.

27:5 Et pelagus Ciliciæ et Pamphyliæ navigantes, venimus Lystram, quæ est Lyciæ :

27:6 et ibi inveniens centurio navem Alexandrinam navigantem in Italiam, transposuit nos in eam.

27:7 Et cum multis diebus tarde navigaremus, et vix devenissemus contra Gnidum, prohibente nos vento, adnavigavimus Cretæ juxta Salmonem :

27:8 et vix juxta navigantes, venimus in locum quemdam qui vocatur Boniportus, cui juxta erat civitas Thalassa.

27:9 Multo autem tempore peracto, et cum jam

lent Festus, but I speak words of truth and soberness.

26:26 For the king knoweth of these things, to whom also I speak with confidence. For I am persuaded that none of these things are hidden from him. For neither was any of these things done in a corner.

26:27 Believest thou the prophets, O king Agrippa? I know that thou believest.

26:28 And Agrippa said to Paul: In a little thou persuadest me to become a Christian.

26:29 And Paul said: I would to God, that both in a little and in much, not only thou, but also all that hear me, this day, should become such as I also am, except these bands.

26:30 And the king rose up, and the governor, and Bernice, and they that sat with them.

26:31 And when they were gone aside, they spoke among themselves, saying: This man hath done nothing worthy of death or of bands.

26:32 And Agrippa said to Festus: This man might have been set at liberty, if he had not appealed to Caesar.

27:1 And when it was determined that he should sail into Italy, and that Paul, with the other prisoners, should be delivered to a centurion, named Julius, of the band Augusta,

27:2 Going on board a ship of Adrumetum, we launched, meaning to sail by the coasts of Asia, Aristarchus, the Macedonian of Thessalonica, continuing with us.

27:3 And the day following we came to Sidon. And Julius treating Paul courteously, permitted him to go to his friends, and to take care of himself.

27:4 And when we had launched from thence, we sailed under Cyprus, because the winds were contrary.

27:5 And sailing over the sea of Cilicia, and Pamphylia, we came to Lystra, which is in Lycia:

27:6 And there the centurion finding a ship of Alexandria sailing into Italy, removed us into it.

27:7 And when for many days we had sailed slowly, and were scarce come over against Gnidus, the wind not suffering us, we sailed near Crete by Salmone:

27:8 And with much ado sailing by it, we came into a certain place, which is called Good havens, nigh to which was the city of Thalassa.

27:9 And when much time was spent, and when

non esset tuta navigatio eo quod et jejunium jam præteriisset, consolabatur eos Paulus,

27:10 dicens eis : Viri, video quoniam cum injuria et multo damno non solum oneris, et navis, sed etiam animarum nostrarum incipit esse navigatio.

27:11 Centurio autem gubernatori et nauclero magis credebat, quam his quæ a Paulo dicebantur.

27:12 Et cum aptus portus non esset ad hiemandum, plurimi statuerunt consilium navigare inde, si quomodo possent, devenientes Phœnicen hiemare, portum Cretæ respicientem ad Africum et ad Corum.

27:13 Aspirante autem austro, æstimantes propositum se tenere, cum sustulissent de Asson, legebant Cretam.

27:14 Non post multum autem misit se contra ipsam ventus typhonicus, qui vocatur Euroaquilo.

27:15 Cumque arrepta esset navis, et non posset conari in ventum, data nave flatibus, ferebamur.

27:16 In insulam autem quamdam decurrentes, quæ vocatur Cauda, potuimus vix obtinere scapham.

27:17 Qua sublata, adjutoriis utebantur, accingentes navem, timentes ne in Syrtim inciderent, summisso vase sic ferebantur.

27:18 Valida autem nobis tempestate jactatis, sequenti die jactum fecerunt :

27:19 et tertia die suis manibus armamenta navis projecerunt.

27:20 Neque autem sole, neque sideribus apparentibus per plures dies, et tempestate non exigua imminente, jam ablata erat spes omnis salutis nostræ.

27:21 Et cum multa jejunatio fuisset, tunc stans Paulus in medio eorum, dixit : Oportebat quidem, o viri, audito me, non tollere a Creta, lucrique facere injuriam hanc et jacturam.

27:22 Et nunc suadeo vobis bono animo esse : amissio enim nullius animæ erit ex vobis, præterquam navis.

27:23 Astitit enim mihi hac nocte angelus Dei, cujus sum ego, et cui deservio,

27:24 dicens : Ne timeas, Paule : Cæsari te oportet assistere : et ecce donavit tibi Deus omnes

sailing now was dangerous, because the fast was now past, Paul comforted them,

27:10 Saying to them: Ye men, I see that the voyage beginneth to be with injury and much damage, not only of the lading and ship, but also of our lives.

27:11 But the centurion believed the pilot and the master of the ship, more than those things which were said by Paul.

27:12 And whereas it was not a commodious haven to winter in, the greatest part gave counsel to sail thence, if by any means they might reach Phenice to winter there, which is a haven of Crete, looking towards the southwest and northwest.

27:13 And the south wind gently blowing, thinking that they had obtained their purpose, when they had loosed from Asson, they sailed close by Crete.

27:14 But not long after, there arose against it a tempestuous wind, called Euroaquilo.

27:15 And when the ship was caught, and could not bear up against the wind, giving up the ship to the winds, we were driven.

27:16 And running under a certain island, that is called Cauda, we had much work to come by the boat.

27:17 Which being taken up, they used helps, undergirding the ship, and fearing lest they should fall into the quicksands, they let down the sail yard, and so were driven.

27:18 And we being mightily tossed with the tempest, the next day they lightened the ship.

27:19 And the third day they cast out with their own hands the tackling of the ship.

27:20 And when neither sun nor stars appeared for many days, and no small storm lay on us, all hope of our being saved was now taken away.

27:21 And after they had fasted a long time, Paul standing forth in the midst of them, said: You should indeed, O ye men, have hearkened unto me, and not have loosed from Crete, and have gained this harm and loss.

27:22 And now I exhort you to be of good cheer. For there shall be no loss of any man's life among you, but only of the ship.

27:23 For an angel of God, whose I am, and whom I serve, stood by me this night,

27:24 Saying: Fear not, Paul, thou must be brought before Caesar; and behold, God hath

qui navigant tecum.

27:25 Propter quod bono animo estote, viri : credo enim Deo quia sic erit, quemadmodum dictum est mihi.

27:26 In insulam autem quamdam oportet nos devenire.

27:27 Sed posteaquam quartadecima nox supervenit, navigantibus nobis in Adria circa mediam noctem, suspicabantur nautæ apparere sibi aliquam regionem.

27:28 Qui et summittentes bolidem, invenerunt passus viginti : et pusillum inde separati, invenerunt passus quindecim.

27:29 Timentes autem ne in aspera loca incideremus, de puppi mittentes anchoras quatuor, optabant diem fieri.

27:30 Nautis vero quærentibus fugere de navi, cum misissent scapham in mare, sub obtentu quasi inciperent a prora anchoras extendere,

27:31 dixit Paulus centurioni et militibus : Nisi hi in navi manserint, vos salvi fieri non potestis.

27:32 Tunc absciderunt milites funes scaphæ, et passi sunt eam excidere.

27:33 Et cum lux inciperet fieri, rogabat Paulus omnes sumere cibum, dicens : Quartadecima die hodie exspectantes jejuni permanetis, nihil accipientes.

27:34 Propter quod rogo vos accipere cibum pro salute vestra : quia nullius vestrum capillus de capite peribit.

27:35 Et cum hæc dixisset, sumens panem, gratias egit Deo in conspectu omnium : et cum fregisset, cœpit manducare.

27:36 Animæquiores autem facti omnes, et ipsi sumpserunt cibum.

27:37 Eramus vero universæ animæ in navi ducentæ septuaginta sex.

27:38 Et satiati cibo alleviabant navem, jactantes triticum in mare.

27:39 Cum autem dies factus esset, terram non agnoscebant : sinum vero quemdam considerabant habentem littus, in quem cogitabant si possent ejicere navem.

27:40 Et cum anchoras sustulissent, committebant se mari, simul laxantes juncturas gubernaculorum : et levato artemone secundum auræ flatum, tendebant ad littus.

27:41 Et cum incidissemus in locum dithalassum,

given thee all them that sail with thee.

27:25 Wherefore, sirs, be of good cheer; for I believe God that it shall so be, as it hath been told me.

27:26 And we must come unto a certain island.

27:27 But after the fourteenth night was come, as we were sailing in Adria, about midnight, the shipmen deemed that they discovered some country.

27:28 Who also sounding, found twenty fathoms; and going on a little further, they found fifteen fathoms.

27:29 Then fearing lest we should fall upon rough places, they cast four anchors out of the stern, and wished for the day.

27:30 But as the shipmen sought to fly out of the ship, having let down the boat into the sea, under colour, as though they would have cast anchors out of the forepart of the ship,

27:31 Paul said to the centurion, and to the soldiers: Except these stay in the ship, you cannot be saved.

27:32 Then the soldiers cut off the ropes of the boat, and let her fall off.

27:33 And when it began to be light, Paul besought them all to take meat, saying: This day is the fourteenth day that you have waited, and continued fasting, taking nothing.

27:34 Wherefore I pray you to take some meat for your health's sake; for there shall not an hair of the head of any of you perish.

27:35 And when he had said these things, taking bread, he gave thanks to God in the sight of them all; and when he had broken it, he began to eat.

27:36 Then were they all of better cheer, and they also took some meat.

27:37 And we were in all in the ship, two hundred threescore and sixteen souls.

27:38 And when they had eaten enough, they lightened the ship, casting the wheat into the sea.

27:39 And when it was day, they knew not the land; but they discovered a certain creek that had a shore, into which they minded, if they could, to thrust in the ship.

27:40 And when they had taken up the anchors, they committed themselves to the sea, loosing withal the rudder bands; and hoisting up the mainsail to the wind, they made towards shore.

27:41 And when we were fallen into a place

impegerunt navem : et prora quidem fixa manebat immobilis, puppis vero solvebatur a vi maris.

27:42 Militum autem consilium fuit ut custodias occiderent, ne quis cum enatasset, effugeret.

27:43 Centurio autem volens servare Paulum, prohibuit fieri : jussitque eos qui possent natare, emittere se primos, et evadere, et ad terram exire :

27:44 et ceteros, alios in tabulis ferebant, quosdam super ea quæ de navi erant. Et sic factum est, ut omnes animæ evaderent ad terram.

28:1 Et cum evasissemus, tunc cognovimus quia Melita insula vocabatur. Barbari vero præstabant non modicam humanitatem nobis.

28:2 Accensa enim pyra, reficiebant nos omnes propter imbrem qui imminebat, et frigus.

28:3 Cum congregasset autem Paulus sarmentorum aliquantam multitudinem, et imposuisset super ignem, vipera a calore cum processisset, invasit manum ejus.

28:4 Ut vero viderunt barbari pendentem bestiam de manu ejus, ad invicem dicebant : Utique homicida est homo hic, qui cum evaserit de mari, ultio non sinit eum vivere.

28:5 Et ille quidem excutiens bestiam in ignem, nihil mali passus est.

28:6 At illi existimabant eum in tumorem convertendum, et subito casurum et mori. Diu autem illis exspectantibus, et videntibus nihil mali in eo fieri, convertentes se, dicebant eum esse deum.

28:7 In locis autem illis erant prædia principis insulæ, nomine Publii, qui nos suscipiens, triduo benigne exhibuit.

28:8 Contigit autem patrem Publii febribus et dysenteria vexatum jacere. Ad quem Paulus intravit : et cum orasset, et imposuisset ei manus, salvavit eum.

28:9 Quo facto, omnes qui in insula habebant infirmitates, accedebant, et curabantur :

28:10 qui etiam multis honoribus nos honoraverunt, et navigantibus imposuerunt quæ necessaria erant.

28:11 Post menses autem tres navigavimus in navi

where two seas met, they run the ship aground; and the forepart indeed, sticking fast, remained unmoveable: but the hinder part was broken with the violence of the sea.

27:42 And the soldiers' counsel was, that they should kill the prisoners, lest any of them, swimming out, should escape.

27:43 But the centurion, willing to save Paul, forbade it to be done; and he commanded that they who could swim, should cast themselves first into the sea, and save themselves, and get to land.

27:44 And the rest, some they carried on boards, and some on those things that belonged to the ship. And so it came to pass, that every soul got safe to land.

28:1 And when we had escaped, then we knew that the island was called Melita. But the barbarians shewed us no small courtesy.

28:2 For kindling a fire, they refreshed us all, because of the present rain, and of the cold.

28:3 And when Paul had gathered together a bundle of sticks, and had laid them on the fire, a viper coming out of the heat, fastened on his hand.

28:4 And when the barbarians saw the beast hanging on his hand, they said one to another: Undoubtedly this man is a murderer, who though he hath escaped the sea, yet vengeance doth not suffer him to live.

28:5 And he indeed shaking off the beast into the fire, suffered no harm.

28:6 But they supposed that he would begin to swell up, and that he would suddenly fall down and die. But expecting long, and seeing that there came no harm to him, changing their minds, they said, that he was a god.

28:7 Now in these places were possessions of the chief man of the island, named Publius, who receiving us, for three days entertained us courteously.

28:8 And it happened that the father of Publius lay sick of a fever, and of a bloody flux. To whom Paul entered in; and when he had prayed, and laid his hands on him, he healed him.

28:9 Which being done, all that had diseases in the island, came and were healed:

28:10 Who also honoured us with many honours, and when we were to set sail, they laded us with such things as were necessary.

28:11 And after three months, we sailed in a ship

Alexandrina, quæ in insula hiemaverat, cui erat insigne Castorum.

28:12 Et cum venissemus Syracusam, mansimus ibi triduo.

28:13 Inde circumlegentes devenimus Rhegium : et post unum diem, flante austro, secunda die venimus Puteolos :

28:14 ubi inventis fratribus rogati sumus manere apud eos dies septem : et sic venimus Romam.

28:15 Et inde cum audissent fratres, occurrerunt nobis usque ad Appii forum, ac tres Tabernas. Quos cum vidisset Paulus, gratias agens Deo, accepit fiduciam.

28:16 Cum autem venissemus Romam, permissum est Paulo manere sibimet cum custodiente se milite.

28:17 Post tertium autem diem convocavit primos Judæorum. Cumque convenissent, dicebat eis : Ego, viri fratres, nihil adversus plebem faciens, aut morem paternum, vinctus ab Jerosolymis traditus sum in manus Romanorum,

28:18 qui cum interrogationem de me habuissent, voluerunt me dimittere, eo quod nulla esset causa mortis in me.

28:19 Contradicentibus autem Judæis, coactus sum appellare Cæsarem, non quasi gentem meam habens aliquid accusare.

28:20 Propter hanc igitur causam rogavi vos videre, et alloqui. Propter spem enim Israël catena hac circumdatus sum.

28:21 At illi dixerunt ad eum : Nos neque litteras accepimus de te a Judæa, neque adveniens aliquis fratrum nuntiavit, aut locutus est quid de te malum.

28:22 Rogamus autem a te audire quæ sentis : nam de secta hac notum est nobis quia ubique ei contradicitur.

28:23 Cum constituissent autem illi diem, venerunt ad eum in hospitium plurimi, quibus exponebat testificans regnum Dei, suadensque eis de Jesu ex lege Moysi et prophetis a mane usque ad vesperam.

28:24 Et quidam credebant his quæ dicebantur : quidam vero non credebant.

28:25 Cumque invicem non essent consentientes, discedebant, dicente Paulo unum verbum : Quia bene Spiritus Sanctus locutus est per

of Alexandria, that had wintered in the island, whose sign was the Castors.

28:12 And when we were come to Syracusa, we tarried there three days.

28:13 From thence, compassing by the shore, we came to Rhegium: and after one day, the south wind blowing, we came the second day to Puteoli;

28:14 Where, finding brethren, we were desired to tarry with them seven days: and so we went to Rome.

28:15 And from thence, when the brethren had heard of us, they came to meet us as far as Appii Forum, and the Three Taverns: whom when Paul saw, he gave thanks to God, and took courage.

28:16 And when we were come to Rome, Paul was suffered to dwell by himself, with a soldier that kept him.

28:17 And after the third day, he called together the chief of the Jews. And when they were assembled, he said to them: Men, brethren, I, having done nothing against the people, or the custom of our fathers, was delivered prisoner from Jerusalem into the hands of the Romans;

28:18 Who, when they had examined me, would have released me, for that there was no cause of death in me;

28:19 But the Jews contradicting it, I was constrained to appeal unto Caesar; not that I had any thing to accuse my nation of.

28:20 For this cause therefore I desired to see you, and to speak to you. Because that for the hope of Israel, I am bound with this chain.

28:21 But they said to him: We neither received letters concerning thee from Judea, neither did any of the brethren that came hither, relate or speak any evil of thee.

28:22 But we desire to hear of thee what thou thinkest; for as concerning this sect, we know that it is every where contradicted.

28:23 And when they had appointed him a day, there came very many to him unto his lodgings; to whom he expounded, testifying the kingdom of God, and persuading them concerning Jesus, out of the law of Moses and the prophets, from morning until evening.

28:24 And some believed the things that were said; but some believed not.

28:25 And when they agreed not among themselves, they departed, Paul speaking this one word: Well did the Holy Ghost speak to our fa-

Isaiam prophetam ad patres nostros,

²⁸:²⁶ dicens : *Vade ad populum istum, et dic ad eos : Aure audietis, et non intelligetis, et videntes videbitis, et non perspicietis.*

²⁸:²⁷ *Incrassatum est enim cor populi hujus, et auribus graviter audierunt, et oculos suos compresserunt : ne forte videant oculis, et auribus audiant, et corde intelligant, et convertantur, et sanem eos.*

²⁸:²⁸ Notum ergo sit vobis, quoniam gentibus missum est hoc salutare Dei, et ipsi audient.

²⁸:²⁹ Et cum hæc dixisset, exierunt ab eo Judæi, multam habentes inter se quæstionem.

²⁸:³⁰ Mansit autem biennio toto in suo conducto : et suscipiebat omnes qui ingrediebantur ad eum,

²⁸:³¹ prædicans regnum Dei, et docens quæ sunt de Domino Jesu Christo cum omni fiducia, sine prohibitione.

thers by Isaias the prophet,

²⁸:²⁶ Saying: *Go to this people, and say to them:With the ear you shall hear, and shall not understand; and seeing you shall see, and shall not perceive.*

²⁸:²⁷ For the heart of this people is grown gross, and with their ears have they heard heavily, and their eyes they have shut; lest perhaps they should see with their eyes, and hear with their ears, and understand with their heart, and should be converted, and I should heal them.

²⁸:²⁸ Be it known therefore to you, that this salvation of God is sent to the Gentiles, and they will hear it.

²⁸:²⁹ And when he had said these things, the Jews went out from him, having much reasoning among themselves.

²⁸:³⁰ And he remained two whole years in his own hired lodging; and he received all that came in to him,

²⁸:³¹ Preaching the kingdom of God, and teaching the things which concern the Lord Jesus Christ, with all confidence, without prohibition.

Epistula Beati Pauli Apostoli ad Romanos

THE EPISTLE OF BLESSED PAUL THE APOSTLE TO THE ROMANS

✠

1:1 PAULUS, SERVUS JESU CHRISTI, vocatus Apostolus, segregatus in Evangelium Dei,

1:2 quod ante promiserat per prophetas suos in Scripturis sanctis

1:3 de Filio suo, qui factus est ei ex semine David secundum carnem,

1:4 qui prædestinatus est Filius Dei in virtute secundum spiritum sanctificationis ex resurrectione mortuorum Jesu Christi Domini nostri :

1:5 per quem accepimus gratiam, et apostolatum ad obediendum fidei in omnibus gentibus pro nomine ejus,

1:6 in quibus estis et vos vocati Jesu Christi :

1:7 omnibus qui sunt Romæ, dilectis Dei, vocatis sanctis. Gratia vobis, et pax a Deo Patre nostro, et Domino Jesu Christo.

1:8 Primum quidem gratias ago Deo meo per Jesum Christum pro omnibus vobis : quia fides vestra annuntiatur in universo mundo.

1:9 Testis enim mihi est Deus, cui servio in spiritu meo in Evangelio Filii ejus, quod sine intermissione memoriam vestri facio

1:10 semper in orationibus meis : obsecrans, si quomodo tandem aliquando prosperum iter habeam in voluntate Dei veniendi ad vos.

1:11 Desidero enim videre vos, ut aliquid impertiar vobis gratiæ spiritualis ad confirmandos vos :

1:12 id est, simul consolari in vobis per eam quæ invicem est, fidem vestram atque meam.

1:13 Nolo autem vos ignorare fratres : quia sæpe proposui venire ad vos (et prohibitus sum usque adhuc) ut aliquem fructum habeam et in vobis, sicut et in ceteris gentibus.

1:14 Græcis ac barbaris, sapientibus, et insipientibus debitor sum :

1:1 PAUL, A SERVANT OF JESUS CHRIST, called to be an apostle, separated unto the gospel of God,

1:2 Which he had promised before, by his prophets, in the holy scriptures,

1:3 Concerning his Son, who was made to him of the seed of David, according to the flesh,

1:4 Who was predestinated the Son of God in power, according to the spirit of sanctification, by the resurrection of our Lord Jesus Christ from the dead;

1:5 By whom we have received grace and apostleship for obedience to the faith, in all nations, for his name;

1:6 Among whom are you also the called of Jesus Christ:

1:7 To all that are at Rome, the beloved of God, called to be saints. Grace to you, and peace from God our Father, and from the Lord Jesus Christ.

1:8 First I give thanks to my God, through Jesus Christ, for you all, because your faith is spoken of in the whole world.

1:9 For God is my witness, whom I serve in my spirit in the gospel of his Son, that without ceasing I make a commemoration of you;

1:10 Always in my prayers making request, if by any means now at length I may have a prosperous journey, by the will of God, to come unto you.

1:11 For I long to see you, that I may impart unto you some spiritual grace, to strengthen you:

1:12 That is to say, that I may be comforted together in you, by that which is common to us both, your faith and mine.

1:13 And I would not have you ignorant, brethren, that I have often purposed to come unto you, (and have been hindered hitherto,) that I might have some fruit among you also, even as among other Gentiles.

1:14 To the Greeks and to the barbarians, to the wise and to the unwise, I am a debtor;

1:15 ita (quod in me) promptum est et vobis, qui Romæ estis, evangelizare.

1:16 Non enim erubesco Evangelium. Virtus enim Dei est in salutem omni credenti, Judæo primum, et Græco.

1:17 Justitia enim Dei in eo revelatur ex fide in fidem : sicut scriptum est : Justus autem ex fide vivit.

1:18 Revelatur enim ira Dei de cælo super omnem impietatem, et injustitiam hominum eorum, qui veritatem Dei in injustitia detinent :

1:19 quia quod notum est Dei, manifestum est in illis. Deus enim illis manifestavit.

1:20 Invisibilia enim ipsius, a creatura mundi, per ea quæ facta sunt, intellecta, conspiciuntur : sempiterna quoque ejus virtus, et divinitas : ita ut sint inexcusabiles.

1:21 Quia cum cognovissent Deum, non sicut Deum glorificaverunt, aut gratias egerunt : sed evanuerunt in cogitationibus suis, et obscuratum est insipiens cor eorum :

1:22 dicentes enim se esse sapientes, stulti facti sunt.

1:23 Et mutaverunt gloriam incorruptibilis Dei in similitudinem imaginis corruptibilis hominis, et volucrum, et quadrupedum, et serpentium.

1:24 Propter quod tradidit illos Deus in desideria cordis eorum, in immunditiam, ut contumeliis afficiant corpora sua in semetipsis :

1:25 qui commutaverunt veritatem Dei in mendacium : et coluerunt, et servierunt creaturæ potius quam Creatori, qui est benedictus in sæcula. Amen.

1:26 Propterea tradidit illos Deus in passiones ignominiæ : nam feminæ eorum immutaverunt naturalem usum in eum usum qui est contra naturam.

1:27 Similiter autem et masculi, relicto naturali usu feminæ, exarserunt in desideriis suis in invicem, masculi in masculos turpitudinem operantes, et mercedem, quam oportuit, erroris sui in semetipsis recipientes.

1:28 Et sicut non probaverunt Deum habere in notitia, tradidit illos Deus in reprobum sensum, ut faciant ea quæ non conveniunt,

1:15 So (as much as is in me) I am ready to preach the gospel to you also that are at Rome.

1:16 For I am not ashamed of the gospel. For it is the power of God unto salvation to every one that believeth, to the Jew first, and to the Greek.

1:17 For the justice of God is revealed therein, from faith unto faith, as it is written: The just man liveth by faith.

1:18 For the wrath of God is revealed from heaven against all ungodliness and injustice of those men that detain the truth of God in injustice:

1:19 Because that which is known of God is manifest in them. For God hath manifested it unto them.

1:20 For the invisible things of him, from the creation of the world, are clearly seen, being understood by the things that are made; his eternal power also, and divinity: so that they are inexcusable.

1:21 Because that, when they knew God, they have not glorified him as God, or given thanks; but became vain in their thoughts, and their foolish heart was darkened.

1:22 For professing themselves to be wise, they became fools.

1:23 And they changed the glory of the incorruptible God into the likeness of the image of a corruptible man, and of birds, and of fourfooted beasts, and of creeping things.

1:24 Wherefore God gave them up to the desires of their heart, unto uncleanness, to dishonour their own bodies among themselves.

1:25 Who changed the truth of God into a lie; and worshipped and served the creature rather than the Creator, who is blessed for ever. Amen.

1:26 For this cause God delivered them up to shameful affections. For their women have changed the natural use into that use which is against nature.

1:27 And, in like manner, the men also, leaving the natural use of the women, have burned in their lusts one towards another, men with men working that which is filthy, and receiving in themselves the recompense which was due to their error.

1:28 And as they liked not to have God in their knowledge, God delivered them up to a reprobate sense, to do those things which are not convenient;

1:29 repletos omni iniquitate, malitia, fornicatione, avaritia, nequitia, plenos invidia, homicidio, contentione, dolo, malignitate : susurrones,

1:30 detractores, Deo odibiles, contumeliosos, superbos, elatos, inventores malorum, parentibus non obedientes,

1:31 insipientes, incompositos, sine affectione, absque fœdere, sine misericordia.

1:32 Qui cum justitiam Dei cognovissent, non intellexerunt quoniam qui talia agunt, digni sunt morte : et non solum qui ea faciunt, sed etiam qui consentiunt facientibus.

2:1 Propter quod inexcusabilis es, o homo omnis qui judicas. In quo enim judicas alterum, teipsum condemnas : eadem enim agis quæ judicas.

2:2 Scimus enim quoniam judicium Dei est secundum veritatem in eos qui talia agunt.

2:3 Existimas autem hoc, o homo, qui judicas eos qui talia agunt, et facis ea, quia tu effugies judicium Dei ?

2:4 an divitias bonitatis ejus, et patientiæ, et longanimitatis contemnis ? ignoras quoniam benignitas Dei ad pœnitentiam te adducit ?

2:5 Secundum autem duritiam tuam, et impœnitens cor, thesaurizas tibi iram in die iræ, et revelationis justi judicii Dei,

2:6 qui reddet unicuique secundum opera ejus :

2:7 iis quidem qui secundum patientiam boni operis, gloriam, et honorem, et incorruptionem quærunt, vitam æternam :

2:8 iis autem qui sunt ex contentione, et qui non acquiescunt veritati, credunt autem iniquitati, ira et indignatio.

2:9 Tribulatio et angustia in omnem animam hominis operantis malum, Judæi primum, et Græci :

2:10 gloria autem, et honor, et pax omni operanti bonum, Judæo primum, et Græco :

2:11 non enim est acceptio personarum apud Deum.

2:12 Quicumque enim sine lege peccaverunt, sine lege peribunt : et quicumque in lege peccaverunt, per legem judicabuntur.

1:29 Being filled with all iniquity, malice, fornication, avarice, wickedness, full of envy, murder, contention, deceit, malignity, whisperers,

1:30 Detractors, hateful to God, contumelious, proud, haughty, inventors of evil things, disobedient to parents,

1:31 Foolish, dissolute, without affection, without fidelity, without mercy.

1:32 Who, having known the justice of God, did not understand that they who do such things, are worthy of death; and not only they that do them, but they also that consent to them that do them.

2:1 Wherefore thou art inexcusable, O man, whosoever thou art that judgest. For wherein thou judgest another, thou condemnest thyself. For thou dost the same things which thou judgest.

2:2 For we know that the judgment of God is, according to truth, against them that do such things.

2:3 And thinkest thou this, O man, that judgest them who do such things, and dost the same, that thou shalt escape the judgment of God?

2:4 Or despisest thou the riches of his goodness, and patience, and longsuffering? Knowest thou not, that the benignity of God leadeth thee to penance?

2:5 But according to thy hardness and impenitent heart, thou treasurest up to thyself wrath, against the day of wrath, and revelation of the just judgment of God.

2:6 Who will render to every man according to his works.

2:7 To them indeed, who according to patience in good work, seek glory and honour and incorruption, eternal life:

2:8 But to them that are contentious, and who obey not the truth, but give credit to iniquity, wrath and indignation.

2:9 Tribulation and anguish upon every soul of man that worketh evil, of the Jew first, and also of the Greek.

2:10 But glory, and honour, and peace to every one that worketh good, to the Jew first, and also to the Greek.

2:11 For there is no respect of persons with God.

2:12 For whosoever have sinned without the law, shall perish without the law; and whosoever have sinned in the law, shall be judged by the

2:13 Non enim auditores legis justi sunt apud Deum, sed factores legis justificabuntur.

2:14 Cum autem gentes, quæ legem non habent, naturaliter ea, quæ legis sunt, faciunt, ejusmodi legem non habentes, ipsi sibi sunt lex :

2:15 qui ostendunt opus legis scriptum in cordibus suis, testimonium reddente illis conscientia ipsorum, et inter se invicem cogitationibus accusantibus, aut etiam defendentibus,

2:16 in die, cum judicabit Deus occulta hominum, secundum Evangelium meum per Jesum Christum.

2:17 Si autem tu Judæus cognominaris, et requiescis in lege, et gloriaris in Deo,

2:18 et nosti voluntatem ejus, et probas utiliora, instructus per legem,

2:19 confidis teipsum esse ducem cæcorum, lumen eorum qui in tenebris sunt,

2:20 eruditorem insipientium, magistrum infantium, habentem formam scientiæ, et veritatis in lege.

2:21 Qui ergo alium doces, teipsum non doces : qui prædicas non furandum, furaris :

2:22 qui dicis non mœchandum, mœcharis : qui abominaris idola, sacrilegium facis :

2:23 qui in lege gloriaris, per prævaricationem legis Deum inhonoras.

2:24 (Nomen enim Dei per vos blasphematur inter gentes, sicut scriptum est.)

2:25 Circumcisio quidem prodest, si legem observes : si autem prævaricator legis sis, circumcisio tua præputium facta est.

2:26 Si igitur præputium justitias legis custodiat, nonne præputium illius in circumcisionem reputabitur ?

2:27 et judicabit id quod ex natura est præputium, legem consummans, te, qui per litteram et circumcisionem prævaricator legis es ?

2:28 Non enim qui in manifesto, Judæus est : neque quæ in manifesto, in carne, est circumcisio :

2:29 sed qui in abscondito, Judæus est : et circumcisio cordis in spiritu, non littera : cujus laus non ex hominibus, sed ex Deo est.

law.

2:13 For not the hearers of the law are just before God, but the doers of the law shall be justified.

2:14 For when the Gentiles, who have not the law, do by nature those things that are of the law; these having not the law are a law to themselves:

2:15 Who shew the work of the law written in their hearts, their conscience bearing witness to them, and their thoughts between themselves accusing, or also defending one another,

2:16 In the day when God shall judge the secrets of men by Jesus Christ, according to my gospel.

2:17 But if thou art called a Jew and restest in the law, and makest thy boast of God,

2:18 And knowest his will, and approvest the more profitable things, being instructed by the law,

2:19 Art confident that thou thyself art a guide of the blind, a light of them that are in darkness,

2:20 An instructor of the foolish, a teacher of infants, having the form of knowledge and of truth in the law.

2:21 Thou therefore that teachest another, teachest not thyself: thou that preachest that men should not steal, stealest:

2:22 Thou that sayest, men should not commit adultery, committest adultery: thou that abhorrest idols, committest sacrilege:

2:23 Thou that makest thy boast of the law, by transgression of the law dishonourest God.

2:24 (For the name of God through you is blasphemed among the Gentiles, as it is written.)

2:25 Circumcision profiteth indeed, if thou keep the law; but if thou be a transgressor of the law, thy circumcision is made uncircumcision.

2:26 If, then, the uncircumcised keep the justices of the law, shall not this uncircumcision be counted for circumcision?

2:27 And shall not that which by nature is uncircumcision, if it fulfil the law, judge thee, who by the letter and circumcision art a transgressor of the law?

2:28 For it is not he is a Jew, who is so outwardly; nor is that circumcision which is outwardly in the flesh:

2:29 But he is a Jew, that is one inwardly; and the circumcision is that of the heart, in the spirit, not in the letter; whose praise is not of men,

but of God.

3:1 Quid ergo amplius Judæo est ? aut quæ utilitas circumcisionis ?

3:2 Multum per omnem modum. Primum quidem quia credita sunt illis eloquia Dei.

3:3 Quid enim si quidam illorum non crediderunt ? numquid incredulitas illorum fidem Dei evacuabit ? Absit.

3:4 Est autem Deus verax : omnis autem homo mendax, sicut scriptum est : *Ut justificeris in sermonibus tuis : et vincas cum judicaris.*

3:5 Si autem iniquitas nostra justitiam Dei commendat, quid dicemus ? Numquid iniquus est Deus, qui infert iram ?

3:6 secundum hominem dico. Absit. Alioquin quomodo judicabit Deus hunc mundum ?

3:7 Si enim veritas Dei in meo mendacio abundavit in gloriam ipsius : quid adhuc et ego tamquam peccator judicor ?

3:8 et non (sicut blasphemamur, et sicut aiunt quidam nos dicere) faciamus mala ut veniant bona : quorum damnatio justa est.

3:9 Quid ergo ? præcellimus eos ? Nequaquam. Causati enim sumus Judæos et Græcos omnes sub peccato esse,

3:10 sicut scriptum est : *Quia non est justus quisquam :*

3:11 *non est intelligens, non est requirens Deum.*

3:12 *Omnes declinaverunt, simul inutiles facti sunt : non est qui faciat bonum, non est usque ad unum.*

3:13 *Sepulchrum patens est guttur eorum, linguis suis dolose agebant : venenum aspidum sub labiis eorum :*

3:14 *quorum os maledictione, et amaritudine plenum est :*

3:15 *veloces pedes eorum ad effundendum sanguinem :*

3:16 *contritio et infelicitas in viis eorum :*

3:17 *et viam pacis non cognoverunt :*

3:18 *non est timor Dei ante oculos eorum.*

3:19 Scimus autem quoniam quæcumque lex loquitur, iis, qui in lege sunt, loquitur : ut omne os obstruatur, et subditus fiat omnis mundus Deo :

3:20 quia ex operibus legis non justificabitur omnis caro coram illo. Per legem enim cognitio peccati.

3:21 Nunc autem sine lege justitia Dei manifestata est : testificata a lege et prophetis.

3:1 What advantage then hath the Jew, or what is the profit of circumcision?

3:2 Much every way. First indeed, because the words of God were committed to them.

3:3 For what if some of them have not believed? shall their unbelief make the faith of God without effect? God forbid.

3:4 But God is true; and every man a liar, as it is written, *That thou mayest be justified in thy words, and mayest overcome when thou art judged.*

3:5 But if our injustice commend the justice of God, what shall we say? Is God unjust, who executeth wrath?

3:6 (I speak according to man.) God forbid: otherwise how shall God judge this world?

3:7 For if the truth of God hath more abounded through my lie, unto his glory, why am I also yet judged as a sinner?

3:8 And not rather (as we are slandered, and as some affirm that we say) let us do evil, that there may come good? whose damnation is just.

3:9 What then? Do we excel them? No, not so. For we have charged both Jews, and Greeks, that they are all under sin.

3:10 As it is written: *There is not any man just.*

3:11 *There is none that understandeth, there is none that seeketh after God.*

3:12 *All have turned out of the way; they are become unprofitable together: there is none that doth good, there is not so much as one.*

3:13 *Their throat is an open sepulchre; with their tongues they have dealt deceitfully. The venom of asps is under their lips.*

3:14 *Whose mouth is full of cursing and bitterness:*

3:15 *Their feet swift to shed blood:*

3:16 *Destruction and misery in their ways:*

3:17 *And the way of peace they have not known:*

3:18 *There is no fear of God before their eyes.*

3:19 Now we know, that what things soever the law speaketh, it speaketh to them that are in the law; that every mouth may be stopped, and all the world may be made subject to God.

3:20 Because by the works of the law no flesh shall be justified before him. For by the law is the knowledge of sin.

3:21 But now without the law the justice of God is made manifest, being witnessed by the law and the prophets.

3:22 Justitia autem Dei per fidem Jesu Christi in omnes et super omnes qui credunt in eum : non enim est distinctio :

3:23 omnes enim peccaverunt, et egent gloria Dei.

3:24 Justificati gratis per gratiam ipsius, per redemptionem quæ est in Christo Jesu,

3:25 quem proposuit Deus propitiationem per fidem in sanguine ipsius, ad ostensionem justitiæ suæ propter remissionem præcedentium delictorum

3:26 in sustentatione Dei, ad ostensionem justitiæ ejus in hoc tempore : ut sit ipse justus, et justificans eum, qui est ex fide Jesu Christi.

3:27 Ubi est ergo gloriatio tua ? Exclusa est. Per quam legem ? Factorum ? Non : sed per legem fidei.

3:28 Arbitramur enim justificari hominem per fidem sine operibus legis.

3:29 An Judæorum Deus tantum ? nonne et gentium ? Immo et gentium :

3:30 quoniam quidem unus est Deus, qui justificat circumcisionem ex fide, et præputium per fidem.

3:31 Legem ergo destruimus per fidem ? Absit : sed legem statuimus.

4:1 Quid ergo dicemus invenisse Abraham patrem nostrum secundum carnem ?

4:2 Si enim Abraham ex operibus justificatus est, habet gloriam, sed non apud Deum.

4:3 Quid enim dicit Scriptura ? Credidit Abraham Deo, et reputatum est illi ad justitiam.

4:4 Ei autem qui operatur, merces non imputatur secundum gratiam, sed secundum debitum.

4:5 Ei vero qui non operatur, credenti autem in eum, qui justificat impium, reputatur fides ejus ad justitiam secundum propositum gratiæ Dei.

4:6 Sicut et David dicit beatitudinem hominis, cui Deus accepto fert justitiam sine operibus :

4:7 *Beati, quorum remissæ sunt iniquitates, et quorum tecta sunt peccata.*

4:8 *Beatus vir, cui non imputavit Dominus peccatum.*

4:9 Beatitudo ergo hæc in circumcisione tantum manet, an etiam in præputio ? Dicimus enim quia reputata est Abrahæ fides ad justitiam.

3:22 Even the justice of God, by faith of Jesus Christ, unto all and upon all them that believe in him: for there is no distinction:

3:23 For all have sinned, and do need the glory of God.

3:24 Being justified freely by his grace, through the redemption, that is in Christ Jesus,

3:25 Whom God hath proposed to be a propitiation, through faith in his blood, to the shewing of his justice, for the remission of former sins,

3:26 Through the forbearance of God, for the shewing of his justice in this time; that he himself may be just, and the justifier of him, who is of the faith of Jesus Christ.

3:27 Where is then thy boasting? It is excluded. By what law? Of works? No, but by the law of faith.

3:28 For we account a man to be justified by faith, without the works of the law.

3:29 Is he the God of the Jews only? Is he not also of the Gentiles? Yes, of the Gentiles also.

3:30 For it is one God, that justifieth circumcision by faith, and uncircumcision through faith.

3:31 Do we, then, destroy the law through faith? God forbid: but we establish the law.

4:1 What shall we say then that Abraham hath found, who is our father according to the flesh.

4:2 For if Abraham were justified by works, he hath whereof to glory, but not before God.

4:3 For what saith the scripture? Abraham believed God, and it was reputed to him unto justice.

4:4 Now to him that worketh, the reward is not reckoned according to grace, but according to debt.

4:5 But to him that worketh not, yet believeth in him that justifieth the ungodly, his faith is reputed to justice, according to the purpose of the grace of God.

4:6 As David also termeth the blessedness of a man, to whom God reputeth justice without works:

4:7 *Blessed are they whose iniquities are forgiven, and whose sins are covered.*

4:8 *Blessed is the man to whom the Lord hath not imputed sin.*

4:9 This blessedness then, doth it remain in the circumcision only, or in the uncircumcision also? For we say that unto Abraham faith was reputed to justice.

4:10 Quomodo ergo reputata est ? in circumcisione, an in præputio ? Non in circumcisione, sed in præputio.

4:11 Et signum accepit circumcisionis, signaculum justitiæ fidei, quæ est in præputio : ut sit pater omnium credentium per præputium, ut reputetur et illis ad justitiam :

4:12 et sit pater circumcisionis non iis tantum, qui sunt ex circumcisione, sed et iis qui sectantur vestigia fidei, quæ est in præputio patris nostri Abrahæ.

4:13 Non enim per legem promissio Abrahæ, aut semini ejus ut hæres esset mundi : sed per justitiam fidei.

4:14 Si enim qui ex lege, hæredes sunt : exinanita est fides, abolita est promissio.

4:15 Lex enim iram operatur. Ubi enim non est lex, nec prævaricatio.

4:16 Ideo ex fide, ut secundum gratiam firma sit promissio omni semini, non ei qui ex lege est solum, sed et ei qui ex fide est Abrahæ, qui pater est omnium nostrum

4:17 (sicut scriptum est : Quia patrem multarum gentium posui te) ante Deum, cui credidit, qui vivificat mortuos, et vocat ea quæ non sunt, tamquam ea quæ sunt :

4:18 qui contra spem in spem credidit, ut fieret pater multarum gentium secundum quod dictum est ei : Sic erit semen tuum.

4:19 Et non infirmatus est fide, nec consideravit corpus suum emortuum, cum jam fere centum esset annorum, et emortuam vulvam Saræ.

4:20 In repromissione etiam Dei non hæsitavit diffidentia, sed confortatus est fide, dans gloriam Deo :

4:21 plenissime sciens, quia quæcumque promisit, potens est et facere.

4:22 Ideo et reputatum est illi ad justitiam.

4:23 Non est autem scriptum tantum propter ipsum quia reputatum est illi ad justitiam :

4:24 sed et propter nos, quibus reputabitur credentibus in eum, qui suscitavit Jesum Christum Dominum nostrum a mortuis,

4:25 qui traditus est propter delicta nostra, et resurrexit propter justificationem nostram.

4:10 How then was it reputed? When he was in circumcision, or in uncircumcision? Not in circumcision, but in uncircumcision.

4:11 And he received the sign of circumcision, a seal of the justice of the faith, which he had, being uncircumcised; that he might be the father of all them that believe, being uncircumcised, that unto them also it may be reputed to justice:

4:12 And might be the father of circumcision; not to them only, that are of the circumcision, but to them also that follow the steps of the faithful, that is in the uncircumcision of our father Abraham.

4:13 For not through the law was the promise to Abraham, or to his seed, that he should be heir of the world; but through the justice of faith.

4:14 For if they who are of the law be heirs, faith is made void, the promise is made of no effect.

4:15 For the law worketh wrath. For where there is no law, neither is there transgression.

4:16 Therefore is it of faith, that according to grace the promise might be firm to all the seed; not to that only which is of the law, but to that also which is of the faith of Abraham, who is the father of us all,

4:17 (As it is written: I have made thee a father of many nations,) before God, whom he believed, who quickeneth the dead; and calleth those things that are not, as those that are.

4:18 Who against hope believed in hope; that he might be made the father of many nations, according to that which was said to him: So shall thy seed be.

4:19 And he was not weak in faith; neither did he consider his own body now dead, whereas he was almost an hundred years old, nor the dead womb of Sara.

4:20 In the promise also of God he staggered not by distrust; but was strengthened in faith, giving glory to God:

4:21 Most fully knowing, that whatsoever he has promised, he is able also to perform.

4:22 And therefore it was reputed to him unto justice.

4:23 Now it is not written only for him, that it was reputed to him unto justice,

4:24 But also for us, to whom it shall be reputed, if we believe in him, that raised up Jesus Christ, our Lord, from the dead,

4:25 Who was delivered up for our sins, and rose again for our justification.

5:1 Justificati ergo ex fide, pacem habeamus ad Deum per Dominum nostrum Jesum Christum :

5:2 per quem et habemus accessum per fidem in gratiam istam, in qua stamus, et gloriamur in spe gloriæ filiorum Dei.

5:3 Non solum autem, sed et gloriamur in tribulationibus : scientes quod tribulatio patientiam operatur :

5:4 patientia autem probationem, probatio vero spem,

5:5 spes autem non confundit : quia caritas Dei diffusa est in cordibus nostris per Spiritum Sanctum, qui datus est nobis.

5:6 Ut quid enim Christus, cum adhuc infirmi essemus, secundum tempus, pro impiis mortuus est ?

5:7 vix enim pro justo quis moritur : nam pro bono forsitan quis audeat mori.

5:8 Commendat autem caritatem suam Deus in nobis : quoniam cum adhuc peccatores essemus, secundum tempus,

5:9 Christus pro nobis mortuus est : multo igitur magis nunc justificati in sanguine ipsius, salvi erimus ab ira per ipsum.

5:10 Si enim cum inimici essemus, reconciliati sumus Deo per mortem filii ejus : multo magis reconciliati, salvi erimus in vita ipsius.

5:11 Non solum autem : sed et gloriamur in Deo per Dominum nostrum Jesum Christum, per quem nunc reconciliationem accepimus.

5:12 Propterea sicut per unum hominem peccatum in hunc mundum intravit, et per peccatum mors, et ita in omnes homines mors pertransiit, in quo omnes peccaverunt.

5:13 Usque ad legem enim peccatum erat in mundo : peccatum autem non imputabatur, cum lex non esset.

5:14 Sed regnavit mors ab Adam usque ad Moysen etiam in eos qui non peccaverunt in similitudinem prævaricationis Adæ, qui est forma futuri.

5:15 Sed non sicut delictum, ita et donum : si enim unius delicto multi mortui sunt : multo magis gratia Dei et donum in gratia unius hominis Jesu Christi in plures abundavit.

5:16 Et non sicut per unum peccatum, ita et donum. Nam judicium quidem ex uno in condemnationem : gratia autem ex multis delictis

5:1 Being justified therefore by faith, let us have peace with God, through our Lord Jesus Christ:

5:2 By whom also we have access through faith into this grace, wherein we stand, and glory in the hope of the glory of the sons of God.

5:3 And not only so; but we glory also in tribulations, knowing that tribulation worketh patience;

5:4 And patience trial; and trial hope;

5:5 And hope confoundeth not: because the charity of God is poured forth in our hearts, by the Holy Ghost, who is given to us.

5:6 For why did Christ, when as yet we were weak, according to the time, die for the ungodly?

5:7 For scarce for a just man will one die; yet perhaps for a good man some one would dare to die.

5:8 But God commendeth his charity towards us; because when as yet we were sinners, according to the time,

5:9 Christ died for us; much more therefore, being now justified by his blood, shall we be saved from wrath through him.

5:10 For if, when we were enemies, we were reconciled to God by the death of his Son; much more, being reconciled, shall we be saved by his life.

5:11 And not only so; but also we glory in God, through our Lord Jesus Christ, by whom we have now received reconciliation.

5:12 Wherefore as by one man sin entered into this world, and by sin death; and so death passed upon all men, in whom all have sinned.

5:13 For until the law sin was in the world; but sin was not imputed, when the law was not.

5:14 But death reigned from Adam unto Moses, even over them also who have not sinned after the similitude of the transgression of Adam, who is a figure of him who was to come.

5:15 But not as the offence, so also the gift. For if by the offence of one, many died; much more the grace of God, and the gift, by the grace of one man, Jesus Christ, hath abounded unto many.

5:16 And not as it was by one sin, so also is the gift. For judgment indeed was by one unto condemnation; but grace is of many offences,

in justificationem.

5:17 Si enim unius delicto mors regnavit per unum : multo magis abundantiam gratiæ, et donationis, et justitiæ accipientes, in vita regnabunt per unum Jesum Christum.

5:18 Igitur sicut per unius delictum in omnes homines in condemnationem : sic et per unius justitiam in omnes homines in justificationem vitæ.

5:19 Sicut enim per inobedientiam unius hominis, peccatores constituti sunt multi : ita et per unius obeditionem, justi constituentur multi.

5:20 Lex autem subintravit ut abundaret delictum. Ubi autem abundavit delictum, superabundavit gratia :

5:21 ut sicut regnavit peccatum in mortem : ita et gratia regnet per justitiam in vitam æternam, per Jesum Christum Dominum nostrum.

6:1 Quid ergo dicemus ? permanebimus in peccato ut gratia abundet ?

6:2 Absit. Qui enim mortui sumus peccato, quomodo adhuc vivemus in illo ?

6:3 an ignoratis quia quicumque baptizati sumus in Christo Jesu, in morte ipsius baptizati sumus ?

6:4 Consepulti enim sumus cum illo per baptismum in mortem : ut quomodo Christus surrexit a mortuis per gloriam Patris, ita et nos in novitate vitæ ambulemus.

6:5 Si enim complantati facti sumus similitudini mortis ejus : simul et resurrectionis erimus.

6:6 Hoc scientes, quia vetus homo noster simul crucifixus est, ut destruatur corpus peccati, et ultra non serviamus peccato.

6:7 Qui enim mortuus est, justificatus est a peccato.

6:8 Si autem mortui sumus cum Christo, credimus quia simul etiam vivemus cum Christo,

6:9 scientes quod Christus resurgens ex mortuis jam non moritur : mors illi ultra non dominabitur.

6:10 Quod enim mortuus est peccato, mortuus est semel : quod autem vivit, vivit Deo.

6:11 Ita et vos existimate vos mortuos quidem esse peccato, viventes autem Deo, in Christo Jesu Domino nostro.

6:12 Non ergo regnet peccatum in vestro mortali corpore ut obediatis concupiscentiis ejus.

6:13 Sed neque exhibeatis membra vestra arma

unto justification.

5:17 For if by one man's offence death reigned through one; much more they who receive abundance of grace, and of the gift, and of justice, shall reign in life through one, Jesus Christ.

5:18 Therefore, as by the offence of one, unto all men to condemnation; so also by the justice of one, unto all men to justification of life.

5:19 For as by the disobedience of one man, many were made sinners; so also by the obedience of one, many shall be made just.

5:20 Now the law entered in, that sin might abound. And where sin abounded, grace did more abound.

5:21 That as sin hath reigned to death; so also grace might reign by justice unto life everlasting, through Jesus Christ our Lord.

6:1 What shall we say, then? shall we continue in sin, that grace may abound?

6:2 God forbid. For we that are dead to sin, how shall we live any longer therein?

6:3 Know you not that all we, who are baptized in Christ Jesus, are baptized in his death?

6:4 For we are buried together with him by baptism into death; that as Christ is risen from the dead by the glory of the Father, so we also may walk in newness of life.

6:5 For if we have been planted together in the likeness of his death, we shall be also in the likeness of his resurrection.

6:6 Knowing this, that our old man is crucified with him, that the body of sin may be destroyed, to the end that we may serve sin no longer.

6:7 For he that is dead is justified from sin.

6:8 Now if we be dead with Christ, we believe that we shall live also together with Christ:

6:9 Knowing that Christ rising again from the dead, dieth now no more, death shall no more have dominion over him.

6:10 For in that he died to sin, he died once; but in that he liveth, he liveth unto God:

6:11 So do you also reckon, that you are dead to sin, but alive unto God, in Christ Jesus our Lord.

6:12 Let not sin therefore reign in your mortal body, so as to obey the lusts thereof.

6:13 Neither yield ye your members as instru-

iniquitatis peccato : sed exhibete vos Deo, tamquam ex mortuis viventes : et membra vestra arma justitiæ Deo.

6:14 Peccatum enim vobis non dominabitur : non enim sub lege estis, sed sub gratia.

6:15 Quid ergo ? peccabimus, quoniam non sumus sub lege, sed sub gratia ? Absit.

6:16 Nescitis quoniam cui exhibetis vos servos ad obediendum, servi estis ejus, cui obeditis, sive peccati ad mortem, sive obeditionis ad justitiam ?

6:17 Gratias autem Deo quod fuistis servi peccati, obedistis autem ex corde in eam formam doctrinæ, in quam traditi estis.

6:18 Liberati autem a peccato, servi facti estis justitiæ.

6:19 Humanum dico, propter infirmitatem carnis vestræ : sicut enim exhibuistis membra vestra servire immunditiæ, et iniquitati ad iniquitatem, ita nunc exhibete membra vestra servire justitiæ in sanctificationem.

6:20 Cum enim servi essetis peccati, liberi fuistis justitiæ.

6:21 Quem ergo fructum habuistis tunc in illis, in quibus nunc erubescitis ? nam finis illorum mors est.

6:22 Nunc vero liberati a peccato, servi autem facti Deo, habetis fructum vestrum in sanctificationem, finem vero vitam æternam.

6:23 Stipendia enim peccati, mors. Gratia autem Dei, vita æterna, in Christo Jesu Domino nostro.

7:1 An ignoratis, fratres (scientibus enim legem loquor), quia lex in homine dominatur quanto tempore vivit ?

7:2 Nam quæ sub viro est mulier, vivente viro, alligata est legi : si autem mortuus fuerit vir ejus, soluta est a lege viri.

7:3 Igitur, vivente viro, vocabitur adultera si fuerit cum alio viro : si autem mortuus fuerit vir ejus, liberata est a lege viri, ut non sit adultera si fuerit cum alio viro.

7:4 Itaque fratres mei, et vos mortificati estis legi per corpus Christi : ut sitis alterius, qui ex mortuis resurrexit, ut fructificemus Deo.

ments of iniquity unto sin; but present yourselves to God, as those that are alive from the dead, and your members as instruments of justice unto God.

6:14 For sin shall not have dominion over you; for you are not under the law, but under grace.

6:15 What then? Shall we sin, because we are not under the law, but under grace? God forbid.

6:16 Know you not, that to whom you yield yourselves servants to obey, his servants you are whom you obey, whether it be of sin unto death, or of obedience unto justice.

6:17 But thanks be to God, that you were the servants of sin, but have obeyed from the heart, unto that form of doctrine, into which you have been delivered.

6:18 Being then freed from sin, we have been made servants of justice.

6:19 I speak an human thing, because of the infirmity of your flesh. For as you have yielded your members to serve uncleanness and iniquity, unto iniquity; so now yield your members to serve justice, unto sanctification.

6:20 For when you were the servants of sin, you were free men to justice.

6:21 What fruit therefore had you then in those things, of which you are now ashamed? For the end of them is death.

6:22 But now being made free from sin, and become servants to God, you have your fruit unto sanctification, and the end life everlasting.

6:23 For the wages of sin is death. But the grace of God, life everlasting, in Christ Jesus our Lord.

7:1 Know you not, brethren, (for I speak to them that know the law,) that the law hath dominion over a man, as long as it liveth?

7:2 For the woman that hath an husband, whilst her husband liveth is bound to the law. But if her husband be dead, she is loosed from the law of her husband.

7:3 Therefore, whilst her husband liveth, she shall be called an adulteress, if she be with another man: but if her husband be dead, she is delivered from the law of her husband; so that she is not an adulteress, if she be with another man.

7:4 Therefore, my brethren, you also are become dead to the law, by the body of Christ; that you may belong to another, who is risen again from the dead, that we may bring forth fruit to God.

7:5 Cum enim essemus in carne, passiones peccatorum, quæ per legem erant, operabantur in membris nostris, ut fructificarent morti.

7:6 Nunc autem soluti sumus a lege mortis, in qua detinebamur, ita ut serviamus in novitate spiritus, et non in vetustate litteræ.

7:7 Quid ergo dicemus ? lex peccatum est ? Absit. Sed peccatum non cognovi, nisi per legem : nam concupiscentiam nesciebam, nisi lex diceret : Non concupisces.

7:8 Occasione autem accepta, peccatum per mandatum operatum est in me omnem concupiscentiam. Sine lege enim peccatum mortuum erat.

7:9 Ego autem vivebam sine lege aliquando : sed cum venisset mandatum, peccatum revixit.

7:10 Ego autem mortuus sum : et inventum est mihi mandatum, quod erat ad vitam, hoc esse ad mortem.

7:11 Nam peccatum occasione accepta per mandatum, seduxit me, et per illud occidit.

7:12 Itaque lex quidem sancta, et mandatum sanctum, et justum, et bonum.

7:13 Quod ergo bonum est, mihi factum est mors ? Absit. Sed peccatum, ut appareat peccatum, per bonum operatum est mihi mortem : ut fiat supra modum peccans peccatum per mandatum.

7:14 Scimus enim quia lex spiritualis est : ego autem carnalis sum, venundatus sub peccato.

7:15 Quod enim operor, non intelligo : non enim quod volo bonum, hoc ago : sed quod odi malum, illud facio.

7:16 Si autem quod nolo, illud facio : consentio legi, quoniam bona est.

7:17 Nunc autem jam non ego operor illud, sed quod habitat in me peccatum.

7:18 Scio enim quia non habitat in me, hoc est in carne mea, bonum. Nam velle, adjacet mihi : perficere autem bonum, non invenio.

7:19 Non enim quod volo bonum, hoc facio : sed quod nolo malum, hoc ago.

7:20 Si autem quod nolo, illud facio : jam non ego operor illud, sed quod habitat in me, peccatum.

7:21 Invenio igitur legem, volenti mihi facere bonum, quoniam mihi malum adjacet :

7:22 condelector enim legi Dei secundum interiorem hominem :

7:23 video autem aliam legem in membris meis,

7:5 For when we were in the flesh, the passions of sins, which were by the law, did work in our members, to bring forth fruit unto death.

7:6 But now we are loosed from the law of death, wherein we were detained; so that we should serve in newness of spirit, and not in the oldness of the letter.

7:7 What shall we say, then? Is the law sin? God forbid. But I do not know sin, but by the law; for I had not known concupiscence, if the law did not say: Thou shalt not covet.

7:8 But sin taking occasion by the commandment, wrought in me all manner of concupiscence. For without the law sin was dead.

7:9 And I lived some time without the law. But when the commandment came, sin revived,

7:10 And I died. And the commandment that was ordained to life, the same was found to be unto death to me.

7:11 For sin, taking occasion by the commandment, seduced me, and by it killed me.

7:12 Wherefore the law indeed is holy, and the commandment holy, and just, and good.

7:13 Was that then which is good, made death unto me? God forbid. But sin, that it may appear sin, by that which is good, wrought death in me; that sin, by the commandment, might become sinful above measure.

7:14 For we know that the law is spiritual; but I am carnal, sold under sin.

7:15 For that which I work, I understand not. For I do not that good which I will; but the evil which I hate, that I do.

7:16 If then I do that which I will not, I consent to the law, that it is good.

7:17 Now then it is no more I that do it, but sin that dwelleth in me.

7:18 For I know that there dwelleth not in me, that is to say, in my flesh, that which is good. For to will, is present with me; but to accomplish that which is good, I find not.

7:19 For the good which I will, I do not; but the evil which I will not, that I do.

7:20 Now if I do that which I will not, it is no more I that do it, but sin that dwelleth in me.

7:21 I find then a law, that when I have a will to do good, evil is present with me.

7:22 For I am delighted with the law of God, according to the inward man:

7:23 But I see another law in my members,

repugnantem legi mentis meæ, et captivantem me in lege peccati, quæ est in membris meis.

7:24 Infelix ego homo, quis me liberabit de corpore mortis hujus ?

7:25 gratia Dei per Jesum Christum Dominum nostrum. Igitur ego ipse mente servio legi Dei : carne autem, legi peccati.

8:1 Nihil ergo nunc damnationis est iis qui sunt in Christo Jesu : qui non secundum carnem ambulant.

8:2 Lex enim spiritus vitæ in Christo Jesu liberavit me a lege peccati et mortis.

8:3 Nam quod impossibile erat legi, in quo infirmabatur per carnem : Deus Filium suum mittens in similitudinem carnis peccati et de peccato, damnavit peccatum in carne,

8:4 ut justificatio legis impleretur in nobis, qui non secundum carnem ambulamus, sed secundum spiritum.

8:5 Qui enim secundum carnem sunt, quæ carnis sunt, sapiunt : qui vero secundum spiritum sunt, quæ sunt spiritus, sentiunt.

8:6 Nam prudentia carnis, mors est : prudentia autem spiritus, vita et pax :

8:7 quoniam sapientia carnis inimica est Deo : legi enim Dei non est subjecta, nec enim potest.

8:8 Qui autem in carne sunt, Deo placere non possunt.

8:9 Vos autem in carne non estis, sed in spiritu : si tamen Spiritus Dei habitat in vobis. Si quis autem Spiritum Christi non habet, hic non est ejus.

8:10 Si autem Christus in vobis est, corpus quidem mortuum est propter peccatum, spiritus vero vivit propter justificationem.

8:11 Quod si Spiritus ejus, qui suscitavit Jesum a mortuis, habitat in vobis : qui suscitavit Jesum Christum a mortuis, vivificabit et mortalia corpora vestra, propter inhabitantem Spiritum ejus in vobis.

8:12 Ergo fratres, debitores sumus non carni, ut secundum carnem vivamus.

8:13 Si enim secundum carnem vixeritis, moriemini : si autem spiritu facta carnis mortificaveritis, vivetis.

8:14 Quicumque enim Spiritu Dei aguntur, ii sunt filii Dei.

8:15 Non enim accepistis spiritum servitutis it-

fighting against the law of my mind, and captivating me in the law of sin, that is in my members.

7:24 Unhappy man that I am, who shall deliver me from the body of this death?

7:25 The grace of God, by Jesus Christ our Lord. Therefore, I myself, with the mind serve the law of God; but with the flesh, the law of sin.

8:1 There is now therefore no condemnation to them that are in Christ Jesus, who walk not according to the flesh.

8:2 For the law of the spirit of life, in Christ Jesus, hath delivered me from the law of sin and of death.

8:3 For what the law could not do, in that it was weak through the flesh; God sending his own Son, in the likeness of sinful flesh and of sin, hath condemned sin in the flesh;

8:4 That the justification of the law might be fulfilled in us, who walk not according to the flesh, but according to the spirit.

8:5 For they that are according to the flesh, mind the things that are of the flesh; but they that are according to the spirit, mind the things that are of the spirit.

8:6 For the wisdom of the flesh is death; but the wisdom of the spirit is life and peace.

8:7 Because the wisdom of the flesh is an enemy to God; for it is not subject to the law of God, neither can it be.

8:8 And they who are in the flesh, cannot please God.

8:9 But you are not in the flesh, but in the spirit, if so be that the Spirit of God dwell in you. Now if any man have not the Spirit of Christ, he is none of his.

8:10 And if Christ be in you, the body indeed is dead, because of sin; but the spirit liveth, because of justification.

8:11 And if the Spirit of him that raised up Jesus from the dead, dwell in you; he that raised up Jesus Christ from the dead, shall quicken also your mortal bodies, because of his Spirit that dwelleth in you.

8:12 Therefore, brethren, we are debtors, not to the flesh, to live according to the flesh.

8:13 For if you live according to the flesh, you shall die: but if by the Spirit you mortify the deeds of the flesh, you shall live.

8:14 For whosoever are led by the Spirit of God, they are the sons of God.

8:15 For you have not received the spirit of

erum in timore, sed accepistis spiritum adoptionis filiorum, in quo clamamus : Abba (Pater).

8:16 Ipse enim Spiritus testimonium reddit spiritui nostro quod sumus filii Dei.

8:17 Si autem filii, et hæredes : hæredes, quidem Dei, cohæredes autem Christi : si tamen compatimur ut et conglorificemur.

8:18 Existimo enim quod non sunt condignæ passiones hujus temporis ad futuram gloriam, quæ revelabitur in nobis.

8:19 Nam exspectatio creaturæ revelationem filiorum Dei exspectat.

8:20 Vanitati enim creatura subjecta est non volens, sed propter eum, qui subjecit eam in spe :

8:21 quia et ipsa creatura liberabitur a servitute corruptionis in libertatem gloriæ filiorum Dei.

8:22 Scimus enim quod omnis creatura ingemiscit, et parturit usque adhuc.

8:23 Non solum autem illa, sed et nos ipsi primitias spiritus habentes : et ipsi intra nos gemimus adoptionem filiorum Dei exspectantes, redemptionem corporis nostri.

8:24 Spe enim salvi facti sumus. Spes autem, quæ videtur, non est spes : nam quod videt quis, quid sperat ?

8:25 Si autem quod non videmus, speramus : per patientiam exspectamus.

8:26 Similiter autem et Spiritus adjuvat infirmitatem nostram : nam quid oremus, sicut oportet, nescimus : sed ipse Spiritus postulat pro nobis gemitibus inenarrabilibus.

8:27 Qui autem scrutatur corda, scit quid desideret Spiritus : quia secundum Deum postulat pro sanctis.

8:28 Scimus autem quoniam diligentibus Deum omnia cooperantur in bonum, iis qui secundum propositum vocati sunt sancti.

8:29 Nam quos præscivit, et prædestinavit conformes fieri imaginis Filii sui, ut sit ipse primogenitus in multis fratribus.

8:30 Quos autem prædestinavit, hos et vocavit : et quos vocavit, hos et justificavit : quos autem justificavit, illos et glorificavit.

8:31 Quid ergo dicemus ad hæc ? si Deus pro

bondage again in fear; but you have received the spirit of adoption of sons, whereby we cry: Abba (Father).

8:16 For the Spirit himself giveth testimony to our spirit, that we are the sons of God.

8:17 And if sons, heirs also; heirs indeed of God, and joint heirs with Christ: yet so, if we suffer with him, that we may be also glorified with him.

8:18 For I reckon that the sufferings of this time are not worthy to be compared with the glory to come, that shall be revealed in us.

8:19 For the expectation of the creature waiteth for the revelation of the sons of God.

8:20 For the creature was made subject to vanity, not willingly, but by reason of him that made it subject, in hope:

8:21 Because the creature also itself shall be delivered from the servitude of corruption, into the liberty of the glory of the children of God.

8:22 For we know that every creature groaneth and travaileth in pain, even till now.

8:23 And not only it, but ourselves also, who have the firstfruits of the Spirit, even we ourselves groan within ourselves, waiting for the adoption of the sons of God, the redemption of our body.

8:24 For we are saved by hope. But hope that is seen, is not hope. For what a man seeth, why doth he hope for?

8:25 But if we hope for that which we see not, we wait for it with patience.

8:26 Likewise the Spirit also helpeth our infirmity. For we know not what we should pray for as we ought; but the Spirit himself asketh for us with unspeakable groanings.

8:27 And he that searcheth the hearts, knoweth what the Spirit desireth; because he asketh for the saints according to God.

8:28 And we know that to them that love God, all things work together unto good, to such as, according to his purpose, are called to be saints.

8:29 For whom he foreknew, he also predestinated to be made conformable to the image of his Son; that he might be the firstborn amongst many brethren.

8:30 And whom he predestinated, them he also called. And whom he called, them he also justified. And whom he justified, them he also glorified.

8:31 What shall we then say to these things? If

nobis, quis contra nos ?

8:32 Qui etiam proprio Filio suo non pepercit, sed pro nobis omnibus tradidit illum : quomodo non etiam cum illo omnia nobis donavit ?

8:33 Quis accusabit adversus electos Dei ? Deus qui justificat,

8:34 quis est qui condemnet ? Christus Jesus, qui mortuus est, immo qui et resurrexit, qui est ad dexteram Dei, qui etiam interpellat pro nobis.

8:35 Quis ergo nos separabit a caritate Christi ? tribulatio ? an angustia ? an fames ? an nuditas ? an periculum ? an persecutio ? an gladius ?

8:36 (Sicut scriptum est : *Quia propter te mortificamur tota die : æstimati sumus sicut oves occisionis.*)

8:37 Sed in his omnibus superamus propter eum qui dilexit nos.

8:38 Certus sum enim quia neque mors, neque vita, neque angeli, neque principatus, neque virtutes, neque instantia, neque futura, neque fortitudo,

8:39 neque altitudo, neque profundum, neque creatura alia poterit nos separare a caritate Dei, quæ est in Christo Jesu Domino nostro.

9:1 Veritatem dico in Christo, non mentior : testimonium mihi perhibente conscientia mea in Spiritu Sancto :

9:2 quoniam tristitia mihi magna est, et continuus dolor cordi meo.

9:3 Optabam enim ego ipse anathema esse a Christo pro fratribus meis, qui sunt cognati mei secundum carnem,

9:4 qui sunt Israëlitæ, quorum adoptio est filiorum, et gloria, et testamentum, et legislatio, et obsequium, et promissa :

9:5 quorum patres, et ex quibus est Christus secundum carnem, qui est super omnia Deus benedictus in sæcula. Amen.

9:6 Non autem quod exciderit verbum Dei. Non enim omnes qui ex Israël sunt, ii sunt Israëlitæ :

9:7 neque qui semen sunt Abrahæ, omnes filii : sed in Isaac vocabitur tibi semen :

9:8 id est, non qui filii carnis, hi filii Dei : sed qui filii sunt promissionis, æstimantur in semine.

9:9 Promissionis enim verbum hoc est : Secun-

God be for us, who is against us?

8:32 He that spared not even his own Son, but delivered him up for us all, how hath he not also, with him, given us all things?

8:33 Who shall accuse against the elect of God? God that justifieth.

8:34 Who is he that shall condemn? Christ Jesus that died, yea that is risen also again; who is at the right hand of God, who also maketh intercession for us.

8:35 Who then shall separate us from the love of Christ? Shall tribulation? or distress? or famine? or nakedness? or danger? or persecution? or the sword?

8:36 (As it is written: *For thy sake we are put to death all the day long. We are accounted as sheep for the slaughter.*)

8:37 But in all these things we overcome, because of him that hath loved us.

8:38 For I am sure that neither death, nor life, nor angels, nor principalities, nor powers, nor things present, nor things to come, nor might,

8:39 Nor height, nor depth, nor any other creature, shall be able to separate us from the love of God, which is in Christ Jesus our Lord.

9:1 I SPEAK the truth in Christ, I lie not, my conscience bearing me witness in the Holy Ghost:

9:2 That I have great sadness, and continual sorrow in my heart.

9:3 For I wished myself to be an anathema from Christ, for my brethren, who are my kinsmen according to the flesh,

9:4 Who are Israelites, to whom belongeth the adoption as of children, and the glory, and the testament, and the giving of the law, and the service of God, and the promises:

9:5 Whose are the fathers, and of whom is Christ, according to the flesh, who is over all things, God blessed for ever. Amen.

9:6 Not as though the word of God hath miscarried. For all are not Israelites that are of Israel:

9:7 Neither are all they that are the seed of Abraham, children; but in Isaac shall thy seed be called:

9:8 That is to say, not they that are the children of the flesh, are the children of God; but they, that are the children of the promise, are accounted for the seed.

9:9 For this is the word of promise: According

dum hoc tempus veniam : et erit Saræ filius.

9:10 Non solum autem illa : sed et Rebecca ex uno concubitu habens, Isaac patris nostri.

9:11 Cum enim nondum nati fuissent, aut aliquid boni egissent, aut mali (ut secundum electionem propositum Dei maneret),

9:12 non ex operibus, sed ex vocante dictum est ei quia major serviet minori,

9:13 sicut scriptum est : Jacob dilexi, Esau autem odio habui.

9:14 Quid ergo dicemus ? numquid iniquitas apud Deum ? Absit.

9:15 Moysi enim dicit : Miserebor cujus misereor : et misericordiam præstabo cujus miserebor.

9:16 Igitur non volentis, neque currentis, sed miserentis est Dei.

9:17 Dicit enim Scriptura Pharaoni : Quia in hoc ipsum excitavi te, ut ostendam in te virtutem meam : et ut annuntietur nomen meum in universa terra.

9:18 Ergo cujus vult miseretur, et quem vult indurat.

9:19 Dicis itaque mihi : Quid adhuc queritur ? voluntati enim ejus quis resistit ?

9:20 O homo, tu quis es, qui respondeas Deo ? numquid dicit figmentum ei qui se finxit : Quid me fecisti sic ?

9:21 an non habet potestatem figulus luti ex eadem massa facere aliud quidem vas in honorem, aliud vero in contumeliam ?

9:22 Quod si Deus volens ostendere iram, et notum facere potentiam suam, sustinuit in multa patientia vasa iræ, apta in interitum,

9:23 ut ostenderet divitias gloriæ suæ in vasa misericordiæ, quæ præparavit in gloriam.

9:24 Quos et vocavit nos non solum ex Judæis, sed etiam in gentibus,

9:25 sicut in Osee dicit : Vocabo non plebem meam, plebem meam : et non dilectam, dilectam : et non misericordiam consecutam, misericordiam consecutam.

9:26 Et erit : in loco, ubi dictum est eis : Non plebs mea vos : ibi vocabuntur filii Dei vivi.

9:27 Isaias autem clamat pro Israël : Si fuerit numerus filiorum Israël tamquam arena maris,

to this time will I come; and Sara shall have a son.

9:10 And not only she. But when Rebecca also had conceived at once, of Isaac our father.

9:11 For when the children were not yet born, nor had done any good or evil (that the purpose of God, according to election, might stand,)

9:12 Not of works, but of him that calleth, it was said to her: The elder shall serve the younger.

9:13 As it is written: Jacob I have loved, but Esau I have hated.

9:14 What shall we say then? Is there injustice with God? God forbid.

9:15 For he saith to Moses: I will have mercy on whom I will have mercy; and I will shew mercy to whom I will shew mercy.

9:16 So then it is not of him that willeth, nor of him that runneth, but of God that sheweth mercy.

9:17 For the scripture saith to Pharao: To this purpose have I raised thee, that I may shew my power in thee, and that my name may be declared throughout all the earth.

9:18 Therefore he hath mercy on whom he will; and whom he will, he hardeneth.

9:19 Thou wilt say therefore to me: Why doth he then find fault? for who resisteth his will?

9:20 O man, who art thou that repliest against God? Shall the thing formed say to him that formed it: Why hast thou made me thus?

9:21 Or hath not the potter power over the clay, of the same lump, to make one vessel unto honour, and another unto dishonour?

9:22 What if God, willing to shew his wrath, and to make his power known, endured with much patience vessels of wrath, fitted for destruction,

9:23 That he might shew the riches of his glory on the vessels of mercy, which he hath prepared unto glory?

9:24 Even us, whom also he hath called, not only of the Jews, but also of the Gentiles.

9:25 As in Osee he saith: I will call that which was not my people, my people; and her that was not beloved, beloved; and her that had not obtained mercy, one that hath obtained mercy.

9:26 And it shall be, in the place where it was said unto them, You are not my people; there they shall be called the sons of the living God.

9:27 And Isaias crieth out concerning Israel: If the number of the children of Israel be as the

reliquiæ salvæ fient.

9:28 Verbum enim consummans, et abbrevians in æquitate : quia verbum breviatum faciet Dominus super terram :

9:29 et sicut prædixit Isaias : Nisi Dominus Sabaoth reliquisset nobis semen, sicut Sodoma facti essemus, et sicut Gomorrha similes fuissemus.

9:30 Quid ergo dicemus ? Quod gentes, quæ non sectabantur justitiam, apprehenderunt justitiam : justitiam autem, quæ ex fide est.

9:31 Israël vero sectando legem justitiæ, in legem justitiæ non pervenit.

9:32 Quare ? Quia non ex fide, sed quasi ex operibus : offenderunt enim in lapidem offensionis,

9:33 sicut scriptum est : Ecce pono in Sion lapidem offensionis, et petram scandali : et omnis qui credit in eum, non confundetur.

10:1 Fratres, voluntas quidem cordis mei, et obsecratio ad Deum, fit pro illis in salutem.

10:2 Testimonium enim perhibeo illis quod æmulationem Dei habent, sed non secundum scientiam.

10:3 Ignorantes enim justitiam Dei, et suam quærentes statuere, justitiæ Dei non sunt subjecti.

10:4 Finis enim legis, Christus, ad justitiam omni credenti.

10:5 Moyses enim scripsit, quoniam justitiam, quæ ex lege est, qui fecerit homo, vivet in ea.

10:6 Quæ autem ex fide est justitia, sic dicit : Ne dixeris in corde tuo : Quis ascendet in cælum ? id est, Christum deducere :

10:7 aut, Quis descendet in abyssum ? hoc est, Christum a mortuis revocare.

10:8 Sed quid dicit Scriptura ? Prope est verbum in ore tuo, et in corde tuo : hoc est verbum fidei, quod prædicamus.

10:9 Quia si confitearis in ore tuo Dominum Jesum, et in corde tuo credideris quod Deus illum suscitavit a mortuis, salvus eris.

10:10 Corde enim creditur ad justitiam : ore autem confessio fit ad salutem.

10:11 Dicit enim Scriptura : Omnis qui credit in illum, non confundetur.

10:12 Non enim est distinctio Judæi et Græci : nam idem Dominus omnium, dives in omnes qui invocant illum.

---

sand of the sea, a remnant shall be saved.

9:28 For he shall finish his word, and cut it short in justice; because a short word shall the Lord make upon the earth.

9:29 And as Isaias foretold: Unless the Lord of Sabaoth had left us a seed, we had been made as Sodom, and we had been like unto Gomorrha.

9:30 What then shall we say? That the Gentiles, who followed not after justice, have attained to justice, even the justice that is of faith.

9:31 But Israel, by following after the law of justice, is not come unto the law of justice.

9:32 Why so? Because they sought it not by faith, but as it were of works. For they stumbled at the stumblingstone.

9:33 As it is written: Behold I lay in Sion a stumblingstone and a rock of scandal; and whosoever believeth in him shall not be confounded.

10:1 Brethren, the will of my heart, indeed, and my prayer to God, is for them unto salvation.

10:2 For I bear them witness, that they have a zeal of God, but not according to knowledge.

10:3 For they, not knowing the justice of God, and seeking to establish their own, have not submitted themselves to the justice of God.

10:4 For the end of the law is Christ, unto justice to every one that believeth.

10:5 For Moses wrote, that the justice which is of the law, the man that shall do it, shall live by it.

10:6 But the justice which is of faith, speaketh thus: Say not in thy heart, Who shall ascend into heaven? that is, to bring Christ down;

10:7 Or who shall descend into the deep? that is, to bring up Christ again from the dead.

10:8 But what saith the scripture? The word is nigh thee, even in thy mouth, and in thy heart. This is the word of faith, which we preach.

10:9 For if thou confess with thy mouth the Lord Jesus, and believe in thy heart that God hath raised him up from the dead, thou shalt be saved.

10:10 For, with the heart, we believe unto justice; but, with the mouth, confession is made unto salvation.

10:11 For the scripture saith: Whosoever believeth in him, shall not be confounded.

10:12 For there is no distinction of the Jew and the Greek: for the same is Lord over all, rich unto all that call upon him.

10:13 Omnis enim quicumque invocaverit nomen Domini, salvus erit.

10:14 Quomodo ergo invocabunt, in quem non crediderunt ? aut quomodo credent ei, quem non audierunt ? quomodo autem audient sine prædicante ?

10:15 quomodo vero prædicabunt nisi mittantur ? sicut scriptum est : Quam speciosi pedes evangelizantium pacem, evangelizantium bona !

10:16 Sed non omnes obediunt Evangelio. Isaias enim dicit : Domine, quis credidit auditui nostro ?

10:17 Ergo fides ex auditu, auditus autem per verbum Christi.

10:18 Sed dico : Numquid non audierunt ? Et quidem in omnem terram exivit sonus eorum, et in fines orbis terræ verba eorum.

10:19 Sed dico : Numquid Israël non cognovit ? Primus Moyses dicit : Ego ad æmulationem vos adducam in non gentem : in gentem insipientem, in iram vos mittam.

10:20 Isaias autem audet, et dicit : Inventus sum a non quærentibus me : palam apparui iis qui me non interrogabant.

10:21 Ad Israël autem dicit : Tota die expandi manus meas ad populum non credentem, et contradicentem.

11:1 Dico ergo : Numquid Deus repulit populum suum ? Absit. Nam et ego Israëlita sum ex semine Abraham, de tribu Benjamin :

11:2 non repulit Deus plebem suam, quam præscivit. An nescitis in Elia quid dicit Scriptura ? quemadmodum interpellat Deum adversum Israël :

11:3 Domine, prophetas tuos occiderunt, altaria tua suffoderunt : et ego relictus sum solus, et quærunt animam meam.

11:4 Sed quid dicit illi divinum responsum ? Reliqui mihi septem millia virorum, qui non curvaverunt genua ante Baal.

11:5 Sic ergo et in hoc tempore reliquiæ secundum electionem gratiæ salvæ factæ sunt.

11:6 Si autem gratia, jam non ex operibus : alioquin gratia jam non est gratia.

11:7 Quid ergo ? Quod quærebat Israël, hoc non est consecutus : electio autem consecuta est : ceteri vero excæcati sunt :

11:8 sicut scriptum est : Dedit illis Deus spiritum compunctionis : oculos ut non videant, et

10:13 For whosoever shall call upon the name of the Lord, shall be saved.

10:14 How then shall they call on him, in whom they have not believed? Or how shall they believe him, of whom they have not heard? And how shall they hear, without a preacher?

10:15 And how shall they preach unless they be sent, as it is written: How beautiful are the feet of them that preach the gospel of peace, of them that bring glad tidings of good things!

10:16 But all do not obey the gospel. For Isaias saith: Lord, who hath believed our report?

10:17 Faith then cometh by hearing; and hearing by the word of Christ.

10:18 But I say: Have they not heard? Yes, verily, their sound hath gone forth into all the earth, and their words unto the ends of the whole world.

10:19 But I say: Hath not Israel known? First, Moses saith: I will provoke you to jealousy by that which is not a nation; by a foolish nation I will anger you.

10:20 But Isaias is bold, and saith: I was found by them that did not seek me: I appeared openly to them that asked not after me.

10:21 But to Israel he saith: All the day long have I spread my hands to a people that believeth not, and contradicteth me.

11:1 I SAY then: Hath God cast away his people? God forbid. For I also am an Israelite of the seed of Abraham, of the tribe of Benjamin.

11:2 God hath not cast away his people, which he foreknew. Know you not what the scripture saith of Elias; how he calleth on God against Israel?

11:3 Lord, they have slain thy prophets, they have dug down thy altars; and I am left alone, and they seek my life.

11:4 But what saith the divine answer to him? I have left me seven thousand men, that have not bowed their knees to Baal.

11:5 Even so then at this present time also, there is a remnant saved according to the election of grace.

11:6 And if by grace, it is not now by works: otherwise grace is no more grace.

11:7 What then? That which Israel sought, he hath not obtained: but the election hath obtained it; and the rest have been blinded.

11:8 As it is written: God hath given them the spirit of insensibility; eyes that they should not

aures ut non audiant, usque in hodiernum diem.

11:9 Et David dicit : Fiat mensa eorum in laqueum, et in captionem, et in scandalum, et in retributionem illis.

11:10 Obscurentur oculi eorum ne videant : et dorsum eorum semper incurva.

11:11 Dico ergo : Numquid sic offenderunt ut caderent ? Absit. Sed illorum delicto, salus est gentibus ut illos æmulentur.

11:12 Quod si delictum illorum divitiæ sunt mundi, et diminutio eorum divitiæ gentium : quanto magis plenitudo eorum ?

11:13 Vobis enim dico gentibus : Quamdiu quidem ego sum gentium Apostolus, ministerium meum honorificabo,

11:14 si quomodo ad æmulandum provocem carnem meam, et salvos faciam aliquos ex illis.

11:15 Si enim amissio eorum, reconciliatio est mundi : quæ assumptio, nisi vita ex mortuis ?

11:16 Quod si delibatio sancta est, et massa : et si radix sancta, et rami.

11:17 Quod si aliqui ex ramis fracti sunt, tu autem cum oleaster esses, insertus es in illis, et socius radicis, et pinguedinis olivæ factus es,

11:18 noli gloriari adversus ramos. Quod si gloriaris : non tu radicem portas, sed radix te.

11:19 Dices ergo : Fracti sunt rami ut ego inserar.

11:20 Bene : propter incredulitatem fracti sunt. Tu autem fide stas : noli altum sapere, sed time.

11:21 Si enim Deus naturalibus ramis non pepercit : ne forte nec tibi parcat.

11:22 Vide ergo bonitatem, et severitatem Dei : in eos quidem qui ceciderunt, severitatem : in te autem bonitatem Dei, si permanseris in bonitate, alioquin et tu excideris.

11:23 Sed et illi, si non permanserint in incredulitate, inserentur : potens est enim Deus iterum inserere illos.

11:24 Nam si tu ex naturali excisus es oleastro, et contra naturam insertus es in bonam olivam :

see; and ears that they should not hear, until this present day.

11:9 And David saith: Let their table be made a snare, and a trap, and a stumblingblock, and a recompense unto them.

11:10 Let their eyes be darkened, that they may not see: and bow down their back always.

11:11 I say then, have they so stumbled, that they should fall? God forbid. But by their offence, salvation is come to the Gentiles, that they may be emulous of them.

11:12 Now if the offence of them be the riches of the world, and the diminution of them, the riches of the Gentiles; how much more the fulness of them?

11:13 For I say to you, Gentiles: as long indeed as I am the apostle of the Gentiles, I will honour my ministry,

11:14 If, by any means, I may provoke to emulation them who are my flesh, and may save some of them.

11:15 For if the loss of them be the reconciliation of the world, what shall the receiving of them be, but life from the dead?

11:16 For if the firstfruit be holy, so is the lump also: and if the root be holy, so are the branches.

11:17 And if some of the branches be broken, and thou, being a wild olive, art ingrafted in them, and art made partaker of the root, and of the fatness of the olive tree,

11:18 Boast not against the branches. But if thou boast, thou bearest not the root, but the root thee.

11:19 Thou wilt say then: The branches were broken off, that I might be grafted in.

11:20 Well: because of unbelief they were broken off. But thou standest by faith: be not highminded, but fear.

11:21 For if God hath not spared the natural branches, fear lest perhaps he also spare not thee.

11:22 See then the goodness and the severity of God: towards them indeed that are fallen, the severity; but towards thee, the goodness of God, if thou abide in goodness, otherwise thou also shalt be cut off.

11:23 And they also, if they abide not still in unbelief, shall be grafted in: for God is able to graft them in again.

11:24 For if thou wert cut out of the wild olive tree, which is natural to thee; and, contrary to

quanto magis ii qui secundum naturam inserentur suæ olivæ ?

11:25 Nolo enim vos ignorare, fratres, mysterium hoc (ut non sitis vobis ipsis sapientes), quia cæcitas ex parte contigit in Israël, donec plenitudo gentium intraret,

11:26 et sic omnis Israël salvus fieret, sicut scriptum est : Veniet ex Sion, qui eripiat, et avertat impietatem a Jacob.

11:27 Et hoc illis a me testamentum : cum abstulero peccata eorum.

11:28 Secundum Evangelium quidem, inimici propter vos : secundum electionem autem, carissimi propter patres.

11:29 Sine pœnitentia enim sunt dona et vocatio Dei.

11:30 Sicut enim aliquando et vos non credidistis Deo, nunc autem misericordiam consecuti estis propter incredulitatem illorum :

11:31 ita et isti nunc non crediderunt in vestram misericordiam : ut et ipsi misericordiam consequantur.

11:32 Conclusit enim Deus omnia in incredulitate, ut omnium misereatur.

11:33 O altitudo divitiarum sapientiæ, et scientiæ Dei : quam incomprehensibilia sunt judicia ejus, et investigabiles viæ ejus !

11:34 Quis enim cognovit sensum Domini ? aut quis consiliarius ejus fuit ?

11:35 aut quis prior dedit illi, et retribuetur ei ?

11:36 Quoniam ex ipso, et per ipsum, et in ipso sunt omnia : ipsi gloria in sæcula. Amen.

12:1 Obsecro itaque vos fratres per misericordiam Dei, ut exhibeatis corpora vestra hostiam viventem, sanctam, Deo placentem, rationabile obsequium vestrum.

12:2 Et nolite conformari huic sæculo, sed reformamini in novitate sensus vestri : ut probetis quæ sit voluntas Dei bona, et beneplacens, et perfecta.

12:3 Dico enim per gratiam quæ data est mihi, omnibus qui sunt inter vos, non plus sapere quam oportet sapere, sed sapere ad sobrietatem : et unicuique sicut Deus divisit mensuram fidei.

12:4 Sicut enim in uno corpore multa membra

nature, were grafted into the good olive tree; how much more shall they that are the natural branches, be grafted into their own olive tree?

11:25 For I would not have you ignorant, brethren, of this mystery, (lest you should be wise in your own conceits), that blindness in part has happened in Israel, until the fulness of the Gentiles should come in.

11:26 And so all Israel should be saved, as it is written: There shall come out of Sion, he that shall deliver, and shall turn away ungodliness from Jacob.

11:27 And this is to them my covenant: when I shall take away their sins.

11:28 As concerning the gospel, indeed, they are enemies for your sake: but as touching the election, they are most dear for the sake of the fathers.

11:29 For the gifts and the calling of God are without repentance.

11:30 For as you also in times past did not believe God, but now have obtained mercy, through their unbelief;

11:31 So these also now have not believed, for your mercy, that they also may obtain mercy.

11:32 For God hath concluded all in unbelief, that he may have mercy on all.

11:33 O the depth of the riches of the wisdom and of the knowledge of God! How incomprehensible are his judgments, and how unsearchable his ways!

11:34 For who hath known the mind of the Lord? Or who hath been his counsellor?

11:35 Or who hath first given to him, and recompense shall be made him?

11:36 For of him, and by him, and in him, are all things: to him be glory for ever. Amen.

12:1 I BESEECH you therefore, brethren, by the mercy of God, that you present your bodies a living sacrifice, holy, pleasing unto God, your reasonable service.

12:2 And be not conformed to this world; but be reformed in the newness of your mind, that you may prove what is the good, and the acceptable, and the perfect will of God.

12:3 For I say, by the grace that is given me, to all that are among you, not to be more wise than it behoveth to be wise, but to be wise unto sobriety, and according as God hath divided to every one the measure of faith.

12:4 For as in one body we have many members,

habemus, omnia autem membra non eumdem actum habent :

12:5 ita multi unum corpus sumus in Christo, singuli autem alter alterius membra.

12:6 Habentes autem donationes secundum gratiam, quæ data est nobis, differentes : sive prophetiam secundum rationem fidei,

12:7 sive ministerium in ministrando, sive qui docet in doctrina,

12:8 qui exhortatur in exhortando, qui tribuit in simplicitate, qui præest in sollicitudine, qui miseretur in hilaritate.

12:9 Dilectio sine simulatione : odientes malum, adhærentes bono :

12:10 caritate fraternitatis invicem diligentes : honore invicem prævenientes :

12:11 sollicitudine non pigri : spiritu ferventes : Domino servientes :

12:12 spe gaudentes : in tribulatione patientes : orationi instantes :

12:13 necessitatibus sanctorum communicantes : hospitalitatem sectantes.

12:14 Benedicite persequentibus vos : benedicite, et nolite maledicere.

12:15 Gaudere cum gaudentibus, flere cum flentibus :

12:16 idipsum invicem sentientes : non alta sapientes, sed humilibus consentientes. Nolite esse prudentes apud vosmetipsos :

12:17 nulli malum pro malo reddentes : providentes bona non tantum coram Deo, sed etiam coram omnibus hominibus.

12:18 Si fieri potest, quod ex vobis est, cum omnibus hominibus pacem habentes :

12:19 non vosmetipsos defendentes carissimi, sed date locum iræ. Scriptum est enim : Mihi vindicta : ego retribuam, dicit Dominus.

12:20 Sed si esurierit inimicus tuus, ciba illum : si sitit, potum da illi : hoc enim faciens, carbones ignis congeres super caput ejus.

12:21 Noli vinci a malo, sed vince in bono malum.

13:1 Omnis anima potestatibus sublimioribus subdita sit : non est enim potestas nisi a Deo : quæ autem sunt, a Deo ordinatæ sunt.

13:2 Itaque qui resistit potestati, Dei ordinationi resistit. Qui autem resistunt, ipsi sibi damnationem acquirunt :

but all the members have not the same office:

12:5 So we being many, are one body in Christ, and every one members one of another.

12:6 And having different gifts, according to the grace that is given us, either prophecy, to be used according to the rule of faith;

12:7 Or ministry, in ministering; or he that teacheth, in doctrine;

12:8 He that exhorteth, in exhorting; he that giveth, with simplicity; he that ruleth, with carefulness; he that sheweth mercy, with cheerfulness.

12:9 Let love be without dissimulation. Hating that which is evil, cleaving to that which is good.

12:10 Loving one another with the charity of brotherhood, with honour preventing one another.

12:11 In carefulness not slothful. In spirit fervent. Serving the Lord.

12:12 Rejoicing in hope. Patient in tribulation. Instant in prayer.

12:13 Communicating to the necessities of the saints. Pursuing hospitality.

12:14 Bless them that persecute you: bless, and curse not.

12:15 Rejoice with them that rejoice; weep with them that weep.

12:16 Being of one mind one towards another. Not minding high things, but consenting to the humble. Be not wise in your own conceits.

12:17 To no man rendering evil for evil. Providing good things, not only in the sight of God, but also in the sight of all men.

12:18 If it be possible, as much as is in you, have peace with all men.

12:19 Revenge not yourselves, my dearly beloved; but give place unto wrath, for it is written: Revenge is mine, I will repay, saith the Lord

12:20 But if thy enemy be hungry, give him to eat; if he thirst, give him to drink. For, doing this, thou shalt heap coals of fire upon his head.

12:21 Be not overcome by evil, but overcome evil by good.

13:1 Let every soul be subject to higher powers: for there is no power but from God: and those that are, are ordained of God.

13:2 Therefore he that resisteth the power, resisteth the ordinance of God. And they that resist, purchase to themselves damnation.

13:3 nam principes non sunt timori boni operis, sed mali. Vis autem non timere potestatem ? Bonum fac : et habebis laudem ex illa :

13:4 Dei enim minister est tibi in bonum. Si autem malum feceris, time : non enim sine causa gladium portat. Dei enim minister est : vindex in iram ei qui malum agit.

13:5 Ideo necessitate subditi estote non solum propter iram, sed etiam propter conscientiam. 13:6 Ideo enim et tributa præstatis : ministri enim Dei sunt, in hoc ipsum servientes.

13:7 Reddite ergo omnibus debita : cui tributum, tributum : cui vectigal, vectigal : cui timorem, timorem : cui honorem, honorem.

13:8 Nemini quidquam debeatis, nisi ut invicem diligatis : qui enim diligit proximum, legem implevit.
13:9 Nam : Non adulterabis : non occides : non furaberis : non falsum testimonium dices : non concupisces : et si quod est aliud mandatum, in hoc verbo instauratur : diliges proximum tuum sicut teipsum.

13:10 Dilectio proximi malum non operatur. Plenitudo ergo legis est dilectio.
13:11 Et hoc scientes tempus : quia hora est jam nos de somno surgere. Nunc enim propior est nostra salus, quam cum credidimus.
13:12 Nox præcessit, dies autem appropinquavit. Abjiciamus ergo opera tenebrarum, et induamur arma lucis.
13:13 Sicut in die honeste ambulemus : non in comessationibus, et ebrietatibus, non in cubilibus, et impudicitiis, non in contentione, et æmulatione :
13:14 sed induimini Dominum Jesum Christum, et carnis curam ne feceritis in desideriis.

14:1 Infirmum autem in fide assumite, non in disceptationibus cogitationum.
14:2 Alius enim credit se manducare omnia : qui autem infirmus est, olus manducet.
14:3 Is qui manducat, non manducantem non spernat : et qui non manducat, manducantem non judicet : Deus enim illum assumpsit.

14:4 Tu quis es, qui judicas alienum servum ? domino suo stat, aut cadit : stabit autem : po-

13:3 For princes are not a terror to the good work, but to the evil. Wilt thou then not be afraid of the power? Do that which is good: and thou shalt have praise from the same.

13:4 For he is God's minister to thee, for good. But if thou do that which is evil, fear: for he beareth not the sword in vain. For he is God's minister: an avenger to execute wrath upon him that doth evil.

13:5 Wherefore be subject of necessity, not only for wrath, but also for conscience' sake.
13:6 For therefore also you pay tribute. For they are the ministers of God, serving unto this purpose.

13:7 Render therefore to all men their dues. Tribute, to whom tribute is due: custom, to whom custom: fear, to whom fear: honour, to whom honour.

13:8 Owe no man any thing, but to love one another. For he that loveth his neighbour, hath fulfilled the law.
13:9 For Thou shalt not commit adultery: Thou shalt not kill: Thou shalt not steal, Thou shalt not bear false witness: Thou shalt not covet: and if there be any other commandment, it is comprised in this word, Thou shalt love thy neighbour as thyself.
13:10 The love of our neighbour worketh no evil. Love therefore is the fulfilling of the law.
13:11 And that knowing the season; that it is now the hour for us to rise from sleep. For now our salvation is nearer than when we believed.
13:12 The night is passed, and the day is at hand. Let us therefore cast off the works of darkness, and put on the armour of light.
13:13 Let us walk honestly, as in the day: not in rioting and drunkenness, not in chambering and impurities, not in contention and envy:

13:14 But put ye on the Lord Jesus Christ, and make not provision for the flesh in its concupiscences.
14:1 Now him that is weak in faith, take unto you: not in disputes about thoughts.
14:2 For one believeth that he may eat all things: but he that is weak, let him eat herbs.
14:3 Let not him that eateth, despise him that eateth not: and he that eateth not, let him not judge him that eateth. For God hath taken him to him.
14:4 Who art thou that judgest another man's servant? To his own lord he standeth or falleth.

tens est enim Deus statuere illum.

14:5 Nam alius judicat diem inter diem : alius autem judicat omnem diem : unusquisque in suo sensu abundet.

14:6 Qui sapit diem, Domino sapit, et qui manducat, Domino manducat : gratias enim agit Deo. Et qui non manducat, Domino non manducat, et gratias agit Deo.

14:7 Nemo enim nostrum sibi vivit, et nemo sibi moritur.

14:8 Sive enim vivemus, Domino vivimus : sive morimur, Domino morimur. Sive ergo vivimus, sive morimur, Domini sumus.

14:9 In hoc enim Christus mortuus est, et resurrexit : ut et mortuorum et vivorum dominetur.

14:10 Tu autem quid judicas fratrem tuum ? aut tu quare spernis fratrem tuum ? omnes enim stabimus ante tribunal Christi.

14:11 Scriptum est enim : Vivo ego, dicit Dominus, quoniam mihi flectetur omne genu : et omnis lingua confitebitur Deo.

14:12 Itaque unusquisque nostrum pro se rationem reddet Deo.

14:13 Non ergo amplius invicem judicemus : sed hoc judicate magis, ne ponatis offendiculum fratri, vel scandalum.

14:14 Scio, et confido in Domino Jesu, quia nihil commune per ipsum, nisi ei qui existimat quid commune esset, illi commune est.

14:15 Si enim propter cibum frater tuus contristatur, jam non secundum caritatem ambulas. Noli cibo tuo illum perdere, pro quo Christus mortuus est.

14:16 Non ergo blasphemetur bonum nostrum.

14:17 Non est enim regnum Dei esca et potus : sed justitia, et pax, et gaudium in Spiritu Sancto :

14:18 qui enim in hoc servit Christo, placet Deo, et probatus est hominibus.

14:19 Itaque quæ pacis sunt, sectemur : et quæ ædificationis sunt, in invicem custodiamus.

14:20 Noli propter escam destruere opus Dei, omnia quidem sunt munda : sed malum est homini, qui per offendiculum manducat.

And he shall stand: for God is able to make him stand.

14:5 For one judgeth between day and day: and another judgeth every day: let every man abound in his own sense.

14:6 He that regardeth the day, regardeth it unto the Lord. And he that eateth, eateth to the Lord: for he giveth thanks to God. And he that eateth not, to the Lord he eateth not, and giveth thanks to God.

14:7 For none of us liveth to himself; and no man dieth to himself.

14:8 For whether we live, we live unto the Lord; or whether we die, we die unto the Lord. Therefore, whether we live, or whether we die, we are the Lord's.

14:9 For to this end Christ died and rose again; that he might be Lord both of the dead and of the living.

14:10 But thou, why judgest thou thy brother? or thou, why dost thou despise thy brother? For we shall all stand before the judgment seat of Christ.

14:11 For it is written: As I live, saith the Lord, every knee shall bow to me, and every tongue shall confess to God.

14:12 Therefore every one of us shall render account to God for himself.

14:13 Let us not therefore judge one another any more. But judge this rather, that you put not a stumblingblock or a scandal in your brother's way.

14:14 I know, and am confident in the Lord Jesus, that nothing is unclean of itself; but to him that esteemeth any thing to be unclean, to him it is unclean.

14:15 For if, because of thy meat, thy brother be grieved, thou walkest not now according to charity. Destroy not him with thy meat, for whom Christ died.

14:16 Let not then our good be evil spoken of.

14:17 For the kingdom of God is not meat and drink; but justice, and peace, and joy in the Holy Ghost.

14:18 For he that in this serveth Christ, pleaseth God, and is approved of men.

14:19 Therefore let us follow after the things that are of peace; and keep the things that are of edification one towards another.

14:20 Destroy not the work of God for meat. All things indeed are clean: but it is evil for that man who eateth with offence.

14:21 Bonum est non manducare carnem, et non bibere vinum, neque in quo frater tuus offenditur, aut scandalizatur, aut infirmatur.

14:22 Tu fidem habes ? penes temetipsum habe coram Deo. Beatus qui non judicat semetipsum in eo quod probat.

14:23 Qui autem discernit, si manducaverit, damnatus est : quia non ex fide. Omne autem, quod non est ex fide, peccatum est.

15:1 Debemus autem nos firmiores imbecillitates infirmorum sustinere, et non nobis placere.

15:2 Unusquisque vestrum proximo suo placeat in bonum, ad ædificationem.

15:3 Etenim Christus non sibi placuit, sed sicut scriptum est : Improperia improperantium tibi ceciderunt super me.

15:4 Quæcumque enim scripta sunt, ad nostram doctrinam scripta sunt : ut per patientiam, et consolationem Scripturarum, spem habeamus.

15:5 Deus autem patientiæ et solatii det vobis idipsum sapere in alterutrum secundum Jesum Christum :

15:6 ut unanimes, uno ore honorificetis Deum et patrem Domini nostri Jesu Christi.

15:7 Propter quod suscipite invicem, sicut et Christus suscepit vos in honorem Dei.

15:8 Dico enim Christum Jesum ministrum fuisse circumcisionis propter veritatem Dei, ad confirmandas promissiones patrum :

15:9 gentes autem super misericordia honorare Deum, sicut scriptum est : Propterea confitebor tibi in gentibus, Domine, et nomini tuo cantabo.

15:10 Et iterum dicit : Lætamini gentes cum plebe ejus.

15:11 Et iterum : Laudate omnes gentes Dominum : et magnificate eum omnes populi.

15:12 Et rursus Isaias ait : Erit radix Jesse, et qui exsurget regere gentes, in eum gentes sperabunt.

15:13 Deus autem spei repleat vos omni gaudio, et pace in credendo : ut abundetis in spe, et virtute Spiritus Sancti.

15:14 Certus sum autem fratres mei et ego ipse de vobis, quoniam et ipsi pleni estis dilectione, repleti omni scientia, ita ut possitis alterutrum monere.

15:15 Audacius autem scripsi vobis fratres ex parte, tamquam in memoriam vos reducens :

14:21 It is good not to eat flesh, and not to drink wine, nor any thing whereby thy brother is offended, or scandalized, or made weak.

14:22 Hast thou faith? Have it to thyself before God. Blessed is he that condemneth not himself in that which he alloweth.

14:23 But he that discerneth, if he eat, is condemned; because not of faith. For all that is not of faith is sin.

15:1 Now we that are stronger, ought to bear the infirmities of the weak, and not to please ourselves.

15:2 Let every one of you please his neighbour unto good, to edification.

15:3 For Christ did not please himself, but as it is written: The reproaches of them that reproached thee, fell upon me.

15:4 For what things soever were written, were written for our learning: that through patience and the comfort of the scriptures, we might have hope.

15:5 Now the God of patience and of comfort grant you to be of one mind one towards another, according to Jesus Christ:

15:6 That with one mind, and with one mouth, you may glorify God and the Father of our Lord Jesus Christ.

15:7 Wherefore receive one another, as Christ also hath received you unto the honour of God.

15:8 For I say that Christ Jesus was minister of the circumcision for the truth of God, to confirm the promises made unto the fathers.

15:9 But that the Gentiles are to glorify God for his mercy, as it is written: Therefore will I confess to thee, O Lord, among the Gentiles, and will sing to thy name.

15:10 And again he saith: Rejoice, ye Gentiles, with his people.

15:11 And again: Praise the Lord, all ye Gentiles; and magnify him, all ye people.

15:12 And again Isaias saith: There shall be a root of Jesse; and he that shall rise up to rule the Gentiles, in him the Gentiles shall hope.

15:13 Now the God of hope fill you with all joy and peace in believing; that you may abound in hope, and in the power of the Holy Ghost.

15:14 And I myself also, my brethren, am assured of you, that you also are full of love, replenished with all knowledge, so that you are able to admonish one another.

15:15 But I have written to you, brethren, more boldly in some sort, as it were putting you in

propter gratiam, quæ data est mihi a Deo,

^{15:16} ut sim minister Christi Jesu in gentibus : sanctificans Evangelium Dei, ut fiat oblatio gentium accepta, et sanctificata in Spiritu Sancto.

^{15:17} Habeo igitur gloriam in Christo Jesu ad Deum.

^{15:18} Non enim audeo aliquid loqui eorum, quæ per me non efficit Christus in obedientiam gentium, verbo et factis :

^{15:19} in virtute signorum, et prodigiorum, in virtute Spiritus Sancti : ita ut ab Jerusalem per circuitum usque ad Illyricum repleverim Evangelium Christi.

^{15:20} Sic autem prædicavi Evangelium hoc, non ubi nominatus est Christus, ne super alienum fundamentum ædificarem :

^{15:21} sed sicut scriptum est : Quibus non est annuntiatum de eo, videbunt : et qui non audierunt, intelligent.

^{15:22} Propter quod et impediebar plurimum venire ad vos, et prohibitus sum usque adhuc.

^{15:23} Nunc vero ulterius locum non habens in his regionibus, cupiditatem autem habens veniendi ad vos ex multis jam præcedentibus annis :

^{15:24} cum in Hispaniam proficisci cœpero, spero quod præteriens videam vos, et a vobis deducar illuc, si vobis primum ex parte fruitus fuero.

^{15:25} Nunc igitur proficiscar in Jerusalem ministrare sanctis.

^{15:26} Probaverunt enim Macedonia et Achaia collationem aliquam facere in pauperes sanctorum, qui sunt in Jerusalem.

^{15:27} Placuit enim eis : et debitores sunt eorum. Nam si spiritualium eorum participes facti sunt gentiles, debent et in carnalibus ministrare illis.

^{15:28} Hoc igitur cum consummavero, et assignavero eis fructum hunc, per vos proficiscar in Hispaniam.

^{15:29} Scio autem quoniam veniens ad vos, in abundantia benedictionis Evangelii Christi veniam.

^{15:30} Obsecro ergo vos fratres per Dominum nostrum Jesum Christum, et per caritatem Sancti Spiritus, ut adjuvetis me in orationibus vestris pro me ad Deum,

mind: because of the grace which is given me from God.

^{15:16} That I should be the minister of Christ Jesus among the Gentiles; sanctifying the gospel of God, that the oblation of the Gentiles may be made acceptable and sanctified in the Holy Ghost.

^{15:17} I have therefore glory in Christ Jesus towards God.

^{15:18} For I dare not to speak of any of those things which Christ worketh not by me, for the obedience of the Gentiles, by word and deed,

^{15:19} By the virtue of signs and wonders, in the power of the Holy Ghost, so that from Jerusalem round about as far as unto Illyricum, I have replenished the gospel of Christ.

^{15:20} And I have so preached this gospel, not where Christ was named, lest I should build upon another man's foundation.

^{15:21} But as it is written: They to whom he was not spoken of, shall see, and they that have not heard shall understand.

^{15:22} For which cause also I was hindered very much from coming to you, and have been kept away till now.

^{15:23} But now having no more place in these countries, and having a great desire these many years past to come unto you,

^{15:24} When I shall begin to take my journey into Spain, I hope that as I pass, I shall see you, and be brought on my way thither by you, if first, in part, I shall have enjoyed you:

^{15:25} But now I shall go to Jerusalem, to minister unto the saints.

^{15:26} For it hath pleased them of Macedonia and Achaia to make a contribution for the poor of the saints that are in Jerusalem.

^{15:27} For it hath pleased them; and they are their debtors. For if the Gentiles have been made partakers of their spiritual things, they ought also in carnal things to minister to them.

^{15:28} When therefore I shall have accomplished this, and consigned to them this fruit, I will come by you into Spain.

^{15:29} And I know, that when I come to you, I shall come in the abundance of the blessing of the gospel of Christ.

^{15:30} I beseech you therefore, brethren, through our Lord Jesus Christ, and by the charity of the Holy Ghost, that you help me in your prayers for me to God,

15:31 ut liberer ab infidelibus, qui sunt in Judæa, et obsequii mei oblatio accepta fiat in Jerusalem sanctis,

15:32 ut veniam ad vos in gaudio per voluntatem Dei, et refrigerer vobiscum.

15:33 Deus autem pacis sit cum omnibus vobis. Amen.

16:1 Commendo autem vobis Phœben sororem nostram, quæ est in ministerio ecclesiæ, quæ est in Cenchris :

16:2 ut eam suscipiatis in Domino digne sanctis : et assistatis ei in quocumque negotio vestri indiguerit : etenim ipsa quoque astitit multis, et mihi ipsi.

16:3 Salutate Priscam et Aquilam, adjutores meos in Christo Jesu

16:4 (qui pro anima mea suas cervices supposuerunt : quibus non solus ego gratias ago, sed et cunctæ ecclesiæ gentium),

16:5 et domesticam ecclesiam eorum. Salutate Epænetum dilectum mihi, qui est primitivus Asiæ in Christo.

16:6 Salutate Mariam, quæ multum laboravit in vobis.

16:7 Salutate Andronicum et Juniam, cognatos, et concaptivos meos : qui sunt nobiles in Apostolis, qui et ante me fuerunt in Christo.

16:8 Salutate Ampliatum dilectissimum mihi in Domino.

16:9 Salutate Urbanum adjutorem nostrum in Christo Jesu, et Stachyn dilectum meum.

16:10 Salutate Apellen probum in Christo.

16:11 Salutate eos qui sunt ex Aristoboli domo. Salutate Herodionem cognatum meum. Salutate eos qui sunt ex Narcisi domo, qui sunt in Domino.

16:12 Salutate Tryphænam et Tryphosam, quæ laborant in Domino. Salutate Persidem carissimam, quæ multum laboravit in Domino.

16:13 Salutate Rufum electum in Domino, et matrem ejus, et meam.

16:14 Salutate Asyncritum, Phlegontem, Hermam, Patrobam, Hermen, et qui cum eis sunt, fratres.

16:15 Salutate Philologum et Juliam, Nereum, et sororem ejus, et Olympiadem, et omnes qui cum eis sunt, sanctos.

16:16 Salutate invicem in osculo sancto. Salutant vos omnes ecclesiæ Christi.

16:17 Rogo autem vos fratres, ut observetis eos

15:31 That I may be delivered from the unbelievers that are in Judea, and that the oblation of my service may be acceptable in Jerusalem to the saints.

15:32 That I may come to you with joy, by the will of God, and may be refreshed with you.

15:33 Now the God of peace be with you all. Amen.

16:1 And I commend to you Phebe, our sister, who is in the ministry of the church, that is in Cenchrae:

16:2 That you receive her in the Lord as becometh saints; and that you assist her in whatsoever business she shall have need of you. For she also hath assisted many, and myself also.

16:3 Salute Prisca and Aquila, my helpers in Christ Jesus,

16:4 (Who have for my life laid down their own necks: to whom not I only give thanks, but also all the churches of the Gentiles,)

16:5 And the church which is in their house. Salute Epenetus, my beloved: who is the firstfruits of Asia in Christ.

16:6 Salute Mary, who hath laboured much among you.

16:7 Salute Andronicus and Junias, my kinsmen and fellow prisoners: who are of note among the apostles, who also were in Christ before me.

16:8 Salute Ampliatus, most beloved to me in the Lord.

16:9 Salute Urbanus, our helper in Christ Jesus, and Stachys, my beloved.

16:10 Salute Apelles, approved in Christ.

16:11 Salute them that are of Aristobulus' household. Salute Herodian, my kinsman. Salute them that are of Narcissus' household, who are in the Lord.

16:12 Salute Tryphaena and Tryphosa, who labour in the Lord. Salute Persis, the dearly beloved, who hath much laboured in the Lord.

16:13 Salute Rufus, elect in the Lord, and his mother and mine.

16:14 Salute Asyncritus, Phlegon, Hermas, Patrobas, Hermes, and the brethren that are with them.

16:15 Salute Philologus and Julia, Nereus and his sister, and Olympias; and all the saints that are with them.

16:16 Salute one another with an holy kiss. All the churches of Christ salute you.

16:17 Now I beseech you, brethren, to mark

qui dissensiones et offendicula, præter doctrinam, quam vos didicistis, faciunt, et declinate ab illis.

16:18 Hujuscemodi enim Christo Domino nostro non serviunt, sed suo ventri : et per dulces sermones et benedictiones seducunt corda innocentium.

16:19 Vestra enim obedientia in omnem locum divulgata est. Gaudeo igitur in vobis. Sed volo vos sapientes esse in bono, et simplices in malo.

16:20 Deus autem pacis conterat Satanam sub pedibus vestris velociter. Gratia Domini nostri Jesu Christi vobiscum.

16:21 Salutat vos Timotheus adjutor meus, et Lucius, et Jason, et Sosipater cognati mei.

16:22 Saluto vos ego Tertius, qui scripsi epistolam, in Domino.

16:23 Salutat vos Cajus hospes meus, et universa ecclesia. Salutat vos Erastus arcarius civitatis, et Quartus, frater.

16:24 Gratia Domini nostri Jesu Christi cum omnibus vobis. Amen.

16:25 Ei autem, qui potens est vos confirmare juxta Evangelium meum, et prædicationem Jesu Christi, secundum revelationem mysterii temporibus æternis taciti

16:26 (quod nunc patefactum est per Scripturas prophetarum secundum præceptum æterni Dei, ad obeditionem fidei), in cunctis gentibus cogniti,

16:27 soli sapienti Deo, per Jesum Christum, cui honor et gloria in sæcula sæculorum. Amen.

them who make dissensions and offences contrary to the doctrine which you have learned, and avoid them.

16:18 For they that are such, serve not Christ our Lord, but their own belly; and by pleasing speeches and good words, seduce the hearts of the innocent.

16:19 For your obedience is published in every place. I rejoice therefore in you. But I would have you to be wise in good, and simple in evil.

16:20 And the God of peace crush Satan under your feet speedily. The grace of our Lord Jesus Christ be with you.

16:21 Timothy, my fellow labourer, saluteth you, and Lucius, and Jason, and Sosipater, my kinsmen.

16:22 I Tertius, who wrote this epistle, salute you in the Lord.

16:23 Caius, my host, and the whole church, saluteth you. Erastus, the treasurer of the city, saluteth you, and Quartus, a brother.

16:24 The grace of our Lord Jesus Christ be with you all. Amen.

16:25 Now to him that is able to establish you, according to my gospel, and the preaching of Jesus Christ, according to the revelation of the mystery, which was kept secret from eternity,

16:26 (Which now is made manifest by the scriptures of the prophets, according to the precept of the eternal God, for the obedience of faith,) known among all nations;

16:27 To God the only wise, through Jesus Christ, to whom be honour and glory for ever and ever. Amen.

Epistula Beati Pauli Apostoli ad Corinthios Prima

THE FIRST EPISTLE OF BLESSED PAUL THE APOSTLE TO THE CORINTHIANS

✠

1:1 PAULUS VOCATUS APOSTOLUS JESU CHRISTI per voluntatem Dei, et Sosthenes frater,

1:2 ecclesiæ Dei, quæ est Corinthi, sanctificatis in Christo Jesu, vocatis sanctis, cum omnibus qui invocant nomen Domini nostri Jesu Christi, in omni loco ipsorum et nostro.

1:3 Gratia vobis, et pax a Deo Patre nostro, et Domino Jesu Christo.

1:4 Gratias ago Deo meo semper pro vobis in gratia Dei, quæ data est vobis in Christo Jesu :

1:5 quod in omnibus divites facti estis in illo, in omni verbo, et in omni scientia.

1:6 Sicut testimonium Christi confirmatum est in vobis :

1:7 ita ut nihil vobis desit in ulla gratia, exspectantibus revelationem Domini nostri Jesu Christi,

1:8 qui et confirmabit vos usque in finem sine crimine, in die adventus Domini nostri Jesu Christi.

1:9 Fidelis Deus : per quem vocati estis in societatem filii ejus Jesu Christi Domini nostri.

1:10 Obsecro autem vos fratres per nomen Domini nostri Jesu Christi : ut idipsum dicatis omnes, et non sint in vobis schismata : sitis autem perfecti in eodem sensu, et in eadem sententia.

1:11 Significatum est enim mihi de vobis fratres mei ab iis, qui sunt Chloës, quia contentiones sunt inter vos.

1:12 Hoc autem dico, quod unusquisque vestrum dicit : Ego quidem sum Pauli : ego autem Apollo : ego vero Cephæ : ego autem Christi.

1:13 Divisus est Christus ? numquid Paulus crucifixus est pro vobis ? aut in nomine Pauli baptizati estis ?

1:14 Gratias ago Deo, quod neminem vestrum baptizavi, nisi Crispum et Caium :

1:1 PAUL, CALLED TO BE AN APOSTLE OF JESUS CHRIST by the will of God, and Sosthenes a brother,

1:2 To the church of God that is at Corinth, to them that are sanctified in Christ Jesus, called to be saints, with all that invoke the name of our Lord Jesus Christ, in every place of theirs and ours.

1:3 Grace to you, and peace from God our Father, and from the Lord Jesus Christ.

1:4 I give thanks to my God always for you, for the grace of God that is given you in Christ Jesus,

1:5 That in all things you are made rich in him, in all utterance, and in all knowledge;

1:6 As the testimony of Christ was confirmed in you,

1:7 So that nothing is wanting to you in any grace, waiting for the manifestation of our Lord Jesus Christ.

1:8 Who also will confirm you unto the end without crime, in the day of the coming of our Lord Jesus Christ.

1:9 God is faithful: by whom you are called unto the fellowship of his Son Jesus Christ our Lord.

1:10 Now I beseech you, brethren, by the name of our Lord Jesus Christ, that you all speak the same thing, and that there be no schisms among you; but that you be perfect in the same mind, and in the same judgment.

1:11 For it hath been signified unto me, my brethren, of you, by them that are of the house of Chloe, that there are contentions among you.

1:12 Now this I say, that every one of you saith: I indeed am of Paul; and I am of Apollo; and I am of Cephas; and I of Christ.

1:13 Is Christ divided? Was Paul then crucified for you? or were you baptized in the name of Paul?

1:14 I give God thanks, that I baptized none of you but Crispus and Caius;

1:15 ne quis dicat quod in nomine meo baptizati estis.

1:16 Baptizavi autem et Stephanæ domum : ceterum nescio si quem alium baptizaverim.

1:17 Non enim misit me Christus baptizare, sed evangelizare : non in sapientia verbi, ut non evacuetur crux Christi.

1:18 Verbum enim crucis pereuntibus quidem stultitia est : iis autem qui salvi fiunt, id est nobis, Dei virtus est.

1:19 Scriptum est enim : Perdam sapientiam sapientium, et prudentiam prudentium reprobabo.

1:20 Ubi sapiens ? ubi scriba ? ubi conquisitor hujus sæculi ? Nonne stultam fecit Deus sapientiam hujus mundi ?

1:21 Nam quia in Dei sapientia non cognovit mundus per sapientiam Deum : placuit Deo per stultitiam prædicationis salvos facere credentes.

1:22 Quoniam et Judæi signa petunt, et Græci sapientiam quærunt :

1:23 nos autem prædicamus Christum crucifixum : Judæis quidem scandalum, gentibus autem stultitiam,

1:24 ipsis autem vocatis Judæis, atque Græcis Christum Dei virtutem, et Dei sapientiam :

1:25 quia quod stultum est Dei, sapientius est hominibus : et quod infirmum est Dei, fortius est hominibus.

1:26 Videte enim vocationem vestram, fratres, quia non multi sapientes secundum carnem, non multi potentes, non multi nobiles :

1:27 sed quæ stulta sunt mundi elegit Deus, ut confundat sapientes : et infirma mundi elegit Deus, ut confundat fortia :

1:28 et ignobilia mundi, et contemptibilia elegit Deus, et ea quæ non sunt, ut ea quæ sunt destrueret :

1:29 ut non glorietur omnis caro in conspectu ejus.

1:30 Ex ipso autem vos estis in Christo Jesu, qui factus est nobis sapientia a Deo, et justitia, et sanctificatio, et redemptio :

1:31 ut quemadmodum scriptum est : Qui gloriatur, in Domino glorietur.

1:15 Lest any should say that you were baptized in my name.

1:16 And I baptized also the household of Stephanus; besides, I know not whether I baptized any other.

1:17 For Christ sent me not to baptize, but to preach the gospel: not in wisdom of speech, lest the cross of Christ should be made void.

1:18 For the word of the cross, to them indeed that perish, is foolishness; but to them that are saved, that is, to us, it is the power of God.

1:19 For it is written: I will destroy the wisdom of the wise, and the prudence of the prudent I will reject.

1:20 Where is the wise? Where is the scribe? Where is the disputer of this world? Hath not God made foolish the wisdom of this world?

1:21 For seeing that in the wisdom of God the world, by wisdom, knew not God, it pleased God, by the foolishness of our preaching, to save them that believe.

1:22 For both the Jews require signs, and the Greeks seek after wisdom:

1:23 But we preach Christ crucified, unto the Jews indeed a stumblingblock, and unto the Gentiles foolishness:

1:24 But unto them that are called, both Jews and Greeks, Christ the power of God, and the wisdom of God.

1:25 For the foolishness of God is wiser than men; and the weakness of God is stronger than men.

1:26 For see your vocation, brethren, that there are not many wise according to the flesh, not many mighty, not many noble:

1:27 But the foolish things of the world hath God chosen, that he may confound the wise; and the weak things of the world hath God chosen, that he may confound the strong.

1:28 And the base things of the world, and the things that are contemptible, hath God chosen, and things that are not, that he might bring to nought things that are:

1:29 That no flesh should glory in his sight.

1:30 But of him are you in Christ Jesus, who of God is made unto us wisdom, and justice, and sanctification, and redemption:

1:31 That, as it is written: He that glorieth, may glory in the Lord.

2:1 Et ego, cum venissem ad vos, fratres, veni non in sublimitate sermonis, aut sapientiæ, annuntians vobis testimonium Christi.

2:2 Non enim judicavi me scire aliquid inter vos, nisi Jesum Christum, et hunc crucifixum.

2:3 Et ego in infirmitate, et timore, et tremore multo fui apud vos :

2:4 et sermo meus, et prædicatio mea non in persuasibilibus humanæ sapientiæ verbis, sed in ostensione spiritus et virtutis :

2:5 ut fides vestra non sit in sapientia hominum, sed in virtute Dei.

2:6 Sapientiam autem loquimur inter perfectos : sapientiam vero non hujus sæculi, neque principum hujus sæculi, qui destruuntur :

2:7 sed loquimur Dei sapientiam in mysterio, quæ abscondita est, quam prædestinavit Deus ante sæcula in gloriam nostram,

2:8 quam nemo principum hujus sæculi cognovit : si enim cognovissent, numquam Dominum gloriæ crucifixissent.

2:9 Sed sicut scriptum est : Quod oculus non vidit, nec auris audivit, nec in cor hominis ascendit, quæ præparavit Deus iis qui diligunt illum :

2:10 nobis autem revelavit Deus per Spiritum suum : Spiritus enim omnia scrutatur, etiam profunda Dei.

2:11 Quis enim hominum scit quæ sunt hominis, nisi spiritus hominis, qui in ipso est ? ita et quæ Dei sunt, nemo cognovit, nisi Spiritus Dei.

2:12 Nos autem non spiritum hujus mundi accepimus, sed Spiritum qui ex Deo est, ut sciamus quæ a Deo donata sunt nobis :

2:13 quæ et loquimur non in doctis humanæ sapientiæ verbis, sed in doctrina Spiritus, spiritualibus spiritualia comparantes.

2:14 Animalis autem homo non percipit ea quæ sunt Spiritus Dei : stultitia enim est illi, et non potest intelligere : quia spiritualiter examinatur.

2:15 Spiritualis autem judicat omnia : et ipse a nemine judicatur.

2:16 Quis enim cognovit sensum Domini, qui instruat eum ? nos autem sensum Christi habemus.

2:1 And I, brethren, when I came to you, came not in loftiness of speech or of wisdom, declaring unto you the testimony of Christ.

2:2 For I judged not myself to know anything among you, but Jesus Christ, and him crucified.

2:3 And I was with you in weakness, and in fear, and in much trembling.

2:4 And my speech and my preaching was not in the persuasive words of human wisdom, but in shewing of the Spirit and power;

2:5 That your faith might not stand on the wisdom of men, but on the power of God.

2:6 Howbeit we speak wisdom among the perfect: yet not the wisdom of this world, neither of the princes of this world that come to nought;

2:7 But we speak the wisdom of God in a mystery, a wisdom which is hidden, which God ordained before the world, unto our glory:

2:8 Which none of the princes of this world knew; for if they had known it, they would never have crucified the Lord of glory.

2:9 But, as it is written: That eye hath not seen, nor ear heard, neither hath it entered into the heart of man, what things God hath prepared for them that love him.

2:10 But to us God hath revealed them, by this Spirit. For the Spirit searcheth all things, yea, the deep things of God.

2:11 For what man knoweth the things of a man, but the spirit of a man that is in him? So the things also that are of God no man knoweth, but the Spirit of God.

2:12 Now we have received not the spirit of this world, but the Spirit that is of God; that we may know the things that are given us from God.

2:13 Which things also we speak, not in the learned words of human wisdom; but in the doctrine of the Spirit, comparing spiritual things with spiritual.

2:14 But the sensual man perceiveth not these things that are of the Spirit of God; for it is foolishness to him, and he cannot understand, because it is spiritually examined.

2:15 But the spiritual man judgeth all things; and he himself is judged of no man.

2:16 For who hath known the mind of the Lord, that we may instruct him? But we have the mind of Christ.

3:1 Et ego, fratres, non potui vobis loqui quasi spiritualibus, sed quasi carnalibus. Tamquam parvulis in Christo,

3:2 lac vobis potum dedi, non escam : nondum enim poteratis : sed nec nunc quidem potestis : adhuc enim carnales estis.

3:3 Cum enim sit inter vos zelus, et contentio : nonne carnales estis, et secundum hominem ambulatis ?

3:4 Cum enim quis dicat : Ego quidem sum Pauli ; alius autem : Ego Apollo : nonne homines estis ? Quid igitur est Apollo ? quid vero Paulus ?

3:5 ministri ejus, cui credidistis, et unicuique sicut Dominus dedit.

3:6 Ego plantavi, Apollo rigavit : sed Deus incrementum dedit.

3:7 Itaque neque qui plantat est aliquid, neque qui rigat : sed qui incrementum dat, Deus.

3:8 Qui autem plantat, et qui rigat, unum sunt. Unusquisque autem propriam mercedem accipiet, secundum suum laborem.

3:9 Dei enim sumus adjutores : Dei agricultura estis, Dei ædificatio estis.

3:10 Secundum gratiam Dei, quæ data est mihi, ut sapiens architectus fundamentum posui : alius autem superædificat. Unusquisque autem videat quomodo superædificet.

3:11 Fundamentum enim aliud nemo potest ponere præter id quod positum est, quod est Christus Jesus.

3:12 Si quis autem superædificat super fundamentum hoc, aurum, argentum, lapides pretiosos, ligna, fœnum, stipulam,

3:13 uniuscujusque opus manifestum erit : dies enim Domini declarabit, quia in igne revelabitur : et uniuscujusque opus quale sit, ignis probabit.

3:14 Si cujus opus manserit quod superædificavit, mercedem accipiet.

3:15 Si cujus opus arserit, detrimentum patietur : ipse autem salvus erit, sic tamen quasi per ignem.

3:16 Nescitis quia templum Dei estis, et Spiritus Dei habitat in vobis ?

3:17 Si quis autem templum Dei violaverit, disperdet illum Deus. Templum enim Dei sanctum est, quod estis vos.

3:18 Nemo se seducat : si quis videtur inter vos

3:1 And I, brethren, could not speak to you as unto spiritual, but as unto carnal. As unto little ones in Christ.

3:2 I gave you milk to drink, not meat; for you were not able as yet. But neither indeed are you now able; for you are yet carnal.

3:3 For, whereas there is among you envying and contention, are you not carnal, and walk according to man?

3:4 For while one saith, I indeed am of Paul; and another, I am of Apollo; are you not men? What then is Apollo, and what is Paul?

3:5 The ministers of him whom you have believed; and to every one as the Lord hath given.

3:6 I have planted, Apollo watered, but God gave the increase.

3:7 Therefore, neither he that planteth is any thing, nor he that watereth; but God that giveth the increase.

3:8 Now he that planteth, and he that watereth, are one. And every man shall receive his own reward, according to his own labour.

3:9 For we are God's coadjutors: you are God's husbandry; you are God's building.

3:10 According to the grace of God that is given to me, as a wise architect, I have laid the foundation; and another buildeth thereon. But let every man take heed how he buildeth thereupon.

3:11 For other foundation no man can lay, but that which is laid; which is Christ Jesus.

3:12 Now if any man build upon this foundation, gold, silver, precious stones, wood, hay, stubble:

3:13 Every man's work shall be manifest; for the day of the Lord shall declare it, because it shall be revealed in fire; and the fire shall try every man's work, of what sort it is.

3:14 If any man's work abide, which he hath built thereupon, he shall receive a reward.

3:15 If any man's work burn, he shall suffer loss; but he himself shall be saved, yet so as by fire.

3:16 Know you not, that you are the temple of God, and that the Spirit of God dwelleth in you?

3:17 But if any man violate the temple of God, him shall God destroy. For the temple of God is holy, which you are.

3:18 Let no man deceive himself: if any man

sapiens esse in hoc sæculo, stultus fiat ut sit sapiens.

3:19 Sapientia enim hujus mundi, stultitia est apud Deum. Scriptum est enim : Comprehendam sapientes in astutia eorum.

3:20 Et iterum : Dominus novit cogitationes sapientium quoniam vanæ sunt.

3:21 Nemo itaque glorietur in hominibus.

3:22 Omnia enim vestra sunt, sive Paulus, sive Apollo, sive Cephas, sive mundus, sive vita, sive mors, sive præsentia, sive futura : omnia enim vestra sunt :

3:23 vos autem Christi : Christus autem Dei.

4:1 Sic nos existimet homo ut ministros Christi, et dispensatores mysteriorum Dei.

4:2 Hic jam quæritur inter dispensatores ut fidelis quis inveniatur.

4:3 Mihi autem pro minimo est ut a vobis judicer, aut ab humano die : sed neque meipsum judico.

4:4 Nihil enim mihi conscius sum, sed non in hoc justificatus sum : qui autem judicat me, Dominus est.

4:5 Itaque nolite ante tempus judicare, quoadusque veniat Dominus : qui et illuminabit abscondita tenebrarum, et manifestabit consilia cordium : et tunc laus erit unicuique a Deo.

4:6 Hæc autem, fratres, transfiguravi in me et Apollo, propter vos : ut in nobis discatis, ne supra quam scriptum est, unus adversus alterum infletur pro alio.

4:7 Quis enim te discernit ? quid autem habes quod non accepisti ? si autem accepisti, quid gloriaris quasi non acceperis ?

4:8 Jam saturati estis, jam divites facti estis : sine nobis regnatis : et utinam regnetis, ut et nos vobiscum regnemus.

4:9 Puto enim quod Deus nos Apostolos novissimos ostendit, tamquam morti destinatos : quia spectaculum facti sumus mundo, et angelis, et hominibus.

4:10 Nos stulti propter Christum, vos autem prudentes in Christo : nos infirmi, vos autem fortes : vos nobiles, nos autem ignobiles.

4:11 Usque in hanc horam et esurimus, et sitimus, et nudi sumus, et colaphis cædimur, et instabiles sumus,

among you seem to be wise in this world, let him become a fool, that he may be wise.

3:19 For the wisdom of this world is foolishness with God. For it is written: I will catch the wise in their own craftiness.

3:20 And again: The Lord knoweth the thoughts of the wise, that they are vain.

3:21 Let no man therefore glory in men.

3:22 For all things are yours, whether it be Paul, or Apollo, or Cephas, or the world, or life, or death, or things present, or things to come; for all are yours;

3:23 And you are Christ's; and Christ is God's.

4:1 Let a man so account of us as of the ministers of Christ, and the dispensers of the mysteries of God.

4:2 Here now it is required among the dispensers, that a man be found faithful.

4:3 But to me it is a very small thing to be judged by you, or by man's day; but neither do I judge my own self.

4:4 For I am not conscious to myself of any thing, yet am I not hereby justified; but he that judgeth me, is the Lord.

4:5 Therefore judge not before the time; until the Lord come, who both will bring to light the hidden things of darkness, and will make manifest the counsels of the hearts; and then shall every man have praise from God.

4:6 But these things, brethren, I have in a figure transferred to myself and to Apollo, for your sakes; that in us you may learn, that one be not puffed up against the other for another, above that which is written.

4:7 For who distinguisheth thee? Or what hast thou that thou hast not received? And if thou hast received, why dost thou glory, as if thou hadst not received it?

4:8 You are now full; you are now become rich; you reign without us; and I would to God you did reign, that we also might reign with you.

4:9 For I think that God hath set forth us apostles, the last, as it were men appointed to death: we are made a spectacle to the world, and to angels, and to men.

4:10 We are fools for Christ's sake, but you are wise in Christ; we are weak, but you are strong; you are honourable, but we without honour.

4:11 Even unto this hour we both hunger and thirst, and are naked, and are buffeted, and have no fixed abode;

4:12 et laboramus operantes manibus nostris : maledicimur, et benedicimus : persecutionem patimur, et sustinemus :

4:13 blasphemamur, et obsecramus : tamquam purgamenta hujus mundi facti sumus, omnium peripsema usque adhuc.

4:14 Non ut confundam vos, hæc scribo, sed ut filios meos carissimos moneo.

4:15 Nam si decem millia pædagogorum habeatis in Christo, sed non multos patres. Nam in Christo Jesu per Evangelium ego vos genui.

4:16 Rogo ergo vos, imitatores mei estote, sicut et ego Christi.

4:17 Ideo misi ad vos Timotheum, qui est filius meus carissimus, et fidelis in Domino : qui vos commonefaciet vias meas, quæ sunt in Christo Jesu, sicut ubique in omni ecclesia doceo.

4:18 Tamquam non venturus sim ad vos, sic inflati sunt quidam.

4:19 Veniam autem ad vos cito, si Dominus voluerit : et cognoscam non sermonem eorum qui inflati sunt, sed virtutem.

4:20 Non enim in sermone est regnum Dei, sed in virtute.

4:21 Quid vultis ? in virga veniam ad vos, an in caritate, et spiritu mansuetudinis ?

5:1 Omnino auditur inter vos fornicatio, et talis fornicatio, qualis nec inter gentes, ita ut uxorem patris sui aliquis habeat.

5:2 Et vos inflati estis : et non magis luctum habuistis ut tollatur de medio vestrum qui hoc opus fecit.

5:3 Ego quidem absens corpore, præsens autem spiritu, jam judicavi ut præsens eum, qui sic operatus est,

5:4 in nomine Domini nostri Jesu Christi, congregatis vobis et meo spiritu, cum virtute Domini nostri Jesu,

5:5 tradere hujusmodi Satanæ in interitum carnis, ut spiritus salvus sit in die Domini nostri Jesu Christi.

5:6 Non est bona gloriatio vestra. Nescitis quia modicum fermentum totam massam corrumpit ?

5:7 Expurgate vetus fermentum, ut sitis nova conspersio, sicut estis azymi. Etenim Pascha nostrum immolatus est Christus.

5:8 Itaque epulemur : non in fermento veteri, neque in fermento malitiæ et nequitiæ : sed in

4:12 And we labour, working with our own hands: we are reviled, and we bless; we are persecuted, and we suffer it.

4:13 We are blasphemed, and we entreat; we are made as the refuse of this world, the offscouring of all even until now.

4:14 I write not these things to confound you; but I admonish you as my dearest children.

4:15 For if you have ten thousand instructors in Christ, yet not many fathers. For in Christ Jesus, by the gospel, I have begotten you.

4:16 Wherefore I beseech you, be ye followers of me, as I also am of Christ.

4:17 For this cause have I sent to you Timothy, who is my dearest son and faithful in the Lord; who will put you in mind of my ways, which are in Christ Jesus; as I teach every where in every church.

4:18 As if I would not come to you, so some are puffed up.

4:19 But I will come to you shortly, if the Lord will: and will know, not the speech of them that are puffed up, but the power.

4:20 For the kingdom of God is not in speech, but in power.

4:21 What will you? shall I come to you with a rod; or in charity, and in the spirit of meekness?

5:1 It is absolutely heard, that there is fornication among you, and such fornication as the like is not among the heathens; that one should have his father's wife.

5:2 And you are puffed up; and have not rather mourned, that he might be taken away from among you, that hath done this deed.

5:3 I indeed, absent in body, but present in spirit, have already judged, as though I were present, him that hath so done,

5:4 In the name of our Lord Jesus Christ, you being gathered together, and my spirit, with the power of our Lord Jesus;

5:5 To deliver such a one to Satan for the destruction of the flesh, that the spirit may be saved in the day of our Lord Jesus Christ.

5:6 Your glorying is not good. Know you not that a little leaven corrupteth the whole lump?

5:7 Purge out the old leaven, that you may be a new paste, as you are unleavened. For Christ our pasch is sacrificed.

5:8 Therefore let us feast, not with the old leaven, nor with the leaven of malice and wicked-

azymis sinceritatis et veritatis.

5:9 Scripsi vobis in epistola : Ne commisceamini fornicariis :

5:10 non utique fornicariis hujus mundi, aut avaris, aut rapacibus, aut idolis servientibus : alioquin debueratis de hoc mundo exiisse.

5:11 Nunc autem scripsi vobis non commisceri : si is qui frater nominatur, est fornicator, aut avarus, aut idolis serviens, aut maledicus, aut ebriosus, aut rapax, cum ejusmodi nec cibum sumere.

5:12 Quid enim mihi de iis qui foris sunt, judicare ? nonne de iis qui intus sunt, vos judicatis ?

5:13 nam eos qui foris sunt, Deus judicabit. Auferte malum ex vobis ipsis.

6:1 Audet aliquis vestrum habens negotium adversus alterum, judicari apud iniquos, et non apud sanctos ?

6:2 an nescitis quoniam sancti de hoc mundo judicabunt ? et si in vobis judicabitur mundus, indigni estis qui de minimis judicetis ?

6:3 Nescitis quoniam angelos judicabimus ? quanto magis sæcularia ?

6:4 Sæcularia igitur judicia si habueritis : contemptibiles, qui sunt in ecclesia, illos constituite ad judicandum.

6:5 Ad verecundiam vestram dico. Sic non est inter vos sapiens quisquam, qui possit judicare inter fratrem suum ?

6:6 Sed frater cum fratre judicio contendit : et hoc apud infideles ?

6:7 Jam quidem omnino delictum est in vobis, quod judicia habetis inter vos. Quare non magis injuriam accipitis ? quare non magis fraudem patimini ?

6:8 Sed vos injuriam facitis, et fraudatis : et hoc fratribus.

6:9 An nescitis quia iniqui regnum Dei non possidebunt ? Nolite errare : neque fornicarii, neque idolis servientes, neque adulteri,

6:10 neque molles, neque masculorum concubitores, neque fures, neque avari, neque ebriosi, neque maledici, neque rapaces regnum Dei possidebunt.

6:11 Et hæc quidam fuistis : sed abluti estis, sed sanctificati estis, sed justificati estis in nomine Domini nostri Jesu Christi, et in Spiritu Dei

ness; but with the unleavened bread of sincerity and truth.

5:9 I wrote to you in an epistle, not to keep company with fornicators.

5:10 I mean not with the fornicators of this world, or with the covetous, or the extortioners, or the servers of idols; otherwise you must needs go out of this world.

5:11 But now I have written to you, not to keep company, if any man that is named a brother, be a fornicator, or covetous, or a server of idols, or a railer, or a drunkard, or an extortioner: with such a one, not so much as to eat.

5:12 For what have I to do to judge them that are without? Do not you judge them that are within?

5:13 For them that are without, God will judge. Put away the evil one from among yourselves.

6:1 Dare any of you, having a matter against another, go to be judged before the unjust, and not before the saints?

6:2 Know you not that the saints shall judge this world? And if the world shall be judged by you, are you unworthy to judge the smallest matters?

6:3 Know you not that we shall judge angels? how much more things of this world?

6:4 If therefore you have judgments of things pertaining to this world, set them to judge, who are the most despised in the church.

6:5 I speak to your shame. Is it so that there is not among you any one wise man, that is able to judge between his brethren?

6:6 But brother goeth to law with brother, and that before unbelievers.

6:7 Already indeed there is plainly a fault among you, that you have lawsuits one with another. Why do you not rather take wrong? Why do you not rather suffer yourselves to be defrauded?

6:8 But you do wrong and defraud, and that to your brethren.

6:9 Know you not that the unjust shall not possess the kingdom of God? Do not err: neither fornicators, nor idolaters, nor adulterers,

6:10 Nor the effeminate, nor liers with mankind, nor thieves, nor covetous, nor drunkards, nor railers, nor extortioners, shall possess the kingdom of God.

6:11 And such some of you were; but you are washed, but you are sanctified, but you are justified in the name of our Lord Jesus Christ, and

nostri.

6:12 Omnia mihi licent, sed non omnia expediunt : omnia mihi licent, sed ego sub nullis redi-
gar potestate.

6:13 Esca ventri, et venter escis : Deus autem et
hunc et has destruet : corpus autem non forni-
cationi, sed Domino : et Dominus corpori.

6:14 Deus vero et Dominum suscitavit : et nos
suscitabit per virtutem suam.

6:15 Nescitis quoniam corpora vestra membra
sunt Christi ? Tollens ergo membra Christi, faciam membra meretricis ? Absit.

6:16 An nescitis quoniam qui adhæret meretrici,
unum corpus efficitur ? Erunt enim (inquit)
duo in carne una.

6:17 Qui autem adhæret Domino, unus spiritus
est.

6:18 Fugite fornicationem. Omne peccatum,
quodcumque fecerit homo, extra corpus est :
qui autem fornicatur, in corpus suum peccat.

6:19 An nescitis quoniam membra vestra, templum sunt Spiritus Sancti, qui in vobis est,
quem habetis a Deo, et non estis vestri ?

6:20 Empti enim estis pretio magno. Glorificate,
et portate Deum in corpore vestro.

7:1 De quibus autem scripsistis mihi : Bonum
est homini mulierem non tangere :

7:2 propter fornicationem autem unusquisque
suam uxorem habeat, et unaquæque suum
virum habeat.

7:3 Uxori vir debitum reddat : similiter autem
et uxor viro.

7:4 Mulier sui corporis potestatem non habet,
sed vir. Similiter autem et vir sui corporis
potestatem non habet, sed mulier.

7:5 Nolite fraudare invicem, nisi forte ex consensu ad tempus, ut vacetis orationi : et iterum
revertimini in idipsum, ne tentet vos Satanas
propter incontinentiam vestram.

7:6 Hoc autem dico secundum indulgentiam,
non secundum imperium.

7:7 Volo enim omnes vos esse sicut meipsum :
sed unusquisque proprium donum habet ex
Deo : alius quidem sic, alius vero sic.

the Spirit of our God.

6:12 All things are lawful to me, but all things
are not expedient. All things are lawful to me,
but I will not be brought under the power of
any.

6:13 Meat for the belly, and the belly for the
meats; but God shall destroy both it and them:
but the body is not for fornication, but for the
Lord, and the Lord for the body.

6:14 Now God hath both raised up the Lord, and
will raise us up also by his power.

6:15 Know you not that your bodies are the
members of Christ? Shall I then take the members of Christ, and make them the members of
an harlot? God forbid.

6:16 Or know you not, that he who is joined to a
harlot, is made one body? For they shall be,
saith he, two in one flesh.

6:17 But he who is joined to the Lord, is one
spirit.

6:18 Fly fornication. Every sin that a man doth,
is without the body; but he that committeth
fornication, sinneth against his own body.

6:19 Or know you not, that your members are
the temple of the Holy Ghost, who is in you,
whom you have from God; and you are not
your own?

6:20 For you are bought with a great price. Glorify and bear God in your body.

7:1 Now concerning the things whereof you
wrote to me: It is good for a man not to touch
a woman.

7:2 But for fear of fornication, let every man
have his own wife, and let every woman have
her own husband.

7:3 Let the husband render the debt to his wife,
and the wife also in like manner to the husband.

7:4 The wife hath not power of her own body,
but the husband. And in like manner the husband also hath not power of his own body, but
the wife.

7:5 Defraud not one another, except, perhaps,
by consent, for a time, that you may give yourselves to prayer; and return together again, lest
Satan tempt you for your incontinency.

7:6 But I speak this by indulgence, not by commandment.

7:7 For I would that all men were even as myself: but every one hath his proper gift from
God; one after this manner, and another after
that.

7:8 Dico autem non nuptis, et viduis : bonum est illis si sic permaneant, sicut et ego.

7:9 Quod si non se continent, nubant. Melius est enim nubere, quam uri.

7:10 Iis autem qui matrimonio juncti sunt, præcipio non ego, sed Dominus, uxorem a viro non discedere :

7:11 quod si discesserit, manere innuptam, aut viro suo reconciliari. Et vir uxorem non dimittat.

7:12 Nam ceteris ego dico, non Dominus. Si quis frater uxorem habet infidelem, et hæc consentit habitare cum illo, non dimittat illam.

7:13 Et si qua mulier fidelis habet virum infidelem, et hic consentit habitare cum illa, non dimittat virum :

7:14 sanctificatus est enim vir infidelis per mulierem fidelem, et sanctificata est mulier infidelis per virum fidelem : alioquin filii vestri immundi essent, nunc autem sancti sunt.

7:15 Quod si infidelis discedit, discedat : non enim servituti subjectus est frater, aut soror in hujusmodi : in pace autem vocavit nos Deus.

7:16 Unde enim scis mulier, si virum salvum facies ? aut unde scis vir, si mulierem salvam facies ?

7:17 Nisi unicuique sicut divisit Dominus, unumquemque sicut vocavit Deus, ita ambulet, et sicut in omnibus ecclesiis doceo.

7:18 Circumcisus aliquis vocatus est ? non adducat præputium. In præputio aliquis vocatus est ? non circumcidatur.

7:19 Circumcisio nihil est, et præputium nihil est : sed observatio mandatorum Dei.

7:20 Unusquisque in qua vocatione vocatus est, in ea permaneat.

7:21 Servus vocatus es ? non sit tibi curæ : sed et si potes fieri liber, magis utere.

7:22 Qui enim in Domino vocatus est servus, libertus est Domini : similiter qui liber vocatus est, servus est Christi.

7:23 Pretio empti estis : nolite fieri servi hominum.

7:24 Unusquisque in quo vocatus est, fratres, in

7:8 But I say to the unmarried, and to the widows: It is good for them if they so continue, even as I.

7:9 But if they do not contain themselves, let them marry. For it is better to marry than to be burnt.

7:10 But to them that are married, not I but the Lord commandeth, that the wife depart not from her husband.

7:11 And if she depart, that she remain unmarried, or be reconciled to her husband. And let not the husband put away his wife.

7:12 For to the rest I speak, not the Lord. If any brother hath a wife that believeth not, and she consent to dwell with him, let him not put her away.

7:13 And if any woman hath a husband that believeth not, and he consent to dwell with her, let her not put away her husband.

7:14 For the unbelieving husband is sanctified by the believing wife; and the unbelieving wife is sanctified by the believing husband: otherwise your children should be unclean; but now they are holy.

7:15 But if the unbeliever depart, let him depart. For a brother or sister is not under servitude in such cases. But God hath called us in peace.

7:16 For how knowest thou, O wife, whether thou shalt save thy husband? Or how knowest thou, O man, whether thou shalt save thy wife?

7:17 But as the Lord hath distributed to every one, as God hath called every one, so let him walk: and so in all churches I teach.

7:18 Is any man called, being circumcised? let him not procure uncircumcision. Is any man called in uncircumcision? let him not be circumcised.

7:19 Circumcision is nothing, and uncircumcision is nothing: but the observance of the commandments of God.

7:20 Let every man abide in the same calling in which he was called.

7:21 Wast thou called, being a bondman? care not for it; but if thou mayest be made free, use it rather.

7:22 For he that is called in the Lord, being a bondman, is the freeman of the Lord. Likewise he that is called, being free, is the bondman of Christ.

7:23 You are bought with a price; be not made the bondslaves of men.

7:24 Brethren, let every man, wherein he was

hoc permaneat apud Deum.

7:25 De virginibus autem præceptum Domini non habeo : consilium autem do, tamquam misericordiam consecutus a Domino, ut sim fidelis.

7:26 Existimo ergo hoc bonum esse propter instantem necessitatem, quoniam bonum est homini sic esse.

7:27 Alligatus es uxori ? noli quærere solutionem. Solutus es ab uxore ? noli quærere uxorem.

7:28 Si autem acceperis uxorem, non peccasti. Et si nupserit virgo, non peccavit : tribulationem tamen carnis habebunt hujusmodi. Ego autem vobis parco.

7:29 Hoc itaque dico, fratres : tempus breve est : reliquum est, ut et qui habent uxores, tamquam non habentes sint :

7:30 et qui flent, tamquam non flentes : et qui gaudent, tamquam non gaudentes : et qui emunt, tamquam non possidentes :

7:31 et qui utuntur hoc mundo, tamquam non utantur : præterit enim figura hujus mundi.

7:32 Volo autem vos sine sollicitudine esse. Qui sine uxore est, sollicitus est quæ Domini sunt, quomodo placeat Deo.

7:33 Qui autem cum uxore est, sollicitus est quæ sunt mundi, quomodo placeat uxori, et divisus est.

7:34 Et mulier innupta, et virgo, cogitat quæ Domini sunt, ut sit sancta corpore, et spiritu. Quæ autem nupta est, cogitat quæ sunt mundi, quomodo placeat viro.

7:35 Porro hoc ad utilitatem vestram dico : non ut laqueum vobis injiciam, sed ad id, quod honestum est, et quod facultatem præbeat sine impedimento Dominum obsecrandi.

7:36 Si quis autem turpem se videri existimat super virgine sua, quod sit superadulta, et ita oportet fieri : quod vult faciat : non peccat, si nubat.

7:37 Nam qui statuit in corde suo firmus, non habens necessitatem, potestatem autem habens suæ voluntatis, et hoc judicavit in corde suo, servare virginem suam, bene facit.

7:38 Igitur et qui matrimonio jungit virginem suam, bene facit : et qui non jungit, melius facit.

called, therein abide with God.

7:25 Now concerning virgins, I have no commandment of the Lord; but I give counsel, as having obtained mercy of the Lord, to be faithful.

7:26 I think therefore that this is good for the present necessity, that it is good for a man so to be.

7:27 Art thou bound to a wife? seek not to be loosed. Art thou loosed from a wife? seek not a wife.

7:28 But if thou take a wife, thou hast not sinned. And if a virgin marry, she hath not sinned: nevertheless, such shall have tribulation of the flesh. But I spare you.

7:29 This therefore I say, brethren; the time is short; it remaineth, that they also who have wives, be as if they had none;

7:30 And they that weep, as though they wept not; and they that rejoice, as if they rejoiced not; and they that buy, as though they possessed not;

7:31 And they that use this world, as if they used it not: for the fashion of this world passeth away.

7:32 But I would have you to be without solicitude. He that is without a wife, is solicitous for the things that belong to the Lord, how he may please God.

7:33 But he that is with a wife, is solicitous for the things of the world, how he may please his wife: and he is divided.

7:34 And the unmarried woman and the virgin thinketh on the things of the Lord, that she may be holy both in body and in spirit. But she that is married thinketh on the things of the world, how she may please her husband.

7:35 And this I speak for your profit: not to cast a snare upon you; but for that which is decent, and which may give you power to attend upon the Lord, without impediment.

7:36 But if any man think that he seemeth dishonoured, with regard to his virgin, for that she is above the age, and it must so be: let him do what he will; he sinneth not, if she marry.

7:37 For he that hath determined being steadfast in his heart, having no necessity, but having power of his own will; and hath judged this in his heart, to keep his virgin, doth well.

7:38 Therefore, both he that giveth his virgin in marriage, doth well; and he that giveth her not, doth better.

7:39 Mulier alligata est legi quanto tempore vir ejus vivit, quod si dormierit vir ejus, liberata est : cui vult nubat, tantum in Domino.

7:40 Beatior autem erit si sic permanserit secundum meum consilium : puto autem quod et ego Spiritum Dei habeam.

8:1 De iis autem quæ idolis sacrificantur, scimus quia omnes scientiam habemus. Scientia inflat, caritas vero ædificat.

8:2 Si quis autem se existimat scire aliquid, nondum cognovit quemadmodum oporteat eum scire.

8:3 Si quis autem diligit Deum, hic cognitus est ab eo.

8:4 De escis autem quæ idolis immolantur, scimus quia nihil est idolum in mundo, et quod nullus est Deus, nisi unus.

8:5 Nam etsi sunt qui dicantur dii sive in cælo, sive in terra (siquidem sunt dii multi, et domini multi) :

8:6 nobis tamen unus est Deus, Pater, ex quo omnia, et nos in illum : et unus Dominus Jesus Christus, per quem omnia, et nos per ipsum.

8:7 Sed non in omnibus est scientia. Quidam autem cum conscientia usque nunc idoli, quasi idolothytum manducant : et conscientia ipsorum cum sit infirma, polluitur.

8:8 Esca autem nos non commendat Deo. Neque enim si manducaverimus, abundabimus : neque si non manducaverimus, deficiemus.

8:9 Videte autem ne forte hæc licentia vestra offendiculum fiat infirmis.

8:10 Si enim quis viderit eum, qui habet scientiam, in idolio recumbentem : nonne conscientia ejus, cum sit infirma, ædificabitur ad manducandum idolothyta ?

8:11 Et peribit infirmus in tua scientia, frater, propter quem Christus mortuus est ?

8:12 Sic autem peccantes in fratres, et percutientes conscientiam eorum infirmam, in Christum peccatis.

8:13 Quapropter si esca scandalizat fratrem meum, non manducabo carnem in æternum, ne fratrem meum scandalizem.

9:1 Non sum liber ? non sum Apostolus ? nonne Christum Jesum Dominum nostrum vidi ? nonne opus meum vos estis in Domino ?

9:2 Et si aliis non sum Apostolus, sed tamen vobis sum : nam signaculum apostolatus mei vos

7:39 A woman is bound by the law as long as her husband liveth; but if her husband die, she is at liberty: let her marry to whom she will; only in the Lord.

7:40 But more blessed shall she be, if she so remain, according to my counsel; and I think that I also have the spirit of God.

8:1 Now concerning those things that are sacrificed to idols, we know that we all have knowledge. Knowledge puffeth up; but charity edifieth.

8:2 And if any man think that he knoweth any thing, he hath not yet known as he ought to know.

8:3 But if any any love God, the same is known by him.

8:4 But as for the meats that are sacrificed to idols, we know that an idol is nothing in the world, and that there is no God but one.

8:5 For although there be that are called gods, either in heaven or on earth (for there be gods many, and lords many);

8:6 Yet to us there is but one God, the Father, of whom are all things, and we unto him; and one Lord Jesus Christ, by whom are all things, and we by him.

8:7 But there is not knowledge in every one. For some until this present, with conscience of the idol: eat as a thing sacrificed to an idol, and their conscience, being weak, is defiled.

8:8 But meat doth not commend us to God. For neither, if we eat, shall we have the more; nor, if we eat not, shall we have the less.

8:9 But take heed lest perhaps this your liberty become a stumblingblock to the weak.

8:10 For if a man see him that hath knowledge sit at meat in the idol's temple, shall not his conscience, being weak, be emboldened to eat those things which are sacrificed to idols?

8:11 And through thy knowledge shall the weak brother perish, for whom Christ hath died?

8:12 Now when you sin thus against the brethren, and wound their weak conscience, you sin against Christ.

8:13 Wherefore, if meat scandalize my brother, I will never eat flesh, lest I should scandalize my brother.

9:1 Am not I free? Am not I an apostle? Have not I seen Christ Jesus our Lord? Are not you my work in the Lord?

9:2 And if unto others I be not an apostle, but yet to you I am. For you are the seal of my

estis in Domino.

9:3 Mea defensio apud eos qui me interrogant, hæc est :

9:4 Numquid non habemus potestatem manducandi et bibendi ?

9:5 numquid non habemus potestatem mulierem sororem circumducendi sicut et ceteri Apostoli, et fratres Domini, et Cephas ?

9:6 aut ego solus, et Barnabas, non habemus potestatem hoc operandi ?

9:7 Quis militat suis stipendiis umquam ? quis plantat vineam, et de fructu ejus non edit ? quis pascit gregem, et de lacte gregis non manducat ?

9:8 Numquid secundum hominem hæc dico ? an et lex hæc non dicit ?

9:9 Scriptum est enim in lege Moysi : Non alligabis os bovi trituranti. Numquid de bobus cura est Deo ?

9:10 an propter nos utique hoc dicit ? Nam propter nos scripta sunt : quoniam debet in spe qui arat, arare : et qui triturat, in spe fructus percipiendi.

9:11 Si nos vobis spiritualia seminavimus, magnum est si nos carnalia vestra metamus ?

9:12 Si alii potestatis vestræ participes sunt, quare non potius nos ? Sed non usi sumus hac potestate : sed omnia sustinemus, ne quod offendiculum demus Evangelio Christi.

9:13 Nescitis quoniam qui in sacrario operantur quæ de sacrario sunt, edunt : et qui altari deserviunt, cum altari participant ?

9:14 Ita et Dominus ordinavit iis qui Evangelium annuntiant, de Evangelio vivere.

9:15 Ego autem nullo horum usus sum. Non autem scripsi hæc ut ita fiant in me : bonum est enim mihi magis mori, quam ut gloriam meam quis evacuet.

9:16 Nam si evangelizavero, non est mihi gloria : necessitas enim mihi incumbit : væ enim mihi est, si non evangelizavero.

9:17 Si enim volens hoc ago, mercedem habeo : si autem invitus, dispensatio mihi credita est.

9:18 Quæ est ergo merces mea ? ut Evangelium prædicans, sine sumptu ponam Evangelium, ut non abutar potestate mea in Evangelio.

apostleship in the Lord.

9:3 My defence with them that do examine me is this.

9:4 Have not we power to eat and to drink?

9:5 Have we not power to carry about a woman, a sister, as well as the rest of the apostles, and the brethren of the Lord, and Cephas?

9:6 Or I only and Barnabas, have not we power to do this?

9:7 Who serveth as a soldier at any time, at his own charges? Who planteth a vineyard, and eateth not of the fruit thereof? Who feedeth the flock, and eateth not of the milk of the flock?

9:8 Speak I these things according to man? Or doth not the law also say these things?

9:9 For it is written in the law of Moses: Thou shalt not muzzle the mouth of the ox that treadeth out the corn. Doth God take care for oxen?

9:10 Or doth he say this indeed for our sakes? For these things are written for our sakes: that he that plougheth, should plough in hope; and he that thrasheth, in hope to receive fruit.

9:11 If we have sown unto you spiritual things, is it a great matter if we reap your carnal things?

9:12 If others be partakers of this power over you, why not we rather? Nevertheless, we have not used this power: but we bear all things, lest we should give any hindrance to the gospel of Christ.

9:13 Know you not, that they who work in the holy place, eat the things that are of the holy place; and they that serve the altar, partake with the altar?

9:14 So also the Lord ordained that they who preach the gospel, should live by the gospel.

9:15 But I have used none of these things. Neither have I written these things, that they should be so done unto me: for it is good for me to die, rather than that any man should make my glory void.

9:16 For if I preach the gospel, it is no glory to me, for a necessity lieth upon me: for woe is unto me if I preach not the gospel.

9:17 For if I do this thing willingly, I have a reward: but if against my will, a dispensation is committed to me:

9:18 What is my reward then? That preaching the gospel, I may deliver the gospel without charge, that I abuse not my power in the gos-

9:19 Nam cum liber essem ex omnibus, omnium me servum feci, ut plures lucrifacerem.

9:20 Et factus sum Judæis tamquam Judæus, ut Judæos lucrarer :

9:21 iis qui sub lege sunt, quasi sub lege essem (cum ipse non essem sub lege) ut eos qui sub lege erant, lucrifacerem : iis qui sine lege erant, tamquam sine lege essem (cum sine lege Dei non essem : sed in lege essem Christi) ut lucrifacerem eos qui sine lege erant.

9:22 Factus sum infirmis infirmus, ut infirmos lucrifacerem. Omnibus omnia factus sum, ut omnes facerem salvos.

9:23 Omnia autem facio propter Evangelium : ut particeps ejus efficiar.

9:24 Nescitis quod ii qui in stadio currunt, omnes quidem currunt, sed unus accipit bravium ? Sic currite ut comprehendatis.

9:25 Omnis autem qui in agone contendit, ab omnibus se abstinet, et illi quidem ut corruptibilem coronam accipiant : nos autem incorruptam.

9:26 Ego igitur sic curro, non quasi in incertum : sic pugno, non quasi aërem verberans :

9:27 sed castigo corpus meum, et in servitutem redigo : ne forte cum aliis prædicaverim, ipse reprobus efficiar.

10:1 Nolo enim vos ignorare fratres, quoniam patres nostri omnes sub nube fuerunt, et omnes mare transierunt,

10:2 et omnes in Moyse baptizati sunt in nube, et in mari :

10:3 et omnes eamdem escam spiritalem manducaverunt,

10:4 et omnes eumdem potum spiritalem biberunt (bibebant autem de spiritali, consequente eos, petra : petra autem erat Christus) :

10:5 sed non in pluribus eorum beneplacitum est Deo : nam prostrati sunt in deserto.

10:6 Hæc autem in figura facta sunt nostri, ut non simus concupiscentes malorum, sicut et illi concupierunt.

10:7 Neque idololatræ efficiamini, sicut quidam ex ipsis : quemadmodum scriptum est : Sedit populus manducare, et bibere, et surrexerunt ludere.

10:8 Neque fornicemur, sicut quidam ex ipsis

pel.

9:19 For whereas I was free as to all, I made myself the servant of all, that I might gain the more.

9:20 And I became to the Jews, a Jew, that I might gain the Jews:

9:21 To them that are under the law, as if I were under the law, (whereas myself was not under the law,) that I might gain them that were under the law. To them that were without the law, as if I were without the law, (whereas I was not without the law of God, but was in the law of Christ,) that I might gain them that were without the law.

9:22 To the weak I became weak, that I might gain the weak. I became all things to all men, that I might save all.

9:23 And I do all things for the gospel's sake: that I may be made partaker thereof.

9:24 Know you not that they that run in the race, all run indeed, but one receiveth the prize? So run that you may obtain.

9:25 And every one that striveth for the mastery, refraineth himself from all things: and they indeed that they may receive a corruptible crown; but we an incorruptible one.

9:26 I therefore so run, not as at an uncertainty: I so fight, not as one beating the air:

9:27 But I chastise my body, and bring it into subjection: lest perhaps, when I have preached to others, I myself should become a castaway.

10:1 For I would not have you ignorant, brethren, that our fathers were all under the cloud, and all passed through the sea.

10:2 And all in Moses were baptized, in the cloud, and in the sea:

10:3 And did all eat the same spiritual food,

10:4 And all drank the same spiritual drink; (and they drank of the spiritual rock that followed them, and the rock was Christ.)

10:5 But with most of them God was not well pleased: for they were overthrown in the desert.

10:6 Now these things were done in a figure of us, that we should not covet evil things as they also coveted.

10:7 Neither become ye idolaters, as some of them, as it is written: The people sat down to eat and drink, and rose up to play.

10:8 Neither let us commit fornication, as some

fornicati sunt, et ceciderunt una die viginti tria millia.

10:9 Neque tentemus Christum, sicut quidam eorum tentaverunt, et a serpentibus perierunt.

10:10 Neque murmuraveritis, sicut quidam eorum murmuraverunt, et perierunt ab exterminatore.

10:11 Hæc autem omnia in figura contingebant illis : scripta sunt autem ad correptionem nostram, in quos fines sæculorum devenerunt.

10:12 Itaque qui se existimat stare, videat ne cadat.

10:13 Tentatio vos non apprehendat nisi humana : fidelis autem Deus est, qui non patietur vos tentari supra id quod potestis, sed faciet etiam cum tentatione proventum ut possitis sustinere.

10:14 Propter quod, carissimi mihi, fugite ab idolorum cultura :

10:15 ut prudentibus loquor, vos ipsi judicate quod dico.

10:16 Calix benedictionis, cui benedicimus, nonne communicatio sanguinis Christi est ? et panis quem frangimus, nonne participatio corporis Domini est ?

10:17 Quoniam unus panis, unum corpus multi sumus, omnes qui de uno pane participamus.

10:18 Videte Israël secundum carnem : nonne qui edunt hostias, participes sunt altaris ?

10:19 Quid ergo ? dico quod idolis immolatum sit aliquid ? aut quod idolum, sit aliquid ?

10:20 Sed quæ immolant gentes, dæmoniis immolant, et non Deo. Nolo autem vos socios fieri dæmoniorum :

10:21 non potestis calicem Domini bibere, et calicem dæmoniorum ; non potestis mensæ Domini participes esse, et mensæ dæmoniorum.

10:22 An æmulamur Dominum ? numquid fortiores illo sumus ? Omnia mihi licent, sed non omnia expediunt.

10:23 Omnia mihi licent, sed non omnia ædificat.

10:24 Nemo quod suum est quærat, sed quod alterius.

10:25 Omne quod in macello venit, manducate, nihil interrogantes propter conscientiam.

10:26 Domini est terra, et plenitudo ejus.

of them committed fornication, and there fell in one day three and twenty thousand.

10:9 Neither let us tempt Christ: as some of them tempted, and perished by the serpents.

10:10 Neither do you murmur: as some of them murmured, and were destroyed by the destroyer.

10:11 Now all these things happened to them in figure: and they are written for our correction, upon whom the ends of the world are come.

10:12 Wherefore he that thinketh himself to stand, let him take heed lest he fall.

10:13 Let no temptation take hold on you, but such as is human. And God is faithful, who will not suffer you to be tempted above that which you are able: but will make also with temptation issue, that you may be able to bear it.

10:14 Wherefore, my dearly beloved, fly from the service of idols.

10:15 I speak as to wise men: judge ye yourselves what I say.

10:16 The chalice of benediction, which we bless, is it not the communion of the blood of Christ? And the bread, which we break, is it not the partaking of the body of the Lord?

10:17 For we, being many, are one bread, one body, all that partake of one bread.

10:18 Behold Israel according to the flesh: are not they, that eat of the sacrifices, partakers of the altar?

10:19 What then? Do I say, that what is offered in sacrifice to idols, is any thing? Or, that the idol is any thing?

10:20 But the things which the heathens sacrifice, they sacrifice to devils, and not to God. And I would not that you should be made partakers with devils.

10:21 You cannot drink the chalice of the Lord, and the chalice of devils: you cannot be partakers of the table of the Lord, and of the table of devils.

10:22 Do we provoke the Lord to jealousy? Are we stronger than he? All things are lawful for me, but all things are not expedient.

10:23 All things are lawful for me, but all things do not edify.

10:24 Let no man seek his own, but that which is another's.

10:25 Whatsoever is sold in the shambles, eat; asking no question for conscience' sake.

10:26 The earth is the Lord's, and the fulness thereof.

10:27 Si quis vocat vos infidelium, et vultis ire : omne quod vobis apponitur, manducate, nihil interrogantes propter conscientiam.

10:28 Si quis autem dixerit : Hoc immolatum est idolis : nolite manducare propter illum qui indicavit, et propter conscientiam :
10:29 conscientiam autem dico non tuam, sed alterius. Ut quid enim libertas mea judicatur ab aliena conscientia ?
10:30 Si ego cum gratia participo, quid blasphemor pro eo quod gratias ago ?
10:31 Sive ergo manducatis, sive bibitis, sive aliud quid facitis : omnia in gloriam Dei facite.

10:32 Sine offensione estote Judæis, et gentibus, et ecclesiæ Dei :
10:33 sicut et ego per omnia omnibus placeo, non quærens quod mihi utile est, sed quod multis : ut salvi fiant.
11:1 Imitatores mei estote, sicut et ego Christi.

11:2 Laudo autem vos fratres quod per omnia mei memores estis : et sicut tradidi vobis, præcepta mea tenetis.
11:3 Volo autem vos scire quod omnis viri caput, Christus est : caput autem mulieris, vir : caput vero Christi, Deus.
11:4 Omnis vir orans, aut prophetans velato capite, deturpat caput suum.
11:5 Omnis autem mulier orans, aut prophetans non velato capite, deturpat caput suum : unum enim est ac si decalvetur.
11:6 Nam si non velatur mulier, tondeatur. Si vero turpe est mulieri tonderi, aut decalvari, velet caput suum.
11:7 Vir quidem non debet velare caput suum : quoniam imago et gloria Dei est, mulier autem gloria viri est.
11:8 Non enim vir ex muliere est, sed mulier ex viro.
11:9 Etenim non est creatus vir propter mulierem, sed mulier propter virum.
11:10 Ideo debet mulier potestatem habere supra caput propter angelos.
11:11 Verumtamen neque vir sine muliere : neque mulier sine viro in Domino.

11:12 Nam sicut mulier de viro, ita et vir per mulierem : omnia autem ex Deo.
11:13 Vos ipsi judicate : decet mulierem non velatam orare Deum ?

10:27 If any of them that believe not, invite you, and you be willing to go; eat of any thing that is set before you, asking no question for conscience' sake.
10:28 But if any man say: This has been sacrificed to idols, do not eat of it for his sake that told it, and for conscience' sake.
10:29 Conscience, I say, not thy own, but the other's. For why is my liberty judged by another man's conscience?
10:30 If I partake with thanksgiving, why am I evil spoken of, for that for which I give thanks?
10:31 Therefore, whether you eat or drink, or whatsoever else you do, do all to the glory of God.

10:32 Be without offence to the Jews, and to the Gentiles, and to the church of God:
10:33 As I also in all things please all men, not seeking that which is profitable to myself, but to many, that they may be saved.
11:1 Be ye followers of me, as I also am of Christ.

11:2 Now I praise you, brethren, that in all things you are mindful of me: and keep my ordinances as I have delivered them to you.
11:3 But I would have you know, that the head of every man is Christ; and the head of the woman is the man; and the head of Christ is God.
11:4 Every man praying or prophesying with his head covered, disgraceth his head.
11:5 But every woman praying or prophesying with her head not covered, disgraceth her head: for it is all one as if she were shaven.
11:6 For if a woman be not covered, let her be shorn. But if it be a shame to a woman to be shorn or made bald, let her cover her head.
11:7 The man indeed ought not to cover his head, because he is the image and glory of God; but the woman is the glory of the man.
11:8 For the man is not of the woman, but the woman of the man.
11:9 For the man was not created for the woman, but the woman for the man.
11:10 Therefore ought the woman to have a power over her head, because of the angels.
11:11 But yet neither is the man without the woman, nor the woman without the man, in the Lord.

11:12 For as the woman is of the man, so also is the man by the woman: but all things of God.
11:13 You yourselves judge: doth it become a woman, to pray unto God uncovered?

11:14 Nec ipsa natura docet vos, quod vir quidem si comam nutriat, ignominia est illi :

11:15 mulier vero si comam nutriat, gloria est illi : quoniam capilli pro velamine ei dati sunt.

11:16 Si quis autem videtur contentiosus esse : nos talem consuetudinem non habemus, neque ecclesia Dei.

11:17 Hoc autem præcipio : non laudans quod non in melius, sed in deterius convenitis.

11:18 Primum quidem convenientibus vobis in ecclesiam, audio scissuras esse inter vos, et ex parte credo.

11:19 Nam oportet et hæreses esse, ut et qui probati sunt, manifesti fiant in vobis.

11:20 Convenientibus ergo vobis in unum, jam non est Dominicam cœnam manducare.

11:21 Unusquisque enim suam cœnam præsumit ad manducandum, et alius quidem esurit, alius autem ebrius est.

11:22 Numquid domos non habetis ad manducandum, et bibendum ? aut ecclesiam Dei contemnitis, et confunditis eos qui non habent ? Quid dicam vobis ? laudo vos ? in hoc non laudo.

11:23 Ego enim accepi a Domino quod et tradidi vobis, quoniam Dominus Jesus in qua nocte tradebatur, accepit panem,

11:24 et gratias agens fregit, et dixit : Accipite, et manducate : hoc est corpus meum, quod pro vobis tradetur : hoc facite in meam commemorationem.

11:25 Similiter et calicem, postquam cœnavit, dicens : Hic calix novum testamentum est in meo sanguine : hoc facite quotiescumque bibetis, in meam commemorationem.

11:26 Quotiescumque enim manducabitis panem hunc, et calicem bibetis, mortem Domini annuntiabitis donec veniat.

11:27 Itaque quicumque manducaverit panem hunc, vel biberit calicem Domini indigne, reus erit corporis et sanguinis Domini.

11:28 Probet autem seipsum homo : et sic de pane illo edat, et de calice bibat.

11:29 Qui enim manducat et bibit indigne, judicium sibi manducat et bibit, non dijudicans

11:14 Doth not even nature itself teach you, that a man indeed, if he nourish his hair, it is a shame unto him?

11:15 But if a woman nourish her hair, it is a glory to her; for her hair is given to her for a covering.

11:16 But if any man seem to be contentious, we have no such custom, nor the church of God.

11:17 Now this I ordain: not praising you, that you come together not for the better, but for the worse.

11:18 For first of all I hear that when you come together in the church, there are schisms among you; and in part I believe it.

11:19 For there must be also heresies: that they also, who are approved, may be made manifest among you.

11:20 When you come therefore together into one place, it is not now to eat the Lord's supper.

11:21 For every one taketh before his own supper to eat. And one indeed is hungry and another is drunk.

11:22 What, have you not houses to eat and to drink in? Or despise ye the church of God; and put them to shame that have not? What shall I say to you? Do I praise you? In this I praise you not.

11:23 For I have received of the Lord that which also I delivered unto you, that the Lord Jesus, the same night in which he was betrayed, took bread.

11:24 And giving thanks, broke, and said: Take ye, and eat: this is my body, which shall be delivered for you: this do for the commemoration of me.

11:25 In like manner also the chalice, after he had supped, saying: This chalice is the new testament in my blood: this do ye, as often as you shall drink, for the commemoration of me.

11:26 For as often as you shall eat this bread, and drink the chalice, you shall shew the death of the Lord, until he come.

11:27 Therefore whosoever shall eat this bread, or drink the chalice of the Lord unworthily, shall be guilty of the body and of the blood of the Lord.

11:28 But let a man prove himself: and so let him eat of that bread, and drink of the chalice.

11:29 For he that eateth and drinketh unworthily, eateth and drinketh judgment to himself, not

corpus Domini.

11:30 Ideo inter vos multi infirmi et imbecilles, et dormiunt multi.

11:31 Quod si nosmetipsos dijudicaremus, non utique judicaremur.

11:32 Dum judicamur autem, a Domino corripimur, ut non cum hoc mundo damnemur.

11:33 Itaque fratres mei, cum convenitis ad manducandum, invicem exspectate.

11:34 Si quis esurit, domi manducet, ut non in judicium conveniatis. Cetera autem, cum venero, disponam.

12:1 De spiritualibus autem, nolo vos ignorare fratres.

12:2 Scitis quoniam cum gentes essetis, ad simulacra muta prout ducebamini euntes.

12:3 Ideo notum vobis facio, quod nemo in Spiritu Dei loquens, dicit anathema Jesu. Et nemo potest dicere, Dominus Jesus, nisi in Spiritu Sancto.

12:4 Divisiones vero gratiarum sunt, idem autem Spiritus :

12:5 et divisiones ministrationum sunt, idem autem Dominus :

12:6 et divisiones operationum sunt, idem vero Deus qui operatur omnia in omnibus.

12:7 Unicuique autem datur manifestatio Spiritus ad utilitatem.

12:8 Alii quidem per Spiritum datur sermo sapientiæ : alii autem sermo scientiæ secundum eumdem Spiritum :

12:9 alteri fides in eodem Spiritu : alii gratia sanitatum in uno Spiritu :

12:10 alii operatio virtutum, alii prophetia, alii discretio spirituum, alii genera linguarum, alii interpretatio sermonum.

12:11 Hæc autem omnia operatur unus atque idem Spiritus, dividens singulis prout vult.

12:12 Sicut enim corpus unum est, et membra habet multa, omnia autem membra corporis cum sint multa, unum tamen corpus sunt : ita et Christus.

12:13 Etenim in uno Spiritu omnes nos in unum corpus baptizati sumus, sive Judæi, sive gentiles, sive servi, sive liberi : et omnes in uno Spiritu potati sumus.

12:14 Nam et corpus non est unum membrum, sed multa.

discerning the body of the Lord.

11:30 Therefore are there many infirm and weak among you, and many sleep.

11:31 But if we would judge ourselves, we should not be judged.

11:32 But whilst we are judged, we are chastised by the Lord, that we be not condemned with this world.

11:33 Wherefore, my brethren, when you come together to eat, wait for one another.

11:34 If any man be hungry, let him eat at home; that you come not together unto judgment. And the rest I will set in order, when I come.

12:1 Now concerning spiritual things, my brethren, I would not have you ignorant.

12:2 You know that when you were heathens, you went to dumb idols, according as you were led.

12:3 Wherefore I give you to understand, that no man, speaking by the Spirit of God, saith Anathema to Jesus. And no man can say the Lord Jesus, but by the Holy Ghost.

12:4 Now there are diversities of graces, but the same Spirit;

12:5 And there are diversities of ministries, but the same Lord;

12:6 And there are diversities of operations, but the same God, who worketh all in all.

12:7 And the manifestation of the Spirit is given to every man unto profit.

12:8 To one indeed, by the Spirit, is given the word of wisdom: and to another, the word of knowledge, according to the same Spirit;

12:9 To another, faith in the same spirit; to another, the grace of healing in one Spirit;

12:10 To another, the working of miracles; to another, prophecy; to another, the discerning of spirits; to another, diverse kinds of tongues; to another, interpretation of speeches.

12:11 But all these things one and the same Spirit worketh, dividing to every one according as he will.

12:12 For as the body is one, and hath many members; and all the members of the body, whereas they are many, yet are one body, so also is Christ.

12:13 For in one Spirit were we all baptized into one body, whether Jews or Gentiles, whether bond or free; and in one Spirit we have all been made to drink.

12:14 For the body also is not one member, but many.

12:15 Si dixerit pes : Quoniam non sum manus, non sum de corpore : num ideo non est de corpore ?

12:16 Et si dixerit auris : Quoniam non sum oculus, non sum de corpore : num ideo est de corpore ?

12:17 Si totum corpus oculus : ubi auditus ? Si totum auditus : ubi odoratus ?

12:18 Nunc autem posuit Deus membra, unumquodque eorum in corpore sicut voluit.

12:19 Quod si essent omnia unum membrum, ubi corpus ?

12:20 Nunc autem multa quidem membra, unum autem corpus.

12:21 Non potest autem oculus dicere manui : Opera tua non indigeo : aut iterum caput pedibus : Non estis mihi necessarii.

12:22 Sed multo magis quæ videntur membra corporis infirmiora esse, necessariora sunt :

12:23 et quæ putamus ignobiliora membra esse corporis, his honorem abundantiorem circumdamus : et quæ inhonesta sunt nostra, abundantiorem honestatem habent.

12:24 Honesta autem nostra nullius egent : sed Deus temperavit corpus, ei cui deerat, abundantiorem tribuendo honorem,

12:25 ut non sit schisma in corpore, sed idipsum pro invicem sollicita sint membra.

12:26 Et si quid patitur unum membrum, compatiuntur omnia membra : sive gloriatur unum membrum, congaudent omnia membra.

12:27 Vos autem estis corpus Christi, et membra de membro.

12:28 Et quosdam quidem posuit Deus in ecclesia primum apostolos, secundo prophetas, exinde doctores, deinde virtutes, exinde gratias curationum, opitulationes, gubernationes, genera linguarum, interpretationes sermonum.

12:29 Numquid omnes apostoli ? numquid omnes prophetæ ? numquid omnes doctores ?

12:30 numquid omnes virtutes ? numquid omnes gratiam habent curationum ? numquid omnes linguis loquuntur ? numquid omnes interpretantur ?

12:31 Æmulamini autem charismata meliora. Et adhuc excellentiorem viam vobis demonstro.

12:15 If the foot should say, because I am not the hand, I am not of the body; is it therefore not of the body?

12:16 And if the ear should say, because I am not the eye, I am not of the body; is it therefore not of the body?

12:17 If the whole body were the eye, where would be the hearing? If the whole were hearing, where would be the smelling?

12:18 But now God hath set the members every one of them in the body as it hath pleased him.

12:19 And if they all were one member, where would be the body?

12:20 But now there are many members indeed, yet one body.

12:21 And the eye cannot say to the hand: I need not thy help; nor again the head to the feet: I have no need of you.

12:22 Yea, much more those that seem to be the more feeble members of the body, are more necessary.

12:23 And such as we think to be the less honourable members of the body, about these we put more abundant honour; and those that are our uncomely parts, have more abundant comeliness.

12:24 But our comely parts have no need: but God hath tempered the body together, giving to that which wanted the more abundant honour,

12:25 That there might be no schism in the body; but the members might be mutually careful one for another.

12:26 And if one member suffer any thing, all the members suffer with it; or if one member glory, all the members rejoice with it.

12:27 Now you are the body of Christ, and members of member.

12:28 And God indeed hath set some in the church; first apostles, secondly prophets, thirdly doctors; after that miracles; then the graces of healings, helps, governments, kinds of tongues, interpretations of speeches.

12:29 Are all apostles? Are all prophets? Are all doctors?

12:30 Are all workers of miracles? Have all the grace of healing? Do all speak with tongues? Do all interpret?

12:31 But be zealous for the better gifts. And I shew unto you yet a more excellent way.

13:1 Si linguis hominum loquar, et angelorum, caritatem autem non habeam, factus sum velut æs sonans, aut cymbalum tinniens.

13:2 Et si habuero prophetiam, et noverim mysteria omnia, et omnem scientiam : et si habuero omnem fidem ita ut montes transferam, caritatem autem non habuero, nihil sum.

13:3 Et si distribuero in cibos pauperum omnes facultates meas, et si tradidero corpus meum ita ut ardeam, caritatem autem non habuero, nihil mihi prodest.

13:4 Caritas patiens est, benigna est. Caritas non æmulatur, non agit perperam, non inflatur,

13:5 non est ambitiosa, non quærit quæ sua sunt, non irritatur, non cogitat malum,

13:6 non gaudet super iniquitate, congaudet autem veritati :

13:7 omnia suffert, omnia credit, omnia sperat, omnia sustinet.

13:8 Caritas numquam excidit : sive prophetiæ evacuabuntur, sive linguæ cessabunt, sive scientia destruetur.

13:9 Ex parte enim cognoscimus, et ex parte prophetamus.

13:10 Cum autem venerit quod perfectum est, evacuabitur quod ex parte est.

13:11 Cum essem parvulus, loquebar ut parvulus, sapiebam ut parvulus, cogitabam ut parvulus. Quando autem factus sum vir, evacuavi quæ erant parvuli.

13:12 Videmus nunc per speculum in ænigmate : tunc autem facie ad faciem. Nunc cognosco ex parte : tunc autem cognoscam sicut et cognitus sum.

13:13 Nunc autem manent fides, spes, caritas, tria hæc : major autem horum est caritas.

14:1 Sectamini caritatem, æmulamini spiritualia : magis autem ut prophetetis.

14:2 Qui enim loquitur lingua, non hominibus loquitur, sed Deo : nemo enim audit. Spiritu autem loquitur mysteria.

14:3 Nam qui prophetat, hominibus loquitur ad ædificationem, et exhortationem, et consolationem.

14:4 Qui loquitur lingua, semetipsum ædificat : qui autem prophetat, ecclesiam Dei ædificat.

14:5 Volo autem omnes vos loqui linguis : magis autem prophetare. Nam major est qui prophetat, quam qui loquitur linguis ; nisi forte

13:1 If I speak with the tongues of men, and of angels, and have not charity, I am become as sounding brass, or a tinkling cymbal.

13:2 And if I should have prophecy and should know all mysteries, and all knowledge, and if I should have all faith, so that I could remove mountains, and have not charity, I am nothing.

13:3 And if I should distribute all my goods to feed the poor, and if I should deliver my body to be burned, and have not charity, it profiteth me nothing.

13:4 Charity is patient, is kind: charity envieth not, dealeth not perversely; is not puffed up;

13:5 Is not ambitious, seeketh not her own, is not provoked to anger, thinketh no evil;

13:6 Rejoiceth not in iniquity, but rejoiceth with the truth;

13:7 Beareth all things, believeth all things, hopeth all things, endureth all things.

13:8 Charity never falleth away: whether prophecies shall be made void, or tongues shall cease, or knowledge shall be destroyed.

13:9 For we know in part, and we prophesy in part.

13:10 But when that which is perfect is come, that which is in part shall be done away.

13:11 When I was a child, I spoke as a child, I understood as a child, I thought as a child. But, when I became a man, I put away the things of a child.

13:12 We see now through a glass in a dark manner; but then face to face. Now I know in part; but then I shall know even as I am known.

13:13 And now there remain faith, hope, and charity, these three: but the greatest of these is charity.

14:1 Follow after charity, be zealous for spiritual gifts; but rather that you may prophesy.

14:2 For he that speaketh in a tongue, speaketh not unto men, but unto God: for no man heareth. Yet by the Spirit he speaketh mysteries.

14:3 But he that prophesieth, speaketh to men unto edification, and exhortation, and comfort.

14:4 He that speaketh in a tongue, edifieth himself: but he that prophesieth, edifieth the church.

14:5 And I would have you all to speak with tongues, but rather to prophesy. For greater is he that prophesieth, than he that speaketh with

interpretetur ut ecclesia ædificationem accipiat.

14:6 Nunc autem, fratres, si venero ad vos linguis loquens : quid vobis prodero, nisi vobis loquar aut in revelatione, aut in scientia, aut in prophetia, aut in doctrina ?

14:7 Tamen quæ sine anima sunt vocem dantia, sive tibia, sive cithara ; nisi distinctionem sonituum dederint, quomodo scietur id quod canitur, aut quod citharizatur ?

14:8 Etenim si incertam vocem det tuba, quis parabit se ad bellum ?

14:9 Ita et vos per linguam nisi manifestum sermonem dederitis : quomodo scietur id quod dicitur ? eritis enim in aëra loquentes.

14:10 Tam multa, ut puta genera linguarum sunt in hoc mundo : et nihil sine voce est.

14:11 Si ergo nesciero virtutem vocis, ero ei, cui loquor, barbarus : et qui loquitur, mihi barbarus.

14:12 Sic et vos, quoniam æmulatores estis spirituum, ad ædificationem ecclesiæ quærite ut abundetis.

14:13 Et ideo qui loquitur lingua, oret ut interpretetur.

14:14 Nam si orem lingua, spiritus meus orat, mens autem mea sine fructu est.

14:15 Quid ergo est ? Orabo spiritu, orabo et mente : psallam spiritu, psallam et mente.

14:16 Ceterum si benedixeris spiritu, qui supplet locum idiotæ, quomodo dicet : Amen, super tuam benedictionem ? quoniam quid dicas, nescit.

14:17 Nam tu quidem bene gratias agis, sed alter non ædificatur.

14:18 Gratias ago Deo meo, quod omnium vestrum lingua loquor.

14:19 Sed in ecclesia volo quinque verba sensu meo loqui, ut et alios instruam : quam decem millia verborum in lingua.

14:20 Fratres, nolite pueri effici sensibus, sed malitia parvuli estote : sensibus autem perfecti estote.

14:21 In lege scriptum est : Quoniam in aliis linguis et labiis aliis loquar populo huic : et nec sic exaudient me, dicit Dominus.

14:22 Itaque linguæ in signum sunt non fidelibus,

tongues: unless perhaps he interpret, that the church may receive edification.

14:6 But now, brethren, if I come to you speaking with tongues, what shall I profit you, unless I speak to you either in revelation, or in knowledge, or in prophecy, or in doctrine?

14:7 Even things without life that give sound, whether pipe or harp, except they give a distinction of sounds, how shall it be known what is piped or harped?

14:8 For if the trumpet give an uncertain sound, who shall prepare himself to the battle?

14:9 So likewise you, except you utter by the tongue plain speech, how shall it be known what is said? For you shall be speaking into the air.

14:10 There are, for example, so many kinds of tongues in this world; and none is without voice.

14:11 If then I know not the power of the voice, I shall be to him to whom I speak a barbarian; and he that speaketh, a barbarian to me.

14:12 So you also, forasmuch as you are zealous of spirits, seek to abound unto the edifying of the church.

14:13 And therefore he that speaketh by a tongue, let him pray that he may interpret.

14:14 For if I pray in a tongue, my spirit prayeth, but my understanding is without fruit.

14:15 What is it then? I will pray with the spirit, I will pray also with the understanding; I will sing with the spirit, I will sing also with the understanding.

14:16 Else if thou shalt bless with the spirit, how shall he that holdeth the place of the unlearned say, Amen, to thy blessing? because he knoweth not what thou sayest.

14:17 For thou indeed givest thanks well, but the other is not edified.

14:18 I thank my God I speak with all your tongues.

14:19 But in the church I had rather speak five words with my understanding, that I may instruct others also; than ten thousand words in a tongue.

14:20 Brethren, do not become children in sense: but in malice be children, and in sense be perfect.

14:21 In the law it is written: In other tongues and other lips I will speak to this people; and neither so will they hear me, saith the Lord.

14:22 Wherefore tongues are for a sign, not to

sed infidelibus : prophetiæ autem non infidelibus, sed fidelibus.

14:23 Si ergo conveniat universa ecclesia in unum, et omnes linguis loquantur, intrent autem idiotæ, aut infideles : nonne dicent quod insanitis ?

14:24 Si autem omnes prophetent, intret autem quis infidelis, vel idiota, convincitur ab omnibus, dijudicatur ab omnibus :

14:25 occulta cordis ejus manifesta fiunt : et ita cadens in faciem adorabit Deum, pronuntians quod vere Deus in vobis sit.

14:26 Quid ergo est, fratres ? Cum convenitis, unusquisque vestrum psalmum habet, doctrinam habet, apocalypsim habet, linguam habet, interpretationem habet : omnia ad ædificationem fiant.

14:27 Sive lingua quis loquitur, secundum duos, aut ut multum tres, et per partes, et unus interpretatur.

14:28 Si autem non fuerit interpres, taceat in ecclesia : sibi autem loquatur, et Deo.

14:29 Prophetæ autem duo, aut tres dicant, et ceteri dijudicent.

14:30 Quod si alii revelatum fuerit sedenti, prior taceat.

14:31 Potestis enim omnes per singulos prophetare : ut omnes discant, et omnes exhortentur :

14:32 et spiritus prophetarum prophetis subjecti sunt.

14:33 Non enim est dissensionis Deus, sed pacis : sicut et in omnibus ecclesiis sanctorum doceo.

14:34 Mulieres in ecclesiis taceant, non enim permittitur eis loqui, sed subditas esse, sicut et lex dicit.

14:35 Si quid autem volunt discere, domi viros suos interrogent. Turpe est enim mulieri loqui in ecclesia.

14:36 An a vobis verbum Dei processit ? aut in vos solos pervenit ?

14:37 Si quis videtur propheta esse, aut spiritualis, cognoscat quæ scribo vobis, quia Domini sunt mandata.

14:38 Si quis autem ignorat, ignorabitur.

14:39 Itaque fratres æmulamini prophetare : et loqui linguis nolite prohibere.

14:40 Omnia autem honeste, et secundum ordinem fiant.

believers, but to unbelievers; but prophecies not to unbelievers, but to believers.

14:23 If therefore the whole church come together into one place, and all speak with tongues, and there come in unlearned persons or infidels, will they not say that you are mad?

14:24 But if all prophesy, and there come in one that believeth not, or an unlearned person, he is convinced of all, he is judged of all.

14:25 The secrets of his heart are made manifest; and so, falling down on his face, he will adore God, affirming that God is among you indeed.

14:26 How is it then, brethren? When you come together, every one of you hath a psalm, hath a doctrine, hath a revelation, hath a tongue, hath an interpretation: let all things be done to edification.

14:27 If any speak with a tongue, let it be by two, or at the most by three, and in course, and let one interpret.

14:28 But if there be no interpreter, let him hold his peace in the church, and speak to himself and to God.

14:29 And let the prophets speak, two or three; and let the rest judge.

14:30 But if any thing be revealed to another sitting, let the first hold his peace.

14:31 For you may all prophesy one by one; that all may learn, and all may be exhorted:

14:32 And the spirits of the prophets are subject to the prophets.

14:33 For God is not the God of dissension, but of peace: as also I teach in all the churches of the saints.

14:34 Let women keep silence in the churches: for it is not permitted them to speak, but to be subject, as also the law saith.

14:35 But if they would learn any thing, let them ask their husbands at home. For it is a shame for a woman to speak in the church.

14:36 Or did the word of God come out from you? Or came it only unto you?

14:37 If any seem to be a prophet, or spiritual, let him know the things that I write to you, that they are the commandments of the Lord.

14:38 But if any man know not, he shall not be known.

14:39 Wherefore, brethren, be zealous to prophesy; and forbid not to speak with tongues.

14:40 But let all things be done decently, and according to order.

15:1 Notum autem vobis facio, fratres, Evangelium, quod prædicavi vobis, quod et accepistis, in quo et statis,

15:2 per quod et salvamini : qua ratione prædicaverim vobis, si tenetis, nisi frustra credidistis.

15:3 Tradidi enim vobis in primis quod et accepi : quoniam Christus mortuus est pro peccatis nostris secundum Scripturas :

15:4 et quia sepultus est, et quia resurrexit tertia die secundum Scripturas :

15:5 et quia visus est Cephæ, et post hoc undecim :

15:6 deinde visus est plus quam quingentis fratribus simul : ex quibus multi manent usque adhuc, quidam autem dormierunt :

15:7 deinde visus est Jacobo, deinde Apostolis omnibus :

15:8 novissime autem omnium tamquam abortivo, visus est et mihi.

15:9 Ego enim sum minimus Apostolorum, qui non sum dignus vocari Apostolus, quoniam persecutus sum ecclesiam Dei.

15:10 Gratia autem Dei sum id quod sum, et gratia ejus in me vacua non fuit, sed abundantius illis omnibus laboravi : non ego autem, sed gratia Dei mecum :

15:11 sive enim ego, sive illi : sic prædicamus, et sic credidistis.

15:12 Si autem Christus prædicatur quod resurrexit a mortuis, quomodo quidam dicunt in vobis, quoniam resurrectio mortuorum non est ?

15:13 Si autem resurrectio mortuorum non est : neque Christus resurrexit.

15:14 Si autem Christus non resurrexit, inanis est ergo prædicatio nostra, inanis est et fides vestra :

15:15 invenimur autem et falsi testes Dei : quoniam testimonium diximus adversus Deum quod suscitaverit Christum, quem non suscitavit, si mortui non resurgunt.

15:16 Nam si mortui non resurgunt, neque Christus resurrexit.

15:17 Quod si Christus non resurrexit, vana est fides vestra : adhuc enim estis in peccatis vestris.

15:18 Ergo et qui dormierunt in Christo, perierunt.

15:19 Si in hac vita tantum in Christo sperantes sumus, miserabiliores sumus omnibus hominibus.

15:1 Now I make known unto you, brethren, the gospel which I preached to you, which also you have received, and wherein you stand;

15:2 By which also you are saved, if you hold fast after what manner I preached unto you, unless you have believed in vain.

15:3 For I delivered unto you first of all, which I also received: how that Christ died for our sins, according to the scriptures:

15:4 And that he was buried, and that he rose again the third day, according to the scriptures:

15:5 And that he was seen by Cephas; and after that by the eleven.

15:6 Then he was seen by more than five hundred brethren at once: of whom many remain until this present, and some are fallen asleep.

15:7 After that, he was seen by James, then by all the apostles.

15:8 And last of all, he was seen also by me, as by one born out of due time.

15:9 For I am the least of the apostles, who am not worthy to be called an apostle, because I persecuted the church of God.

15:10 But by the grace of God, I am what I am; and his grace in me hath not been void, but I have laboured more abundantly than all they: yet not I, but the grace of God with me.

15:11 For whether I, or they, so we preach, and so you have believed.

15:12 Now if Christ be preached, that he arose again from the dead, how do some among you say, that there is no resurrection of the dead?

15:13 But if there be no resurrection of the dead, then Christ is not risen again.

15:14 And if Christ be not risen again, then is our preaching vain, and your faith is also vain.

15:15 Yea, and we are found false witnesses of God: because we have given testimony against God, that he hath raised up Christ; whom he hath not raised up, if the dead rise not again.

15:16 For if the dead rise not again, neither is Christ risen again.

15:17 And if Christ be not risen again, your faith is vain, for you are yet in your sins.

15:18 Then they also that are fallen asleep in Christ, are perished.

15:19 If in this life only we have hope in Christ, we are of all men most miserable.

15:20 Nunc autem Christus resurrexit a mortuis primitiæ dormientium,

15:21 quoniam quidem per hominem mors, et per hominem resurrectio mortuorum.

15:22 Et sicut in Adam omnes moriuntur, ita et in Christo omnes vivificabuntur.

15:23 Unusquisque autem in suo ordine, primitiæ Christus : deinde ii qui sunt Christi, qui in adventu ejus crediderunt.

15:24 Deinde finis : cum tradiderit regnum Deo et Patri, cum evacuaverit omnem principatum, et potestatem, et virtutem.

15:25 Oportet autem illum regnare donec ponat omnes inimicos sub pedibus ejus.

15:26 Novissima autem inimica destruetur mors : omnia enim subjecit pedibus ejus. Cum autem dicat :

15:27 Omnia subjecta sunt ei, sine dubio præter eum qui subjecit ei omnia.

15:28 Cum autem subjecta fuerint illi omnia : tunc et ipse Filius subjectus erit ei, qui subjecit sibi omnia, ut sit Deus omnia in omnibus.

15:29 Alioquin quid facient qui baptizantur pro mortuis, si omnino mortui non resurgunt ? ut quid et baptizantur pro illis ?

15:30 ut quid et nos periclitamur omni hora ?

15:31 Quotidie morior per vestram gloriam, fratres, quam habeo in Christo Jesu Domino nostro.

15:32 Si secundum hominem ad bestias pugnavi Ephesi, quid mihi prodest, si mortui non resurgunt ? Manducemus, et bibamus, cras enim moriemur.

15:33 Nolite seduci : corrumpunt mores bonos colloquia mala.

15:34 Evigilate justi, et nolite peccare : ignorantiam enim Dei quidam habent, ad reverentiam vobis loquor.

15:35 Sed dicet aliquis : Quomodo resurgunt mortui ? qualive corpore venient ?

15:36 Insipiens, tu quod seminas non vivificatur, nisi prius moriatur :

15:37 et quod seminas, non corpus, quod futurum est, seminas, sed nudum granum, ut puta tritici, aut alicujus ceterorum.

15:38 Deus autem dat illi corpus sicut vult : ut unicuique seminum proprium corpus.

15:39 Non omnis caro, eadem caro : sed alia quidem hominum, alia vero pecorum, alia vo-

15:20 But now Christ is risen from the dead, the firstfruits of them that sleep:

15:21 For by a man came death, and by a man the resurrection of the dead.

15:22 And as in Adam all die, so also in Christ all shall be made alive.

15:23 But every one in his own order: the firstfruits Christ, then they that are of Christ, who have believed in his coming.

15:24 Afterwards the end, when he shall have delivered up the kingdom to God and the Father, when he shall have brought to nought all principality, and power, and virtue.

15:25 For he must reign, until he hath put all his enemies under his feet.

15:26 And the enemy death shall be destroyed last: For he hath put all things under his feet. And whereas he saith,

15:27 All things are put under him; undoubtedly, he is excepted, who put all things under him.

15:28 And when all things shall be subdued unto him, then the Son also himself shall be subject unto him that put all things under him, that God may be all in all.

15:29 Otherwise what shall they do that are baptized for the dead, if the dead rise not again at all? why are they then baptized for them?

15:30 Why also are we in danger every hour?

15:31 I die daily, I protest by your glory, brethren, which I have in Christ Jesus our Lord.

15:32 If (according to man) I fought with beasts at Ephesus, what doth it profit me, if the dead rise not again? Let us eat and drink, for to morrow we shall die.

15:33 Be not seduced: Evil communications corrupt good manners.

15:34 Awake, ye just, and sin not. For some have not the knowledge of God, I speak it to your shame.

15:35 But some man will say: How do the dead rise again? or with what manner of body shall they come?

15:36 Senseless man, that which thou sowest is not quickened, except it die first.

15:37 And that which thou sowest, thou sowest not the body that shall be; but bare grain, as of wheat, or of some of the rest.

15:38 But God giveth it a body as he will: and to every seed its proper body.

15:39 All flesh is not the same flesh: but one is the flesh of men, another of beasts, another of

lucrum, alia autem piscium.

15:40 Et corpora cælestia, et corpora terrestria : sed alia quidem cælestium gloria, alia autem terrestrium.

15:41 Alia claritas solis, alia claritas lunæ, et alia claritas stellarum. Stella enim a stella differt in claritate :

15:42 sic et resurrectio mortuorum. Seminatur in corruptione, surget in incorruptione.

15:43 Seminatur in ignobilitate, surget in gloria : seminatur in infirmitate, surget in virtute :

15:44 seminatur corpus animale, surget corpus spirituale. Si est corpus animale, est et spiritale, sicut scriptum est :

15:45 Factus est primus homo Adam in animam viventem, novissimus Adam in spiritum vivificantem.

15:46 Sed non prius quod spiritale est, sed quod animale : deinde quod spiritale.

15:47 Primus homo de terra, terrenus : secundus homo de cælo, cælestis.

15:48 Qualis terrenus, tales et terreni : et qualis cælestis, tales et cælestes.

15:49 Igitur, sicut portavimus imaginem terreni, portemus et imaginem cælestis.

15:50 Hoc autem dico, fratres : quia caro et sanguis regnum Dei possidere non possunt : neque corruptio incorruptelam possidebit.

15:51 Ecce mysterium vobis dico : omnes quidem resurgemus, sed non omnes immutabimur.

15:52 In momento, in ictu oculi, in novissima tuba : canet enim tuba, et mortui resurgent incorrupti : et nos immutabimur.

15:53 Oportet enim corruptibile hoc induere incorruptionem : et mortale hoc induere immortalitatem.

15:54 Cum autem mortale hoc induerit immortalitatem, tunc fiet sermo, qui scriptus est : Absorpta est mors in victoria.

15:55 Ubi est mors victoria tua ? ubi est mors stimulus tuus ?

15:56 Stimulus autem mortis peccatum est : virtus vero peccati lex.

15:57 Deo autem gratias, qui dedit nobis victoriam per Dominum nostrum Jesum Christum.

15:58 Itaque fratres mei dilecti, stabiles estote, et

birds, another of fishes.

15:40 And there are bodies celestial, and bodies terrestrial: but, one is the glory of the celestial, and another of the terrestrial.

15:41 One is the glory of the sun, another the glory of the moon, and another the glory of the stars. For star differeth from star in glory.

15:42 So also is the resurrection of the dead. It is sown in corruption, it shall rise in incorruption.

15:43 It is sown in dishonour, it shall rise in glory. It is sown in weakness, it shall rise in power.

15:44 It is sown a natural body, it shall rise a spiritual body. If there be a natural body, there is also a spiritual body, as it is written:

15:45 The first man Adam was made into a living soul; the last Adam into a quickening spirit.

15:46 Yet that was not first which is spiritual, but that which is natural; afterwards that which is spiritual.

15:47 The first man was of the earth, earthly: the second man, from heaven, heavenly.

15:48 Such as is the earthly, such also are the earthly: and such as is the heavenly, such also are they that are heavenly.

15:49 Therefore as we have borne the image of the earthly, let us bear also the image of the heavenly.

15:50 Now this I say, brethren, that flesh and blood cannot possess the kingdom of God: neither shall corruption possess incorruption.

15:51 Behold, I tell you a mystery. We shall all indeed rise again: but we shall not all be changed.

15:52 In a moment, in the twinkling of an eye, at the last trumpet: for the trumpet shall sound, and the dead shall rise again incorruptible: and we shall be changed.

15:53 For this corruptible must put on incorruption; and this mortal must put on immortality.

15:54 And when this mortal hath put on immortality, then shall come to pass the saying that is written: Death is swallowed up in victory.

15:55 O death, where is thy victory? O death, where is thy sting?

15:56 Now the sting of death is sin: and the power of sin is the law.

15:57 But thanks be to God, who hath given us the victory through our Lord Jesus Christ.

15:58 Therefore, my beloved brethren, be ye

immobiles : abundantes in opere Domini semper, scientes quod labor vester non est inanis in Domino.

16:1 De collectis autem, quæ fiunt in sanctos, sicut ordinavi ecclesiis Galatiæ, ita et vos facite.

16:2 Per unam sabbati unusquisque vestrum apud se seponat, recondens quod ei bene placuerit : ut non, cum venero, tunc collectæ fiant.

16:3 Cum autem præsens fuero, quos probaveritis per epistolas, hos mittam perferre gratiam vestram in Jerusalem.

16:4 Quod si dignum fuerit ut et ego eam, mecum ibunt.

16:5 Veniam autem ad vos, cum Macedoniam pertransiero : nam Macedoniam pertransibo.

16:6 Apud vos autem forsitan manebo, vel etiam hiemabo : ut vos me deducatis quocumque iero.

16:7 Nolo enim vos modo in transitu videre, spero enim me aliquantulum temporis manere apud vos, si Dominus permiserit.

16:8 Permanebo autem Ephesi usque ad Pentecosten.

16:9 Ostium enim mihi apertum est magnum, et evidens : et adversarii multi.

16:10 Si autem venerit Timotheus, videte ut sine timore sit apud vos : opus enim Domini operatur, sicut et ego.

16:11 Ne quis ergo illum spernat : deducite autem illum in pace, ut veniat ad me : exspecto enim illum cum fratribus.

16:12 De Apollo autem fratre vobis notum facio, quoniam multum rogavi eum ut veniret ad vos cum fratribus : et utique non fuit voluntas ut nunc veniret : veniet autem, cum ei vacuum fuerit.

16:13 Vigilate, state in fide, viriliter agite, et confortamini.

16:14 Omnia vestra in caritate fiant.

16:15 Obsecro autem vos fratres, nostis domum Stephanæ, et Fortunati, et Achaici : quoniam sunt primitiæ Achaiæ, et in ministerium sanctorum ordinaverunt seipsos :

16:16 ut et vos subditi sitis ejusmodi, et omni cooperanti, et laboranti.

16:17 Gaudeo autem in præsentia Stephanæ, et

steadfast and unmoveable; always abounding in the work of the Lord, knowing that your labour is not in vain in the Lord.

16:1 Now concerning the collections that are made for the saints, as I have given order to the churches of Galatia, so do ye also.

16:2 On the first day of the week let every one of you put apart with himself, laying up what it shall well please him; that when I come, the collections be not then to be made.

16:3 And when I shall be with you, whomsoever you shall approve by letters, them will I send to carry your grace to Jerusalem.

16:4 And if it be meet that I also go, they shall go with me.

16:5 Now I will come to you, when I shall have passed through Macedonia. For I shall pass through Macedonia.

16:6 And with you perhaps I shall abide, or even spend the winter: that you may bring me on my way whithersoever I shall go.

16:7 For I will not see you now by the way, for I trust that I shall abide with you some time, if the Lord permit.

16:8 But I will tarry at Ephesus until Pentecost.

16:9 For a great door and evident is opened unto me: and many adversaries.

16:10 Now if Timothy come, see that he be with you without fear, for he worketh the work of the Lord, as I also do.

16:11 Let no man therefore despise him, but conduct ye him on his way in peace: that he may come to me. For I look for him with the brethren.

16:12 And touching our brother Apollo, I give you to understand, that I much entreated him to come unto you with the brethren: and indeed it was not his will at all to come at this time. But he will come when he shall have leisure.

16:13 Watch ye, stand fast in the faith, do manfully, and be strengthened.

16:14 Let all your things be done in charity.

16:15 And I beseech you, brethren, you know the house of Stephanas, and of Fortunatus, and of Achaicus, that they are the firstfruits of Achaia, and have dedicated themselves to the ministry of the saints:

16:16 That you also be subject to such, and to every one that worketh with us, and laboureth.

16:17 And I rejoice in the presence of Stephanas,

Fortunati, et Achaici : quoniam id, quod vobis deerat, ipsi suppleverunt :

16:18 refecerunt enim et meum spiritum, et vestrum. Cognoscite ergo qui hujusmodi sunt.
16:19 Salutant vos ecclesiæ Asiæ. Salutant vos in Domino multum, Aquila et Priscilla cum domestica sua ecclesia : apud quos et hospitor.

16:20 Salutant vos omnes fratres. Salutate invicem in osculo sancto.
16:21 Salutatio, mea manu Pauli.

16:22 Si quis non amat Dominum nostrum Jesum Christum, sit anathema, Maran Atha.
16:23 Gratia Domini nostri Jesu Christi vobiscum.
16:24 Caritas mea cum omnibus vobis in Christo Jesu. Amen.

and Fortunatus, and Achaicus, because that which was wanting on your part, they have supplied.

16:18 For they have refreshed both my spirit and yours. Know them, therefore, that are such.
16:19 The churches of Asia salute you. Aquila and Priscilla salute you much in the Lord, with the church that is in their house, with whom I also lodge.

16:20 All the brethren salute you. Salute one another with a holy kiss.
16:21 The salutation of me Paul, with my own hand.

16:22 If any man love not our Lord Jesus Christ, let him be anathema, maran-atha.
16:23 The grace of our Lord Jesus Christ be with you.
16:24 My charity be with you all in Christ Jesus. Amen.

Epistula Beati Pauli Apostoli ad Corinthios Secunda

THE SECOND EPISTLE OF BLESSED PAUL THE APOSTLE TO THE CORINTHIANS

✠

1:1 PAULUS, APOSTOLUS JESU CHRISTI per voluntatem Dei, et Timotheus frater, ecclesiæ Dei, quæ est Corinthi cum omnibus sanctis, qui sunt in universa Achaia.

1:2 Gratia vobis, et pax a Deo Patre nostro, et Domino Jesu Christo.

1:3 Benedictus Deus et Pater Domini nostri Jesu Christi, Pater misericordiarum, et Deus totius consolationis,

1:4 qui consolatur nos in omni tribulatione nostra : ut possimus et ipsi consolari eos qui in omni pressura sunt, per exhortationem, qua exhortamur et ipsi a Deo.

1:5 Quoniam sicut abundant passiones Christi in nobis : ita et per Christum abundat consolatio nostra.

1:6 Sive autem tribulamur pro vestra exhortatione et salute, sive consolamur pro vestra consolatione, sive exhortamur pro vestra exhortatione et salute, quæ operatur tolerantiam earumdem passionum, quas et nos patimur :

1:7 ut spes nostra firma sit pro vobis : scientes quod sicut socii passionum estis, sic eritis et consolationis.

1:8 Non enim volumus ignorare vos, fratres, de tribulatione nostra, quæ facta est in Asia, quoniam supra modum gravati sumus supra virtutem, ita ut tæderet nos etiam vivere.

1:9 Sed ipsi in nobismetipsis responsum mortis habuimus, ut non simus fidentes in nobis, sed in Deo, qui suscitat mortuos :

1:10 qui de tantis periculis nos eripuit, et eruit : in quem speramus quoniam et adhuc eripiet,

1:11 adjuvantibus et vobis in oratione pro nobis : ut ex multorum personis, ejus quæ in nobis est donationis, per multos gratiæ agantur pro nobis.

1:12 Nam gloria nostra hæc est : testimonium conscientiæ nostræ, quod in simplicitate cordis

1:1 PAUL, AN APOSTLE OF JESUS CHRIST by the will of God, and Timothy our brother: to the church of God that is at Corinth, with all the saints that are in all Achaia:

1:2 Grace unto you and peace from God our Father, and from the Lord Jesus Christ.

1:3 Blessed be the God and Father of our Lord Jesus Christ, the Father of mercies, and the God of all comfort.

1:4 Who comforteth us in all our tribulation; that we also may be able to comfort them who are in all distress, by the exhortation wherewith we also are exhorted by God.

1:5 For as the sufferings of Christ abound in us: so also by Christ doth our comfort abound.

1:6 Now whether we be in tribulation, it is for your exhortation and salvation: or whether we be comforted, it is for your consolation: or whether we be exhorted, it is for your exhortation and salvation, which worketh the enduring of the same sufferings which we also suffer.

1:7 That our hope for you may be steadfast: knowing that as you are partakers of the sufferings, so shall you be also of the consolation.

1:8 For we would not have you ignorant,brethren, of our tribulation, which came to us in Asia, that we were pressed out of measure above our strength, so that we were weary even of life.

1:9 But we had in ourselves the answer of death, that we should not trust in ourselves, but in God who raiseth the dead.

1:10 Who hath delivered and doth deliver us out of so great dangers: in whom we trust that he will yet also deliver us.

1:11 You helping withal in prayer for us: that for this gift obtained for us, by the means of many persons, thanks may be given by many in our behalf.

1:12 For our glory is this, the testimony of our conscience, that in simplicity of heart and sin-

et sinceritate Dei, et non in sapientia carnali, sed in gratia Dei, conversati sumus in hoc mundo : abundantius autem ad vos.

1:13 Non enim alia scribimus vobis, quam quæ legistis, et cognovistis. Spero autem quod usque in finem cognoscetis,

1:14 sicut et cognovistis nos ex parte, quod gloria vestra sumus, sicut et vos nostra, in die Domini nostri Jesu Christi.

1:15 Et hac confidentia volui prius venire ad vos, ut secundam gratiam haberetis :

1:16 et per vos transire in Macedoniam, et iterum a Macedonia venire ad vos, et a vobis deduci in Judæam.

1:17 Cum ergo hoc voluissem, numquid levitate usus sum ? aut quæ cogito, secundum carnem cogito, ut sit apud me Est et Non ?

1:18 Fidelis autem Deus, quia sermo noster, qui fuit apud vos, non est in illo Est et Non.

1:19 Dei enim Filius Jesus Christus, qui in vobis per nos prædicatus est, per me, et Silvanum, et Timotheum, non fuit Est et Non, sed Est in illo fuit.

1:20 Quotquot enim promissiones Dei sunt, in illo Est : ideo et per ipsum Amen Deo ad gloriam nostram.

1:21 Qui autem confirmat nos vobiscum in Christo, et qui unxit nos Deus :

1:22 qui et signavit nos, et dedit pignus Spiritus in cordibus nostris.

1:23 Ego autem testem Deum invoco in animam meam, quod parcens vobis, non veni ultra Corinthum :

1:24 non quia dominamur fidei vestæ, sed adjutores sumus gaudii vestri : nam fide statis.

2:1 Statui autem hoc ipsum apud me, ne iterum in tristitia venirem ad vos.

2:2 Si enim ego contristo vos : et quis est, qui me lætificet, nisi qui contristatur ex me ?

2:3 Et hoc ipsum scripsi vobis, ut non cum venero, tristitiam super tristitiam habeam, de quibus oportuerat me gaudere : confidens in omnibus vobis, quia meum gaudium, omnium vestrum est.

2:4 Nam ex multa tribulatione et angustia cordis scripsi vobis per multas lacrimas : non ut contristemini, sed ut sciatis, quam caritatem habeam abundantius in vobis.

cerity of God, and not in carnal wisdom, but in the grace of God, we have conversed in this world: and more abundantly towards you.

1:13 For we write no other things to you than what you have read and known. And I hope that you shall know unto the end:

1:14 As also you have known us in part, that we are your glory, as you also are ours, in the day of our Lord Jesus Christ.

1:15 And in this confidence I had a mind to come to you before, that you might have a second grace:

1:16 And to pass by you into Macedonia, and again from Macedonia to come to you, and by you to be brought on my way towards Judea.

1:17 Whereas then I was thus minded, did I use lightness? Or, the things that I purpose, do I purpose according to the flesh, that there should be with me, It is, and It is not?

1:18 But God is faithful, for our preaching which was to you, was not, It is, and It is not.

1:19 For the Son of God, Jesus Christ who was preached among you by us, by me, and Sylvanus, and Timothy, was not, It is and It is not, but, It is, was in him.

1:20 For all the promises of God are in him, It is; therefore also by him, amen to God, unto our glory.

1:21 Now he that confirmeth us with you in Christ, and that hath anointed us, is God:

1:22 Who also hath sealed us, and given the pledge of the Spirit in our hearts.

1:23 But I call God to witness upon my soul, that to spare you, I came not any more to Corinth:

1:24 not because we exercise dominion over your faith: but we are helpers of your joy: for in faith you stand.

2:1 But I determined this with myself, not to come to you again in sorrow.

2:2 For if I make you sorrowful, who is he then that can make me glad, but the same who is made sorrowful by me?

2:3 And I wrote this same to you; that I may not, when I come, have sorrow upon sorrow, from them of whom I ought to rejoice: having confidence in you all, that my joy is the joy of you all.

2:4 For out of much affliction and anguish of heart, I wrote to you with many tears: not that you should be made sorrowful: but that you might know the charity I have more abundantly

2:5 Si quis autem contristavit, non me contristavit : sed ex parte, ut non onerem omnes vos.

2:6 Sufficit illi, qui ejusmodi est, objurgatio hæc, quæ fit a pluribus :

2:7 ita ut e contrario magis donetis, et consolemini, ne forte abundantiori tristitia absorbeatur qui ejusmodi est.

2:8 Propter quod obsecro vos, ut confirmetis in illum caritatem.

2:9 Ideo enim et scripsi, ut cognoscam experimentum vestrum, an in omnibus obedientes sitis.

2:10 Cui autem aliquid donastis, et ego : nam et ego quod donavi, si quid donavi, propter vos in persona Christi,

2:11 ut non circumveniamur a Satana : non enim ignoramus cogitationes ejus.

2:12 Cum venissem autem Troadem propter Evangelium Christi, et ostium mihi apertum esset in Domino,

2:13 non habui requiem spiritui meo, eo quod non invenerim Titum fratrem meum, sed valefaciens eis, profectus sum in Macedoniam.

2:14 Deo autem gratias, qui semper triumphat nos in Christo Jesu, et odorem notitiæ suæ manifestat per nos in omni loco :

2:15 quia Christi bonus odor sumus Deo in iis qui salvi fiunt, et in iis qui pereunt :

2:16 aliis quidem odor mortis in mortem : aliis autem odor vitæ in vitam. Et ad hæc quis tam idoneus ?

2:17 non enim sumus sicut plurimi, adulterantes verbum Dei, sed ex sinceritate, sed sicut ex Deo, coram Deo, in Christo loquimur.

3:1 Incipimus iterum nosmetipsos commendare ? aut numquid egemus (sicut quidam) commendatitiis epistolis ad vos, aut ex vobis ?

3:2 Epistola nostra vos estis, scripta in cordibus nostris, quæ scitur, et legitur ab omnibus hominibus :

3:3 manifestati quod epistola estis Christi, ministrata a nobis, et scripta non atramento, sed Spiritu Dei vivi : non in tabulis lapideis, sed in tabulis cordis carnalibus.

3:4 Fiduciam autem talem habemus per Christum ad Deum :

towards you.

2:5 And if any one have caused grief, he hath not grieved me; but in part, that I may not burden you all.

2:6 To him who is such a one, this rebuke is sufficient, which is given by many:

2:7 So that on the contrary, you should rather forgive him and comfort him, lest perhaps such a one be swallowed up with overmuch sorrow.

2:8 Wherefore, I beseech you, that you would confirm your charity towards him.

2:9 For to this end also did I write, that I may know the experiment of you, whether you be obedient in all things.

2:10 And to whom you have pardoned any thing, I also. For, what I have pardoned, if I have pardoned any thing, for your sakes have I done it in the person of Christ.

2:11 That we be not overreached by Satan. For we are not ignorant of his devices.

2:12 And when I was come to Troas for the gospel of Christ, and a door was opened unto me in the Lord,

2:13 I had no rest in my spirit, because I found not Titus my brother; but bidding them farewell, I went into Macedonia.

2:14 Now thanks be to God, who always maketh us to triumph in Christ Jesus, and manifesteth the odour of his knowledge by us in every place.

2:15 For we are the good odour of Christ unto God, in them that are saved, and in them that perish.

2:16 To the one indeed the odour of death unto death: but to the others the odour of life unto life. And for these things who is so sufficient?

2:17 For we are not as many, adulterating the word of God; but with sincerity, but as from God, before God, in Christ we speak.

3:1 Do we begin again to commend ourselves? Or do we need (as some do) epistles of commendation to you, or from you?

3:2 You are our epistle, written in our hearts, which is known and read by all men:

3:3 Being manifested, that you are the epistle of Christ, ministered by us, and written not with ink, but with the Spirit of the living God; not in tables of stone, but in the fleshly tables of the heart.

3:4 And such confidence we have, through Christ, towards God.

3:5 non quod sufficientes simus cogitare aliquid a nobis, quasi ex nobis : sed sufficientia nostra ex Deo est :

3:6 qui et idoneos nos fecit ministros novi testamenti : non littera, sed Spiritu : littera enim occidit, Spiritus autem vivificat.

3:7 Quod si ministratio mortis litteris deformata in lapidibus fuit in gloria, ita ut non possent intendere filii Israël in faciem Moysi propter gloriam vultus ejus, quæ evacuatur :

3:8 quomodo non magis ministratio Spiritus erit in gloria ?

3:9 Nam si ministratio damnationis gloria est : multo magis abundat ministerium justitiæ in gloria.

3:10 Nam nec glorificatum est, quod claruit in hac parte, propter excellentem gloriam.

3:11 Si enim quod evacuatur, per gloriam est : multo magis quod manet, in gloria est.

3:12 Habentes igitur talem spem, multa fiducia utimur :

3:13 et non sicut Moyses ponebat velamen super faciem suam, ut non intenderent filii Israël in faciem ejus, quod evacuatur,

3:14 sed obtusi sunt sensus eorum. Usque in hodiernum enim diem, idipsum velamen in lectione veteris testamenti manet non revelatum (quoniam in Christo evacuatur),

3:15 sed usque in hodiernum diem, cum legitur Moyses, velamen positum est super cor eorum.

3:16 Cum autem conversus fuerit ad Dominum, auferetur velamen.

3:17 Dominus autem Spiritus est : ubi autem Spiritus Domini, ibi libertas.

3:18 Nos vero omnes, revelata facie gloriam Domini speculantes, in eamdem imaginem transformamur a claritate in claritatem, tamquam a Domini Spiritu.

4:1 Ideo habentes administrationem, juxta quod misericordiam consecuti sumus, non deficimus,

4:2 sed abdicamus occulta dedecoris, non ambulantes in astutia, neque adulterantes verbum Dei, sed in manifestatione veritatis commendantes nosmetipsos ad omnem conscientiam hominum coram Deo.

4:3 Quod si etiam opertum est Evangelium nostrum, in iis, qui pereunt, est opertum :

4:4 in quibus Deus hujus sæculi excæcavit

3:5 Not that we are sufficient to think any thing of ourselves, as of ourselves: but our sufficiency is from God.

3:6 Who also hath made us fit ministers of the new testament, not in the letter, but in the spirit. For the letter killeth, but the spirit quickeneth.

3:7 Now if the ministration of death, engraven with letters upon stones, was glorious; so that the children of Israel could not steadfastly behold the face of Moses, for the glory of his countenance, which is made void:

3:8 How shall not the ministration of the spirit be rather in glory?

3:9 For if the ministration of condemnation be glory, much more the ministration of justice aboundeth in glory.

3:10 For even that which was glorious in this part was not glorified, by reason of the glory that excelleth.

3:11 For if that which is done away was glorious, much more that which remaineth is in glory.

3:12 Having therefore such hope, we use much confidence:

3:13 And not as Moses put a veil upon his face, that the children of Israel might not steadfastly look on the face of that which is made void.

3:14 But their senses were made dull. For, until this present day, the selfsame veil, in the reading of the old testament, remaineth not taken away (because in Christ it is made void).

3:15 But even until this day, when Moses is read, the veil is upon their heart.

3:16 But when they shall be converted to the Lord, the veil shall be taken away.

3:17 Now the Lord is a Spirit. And where the Spirit of the Lord is, there is liberty.

3:18 But we all beholding the glory of the Lord with open face, are transformed into the same image from glory to glory, as by the Spirit of the Lord.

4:1 Therefore, seeing we have this ministration, according as we have obtained mercy, we faint not;

4:2 But we renounce the hidden things of dishonesty, not walking in craftiness, nor adulterating the word of God; but by manifestation of the truth commending ourselves to every man's conscience, in the sight of God.

4:3 And if our gospel be also hid, it is hid to them that are lost,

4:4 In whom the god of this world hath blinded

mentes infidelium, ut non fulgeat illis illuminatio Evangelii gloriæ Christi, qui est imago Dei.

4:5 Non enim nosmetipsos prædicamus, sed Jesum Christum Dominum nostrum : nos autem servos vestros per Jesum :

4:6 quoniam Deus, qui dixit de tenebris lucem splendescere, ipse illuxit in cordibus nostris ad illuminationem scientiæ claritatis Dei, in facie Christi Jesu.

4:7 Habemus autem thesaurum istum in vasis fictilibus : ut sublimitas sit virtutis Dei, et non ex nobis.

4:8 In omnibus tribulationem patimur, sed non angustiamur : aporiamur, sed non destituimur :

4:9 persecutionem patimur, sed non derelinquimur : dejicimur, sed non perimus :

4:10 semper mortificationem Jesu in corpore nostro circumferentes, ut et vita Jesu manifestetur in corporibus nostris.

4:11 Semper enim nos, qui vivimus, in mortem tradimur propter Jesum : ut et vita Jesu manifestetur in carne nostra mortali.

4:12 Ergo mors in nobis operatur, vita autem in vobis.

4:13 Habentes autem eumdem spiritum fidei, sicut scriptum est : Credidi, propter quod locutus sum : et nos credimus, propter quod et loquimur :

4:14 scientes quoniam qui suscitavit Jesum, et nos cum Jesu suscitabit, et constituet vobiscum.

4:15 Omnia enim propter vos : ut gratia abundans, per multos in gratiarum actione, abundet in gloriam Dei.

4:16 Propter quod non deficimus : sed licet is, qui foris est, noster homo corrumpatur, tamen is, qui intus est, renovatur de die in diem.

4:17 Id enim, quod in præsenti est momentaneum et leve tribulationis nostræ, supra modum in sublimitate æternum gloriæ pondus operatur in nobis,

4:18 non contemplantibus nobis quæ videntur, sed quæ non videntur. Quæ enim videntur, temporalia sunt : quæ autem non videntur, æterna sunt.

5:1 Scimus enim quoniam si terrestris domus nostra hujus habitationis dissolvatur, quod ædificationem ex Deo habemus, domum non manufactam, æternam in cælis.

5:2 Nam et in hoc ingemiscimus, habitationem

the minds of unbelievers, that the light of the gospel of the glory of Christ, who is the image of God, should not shine unto them.

4:5 For we preach not ourselves, but Jesus Christ our Lord; and ourselves your servants through Jesus.

4:6 For God, who commanded the light to shine out of darkness, hath shined in our hearts, to give the light of the knowledge of the glory of God, in the face of Christ Jesus.

4:7 But we have this treasure in earthen vessels, that the excellency may be of the power of God, and not of us.

4:8 In all things we suffer tribulation, but are not distressed; we are straitened, but are not destitute;

4:9 We suffer persecution, but are not forsaken; we are cast down, but we perish not:

4:10 Always bearing about in our body the mortification of Jesus, that the life also of Jesus may be made manifest in our bodies.

4:11 For we who live are always delivered unto death for Jesus' sake; that the life also of Jesus may be made manifest in our mortal flesh.

4:12 So then death worketh in us, but life in you.

4:13 But having the same spirit of faith, as it is written: I believed, for which cause I have spoken; we also believe, for which cause we speak also:

4:14 Knowing that he who raised up Jesus, will raise us up also with Jesus, and place us with you.

4:15 For all things are for your sakes; that the grace abounding through many, may abound in thanksgiving unto the glory of God.

4:16 For which cause we faint not; but though our outward man is corrupted, yet the inward man is renewed day by day.

4:17 For that which is at present momentary and light of our tribulation, worketh for us above measure exceedingly an eternal weight of glory.

4:18 While we look not at the things which are seen, but at the things which are not seen. For the things which are seen, are temporal; but the things which are not seen, are eternal.

5:1 For we know, if our earthly house of this habitation be dissolved, that we have a building of God, a house not made with hands, eternal in heaven.

5:2 For in this also we groan, desiring to be

nostram, quæ de cælo est, superindui cupientes :

5:3 si tamen vestiti, non nudi inveniamur.

5:4 Nam et qui sumus in hoc tabernaculo, ingemiscimus gravati : eo quod nolumus expoliari, sed supervestiri, ut absorbeatur quod mortale est, a vita.

5:5 Qui autem efficit nos in hoc ipsum, Deus, qui dedit nobis pignus Spiritus.

5:6 Audentes igitur semper, scientes quoniam dum sumus in corpore, peregrinamur a Domino

5:7 (per fidem enim ambulamus, et non per speciem) :

5:8 audemus autem, et bonam voluntatem habemus magis peregrinari a corpore, et præsentes esse ad Dominum.

5:9 Et ideo contendimus, sive absentes, sive præsentes, placere illi.

5:10 Omnes enim nos manifestari oportet ante tribunal Christi, ut referat unusquisque propria corporis, prout gessit, sive bonum, sive malum.

5:11 Scientes ergo timorem Domini, hominibus suademus, Deo autem manifesti sumus. Spero autem et in conscientiis vestris manifestos nos esse.

5:12 Non iterum commendamus nos vobis, sed occasionem damus vobis gloriandi pro nobis : ut habeatis ad eos qui in facie gloriantur, et non in corde.

5:13 Sive enim mente excedimus Deo : sive sobrii sumus, vobis.

5:14 Caritas enim Christi urget nos : æstimantes hoc, quoniam si unus pro omnibus mortuus est, ergo omnes mortui sunt :

5:15 et pro omnibus mortuus est Christus : ut, et qui vivunt, jam non sibi vivant, sed ei qui pro ipsis mortuus est et resurrexit.

5:16 Itaque nos ex hoc neminem novimus secundum carnem. Et si cognovimus secundum carnem Christum, sed nunc jam non novimus.

5:17 Si qua ergo in Christo nova creatura, vetera transierunt : ecce facta sunt omnia nova.

5:18 Omnia autem ex Deo, qui nos reconciliavit sibi per Christum : et dedit nobis ministerium reconciliationis,

5:19 quoniam quidem Deus erat in Christo

clothed upon with our habitation that is from heaven.

5:3 Yet so that we be found clothed, not naked.

5:4 For we also, who are in this tabernacle, do groan, being burthened; because we would not be unclothed, but clothed upon, that that which is mortal may be swallowed up by life.

5:5 Now he that maketh us for this very thing, is God, who hath given us the pledge of the Spirit.

5:6 Therefore having always confidence, knowing that, while we are in the body, we are absent from the Lord.

5:7 (For we walk by faith, and not by sight.)

5:8 But we are confident, and have a good will to be absent rather from the body, and to be present with the Lord.

5:9 And therefore we labour, whether absent or present, to please him.

5:10 For we must all be manifested before the judgement seat of Christ, that every one may receive the proper things of the body, according as he hath done, whether it be good or evil.

5:11 Knowing therefore the fear of the Lord, we use persuasion to men; but to God we are manifest. And I trust also that in your consciences we are manifest.

5:12 We commend not ourselves again to you, but give you occasion to glory in our behalf; that you may have somewhat to answer them who glory in face, and not in heart.

5:13 For whether we be transported in mind, it is to God; or whether we be sober, it is for you.

5:14 For the charity of Christ presseth us: judging this, that if one died for all, then all were dead.

5:15 And Christ died for all; that they also who live, may not now live to themselves, but unto him who died for them, and rose again.

5:16 Wherefore henceforth, we know no man according to the flesh. And if we have known Christ according to the flesh; but now we know him so no longer.

5:17 If then any be in Christ a new creature, the old things are passed away, behold all things are made new.

5:18 But all things are of God, who hath reconciled us to himself by Christ; and hath given to us the ministry of reconciliation.

5:19 For God indeed was in Christ, reconciling

mundum reconcilians sibi, non reputans illis delicta ipsorum, et posuit in nobis verbum reconciliationis.

5:20 Pro Christo ergo legatione fungimur, tamquam Deo exhortante per nos. Obsecramus pro Christo, reconciliamini Deo.

5:21 Eum, qui non noverat peccatum, pro nobis peccatum fecit, ut nos efficeremur justitia Dei in ipso.

6:1 Adjuvantes autem exhortamur ne in vacuum gratiam Dei recipiatis.

6:2 Ait enim : Tempore accepto exaudivi te, et in die salutis adjuvi te. Ecce nunc tempus acceptabile, ecce nunc dies salutis.

6:3 Nemini dantes ullam offensionem, ut non vituperetur ministerium nostrum :

6:4 sed in omnibus exhibeamus nosmetipsos sicut Dei ministros in multa patientia, in tribulationibus, in necessitatibus, in angustiis,

6:5 in plagis, in carceribus, in seditionibus, in laboribus, in vigiliis, in jejuniis,

6:6 in castitate, in scientia, in longanimitate, in suavitate, in Spiritu Sancto, in caritate non ficta,

6:7 in verbo veritatis, in virtute Dei, per arma justitiæ a dextris et a sinistris,

6:8 per gloriam, et ignobilitatem, per infamiam, et bonam famam : ut seductores, et veraces, sicut qui ignoti, et cogniti :

6:9 quasi morientes, et ecce vivimus : ut castigati, et non mortificati :

6:10 quasi tristes, semper autem gaudentes : sicut egentes, multos autem locupletantes : tamquam nihil habentes, et omnia possidentes.

6:11 Os nostrum patet ad vos, o Corinthii ; cor nostrum dilatatum est.

6:12 Non angustiamini in nobis : angustiamini autem in visceribus vestris :

6:13 eamdem autem habentes remunerationem, tamquam filiis dico, dilatamini et vos.

6:14 Nolite jugum ducere cum infidelibus. Quæ enim participatio justitiæ cum iniquitate ? aut quæ societas luci ad tenebras ?

6:15 quæ autem conventio Christi ad Belial ? aut quæ pars fideli cum infideli ?

6:16 qui autem consensus templo Dei cum idolis ? vos enim estis templum Dei vivi, sicut dicit Deus : *Quoniam inhabitabo in illis, et inambulabo inter eos, et ero illorum Deus, et ipsi erunt mihi pop-*

the world to himself, not imputing to them their sins; and he hath placed in us the word of reconciliation.

5:20 For Christ therefore we are ambassadors, God as it were exhorting by us. For Christ, we beseech you, be reconciled to God.

5:21 Him, who knew no sin, he hath made sin for us, that we might be made the justice of God in him.

6:1 And we helping do exhort you, that you receive not the grace of God in vain.

6:2 For he saith: In an accepted time have I heard thee; and in the day of salvation have I helped thee. Behold, now is the acceptable time; behold, now is the day of salvation.

6:3 Giving no offence to any man, that our ministry be not blamed:

6:4 But in all things let us exhibit ourselves as the ministers of God, in much patience, in tribulation, in necessities, in distresses,

6:5 In stripes, in prisons, in seditions, in labours, in watchings, in fastings,

6:6 In chastity, in knowledge, in longsuffering, in sweetness, in the Holy Ghost, in charity unfeigned,

6:7 In the word of truth, in the power of God; by the armour of justice on the right hand and on the left;

6:8 By honour and dishonour, by evil report and good report; as deceivers, and yet true; as unknown, and yet known;

6:9 As dying, and behold we live; as chastised, and not killed;

6:10 As sorrowful, yet always rejoicing; as needy, yet enriching many; as having nothing, and possessing all things.

6:11 Our mouth is open to you, O ye Corinthians, our heart is enlarged.

6:12 You are not straitened in us, but in your own bowels you are straitened.

6:13 But having the same recompense, (I speak as to my children,) be you also enlarged.

6:14 Bear not the yoke with unbelievers. For what participation hath justice with injustice? Or what fellowship hath light with darkness?

6:15 And what concord hath Christ with Belial? Or what part hath the faithful with the unbeliever?

6:16 And what agreement hath the temple of God with idols? For you are the temple of the living God; as God saith: *I will dwell in them, and walk among them; and I will be their God, and they*

ulus.

6:17 *Propter quod exite de medio eorum, et separamini, dicit Dominus, et immundum ne tetigeritis :*

6:18 *et ego recipiam vos : et ero vobis in patrem, et vos eritis mihi in filios et filias, dicit Dominus omnipotens.*

7:1 Has ergo habentes promissiones, carissimi, mundemus nos ab omni inquinamento carnis et spiritus, perficientes sanctificationem in timore Dei.

7:2 Capite nos. Neminem læsimus, neminem corrupimus, neminem circumvenimus.

7:3 Non ad condemnationem vestram dico : prædiximus enim quod in cordibus nostris estis ad commoriendum et ad convivendum.

7:4 Multa mihi fiducia est apud vos, multa mihi gloriatio pro vobis : repletus sum consolatione ; superabundo gaudio in omni tribulatione nostra.

7:5 Nam et cum venissemus in Macedoniam, nullam requiem habuit caro nostra, sed omnem tribulationem passi sumus : foris pugnæ, intus timores.

7:6 Sed qui consolatur humiles, consolatus est nos Deus in adventu Titi.

7:7 Non solum autem in adventu ejus, sed etiam in consolatione, qua consolatus est in vobis, referens nobis vestrum desiderium, vestrum fletum, vestram æmulationem pro me, ita ut magis gauderem.

7:8 Quoniam etsi contristavi vos in epistola, non me pœnitet : etsi pœniteret, videns quod epistola illa (etsi ad horam) vos contristavit,

7:9 nunc gaudeo : non quia contristati estis, sed quia contristati estis ad pœnitentiam. Contristati enim estis ad Deum, ut in nullo detrimentum patiamini ex nobis.

7:10 Quæ enim secundum Deum tristitia est, pœnitentiam in salutem stabilem operatur : sæculi autem tristitia mortem operatur.

7:11 Ecce enim hoc ipsum, secundum Deum contristari vos, quantam in vobis operatur sollicitudinem : sed defensionem, sed indignationem, sed timorem, sed desiderium, sed æmulationem, sed vindictam : in omnibus exhibuistis vos incontaminatos esse negotio.

7:12 Igitur, etsi scripsi vobis, non propter eum qui fecit injuriam, nec propter eum qui passus

shall be my people.

6:17 *Wherefore, Go out from among them, and be ye separate, saith the Lord, and touch not the unclean thing:*

6:18 *And I will receive you; and I will be a Father to you; and you shall be my sons and daughters, saith the Lord Almighty.*

7:1 Having therefore these promises, dearly beloved, let us cleanse ourselves from all defilement of the flesh and of the spirit, perfecting sactification in the fear of God.

7:2 Receive us. We have injured no man, we have corrupted no man, we have overreached no man.

7:3 I speak not this to your condemnation. For we have said before, that you are in our hearts, to die together, and to live together.

7:4 Great is my confidence for you, great is my glorying for you. I am filled with comfort: I exceedingly abound with joy in all our tribulation.

7:5 For also when we were come into Macedonia, our flesh had no rest, but we suffered all tribulation; combats without, fears within.

7:6 But God, who comforteth the humble, comforted us by the coming of Titus.

7:7 And not by his coming only, but also by the consolation, wherewith he was comforted in you, relating to us your desire, your mourning, your zeal for me, so that I rejoiced the more.

7:8 For although I made you sorrowful by my epistle, I do not repent; and if I did repent, seeing that the same epistle (although but for a time) did make you sorrowful;

7:9 Now I am glad: not because you were made sorrowful; but because you were made sorrowful unto penance. For you were made sorrowful according to God, that you might suffer damage by us in nothing.

7:10 For the sorrow that is according to God worketh penance, steadfast unto salvation; but the sorrow of the world worketh death.

7:11 For behold this selfsame thing, that you were made sorrowful according to God, how great carefulness it worketh in you; yea defence, yea indignation, yea fear, yea desire, yea zeal, yea revenge: in all things you have shewed yourselves to be undefiled in the matter.

7:12 Wherefore although I wrote to you, it was not for his sake that I did the wrong, nor for

est : sed ad manifestandam sollicitudinem nostram, quam habemus pro vobis

7:13 coram Deo : ideo consolati sumus. In consolatione autem nostra, abundantius magis gavisi sumus super gaudio Titi, quia refectus est spiritus ejus ab omnibus vobis :

7:14 et si quid apud illum de vobis gloriatus sum, non sum confusus : sed sicut omnia vobis in veritate locuti sumus, ita et gloriatio nostra, quæ fuit ad Titum, veritas facta est,

7:15 et viscera ejus abundantius in vobis sunt, reminiscentis omnium vestrum obedientiam : quomodo cum timore et tremore excepistis illum.

7:16 Gaudeo quod in omnibus confido in vobis.

8:1 Notam autem facimus vobis, fratres, gratiam Dei, quæ data est in ecclesiis Macedoniæ :

8:2 quod in multo experimento tribulationis abundantia gaudii ipsorum fuit, et altissima paupertas eorum, abundavit in divitias simplicitatis eorum :

8:3 quia secundum virtutem testimonium illis reddo, et supra virtutem voluntarii fuerunt,

8:4 cum multa exhortatione obsecrantes nos gratiam, et communicationem ministerii, quod fit in sanctos.

8:5 Et non sicut speravimus, sed semetipsos dederunt primum Domino, deinde nobis per voluntatem Dei,

8:6 ita ut rogaremus Titum, ut quemadmodum cœpit, ita et perficiat in vobis etiam gratiam istam.

8:7 Sed sicut in omnibus abundatis fide, et sermone, et scientia, et omni sollicitudine, insuper et caritate vestra in nos, ut et in hac gratia abundetis.

8:8 Non quasi imperans dico : sed per aliorum sollicitudinem, etiam vestræ caritatis ingenium bonum comprobans.

8:9 Scitis enim gratiam Domini nostri Jesu Christi, quoniam propter vos egenus factus est, cum esset dives, ut illius inopia vos divites essetis.

8:10 Et consilium in hoc do : hoc enim vobis utile est, qui non solum facere, sed et velle cœpistis ab anno priore :

8:11 nunc vero et facto perficite : ut quemadmodum promptus est animus voluntatis, ita sit

him that suffered it; but to manifest our carefulness that we have for you

7:13 Before God: therefore we were comforted. But in our consolation, we did the more abundantly rejoice for the joy of Titus, because his spirit was refreshed by you all.

7:14 And if I have boasted any thing to him of you, I have not been put to shame; but as we have spoken all things to you in truth, so also our boasting that was made to Titus is found a truth.

7:15 And his bowels are more abundantly towards you; remembering the obedience of you all, how with fear and trembling you received him.

7:16 I rejoice that in all things I have confidence in you.

8:1 Now we make known unto you, brethren, the grace of God, that hath been given in the churches of Macedonia.

8:2 That in much experience of tribulation, they have had abundance of joy; and their very deep poverty hath abounded unto the riches of their simplicity.

8:3 For according to their power (I bear them witness), and beyond their power, they were willing.

8:4 With much entreaty begging of us the grace and communication of the ministry that is done toward the saints.

8:5 And not as we hoped, but they gave their own selves first to the Lord, then to us by the will of God:

8:6 Insomuch, that we desired Titus, that as he had begun, so also he would finish among you this same grace.

8:7 That as in all things you abound in faith, and word, and knowledge, and all carefulness; moreover also in your charity towards us, so in this grace also you may abound.

8:8 I speak not as commanding; but by the carefulness of others, approving also the good disposition of your charity.

8:9 For you know the grace of our Lord Jesus Christ, that being rich he became poor, for your sakes; that through his poverty you might be rich.

8:10 And herein I give my advice; for this is profitable for you, who have begun not only to do, but also to be willing, a year ago.

8:11 Now therefore perform ye it also in deed; that as your mind is forward to be willing, so it

et perficiendi ex eo quod habetis.

8:12 Si enim voluntas prompta est, secundum id quod habet, accepta est, non secundum id quod non habet.

8:13 Non enim ut aliis sit remissio, vobis autem tribulatio, sed ex æqualitate.

8:14 In præsenti tempore vestra abundantia illorum inopiam suppleat : ut et illorum abundantia vestræ inopiæ sit supplementum, ut fiat æqualitas, sicut scriptum est :

8:15 Qui multum, non abundavit : et qui modicum, non minoravit.

8:16 Gratias autem Deo, qui dedit eamdem sollicitudinem pro vobis in corde Titi,

8:17 quoniam exhortationem quidem suscepit : sed cum sollicitior esset, sua voluntate profectus est ad vos.

8:18 Misimus etiam cum illo fratrem, cujus laus est in Evangelio per omnes ecclesias :

8:19 non solum autem, sed et ordinatus est ab ecclesiis comes peregrinationis nostræ in hanc gratiam, quæ ministratur a nobis ad Domini gloriam, et destinatam voluntatem nostram :

8:20 devitantes hoc, ne quis nos vituperet in hac plenitudine, quæ ministratur a nobis.

8:21 Providemus enim bona non solum coram Deo, sed etiam coram hominibus.

8:22 Misimus autem cum illis et fratrem nostrum, quem probavimus in multis sæpe sollicitum esse : nunc autem multo sollicitiorem, confidentia multa in vos,

8:23 sive pro Tito, qui est socius meus, et in vos adjutor, sive fratres nostri, Apostoli ecclesiarum, gloria Christi.

8:24 Ostensionem ergo, quæ est caritatis vestræ, et nostræ gloriæ pro vobis, in illos ostendite in faciem ecclesiarum.

9:1 Nam de ministerio, quod fit in sanctos ex abundanti est mihi scribere vobis.

9:2 Scio enim promptum animum vestrum : pro quo de vobis glorior apud Macedones. Quoniam et Achaia parata est ab anno præterito, et vestra æmulatio provocavit plurimos.

9:3 Misi autem fratres : ut ne quod gloriamur de vobis, evacuetur in hac parte, ut (quemadmodum dixi) parati sitis :

may be also to perform, out of that which you have.

8:12 For if the will be forward, it is accepted according to that which a man hath, not according to that which he hath not.

8:13 For I mean not that others should be eased, and you burthened, but by an equality.

8:14 In this present time let your abundance supply their want, that their abundance also may supply your want, that there may be an equality,

8:15 As it is written: He that had much, had nothing over; and he that had little, had no want.

8:16 And thanks be to God, who hath given the same carefulness for you in the heart of Titus.

8:17 For indeed he accepted the exhortation; but being more careful, of his own will he went unto you.

8:18 We have sent also with him the brother, whose praise is in the gospel through all the churches.

8:19 And not that only, but he was also ordained by the churches companion of our travels, for this grace, which is administered by us, to the glory of the Lord, and our determined will:

8:20 Avoiding this, lest any man should blame us in this abundance which is administered by us.

8:21 For we forecast what may be good not only before God, but also before men.

8:22 And we have sent with them our brother also, whom we have often proved diligent in many things; but now much more diligent, with much confidence in you,

8:23 Either for Titus, who is my companion and fellow labourer towards you, or our brethren, the apostles of the churches, the glory of Christ.

8:24 Wherefore shew ye to them, in the sight of the churches, the evidence of your charity, and of our boasting on your behalf.

9:1 For concerning the ministry that is done towards the saints, it is superfluous for me to write unto you.

9:2 For I know your forward mind: for which I boast of you to the Macedonians. That Achaia also is ready from the year past, and your emulation hath provoked very many.

9:3 Now I have sent the brethren, that the thing which we boast of concerning you, be not made void in this behalf, that (as I have said) you may be ready:

9:4 ne cum venerint Macedones mecum, et invenerint vos imparatos, erubescamus nos (ut non dicamus vos) in hac substantia.

9:5 Necessarium ergo existimavi rogare fratres, ut præveniant ad vos, et præparent repromissam benedictionem hanc paratam esse sic, quasi benedictionem, non tamquam avaritiam.

9:6 Hoc autem dico : qui parce seminat, parce et metet : et qui seminat in benedictionibus, de benedictionibus et metet.

9:7 Unusquisque, prout destinavit in corde suo, non ex tristitia, aut ex necessitate : hilarem enim datorem diligit Deus.

9:8 Potens est autem Deus omnem gratiam abundare facere in vobis : ut in omnibus semper omnem sufficientiam habentes, abundetis in omne opus bonum,

9:9 sicut scriptum est : Dispersit, dedit pauperibus : justitia ejus manet in sæculum sæculi.

9:10 Qui autem administrat semen seminanti : et panem ad manducandum præstabit, et multiplicabit semen vestrum, et augebit incrementa frugum justitiæ vestræ :

9:11 ut in omnibus locupletati abundetis in omnem simplicitatem, quæ operatur per nos gratiarum actionem Deo.

9:12 Quoniam ministerium hujus officii non solum supplet ea quæ desunt sanctis, sed etiam abundat per multas gratiarum actiones in Domino,

9:13 per probationem ministerii hujus, glorificantes Deum in obedientia confessionis vestræ, in Evangelium Christi, et simplicitate communicationis in illos, et in omnes,

9:14 et in ipsorum obsecratione pro vobis, desiderantium vos propter eminentem gratiam Dei in vobis.

9:15 Gratias Deo super inenarrabili dono ejus.

10:1 Ipse autem ego Paulus obsecro vos per mansuetudinem et modestiam Christi, qui in facie quidem humilis sum inter vos, absens autem confido in vos.

10:2 Rogo autem vos ne præsens audeam per eam confidentiam, qua existimor audere in quosdam, qui arbitrantur nos tamquam secundum carnem ambulemus.

10:3 In carne enim ambulantes, non secundum carnem militamus.

10:4 Nam arma militiæ nostræ non carnalia sunt, sed potentia Deo ad destructionem muni-

9:4 Lest, when the Macedonians shall come with me, and find you unprepared, we (not to say ye) should be ashamed in this matter.

9:5 Therefore I thought it necessary to desire the brethren that they would go to you before, and prepare this blessing before promised, to be ready, so as a blessing, not as covetousness.

9:6 Now this I say: He who soweth sparingly, shall also reap sparingly: and he who soweth in blessings, shall also reap blessings.

9:7 Every one as he hath determined in his heart, not with sadness, or of necessity: for God loveth a cheerful giver.

9:8 And God is able to make all grace abound in you; that ye always, having all sufficiency in all things, may abound to every good work,

9:9 As it is written: He hath dispersed abroad, he hath given to the poor: his justice remaineth for ever.

9:10 And he that ministereth seed to the sower, will both give you bread to eat, and will multiply your seed, and increase the growth of the fruits of your justice:

9:11 That being enriched in all things, you may abound unto all simplicity, which worketh through us thanksgiving to God.

9:12 Because the administration of this office doth not only supply the want of the saints, but aboundeth also by many thanksgivings in the Lord,

9:13 By the proof of this ministry, glorifying God for the obedience of your confession unto the gospel of Christ, and for the simplicity of your communicating unto them, and unto all.

9:14 And in their praying for you, being desirous of you, because of the excellent grace of God in you.

9:15 Thanks be to God for his unspeakable gift.

10:1 Now I Paul myself beseech you, by the mildness and modesty of Christ, who in presence indeed am lowly among you, but being absent, am bold toward you.

10:2 But I beseech you, that I may not be bold when I am present, with that confidence wherewith I am thought to be bold, against some, who reckon us as if we walked according to the flesh.

10:3 For though we walk in the flesh, we do not war according to the flesh.

10:4 For the weapons of our warfare are not carnal, but mighty to God unto the pulling down

tionum, consilia destruentes,

10:5 et omnem altitudinem extollentem se adversus scientiam Dei, et in captivitatem redigentes omnem intellectum in obsequium Christi,

10:6 et in promptu habentes ulcisci omnem inobedientiam, cum impleta fuerit vestra obedientia.

10:7 Quæ secundum faciem sunt, videte. Si quis confidit sibi Christi se esse, hoc cogitet iterum apud se : quia sicut ipse Christi est, ita et nos.

10:8 Nam etsi amplius aliquid gloriatus fuero de potestate nostra, quam dedit nobis Dominus in ædificationem, et non in destructionem vestram, non erubescam.

10:9 Ut autem non existimer tamquam terrere vos per epistolas :

10:10 quoniam quidem epistolæ, inquiunt, graves sunt et fortes : præsentia autem corporis infirma, et sermo contemptibilis :

10:11 hoc cogitet qui ejusmodi est, quia quales sumus verbo per epistolas absentes, tales et præsentes in facto.

10:12 Non enim audemus inserere, aut comparare nos quibusdam, qui seipsos commendant : sed ipsi in nobis nosmetipsos metientes, et comparantes nosmetipsos nobis.

10:13 Nos autem non in immensum gloriabimur, sed secundum mensuram regulæ, qua mensus est nobis Deus, mensuram pertingendi usque ad vos.

10:14 Non enim quasi non pertingentes ad vos, superextendimus nos : usque ad vos enim pervenimus in Evangelio Christi.

10:15 Non in immensum gloriantes in alienis laboribus : spem autem habentes crescentis fidei vestræ, in vobis magnificari secundum regulam nostram in abundantiam,

10:16 etiam in illa, quæ ultra vos sunt, evangelizare, non in aliena regula in iis quæ præparata sunt gloriari.

10:17 Qui autem gloriatur, in Domino glorietur.

10:18 Non enim qui seipsum commendat, ille probatus est : sed quem Deus commendat.

11:1 Utinam sustineretis modicum quid insipientiæ meæ, sed et supportare me :

11:2 æmulor enim vos Dei æmulatione. Despondi enim vos uni viro, virginem castam ex-

of fortifications, destroying counsels,

10:5 And every height that exhalteth itself against the knowledge of God, and bringing into captivity every understanding unto the obedience of Christ;

10:6 And having in readiness to revenge all disobedience, when your obedience shall be fulfilled.

10:7 See the things that are according to outward appearance. If any man trust to himself, that he is Christ's, let him think this again with himself, that as he is Christ's, so are we also.

10:8 For if also I should boast somewhat more of our power, which the Lord hath given us unto edification, and not for your destruction, I should not be ashamed.

10:9 But that I may not be thought as it were to terrify you by epistles,

10:10 (For his epistles indeed, say they, are weighty and strong; but his bodily presence is weak, and his speech contemptible,)

10:11 Let such a one think this, that such as we are in word by epistles, when absent, such also we will be indeed when present.

10:12 For we dare not match, or compare ourselves with some, that commend themselves; but we measure ourselves by ourselves, and compare ourselves with ourselves.

10:13 But we will not glory beyond our measure; but according to the measure of the rule, which God hath measured to us, a measure to reach even unto you.

10:14 For we stretch not ourselves beyond our measure, as if we reached not unto you. For we are come as far as to you in the gospel of Christ.

10:15 Not glorying beyond measure in other men's labours; but having hope of your increasing faith, to be magnified in you according to our rule abundantly;

10:16 Yea, unto those places that are beyond you, to preach the gospel, not to glory in another man's rule, in those things that are made ready to our hand.

10:17 But he that glorieth, let him glory in the Lord.

10:18 For not he who commendeth himself, is approved, but he, whom God commendeth.

11:1 Would to God you could bear with some little of my folly: but do bear with me.

11:2 For I am jealous of you with the jealousy of God. For I have espoused you to one husband

hibere Christo.

11:3 Timeo autem ne sicut serpens Hevam seduxit astutia sua, ita corrumpantur sensus vestri, et excidant a simplicitate, quæ est in Christo.

11:4 Nam si is qui venit, alium Christum prædicat, quem non prædicavimus, aut alium spiritum accipitis, quem non accepistis : aut aliud Evangelium, quod non recepistis : recte pateremini.

11:5 Existimo enim nihil me minus fecisse a magnis Apostolis.

11:6 Nam etsi imperitus sermone, sed non scientia, in omnibus autem manifestati sumus vobis.

11:7 Aut numquid peccatum feci, meipsum humilians, ut vos exaltemini ? quoniam gratis Evangelium Dei evangelizavi vobis ?

11:8 Alias ecclesias expoliavi, accipiens stipendium ad ministerium vestrum.

11:9 Et cum essem apud vos, et egerem, nulli onerosus fui : nam quod mihi deerat, suppleverunt fratres, qui venerunt a Macedonia : et in omnibus sine onere me vobis servavi, et servabo.

11:10 Est veritas Christi in me, quoniam hæc gloriatio non infringetur in me in regionibus Achaiæ.

11:11 Quare ? quia non diligo vos ? Deus scit.

11:12 Quod autem facio, et faciam : ut amputem occasionem eorum qui volunt occasionem, ut in quo gloriantur, inveniantur sicut et nos.

11:13 Nam ejusmodi pseudoapostoli sunt operarii subdoli, transfigurantes se in apostolos Christi.

11:14 Et non mirum : ipse enim Satanas transfigurat se in angelum lucis.

11:15 Non est ergo magnum, si ministri ejus transfigurentur velut ministri justitiæ : quorum finis erit secundum opera ipsorum.

11:16 Iterum dico (ne quis me putet insipientem esse, alioquin velut insipientem accipite me, ut et ego modicum quid glorier),

11:17 quod loquor, non loquor secundum Deum, sed quasi in insipientia, in hac substantia gloriæ.

11:18 Quoniam multi gloriantur secundum carnem : et ego gloriabor.

that I may present you as a chaste virgin to Christ.

11:3 But I fear lest, as the serpent seduced Eve by his subtilty, so your minds should be corrupted, and fall from the simplicity that is in Christ.

11:4 For if he that cometh preacheth another Christ, whom we have not preached; or if you receive another Spirit, whom you have not received; or another gospel which you have not received; you might well bear with him.

11:5 For I suppose that I have done nothing less than the great apostles.

11:6 For although I be rude in speech, yet not in knowledge; but in all things we have been made manifest to you.

11:7 Or did I commit a fault, humbling myself, that you might be exalted? Because I preached unto you the gospel of God freely?

11:8 I have taken from other churches, receiving wages of them for your ministry.

11:9 And, when I was present with you, and wanted, I was chargeable to no man: for that which was wanting to me, the brethren supplied who came from Macedonia; and in all things I have kept myself from being burthensome to you, and so I will keep myself.

11:10 The truth of Christ is in me, that this glorying shall not be broken off in me in the regions of Achaia.

11:11 Wherefore? Because I love you not? God knoweth it.

11:12 But what I do, that I will do, that I may cut off the occasion from them that desire occasion, that wherein they glory, they may be found even as we.

11:13 For such false apostles are deceitful workmen, transforming themselves into the apostles of Christ.

11:14 And no wonder: for Satan himself transformeth himself into an angel of light.

11:15 Therefore it is no great thing if his ministers be transformed as the ministers of justice, whose end shall be according to their works.

11:16 I say again, (let no man think me to be foolish, otherwise take me as one foolish, that I also may glory a little.)

11:17 That which I speak, I speak not according to God, but as it were in foolishness, in this matter of glorying.

11:18 Seeing that many glory according to the flesh, I will glory also.

11:19 Libenter enim suffertis insipientes, cum sitis ipsi sapientes.

11:20 Sustinetis enim si quis vos in servitutem redigit, si quis devorat, si quis accipit, si quis extollitur, si quis in faciem vos cædit.

11:21 Secundum ignobilitatem dico, quasi nos infirmi fuerimus in hac parte. In quo quis audet (in insipientia dico) audeo et ego :

11:22 Hebræi sunt, et ego : Israëlitæ sunt, et ego : semen Abrahæ sunt, et ego.

11:23 Ministri Christi sunt (ut minus sapiens dico), plus ego : in laboribus plurimis, in carceribus abundantius, in plagis supra modum, in mortibus frequenter.

11:24 A Judæis quinquies, quadragenas, una minus, accepi.

11:25 Ter virgis cæsus sum, semel lapidatus sum : ter naufragium feci, nocte et die in profundo maris fui,

11:26 in itineribus sæpe, periculis fluminum, periculis latronum, periculis ex genere, periculis ex gentibus, periculis in civitate, periculis in solitudine, periculis in mari, periculis in falsis fratribus :

11:27 in labore et ærumna, in vigiliis multis, in fame et siti, in jejuniis multis, in frigore et nuditate,

11:28 præter illa quæ extrinsecus sunt, instantia mea quotidiana, sollicitudo omnium ecclesiarum.

11:29 Quis infirmatur, et ego non infirmor ? quis scandalizatur, et ego non uror ?

11:30 Si gloriari oportet, quæ infirmitatis meæ sunt, gloriabor.

11:31 Deus et Pater Domini nostri Jesu Christi, qui est benedictus in sæcula, scit quod non mentior.

11:32 Damasci præpositus gentis Aretæ regis custodiebat civitatem Damascenorum ut me comprehenderet :

11:33 et per fenestram in sporta dimissus sum per murum, et sic effugi manus ejus.

12:1 Si gloriari oportet (non expedit quidem), veniam autem ad visiones et revelationes Domini.

12:2 Scio hominem in Christo ante annos quatuordecim, sive in corpore nescio, sive extra corpus nescio, Deus scit, raptum hujusmodi usque ad tertium cælum.

12:3 Et scio hujusmodi hominem sive in corpore,

11:19 For you gladly suffer the foolish; whereas yourselves are wise.

11:20 For you suffer if a man bring you into bondage, if a man devour you, if a man take from you, if a man be lifted up, if a man strike you on the face.

11:21 I speak according to dishonour, as if we had been weak in this part. Wherein if any man dare (I speak foolishly), I dare also.

11:22 They are Hebrews: so am I. They are Israelites: so am I. They are the seed of Abraham: so am I.

11:23 They are the ministers of Christ (I speak as one less wise): I am more; in many more labours, in prisons more frequently, in stripes above measure, in deaths often.

11:24 Of the Jews five times did I receive forty stripes, save one.

11:25 Thrice was I beaten with rods, once I was stoned, thrice I suffered shipwreck, a night and a day I was in the depth of the sea.

11:26 In journeying often, in perils of waters, in perils of robbers, in perils from my own nation, in perils from the Gentiles, in perils in the city, in perils in the wilderness, in perils in the sea, in perils from false brethren.

11:27 In labour and painfulness, in much watchings, in hunger and thirst, in fastings often, in cold and nakedness.

11:28 Besides those things which are without: my daily instance, the solicitude for all the churches.

11:29 Who is weak, and I am not weak? Who is scandalized, and I am not on fire?

11:30 If I must needs glory, I will glory of the things that concern my infirmity.

11:31 The God and Father of our Lord Jesus Christ, who is blessed for ever, knoweth that I lie not.

11:32 At Damascus, the governor of the nation under Aretas the king, guarded the city of the Damascenes, to apprehend me.

11:33 And through a window in a basket was I let down by the wall, and so escaped his hands.

12:1 If I must glory (it is not expedient indeed): but I will come to visions and revelations of the Lord.

12:2 I know a man in Christ above fourteen years ago (whether in the body, I know not, or out of the body, I know not; God knoweth), such a one caught up to the third heaven.

12:3 And I know such a man (whether in the

sive extra corpus nescio, Deus scit :

12:4 quoniam raptus est in paradisum : et audivit arcana verba, quæ non licet homini loqui.

12:5 Pro hujusmodi gloriabor : pro me autem nihil gloriabor nisi in infirmitatibus meis.

12:6 Nam etsi voluero gloriari, non ero insipiens : veritatem enim dicam : parco autem, ne quis me existimet supra id quod videt in me, aut aliquid audit ex me.

12:7 Et ne magnitudo revelationum extollat me, datus est mihi stimulus carnis meæ angelus Satanæ, qui me colaphizet.

12:8 Propter quod ter Dominum rogavi ut discederet a me :

12:9 et dixit mihi : Sufficit tibi gratia mea : nam virtus in infirmitate perficitur. Libenter igitur gloriabor in infirmitatibus meis, ut inhabitet in me virtus Christi.

12:10 Propter quod placeo mihi in infirmitatibus meis, in contumeliis, in necessitatibus, in persecutionibus, in angustiis pro Christo : cum enim infirmor, tunc potens sum.

12:11 Factus sum insipiens, vos me coëgistis. Ego enim a vobis debui commendari : nihil enim minus fui ab iis, qui sunt supra modum Apostoli : tametsi nihil sum :

12:12 signa tamen apostolatus mei facta sunt super vos in omni patientia, in signis, et prodigiis, et virtutibus.

12:13 Quid est enim, quod minus habuistis præ ceteris ecclesiis, nisi quod ego ipse non gravavi vos ? donate mihi hanc injuriam.

12:14 Ecce tertio hoc paratus sum venire ad vos : et non ero gravis vobis. Non enim quæro quæ vestra sunt, sed vos. Nec enim debent filii parentibus thesaurizare, sed parentes filiis.

12:15 Ego autem libentissime impendam, et super impendar ipse pro animabus vestris : licet plus vos diligens, minus diligar.

12:16 Sed esto : ego vos non gravavi : sed cum essem astutus, dolo vos cepi.

12:17 Numquid per aliquem eorum, quod misi ad vos, circumveni vos ?

12:18 Rogavi Titum, et misi cum illo fratrem. Numquid Titus vos circumvenit ? nonne eodem

body, or out of the body, I know not: God knoweth):

12:4 That he was caught up into paradise, and heard secret words, which it is not granted to man to utter.

12:5 For such an one I will glory; but for myself I will glory nothing, but in my infirmities.

12:6 For though I should have a mind to glory, I shall not be foolish; for I will say the truth. But I forbear, lest any man should think of me above that which he seeth in me, or any thing he heareth from me.

12:7 And lest the greatness of the revelations should exalt me, there was given me a sting of my flesh, an angel of Satan, to buffet me.

12:8 For which thing thrice I besought the Lord, that it might depart from me.

12:9 And he said to me: My grace is sufficient for thee; for power is made perfect in infirmity. Gladly therefore will I glory in my infirmities, that the power of Christ may dwell in me.

12:10 For which cause I please myself in my infirmities, in reproaches, in necessities, in persecutions, in distresses, for Christ. For when I am weak, then am I powerful.

12:11 I am become foolish: you have compelled me. For I ought to have been commended by you: for I have no way come short of them that are above measure apostles, although I be nothing.

12:12 Yet the signs of my apostleship have been wrought on you, in all patience, in signs, and wonders, and mighty deeds.

12:13 For what is there that you have had less than the other churches, but that I myself was not burthensome to you? Pardon me this injury.

12:14 Behold now the third time I am ready to come to you; and I will not be burthensome unto you. For I seek not the things that are yours, but you. For neither ought the children to lay up for the parents, but the parents for the children.

12:15 But I most gladly will spend and be spent myself for your souls; although loving you more, I be loved less.

12:16 But be it so: I did not burthen you: but being crafty, I caught you by guile.

12:17 Did I overreach you by any of them whom I sent to you?

12:18 I desired Titus, and I sent with him a brother. Did Titus overreach you? Did we not

spiritu ambulavimus ? nonne iisdem vestigiis ?

12:19 Olim putatis quod excusemus nos apud vos ? coram Deo in Christo loquimur : omnia autem, carissimi, propter ædificationem vestram.

12:20 Timeo enim ne forte cum venero, non quales volo, inveniam vos : et ego inveniar a vobis, qualem non vultis : ne forte contentiones, æmulationes, animositates, dissensiones, detractiones, susurrationes, inflationes, seditiones sint inter vos :

12:21 ne iterum cum venero, humiliet me Deus apud vos, et lugeam multos ex iis qui ante peccaverunt, et non egerunt pœnitentiam super immunditia, et fornicatione, et impudicitia, quam gesserunt.

13:1 Ecce tertio hoc venio ad vos : in ore duorum vel trium testium stabit omne verbum.

13:2 Prædixi, et prædico, ut præsens, et nunc absens iis qui ante peccaverunt, et ceteris omnibus, quoniam si venero iterum, non parcam.

13:3 An experimentum quæritis ejus, qui in me loquitur Christus, qui in vobis non infirmatur, sed potens est in vobis ?

13:4 Nam etsi crucifixus est ex infirmitate : sed vivit ex virtute Dei. Nam et nos infirmi sumus in illo : sed vivemus cum eo ex virtute Dei in vobis.

13:5 Vosmetipsos tentate si estis in fide : ipsi vos probate. An non cognoscitis vosmetipsos quia Christus Jesus in vobis est ? nisi forte reprobi estis.

13:6 Spero autem quod cognoscetis, quia nos non sumus reprobi.

13:7 Oramus autem Deum ut nihil mali faciatis, non ut nos probati appareamus, sed ut vos quod bonum est faciatis : nos autem ut reprobi simus.

13:8 Non enim possumus aliquid adversus veritatem, sed pro veritate.

13:9 Gaudemus enim, quoniam nos infirmi sumus, vos autem potentes estis. Hoc et oramus, vestram consummationem.

13:10 Ideo hæc absens scribo, ut non præsens durius agam secundum potestatem, quam Dominus dedit mihi in ædificationem, et non in destructionem.

13:11 De cetero, fratres, gaudete, perfecti estote,

walk with the same spirit? did we not in the same steps?

12:19 Of old, think you that we excuse ourselves to you? We speak before God in Christ; but all things, my dearly beloved, for your edification.

12:20 For I fear lest perhaps when I come I shall not find you such as I would, and that I shall be found by you such as you would not. Lest perhaps contentions, envyings, animosities, dissensions, detractions, whisperings, swellings, seditions, be among you.

12:21 Lest again, when I come, God humble me among you: and I mourn many of them that sinned before, and have not done penance for the uncleanness, and fornication, and lasciviousness, that they have committed.

13:1 Behold, this is the third time I am coming to you: In the mouth of two or three witnesses shall every word stand.

13:2 I have told before, and foretell, as present, and now absent, to them that sinned before, and to all the rest, that if I come again, I will not spare.

13:3 Do you seek a proof of Christ that speaketh in me, who towards you is not weak, but is mighty in you?

13:4 For although he was crucified through weakness, yet he liveth by the power of God. For we also are weak in him: but we shall live with him by the power of God towards you.

13:5 Try your own selves if you be in the faith; prove ye yourselves. Know you not your own selves, that Christ Jesus is in you, unless perhaps you be reprobates?

13:6 But I trust that you shall know that we are not reprobates.

13:7 Now we pray God, that you may do no evil, not that we may appear approved, but that you may do that which is good, and that we may be as reprobates.

13:8 For we can do nothing against the truth; but for the truth.

13:9 For we rejoice that we are weak, and you are strong. This also we pray for, your perfection.

13:10 Therefore I write these things, being absent, that, being present, I may not deal more severely, according to the power which the Lord hath given me unto edification, and not unto destruction.

13:11 For the rest, brethren, rejoice, be perfect,

exhortamini, idem sapite, pacem habete, et Deus pacis et dilectionis erit vobiscum.

13:12 Salutate invicem in osculo sancto. Salutant vos omnes sancti.

13:13 Gratia Domini nostri Jesu Christi, et caritas Dei, et communicatio Sancti Spiritus sit cum omnibus vobis. Amen.

take exhortation, be of one mind, have peace; and the God of peace and of love shall be with you.

13:12 Salute one another with a holy kiss. All the saints salute you.

13:13 The grace of our Lord Jesus Christ, and the charity of God, and the communication of the Holy Ghost be with you all. Amen.

Epistula Beati Pauli Apostoli ad Galatas

THE EPISTLE OF BLESSED PAUL THE APOSTLE TO THE GALATIANS

✠

1:1 PAULUS, APOSTOLUS non ab hominibus, neque per hominem, sed per Jesum Christum, et Deum Patrem, qui suscitavit eum a mortuis :

1:2 et qui mecum sunt omnes fratres, ecclesiis Galatiæ.

1:3 Gratia vobis, et pax a Deo Patre, et Domino nostro Jesu Christo,

1:4 qui dedit semetipsum pro peccatis nostris, ut eriperet nos de præsenti sæculo nequam, secundum voluntatem Dei et Patris nostri,

1:5 cui est gloria in sæcula sæculorum. Amen.

1:6 Miror quod sic tam cito transferimini ab eo qui vos vocavit in gratiam Christi in aliud Evangelium :

1:7 quod non est aliud, nisi sunt aliqui qui vos conturbant, et volunt convertere Evangelium Christi.

1:8 Sed licet nos aut angelus de cælo evangelizet vobis præterquam quod evangelizavimus vobis, anathema sit.

1:9 Sicut prædiximus, et nunc iterum dico : si quis vobis evangelizaverit præter id quod accepistis, anathema sit.

1:10 Modo enim hominibus suadeo, an Deo ? an quæro hominibus placere ? si adhuc hominibus placerem, Christi servus non essem.

1:11 Notum enim vobis facio, fratres, Evangelium, quod evangelizatum est a me, quia non est secundum hominem :

1:12 neque enim ego ab homine accepi illud, neque didici, sed per revelationem Jesu Christi.

1:13 Audistis enim conversationem meam aliquando in Judaismo : quoniam supra modum persequebar Ecclesiam Dei, et expugnabam illam,

1:14 et proficiebam in Judaismo supra multos coætaneos meos in genere meo, abundantius æmulator existens paternarum mearum traditionum.

1:15 Cum autem placuit ei, qui me segregavit ex utero matris meæ, et vocavit per gratiam

1:1 PAUL, AN APOSTLE, not of men, neither by man, but by Jesus Christ, and God the Father, who raised him from the dead,

1:2 And all the brethren who are with me, to the churches of Galatia.

1:3 Grace be to you, and peace from God the Father, and from our Lord Jesus Christ,

1:4 Who gave himself for our sins, that he might deliver us from this present wicked world, according to the will of God and our Father:

1:5 To whom is glory for ever and ever. Amen.

1:6 I wonder that you are so soon removed from him that called you into the grace of Christ, unto another gospel.

1:7 Which is not another, only there are some that trouble you, and would pervert the gospel of Christ.

1:8 But though we, or an angel from heaven, preach a gospel to you besides that which we have preached to you, let him be anathema.

1:9 As we said before, so now I say again: If any one preach to you a gospel, besides that which you have received, let him be anathema.

1:10 For do I now persuade men, or God? Or do I seek to please men? If I yet pleased men, I should not be the servant of Christ.

1:11 For I give you to understand, brethren, that the gospel which was preached by me is not according to man.

1:12 For neither did I receive it of man, nor did I learn it; but by the revelation of Jesus Christ.

1:13 For you have heard of my conversation in time past in the Jews' religion: how that, beyond measure, I persecuted the church of God, and wasted it.

1:14 And I made progress in the Jews' religion above many of my equals in my own nation, being more abundantly zealous for the traditions of my fathers.

1:15 But when it pleased him, who separated me from my mother's womb, and called me by his

suam,

1:16 ut revelaret Filium suum in me, ut evangelizarem illum in gentibus : continuo non acquievi carni et sanguini,

1:17 neque veni Jerosolymam ad antecessores meos Apostolos : sed abii in Arabiam, et iterum reversus sum Damascum :

1:18 deinde post annos tres veni Jerosolymam videre Petrum, et mansi apud eum diebus quindecim :

1:19 alium autem Apostolorum vidi neminem, nisi Jacobum fratrem Domini.

1:20 Quæ autem scribo vobis, ecce coram Deo, quia non mentior.

1:21 Deinde veni in partes Syriæ, et Ciliciæ.

1:22 Eram autem ignotus facie ecclesiis Judææ, quæ erant in Christo :

1:23 tantum autem auditum habebant quoniam qui persequebatur nos aliquando, nunc evangelizat fidem, quam aliquando expugnabat :

1:24 et in me clarificabant Deum.

2:1 Deinde post annos quatuordecim, iterum ascendi Jerosolymam cum Barnaba, assumpto et Tito.

2:2 Ascendi autem secundum revelationem : et contuli cum illis Evangelium, quod prædico in gentibus, seorsum autem iis qui videbantur aliquid esse : ne forte in vacuum currerem, aut cucurrissem.

2:3 Sed neque Titus, qui mecum erat, cum esset gentilis, compulsus est circumcidi :

2:4 sed propter subintroductos falsos fratres, qui subintroierunt explorare libertatem nostram, quam habemus in Christo Jesu, ut nos in servitutem redigerent.

2:5 Quibus neque ad horam cessimus subjectione, ut veritas Evangelii permaneat apud vos :

2:6 ab iis autem, qui videbantur esse aliquid (quales aliquando fuerint, nihil mea interest : Deus personam hominis non accipit) : mihi enim qui videbantur esse aliquid, nihil contulerunt.

2:7 Sed e contra cum vidissent quod creditum est mihi Evangelium præputii, sicut et Petro circumcisionis

2:8 (qui enim operatus est Petro in apostolatum circumcisionis, operatus est et mihi inter gentes) :

2:9 et cum cognovissent gratiam, quæ data est

grace,

1:16 To reveal his Son in me, that I might preach him among the Gentiles, immediately I condescended not to flesh and blood.

1:17 Neither went I to Jerusalem, to the apostles who were before me: but I went into Arabia, and again I returned to Damascus.

1:18 Then, after three years, I went to Jerusalem, to see Peter, and I tarried with him fifteen days.

1:19 But other of the apostles I saw none, saving James the brother of the Lord.

1:20 Now the things which I write to you, behold, before God, I lie not.

1:21 Afterwards I came into the regions of Syria and Cilicia.

1:22 And I was unknown by face to the churches of Judea, which were in Christ:

1:23 But they had heard only: He, who persecuted us in times past, doth now preach the faith which once he impugned:

1:24 And they glorified God in me.

2:1 Then, after fourteen years, I went up again to Jerusalem with Barnabas, taking Titus also with me.

2:2 And I went up according to revelation; and communicated to them the gospel, which I preach among the Gentiles, but apart to them who seemed to be some thing: lest perhaps I should run, or had run in vain.

2:3 But neither Titus, who was with me, being a Gentile, was compelled to be circumcised.

2:4 But because of false brethren unawares brought in, who came in privately to spy our liberty, which we have in Christ Jesus, that they might bring us into servitude.

2:5 To whom we yielded not by subjection, no not for an hour, that the truth of the gospel might continue with you.

2:6 But of them who seemed to be some thing, (what they were some time, it is nothing to me, God accepteth not the person of man,) for to me they that seemed to be some thing added nothing.

2:7 But contrariwise, when they had seen that to me was committed the gospel of the uncircumcision, as to Peter was that of the circumcision.

2:8 (For he who wrought in Peter to the apostleship of the circumcision, wrought in me also among the Gentiles.)

2:9 And when they had known the grace that

mihi, Jacobus, et Cephas, et Joannes, qui videbantur columnæ esse, dextras dederunt mihi, et Barnabæ societatis : ut nos in gentes, ipsi autem in circumcisionem :

2:10 tantum ut pauperum memores essemus, quod etiam sollicitus fui hoc ipsum facere.

2:11 Cum autem venisset Cephas Antiochiam, in faciem ei restiti, quia reprehensibilis erat.

2:12 Prius enim quam venirent quidam a Jacobo, cum gentibus edebat : cum autem venissent, subtrahebat, et segregabat se, timens eos qui ex circumcisione erant.

2:13 Et simulationi ejus consenserunt ceteri Judæi, ita ut et Barnabas duceretur ab eis in illam simulationem.

2:14 Sed cum vidissem quod non recte ambularent ad veritatem Evangelii, dixi Cephæ coram omnibus : Si tu, cum Judæus sis, gentiliter vivis, et non judaice : quomodo gentes cogis judaizare ?

2:15 Nos natura Judæi, et non ex gentibus peccatores.

2:16 Scientes autem quod non justificatur homo ex operibus legis, nisi per fidem Jesu Christi : et nos in Christo Jesu credimus, ut justificemur ex fide Christi, et non ex operibus legis : propter quod ex operibus legis non justificabitur omnis caro.

2:17 Quod si quærentes justificari in Christo, inventi sumus et ipsi peccatores, numquid Christus peccati minister est ? Absit.

2:18 Si enim quæ destruxi, iterum hæc ædifico : prævaricatorem me constituo.

2:19 Ego enim per legem, legi mortuus sum, ut Deo vivam : Christo confixus sum cruci.

2:20 Vivo autem, jam non ego : vivit vero in me Christus. Quod autem nunc vivo in carne : in fide vivo Filii Dei, qui dilexit me, et tradidit semetipsum pro me.

2:21 Non abjicio gratiam Dei. Si enim per legem justitia, ergo gratis Christus mortuus est.

3:1 O insensati Galatæ, quis vos fascinavit non obedire veritati, ante quorum oculos Jesus Christus præscriptus est, in vobis crucifixus ?

3:2 Hoc solum a vobis volo discere : ex operibus legis Spiritum accepistis, an ex auditu fidei ?

was given to me, James and Cephas and John, who seemed to be pillars, gave to me and Barnabas the right hands of fellowship: that we should go unto the Gentiles, and they unto the circumcision:

2:10 Only that we should be mindful of the poor: which same thing also I was careful to do.

2:11 But when Cephas was come to Antioch, I withstood him to the face, because he was to be blamed.

2:12 For before that some came from James, he did eat with the Gentiles: but when they were come, he withdrew and separated himself, fearing them who were of the circumcision.

2:13 And to his dissimulation the rest of the Jews consented, so that Barnabas also was led by them into that dissimulation.

2:14 But when I saw that they walked not uprightly unto the truth of the gospel, I said to Cephas before them all: If thou, being a Jew, livest after the manner of the Gentiles, and not as the Jews do, how dost thou compel the Gentiles to live as do the Jews?

2:15 We by nature are Jews, and not of the Gentiles sinners.

2:16 But knowing that man is not justified by the works of the law, but by the faith of Jesus Christ; we also believe in Christ Jesus, that we may be justified by the faith of Christ, and not by the works of the law: because by the works of the law no flesh shall be justified.

2:17 But if while we seek to be justified in Christ, we ourselves also are found sinners; is Christ then the minister of sin? God forbid.

2:18 For if I build up again the things which I have destroyed, I make myself a prevaricator.

2:19 For I, through the law, am dead to the law, that I may live to God: with Christ I am nailed to the cross.

2:20 And I live, now not I; but Christ liveth in me. And that I live now in the flesh: I live in the faith of the Son of God, who loved me, and delivered himself for me.

2:21 I cast not away the grace of God. For if justice be by the law, then Christ died in vain.

3:1 O SENSELESS Galatians, who hath bewitched you that you should not obey the truth, before whose eyes Jesus Christ hath been set forth, crucified among you?

3:2 This only would I learn of you: Did you receive the Spirit by the works of the law, or by

3:3 sic stulti estis, ut cum Spiritu cœperitis, nunc carne consummemini ?

3:4 tanta passi estis sine causa ? si tamen sine causa.

3:5 Qui ergo tribuit vobis Spiritum, et operatur virtutes in vobis : ex operibus legis, an ex auditu fidei ?

3:6 Sicut scriptum est : Abraham credidit Deo, et reputatum est illi ad justitiam :

3:7 cognoscite ergo quia qui ex fide sunt, ii sunt filii Abrahæ.

3:8 Providens autem Scriptura quia ex fide justificat gentes Deus, prænuntiavit Abrahæ : Quia benedicentur in te omnes gentes.

3:9 Igitur qui ex fide sunt, benedicentur cum fideli Abraham.

3:10 Quicumque enim ex operibus legis sunt, sub maledicto sunt. Scriptum est enim : Maledictus omnis qui non permanserit in omnibus quæ scripta sunt in libro legis ut faciat ea.

3:11 Quoniam autem in lege nemo justificatur apud Deum, manifestum est : quia justus ex fide vivit.

3:12 Lex autem non est ex fide, sed : Qui fecerit ea, vivet in illis.

3:13 Christus nos redemit de maledicto legis, factus pro nobis maledictum : quia scriptum est : Maledictus omnis qui pendet in ligno :

3:14 ut in gentibus benedictio Abrahæ fieret in Christo Jesu, ut pollicitationem Spiritus accipiamus per fidem.

3:15 Fratres (secundum hominem dico) tamen hominis confirmatum testamentum nemo spernit, aut superordinat.

3:16 Abrahæ dictæ sunt promissiones, et semini ejus. Non dicit : Et seminibus, quasi in multis : sed quasi in uno : Et semini tuo, qui est Christus.

3:17 Hoc autem dico, testamentum confirmatum a Deo : quæ post quadringentos et triginta annos facta est lex, non irritum facit ad evacuandam promissionem.

3:18 Nam si ex lege hæreditas, jam non ex promissione. Abrahæ autem per repromissionem donavit Deus.

3:19 Quid igitur lex ? Propter transgressiones posita est donec veniret semen, cui promiserat, ordinata per angelos in manu mediatoris.

the hearing of faith?

3:3 Are you so foolish, that, whereas you began in the Spirit, you would now be made perfect by the flesh?

3:4 Have you suffered so great things in vain? If it be yet in vain.

3:5 He therefore who giveth to you the Spirit, and worketh miracles among you; doth he do it by the works of the law, or by the hearing of the faith?

3:6 As it is written: Abraham believed God, and it was reputed to him unto justice.

3:7 Know ye therefore, that they who are of faith, the same are the children of Abraham.

3:8 And the scripture, foreseeing, that God justifieth the Gentiles by faith, told unto Abraham before: In thee shall all nations be blessed.

3:9 Therefore they that are of faith, shall be blessed with faithful Abraham.

3:10 For as many as are of the works of the law, are under a curse. For it is written: Cursed is every one, that abideth not in all things, which are written in the book of the law to do them.

3:11 But that in the law no man is justified with God, it is manifest: because the just man liveth by faith.

3:12 But the law is not of faith: but, He that doth those things, shall live in them.

3:13 Christ hath redeemed us from the curse of the law, being made a curse for us: for it is written: Cursed is every one that hangeth on a tree:

3:14 That the blessing of Abraham might come on the Gentiles through Christ Jesus: that we may receive the promise of the Spirit by faith.

3:15 Brethren (I speak after the manner of man,) yet a man's testament, if it be confirmed, no man despiseth, nor addeth to it.

3:16 To Abraham were the promises made and to his seed. He saith not, And to his seeds, as of many: but as of one, And to thy seed, which is Christ.

3:17 Now this I say, that the testament which was confirmed by God, the law which was made after four hundred and thirty years, doth not disannul, to make the promise of no effect.

3:18 For if the inheritance be of the law, it is no more of promise. But God gave it to Abraham by promise.

3:19 Why then was the law? It was set because of transgressions, until the seed should come, to whom he made the promise, being ordained by

3:20 Mediator autem unius non est : Deus autem unus est.

3:21 Lex ergo adversus promissa Dei ? Absit. Si enim data esset lex, quæ posset vivificare, vere ex lege esset justitia.

3:22 Sed conclusit Scriptura omnia sub peccato, ut promissio ex fide Jesu Christi daretur credentibus.

3:23 Prius autem quam veniret fides, sub lege custodiebamur conclusi in eam fidem quæ revelanda erat.

3:24 Itaque lex pædagogus noster fuit in Christo, ut ex fide justificemur.

3:25 At ubi venit fides, jam non sumus sub pædagogo.

3:26 Omnes enim filii Dei estis per fidem, quæ est in Christo Jesu.

3:27 Quicumque enim in Christo baptizati estis, Christum induistis.

3:28 Non est Judæus, neque Græcus : non est servus, neque liber : non est masculus, neque femina. Omnes enim vos unum estis in Christo Jesu.

3:29 Si autem vos Christi, ergo semen Abrahæ estis, secundum promissionem hæredes.

4:1 Dico autem : quanto tempore hæres parvulus est, nihil differt a servo, cum sit dominus omnium :

4:2 sed sub tutoribus et actoribus est usque ad præfinitum tempus a patre :

4:3 ita et nos cum essemus parvuli, sub elementis mundi eramus servientes.

4:4 At ubi venit plenitudo temporis, misit Deus Filium suum factum ex muliere, factum sub lege,

4:5 ut eos, qui sub lege erant, redimeret, ut adoptionem filiorum reciperemus.

4:6 Quoniam autem estis filii, misit Deus Spiritum Filii sui in corda vestra, clamantem : Abba, Pater.

4:7 Itaque jam non est servus, sed filius : quod si filius, et hæres per Deum.

4:8 Sed tunc quidem ignorantes Deum, iis, qui natura non sunt dii, serviebatis.

4:9 Nunc autem cum cognoveritis Deum, immo cogniti sitis a Deo : quomodo convertimini iterum ad infirma et egena elementa, quibus denuo servire vultis ?

3:20 Now a mediator is not of one: but God is one.

3:21 Was the law then against the promises of God? God forbid. For if there had been a law given which could give life, verily justice should have been by the law.

3:22 But the scripture hath concluded all under sin, that the promise, by the faith of Jesus Christ, might be given to them that believe.

3:23 But before the faith came, we were kept under the law shut up, unto that faith which was to be revealed.

3:24 Wherefore the law was our pedagogue in Christ, that we might be justified by faith.

3:25 But after the faith is come, we are no longer under a pedagogue.

3:26 For you are all the children of God by faith, in Christ Jesus.

3:27 For as many of you as have been baptized in Christ, have put on Christ.

3:28 There is neither Jew nor Greek: there is neither bond nor free: there is neither male nor female. For you are all one in Christ Jesus.

3:29 And if you be Christ's, then are you the seed of Abraham, heirs according to the promise.

4:1 Now I say, as long as the heir is a child, he differeth nothing from a servant, though he be lord of all;

4:2 But is under tutors and governors until the time appointed by the father:

4:3 So we also, when we were children, were serving under the elements of the world.

4:4 But when the fulness of the time was come, God sent his Son, made of a woman, made under the law:

4:5 That he might redeem them who were under the law: that we might receive the adoption of sons.

4:6 And because you are sons, God hath sent the Spirit of his Son into your hearts, crying: Abba, Father.

4:7 Therefore now he is not a servant, but a son. And if a son, an heir also through God.

4:8 But then indeed, not knowing God, you served them, who, by nature, are not gods.

4:9 But now, after that you have known God, or rather are known by God: how turn you again to the weak and needy elements, which you desire to serve again?

4:10 Dies observatis, et menses, et tempora, et annos.

4:11 Timeo vos, ne forte sine causa laboraverim in vobis.

4:12 Estote sicut ego, quia et ego sicut vos : fratres, obsecro vos. Nihil me læsistis.

4:13 Scitis autem quia per infirmitatem carnis evangelizavi vobis jampridem : et tentationem vestram in carne mea

4:14 non sprevistis, neque respuistis : sed sicut angelum Dei excepistis me, sicut Christum Jesum.

4:15 Ubi est ergo beatitudo vestra ? testimonium enim perhibeo vobis, quia, si fieri posset, oculos vestros eruissetis, et dedissetis mihi.

4:16 Ergo inimicus vobis factus sum, verum dicens vobis ?

4:17 Æmulantur vos non bene : sed excludere vos volunt, ut illos æmulemini.

4:18 Bonum autem æmulamini in bono semper : et non tantum cum præsens sum apud vos.

4:19 Filioli mei, quos iterum parturio, donec formetur Christus in vobis :

4:20 vellem autem esse apud vos modo, et mutare vocem meam : quoniam confundor in vobis.

4:21 Dicite mihi qui sub lege vultis esse : legem non legistis ?

4:22 Scriptum est enim : Quoniam Abraham duos filios habuit : unum de ancilla, et unum de libera.

4:23 Sed qui de ancilla, secundum carnem natus est : qui autem de libera, per repromissionem :

4:24 quæ sunt per allegoriam dicta. Hæc enim sunt duo testamenta. Unum quidem in monte Sina, in servitutem generans, quæ est Agar :

4:25 Sina enim mons est in Arabia, qui conjunctus est ei quæ nunc est Jerusalem, et servit cum filiis suis.

4:26 Illa autem, quæ sursum est Jerusalem, libera est, quæ est mater nostra.

4:27 Scriptum est enim : *Lætare, sterilis, quæ non paris ; erumpe et clama, quæ non parturis : quia multi filii desertæ, magis quam ejus quæ habet virum.*

4:28 Nos autem, fratres, secundum Isaac promis-

4:10 You observe days, and months, and times, and years.

4:11 I am afraid of you, lest perhaps I have laboured in vain among you.

4:12 Be ye as I, because I also am as you: brethren, I beseech you: you have not injured me at all.

4:13 And you know, how through infirmity of the flesh, I preached the gospel to you heretofore: and your temptation in my flesh,

4:14 You despised not, nor rejected: but received me as an angel of God, even as Christ Jesus.

4:15 Where is then your blessedness? For I bear you witness, that, if it could be done, you would have plucked out your own eyes, and would have given them to me.

4:16 Am I then become your enemy, because I tell you the truth?

4:17 They are zealous in your regard not well: but they would exclude you, that you might be zealous for them.

4:18 But be zealous for that which is good in a good thing always: and not only when I am present with you.

4:19 My little children, of whom I am in labour again, until Christ be formed in you.

4:20 And I would willingly be present with you now, and change my voice: because I am ashamed for you.

4:21 Tell me, you that desire to be under the law, have you not read the law?

4:22 For it is written that Abraham had two sons: the one by a bondwoman, and the other by a free woman.

4:23 But he who was of the bondwoman, was born according to the flesh: but he of the free woman, was by promise.

4:24 Which things are said by an allegory. For these are the two testaments. The one from mount Sina, engendering unto bondage; which is Agar:

4:25 For Sina is a mountain in Arabia, which hath affinity to that Jerusalem which now is, and is in bondage with her children.

4:26 But that Jerusalem, which is above, is free: which is our mother.

4:27 For it is written: *Rejoice, thou barren, that bearest not: break forth and cry, thou that travailest not: for many are the children of the desolate, more than of her that hath a husband.*

4:28 Now we, brethren, as Isaac was, are the

sionis filii sumus.

4:29 Sed quomodo tunc is, qui secundum carnem natus fuerat, persequebatur eum qui secundum spiritum : ita et nunc.

4:30 Sed quid dicit Scriptura ? Ejice ancillam, et filium ejus : non enim hæres erit filius ancillæ cum filio liberæ.

4:31 Itaque, fratres, non sumus ancillæ filii, sed liberæ : qua libertate Christus nos liberavit.

5:1 State, et nolite iterum jugo servitutis contineri.

5:2 Ecce ego Paulus dico vobis : quoniam si circumcidamini, Christus vobis nihil proderit.

5:3 Testificor autem rursus omni homini circumcidenti se, quoniam debitor est universæ legis faciendæ.

5:4 Evacuati estis a Christo, qui in lege justificamini : a gratia excidistis.

5:5 Nos enim spiritu ex fide, spem justitiæ exspectamus.

5:6 Nam in Christo Jesu neque circumcisio aliquid valet, neque præputium : sed fides, quæ per caritatem operatur.

5:7 Currebatis bene : quis vos impedivit veritati non obedire ?

5:8 persuasio hæc non est ex eo, qui vocat vos.

5:9 Modicum fermentum totam massam corrumpit.

5:10 Ego confido in vobis in Domino, quod nihil aliud sapietis : qui autem conturbat vos, portabit judicium, quicumque est ille.

5:11 Ego autem, fratres, si circumcisionem adhuc prædico : quid adhuc persecutionem patior ? ergo evacuatum est scandalum crucis.

5:12 Utinam et abscindantur qui vos conturbant.

5:13 Vos enim in libertatem vocati estis, fratres : tantum ne libertatem in occasionem detis carnis, sed per caritatem Spiritus servite invicem.

5:14 Omnis enim lex in uno sermone impletur : Diliges proximum tuum sicut teipsum.

5:15 Quod si invicem mordetis, et comeditis : videte ne ab invicem consumamini.

5:16 Dico autem : Spiritu ambulate, et desideria carnis non perficietis.

5:17 Caro enim concupiscit adversus spiritum, spiritus autem adversus carnem : hæc enim sibi

children of promise.

4:29 But as then he, that was born according to the flesh, persecuted him that was after the spirit; so also it is now.

4:30 But what saith the scripture? Cast out the bondwoman and her son; for the son of the bondwoman shall not be heir with the son of the free woman.

4:31 So then, brethren, we are not the children of the bondwoman, but of the free: by the freedom wherewith Christ has made us free.

5:1 Stand fast, and be not held again under the yoke of bondage.

5:2 Behold, I Paul tell you, that if you be circumcised, Christ shall profit you nothing.

5:3 And I testify again to every man circumcising himself, that he is a debtor to the whole law.

5:4 You are made void of Christ, you who are justified in the law: you are fallen from grace.

5:5 For we in spirit, by faith, wait for the hope of justice.

5:6 For in Christ Jesus neither circumcision availeth any thing, nor uncircumcision: but faith that worketh by charity.

5:7 You did run well, who hath hindered you, that you should not obey the truth?

5:8 This persuasion is not from him that calleth you.

5:9 A little leaven corrupteth the whole lump.

5:10 I have confidence in you in the Lord: that you will not be of another mind: but he that troubleth you, shall bear the judgment, whosoever he be.

5:11 And I, brethren, if I yet preach circumcision, why do I yet suffer persecution? Then is the scandal of the cross made void.

5:12 I would they were even cut off, who trouble you.

5:13 For you, brethren, have been called unto liberty: only make not liberty an occasion to the flesh, but by charity of the spirit serve one another.

5:14 For all the law is fulfilled in one word: Thou shalt love thy neighbour as thyself.

5:15 But if you bite and devour one another; take heed you be not consumed one of another.

5:16 I say then, walk in the spirit, and you shall not fulfil the lusts of the flesh.

5:17 For the flesh lusteth against the spirit: and the spirit against the flesh; for these are contra-

invicem adversantur, ut non quæcumque vultis, illa faciatis.

5:18 Quod si Spiritu ducimini, non estis sub lege.

5:19 Manifesta sunt autem opera carnis, quæ sunt fornicatio, immunditia, impudicitia, luxuria,

5:20 idolorum servitus, veneficia, inimicitiæ, contentiones, æmulationes, iræ, rixæ, dissensiones, sectæ,

5:21 invidiæ, homicidia, ebrietates, comessationes, et his similia, quæ prædico vobis, sicut prædixi : quoniam qui talia agunt, regnum Dei non consequentur.

5:22 Fructus autem Spiritus est caritas, gaudium, pax, patientia, benignitas, bonitas, longanimitas,

5:23 mansuetudo, fides, modestia, continentia, castitas. Adversus hujusmodi non est lex.

5:24 Qui autem sunt Christi, carnem suam crucifixerunt cum vitiis et concupiscentiis.

5:25 Si Spiritu vivimus, Spiritu et ambulemus.

5:26 Non efficiamur inanis gloriæ cupidi, invicem provocantes, invicem invidentes.

6:1 Fratres, etsi præoccupatus fuerit homo in aliquo delicto, vos, qui spirituales estis, hujusmodi instruite in spiritu lenitatis, considerans teipsum, ne et tu tenteris.

6:2 Alter alterius onera portate, et sic adimplebitis legem Christi.

6:3 Nam si quis existimat se aliquid esse, cum nihil sit, ipse se seducit.

6:4 Opus autem suum probet unusquisque, et sic in semetipso tantum gloriam habebit, et non in altero.

6:5 Unusquisque enim onus suum portabit.

6:6 Communicet autem is qui catechizatur verbo, ei qui se catechizat, in omnibus bonis.

6:7 Nolite errare : Deus non irridetur.

6:8 Quæ enim seminaverit homo, hæc et metet. Quoniam qui seminat in carne sua, de carne et metet corruptionem : qui autem seminat in spiritu, de spiritu metet vitam æternam.

6:9 Bonum autem facientes, non deficiamus : tempore enim suo metemus non deficientes.

6:10 Ergo dum tempus habemus, operemur bonum ad omnes, maxime autem ad domesticos fidei.

ry one to another: so that you do not the things that you would.

5:18 But if you are led by the spirit, you are not under the law.

5:19 Now the works of the flesh are manifest, which are fornication, uncleanness, immodesty, luxury,

5:20 Idolatry, witchcrafts, enmities, contentions, emulations, wraths, quarrels, dissensions, sects,

5:21 Envies, murders, drunkenness, revellings, and such like. Of the which I foretell you, as I have foretold to you, that they who do such things shall not obtain the kingdom of God.

5:22 But the fruit of the Spirit is, charity, joy, peace, patience, benignity, goodness, longanimity,

5:23 Mildness, faith, modesty, continency, chastity. Against such there is no law.

5:24 And they that are Christ's, have crucified their flesh, with the vices and concupiscences.

5:25 If we live in the Spirit, let us also walk in the Spirit.

5:26 Let us not be made desirous of vain glory, provoking one another, envying one another.

6:1 Brethren, and if a man be overtaken in any fault, you, who are spiritual, instruct such a one in the spirit of meekness, considering thyself, lest thou also be tempted.

6:2 Bear ye one another's burdens; and so you shall fulfil the law of Christ.

6:3 For if any man think himself to be something, whereas he is nothing, he deceiveth himself.

6:4 But let every one prove his own work, and so he shall have glory in himself only, and not in another.

6:5 For every one shall bear his own burden.

6:6 And let him that is instructed in the word, communicate to him that instructeth him, in all good things.

6:7 Be not deceived, God is not mocked.

6:8 For what things a man shall sow, those also shall he reap. For he that soweth in his flesh, of the flesh also shall reap corruption. But he that soweth in the spirit, of the spirit shall reap life everlasting.

6:9 And in doing good, let us not fail. For in due time we shall reap, not failing.

6:10 Therefore, whilst we have time, let us work good to all men, but especially to those who are of the household of the faith.

6:11 Videte qualibus litteris scripsi vobis mea manu.

6:12 Quicumque enim volunt placere in carne, hi cogunt vos circumcidi, tantum ut crucis Christi persecutionem non patiantur.

6:13 Neque enim qui circumciduntur, legem custodiunt : sed volunt vos circumcidi, ut in carne vestra glorientur.

6:14 Mihi autem absit gloriari, nisi in cruce Domini nostri Jesu Christi : per quem mihi mundus crucifixus est, et ego mundo.

6:15 In Christo enim Jesu neque circumcisio aliquid valet, neque præputium, sed nova creatura.

6:16 Et quicumque hanc regulam secuti fuerint, pax super illos, et misericordia, et super Israël Dei.

6:17 De cetero, nemo mihi molestus sit : ego enim stigmata Domini Jesu in corpore meo porto.

6:18 Gratia Domini nostri Jesu Christi cum spiritu vestro, fratres. Amen.

6:11 See what a letter I have written to you with my own hand.

6:12 For as many as desire to please in the flesh, they constrain you to be circumcised, only that they may not suffer the persecution of the cross of Christ.

6:13 For neither they themselves who are circumcised, keep the law; but they will have you to be circumcised, that they may glory in your flesh.

6:14 But God forbid that I should glory, save in the cross of our Lord Jesus Christ; by whom the world is crucified to me, and I to the world.

6:15 For in Christ Jesus neither circumcision availeth any thing, nor uncircumcision, but a new creature.

6:16 And whosoever shall follow this rule, peace on them, and mercy, and upon the Israel of God.

6:17 From henceforth let no man be troublesome to me; for I bear the marks of the Lord Jesus in my body.

6:18 The grace of our Lord Jesus Christ be with your spirit, brethren. Amen.

Epistula Beati Pauli Apostoli ad Ephesios

THE EPISTLE OF BLESSED PAUL THE APOSTLE TO THE EPHESIANS

✠

1:1 PAULUS APOSTOLUS JESU CHRISTI per voluntatem Dei, omnibus sanctis qui sunt Ephesi, et fidelibus in Christo Jesu.

1:2 Gratia vobis, et pax a Deo Patre nostro, et Domino Jesu Christo.

1:3 Benedictus Deus et Pater Domini nostri Jesu Christi, qui benedixit nos in omni benedictione spirituali in cælestibus in Christo,

1:4 sicut elegit nos in ipso ante mundi constitutionem, ut essemus sancti et immaculati in conspectu ejus in caritate.

1:5 Qui prædestinavit nos in adoptionem filiorum per Jesum Christum in ipsum : secundum propositum voluntatis suæ,

1:6 in laudem gloriæ gratiæ suæ, in qua gratificavit nos in dilecto Filio suo.

1:7 In quo habemus redemptionem per sanguinem ejus, remissionem peccatorum secundum divitias gratiæ ejus,

1:8 quæ superabundavit in nobis in omni sapientia et prudentia :

1:9 ut notum faceret nobis sacramentum voluntatis suæ, secundum beneplacitum ejus, quod proposuit in eo,

1:10 in dispensatione plenitudinis temporum, instaurare omnia in Christo, quæ in cælis et quæ in terra sunt, in ipso ;

1:11 in quo etiam et nos sorte vocati sumus prædestinati secundum propositum ejus qui operatur omnia secundum consilium voluntatis suæ :

1:12 ut simus in laudem gloriæ ejus nos, qui ante speravimus in Christo ;

1:13 in quo et vos, cum audissetis verbum veritatis, Evangelium salutis vestræ, in quo et credentes signati estis Spiritu promissionis Sancto,

1:14 qui est pignus hæreditatis nostræ, in redemptionem acquisitionis, in laudem gloriæ ipsius.

1:15 Propterea et ego audiens fidem vestram, quæ est in Domino Jesu, et dilectionem in omnes sanctos,

1:1 PAUL, AN APOSTLE OF JESUS CHRIST, by the will of God, to all the saints who are at Ephesus, and to the faithful in Christ Jesus.

1:2 Grace be to you, and peace from God the Father, and from the Lord Jesus Christ.

1:3 Blessed be the God and Father of our Lord Jesus Christ, who hath blessed us with spiritual blessings in heavenly places, in Christ:

1:4 As he chose us in him before the foundation of the world, that we should be holy and unspotted in his sight in charity.

1:5 Who hath predestinated us unto the adoption of children through Jesus Christ unto himself: according to the purpose of his will:

1:6 Unto the praise of the glory of his grace, in which he hath graced us in his beloved son.

1:7 In whom we have redemption through his blood, the remission of sins, according to the riches of his grace,

1:8 Which hath superabounded in us in all wisdom and prudence,

1:9 That he might make known unto us the mystery of his will, according to his good pleasure, which he hath purposed in him,

1:10 In the dispensation of the fulness of times, to re-establish all things in Christ, that are in heaven and on earth, in him.

1:11 In whom we also are called by lot, being predestinated according to the purpose of him who worketh all things according to the counsel of his will.

1:12 That we may be unto the praise of his glory, we who before hoped in Christ:

1:13 In whom you also, after you had heard the word of truth, (the gospel of your salvation;) in whom also believing, you were signed with the holy Spirit of promise,

1:14 Who is the pledge of our inheritance, unto the redemption of acquisition, unto the praise of his glory.

1:15 Wherefore I also, hearing of your faith that is in the Lord Jesus, and of your love towards all the saints,

1:16 non cesso gratias agens pro vobis, memoriam vestri faciens in orationibus meis :

1:17 ut Deus Domini nostri Jesu Christi, Pater gloriæ, det vobis spiritum sapientiæ et revelationis in agnitione ejus,

1:18 illuminatos oculos cordis vestri, ut sciatis quæ sit spes vocationis ejus, et quæ divitiæ gloriæ hæreditatis ejus in sanctis,

1:19 et quæ sit supereminens magnitudo virtutis ejus in nos, qui credimus secundum operationem potentiæ virtutis ejus,

1:20 quam operatus est in Christo, suscitans illum a mortuis, et constituens ad dexteram suam in cælestibus :

1:21 supra omnem principatum, et potestatem, et virtutem, et dominationem, et omne nomen, quod nominatur non solum in hoc sæculo, sed etiam in futuro.

1:22 Et omnia subjecit sub pedibus ejus : et ipsum dedit caput supra omnem ecclesiam,

1:23 quæ est corpus ipsius, et plenitudo ejus, qui omnia in omnibus adimpletur.

2:1 Et vos, cum essetis mortui delictis et peccatis vestris,

2:2 in quibus aliquando ambulastis secundum sæculum mundi hujus, secundum principem potestatis aëris hujus, spiritus, qui nunc operatur in filios diffidentiæ,

2:3 in quibus et nos omnes aliquando conversati sumus in desideriis carnis nostræ, facientes voluntatem carnis et cogitationum, et eramus natura filii iræ, sicut et ceteri :

2:4 Deus autem, qui dives est in misericordia, propter nimiam caritatem suam, qua dilexit nos,

2:5 et cum essemus mortui peccatis, convivificavit nos in Christo (cujus gratia estis salvati),

2:6 et conresuscitavit, et consedere fecit in cælestibus in Christo Jesu :

2:7 ut ostenderet in sæculis supervenientibus abundantes divitias gratiæ suæ, in bonitate super nos in Christo Jesu.

2:8 Gratia enim estis salvati per fidem, et hoc non ex vobis : Dei enim donum est :

2:9 non ex operibus, ut ne quis glorietur.

2:10 Ipsius enim sumus factura, creati in Christo Jesu in operibus bonis, quæ præparavit Deus ut

1:16 Cease not to give thanks for you, making commemoration of you in my prayers,

1:17 That the God of our Lord Jesus Christ, the Father of glory, may give unto you the spirit of wisdom and of revelation, in the knowledge of him:

1:18 The eyes of your heart enlightened, that you may know what the hope is of his calling, and what are the riches of the glory of his inheritance in the saints.

1:19 And what is the exceeding greatness of his power towards us, who believe according to the operation of the might of his power,

1:20 Which he wrought in Christ, raising him up from the dead, and setting him on his right hand in the heavenly places.

1:21 Above all principality, and power, and virtue, and dominion, and every name that is named, not only in this world, but also in that which is to come.

1:22 And he hath subjected all things under his feet, and hath made him head over all the church,

1:23 Which is his body, and the fulness of him who is filled all in all.

2:1 And you, when you were dead in your offences, and sins,

2:2 Wherein in time past you walked according to the course of this world, according to the prince of the power of this air, of the spirit that now worketh on the children of unbelief:

2:3 In which also we all conversed in time past, in the desires of our flesh, fulfilling the will of the flesh and of our thoughts, and were by nature children of wrath, even as the rest:

2:4 But God, (who is rich in mercy,) for his exceeding charity wherewith he loved us,

2:5 Even when we were dead in sins, hath quickened us together in Christ, (by whose grace you are saved,)

2:6 And hath raised us up together, and hath made us sit together in the heavenly places, through Christ Jesus.

2:7 That he might shew in the ages to come the abundant riches of his grace, in his bounty towards us in Christ Jesus.

2:8 For by grace you are saved through faith, and that not of yourselves, for it is the gift of God;

2:9 Not of works, that no man may glory.

2:10 For we are his workmanship, created in Christ Jesus in good works, which God hath

in illis ambulemus.

2:11 Propter quod memores estote quod aliquando vos gentes in carne, qui dicimini præputium ab ea quæ dicitur circumcisio in carne, manu facta :

2:12 quia eratis illo in tempore sine Christo, alienati a conversatione Israël, et hospites testamentorum, promissionis spem non habentes, et sine Deo in hoc mundo.

2:13 Nunc autem in Christo Jesu, vos, qui aliquando eratis longe, facti estis prope in sanguine Christi.

2:14 Ipse enim est pax nostra, qui fecit utraque unum, et medium parietem maceriæ solvens, inimicitias in carne sua,

2:15 legem mandatorum decretis evacuans, ut duos condat in semetipso in unum novum hominem, faciens pacem :

2:16 et reconciliet ambos in uno corpore, Deo per crucem, interficiens inimicitias in semetipso.

2:17 Et veniens evangelizavit pacem vobis, qui longe fuistis, et pacem iis, qui prope.

2:18 Quoniam per ipsum habemus accessum ambo in uno Spiritu ad Patrem.

2:19 Ergo jam non estis hospites, et advenæ : sed estis cives sanctorum, et domestici Dei,

2:20 superædificati super fundamentum apostolorum, et prophetarum, ipso summo angulari lapide Christo Jesu :

2:21 in quo omnis ædificatio constructa crescit in templum sanctum in Domino,

2:22 in quo et vos coædificamini in habitaculum Dei in Spiritu.

3:1 Hujus rei gratia, ego Paulus vinctus Christi Jesu, pro vobis gentibus,

3:2 si tamen audistis dispensationem gratiæ Dei, quæ data est mihi in vobis :

3:3 quoniam secundum revelationem notum mihi factum est sacramentum, sicut supra scripsi in brevi,

3:4 prout potestis legentes intelligere prudentiam meam in mysterio Christi :

3:5 quod aliis generationibus non est agnitum filiis hominum, sicuti nunc revelatum est sanctis apostolis ejus et prophetis in Spiritu,

3:6 gentes esse cohæredes, et concorporales, et

prepared that we should walk in them.

2:11 For which cause be mindful that you, being heretofore Gentiles in the flesh, who are called uncircumcision by that which is called circumcision in the flesh, made by hands;

2:12 That you were at that time without Christ, being aliens from the conversation of Israel, and strangers to the testament, having no hope of the promise, and without God in this world.

2:13 But now in Christ Jesus, you, who some time were afar off, are made nigh by the blood of Christ.

2:14 For he is our peace, who hath made both one, and breaking down the middle wall of partition, the enmities in his flesh:

2:15 Making void the law of commandments contained in decrees; that he might make the two in himself into one new man, making peace;

2:16 And might reconcile both to God in one body by the cross, killing the enmities in himself.

2:17 And coming, he preached peace to you that were afar off, and peace to them that were nigh.

2:18 For by him we have access both in one Spirit to the Father.

2:19 Now therefore you are no more strangers and foreigners; but you are fellow citizens with the saints, and the domestics of God,

2:20 Built upon the foundation of the apostles and prophets, Jesus Christ himself being the chief corner stone:

2:21 In whom all the building, being framed together, groweth up into an holy temple in the Lord.

2:22 In whom you also are built together into an habitation of God in the Spirit.

3:1 For this cause, I Paul, the prisoner of Jesus Christ, for you Gentiles;

3:2 If yet you have heard of the dispensation of the grace of God which is given me towards you:

3:3 How that, according to revelation, the mystery has been made known to me, as I have written above in a few words;

3:4 As you reading, may understand my knowledge in the mystery of Christ,

3:5 Which in other generations was not known to the sons of men, as it is now revealed to his holy apostles and prophets in the Spirit:

3:6 That the Gentiles should be fellow heirs, and

comparticipes promissionis ejus in Christo Jesu per Evangelium :

3:7 cujus factus sum minister secundum donum gratiæ Dei, quæ data est mihi secundum operationem virtutis ejus.

3:8 Mihi omnium sanctorum minimo data est gratia hæc, in gentibus evangelizare investigabiles divitias Christi,

3:9 et illuminare omnes, quæ sit dispensatio sacramenti absconditi a sæculis in Deo, qui omnia creavit :

3:10 ut innotescat principatibus et potestatibus in cælestibus per Ecclesiam, multiformis sapientia Dei,

3:11 secundum præfinitionem sæculorum, quam fecit in Christo Jesu Domino nostro :

3:12 in quo habemus fiduciam, et accessum in confidentia per fidem ejus.

3:13 Propter quod peto ne deficiatis in tribulationibus meis pro vobis : quæ est gloria vestra.

3:14 Hujus rei gratia flecto genua mea ad Patrem Domini nostri Jesu Christi,

3:15 ex quo omnis paternitas in cælis et in terra nominatur,

3:16 ut det vobis secundum divitias gloriæ suæ, virtute corroborari per Spiritum ejus in interiorem hominem,

3:17 Christum habitare per fidem in cordibus vestris : in caritate radicati, et fundati,

3:18 ut possitis comprehendere cum omnibus sanctis, quæ sit latitudo, et longitudo, et sublimitas, et profundum :

3:19 scire etiam supereminentem scientiæ caritatem Christi, ut impleamini in omnem plenitudinem Dei.

3:20 Ei autem, qui potens est omnia facere superabundanter quam petimus aut intelligimus, secundum virtutem, quæ operatur in nobis :

3:21 ipsi gloria in Ecclesia, et in Christo Jesu, in omnes generationes sæculi sæculorum. Amen.

4:1 Obsecro itaque vos ego vinctus in Domino, ut digne ambuletis vocatione, qua vocati estis,

4:2 cum omni humilitate, et mansuetudine, cum patientia, supportantes invicem in caritate,

4:3 solliciti servare unitatem Spiritus in vinculo pacis.

4:4 Unum corpus, et unus Spiritus, sicut vocati estis in una spe vocationis vestræ.

of the same body, and co-partners of his promise in Christ Jesus, by the gospel:

3:7 Of which I am made a minister, according to the gift of the grace of God, which is given to me according to the operation of his power:

3:8 To me, the least of all the saints, is given this grace, to preach among the Gentiles, the unsearchable riches of Christ,

3:9 And to enlighten all men, that they may see what is the dispensation of the mystery which hath been hidden from eternity in God, who created all things:

3:10 That the manifold wisdom of God may be made known to the principalities and powers in heavenly places through the church,

3:11 According to the eternal purpose, which he made, in Christ Jesus our Lord:

3:12 In whom we have boldness and access with confidence by the faith of him.

3:13 Wherefore I pray you not to faint at my tribulations for you, which is your glory.

3:14 For this cause I bow my knees to the Father of our Lord Jesus Christ,

3:15 Of whom all paternity in heaven and earth is named,

3:16 That he would grant you, according to the riches of his glory, to be strengthened by his Spirit with might unto the inward man,

3:17 That Christ may dwell by faith in your hearts; that being rooted and founded in charity,

3:18 You may be able to comprehend, with all the saints, what is the breadth, and length, and height, and depth:

3:19 To know also the charity of Christ, which surpasseth all knowledge, that you may be filled unto all the fulness of God.

3:20 Now to him who is able to do all things more abundantly than we desire or understand, according to the power that worketh in us;

3:21 To him be glory in the church, and in Christ Jesus unto all generations, world without end. Amen.

4:1 I THEREFORE, a prisoner in the Lord, beseech you that you walk worthy of the vocation in which you are called,

4:2 With all humility and mildness, with patience, supporting one another in charity,

4:3 Careful to keep the unity of the Spirit in the bond of peace.

4:4 One body and one Spirit; as you are called in one hope of your calling.

4:5 Unus Dominus, una fides, unum baptisma.

4:6 Unus Deus et Pater omnium, qui est super omnes, et per omnia, et in omnibus nobis.

4:7 Unicuique autem nostrum data est gratia secundum mensuram donationis Christi.

4:8 Propter quod dicit : Ascendens in altum, captivam duxit captivitatem : dedit dona hominibus.

4:9 Quod autem ascendit, quid est, nisi quia et descendit primum in inferiores partes terræ ?

4:10 Qui descendit, ipse est et qui ascendit super omnes cælos, ut impleret omnia.

4:11 Et ipse dedit quosdam quidem apostolos, quosdam autem prophetas, alios vero evangelistas, alios autem pastores et doctores,

4:12 ad consummationem sanctorum in opus ministerii, in ædificationem corporis Christi :

4:13 donec occurramus omnes in unitatem fidei, et agnitionis Filii Dei, in virum perfectum, in mensuram ætatis plenitudinis Christi :

4:14 ut jam non simus parvuli fluctuantes, et circumferamur omni vento doctrinæ in nequitia hominum, in astutia ad circumventionem erroris.

4:15 Veritatem autem facientes in caritate, crescamus in illo per omnia, qui est caput Christus :

4:16 ex quo totum corpus compactum et connexum per omnem juncturam subministrationis, secundum operationem in mensuram uniuscujusque membri, augmentum corporis facit in ædificationem sui in caritate.

4:17 Hoc igitur dico, et testificor in Domino, ut jam non ambuletis, sicut et gentes ambulant in vanitate sensus sui,

4:18 tenebris obscuratum habentes intellectum, alienati a vita Dei per ignorantiam, quæ est in illis, propter cæcitatem cordis ipsorum,

4:19 qui desperantes, semetipsos tradiderunt impudicitiæ, in operationem immunditiæ omnis in avaritiam.

4:20 Vos autem non ita didicistis Christum,

4:21 si tamen illum audistis, et in ipso edocti estis, sicut est veritas in Jesu,

4:22 deponere vos secundum pristinam conversationem veterem hominem, qui corrumpitur

4:5 One Lord, one faith, one baptism.

4:6 One God and Father of all, who is above all, and through all, and in us all.

4:7 But to every one of us is given grace, according to the measure of the giving of Christ.

4:8 Wherefore he saith: Ascending on high, he led captivity captive; he gave gifts to men.

4:9 Now that he ascended, what is it, but because he also descended first into the lower parts of the earth?

4:10 He that descended is the same also that ascended above all the heavens, that he might fill all things.

4:11 And he gave some apostles, and some prophets, and other some evangelists, and other some pastors and doctors,

4:12 For the perfecting of the saints, for the work of the ministry, for the edifying of the body of Christ:

4:13 Until we all meet into the unity of faith, and of the knowledge of the Son of God, unto a perfect man, unto the measure of the age of the fulness of Christ;

4:14 That henceforth we be no more children tossed to and fro, and carried about with every wind of doctrine by the wickedness of men, by cunning craftiness, by which they lie in wait to deceive

4:15 But doing the truth in charity, we may in all things grow up in him who is the head, even Christ:

4:16 From whom the whole body, being compacted and fitly joined together, by what every joint supplieth, according to the operation in the measure of every part, maketh increase of the body, unto the edifying of itself in charity.

4:17 This then I say and testify in the Lord: That henceforward you walk not as also the Gentiles walk in the vanity of their mind,

4:18 Having their understanding darkened, being alienated from the life of God through the ignorance that is in them, because of the blindness of their hearts.

4:19 Who despairing, have given themselves up to lasciviousness, unto the working of all uncleanness, unto covetousness.

4:20 But you have not so learned Christ;

4:21 If so be that you have heard him, and have been taught in him, as the truth is in Jesus:

4:22 To put off, according to former conversation, the old man, who is corrupted according

secundum desideria erroris.

4:23 Renovamini autem spiritu mentis vestræ,

4:24 et induite novum hominem, qui secundum Deum creatus est in justitia, et sanctitate veritatis.

4:25 Propter quod deponentes mendacium, loquimini veritatem unusquisque cum proximo suo : quoniam sumus invicem membra.

4:26 Irascimini, et nolite peccare : sol non occidat super iracundiam vestram.

4:27 Nolite locum dare diabolo :

4:28 qui furabatur, jam non furetur : magis autem laboret, operando manibus suis, quod bonum est, ut habeat unde tribuat necessitatem patienti.

4:29 Omnis sermo malus ex ore vestro non procedat : sed si quis bonus ad ædificationem fidei ut det gratiam audientibus.

4:30 Et nolite contristare Spiritum Sanctum Dei : in quo signati estis in diem redemptionis.

4:31 Omnis amaritudo, et ira, et indignatio, et clamor, et blasphemia tollatur a vobis cum omni malitia.

4:32 Estote autem invicem benigni, misericordes, donantes invicem sicut et Deus in Christo donavit vobis.

5:1 Estote ergo imitatores Dei, sicut filii carissimi,

5:2 et ambulate in dilectione, sicut et Christus dilexit nos, et tradidit semetipsum pro nobis, oblationem et hostiam Deo in odorem suavitatis.

5:3 Fornicatio autem, et omnis immunditia, aut avaritia, nec nominetur in vobis, sicut decet sanctos :

5:4 aut turpitudo, aut stultiloquium, aut scurrilitas, quæ ad rem non pertinet : sed magis gratiarum actio.

5:5 Hoc enim scitote intelligentes : quod omnis fornicator, aut immundus, aut avarus, quod est idolorum servitus, non habet hæreditatem in regno Christi et Dei.

5:6 Nemo vos seducat inanibus verbis : propter hæc enim venit ira Dei in filios diffidentiæ.

5:7 Nolite ergo effici participes eorum.

5:8 Eratis enim aliquando tenebræ : nunc autem lux in Domino. Ut filii lucis ambulate :

to the desire of error.

4:23 And be renewed in the spirit of your mind:

4:24 And put on the new man, who according to God is created in justice and holiness of truth.

4:25 Wherefore putting away lying, speak ye the truth every man with his neighbour; for we are members one of another.

4:26 Be angry, and sin not. Let not the sun go down upon your anger.

4:27 Give not place to the devil.

4:28 He that stole, let him now steal no more; but rather let him labour, working with his hands the thing which is good, that he may have something to give to him that suffereth need.

4:29 Let no evil speech proceed from your mouth; but that which is good, to the edification of faith, that it may administer grace to the hearers.

4:30 And grieve not the holy Spirit of God: whereby you are sealed unto the day of redemption.

4:31 Let all bitterness, and anger, and indignation, and clamour, and blasphemy, be put away from you, with all malice.

4:32 And be ye kind one to another; merciful, forgiving one another, even as God hath forgiven you in Christ.

5:1 Be ye therefore followers of God, as most dear children;

5:2 And walk in love, as Christ also hath loved us, and hath delivered himself for us, an oblation and a sacrifice to God for an odour of sweetness.

5:3 But fornication, and all uncleanness, or covetousness, let it not so much as be named among you, as becometh saints:

5:4 Or obscenity, or foolish talking, or scurrility, which is to no purpose; but rather giving of thanks.

5:5 For know you this and understand, that no fornicator, or unclean, or covetous person (which is a serving of idols), hath inheritance in the kingdom of Christ and of God.

5:6 Let no man deceive you with vain words. For because of these things cometh the anger of God upon the children of unbelief.

5:7 Be ye not therefore partakers with them.

5:8 For you were heretofore darkness, but now light in the Lord. Walk then as children of the light.

5:9 fructus enim lucis est in omni bonitate, et justitia, et veritate :

5:10 probantes quid sit beneplacitum Deo :

5:11 et nolite communicare operibus infructuosis tenebrarum, magis autem redarguite.

5:12 Quæ enim in occulto fiunt ab ipsis, turpe est et dicere.

5:13 Omnia autem, quæ arguuntur, a lumine manifestantur : omne enim, quod manifestatur, lumen est.

5:14 Propter quod dicit : Surge qui dormis, et exsurge a mortuis, et illuminabit te Christus.

5:15 Videte itaque, fratres, quomodo caute ambuletis : non quasi insipientes,

5:16 sed ut sapientes : redimentes tempus, quoniam dies mali sunt.

5:17 Propterea nolite fieri imprudentes, sed intelligentes quæ sit voluntas Dei.

5:18 Et nolite inebriari vino, in quo est luxuria, sed implemini Spiritu Sancto,

5:19 loquentes vobismetipsis in psalmis, et hymnis, et canticis spiritualibus, cantantes et psallentes in cordibus vestris Domino,

5:20 gratias agentes semper pro omnibus in nomine Domini nostri Jesu Christi Deo et Patri,

5:21 subjecti invicem in timore Christi.

5:22 Mulieres viris suis subditæ sint, sicut Domino :

5:23 quoniam vir caput est mulieris, sicut Christus caput est Ecclesiæ : ipse, salvator corporis ejus.

5:24 Sed sicut Ecclesia subjecta est Christo, ita et mulieres viris suis in omnibus.

5:25 Viri, diligite uxores vestras, sicut et Christus dilexit Ecclesiam, et seipsum tradidit pro ea,

5:26 ut illam sanctificaret, mundans lavacro aquæ in verbo vitæ,

5:27 ut exhiberet ipse sibi gloriosam Ecclesiam, non habentem maculam, aut rugam, aut aliquid hujusmodi, sed ut sit sancta et immaculata.

5:28 Ita et viri debent diligere uxores suas ut corpora sua. Qui suam uxorem diligit, seipsum diligit.

5:29 Nemo enim umquam carnem suam odio habuit : sed nutrit et fovet eam, sicut et Christus Ecclesiam :

5:9 For the fruit of the light is in all goodness, and justice, and truth;

5:10 Proving what is well pleasing to God:

5:11 And have no fellowship with the unfruitful works of darkness, but rather reprove them.

5:12 For the things that are done by them in secret, it is a shame even to speak of.

5:13 But all things that are reproved, are made manifest by the light; for all that is made manifest is light.

5:14 Wherefore he saith: Rise thou that sleepest, and arise from the dead: and Christ shall enlighten thee.

5:15 See therefore, brethren, how you walk circumspectly: not as unwise,

5:16 But as wise: redeeming the time, because the days are evil.

5:17 Wherefore become not unwise, but understanding what is the will of God.

5:18 And be not drunk with wine, wherein is luxury; but be ye filled with the holy Spirit,

5:19 Speaking to yourselves in psalms, and hymns, and spiritual canticles, singing and making melody in your hearts to the Lord;

5:20 Giving thanks always for all things, in the name of our Lord Jesus Christ, to God and the Father:

5:21 Being subject one to another, in the fear of Christ.

5:22 Let women be subject to their husbands, as to the Lord:

5:23 Because the husband is the head of the wife, as Christ is the head of the church. He is the saviour of his body.

5:24 Therefore as the church is subject to Christ, so also let the wives be to their husbands in all things.

5:25 Husbands, love your wives, as Christ also loved the church, and delivered himself up for it:

5:26 That he might sanctify it, cleansing it by the laver of water in the word of life:

5:27 That he might present it to himself a glorious church, not having spot or wrinkle, or any such thing; but that it should be holy, and without blemish.

5:28 So also ought men to love their wives as their own bodies. He that loveth his wife, loveth himself.

5:29 For no man ever hated his own flesh; but nourisheth and cherisheth it, as also Christ doth the church:

5:30 quia membra sumus corporis ejus, de carne ejus et de ossibus ejus.

5:31 Propter hoc relinquet homo patrem et matrem suam, et adhærebit uxori suæ, et erunt duo in carne una.

5:32 Sacramentum hoc magnum est, ego autem dico in Christo et in Ecclesia.

5:33 Verumtamen et vos singuli, unusquisque uxorem suam sicut seipsum diligat : uxor autem timeat virum suum.

6:1 Filii, obedite parentibus vestris in Domino : hoc enim justum est.

6:2 Honora patrem tuum, et matrem tuam, quod est mandatum primum in promissione :

6:3 ut bene sit tibi, et sis longævus super terram.

6:4 Et vos patres, nolite ad iracundiam provocare filios vestros : sed educate illos in disciplina et correptione Domini.

6:5 Servi, obedite dominis carnalibus cum timore et tremore, in simplicitate cordis vestri, sicut Christo :

6:6 non ad oculum servientes, quasi hominibus placentes, sed ut servi Christi, facientes voluntatem Dei ex animo,

6:7 cum bona voluntate servientes, sicut Domino, et non hominibus :

6:8 scientes quoniam unusquisque quodcumque fecerit bonum, hoc recipiet a Domino, sive servus, sive liber.

6:9 Et vos domini, eadem facite illis, remittentes minas : scientes quia et illorum et vester Dominus est in cælis : et personarum acceptio non est apud eum.

6:10 De cetero, fratres, confortamini in Domino, et in potentia virtutis ejus.

6:11 Induite vos armaturam Dei, ut possitis stare adversus insidias diaboli :

6:12 quoniam non est nobis colluctatio adversus carnem et sanguinem, sed adversus principes, et potestates, adversus mundi rectores tenebrarum harum, contra spiritualia nequitiæ, in cælestibus.

6:13 Propterea accipite armaturam Dei, ut possitis resistere in die malo, et in omnibus perfecti stare.

6:14 State ergo succincti lumbos vestros in veritate, et induti loricam justitiæ,

6:15 et calceati pedes in præparatione Evangelii

5:30 Because we are members of his body, of his flesh, and of his bones.

5:31 For this cause shall a man leave his father and mother, and shall cleave to his wife, and they shall be two in one flesh.

5:32 This is a great sacrament; but I speak in Christ and in the church.

5:33 Nevertheless let every one of you in particular love his wife as himself: and let the wife fear her husband.

6:1 Children, obey your parents in the Lord, for this is just.

6:2 Honour thy father and thy mother, which is the first commandment with a promise:

6:3 That it may be well with thee, and thou mayest be long lived upon earth.

6:4 And you, fathers, provoke not your children to anger; but bring them up in the discipline and correction of the Lord.

6:5 Servants, be obedient to them that are your lords according to the flesh, with fear and trembling, in the simplicity of your heart, as to Christ:

6:6 Not serving to the eye, as it were pleasing men, but, as the servants of Christ doing the will of God from the heart,

6:7 With a good will serving, as to the Lord, and not to men.

6:8 Knowing that whatsoever good thing any man shall do, the same shall he receive from the Lord, whether he be bond, or free.

6:9 And you, masters, do the same things to them, forbearing threatenings, knowing that the Lord both of them and you is in heaven; and there is no respect of persons with him.

6:10 Finally, brethren, be strengthened in the Lord, and in the might of his power.

6:11 Put you on the armour of God, that you may be able to stand against the deceits of the devil.

6:12 For our wrestling is not against flesh and blood; but against principalities and power, against the rulers of the world of this darkness, against the spirits of wickedness in the high places.

6:13 Therefore take unto you the armour of God, that you may be able to resist in the evil day, and to stand in all things perfect.

6:14 Stand therefore, having your loins girt about with truth, and having on the breastplate of justice,

6:15 And your feet shod with the preparation of

pacis,

6:16 in omnibus sumentes scutum fidei, in quo possitis omnia tela nequissimi ignea extinguere :

6:17 et galeam salutis assumite, et gladium spiritus (quod est verbum Dei),

6:18 per omnem orationem et obsecrationem orantes omni tempore in spiritu : et in ipso vigilantes in omni instantia et obsecratione pro omnibus sanctis :

6:19 et pro me, ut detur mihi sermo in apertione oris mei cum fiducia, notum facere mysterium Evangelii :

6:20 pro quo legatione fungor in catena, ita ut in ipso audeam, prout oportet me loqui.

6:21 Ut autem et vos sciatis quæ circa me sunt, quid agam, omnia vobis nota faciet Tychicus, carissimus frater, et fidelis minister in Domino :

6:22 quem misi ad vos in hoc ipsum, ut cognoscatis quæ circa nos sunt, et consoletur corda vestra.

6:23 Pax fratribus, et caritas cum fide a Deo Patre et Domino Jesu Christo.

6:24 Gratia cum omnibus qui diligunt Dominum nostrum Jesum Christum in incorruptione. Amen.

the gospel of peace:

6:16 In all things taking the shield of faith, wherewith you may be able to extinguish all the fiery darts of the most wicked one.

6:17 And take unto you the helmet of salvation, and the sword of the Spirit (which is the word of God).

6:18 By all prayer and supplication praying at all times in the spirit; and in the same watching with all instance and supplication for all the saints:

6:19 And for me, that speech may be given me, that I may open my mouth with confidence, to make known the mystery of the gospel.

6:20 For which I am an ambassador in a chain, so that therein I may be bold to speak according as I ought.

6:21 But that you also may know the things that concern me, and what I am doing, Tychicus, my dearest brother and faithful minister in the Lord, will make known to you all things:

6:22 Whom I have sent to you for this same purpose, that you may know the things concerning us, and that he may comfort your hearts.

6:23 Peace be to the brethren and charity with faith, from God the Father, and the Lord Jesus Christ.

6:24 Grace be with all them that love our Lord Jesus Christ in incorruption. Amen.

Epistula Beati Pauli Apostoli ad Philippenses

THE EPISTLE OF BLESSED PAUL THE APOSTLE TO THE PHILIPPIANS

✠

1:1 PAULUS ET TIMOTHEUS, SERVI JESU CHRISTI, omnibus sanctis in Christo Jesu, qui sunt Philippis, cum episcopis et diaconibus.

1:2 Gratia vobis, et pax a Deo Patre nostro, et Domino Jesu Christo.

1:3 Gratias ago Deo meo in omni memoria vestri,

1:4 semper in cunctis orationibus meis pro omnibus vobis, cum gaudio deprecationem faciens,

1:5 super communicatione vestra in Evangelio Christi a prima die usque nunc.

1:6 Confidens hoc ipsum, quia qui cœpit in vobis opus bonum, perficiet usque in diem Christi Jesu :

1:7 sicut est mihi justum hoc sentire pro omnibus vobis : eo quod habeam vos in corde, et in vinculis meis, et in defensione, et confirmatione Evangelii, socios gaudii mei omnes vos esse.

1:8 Testis enim mihi est Deus, quomodo cupiam omnes vos in visceribus Jesu Christi.

1:9 Et hoc oro, ut caritas vestra magis ac magis abundet in scientia, et in omni sensu :

1:10 ut probetis potiora, ut sitis sinceri, et sine offensa in diem Christi,

1:11 repleti fructu justitiæ per Jesum Christum, in gloriam et laudem Dei.

1:12 Scire autem vos volo fratres, quia quæ circa me sunt, magis ad profectum venerunt Evangelii :

1:13 ita ut vincula mea manifesta fierent in Christo in omni prætorio, et in ceteris omnibus,

1:14 et plures e fratribus in Domino confidentes vinculis meis, abundantius auderent sine timore verbum Dei loqui.

1:15 Quidam quidem et propter invidiam et contentionem : quidam autem et propter

1:1 PAUL AND TIMOTHY, THE SERVANTS OF JESUS CHRIST; to all the saints in Christ Jesus, who are at Philippi, with the bishops and deacons.

1:2 Grace be unto you, and peace from God our Father, and from the Lord Jesus Christ.

1:3 I give thanks to my God in every remembrance of you,

1:4 Always in all my prayers making supplication for you all, with joy;

1:5 For your communication in the gospel of Christ from the first day until now.

1:6 Being confident of this very thing, that he, who hath begun a good work in you, will perfect it unto the day of Christ Jesus.

1:7 As it is meet for me to think this for you all, for that I have you in my heart; and that in my bands, and in the defence and confirmation of the gospel, you all are partakers of my joy.

1:8 For God is my witness, how I long after you all in the bowels of Jesus Christ.

1:9 And this I pray, that your charity may more and more abound in knowledge, and in all understanding:

1:10 That you may approve the better things, that you may be sincere and without offence unto the day of Christ,

1:11 Filled with the fruit of justice, through Jesus Christ, unto the glory and praise of God.

1:12 Now, brethren, I desire you should know, that the things which have happened to me, have fallen out rather to the furtherance of the gospel:

1:13 So that my bands are made manifest in Christ, in all the court, and in all other places;

1:14 And many of the brethren in the Lord, growing confident by my bands, are much more bold to speak the word of God without fear.

1:15 Some indeed, even out of envy and contention; but some also for good will preach

bonam voluntatem Christum prædicant :

1:16 quidam ex caritate, scientes quoniam in defensionem Evangelii positus sum.

1:17 Quidam autem ex contentione Christum annuntiant non sincere, existimantes pressuram se suscitare vinculis meis.

1:18 Quid enim ? Dum omni modo sive per occasionem, sive per veritatem, Christus annuntietur : et in hoc gaudeo, sed et gaudebo.

1:19 Scio enim quia hoc mihi proveniet ad salutem, per vestram orationem, et subministrationem Spiritus Jesu Christi,

1:20 secundum exspectationem et spem meam, quia in nullo confundar : sed in omni fiducia sicut semper, et nunc magnificabitur Christus in corpore meo, sive per vitam, sive per mortem.

1:21 Mihi enim vivere Christus est, et mori lucrum.

1:22 Quod si vivere in carne, hic mihi fructus operis est, et quid eligam ignoro.

1:23 Coarctor autem e duobus : desiderium habens dissolvi, et esse cum Christo, multo magis melius :

1:24 permanere autem in carne, necessarium propter vos.

1:25 Et hoc confidens scio quia manebo, et permanebo omnibus vobis ad profectum vestrum, et gaudium fidei :

1:26 ut gratulatio vestra abundet in Christo Jesu in me, per meum adventum iterum ad vos.

1:27 Tantum digne Evangelio Christi conversamini : ut sive cum venero, et videro vos, sive absens audiam de vobis, quia statis in uno spiritu unanimes, collaborantes fidei Evangelii :

1:28 et in nullo terreamini ab adversariis : quæ illis est causa perditionis, vobis autem salutis, et hoc a Deo :

1:29 quia vobis donatum est pro Christo, non solum ut in eum credatis, sed ut etiam pro illo patiamini :

1:30 idem certamen habentes, quale et vidistis in me, et nunc audistis de me.

2:1 Si qua ergo consolatio in Christo, si quod solatium caritatis, si qua societas spiritus, si qua viscera miserationis :

2:2 implete gaudium meum ut idem sapiatis, eamdem caritatem habentes, unanimes, idipsum sentientes,

Christ.

1:16 Some out of charity, knowing that I am set for the defence of the gospel.

1:17 And some out of contention preach Christ not sincerely: supposing that they raise affliction to my bands.

1:18 But what then? So that by all means, whether by occasion, or by truth, Christ be preached: in this also I rejoice, yea, and will rejoice.

1:19 For I know that this shall fall out to me unto salvation, through your prayer, and the supply of the Spirit of Jesus Christ,

1:20 According to my expectation and hope; that in nothing I shall be confounded, but with all confidence, as always, so now also shall Christ be magnified in my body, wither it be by life, or by death.

1:21 For to me, to live is Christ; and to die is gain.

1:22 And if to live in the flesh, this is to me the fruit of labour, and what I shall choose I know not.

1:23 But I am straitened between two: having a desire to be dissolved and to be with Christ, a thing by far the better.

1:24 But to abide still in the flesh, is needful for you.

1:25 And having this confidence, I know that I shall abide, and continue with you all, for your furtherance and joy of faith:

1:26 That your rejoicing may abound in Christ Jesus for me, by my coming to you again.

1:27 Only let your conversation be worthy of the gospel of Christ: that, whether I come and see you, or, being absent, may hear of you, that you stand fast in one spirit, with one mind labouring together for the faith of the gospel.

1:28 And in nothing be ye terrified by the adversaries: which to them is a cause of perdition, but to you of salvation, and this from God:

1:29 For unto you it is given for Christ, not only to believe in him, but also to suffer for him.

1:30 Having the same conflict as that which you have seen in me, and now have heard of me.

2:1 If there be therefore any consolation in Christ, if any comfort of charity, if any society of the spirit, if any bowels of commiseration:

2:2 Fulfil ye my joy, that you may be of one mind, having the same charity, being of one accord, agreeing in sentiment.

2:3 nihil per contentionem, neque per inanem gloriam : sed in humilitate superiores sibi invicem arbitrantes,

2:4 non quæ sua sunt singuli considerantes, sed ea quæ aliorum.

2:5 Hoc enim sentite in vobis, quod et in Christo Jesu :

2:6 qui cum in forma Dei esset, non rapinam arbitratus est esse se æqualem Deo :

2:7 sed semetipsum exinanivit, formam servi accipiens, in similitudinem hominum factus, et habitu inventus ut homo.

2:8 Humiliavit semetipsum factus obediens usque ad mortem, mortem autem crucis.

2:9 Propter quod et Deus exaltavit illum, et donavit illi nomen, quod est super omne nomen :

2:10 ut in nomine Jesu omne genu flectatur cælestium, terrestrium et infernorum,

2:11 et omnis lingua confiteatur, quia Dominus Jesus Christus in gloria est Dei Patris.

2:12 Itaque carissimi mei (sicut semper obedistis), non ut in præsentia mei tantum, sed multo magis nunc in absentia mea, cum metu et tremore vestram salutem operamini.

2:13 Deus est enim, qui operatur in vobis et velle, et perficere pro bona voluntate.

2:14 Omnia autem facite sine murmurationibus et hæsitationibus :

2:15 ut sitis sine querela, et simplices filii Dei, sine reprehensione in medio nationis pravæ et perversæ : inter quos lucetis sicut luminaria in mundo,

2:16 verbum vitæ continentes ad gloriam meam in die Christi, quia non in vacuum cucurri, neque in vacuum laboravi.

2:17 Sed et si immolor supra sacrificium, et obsequium fidei vestræ, gaudeo, et congratulor omnibus vobis.

2:18 Idipsum autem et vos gaudete, et congratulamini mihi.

2:19 Spero autem in Domino Jesu, Timotheum me cito mittere ad vos : ut et ego bono animo sim, cognitis quæ circa vos sunt.

2:20 Neminem enim habeo tam unanimem, qui sincera affectione pro vobis sollicitus sit.

2:21 Omnes enim quæ sua sunt quærunt, non quæ sunt Jesu Christi.

2:3 Let nothing be done through contention, neither by vain glory: but in humility, let each esteem others better than themselves:

2:4 Each one not considering the things that are his own, but those that are other men's.

2:5 For let this mind be in you, which was also in Christ Jesus:

2:6 Who being in the form of God, thought it not robbery to be equal with God:

2:7 But emptied himself, taking the form of a servant, being made in the likeness of men, and in habit found as a man.

2:8 He humbled himself, becoming obedient unto death, even to the death of the cross.

2:9 For which cause God also hath exalted him, and hath given him a name which is above all names:

2:10 That in the name of Jesus every knee should bow, of those that are in heaven, on earth, and under the earth:

2:11 And that every tongue should confess that the Lord Jesus Christ is in the glory of God the Father.

2:12 Wherefore, my dearly beloved, (as you have always obeyed, not as in my presence only, but much more now in my absence,) with fear and trembling work out your salvation.

2:13 For it is God who worketh in you, both to will and to accomplish, according to his good will.

2:14 And do ye all things without murmurings and hesitations;

2:15 That you may be blameless, and sincere children of God, without reproof, in the midst of a crooked and perverse generation; among whom you shine as lights in the world.

2:16 Holding forth the word of life to my glory in the day of Christ, because I have not run in vain, nor laboured in vain.

2:17 Yea, and if I be made a victim upon the sacrifice and service of your faith, I rejoice, and congratulate with you all.

2:18 And for the selfsame thing do you also rejoice, and congratulate with me.

2:19 And I hope in the Lord Jesus to send Timothy unto you shortly, that I also may be of good comfort, when I know the things concerning you.

2:20 For I have no man so of the same mind, who with sincere affection is solicitous for you.

2:21 For all seek the things that are their own; not the things that are Jesus Christ's.

2:22 Experimentum autem ejus cognoscite, quia sicut patri filius, mecum servivit in Evangelio.

2:23 Hunc igitur spero me mittere ad vos, mox ut videro quæ circa me sunt.

2:24 Confido autem in Domino quoniam et ipse veniam ad vos cito.

2:25 Necessarium autem existimavi Epaphroditum fratrem, et cooperatorem, et commilitonem meum, vestrum autem apostolum, et ministrum necessitatis meæ, mittere ad vos :

2:26 quoniam quidem omnes vos desiderabat : et mœstus erat, propterea quod audieratis illum infirmatum.

2:27 Nam et infirmatus est usque ad mortem : sed Deus misertus est ejus : non solum autem ejus, verum etiam et mei, ne tristitiam super tristitiam haberem.

2:28 Festinantius ergo misi illum, ut viso eo iterum gaudeatis, et ego sine tristitia sim.

2:29 Excipite itaque illum cum omni gaudio in Domino, et ejusmodi cum honore habetote ;

2:30 quoniam propter opus Christi usque ad mortem accessit, tradens animam suam ut impleret id quod ex vobis deerat erga meum obsequium.

3:1 De cetero, fratres mei, gaudete in Domino. Eadem vobis scribere, mihi quidem non pigrum, vobis autem necessarium.

3:2 Videte canes, videte malos operarios, videte concisionem.

3:3 Nos enim sumus circumcisio, qui spiritu servimus Deo, et gloriamur in Christo Jesu, et non in carne fiduciam habentes,

3:4 quamquam ego habeam confidentiam et in carne. Si quis alius videtur confidere in carne, ego magis,

3:5 circumcisus octavo die, ex genere Israël, de tribu Benjamin, Hebræus ex Hebræis, secundum legem pharisæus,

3:6 secundum æmulationem persequens Ecclesiam Dei, secundum justitiam, quæ in lege est, conversatus sine querela.

3:7 Sed quæ mihi fuerunt lucra, hæc arbitratus sum propter Christum detrimenta.

3:8 Verumtamen existimo omnia detrimentum esse propter eminentem scientiam Jesu Christi Domini mei : propter quem omnia detrimen-

2:22 Now know ye the proof of him, that as a son with the father, so hath he served with me in the gospel.

2:23 Him therefore I hope to send unto you immediately, so soon as I shall see how it will go with me.

2:24 And I trust in the Lord, that I myself also shall come to you shortly.

2:25 But I have thought it necessary to send to you Epaphroditus, my brother and fellow labourer, and fellow soldier, but your apostle, and he that hath ministered to my wants.

2:26 For indeed he longed after you all: and was sad, for that you had heard that he was sick.

2:27 For indeed he was sick, nigh unto death; but God had mercy on him; and not only on him, but on me also, lest I should have sorrow upon sorrow.

2:28 Therefore I sent him the more speedily: that seeing him again, you may rejoice, and I may be without sorrow.

2:29 Receive him therefore with all joy in the Lord; and treat with honour such as he is.

2:30 Because for the work of Christ he came to the point of death: delivering his life, that he might fulfil that which on your part was wanting towards my service.

3:1 As to the rest, my brethren, rejoice in the Lord. To write the same things to you, to me indeed is not wearisome, but to you it is necessary.

3:2 Beware of dogs, beware of evil workers, beware of the concision.

3:3 For we are the circumcision, who in spirit serve God; and glory in Christ Jesus, not having confidence in the flesh.

3:4 Though I might also have confidence in the flesh. If any other thinketh he may have confidence in the flesh, I more,

3:5 Being circumcised the eighth day, of the stock of Israel, of the tribe of Benjamin, an Hebrew of the Hebrews; according to the law, a Pharisee:

3:6 According to zeal, persecuting the church of God; according to the justice that is in the law, conversing without blame.

3:7 But the things that were gain to me, the same I have counted loss for Christ.

3:8 Furthermore I count all things to be but loss for the excellent knowledge of Jesus Christ my Lord; for whom I have suffered the loss of all

tum feci, et arbitror ut stercora, ut Christum lucrifaciam,

3:9 et inveniar in illo non habens meam justitiam, quæ ex lege est, sed illam, quæ ex fide est Christi Jesu : quæ ex Deo est justitia in fide,

3:10 ad cognoscendum illum, et virtutem resurrectionis ejus, et societatem passionum illius : configuratus morti ejus :

3:11 si quo modo occurram ad resurrectionem, quæ est ex mortuis :

3:12 non quod jam acceperim, aut jam perfectus sim : sequor autem, si quomodo comprehendam in quo et comprehensus sum a Christo Jesu.

3:13 Fratres, ego me non arbitror comprehendisse. Unum autem, quæ quidem retro sunt obliviscens, ad ea vero quæ sunt priora, extendens meipsum,

3:14 ad destinatum persequor, ad bravium supernæ vocationis Dei in Christo Jesu.

3:15 Quicumque ergo perfecti sumus, hoc sentiamus : et si quid aliter sapitis, et hoc vobis Deus revelabit.

3:16 Verumtamen ad quod pervenimus ut idem sapiamus, et in eadem permaneamus regula.

3:17 Imitatores mei estote, fratres, et observate eos qui ita ambulant, sicut habetis formam nostram.

3:18 Multi enim ambulant, quos sæpe dicebam vobis (nunc autem et flens dico) inimicos crucis Christi :

3:19 quorum finis interitus : quorum Deus venter est : et gloria in confusione ipsorum, qui terrena sapiunt.

3:20 Nostra autem conversatio in cælis est : unde etiam Salvatorem exspectamus Dominum nostrum Jesum Christum,

3:21 qui reformabit corpus humilitatis nostræ, configuratum corpori claritatis suæ, secundum operationem, qua etiam possit subjicere sibi omnia.

4:1 Itaque fratres mei carissimi, et desideratissimi, gaudium meum, et corona mea : sic state in Domino, carissimi.

4:2 Evodiam rogo, et Syntychen deprecor, idipsum sapere in Domino.

4:3 Etiam rogo et te, germane compar, adjuva illas, quæ mecum laboraverunt in Evangelio cum Clemente, et ceteris adjutoribus meis, quorum nomina sunt in libro vitæ.

things, and count them but as dung, that I may gain Christ:

3:9 And may be found in him, not having my justice, which is of the law, but that which is of the faith of Christ Jesus, which is of God, justice in faith:

3:10 That I may know him, and the power of his resurrection, and the fellowship of his sufferings, being made conformable to his death,

3:11 If by any means I may attain to the resurrection which is from the dead.

3:12 Not as though I had already attained, or were already perfect; but I follow after, if I may by any means apprehend, wherein I am also apprehended by Christ Jesus.

3:13 Brethren, I do not count myself to have apprehended. But one thing I do: forgetting the things that are behind, and stretching forth myself to those that are before,

3:14 I press towards the mark, to the prize of the supernal vocation of God in Christ Jesus.

3:15 Let us therefore, as many as are perfect, be thus minded; and if in any thing you be otherwise minded, this also God will reveal to you.

3:16 Nevertheless whereunto we are come, that we be of the same mind, let us also continue in the same rule.

3:17 Be ye followers of me, brethren, and observe them who walk so as you have our model.

3:18 For many walk, of whom I have told you often (and now tell you weeping), that they are enemies of the cross of Christ;

3:19 Whose end is destruction; whose God is their belly; and whose glory is in their shame; who mind earthly things.

3:20 But our conversation is in heaven; from whence also we look for the Saviour, our Lord Jesus Christ,

3:21 Who will reform the body of our lowness, made like to the body of his glory, according to the operation whereby also he is able to subdue all things unto himself.

4:1 Therefore, my dearly beloved brethren, and most desired, my joy and my crown; so stand fast in the Lord, my dearly beloved.

4:2 I beg of Evodia, and I beseech Syntyche, to be of one mind in the Lord.

4:3 And I entreat thee also, my sincere companion, help those women who have laboured with me in the gospel, with Clement and the rest of my fellow labourers, whose names are in the

book of life.

4:4 Gaudete in Domino semper : iterum dico gaudete.

4:5 Modestia vestra nota sit omnibus hominibus : Dominus prope est.

4:6 Nihil solliciti sitis : sed in omni oratione, et obsecratione, cum gratiarum actione petitiones vestræ innotescant apud Deum.

4:7 Et pax Dei, quæ exuperat omnem sensum, custodiat corda vestra, et intelligentias vestras in Christo Jesu.

4:8 De cetero fratres, quæcumque sunt vera, quæcumque pudica, quæcumque justa, quæcumque sancta, quæcumque amabilia, quæcumque bonæ famæ, siqua virtus, siqua laus disciplinæ, hæc cogitate.

4:9 Quæ et didicistis, et accepistis, et audistis, et vidistis in me, hæc agite : et Deus pacis erit vobiscum.

4:10 Gavisus sum autem in Domino vehementer, quoniam tandem aliquando refloruistis pro me sentire, sicut et sentiebatis : occupati autem eratis.

4:11 Non quasi propter penuriam dico : ego enim didici, in quibus sum, sufficiens esse.

4:12 Scio et humiliari, scio et abundare (ubique et in omnibus institutus sum) : et satiari, et esurire, et abundare, et penuriam pati.

4:13 Omnia possum in eo qui me confortat.

4:14 Verumtamen bene fecistis, communicantes tribulationi meæ.

4:15 Scitis autem et vos Philippenses, quod in principio Evangelii, quando profectus sum a Macedonia, nulla mihi ecclesia communicavit in ratione dati et accepti, nisi vos soli :

4:16 quia et Thessalonicam semel et bis in usum mihi misistis.

4:17 Non quia quæro datum, sed requiro fructum abundantem in ratione vestra.

4:18 Habeo autem omnia, et abundo : repletus sum, acceptis ab Epaphrodito quæ misistis odorem suavitatis, hostiam acceptam, placentem Deo.

4:19 Deus autem meus impleat omne desiderium vestrum secundum divitias suas in gloria in Christo Jesu.

4:20 Deo autem et Patri nostro gloria in sæcula sæculorum. Amen.

4:4 Rejoice in the Lord always; again, I say, rejoice.

4:5 Let your modesty be known to all men. The Lord is nigh.

4:6 Be nothing solicitous; but in every thing, by prayer and supplication, with thanksgiving, let your petitions be made known to God.

4:7 And the peace of God, which surpasseth all understanding, keep your hearts and minds in Christ Jesus.

4:8 For the rest, brethren, whatsoever things are true, whatsoever modest, whatsoever just, whatsoever holy, whatsoever lovely, whatsoever of good fame, if there be any virtue, if any praise of discipline, think on these things.

4:9 The things which you have both learned, and received, and heard, and seen in me, these do ye, and the God of peace shall be with you.

4:10 Now I rejoice in the Lord exceedingly, that now at length your thought for me hath flourished again, as you did also think; but you were busied.

4:11 I speak not as it were for want. For I have learned, in whatsoever state I am, to be content therewith.

4:12 I know both how to be brought low, and I know how to abound: (every where, and in all things I am instructed) both to be full, and to be hungry; both to abound, and to suffer need.

4:13 I can do all things in him who strengtheneth me.

4:14 Nevertheless you have done well in communicating to my tribulation.

4:15 And you also know, O Philippians, that in the beginning of the gospel, when I departed from Macedonia, no church communicated with me as concerning giving and receiving, but you only:

4:16 For unto Thessalonica also you sent once and again for my use.

4:17 Not that I seek the gift, but I seek the fruit that may abound to your account.

4:18 But I have all, and abound: I am filled, having received from Epaphroditus the things you sent, an odour of sweetness, an acceptable sacrifice, pleasing to God.

4:19 And may my God supply all your want, according to his riches in glory in Christ Jesus.

4:20 Now to God and our Father be glory world without end. Amen.

4:21 Salutate omnem sanctum in Christo Jesu.

4:22 Salutant vos, qui mecum sunt, fratres. Salutant vos omnes sancti, maxime autem qui de Cæsaris domo sunt.

4:23 Gratia Domini nostri Jesu Christi cum spiritu vestro. Amen.

4:21 Salute ye every saint in Christ Jesus.

4:22 The brethren who are with me, salute you. All the saints salute you; especially they that are of Caesar's household.

4:23 The grace of our Lord Jesus Christ be with your spirit. Amen.

Epistula Beati Pauli Apostoli ad Colossenses

THE EPISTLE OF BLESSED PAUL THE APOSTLE TO THE COLOSSIANS

✠

1:1 PAULUS APOSTOLUS JESU CHRISTI per voluntatem Dei, et Timotheus frater :

1:2 eis, qui sunt Colossis, sanctis, et fidelibus fratribus in Christo Jesu.

1:3 Gratia vobis, et pax a Deo Patre nostro, et Domino Jesu Christo. Gratias agimus Deo, et Patri Domini nostri Jesu Christi semper pro vobis orantes :

1:4 audientes fidem vestram in Christo Jesu, et dilectionem quam habetis in sanctos omnes

1:5 propter spem, quæ reposita est vobis in cælis : quam audistis in verbo veritatis Evangelii :

1:6 quod pervenit ad vos, sicut et in universo mundo est, et fructificat, et crescit sicut in vobis, ex ea die, qua audistis, et cognovistis gratiam Dei in veritate,

1:7 sicut didicistis ab Epaphra carissimo conservo nostro, qui est fidelis pro vobis minister Christi Jesu,

1:8 qui etiam manifestavit nobis dilectionem vestram in spiritu.

1:9 Ideo et nos ex qua die audivimus, non cessamus pro vobis orantes, et postulantes ut impleamini agnitione voluntatis ejus, in omni sapientia et intellectu spirituali :

1:10 ut ambuletis digne Deo per omnia placentes : in omni opere bono fructificantes, et crescentes in scientia Dei :

1:11 in omni virtute confortati secundum potentiam claritatis ejus, in omni patientia et longanimitate cum gaudio,

1:12 gratias agentes Deo Patri, qui dignos nos fecit in partem sortis sanctorum in lumine :

1:13 qui eripuit nos de potestate tenebrarum, et transtulit in regnum filii dilectionis suæ,

1:14 in quo habemus redemptionem per sanguinem ejus, remissionem peccatorum :

1:15 qui est imago Dei invisibilis, primogenitus omnis creaturæ :

1:1 PAUL, AN APOSTLE OF JESUS CHRIST, by the will of God, and Timothy, a brother,

1:2 To the saints and faithful brethren in Christ Jesus, who are at Colossa.

1:3 Grace be to you and peace from God our Father, and from the Lord Jesus Christ. We give thanks to God, and the Father of our Lord Jesus Christ, praying always for you.

1:4 Hearing your faith in Christ Jesus, and the love which you have towards all the saints.

1:5 For the hope that is laid up for you in heaven, which you have heard in the word of the truth of the gospel,

1:6 Which is come unto you, as also it is in the whole world, and bringeth forth fruit and groweth, even as it doth in you, since the day you heard and knew the grace of God in truth.

1:7 As you learned of Epaphras, our most beloved fellow servant, who is for you a faithful minister of Christ Jesus;

1:8 Who also hath manifested to us your love in the spirit.

1:9 Therefore we also, from the day that we heard it, cease not to pray for you, and to beg that you may be filled with the knowledge of his will, in all wisdom, and spiritual understanding:

1:10 That you may walk worthy of God, in all things pleasing; being fruitful in every good work, and increasing in the knowledge of God:

1:11 Strengthened with all might, according to the power of his glory, in all patience and longsuffering with joy,

1:12 Giving thanks to God the Father, who hath made us worthy to be partakers of the lot of the saints in light:

1:13 Who hath delivered us from the power of darkness, and hath translated us into the kingdom of the Son of his love,

1:14 In whom we have redemption through his blood, the remission of sins;

1:15 Who is the image of the invisible God, the firstborn of every creature:

1:16 quoniam in ipso condita sunt universa in cælis, et in terra, visibilia, et invisibilia, sive throni, sive dominationes, sive principatus, sive potestates : omnia per ipsum et in ipso creata sunt :

1:17 et ipse est ante omnes, et omnia in ipso constant.

1:18 Et ipse est caput corporis Ecclesiæ, qui est principium, primogenitus ex mortuis : ut sit in omnibus ipse primatum tenens :

1:19 quia in ipso complacuit, omnem plenitudinem inhabitare :

1:20 et per eum reconciliare omnia in ipsum, pacificans per sanguinem crucis ejus, sive quæ in terris, sive quæ in cælis sunt.

1:21 Et vos cum essetis aliquando alienati, et inimici sensu in operibus malis :

1:22 nunc autem reconciliavit in corpore carnis ejus per mortem, exhibere vos sanctos, et immaculatos, et irreprehensibiles coram ipso :

1:23 si tamen permanetis in fide fundati, et stabiles, et immobiles a spe Evangelii, quod audistis, quod prædicatum est in universa creatura, quæ sub cælo est, cujus factus sum ego Paulus minister.

1:24 Qui nunc gaudeo in passionibus pro vobis, et adimpleo ea quæ desunt passionum Christi, in carne mea pro corpore ejus, quod est Ecclesia :

1:25 cujus factus sum ego minister secundum dispensationem Dei, quæ data est mihi in vos, ut impleam verbum Dei :

1:26 mysterium, quod absconditum fuit a sæculis, et generationibus, nunc autem manifestatum est sanctis ejus,

1:27 quibus voluit Deus notas facere divitias gloriæ sacramenti hujus in gentibus, quod est Christus, in vobis spes gloriæ,

1:28 quem nos annuntiamus, corripientes omnem hominem, et docentes omnem hominem, in omni sapientia, ut exhibeamus omnem hominem perfectum in Christo Jesu :

1:29 in quo et laboro, certando secundum operationem ejus, quam operatur in me in virtute.

2:1 Volo enim vos scire qualem sollicitudinem habeam pro vobis, et pro iis qui sunt Laodiciæ, et quicumque non viderunt faciem meam in carne :

2:2 ut consolentur corda ipsorum, instructi in

1:16 For in him were all things created in heaven and on earth, visible and invisible, whether thrones, or dominations, or principalities, or powers: all things were created by him and in him.

1:17 And he is before all, and by him all things consist.

1:18 And he is the head of the body, the church, who is the beginning, the firstborn from the dead; that in all things he may hold the primacy:

1:19 Because in him, it hath well pleased the Father, that all fullness should dwell;

1:20 And through him to reconcile all things unto himself, making peace through the blood of his cross, both as to the things that are on earth, and the things that are in heaven.

1:21 And you, whereas you were some time alienated and enemies in mind in evil works:

1:22 Yet now he hath reconciled in the body of his flesh through death, to present you holy and unspotted, and blameless before him:

1:23 If so ye continue in the faith, grounded and settled, and immoveable from the hope of the gospel which you have heard, which is preached in all the creation that is under heaven, whereof I Paul am made a minister.

1:24 Who now rejoice in my sufferings for you, and fill up those things that are wanting of the sufferings of Christ, in my flesh, for his body, which is the church:

1:25 Whereof I am made a minister according to the dispensation of God, which is given me towards you, that I may fulfil the word of God:

1:26 The mystery which hath been hidden from ages and generations, but now is manifested to his saints,

1:27 To whom God would make known the riches of the glory of this mystery among the Gentiles, which is Christ, in you the hope of glory.

1:28 Whom we preach, admonishing every man, and teaching every man in all wisdom, that we may present every man perfect in Christ Jesus.

1:29 Wherein also I labour, striving according to his working which he worketh in me in power.

2:1 For I would have you know, what manner of care I have for you and for them that are at Laodicea, and whosoever have not seen my face in the flesh:

2:2 That their hearts may be comforted, being

caritate, et in omnes divitias plenitudinis intellectus, in agnitionem mysterii Dei Patris et Christi Jesu :

2:3 in quo sunt omnes thesauri sapientiæ et scientiæ absconditi.

2:4 Hoc autem dico, ut nemo vos decipiat in sublimitate sermonum.

2:5 Nam etsi corpore absens sum, sed spiritu vobiscum sum : gaudens, et videns ordinem vestrum, et firmamentum ejus, quæ in Christo est, fidei vestræ.

2:6 Sicut ergo accepistis Jesum Christum Dominum, in ipso ambulate,

2:7 radicati, et superædificati in ipso, et confirmati fide, sicut et didicistis, abundantes in illo in gratiarum actione.

2:8 Videte ne quis vos decipiat per philosophiam, et inanem fallaciam secundum traditionem hominum, secundum elementa mundi, et non secundum Christum :

2:9 quia in ipso inhabitat omnis plenitudo divinitatis corporaliter :

2:10 et estis in illo repleti, qui est caput omnis principatus et potestatis :

2:11 in quo et circumcisi estis circumcisione non manu facta in expoliatione corporis carnis, sed in circumcisione Christi :

2:12 consepulti ei in baptismo, in quo et resurrexistis per fidem operationis Dei, qui suscitavit illum a mortuis.

2:13 Et vos cum mortui essetis in delictis, et præputio carnis vestræ, convivificavit cum illo, donans vobis omnia delicta :

2:14 delens quod adversus nos erat chirographum decreti, quod erat contrarium nobis, et ipsum tulit de medio, affigens illud cruci :

2:15 et expolians principatus, et potestates traduxit confidenter, palam triumphans illos in semetipso.

2:16 Nemo ergo vos judicet in cibo, aut in potu, aut in parte diei festi, aut neomeniæ, aut sabbatorum :

2:17 quæ sunt umbra futurorum : corpus autem Christi.

2:18 Nemo vos seducat, volens in humilitate, et religione angelorum, quæ non vidit ambulans, frustra inflatus sensu carnis suæ,

instructed in charity, and unto all riches of fulness of understanding, unto the knowledge of the mystery of God the Father and of Christ Jesus:

2:3 In whom are hid all the treasures of wisdom and knowledge.

2:4 Now this I say, that no man may deceive you by loftiness of words.

2:5 For though I be absent in body, yet in spirit I am with you; rejoicing, and beholding your order, and the steadfastness of your faith which is in Christ.

2:6 As therefore you have received Jesus Christ the Lord, walk ye in him;

2:7 Rooted and built up in him, and confirmed in the faith, as also you have learned, abounding in him in thanksgiving.

2:8 Beware lest any man cheat you by philosophy, and vain deceit; according to the tradition of men, according to the elements of the world, and not according to Christ:

2:9 For in him dwelleth all the fulness of the Godhead corporeally;

2:10 And you are filled in him, who is the head of all principality and power:

2:11 In whom also you are circumcised with circumcision not made by hand, in despoiling of the body of the flesh, but in the circumcision of Christ:

2:12 Buried with him in baptism, in whom also you are risen again by the faith of the operation of God, who hath raised him up from the dead.

2:13 And you, when you were dead in your sins, and the uncircumcision of your flesh; he hath quickened together with him, forgiving you all offences:

2:14 Blotting out the handwriting of the decree that was against us, which was contrary to us. And he hath taken the same out of the way, fastening it to the cross:

2:15 And despoiling the principalities and powers, he hath exposed them confidently in open shew, triumphing over them in himself.

2:16 Let no man therefore judge you in meat or in drink, or in respect of a festival day, or of the new moon, or of the sabbaths,

2:17 Which are a shadow of things to come, but the body is of Christ.

2:18 Let no man seduce you, willing in humility, and religion of angels, walking in the things which he hath not seen, in vain puffed up by the sense of his flesh,

2:19 et non tenens caput, ex quo totum corpus per nexus, et conjunctiones subministratum, et constructum crescit in augmentum Dei.

2:20 Si ergo mortui estis cum Christo ab elementis hujus mundi : quid adhuc tamquam viventes in mundo decernitis ?

2:21 Ne tetigeritis, neque gustaveritis, neque contrectaveritis :

2:22 quæ sunt omnia in interitum ipso usu, secundum præcepta et doctrinas hominum :

2:23 quæ sunt rationem quidem habentia sapientiæ in superstitione, et humilitate, et non ad parcendum corpori, non in honore aliquo ad saturitatem carnis.

3:1 Igitur, si consurrexistis cum Christo : quæ sursum sunt quærite, ubi Christus est in dextera Dei sedens :

3:2 quæ sursum sunt sapite, non quæ super terram.

3:3 Mortui enim estis, et vita vestra est abscondita cum Christo in Deo.

3:4 Cum Christus apparuerit, vita vestra : tunc et vos apparebitis cum ipso in gloria.

3:5 Mortificate ergo membra vestra, quæ sunt super terram : fornicationem, immunditiam, libidinem, concupiscentiam malam, et avaritiam, quæ est simulacrorum servitus :

3:6 propter quæ venit ira Dei super filios incredulitatis :

3:7 in quibus et vos ambulastis aliquando, cum viveretis in illis.

3:8 Nunc autem deponite et vos omnia : iram, indignationem, malitiam, blasphemiam, turpem sermonem de ore vestro.

3:9 Nolite mentiri invicem, expoliantes vos veterem hominem cum actibus suis,

3:10 et induentes novum eum, qui renovatur in agnitionem secundum imaginem ejus qui creavit illum :

3:11 ubi non est gentilis et Judæus, circumcisio et præputium, Barbarus et Scytha, servus et liber : sed omnia, et in omnibus Christus.

3:12 Induite vos ergo, sicut electi Dei, sancti, et dilecti, viscera misericordiæ, benignitatem, humilitatem, modestiam, patientiam :

3:13 supportantes invicem, et donantes vobismetipsis si quis adversus aliquem habet querelam : sicut et Dominus donavit vobis, ita et vos.

2:19 And not holding the head, from which the whole body, by joints and bands, being supplied with nourishment and compacted, groweth unto the increase of God.

2:20 If then you be dead with Christ from the elements of this world, why do you yet decree as though living in the world?

2:21 Touch not, taste not, handle not:

2:22 Which all are unto destruction by the very use, according to the precepts and doctrines of men.

2:23 Which things have indeed a shew of wisdom in superstition and humility, and not sparing the body; not in any honour to the filling of the flesh.

3:1 Therefore, if you be risen with Christ, seek the things that are above; where Christ is sitting at the right hand of God:

3:2 Mind the things that are above, not the things that are upon the earth.

3:3 For you are dead; and your life is hid with Christ in God.

3:4 When Christ shall appear, who is your life, then you also shall appear with him in glory.

3:5 Mortify therefore your members which are upon the earth; fornication, uncleanness, lust, evil concupiscence, and covetousness, which is the service of idols.

3:6 For which things the wrath of God cometh upon the children of unbelief,

3:7 In which you also walked some time, when you lived in them.

3:8 But now put you also all away: anger, indignation, malice, blasphemy, filthy speech out of your mouth.

3:9 Lie not one to another: stripping yourselves of the old man with his deeds,

3:10 And putting on the new, him who is renewed unto knowledge, according to the image of him that created him.

3:11 Where there is neither Gentile nor Jew, circumcision nor uncircumcision, Barbarian nor Scythian, bond nor free. But Christ is all, and in all.

3:12 Put ye on therefore, as the elect of God, holy, and beloved, the bowels of mercy, benignity, humility, modesty, patience:

3:13 Bearing with one another, and forgiving one another, if any have a complaint against another: even as the Lord hath forgiven you, so do you also.

3:14 Super omnia autem hæc, caritatem habete, quod est vinculum perfectionis :

3:15 et pax Christi exsultet in cordibus vestris, in qua et vocati estis in uno corpore : et grati estote.

3:16 Verbum Christi habitet in vobis abundanter, in omni sapientia, docentes, et commonentes vosmetipsos, psalmis, hymnis, et canticis spiritualibus, in gratia cantantes in cordibus vestris Deo.

3:17 Omne, quodcumque facitis in verbo aut in opere, omnia in nomine Domini Jesu Christi, gratias agentes Deo et Patri per ipsum.

3:18 Mulieres, subditæ estote viris, sicut oportet, in Domino.

3:19 Viri, diligite uxores vestras, et nolite amari esse ad illas.

3:20 Filii, obedite parentibus per omnia : hoc enim placitum est in Domino.

3:21 Patres, nolite ad indignationem provocare filios vestros, ut non pusillo animo fiant.

3:22 Servi, obedite per omnia dominis carnalibus, non ad oculum servientes, quasi hominibus placentes, sed in simplicitate cordis, timentes Deum.

3:23 Quodcumque facitis, ex animo operamini sicut Domino, et non hominibus :

3:24 scientes quod a Domino accipietis retributionem hæreditatis. Domino Christo servite.

3:25 Qui enim injuriam facit, recipiet id quod inique gessit : et non est personarum acceptio apud Deum.

4:1 Domini, quod justum est et æquum, servis præstate : scientes quod et vos Dominum habetis in cælo.

4:2 Orationi instate, vigilantes in ea in gratiarum actione :

4:3 orantes simul et pro nobis, ut Deus aperiat nobis ostium sermonis ad loquendum mysterium Christi (propter quod etiam vinctus sum),

4:4 ut manifestem illud ita ut oportet me loqui.

4:5 In sapientia ambulate ad eos, qui foris sunt : tempus redimentes.

4:6 Sermo vester semper in gratia sale sit conditus, ut sciatis quomodo oporteat vos unicuique respondere.

4:7 Quæ circa me sunt, omnia vobis nota faciet Tychicus, carissimus frater, et fidelis minister, et conservus in Domino :

3:14 But above all these things have charity, which is the bond of perfection:

3:15 And let the peace of Christ rejoice in your hearts, wherein also you are called in one body: and be ye thankful.

3:16 Let the word of Christ dwell in you abundantly, in all wisdom: teaching and admonishing one another in psalms, hymns, and spiritual canticles, singing in grace in your hearts to God.

3:17 All whatsoever you do in word or in work, do all in the name of the Lord Jesus Christ, giving thanks to God and the Father by him.

3:18 Wives, be subject to your husbands, as it behoveth in the Lord.

3:19 Husbands, love your wives, and be not bitter towards them.

3:20 Children, obey your parents in all things: for this is well pleasing to the Lord.

3:21 Fathers, provoke not your children to indignation, lest they be discouraged.

3:22 Servants, obey in all things your masters according to the flesh, not serving to the eye, as pleasing men, but in simplicity of heart, fearing God.

3:23 Whatsoever you do, do it from the heart, as to the Lord, and not to men:

3:24 Knowing that you shall receive of the Lord the reward of inheritance. Serve ye the Lord Christ.

3:25 For he that doth wrong, shall receive for that which he hath done wrongfully: and there is no respect of persons with God.

4:1 Masters, do to your servants that which is just and equal: knowing that you also have a master in heaven.

4:2 Be instant in prayer; watching in it with thanksgiving:

4:3 Praying withal for us also, that God may open unto us a door of speech to speak the mystery of Christ (for which also I am bound;)

4:4 That I may make it manifest as I ought to speak.

4:5 Walk with wisdom towards them that are without, redeeming the time.

4:6 Let your speech be always in grace seasoned with salt: that you may know how you ought to answer every man.

4:7 All the things that concern me, Tychicus, our dearest brother, and faithful minister and fellow servant in the Lord, will make known to you,

4:8 quem misi ad vos ad hoc ipsum, ut cognoscat quæ circa vos sunt, et consoletur corda vestra,

4:9 cum Onesimo carissimo, et fideli fratre, qui ex vobis est. Omnia, quæ hic aguntur, nota facient vobis.

4:10 Salutat vos Aristarchus concaptivus meus, et Marcus consobrinus Barnabæ, de quo accepistis mandata : si venerit ad vos, excipite illum :

4:11 et Jesus, qui dicitur Justus : qui sunt ex circumcisione : hi soli sunt adjutores mei in regno Dei, qui mihi fuerunt solatio.

4:12 Salutat vos Epaphras, qui ex vobis est, servus Christi Jesu, semper sollicitus pro vobis in orationibus, ut stetis perfecti, et pleni in omni voluntate Dei.

4:13 Testimonium enim illi perhibeo quod habet multum laborem pro vobis, et pro iis qui sunt Laodiciæ, et qui Hierapoli.

4:14 Salutat vos Lucas, medicus carissimus, et Demas.

4:15 Salutate fratres, qui sunt Laodiciæ, et Nympham, et quæ in domo ejus est, ecclesiam.

4:16 Et cum lecta fuerit apud vos epistola hæc, facite ut et in Laodicensium ecclesia legatur : et eam, quæ Laodicensium est, vos legatis.

4:17 Et dicite Archippo : Vide ministerium, quod accepisti in Domino, ut illud impleas.

4:18 Salutatio, mea manu Pauli. Memores estote vinculorum meorum. Gratia vobiscum. Amen.

4:8 Whom I have sent to you for this same purpose, that he may know the things that concern you, and comfort your hearts,

4:9 With Onesimus, a most beloved and faithful brother, who is one of you. All things that are done here, they shall make known to you.

4:10 Aristarchus, my fellow prisoner, saluteth you, and Mark, the cousin german of Barnabus, touching whom you have received commandments; if he come unto you, receive him:

4:11 And Jesus, that is called Justus: who are of the circumcision: these only are my helpers in the kingdom of God; who have been a comfort to me.

4:12 Epaphras saluteth you, who is one of you, a servant of Christ Jesus, who is always solicitous for you in prayers, that you may stand perfect, and full in all the will of God.

4:13 For I bear him testimony that he hath much labour for you, and for them that are at Laodicea, and them at Hierapolis.

4:14 Luke, the most dear physician, saluteth you: and Demas.

4:15 Salute the brethren who are at Laodicea, and Nymphas, and the church that is in his house.

4:16 And when this epistle shall have been read with you, cause that it be read also in the church of the Laodiceans: and that you read that which is of the Laodiceans.

4:17 And say to Archippus: Take heed to the ministry which thou hast received in the Lord, that thou fulfil it.

4:18 The salutation of Paul with my own hand. Be mindful of my bands. Grace be with you. Amen

Epistula Beati Pauli Apostoli ad Thessalonicenses Prima

THE FIRST EPISTLE OF BLESSED PAUL THE APOSTLE TO THE THESSALONIANS

✠

1:1 PAULUS, ET SILVANUS, ET TIMOTHEUS ecclesiæ Thessalonicensium in Deo Patre, et Domino Jesu Christo.

1:2 Gratia vobis, et pax. Gratias agimus Deo semper pro omnibus vobis, memoriam vestri facientes in orationibus nostris sine intermissione,

1:3 memores operis fidei vestræ, et laboris, et caritatis, et sustinentiæ spei Domini nostri Jesu Christi, ante Deum et Patrem nostrum :

1:4 scientes, fratres dilecti a Deo, electionem vestram :

1:5 quia Evangelium nostrum non fuit ad vos in sermone tantum, sed et in virtute, et in Spiritu Sancto, et in plenitudine multa, sicut scitis quales fuerimus in vobis propter vos.

1:6 Et vos imitatores nostri facti estis, et Domini, excipientes verbum in tribulatione multa, cum gaudio Spiritus Sancti :

1:7 ita ut facti sitis forma omnibus credentibus in Macedonia, et in Achaia.

1:8 A vobis enim diffamatus est sermo Domini, non solum in Macedonia, et in Achaia, sed et in omni loco fides vestra, quæ est ad Deum, profecta est ita ut non sit nobis necesse quidquam loqui.

1:9 Ipsi enim de nobis annuntiant qualem introitum habuerimus ad vos : et quomodo conversi estis ad Deum a simulacris, servire Deo vivo, et vero,

1:10 et exspectare Filium ejus de cælis (quem suscitavit a mortuis) Jesum, qui eripuit nos ab ira ventura.

2:1 Nam ipsi scitis, fratres, introitum nostrum ad vos, quia non inanis fuit :

2:2 sed ante passi, et contumeliis affecti (sicut scitis) in Philippis, fiduciam habuimus in Deo nostro, loqui ad vos Evangelium Dei in multa sollicitudine.

1:1 PAUL AND SYLVANUS AND TIMOTHY: to the church of the Thessalonians, in God the Father, and in the Lord Jesus Christ.

1:2 Grace be to you and peace. We give thanks to God always for you all; making a remembrance of you in our prayers without ceasing,

1:3 Being mindful of the work of your faith, and labour, and charity, and of the enduring of the hope of our Lord Jesus Christ before God and our Father:

1:4 Knowing, brethren beloved of God, your election:

1:5 For our gospel hath not been unto you in word only, but in power also, and in the Holy Ghost, and in much fulness, as you know what manner of men we have been among you for your sakes.

1:6 And you became followers of us, and of the Lord; receiving the word in much tribulation, with joy of the Holy Ghost:

1:7 So that you were made a pattern to all that believe in Macedonia and in Achaia.

1:8 For from you was spread abroad the word of the Lord, not only in Macedonia, and in Achaia, but also in every place, your faith which is towards God, is gone forth, so that we need not to speak any thing.

1:9 For they themselves relate of us, what manner of entering in we had unto you; and how you turned to God from idols, to serve the living and true God.

1:10 And to wait for his Son from heaven (whom he raised up from the dead,) Jesus, who hath delivered us from the wrath to come.

2:1 For yourselves know, brethren, our entrance in unto you, that it was not in vain:

2:2 But having suffered many things before, and been shamefully treated (as you know) at Philippi, we had confidence in our God, to speak unto you the gospel of God in much carefulness.

2:3 Exhortatio enim nostra non de errore, neque de immunditia, neque in dolo,

2:4 sed sicut probati sumus a Deo ut crederetur nobis Evangelium : ita loquimur non quasi hominibus placentes, sed Deo, qui probat corda nostra.

2:5 Neque enim aliquando fuimus in sermone adulationis, sicut scitis : neque in occasione avaritiæ : Deus testis est :

2:6 nec quærentes ab hominibus gloriam, neque a vobis, neque ab aliis.

2:7 Cum possemus vobis oneri esse ut Christi apostoli : sed facti sumus parvuli in medio vestrum, tamquam si nutrix foveat filios suos.

2:8 Ita desiderantes vos, cupide volebamus tradere vobis non solum Evangelium Dei, sed etiam animas nostras : quoniam carissimi nobis facti estis.

2:9 Memores enim estis, fratres, laboris nostri, et fatigationis : nocte ac die operantes, ne quem vestrum gravaremus, prædicavimus in vobis Evangelium Dei.

2:10 Vos testes estis, et Deus, quam sancte, et juste, et sine querela, vobis, qui credidistis, fuimus :

2:11 sicut scitis, qualiter unumquemque vestrum (sicut pater filios suos)

2:12 deprecantes vos, et consolantes, testificati sumus, ut ambularetis digne Deo, qui vocavit vos in suum regnum et gloriam.

2:13 Ideo et nos gratias agimus Deo sine intermissione : quoniam cum accepissetis a nobis verbum auditus Dei, accepistis illud, non ut verbum hominum, sed (sicut est vere) verbum Dei, qui operatur in vobis, qui credidistis :

2:14 vos enim imitatores facti estis, fratres, ecclesiarum Dei, quæ sunt in Judæa in Christo Jesu : quia eadem passi estis et vos a contribulibus vestris, sicut et ipsi a Judæis :

2:15 qui et Dominum occiderunt Jesum, et prophetas, et nos persecuti sunt, et Deo non placent, et omnibus hominibus adversantur,

2:16 prohibentes nos gentibus loqui ut salvæ fiant, ut impleant peccata sua semper : pervenit enim ira Dei super illos usque in finem.

2:17 Nos autem fratres desolati a vobis ad tempus horæ, aspectu, non corde, abundantius fes-

2:3 For our exhortation was not of error, nor of uncleanness, nor in deceit:

2:4 But as we were approved by God that the gospel should be committed to us: even so we speak, not as pleasing men, but God, who proveth our hearts.

2:5 For neither have we used, at any time, the speech of flattery, as you know; nor taken an occasion of covetousness, God is witness:

2:6 Nor sought we glory of men, neither of you, nor of others.

2:7 Whereas we might have been burdensome to you, as the apostles of Christ: but we became little ones in the midst of you, as if a nurse should cherish her children:

2:8 So desirous of you, we would gladly impart unto you not only the gospel of God, but also our own souls: because you were become most dear unto us.

2:9 For you remember, brethren, our labour and toil: working night and day, lest we should be chargeable to any of you, we preached among you the gospel of God.

2:10 You are witnesses, and God also, how holily, and justly, and without blame, we have been to you that have believed:

2:11 As you know in what manner, entreating and comforting you, (as a father doth his children,)

2:12 We testified to every one of you, that you would walk worthy of God, who hath called you unto his kingdom and glory.

2:13 Therefore, we also give thanks to God without ceasing: because, that when you had received of us the word of the hearing of God, you received it not as the word of men, but (as it is indeed) the word of God, who worketh in you that have believed.

2:14 For you, brethren, are become followers of the churches of God which are in Judea, in Christ Jesus: for you also have suffered the same things from your own coutrymen, even as they have from the Jews,

2:15 Who both killed the Lord Jesus, and the prophets, and have persecuted us, and please not God, and are adversaries to all men;

2:16 Prohibiting us to speak to the Gentiles, that they may be saved, to fill up their sins always: for the wrath of God is come upon them to the end.

2:17 But we, brethren, being taken away from you for a short time, in sight, not in heart, have

tinavimus faciem vestram videre cum multo desiderio :

2:18 quoniam voluimus venire ad vos, ego quidem Paulus, et semel, et iterum : sed impedivit nos Satanas.

2:19 Quæ est enim nostra spes aut gaudium, aut corona gloriæ ? nonne vos ante Dominum nostrum Jesum Christum estis in adventu ejus ?

2:20 vos enim estis gloria nostra et gaudium.

3:1 Propter quod non sustinentes amplius, placuit nobis remanere Athenis, solis :

3:2 et misimus Timotheum fratrem nostrum, et ministrum Dei in Evangelio Christi, ad confirmandos vos, et exhortandos pro fide vestra :

3:3 ut nemo moveatur in tribulationibus istis : ipsi enim scitis quod in hoc positi sumus.

3:4 Nam et cum apud vos essemus, prædicebamus vobis passuros nos tribulationes, sicut et factum est, et scitis.

3:5 Propterea et ego amplius non sustinens, misi ad cognoscendam fidem vestram : ne forte tentaverit vos is qui tentat, et inanis fiat labor noster.

3:6 Nunc autem veniente Timotheo ad nos a vobis, et annuntiante nobis fidem et caritatem vestram, et quia memoriam nostri habetis bonam semper, desiderantes nos videre, sicut et nos quoque vos :

3:7 ideo consolati sumus, fratres, in vobis in omni necessitate et tribulatione nostra, per fidem vestram,

3:8 quoniam nunc vivimus, si vos statis in Domino.

3:9 Quam enim gratiarum actionem possumus Deo retribuere pro vobis in omni gaudio, quo gaudemus propter vos ante Deum nostrum,

3:10 nocte ac die abundantius orantes, ut videamus faciem vestram, et compleamus ea quæ desunt fidei vestræ ?

3:11 Ipse autem Deus, et Pater noster, et Dominus noster Jesus Christus, dirigat viam nostram ad vos.

3:12 Vos autem Dominus multiplicet, et abundare faciat caritatem vestram in invicem, et in omnes, quemadmodum et nos in vobis :

3:13 ad confirmanda corda vestra sine querela in sanctitate, ante Deum et Patrem nostrum, in adventu Domini nostri Jesu Christi cum omnibus sanctis ejus. Amen.

hastened the more abundantly to see your face with great desire.

2:18 For we would have come unto you, I Paul indeed, once and again: but Satan hath hindered us.

2:19 For what is our hope, or joy, or crown of glory? Are not you, in the presence of our Lord Jesus Christ at his coming?

2:20 For you are our glory and joy.

3:1 For which cause, forbearing no longer, we thought it good to remain at Athens alone:

3:2 And we sent Timothy, our brother, and the minister of God in the gospel of Christ, to confirm you and exhort you concerning your faith:

3:3 That no man should be moved in these tribulations: for yourselves know, that we are appointed thereunto.

3:4 For even when we were with you, we foretold you that we should suffer tribulations, as also it is come to pass, and you know.

3:5 For this cause also, I, forbearing no longer, sent to know your faith: lest perhaps he that tempteth should have tempted you, and our labour should be made vain.

3:6 But now when Timothy came to us from you, and related to us your faith and charity, and that you have a good remembrance of us always, desiring to see us as we also to see you;

3:7 Therefore we were comforted, brethren, in you, in all our necessity and tribulation, by your faith,

3:8 Because now we live, if you stand in the Lord.

3:9 For what thanks can we return to God for you, in all the joy wherewith we rejoice for you before our God,

3:10 Night and day more abundantly praying that we may see your face, and may accomplish those things that are wanting to your faith?

3:11 Now God himself and our Father, and our Lord Jesus Christ, direct our way unto you.

3:12 And may the Lord multiply you, and make you abound in charity towards one another, and towards all men: as we do also towards you,

3:13 To confirm your hearts without blame, in holiness, before God and our Father, at the coming of our Lord Jesus Christ, with all his saints. Amen.

4:1 De cetero ergo, fratres, rogamus vos et obsecramus in Domino Jesu, ut quemadmodum accepistis a nobis quomodo oporteat vos ambulare, et placere Deo, sic et ambuletis ut abundetis magis.

4:2 Scitis enim quæ præcepta dederim vobis per Dominum Jesum.

4:3 Hæc est enim voluntas Dei, sanctificatio vestra : ut abstineatis vos a fornicatione,

4:4 ut sciat unusquisque vestrum vas suum possidere in sanctificatione, et honore :

4:5 non in passione desiderii, sicut et gentes, quæ ignorant Deum :

4:6 et ne quis supergrediatur, neque circumveniat in negotio fratrem suum : quoniam vindex est Dominus de his omnibus, sicut prædiximus vobis, et testificati sumus.

4:7 Non enim vocavit nos Deus in immunditiam, sed in sanctificationem.

4:8 Itaque qui hæc spernit, non hominem spernit, sed Deum : qui etiam dedit Spiritum suum Sanctum in nobis.

4:9 De caritate autem fraternitatis non necesse habemus scribere vobis : ipsi enim vos a Deo didicistis ut diligatis invicem.

4:10 Etenim illud facitis in omnes fratres in universa Macedonia. Rogamus autem vos, fratres, ut abundetis magis,

4:11 et operam detis ut quieti sitis, et ut vestrum negotium agatis, et operemini manibus vestris, sicut præcepimus vobis :

4:12 et ut honeste ambuletis ad eos qui foris sunt : et nullius aliquid desideretis.

4:13 Nolumus autem vos ignorare fratres de dormientibus, ut non contristemini sicut et ceteri, qui spem non habent.

4:14 Si enim credimus quod Jesus mortuus est, et resurrexit : ita et Deus eos qui dormierunt per Jesum, adducet cum eo.

4:15 Hoc enim vobis dicimus in verbo Domini, quia nos, qui vivimus, qui residui sumus in adventum Domini, non præveniemus eos qui dormierunt.

4:16 Quoniam ipse Dominus in jussu, et in voce archangeli, et in tuba Dei descendet de cælo : et mortui, qui in Christo sunt, resurgent primi.

4:17 Deinde nos, qui vivimus, qui relinquimur, simul rapiemur cum illis in nubibus obviam

4:1 For the rest therefore, brethren, we pray and beseech you in the Lord Jesus, that as you have received from us, how you ought to walk, and to please God, so also you would walk, that you may abound the more.

4:2 For you know what precepts I have given to you by the Lord Jesus.

4:3 For this is the will of God, your sanctification; that you should abstain from fornication;

4:4 That every one of you should know how to possess his vessel in sanctification and honour:

4:5 Not in the passion of lust, like the Gentiles that know not God:

4:6 And that no man overreach, nor circumvent his brother in business: because the Lord is the avenger of all these things, as we have told you before, and have testified.

4:7 For God hath not called us unto uncleanness, but unto sanctification.

4:8 Therefore, he that despiseth these things, despiseth not man, but God, who also hath given his holy Spirit in us.

4:9 But as touching the charity of brotherhood, we have no need to write to you: for yourselves have learned of God to love one another.

4:10 For indeed you do it towards all the brethren in all Macedonia. But we entreat you, brethren, that you abound more:

4:11 And that you use your endeavour to be quiet, and that you do your own business, and work with your own hands, as we commanded you:

4:12 and that you walk honestly towards them that are without; and that you want nothing of any man's.

4:13 And we will not have you ignorant, brethren, concerning them that are asleep, that you be not sorrowful, even as others who have no hope.

4:14 For if we believe that Jesus died, and rose again; even so them who have slept through Jesus, will God bring with him.

4:15 For this we say unto you in the word of the Lord, that we who are alive, who remain unto the coming of the Lord, shall not prevent them who have slept.

4:16 For the Lord himself shall come down from heaven with commandment, and with the voice of an archangel, and with the trumpet of God: and the dead who are in Christ, shall rise first.

4:17 Then we who are alive, who are left, shall be taken up together with them in the clouds

Christo in aëra, et sic semper cum Domino erimus.

4:18 Itaque consolamini invicem in verbis istis.

5:1 De temporibus autem, et momentis, fratres, non indigetis ut scribamus vobis.

5:2 Ipsi enim diligenter scitis quia dies Domini, sicut fur in nocte, ita veniet :

5:3 cum enim dixerint : Pax et securitas : tunc repentinus eis superveniet interitus, sicut dolor in utero habenti, et non effugient.

5:4 Vos autem, fratres, non estis in tenebris, ut vos dies illa tamquam fur comprehendat :

5:5 omnes enim vos filii lucis estis, et filii diei : non sumus noctis, neque tenebrarum.

5:6 Igitur non dormiamus sicut et ceteri, sed vigilemus, et sobrii simus.

5:7 Qui enim dormiunt, nocte dormiunt : et qui ebrii sunt, nocte ebrii sunt.

5:8 Nos autem, qui diei sumus, sobrii simus, induti loricam fidei et caritatis, et galeam spem salutis :

5:9 quoniam non posuit nos Deus in iram, sed in acquisitionem salutis per Dominum nostrum Jesum Christum,

5:10 qui mortuus est pro nobis : ut sive vigilemus, sive dormiamus, simul cum illo vivamus.

5:11 Propter quod consolamini invicem, et ædificate alterutrum, sicut et facitis.

5:12 Rogamus autem vos, fratres, ut noveritis eos qui laborant inter vos, et præsunt vobis in Domino, et monent vos,

5:13 ut habeatis illos abundantius in caritate propter opus illorum : pacem habete cum eis.

5:14 Rogamus autem vos, fratres, corripite inquietos, consolamini pusillanimes, suscipite infirmos, patientes estote ad omnes.

5:15 Videte ne quis malum pro malo alicui reddat : sed semper quod bonum est sectamini in invicem, et in omnes.

5:16 Semper gaudete.

5:17 Sine intermissione orate.

5:18 In omnibus gratias agite : hæc est enim voluntas Dei in Christo Jesu in omnibus vobis.

5:19 Spiritum nolite extinguere.

5:20 Prophetias nolite spernere.

5:21 Omnia autem probate : quod bonum est

to meet Christ, into the air, and so shall we be always with the Lord.

4:18 Wherefore, comfort ye one another with these words.

5:1 But of the times and moments, brethren, you need not, that we should write to you;

5:2 For yourselves know perfectly, that the day of the Lord shall so come, as a thief in the night.

5:3 For when they shall say, peace and security; then shall sudden destruction come upon them, as the pains upon her that is with child, and they shall not escape.

5:4 But you, brethren, are not in darkness, that that day should overtake you as a thief.

5:5 For all you are the children of light, and children of the day: we are not of the night, nor of darkness.

5:6 Therefore, let us not sleep, as others do; but let us watch, and be sober.

5:7 For they that sleep, sleep in the night; and they that are drunk, are drunk in the night.

5:8 But let us, who are of the day, be sober, having on the breastplate of faith and charity, and for a helmet the hope of salvation.

5:9 For God hath not appointed us unto wrath, but unto the purchasing of salvation by our Lord Jesus Christ,

5:10 Who died for us; that, whether we watch or sleep, we may live together with him.

5:11 For which cause comfort one another; and edify one another, as you also do.

5:12 And we beseech you, brethren, to know them who labour among you, and are over you in the Lord, and admonish you:

5:13 That you esteem them more abundantly in charity, for their work's sake. Have peace with them.

5:14 And we beseech you, brethren, rebuke the unquiet, comfort the feeble minded, support the weak, be patient towards all men.

5:15 See that none render evil for evil to any man; but ever follow that which is good towards each other, and towards all men.

5:16 Always rejoice.

5:17 Pray without ceasing.

5:18 In all things give thanks; for this is the will of God in Christ Jesus concerning you all.

5:19 Extinguish not the spirit.

5:20 Despise not prophecies.

5:21 But prove all things; hold fast that which is

tenete.

5:22 Ab omni specie mala abstinete vos.

5:23 Ipse autem Deus pacis sanctificet vos per omnia : ut integer spiritus vester, et anima, et corpus sine querela in adventu Domini nostri Jesu Christi servetur.

5:24 Fidelis est, qui vocavit vos : qui etiam faciet.

5:25 Fratres, orate pro nobis.

5:26 Salutate fratres omnes in osculo sancto.

5:27 Adjuro vos per Dominum ut legatur epistola hæc omnibus sanctis fratribus.

5:28 Gratia Domini nostri Jesu Christi vobiscum. Amen.

good.

5:22 From all appearance of evil refrain yourselves.

5:23 And may the God of peace himself sanctify you in all things; that your whole spirit, and soul, and body, may be preserved blameless in the coming of our Lord Jesus Christ.

5:24 He is faithful who hath called you, who also will do it.

5:25 Brethren, pray for us.

5:26 Salute all the brethren with a holy kiss.

5:27 I charge you by the Lord, that this epistle be read to all the holy brethren.

5:28 The grace of our Lord Jesus Christ be with you. Amen.

Epistula Beati Pauli Apostoli ad Thessalonicenses Secunda

THE SECOND EPISTLE OF BLESSED PAUL THE APOSTLE TO THE THESSALONIANS

✠

1:1 PAULUS, ET SYLVANUS, ET TIMOTHEUS, ecclesiæ Thessalonicensium in Deo Patre nostro, et Domino Jesu Christo.

1:2 Gratia vobis, et pax a Deo Patre nostro, et Domino Jesu Christo.

1:3 Gratias agere debemus semper Deo pro vobis, fratres, ita ut dignum est, quoniam supercrescit fides vestra, et abundat caritas uniuscujusque vestrum in invicem :

1:4 ita ut et nos ipsi in vobis gloriemur in ecclesiis Dei, pro patientia vestra, et fide, et in omnibus persecutionibus vestris, et tribulationibus, quas sustinetis

1:5 in exemplum justi judicii Dei, ut digni habeamini in regno Dei, pro quo et patimini.

1:6 Si tamen justum est apud Deum retribuere tribulationem iis qui vos tribulant :

1:7 et vobis, qui tribulamini, requiem nobiscum in revelatione Domini Jesu de cælo cum angelis virtutis ejus,

1:8 in flamma ignis dantis vindictam iis qui non noverunt Deum, et qui non obediunt Evangelio Domini nostri Jesu Christi,

1:9 qui pœnas dabunt in interitu æternas a facie Domini, et a gloria virtutis ejus :

1:10 cum venerit glorificari in sanctis suis, et admirabilis fieri in omnibus, qui crediderunt, quia creditum est testimonium nostrum super vos in die illo.

1:11 In quo etiam oramus semper pro vobis : ut dignetur vos vocatione sua Deus noster, et impleat omnem voluntatem bonitatis, et opus fidei in virtute,

1:12 ut clarificetur nomen Domini nostri Jesu Christi in vobis, et vos in illo secundum gratiam Dei nostri, et Domini Jesu Christi.

1:1 PAUL, AND SYLVANUS, AND TIMOTHY, to the church of the Thessalonians in God our Father, and the Lord Jesus Christ.

1:2 Grace unto you, and peace from God our Father, and from the Lord Jesus Christ.

1:3 We are bound to give thanks always to God for you, brethren, as it is fitting, because your faith groweth exceedingly, and the charity of every one of you towards each other, aboundeth:

1:4 So that we ourselves also glory in you in the churches of God, for your patience and faith, and in all your persecutions and tribulations, which you endure,

1:5 For an example of the just judgment of God, that you may be counted worthy of the kingdom of God, for which also you suffer.

1:6 Seeing it is a just thing with God to repay tribulation to them that trouble you:

1:7 And to you who are troubled, rest with us when the Lord Jesus shall be revealed from heaven, with the angels of his power:

1:8 In a flame of fire, giving vengeance to them who know not God, and who obey not the gospel of our Lord Jesus Christ.

1:9 Who shall suffer eternal punishment in destruction, from the face of the Lord, and from the glory of his power:

1:10 When he shall come to be glorified in his saints, and to be made wonderful in all them who have believed; because our testimony was believed upon you in that day.

1:11 Wherefore also we pray always for you; that our God would make you worthy of his vocation, and fulfill all the good pleasure of his goodness and the work of faith in power;

1:12 That the name of our Lord Jesus may be glorified in you, and you in him, according to the grace of our God, and of the Lord Jesus Christ.

2:1 Rogamus autem vos, fratres, per adventum Domini nostri Jesu Christi, et nostræ congregationis in ipsum :

2:2 ut non cito moveamini a vestro sensu, neque terreamini, neque per spiritum, neque per sermonem, neque per epistolam tamquam per nos missam, quasi instet dies Domini.

2:3 Ne quis vos seducat ullo modo : quoniam nisi venerit discessio primum, et revelatus fuerit homo peccati filius perditionis,

2:4 qui adversatur, et extollitur supra omne, quod dicitur Deus, aut quod colitur, ita ut in templo Dei sedeat ostendens se tamquam sit Deus.

2:5 Non retinetis quod cum adhuc essem apud vos, hæc dicebam vobis ?

2:6 et nunc quid detineat scitis, ut reveletur in suo tempore.

2:7 Nam mysterium jam operatur iniquitatis : tantum ut qui tenet nunc, teneat, donec de medio fiat.

2:8 Et tunc revelabitur ille iniquus, quem Dominus Jesus interficiet spiritu oris sui, et destruet illustratione adventus sui eum :

2:9 cujus est adventus secundum operationem Satanæ in omni virtute, et signis, et prodigiis mendacibus,

2:10 et in omni seductione iniquitatis iis qui pereunt : eo quod caritatem veritatis non receperunt ut salvi fierent.

2:11 Ideo mittet illis Deus operationem erroris ut credant mendacio,

2:12 ut judicentur omnes qui non crediderunt veritati, sed consenserunt iniquitati.

2:13 Nos autem debemus gratias agere Deo semper pro vobis, fratres dilecti a Deo, quod elegerit vos Deus primitias in salutem in sanctificatione spiritus, et in fide veritatis :

2:14 in qua et vocavit vos per Evangelium nostrum in acquisitionem gloriæ Domini nostri Jesu Christi.

2:15 Itaque fratres, state : et tenete traditiones, quas didicistis, sive per sermonem, sive per epistolam nostram.

2:16 Ipse autem Dominus noster Jesus Christus, et Deus et Pater noster, qui dilexit nos, et dedit consolationem æternam, et spem bonam in gratia,

2:17 exhortetur corda vestra, et confirmet in omni opere et sermone bono.

2:1 And we beseech you, brethren, by the coming of our Lord Jesus Christ, and of our gathering together unto him:

2:2 That you be not easily moved from your sense, nor be terrified, neither by spirit, nor by word, nor by epistle, as sent from us, as if the day of the Lord were at hand.

2:3 Let no man deceive you by any means, for unless there come a revolt first, and the man of sin be revealed, the son of perdition,

2:4 Who opposeth, and is lifted up above all that is called God, or that is worshipped, so that he sitteth in the temple of God, shewing himself as if he were God.

2:5 Remember you not, that when I was yet with you, I told you these things?

2:6 And now you know what withholdeth, that he may be revealed in his time.

2:7 For the mystery of iniquity already worketh; only that he who now holdeth, do hold, until he be taken out of the way.

2:8 And then that wicked one shall be revealed whom the Lord Jesus shall kill with the spirit of his mouth; and shall destroy with the brightness of his coming, him,

2:9 Whose coming is according to the working of Satan, in all power, and signs, and lying wonders,

2:10 And in all seduction of iniquity to them that perish; because they receive not the love of the truth, that they might be saved.

2:11 Therefore God shall send them the operation of error, to believe lying:

2:12 That all may be judged who have not believed the truth, but have consented to iniquity.

2:13 But we ought to give thanks to God always for you, brethren, beloved of God, for that God hath chosen you firstfruits unto salvation, in sanctification of the spirit, and faith of the truth:

2:14 Whereunto also he hath called you by our gospel, unto the purchasing of the glory of our Lord Jesus Christ.

2:15 Therefore, brethren, stand fast; and hold the traditions which you have learned, whether by word, or by our epistle.

2:16 Now our Lord Jesus Christ himself, and God and our Father, who hath loved us, and hath given us everlasting consolation, and good hope in grace,

2:17 Exhort your hearts, and confirm you in every good work and word.

3:1 De cetero fratres, orate pro nobis ut sermo Dei currat, et clarificetur, sicut et apud vos :

3:2 et ut liberemur ab importunis, et malis hominibus : non enim omnium est fides.

3:3 Fidelis autem Deus est, qui confirmabit vos, et custodiet a malo.

3:4 Confidimus autem de vobis, in Domino, quoniam quæ præcepimus, et facitis, et facietis.

3:5 Dominus autem dirigat corda vestra in caritate Dei, et patientia Christi.

3:6 Denuntiamus autem vobis, fratres, in nomine Domini nostri Jesu Christi, ut subtrahatis vos ab omni fratre ambulante inordinate, et non secundum traditionem, quam acceperunt a nobis.

3:7 Ipsi enim scitis quemadmodum oporteat imitari nos : quoniam non inquieti fuimus inter vos :

3:8 neque gratis panem manducavimus ab aliquo, sed in labore, et in fatigatione, nocte et die operantes, ne quem vestrum gravaremus.

3:9 Non quasi non habuerimus potestatem, sed ut nosmetipsos formam daremus vobis ad imitandum nos.

3:10 Nam et cum essemus apud vos, hoc denuntiabamus vobis : quoniam si quis non vult operari, nec manducet.

3:11 Audivimus enim inter vos quosdam ambulare inquiete, nihil operantes, sed curiose agentes.

3:12 Iis autem, qui ejusmodi sunt, denuntiemus, et obsecramus in Domino Jesu Christo, ut cum silentio operantes, suum panem manducent.

3:13 Vos autem, fratres, nolite deficere benefacientes.

3:14 Quod si quis non obedit verbo nostro per epistolam, hunc notate, et ne commisceamini cum illo ut confundatur :

3:15 et nolite quasi inimicum existimare, sed corripite ut fratrem.

3:16 Ipse autem Dominus pacis det vobis pacem sempiternam in omni loco. Dominus sit cum omnibus vobis.

3:17 Salutatio, mea manu Pauli : quod est signum in omni epistola, ita scribo.

3:18 Gratia Domini nostri Jesu Christi cum omnibus vobis. Amen.

3:1 For the rest, brethren, pray for us, that the word of God may run, and may be glorified, even as among you;

3:2 And that we may be delivered from importunate and evil men; for all men have not faith.

3:3 But God is faithful, who will strengthen and keep you from evil.

3:4 And we have confidence concerning you in the Lord, that the things which we command, you both do, and will do.

3:5 And the Lord direct your hearts, in the charity of God, and the patience of Christ.

3:6 And we charge you, brethren, in the name of our Lord Jesus Christ, that you withdraw yourselves from every brother walking disorderly, and not according to the tradition which they have received of us.

3:7 For yourselves know how you ought to imitate us: for we were not disorderly among you;

3:8 Neither did we eat any man's bread for nothing, but in labour and in toil we worked night and day, lest we should be chargeable to any of you.

3:9 Not as if we had not power: but that we might give ourselves a pattern unto you, to imitate us.

3:10 For also when we were with you, this we declared to you: that, if any man will not work, neither let him eat.

3:11 For we have heard there are some among you who walk disorderly, working not at all, but curiously meddling.

3:12 Now we charge them that are such, and beseech them by the Lord Jesus Christ, that, working with silence, they would eat their own bread.

3:13 But you, brethren, be not weary in well doing.

3:14 And if any man obey not our word by this epistle, note that man, and do not keep company with him, that he may be ashamed:

3:15 Yet do not esteem him as an enemy, but admonish him as a brother.

3:16 Now the Lord of peace himself give you everlasting peace in every place. The Lord be with you all.

3:17 The salutation of Paul with my own hand; which is the sign in every epistle. So I write.

3:18 The grace of our Lord Jesus Christ be with you all. Amen.

Epistula Beati Pauli Apostoli ad Timotheum Prima

THE FIRST EPISTLE OF BLESSED PAUL THE APOSTLE TO SAINT TIMOTHY

✠

1:1 PAULUS APOSTOLUS JESU CHRISTI secundum imperium Dei Salvatoris nostri, et Christi Jesu spei nostræ,

1:2 Timotheo dilecto filio in fide. Gratia, misericordia, et pax a Deo Patre, et Christo Jesu Domino nostro.

1:3 Sicut rogavi te ut remaneres Ephesi cum irem in Macedoniam, ut denuntiares quibusdam ne aliter docerent,

1:4 neque intenderent fabulis, et genealogiis interminatis : quæ quæstiones præstant magis quam ædificationem Dei, quæ est in fide.

1:5 Finis autem præcepti est caritas de corde puro, et conscientia bona, et fide non ficta.

1:6 A quibus quidam aberrantes, conversi sunt in vaniloquium,

1:7 volentes esse legis doctores, non intelligentes neque quæ loquuntur, neque de quibus affirmant.

1:8 Scimus autem quia bona est lex si quis ea legitime utatur :

1:9 sciens hoc quia lex justo non est posita, sed injustis, et non subditis, impiis, et peccatoribus, sceleratis, et contaminatis, parricidis, et matricidis, homicidis,

1:10 fornicariis, masculorum concubitoribus, plagiariis, mendacibus, et perjuris, et si quid aliud sanæ doctrinæ adversatur,

1:11 quæ est secundum Evangelium gloriæ beati Dei, quod creditum est mihi.

1:12 Gratias ago ei, qui me confortavit, Christo Jesu Domino nostro, quia fidelem me existimavit, ponens in ministerio :

1:13 qui prius blasphemus fui, et persecutor, et contumeliosus : sed misericordiam Dei consecutus sum, quia ignorans feci in incredulitate.

1:1 PAUL, AN APOSTLE OF JESUS CHRIST, according to the commandment of God our Savior, and of Christ Jesus our hope:

1:2 To Timothy, his beloved son in faith. Grace, mercy, and peace from God the Father, and from Christ Jesus our Lord.

1:3 As I desired thee to remain at Ephesus when I went into Macedonia, that thou mightest charge some not to teach otherwise,

1:4 Not to give heed to fables and endless genealogies: which furnish questions rather than the edification of God, which is in faith.

1:5 Now the end of the commandment is charity, from a pure heart, and a good conscience, and an unfeigned faith.

1:6 From which things some going astray, are turned aside unto vain babbling:

1:7 Desiring to be teachers of the law, understanding neither the things they say, nor whereof they affirm.

1:8 But we know that the law is good, if a man use it lawfully:

1:9 Knowing this, that the law is not made for the just man, but for the unjust and disobedient, for the ungodly, and for sinners, for the wicked and defiled, for murderers of fathers, and murderers of mothers, for manslayers,

1:10 For fornicators, for them who defile themselves with mankind, for menstealers, for liars, for perjured persons, and whatever other thing is contrary to sound doctrine,

1:11 Which is according to the gospel of the glory of the blessed God, which hath been committed to my trust.

1:12 I give thanks who hath strengthened me, even to Christ Jesus our Lord, for that he hath counted me faithful, putting me in the ministry;

1:13 Who before was a blasphemer, and a persecutor, and contumelious. But I obtained the mercy of God, because I did it ignorantly in unbelief.

1:14 Superabundavit autem gratia Domini nostri cum fide, et dilectione, quæ est in Christo Jesu.

1:15 Fidelis sermo, et omni acceptione dignus : quod Christus Jesus venit in hunc mundum peccatores salvos facere, quorum primus ego sum.

1:16 Sed ideo misericordiam consecutus sum : ut in me primo ostenderet Christus Jesus omnem patientiam ad informationem eorum, qui credituri sunt illi, in vitam æternam.

1:17 Regi autem sæculorum immortali, invisibili, soli Deo honor et gloria in sæcula sæculorum. Amen.

1:18 Hoc præceptum commendo tibi, fili Timothee, secundum præcedentes in te prophetias, ut milites in illis bonam militiam,

1:19 habens fidem, et bonam conscientiam, quam quidam repellentes, circa fidem naufragaverunt :

1:20 ex quibus est Hymenæus, et Alexander : quos tradidi Satanæ, ut discant non blasphemare.

2:1 Obsecro igitur primum omnium fieri obsecrationes, orationes, postulationes, gratiarum actiones, pro omnibus hominibus :

2:2 pro regibus, et omnibus qui in sublimitate sunt, ut quietam et tranquillam vitam agamus in omni pietate, et castitate :

2:3 hoc enim bonum est, et acceptum coram Salvatore nostro Deo,

2:4 qui omnes homines vult salvos fieri, et ad agnitionem veritatis venire.

2:5 Unus enim Deus, unus et mediator Dei et hominum homo Christus Jesus :

2:6 qui dedit redemptionem semetipsum pro omnibus, testimonium temporibus suis :

2:7 in quo positus sum ego prædicator, et Apostolus (veritatem dico, non mentior) doctor gentium in fide, et veritate.

2:8 Volo ergo viros orare in omni loco, levantes puras manus sine ira et disceptatione.

2:9 Similiter et mulieres in habitu ornato, cum verecundia et sobrietate ornantes se, et non in tortis crinibus, aut auro, aut margaritis, vel veste pretiosa :

2:10 sed quod decet mulieres, promittentes pietatem per opera bona.

2:11 Mulier in silentio discat cum omni subjectione.

1:14 Now the grace of our Lord hath abounded exceedingly with faith and love, which is in Christ Jesus.

1:15 A faithful saying, and worthy of all acceptation, that Christ Jesus came into this world to save sinners, of whom I am the chief.

1:16 But for this cause have I obtained mercy: that in me first Christ Jesus might shew forth all patience, for the information of them that shall believe in him unto life everlasting.

1:17 Now to the king of ages, immortal, invisible, the only God, be honour and glory for ever and ever. Amen.

1:18 This precept I commend to thee, O son Timothy; according to the prophecies going before on thee, that thou war in them a good warfare,

1:19 Having faith and a good conscience, which some rejecting have made shipwreck concerning the faith.

1:20 Of whom is Hymeneus and Alexander, whom I have delivered up to Satan, that they may learn not to blaspheme.

2:1 I desire therefore, first of all, that supplications, prayers, intercessions, and thanksgivings be made for all men:

2:2 For kings, and for all that are in high station: that we may lead a quiet and a peaceable life in all piety and chastity.

2:3 For this is good and acceptable in the sight of God our Saviour,

2:4 Who will have all men to be saved, and to come to the knowledge of the truth.

2:5 For there is one God, and one mediator of God and men, the man Christ Jesus:

2:6 Who gave himself a redemption for all, a testimony in due times.

2:7 Whereunto I am appointed a preacher and an apostle, (I say the truth, I lie not,) a doctor of the Gentiles in faith and truth.

2:8 I will therefore that men pray in every place, lifting up pure hands, without anger and contention.

2:9 In like manner women also in decent apparel: adorning themselves with modesty and sobriety, not with plaited hair, or gold, or pearls, or costly attire,

2:10 But as it becometh women professing godliness, with good works.

2:11 Let the woman learn in silence, with all subjection.

2:12 Docere autem mulieri non permitto, neque dominari in virum : sed esse in silentio.

2:13 Adam enim primus formatus est : deinde Heva :

2:14 et Adam non est seductus : mulier autem seducta in prævaricatione fuit.

2:15 Salvabitur autem per filiorum generationem, si permanserit in fide, et dilectione, et sanctificatione cum sobrietate.

3:1 Fidelis sermo : si quis episcopatum desiderat, bonum opus desiderat.

3:2 Oportet ergo episcopum irreprehensibilem esse, unius uxoris virum, sobrium, prudentem, ornatum, pudicum, hospitalem, doctorem,

3:3 non vinolentum, non percussorem, sed modestum : non litigiosum, non cupidum, sed

3:4 suæ domui bene præpositum : filios habentem subditos cum omni castitate.

3:5 Si quis autem domui suæ præesse nescit, quomodo ecclesiæ Dei diligentiam habebit ?

3:6 Non neophytum : ne in superbiam elatus, in judicium incidat diaboli.

3:7 Oportet autem illum et testimonium habere bonum ab iis qui foris sunt, ut non in opprobrium incidat, et in laqueum diaboli.

3:8 Diaconos similiter pudicos, non bilingues, non multo vino deditos, non turpe lucrum sectantes :

3:9 habentes mysterium fidei in conscientia pura.

3:10 Et hi autem probentur primum : et sic ministrent, nullum crimen habentes.

3:11 Mulieres similiter pudicas, non detrahentes, sobrias, fideles in omnibus.

3:12 Diaconi sint unius uxoris viri, qui filiis suis bene præsint, et suis domibus.

3:13 Qui enim bene ministraverint, gradum bonum sibi acquirent, et multam fiduciam in fide, quæ est in Christo Jesu.

3:14 Hæc tibi scribo, sperans me ad te venire cito :

3:15 si autem tardavero, ut scias quomodo oporteat te in domo Dei conversari, quæ est ecclesia Dei vivi, columna et firmamentum veritatis.

3:16 Et manifeste magnum est pietatis sacramentum, quod manifestatum est in carne, justifica-

2:12 But I suffer not a woman to teach, nor to use authority over the man: but to be in silence.

2:13 For Adam was first formed; then Eve.

2:14 And Adam was not seduced; but the woman being seduced, was in the transgression.

2:15 Yet she shall be saved through childbearing; if she continue in faith, and love, and sanctification, with sobriety.

3:1 A FAITHFUL saying: if a man desire the office of a bishop, he desireth a good work.

3:2 It behoveth therefore a bishop to be blameless, the husband of one wife, sober, prudent, of good behaviour, chaste, given to hospitality, a teacher,

3:3 Not given to wine, no striker, but modest, not quarrelsome, not covetous, but

3:4 One that ruleth well his own house, having his children in subjection with all chastity.

3:5 But if a man know not how to rule his own house, how shall he take care of the church of God?

3:6 Not a neophyte: lest being puffed up with pride, he fall into the judgment of the devil.

3:7 Moreover he must have a good testimony of them who are without: lest he fall into reproach and the snare of the devil.

3:8 Deacons in like manner chaste, not double tongued, not given to much wine, not greedy of filthy lucre:

3:9 Holding the mystery of faith in a pure conscience.

3:10 And let these also first be proved: and so let them minister, having no crime.

3:11 The women in like manner chaste, not slanderers, but sober, faithful in all things.

3:12 Let deacons be the husbands of one wife: who rule well their children, and their own houses.

3:13 For they that have ministered well, shall purchase to themselves a good degree, and much confidence in the faith which is in Christ Jesus.

3:14 These things I write to thee, hoping that I shall come to thee shortly.

3:15 But if I tarry long, that thou mayest know how thou oughtest to behave thyself in the house of God, which is the church of the living God, the pillar and ground of the truth.

3:16 And evidently great is the mystery of godliness, which was manifested in the flesh, was

tum est in spiritu, apparuit angelis, prædicatum est gentibus, creditum est in mundo, assumptum est in gloria.

4:1 Spiritus autem manifeste dicit, quia in novissimis temporibus discedent quidam a fide, attendentes spiritibus erroris, et doctrinis dæmoniorum,

4:2 in hypocrisi loquentium mendacium, et cauteriatam habentium suam conscientiam,

4:3 prohibentium nubere, abstinere a cibis, quod Deus creavit ad percipiendum cum gratiarum actione fidelibus, et iis qui cognoverunt veritatem.

4:4 Quia omnis creatura Dei bona est, et nihil rejiciendum quod cum gratiarum actione percipitur :

4:5 sanctificatur enim per verbum Dei, et orationem.

4:6 Hæc proponens fratribus, bonus eris minister Christi Jesu enutritus verbis fidei, et bonæ doctrinæ, quam assecutus es.

4:7 Ineptas autem, et aniles fabulas devita : exerce autem teipsum ad pietatem.

4:8 Nam corporalis exercitatio, ad modicum utilis est : pietas autem ad omnia utilis est, promissionem habens vitæ, quæ nunc est, et futuræ.

4:9 Fidelis sermo, et omni acceptione dignus.

4:10 In hoc enim laboramus, et maledicimur, quia speramus in Deum vivum, qui est Salvator omnium hominum, maxime fidelium.

4:11 Præcipe hæc, et doce.

4:12 Nemo adolescentiam tuam contemnat : sed exemplum esto fidelium in verbo, in conversatione, in caritate, in fide, in castitate.

4:13 Dum venio, attende lectioni, exhortationi, et doctrinæ.

4:14 Noli negligere gratiam, quæ in te est, quæ data est tibi per prophetiam, cum impositione manuum presbyterii.

4:15 Hæc meditare, in his esto : ut profectus tuus manifestus sit omnibus.

4:16 Attende tibi, et doctrinæ : insta in illis. Hoc enim faciens, et teipsum salvum facies, et eos qui te audiunt.

5:1 Seniorem ne increpaveris, sed obsecra ut patrem : juvenes, ut fratres :

5:2 anus, ut matres : juvenculas, ut sorores in omni castitate :

justified in the spirit, appeared unto angels, hath been preached unto the Gentiles, is believed in the world, is taken up in glory.

4:1 Now the Spirit manifestly saith, that in the last times some shall depart from the faith, giving heed to spirits of error, and doctrines of devils,

4:2 Speaking lies in hypocrisy, and having their conscience seared,

4:3 Forbidding to marry, to abstain from meats, which God hath created to be received with thanksgiving by the faithful, and by them that have known the truth.

4:4 For every creature of God is good, and nothing to be rejected that is received with thanksgiving:

4:5 For it is sanctified by the word of God and prayer.

4:6 These things proposing to the brethren, thou shalt be a good minister of Christ Jesus, nourished up in the words of faith, and of the good doctrine which thou hast attained unto.

4:7 But avoid foolish and old wives' fables: and exercise thyself unto godliness.

4:8 For bodily exercise is profitable to little: but godliness is profitable to all things, having promise of the life that now is, and of that which is to come.

4:9 A faithful saying and worthy of all acceptation.

4:10 For therefore we labor and are reviled, because we hope in the living God, who is the Saviour of all men, especially of the faithful.

4:11 These things command and teach.

4:12 Let no man despise thy youth: but be thou an example of the faithful in word, in conversation, in charity, in faith, in chastity.

4:13 Till I come, attend unto reading, to exhortation, and to doctrine.

4:14 Neglect not the grace that is in thee, which was given thee by prophesy, with imposition of the hands of the priesthood.

4:15 Meditate upon these things, be wholly in these things: that thy profiting may be manifest to all.

4:16 Take heed to thyself and to doctrine: be earnest in them. For in doing this thou shalt both save thyself and them that hear thee.

5:1 An ancient man rebuke not, but entreat him as a father: young men, as brethren:

5:2 Old women, as mothers: young women, as sisters, in all chastity.

5:3 viduas honora, quæ vere viduæ sunt.

5:4 Si qua autem vidua filios, aut nepotes habet : discat primum domum suam regere, et mutuam vicem reddere parentibus : hoc enim acceptum est coram Deo.

5:5 Quæ autem vere vidua est, et desolata, speret in Deum, et instet obsecrationibus, et orationibus nocte ac die.

5:6 Nam quæ in deliciis est, vivens mortua est.

5:7 Et hoc præcipe, ut irreprehensibiles sint.

5:8 Si quis autem suorum, et maxime domesticorum, curam non habet, fidem negavit, et est infideli deterior.

5:9 Vidua eligatur non minus sexaginta annorum, quæ fuerit unius viri uxor,

5:10 in operibus bonis testimonium habens, si filios educavit, si hospitio recepit, si sanctorum pedes lavit, si tribulationem patientibus subministravit, si omne opus bonum subsecuta est.

5:11 Adolescentiores autem viduas devita : cum enim luxuriatæ fuerint in Christo, nubere volunt :

5:12 habentes damnationem, quia primam fidem irritam fecerunt ;

5:13 simul autem et otiosæ discunt circuire domos : non solum otiosæ, sed et verbosæ, et curiosæ, loquentes quæ non oportet.

5:14 Volo ergo juniores nubere, filios procreare, matresfamilias esse, nullam occasionem dare adversario maledicti gratia.

5:15 Jam enim quædam conversæ sunt retro Satanam.

5:16 Si quis fidelis habet viduas, subministret illis, et non gravetur ecclesia : ut iis quæ vere viduæ sunt, sufficiat.

5:17 Qui bene præsunt presbyteri, duplici honore digni habeantur : maxime qui laborant in verbo et doctrina.

5:18 Dicit enim Scriptura : Non alligabis os bovi trituranti. Et : Dignus est operarius mercede sua.

5:19 Adversus presbyterum accusationem noli recipere, nisi sub duobus aut tribus testibus.

5:20 Peccantes coram omnibus argue : ut et ceteri timorem habeant.

5:3 Honour widows, that are widows indeed.

5:4 But if any widow have children, or grandchildren, let her learn first to govern her own house, and to make a return of duty to her parents: for this is acceptable before God.

5:5 But she that is a widow indeed, and desolate, let her trust in God, and continue in supplications and prayers night and day.

5:6 For she that liveth in pleasures, is dead while she is living.

5:7 And this give in charge, that they may be blameless.

5:8 But if any man have not care of his own, and especially of those of his house, he hath denied the faith, and is worse than an infidel.

5:9 Let a widow be chosen of no less than threescore years of age, who hath been the wife of one husband.

5:10 Having testimony for her good works, if she have brought up children, if she have received to harbour, if she have washed the saints' feet, if she have ministered to them that suffer tribulation, if she have diligently followed every good work.

5:11 But the younger widows avoid. For when they have grown wanton in Christ, they will marry:

5:12 Having damnation, because they have made void their first faith.

5:13 And withal being idle they learn to go about from house to house: and are not only idle, but tattlers also, and busybodies, speaking things which they ought not.

5:14 I will therefore that the younger should marry, bear children, be mistresses of families, give no occasion to the adversary to speak evil.

5:15 For some are already turned aside after Satan.

5:16 If any of the faithful have widows, let him minister to them, and let not the church be charged: that there may be sufficient for them that are widows indeed.

5:17 Let the priests that rule well, be esteemed worthy of double honour: especially they who labour in the word and doctrine:

5:18 For the scripture saith: Thou shalt not muzzle the ox that treadeth out the corn: and, The labourer is worthy of his reward.

5:19 Against a priest receive not an accusation, but under two or three witnesses.

5:20 Them that sin reprove before all: that the rest also may have fear.

5:21 Testor coram Deo et Christo Jesu, et electis angelis, ut hæc custodias sine præjudicio, nihil faciens in alteram partem declinando.

5:22 Manus cito nemini imposueris, neque communicaveris peccatis alienis. Teipsum castum custodi.

5:23 Noli adhuc aquam bibere, sed modico vino utere propter stomachum tuum, et frequentes tuas infirmitates.

5:24 Quorumdam hominum peccata manifesta sunt, præcedentia ad judicium : quosdam autem et subsequuntur.

5:25 Similiter et facta bona, manifesta sunt : et quæ aliter se habent, abscondi non possunt.

6:1 Quicumque sunt sub jugo servi, dominos suos omni honore dignos arbitrentur, ne nomen Domini et doctrina blasphemetur.

6:2 Qui autem fideles habent dominos, non contemnant, quia fratres sunt : sed magis serviant, quia fideles sunt et dilecti, qui beneficii participes sunt. Hæc doce, et exhortare.

6:3 Si quis aliter docet, et non acquiescit sanis sermonibus Domini nostri Jesu Christi, et ei, quæ secundum pietatem est, doctrinæ :

6:4 superbus est, nihil sciens, sed languens circa quæstiones, et pugnas verborum : ex quibus oriuntur invidiæ, contentiones, blasphemiæ, suspiciones malæ,

6:5 conflictationes hominum mente corruptorum, et qui veritate privati sunt, existimantium quæstum esse pietatem.

6:6 Est autem quæstus magnus pietas cum sufficientia.

6:7 Nihil enim intulimus in hunc mundum : haud dubium quod nec auferre quid possumus.

6:8 Habentes autem alimenta, et quibus tegamur, his contenti simus.

6:9 Nam qui volunt divites fieri, incidunt in tentationem, et in laqueum diaboli, et desideria multa inutilia, et nociva, quæ mergunt homines in interitum et perditionem.

6:10 Radix enim omnium malorum est cupiditas : quam quidam appetentes erraverunt a fide, et inseruerunt se doloribus multis.

6:11 Tu autem, o homo Dei, hæc fuge : sectare

5:21 I charge thee before God, and Christ Jesus, and the elect angels, that thou observe these things without prejudice, doing nothing by declining to either side.

5:22 Impose not hands lightly upon any man, neither be partaker of other men's sins. Keep thyself chaste.

5:23 Do not still drink water, but use a little wine for thy stomach's sake, and thy frequent infirmities.

5:24 Some men's sins are manifest, going before to judgment: and some men they follow after.

5:25 In like manner also good deeds are manifest: and they that are otherwise, cannot be hid.

6:1 Whosoever are servants under the yoke, let them count their masters worthy of all honour; lest the name of the Lord and his doctrine be blasphemed.

6:2 But they that have believing masters, let them not despise them, because they are brethren; but serve them the rather, because they are faithful and beloved, who are partakers of the benefit. These things teach and exhort.

6:3 If any man teach otherwise, and consent not to the sound words of our Lord Jesus Christ, and to that doctrine which is according to godliness,

6:4 He is proud, knowing nothing, but sick about questions and strifes of words; from which arise envies, contentions, blasphemies, evil suspicions,

6:5 Conflicts of men corrupted in mind, and who are destitute of the truth, supposing gain to be godliness.

6:6 But godliness with contentment is great gain.

6:7 For we brought nothing into this world: and certainly we can carry nothing out.

6:8 But having food, and wherewith to be covered, with these we are content.

6:9 For they that will become rich, fall into temptation, and into the snare of the devil, and into many unprofitable and hurtful desires, which drown men into destruction and perdition.

6:10 For the desire of money is the root of all evils; which some coveting have erred from the faith, and have entangled themselves in many sorrows.

6:11 But thou, O man of God, fly these things:

vero justitiam, pietatem, fidem, caritatem, patientiam, mansuetudinem.

6:12 Certa bonum certamen fidei, apprehende vitam æternam, in qua vocatus es, et confessus bonam confessionem coram multis testibus.

6:13 Præcipio tibi coram Deo, qui vivificat omnia, et Christo Jesu, qui testimonium reddidit sub Pontio Pilato, bonam confessionem,

6:14 ut serves mandatum sine macula, irreprehensibile usque in adventum Domini nostri Jesu Christi,

6:15 quem suis temporibus ostendet beatus et solus potens, Rex regum, et Dominus dominantium :

6:16 qui solus habet immortalitatem, et lucem inhabitat inaccessibilem : quem nullus hominum vidit, sed nec videre potest : cui honor, et imperium sempiternum. Amen.

6:17 Divitibus hujus sæculi præcipe non sublime sapere, neque sperare in incerto divitiarum, sed in Deo vivo (qui præstat nobis omnia abunde ad fruendum)

6:18 bene agere, divites fieri in bonis operibus, facile tribuere, communicare,

6:19 thesaurizare sibi fundamentum bonum in futurum, ut apprehendant veram vitam.

6:20 O Timothee, depositum custodi, devitans profanas vocum novitates, et oppositiones falsi nominis scientiæ,

6:21 quam quidam promittentes, circa fidem exciderunt. Gratia tecum. Amen.

and pursue justice, godliness, faith, charity, patience, mildness.

6:12 Fight the good fight of faith: lay hold on eternal life, whereunto thou art called, and hast confessed a good confession before many witnesses.

6:13 I charge thee before God, who quickeneth all things, and before Christ Jesus, who gave testimony under Pontius Pilate, a good confession,

6:14 That thou keep the commandment without spot, blameless, unto the coming of our Lord Jesus Christ,

6:15 Which in his times he shall shew who is the Blessed and only Mighty, the King of kings, and Lord of lords;

6:16 Who only hath immortality, and inhabiteth light inaccessible, whom no man hath seen, nor can see: to whom be honour and empire everlasting. Amen.

6:17 Charge the rich of this world not to be highminded, nor to trust in the uncertainty of riches, but in the living God, (who giveth us abundantly all things to enjoy,)

6:18 To do good, to be rich in good works, to give easily, to communicate to others,

6:19 To lay up in store for themselves a good foundation against the time to come, that they may lay hold on the true life.

6:20 O Timothy, keep that which is committed to thy trust, avoiding the profane novelties of words, and oppositions of knowledge falsely so called.

6:21 Which some promising, have erred concerning the faith. Grace be with thee. Amen.

Epistula Beati Pauli Apostoli ad Timotheum Secunda

THE SECOND EPISTLE OF BLESSED PAUL THE APOSTLE TO SAINT TIMOTHY

✠

1:1 PAULUS APOSTOLUS JESU CHRISTI per voluntatem Dei, secundum promissionem vitæ, quæ est in Christo Jesu,

1:2 Timotheo carissimo filio : gratia, misericordia, pax a Deo Patre, et Christo Jesu Domino nostro.

1:3 Gratias ago Deo, cui servio a progenitoribus in conscientia pura, quod sine intermissione habeam tui memoriam in orationibus meis, nocte ac die

1:4 desiderans te videre, memor lacrimarum tuarum, ut gaudio implear,

1:5 recordationem accipiens ejus fidei, quæ est in te non ficta, quæ et habitavit primum in avia tua Loide, et matre tua Eunice, certus sum autem quod et in te.

1:6 Propter quam causam admoneo te ut resuscites gratiam Dei, quæ est in te per impositionem manuum mearum.

1:7 Non enim dedit nobis Deus spiritum timoris : sed virtutis, et dilectionis, et sobrietatis.

1:8 Noli itaque erubescere testimonium Domini nostri, neque me vinctum ejus : sed collabora Evangelio secundum virtutem Dei :

1:9 qui nos liberavit, et vocavit vocatione sua sancta, non secundum opera nostra, sed secundum propositum suum, et gratiam, quæ data est nobis in Christo Jesu ante tempora sæcularia.

1:10 Manifestata est autem nunc per illuminationem Salvatoris nostri Jesu Christi, qui destruxit quidem mortem, illuminavit autem vitam, et incorruptionem per Evangelium :

1:11 in quo positus sum ego prædicator, et Apostolus, et magister gentium.

1:12 Ob quam causam etiam hæc patior, sed non confundor. Scio enim cui credidi, et certus sum quia potens est depositum meum servare in illum diem.

1:1 PAUL, AN APOSTLE OF JESUS CHRIST, by the will of God, according to the promise of life, which is in Christ Jesus.

1:2 To Timothy my dearly beloved son, grace, mercy, and peace, from God the Father, and from Christ Jesus our Lord.

1:3 I give thanks to God, whom I serve from my forefathers with a pure conscience, that without ceasing, I have a remembrance of thee in my prayers, night and day.

1:4 Desiring to see thee, being mindful of thy tears, that I may be filled with joy,

1:5 Calling to mind that faith which is in thee unfeigned, which also dwelt first in thy grandmother Lois, and in thy mother Eunice, and I am certain that in thee also.

1:6 For which cause I admonish thee, that thou stir up the grace of God which is in thee, by the imposition of my hands.

1:7 For God hath not given us the spirit of fear: but of power, and of love, and of sobriety.

1:8 Be not thou therefore ashamed of the testimony of our Lord, nor of me his prisoner: but labour with the gospel, according to the power of God,

1:9 Who hath delivered us and called us by his holy calling, not according to our works, but according to his own purpose and grace, which was given us in Christ Jesus before the times of the world.

1:10 But is now made manifest by the illumination of our Saviour Jesus Christ, who hath destroyed death, and hath brought to light life and incorruption by the gospel:

1:11 Wherein I am appointed a preacher, and an apostle, and teacher of the Gentiles.

1:12 For which cause I also suffer these things: but I am not ashamed. For I know whom I have believed, and I am certain that he is able to keep that which I have committed unto him, against that day.

1:13 Formam habe sanorum verborum, quæ a me audisti in fide, et in dilectione in Christo Jesu.

1:14 Bonum depositum custodi per Spiritum Sanctum, qui habitat in nobis.

1:15 Scis hoc, quod aversi sunt a me omnes, qui in Asia sunt, ex quibus est Phigellus, et Hermogenes.

1:16 Det misericordiam Dominus Onesiphori domui : quia sæpe me refrigeravit, et catenam meam non erubuit :

1:17 sed cum Romam venisset, sollicite me quæsivit, et invenit.

1:18 Det illi Dominus invenire misericordiam a Domino in illa die. Et quanta Ephesi ministravit mihi, tu melius nosti.

2:1 Tu ergo fili mi, confortare in gratia, quæ est in Christo Jesu :

2:2 et quæ audisti a me per multos testes, hæc commenda fidelibus hominibus, qui idonei erant et alios docere.

2:3 Labora sicut bonus miles Christi Jesu.

2:4 Nemo militans Deo implicat se negotiis sæcularibus : ut ei placeat, cui se probavit.

2:5 Nam et qui certat in agone, non coronatur nisi legitime certaverit.

2:6 Laborantem agricolam oportet primum de fructibus percipere.

2:7 Intellige quæ dico : dabit enim tibi Dominus in omnibus intellectum.

2:8 Memor esto Dominum Jesum Christum resurrexisse a mortuis ex semine David, secundum Evangelium meum,

2:9 in quo laboro usque ad vincula, quasi male operans : sed verbum Dei non est alligatum.

2:10 Ideo omnia sustineo propter electos, ut et ipsi salutem consequantur, quæ est in Christo Jesu, cum gloria cælesti.

2:11 Fidelis sermo : nam si commortui sumus, et convivemus :

2:12 si sustinebimus, et conregnabimus : si negaverimus, et ille negabit nos :

2:13 si non credimus, ille fidelis permanet, negare seipsum non potest.

2:14 Hæc commone, testificans coram Domino. Noli contendere verbis : ad nihil enim utile est, nisi ad subversionem audientium.

1:13 Hold the form of sound words, which thou hast heard of me in faith, and in the love which is in Christ Jesus.

1:14 Keep the good thing committed to thy trust by the Holy Ghost, who dwelleth in us.

1:15 Thou knowest this, that all they who are in Asia, are turned away from me: of whom are Phigellus and Hermogenes.

1:16 The Lord give mercy to the house of Onesiphorus: because he hath often refreshed me, and hath not been ashamed of my chain:

1:17 But when he was come to Rome, he carefully sought me, and found me.

1:18 The Lord grant unto him to find mercy of the Lord in that day: and in how many things he ministered unto me at Ephesus, thou very well knowest.

2:1 Thou therefore, my son, be strong in the grace which is in Christ Jesus:

2:2 And the things which thou hast heard of me by many witnesses, the same commend to faithful men, who shall be fit to teach others also.

2:3 Labour as a good soldier of Christ Jesus.

2:4 No man, being a soldier to God, entangleth himself with secular businesses; that he may please him to whom he hath engaged himself.

2:5 For he also that striveth for the mastery, is not crowned, except he strive lawfully.

2:6 The husbandman, that laboureth, must first partake of the fruits.

2:7 Understand what I say: for the Lord will give thee in all things understanding.

2:8 Be mindful that the Lord Jesus Christ is risen again from the dead, of the seed of David, according to my gospel.

2:9 Wherein I labour even unto bands, as an evildoer; but the word of God is not bound.

2:10 Therefore I endure all things for the sake of the elect, that they also may obtain the salvation, which is in Christ Jesus, with heavenly glory.

2:11 A faithful saying: for if we be dead with him, we shall live also with him.

2:12 If we suffer, we shall also reign with him. If we deny him, he will also deny us.

2:13 If we believe not, he continueth faithful, he can not deny himself.

2:14 Of these things put them in mind, charging them before the Lord. Contend not in words, for it is to no profit, but to the subverting of the hearers.

2:15 Sollicite cura teipsum probabilem exhibere Deo, operarium inconfusibilem, recte tractantem verbum veritatis.

2:16 Profana autem et vaniloquia devita : multum enim proficiunt ad impietatem :

2:17 et sermo eorum ut cancer serpit : ex quibus est Hymenæus et Philetus,

2:18 qui a veritate exciderunt, dicentes resurrectionem esse jam factam, et subverterunt quorumdam fidem.

2:19 Sed firmum fundamentum Dei stat, habens signaculum hoc : cognovit Dominus qui sunt ejus, et discedat ab iniquitate omnis qui nominat nomen Domini.

2:20 In magna autem domo non solum sunt vasa aurea, et argentea, sed et lignea, et fictilia : et quædam quidem in honorem, quædam autem in contumeliam.

2:21 Si quis ergo emundaverit se ab istis, erit vas in honorem sanctificatum, et utile Domino ad omne opus bonum paratum.

2:22 Juvenilia autem desideria fuge, sectare vero justitiam, fidem, spem, caritatem, et pacem cum iis qui invocant Dominum de corde puro.

2:23 Stultas autem et sine disciplina quæstiones devita : sciens quia generant lites.

2:24 Servum autem Domini non oportet litigare : sed mansuetum esse ad omnes, docibilem, patientem,

2:25 cum modestia corripientem eos qui resistunt veritati, nequando Deus det illis pœnitentiam ad cognoscendam veritatem,

2:26 et resipiscant a diaboli laqueis, a quo captivi tenentur ad ipsius voluntatem.

3:1 Hoc autem scito, quod in novissimis diebus instabunt tempora periculosa :

3:2 erunt homines seipsos amantes, cupidi, elati, superbi, blasphemi, parentibus non obedientes, ingrati, scelesti,

3:3 sine affectione, sine pace, criminatores, incontinentes, immites, sine benignitate,

3:4 proditores, protervi, tumidi, et voluptatum amatores magis quam Dei :

3:5 habentes speciem quidem pietatis, virtutem autem ejus abnegantes. Et hos devita :

3:6 ex his enim sunt qui penetrant domos, et captivas ducunt mulierculas oneratas peccatis, quæ ducuntur variis desideriis :

3:7 semper discentes, et numquam ad scientiam

2:15 Carefully study to present thyself approved unto God, a workman that needeth not to be ashamed, rightly handling the word of truth.

2:16 But shun profane and vain babblings: for they grow much towards ungodliness.

2:17 And their speech spreadeth like a canker: of whom are Hymeneus and Philetus:

2:18 Who have erred from the truth, saying, that the resurrection is past already, and have subverted the faith of some.

2:19 But the sure foundation of God standeth firm, having this seal: the Lord knoweth who are his; and let every one depart from iniquity who nameth the name of the Lord.

2:20 But in a great house there are not only vessels of gold and of silver, but also of wood and earth: and some indeed unto honour, but some unto dishonour.

2:21 If any man therefore shall cleanse himself from these, he shall be a vessel unto honour, sanctified and profitable to the Lord, prepared unto every good work.

2:22 But flee thou youthful desires, and pursue justice, faith, charity, and peace, with them that call on the Lord out of a pure heart.

2:23 And avoid foolish and unlearned questions, knowing that they beget strifes.

2:24 But the servant of the Lord must not wrangle: but be mild towards all men, apt to teach, patient,

2:25 With modesty admonishing them that resist the truth: if peradventure God may give them repentance to know the truth,

2:26 And they may recover themselves from the snares of the devil, by whom they are held captive at his will.

3:1 Know also this, that, in the last days, shall come dangerous times.

3:2 Men shall be lovers of themselves, covetous, haughty, proud, blasphemers, disobedient to parents, ungrateful, wicked,

3:3 Without affection, without peace, slanderers, incontinent, unmerciful, without kindness,

3:4 Traitors, stubborn, puffed up, and lovers of pleasures more than of God:

3:5 Having an appearance indeed of godliness, but denying the power thereof. Now these avoid.

3:6 For of these sort are they who creep into houses, and lead captive silly women laden with sins, who are led away with divers desires:

3:7 Ever learning, and never attaining to the

veritatis pervenientes.

3:8 Quemadmodum autem Jannes et Mambres restiterunt Moysi : ita et hi resistunt veritati, homines corrupti mente, reprobi circa fidem ;

3:9 sed ultra non proficient : insipientia enim eorum manifesta erit omnibus, sicut et illorum fuit.

3:10 Tu autem assecutus es meam doctrinam, institutionem, propositum, fidem, longanimitatem, dilectionem, patientiam,

3:11 persecutiones, passiones : qualia mihi facta sunt Antiochiæ, Iconii, et Lystris : quales persecutiones sustinui, et ex omnibus eripuit me Dominus.

3:12 Et omnes, qui pie volunt vivere in Christo Jesu, persecutionem patientur.

3:13 Mali autem homines et seductores proficient in pejus, errantes, et in errorem mittentes.

3:14 Tu vero permane in iis quæ didicisti, et credita sunt tibi : sciens a quo didiceris :

3:15 et quia ab infantia sacras litteras nosti, quæ te possunt instruere ad salutem, per fidem quæ est in Christo Jesu.

3:16 Omnis Scriptura divinitus inspirata utilis est ad docendum, ad arguendum, ad corripiendum, et erudiendum in justitia :

3:17 ut perfectus sit homo Dei, ad omne opus bonum instructus.

4:1 Testificor coram Deo, et Jesu Christo, qui judicaturus est vivos et mortuos, per adventum ipsius, et regnum ejus :

4:2 prædica verbum, insta opportune, importune : argue, obsecra, increpa in omni patientia, et doctrina.

4:3 Erit enim tempus, cum sanam doctrinam non sustinebunt, sed ad sua desideria coacervabunt sibi magistros, prurientes auribus,

4:4 et a veritate quidem auditum avertent, ad fabulas autem convertentur.

4:5 Tu vero vigila, in omnibus labora, opus fac evangelistæ, ministerium tuum imple. Sobrius esto.

4:6 Ego enim jam delibor, et tempus resolutionis meæ instat.

4:7 Bonum certamen certavi, cursum consummavi, fidem servavi.

4:8 In reliquo reposita est mihi corona justitiæ,

knowledge of the truth.

3:8 Now as Jannes and Mambres resisted Moses, so these also resist the truth, men corrupted in mind, reprobate concerning the faith.

3:9 But they shall proceed no farther; for their folly shall be manifest to all men, as theirs also was.

3:10 But thou hast fully known my doctrine, manner of life, purpose, faith, longsuffering, love, patience,

3:11 Persecutions, afflictions: such as came upon me at Antioch, at Iconium, and at Lystra: what persecutions I endured, and out of them all the Lord delivered me.

3:12 And all that will live godly in Christ Jesus, shall suffer persecution.

3:13 But evil men and seducers shall grow worse and worse: erring, and driving into error.

3:14 But continue thou in those things which thou hast learned, and which have been committed to thee: knowing of whom thou hast learned them;

3:15 And because from thy infancy thou hast known the holy scriptures, which can instruct thee to salvation, by the faith which is in Christ Jesus.

3:16 All scripture, inspired of God, is profitable to teach, to reprove, to correct, to instruct in justice,

3:17 That the man of God may be perfect, furnished to every good work.

4:1 I charge thee, before God and Jesus Christ, who shall judge the living and the dead, by his coming, and his kingdom:

4:2 Preach the word: be instant in season, out of season: reprove, entreat, rebuke in all patience and doctrine.

4:3 For there shall be a time, when they will not endure sound doctrine; but, according to their own desires, they will heap to themselves teachers, having itching ears:

4:4 And will indeed turn away their hearing from the truth, but will be turned unto fables.

4:5 But be thou vigilant, labour in all things, do the work of an evangelist, fulfil thy ministry. Be sober.

4:6 For I am even now ready to be sacrificed: and the time of my dissolution is at hand.

4:7 I have fought a good fight, I have finished my course, I have kept the faith.

4:8 As to the rest, there is laid up for me a

quam reddet mihi Dominus in illa die, justus judex : non solum autem mihi, sed et iis, qui diligunt adventum ejus. Festina ad me venire cito.

4:9 Demas enim me reliquit, diligens hoc sæculum, et abiit Thessalonicam :

4:10 Crescens in Galatiam, Titus in Dalmatiam.

4:11 Lucas est mecum solus. Marcum assume, et adduc tecum : est enim mihi utilis in ministerium.

4:12 Tychicum autem misi Ephesum.

4:13 Penulam, quam reliqui Troade apud Carpum, veniens affer tecum, et libros, maxime autem membranas.

4:14 Alexander ærarius multa mala mihi ostendit : reddet illi Dominus secundum opera ejus :

4:15 quem et tu devita : valde enim restitit verbis nostris.

4:16 In prima mea defensione nemo mihi affuit, sed omnes me dereliquerunt : non illis imputetur.

4:17 Dominus autem mihi astitit, et confortavit me, ut per me prædicatio impleatur, et audiant omnes gentes : et liberatus sum de ore leonis.

4:18 Liberavit me Dominus ab omni opere malo : et salvum faciet in regnum suum cæleste, cui gloria in sæcula sæculorum. Amen.

4:19 Saluta Priscam, et Aquilam, et Onesiphori domum.

4:20 Erastus remansit Corinthi. Trophimum autem reliqui infirmum Mileti.

4:21 Festina ante hiemem venire. Salutant te Eubulus, et Pudens, et Linus, et Claudia, et fratres omnes.

4:22 Dominus Jesus Christus cum spiritu tuo. Gratia vobiscum. Amen.

crown of justice, which the Lord the just judge will render to me in that day: and not only to me, but to them also that love his coming. Make haste to come to me quickly.

4:9 For Demas hath left me, loving this world, and is gone to Thessalonica:

4:10 Crescens into Galatia, Titus into Dalmatia.

4:11 Only Luke is with me. Take Mark, and bring him with thee: for he is profitable to me for the ministry.

4:12 But Tychicus I have sent to Ephesus.

4:13 The cloak that I left at Troas, with Carpus, when thou comest, bring with thee, and the books, especially the parchments.

4:14 Alexander the coppersmith hath done me much evil: the Lord will reward him according to his works:

4:15 Whom do thou also avoid, for he hath greatly withstood our words.

4:16 At my first answer no man stood with me, but all forsook me: may it not be laid to their charge.

4:17 But the Lord stood by me, and strengthened me, that by me the preaching may be accomplished, and that all the Gentiles may hear: and I was delivered out of the mouth of the lion.

4:18 The Lord hath delivered me from every evil work: and will preserve me unto his heavenly kingdom, to whom be glory for ever and ever. Amen.

4:19 Salute Prisca and Aquila, and the household of Onesiphorus.

4:20 Erastus remained at Corinth. And Trophimus I left sick at Miletus.

4:21 Make haste to come before winter Eubulus and Pudens, and Linus and Claudia, and all the brethren, salute thee.

4:22 The Lord Jesus Christ be with thy spirit. Grace be with you. Amen.

Epistula Beati Pauli Apostoli ad Titum

THE EPISTLE OF BLESSED PAUL THE APOSTLE TO TITUS

✠

1:1 PAULUS SERVUS DEI, APOSTOLUS autem JESU CHRISTI secundum fidem electorum Dei, et agnitionem veritatis, quæ secundum pietatem est

1:2 in spem vitæ æternæ, quam promisit qui non mentitur, Deus, ante tempora sæcularia :

1:3 manifestavit autem temporibus suis verbum suum in prædicatione, quæ credita est mihi secundum præceptum Salvatoris nostri Dei :

1:4 Tito dilecto filio secundum communem fidem, gratia, et pax a Deo Patre, et Christo Jesu Salvatore nostro.

1:5 Hujus rei gratia reliqui te Cretæ, ut ea quæ desunt, corrigas, et constituas per civitates presbyteros, sicut et ego disposui tibi,

1:6 si quis sine crimine est, unius uxoris vir, filios habens fideles, non in accusatione luxuriæ, aut non subditos.

1:7 Oportet enim episcopum sine crimine esse, sicut Dei dispensatorem : non superbum, non iracundum, non vinolentum, non percussorem, non turpis lucri cupidum :

1:8 sed hospitalem, benignum, sobrium, justum, sanctum, continentem,

1:9 amplectentem eum, qui secundum doctrinam est, fidelem sermonem : ut potens sit exhortari in doctrina sana, et eos qui contradicunt, arguere.

1:10 Sunt enim multi etiam inobedientes, vaniloqui, et seductores : maxime qui de circumcisione sunt :

1:11 quos oportet redargui : qui universas domos subvertunt, docentes quæ non oportet, turpis lucri gratia.

1:12 Dixit quidam ex illis, proprius ipsorum propheta : Cretenses semper mendaces, malæ bestiæ, ventres pigri.

1:13 Testimonium hoc verum est. Quam ob causam increpa illos dure, ut sani sint in fide,

1:14 non intendentes judaicis fabulis, et mandatis hominum, aversantium se a veritate.

1:1 PAUL, A SERVANT OF GOD, AND AN APOSTLE OF JESUS CHRIST, according to the faith of the elect of God and the acknowledging of the truth, which is according to godliness:

1:2 Unto the hope of life everlasting, which God, who lieth not, hath promised before the times of the world:

1:3 But hath in due times manifested his word in preaching, which is committed to me according to the commandment of God our Savior:

1:4 To Titus my beloved son, according to the common faith, grace and peace from God the Father, and from Christ Jesus our Savior.

1:5 For this cause I left thee in Crete, that thou shouldest set in order the things that are wanting, and shouldest ordain priests in every city, as I also appointed thee:

1:6 If any be without crime, the husband of one wife, having faithful children, not accused of riot, or unruly.

1:7 For a bishop must be without crime, as the steward of God: not proud, not subject to anger, not given to wine, no striker, not greedy of filthy lucre:

1:8 But given to hospitality, gentle, sober, just, holy, continent:

1:9 Embracing that faithful word which is according to doctrine, that he may be able to exhort in sound doctrine, and to convince the gainsayers.

1:10 For there are also many disobedient, vain talkers, and seducers: especially they who are of the circumcision:

1:11 Who must be reproved, who subvert whole houses, teaching things which they ought not, for filthy lucre's sake.

1:12 One of them a prophet of their own, said, The Cretians are always liars, evil beasts, slothful bellies.

1:13 This testimony is true. Wherefore rebuke them sharply, that they may be sound in the faith;

1:14 Not giving heed to Jewish fables and commandments of men, who turn themselves away from the truth.

1:15 Omnia munda mundis : coinquinatis autem et infidelibus, nihil est mundum, sed inquinatæ sunt eorum et mens et conscientia.

1:16 Confitentur se nosse Deum, factis autem negant : cum sint abominati, et incredibiles, et ad omne opus bonum reprobi.

2:1 Tu autem loquere quæ decent sanam doctrinam :

2:2 senes ut sobrii sint, pudici, prudentes, sani in fide, in dilectione, in patientia :

2:3 anus similiter in habitu sancto, non criminatrices, non multo vino servientes, bene docentes :

2:4 ut prudentiam doceant adolescentulas, ut viros suos ament, filios suos diligant,

2:5 prudentes, castas, sobrias, domus curam habentes, benignas, subditas viris suis, ut non blasphemetur verbum Dei.

2:6 Juvenes similiter hortare ut sobrii sint.

2:7 In omnibus teipsum præbe exemplum bonorum operum, in doctrina, in integritate, in gravitate,

2:8 verbum sanum, irreprehensibile : ut is qui ex adverso est, vereatur, nihil habens malum dicere de nobis.

2:9 Servos dominis suis subditos esse, in omnibus placentes, non contradicentes,

2:10 non fraudantes, sed in omnibus fidem bonam ostendentes : ut doctrinam Salvatoris nostri Dei ornent in omnibus.

2:11 Apparuit enim gratia Dei Salvatoris nostri omnibus hominibus,

2:12 erudiens nos, ut abnegantes impietatem, et sæcularia desideria, sobrie, et juste, et pie vivamus in hoc sæculo,

2:13 exspectantes beatam spem, et adventum gloriæ magni Dei, et Salvatoris nostri Jesu Christi :

2:14 qui dedit semetipsum pro nobis, ut nos redimeret ab omni iniquitate, et mundaret sibi populum acceptabilem, sectatorem bonorum operum.

2:15 Hæc loquere, et exhortare, et argue cum omni imperio. Nemo te contemnat.

3:1 Admone illos principibus, et potestatibus subditos esse, dicto obedire, ad omne opus bonum paratos esse :

3:2 neminem blasphemare, non litigiosos esse,

1:15 All things are clean to the clean: but to them that are defiled, and to unbelievers, nothing is clean: but both their mind and their conscience are defiled.

1:16 They profess that they know God: but in their works they deny him; being abominable, and incredulous, and to every good work reprobate.

2:1 But speak thou the things that become sound doctrine:

2:2 That the aged men be sober, chaste, prudent, sound in faith, in love, in patience.

2:3 The aged women, in like manner, in holy attire, not false accusers, not given to much wine, teaching well:

2:4 That they may teach the young women to be wise, to love their husbands, to love their children,

2:5 To be discreet, chaste, sober, having a care of the house, gentle, obedient to their husbands, that the word of God be not blasphemed.

2:6 Young men, in like manner, exhort that they be sober.

2:7 In all things shew thyself an example of good works, in doctrine, in integrity, in gravity,

2:8 The sound word that can not be blamed: that he, who is on the contrary part, may be afraid, having no evil to say of us.

2:9 Exhort servants to be obedient to their masters, in all things pleasing, not gainsaying:

2:10 Not defrauding, but in all things shewing good fidelity, that they may adorn the doctrine of God our Savior in all things.

2:11 For the grace of God our Savior hath appeared to all men;

2:12 Instructing us, that, denying ungodliness and worldly desires, we should live soberly, and justly, and godly in this world,

2:13 Looking for the blessed hope and coming of the glory of the great God and our Savior Jesus Christ,

2:14 Who gave himself for us, that he might redeem us from all iniquity, and might cleanse to himself a people acceptable, a pursuer of good works.

2:15 These things speak, and exhort and rebuke with all authority. Let no man despise thee.

3:1 Admonish them to be subject to princes and powers, to obey at a word, to be ready to every good work.

3:2 To speak evil of no man, not to be litigious,

sed modestos, omnem ostendentes mansuetu-dinem ad omnes homines.

3:3 Eramus enim aliquando et nos insipientes, increduli, errantes, servientes desideriis, et vo-luptatibus variis, in malitia et invidia agentes, odibiles, odientes invicem.

3:4 Cum autem benignitas et humanitas apparuit Salvatoris nostri Dei,

3:5 non ex operibus justitiæ, quæ fecimus nos, sed secundum suam misericordiam salvos nos fecit per lavacrum regenerationis et renova-tionis Spiritus Sancti,

3:6 quem effudit in nos abunde per Jesum Christum Salvatorem nostrum :

3:7 ut justificati gratia ipsius, hæredes simus secundum spem vitæ æternæ.

3:8 Fidelis sermo est : et de his volo te confir-mare : ut curent bonis operibus præesse qui credunt Deo. Hæc sunt bona, et utilia homini-bus.

3:9 Stultas autem quæstiones, et genealogias, et contentiones, et pugnas legis devita : sunt enim inutiles, et vanæ.

3:10 Hæreticum hominem post unam et secun-dam correptionem devita :

3:11 sciens quia subversus est, qui ejusmodi est, et delinquit, cum sit proprio judicio condem-natus.

3:12 Cum misero ad te Artemam, aut Tychicum, festina ad me venire Nicopolim : ibi enim statui hiemare.

3:13 Zenam legisperitum et Apollo sollicite præmitte, ut nihil illis desit.

3:14 Discant autem et nostri bonis operibus præesse ad usus necessarios : ut non sint in-fructuosi.

3:15 Salutant te qui mecum sunt omnes : saluta eos qui nos amant in fide. Gratia Dei cum om-nibus vobis. Amen.

but gentle: shewing all mildness towards all men.

3:3 For we ourselves also were some time un-wise, incredulous, erring, slaves to divers de-sires and pleasures, living in malice and envy, hateful, and hating one another.

3:4 But when the goodness and kindness of God our Savior appeared:

3:5 Not by the works of justice, which we have done, but according to his mercy, he saved us, by the laver of regeneration, and renovation of the Holy Ghost;

3:6 Whom he hath poured forth upon us abun-dantly, through Jesus Christ our Savior:

3:7 That, being justified by his grace, we may be heirs, according to hope of life everlasting.

3:8 It is a faithful saying: and these things I will have thee affirm constantly: that they, who be-lieve in God, may be careful to excel in good works. These things are good and profitable un-to men.

3:9 But avoid foolish questions, and genealogies, and contentions, and strivings about the law. For they are unprofitable and vain.

3:10 A man that is a heretic, after the first and second admonition, avoid:

3:11 Knowing that he, that is such an one, is sub-verted, and sinneth, being condemned by his own judgment.

3:12 When I shall send to thee Artemas or Tychi-cus, make haste to come unto me to Nicopolis. For there I have determined to winter.

3:13 Send forward Zenas, the lawyer, and Apol-lo, with care, that nothing be wanting to them.

3:14 And let our men also learn to excel in good works for necessary uses: that they be not un-fruitful.

3:15 All that are with me salute thee: salute them that love us in the faith. The grace of God be with you all. Amen.

Epistula Beati Pauli Apostoli ad Philemonem

THE EPISTLE OF BLESSED PAUL THE APOSTLE TO PHILEMON

✠

1:1 PAULUS VINCTUS CHRISTI JESU, ET TIMOTHEUS FRATER, Philemoni dilecto, et adjutori nostro,

1:2 et Appiæ sorori carissimæ, et Archippo commilitoni nostro, et ecclesiæ, quæ in domo tua est.

1:3 Gratia vobis, et pax a Deo Patre nostro, et Domino Jesu Christo.

1:4 Gratias ago Deo meo, semper memoriam tui faciens in orationibus meis,

1:5 audiens caritatem tuam, et fidem, quam habes in Domino Jesu, et in omnes sanctos :

1:6 ut communicatio fidei tuæ evidens fiat in agnitione omnis operis boni, quod est in vobis in Christo Jesu.

1:7 Gaudium enim magnum habui, et consolationem in caritate tua : quia viscera sanctorum requieverunt per te, frater.

1:8 Propter quod multam fiduciam habens in Christo Jesu imperandi tibi quod ad rem pertinet :

1:9 propter caritatem magis obsecro, cum sis talis, ut Paulus senex, nunc autem et vinctus Jesu Christi :

1:10 obsecro te pro meo filio, quem genui in vinculis, Onesimo,

1:11 qui tibi aliquando inutilis fuit, nunc autem et mihi et tibi utilis,

1:12 quem remisi tibi. Tu autem illum, ut mea viscera, suscipe :

1:13 quem ego volueram mecum detinere, ut pro te mihi ministraret in vinculis Evangelii :

1:14 sine consilio autem tuo nihil volui facere, uti ne velut ex necessitate bonum tuum esset, sed voluntarium.

1:15 Forsitan enim ideo discessit ad horam a te, ut æternum illum reciperes :

1:16 jam non ut servum, sed pro servo carissimum fratrem, maxime mihi : quanto autem

1:1 PAUL, A PRISONER OF CHRIST JESUS, AND TIMOTHY, A BROTHER: to Philemon, our beloved and fellow labourer;

1:2 And to Appia, our dearest sister, and to Archippus, our fellow soldier, and to the church which is in thy house:

1:3 Grace to you and peace from God our Father, and from the Lord Jesus Christ.

1:4 I give thanks to my God, always making a remembrance of thee in my prayers.

1:5 Hearing of thy charity and faith, which thou hast in the Lord Jesus, and towards all the saints:

1:6 That the communication of thy faith may be made evident in the acknowledgment of every good work, that is in you in Christ Jesus.

1:7 For I have had great joy and consolation in thy charity, because the bowels of the saints have been refreshed by thee, brother.

1:8 Wherefore though I have much confidence in Christ Jesus, to command thee that which is to the purpose:

1:9 For charity sake I rather beseech, whereas thou art such a one, as Paul an old man, and now a prisoner also of Jesus Christ.

1:10 I beseech thee for my son, whom I have begotten in my bands, Onesimus,

1:11 Who hath been heretofore unprofitable to thee, but now is profitable both to me and thee,

1:12 Whom I have sent back to thee. And do thou receive him as my own bowels.

1:13 Whom I would have retained with me, that in thy stead he might have ministered to me in the bands of the gospel:

1:14 But without thy counsel I would do nothing: that thy good deed might not be as it were of necessity, but voluntary.

1:15 For perhaps he therefore departed for a season from thee, that thou mightest receive him again for ever:

1:16 Not now as a servant, but instead of a servant, a most dear brother, especially to me: but

magis tibi et in carne, et in Domino ?

1:17 Si ergo habes me socium, suscipe illum sicut me :

1:18 si autem aliquid nocuit tibi, aut debet, hoc mihi imputa.

1:19 Ego Paulus scripsi mea manu : ego reddam, ut non dicam tibi, quod et teipsum mihi debes :

1:20 ita, frater. Ego te fruar in Domino : refice viscera mea in Domino.

1:21 Confidens in obedientia tua scripsi tibi : sciens quoniam et super id, quod dico, facies.

1:22 Simul autem et para mihi hospitium : nam spero per orationes vestras donari me vobis.

1:23 Salutat te Epaphras concaptivus meus in Christo Jesu,

1:24 Marcus, Aristarchus, Demas, et Lucas, adjutores mei.

1:25 Gratia Domini nostri Jesu Christi cum spiritu vestro. Amen.

how much more to thee both in the flesh and in the Lord?

1:17 If therefore thou count me a partner, receive him as myself.

1:18 And if he hath wronged thee in any thing, or is in thy debt, put that to my account.

1:19 I Paul have written it with my own hand: I will repay it: not to say to thee, that thou owest me thy own self also.

1:20 Yea, brother. May I enjoy thee in the Lord. Refresh my bowels in the Lord.

1:21 Trusting in thy obedience, I have written to thee: knowing that thou wilt also do more than I say.

1:22 But withal prepare me also a lodging. For I hope that through your prayers I shall be given unto you.

1:23 There salute thee Epaphras, my fellow prisoner in Christ Jesus;

1:24 Mark, Aristarchus, Demas, and Luke my fellow labourers.

1:25 The grace of our Lord Jesus Christ be with your spirit. Amen.

Epistula Beati Pauli Apostoli ad Hebræos

THE EPISTLE OF BLESSED PAUL THE APOSTLE TO THE HEBREWS

✠

1:1 MULTIFARIAM, MULTISQUE MODIS OLIM DEUS loquens patribus in prophetis :

1:2 novissime, diebus istis locutus est nobis in Filio, quem constituit hæredem universorum, per quem fecit et sæcula :

1:3 qui cum sit splendor gloriæ, et figura substantiæ ejus, portansque omnia verbo virtutis suæ, purgationem peccatorum faciens, sedet ad dexteram majestatis in excelsis :

1:4 tanto melior angelis effectus, quanto differentius præ illis nomen hæreditavit.

1:5 Cui enim dixit aliquando angelorum : Filius meus es tu, ego hodie genui te ? Et rursum : Ego ero illi in patrem, et ipse erit mihi in filium ?

1:6 Et cum iterum introducit primogenitum in orbem terræ, dicit : Et adorent eum omnes angeli Dei.

1:7 Et ad angelos quidem dicit : Qui facit angelos suos spiritus, et ministros suos flammam ignis.

1:8 Ad Filium autem : Thronus tuus Deus in sæculum sæculi : virga æquitatis, virga regni tui.

1:9 Dilexisti justitiam, et odisti iniquitatem : propterea unxit te Deus, Deus tuus, oleo exultationis præ participibus tuis.

1:10 Et : Tu in principio, Domine, terram fundasti : et opera manuum tuarum sunt cæli.

1:11 Ipsi peribunt, tu autem permanebis, et omnes ut vestimentum veterascent :

1:12 et velut amictum mutabis eos, et mutabuntur : tu autem idem ipse es, et anni tui non deficient.

1:13 Ad quem autem angelorum dixit aliquando : Sede a dextris meis, quoadusque ponam inimicos tuos scabellum pedum tuorum ?

1:14 Nonne omnes sunt administratorii spiritus, in ministerium missi propter eos, qui hæredi-

1:1 GOD, WHO, AT SUNDRY TIMES AND IN DIVERS MANNERS, spoke in times past to the fathers by the prophets, last of all,

1:2 In these days hath spoken to us by his Son, whom he hath appointed heir of all things, by whom also he made the world.

1:3 Who being the brightness of his glory, and the figure of his substance, and upholding all things by the word of his power, making purgation of sins, sitteth on the right hand of the majesty on high.

1:4 Being made so much better than the angels, as he hath inherited a more excellent name than they.

1:5 For to which of the angels hath he said at any time, Thou art my Son, to day have I begotten thee? And again, I will be to him a Father, and he shall be to me a Son?

1:6 And again, when he bringeth in the first begotten into the world, he saith: And let all the angels of God adore him.

1:7 And to the angels indeed he saith: He that maketh his angels spirits, and his ministers a flame of fire.

1:8 But to the Son: Thy throne, O God, is for ever and ever: a sceptre of justice is the sceptre of thy kingdom.

1:9 Thou hast loved justice, and hated iniquity: therefore God, thy God, hath anointed thee with the oil of gladness above thy fellows.

1:10 And: Thou in the beginning, O Lord, didst found the earth: and the works of thy hands are the heavens.

1:11 They shall perish, but thou shalt continue: and they shall all grow old as a garment.

1:12 And as a vesture shalt thou change them, and they shall be changed: but thou art the self-same, and thy years shall not fail.

1:13 But to which of the angels said he at any time: Sit on my right hand, until I make thy enemies thy footstool?

1:14 Are they not all ministering spirits, sent to minister for them, who shall receive the inher-

tatem capient salutis ?

2:1 Propterea abundantius oportet observare nos ea quæ audivimus, ne forte pereffluamus.

2:2 Si enim qui per angelos dictus est sermo, factus est firmus, et omnis prævaricatio, et inobedientia accepit justam mercedis retributionem :

2:3 quomodo nos effugiemus si tantam neglexerimus salutem ? quæ cum initium accepisset enarrari per Dominum ab eis, qui audierunt, in nos confirmata est,

2:4 contestante Deo signis et portentis, et variis virtutibus, et Spiritus Sancti distributionibus secundum suam voluntatem.

2:5 Non enim angelis subjecit Deus orbem terræ futurum, de quo loquimur.

2:6 Testatus est autem in quodam loco quis, dicens : Quid est homo quod memor es ejus, aut filius hominis quoniam visitas eum ?

2:7 Minuisti eum paulo minus ab angelis : gloria et honore coronasti eum : et constituisti eum super opera manuum tuarum.

2:8 Omnia subjecisti sub pedibus ejus. In eo enim quod omnia ei subjecit, nihil dimisit non subjectum ei. Nunc autem necdum videmus omnia subjecta ei.

2:9 Eum autem, qui modico quam angeli minoratus est, videmus Jesum propter passionem mortis, gloria et honore coronatum : ut, gratia Dei, pro omnibus gustaret mortem.

2:10 Decebat enim eum, propter quem omnia, et per quem omnia, qui multos filios in gloriam adduxerat, auctorem salutis eorum per passionem consummare.

2:11 Qui enim sanctificat, et qui sanctificantur, ex uno omnes. Propter quam causam non confunditur fratres eos vocare, dicens :

2:12 Nuntiabo nomen tuum fratribus meis : in medio ecclesiæ laudabo te.

2:13 Et iterum : Ego ero fidens in eum. Et iterum : Ecce ego, et pueri mei, quos dedit mihi Deus.

2:14 Quia ergo pueri communicaverunt carni, et sanguini, et ipse similiter participavit eisdem : ut per mortem destrueret eum qui habebat mortis imperium, id est, diabolum :

2:15 et liberaret eos qui timore mortis per totam vitam obnoxii erant servituti.

itance of salvation?

2:1 Therefore ought we more diligently to observe the things which we have heard, lest perhaps we should let them slip.

2:2 For if the word, spoken by angels, became steadfast, and every transgression and disobedience received a just recompense of reward:

2:3 How shall we escape if we neglect so great salvation? which having begun to be declared by the Lord, was confirmed unto us by them that heard him.

2:4 God also bearing them witness by signs, and wonders, and divers miracles, and distributions of the Holy Ghost, according to his own will.

2:5 For God hath not subjected unto angels the world to come, whereof we speak.

2:6 But one in a certain place hath testified, saying: What is man, that thou art mindful of him: or the son of man, that thou visitest him?

2:7 Thou hast made him a little lower than the angels: thou hast crowned him with glory and honour, and hast set him over the works of thy hands:

2:8 Thou hast subjected all things under his feet. For in that he hath subjected all things to him, he left nothing not subject to him. But now we see not as yet all things subject to him.

2:9 But we see Jesus, who was made a little lower than the angels, for the suffering of death, crowned with glory and honour: that, through the grace of God, he might taste death for all.

2:10 For it became him, for whom are all things, and by whom are all things, who had brought many children into glory, to perfect the author of their salvation, by his passion.

2:11 For both he that sanctifieth, and they who are sanctified, are all of one. For which cause he is not ashamed to call them brethren, saying:

2:12 I will declare thy name to my brethren; in the midst of the church will I praise thee.

2:13 And again: I will put my trust in him. And again: Behold I and my children, whom God hath given me.

2:14 Therefore because the children are partakers of flesh and blood, he also himself in like manner hath been partaker of the same: that, through death, he might destroy him who had the empire of death, that is to say, the devil:

2:15 And might deliver them, who through the fear of death were all their lifetime subject to

2:16 Nusquam enim angelos apprehendit, sed semen Abrahæ apprehendit.

2:17 Unde debuit per omnia fratribus similari, ut misericors fieret, et fidelis pontifex ad Deum, ut repropitiaret delicta populi.

2:18 In eo enim, in quo passus est ipse et tentatus, potens est et eis, qui tentantur, auxiliari.

3:1 Unde, fratres sancti, vocationis cælestis participes, considerate Apostolum, et pontificem confessionis nostræ Jesum :

3:2 qui fidelis est ei, qui fecit illum, sicut et Moyses in omni domo ejus.

3:3 Amplioris enim gloriæ iste præ Moyse dignus est habitus, quanto ampliorem honorem habet domus, qui fabricavit illam.

3:4 Omnis namque domus fabricatur ab aliquo : qui autem omnia creavit, Deus est.

3:5 Et Moyses quidem fidelis erat in tota domo ejus tamquam famulus, in testimonium eorum, quæ dicenda erant :

3:6 Christus vero tamquam filius in domo sua : quæ domus sumus nos, si fiduciam, et gloriam spei usque ad finem, firmam retineamus.

3:7 Quapropter sicut dicit Spiritus Sanctus : Hodie si vocem ejus audieritis,

3:8 nolite obdurare corda vestra, sicut in exacerbatione secundum diem tentationis in deserto,

3:9 ubi tentaverunt me patres vestri : probaverunt, et viderunt opera mea

3:10 quadraginta annis : propter quod infensus fui generationi huic, et dixi : Semper errant corde. Ipsi autem non cognoverunt vias meas,

3:11 sicut juravi in ira mea : Si introibunt in requiem meam.

3:12 Videte fratres, ne forte sit in aliquo vestrum cor malum incredulitatis, discedendi a Deo vivo :

3:13 sed adhortamini vosmetipsos per singulos dies, donec hodie cognominatur, ut non obduretur quis ex vobis fallacia peccati.

3:14 Participes enim Christi effecti sumus, si tamen initium substantiæ ejus usque ad finem firmum retineamus.

3:15 Dum dicitur : Hodie si vocem ejus audieritis, nolite obdurare corda vestra, quemad-

servitude.

2:16 For no where doth he take hold of the angels: but of the seed of Abraham he taketh hold.

2:17 Wherefore it behoved him in all things to be made like unto his brethren, that he might become a merciful and faithful high priest before God, that he might be a propitiation for the sins of the people.

2:18 For in that, wherein he himself hath suffered and been tempted, he is able to succour them also that are tempted.

3:1 Wherefore, holy brethren, partakers of the heavenly vocation, consider the apostle and high priest of our confession, Jesus:

3:2 Who is faithful to him that made him, as was also Moses in all his house.

3:3 For this man was counted worthy of greater glory than Moses, by so much as he that hath built the house, hath greater honour than the house.

3:4 For every house is built by some man: but he that created all things, is God.

3:5 And Moses indeed was faithful in all his house as a servant, for a testimony of those things which were to be said:

3:6 But Christ as the Son in his own house: which house are we, if we hold fast the confidence and glory of hope unto the end.

3:7 Wherefore, as the Holy Ghost saith: To day if you shall hear his voice,

3:8 Harden not your hearts, as in the provocation; in the day of temptation in the desert,

3:9 Where your fathers tempted me, proved and saw my works,

3:10 Forty years: for which cause I was offended with this generation, and I said: They always err in heart. And they have not known my ways,

3:11 As I have sworn in my wrath: If they shall enter into my rest.

3:12 Take heed, brethren, lest perhaps there be in any of you an evil heart of unbelief, to depart from the living God.

3:13 But exhort one another every day, whilst it is called to day, that none of you be hardened through the deceitfulness of sin.

3:14 For we are made partakers of Christ: yet so, if we hold the beginning of his substance firm unto the end.

3:15 While it is said, To day if you shall hear his voice, harden not your hearts, as in that provo-

modum in illa exacerbatione.

3:16 Quidam enim audientes exacerbaverunt : sed non universi qui profecti sunt ex Ægypto per Moysen.

3:17 Quibus autem infensus est quadraginta annis ? nonne illis qui peccaverunt, quorum cadavera prostrata sunt in deserto ?

3:18 Quibus autem juravit non introire in requiem ipsius, nisi illis qui increduli fuerunt ?

3:19 Et videmus, quia non potuerunt introire propter incredulitatem.

4:1 Timeamus ergo ne forte relicta pollicitatione introëundi in requiem ejus, existimetur aliquis ex vobis deesse.

4:2 Etenim et nobis nuntiatum est, quemadmodum et illis : sed non profuit illis sermo auditus, non admistus fidei ex iis quæ audierunt.

4:3 Ingrediemur enim in requiem, qui credidimus : quemadmodum dixit : Sicut juravi in ira mea : Si introibunt in requiem meam : et quidem operibus ab institutione mundi perfectis.

4:4 Dixit enim in quodam loco de die septima sic : Et requievit Deus die septima ab omnibus operibus suis.

4:5 Et in isto rursum : Si introibunt in requiem meam.

4:6 Quoniam ergo superest introire quosdam in illam, et ii, quibus prioribus annuntiatum est, non introierunt propter incredulitatem :

4:7 iterum terminat diem quemdam, Hodie, in David dicendo, post tantum temporis, sicut supra dictum est : Hodie si vocem ejus audieritis, nolite obdurare corda vestra.

4:8 Nam si eis Jesus requiem præstitisset, numquam de alia loqueretur, posthac, die.

4:9 Itaque relinquitur sabbatismus populo Dei.

4:10 Qui enim ingressus est in requiem ejus, etiam ipse requievit ab operibus suis, sicut a suis Deus.

4:11 Festinemus ergo ingredi in illam requiem : ut ne in idipsum quis incidat incredulitatis exemplum.

4:12 Vivus est enim sermo Dei, et efficax et penetrabilior omni gladio ancipiti : et pertingens usque ad divisionem animæ ac spiritus : compagum quoque ac medullarum, et discretor cogitationum et intentionum cordis.

cation.

3:16 For some who heard did provoke: but not all that came out of Egypt by Moses.

3:17 And with whom was he offended forty years? Was it not with them that sinned, whose carcasses were overthrown in the desert?

3:18 And to whom did he swear, that they should not enter into his rest: but to them that were incredulous?

3:19 And we see that they could not enter in, because of unbelief.

4:1 Let us fear therefore lest the promise being left of entering into his rest, any of you should be thought to be wanting.

4:2 For unto us also it hath been declared, in like manner as unto them. But the word of hearing did not profit them, not being mixed with faith of those things they heard.

4:3 For we, who have believed, shall enter into rest; as he said: As I have sworn in my wrath; If they shall enter into my rest; and this indeed when the works from the foundation of the world were finished.

4:4 For in a certain place he spoke of the seventh day thus: And God rested the seventh day from all his works.

4:5 And in this place again: If they shall enter into my rest.

4:6 Seeing then it remaineth that some are to enter into it, and they, to whom it was first preached, did not enter because of unbelief:

4:7 Again he limiteth a certain day, saying in David, To day, after so long a time, as it is above said: To day if you shall hear his voice, harden not your hearts.

4:8 For if Jesus had given them rest, he would never have afterwards spoken of another day.

4:9 There remaineth therefore a day of rest for the people of God.

4:10 For he that is entered into his rest, the same also hath rested from his works, as God did from his.

4:11 Let us hasten therefore to enter into that rest; lest any man fall into the same example of unbelief.

4:12 For the word of God is living and effectual, and more piercing than any two edged sword; and reaching unto the division of the soul and the spirit, of the joints also and the marrow, and is a discerner of the thoughts and intents of the heart.

4:13 Et non est ulla creatura invisibilis in conspectu ejus : omnia autem nuda et aperta sunt oculis ejus, ad quem nobis sermo.

4:14 Habentes ergo pontificem magnum qui penetravit cælos, Jesum Filium Dei, teneamus confessionem.

4:15 Non enim habemus pontificem qui non possit compati infirmitatibus nostris : tentatum autem per omnia pro similitudine absque peccato.

4:16 Adeamus ergo cum fiducia ad thronum gratiæ : ut misericordiam consequamur, et gratiam inveniamus in auxilio opportuno.

5:1 Omnis namque pontifex ex hominibus assumptus, pro hominibus constituitur in iis quæ sunt ad Deum, ut offerat dona, et sacrificia pro peccatis :

5:2 qui condolere possit iis qui ignorant et errant : quoniam et ipse circumdatus est infirmitate :

5:3 et propterea debet, quemadmodum pro populo, ita etiam et pro semetipso offerre pro peccatis.

5:4 Nec quisquam sumit sibi honorem, sed qui vocatur a Deo, tamquam Aaron.

5:5 Sic et Christus non semetipsum clarificavit ut pontifex fieret : sed qui locutus est ad eum : Filius meus es tu, ego hodie genui te.

5:6 Quemadmodum et in alio loco dicit : Tu es sacerdos in æternum, secundum ordinem Melchisedech.

5:7 Qui in diebus carnis suæ preces, supplicationesque ad eum qui possit illum salvum facere a morte cum clamore valido, et lacrimis offerens, exauditus est pro sua reverentia.

5:8 Et quidem cum esset Filius Dei, didicit ex iis, quæ passus est, obedientiam :

5:9 et consummatus, factus est omnibus obtemperantibus sibi, causa salutis æternæ,

5:10 appellatus a Deo pontifex juxta ordinem Melchisedech.

5:11 De quo nobis grandis sermo, et ininterpretabilis ad dicendum : quoniam imbecilles facti estis ad audiendum.

5:12 Etenim cum deberetis magistri esse propter tempus, rursum indigetis ut vos doceamini quæ sint elementa exordii sermonum Dei : et facti estis quibus lacte opus sit, non solido cibo.

4:13 Neither is there any creature invisible in his sight: but all things are naked and open to his eyes, to whom our speech is.

4:14 Having therefore a great high priest that hath passed into the heavens, Jesus the Son of God: let us hold fast our confession.

4:15 For we have not a high priest, who can not have compassion on our infirmities: but one tempted in all things like as we are, without sin.

4:16 Let us go therefore with confidence to the throne of grace: that we may obtain mercy, and find grace in seasonable aid.

5:1 For every high priest taken from among men, is ordained for men in the things that appertain to God, that he may offer up gifts and sacrifices for sins:

5:2 Who can have compassion on them that are ignorant and that err: because he himself also is compassed with infirmity.

5:3 And therefore he ought, as for the people, so also for himself, to offer for sins.

5:4 Neither doth any man take the honour to himself, but he that is called by God, as Aaron was.

5:5 So Christ also did not glorify himself, that he might be made a high priest: but he that said unto him: Thou art my Son, this day have I begotten thee.

5:6 As he saith also in another place: Thou art a priest for ever, according to the order of Melchisedech.

5:7 Who in the days of his flesh, with a strong cry and tears, offering up prayers and supplications to him that was able to save him from death, was heard for his reverence.

5:8 And whereas indeed he was the Son of God, he learned obedience by the things which he suffered:

5:9 And being consummated, he became, to all that obey him, the cause of eternal salvation.

5:10 Called by God a high priest according to the order of Melchisedech.

5:11 Of whom we have much to say, and hard to be intelligibly uttered: because you are become weak to hear.

5:12 For whereas for the time you ought to be masters, you have need to be taught again what are the first elements of the words of God: and you are become such as have need of milk, and not of strong meat.

5:13 Omnis enim, qui lactis est particeps, expers est sermonis justitiæ : parvulus enim est.

5:14 Perfectorum autem est solidus cibus : eorum, qui pro consuetudine exercitatos habent sensus ad discretionem boni ac mali.

6:1 Quapropter intermittentes inchoationis Christi sermonem, ad perfectiora feramur, non rursum jacientes fundamentum pœnitentiæ ab operibus mortuis, et fidei ad Deum,

6:2 baptismatum doctrinæ, impositionis quoque manuum, ac resurrectionis mortuorum, et judicii æterni.

6:3 Et hoc faciemus, si quidem permiserit Deus.

6:4 Impossibile est enim eos qui semel sunt illuminati, gustaverunt etiam donum cæleste, et participes facti sunt Spiritus Sancti,

6:5 gustaverunt nihilominus bonum Dei verbum, virtutesque sæculi venturi,

6:6 et prolapsi sunt ; rursus renovari ad pœnitentiam, rursum crucifigentes sibimetipsis Filium Dei, et ostentui habentes.

6:7 Terra enim sæpe venientem super se bibens imbrem, et generans herbam opportunam illis, a quibus colitur, accipit benedictionem a Deo :

6:8 proferens autem spinas ac tribulos, reproba est, et maledicto proxima : cujus consummatio in combustionem.

6:9 Confidimus autem de vobis dilectissimi meliora, et viciniora saluti : tametsi ita loquimur.

6:10 Non enim injustus Deus, ut obliviscatur operis vestri, et dilectionis, quam ostendistis in nomine ipsius, qui ministrastis sanctis, et ministratis.

6:11 Cupimus autem unumquemque vestrum eamdem ostentare sollicitudinem ad expletionem spei usque in finem :

6:12 ut non segnes efficiamini, verum imitatores eorum, qui fide, et patientia hæreditabunt promissiones.

6:13 Abrahæ namque promittens Deus, quoniam neminem habuit, per quem juraret, majorem, juravit per semetipsum,

6:14 dicens : Nisi benedicens benedicam te, et multiplicans multiplicabo te.

6:15 Et sic longanimiter ferens, adeptus est repromissionem.

6:16 Homines enim per majorem sui jurant : et omnis controversiæ eorum finis, ad confirmationem, est juramentum.

5:13 For every one that is a partaker of milk, is unskillful in the word of justice: for he is a little child.

5:14 But strong meat is for the perfect; for them who by custom have their senses exercised to the discerning of good and evil.

6:1 Wherefore leaving the word of the beginning of Christ, let us go on to things more perfect, not laying again the foundation of penance from dead works, and of faith towards God,

6:2 Of the doctrine of baptisms, and imposition of hands, and of the resurrection of the dead, and of eternal judgment.

6:3 And this will we do, if God permit.

6:4 For it is impossible for those who were once illuminated, have tasted also the heavenly gift, and were made partakers of the Holy Ghost,

6:5 Have moreover tasted the good word of God, and the powers of the world to come,

6:6 And are fallen away: to be renewed again to penance, crucifying again to themselves the Son of God, and making him a mockery.

6:7 For the earth that drinketh in the rain which cometh often upon it, and bringeth forth herbs meet for them by whom it is tilled, receiveth blessing from God.

6:8 But that which bringeth forth thorns and briers, is reprobate, and very near unto a curse, whose end is to be burnt.

6:9 But, my dearly beloved, we trust better things of you, and nearer to salvation; though we speak thus.

6:10 For God is not unjust, that he should forget your work, and the love which you have shewn in his name, you who have ministered, and do minister to the saints.

6:11 And we desire that every one of you shew forth the same carefulness to the accomplishing of hope unto the end:

6:12 That you become not slothful, but followers of them, who through faith and patience shall inherit the promises.

6:13 For God making promise to Abraham, because he had no one greater by whom he might swear, swore by himself,

6:14 Saying: Unless blessing I shall bless thee, and multiplying I shall multiply thee.

6:15 And so patiently enduring he obtained the promise.

6:16 For men swear by one greater than themselves: and an oath for confirmation is the end of all their controversy.

6:17 In quo abundantius volens Deus ostendere pollicitationis hæredibus, immobilitatem consilii sui, interposuit jusjurandum :

6:18 ut per duas res immobiles, quibus impossibile est mentiri Deum, fortissimum solatium habeamus, qui confugimus ad tenendam propositam spem,

6:19 quam sicut anchoram habemus animæ tutam ac firmam, et incedentem usque ad interiora velaminis,

6:20 ubi præcursor pro nobis introivit Jesus, secundum ordinem Melchisedech pontifex factus in æternum.

7:1 Hic enim Melchisedech, rex Salem, sacerdos Dei summi, qui obviavit Abrahæ regresso a cæde regum, et benedixit ei :

7:2 cui et decimas omnium divisit Abraham : primum quidem qui interpretatur rex justitiæ : deinde autem et rex Salem, quod est, rex pacis,

7:3 sine patre, sine matre, sine genealogia, neque initium dierum, neque finem vitæ habens, assimilatus autem Filio Dei, manet sacerdos in perpetuum.

7:4 Intuemini autem quantus sit hic, cui et decimas dedit de præcipuis Abraham patriarcha.

7:5 Et quidem de filiis Levi sacerdotium accipientes, mandatum habent decimas sumere a populo secundum legem, id est, a fratribus suis : quamquam et ipsi exierint de lumbis Abrahæ.

7:6 Cujus autem generatio non annumeratur in eis, decimas sumpsit ab Abraham, et hunc, qui habebat repromissiones, benedixit.

7:7 Sine ulla autem contradictione, quod minus est, a meliore benedicitur.

7:8 Et hic quidem, decimas morientes homines accipiunt : ibi autem contestatur, quia vivit.

7:9 Et (ut ita dictum sit) per Abraham, et Levi, qui decimas accepit, decimatus est :

7:10 adhuc enim in lumbis patris erat, quando obviavit ei Melchisedech.

7:11 Si ergo consummatio per sacerdotium Leviticum erat (populus enim sub ipso legem accepit) quid adhuc necessarium fuit secundum ordinem Melchisedech, alium surgere sacerdotem, et non secundum ordinem Aaron dici ?

6:17 Wherein God, meaning more abundantly to shew to the heirs of the promise the immutability of his counsel, interposed an oath:

6:18 That by two immutable things, in which it is impossible for God to lie, we may have the strongest comfort, who have fled for refuge to hold fast the hope set before us.

6:19 Which we have as an anchor of the soul, sure and firm, and which entereth in even within the veil;

6:20 Where the forerunner Jesus is entered for us, made a high priest for ever according to the order of Melchisedech.

7:1 For this Melchisedech was king of Salem, priest of the most high God, who met Abraham returning from the slaughter of the kings, and blessed him:

7:2 To whom also Abraham divided the tithes of all: who first indeed by interpretation, is king of justice: and then also king of Salem, that is, king of peace:

7:3 Without father, without mother, without genealogy, having neither beginning of days nor end of life, but likened unto the Son of God, continueth a priest for ever.

7:4 Now consider how great this man is, to whom also Abraham the patriarch gave tithes out of the principal things.

7:5 And indeed they that are of the sons of Levi, who receive the priesthood, have a commandment to take tithes of the people according to the law, that is to say, of their brethren: though they themselves also came out of the loins of Abraham.

7:6 But he, whose pedigree is not numbered among them, received tithes of Abraham, and blessed him that had the promises.

7:7 And without all contradiction, that which is less, is blessed by the better.

7:8 And here indeed, men that die, receive thithes: but there he hath witness, that he liveth.

7:9 And (as it may be said) even Levi who received tithes, paid tithes in Abraham:

7:10 For he was yet in the loins of his father, when Melchisedech met him.

7:11 If then perfection was by the Levitical priesthood, (for under it the people received the law,) what further need was there that another priest should rise according to the order of Melchisedech, and not be called according to the order of Aaron?

7:12 Translato enim sacerdotio, necesse est ut et legis translatio fiat.

7:13 In quo enim hæc dicuntur, de alia tribu est, de qua nullus altari præsto fuit.

7:14 Manifestum est enim quod ex Juda ortus sit Dominus noster : in qua tribu nihil de sacerdotibus Moyses locutus est.

7:15 Et amplius adhuc manifestum est : si secundum similitudinem Melchisedech exsurgat alius sacerdos,

7:16 qui non secundum legem mandati carnalis factus est, sed secundum virtutem vitæ insolubilis.

7:17 Contestatur enim : Quoniam tu es sacerdos in æternum, secundum ordinem Melchisedech.

7:18 Reprobatio quidem fit præcedentis mandati, propter infirmitatem ejus, et inutilitatem :

7:19 nihil enim ad perfectum adduxit lex : introductio vero melioris spei, per quam proximamus ad Deum.

7:20 Et quantum est non sine jurejurando (alii quidem sine jurejurando sacerdotes facti sunt,

7:21 hic autem cum jurejurando per eum, qui dixit ad illum : Juravit Dominus, et non pœnitebit eum : tu es sacerdos in æternum) :

7:22 in tantum melioris testamenti sponsor factus est Jesus.

7:23 Et alii quidem plures facti sunt sacerdotes, idcirco quod morte prohiberentur permanere :

7:24 hic autem eo quod maneat in æternum, sempiternum habet sacerdotium.

7:25 Unde et salvare in perpetuum potest accedentes per semetipsum ad Deum : semper vivens ad interpellandum pro nobis.

7:26 Talis enim decebat ut nobis esset pontifex, sanctus, innocens, impollutus, segregatus a peccatoribus, et excelsior cælis factus :

7:27 qui non habet necessitatem quotidie, quemadmodum sacerdotes, prius pro suis delictis hostias offerre, deinde pro populi : hoc enim fecit semel, seipsum offerendo.

7:28 Lex enim homines constituit sacerdotes infirmitatem habentes : sermo autem jurisjurandi, qui post legem est, Filium in æternum perfectum.

7:12 For the priesthood being translated, it is necessary that a translation also be made of the law.

7:13 For he, of whom these things are spoken, is of another tribe, of which no one attended on the altar.

7:14 For it is evident that our Lord sprung out of Juda: in which tribe Moses spoke nothing concerning priests.

7:15 And it is yet far more evident: if according to the similitude of Melchisedech there ariseth another priest,

7:16 Who is made not according to the law of a carnal commandment, but according to the power of an indissoluble life:

7:17 For he testifieth: Thou art a priest for ever, according to the order of Melchisedech.

7:18 There is indeed a setting aside of the former commandment, because of the weakness and unprofitableness thereof:

7:19 (For the law brought nothing to perfection,) but a bringing in of a better hope, by which we draw nigh to God.

7:20 And inasmuch as it is not without an oath, (for the others indeed were made priests without an oath;

7:21 But this with an oath, by him that said unto him: The Lord hath sworn, and he will not repent, Thou art a priest for ever.)

7:22 By so much is Jesus made a surety of a better testament.

7:23 And the others indeed were made many priests, because by reason of death they were not suffered to continue:

7:24 But this, for that he continueth for ever, hath an everlasting priesthood,

7:25 Whereby he is able also to save for ever them that come to God by him; always living to make intercession for us.

7:26 For it was fitting that we should have such a high priest, holy, innocent, undefiled, separated from sinners, and made higher than the heavens;

7:27 Who needeth not daily (as the other priests) to offer sacrifices first for his own sins, and then for the people's: for this he did once, in offering himself.

7:28 For the law maketh men priests, who have infirmity: but the word of the oath, which was since the law, the Son who is perfected for evermore.

8:1 Capitulum autem super ea quæ dicuntur : Talem habemus pontificem, qui consedit in dextera sedis magnitudinis in cælis,

8:2 sanctorum minister, et tabernaculi veri, quod fixit Dominus, et non homo.

8:3 Omnis enim pontifex ad offerendum munera, et hostias constituitur : unde necesse est et hunc habere aliquid, quod offerat.

8:4 Si ergo esset super terram, nec esset sacerdos : cum essent qui offerent secundum legem munera,

8:5 qui exemplari, et umbræ deserviunt cælestium. Sicut responsum est Moysi, cum consummaret tabernaculum : Vide (inquit) omnia facito secundum exemplar, quod tibi ostensum est in monte.

8:6 Nunc autem melius sortitus est ministerium, quanto et melioris testamenti mediator est, quod in melioribus repromissionibus sancitum est.

8:7 Nam si illud prius culpa vacasset, non utique secundi locus inquireretur.

8:8 Vituperans enim eos dicit : Ecce dies venient, dicit Dominus : et consummabo super domum Israël, et super domum Juda, testamentum novum,

8:9 non secundum testamentum quod feci patribus eorum in die qua apprehendi manum eorum ut educerem illos de terra Ægypti : quoniam ipsi non permanserunt in testamento meo : et ego neglexi eos, dicit Dominus.

8:10 Quia hoc est testamentum quod disponam domui Israël post dies illos, dicit Dominus : dando leges meas in mentem eorum, et in corde eorum superscribam eas : et ero eis in Deum, et ipsi erunt mihi in populum :

8:11 et non docebit unusquisque proximum suum, et unusquisque fratrem suum, dicens : Cognosce Dominum : quoniam omnes scient me a minore usque ad majorem eorum :

8:12 quia propitius ero iniquitatibus eorum, et peccatorum eorum jam non memorabor.

8:13 Dicendo autem novum : veteravit prius. Quod autem antiquatur, et senescit, prope interitum est.

9:1 Habuit quidem et prius justificationes culturæ, et Sanctum sæculare.

9:2 Tabernaculum enim factum est primum, in

8:1 Now of the things which we have spoken, this is the sum: We have such an high priest, who is set on the right hand of the throne of majesty in the heavens,

8:2 A minister of the holies, and of the true tabernacle, which the Lord hath pitched, and not man.

8:3 For every high priest is appointed to offer gifts and sacrifices: wherefore it is necessary that he also should have some thing to offer.

8:4 If then he were on earth, he would not be a priest: seeing that there would be others to offer gifts according to the law,

8:5 Who serve unto the example and shadow of heavenly things. As it was answered to Moses, when he was to finish the tabernacle: See (saith he) that thou make all things according to the pattern which was shewn thee on the mount.

8:6 But now he hath obtained a better ministry, by how much also he is a mediator of a better testament, which is established on better promises.

8:7 For if that former had been faultless, there should not indeed a place have been sought for a second.

8:8 For finding fault with them, he saith: Behold, the days shall come, saith the Lord: and I will perfect unto the house of Israel, and unto the house of Juda, a new testament:

8:9 Not according to the testament which I made to their fathers, on the day when I took them by the hand to lead them out of the land of Egypt: because they continued not in my testament: and I regarded them not, saith the Lord.

8:10 For this is the testament which I will make to the house of Israel after those days, saith the Lord: I will give my laws into their mind, and in their heart will I write them: and I will be their God, and they shall be my people:

8:11 And they shall not teach every man his neighbour and every man his brother, saying, Know the Lord: for all shall know me from the least to the greatest of them:

8:12 Because I will be merciful to their iniquities, and their sins I will remember no more.

8:13 Now in saying a new, he hath made the former old. And that which decayeth and groweth old, is near its end.

9:1 The former indeed had also justifications of divine service, and a worldly sanctuary.

9:2 For there was a tabernacle made the first,

quo erant candelabra, et mensa, et propositio panum, quæ dicitur Sancta.

9:3 Post velamentum autem secundum, tabernaculum, quod dicitur Sancta sanctorum :

9:4 aureum habens thuribulum, et arcam testamenti circumtectam ex omni parte auro, in qua urna aurea habens manna, et virga Aaron, quæ fronduerat, et tabulæ testamenti,

9:5 superque eam erant cherubim gloriæ obumbrantia propitiatorium : de quibus non est modo dicendum per singula.

9:6 His vero ita compositis, in priori quidem tabernaculo semper introibant sacerdotes, sacrificiorum officia consummantes :

9:7 in secundo autem semel in anno solus pontifex non sine sanguine, quem offert pro sua et populi ignorantia :

9:8 hoc significante Spiritu Sancto, nondum propalatam esse sanctorum viam, adhuc priore tabernaculo habente statum :

9:9 quæ parabola est temporis instantis : juxta quam munera, et hostiæ offeruntur, quæ non possunt juxta conscientiam perfectum facere servientem, solummodo in cibis, et in potibus,

9:10 et variis baptismatibus, et justitiis carnis usque ad tempus correctionis impositis.

9:11 Christus autem assistens pontifex futurorum bonorum, per amplius et perfectius tabernaculum, non manufactum, id est, non hujus creationis :

9:12 neque per sanguinem hircorum aut vitulorum, sed per proprium sanguinem introivit semel in Sancta, æterna redemptione inventa.

9:13 Si enim sanguis hircorum et taurorum, et cinis vitulæ aspersus inquinatos sanctificat ad emundationem carnis :

9:14 quanto magis sanguis Christi, qui per Spiritum Sanctum semetipsum obtulit immaculatum Deo, emundabit conscientiam nostram ab operibus mortuis, ad serviendum Deo viventi ?

9:15 Et ideo novi testamenti mediator est : ut morte intercedente, in redemptionem earum prævaricationum, quæ erant sub priori testamento, repromissionem accipiant qui vocati sunt æternæ hæreditatis.

9:16 Ubi enim testamentum est, mors necesse est intercedat testatoris.

wherein were the candlesticks, and the table, and the setting forth of loaves, which is called the holy.

9:3 And after the second veil, the tabernacle, which is called the holy of holies:

9:4 Having a golden censer, and the ark of the testament covered about on every part with gold, in which was a golden pot that had manna, and the rod of Aaron, that had blossomed, and the tables of the testament.

9:5 And over it were the cherubims of glory overshadowing the propitiatory: of which it is not needful to speak now particularly.

9:6 Now these things being thus ordered, into the first tabernacle the priests indeed always entered, accomplishing the offices of sacrifices.

9:7 But into the second, the high priest alone, once a year: not without blood, which he offereth for his own, and the people's ignorance:

9:8 The Holy Ghost signifying this, that the way into the holies was not yet made manifest, whilst the former tabernacle was yet standing.

9:9 Which is a parable of the time present: according to which gifts and sacrifices are offered, which can not, as to the conscience, make him perfect that serveth, only in meats and in drinks,

9:10 And divers washings, and justices of the flesh laid on them until the time of correction.

9:11 But Christ, being come an high priest of the good things to come, by a greater and more perfect tabernacle not made with hand, that is, not of this creation:

9:12 Neither by the blood of goats, or of calves, but by his own blood, entered once into the holies, having obtained eternal redemption.

9:13 For if the blood of goats and of oxen, and the ashes of an heifer being sprinkled, sanctify such as are defiled, to the cleansing of the flesh:

9:14 How much more shall the blood of Christ, who by the Holy Ghost offered himself unspotted unto God, cleanse our conscience from dead works, to serve the living God?

9:15 And therefore he is the mediator of the new testament: that by means of his death, for the redemption of those trangressions, which were under the former testament, they that are called may receive the promise of eternal inheritance.

9:16 For where there is a testament, the death of the testator must of necessity come in.

9:17 Testamentum enim in mortuis confirmatum est : alioquin nondum valet, dum vivit qui testatus est.

9:18 Unde nec primum quidem sine sanguine dedicatum est.

9:19 Lecto enim omni mandato legis a Moyse universo populo, accipiens sanguinem vitulorum et hircorum cum aqua, et lana coccinea, et hyssopo, ipsum quoque librum, et omnem populum aspersit,

9:20 dicens : Hic sanguis testamenti, quod mandavit ad vos Deus.

9:21 Etiam tabernaculum et omnia vasa ministerii sanguine similiter aspersit.

9:22 Et omnia pene in sanguine secundum legem mundantur : et sine sanguinis effusione non fit remissio.

9:23 Necesse est ergo exemplaria quidem cælestium his mundari : ipsa autem cælestia melioribus hostiis quam istis.

9:24 Non enim in manufacta Sancta Jesus introivit exemplaria verorum : sed in ipsum cælum, ut appareat nunc vultui Dei pro nobis :

9:25 neque ut sæpe offerat semetipsum, quemadmodum pontifex intrat in Sancta per singulos annos in sanguine alieno :

9:26 alioquin oportebat eum frequenter pati ab origine mundi : nunc autem semel in consummatione sæculorum, ad destitutionem peccati, per hostiam suam apparuit.

9:27 Et quemadmodum statutum est hominibus semel mori, post hoc autem judicium :

9:28 sic et Christus semel oblatus est ad multorum exhaurienda peccata : secundo sine peccato apparebit exspectantibus se, in salutem.

10:1 Umbram enim habens lex futurorum bonorum, non ipsam imaginem rerum : per singulos annos, eisdem ipsis hostiis quas offerunt indesinenter, numquam potest accedentes perfectos facere :

10:2 alioquin cessassent offerri : ideo quod nullam haberent ultra conscientiam peccati, cultores semel mundati :

10:3 sed in ipsis commemoratio peccatorum per singulos annos fit.

10:4 Impossibile enim est sanguine taurorum et hircorum auferri peccata.

10:5 Ideo ingrediens mundum dicit : Hostiam et

9:17 For a testament is of force, after men are dead: otherwise it is as yet of no strength, whilst the testator liveth.

9:18 Whereupon neither was the first indeed dedicated without blood.

9:19 For when every commandment of the law had been read by Moses to all the people, he took the blood of calves and goats, with water, and scarlet wool and hyssop, and sprinkled both the book itself and all the people,

9:20 Saying: This is the blood of the testament, which God hath enjoined unto you.

9:21 The tabernacle also and all the vessels of the ministry, in like manner, he sprinkled with blood.

9:22 And almost all things, according to the law, are cleansed with blood: and without shedding of blood there is no remission.

9:23 It is necessary therefore that the patterns of heavenly things should be cleansed with these: but the heavenly things themselves with better sacrifices than these.

9:24 For Jesus is not entered into the holies made with hands, the patterns of the true: but into heaven itself, that he may appear now in the presence of God for us.

9:25 Nor yet that he should offer himself often, as the high priest entereth into the holies, every year with the blood of others:

9:26 For then he ought to have suffered often from the beginning of the world: but now once at the end of ages, he hath appeared for the destruction of sin, by the sacrifice of himself.

9:27 And as it is appointed unto men once to die, and after this the judgment:

9:28 So also Christ was offered once to exhaust the sins of many; the second time he shall appear without sin to them that expect him unto salvation.

10:1 For the law having a shadow of the good things to come, not the very image of the things; by the selfsame sacrifices which they offer continually every year, can never make the comers thereunto perfect:

10:2 For then they would have ceased to be offered: because the worshippers once cleansed should have no conscience of sin any longer:

10:3 But in them there is made a commemoration of sins every year.

10:4 For it is impossible that with the blood of oxen and goats sin should be taken away.

10:5 Wherefore when he cometh into the world,

oblationem noluisti : corpus autem aptasti mihi :

10:6 holocautomata pro peccato non tibi placuerunt.

10:7 Tunc dixi : Ecce venio : in capite libri scriptum est de me : Ut faciam, Deus, voluntatem tuam.

10:8 Superius dicens : Quia hostias, et oblationes, et holocautomata pro peccato noluisti, nec placita sunt tibi, quæ secundum legem offeruntur,

10:9 tunc dixi : Ecce venio, ut faciam, Deus, voluntatem tuam : aufert primum, ut sequens statuat.

10:10 In qua voluntate sanctificati sumus per oblationem corporis Jesu Christi semel.

10:11 Et omnis quidem sacerdos præsto est quotidie ministrans, et easdem sæpe offerens hostias, quæ numquam possunt auferre peccata :

10:12 hic autem unam pro peccatis offerens hostiam, in sempiternum sedet in dextera Dei,

10:13 de cetero exspectans donec ponantur inimici ejus scabellum pedum ejus.

10:14 Una enim oblatione, consummavit in sempiternum sanctificatos.

10:15 Contestatur autem nos et Spiritus Sanctus. Postquam enim dixit :

10:16 Hoc autem testamentum, quod testabor ad illos post dies illos, dicit Dominus, dando leges meas in cordibus eorum, et in mentibus eorum superscribam eas :

10:17 et peccatorum, et iniquitatum eorum jam non recordabor amplius.

10:18 Ubi autem horum remissio : jam non est oblatio pro peccato.

10:19 Habentes itaque, fratres, fiduciam in introitu sanctorum in sanguine Christi,

10:20 quam initiavit nobis viam novam, et viventem per velamen, id est, carnem suam,

10:21 et sacerdotem magnum super domum Dei :

10:22 accedamus cum vero corde in plenitudine fidei, aspersi corda a conscientia mala, et abluti corpus aqua munda,

10:23 teneamus spei nostræ confessionem indeclinabilem (fidelis enim est qui repromisit),

10:24 et consideremus invicem in provocationem

he saith: Sacrifice and oblation thou wouldest not: but a body thou hast fitted to me:

10:6 Holocausts for sin did not please thee.

10:7 Then said I: Behold I come: in the head of the book it is written of me: that I should do thy will, O God.

10:8 In saying before, Sacrifices, and oblations, and holocausts for sin thou wouldest not, neither are they pleasing to thee, which are offered according to the law.

10:9 Then said I: Behold, I come to do thy will, O God: he taketh away the first, that he may establish that which followeth.

10:10 In the which will, we are sanctified by the oblation of the body of Jesus Christ once.

10:11 And every priest indeed standeth daily ministering, and often offering the same sacrifices, which can never take away sins.

10:12 But this man offering one sacrifice for sins, for ever sitteth on the right hand of God,

10:13 From henceforth expecting, until his enemies be made his footstool.

10:14 For by one oblation he hath perfected for ever them that are sanctified.

10:15 And the Holy Ghost also doth testify this to us. For after that he said:

10:16 And this is the testament which I will make unto them after those days, saith the Lord. I will give my laws in their hearts, and on their minds will I write them:

10:17 And their sins and iniquities I will remember no more.

10:18 Now where there is a remission of these, there is no more an oblation for sin.

10:19 Having therefore, brethren, a confidence in the entering into the holies by the blood of Christ;

10:20 A new and living way which he hath dedicated for us through the veil, that is to say, his flesh,

10:21 And a high priest over the house of God:

10:22 Let us draw near with a true heart in fulness of faith, having our hearts sprinkled from an evil conscience, and our bodies washed with clean water.

10:23 Let us hold fast the confession of our hope without wavering (for he is faithful that hath promised),

10:24 And let us consider one another, to pro-

caritatis, et bonorum operum :

10:25 non deserentes collectionem nostram, sicut consuetudinis est quibusdam, sed consolantes, et tanto magis quanto videritis appropinquantem diem.

10:26 Voluntarie enim peccantibus nobis post acceptam notitiam veritatis, jam non relinquitur pro peccatis hostia,

10:27 terribilis autem quædam exspectatio judicii, et ignis æmulatio, quæ consumptura est adversarios.

10:28 Irritam quis faciens legem Moysi, sine ulla miseratione duobus vel tribus testibus moritur :

10:29 quanto magis putatis deteriora mereri supplicia qui Filium Dei conculcaverit, et sanguinem testamenti pollutum duxerit, in quo sanctificatus est, et spiritui gratiæ contumeliam fecerit ?

10:30 Scimus enim qui dixit : Mihi vindicta, et ego retribuam. Et iterum : Quia judicabit Dominus populum suum.

10:31 Horrendum est incidere in manus Dei viventis.

10:32 Rememoramini autem pristinos dies, in quibus illuminati, magnum certamen sustinuistis passionum :

10:33 et in altero quidem opprobriis et tribulationibus spectaculum facti : in altero autem socii taliter conversantium effecti.

10:34 Nam et vinctis compassi estis, et rapinam bonorum vestrorum cum gaudio suscepistis, cognoscentes vos habere meliorem et manentem substantiam.

10:35 Nolite itaque amittere confidentiam vestram, quæ magnam habet remunerationem.

10:36 Patientia enim vobis necessaria est : ut voluntatem Dei facientes, reportetis promissionem.

10:37 Adhuc enim modicum aliquantulum, qui venturus est, veniet, et non tardabit.

10:38 Justus autem meus ex fide vivit : quod si subtraxerit se, non placebit animæ meæ.

10:39 Nos autem non sumus subtractionis filii in perditionem, sed fidei in acquisitionem animæ.

voke unto charity and to good works:

10:25 Not forsaking our assembly, as some are accustomed; but comforting one another, and so much the more as you see the day approaching.

10:26 For if we sin wilfully after having the knowledge of the truth, there is now left no sacrifice for sins,

10:27 But a certain dreadful expectation of judgment, and the rage of a fire which shall consume the adversaries.

10:28 A man making void the law of Moses, dieth without any mercy under two or three witnesses:

10:29 How much more, do you think he deserveth worse punishments, who hath trodden under foot the Son of God, and hath esteemed the blood of the testament unclean, by which he was sanctified, and hath offered an affront to the Spirit of grace?

10:30 For we know him that hath said: Vengeance belongeth to me, and I will repay. And again: The Lord shall judge his people.

10:31 It is a fearful thing to fall into the hands of the living God.

10:32 But call to mind the former days, wherein, being illuminated, you endured a great fight of afflictions.

10:33 And on the one hand indeed, by reproaches and tribulations, were made a gazingstock; and on the other, became companions of them that were used in such sort.

10:34 For you both had compassion on them that were in bands, and took with joy the being stripped of your own goods, knowing that you have a better and a lasting substance.

10:35 Do not therefore lose your confidence, which hath a great reward.

10:36 For patience is necessary for you; that, doing the will of God, you may receive the promise.

10:37 For yet a little and a very little while, and he that is to come, will come, and will not delay.

10:38 But my just man liveth by faith; but if he withdraw himself, he shall not please my soul.

10:39 But we are not the children of withdrawing unto perdition, but of faith to the saving of the soul.

11:1 Est autem fides sperandarum substantia rerum, argumentum non apparentium.

11:2 In hac enim testimonium consecuti sunt senes.

11:3 Fide intelligimus aptata esse sæcula verbo Dei : ut ex invisibilibus visibilia fierent.

11:4 Fide plurimam hostiam Abel, quam Cain, obtulit Deo, per quam testimonium consecutus est esse justus, testimonium perhibente muneribus ejus Deo, et per illam defunctus adhuc loquitur.

11:5 Fide Henoch translatus est ne videret mortem, et non inveniebatur, quia transtulit illum Deus : ante translationem enim testimonium habuit placuisse Deo.

11:6 Sine fide autem impossibile est placere Deo. Credere enim oportet accedentem ad Deum quia est, et inquirentibus se remunerator sit.

11:7 Fide Noë responso accepto de iis quæ adhuc non videbantur, metuens aptavit arcam in salutem domus suæ, per quam damnavit mundum : et justitiæ, quæ per fidem est, hæres est institutus.

11:8 Fide qui vocatur Abraham obedivit in locum exire, quem accepturus erat in hæreditatem : et exiit, nesciens quo iret.

11:9 Fide demoratus est in terra repromissionis, tamquam in aliena, in casulis habitando cum Isaac et Jacob cohæredibus repromissionis ejusdem.

11:10 Exspectabat enim fundamenta habentem civitatem : cujus artifex et conditor Deus.

11:11 Fide et ipsa Sara sterilis virtutem in conceptionem seminis accepit, etiam præter tempus ætatis : quoniam fidelem credidit esse eum qui repromiserat.

11:12 Propter quod et ab uno orti sunt (et hoc emortuo) tamquam sidera cæli in multitudinem, et sicut arena, quæ est ad oram maris, innumerabilis.

11:13 Juxta fidem defuncti sunt omnes isti, non acceptis repromissionibus, sed a longe eas aspicientes, et salutantes, et confitentes quia peregrini et hospites sunt super terram.

11:14 Qui enim hæc dicunt, significant se patriam inquirere.

11:1 Now faith is the substance of things to be hoped for, the evidence of things that appear not.

11:2 For by this the ancients obtained a testimony.

11:3 By faith we understand that the world was framed by the word of God; that from invisible things visible things might be made.

11:4 By faith Abel offered to God a sacrifice exceeding that of Cain, by which he obtained a testimony that he was just, God giving testimony to his gifts; and by it he being dead yet speaketh.

11:5 By faith Henoch was translated, that he should not see death; and he was not found, because God had translated him: for before his translation he had testimony that he pleased God.

11:6 But without faith it is impossible to please God. For he that cometh to God, must believe that he is, and is a rewarder to them that seek him.

11:7 By faith Noe, having received an answer concerning those things which as yet were not seen, moved with fear, framed the ark for the saving of his house, by the which he condemned the world; and was instituted heir of the justice which is by faith.

11:8 By faith he that is called Abraham, obeyed to go out into a place which he was to receive for an inheritance; and he went out, not knowing whither he went.

11:9 By faith he abode in the land, dwelling in cottages, with Isaac and Jacob, the co-heirs of the same promise.

11:10 For he looked for a city that hath foundations; whose builder and maker is God.

11:11 By faith also Sara herself, being barren, received strength to conceive seed, even past the time of age; because she believed that he was faithful who had promised,

11:12 For which cause there sprung even from one (and him as good as dead) as the stars of heaven in multitude, and as the sand which is by the sea shore innumerable.

11:13 All these died according to faith, not having received the promises, but beholding them afar off, and saluting them, and confessing that they are pilgrims and strangers on the earth.

11:14 For they that say these things, do signify that they seek a country.

11:15 Et si quidem ipsius meminissent de qua exierunt, habebant utique tempus revertendi :

11:16 nunc autem meliorem appetunt, id est, cælestem. Ideo non confunditur Deus vocari Deus eorum : paravit enim illis civitatem.

11:17 Fide obtulit Abraham Isaac, cum tentaretur, et unigenitum offerebat, qui susceperat repromissiones :

11:18 ad quem dictum est : Quia in Isaac vocabitur tibi semen :

11:19 arbitrans quia et a mortuis suscitare potens est Deus : unde eum et in parabolam accepit.

11:20 Fide et de futuris benedixit Isaac Jacob et Esau.

11:21 Fide Jacob, moriens, singulos filiorum Joseph benedixit : et adoravit fastigium virgæ ejus.

11:22 Fide Joseph, moriens, de profectione filiorum Israël memoratus est, et de ossibus suis mandavit.

11:23 Fide Moyses, natus, occultatus est mensibus tribus a parentibus suis, eo quod vidissent elegantem infantem, et non timuerunt regis edictum.

11:24 Fide Moyses grandis factus negavit se esse filium filiæ Pharaonis,

11:25 magis eligens affligi cum populo Dei, quam temporalis peccati habere jucunditatem,

11:26 majores divitias æstimans thesauro Ægyptiorum, improperium Christi : aspiciebat enim in remunerationem.

11:27 Fide reliquit Ægyptum, non veritus animositatem regis : invisibilem enim tamquam videns sustinuit.

11:28 Fide celebravit Pascha, et sanguinis effusionem : ne qui vastabat primitiva, tangeret eos.

11:29 Fide transierunt mare Rubrum tamquam per aridam terram : quod experti Ægyptii, devorati sunt.

11:30 Fide muri Jericho corruerunt, circuitu dierum septem.

11:31 Fide Rahab meretrix non periit cum incredulis, excipiens exploratores cum pace.

11:32 Et quid adhuc dicam ? deficiet enim me tempus enarrantem de Gedeon, Barac, Sam-

11:15 And truly if they had been mindful of that from whence they came out, they had doubtless time to return.

11:16 But now they desire a better, that is to say, a heavenly country. Therefore God is not ashamed to be called their God; for he hath prepared for them a city.

11:17 By faith Abraham, when he was tried, offered Isaac: and he that had received the promises, offered up his only begotten son;

11:18 (To whom it was said: In Isaac shall thy seed be called.)

11:19 Accounting that God is able to raise up even from the dead. Whereupon also he received him for a parable.

11:20 By faith also of things to come, Isaac blessed Jacob and Esau.

11:21 By faith Jacob dying, blessed each of the sons of Joseph, and adored the top of his rod.

11:22 By faith Joseph, when he was dying, made mention of the going out of the children of Israel; and gave commandment concerning his bones.

11:23 By faith Moses, when he was born, was hid three months by his parents; because they saw he was a comely babe, and they feared not the king's edict.

11:24 By faith Moses, when he was grown up, denied himself to be the son of Pharao's daughter;

11:25 Rather choosing to be afflicted with the people of God, than to have the pleasure of sin for a time,

11:26 Esteeming the reproach of Christ greater riches than the treasure of the Egyptians. For he looked unto the reward.

11:27 By faith he left Egypt, not fearing the fierceness of the king: for he endured as seeing him that is invisible.

11:28 By faith he celebrated the pasch, and the shedding of the blood; that he, who destroyed the firstborn, might not touch them.

11:29 By faith they passed through the Red Sea, as by dry land: which the Egyptians attempting, were swallowed up.

11:30 By faith the walls of Jericho fell down, by the going round them seven days.

11:31 By faith Rahab the harlot perished not with the unbelievers, receiving the spies with peace.

11:32 And what shall I yet say? For the time would fail me to tell of Gedeon, Barac, Sam-

son, Jephte, David, Samuel, et prophetis :

11:33 qui per fidem vicerunt regna, operati sunt justitiam, adepti sunt repromissiones, obturaverunt ora leonum,

11:34 extinxerunt impetum ignis, effugerunt aciem gladii, convaluerunt de infirmitate, fortes facti sunt in bello, castra verterunt exterorum :

11:35 acceperunt mulieres de resurrectione mortuos suos : alii autem distenti sunt non suscipientes redemptionem ut meliorem invenirent resurrectionem.

11:36 Alii vero ludibria, et verbera experti, insuper et vincula, et carceres :

11:37 lapidati sunt, secti sunt, tentati sunt, in occisione gladii mortui sunt, circuierunt in melotis, in pellibus caprinis, egentes, angustiati, afflicti :

11:38 quibus dignus non erat mundus : in solitudinibus errantes, in montibus, in speluncis, et in cavernis terræ.

11:39 Et hi omnes testimonio fidei probati, non acceperunt repromissionem,

11:40 Deo pro nobis melius aliquid providente, ut non sine nobis consummarentur.

12:1 Ideoque et nos tantam habentes impositam nubem testium, deponentes omne pondus, et circumstans nos peccatum, per patientiam curramus ad propositum nobis certamen :

12:2 aspicientes in auctorem fidei, et consummatorem Jesum, qui proposito sibi gaudio sustinuit crucem, confusione contempta, atque in dextera sedis Dei sedet.

12:3 Recogitate enim eum qui talem sustinuit a peccatoribus adversum semetipsum contradictionem : ut ne fatigemini, animis vestris deficientes.

12:4 Nondum enim usque ad sanguinem restitistis, adversus peccatum repugnantes :

12:5 et obliti estis consolationis, quæ vobis tamquam filiis loquitur, dicens : Fili mi, noli negligere disciplinam Domini : neque fatigeris dum ab eo argueris.

12:6 Quem enim diligit Dominus, castigat : flagellat autem omnem filium, quem recipit.

12:7 In disciplina perseverate. Tamquam filiis vobis offert se Deus : quis enim filius, quem non corripit pater ?

12:8 quod si extra disciplinam estis, cujus par-

son, Jephthe, David, Samuel, and the prophets:

11:33 Who by faith conquered kingdoms, wrought justice, obtained promises, stopped the mouths of lions,

11:34 Quenched the violence of fire, escaped the edge of the sword, recovered strength from weakness, became valiant in battle, put to flight the armies of foreigners:

11:35 Women received their dead raised to life again. But others were racked, not accepting deliverance, that they might find a better resurrection.

11:36 And others had trial of mockeries and stripes, moreover also of bands and prisons.

11:37 They were stoned, they were cut asunder, they were tempted, they were put to death by the sword, they wandered about in sheepskins, in goatskins, being in want, distressed, afflicted:

11:38 Of whom the world was not worthy; wandering in deserts, in mountains, and in dens, and in caves of the earth.

11:39 And all these being approved by the testimony of faith, received not the promise;

11:40 God providing some better thing for us, that they should not be perfected without us.

12:1 And therefore we also having so great a cloud of witnesses over our head, laying aside every weight and sin which surrounds us, let us run by patience to the fight proposed to us:

12:2 Looking on Jesus, the author and finisher of faith, who having joy set before him, endured the cross, despising the shame, and now sitteth on the right hand of the throne of God.

12:3 For think diligently upon him that endured such opposition from sinners against himself; that you be not wearied, fainting in your minds.

12:4 For you have not yet resisted unto blood, striving against sin:

12:5 And you have forgotten the consolation, which speaketh to you, as unto children, saying: My son, neglect not the discipline of the Lord; neither be thou wearied whilst thou art rebuked by him.

12:6 For whom the Lord loveth, he chastiseth; and he scourgeth every son whom he receiveth.

12:7 Persevere under discipline. God dealeth with you as with his sons; for what son is there, whom the father doth not correct?

12:8 But if you be without chastisement, where-

ticipes facti sunt omnes : ergo adulteri, et non filii estis.

12:9 Deinde patres quidem carnis nostræ, eruditores habuimus, et reverebamur eos, non multo magis obtemperabimus Patri spirituum, et vivemus ?

12:10 Et illi quidem in tempore paucorum dierum, secundum voluntatem suam erudiebant nos : hic autem ad id quod utile est in recipiendo sanctificationem ejus.

12:11 Omnis autem disciplina in præsenti quidem videtur non esse gaudii, sed mœroris : postea autem fructum pacatissimum exercitatis per eam, reddet justitiæ.

12:12 Propter quod remissas manus, et soluta genua erigite,

12:13 et gressus rectos facite pedibus vestris : ut non claudicans quis erret, magis autem sanetur.

12:14 Pacem sequimini cum omnibus, et sanctimoniam, sine qua nemo videbit Deum :

12:15 contemplantes nequis desit gratiæ Dei : ne qua radix amaritudinis sursum germinans impediat, et per illam inquinentur multi.

12:16 Ne quis fornicator, aut profanus ut Esau : qui propter unam escam vendidit primitiva sua :

12:17 scitote enim quoniam et postea cupiens hæreditare benedictionem, reprobatus est : non enim invenit pœnitentiæ locum, quamquam cum lacrimis inquisisset eam.

12:18 Non enim accessistis ad tractabilem montem, et accensibilem ignem, et turbinem, et caliginem, et procellam,

12:19 et tubæ sonum, et vocem verborum, quam qui audierunt, excusaverunt se, ne eis fieret verbum.

12:20 Non enim portabant quod dicebatur : Et si bestia tetigerit montem, lapidabitur.

12:21 Et ita terribile erat quod videbatur. Moyses dixit : Exterritus sum, et tremebundus.

12:22 Sed accessistis ad Sion montem, et civitatem Dei viventis, Jerusalem cælestem, et multorum millium angelorum frequentiam,

12:23 et ecclesiam primitivorum, qui conscripti sunt in cælis, et judicem omnium Deum, et spiritus justorum perfectorum,

of all are made partakers, then are you bastards, and not sons.

12:9 Moreover we have had fathers of our flesh, for instructors, and we reverenced them: shall we not much more obey the Father of spirits, and live?

12:10 And they indeed for a few days, according to their own pleasure, instructed us: but he, for our profit, that we might receive his sanctification.

12:11 Now all chastisement for the present indeed seemeth not to bring with it joy, but sorrow: but afterwards it will yield, to them that are exercised by it, the most peaceable fruit of justice.

12:12 Wherefore lift up the hands which hang down, and the feeble knees,

12:13 And make straight steps with your feet: that no one, halting, may go out of the way; but rather be healed.

12:14 Follow peace with all men, and holiness: without which no man shall see God.

12:15 Looking diligently, lest any man be wanting to the grace of God; lest any root of bitterness springing up do hinder, and by it many be defiled.

12:16 Lest there be any fornicator, or profane person, as Esau; who for one mess, sold his first birthright.

12:17 For know ye that afterwards, when he desired to inherit the benediction, he was rejected; for he found no place of repentance, although with tears he had sought it.

12:18 For you are not come to a mountain that might be touched, and a burning fire, and a whirlwind, and darkness, and storm,

12:19 And the sound of a trumpet, and the voice of words, which they that heard excused themselves, that the word might not be spoken to them:

12:20 For they did not endure that which was said: And if so much as a beast shall touch the mount, it shall be stoned.

12:21 And so terrible was that which was seen, Moses said: I am frighted, and tremble.

12:22 But you are come to mount Sion, and to the city of the living God, the heavenly Jerusalem, and to the company of many thousands of angels,

12:23 And to the church of the firstborn, who are written in the heavens, and to God the judge of all, and to the spirits of the just made

perfect,

12:24 et testamenti novi mediatorem Jesum, et sanguinis aspersionem melius loquentem quam Abel.

12:25 Videte ne recusetis loquentem. Si enim illi non effugerunt, recusantes eum, qui super terram loquebatur : multo magis nos, qui de cælis loquentem nobis avertimus.

12:26 Cujus vox movit terram tunc : nunc autem repromittit, dicens : Adhuc semel, et ego movebo non solum terram, sed et cælum.

12:27 Quod autem, Adhuc semel, dicit : declarat mobilium translationem tamquam factorum, ut maneant ea quæ sunt immobilia.

12:28 Itaque regnum immobile suscipientes, habemus gratiam : per quam serviamus placentes Deo, cum metu et reverentia.

12:29 Etenim Deus noster ignis consumens est.

13:1 Caritas fraternitatis maneat in vobis,

13:2 et hospitalitatem nolite oblivisci : per hanc enim latuerunt quidam, angelis hospitio receptis.

13:3 Mementote vinctorum, tamquam simul vincti : et laborantium, tamquam et ipsi in corpore morantes.

13:4 Honorabile connubium in omnibus, et thorus immaculatus. Fornicatores enim, et adulteros judicabit Deus.

13:5 Sint mores sine avaritia, contenti præsentibus : ipse enim dixit : Non te deseram, neque derelinquam :

13:6 ita ut confidenter dicamus : Dominus mihi adjutor : non timebo quid faciat mihi homo.

13:7 Mementote præpositorum vestrorum, qui vobis locuti sunt verbum Dei : quorum intuentes exitum conversationis, imitamini fidem.

13:8 Jesus Christus heri, et hodie : ipse et in sæcula.

13:9 Doctrinis variis et peregrinis nolite abduci. Optimum est enim gratia stabilire cor, non escis : quæ non profuerunt ambulantibus in eis.

13:10 Habemus altare, de quo edere non habent potestatem, qui tabernaculo deserviunt.

13:11 Quorum enim animalium infertur sanguis pro peccato in Sancta per pontificem, horum

12:24 And to Jesus the mediator of the new testament, and to the sprinkling of blood which speaketh better than that of Abel.

12:25 See that you refuse him not that speaketh. For if they escaped not who refused him that spoke upon the earth, much more shall not we, that turn away from him that speaketh to us from heaven.

12:26 Whose voice then moved the earth; but now he promiseth, saying: Yet once more, and I will move not only the earth, but heaven also.

12:27 And in that he saith, Yet once more, he signifieth the translation of the moveable things as made, that those things may remain which are immoveable.

12:28 Therefore receiving an immoveable kingdom, we have grace; whereby let us serve, pleasing God, with fear and reverence.

12:29 For our God is a consuming fire.

13:1 Let the charity of the brotherhood abide in you.

13:2 And hospitality do not forget; for by this some, being not aware of it, have entertained angels.

13:3 Remember them that are in bands, as if you were bound with them; and them that labour, as being yourselves also in the body.

13:4 Marriage honourable in all, and the bed undefiled. For fornicators and adulterers God will judge.

13:5 Let your manners be without covetousness, contented with such things as you have; for he hath said: I will not leave thee, neither will I forsake thee.

13:6 So that we may confidently say: The Lord is my helper: I will not fear what man shall do to me.

13:7 Remember your prelates who have spoken the word of God to you; whose faith follow, considering the end of their conversation,

13:8 Jesus Christ, yesterday, and to day; and the same for ever.

13:9 Be not led away with various and strange doctrines. For it is best that the heart be established with grace, not with meats; which have not profited those that walk in them.

13:10 We have an altar, whereof they have no power to eat who serve the tabernacle.

13:11 For the bodies of those beasts, whose blood is brought into the holies by the high

corpora cremantur extra castra.

13:12 Propter quod et Jesus, ut sanctificaret per suum sanguinem populum, extra portam passus est.

13:13 Exeamus igitur ad eum extra castra, improperium ejus portantes.

13:14 Non enim habemus hic manentem civitatem, sed futuram inquirimus.

13:15 Per ipsum ergo offeramus hostiam laudis semper Deo, id est, fructum labiorum confitentium nomini ejus.

13:16 Beneficentiæ autem et communionis nolite oblivisci : talibus enim hostiis promeretur Deus.

13:17 Obedite præpositis vestris, et subjacete eis. Ipsi enim pervigilant quasi rationem pro animabus vestris reddituri, ut cum gaudio hoc faciant, et non gementes : hoc enim non expedit vobis.

13:18 Orate pro nobis : confidimus enim quia bonam conscientiam habemus in omnibus bene volentes conversari.

13:19 Amplius autem deprecor vos hoc facere, quo celerius restituar vobis.

13:20 Deus autem pacis, qui eduxit de mortuis pastorem magnum ovium, in sanguine testamenti æterni, Dominum nostrum Jesum Christum,

13:21 aptet vos in omni bono, ut faciatis ejus voluntatem : faciens in vobis quod placeat coram se per Jesum Christum : cui est gloria in sæcula sæculorum. Amen.

13:22 Rogo autem vos fratres, ut sufferatis verbum solatii. Etenim perpaucis scripsi vobis.

13:23 Cognoscite fratrem nostrum Timotheum dimissum : cum quo (si celerius venerit) videbo vos.

13:24 Salutate omnes præpositos vestros, et omnes sanctos. Salutant vos de Italia fratres.

13:25 Gratia cum omnibus vobis. Amen.

---

priest for sin, are burned without the camp.

13:12 Wherefore Jesus also, that he might sanctify the people by his own blood, suffered without the gate.

13:13 Let us go forth therefore to him without the camp, bearing his reproach.

13:14 For we have not here a lasting city, but we seek one that is to come.

13:15 By him therefore let us offer the sacrifice of praise always to God, that is to say, the fruit of lips confessing to his name.

13:16 And do not forget to do good, and to impart; for by such sacrifices God's favour is obtained.

13:17 Obey your prelates, and be subject to them. For they watch as being to render an account of your souls; that they may do this with joy, and not with grief. For this is not expedient for you.

13:18 Pray for us. For we trust we have a good conscience, being willing to behave ourselves well in all things.

13:19 And I beseech you the more to do this, that I may be restored to you the sooner.

13:20 And may the God of peace, who brought again from the dead the great pastor of the sheep, our Lord Jesus Christ, in the blood of the everlasting testament,

13:21 Fit you in all goodness, that you may do his will; doing in you that which is well pleasing in his sight, through Jesus Christ, to whom is glory for ever and ever. Amen.

13:22 And I beseech you, brethren, that you suffer this word of consolation. For I have written to you in a few words.

13:23 Know ye that our brother Timothy is set at liberty: with whom (if he come shortly) I will see you.

13:24 Salute all your prelates, and all the saints. The brethren from Italy salute you.

13:25 Grace be with you all. Amen.

Epistula Catholica Beati Jacobi Apostoli

THE CATHOLIC EPISTLE OF BLESSED JAMES THE APOSTLE

✠

1:1 JACOBUS, DEI ET DOMINI NOSTRI JESU CHRISTI SERVUS, duodecim tribubus, quæ sunt in dispersione, salutem.

1:2 Omne gaudium existimate fratres mei, cum in tentationes varias incideritis :

1:3 scientes quod probatio fidei vestræ patientiam operatur.

1:4 Patientia autem opus perfectum habet : ut sitis perfecti et integri in nullo deficientes.

1:5 Si quis autem vestrum indiget sapientia, postulet a Deo, qui dat omnibus affluenter, et non improperat : et dabitur ei.

1:6 Postulet autem in fide nihil hæsitans : qui enim hæsitat, similis est fluctui maris, qui a vento movetur et circumfertur :

1:7 non ergo æstimet homo ille quod accipiat aliquid a Domino.

1:8 Vir duplex animo inconstans est in omnibus viis suis.

1:9 Glorietur autem frater humilis in exaltatione sua :

1:10 dives autem in humilitate sua, quoniam sicut flos fœni transibit ;

1:11 exortus est enim sol cum ardore, et arefecit fœnum, et flos ejus decidit, et decor vultus ejus deperiit : ita et dives in itineribus suis marcescet.

1:12 Beatus vir qui suffert tentationem : quoniam cum probatus fuerit, accipiet coronam vitæ, quam repromisit Deus diligentibus se.

1:13 Nemo cum tentatur, dicat quoniam a Deo tentatur : Deus enim intentator malorum est : ipse autem neminem tentat.

1:14 Unusquisque vero tentatur a concupiscentia sua abstractus, et illectus.

1:15 Deinde concupiscentia cum conceperit, parit peccatum : peccatum vero cum consummatum fuerit, generat mortem.

1:16 Nolite itaque errare, fratres mei dilectissimi.

1:17 Omne datum optimum, et omne donum perfectum desursum est, descendens a Patre luminum, apud quem non est transmutatio,

1:1 JAMES THE SERVANT OF GOD, AND OF OUR LORD JESUS CHRIST, to the twelve tribes which are scattered abroad, greeting.

1:2 My brethren, count it all joy, when you shall fall into divers temptations;

1:3 Knowing that the trying of your faith worketh patience.

1:4 And patience hath a perfect work; that you may be perfect and entire, failing in nothing.

1:5 But if any of you want wisdom, let him ask of God, who giveth to all men abundantly, and upbraideth not; and it shall be given him.

1:6 But let him ask in faith, nothing wavering. For he that wavereth is like a wave of the sea, which is moved and carried about by the wind.

1:7 Therefore let not that man think that he shall receive any thing of the Lord.

1:8 A double minded man is inconstant in all his ways.

1:9 But let the brother of low condition glory in his exaltation:

1:10 And the rich, in his being low; because as the flower of the grass shall he pass away.

1:11 For the sun rose with a burning heat, and parched the grass, and the flower thereof fell off, and the beauty of the shape thereof perished: so also shall the rich man fade away in his ways.

1:12 Blessed is the man that endureth temptation; for when he hath been proved, he shall receive a crown of life, which God hath promised to them that love him.

1:13 Let no man, when he is tempted, say that he is tempted by God. For God is not a tempter of evils, and he tempteth no man.

1:14 But every man is tempted by his own concupiscence, being drawn away and allured.

1:15 Then when concupiscence hath conceived, it bringeth forth sin. But sin, when it is completed, begetteth death.

1:16 Do not err, therefore, my dearest brethren.

1:17 Every best gift, and every perfect gift, is from above, coming down from the Father of lights, with whom there is no change, nor

nec vicissitudinis obumbratio.

1:18 Voluntarie enim genuit nos verbo veritatis, ut simus initium aliquod creaturæ ejus.

1:19 Scitis, fratres mei dilectissimi. Sit autem omnis homo velox ad audiendum : tardus autem ad loquendum, et tardus ad iram.

1:20 Ira enim viri justitiam Dei non operatur.

1:21 Propter quod abjicientes omnem immunditiam, et abundantiam malitiæ, in mansuetudine suscipite insitum verbum, quod potest salvare animas vestras.

1:22 Estote autem factores verbi, et non auditores tantum : fallentes vosmetipsos.

1:23 Quia si quis auditor est verbi, et non factor, hic comparabitur viro consideranti vultum nativitatis suæ in speculo :

1:24 consideravit enim se, et abiit, et statim oblitus est qualis fuerit.

1:25 Qui autem perspexerit in legem perfectam libertatis, et permanserit in ea, non auditor obliviosus factus, sed factor operis : hic beatus in facto suo erit.

1:26 Si quis autem putat se religiosum esse, non refrenans linguam suam, sed seducens cor suum, hujus vana est religio.

1:27 Religio munda et immaculata apud Deum et Patrem, hæc est : visitare pupillos et viduas in tribulatione eorum, et immaculatum se custodire ab hoc sæculo.

2:1 Fratres mei, nolite in personarum acceptione habere fidem Domini nostri Jesu Christi gloriæ.

2:2 Etenim si introierit in conventum vestrum vir aureum annulum habens in veste candida, introierit autem et pauper in sordido habitu,

2:3 et intendatis in eum qui indutus est veste præclara, et dixeritis ei : Tu sede hic bene : pauperi autem dicatis : Tu sta illic ; aut sede sub scabello pedum meorum :

2:4 nonne judicatis apud vosmetipsos, et facti estis judices cogitationum iniquarum ?

2:5 Audite, fratres mei dilectissimi : nonne Deus elegit pauperes in hoc mundo, divites in fide, et hæredes regni, quod repromisit Deus diligentibus se ?

2:6 vos autem exhonorastis pauperem. Nonne divites per potentiam opprimunt vos, et ipsi trahunt vos ad judicia ?

shadow of alteration.

1:18 For of his own will hath he begotten us by the word of truth, that we might be some beginning of his creature.

1:19 You know, my dearest brethren. And let every man be swift to hear, but slow to speak, and slow to anger.

1:20 For the anger of man worketh not the justice of God.

1:21 Wherefore casting away all uncleanness, and abundance of naughtiness, with meekness receive the ingrafted word, which is able to save your souls.

1:22 But be ye doers of the word, and not hearers only, deceiving your own selves.

1:23 For if a man be a hearer of the word, and not a doer, he shall be compared to a man beholding his own countenance in a glass.

1:24 For he beheld himself, and went his way, and presently forgot what manner of man he was.

1:25 But he that hath looked into the perfect law of liberty, and hath continued therein, not becoming a forgetful hearer, but a doer of the work; this man shall be blessed in his deed.

1:26 And if any man think himself to be religious, not bridling his tongue, but deceiving his own heart, this man's religion is vain.

1:27 Religion clean and undefiled before God and the Father, is this: to visit the fatherless and widows in their tribulation: and to keep one's self unspotted from this world.

2:1 My brethren, have not the faith of our Lord Jesus Christ of glory with respect of persons.

2:2 For if there shall come into your assembly a man having a golden ring, in fine apparel, and there shall come in also a poor man in mean attire,

2:3 And you have respect to him that is clothed with the fine apparel, and shall say to him: Sit thou here well; but say to the poor man: Stand thou there, or sit under my footstool:

2:4 Do you not judge within yourselves, and are become judges of unjust thoughts?

2:5 Hearken, my dearest brethren: hath not God chosen the poor in this world, rich in faith, and heirs of the kingdom which God hath promised to them that love him?

2:6 But you have dishonoured the poor man. Do not the rich oppress you by might? and do not they draw you before the judgment seats?

2:7 nonne ipsi blasphemant bonum nomen, quod invocatum est super vos ?

2:8 Si tamen legem perficitis regalem secundum Scripturas : Diliges proximum tuum sicut teipsum : bene facitis :

2:9 si autem personas accipitis, peccatum operamini, redarguti a lege quasi transgressores.

2:10 Quicumque autem totam legem servaverit, offendat autem in uno, factus est omnium reus.

2:11 Qui enim dixit : Non mœchaberis, dixit et : Non occides. Quod si non mœchaberis, occides autem, factus es transgressor legis.

2:12 Sic loquimini, et sic facite sicut per legem libertatis incipientes judicari.

2:13 Judicium enim sine misericordia illi qui non fecit misericordiam : superexaltat autem misericordia judicium.

2:14 Quid proderit, fratres mei, si fidem quis dicat se habere, opera autem non habeat ? numquid poterit fides salvare eum ?

2:15 Si autem frater et soror nudi sint, et indigeant victu quotidiano,

2:16 dicat autem aliquis ex vobis illis : Ite in pace, calefacimini et saturamini : non dederitis autem eis quæ necessaria sunt corpori, quid proderit ?

2:17 Sic et fides, si non habeat opera, mortua est in semetipsa.

2:18 Sed dicet quis : Tu fidem habes, et ego opera habeo : ostende mihi fidem tuam sine operibus : et ego ostendam tibi ex operibus fidem meam.

2:19 Tu credis quoniam unus est Deus : bene facis : et dæmones credunt, et contremiscunt.

2:20 Vis autem scire, o homo inanis, quoniam fides sine operibus mortua est ?

2:21 Abraham pater noster nonne ex operibus justificatus est, offerens Isaac filium suum super altare ?

2:22 Vides quoniam fides cooperabatur operibus illius : et ex operibus fides consummata est ?

2:23 Et suppleta est Scriptura, dicens : Credidit Abraham Deo, et reputatum est illi ad justitiam, et amicus Dei appellatus est.

2:24 Videtis quoniam ex operibus justificatur homo, et non ex fide tantum ?

2:25 Similiter et Rahab meretrix, nonne ex operibus justificata est, suscipiens nuntios, et

2:7 Do not they blaspheme the good name that is invoked upon you?

2:8 If then you fulfil the royal law, according to the scriptures, Thou shalt love thy neighbour as thyself; you do well.

2:9 But if you have respect to persons, you commit sin, being reproved by the law as transgressors.

2:10 And whosoever shall keep the whole law, but offend in one point, is become guilty of all.

2:11 For he that said, Thou shalt not commit adultery, said also, Thou shalt not kill. Now if thou do not commit adultery, but shalt kill, thou art become a transgressor of the law.

2:12 So speak ye, and so do, as being to be judged by the law of liberty.

2:13 For judgment without mercy to him that hath not done mercy. And mercy exalteth itself above judgment.

2:14 What shall it profit, my brethren, if a man say he hath faith, but hath not works? Shall faith be able to save him?

2:15 And if a brother or sister be naked, and want daily food:

2:16 And one of you say to them: Go in peace, be ye warmed and filled; yet give them not those things that are necessary for the body, what shall it profit?

2:17 So faith also, if it have not works, is dead in itself.

2:18 But some man will say: Thou hast faith, and I have works: shew me thy faith without works; and I will shew thee, by works, my faith.

2:19 Thou believest that there is one God. Thou dost well: the devils also believe and tremble.

2:20 But wilt thou know, O vain man, that faith without works is dead?

2:21 Was not Abraham our father justified by works, offering up Isaac his son upon the altar?

2:22 Seest thou, that faith did co-operate with his works; and by works faith was made perfect?

2:23 And the scripture was fulfilled, saying: Abraham believed God, and it was reputed to him to justice, and he was called the friend of God.

2:24 Do you see that by works a man is justified; and not by faith only?

2:25 And in like manner also Rahab the harlot, was not she justified by works, receiving the

alia via ejiciens ?

2:26 Sicut enim corpus sine spiritu mortuum est, ita et fides sine operibus mortua est.

3:1 Nolite plures magistri fieri fratres mei, scientes quoniam majus judicium sumitis.

3:2 In multis enim offendimus omnes. Si quis in verbo non offendit, hic perfectus est vir : potest etiam freno circumducere totum corpus.

3:3 Si autem equis frena in ora mittimus ad consentiendum nobis, et omne corpus illorum circumferimus.

3:4 Ecce et naves, cum magnæ sint, et a ventis validis minentur, circumferuntur a modico gubernaculo ubi impetus dirigentis voluerit.

3:5 Ita et lingua modicum quidem membrum est, et magna exaltat. Ecce quantus ignis quam magnam silvam incendit !

3:6 Et lingua ignis est, universitas iniquitatis. Lingua constituitur in membris nostris, quæ maculat totum corpus, et inflammat rotam nativitatis nostræ inflammata a gehenna.

3:7 Omnis enim natura bestiarum, et volucrum, et serpentium, et ceterorum domantur, et domita sunt a natura humana :

3:8 linguam autem nullus hominum domare potest : inquietum malum, plena veneno mortifero.

3:9 In ipsa benedicimus Deum et Patrem : et in ipsa maledicimus homines, qui ad similitudinem Dei facti sunt.

3:10 Ex ipso ore procedit benedictio et maledictio. Non oportet, fratres mei, hæc ita fieri.

3:11 Numquid fons de eodem foramine emanat dulcem et amaram aquam ?

3:12 Numquid potest, fratres mei, ficus uvas facere, aut vitis ficus ? Sic neque salsa dulcem potest facere aquam.

3:13 Quis sapiens et disciplinatus inter vos ? Ostendat ex bona conversatione operationem suam in mansuetudine sapientiæ.

3:14 Quod si zelum amarum habetis, et contentiones sint in cordibus vestris : nolite gloriari, et mendaces esse adversus veritatem :

3:15 non est enim ista sapientia desursum descendens : sed terrena, animalis, diabolica.

messengers, and sending them out another way?

2:26 For even as the body without the spirit is dead; so also faith without works is dead.

3:1 Be ye not many masters, my brethren, knowing that you receive the greater judgment.

3:2 For in many things we all offend. If any man offend not in word, the same is a perfect man. He is able also with a bridle to lead about the whole body.

3:3 For if we put bits into the mouths of horses, that they may obey us, and we turn about their whole body.

3:4 Behold also ships, whereas they are great, and are driven by strong winds, yet are they turned about with a small helm, whithersoever the force of the governor willeth.

3:5 Even so the tongue is indeed a little member, and boasteth great things. Behold how small a fire kindleth a great wood.

3:6 And the tongue is a fire, a world of iniquity. The tongue is placed among our members, which defileth the whole body, and inflameth the wheel of our nativity, being set on fire by hell.

3:7 For every nature of beasts, and of birds, and of serpents, and of the rest, is tamed, and hath been tamed, by the nature of man:

3:8 But the tongue no man can tame, an unquiet evil, full of deadly poison.

3:9 By it we bless God and the Father: and by it we curse men, who are made after the likeness of God.

3:10 Out of the same mouth proceedeth blessing and cursing. My brethren, these things ought not so to be.

3:11 Doth a fountain send forth, out of the same hole, sweet and bitter water?

3:12 Can the fig tree, my brethren, bear grapes; or the vine, figs? So neither can the salt water yield sweet.

3:13 Who is a wise man, and endued with knowledge among you? Let him shew, by a good conversation, his work in the meekness of wisdom.

3:14 But if you have bitter zeal, and there be contentions in your hearts; glory not, and be not liars against the truth.

3:15 For this is not wisdom, descending from above: but earthly, sensual, devilish.

3:16 Ubi enim zelus et contentio, ibi inconstantia et omne opus pravum.

3:17 Quæ autem desursum est sapientia, primum quidem pudica est, deinde pacifica, modesta, suadibilis, bonis consentiens, plena misericordia et fructibus bonis, non judicans, sine simulatione.

3:18 Fructus autem justitiæ, in pace seminatur, facientibus pacem.

4:1 Unde bella et lites in vobis ? nonne hinc : ex concupiscentiis vestris, quæ militant in membris vestris ?

4:2 concupiscitis, et non habetis : occiditis, et zelatis : et non potestis adipisci : litigatis, et belligeratis, et non habetis, propter quod non postulatis.

4:3 Petitis, et non accipitis : eo quod male petatis : ut in concupiscentiis vestris insumatis.

4:4 Adulteri, nescitis quia amicitia hujus mundi inimica est Dei ? quicumque ergo voluerit amicus esse sæculi hujus, inimicus Dei constituitur.

4:5 An putatis quia inaniter Scriptura dicat : Ad invidiam concupiscit spiritus qui habitat in vobis ?

4:6 majorem autem dat gratiam. Propter quod dicit : Deus superbis resistit, humilibus autem dat gratiam.

4:7 Subditi ergo estote Deo, resistite autem diabolo, et fugiet a vobis.

4:8 Appropinquate Deo, et appropinquabit vobis. Emundate manus, peccatores : et purificate corda, duplices animo.

4:9 Miseri estote, et lugete, et plorate : risus vester in luctum convertatur, et gaudium in mœrorem.

4:10 Humiliamini in conspectu Domini, et exaltabit vos.

4:11 Nolite detrahere alterutrum fratres. Qui detrahit fratri, aut qui judicat fratrem suum, detrahit legi, et judicat legem. Si autem judicas legem, non es factor legis, sed judex.

4:12 Unus est legislator et judex, qui potest perdere et liberare.

4:13 Tu autem quis es, qui judicas proximum ? Ecce nunc qui dicitis : Hodie, aut crastino ibimus in illam civitatem, et faciemus ibi quidem annum, et mercabimur, et lucrum faciemus :

4:14 qui ignoratis quid erit in crastino.

3:16 For where envying and contention is, there is inconstancy, and every evil work.

3:17 But the wisdom, that is from above, first indeed is chaste, then peaceable, modest, easy to be persuaded, consenting to the good, full of mercy and good fruits, without judging, without dissimulation.

3:18 And the fruit of justice is sown in peace, to them that make peace.

4:1 From whence are wars and contentions among you? Are they not hence, from your concupiscences, which war in your members?

4:2 You covet, and have not: you kill, and envy, and can not obtain. You contend and war, and you have not, because you ask not.

4:3 You ask, and receive not; because you ask amiss: that you may consume it on your concupiscences.

4:4 Adulterers, know you not that the friendship of this world is the enemy of God? Whosoever therefore will be a friend of this world, becometh an enemy of God.

4:5 Or do you think that the scripture saith in vain: To envy doth the spirit covet which dwelleth in you?

4:6 But he giveth greater grace. Wherefore he saith: God resisteth the proud, and giveth grace to the humble.

4:7 Be subject therefore to God, but resist the devil, and he will fly from you.

4:8 Draw nigh to God, and he will draw nigh to you. Cleanse your hands, ye sinners: and purify your hearts, ye double minded.

4:9 Be afflicted, and mourn, and weep: let your laughter be turned into mourning, and your joy into sorrow.

4:10 Be humbled in the sight of the Lord, and he will exalt you.

4:11 Detract not one another, my brethren. He that detracteth his brother, or he that judgeth his brother, detracteth the law, and judgeth the law. But if thou judge the law, thou art not a doer of the law, but a judge.

4:12 There is one lawgiver, and judge, that is able to destroy and to deliver.

4:13 But who art thou that judgest thy neighbour? Behold, now you that say: To day or to morrow we will go into such a city, and there we will spend a year, and will traffic, and make our gain.

4:14 Whereas you know not what shall be on the

4:15 Quæ est enim vita vestra ? vapor est ad modicum parens, et deinceps exterminabitur ; pro eo ut dicatis : Si Dominus voluerit. Et : Si vixerimus, faciemus hoc, aut illud.

4:16 Nunc autem exsultatis in superbiis vestris. Omnis exsultatio talis, maligna est.

4:17 Scienti igitur bonum facere, et non facienti, peccatum est illi.

5:1 Agite nunc divites, plorate ululantes in miseriis vestris, quæ advenient vobis.

5:2 Divitiæ vestræ putrefactæ sunt, et vestimenta vestra a tineis comesta sunt.

5:3 Aurum et argentum vestrum æruginavit : et ærugo eorum in testimonium vobis erit, et manducabit carnes vestras sicut ignis. Thesaurizastis vobis iram in novissimis diebus.

5:4 Ecce merces operariorum, qui messuerunt regiones vestras, quæ fraudata est a vobis, clamat : et clamor eorum in aures Domini sabbaoth introivit.

5:5 Epulati estis super terram, et in luxuriis enutristis corda vestra in die occisionis.

5:6 Addixistis, et occidistis justum, et non restitit vobis.

5:7 Patientes igitur estote, fratres, usque ad adventum Domini. Ecce agricola exspectat pretiosum fructum terræ, patienter ferens donec accipiat temporaneum et serotinum.

5:8 Patientes igitur estote et vos, et confirmate corda vestra : quoniam adventus Domini appropinquavit.

5:9 Nolite ingemiscere, fratres, in alterutrum, ut non judicemini. Ecce judex ante januam assistit.

5:10 Exemplum accipite, fratres, exitus mali, laboris, et patientiæ, prophetas qui locuti sunt in nomine Domini.

5:11 Ecce beatificamus eos qui sustinuerunt. Sufferentiam Job audistis, et finem Domini vidistis, quoniam misericors Dominus est, et miserator.

5:12 Ante omnia autem, fratres mei, nolite jurare, neque per cælum, neque per terram, neque aliud quodcumque juramentum. Sit autem sermo vester : Est, est : Non, non : ut non sub judicio decidatis.

morrow.

4:15 For what is your life? It is a vapour which appeareth for a little while, and afterwards shall vanish away. For that you should say: If the Lord will, and if we shall live, we will do this or that.

4:16 But now you rejoice in your arrogancies. All such rejoicing is wicked.

4:17 To him therefore who knoweth to do good, and doth it not, to him it is sin.

5:1 Go to now, ye rich men, weep and howl in your miseries, which shall come upon you.

5:2 Your riches are corrupted: and your garments are motheaten.

5:3 Your gold and silver is cankered: and the rust of them shall be for a testimony against you, and shall eat your flesh like fire. You have stored up to yourselves wrath against the last days.

5:4 Behold the hire of the labourers, who have reaped down your fields, which by fraud has been kept back by you, crieth: and the cry of them hath entered into the ears of the Lord of sabaoth.

5:5 You have feasted upon earth: and in riotousness you have nourished your hearts, in the day of slaughter.

5:6 You have condemned and put to death the Just One, and he resisted you not.

5:7 Be patient therefore, brethren, until the coming of the Lord. Behold, the husbandman waiteth for the precious fruit of the earth: patiently bearing till he receive the early and latter rain.

5:8 Be you therefore also patient, and strengthen your hearts: for the coming of the Lord is at hand.

5:9 Grudge not, brethren, one against another, that you may not be judged. Behold the judge standeth before the door.

5:10 Take, my brethren, for an example of suffering evil, of labour and patience, the prophets, who spoke in the name of the Lord.

5:11 Behold, we account them blessed who have endured. You have heard of the patience of Job, and you have seen the end of the Lord, that the Lord is merciful and compassionate.

5:12 But above all things, my brethren, swear not, neither by heaven, nor by the earth, nor by any other oath. But let your speech be, yea, yea: no, no: that you fall not under judgment.

5:13 Tristatur aliquis vestrum ? oret. Æquo animo est ? psallat.

5:14 Infirmatur quis in vobis ? inducat presbyteros ecclesiæ, et orent super eum, ungentes eum oleo in nomine Domini :

5:15 et oratio fidei salvabit infirmum, et alleviabit eum Dominus : et si in peccatis sit, remittentur ei.

5:16 Confitemini ergo alterutrum peccata vestra, et orate pro invicem ut salvemini : multum enim valet deprecatio justi assidua.

5:17 Elias homo erat similis nobis passibilis : et oratione oravit ut non plueret super terram, et non pluit annos tres, et menses sex.

5:18 Et rursum oravit : et cælum dedit pluviam, et terra dedit fructum suum.

5:19 Fratres mei, si quis ex vobis erraverit a veritate, et converterit quis eum :

5:20 scire debet quoniam qui converti fecerit peccatorem ab errore viæ suæ, salvabit animam ejus a morte, et operiet multitudinem peccatorum.

5:13 Is any of you sad? Let him pray. Is he cheerful in mind? Let him sing.

5:14 Is any man sick among you? Let him bring in the priests of the church, and let them pray over him, anointing him with oil in the name of the Lord.

5:15 And the prayer of faith shall save the sick man: and the Lord shall raise him up: and if he be in sins, they shall be forgiven him.

5:16 Confess therefore your sins one to another: and pray one for another, that you may be saved. For the continual prayer of a just man availeth much.

5:17 Elias was a man passible like unto us: and with prayer he prayed that it might not rain upon the earth, and it rained not for three years and six months.

5:18 And he prayed again: and the heaven gave rain, and the earth brought forth her fruit.

5:19 My brethren, if any of you err from the truth, and one convert him:

5:20 He must know that he who causeth a sinner to be converted from the error of his way, shall save his soul from death, and shall cover a multitude of sins.

Beati Petri Apostoli Epistula Prima

THE FIRST EPISTLE OF BLESSED PETER THE APOSTLE

✠

1:1 PETRUS APOSTOLUS JESU CHRISTI, electis advenis dispersionis Ponti, Galatiæ, Cappadociæ, Asiæ, et Bithyniæ,

1:2 secundum præscientiam Dei Patris, in sanctificationem Spiritus, in obedientiam, et aspersionem sanguinis Jesu Christi. Gratia vobis, et pax multiplicetur.

1:3 Benedictus Deus et Pater Domini nostri Jesu Christi, qui secundum misericordiam suam magnam regeneravit nos in spem vivam, per resurrectionem Jesu Christi ex mortuis,

1:4 in hæreditatem incorruptibilem, et incontaminatam, et immarcescibilem, conservatam in cælis in vobis,

1:5 qui in virtute Dei custodimini per fidem in salutem, paratam revelari in tempore novissimo.

1:6 In quo exsultabis, modicum nunc si oportet contristari in variis tentationibus :

1:7 ut probatio vestræ fidei multo pretiosior auro (quod per ignem probatur) inveniatur in laudem, et gloriam, et honorem in revelatione Jesu Christi :

1:8 quem cum non videritis, diligitis : in quem nunc quoque non videntes creditis : credentes autem exsultabitis lætitia inenarrabili, et glorificata :

1:9 reportantes finem fidei vestræ, salutem animarum.

1:10 De qua salute exquisierunt, atque scrutati sunt prophetæ, qui de futura in vobis gratia prophetaverunt :

1:11 scrutantes in quod vel quale tempus significaret in eis Spiritus Christi : prænuntians eas quæ in Christo sunt passiones, et posteriores glorias :

1:12 quibus revelatum est quia non sibimetipsis, vobis autem ministrabant ea quæ nunc nuntiata sunt vobis per eos qui evangelizaverunt vobis, Spiritu Sancto misso de cælo, in quem desiderant angeli prospicere.

1:13 Propter quod succincti lumbos mentis ves-

1:1 PETER, AN APOSTLE OF JESUS CHRIST, to the strangers dispersed through Pontus, Galatia, Cappadocia, Asia, and Bithynia, elect,

1:2 According to the foreknowledge of God the Father, unto the sanctification of the Spirit, unto obedience and sprinkling of the blood of Jesus Christ: Grace unto you and peace be multiplied.

1:3 Blessed be the God and Father of our Lord Jesus Christ, who according to his great mercy hath regenerated us unto a lively hope, by the resurrection of Jesus Christ from the dead,

1:4 Unto an inheritance incorruptible, and undefiled, and that can not fade, reserved in heaven for you,

1:5 Who, by the power of God, are kept by faith unto salvation, ready to be revealed in the last time.

1:6 Wherein you shall greatly rejoice, if now you must be for a little time made sorrowful in divers temptations:

1:7 That the trial of your faith (much more precious than gold which is tried by the fire) may be found unto praise and glory and honour at the appearing of Jesus Christ:

1:8 Whom having not seen, you love: in whom also now, though you see him not, you believe: and believing shall rejoice with joy unspeakable and glorified;

1:9 Receiving the end of your faith, even the salvation of your souls.

1:10 Of which salvation the prophets have inquired and diligently searched, who prophesied of the grace to come in you.

1:11 Searching what or what manner of time the Spirit of Christ in them did signify: when it foretold those sufferings that are in Christ, and the glories that should follow:

1:12 To whom it was revealed, that not to themselves, but to you they ministered those things which are now declared to you by them that have preached the gospel to you, the Holy Ghost being sent down from heaven, on whom the angels desire to look.

1:13 Wherefore having the loins of your mind

træ, sobrii, perfecte sperate in eam, quæ offertur vobis, gratiam, in revelationem Jesu Christi :

1:14 quasi filii obedientiæ, non configurati prioribus ignorantiæ vestræ desideriis :

1:15 sed secundum eum qui vocavit vos, Sanctum : et ipsi in omni conversatione sancti sitis :

1:16 quoniam scriptum est : Sancti eritis, quoniam ego sanctus sum.

1:17 Et si patrem invocatis eum, qui sine acceptione personarum judicat secundum uniuscujusque opus, in timore incolatus vestri tempore conversamini.

1:18 Scientes quod non corruptibilibus, auro vel argento, redempti estis de vana vestra conversatione paternæ traditionis :

1:19 sed pretioso sanguine quasi agni immaculati Christi, et incontaminati :

1:20 præcogniti quidem ante mundi constitutionem, manifestati autem novissimis temporibus propter vos,

1:21 qui per ipsum fideles estis in Deo, qui suscitavit eum a mortuis, et dedit ei gloriam, ut fides vestra et spes esset in Deo :

1:22 animas vestras castificantes in obedientia caritatis, in fraternitatis amore, simplici ex corde invicem diligite attentius :

1:23 renati non ex semine corruptibili, sed incorruptibili per verbum Dei vivi, et permanentis in æternum :

1:24 quia omnis caro ut fœnum : et omnis gloria ejus tamquam flos fœni : exaruit fœnum, et flos ejus decidit.

1:25 Verbum autem Domini manet in æternum : hoc est autem verbum, quod evangelizatum est in vos.

2:1 Deponentes igitur omnem malitiam, et omnem dolum, et simulationes, et invidias, et omnes detractiones,

2:2 sicut modo geniti infantes, rationabile, sine dolo lac concupiscite : ut in eo crescatis in salutem :

2:3 si tamen gustastis quoniam dulcis est Dominus.

2:4 Ad quem accedentes lapidem vivum, ab hominibus quidem reprobatum, a Deo autem electum, et honorificatum :

2:5 et ipsi tamquam lapides vivi superædifi-

girt up, being sober, trust perfectly in the grace which is offered you in the revelation of Jesus Christ,

1:14 As children of obedience, not fashioned according to the former desires of your ignorance:

1:15 But according to him that hath called you, who is holy, be you also in all manner of conversation holy:

1:16 Because it is written: You shall be holy, for I am holy.

1:17 And if you invoke as Father him who, without respect of persons, judgeth according to every one's work: converse in fear during the time of your sojourning here.

1:18 Knowing that you were not redeemed with corruptible things as gold or silver, from your vain conversation of the tradition of your fathers:

1:19 But with the precious blood of Christ, as of a lamb unspotted and undefiled,

1:20 Foreknown indeed before the foundation of the world, but manifested in the last times for you,

1:21 Who through him are faithful in God, who raised him up from the dead, and hath given him glory, that your faith and hope might be in God.

1:22 Purifying your souls in the obedience of charity, with a brotherly love, from a sincere heart love one another earnestly:

1:23 Being born again not of corruptible seed, but incorruptible, by the word of God who liveth and remaineth for ever.

1:24 For all flesh is as grass; and all the glory thereof as the flower of grass. The grass is withered, and the flower thereof is fallen away.

1:25 But the word of the Lord endureth for ever. And this is the word which by the gospel hath been preached unto you.

2:1 Wherefore laying away all malice, and all guile, and dissimulations, and envies, and all detractions,

2:2 As newborn babes, desire the rational milk without guile, that thereby you may grow unto salvation:

2:3 If so be you have tasted that the Lord is sweet.

2:4 Unto whom coming, as to a living stone, rejected indeed by men, but chosen and made honourable by God:

2:5 Be you also as living stones built up, a spir-

camini, domus spiritualis, sacerdotium sanctum, offerre spirituales hostias, acceptabiles Deo per Jesum Christum.

2:6 Propter quod continet Scriptura : Ecce pono in Sion lapidem summum angularem, electum, pretiosum : et qui crediderit in eum, non confundetur.

2:7 Vobis igitur honor credentibus : non credentibus autem lapis, quem reprobaverunt ædificantes : hic factus est in caput anguli,

2:8 et lapis offensionis, et petra scandali, his qui offendunt verbo, nec credunt in quo et positi sunt.

2:9 Vos autem genus electum, regale sacerdotium, gens sancta, populus acquisitionis : ut virtutes annuntietis ejus qui de tenebris vos vocavit in admirabile lumen suum.

2:10 Qui aliquando non populus, nunc autem populus Dei : qui non consecuti misericordiam, nunc autem misericordiam consecuti.

2:11 Carissimi, obsecro vos tamquam advenas et peregrinos abstinere vos a carnalibus desideriis, quæ militant adversus animam,

2:12 conversationem vestram inter gentes habentes bonam : ut in eo quod detrectant de vobis tamquam de malefactoribus, ex bonis operibus vos considerantes, glorificent Deum in die visitationis.

2:13 Subjecti igitur estote omni humanæ creaturæ propter Deum : sive regi quasi præcellenti :

2:14 sive ducibus tamquam ab eo missis ad vindictam malefactorum, laudem vero bonorum :

2:15 quia sic est voluntas Dei, ut benefacientes obmutescere faciatis imprudentium hominum ignorantiam :

2:16 quasi liberi, et non quasi velamen habentes malitiæ libertatem, sed sicut servi Dei.

2:17 Omnes honorate : fraternitatem diligite : Deum timete : regem honorificate.

2:18 Servi, subditi estote in omni timore dominis, non tantum bonis et modestis, sed etiam dyscolis.

2:19 Hæc est enim gratia, si propter Dei conscientiam sustinet quis tristitias, patiens injuste.

2:20 Quæ enim est gloria, si peccantes, et colaphizati suffertis ? sed si bene facientes patienter sustinetis, hæc est gratia apud Deum.

itual house, a holy priesthood, to offer up spiritual sacrifices, acceptable to God by Jesus Christ.

2:6 Wherefore it is said in the scripture: Behold, I lay in Sion a chief corner stone, elect, precious. And he that shall believe in him, shall not be confounded.

2:7 To you therefore that believe, he is honour: but to them that believe not, the stone which the builders rejected, the same is made the head of the corner:

2:8 And a stone of stumbling, and a rock of scandal, to them who stumble at the word, neither do believe, whereunto also they are set.

2:9 But you are a chosen generation, a kingly priesthood, a holy nation, a purchased people: that you may declare his virtues, who hath called you out of darkness into his marvellous light:

2:10 Who in time past were not a people: but are now the people of God. Who had not obtained mercy; but now have obtained mercy.

2:11 Dearly beloved, I beseech you as strangers and pilgrims, to refrain yourselves from carnal desires which war against the soul,

2:12 Having your conversation good among the Gentiles: that whereas they speak against you as evildoers, they may, by the good works, which they shall behold in you, glorify God in the day of visitation.

2:13 Be ye subject therefore to every human creature for God's sake: whether it be to the king as excelling;

2:14 Or to governors as sent by him for the punishment of evildoers, and for the praise of the good:

2:15 For so is the will of God, that by doing well you may put to silence the ignorance of foolish men:

2:16 As free, and not as making liberty a cloak for malice, but as the servants of God.

2:17 Honour all men. Love the brotherhood. Fear God. Honour the king.

2:18 Servants, be subject to your masters with all fear, not only to the good and gentle, but also to the froward.

2:19 For this is thankworthy, if for conscience towards God, a man endure sorrows, suffering wrongfully.

2:20 For what glory is it, if committing sin, and being buffeted for it, you endure? But if doing well you suffer patiently; this is thankworthy

2:21 In hoc enim vocati estis : quia et Christus passus est pro nobis, vobis relinquens exemplum ut sequamini vestigia ejus :

2:22 qui peccatum non fecit, nec inventus est dolus in ore ejus :

2:23 qui cum malediceretur, non maledicebat : cum pateretur, non comminabatur : tradebat autem judicanti se injuste :

2:24 qui peccata nostra ipse pertulit in corpore suo super lignum ; ut peccatis mortui, justitiæ vivamus : cujus livore sanati estis.

2:25 Eratis enim sicut oves errantes, sed conversi estis nunc ad pastorem, et episcopum animarum vestrarum.

3:1 Similiter et mulieres subditæ sint viris suis : ut etsi qui non credunt verbo, per mulierem conversationem sine verbo lucrifiant :

3:2 considerantes in timore castam conversationem vestram.

3:3 Quarum non sit extrinsecus capillatura, aut circumdatio auri, aut indumenti vestimentorum cultus :

3:4 sed qui absconditus est cordis homo, in incorruptibilitate quieti, et modesti spiritus, qui est in conspectu Dei locuples.

3:5 Sic enim aliquando et sanctæ mulieres, sperantes in Deo, ornabant se, subjectæ propriis viris.

3:6 Sicut Sara obediebat Abrahæ, dominum eum vocans : cujus estis filiæ benefacientes, et non pertimentes ullam perturbationem.

3:7 Viri similiter cohabitantes secundum scientiam, quasi infirmiori vasculo muliebri impartientes honorem, tamquam et cohæredibus gratiæ vitæ : ut non impediantur orationes vestræ.

3:8 In fine autem omnes unanimes, compatientes fraternitatis amatores, misericordes, modesti, humiles :

3:9 non reddentes malum pro malo, nec maledictum pro maledicto, sed e contrario benedicentes : quia in hoc vocati estis, ut benedictionem hæreditate possideatis.

3:10 Qui enim vult vitam diligere, et dies videre bonos, coërceat linguam suam a malo, et labia ejus ne loquantur dolum.

3:11 Declinet a malo, et faciat bonum : inquirat pacem, et sequatur eam :

before God.

2:21 For unto this are you called: because Christ also suffered for us, leaving you an example that you should follow his steps.

2:22 Who did no sin, neither was guile found in his mouth.

2:23 Who, when he was reviled, did not revile: when he suffered, he threatened not: but delivered himself to him that judged him unjustly.

2:24 Who his own self bore our sins in his body upon the tree: that we, being dead to sins, should live to justice: by whose stripes you were healed.

2:25 For you were as sheep going astray; but you are now converted to the shepherd and bishop of your souls.

3:1 In like manner also let wives be subject to their husbands: that if any believe not the word, they may be won without the word, by the conversation of the wives.

3:2 Considering your chaste conversation with fear.

3:3 Whose adorning let it not be the outward plaiting of the hair, or the wearing of gold, or the putting on of apparel:

3:4 But the hidden man of the heart in the incorruptibility of a quiet and a meek spirit, which is rich in the sight of God.

3:5 For after this manner heretofore the holy women also, who trusted in God, adorned themselves, being in subjection to their own husbands:

3:6 As Sara obeyed Abraham, calling him lord: whose daughters you are, doing well, and not fearing any disturbance.

3:7 Ye husbands, likewise dwelling with them according to knowledge, giving honour to the female as to the weaker vessel, and as to the co-heirs of the grace of life: that your prayers be not hindered.

3:8 And in fine, be ye all of one mind, having compassion one of another, being lovers of the brotherhood, merciful, modest, humble:

3:9 Not rendering evil for evil, nor railing for railing, but contrariwise, blessing: for unto this are you called, that you may inherit a blessing.

3:10 For he that will love life, and see good days, let him refrain his tongue from evil, and his lips that they speak no guile.

3:11 Let him decline from evil, and do good: let him seek after peace and pursue it:

3:12 quia oculi Domini super justos, et aures ejus in preces eorum : vultus autem Domini super facientes mala.

3:13 Et quis est qui vobis noceat, si boni æmulatores fueritis ?

3:14 Sed et si quid patimini propter justitiam, beati. Timorem autem eorum ne timueritis, et non conturbemini.

3:15 Dominum autem Christum sanctificate in cordibus vestris, parati semper ad satisfactionem omni poscenti vos rationem de ea, quæ in vobis est, spe.

3:16 Sed cum modestia, et timore, conscientiam habentes bonam : ut in eo, quod detrahunt vobis, confundantur, qui calumniantur vestram bonam in Christo conversationem.

3:17 Melius est enim benefacientes (si voluntas Dei velit) pati, quam malefacientes.

3:18 Quia et Christus semel pro peccatis nostris mortuus est, justus pro injustis, ut nos offerret Deo, mortificatus quidem carne, vivificatus autem spiritu.

3:19 In quo et his, qui in carcere erant, spiritibus veniens prædicavit :

3:20 qui increduli fuerant aliquando, quando exspectabant Dei patientiam in diebus Noë, cum fabricaretur arca : in qua pauci, id est octo animæ, salvæ factæ sunt per aquam.

3:21 Quod et vos nunc similis formæ salvos fecit baptisma : non carnis depositio sordium, sed conscientiæ bonæ interrogatio in Deum per resurrectionem Jesu Christi.

3:22 Qui est in dextera Dei, deglutiens mortem ut vitæ æternæ hæredes efficeremur : profectus in cælum subjectis sibi angelis, et potestatibus, et virtutibus.

4:1 Christo igitur passo in carne, et vos eadem cogitatione armamini : quia qui passus est in carne, desiit a peccatis :

4:2 ut jam non desideriis hominum, sed voluntati Dei, quod reliquum est in carne vivat temporis.

4:3 Sufficit enim præteritum tempus ad voluntatem gentium consummandam his qui ambulaverunt in luxuriis, desideriis, vinolentiis, comessationibus, potationibus, et illicitis idolorum cultibus.

3:12 Because the eyes of the Lord are upon the just, and his ears unto their prayers: but the countenance of the Lord upon them that do evil things.

3:13 And who is he that can hurt you, if you be zealous of good?

3:14 But if also you suffer any thing for justice' sake, blessed are ye. And be not afraid of their fear, and be not troubled.

3:15 But sanctify the Lord Christ in your hearts, being ready always to satisfy every one that asketh you a reason of that hope which is in you.

3:16 But with modesty and fear, having a good conscience: that whereas they speak evil of you, they may be ashamed who falsely accuse your good conversation in Christ.

3:17 For it is better doing well (if such be the will of God) to suffer, than doing ill.

3:18 Because Christ also died once for our sins, the just for the unjust: that he might offer us to God, being put to death indeed in the flesh, but enlivened in the spirit,

3:19 In which also coming he preached to those spirits that were in prison:

3:20 Which had been some time incredulous, when they waited for the patience of God in the days of Noe, when the ark was a building: wherein a few, that is, eight souls, were saved by water.

3:21 Whereunto baptism being of the like form, now saveth you also: not the putting away of the filth of the flesh, but the examination of a good conscience towards God by the resurrection of Jesus Christ.

3:22 Who is on the right hand of God, swallowing down death, that we might be made heirs of life everlasting: being gone into heaven, the angels and powers and virtues being made subject to him.

4:1 Christ therefore having suffered in the flesh, be you also armed with the same thought: for he that hath suffered in the flesh, hath ceased from sins:

4:2 That now he may live the rest of his time in the flesh, not after the desires of men, but according to the will of God.

4:3 For the time past is sufficient to have fulfilled the will of the Gentiles, for them who have walked in riotousness, lusts, excess of wine, revellings, banquetings, and unlawful worshipping of idols.

4:4 In quo admirantur non concurrentibus vobis in eamdem luxuriæ confusionem, blasphemantes.

4:5 Qui reddent rationem ei qui paratus est judicare vivos et mortuos.

4:6 Propter hoc enim et mortuis evangelizatum est : ut judicentur quidem secundum homines in carne, vivant autem secundum Deum in spiritu.

4:7 Omnium autem finis appropinquavit. Estote itaque prudentes, et vigilate in orationibus.

4:8 Ante omnia autem, mutuam in vobismetipsis caritatem continuam habentes : quia caritas operit multitudinem peccatorum.

4:9 Hospitales invicem sine murmuratione.

4:10 Unusquisque, sicut accepit gratiam, in alterutrum illam administrantes, sicut boni dispensatores multiformis gratiæ Dei.

4:11 Si quis loquitur, quasi sermones Dei : si quis ministrat, tamquam ex virtute, quam administrat Deus : ut in omnibus honorificetur Deus per Jesum Christum : cui est gloria et imperium in sæcula sæculorum. Amen.

4:12 Carissimi, nolite peregrinari in fervore, qui ad tentationem vobis fit, quasi novi aliquid vobis contingat :

4:13 sed communicantes Christi passionibus gaudete, ut et in revelatione gloriæ ejus gaudeatis exsultantes.

4:14 Si exprobramini in nomine Christi, beati eritis : quoniam quod est honoris, gloriæ, et virtutis Dei, et qui est ejus Spiritus, super vos requiescit.

4:15 Nemo autem vestrum patiatur ut homicida, aut fur, aut maledicus, aut alienorum appetitor.

4:16 Si autem ut christianus, non erubescat : glorificet autem Deum in isto nomine :

4:17 quoniam tempus est ut incipiat judicium a domo Dei. Si autem primum a nobis, quis finis eorum, qui non credunt Dei Evangelio ?

4:18 et si justus vix salvabitur, impius et peccator ubi parebunt ?

4:19 Itaque et hi, qui patiuntur secundum voluntatem Dei, fideli Creatori commendent animas suas in benefactis.

4:4 Wherein they think it strange, that you run not with them into the same confusion of riotousness, speaking evil of you.

4:5 Who shall render account to him, who is ready to judge the living and the dead.

4:6 For, for this cause was the gospel preached also to the dead: that they might be judged indeed according to men, in the flesh; but may live according to God, in the Spirit.

4:7 But the end of all is at hand. Be prudent therefore, and watch in prayers.

4:8 But before all things have a constant mutual charity among yourselves: for charity covereth a multitude of sins.

4:9 Using hospitality one towards another, without murmuring,

4:10 As every man hath received grace, ministering the same one to another: as good stewards of the manifold grace of God.

4:11 If any man speak, let him speak, as the words of God. If any man minister, let him do it, as of the power, which God administereth: that in all things God may be honoured through Jesus Christ: to whom is glory and empire for ever and ever. Amen.

4:12 Dearly beloved, think not strange the burning heat which is to try you, as if some new thing happened to you;

4:13 But if you partake of the sufferings of Christ, rejoice that when his glory shall be revealed, you may also be glad with exceeding joy.

4:14 If you be reproached for the name of Christ, you shall be blessed: for that which is of the honour, glory, and power of God, and that which is his Spirit, resteth upon you.

4:15 But let none of you suffer as a murderer, or a thief, or a railer, or a coveter of other men's things.

4:16 But if as a Christian, let him not be ashamed, but let him glorify God in that name.

4:17 For the time is, that judgment should begin at the house of God. And if first at us, what shall be the end of them that believe not the gospel of God?

4:18 And if the just man shall scarcely be saved, where shall the ungodly and the sinner appear?

4:19 Wherefore let them also that suffer according to the will of God, commend their souls in good deeds to the faithful Creator.

5:1 Seniores ergo, qui in vobis sunt, obsecro, consenior et testis Christi passionum : qui et ejus, quæ in futuro revelanda est, gloriæ communicator :

5:2 pascite qui in vobis est gregem Dei, providentes non coacte, sed spontanee secundum Deum : neque turpis lucri gratia, sed voluntarie :

5:3 neque ut dominantes in cleris, sed forma facti gregis ex animo.

5:4 Et cum apparuerit princeps pastorum, percipietis immarcescibilem gloriæ coronam.

5:5 Similiter adolescentes subditi estote senioribus. Omnes autem invicem humilitatem insinuate, quia Deus superbis resistit, humilibus autem dat gratiam.

5:6 Humiliamini igitur sub potenti manu Dei, ut vos exaltet in tempore visitationis :

5:7 omnem sollicitudinem vestram projicientes in eum, quoniam ipsi cura est de vobis.

5:8 Sobrii estote, et vigilate : quia adversarius vester diabolus tamquam leo rugiens circuit, quærens quem devoret :

5:9 cui resistite fortes in fide : scientes eamdem passionem ei quæ in mundo est vestræ fraternitati fieri.

5:10 Deus autem omnis gratiæ, qui vocavit nos in æternam suam gloriam in Christo Jesu, modicum passos ipse perficiet, confirmabit, solidabitque.

5:11 Ipsi gloria, et imperium in sæcula sæculorum. Amen.

5:12 Per Silvanum fidelem fratrem vobis, ut arbitror, breviter scripsi : obsecrans et contestans, hanc esse veram gratiam Dei, in qua statis.

5:13 Salutat vos ecclesia quæ est in Babylone coëlecta, et Marcus filius meus.

5:14 Salutate invicem in osculo sancto. Gratia vobis omnibus qui estis in Christo Jesu. Amen.

5:1 The ancients therefore that are among you, I beseech, who am myself also an ancient, and a witness of the sufferings of Christ: as also a partaker of that glory which is to be revealed in time to come:

5:2 Feed the flock of God which is among you, taking care of it, not by constraint, but willingly, according to God: not for filthy lucre's sake, but voluntarily:

5:3 Neither as lording it over the clergy, but being made a pattern of the flock from the heart.

5:4 And when the prince of pastors shall appear, you shall receive a never fading crown of glory.

5:5 In like manner, ye young men, be subject to the ancients. And do you all insinuate humility one to another, for God resisteth the proud, but to the humble he giveth grace.

5:6 Be you humbled therefore under the mighty hand of God, that he may exalt you in the time of visitation:

5:7 Casting all your care upon him, for he hath care of you.

5:8 Be sober and watch: because your adversary the devil, as a roaring lion, goeth about seeking whom he may devour.

5:9 Whom resist ye, strong in faith: knowing that the same affliction befalls your brethren who are in the world.

5:10 But the God of all grace, who hath called us unto his eternal glory in Christ Jesus, after you have suffered a little, will himself perfect you, and confirm you, and establish you.

5:11 To him be glory and empire for ever and ever. Amen.

5:12 By Sylvanus, a faithful brother unto you, as I think, I have written briefly: beseeching and testifying that this is the true grace of God, wherein you stand.

5:13 The church that is in Babylon, elected together with you, saluteth you: and so doth my son Mark.

5:14 Salute one another with a holy kiss. Grace be to all you, who are in Christ Jesus. Amen.

Beati Petri Apostoli Epistula Secunda

THE SECOND EPISTLE OF BLESSED PETER THE APOSTLE

✠

1:1 SIMON PETRUS, SERVUS ET APOSTOLUS JESU CHRISTI, iis qui coæqualem nobiscum sortiti sunt fidem in justitia Dei nostri, et Salvatoris Jesu Christi.

1:2 Gratia vobis, et pax adimpleatur in cognitione Dei, et Christi Jesu Domini nostri :

1:3 Quomodo omnia nobis divinæ virtutis suæ, quæ ad vitam et pietatem donata sunt, per cognitionem ejus, qui vocavit nos propria gloria, et virtute,

1:4 per quem maxima, et pretiosa nobis promissa donavit : ut per hæc efficiamini divinæ consortes naturæ : fugientes ejus, quæ in mundo est, concupiscentiæ corruptionem.

1:5 Vos autem curam omnem subinferentes, ministrate in fide vestra virtutem, in virtute autem scientiam,

1:6 in scientia autem abstinentiam, in abstinentia autem patientiam, in patientia autem pietatem,

1:7 in pietate autem amorem fraternitatis, in amore autem fraternitatis caritatem.

1:8 Hæc enim si vobiscum adsint, et superent, non vacuos nec sine fructu vos constituent in Domini nostri Jesu Christi cognitione.

1:9 Cui enim non præsto sunt hæc, cæcus est, et manu tentans, oblivionem accipiens purgationis veterum suorum delictorum.

1:10 Quapropter fratres, magis satagite ut per bona opera certam vestram vocationem, et electionem faciatis : hæc enim facientes, non peccabitis aliquando.

1:11 Sic enim abundanter ministrabitur vobis introitus in æternum regnum Domini nostri et Salvatoris Jesu Christi.

1:12 Propter quod incipiam vos semper commonere de his : et quidem scientes et confirmatos vos in præsenti veritate.

1:13 Justum autem arbitror quamdiu sum in hoc tabernaculo, suscitare vos in commonitione :

1:14 certus quod velox est depositio tabernaculi

1:1 SIMON PETER, SERVANT AND APOSTLE OF JESUS CHRIST, to them that have obtained equal faith with us in the justice of our God and Saviour Jesus Christ.

1:2 Grace to you and peace be accomplished in the knowledge of God and of Christ Jesus our Lord:

1:3 As all things of his divine power which appertain to life and godliness, are given us, through the knowledge of him who hath called us by his own proper glory and virtue.

1:4 By whom he hath given us most great and precious promises: that by these you may be made partakers of the divine nature: flying the corruption of that concupiscence which is in the world.

1:5 And you, employing all care, minister in your faith, virtue; and in virtue, knowledge;

1:6 And in knowledge, abstinence; and in abstinence, patience; and in patience, godliness;

1:7 And in godliness, love of brotherhood; and in love of brotherhood, charity.

1:8 For if these things be with you and abound, they will make you to be neither empty nor unfruitful in the knowledge of our Lord Jesus Christ.

1:9 For he that hath not these things with him, is blind, and groping, having forgotten that he was purged from his old sins.

1:10 Wherefore, brethren, labour the more, that by good works you may make sure your calling and election. For doing these things, you shall not sin at any time.

1:11 For so an entrance shall be ministered to you abundantly into the everlasting kingdom of our Lord and Saviour Jesus Christ.

1:12 For which cause I will begin to put you always in remembrance of these things: though indeed you know them, and are confirmed in the present truth.

1:13 But I think it meet as long as I am in this tabernacle, to stir you up by putting you in remembrance.

1:14 Being assured that the laying away of this

mei secundum quod et Dominus noster Jesus Christus significavit mihi.

1:15 Dabo autem operam et frequenter habere vos post obitum meum, ut horum memoriam faciatis.

1:16 Non enim doctas fabulas secuti notam fecimus vobis Domini nostri Jesu Christi virtutem et præsentiam : sed speculatores facti illius magnitudinis.

1:17 Accipiens enim a Deo Patre honorem et gloriam, voce delapsa ad eum hujuscemodi a magnifica gloria : Hic est Filius meus dilectus, in quo mihi complacui, ipsum audite.

1:18 Et hanc vocem nos audivimus de cælo allatam, cum essemus cum ipso in monte sancto.

1:19 Et habemus firmiorem propheticum sermonem : cui benefacitis attendentes quasi lucernæ lucenti in caliginoso loco donec dies elucescat, et lucifer oriatur in cordibus vestris :

1:20 hoc primum intelligentes quod omnis prophetia Scripturæ propria interpretatione non fit.

1:21 Non enim voluntate humana allata est aliquando prophetia : sed Spiritu Sancto inspirati, locuti sunt sancti Dei homines.

2:1 Fuerunt vero et pseudoprophetæ in populo, sicut et in vobis erunt magistri mendaces, qui introducent sectas perditionis : et eum qui emit eos, Dominum negant, superducentes sibi celerem perditionem.

2:2 Et multi sequentur eorum luxurias, per quos via veritatis blasphemabitur :

2:3 et in avaritia fictis verbis de vobis negotiabuntur : quibus judicium jam olim non cessat : et perditio eorum non dormitat.

2:4 Si enim Deus angelis peccantibus non pepercit, sed rudentibus inferni detractos in tartarum tradidit cruciandos, in judicium reservari.

2:5 Et originali mundo non pepercit, sed octavum Noë justitiæ præconem custodivit, diluvium mundo impiorum inducens.

2:6 Et civitates Sodomorum et Gomorrhæorum in cinerem redigens, eversione damnavit : exemplum eorum, qui impie acturi sunt, ponens :

2:7 et justum Lot oppressum a nefandorum in-

my tabernacle is at hand, according as our Lord Jesus Christ also hath signified to me.

1:15 And I will endeavour, that you frequently have after my decease, whereby you may keep a memory of these things.

1:16 For we have not by following artificial fables, made known to you the power, and presence of our Lord Jesus Christ; but we were eyewitnesses of his greatness.

1:17 For he received from God the Father, honour and glory: this voice coming down to him from the excellent glory: This is my beloved Son, in whom I am well pleased; hear ye him.

1:18 And this voice we heard brought from heaven, when we were with him in the holy mount.

1:19 And we have the more firm prophetical word: whereunto you do well to attend, as to a light that shineth in a dark place, until the day dawn, and the day star arise in your hearts:

1:20 Understanding this first, that no prophecy of scripture is made by private interpretation.

1:21 For prophecy came not by the will of man at any time: but the holy men of God spoke, inspired by the Holy Ghost.

2:1 But there were also false prophets among the people, even as there shall be among you lying teachers, who shall bring in sects of perdition, and deny the Lord who bought them: bringing upon themselves swift destruction.

2:2 And many shall follow their riotousnesses, through whom the way of truth shall be evil spoken of.

2:3 And through covetousness shall they with feigned words make merchandise of you. Whose judgment now of a long time lingereth not, and their perdition slumbereth not.

2:4 For if God spared not the angels that sinned, but delivered them, drawn down by infernal ropes to the lower hell, unto torments, to be reserved unto judgment:

2:5 And spared not the original world, but preserved Noe, the eighth person, the preacher of justice, bringing in the flood upon the world of the ungodly.

2:6 And reducing the cities of the Sodomites, and of the Gomorrhites, into ashes, condemned them to be overthrown, making them an example to those that should after act wickedly.

2:7 And delivered just Lot, oppressed by the in-

juria, ac luxuriosa conversatione eripuit :

2:8 aspectu enim, et auditu justus erat : habitans apud eos, qui de die in diem animam justam iniquis operibus cruciabant.

2:9 Novit Dominus pios de tentatione eripere : iniquos vero in diem judicii reservare cruciandos.

2:10 Magis autem eos, qui post carnem in concupiscentia immunditiæ ambulant, dominationemque contemnunt, audaces, sibi placentes, sectas non metuunt introducere blasphemantes :

2:11 ubi angeli fortitudine, et virtute cum sint majores, non portant adversum se execrabile judicium.

2:12 Hi vero velut irrationabilia pecora, naturaliter in captionem, et in perniciem in his quæ ignorant blasphemantes in corruptione sua peribunt,

2:13 percipientes mercedem injustitiæ, voluptatem existimantes diei delicias : coinquinationes, et maculæ deliciis affluentes, in conviviis suis luxuriantes vobiscum,

2:14 oculos habentes plenos adulterii, et incessabilis delicti. Pellicientes animas instabiles, cor exercitatum avaritia habentes, maledictionis filii :

2:15 derelinquentes rectam viam erraverunt, secuti viam Balaam ex Bosor, qui mercedem iniquitatis amavit :

2:16 correptionem vero habuit suæ vesaniæ : subjugale mutum animal, hominis voce loquens, prohibuit prophetæ insipientiam.

2:17 Hi sunt fontes sine aqua, et nebulæ turbinibus exagitatæ, quibus caligo tenebrarum reservatur.

2:18 Superba enim vanitatis loquentes, pelliciunt in desideriis carnis luxuriæ eos, qui paululum effugiunt, qui in errore conversantur :

2:19 libertatem illis promittentes, cum ipsi servi sint corruptionem : a quo enim quis superatus est, hujus et servus est.

2:20 Si enim refugientes coinquinationes mundi in cognitione Domini nostri, et Salvatoris Jesu Christi, his rursus implicati superantur : facta sunt eis posteriora deteriora prioribus.

2:21 Melius enim erat illis non cognoscere viam justitiæ, quam post agnitionem, retrorsum converti ab eo, quod illis traditum est, sancto

justice and lewd conversation of the wicked.

2:8 For in sight and hearing he was just: dwelling among them, who from day to day vexed the just soul with unjust works.

2:9 The Lord knoweth how to deliver the godly from temptation, but to reserve the unjust unto the day of judgment to be tormented.

2:10 And especially them who walk after the flesh in the lust of uncleanness, and despise government, audacious, self willed, they fear not to bring in sects, blaspheming.

2:11 Whereas angels who are greater in strength and power, bring not against themselves a railing judgment.

2:12 But these men, as irrational beasts, naturally tending to the snare and to destruction, blaspheming those things which they know not, shall perish in their corruption,

2:13 Receiving the reward of their injustice, counting for a pleasure the delights of a day: stains and spots, sporting themselves to excess, rioting in their feasts with you:

2:14 Having eyes full of adultery and of sin that ceaseth not: alluring unstable souls, having their heart exercised with covetousness, children of malediction:

2:15 Leaving the right way they have gone astray, having followed the way of Balaam of Bosor, who loved the wages of iniquity,

2:16 But had a check of his madness, the dumb beast used to the yoke, which speaking with man's voice, forbade the folly of the prophet.

2:17 These are fountains without water, and clouds tossed with whirlwinds, to whom the mist of darkness is reserved.

2:18 For, speaking proud words of vanity, they allure by the desires of fleshly riotousness, those who for a little while escape, such as converse in error:

2:19 Promising them liberty, whereas they themselves are the slaves of corruption. For by whom a man is overcome, of the same also he is the slave.

2:20 For if, flying from the pollutions of the world, through the knowledge of our Lord and Saviour Jesus Christ, they be again entangled in them and overcome: their latter state is become unto them worse than the former.

2:21 For it had been better for them not to have known the way of justice, than after they have known it, to turn back from that holy com-

mandato.

2:22 Contigit enim eis illud veri proverbii : Canis reversus ad suum vomitum : et, Sus lota in volutabro luti.

3:1 Hanc ecce vobis, carissimi, secundam scribo epistolam, in quibus vestram excito in commonitione sinceram mentem :

3:2 ut memores sitis eorum, quæ prædixi, verborum, a sanctis prophetis et apostolorum vestrorum, præceptorum Domini et Salvatoris.

3:3 Hoc primum scientes, quod venient in novissimis diebus in deceptione illusores, juxta proprias concupiscentias ambulantes,

3:4 dicentes : Ubi est promissio, aut adventus ejus ? ex quo enim patres dormierunt, omnia sic perseverant ab initio creaturæ.

3:5 Latet enim eos hoc volentes, quod cæli erant prius, et terra de aqua, et per aquam consistens Dei verbo :

3:6 per quæ, ille tunc mundus aqua inundatus, periit.

3:7 Cæli autem, qui nunc sunt, et terra eodem verbo repositi sunt, igni reservati in diem judicii, et perditionis impiorum hominum.

3:8 Unum vero hoc non lateat vos, carissimi, quia unus dies apud Dominum sicut mille anni, et mille anni sicut dies unus.

3:9 Non tardat Dominus promissionem suam, sicut quidam existimant : sed patienter agit propter vos, nolens aliquos perire, sed omnes ad pœnitentiam reverti.

3:10 Adveniet autem dies Domini ut fur : in quo cæli magno impetu transient, elementa vero calore solventur, terra autem et quæ in ipsa sunt opera, exurentur.

3:11 Cum igitur hæc omnia dissolvenda sunt, quales oportet vos esse in sanctis conversationibus, et pietatibus,

3:12 exspectantes, et properantes in adventum diei Domini, per quem cæli ardentes solventur, et elementa ignis ardore tabescent ?

3:13 Novos vero cælos, et novam terram secundum promissa ipsius exspectamus, in quibus justitia habitat.

3:14 Propter quod, carissimi, hæc exspectantes,

mandment which was delivered to them.

2:22 For, that of the true proverb has happened to them: The dog is returned to his vomit: and, The sow that was washed, to her wallowing in the mire.

3:1 Behold this second epistle I write to you, my dearly beloved, in which I stir up by way of admonition your sincere mind:

3:2 That you may be mindful of those words which I told you before from the holy prophets, and of your apostles, of the precepts of the Lord and Saviour.

3:3 Knowing this first, that in the last days there shall come deceitful scoffers, walking after their own lusts,

3:4 Saying: Where is his promise or his coming? for since the time that the fathers slept, all things continue as they were from the beginning of the creation.

3:5 For this they are wilfully ignorant of, that the heavens were before, and the earth out of water, and through water, consisting by the word of God.

3:6 Whereby the world that then was, being overflowed with water, perished.

3:7 But the heavens and the earth which are now, by the same word are kept in store, reserved unto fire against the day of judgment and perdition of the ungodly men.

3:8 But of this one thing be not ignorant, my beloved, that one day with the Lord is as a thousand years, and a thousand years as one day.

3:9 The Lord delayeth not his promise, as some imagine, but dealeth patiently for your sake, not willing that any should perish, but that all should return to penance.

3:10 But the day of the Lord shall come as a thief, in which the heavens shall pass away with great violence, and the elements shall be melted with heat, and the earth and the works which are in it, shall be burnt up.

3:11 Seeing then that all these things are to be dissolved, what manner of people ought you to be in holy conversation and godliness?

3:12 Looking for and hasting unto the coming of the day of the Lord, by which the heavens being on fire shall be dissolved, and the elements shall melt with the burning heat?

3:13 But we look for new heavens and a new earth according to his promises, in which justice dwelleth.

3:14 Wherefore, dearly beloved, waiting for

satagite immaculati, et inviolati ei inveniri in pace :

3:15 et Domini nostri longanimitatem, salutem arbitremini : sicut et carissimus frater noster Paulus secundum datam sibi sapientiam scripsit vobis,

3:16 sicut et omnibus epistolis, loquens in eis de his in quibus sunt quædam difficilia intellectu, quæ indocti et instabiles depravant, sicut et ceteras Scripturas, ad suam ipsorum perditionem.

3:17 Vos igitur fratres, præscientes custodite, ne insipientium errore traducti excidatis a propria firmitate :

3:18 crescite vero in gratia, et in cognitione Domini nostri, et Salvatoris Jesu Christi. Ipsi gloria et nunc, et in diem æternitatis. Amen.

these things, be diligent that you may be found before him unspotted and blameless in peace.

3:15 And account the longsuffering of our Lord, salvation; as also our most dear brother Paul, according to the wisdom given him, hath written to you:

3:16 As also in all his epistles, speaking in them of these things; in which are certain things hard to be understood, which the unlearned and unstable wrest, as they do also the other scriptures, to their own destruction.

3:17 You therefore, brethren, knowing these things before, take heed, lest being led aside by the error of the unwise, you fall from your own steadfastness.

3:18 But grow in grace, and in the knowledge of our Lord and Saviour Jesus Christ. To him be glory both now and unto the day of eternity. Amen.

Beati Joannis Apostoli Epistula Prima

THE FIRST EPISTLE OF BLESSED JOHN THE APOSTLE

✠

1:1 QUOD FUIT AB INITIO, quod audivimus, quod vidimus oculis nostris, quod perspeximus, et manus nostræ contrectaverunt de verbo vitæ :

1:2 et vita manifestata est, et vidimus, et testamur, et annuntiamus vobis vitam æternam, quæ erat apud Patrem, et apparuit nobis :

1:3 quod vidimus et audivimus, annuntiamus vobis, ut et vos societatem habeatis nobiscum, et societas nostra sit cum Patre, et cum Filio ejus Jesu Christo.

1:4 Et hæc scribimus vobis ut gaudeatis, et gaudium vestrum sit plenum.

1:5 Et hæc est annuntiatio, quam audivimus ab eo, et annuntiamus vobis : quoniam Deus lux est, et tenebræ in eo non sunt ullæ.

1:6 Si dixerimus quoniam societatem habemus cum eo, et in tenebris ambulamus, mentimur, et veritatem non facimus.

1:7 Si autem in luce ambulamus sicut et ipse est in luce, societatem habemus ad invicem, et sanguis Jesu Christi, Filii ejus, emundat nos ab omni peccato.

1:8 Si dixerimus quoniam peccatum non habemus, ipsi nos seducimus, et veritas in nobis non est.

1:9 Si confiteamur peccata nostra : fidelis est, et justus, ut remittat nobis peccata nostra, et emundet nos ab omni iniquitate.

1:10 Si dixerimus quoniam non peccavimus, mendacem facimus eum, et verbum ejus non est in nobis.

2:1 Filioli mei, hæc scribo vobis, ut non peccetis. Sed et si quis peccaverit, advocatum habemus apud Patrem, Jesum Christum justum :

2:2 et ipse est propitiatio pro peccatis nostris : non pro nostris autem tantum, sed etiam pro totius mundi.

2:3 Et in hoc scimus quoniam cognovimus eum, si mandata ejus observemus.

2:4 Qui dicit se nosse eum, et mandata ejus non custodit, mendax est, et in hoc veritas non est.

1:1 THAT WHICH WAS FROM THE BEGINNING, which we have heard, which we have seen with our eyes, which we have looked upon, and our hands have handled, of the word of life:

1:2 For the life was manifested; and we have seen and do bear witness, and declare unto you the life eternal, which was with the Father, and hath appeared to us:

1:3 That which we have seen and have heard, we declare unto you, that you also may have fellowship with us, and our fellowship may be with the Father, and with his Son Jesus Christ.

1:4 And these things we write to you, that you may rejoice, and your joy may be full.

1:5 And this is the declaration which we have heard from him, and declare unto you: That God is light, and in him there is no darkness.

1:6 If we say that we have fellowship with him, and walk in darkness, we lie, and do not the truth.

1:7 But if we walk in the light, as he also is in the light, we have fellowship one with another, and the blood of Jesus Christ his Son cleanseth us from all sin.

1:8 If we say that we have no sin, we deceive ourselves, and the truth is not in us.

1:9 If we confess our sins, he is faithful and just, to forgive us our sins, and to cleanse us from all iniquity.

1:10 If we say that we have not sinned, we make him a liar, and his word is not in us.

2:1 My little children, these things I write to you, that you may not sin. But if any man sin, we have an advocate with the Father, Jesus Christ the just:

2:2 And he is the propitiation for our sins: and not for ours only, but also for those of the whole world.

2:3 And by this we know that we have known him, if we keep his commandments.

2:4 He who saith that he knoweth him, and keepeth not his commandments, is a liar, and the truth is not in him.

2:5 Qui autem servat verbum ejus, vere in hoc caritas Dei perfecta est : et in hoc scimus quoniam in ipso sumus.

2:6 Qui dicit se in ipso manere, debet, sicut ille ambulavit, et ipse ambulare.

2:7 Carissimi, non mandatum novum scribo vobis, sed mandatum vetus, quod habuistis ab initio. Mandatum vetus est verbum, quod audistis.

2:8 Iterum mandatum novum scribo vobis, quod verum est et in ipso, et in vobis : quia tenebræ transierunt, et verum lumen jam lucet.

2:9 Qui dicit se in luce esse, et fratrem suum odit, in tenebris est usque adhuc.

2:10 Qui diligit fratrem suum, in lumine manet, et scandalum in eo non est.

2:11 Qui autem odit fratrem suum, in tenebris est, et in tenebris ambulat, et nescit quo eat : quia tenebræ obcæcaverunt oculos ejus.

2:12 Scribo vobis, filioli, quoniam remittuntur vobis peccata propter nomen ejus.

2:13 Scribo vobis, patres, quoniam cognovistis eum, qui ab initio est. Scribo vobis, adolescentes, quoniam vicistis malignum.

2:14 Scribo vobis, infantes, quoniam cognovistis patrem. Scribo vobis juvenes, quoniam fortes estis, et verbum Dei manet in vobis, et vicistis malignum.

2:15 Nolite diligere mundum, neque ea quæ in mundo sunt. Si quis diligit mundum, non est caritas Patris in eo :

2:16 quoniam omne quod est in mundo, concupiscentia carnis est, et concupiscentia oculorum, et superbia vitæ : quæ non est ex Patre, sed ex mundo est.

2:17 Et mundus transit, et concupiscentia ejus : qui autem facit voluntatem Dei manet in æternum.

2:18 Filioli, novissima hora est : et sicut audistis quia antichristus venit, et nunc antichristi multi facti sunt ; unde scimus, quia novissima hora est.

2:19 Ex nobis prodierunt, sed non erant ex nobis, nam, si fuissent ex nobis, permansissent utique nobiscum : sed ut manifesti sint quoniam non sunt omnes ex nobis.

2:20 Sed vos unctionem habetis a Sancto, et nos-

2:5 But he that keepeth his word, in him in very deed the charity of God is perfected; and by this we know that we are in him.

2:6 He that saith he abideth in him, ought himself also to walk, even as he walked.

2:7 Dearly beloved, I write not a new commandment to you, but an old commandment which you had from the beginning. The old commandment is the word which you have heard.

2:8 Again a new commandment I write unto you, which thing is true both in him and in you; because the darkness is passed, and the true light now shineth.

2:9 He that saith he is in the light, and hateth his brother, is in darkness even until now.

2:10 He that loveth his brother, abideth in the light, and there is no scandal in him.

2:11 But he that hateth his brother, is in darkness, and walketh in darkness, and knoweth not whither he goeth; because the darkness hath blinded his eyes.

2:12 I write unto you, little children, because your sins are forgiven you for his name's sake.

2:13 I write unto you, fathers, because you have known him, who is from the beginning. I write unto you, young men, because you have overcome the wicked one.

2:14 I write unto you, babes, because you have known the Father. I write unto you, young men, because you are strong, and the word of God abideth in you, and you have overcome the wicked one.

2:15 Love not the world, nor the things which are in the world. If any man love the world, the charity of the Father is not in him.

2:16 For all that is in the world, is the concupiscence of the flesh, and the concupiscence of the eyes, and the pride of life, which is not of the Father, but is of the world.

2:17 And the world passeth away, and the concupiscence thereof: but he that doth the will of God, abideth for ever.

2:18 Little children, it is the last hour; and as you have heard that Antichrist cometh, even now there are become many Antichrists: whereby we know that it is the last hour.

2:19 They went out from us, but they were not of us. For if they had been of us, they would no doubt have remained with us; but that they may be manifest, that they are not all of us.

2:20 But you have the unction from the Holy

tis omnia.

2:21 Non scripsi vobis quasi ignorantibus veritatem, sed quasi scientibus eam : et quoniam
omne mendacium ex veritate non est.

2:22 Quis est mendax, nisi is qui negat quoniam
Jesus est Christus ? Hic est antichristus, qui
negat Patrem, et Filium.

2:23 Omnis qui negat Filium, nec Patrem habet :
qui confitetur Filium, et Patrem habet.

2:24 Vos quod audistis ab initio, in vobis permaneat : si in vobis permanserit quod audistis
ab initio, et vos in Filio et Patre manebitis.

2:25 Et hæc est repromissio, quam ipse pollicitus
est nobis, vitam æternam.

2:26 Hæc scripsi vobis de his, qui seducant vos.

2:27 Et vos unctionem, quam accepistis ab eo,
maneat in vobis. Et non necesse habetis ut aliquis doceat vos : sed sicut unctio ejus docet vos
de omnibus, et verum est, et non est mendacium. Et sicut docuit vos : manete in eo.

2:28 Et nunc, filioli, manete in eo : ut cum apparuerit, habeamus fiduciam, et non confunda-
mur ab eo in adventu ejus.

2:29 Si scitis quoniam justus est, scitote quoniam
et omnis, qui facit justitiam, ex ipso natus est.

3:1 Videte qualem caritatem dedit nobis Pater,
ut filii Dei nominemur et simus. Propter hoc
mundus non novit nos : quia non novit eum.

3:2 Carissimi, nunc filii Dei sumus : et nondum
apparuit quid erimus. Scimus quoniam cum
apparuerit, similes ei erimus : quoniam videbimus eum sicuti est.

3:3 Et omnis qui habet hanc spem in eo, sanctificat se, sicut et ille sanctus est.

3:4 Omnis qui facit peccatum, et iniquitatem
facit : et peccatum est iniquitas.

3:5 Et scitis quia ille apparuit ut peccata nostra
tolleret : et peccatum in eo non est.

3:6 Omnis qui in eo manet, non peccat : et omnis qui peccat, non vidit eum, nec cognovit
eum.

3:7 Filioli, nemo vos seducat. Qui facit justitiam,
justus est, sicut et ille justus est.

One, and know all things.

2:21 I have not written to you as to them that
know not the truth, but as to them that know
it: and that no lie is of the truth.

2:22 Who is a liar, but he who denieth that Jesus
is the Christ? This is Antichrist, who denieth
the Father, and the Son.

2:23 Whosoever denieth the Son, the same hath
not the Father. He that confesseth the Son, hath
the Father also.

2:24 As for you, let that which you have heard
from the beginning, abide in you. If that abide
in you, which you have heard from the beginning, you also shall abide in the Son, and in the
Father.

2:25 And this is the promise which he hath
promised us, life everlasting.

2:26 These things have I written to you, concerning them that seduce you.

2:27 And as for you, let the unction, which you
have received from him, abide in you. And you
have no need that any man teach you; but as his
unction teacheth you of all things, and is truth,
and is no lie. And as it hath taught you, abide in
him.

2:28 And now, little children, abide in him, that
when he shall appear, we may have confidence,
and not be confounded by him at his coming.

2:29 If you know, that he is just, know ye, that
every one also, who doth justice, is born of
him.

3:1 Behold what manner of charity the Father
hath bestowed upon us, that we should be
called, and should be the sons of God. Therefore the world knoweth not us, because it
knew not him.

3:2 Dearly beloved, we are now the sons of
God; and it hath not yet appeared what we
shall be. We know, that, when he shall appear,
we shall be like to him: because we shall see
him as he is.

3:3 And every one that hath this hope in him,
sanctifieth himself, as he also is holy.

3:4 Whosoever committeth sin commmitteth also iniquity; and sin is iniquity.

3:5 And you know that he appeared to take away
our sins, and in him there is no sin.

3:6 Whosoever abideth in him, sinneth not; and
whosoever sinneth, hath not seen him, nor
known him.

3:7 Little children, let no man deceive you. He
that doth justice is just, even as he is just.

3:8 Qui facit peccatum, ex diabolo est : quoniam ab initio diabolus peccat. In hoc apparuit Filius Dei, ut dissolvat opera diaboli.

3:9 Omnis qui natus est ex Deo, peccatum non facit : quoniam semen ipsius in eo manet, et non potest peccare, quoniam ex Deo natus est.

3:10 In hoc manifesti sunt filii Dei, et filii diaboli. Omnis qui non est justus, non est ex Deo, et qui non diligit fratrem suum :

3:11 quoniam hæc est annuntiatio, quam audistis ab initio, ut diligatis alterutrum.

3:12 Non sicut Cain, qui ex maligno erat, et occidit fratrem suum. Et propter quid occidit eum ? Quoniam opera ejus maligna erant : fratris autem ejus, justa.

3:13 Nolite mirari, fratres, si odit vos mundus.

3:14 Nos scimus quoniam translati sumus de morte ad vitam, quoniam diligimus fratres. Qui non diligit, manet in morte :

3:15 omnis qui odit fratrem suum, homicida est. Et scitis quoniam omnis homicida non habet vitam æternam in semetipso manentem.

3:16 In hoc cognovimus caritatem Dei, quoniam ille animam suam pro nobis posuit : et nos debemus pro fratribus animas ponere.

3:17 Qui habuerit substantiam hujus mundi, et viderit fratrem suum necessitatem habere, et clauserit viscera sua ab eo : quomodo caritas Dei manet in eo ?

3:18 Filioli mei, non diligamus verbo neque lingua, sed opere et veritate :

3:19 in hoc cognoscimus quoniam ex veritate sumus : et in conspectu ejus suadebimus corda nostra.

3:20 Quoniam si reprehenderit nos cor nostrum : major est Deus corde nostro, et novit omnia.

3:21 Carissimi, si cor nostrum non reprehenderit nos, fiduciam habemus ad Deum :

3:22 et quidquid petierimus, accipiemus ab eo : quoniam mandata ejus custodimus, et ea, quæ sunt placita coram eo, facimus.

3:23 Et hoc est mandatum ejus : ut credamus in nomine Filii ejus Jesu Christi : et diligamus alterutrum, sicut dedit mandatum nobis.

3:8 He that commmitteth sin is of the devil: for the devil sinneth from the beginning. For this purpose, the Son of God appeared, that he might destroy the works of the devil.

3:9 Whosoever is born of God, commmitteth not sin: for his seed abideth in him, and he can not sin, because he is born of God.

3:10 In this the children of God are manifest, and the children of the devil. Whosoever is not just, is not of God, nor he that loveth not his brother.

3:11 For this is the declaration, which you have heard from the beginning, that you should love one another.

3:12 Not as Cain, who was of the wicked one, and killed his brother. And wherefore did he kill him? Because his own works were wicked: and his brother's just.

3:13 Wonder not, brethren, if the world hate you.

3:14 We know that we have passed from death to life, because we love the brethren. He that loveth not, abideth in death.

3:15 Whosoever hateth his brother is a murderer. And you know that no murderer hath eternal life abiding in himself.

3:16 In this we have known the charity of God, because he hath laid down his life for us: and we ought to lay down our lives for the brethren.

3:17 He that hath the substance of this world, and shall see his brother in need, and shall shut up his bowels from him: how doth the charity of God abide in him?

3:18 My little children, let us not love in word, nor in tongue, but in deed, and in truth.

3:19 In this we know that we are of the truth: and in his sight shall persuade our hearts.

3:20 For if our heart reprehend us, God is greater than our heart, and knoweth all things.

3:21 Dearly beloved, if our heart do not reprehend us, we have confidence towards God:

3:22 And whatsoever we shall ask, we shall receive of him: because we keep his commandments, and do those things which are pleasing in his sight.

3:23 And this is his commandment, that we should believe in the name of his Son Jesus Christ: and love one another, as he hath given commandment unto us.

3:24 Et qui servat mandata ejus, in illo manet, et ipse in eo : et in hoc scimus quoniam manet in nobis, de Spiritu quem dedit nobis.

4:1 Carissimi, nolite omni spiritui credere, sed probate spiritus si ex Deo sint : quoniam multi pseudoprophetæ exierunt in mundum.

4:2 In hoc cognoscitur Spiritus Dei : omnis spiritus qui confitetur Jesum Christum in carne venisse, ex Deo est :

4:3 et omnis spiritus qui solvit Jesum, ex Deo non est, et hic est antichristus, de quo audistis quoniam venit, et nunc jam in mundo est.

4:4 Vos ex Deo estis filioli, et vicistis eum, quoniam major est qui in vobis est, quam qui in mundo.

4:5 Ipsi de mundo sunt : ideo de mundo loquuntur, et mundus eos audit.

4:6 Nos ex Deo sumus. Qui novit Deum, audit nos ; qui non est ex Deo, non audit nos : in hoc cognoscimus Spiritum veritatis, et spiritum erroris.

4:7 Carissimi, diligamus nos invicem : quia caritas ex Deo est. Et omnis qui diligit, ex Deo natus est, et cognoscit Deum.

4:8 Qui non diligit, non novit Deum : quoniam Deus caritas est.

4:9 In hoc apparuit caritas Dei in nobis, quoniam Filium suum unigenitum misit Deus in mundum, ut vivamus per eum.

4:10 In hoc est caritas : non quasi nos dilexerimus Deum, sed quoniam ipse prior dilexit nos, et misit Filium suum propitiationem pro peccatis nostris.

4:11 Carissimi, si sic Deus dilexit nos : et nos debemus alterutrum diligere.

4:12 Deum nemo vidit umquam. Si diligamus invicem, Deus in nobis manet, et caritas ejus in nobis perfecta est.

4:13 In hoc cognoscimus quoniam in eo manemus, et ipse in nobis : quoniam de Spiritu suo dedit nobis.

4:14 Et nos vidimus, et testificamur quoniam Pater misit Filium suum Salvatorem mundi.

4:15 Quisquis confessus fuerit quoniam Jesus est Filius Dei, Deus in eo manet, et ipse in Deo.

4:16 Et nos cognovimus, et credidimus caritati, quam habet Deus in nobis. Deus caritas est : et

3:24 And he that keepeth his commandments, abideth in him, and he in him. And in this we know that he abideth in us, by the Spirit which he hath given us.

4:1 Dearly beloved, believe not every spirit, but try the spirits if they be of God: because many false prophets are gone out into the world.

4:2 By this is the spirit of God known. Every spirit which confesseth that Jesus Christ is come in the flesh, is of God:

4:3 And every spirit that dissolveth Jesus, is not of God: and this is Antichrist, of whom you have heard that he cometh, and he is now already in the world.

4:4 You are of God, little children, and have overcome him. Because greater is he that is in you, than he that is in the world.

4:5 They are of the world: therefore of the world they speak, and the world heareth them.

4:6 We are of God. He that knoweth God, heareth us. He that is not of God, heareth us not. By this we know the spirit of truth, and the spirit of error.

4:7 Dearly beloved, let us love one another, for charity is of God. And every one that loveth, is born of God, and knoweth God.

4:8 He that loveth not, knoweth not God: for God is charity.

4:9 By this hath the charity of God appeared towards us, because God hath sent his only begotten Son into the world, that we may live by him.

4:10 In this is charity: not as though we had loved God, but because he hath first loved us, and sent his Son to be a propitiation for our sins.

4:11 My dearest, if God hath so loved us; we also ought to love one another.

4:12 No man hath seen God at any time. If we love one another, God abideth in us, and his charity is perfected in us.

4:13 In this we know that we abide in him, and he in us: because he hath given us of his spirit.

4:14 And we have seen, and do testify, that the Father hath sent his Son to be the Saviour of the world.

4:15 Whosoever shall confess that Jesus is the Son of God, God abideth in him, and he in God.

4:16 And we have known, and have believed the charity, which God hath to us. God is charity:

qui manet in caritate, in Deo manet, et Deus in eo.

4:17 In hoc perfecta est caritas Dei nobiscum, ut fiduciam habeamus in die judicii : quia sicut ille est, et nos sumus in hoc mundo.

4:18 Timor non est in caritate : sed perfecta caritas foras mittit timorem, quoniam timor pœnam habet : qui autem timet, non est perfectus in caritate.

4:19 Nos ergo diligamus Deum, quoniam Deus prior dilexit nos.

4:20 Si quis dixerit : Quoniam diligo Deum, et fratrem suum oderit, mendax est. Qui enim non diligit fratrem suum quem vidit, Deum, quem non vidit, quomodo potest diligere ?

4:21 Et hoc mandatum habemus a Deo : ut qui diligit Deum, diligat et fratrem suum.

5:1 Omnis qui credit quoniam Jesus est Christus, ex Deo natus est. Et omnis qui diligit eum qui genuit, diligit et eum qui natus est ex eo.

5:2 In hoc cognoscimus quoniam diligamus natos Dei, cum Deum diligamus, et mandata ejus faciamus.

5:3 Hæc est enim caritas Dei, ut mandata ejus custodiamus : et mandata ejus gravia non sunt.

5:4 Quoniam omne quod natum est ex Deo, vincit mundum : et hæc est victoria, quæ vincit mundum, fides nostra.

5:5 Quis est, qui vincit mundum, nisi qui credit quoniam Jesus est Filius Dei ?

5:6 Hic est, qui venit per aquam et sanguinem, Jesus Christus : non in aqua solum, sed in aqua et sanguine. Et Spiritus est, qui testificatur quoniam Christus est veritas.

5:7 Quoniam tres sunt, qui testimonium dant in cælo : Pater, Verbum, et Spiritus Sanctus : et hi tres unum sunt.

5:8 Et tres sunt, qui testimonium dant in terra : spiritus, et aqua, et sanguis : et hi tres unum sunt.

5:9 Si testimonium hominum accipimus, testimonium Dei majus est : quoniam hoc est testimonium Dei, quod majus est, quoniam testificatus est de Filio suo.

5:10 Qui credit in Filium Dei, habet testimonium Dei in se. Qui non credit Filio, mendacem facit eum : quia non credit in testimonium quod testificatus est Deus de Filio suo.

and he that abideth in charity, abideth in God, and God in him.

4:17 In this is the charity of God perfected with us, that we may have confidence in the day of judgment: because as he is, we also are in this world.

4:18 Fear is not in charity: but perfect charity casteth out fear, because fear hath pain. And he that feareth, is not perfected in charity.

4:19 Let us therefore love God, because God first hath loved us.

4:20 If any man say, I love God, and hateth his brother; he is a liar. For he that loveth not his brother, whom he seeth, how can he love God, whom he seeth not?

4:21 And this commandment we have from God, that he, who loveth God, love also his brother.

5:1 Whosoever believeth that Jesus is the Christ, is born of God. And every one that loveth him who begot, loveth him also who is born of him.

5:2 In this we know that we love the children of God: when we love God, and keep his commandments.

5:3 For this is the charity of God, that we keep his commandments: and his commandments are not heavy.

5:4 For whatsoever is born of God, overcometh the world: and this is the victory which overcometh the world, our faith.

5:5 Who is he that overcometh the world, but he that believeth that Jesus is the Son of God?

5:6 This is he that came by water and blood, Jesus Christ: not by water only, but by water and blood. And it is the Spirit which testifieth, that Christ is the truth.

5:7 And there are three who give testimony in heaven, the Father, the Word, and the Holy Ghost. And these three are one.

5:8 And there are three that give testimony on earth: the spirit, and the water, and the blood: and these three are one.

5:9 If we receive the testimony of men, the testimony of God is greater. For this is the testimony of God, which is greater, because he hath testified of his Son.

5:10 He that believeth in the Son of God, hath the testimony of God in himself. He that believeth not the Son, maketh him a liar: because he believeth not in the testimony which God hath testified of his Son.

5:11 Et hoc est testimonium, quoniam vitam æternam dedit nobis Deus : et hæc vita in Filio ejus est.

5:12 Qui habet Filium, habet vitam : qui non habet Filium, vitam non habet.

5:13 Hæc scribo vobis ut sciatis quoniam vitam habetis æternam, qui creditis in nomine Filii Dei.

5:14 Et hæc est fiducia, quam habemus ad eum : quia quodcumque petierimus, secundum voluntatem ejus, audit nos.

5:15 Et scimus quia audit nos quidquid petierimus : scimus quoniam habemus petitiones quas postulamus ab eo.

5:16 Qui scit fratrem suum peccare peccatum non ad mortem, petat, et dabitur ei vita peccanti non ad mortem. Est peccatum ad mortem : non pro illo dico ut roget quis.

5:17 Omnis iniquitas, peccatum est : et est peccatum ad mortem.

5:18 Scimus quia omnis qui natus est ex Deo, non peccat : sed generatio Dei conservat eum, et malignus non tangit eum.

5:19 Scimus quoniam ex Deo sumus : et mundus totus in maligno positus est.

5:20 Et scimus quoniam Filius Dei venit, et dedit nobis sensum ut cognoscamus verum Deum, et simus in vero Filio ejus. Hic est verus Deus, et vita æterna.

5:21 Filioli, custodite vos a simulacris. Amen.

5:11 And this is the testimony, that God hath given to us eternal life. And this life is in his Son.

5:12 He that hath the Son, hath life. He that hath not the Son, hath not life.

5:13 These things I write to you, that you may know that you have eternal life, you who believe in the name of the Son of God.

5:14 And this is the confidence which we have towards him: That, whatsoever we shall ask according to his will, he heareth us.

5:15 And we know that he heareth us whatsoever we ask: we know that we have the petitions which we request of him.

5:16 He that knoweth his brother to sin a sin which is not to death, let him ask, and life shall be given to him, who sinneth not to death. There is a sin unto death: for that I say not that any man ask.

5:17 All iniquity is sin. And there is a sin unto death.

5:18 We know that whosoever is born of God, sinneth not: but the generation of God preserveth him, and the wicked one toucheth him not.

5:19 We know that we are of God, and the whole world is seated in wickedness.

5:20 And we know that the Son of God is come: and he hath given us understanding that we may know the true God, and may be in his true Son. This is the true God and life eternal.

5:21 Little children, keep yourselves from idols. Amen.

Beati Joannis Apostoli Epistula Secunda

THE SECOND EPISTLE OF BLESSED JOHN THE APOSTLE

✠

1:1 SENIOR ELECTÆ DOMINÆ, et natis ejus, quos ego diligo in veritate, et non ego solus, sed et omnes qui cognoverunt veritatem,

1:2 propter veritatem, quæ permanet in nobis, et nobiscum erit in æternum.

1:3 Sit vobiscum gratia, misericordia, pax a Deo Patre, et a Christo Jesu Filio Patris in veritate, et caritate.

1:4 Gavisus sum valde, quoniam inveni de filiis tuis ambulantes in veritate, sicut mandatum accepimus a Patre.

1:5 Et nunc rogo te domina, non tamquam mandatum novum scribens tibi, sed quod habuimus ab initio, ut diligamus alterutrum.

1:6 Et hæc est caritas, ut ambulemus secundum mandata ejus. Hoc est enim mandatum, ut quemadmodum audistis ab initio, in eo ambuletis.

1:7 Quoniam multi seductores exierunt in mundum, qui non confitentur Jesum Christum venisse in carnem : hic est seductor, et antichristus.

1:8 Videte vosmetipsos, ne perdatis quæ operati estis : sed ut mercedem plenam accipiatis.

1:9 Omnis qui recedit, et non permanet in doctrina Christi, Deum non habet : qui permanet in doctrina, hic et Patrem et Filium habet.

1:10 Si quis venit ad vos, et hanc doctrinam non affert, nolite recipere eum in domum, nec Ave ei dixeritis.

1:11 Qui enim dicit illi Ave, communicat operibus ejus malignis.

1:12 Plura habens vobis scribere, nolui per cartam et atramentum : spero enim me futurum apud vos, et os ad os loqui : ut gaudium vestrum plenum sit.

1:13 Salutant te filii sororis tuæ Electæ.

1:1 THE ANCIENT TO THE LADY ELECT, and her children, whom I love in the truth, and not I only, but also all they that have known the truth,

1:2 For the sake of the truth which dwelleth in us, and shall be with us for ever.

1:3 Grace be with you, mercy, and peace from God the Father, and from Christ Jesus the Son of the Father; in truth and charity.

1:4 I was exceeding glad, that I found of thy children walking in truth, as we have received a commandment from the Father.

1:5 And now I beseech thee, lady, not as writing a new commandment to thee, but that which we have had from the beginning, that we love one another.

1:6 And this is charity, that we walk according to his commandments. For this is the commandment, that, as you have heard from the beginning, you should walk in the same:

1:7 For many seducers are gone out into the world, who confess not that Jesus Christ is come in the flesh: this is a seducer and an antichrist.

1:8 Look to yourselves, that you lose not the things which you have wrought: but that you may receive a full reward.

1:9 Whosoever revolteth, and continueth not in the doctrine of Christ, hath not God. He that continueth in the doctrine, the same hath both the Father and the Son.

1:10 If any man come to you, and bring not this doctrine, receive him not into the house nor say to him, God speed you.

1:11 For he that saith unto him, God speed you, communicateth with his wicked works.

1:12 Having more things to write unto you, I would not by paper and ink: for I hope that I shall be with you, and speak face to face: that your joy may be full.

1:13 The children of thy sister Elect salute thee.

Beati Joannis Apostoli Epistula Tertia

THE THIRD EPISTLE OF BLESSED JOHN THE APOSTLE

✠

1:1 SENIOR GAJO CARISSIMO, quem ego diligo in veritate.

1:2 Carissime, de omnibus orationem facio prospere te ingredi, et valere sicut prospere agit anima tua.

1:3 Gavisus sum valde venientibus fratribus, et testimonium perhibentibus veritati tuæ, sicut tu in veritate ambulas.

1:4 Majorem horum non habeo gratiam, quam ut audiam filios meos in veritate ambulare.

1:5 Carissime, fideliter facis quidquid operaris in fratres, et hoc in peregrinos,

1:6 qui testimonium reddiderunt caritati tuæ in conspectu ecclesiæ : quos, benefaciens, deduces digne Deo.

1:7 Pro nomine enim ejus profecti sunt, nihil accipientes a gentibus.

1:8 Nos ergo debemus suscipere hujusmodi, ut cooperatores simus veritatis.

1:9 Scripsissem forsitan ecclesiæ : sed is qui amat primatum gerere in eis, Diotrephes, non recipit nos :

1:10 propter hoc si venero, commonebo ejus opera, quæ facit, verbis malignis garriens in nos : et quasi non ei ista sufficiant, neque ipse suscipit fratres : et eos qui suscipiunt, prohibet, et de ecclesia ejicit.

1:11 Carissime, noli imitari malum, sed quod bonum est. Qui benefacit, ex Deo est : qui malefacit, non vidit Deum.

1:12 Demetrio testimonium redditur ab omnibus, et ab ipsa veritate, sed et nos testimonium perhibemus : et nosti quoniam testimonium nostrum verum est.

1:13 Multa habui tibi scribere : sed nolui per atramentum et calamum scribere tibi.

1:14 Spero autem protinus te videre, et os ad os loquemur. Pax tibi. Salutant te amici. Saluta amicos nominatim.

1:1 THE ANCIENT TO THE DEARLY BELOVED GAIUS, whom I love in truth.

1:2 Dearly beloved, concerning all things I make it my prayer that thou mayest proceed prosperously, and fare well as thy soul doth prosperously.

1:3 I was exceedingly glad when the brethren came and gave testimony to the truth in thee, even as thou walkest in the truth.

1:4 I have no greater grace than this, to hear that my children walk in truth.

1:5 Dearly beloved, thou dost faithfully whatever thou dost for the brethren, and that for strangers,

1:6 Who have given testimony to thy charity in the sight of the church: whom thou shalt do well to bring forward on their way in a manner worthy of God.

1:7 Because, for his name they went out, taking nothing of the Gentiles.

1:8 We therefore ought to receive such, that we may be fellow helpers of the truth.

1:9 I had written perhaps to the church: but Diotrephes, who loveth to have the pre-eminence among them, doth not receive us.

1:10 For this cause, if I come, I will advertise his works which he doth, with malicious words prating against us. And as if these things were not enough for him, neither doth he himself receive the brethren, and them that do receive them he forbiddeth, and casteth out of the church.

1:11 Dearly beloved, follow not that which is evil, but that which is good. He that doth good, is of God: he that doth evil, hath not seen God.

1:12 To Demetrius testimony is given by all, and by the truth itself, yea and we also give testimony: and thou knowest that our testimony is true.

1:13 I had many things to write unto thee: but I would not by ink and pen write to thee.

1:14 But I hope speedily to see thee, and we will speak mouth to mouth. Peace be to thee. Our friends salute thee. Salute the friends by name.

Beati Judæ Apostoli Epistula Catholica

THE CATHOLIC EPISTLE OF BLESSED JUDE THE APOSTLE

✠

1:1 JUDAS JESU CHRISTI SERVUS, frater autem Jacobi, his qui sunt in Deo Patre dilectis, et Christo Jesu conservatis, et vocatis.

1:2 Misericordia vobis, et pax, et caritas adimpleatur.

1:3 Carissimi, omnem sollicitudinem faciens scribendi vobis de communi vestra salute, necesse habui scribere vobis : deprecans supercertari semel traditæ sanctis fidei.

1:4 Subintroierunt enim quidam homines (qui olim præscripti sunt in hoc judicium) impii, Dei nostri gratiam transferentes in luxuriam, et solum Dominatorem, et Dominum nostrum Jesum Christum negantes.

1:5 Commonere autem vos volo, scientes semel omnia, quoniam Jesus populum de terra Ægypti salvans, secundo eos, qui non crediderunt, perdidit :

1:6 angelos vero, qui non servaverunt suum principatum, sed dereliquerunt suum domicilium, in judicium magni diei, vinculis æternis sub caligine reservavit.

1:7 Sicut Sodoma, et Gomorrha, et finitimæ civitates simili modo exfornicatæ, et abeuntes post carnem alteram, factæ sunt exemplum, ignis æterni pœnam sustinentes.

1:8 Similiter et hi carnem quidem maculant, dominationem autem spernunt, majestatem autem blasphemant.

1:9 Cum Michaël Archangelus cum diabolo disputans altercaretur de Moysi corpore, non est ausus judicium inferre blasphemiæ : sed dixit : Imperet tibi Dominus.

1:10 Hi autem quæcumque quidem ignorant, blasphemant : quæcumque autem naturaliter, tamquam muta animalia, norunt, in his corrumpuntur.

1:11 Væ illis, quia in via Cain abierunt, et errore Balaam mercede effusi sunt, et in contradictione Core perierunt !

1:1 JUDE, THE SERVANT OF JESUS CHRIST, and brother of James: to them that are beloved in God the Father, and preserved in Jesus Christ, and called.

1:2 Mercy unto you, and peace, and charity be fulfilled.

1:3 Dearly beloved, taking all care to write unto you concerning your common salvation, I was under a necessity to write unto you: to beseech you to contend earnestly for the faith once delivered to the saints.

1:4 For certain men are secretly entered in, (who were written of long ago unto this judgment,) ungodly men, turning the grace of our Lord God into riotousness, and denying the only sovereign Ruler, and our Lord Jesus Christ.

1:5 I will therefore admonish you, though ye once knew all things, that Jesus, having saved the people out of the land of Egypt, did afterwards destroy them that believed not:

1:6 And the angels who kept not their principality, but forsook their own habitation, he hath reserved under darkness in everlasting chains, unto the judgment of the great day.

1:7 As Sodom and Gomorrha, and the neighbouring cities, in like manner, having given themselves to fornication, and going after other flesh, were made an example, suffering the punishment of eternal fire.

1:8 In like manner these men also defile the flesh, and despise dominion, and blaspheme majesty.

1:9 When Michael the archangel, disputing with the devil, contended about the body of Moses, he durst not bring against him the judgment of railing speech, but said: The Lord command thee.

1:10 But these men blaspheme whatever things they know not: and what things soever they naturally know, like dumb beasts, in these they are corrupted.

1:11 Woe unto them, for they have gone in the way of Cain: and after the error of Balaam they have for reward poured out themselves, and

1:12 Hi sunt in epulis suis maculæ, convivantes sine timore, semetipsos pascentes, nubes sine aqua, quæ a ventis circumferentur, arbores autumnales, infructuosæ, bis mortuæ, eradicatæ,

1:13 fluctus feri maris, despumantes suas confusiones, sidera errantia : quibus procella tenebrarum servata est in æternum.

1:14 Prophetavit autem et de his septimus ab Adam Enoch, dicens : Ecce venit Dominus in sanctis millibus suis

1:15 facere judicium contra omnes, et arguere omnes impios de omnibus operibus impietatis eorum, quibus impie egerunt, et de omnibus duris, quæ locuti sunt contra Deum peccatores impii.

1:16 Hi sunt murmuratores querulosi, secundum desideria sua ambulantes, et os eorum loquitur superba, mirantes personas quæstus causa.

1:17 Vos autem carissimi, memores estote verborum, quæ prædicta sunt ab apostolis Domini nostri Jesu Christi,

1:18 qui dicebant vobis, quoniam in novissimo tempore venient illusores, secundum desideria sua ambulantes in impietatibus.

1:19 Hi sunt, qui segregant semetipsos, animales, Spiritum non habentes.

1:20 Vos autem carissimi superædificantes vosmetipsos sanctissimæ vestræ fidei, in Spiritu Sancto orantes,

1:21 vosmetipsos in dilectione Dei servate, exspectantes misericordiam Domini nostri Jesu Christi in vitam æternam.

1:22 Et hos quidem arguite judicatos :

1:23 illos vero salvate, de igne rapientes. Aliis autem miseremini in timore : odientes et eam, quæ carnalis est, maculatam tunicam.

1:24 Ei autem qui potens est vos conservare sine peccato et constituere ante conspectum gloriæ suæ immaculatos in exsultatione in adventu Domini nostri Jesu Christi,

1:25 soli Deo Salvatori nostro, per Jesum Christum Dominum nostrum, gloria et magnificentia, imperium et potestas ante omne sæculum, et nunc, et in omnia sæcula sæculorum. Amen.

have perished in the contradiction of Core.

1:12 These are spots in their banquets, feasting together without fear, feeding themselves, clouds without water, which are carried about by winds, trees of the autumn, unfruitful, twice dead, plucked up by the roots,

1:13 Raging waves of the sea, foaming out their own confusion; wandering stars, to whom the storm of darkness is reserved for ever.

1:14 Now of these Enoch also, the seventh from Adam, prophesied, saying: Behold, the Lord cometh with thousands of his saints,

1:15 To execute judgment upon all, and to reprove all the ungodly for all the works of their ungodliness, whereby they have done ungodly, and of all the hard things which ungodly sinners have spoken against God.

1:16 These are murmurers, full of complaints, walking according to their own desires, and their mouth speaketh proud things, admiring persons for gain's sake.

1:17 But you, my dearly beloved, be mindful of the words which have been spoken before by the apostles of our Lord Jesus Christ,

1:18 Who told you, that in the last time there should come mockers, walking according to their own desires in ungodlinesses.

1:19 These are they, who separate themselves, sensual men, having not the Spirit.

1:20 But you, my beloved, building yourselves upon your most holy faith, praying in the Holy Ghost,

1:21 Keep yourselves in the love of God, waiting for the mercy of our Lord Jesus Christ, unto life everlasting.

1:22 And some indeed reprove, being judged:

1:23 But others save, pulling them out of the fire. And on others have mercy, in fear, hating also the spotted garment which is carnal.

1:24 Now to him who is able to preserve you without sin, and to present you spotless before the presence of his glory with exceeding joy, in the coming of our Lord Jesus Christ,

1:25 To the only God our Saviour through Jesus Christ our Lord, be glory and magnificence, empire and power, before all ages, and now, and for all ages of ages. Amen.

Apocalypsis Beati Joannis Apostoli

THE REVELATION TO BLESSED JOHN THE APOSTLE

1:1 APOCALYPSIS JESU CHRISTI, quam dedit illi Deus palam facere servis suis, quæ oportet fieri cito : et significavit, mittens per angelum suum servo suo Joanni,

1:2 qui testimonium perhibuit verbo Dei, et testimonium Jesu Christi, quæcumque vidit.

1:3 Beatus qui legit, et audit verba prophetiæ hujus, et servat ea, quæ in ea scripta sunt : tempus enim prope est.

1:4 Joannes septem ecclesiis, quæ sunt in Asia. Gratia vobis, et pax ab eo, qui est, et qui erat, et qui venturus est : et a septem spiritibus qui in conspectu throni ejus sunt :

1:5 et a Jesu Christo, qui est testis fidelis, primogenitus mortuorum, et princeps regum terræ, qui dilexit nos, et lavit nos a peccatis nostris in sanguine suo,

1:6 et fecit nos regnum, et sacerdotes Deo et Patri suo : ipsi gloria et imperium in sæcula sæculorum. Amen.

1:7 Ecce venit cum nubibus, et videbit eum omnis oculus, et qui eum pupugerunt. Et plangent se super eum omnes tribus terræ. Etiam : amen.

1:8 Ego sum alpha et omega, principium et finis, dicit Dominus Deus : qui est, et qui erat, et qui venturus est, omnipotens.

1:9 Ego Joannes frater vester, et particeps in tribulatione, et regno, et patientia in Christo Jesu : fui in insula, quæ appellatur Patmos, propter verbum Dei, et testimonium Jesu :

1:1 THE REVELATION OF JESUS CHRIST, which God gave unto him, to make known to his servants the things which must shortly come to pass: and signified, sending by his angel to his servant John,

1:2 Who hath given testimony to the word of God, and the testimony of Jesus Christ, what things soever he hath seen.

1:3 Blessed is he, that readeth and heareth the words of this prophecy; and keepeth those things which are written in it; for the time is at hand.

1:4 John to the seven churches which are in Asia. Grace be unto you and peace from him that is, and that was, and that is to come, and from the seven spirits which are before his throne,

1:5 And from Jesus Christ, who is the faithful witness, the first begotten of the dead, and the prince of the kings of the earth, who hath loved us, and washed us from our sins in his own blood,

1:6 And hath made us a kingdom, and priests to God and his Father, to him be glory and empire for ever and ever. Amen.

1:7 Behold, he cometh with the clouds, and every eye shall see him, and they also that pierced him. And all the tribes of the earth shall bewail themselves because of him. Even so. Amen.

1:8 I am Alpha and Omega, the beginning and the end, saith the Lord God, who is, and who was, and who is to come, the Almighty.

1:9 I John, your brother and your partner in tribulation, and in the kingdom, and patience in Christ Jesus, was in the island, which is called Patmos, for the word of God, and for

the testimony of Jesus.

1:10 fui in spiritu in dominica die, et audivi post me vocem magnam tamquam tubæ,

1:10 I was in the spirit on the Lord's day, and heard behind me a great voice, as of a trumpet,

1:11 dicentis : Quod vides, scribe in libro : et mitte septem ecclesiis, quæ sunt in Asia, Epheso, et Smyrnæ, et Pergamo, et Thyatiræ, et Sardis, et Philadelphiæ, et Laodiciæ.

1:11 Saying: What thou seest, write in a book, and send to the seven churches which are in Asia, to Ephesus, and to Smyrna, and to Pergamus, and to Thyatira, and to Sardis, and to Philadelphia, and to Laodicea.

1:12 Et conversus sum ut viderem vocem, quæ loquebatur mecum : et conversus vidi septem candelabra aurea :

1:12 And I turned to see the voice that spoke with me. And being turned, I saw seven golden candlesticks:

1:13 et in medio septem candelabrorum aureorum, similem Filio hominis vestitum podere, et præcinctum ad mamillas zona aurea :

1:13 And in the midst of the seven golden candlesticks, one like to the Son of man, clothed with a garment down to the feet, and girt about the paps with a golden girdle.

1:14 caput autem ejus, et capilli erant candidi tamquam lana alba, et tamquam nix, et oculi ejus tamquam flamma ignis :

1:14 And his head and his hairs were white, as white wool, and as snow, and his eyes were as a flame of fire,

1:15 et pedes ejus similes auricalco, sicut in camino ardenti, et vox illius tamquam vox aquarum multarum :

1:15 And his feet like unto fine brass, as in a burning furnace. And his voice as the sound of many waters.

1:16 et habebat in dextera sua stellas septem : et de ore ejus gladius utraque parte acutus exibat : et facies ejus sicut sol lucet in virtute sua.

1:16 And he had in his right hand seven stars. And from his mouth came out a sharp two edged sword: and his face was as the sun shineth in his power.

1:17 Et cum vidissem eum, cecidi ad pedes ejus tamquam mortuus. Et posuit dexteram suam super me, dicens : Noli timere : ego sum primus, et novissimus,

1:17 And when I had seen him, I fell at his feet as dead. And he laid his right hand upon me, saying: Fear not. I am the First and the Last,

1:18 et vivus, et fui mortuus, et ecce sum vivens in sæcula sæculorum : et habeo claves mortis, et inferni.

1:18 And alive, and was dead, and behold I am living for ever and ever, and have the keys of death and of hell.

1:19 Scribe ergo quæ vidisti, et quæ sunt, et quæ oportet fieri post hæc.

1:19 Write therefore the things which thou hast seen, and which are, and which must be done hereafter.

1:20 Sacramentum septem stellarum, quas vidisti in dextera mea, et septem candelabra aurea : septem stellæ, angeli sunt septem ecclesiarum : et candelabra septem, septem ecclesiæ sunt.

1:20 The mystery of the seven stars, which thou sawest in my right hand, and the seven golden candlesticks. The seven stars are the angels of the seven churches. And the seven candlesticks are the seven churches.

2:1 Angelo Ephesi ecclesiæ scribe : Hæc dicit, qui tenet septem stellas in dextera sua, qui ambulat in medio septem candelabrorum aureorum :

2:1 Unto the angel of the church of Ephesus write: These things saith he, who holdeth the seven stars in his right hand, who walketh in the midst of the seven golden candlesticks:

2:2 Scio opera tua, et laborem, et patientiam tuam, et quia non potes sustinere malos : et tentasti eos, qui se dicunt apostolos esse, et non sunt : et invenisti eos mendaces :

2:2 I know thy works, and thy labour, and thy patience, and how thou canst not bear them that are evil, and thou hast tried them, who say they are apostles, and are not, and hast found them liars:

2:3 et patientiam habes, et sustinuisti propter nomen meum, et non defecisti.

2:3 And thou hast patience, and hast endured for my name, and hast not fainted.

2:4 Sed habeo adversum te, quod caritatem tu-

2:4 But I have somewhat against thee, because

am primam reliquisti.

2:5 Memor esto itaque unde excideris : et age pœnitentiam, et prima opera fac : sin autem, venio tibi, et movebo candelabrum tuum de loco suo, nisi pœnitentiam egeris.

2:6 Sed hoc habes, quia odisti facta Nicolaitarum, quæ et ego odi.

2:7 Qui habet aurem, audiat quid Spiritus dicat ecclesiis : Vincenti dabo edere de ligno vitæ, quod est in paradiso Dei mei.

2:8 Et angelo Smyrnæ ecclesiæ scribe : Hæc dicit primus, et novissimus, qui fuit mortuus, et vivit :

2:9 Scio tribulationem tuam, et paupertatem tuam, sed dives es : et blasphemaris ab his, qui se dicunt Judæos esse, et non sunt, sed sunt synagoga Satanæ.

2:10 Nihil horum timeas quæ passurus es. Ecce missurus est diabolus aliquos ex vobis in carcerem ut tentemini : et habebitis tribulationem diebus decem. Esto fidelis usque ad mortem, et dabo tibi coronam vitæ.

2:11 Qui habet aurem, audiat quid Spiritus dicat ecclesiis : Qui vicerit, non lædetur a morte secunda.

2:12 Et angelo Pergami ecclesiæ scribe : Hæc dicit qui habet rhomphæam utraque parte acutam :

2:13 Scio ubi habitas, ubi sedes est Satanæ : et tenes nomen meum, et non negasti fidem meam. Et in diebus illis Antipas testis meus fidelis, qui occisus est apud vos ubi Satanas habitat.

2:14 Sed habeo adversus te pauca : quia habes illic tenentes doctrinam Balaam, qui docebat Balac mittere scandalum coram filiis Israël, edere, et fornicari :

2:15 ita habes et tu tenentes doctrinam Nicolaitarum.

2:16 Similiter pœnitentiam age : si quominus veniam tibi cito, et pugnabo cum illis in gladio oris mei.

2:17 Qui habet aurem, audiat quid Spiritus dicat ecclesiis : Vincenti dabo manna absconditum, et dabo illi calculum candidum : et in calculo nomen novum scriptum, quod nemo scit, nisi qui accipit.

2:18 Et angelo Thyatiræ ecclesiæ scribe : Hæc

thou hast left thy first charity.

2:5 Be mindful therefore from whence thou art fallen: and do penance, and do the first works. Or else I come to thee, and will move thy candlestick out of its place, except thou do penance.

2:6 But this thou hast, that thou hatest the deeds of the Nicolaites, which I also hate.

2:7 He, that hath an ear, let him hear what the Spirit saith to the churches: To him, that overcometh, I will give to eat of the tree of life, which is in the paradise of my God.

2:8 And to the angel of the church of Smyrna write: These things saith the First and the Last, who was dead, and is alive:

2:9 I know thy tribulation and thy poverty, but thou art rich: and thou art blasphemed by them that say they are Jews and are not, but are the synagogue of Satan.

2:10 Fear none of those things which thou shalt suffer. Behold, the devil will cast some of you into prison that you may be tried: and you shall have tribulation ten days. Be thou faithful until death: and I will give thee the crown of life.

2:11 He, that hath an ear, let him hear what the Spirit saith to the churches: He that shall overcome, shall not be hurt by the second death.

2:12 And to the angel of the church of Pergamus write: These things, saith he, that hath the sharp two edged sword:

2:13 I know where thou dwellest, where the seat of Satan is: and thou holdest fast my name, and hast not denied my faith. Even in those days when Antipas was my faithful witness, who was slain among you, where Satan dwelleth.

2:14 But I have against thee a few things: because thou hast there them that hold the doctrine of Balaam, who taught Balac to cast a stumblingblock before the children of Israel, to eat, and to commit fornication:

2:15 So hast thou also them that hold the doctrine of the Nicolaites.

2:16 In like manner do penance: if not, I will come to thee quickly, and will fight against them with the sword of my mouth.

2:17 He, that hath an ear, let him hear what the Spirit saith to the churches: To him that overcometh, I will give the hidden manna, and will give him a white counter, and in the counter, a new name written, which no man knoweth, but he that receiveth it.

2:18 And to the angel of the church of Thyatira

dicit Filius Dei, qui habet oculos tamquam flammam ignis, et pedes ejus similes auricalco :

2:19 Novi opera tua, et fidem, et caritatem tuam, et ministerium, et patientiam tuam, et opera tua novissima plura prioribus.

2:20 Sed habeo adversus te pauca : quia permittis mulierem Jezabel, quæ se dicit propheten, docere, et seducere servos meos, fornicari, et manducare de idolothytis.

2:21 Et dedi illi tempus ut pœnitentiam ageret : et non vult pœnitere a fornicatione sua.

2:22 Ecce mittam eam in lectum : et qui mœchantur cum ea, in tribulatione maxima erunt, nisi pœnitentiam ab operibus suis egerint.

2:23 Et filios ejus interficiam in morte, et scient omnes ecclesiæ, quia ego sum scrutans renes, et corda : et dabo unicuique vestrum secundum opera sua. Vobis autem dico,

2:24 et ceteris qui Thyatiræ estis : quicumque non habent doctrinam hanc, et qui non cognoverunt altitudines Satanæ, quemadmodum dicunt, non mittam super vos aliud pondus :

2:25 tamen id quod habetis, tenete donec veniam.

2:26 Et qui vicerit, et custodierit usque in finem opera mea, dabo illi potestatem super gentes,

2:27 et reget eas in virga ferrea, et tamquam vas figuli confringentur,

2:28 sicut et ego accepi a Patre meo : et dabo illi stellam matutinam.

2:29 Qui habet aurem, audiat quid Spiritus dicat ecclesiis.

3:1 Et angelo ecclesiæ Sardis scribe : Hæc dicit qui habet septem spiritus Dei, et septem stellas : Scio opera tua, quia nomen habes quod vivas, et mortuus es.

3:2 Esto vigilans, et confirma cetera, quæ moritura erant. Non enim invenio opera tua plena coram Deo meo.

3:3 In mente ergo habe qualiter acceperis, et audieris, et serva, et pœnitentiam age. Si ergo non vigilaveris, veniam ad te tamquam fur et nescies qua hora veniam ad te.

write: These things saith the Son of God, who hath his eyes like to a flame of fire, and his feet like to fine brass.

2:19 I know thy works, and thy faith, and thy charity, and thy ministry, and thy patience, and thy last works which are more than the former.

2:20 But I have against thee a few things: because thou sufferest the woman Jezabel, who calleth herself a prophetess, to teach, and to seduce my servants, to commit fornication, and to eat of things sacrificed to idols.

2:21 And I gave her a time that she might do penance, and she will not repent of her fornication.

2:22 Behold, I will cast her into a bed: and they that commit adultery with her shall be in very great tribulation, except they do penance from their deeds.

2:23 And I will kill her children with death, and all the churches shall know that I am he that searcheth the reins and hearts, and I will give to every one of you according to your works. But to you I say,

2:24 And to the rest who are at Thyatira: Whosoever have not this doctrine, and who have not known the depths of Satan, as they say, I will not put upon you any other burthen.

2:25 Yet that, which you have, hold fast till I come.

2:26 And he that shall overcome, and keep my works unto the end, I will give him power over the nations.

2:27 And he shall rule them with a rod of iron, and as the vessel of a potter they shall be broken,

2:28 As I also have received of my Father: and I will give him the morning star.

2:29 He that hath an ear, let him hear what the Spirit saith to the churches.

3:1 And to the angel of the church of Sardis, write: These things saith he, that hath the seven spirits of God, and the seven stars: I know thy works, that thou hast the name of being alive: and thou art dead.

3:2 Be watchful and strengthen the things that remain, which are ready to die. For I find not thy works full before my God.

3:3 Have in mind therefore in what manner thou hast received and heard: and observe, and do penance. If then thou shalt not watch, I will come to thee as a thief, and thou shalt not

3:4 Sed habes pauca nomina in Sardis qui non inquinaverunt vestimenta sua : et ambulabunt mecum in albis, quia digni sunt.

3:5 Qui vicerit, sic vestietur vestimentis albis, et non delebo nomen ejus de libro vitæ, et confitebor nomen ejus coram Patre meo, et coram angelis ejus.

3:6 Qui habet aurem, audiat quid Spiritus dicat ecclesiis.

3:7 Et angelo Philadelphiæ ecclesiæ scribe : Hæc dicit Sanctus et Verus, qui habet clavem David : qui aperit, et nemo claudit : claudit, et nemo aperit :

3:8 Scio opera tua. Ecce dedi coram te ostium apertum, quod nemo potest claudere : quia modicam habes virtutem, et servasti verbum meum, et non negasti nomen meum.

3:9 Ecce dabo de synagoga Satanæ, qui dicunt se Judæos esse, et non sunt, sed mentiuntur : ecce faciam illos ut veniant, et adorent ante pedes tuos : et scient quia ego dilexi te,

3:10 quoniam servasti verbum patientiæ meæ, et ego servabo te ab hora tentationis, quæ ventura est in orbem universum tentare habitantes in terra.

3:11 Ecce venio cito : tene quod habes, ut nemo accipiat coronam tuam.

3:12 Qui vicerit, faciam illum columnam in templo Dei mei, et foras non egredietur amplius : et scribam super eum nomen Dei mei, et nomen civitatis Dei mei novæ Jerusalem, quæ descendit de cælo a Deo meo, et nomen meum novum.

3:13 Qui habet aurem, audiat quid Spiritus dicat ecclesiis.

3:14 Et angelo Laodiciæ ecclesiæ scribe : Hæc dicit : Amen, testis fidelis et verus, qui est principium creaturæ Dei.

3:15 Scio opera tua : quia neque frigidus es, neque calidus : utinam frigidus esses, aut calidus :

3:16 sed quia tepidus es, et nec frigidus, nec calidus, incipiam te evomere ex ore meo :

know at what hour I will come to thee.

3:4 But thou hast a few names in Sardis, which have not defiled their garments: and they shall walk with me in white, because they are worthy.

3:5 He that shall overcome, shall thus be clothed in white garments, and I will not blot out his name out of the book of life, and I will confess his name before my Father, and before his angels.

3:6 He that hath an ear, let him hear what the Spirit saith to the churches.

3:7 And to the angel of the church of Philadelphia, write: These things saith the Holy One and the true one, he that hath the key of David; he that openeth, and no man shutteth; shutteth, and no man openeth:

3:8 I know thy works. Behold, I have given before thee a door opened, which no man can shut: because thou hast a little strength, and hast kept my word, and hast not denied my name.

3:9 Behold, I will bring of the synagogue of Satan, who say they are Jews, and are not, but do lie. Behold, I will make them to come and adore before thy feet. And they shall know that I have loved thee.

3:10 Because thou hast kept the word of my patience, I will also keep thee from the hour of the temptation, which shall come upon the whole world to try them that dwell upon the earth.

3:11 Behold, I come quickly: hold fast that which thou hast, that no man take thy crown.

3:12 He that shall overcome, I will make him a pillar in the temple of my God; and he shall go out no more; and I will write upon him the name of my God, and the name of the city of my God, the new Jerusalem, which cometh down out of heaven from my God, and my new name.

3:13 He that hath an ear, let him hear what the Spirit saith to the churches.

3:14 And to the angel of the church of Laodicea, write: These things saith the Amen, the faithful and true witness, who is the beginning of the creation of God:

3:15 I know thy works, that thou art neither cold, nor hot. I would thou wert cold, or hot.

3:16 But because thou art lukewarm, and neither cold, nor hot, I will begin to vomit thee out of

3:17 quia dicis : Quod dives sum, et locupletatus, et nullius egeo : et nescis quia tu es miser, et miserabilis, et pauper, et cæcus, et nudus.

3:18 Suadeo tibi emere a me aurum ignitum probatum, ut locuples fias, et vestimentis albis induaris, et non appareat confusio nuditatis tuæ, et collyrio inunge oculos tuos ut videas.

3:19 Ego quos amo, arguo, et castigo. Æmulare ergo, et pœnitentiam age.

3:20 Ecce sto ad ostium, et pulso : si quis audierit vocem meam, et aperuerit mihi januam, intrabo ad illum, et cœnabo cum illo, et ipse mecum.

3:21 Qui vicerit, dabo ei sedere mecum in throno meo : sicut et ego vici, et sedi cum Patre meo in throno ejus.

3:22 Qui habet aurem, audiat quid Spiritus dicat ecclesiis.

4:1 Post hæc vidi : et ecce ostium apertum in cælo, et vox prima, quam audivi tamquam tubæ loquentis mecum, dicens : Ascende huc, et ostendam tibi quæ oportet fieri post hæc.

4:2 Et statim fui in spiritu : et ecce sedes posita erat in cælo, et supra sedem sedens.

4:3 Et qui sedebat similis erat aspectui lapidis jaspidis, et sardinis : et iris erat in circuitu sedis similis visioni smaragdinæ.

4:4 Et in circuitu sedis sedilia viginti quatuor : et super thronos viginti quatuor seniores sedentes, circumamicti vestimentis albis, et in capitibus eorum coronæ aureæ.

4:5 Et de throno procedebant fulgura, et voces, et tonitrua : et septem lampades ardentes ante thronum, qui sunt septem spiritus Dei.

4:6 Et in conspectu sedis tamquam mare vitreum simile crystallo : et in medio sedis, et in circuitu sedis quatuor animalia plena oculis ante et retro.

4:7 Et animal primum simile leoni, et secundum animal simile vitulo, et tertium animal habens faciem quasi hominis, et quartum animal simile aquilæ volanti.

my mouth.

3:17 Because thou sayest: I am rich, and made wealthy, and have need of nothing: and knowest not, that thou art wretched, and miserable, and poor, and blind, and naked.

3:18 I counsel thee to buy of me gold fire tried, that thou mayest be made rich; and mayest be clothed in white garments, and that the shame of thy nakedness may not appear; and anoint thy eyes with eyesalve, that thou mayest see.

3:19 Such as I love, I rebuke and chastise. Be zealous therefore, and do penance.

3:20 Behold, I stand at the gate, and knock. If any man shall hear my voice, and open to me the door, I will come in to him, and will sup with him, and he with me.

3:21 To him that shall overcome, I will give to sit with me in my throne: as I also have overcome, and am set down with my Father in his throne.

3:22 He that hath an ear, let him hear what the Spirit saith to the churches.

4:1 After these things I looked, and behold a door was opened in heaven, and the first voice which I heard, as it were, of a trumpet speaking with me, said: Come up hither, and I will shew thee the things which must be done hereafter.

4:2 And immediately I was in the spirit: and behold there was a throne set in heaven, and upon the throne one sitting.

4:3 And he that sat, was to the sight like the jasper and the sardine stone; and there was a rainbow round about the throne, in sight like unto an emerald.

4:4 And round about the throne were four and twenty seats; and upon the seats, four and twenty ancients sitting, clothed in white garments, and on their heads were crowns of gold.

4:5 And from the throne proceeded lightnings, and voices, and thunders; and there were seven lamps burning before the throne, which are the seven spirits of God.

4:6 And in the sight of the throne was, as it were, a sea of glass like to crystal; and in the midst of the throne, and round about the throne, were four living creatures, full of eyes before and behind.

4:7 And the first living creature was like a lion: and the second living creature like a calf: and the third living creature, having the face, as it were, of a man: and the fourth living creature

4:8 Et quatuor animalia, singula eorum habebant alas senas : et in circuitu, et intus plena sunt oculis : et requiem non habebant die ac nocte, dicentia : Sanctus, Sanctus, Sanctus Dominus Deus omnipotens, qui erat, et qui est, et qui venturus est.

4:9 Et cum darent illa animalia gloriam, et honorem, et benedictionem sedenti super thronum, viventi in sæcula sæculorum,

4:10 procidebant viginti quatuor seniores ante sedentem in throno, et adorabant viventem in sæcula sæculorum, et mittebant coronas suas ante thronum, dicentes :

4:11 Dignus es Domine Deus noster accipere gloriam, et honorem, et virtutem : quia tu creasti omnia, et propter voluntatem tuam erant, et creata sunt.

5:1 Et vidi in dextera sedentis supra thronum, librum scriptum intus et foris, signatum sigillis septem.

5:2 Et vidi angelum fortem, prædicantem voce magna : Quis est dignus aperire librum, et solvere signacula ejus ?

5:3 Et nemo poterat neque in cælo, neque in terra, neque subtus terram aperire librum, neque respicere illum.

5:4 Et ego flebam multum, quoniam nemo dignus inventus est aperire librum, nec videre eum.

5:5 Et unus de senioribus dixit mihi : Ne fleveris : ecce vicit leo de tribu Juda, radix David, aperire librum, et solvere septem signacula ejus.

5:6 Et vidi : et ecce in medio throni et quatuor animalium, et in medio seniorum, Agnum stantem tamquam occisum, habentem cornua septem, et oculos septem : qui sunt septem spiritus Dei, missi in omnem terram.

5:7 Et venit : et accepit de dextera sedentis in throno librum.

5:8 Et cum aperuisset librum, quatuor animalia, et viginti quatuor seniores ceciderunt coram Agno, habentes singuli citharas, et phialas aureas plenas odoramentorum, quæ sunt orationes sanctorum :

5:9 et cantabant canticum novum, dicentes : Dignus es, Domine, accipere librum, et aperire signacula ejus : quoniam occisus es, et redemisti nos Deo in sanguine tuo ex omni tribu, et lingua, et populo, et natione :

was like an eagle flying.

4:8 And the four living creatures had each of them six wings; and round about and within they are full of eyes. And they rested not day and night, saying: Holy, holy, holy, Lord God Almighty, who was, and who is, and who is to come.

4:9 And when those living creatures gave glory, and honour, and benediction to him that sitteth on the throne, who liveth for ever and ever;

4:10 The four and twenty ancients fell down before him that sitteth on the throne, and adored him that liveth for ever and ever, and cast their crowns before the throne, saying:

4:11 Thou art worthy, O Lord our God, to receive glory, and honour, and power: because thou hast created all things; and for thy will they were, and have been created.

5:1 And I saw in the right hand of him that sat on the throne, a book written within and without, sealed with seven seals.

5:2 And I saw a strong angel, proclaiming with a loud voice: Who is worthy to open the book, and to loose the seals thereof?

5:3 And no man was able, neither in heaven, nor on earth, nor under the earth, to open the book, nor to look on it.

5:4 And I wept much, because no man was found worthy to open the book, nor to see it.

5:5 And one of the ancients said to me: Weep not; behold the lion of the tribe of Juda, the root of David, hath prevailed to open the book, and to loose the seven seals thereof.

5:6 And I saw: and behold in the midst of the throne and of the four living creatures, and in the midst of the ancients, a Lamb standing as it were slain, having seven horns and seven eyes: which are the seven Spirits of God, sent forth into all the earth.

5:7 And he came and took the book out of the right hand of him that sat on the throne.

5:8 And when he had opened the book, the four living creatures, and the four and twenty ancients fell down before the Lamb, having every one of them harps, and golden vials full of odours, which are the prayers of saints:

5:9 And they sung a new canticle, saying: Thou art worthy, O Lord, to take the book, and to open the seals thereof; because thou wast slain, and hast redeemed us to God, in thy blood, out of every tribe, and tongue, and people, and na-

5:10 et fecisti nos Deo nostro regnum, et sacerdotes : et regnabimus super terram.

5:11 Et vidi, et audivi vocem angelorum multorum in circuitu throni, et animalium, et seniorum : et erat numerus eorum millia millium,

5:12 dicentium voce magna : Dignus est Agnus, qui occisus est, accipere virtutem, et divinitatem, et sapientiam, et fortitudinem, et honorem, et gloriam, et benedictionem.

5:13 Et omnem creaturam, quæ in cælo est, et super terram, et sub terra, et quæ sunt in mari, et quæ in eo : omnes audivi dicentes : Sedenti in throno, et Agno, benedictio et honor, et gloria, et potestas in sæcula sæculorum.

5:14 Et quatuor animalia dicebant : Amen. Et viginti quatuor seniores ceciderunt in facies suas : et adoraverunt viventem in sæcula sæculorum.

6:1 Et vidi quod aperuisset Agnus unum de septem sigillis, et audivi unum de quatuor animalibus, dicens tamquam vocem tonitrui : Veni, et vide.

6:2 Et vidi : et ecce equus albus, et qui sedebat super illum, habebat arcum, et data est ei corona, et exivit vincens ut vinceret.

6:3 Et cum aperuisset sigillum secundum, audivi secundum animal, dicens : Veni, et vide.

6:4 Et exivit alius equus rufus : et qui sedebat super illum, datum est ei ut sumeret pacem de terra, et ut invicem se interficiant, et datus est ei gladius magnus.

6:5 Et cum aperuisset sigillum tertium, audivi tertium animal, dicens : Veni, et vide. Et ecce equus niger : et qui sedebat super illum, habebat stateram in manu sua.

6:6 Et audivi tamquam vocem in medio quatuor animalium dicentium : Bilibris tritici denario et tres bilibres hordei denario, et vinum, et oleum ne læseris.

6:7 Et cum aperuisset sigillum quartum, audivi vocem quarti animalis dicentis : Veni, et vide.

6:8 Et ecce equus pallidus : et qui sedebat super eum, nomen illi Mors, et infernus sequebatur eum, et data est illi potestas super quatuor

tion.

5:10 And hast made us to our God a kingdom and priests, and we shall reign on the earth.

5:11 And I beheld, and I heard the voice of many angels round about the throne, and the living creatures, and the ancients; and the number of them was thousands of thousands,

5:12 Saying with a loud voice: The Lamb that was slain is worthy to receive power, and divinity, and wisdom, and strength, and honour, and glory, and benediction.

5:13 And every creature, which is in heaven, and on the earth, and under the earth, and such as are in the sea, and all that are in them: I heard all saying: To him that sitteth on the throne, and to the Lamb, benediction, and honour, and glory, and power, for ever and ever.

5:14 And the four living creatures said: Amen. And the four and twenty ancients fell down on their faces, and adored him that liveth for ever and ever.

6:1 And I saw that the Lamb had opened one of the seven seals, and I heard one of the four living creatures, as it were the voice of thunder, saying: Come, and see.

6:2 And I saw: and behold a white horse, and he that sat on him had a bow, and there was a crown given him, and he went forth conquering that he might conquer.

6:3 And when he had opened the second seal, I heard the second living creature, saying: Come, and see.

6:4 And there went out another horse that was red: and to him that sat thereon, it was given that he should take peace from the earth, and that they should kill one another, and a great sword was given to him.

6:5 And when he had opened the third seal, I heard the third living creature saying: Come, and see. And behold a black horse, and he that sat on him had a pair of scales in his hand.

6:6 And I heard as it were a voice in the midst of the four living creatures, saying: Two pounds of wheat for a penny, and thrice two pounds of barley for a penny, and see thou hurt not the wine and the oil.

6:7 And when he had opened the fourth seal, I heard the voice of the fourth living creature, saying: Come, and see.

6:8 And behold a pale horse, and he that sat upon him, his name was Death, and hell followed him. And power was given to him over the four

partes terræ, interficere gladio, fame, et morte, et bestiis terræ.

6:9 Et cum aperuisset sigillum quintum, vidi subtus altare animas interfectorum propter verbum Dei, et propter testimonium, quod habebant :

6:10 et clamabant voce magna, dicentes : Usquequo Domine (sanctus et verus), non judicas, et non vindicas sanguinem nostrum de iis qui habitant in terra ?

6:11 Et datæ sunt illis singulæ stolæ albæ : et dictum est illis ut requiescerent adhuc tempus modicum donec compleantur conservi eorum, et fratres eorum, qui interficiendi sunt sicut et illi.

6:12 Et vidi cum aperuisset sigillum sextum : et ecce terræmotus magnus factus est, et sol factus est niger tamquam saccus cilicinus : et luna tota facta est sicut sanguis :

6:13 et stellæ de cælo ceciderunt super terram, sicut ficus emittit grossos suos cum a vento magno movetur :

6:14 et cælum recessit sicut liber involutus : et omnis mons, et insulæ de locis suis motæ sunt :

6:15 et reges terræ, et principes, et tribuni, et divites, et fortes, et omnis servus, et liber absconderunt se in speluncis, et in petris montium :

6:16 et dicunt montibus, et petris : Cadite super nos, et abscondite nos a facie sedentis super thronum, et ab ira Agni :

6:17 quoniam venit dies magnus iræ ipsorum : et quis poterit stare ?

7:1 Post hæc vidi quatuor angelos stantes super quatuor angulos terræ, tenentes quatuor ventos terræ, ne flarent super terram, neque super mare, neque in ullam arborem.

7:2 Et vidi alterum angelum ascendentem ab ortu solis, habentem signum Dei vivi : et clamavit voce magna quatuor angelis, quibus datum est nocere terræ et mari,

7:3 dicens : Nolite nocere terræ, et mari, neque arboribus, quoadusque signemus servos Dei nostri in frontibus eorum.

7:4 Et audivi numerum signatorum, centum quadraginta quatuor millia signati, ex omni tri-

parts of the earth, to kill with sword, with famine, and with death, and with the beasts of the earth.

6:9 And when he had opened the fifth seal, I saw under the altar the souls of them that were slain for the word of God, and for the testimony which they held.

6:10 And they cried with a loud voice, saying: How long, O Lord (holy and true) dost thou not judge and revenge our blood on them that dwell on the earth?

6:11 And white robes were given to every one of them one; and it was said to them, that they should rest for a little time, till their fellow servants, and their brethren, who are to be slain, even as they, should be filled up.

6:12 And I saw, when he had opened the sixth seal, and behold there was a great earthquake, and the sun became black as sackcloth of hair: and the whole moon became as blood:

6:13 And the stars from heaven fell upon the earth, as the fig tree casteth its green figs when it is shaken by a great wind:

6:14 And the heaven departed as a book folded up: and every mountain, and the islands were moved out of their places.

6:15 And the kings of the earth, and the princes, and tribunes, and the rich, and the strong, and every bondman, and every freeman, hid themselves in the dens and in the rocks of mountains:

6:16 And they say to the mountains and the rocks: Fall upon us, and hide us from the face of him that sitteth upon the throne and from the wrath of the Lamb:

6:17 For the great day of their wrath is come, and who shall be able to stand?

7:1 After these things, I saw four angels standing on the four corners of the earth, holding the four winds of the earth, that they should not blow upon the earth, nor upon the sea, nor on any tree.

7:2 And I saw another angel ascending from the rising of the sun, having the sign of the living God; and he cried with a loud voice to the four angels, to whom it was given to hurt the earth and the sea,

7:3 Saying: Hurt not the earth, nor the sea, nor the trees, till we sign the servants of our God in their foreheads.

7:4 And I heard the number of them that were signed, an hundred forty-four thousand were

bu filiorum Israël.

7:5 Ex tribu Juda duodecim millia signati : ex tribu Ruben duodecim millia signati : ex tribu Gad duodecim millia signati :

7:6 ex tribu Aser duodecim millia signati : ex tribu Nephthali duodecim millia signati : ex tribu Manasse duodecim millia signati :

7:7 ex tribu Simeon duodecim millia signati : ex tribu Levi duodecim millia signati : ex tribu Issachar duodecim millia signati :

7:8 ex tribu Zabulon duodecim millia signati : ex tribu Joseph duodecim millia signati : ex tribu Benjamin duodecim millia signati.

7:9 Post hæc vidi turbam magnam, quam dinumerare nemo poterat, ex omnibus gentibus, et tribubus, et populis, et linguis : stantes ante thronum, et in conspectu Agni, amicti stolis albis, et palmæ in manibus eorum :

7:10 et clamabant voce magna, dicentes : Salus Deo nostro, qui sedet super thronum, et Agno.

7:11 Et omnes angeli stabant in circuitu throni, et seniorum, et quatuor animalium : et ceciderunt in conspectu throni in facies suas, et adoraverunt Deum,

7:12 dicentes : Amen. Benedictio, et claritas, et sapientia, et gratiarum actio, honor, et virtus, et fortitudo Deo nostro in sæcula sæculorum. Amen.

7:13 Et respondit unus de senioribus et dixit mihi : Hi, qui amicti sunt stolis albis, qui sunt ? et unde venerunt ?

7:14 Et dixi illi : Domine mi, tu scis. Et dixit mihi : Hi sunt, qui venerunt de tribulatione magna, et laverunt stolas suas, et dealbaverunt eas in sanguine Agni.

7:15 Ideo sunt ante thronum Dei, et serviunt ei die ac nocte in templo ejus : et qui sedet in throno, habitabit super illos :

7:16 non esurient, neque sitient amplius, nec cadet super illos sol, neque ullus æstus :

7:17 quoniam Agnus, qui in medio throni est, reget illos et deducet eos ad vitæ fontes aquarum, et absterget Deus omnem lacrimam ab oculis eorum.

---

signed, of every tribe of the children of Israel.

7:5 Of the tribe of Juda, were twelve thousand signed: Of the tribe of Ruben, twelve thousand signed: Of the tribe of Gad, twelve thousand signed:

7:6 Of the tribe of Aser, twelve thousand signed: Of the tribe of Nephthali, twelve thousand signed: Of the tribe of Manasses, twelve thousand signed:

7:7 Of the tribe of Simeon, twelve thousand signed: Of the tribe of Levi, twelve thousand signed: Of the tribe of Issachar, twelve thousand signed:

7:8 Of the tribe of Zabulon, twelve thousand signed: Of the tribe of Joseph, twelve thousand signed: Of the tribe of Benjamin, twelve thousand signed.

7:9 After this I saw a great multitude, which no man could number, of all nations, and tribes, and peoples, and tongues, standing before the throne, and in sight of the Lamb, clothed with white robes, and palms in their hands:

7:10 And they cried with a loud voice, saying: Salvation to our God, who sitteth upon the throne, and to the Lamb.

7:11 And all the angels stood round about the throne, and the ancients, and the four living creatures; and they fell down before the throne upon their faces, and adored God,

7:12 Saying: Amen. Benediction, and glory, and wisdom, and thanksgiving, honour, and power, and strength to our God for ever and ever. Amen.

7:13 And one of the ancients answered, and said to me: These that are clothed in white robes, who are they? and whence came they?

7:14 And I said to him: My Lord, thou knowest. And he said to me: These are they who are come out of great tribulation, and have washed their robes, and have made them white in the blood of the Lamb.

7:15 Therefore they are before the throne of God, and they serve him day and night in his temple: and he, that sitteth on the throne, shall dwell over them.

7:16 They shall no more hunger nor thirst, neither shall the sun fall on them, nor any heat.

7:17 For the Lamb, which is in the midst of the throne, shall rule them, and shall lead them to the fountains of the waters of life, and God shall wipe away all tears from their eyes.

8:1 Et cum aperuisset sigillum septimum, factum est silentium in cælo, quasi media hora.

8:2 Et vidi septem angelos stantes in conspectu Dei : et datæ sunt illis septem tubæ.

8:3 Et alius angelus venit, et stetit ante altare habens thuribulum aureum : et data sunt illi incensa multa, ut daret de orationibus sanctorum omnium super altare aureum, quod est ante thronum Dei.
8:4 Et ascendit fumus incensorum de orationibus sanctorum de manu angeli coram Deo.

8:5 Et accepit angelus thuribulum, et implevit illud de igne altaris, et misit in terram : et facta sunt tonitrua, et voces, et fulgura, et terræmotus magnus.
8:6 Et septem angeli, qui habebant septem tubas, præparaverunt se ut tuba canerent.

8:7 Et primus angelus tuba cecinit, et facta est grando, et ignis, mista in sanguine, et missum est in terram, et tertia pars terræ combusta est, et tertia pars arborum concremata est, et omne fœnum viride combustum est.

8:8 Et secundus angelus tuba cecinit : et tamquam mons magnus igne ardens missus est in mare, et facta est tertia pars maris sanguis,

8:9 et mortua est tertia pars creaturæ eorum, quæ habebant animas in mari, et tertia pars navium interiit.
8:10 Et tertius angelus tuba cecinit : et cecidit de cælo stella magna, ardens tamquam facula, et cecidit in tertiam partem fluminum, et in fontes aquarum :
8:11 et nomen stellæ dicitur Absinthium, et facta est tertia pars aquarum in absinthium ; et multi hominum mortui sunt de aquis, quia amaræ factæ sunt.
8:12 Et quartus angelus tuba cecinit : et percussa est tertia pars solis, et tertia pars lunæ, et tertia pars stellarum, ita ut obscuraretur tertia pars eorum, et diei non luceret pars tertia, et noctis similiter.

8:13 Et vidi, et audivi vocem unius aquilæ volantis per medium cæli dicentis voce magna : Væ, væ, væ habitantibus in terra de ceteris vocibus trium angelorum, qui erant tuba cani-

8:1 And when he had opened the seventh seal, there was silence in heaven, as it were for half an hour.

8:2 And I saw seven angels standing in the presence of God; and there were given to them seven trumpets.

8:3 And another angel came, and stood before the altar, having a golden censer; and there was given to him much incense, that he should offer of the prayers of all saints upon the golden altar, which is before the throne of God.
8:4 And the smoke of the incense of the prayers of the saints ascended up before God from the hand of the angel.

8:5 And the angel took the censer, and filled it with the fire of the altar, and cast it on the earth, and there were thunders and voices and lightnings, and a great earthquake.
8:6 And the seven angels, who had the seven trumpets, prepared themselves to sound the trumpet.

8:7 And the first angel sounded the trumpet, and there followed hail and fire, mingled with blood, and it was cast on the earth, and the third part of the earth was burnt up, and the third part of the trees was burnt up, and all green grass was burnt up.

8:8 And the second angel sounded the trumpet: and as it were a great mountain, burning with fire, was cast into the sea, and the third part of the sea became blood:

8:9 And the third part of those creatures died, which had life in the sea, and the third part of the ships was destroyed.
8:10 And the third angel sounded the trumpet, and a great star fell from heaven, burning as it were a torch, and it fell on the third part of the rivers, and upon the fountains of waters:
8:11 And the name of the star is called Wormwood. And the third part of the waters became wormwood; and many men died of the waters, because they were made bitter.
8:12 And the fourth angel sounded the trumpet, and the third part of the sun was smitten, and the third part of the moon, and the third part of the stars, so that the third part of them was darkened, and the day did not shine for a third part of it, and the night in like manner.
8:13 And I beheld, and heard the voice of one eagle flying through the midst of heaven, saying with a loud voice: Woe, woe, woe to the inhabitants of the earth: by reason of the rest of the

turi.

9:1 Et quintus angelus tuba cecinit : et vidi stellam de cælo cecidisse in terram, et data est ei clavis putei abyssi.

9:2 Et aperuit puteum abyssi : et ascendit fumus putei, sicut fumus fornacis magnæ : et obscuratus est sol, et aër de fumo putei :

9:3 et de fumo putei exierunt locustæ in terram, et data est illis potestas, sicut habent potestatem scorpiones terræ :

9:4 et præceptum est illis ne læderent fœnum terræ, neque omne viride, neque omnem arborem : nisi tantum homines, qui non habent signum Dei in frontibus suis :

9:5 et datum est illis ne occiderent eos : sed ut cruciarent mensibus quinque : et cruciatus eorum, ut cruciatus scorpii cum percutit hominem.

9:6 Et in diebus illis quærent homines mortem, et non invenient eam : et desiderabunt mori, et fugiet mors ab eis.

9:7 Et similitudines locustarum, similes equis paratis in prælium : et super capita earum tamquam coronæ similes auro : et facies earum tamquam facies hominum.

9:8 Et habebant capillos sicut capillos mulierum. Et dentes earum, sicut dentes leonum erant :

9:9 et habebant loricas sicut loricas ferreas, et vox alarum earum sicut vox curruum equorum multorum currentium in bellum :

9:10 et habebant caudas similes scorpionum, et aculei erant in caudis earum : et potestas earum nocere hominibus mensibus quinque :

9:11 et habebant super se regem angelum abyssi cui nomen hebraice Abaddon, græce autem Apollyon, latine habens nomen Exterminans.

9:12 Væ unum abiit, et ecce veniunt adhuc duo væ post hæc.

9:13 Et sextus angelus tuba cecinit : et audivi vocem unam ex quatuor cornibus altaris aurei, quod est ante oculos Dei,

9:14 dicentem sexto angelo, qui habebat tubam : Solve quatuor angelos, qui alligati sunt in flumine magno Euphrate.

9:15 Et soluti sunt quatuor angeli, qui parati er-

voices of the three angels, who are yet to sound the trumpet.

9:1 And the fifth angel sounded the trumpet, and I saw a star fall from heaven upon the earth, and there was given to him the key of the bottomless pit.

9:2 And he opened the bottomless pit: and the smoke of the pit arose, as the smoke of a great furnace; and the sun and the air were darkened with the smoke of the pit.

9:3 And from the smoke of the pit there came out locusts upon the earth. And power was given to them, as the scorpions of the earth have power:

9:4 And it was commanded them that they should not hurt the grass of the earth, nor any green thing, nor any tree: but only the men who have not the sign of God on their foreheads.

9:5 And it was given unto them that they should not kill them; but that they should torment them five months: and their torment was as the torment of a scorpion when he striketh a man.

9:6 And in those days men shall seek death, and shall not find it: and they shall desire to die, and death shall fly from them.

9:7 And the shapes of the locusts were like unto horses prepared unto battle: and on their heads were, as it were, crowns like gold: and their faces were as the faces of men.

9:8 And they had hair as the hair of women; and their teeth were as lions:

9:9 And they had breastplates as breastplates of iron, and the noise of their wings was as the noise of chariots and many horses running to battle.

9:10 And they had tails like to scorpions, and there were stings in their tails; and their power was to hurt men five months. And they had over them

9:11 A king, the angel of the bottomless pit; whose name in Hebrew is Abaddon, and in Greek Apollyon; in Latin Exterminans,

9:12 One woe is past, and behold there come yet two woes more hereafter.

9:13 And the sixth angel sounded the trumpet: and I heard a voice from the four horns of the great altar, which is before the eyes of God,

9:14 Saying to the sixth angel, who had the trumpet: Loose the four angels, who are bound in the great river Euphrates.

9:15 And the four angels were loosed, who were

ant in horam, et diem, et mensem, et annum, ut occiderent tertiam partem hominum.

9:16 Et numerus equestris exercitus vicies millies dena millia. Et audivi numerum eorum.

9:17 Et ita vidi equos in visione : et qui sedebant super eos, habebant loricas igneas, et hyacinthinas, et sulphureas, et capita equorum erant tamquam capita leonum : et de ore eorum procedit ignis, et fumus, et sulphur.

9:18 Et ab his tribus plagis occisa est tertia pars hominum de igne, et de fumo, et sulphure, quæ procedebant de ore ipsorum.

9:19 Potestas enim equorum in ore eorum est, et in caudis eorum, nam caudæ eorum similes serpentibus, habentes capita : et in his nocent.

9:20 Et ceteri homines, qui non sunt occisi in his plagis, neque pœnitentiam egerunt de operibus manuum suarum, ut non adorarent dæmonia, et simulacra aurea, et argentea, et ærea, et lapidea, et lignea, quæ neque videre possunt, neque audire, neque ambulare,

9:21 et non egerunt pœnitentiam ab homicidiis suis, neque a veneficiis suis, neque a fornicatione sua, neque a furtis suis.

10:1 Et vidi alium angelum fortem descendentem de cælo amictum nube, et iris in capite ejus, et facies ejus erat ut sol, et pedes ejus tamquam columnæ ignis :

10:2 et habebat in manu sua libellum apertum : et posuit pedem suum dextrum super mare, sinistrum autem super terram :

10:3 et clamavit voce magna, quemadmodum cum leo rugit. Et cum clamasset, locuta sunt septem tonitrua voces suas.

10:4 Et cum locuta fuissent septem tonitrua voces suas, ego scripturus eram : et audivi vocem de cælo dicentem mihi : Signa quæ locuta sunt septem tonitrua : et noli ea scribere.

10:5 Et angelus, quem vidi stantem super mare et super terram, levavit manum suam ad cælum :

10:6 et juravit per viventem in sæcula sæculorum, qui creavit cælum, et ea quæ in eo sunt : et terram, et ea quæ in ea sunt : et mare, et ea quæ in eo sunt : Quia tempus non erit amplius :

10:7 sed in diebus vocis septimi angeli, cum

prepared for an hour, and a day, and a month, and a year: for to kill the third part of men.

9:16 And the number of the army of horsemen was twenty thousand times ten thousand. And I heard the number of them.

9:17 And thus I saw the horses in the vision: and they that sat on them, had breastplates of fire and of hyacinth and of brimstone, and the heads of the horses were as the heads of lions: and from their mouths proceeded fire, and smoke, and brimstone.

9:18 And by these three plagues was slain the third part of men, by the fire and by the smoke and by the brimstone, which issued out of their mouths.

9:19 For the power of the horses is in their mouths, and in their tails. For, their tails are like to serpents, and have heads: and with them they hurt.

9:20 And the rest of the men, who were not slain by these plagues, did not do penance from the works of their hands, that they should not adore devils, and idols of gold, and silver, and brass, and stone, and wood, which neither can see, nor hear, nor walk:

9:21 Neither did they penance from their murders, nor from their sorceries, nor from their fornication, nor from their thefts.

10:1 And I saw another mighty angel come down from heaven, clothed with a cloud, and a rainbow was on his head, and his face was as the sun, and his feet as pillars of fire.

10:2 And he had in his hand a little book open: and he set his right foot upon the sea, and his left foot upon the earth.

10:3 And he cried with a loud voice as when a lion roareth. And when he had cried, seven thunders uttered their voices.

10:4 And when the seven thunders had uttered their voices, I was about to write: and I heard a voice from heaven saying to me: Seal up the things which the seven thunders have spoken; and write them not.

10:5 And the angel, whom I saw standing upon the sea and upon the earth, lifted up his hand to heaven,

10:6 And he swore by him that liveth for ever and ever, who created heaven, and the things which are therein; and the earth, and the things which are in it; and the sea, and the things which are therein: That time shall be no longer.

10:7 But in the days of the voice of the seventh

cœperit tuba canere, consummabitur mysterium Dei sicut evangelizavit per servos suos prophetas.

10:8 Et audivi vocem de cælo iterum loquentem mecum, et dicentem : Vade, et accipe librum apertum de manu angeli stantis super mare, et super terram.

10:9 Et abii ad angelum, dicens ei, ut daret mihi librum. Et dixit mihi : Accipe librum, et devora illum : et faciet amaricari ventrem tuum, sed in ore tuo erit dulce tamquam mel.

10:10 Et accepi librum de manu angeli, et devoravi illum : et erat in ore meo tamquam mel dulce, et cum devorassem eum, amaricatus est venter meus :

10:11 et dixit mihi : Oportet te iterum prophetare gentibus, et populis, et linguis, et regibus multis.

11:1 Et datus est mihi calamus similis virgæ, et dictum est mihi : Surge, et metire templum Dei, et altare, et adorantes in eo :

11:2 atrium autem, quod est foris templum, ejice foras, et ne metiaris illud : quoniam datum est gentibus, et civitatem sanctam calcabunt mensibus quadraginta duobus :

11:3 et dabo duobus testibus meis, et prophetabunt diebus mille ducentis sexaginta, amicti saccis.

11:4 Hi sunt duæ olivæ et duo candelabra in conspectu Domini terræ stantes.

11:5 Et si quis voluerit eos nocere, ignis exiet de ore eorum, et devorabit inimicos eorum : et si quis voluerit eos lædere, sic oportet eum occidi.

11:6 Hi habent potestatem claudendi cælum, ne pluat diebus prophetiæ ipsorum : et potestatem habent super aquas convertendi eas in sanguinem, et percutere terram omni plaga quotiescumque voluerint.

11:7 Et cum finierint testimonium suum, bestia, quæ ascendit de abysso, faciet adversum eos bellum, et vincet illos, et occidet eos.

11:8 Et corpora eorum jacebunt in plateis civitatis magnæ, quæ vocatur spiritualiter Sodoma, et Ægyptus, ubi et Dominus eorum crucifixus est.

11:9 Et videbunt de tribubus, et populis, et lin-

angel, when he shall begin to sound the trumpet, the mystery of God shall be finished, as he hath declared by his servants the prophets.

10:8 And I heard a voice from heaven again speaking to me, and saying: Go, and take the book that is open, from the hand of the angel who standeth upon the sea, and upon the earth.

10:9 And I went to the angel, saying unto him, that he should give me the book. And he said to me: Take the book, and eat it up: and it shall make thy belly bitter, but in thy mouth it shall be sweet as honey.

10:10 And I took the book from the hand of the angel, and ate it up: and it was in my mouth, sweet as honey: and when I had eaten it, my belly was bitter.

10:11 And he said to me: Thou must prophesy again to many nations, and peoples, and tongues, and kings.

11:1 And there was given me a reed like unto a rod: and it was said to me: Arise, and measure the temple of God, and the altar and them that adore therein.

11:2 But the court, which is without the temple, cast out, and measure it not: because it is given unto the Gentiles, and the holy city they shall tread under foot two and forty months:

11:3 And I will give unto my two witnesses, and they shall prophesy a thousand two hundred sixty days, clothed in sackcloth.

11:4 These are the two olive trees, and the two candlesticks, that stand before the Lord of the earth.

11:5 And if any man will hurt them, fire shall come out of their mouths, and shall devour their enemies. And if any man will hurt them, in this manner must he be slain.

11:6 These have power to shut heaven, that it rain not in the days of their prophecy: and they have power over waters to turn them into blood, and to strike the earth with all plagues as often as they will.

11:7 And when they shall have finished their testimony, the beast, that ascendeth out of the abyss, shall make war against them, and shall overcome them, and kill them.

11:8 And their bodies shall lie in the streets of the great city, which is called spiritually, Sodom and Egypt, where their Lord also was crucified.

11:9 And they of the tribes, and peoples, and

guis, et gentibus corpora eorum per tres dies et dimidium : et corpora eorum non sinent poni in monumentis :

11:10 et inhabitantes terram gaudebunt super illos, et jucundabuntur : et munera mittent invicem, quoniam hi duo prophetæ cruciaverunt eos, qui habitabant super terram.

11:11 Et post dies tres et dimidium, spiritus vitæ a Deo intravit in eos. Et steterunt super pedes suos, et timor magnus cecidit super eos qui viderunt eos.

11:12 Et audierunt vocem magnam de cælo, dicentem eis : Ascendite huc. Et ascenderunt in cælum in nube : et viderunt illos inimici eorum.

11:13 Et in illa hora factus est terræmotus magnus, et decima pars civitatis cecidit : et occisa sunt in terræmotu nomina hominum septem millia : et reliqui in timorem sunt missi, et dederunt gloriam Deo cæli.

11:14 Væ secundum abiit : et ecce væ tertium veniet cito.

11:15 Et septimus angelus tuba cecinit : et factæ sunt voces magnæ in cælo dicentes : Factum est regnum hujus mundi, Domini nostri et Christi ejus, et regnabit in sæcula sæculorum. Amen.

11:16 Et viginti quatuor seniores, qui in conspectu Dei sedent in sedibus suis, ceciderunt in facies suas, et adoraverunt Deum, dicentes :

11:17 Gratias agimus tibi, Domine Deus omnipotens, qui es, et qui eras, et qui venturus es : quia accepisti virtutem tuam magnam, et regnasti.

11:18 Et iratæ sunt gentes, et advenit ira tua et tempus mortuorum judicari, et reddere mercedem servis tuis prophetis, et sanctis, et timentibus nomen tuum pusillis et magnis, et exterminandi eos qui corruperunt terram.

11:19 Et apertum est templum Dei in cælo : et visa est arca testamenti ejus in templo ejus, et facta sunt fulgura, et voces, et terræmotus, et grando magna.

12:1 Et signum magnum apparuit in cælo : mulier amicta sole, et luna sub pedibus ejus, et in capite ejus corona stellarum duodecim :

12:2 et in utero habens, clamabat parturiens, et

tongues, and nations, shall see their bodies for three days and a half: and they shall not suffer their bodies to be laid in sepulchres.

11:10 And they that dwell upon the earth shall rejoice over them, and make merry: and shall send gifts one to another, because these two prophets tormented them that dwelt upon the earth.

11:11 And after three days and a half, the spirit of life from God entered into them. And they stood upon their feet, and great fear fell upon them that saw them.

11:12 And they heard a great voice from heaven, saying to them: Come up hither. And they went up to heaven in a cloud: and their enemies saw them.

11:13 And at that hour there was made a great earthquake, and the tenth part of the city fell: and there were slain in the earthquake names of men seven thousand: and the rest were cast into a fear, and gave glory to the God of heaven.

11:14 The second woe is past: and behold the third woe will come quickly.

11:15 And the seventh angel sounded the trumpet: and there were great voices in heaven, saying: The kingdom of this world is become our Lord's and his Christ's, and he shall reign for ever and ever. Amen.

11:16 And the four and twenty ancients, who sit on their seats in the sight of God, fell on their faces and adored God, saying:

11:17 We give thee thanks, O Lord God Almighty, who art, and who wast, and who art to come: because thou hast taken to thee thy great power, and thou hast reigned.

11:18 And the nations were angry, and thy wrath is come, and the time of the dead, that they should be judged, and that thou shouldest render reward to thy servants the prophets and the saints, and to them that fear thy name, little and great, and shouldest destroy them who have corrupted the earth.

11:19 And the temple of God was opened in heaven: and the ark of his testament was seen in his temple, and there were lightnings, and voices, and an earthquake, and great hail.

12:1 And a great sign appeared in heaven: A woman clothed with the sun, and the moon under her feet, and on her head a crown of twelve stars:

12:2 And being with child, she cried travailing in

cruciabatur ut pariat.

12:3 Et visum est aliud signum in cælo : et ecce draco magnus rufus habens capita septem, et cornua decem : et in capitibus ejus diademata septem,

12:4 et cauda ejus trahebat tertiam partem stellarum cæli, et misit eas in terram : et draco stetit ante mulierem, quæ erat paritura, ut cum peperisset, filium ejus devoraret.

12:5 Et peperit filium masculum, qui recturus erat omnes gentes in virga ferrea : et raptus est filius ejus ad Deum, et ad thronum ejus,

12:6 et mulier fugit in solitudinem ubi habebat locum paratum a Deo, ut ibi pascant eam diebus mille ducentis sexaginta.

12:7 Et factum est prælium magnum in cælo : Michaël et angeli ejus præliabantur cum dracone, et draco pugnabat, et angeli ejus :

12:8 et non valuerunt, neque locus inventus est eorum amplius in cælo.

12:9 Et projectus est draco ille magnus, serpens antiquus, qui vocatur diabolus, et Satanas, qui seducit universum orbem : et projectus est in terram, et angeli ejus cum illo missi sunt.

12:10 Et audivi vocem magnam in cælo dicentem : Nunc facta est salus, et virtus, et regnum Dei nostri, et potestas Christi ejus : quia projectus est accusator fratrum nostrorum, qui accusabat illos ante conspectum Dei nostri die ac nocte.

12:11 Et ipsi vicerunt eum propter sanguinem Agni, et propter verbum testimonii sui, et non dilexerunt animas suas usque ad mortem.

12:12 Propterea lætamini cæli, et qui habitatis in eis. Væ terræ, et mari, quia descendit diabolus ad vos habens iram magnam, sciens quod modicum tempus habet.

12:13 Et postquam vidit draco quod projectus esset in terram, persecutus est mulierem, quæ peperit masculum :

12:14 et datæ sunt mulieri alæ duæ aquilæ magnæ ut volaret in desertum in locum suum, ubi alitur per tempus et tempora, et dimidium temporis a facie serpentis.

12:15 Et misit serpens ex ore suo post mulierem, aquam tamquam flumen, ut eam faceret trahi a

birth, and was in pain to be delivered.

12:3 And there was seen another sign in heaven: and behold a great red dragon, having seven heads, and ten horns: and on his head seven diadems:

12:4 And his tail drew the third part of the stars of heaven, and cast them to the earth: and the dragon stood before the woman who was ready to be delivered; that, when she should be delivered, he might devour her son.

12:5 And she brought forth a man child, who was to rule all nations with an iron rod: and her son was taken up to God, and to his throne.

12:6 And the woman fled into the wilderness, where she had a place prepared by God, that there they should feed her a thousand two hundred sixty days.

12:7 And there was a great battle in heaven, Michael and his angels fought with the dragon, and the dragon fought and his angels:

12:8 And they prevailed not, neither was their place found any more in heaven.

12:9 And that great dragon was cast out, that old serpent, who is called the devil and Satan, who seduceth the whole world; and he was cast unto the earth, and his angels were thrown down with him.

12:10 And I heard a loud voice in heaven, saying: Now is come salvation, and strength, and the kingdom of our God, and the power of his Christ: because the accuser of our brethren is cast forth, who accused them before our God day and night.

12:11 And they overcame him by the blood of the Lamb, and by the word of the testimony, and they loved not their lives unto death.

12:12 Therefore rejoice, O heavens, and you that dwell therein. Woe to the earth, and to the sea, because the devil is come down unto you, having great wrath, knowing that he hath but a short time.

12:13 And when the dragon saw that he was cast unto the earth, he persecuted the woman, who brought forth the man child:

12:14 And there were given to the woman two wings of a great eagle, that she might fly into the desert unto her place, where she is nourished for a time and times, and half a time, from the face of the serpent.

12:15 And the serpent cast out of his mouth after the woman, water as it were a river; that he

flumine.

12:16 Et adjuvit terra mulierem, et aperuit terra os suum, et absorbuit flumen, quod misit draco de ore suo.

12:17 Et iratus est draco in mulierem : et abiit facere prælium cum reliquis de semine ejus, qui custodiunt mandata Dei, et habent testimonium Jesu Christi.

12:18 Et stetit supra arenam maris.

13:1 Et vidi de mari bestiam ascendentem habentem capita septem, et cornua decem, et super cornua ejus decem diademata, et super capita ejus nomina blasphemiæ.

13:2 Et bestia, quam vidi, similis erat pardo, et pedes ejus sicut pedes ursi, et os ejus sicut os leonis. Et dedit illi draco virtutem suam, et potestatem magnam.

13:3 Et vidi unum de capitibus suis quasi occisum in mortem : et plaga mortis ejus curata est. Et admirata est universa terra post bestiam.

13:4 Et adoraverunt draconem, qui dedit potestatem bestiæ : et adoraverunt bestiam, dicentes : Quis similis bestiæ ? et quis poterit pugnare cum ea ?

13:5 Et datum est ei os loquens magna et blasphemias : et data est ei potestas facere menses quadraginta duos.

13:6 Et aperuit os suum in blasphemias ad Deum, blasphemare nomen ejus, et tabernaculum ejus, et eos qui in cælo habitant.

13:7 Et est datum illi bellum facere cum sanctis, et vincere eos. Et data est illi potestas in omnem tribum, et populum, et linguam, et gentem,

13:8 et adoraverunt eam omnes, qui inhabitant terram : quorum non sunt scripta nomina in libro vitæ Agni, qui occisus est ab origine mundi.

13:9 Si quis habet aurem, audiat.

13:10 Qui in captivitatem duxerit, in captivitatem vadet : qui in gladio occiderit, oportet eum gladio occidi. Hic est patientia, et fides sanctorum.

13:11 Et vidi aliam bestiam ascendentem de terra, et habebat cornua duo similia Agni, et loquebatur sicut draco.

13:12 Et potestatem prioris bestiæ omnem faciebat in conspectu ejus : et fecit terram, et habitantes in ea, adorare bestiam primam,

might cause her to be carried away by the river.

12:16 And the earth helped the woman, and the earth opened her mouth, and swallowed up the river, which the dragon cast out of his mouth.

12:17 And the dragon was angry against the woman: and went to make war with the rest of her seed, who keep the commandments of God, and have the testimony of Jesus Christ.

12:18 And he stood upon the sand of the sea.

13:1 And I saw a beast coming up out of the sea, having seven heads and ten horns, and upon his horns ten diadems, and upon his heads names of blasphemy.

13:2 And the beast, which I saw, was like to a leopard, and his feet were as the feet of a bear, and his mouth as the mouth of a lion. And the dragon gave him his own strength, and great power.

13:3 And I saw one of his heads as it were slain to death: and his death's wound was healed. And all the earth was in admiration after the beast.

13:4 And they adored the dragon, which gave power to the beast: and they adored the beast, saying: Who is like to the beast? and who shall be able to fight with him?

13:5 And there was given to him a mouth speaking great things, and blasphemies: and power was given to him to do two and forty months.

13:6 And he opened his mouth unto blasphemies against God, to blaspheme his name, and his tabernacle, and them that dwell in heaven.

13:7 And it was given unto him to make war with the saints, and to overcome them. And power was given him over every tribe, and people, and tongue, and nation.

13:8 And all that dwell upon the earth adored him, whose names are not written in the book of life of the Lamb, which was slain from the beginning of the world.

13:9 If any man have an ear, let him hear.

13:10 He that shall lead into captivity, shall go into captivity: he that shall kill by the sword, must be killed by the sword. Here is the patience and the faith of the saints.

13:11 And I saw another beast coming up out of the earth, and he had two horns, like a lamb, and he spoke as a dragon.

13:12 And he executed all the power of the former beast in his sight; and he caused the earth, and them that dwell therein, to adore the first

cujus curata est plaga mortis.

13:13 Et fecit signa magna, ut etiam ignem faceret de cælo descendere in terram in conspectu hominum.

13:14 Et seduxit habitantes in terra propter signa, quæ data sunt illi facere in conspectu bestiæ, dicens habitantibus in terra, ut faciant imaginem bestiæ, quæ habet plagam gladii, et vixit.

13:15 Et datum est illi ut daret spiritum imagini bestiæ, et ut loquatur imago bestiæ : et faciat ut quicumque non adoraverint imaginem bestiæ, occidantur.

13:16 Et faciet omnes pusillos, et magnos, et divites, et pauperes, et liberos, et servos habere caracterem in dextera manu sua, aut in frontibus suis :

13:17 et nequis possit emere, aut vendere, nisi qui habet caracterem, aut nomen bestiæ, aut numerum nominis ejus.

13:18 Hic sapientia est. Qui habet intellectum, computet numerum bestiæ. Numerus enim hominis est : et numerus ejus sexcenti sexaginta sex.

14:1 Et vidi : et ecce Agnus stabat supra montem Sion, et cum eo centum quadraginta quatuor millia, habentes nomen ejus, et nomen Patris ejus scriptum in frontibus suis.

14:2 Et audivi vocem de cælo, tamquam vocem aquarum multarum, et tamquam vocem tonitrui magni : et vocem, quam audivi, sicut citharœdorum citharizantium in citharis suis.

14:3 Et cantabant quasi canticum novum ante sedem, et ante quatuor animalia, et seniores : et nemo poterat dicere canticum, nisi illa centum quadraginta quatuor millia, qui empti sunt de terra.

14:4 Hi sunt, qui cum mulieribus non sunt coinquinati : virgines enim sunt. Hi sequuntur Agnum quocumque ierit. Hi empti sunt ex hominibus primitiæ Deo, et Agno :

14:5 et in ore eorum non est inventum mendacium : sine macula enim sunt ante thronum Dei.

14:6 Et vidi alterum angelum volantem per medium cæli, habentem Evangelium æternum, ut evangelizaret sedentibus super terram, et super omnem gentem, et tribum, et linguam, et populum :

beast, whose wound to death was healed.

13:13 And he did great signs, so that he made also fire to come down from heaven unto the earth in the sight of men.

13:14 And he seduced them that dwell on the earth, for the signs, which were given him to do in the sight of the beast, saying to them that dwell on the earth, that they should make the image of the beast, which had the wound by the sword, and lived.

13:15 And it was given him to give life to the image of the beast, and that the image of the beast should speak; and should cause, that whosoever will not adore the image of the beast, should be slain.

13:16 And he shall make all, both little and great, rich and poor, freemen and bondmen, to have a character in their right hand, or on their foreheads.

13:17 And that no man might buy or sell, but he that hath the character, or the name of the beast, or the number of his name.

13:18 Here is wisdom. He that hath understanding, let him count the number of the beast. For it is the number of a man: and the number of him is six hundred sixty-six.

14:1 And I beheld, and lo a lamb stood upon mount Sion, and with him an hundred forty-four thousand, having his name, and the name of his Father, written on their foreheads.

14:2 And I heard a voice from heaven, as the noise of many waters, and as the voice of great thunder; and the voice which I heard, was as the voice of harpers, harping on their harps.

14:3 And they sung as it were a new canticle, before the throne, and before the four living creatures, and the ancients; and no man could say the canticle, but those hundred forty-four thousand, who were purchased from the earth.

14:4 These are they who were not defiled with women: for they are virgins. These follow the Lamb whithersoever he goeth. These were purchased from among men, the firstfruits to God and to the Lamb:

14:5 And in their mouth there was found no lie; for they are without spot before the throne of God.

14:6 And I saw another angel flying through the midst of heaven, having the eternal gospel, to preach unto them that sit upon the earth, and over every nation, and tribe, and tongue, and people:

14:7 dicens magna voce : Timete Dominum, et date illi honorem, quia venit hora judicii ejus : et adorate eum, qui fecit cælum, et terram, mare, et fontes aquarum.

14:8 Et alius angelus secutus est dicens : Cecidit, cecidit Babylon illa magna : quæ a vino iræ fornicationis suæ potavit omnes gentes.

14:9 Et tertius angelus secutus est illos, dicens voce magna : Si quis adoraverit bestiam, et imaginem ejus, et acceperit caracterem in fronte sua, aut in manu sua :

14:10 et hic bibet de vino iræ Dei, quod mistum est mero in calice iræ ipsius, et cruciabitur igne, et sulphure in conspectu angelorum sanctorum, et ante conspectum Agni :

14:11 et fumus tormentorum eorum ascendet in sæcula sæculorum : nec habent requiem die ac nocte, qui adoraverunt bestiam, et imaginem ejus, et si quis acceperit caracterem nominis ejus.

14:12 Hic patientia sanctorum est, qui custodiunt mandata Dei, et fidem Jesu.

14:13 Et audivi vocem de cælo, dicentem mihi : Scribe : Beati mortui qui in Domino moriuntur. Amodo jam dicit Spiritus, ut requiescant a laboribus suis : opera enim illorum sequuntur illos.

14:14 Et vidi : et ecce nubem candidam, et super nubem sedentem similem Filio hominis, habentem in capite suo coronam auream, et in manu sua falcem acutam.

14:15 Et alius angelus exivit de templo, clamans voce magna ad sedentem super nubem : Mitte falcem tuam, et mete, quia venit hora ut metatur, quoniam aruit messis terræ.

14:16 Et misit qui sedebat super nubem, falcem suam in terram, et demessa est terra.

14:17 Et alius angelus exivit de templo, quod est in cælo, habens et ipse falcem acutam.

14:18 Et alius angelus exivit de altari, qui habebat potestatem supra ignem : et clamavit voce magna ad eum qui habebat falcem acutam, dicens : Mitte falcem tuam acutam, et vindemia botros vineæ terræ : quoniam maturæ sunt uvæ ejus.

14:19 Et misit angelus falcem suam acutam in

14:7 Saying with a loud voice: Fear the Lord, and give him honour, because the hour of his judgment is come; and adore ye him, that made heaven and earth, the sea, and the fountains of waters.

14:8 And another angel followed, saying: That great Babylon is fallen, is fallen; which made all nations to drink of the wine of the wrath of her fornication.

14:9 And the third angel followed them, saying with a loud voice: If any man shall adore the beast and his image, and receive his character in his forehead, or in his hand;

14:10 He also shall drink of the wine of the wrath of God, which is mingled with pure wine in the cup of his wrath, and shall be tormented with fire and brimstone in the sight of the holy angels, and in the sight of the Lamb.

14:11 And the smoke of their torments shall ascend up for ever and ever: neither have they rest day nor night, who have adored the beast, and his image, and whoever receiveth the character of his name.

14:12 Here is the patience of the saints, who keep the commandments of God, and the faith of Jesus.

14:13 And I heard a voice from heaven, saying to me: Write: Blessed are the dead, who die in the Lord. From henceforth now, saith the Spirit, that they may rest from their labours; for their works follow them.

14:14 And I saw, and behold a white cloud; and upon the cloud one sitting like to the Son of man, having on his head a crown of gold, and in his hand a sharp sickle.

14:15 And another angel came out from the temple crying with a loud voice to him that sat upon the cloud: Thrust in thy sickle, and reap, because the hour is come to reap: for the harvest of the earth is ripe.

14:16 And he that sat on the cloud thrust his sickle into the earth, and the earth was reaped.

14:17 And another angel came out of the temple which is in heaven, he also having a sharp sickle.

14:18 And another angel came out from the altar, who had power over fire; and he cried with a loud voice to him that had the sharp sickle, saying: Thrust in thy sharp sickle, and gather the clusters of the vineyard of the earth; because the grapes thereof are ripe.

14:19 And the angel thrust in his sharp sickle into

terram, et vindemiavit vineam terræ, et misit in lacum iræ Dei magnum :

14:20 et calcatus est lacus extra civitatem, et exivit sanguis de lacu usque ad frenos equorum per stadia mille sexcenta.

15:1 Et vidi aliud signum in cælo magnum et mirabile, angelos septem, habentes plagas septem novissimas : quoniam in illis consummata est ira Dei.

15:2 Et vidi tamquam mare vitreum mistum igne, et eos, qui vicerunt bestiam, et imaginem ejus, et numerum nominis ejus, stantes super mare vitreum, habentes citharas Dei :

15:3 et cantantes canticum Moysi servi Dei, et canticum Agni, dicentes : Magna et mirabilia sunt opera tua, Domine Deus omnipotens : justæ et veræ sunt viæ tuæ, Rex sæculorum.

15:4 Quis non timebit te, Domine, et magnificabit nomen tuum ? quia solus pius es : quoniam omnes gentes venient, et adorabunt in conspectu tuo, quoniam judicia tua manifesta sunt.

15:5 Et post hæc vidi : et ecce apertum est templum tabernaculi testimonii in cælo,

15:6 et exierunt septem angeli habentes septem plagas de templo, vestiti lino mundo et candido, et præcincti circa pectora zonis aureis.

15:7 Et unum de quatuor animalibus dedit septem angelis septem phialas aureas, plenas iracundiæ Dei viventis in sæcula sæculorum.

15:8 Et impletum est templum fumo a majestate Dei, et de virtute ejus : et nemo poterat introire in templum, donec consummarentur septem plagæ septem angelorum.

16:1 Et audivi vocem magnam de templo, dicentem septem angelis : Ite, et effundite septem phialas iræ Dei in terram.

16:2 Et abiit primus, et effudit phialam suam in terram, et factum est vulnus sævum et pessimum in homines, qui habebant caracterem bestiæ, et in eos qui adoraverunt imaginem ejus.

16:3 Et secundus angelus effudit phialam suam in mare, et factus est sanguis tamquam mortui : et omnis anima vivens mortua est in mari.

the earth, and gathered the vineyard of the earth, and cast it into the great press of the wrath of God:

14:20 And the press was trodden without the city, and blood came out of the press, up to the horses' bridles, for a thousand and six hundred furlongs.

15:1 And I saw another sign in heaven, great and wonderful: seven angels having the seven last plagues. For in them is filled up the wrath of God.

15:2 And I saw as it were a sea of glass mingled with fire, and them that had overcome the beast, and his image, and the number of his name, standing on the sea of glass, having the harps of God:

15:3 And singing the canticle of Moses, the servant of God, and the canticle of the Lamb, saying: Great and wonderful are thy works, O Lord God Almighty; just and true are thy ways, O King of ages.

15:4 Who shall not fear thee, O Lord, and magnify thy name? For thou only art holy: for all nations shall come, and shall adore in thy sight, because thy judgments are manifest.

15:5 And after these things I looked; and behold, the temple of the tabernacle of the testimony in heaven was opened:

15:6 And the seven angels came out of the temple, having the seven plagues, clothed with clean and white linen, and girt about the breasts with golden girdles.

15:7 And one of the four living creatures gave to the seven angels seven golden vials, full of the wrath of God, who liveth for ever and ever.

15:8 And the temple was filled with smoke from the majesty of God, and from his power; and no man was able to enter into the temple, till the seven plagues of the seven angels were fulfilled.

16:1 And I heard a great voice out of the temple, saying to the seven angels: Go, and pour out the seven vials of the wrath of God upon the earth.

16:2 And the first went, and poured out his vial upon the earth, and there fell a sore and grievous wound upon men, who had the character of the beast; and upon them that adored the image thereof.

16:3 And the second angel poured out his vial upon the sea, and there came blood as it were of a dead man; and every living soul died in the

16:4 Et tertius effudit phialam suam super flumina, et super fontes aquarum, et factus est sanguis.

16:5 Et audivi angelum aquarum dicentem : Justus es, Domine, qui es, et qui eras sanctus, qui hæc judicasti :

16:6 quia sanguinem sanctorum et prophetarum effuderunt, et sanguinem eis dedisti bibere : digni enim sunt.

16:7 Et audivi alterum ab altari dicentem : Etiam Domine Deus omnipotens, vera et justa judicia tua.

16:8 Et quartus angelus effudit phialam suam in solem, et datum est illi æstu affligere homines, et igni :

16:9 et æstuaverunt homines æstu magno, et blasphemaverunt nomen Dei habentis potestatem super has plagas, neque egerunt pœnitentiam ut darent illi gloriam.

16:10 Et quintus angelus effudit phialam suam super sedem bestiæ : et factum est regnum ejus tenebrosum, et commanducaverunt linguas suas præ dolore :

16:11 et blasphemaverunt Deum cæli præ doloribus, et vulneribus suis, et non egerunt pœnitentiam ex operibus suis.

16:12 Et sextus angelus effudit phialam suam in flumen illud magnum Euphraten : et siccavit aquam ejus, ut præpararetur via regibus ab ortu solis.

16:13 Et vidi de ore draconis, et de ore bestiæ, et de ore pseudoprophetæ spiritus tres immundos in modum ranarum.

16:14 Sunt enim spiritus dæmoniorum facientes signa, et procedunt ad reges totius terræ congregare illos in prælium ad diem magnum omnipotentis Dei.

16:15 Ecce venio sicut fur. Beatus qui vigilat, et custodit vestimenta sua, ne nudus ambulet, et videant turpitudinem ejus.

16:16 Et congregabit illos in locum qui vocatur hebraice Armagedon.

16:17 Et septimus angelus effudit phialam suam in aërem, et exivit vox magna de templo a throno, dicens : Factum est.

16:18 Et facta sunt fulgura, et voces, et tonitrua, et terræmotus factus est magnus, qualis numquam fuit ex quo homines fuerunt super ter-

sea.

16:4 And the third poured out his vial upon the rivers and the fountains of waters; and there was made blood.

16:5 And I heard the angel of the waters saying: Thou art just, O Lord, who art, and who wast, the Holy One, because thou hast judged these things:

16:6 For they have shed the blood of saints and prophets, and thou hast given them blood to drink; for they are worthy.

16:7 And I heard another, from the altar, saying: Yea, O Lord God Almighty, true and just are thy judgments.

16:8 And the fourth angel poured out his vial upon the sun, and it was given unto him to afflict men with heat and fire:

16:9 And men were scorched with great heat, and they blasphemed the name of God, who hath power over these plagues, neither did they penance to give him glory.

16:10 And the fifth angel poured out his vial upon the seat of the beast; and his kingdom became dark, and they gnawed their tongues for pain:

16:11 And they blasphemed the God of heaven, because of their pains and wounds, and did not penance for their works.

16:12 And the sixth angel poured out his vial upon that great river Euphrates; and dried up the water thereof, that a way might be prepared for the kings from the rising of the sun.

16:13 And I saw from the mouth of the dragon, and from the mouth of the beast, and from the mouth of the false prophet, three unclean spirits like frogs.

16:14 For they are the spirits of devils working signs, and they go forth unto the kings of the whole earth, to gather them to battle against the great day of the Almighty God.

16:15 Behold, I come as a thief. Blessed is he that watcheth, and keepeth his garments, lest he walk naked, and they see his shame.

16:16 And he shall gather them together into a place, which in Hebrew is called Armagedon.

16:17 And the seventh angel poured out his vial upon the air, and there came a great voice out of the temple from the throne, saying: It is done.

16:18 And there were lightnings, and voices, and thunders, and there was a great earthquake, such an one as never had been since men were

ram : talis terræmotus, sic magnus.

16:19 Et facta est civitas magna in tres partes : et civitates gentium ceciderunt. Et Babylon magna venit in memoriam ante Deum, dare illi calicem vini indignationis iræ ejus.

16:20 Et omnis insula fugit, et montes non sunt inventi.

16:21 Et grando magna sicut talentum descendit de cælo in homines : et blasphemaverunt Deum homines propter plagam grandinis : quoniam magna facta est vehementer.

17:1 Et venit unus de septem angelis, qui habebant septem phialas, et locutus est mecum, dicens : Veni, ostendam tibi damnationem meretricis magnæ, quæ sedet super aquas multas,

17:2 cum qua fornicati sunt reges terræ, et inebriati sunt qui inhabitant terram de vino prostitutionis ejus.

17:3 Et abstulit me in spiritu in desertum. Et vidi mulierem sedentem super bestiam coccineam, plenam nominibus blasphemiæ, habentem capita septem, et cornua decem.

17:4 Et mulier erat circumdata purpura, et coccino, et inaurata auro, et lapide pretioso, et margaritis, habens poculum aureum in manu sua, plenum abominatione, et immunditia fornicationis ejus.

17:5 Et in fronte ejus nomen scriptum : Mysterium : Babylon magna, mater fornicationum, et abominationum terræ.

17:6 Et vidi mulierem ebriam de sanguine sanctorum, et de sanguine martyrum Jesu. Et miratus sum cum vidissem illam admiratione magna.

17:7 Et dixit mihi angelus : Quare miraris ? ego dicam tibi sacramentum mulieris, et bestiæ, quæ portat eam, quæ habet capita septem, et cornua decem.

17:8 Bestia, quam vidisti, fuit, et non est, et ascensura est de abysso, et in interitum ibit : et mirabuntur inhabitantes terram (quorum non sunt scripta nomina in libro vitæ a constitutione mundi) videntes bestiam, quæ erat, et non est.

17:9 Et hic est sensus, qui habet sapientiam. Septem capita, septem montes sunt, super quos mulier sedet, et reges septem sunt.

upon the earth, such an earthquake, so great.

16:19 And the great city was divided into three parts; and the cities of the Gentiles fell. And great Babylon came in remembrance before God, to give her the cup of the wine of the indignation of his wrath.

16:20 And every island fled away, and the mountains were not found.

16:21 And great hail, like a talent, came down from heaven upon men: and men blasphemed God for the plague of the hail: because it was exceeding great.

17:1 And there came one of the seven angels, who had the seven vials, and spoke with me, saying: Come, I will shew thee the condemnation of the great harlot, who sitteth upon many waters,

17:2 With whom the kings of the earth have committed fornication; and they who inhabit the earth, have been made drunk with the whine of her whoredom.

17:3 And he took me away in spirit into the desert. And I saw a woman sitting upon a scarlet coloured beast, full of names of blasphemy, having seven heads and ten horns.

17:4 And the woman was clothed round about with purple and scarlet, and gilt with gold, and precious stones and pearls, having a golden cup in her hand, full of the abomination and filthiness of her fornication.

17:5 And on her forehead a name was written: A mystery; Babylon the great, the mother of the fornications, and the abominations of the earth.

17:6 And I saw the woman drunk with the blood of the saints, and with the blood of the martyrs of Jesus. And I wondered, when I had seen her, with great admiration.

17:7 And the angel said to me: Why dost thou wonder? I will tell thee the mystery of the woman, and of the beast which carrieth her, which hath the seven heads and ten horns.

17:8 The beast, which thou sawest, was, and is not, and shall come up out of the bottomless pit, and go into destruction: and the inhabitants on the earth (whose names are not written in the book of life from the foundation of the world) shall wonder, seeing the beast that was, and is not.

17:9 And here is the understanding that hath wisdom. The seven heads are seven mountains, upon which the woman sitteth, and they are

17:10 Quinque ceciderunt, unus est, et alius nondum venit : et cum venerit, oportet illum breve tempus manere.

17:11 Et bestia, quæ erat, et non est : et ipsa octava est : et de septem est, et in interitum vadit.

17:12 Et decem cornua, quæ vidisti, decem reges sunt : qui regnum nondum acceperunt, sed potestatem tamquam reges una hora accipient post bestiam.

17:13 Hi unum consilium habent, et virtutem, et potestatem suam bestiæ tradent.

17:14 Hi cum Agno pugnabunt, et Agnus vincet illos : quoniam Dominus dominorum est, et Rex regum, et qui cum illo sunt, vocati, electi, et fideles.

17:15 Et dixit mihi : Aquæ, quas vidisti ubi meretrix sedet, populi sunt, et gentes, et linguæ.

17:16 Et decem cornua, quæ vidisti in bestia : hi odient fornicariam, et desolatam facient illam, et nudam, et carnes ejus manducabunt, et ipsam igni concremabunt.

17:17 Deus enim dedit in corda eorum ut faciant quod placitum est illi : ut dent regnum suum bestiæ donec consummentur verba Dei.

17:18 Et mulier, quam vidisti, est civitas magna, quæ habet regnum super reges terræ.

18:1 Et post hæc vidi alium angelum descendentem de cælo, habentem potestatem magnam : et terra illuminata est a gloria ejus.

18:2 Et exclamavit in fortitudine, dicens : Cecidit, cecidit Babylon magna : et facta est habitatio dæmoniorum, et custodia omnis spiritus immundi, et custodia omnis volucris immundæ, et odibilis :

18:3 quia de vino iræ fornicationis ejus biberunt omnes gentes : et reges terræ cum illa fornicati sunt : et mercatores terræ de virtute deliciarum ejus divites facti sunt.

18:4 Et audivi aliam vocem de cælo, dicentem : Exite de illa populus meus : ut ne participes sitis delictorum ejus, et de plagis ejus non accipiatis.

18:5 Quoniam pervenerunt peccata ejus usque ad cælum, et recordatus est Dominus iniquitatum ejus.

18:6 Reddite illi sicut et ipsa reddidit vobis : et

seven kings:

17:10 Five are fallen, one is, and the other is not yet come: and when he is come, he must remain a short time.

17:11 And the beast which was, and is not: the same also is the eighth, and is of the seven, and goeth into destruction.

17:12 And the ten horns which thou sawest, are ten kings, who have not yet received a kingdom, but shall receive power as kings one hour after the beast.

17:13 These have one design: and their strength and power they shall deliver to the beast.

17:14 These shall fight with the Lamb, and the Lamb shall overcome them, because he is Lord of lords, and King of kings, and they that are with him are called, and elect, and faithful.

17:15 And he said to me: The waters which thou sawest, where the harlot sitteth, are peoples, and nations, and tongues.

17:16 And the ten horns which thou sawest in the beast: these shall hate the harlot, and shall make her desolate and naked, and shall eat her flesh, and shall burn her with fire.

17:17 For God hath given into their hearts to do that which pleaseth him: that they give their kingdom to the beast, till the words of God be fulfilled.

17:18 And the woman which thou sawest, is the great city, which hath kingdom over the kings of the earth.

18:1 And after these things, I saw another angel come down from heaven, having great power: and the earth was enlightened with his glory.

18:2 And he cried out with a strong voice, saying: Babylon the great is fallen, is fallen; and is become the habitation of devils, and the hold of every unclean spirit, and the hold of every unclean and hateful bird:

18:3 Because all nations have drunk of the wine of the wrath of her fornication; and the kings of the earth have committed fornication with her; and the merchants of the earth have been made rich by the power of her delicacies.

18:4 And I heard another voice from heaven, saying: Go out from her, my people; that you be not partakers of her sins, and that you receive not of her plagues.

18:5 For her sins have reached unto heaven, and the Lord hath remembered her iniquities.

18:6 Render to her as she also hath rendered to

duplicate duplicia secundum opera ejus : in poculo, quo miscuit, miscete illi duplum.

18:7 Quantum glorificavit se, et in deliciis fuit, tantum date illi tormentum et luctum : quia in corde suo dicit : Sedeo regina : et vidua non sum, et luctum non videbo.

18:8 Ideo in una die venient plagæ ejus, mors, et luctus, et fames, et igne comburetur : quia fortis est Deus, qui judicabit illam.

18:9 Et flebunt, et plangent se super illam reges terræ, qui cum illa fornicati sunt, et in deliciis vixerunt, cum viderint fumum incendii ejus :

18:10 longe stantes propter timorem tormentorum ejus, dicentes : Væ, væ civitas illa magna Babylon, civitas illa fortis : quoniam una hora venit judicium tuum.

18:11 Et negotiatores terræ flebunt, et lugebunt super illam : quoniam merces eorum nemo emet amplius :

18:12 merces auri, et argenti, et lapidis pretiosi, et margaritæ, et byssi, et purpuræ, et serici, et cocci (et omne lignum thyinum, et omnia vasa eboris, et omnia vasa de lapide pretioso, et æramento, et ferro, et marmore,

18:13 et cinnamomum) et odoramentorum, et unguenti, et thuris, et vini, et olei, et similæ, et tritici, et jumentorum, et ovium, et equorum, et rhedarum, et mancipiorum, et animarum hominum.

18:14 Et poma desiderii animæ tuæ discesserunt a te, et omnia pinguia et præclara perierunt a te, et amplius illa jam non invenient.

18:15 Mercatores horum, qui divites facti sunt, ab ea longe stabunt propter timorem tormentorum ejus, flentes, ac lugentes,

18:16 et dicentes : Væ, væ civitas illa magna, quæ amicta erat bysso, et purpura, et cocco, et deaurata erat auro, et lapide pretioso, et margaritis :

18:17 quoniam una hora destitutæ sunt tantæ divitiæ, et omnis gubernator, et omnis qui in lacum navigat, et nautæ, et qui in mari operantur, longe steterunt,

18:18 et clamaverunt videntes locum incendii ejus, dicentes : Quæ similis civitati huic magnæ

you; and double unto her double according to her works: in the cup wherein she hath mingled, mingle ye double unto her.

18:7 As much as she hath glorified herself, and lived in delicacies, so much torment and sorrow give ye to her; because she saith in her heart: I sit a queen, and am no widow; and sorrow I shall not see.

18:8 Therefore shall her plagues come in one day, death, and mourning, and famine, and she shall be burnt with the fire; because God is strong, who shall judge her.

18:9 And the kings of the earth, who have committed fornication, and lived in delicacies with her, shall weep, and bewail themselves over her, when they shall see the smoke of her burning:

18:10 Standing afar off for fear of her torments, saying: Alas! alas! that great city Babylon, that mighty city: for in one hour is thy judgment come.

18:11 And the merchants of the earth shall weep, and mourn over her: for no man shall buy their merchandise any more.

18:12 Merchandise of gold and silver, and precious stones; and of pearls, and fine linen, and purple, and silk, and scarlet, and all thyine wood, and all manner of vessels of ivory, and all manner of vessels of precious stone, and of brass, and of iron, and of marble,

18:13 And cinnamon, and odours, and ointment, and frankincense, and wine, and oil, and fine flour, and wheat, and beasts, and sheep, and horses, and chariots, and slaves, and souls of men.

18:14 And the fruits of the desire of thy soul are departed from thee, and all fat and goodly things are perished from thee, and they shall find them no more at all.

18:15 The merchants of these things, who were made rich, shall stand afar off from her, for fear of her torments, weeping and mourning.

18:16 And saying: Alas! alas! that great city, which was clothed with fine linen, and purple, and scarlet, and was gilt with gold, and precious stones, and pearls.

18:17 For in one hour are so great riches come to nought; and every shipmaster, and all that sail into the lake, and mariners, and as many as work in the sea, stood afar off.

18:18 And cried, seeing the place of her burning, saying: What city is like to this great city?

?

18:19 et miserunt pulverem super capita sua, et clamaverunt flentes, et lugentes, dicentes : Væ, væ civitas illa magna, in qua divites facti sunt omnes, qui habebant naves in mari de pretiis ejus : quoniam una hora desolata est.

18:20 Exsulta super eam cælum, et sancti apostoli, et prophetæ : quoniam judicavit Deus judicium vestrum de illa.

18:21 Et sustulit unus angelus fortis lapidem quasi molarem magnum, et misit in mare, dicens : Hoc impetu mittetur Babylon civitas illa magna, et ultra jam non invenietur.

18:22 Et vox citharœdorum, et musicorum, et tibia canentium, et tuba non audietur in te amplius : et omnis artifex omnis artis non invenietur in te amplius : et vox molæ non audietur in te amplius :

18:23 et lux lucernæ non lucebit in te amplius : et vox sponsi et sponsæ non audietur adhuc in te : quia mercatores tui erant principes terræ, quia in veneficiis tuis erraverunt omnes gentes.

18:24 Et in ea sanguis prophetarum et sanctorum inventus est : et omnium qui interfecti sunt in terra.

19:1 Post hæc audivi quasi vocem turbarum multarum in cælo dicentium : Alleluja : salus, et gloria, et virtus Deo nostro est :

19:2 quia vera et justa judicia sunt ejus, qui judicavit de meretrice magna, quæ corrupit terram in prostitutione sua, et vindicavit sanguinem servorum suorum de manibus ejus.

19:3 Et iterum dixerunt : Alleluja. Et fumus ejus ascendit in sæcula sæculorum.

19:4 Et ceciderunt seniores viginti quatuor, et quatuor animalia, et adoraverunt Deum sedentem super thronum, dicentes : Amen : alleluja.

19:5 Et vox de throno exivit, dicens : Laudem dicite Deo nostro omnes servi ejus : et qui timetis eum pusilli et magni.

19:6 Et audivi quasi vocem turbæ magnæ, et sicut vocem aquarum multarum, et sicut vocem tonitruorum magnorum, dicentium : Alleluja : quoniam regnavit Dominus Deus noster omnipotens.

19:7 Gaudeamus, et exsultemus : et demus glo-

18:19 And they cast dust upon their heads, and cried, weeping and mourning, saying: Alas! alas! that great city, wherein all were made rich, that had ships at sea, by reason of her prices: for in one hour she is made desolate.

18:20 Rejoice over her, thou heaven, and ye holy apostles and prophets; for God hath judged your judgment on her.

18:21 And a mighty angel took up a stone, as it were a great millstone, and cast it into the sea, saying: With such violence as this shall Babylon, that great city, be thrown down, and shall be found no more at all.

18:22 And the voice of harpers, and of musicians, and of them that play on the pipe, and on the trumpet, shall no more be heard at all in thee; and no craftsman of any art whatsoever shall be found any more at all in thee; and the sound of the mill shall be heard no more at all in thee;

18:23 And the light of the lamp shall shine no more at all in thee; and the voice of the bridegroom and the bride shall be heard no more at all in thee: for thy merchants were the great men of the earth, for all nations have been deceived by thy enchantments.

18:24 And in her was found the blood of prophets and of saints, and of all that were slain upon the earth.

19:1 After these things I heard as it were the voice of much people in heaven, saying: Alleluia. Salvation, and glory, and power is to our God.

19:2 For true and just are his judgments, who hath judged the great harlot which corrupted the earth with her fornication, and hath revenged the blood of his servants, at her hands.

19:3 And again they said: Alleluia. And her smoke ascendeth for ever and ever.

19:4 And the four and twenty ancients, and the four living creatures fell down and adored God that sitteth upon the throne, saying: Amen; Alleluia.

19:5 And a voice came out from the throne, saying: Give praise to our God, all ye his servants; and you that fear him, little and great.

19:6 And I heard as it were the voice of a great multitude, and as the voice of many waters, and as the voice of great thunders, saying, Alleluia: for the Lord our God the Almighty hath reigned.

19:7 Let us be glad and rejoice, and give glory to

riam ei : quia venerunt nuptiæ Agni, et uxor ejus præparavit se.

19:8 Et datum est illi ut cooperiat se byssino splendenti et candido. Byssinum enim justificationes sunt sanctorum.

19:9 Et dixit mihi : Scribe : Beati qui ad cœnam nuptiarum Agni vocati sunt ; et dixit mihi : Hæc verba Dei vera sunt.

19:10 Et cecidi ante pedes ejus, ut adorarem eum. Et dicit mihi : Vide ne feceris : conservus tuus sum, et fratrum tuorum habentium testimonium Jesu. Deum adora. Testimonium enim Jesu est spiritus prophetiæ.

19:11 Et vidi cælum apertum, et ecce equus albus, et qui sedebat super eum, vocabatur Fidelis, et Verax, et cum justitia judicat et pugnat.

19:12 Oculi autem ejus sicut flamma ignis, et in capite ejus diademata multa, habens nomen scriptum, quod nemo novit nisi ipse.

19:13 Et vestitus erat veste aspersa sanguine : et vocatur nomen ejus : Verbum Dei.

19:14 Et exercitus qui sunt in cælo, sequebantur eum in equis albis, vestiti byssino albo et mundo.

19:15 Et de ore ejus procedit gladius ex utraque parte acutus, ut in ipso percutiat gentes. Et ipse reget eas in virga ferrea : et ipse calcat torcular vini furoris iræ Dei omnipotentis.

19:16 Et habet in vestimento et in femore suo scriptum : Rex regum et Dominus dominantium.

19:17 Et vidi unum angelum stantem in sole, et clamavit voce magna, dicens omnibus avibus, quæ volabant per medium cæli : Venite, et congregamini ad cœnam magnam Dei :

19:18 ut manducetis carnes regum, et carnes tribunorum, et carnes fortium, et carnes equorum, et sedentium in ipsis, et carnes omnium liberorum, et servorum, et pusillorum et magnorum.

19:19 Et vidi bestiam, et reges terræ, et exercitus eorum congregatos ad faciendum prælium cum illo, qui sedebat in equo, et cum exercitu ejus.

him; for the marriage of the Lamb is come, and his wife hath prepared herself.

19:8 And it is granted to her that she should clothe herself with fine linen, glittering and white. For the fine linen are the justifications of saints.

19:9 And he said to me: Write: Blessed are they that are called to the marriage supper of the Lamb. And he saith to me: These words of God are true.

19:10 And I fell down before his feet, to adore him. And he saith to me: See thou do it not: I am thy fellow servant, and of thy brethren, who have the testimony of Jesus. Adore God. For the testimony of Jesus is the spirit of prophecy.

19:11 And I saw heaven opened, and behold a white horse; and he that sat upon him was called faithful and true, and with justice doth he judge and fight.

19:12 And his eyes were as a flame of fire, and on his head were many diadems, and he had a name written, which no man knoweth but himself.

19:13 And he was clothed with a garment sprinkled with blood; and his name is called, THE WORD OF GOD.

19:14 And the armies that are in heaven followed him on white horses, clothed in fine linen, white and clean.

19:15 And out of his mouth proceedeth a sharp two edged sword; that with it he may strike the nations. And he shall rule them with a rod of iron; and he treadeth the winepress of the fierceness of the wrath of God the Almighty.

19:16 And he hath on his garment, and on his thigh written: KING OF KINGS , AND LORD OF LORDS.

19:17 And I saw an angel standing in the sun, and he cried with a loud voice, saying to all the birds that did fly through the midst of heaven: Come, gather yourselves together to the great supper of God:

19:18 That you may eat the flesh of kings, and the flesh of tribunes, and the flesh of mighty men, and the flesh of horses, and of them that sit on them, and the flesh of all freemen and bondmen, and of little and of great.

19:19 And I saw the beast, and the kings of the earth, and their armies gathered together to make war with him that sat upon the horse, and with his army.

19:20 Et apprehensa est bestia, et cum ea pseudopropheta : qui fecit signa coram ipso, quibus seduxit eos, qui acceperunt caracterem bestiæ, et qui adoraverunt imaginem ejus. Vivi missi sunt hi duo in stagnum ignis ardentis sulphure :

19:21 et ceteri occisi sunt in gladio sedentis super equum, qui procedit de ore ipsius : et omnes aves saturatæ sunt carnibus eorum.

20:1 Et vidi angelum descendentem de cælo, habentem clavem abyssi, et catenam magnam in manu sua.

20:2 Et apprehendit draconem, serpentem antiquum, qui est diabolus, et Satanas, et ligavit eum per annos mille :

20:3 et misit eum in abyssum, et clausit, et signavit super illum ut non seducat amplius gentes, donec consummentur mille anni : et post hæc oportet illum solvi modico tempore.

20:4 Et vidi sedes, et sederunt super eas, et judicium datum est illis : et animas decollatorum propter testimonium Jesu, et propter verbum Dei, et qui non adoraverunt bestiam, neque imaginem ejus, nec acceperunt caracterem ejus in frontibus, aut in manibus suis, et vixerunt, et regnaverunt cum Christo mille annis.

20:5 Ceteri mortuorum non vixerunt, donec consummentur mille anni. Hæc est resurrectio prima.

20:6 Beatus, et sanctus, qui habet partem in resurrectione prima : in his secunda mors non habet potestatem : sed erunt sacerdotes Dei et Christi, et regnabunt cum illo mille annis.

20:7 Et cum consummati fuerint mille anni, solvetur Satanas de carcere suo, et exibit, et seducet gentes, quæ sunt super quatuor angulos terræ, Gog, et Magog, et congregabit eos in prælium, quorum numerus est sicut arena maris.

20:8 Et ascenderunt super latitudinem terræ, et circuierunt castra sanctorum, et civitatem dilectam.

20:9 Et descendit ignis a Deo de cælo, et devoravit eos : et diabolus, qui seducebat eos, missus est in stagnum ignis, et sulphuris, ubi et bestia

20:10 et pseudopropheta cruciabuntur die ac

19:20 And the beast was taken, and with him the false prophet, who wrought signs before him, wherewith he seduced them who received the character of the beast, and who adored his image. These two were cast alive into the pool of fire, burning with brimstone.

19:21 And the rest were slain by the sword of him that sitteth upon the horse, which proceedeth out of his mouth; and all the birds were filled with their flesh.

20:1 And I saw an angel coming down from heaven, having the key of the bottomless pit, and a great chain in his hand.

20:2 And he laid hold on the dragon the old serpent, which is the devil and Satan, and bound him for a thousand years.

20:3 And he cast him into the bottomless pit, and shut him up, and set a seal upon him, that he should no more seduce the nations, till the thousand years be finished. And after that, he must be loosed a little time.

20:4 And I saw seats; and they sat upon them; and judgment was given unto them; and the souls of them that were beheaded for the testimony of Jesus, and for the word of God, and who had not adored the beast nor his image, nor received his character on their foreheads, or in their hands; and they lived and reigned with Christ a thousand years.

20:5 The rest of the dead lived not, till the thousand years were finished. This is the first resurrection.

20:6 Blessed and holy is he that hath part in the first resurrection. In these the second death hath no power; but they shall be priests of God and of Christ; and shall reign with him a thousand years.

20:7 And when the thousand years shall be finished, Satan shall be loosed out of his prison, and shall go forth, and seduce the nations, which are over the four quarters of the earth, Gog, and Magog, and shall gather them together to battle, the number of whom is as the sand of the sea.

20:8 And they came upon the breadth of the earth, and encompassed the camp of the saints, and the beloved city.

20:9 And there came down fire from God out of heaven, and devoured them; and the devil, who seduced them, was cast into the pool of fire and brimstone, where both the beast

20:10 And the false prophet shall be tormented

nocte in sæcula sæculorum.

20:11 Et vidi thronum magnum candidum, et sedentem super eum, a cujus conspectu fugit terra, et cælum, et locus non est inventus eis.

20:12 Et vidi mortuos, magnos et pusillos, stantes in conspectu throni, et libri aperti sunt : et alius liber apertus est, qui est vitæ : et judicati sunt mortui ex his, quæ scripta erant in libris, secundum opera ipsorum :

20:13 et dedit mare mortuos, qui in eo erant : et mors et infernus dederunt mortuos suos, qui in ipsis erant : et judicatum est de singulis secundum opera ipsorum.

20:14 Et infernus et mors missi sunt in stagnum ignis. Hæc est mors secunda.

20:15 Et qui non inventus est in libro vitæ scriptus, missus est in stagnum ignis.

21:1 Et vidi cælum novum et terram novam. Primum enim cælum, et prima terra abiit, et mare jam non est.

21:2 Et ego Joannes vidi sanctam civitatem Jerusalem novam descendentem de cælo a Deo, paratam sicut sponsam ornatam viro suo.

21:3 Et audivi vocem magnam de throno dicentem : Ecce tabernaculum Dei cum hominibus, et habitabit cum eis. Et ipsi populus ejus erunt, et ipse Deus cum eis erit eorum Deus :

21:4 et absterget Deus omnem lacrimam ab oculis eorum : et mors ultra non erit, neque luctus, neque clamor, neque dolor erit ultra, quia prima abierunt.

21:5 Et dixit qui sedebat in throno : Ecce nova facio omnia. Et dixit mihi : Scribe, quia hæc verba fidelissima sunt, et vera.

21:6 Et dixit mihi : Factum est : ego sum alpha et omega, initium et finis. Ego sitienti dabo de fonte aquæ vitæ, gratis.

21:7 Qui vicerit, possidebit hæc : et ero illi Deus, et ille erit mihi filius.

21:8 Timidis autem, et incredulis, et execratis, et homicidis, et fornicatoribus, et veneficis, et idolatris, et omnibus mendacibus, pars illorum erit in stagno ardenti igne et sulphure : quod est mors secunda.

21:9 Et venit unus de septem angelis habentibus

day and night for ever and ever.

20:11 And I saw a great white throne, and one sitting upon it, from whose face the earth and heaven fled away, and there was no place found for them.

20:12 And I saw the dead, great and small, standing in the presence of the throne, and the books were opened; and another book was opened, which is the book of life; and the dead were judged by those things which were written in the books, according to their works.

20:13 And the sea gave up the dead that were in it, and death and hell gave up their dead that were in them; and they were judged every one according to their works.

20:14 And hell and death were cast into the pool of fire. This is the second death.

20:15 And whosoever was not found written in the book of life, was cast into the pool of fire.

21:1 And I saw a new heaven and a new earth. For the first heaven and the first earth was gone, and the sea is now no more.

21:2 And I John saw the holy city, the new Jerusalem, coming down out of heaven from God, prepared as a bride adorned for her husband.

21:3 And I heard a great voice from the throne, saying: Behold the tabernacle of God with men, and he will dwell with them. And they shall be his people; and God himself with them shall be their God.

21:4 And God shall wipe away all tears from their eyes: and death shall be no more, nor mourning, nor crying, nor sorrow shall be any more, for the former things are passed away.

21:5 And he that sat on the throne, said: Behold, I make all things new. And he said to me: Write, for these words are most faithful and true.

21:6 And he said to me: It is done. I am Alpha and Omega; the beginning and the end. To him that thirsteth, I will give of the fountain of the water of life, freely.

21:7 He that shall overcome shall possess these things, and I will be his God; and he shall be my son.

21:8 But the fearful, and unbelieving, and the abominable, and murderers, and whore-mongers, and sorcerers, and idolaters, and all liars, they shall have their portion in the pool burning with fire and brimstone, which is the second death.

21:9 And there came one of the seven angels,

phialas plenas septem plagis novissimis, et locutus est mecum, dicens : Veni, et ostendam tibi sponsam, uxorem Agni.

21:10 Et sustulit me in spiritu in montem magnum et altum, et ostendit mihi civitatem sanctam Jerusalem descendentem de cælo a Deo,

21:11 habentem claritatem Dei : et lumen ejus simile lapidi pretioso tamquam lapidi jaspidis, sicut crystallum.

21:12 Et habebat murum magnum, et altum, habentem portas duodecim : et in portis angelos duodecim, et nomina inscripta, quæ sunt nomina duodecim tribuum filiorum Israël :

21:13 ab oriente portæ tres, et ab aquilone portæ tres, et ab austro portæ tres, et ab occasu portæ tres.

21:14 Et murus civitatis habens fundamenta duodecim, et in ipsis duodecim nomina duodecim apostolorum Agni.

21:15 Et qui loquebatur mecum, habebat mensuram arundineam auream, ut metiretur civitatem, et portas ejus, et murum.

21:16 Et civitas in quadro posita est, et longitudo ejus tanta est quanta et latitudo : et mensus est civitatem de arundine aurea per stadia duodecim millia : et longitudo, et altitudo, et latitudo ejus æqualia sunt.

21:17 Et mensus est murum ejus centum quadraginta quatuor cubitorum, mensura hominis, quæ est angeli.

21:18 Et erat structura muri ejus ex lapide jaspide : ipsa vero civitas aurum mundum simile vitro mundo.

21:19 Et fundamenta muri civitatis omni lapide pretioso ornata. Fundamentum primum, jaspis : secundum, sapphirus : tertium, calcedonius : quartum, smaragdus :

21:20 quintum, sardonyx : sextum, sardius : septimum, chrysolithus : octavum, beryllus : nonum, topazius : decimum, chrysoprasus : undecimum, hyacinthus : duodecimum, amethystus.

21:21 Et duodecim portæ, duodecim margaritæ sunt, per singulas : et singulæ portæ erant ex singulis margaritis : et platea civitatis aurum mundum, tamquam vitrum perlucidum.

21:22 Et templum non vidi in ea : Dominus enim Deus omnipotens templum illius est, et Agnus.

21:23 Et civitas non eget sole neque luna ut luce-

who had the vials full of the seven last plagues, and spoke with me, saying: Come, and I will shew thee the bride, the wife of the Lamb.

21:10 And he took me up in spirit to a great and high mountain: and he shewed me the holy city Jerusalem coming down out of heaven from God,

21:11 Having the glory of God, and the light thereof was like to a precious stone, as to the jasper stone, even as crystal.

21:12 And it had a wall great and high, having twelve gates, and in the gates twelve angels, and names written thereon, which are the names of the twelve tribes of the children of Israel.

21:13 On the east, three gates: and on the north, three gates: and on the south, three gates: and on the west, three gates.

21:14 And the wall of the city had twelve foundations, and in them, the twelve names of the twelve apostles of the Lamb.

21:15 And he that spoke with me, had a measure of a reed of gold, to measure the city and the gates thereof, and the wall.

21:16 And the city lieth in a foursquare, and the length thereof is as great as the breadth: and he measured the city with the golden reed for twelve thousand furlongs, and the length and the height and the breadth thereof are equal.

21:17 And he measured the wall thereof an hundred and forty-four cubits, the measure of a man, which is of an angel.

21:18 And the building of the wall thereof was of jasper stone: but the city itself pure gold, like to clear glass.

21:19 And the foundations of the wall of the city were adorned with all manner of precious stones. The first foundation was jasper: the second, sapphire: the third, a chalcedony: the fourth, an emerald:

21:20 The fifth, sardonyx: the sixth, sardius: the seventh, chrysolite: the eighth, beryl: the ninth, a topaz: the tenth, a chrysoprasus: the eleventh, a jacinth: the twelfth, an amethyst.

21:21 And the twelve gates are twelve pearls, one to each: and every several gate was of one several pearl. And the street of the city was pure gold, as it were transparent glass.

21:22 And I saw no temple therein. For the Lord God Almighty is the temple thereof, and the Lamb.

21:23 And the city hath no need of the sun, nor

ant in ea, nam claritas Dei illuminavit eam, et lucerna ejus est Agnus.

21:24 Et ambulabunt gentes in lumine ejus : et reges terræ afferent gloriam suam et honorem in illam.

21:25 Et portæ ejus non claudentur per diem : nox enim non erit illic.

21:26 Et afferent gloriam et honorem gentium in illam.

21:27 Non intrabit in eam aliquod coinquinatum, aut abominationem faciens et mendacium, nisi qui scripti sunt in libro vitæ Agni.

22:1 Et ostendit mihi fluvium aquæ vitæ, splendidum tamquam crystallum, procedentem de sede Dei et Agni.

22:2 In medio plateæ ejus, et ex utraque parte fluminis, lignum vitæ, afferens fructus duodecim per menses singulos, reddens fructum suum et folia ligni ad sanitatem gentium.

22:3 Et omne maledictum non erit amplius : sed sedes Dei et Agni in illa erunt, et servi ejus servient illi.

22:4 Et videbunt faciem ejus : et nomen ejus in frontibus eorum.

22:5 Et nox ultra non erit : et non egebunt lumine lucernæ, neque lumine solis, quoniam Dominus Deus illuminabit illos, et regnabunt in sæcula sæculorum.

22:6 Et dixit mihi : Hæc verba fidelissima sunt, et vera. Et Dominus Deus spirituum prophetarum misit angelum suum ostendere servis suis quæ oportet fieri cito.

22:7 Et ecce venio velociter. Beatus, qui custodit verba prophetiæ libri hujus.

22:8 Et ego Joannes, qui audivi, et vidi hæc. Et postquam audissem, et vidissem, cecidi ut adorarem ante pedes angeli, qui mihi hæc ostendebat :

22:9 et dixit mihi : Vide ne feceris : conservus enim tuus sum, et fratrum tuorum prophetarum, et eorum qui servant verba prophetiæ libri hujus : Deum adora.

22:10 Et dicit mihi : Ne signaveris verba prophetiæ libri hujus : tempus enim prope est.

22:11 Qui nocet, noceat adhuc : et qui in sordibus est, sordescat adhuc : et qui justus est, jus-

of the moon, to shine in it. For the glory of God hath enlightened it, and the Lamb is the lamp thereof.

21:24 And the nations shall walk in the light of it: and the kings of the earth shall bring their glory and honour into it.

21:25 And the gates thereof shall not be shut by day: for there shall be no night there.

21:26 And they shall bring the glory and honour of the nations into it.

21:27 There shall not enter into it any thing defiled, or that worketh abomination or maketh a lie, but they that are written in the book of life of the Lamb.

22:1 And he showed me a river of water of life, clear as crystal, proceeding from the throne of God and of the Lamb.

22:2 In the midst of the street thereof, and on both sides of the river, was the tree of life, bearing twelve fruits, yielding its fruits every month, and the leaves of the tree were for the healing of the nations.

22:3 And there shall be no curse any more; but the throne of God and of the Lamb shall be in it, and his servants shall serve him.

22:4 And they shall see his face: and his name shall be on their foreheads.

22:5 And night shall be no more: and they shall not need the light of the lamp, nor the light of the sun, because the Lord God shall enlighten them, and they shall reign for ever and ever.

22:6 And he said to me: These words are most faithful and true. And the Lord God of the spirits of the prophets sent his angel to shew his servants the things which must be done shortly.

22:7 And, Behold I come quickly. Blessed is he that keepeth the words of the prophecy of this book.

22:8 And I, John, who have heard and seen these things. And after I had heard and seen, I fell down to adore before the feet of the angel, who shewed me these things.

22:9 And he said to me: See thou do it not: for I am thy fellow servant, and of thy brethren the prophets, and of them that keep the words of the prophecy of this book. Adore God.

22:10 And he saith to me: Seal not the words of the prophecy of this book: for the time is at hand.

22:11 He that hurteth, let him hurt still: and he that is filthy, let him be filthy still: and he that is

tificetur adhuc : et sanctus, sanctificetur adhuc.

22:12 Ecce venio cito, et merces mea mecum est, reddere unicuique secundum opera sua.

22:13 Ego sum alpha et omega, primus et novissimus, principium et finis.

22:14 Beati, qui lavant stolas suas in sanguine Agni : ut sit potestas eorum in ligno vitæ, et per portas intrent in civitatem.

22:15 Foris canes, et venefici, et impudici, et homicidæ, et idolis servientes, et omnis qui amat et facit mendacium.

22:16 Ego Jesus misi angelum meum testificari vobis hæc in ecclesiis. Ego sum radix, et genus David, stella splendida et matutina.

22:17 Et spiritus, et sponsa dicunt : Veni. Et qui audit, dicat : Veni. Et qui sitit, veniat : et qui vult, accipiat aquam vitæ, gratis.

22:18 Contestor enim omni audienti verba prophetiæ libri hujus : si quis apposuerit ad hæc, apponet Deus super illum plagas scriptas in libro isto.

22:19 Et si quis diminuerit de verbis libri prophetiæ hujus, auferet Deus partem ejus de libro vitæ, et de civitate sancta, et de his quæ scripta sunt in libro isto :

22:20 dicit qui testimonium perhibet istorum. Etiam venio cito : amen. Veni, Domine Jesu.

22:21 Gratia Domini nostri Jesu Christi cum omnibus vobis. Amen.

just, let him be justified still: and he that is holy, let him be sanctified still.

22:12 Behold, I come quickly; and my reward is with me, to render to every man according to his works.

22:13 I am Alpha and Omega, the first and the last, the beginning and the end.

22:14 Blessed are they that wash their robes in the blood of the Lamb: that they may have a right to the tree of life, and may enter in by the gates into the city.

22:15 Without are dogs, and sorcerers, and unchaste, and murderers, and servers of idols, and every one that loveth and maketh a lie.

22:16 I Jesus have sent my angel, to testify to you these things in the churches. I am the root and stock of David, the bright and morning star.

22:17 And the spirit and the bride say: Come. And he that heareth, let him say: Come. And he that thirsteth, let him come: and he that will, let him take the water of life, freely.

22:18 For I testify to every one that heareth the words of the prophecy of this book: If any man shall add to these things, God shall add unto him the plagues written in this book.

22:19 And if any man shall take away from the words of the book of this prophecy, God shall take away his part out of the book of life, and out of the holy city, and from these things that are written in this book.

22:20 He that giveth testimony of these things, saith, Surely I come quickly: Amen. Come, Lord Jesus.

22:21 The grace of our Lord Jesus Christ be with you all. Amen.

Within the illustration:
Deus in adjutorium meum intende. Domine ad adjuvandum me festina. Gloria Patri.

Liber Psalmorum

THE BOOK OF PSALMS

✠

I.

EATUS VIR qui non abiit in consilio impiorum, et in via peccatorum non stetit, et in cathedra pestilentiæ non sedit ;

1:2 sed in lege Domini voluntas ejus, et in lege ejus meditabitur die ac nocte.

1:3 Et erit tamquam lignum quod plantatum est secus decursus aquarum, quod fructum suum dabit in tempore suo : et folium ejus non defluet ; et omnia quæcumque faciet prosperabuntur.

1:4 Non sic impii, non sic ; sed tamquam pulvis quem projicit ventus a facie terræ.

1:5 Ideo non resurgent impii in judicio, neque peccatores in concilio justorum :

1:6 quoniam novit Dominus viam justorum, et iter impiorum peribit.

BLESSED IS THE MAN who hath not walked in the counsel of the ungodly, nor stood in the way of sinners, nor sat in the chair of pestilence.

1:2 But his will is in the law of the Lord, and on his law he shall meditate day and night.

1:3 And he shall be like a tree which is planted near the running waters, which shall bring forth its fruit, in due season. And his leaf shall not fall off: and all whatsoever he shall do shall prosper.

1:4 Not so the wicked, not so: but like the dust, which the wind driveth from the face of the earth.

1:5 Therefore the wicked shall not rise again in judgment: nor sinners in the council of the just.

1:6 For the Lord knoweth the way of the just: and the way of the wicked shall perish.

II.

2:1 QUARE FREMUERUNT GENTES, et populi meditati sunt inania ?

2:2 Astiterunt reges terræ, et principes con-

2:1 WHY HAVE THE GENTILES RAGED, and the people devised vain things?

2:2 The kings of the earth stood up, and the

venerunt in unum adversus Dominum, et adversus christum ejus.

2:3 Dirumpamus vincula eorum, et projiciamus a nobis jugum ipsorum.

2:4 Qui habitat in cælis irridebit eos, et Dominus subsannabit eos.

2:5 Tunc loquetur ad eos in ira sua, et in furore suo conturbabit eos.

2:6 Ego autem constitutus sum rex ab eo super Sion, montem sanctum ejus, prædicans præceptum ejus.

2:7 Dominus dixit ad me : Filius meus es tu ; ego hodie genui te.

2:8 Postula a me, et dabo tibi gentes hæreditatem tuam, et possessionem tuam terminos terræ.

2:9 Reges eos in virga ferrea, et tamquam vas figuli confringes eos.

2:10 Et nunc, reges, intelligite ; erudimini, qui judicatis terram.

2:11 Servite Domino in timore, et exsultate ei cum tremore.

2:12 Apprehendite disciplinam, nequando irascatur Dominus, et pereatis de via justa.

2:13 Cum exarserit in brevi ira ejus, beati omnes qui confidunt in eo.

princes met together, against the Lord and against his Christ.

2:3 Let us break their bonds asunder: and let us cast away their yoke from us.

2:4 He that dwelleth in heaven shall laugh at them: and the Lord shall deride them.

2:5 Then shall he speak to them in his anger, and trouble them in his rage.

2:6 But I am appointed king by him over Sion his holy mountain, preaching his commandment.

2:7 The Lord hath said to me: Thou art my son, this day have I begotten thee.

2:8 Ask of me, and I will give thee the Gentiles for thy inheritance, and the utmost parts of the earth for thy possession.

2:9 Thou shalt rule them with a rod of iron, and shalt break them in pieces like a potter's vessel.

2:10 And now, O ye kings, understand: receive instruction, you that judge the earth.

2:11 Serve ye the Lord with fear: and rejoice unto him with trembling.

2:12 Embrace discipline, lest at any time the Lord be angry, and you perish from the just way.

2:13 When his wrath shall be kindled in a short time, blessed are all they that trust in him.

III.

3:1 *Psalmus David, cum fugeret a facie Absalom filii sui.*

3:2 DOMINE, QUID multiplicati sunt qui tribulant me ? Multi insurgunt adversum me ;

3:3 multi dicunt animæ meæ : Non est salus ipsi in Deo ejus.

3:4 Tu autem Domine, susceptor meus es, gloria mea, et exaltans caput meum.

3:5 Voce mea ad Dominum clamavi ; et exaudivit me de monte sancto suo.

3:6 Ego dormivi, et soporatus sum ; et exsurrexi, quia Dominus suscepit me.

3:7 Non timebo millia populi circumdantis me. Exsurge, Domine ; salvum me fac, Deus meus.

3:8 Quoniam tu percussisti omnes adversantes mihi sine causa ; dentes peccatorum contrivisti.

3:9 Domini est salus ; et super populum tuum benedictio tua.

3:1 *The psalm of David when he fled from the face of his son Absalom.*

3:2 WHY, O LORD, are they multiplied that afflict me? many are they who rise up against me.

3:3 Many say to my soul: There is no salvation for him in his God.

3:4 But thou, O Lord art my protector, my glory, and the lifter up of my head.

3:5 I have cried to the Lord with my voice: and he hath heard me from his holy hill.

3:6 I have slept and taken my rest: and I have risen up, because the Lord hath protected me.

3:7 I will not fear thousands of the people, surrounding me: arise, O Lord; save me, O my God.

3:8 For thou hast struck all them who are my adversaries without cause: thou hast broken the teeth of sinners.

3:9 Salvation is of the Lord: and thy blessing is upon thy people.

IV.

4:1 *In finem, in carminibus. Psalmus David.*

4:2 CUM INVOCAREM exaudivit me Deus justitiæ meæ, in tribulatione dilatasti mihi. Miserere mei, et exaudi orationem meam.

4:3 Filii hominum, usquequo gravi corde ? ut quid diligitis vanitatem, et quæritis mendacium ?

4:4 Et scitote quoniam mirificavit Dominus sanctum suum ; Dominus exaudiet me cum clamavero ad eum.

4:5 Irascimini, et nolite peccare ; quæ dicitis in cordibus vestris, in cubilibus vestris compungimini.

4:6 Sacrificate sacrificium justitiæ, et sperate in Domino. Multi dicunt : Quis ostendit nobis bona ?

4:7 Signatum est super nos lumen vultus tui, Domine : dedisti lætitiam in corde meo.

4:8 A fructu frumenti, vini, et olei sui, multiplicati sunt.

4:9 In pace in idipsum dormiam, et requiescam ;

4:10 quoniam tu, Domine, singulariter in spe constituisti me.

4:1 *Unto the end, in verses. A psalm for David.*

4:2 WHEN I CALLED UPON HIM, the God of my justice heard me: when I was in distress, thou hast enlarged me. Have mercy on me: and hear my prayer.

4:3 O ye sons of men, how long will you be dull of heart? why do you love vanity, and seek after lying?

4:4 Know ye also that the Lord hath made his holy one wonderful: the Lord will hear me when I shall cry unto him.

4:5 Be ye angry, and sin not: the things you say in your hearts, be sorry for them upon your beds.

4:6 Offer up the sacrifice of justice, and trust in the Lord: many say, Who sheweth us good things?

4:7 The light of thy countenance O Lord, is signed upon us: thou hast given gladness in my heart.

4:8 By the fruit of their corn, their wine and oil, they are multiplied.

4:9 In peace in the selfsame I will sleep, and I will rest:

4:10 For thou, O Lord, singularly hast settled me in hope.

V.

5:1 *In finem, pro ea quæ hæreditatem consequitur. Psalmus David.*

5:2 VERBA MEA AURIBUS PERCIPE, DOMINE ; intellige clamorem meum.

5:3 Intende voci orationis meæ, rex meus et Deus meus.

5:4 Quoniam ad te orabo, Domine : mane exaudies vocem meam.

5:5 Mane astabo tibi, et videbo quoniam non Deus volens iniquitatem tu es.

5:6 Neque habitabit juxta te malignus, neque permanebunt injusti ante oculos tuos.

5:7 Odisti omnes qui operantur iniquitatem ; perdes omnes qui loquuntur mendacium. Virum sanguinum et dolosum abominabitur Dominus.

5:8 Ego autem in multitudine misericordiæ tuæ introibo in domum tuam ; adorabo ad templum sanctum tuum in timore tuo.

5:9 Domine, deduc me in justitia tua : propter inimicos meos dirige in conspectu tuo viam meam.

5:1 *Unto the end, for her that obtaineth the inheritance. A psalm of David.*

5:2 GIVE EAR, O LORD, TO MY WORDS, understand my cry.

5:3 Hearken to the voice of my prayer, O my King and my God.

5:4 For to thee will I pray: O Lord, in the morning thou shalt hear my voice.

5:5 In the morning I will stand before thee, and will see: because thou art not a God that willest iniquity.

5:6 Neither shall the wicked dwell near thee: nor shall the unjust abide before thy eyes.

5:7 Thou hatest all the workers of iniquity: Thou wilt destroy all that speak a lie. The bloody and the deceitful man the Lord will abhor.

5:8 But as for me in the multitude of thy mercy, I will come into thy house; I will worship towards thy holy temple, in thy fear.

5:9 Conduct me, O Lord, in thy justice: because of my enemies, direct my way in thy sight.

5:10 Quoniam non est in ore eorum veritas ; cor eorum vanum est.

5:11 Sepulchrum patens est guttur eorum ; linguis suis dolose agebant : judica illos, Deus. Decidant a cogitationibus suis ; secundum multitudinem impietatum eorum expelle eos, quoniam irritaverunt te, Domine.

5:12 Et lætentur omnes qui sperant in te ; in æternum exsultabunt, et habitabis in eis. Et gloriabuntur in te omnes qui diligunt nomen tuum,

5:13 quoniam tu benedices justo. Domine, ut scuto bonæ voluntatis tuæ coronasti nos.

5:10 for there is no truth in their mouth; their heart is vain.

5:11 Their throat is an open sepulchre: they dealt deceitfully with their tongues: judge them, O God. Let them fall from their devices: according to the multitude of their wickedness cast them out: for they have provoked thee, O Lord.

5:12 But let all them be glad that hope in thee: they shall rejoice for ever, and thou shalt dwell in them. And all they that love thy name shall glory in thee:

5:13 For thou wilt bless the just. O Lord, thou hast crowned us, as with a shield of thy good will.

VI.

6:1 *In finem, in carminibus. Psalmus David. Pro octava.*

6:2 DOMINE, NE IN FURORE TUO ARGUAS ME, neque in ira tua corripias me.

6:3 Miserere mei, Domine, quoniam infirmus sum ; sana me, Domine, quoniam conturbata sunt ossa mea.

6:4 Et anima mea turbata est valde ; sed tu, Domine, usquequo ?

6:5 Convertere, Domine, et eripe animam meam ; salvum me fac propter misericordiam tuam.

6:6 Quoniam non est in morte qui memor sit tui ; in inferno autem quis confitebitur tibi ?

6:7 Laboravi in gemitu meo ; lavabo per singulas noctes lectum meum : lacrimis meis stratum meum rigabo.

6:8 Turbatus est a furore oculus meus ; inveteravi inter omnes inimicos meos.

6:9 Discedite a me omnes qui operamini iniquitatem, quoniam exaudivit Dominus vocem fletus mei.

6:10 Exaudivit Dominus deprecationem meam ; Dominus orationem meam suscepit.

6:11 Erubescant, et conturbentur vehementer, omnes inimici mei ; convertantur, et erubescant valde velociter.

6:1 *Unto the end, in verses, a psalm for David, for the octave.*

6:2 O LORD, REBUKE ME NOT IN THY INDIGNATION, nor chastise me in thy wrath.

6:3 Have mercy on me, O Lord, for I am weak: heal me, O Lord, for my bones are troubled.

6:4 And my soul is troubled exceedingly: but thou, O Lord, how long?

6:5 Turn to me, O Lord, and deliver my soul: O save me for thy mercy's sake.

6:6 For there is no one in death, that is mindful of thee: and who shall confess to thee in hell?

6:7 I have laboured in my groanings, every night I will wash my bed: I will water my couch with my tears.

6:8 My eye is troubled through indignation: I have grown old amongst all my enemies.

6:9 Depart from me, all ye workers of iniquity: for the Lord hath heard the voice of my weeping.

6:10 The Lord hath heard my supplication: the Lord hath received my prayer.

6:11 Let all my enemies be ashamed, and be very much troubled: let them be turned back, and be ashamed very speedily.

VII.

7:1 *Psalmus David, quem cantavit Domino pro verbis Chusi, filii Jemini.*

7:2 DOMINE DEUS MEUS, in te speravi ; salvum me fac ex omnibus persequentibus me, et libera me :

7:3 nequando rapiat ut leo animam meam, dum

7:1 *The psalm of David which he sung to the Lord for the words of Chusi the son of Jemini.*

7:2 O LORD MY GOD, in thee have I put my trust: save me from all them that persecute me, and deliver me.

7:3 Lest at any time he seize upon my soul like a

non est qui redimat, neque qui salvum faciat.

7:4 Domine Deus meus, si feci istud, si est iniquitas in manibus meis,

7:5 si reddidi retribuentibus mihi mala, decidam merito ab inimicis meis inanis.

7:6 Persequatur inimicus animam meam, et comprehendat ; et conculcet in terra vitam meam, et gloriam meam in pulverem deducat.

7:7 Exsurge, Domine, in ira tua, et exaltare in finibus inimicorum meorum : et exsurge, Domine Deus meus, in præcepto quod mandasti,

7:8 et synagoga populorum circumdabit te : et propter hanc in altum regredere :

7:9 Dominus judicat populos. Judica me, Domine, secundum justitiam meam, et secundum innocentiam meam super me.

7:10 Consumetur nequitia peccatorum, et diriges justum, scrutans corda et renes, Deus.

7:11 Justum adjutorium meum a Domino, qui salvos facit rectos corde.

7:12 Deus judex justus, fortis, et patiens ; numquid irascitur per singulos dies ?

7:13 Nisi conversi fueritis, gladium suum vibrabit ; arcum suum tetendit, et paravit illum.

7:14 Et in eo paravit vasa mortis, sagittas suas ardentibus effecit.

7:15 Ecce parturiit injustitiam ; concepit dolorem, et peperit iniquitatem.

7:16 Lacum aperuit, et effodit eum ; et incidit in foveam quam fecit.

7:17 Convertetur dolor ejus in caput ejus, et in verticem ipsius iniquitas ejus descendet.

7:18 Confitebor Domino secundum justitiam ejus, et psallam nomini Domini altissimi.

VIII.

8:1 *In finem, pro torcularibus. Psalmus David.*

8:2 DOMINE, DOMINUS NOSTER, quam admirabile est nomen tuum in universa terra ! quoniam elevata est magnificentia tua super cælos.

8:3 Ex ore infantium et lactentium perfecisti laudem propter inimicos tuos, ut destruas inimicum et ultorem.

lion, while there is no one to redeem me, nor to save.

7:4 O Lord my God, if I have done this thing, if there be iniquity in my hands:

7:5 If I have rendered to them that repaid me evils, let me deservedly fall empty before my enemies.

7:6 Let the enemy pursue my soul, and take it, and tread down my life on the earth, and bring down my glory to the dust.

7:7 Rise up, O Lord, in thy anger: and be thou exalted in the borders of my enemies. And arise, O Lord my God, in the precept which thou hast commanded:

7:8 and a congregation of people shall surround thee. And for their sakes return thou on high.

7:9 The Lord judgeth the people. Judge me, O Lord, according to my justice, and according to my innocence in me.

7:10 The wickedness of sinners shall be brought to nought: and thou shalt direct the just: the searcher of hearts and reins is God.

7:11 Just is my help from the Lord: who saveth the upright of heart.

7:12 God is a just judge, strong and patient: is he angry every day?

7:13 Except you will be converted, he will brandish his sword: he hath bent his bow and made it ready.

7:14 And in it he hath prepared the instruments of death, he hath made ready his arrows for them that burn.

7:15 Behold he hath been in labour with injustice; he hath conceived sorrow, and brought forth iniquity.

7:16 He hath opened a pit and dug it: and he is fallen into the hole he made.

7:17 His sorrow shall be turned on his own head: and his iniquity shall come down upon his crown.

7:18 I will give glory to the Lord according to his justice: and will sing to the name of the Lord the most high.

8:1 *Unto the end, for the presses: a psalm for David.*

8:2 O LORD OUR LORD, how admirable is thy name in the whole earth! For thy magnificence is elevated above the heavens.

8:3 Out of the mouth of infants and of sucklings thou hast perfected praise, because of thy enemies, that thou mayst destroy the enemy and

8:4 Quoniam videbo cælos tuos, opera digitorum tuorum, lunam et stellas quæ tu fundasti.

8:5 Quid est homo, quod memor es ejus ? aut filius hominis, quoniam visitas eum ?

8:6 Minuisti eum paulominus ab angelis ; gloria et honore coronasti eum ;

8:7 et constituisti eum super opera manuum tuarum.

8:8 Omnia subjecisti sub pedibus ejus, oves et boves universas, insuper et pecora campi,

8:9 volucres cæli, et pisces maris qui perambulant semitas maris.

8:10 Domine, Dominus noster, quam admirabile est nomen tuum in universa terra !

the avenger.

8:4 For I will behold thy heavens, the works of thy fingers: the moon and the stars which thou hast founded.

8:5 What is man that thou art mindful of him? or the son of man that thou visitest him?

8:6 Thou hast made him a little less than the angels, thou hast crowned him with glory and honour:

8:7 and hast set him over the works of thy hands.

8:8 Thou hast subjected all things under his feet, all sheep and oxen: moreover the beasts also of the fields.

8:9 The birds of the air, and the fishes of the sea, that pass through the paths of the sea.

8:10 O Lord our Lord, how admirable is thy name in all the earth!

IX.

9:1 *In finem, pro occultis filii. Psalmus David.*

9:2 CONFITEBOR TIBI, Domine, in toto corde meo ; narrabo omnia mirabilia tua.

9:3 Lætabor et exsultabo in te ; psallam nomini tuo, Altissime.

9:4 In convertendo inimicum meum retrorsum ; infirmabuntur, et peribunt a facie tua.

9:5 Quoniam fecisti judicium meum et causam meam ; sedisti super thronum, qui judicas justitiam.

9:6 Increpasti gentes, et periit impius : nomen eorum delesti in æternum, et in sæculum sæculi.

9:7 Inimici defecerunt frameæ in finem, et civitates eorum destruxisti. Periit memoria eorum cum sonitu ;

9:8 et Dominus in æternum permanet. Paravit in judicio thronum suum,

9:9 et ipse judicabit orbem terræ in æquitate : judicabit populos in justitia.

9:10 Et factus est Dominus refugium pauperi ; adjutor in opportunitatibus, in tribulatione.

9:11 Et sperent in te qui noverunt nomen tuum, quoniam non dereliquisti quærentes te, Domine.

9:12 Psallite Domino qui habitat in Sion ; annuntiate inter gentes studia ejus :

9:13 quoniam requirens sanguinem eorum recordatus est ; non est oblitus clamorem pauperum.

9:14 Miserere mei, Domine : vide humilitatem

9:1 *Unto the end, for the hidden things of the Son. A psalm for David.*

9:2 I WILL GIVE PRAISE TO THEE, O Lord, with my whole heart: I will relate all thy wonders.

9:3 I will be glad and rejoice in thee: I will sing to thy name, O thou most high.

9:4 When my enemy shall be turned back: they shall be weakened and perish before thy face.

9:5 For thou hast maintained my judgment and my cause: thou hast sat on the throne, who judgest justice.

9:6 Thou hast rebuked the Gentiles, and the wicked one hath perished: thou hast blotted out their name for ever and ever.

9:7 The swords of the enemy have failed unto the end: and their cities thou hast destroyed. Their memory hath perished with a noise:

9:8 but the Lord remaineth for ever. He hath prepared his throne in judgment:

9:9 and he shall judge the world in equity, he shall judge the people in justice.

9:10 And the Lord is become a refuge for the poor: a helper in due time in tribulation.

9:11 And let them trust in thee who know thy name: for thou hast not forsaken them that seek thee, O Lord.

9:12 Sing ye to the Lord, who dwelleth in Sion: declare his ways among the Gentiles:

9:13 For requiring their blood he hath remembered them: he hath not forgotten the cry of the poor.

9:14 Have mercy on me, O Lord: see my humili-

meam de inimicis meis,

9:15 qui exaltas me de portis mortis, ut annuntiem omnes laudationes tuas in portis filiæ Sion :

9:16 exultabo in salutari tuo. Infixæ sunt gentes in interitu quem fecerunt ; in laqueo isto quem absconderunt comprehensus est pes eorum.

9:17 Cognoscetur Dominus judicia faciens ; in operibus manuum suarum comprehensus est peccator.

9:18 Convertantur peccatores in infernum, omnes gentes quæ obliviscuntur Deum.

9:19 Quoniam non in finem oblivio erit pauperis ; patientia pauperum non peribit in finem.

9:20 Exsurge, Domine ; non confortetur homo : judicentur gentes in conspectu tuo.

9:21 Constitue, Domine, legislatorem super eos, ut sciant gentes quoniam homines sunt.

9:22 Ut quid, Domine, recessisti longe ; despicis in opportunitatibus, in tribulatione ?

9:23 Dum superbit impius, incenditur pauper : comprehenduntur in consiliis quibus cogitant.

9:24 Quoniam laudatur peccator in desideriis animæ suæ, et iniquus benedicitur.

9:25 Exacerbavit Dominum peccator : secundum multitudinem iræ suæ, non quæret.

9:26 Non est Deus in conspectu ejus ; inquinatæ sunt viæ illius in omni tempore. Auferuntur judicia tua a facie ejus ; omnium inimicorum suorum dominabitur.

9:27 Dixit enim in corde suo : Non movebor a generatione in generationem, sine malo.

9:28 Cujus maledictione os plenum est, et amaritudine, et dolo ; sub lingua ejus labor et dolor.

9:29 Sedet in insidiis cum divitibus in occultis, ut interficiat innocentem.

9:30 Oculi ejus in pauperem respiciunt ; insidiatur in abscondito, quasi leo in spelunca sua. Insidiatur ut rapiat pauperem ; rapere pauperem dum attrahit eum.

9:31 In laqueo suo humiliabit eum ; inclinabit se, et cadet cum dominatus fuerit pauperum.

9:32 Dixit enim in corde suo : Oblitus est Deus ;

ation which I suffer from my enemies.

9:15 Thou that liftest me up from the gates of death, that I may declare all thy praises in the gates of the daughter of Sion.

9:16 I will rejoice in thy salvation: the Gentiles have stuck fast in the destruction which they have prepared. Their foot hath been taken in the very snare which they hid.

9:17 The Lord shall be known when he executeth judgments: the sinner hath been caught in the works of his own hands.

9:18 The wicked shall be turned into hell, all the nations that forget God.

9:19 For the poor man shall not be forgotten to the end: the patience of the poor shall not perish for ever.

9:20 Arise, O Lord, let not man be strengthened: let the Gentiles be judged in thy sight.

9:21 Appoint, O Lord, a lawgiver over them: that the Gentiles may know themselves to be but men.

9:22 Why, O Lord, hast thou retired afar off? why dost thou slight us in our wants, in the time of trouble?

9:23 Whilst the wicked man is proud, the poor is set on fire: they are caught in the counsels which they devise.

9:24 For the sinner is praised in the desires of his soul: and the unjust man is blessed.

9:25 The sinner hath provoked the Lord according to the multitude of his wrath he will not seek him:

9:26 God is not before his eyes: his ways are filthy at all times. Thy judgments are removed from his sight: he shall rule over all his enemies.

9:27 For he hath said in his heart: I shall not be moved from generation to generation, and shall be without evil.

9:28 His mouth is full of cursing, and of bitterness, and of deceit: under his tongue are labour and sorrow.

9:29 He sitteth in ambush with the rich in private places, that he may kill the innocent.

9:30 His eyes are upon the poor man: He lieth in wait in secret like a lion in his den. He lieth in ambush that he may catch the poor man: to catch the poor, whilst he draweth him to him.

9:31 In his net he will bring him down, he will crouch and fall, when he shall have power over the poor.

9:32 For he hath said in his heart: God hath for-

avertit faciem suam, ne videat in finem.

9:33 Exsurge, Domine Deus, exaltetur manus tua ; ne obliviscaris pauperum.
9:34 Propter quid irritavit impius Deum ? dixit enim in corde suo : Non requiret.

9:35 Vides, quoniam tu laborem et dolorem consideras, ut tradas eos in manus tuas. Tibi derelictus est pauper ; orphano tu eris adjutor.

9:36 Contere brachium peccatoris et maligni ; quæretur peccatum illius, et non invenietur.

9:37 Dominus regnabit in æternum, et in sæculum sæculi ; peribitis, gentes, de terra illius.

9:38 Desiderium pauperum exaudivit Dominus ; præparationem cordis eorum audivit auris tua :

9:39 judicare pupillo et humili, ut non apponat ultra magnificare se homo super terram.

gotten, he hath turned away his face not to see to the end.

9:33 Arise, O Lord God, let thy hand be exalted: forget not the poor.
9:34 Wherefore hath the wicked provoked God? for he hath said in his heart: He will not require it.

9:35 Thou seest it, for thou considerest labour and sorrow: that thou mayst deliver them into thy hands. To thee is the poor man left: thou wilt be a helper to the orphan.

9:36 Break thou the arm of the sinner and of the malignant: his sin shall be sought, and shall not be found.

9:37 The Lord shall reign to eternity, yea, for ever and ever: ye Gentiles shall perish from his land.

9:38 The Lord hath heard the desire of the poor: thy ear hath heard the preparation of their heart.

9:39 To judge for the fatherless and for the humble, that man may no more presume to magnify himself upon earth.

X.

10:1 *In finem. Psalmus David.*
10:2 IN DOMINO CONFIDO ; quomodo dicitis animæ meæ : Transmigra in montem sicut passer ?
10:3 Quoniam ecce peccatores intenderunt arcum ; paraverunt sagittas suas in pharetra, ut sagittent in obscuro rectos corde :
10:4 quoniam quæ perfecisti destruxerunt ; justus autem, quid fecit ?

10:5 Dominus in templo sancto suo ; Dominus in cælo sedes ejus. Oculi ejus in pauperem respiciunt ; palpebræ ejus interrogant filios hominum.
10:6 Dominus interrogat justum et impium ; qui autem diligit iniquitatem, odit animam suam.
10:7 Pluet super peccatores laqueos ; ignis et sulphur, et spiritus procellarum, pars calicis eorum.
10:8 Quoniam justus Dominus, et justitias dilexit : æquitatem vidit vultus ejus.

10:1 *Unto the end. A psalm for David.*
10:2 IN THE LORD I PUT MY TRUST: how then do you say to my soul: Get thee away from hence to the mountain like a sparrow?
10:3 For, lo, the wicked have bent their bow; they have prepared their arrows in the quiver; to shoot in the dark the upright of heart.
10:4 For they have destroyed the things which thou hast made: but what has the just man done?

10:5 The Lord is in his holy temple, the Lord's throne is in heaven. His eyes look on the poor man: his eyelids examine the sons of men.

10:6 The Lord trieth the just and the wicked: but he that loveth iniquity hateth his own soul.
10:7 He shall rain snares upon sinners: fire and brimstone and storms of winds shall be the portion of their cup.
10:8 For the Lord is just, and hath loved justice: his countenance hath beheld righteousness.

XI.

11:1 *In finem, pro octava. Psalmus David.*
11:2 SALVUM ME FAC, DOMINE, quoniam defecit sanctus, quoniam diminutæ sunt veritates a filiis hominum.

11:1 *Unto the end; for the octave, a psalm for David.*
11:2 SAVE ME, O LORD, for there is now no saint: truths are decayed from among the children of men.

11:3 Vana locuti sunt unusquisque ad proximum suum ; labia dolosa, in corde et corde locuti sunt.

11:4 Disperdat Dominus universa labia dolosa, et linguam magniloquam.

11:5 Qui dixerunt : Linguam nostram magnificabimus ; labia nostra a nobis sunt. Quis noster dominus est ?

11:6 Propter miseriam inopum, et gemitum pauperum, nunc exsurgam, dicit Dominus. Ponam in salutari ; fiducialiter agam in eo.

11:7 Eloquia Domini, eloquia casta ; argentum igne examinatum, probatum terræ, purgatum septuplum.

11:8 Tu, Domine, servabis nos, et custodies nos a generatione hac in æternum.

11:9 In circuitu impii ambulant : secundum altitudinem tuam multiplicasti filios hominum.

11:3 They have spoken vain things every one to his neighbour: with deceitful lips, and with a double heart have they spoken.

11:4 May the Lord destroy all deceitful lips, and the tongue that speaketh proud things.

11:5 Who have said: We will magnify our tongue; our lips are our own; who is Lord over us?

11:6 By reason of the misery of the needy, and the groans of the poor, now will I arise, saith the Lord. I will set him in safety; I will deal confidently in his regard.

11:7 The words of the Lord are pure words: as silver tried by the fire, purged from the earth, refined seven times.

11:8 Thou, O Lord, wilt preserve us.: and keep us from this generation for ever.

11:9 The wicked walk round about: according to thy highness, thou hast multiplied the children of men.

XII.

12:1 *In finem. Psalmus David.* USQUEQUO, DOMINE, oblivisceris me in finem ? usquequo avertis faciem tuam a me ?

12:2 quamdiu ponam consilia in anima mea ; dolorem in corde meo per diem ?

12:3 usquequo exaltabitur inimicus meus super me ?

12:4 Respice, et exaudi me, Domine Deus meus. Illumina oculos meos, ne umquam obdormiam in morte ;

12:5 nequando dicat inimicus meus : Prævalui adversus eum. Qui tribulant me exsultabunt si motus fuero ;

12:6 ego autem in misericordia tua speravi. Exsultabit cor meum in salutari tuo. Cantabo Domino qui bona tribuit mihi ; et psallam nomini Domini altissimi.

12:1 *Unto the end, a psalm for David.* HOW LONG, O LORD, wilt thou forget me unto the end? how long dost thou turn away thy face from me?

12:2 How long shall I take counsels in my soul, sorrow in my heart all the day?

12:3 How long shall my enemy be exalted over me?

12:4 Consider, and hear me, O Lord my God. Enlighten my eyes that I never sleep in death:

12:5 lest at any time my enemy say: I have prevailed against him. They that trouble me will rejoice when I am moved:

12:6 but I have trusted in thy mercy. My heart shall rejoice in thy salvation: I will sing to the Lord, who giveth me good things: yea I will sing to the name of the Lord the most high.

XIII.

13:1 *In finem. Psalmus David.* DIXIT INSIPIENS in corde suo : Non est Deus. Corrupti sunt, et abominabiles facti sunt in studiis suis ; non est qui faciat bonum, non est usque ad unum.

13:2 Dominus de cælo prospexit super filios hominum, ut videat si est intelligens, aut requirens Deum.

13:3 Omnes declinaverunt, simul inutiles facti sunt. Non est qui faciat bonum, non est usque

13:1 *Unto the end, a psalm for David.* THE FOOL HATH SAID in his heart: There is no God. They are corrupt, and are become abominable in their ways: there is none that doth good, no not one.

13:2 The Lord hath looked down from heaven upon the children of men, to see if there be any that understand and seek God.

13:3 They are all gone aside, they are become unprofitable together: there is none that doth

ad unum. Sepulchrum patens est guttur eorum ; linguis suis dolose agebant. Venenum aspidum sub labiis eorum, quorum os maledictione et amaritudine plenum est ; veloces pedes eorum ad effundendum sanguinem. Contritio et infelicitas in viis eorum, et viam pacis non cognoverunt ; non est timor Dei ante oculos eorum.

13:4 Nonne cognoscent omnes qui operantur iniquitatem, qui devorant plebem meam sicut escam panis ?

13:5 Dominum non invocaverunt ; illic trepidaverunt timore, ubi non erat timor.

13:6 Quoniam Dominus in generatione justa est : consilium inopis confudistis, quoniam Dominus spes ejus est.

13:7 Quis dabit ex Sion salutare Israël ? Cum averterit Dominus captivitatem plebis suæ, exsultabit Jacob, et lætabitur Israël.

good, no not one. Their throat is an open sepulchre: with their tongues they acted deceitfully; the poison of asps is under their lips. Their mouth is full of cursing and bitterness; their feet are swift to shed blood. Destruction and unhappiness in their ways: and the way of peace they have not known: there is no fear of God before their eyes.

13:4 Shall not all they know that work iniquity, who devour my people as they eat bread?

13:5 They have not called upon the Lord: there have they trembled for fear, where there was no fear.

13:6 For the Lord is in the just generation: you have confounded the counsel of the poor man, but the Lord is his hope.

13:7 Who shall give out of Sion the salvation of Israel? when the Lord shall have turned away the captivity of his people, Jacob shall rejoice and Israel shall be glad.

XIV.

14:1 *Psalmus David.* DOMINE, QUIS HABITABIT in tabernaculo tuo ? aut quis requiescet in monte sancto tuo ?

14:2 Qui ingreditur sine macula, et operatur justitiam ;

14:3 qui loquitur veritatem in corde suo : qui non egit dolum in lingua sua, nec fecit proximo suo malum, et opprobrium non accepit adversus proximos suos.

14:4 Ad nihilum deductus est in conspectu ejus malignus ; timentes autem Dominum glorificat. Qui jurat proximo suo, et non decipit ;

14:5 qui pecuniam suam non dedit ad usuram, et munera super innocentem non accepit : qui facit hæc non movebitur in æternum.

14:1 *A psalm of David.* LORD, WHO SHALL DWELL in thy tabernacle? or who shall rest in thy holy hill?

14:2 He that walketh without blemish, and worketh justice:

14:3 He that speaketh truth in his heart, who hath not used deceit in his tongue: Nor hath done evil to his neighbour: nor taken up a reproach against his neighbours.

14:4 In his sight the malignant is brought to nothing: but he glorifieth them that fear the Lord. He that sweareth to his neighbour, and deceiveth not;

14:5 he that hath not put out his money to usury, nor taken bribes against the innocent: He that doth these things shall not be moved for ever.

XV.

15:1 *Tituli inscriptio, ipsi David.* CONSERVA ME, DOMINE, quoniam speravi in te.

15:2 Dixi Domino : Deus meus es tu, quoniam bonorum meorum non eges.

15:3 Sanctis qui sunt in terra ejus, mirificavit omnes voluntates meas in eis.

15:4 Multiplicatæ sunt infirmitates eorum : postea acceleraverunt. Non congregabo conventicula eorum de sanguinibus, nec memor ero nominum eorum per labia mea.

15:1 *The inscription of a title to David himself.* PRESERVE ME, O LORD, for I have put my trust in thee.

15:2 I have said to the Lord, thou art my God, for thou hast no need of my goods.

15:3 To the saints, who are in his land, he hath made wonderful all my desires in them.

15:4 Their infirmities were multiplied: afterwards they made haste. I will not gather together their meetings for blood offerings: nor will I be mindful of their names by my lips.

15:5 Dominus pars hæreditatis meæ, et calicis mei : tu es qui restitues hæreditatem meam mihi.

15:6 Funes ceciderunt mihi in præclaris ; etenim hæreditas mea præclara est mihi.

15:7 Benedicam Dominum qui tribuit mihi intellectum ; insuper et usque ad noctem increpuerunt me renes mei.

15:8 Providebam Dominum in conspectu meo semper : quoniam a dextris est mihi, ne commovear.

15:9 Propter hoc lætatum est cor meum, et exsultavit lingua mea ; insuper et caro mea requiescet in spe.

15:10 Quoniam non derelinques animam meam in inferno, nec dabis sanctum tuum videre corruptionem. Notas mihi fecisti vias vitæ ; adimplebis me lætitia cum vultu tuo : delectationes in dextera tua usque in finem.

15:5 The Lord is the portion of my inheritance and of my cup: it is thou that wilt restore my inheritance to me.

15:6 The lines are fallen unto me in goodly places: for my inheritance is goodly to me.

15:7 I will bless the Lord, who hath given me understanding: moreover my reins also have corrected me even till night.

15:8 I set the Lord always in my sight: for he is at my right hand, that I be not moved.

15:9 Therefore my heart hath been glad, and my tongue hath rejoiced: moreover my flesh also shall rest in hope.

15:10 Because thou wilt not leave my soul in hell; nor wilt then give thy holy one to see corruption. Thou hast made known to me the ways of life, thou shalt fill me with joy with thy countenance: at thy right hand are delights even to the end.

XVI.

16:1 *Oratio David.* EXAUDI, DOMINE, justitiam meam ; intende deprecationem meam. Auribus percipe orationem meam, non in labiis dolosis.

16:2 De vultu tuo judicium meum prodeat ; oculi tui videant æquitates.

16:3 Probasti cor meum, et visitasti nocte ; igne me examinasti, et non est inventa in me iniquitas.

16:4 Ut non loquatur os meum opera hominum : propter verba labiorum tuorum, ego custodivi vias duras.

16:5 Perfice gressus meos in semitis tuis, ut non moveantur vestigia mea.

16:6 Ego clamavi, quoniam exaudisti me, Deus ; inclina aurem tuam mihi, et exaudi verba mea.

16:7 Mirifica misericordias tuas, qui salvos facis sperantes in te.

16:8 A resistentibus dexteræ tuæ custodi me ut pupillam oculi. Sub umbra alarum tuarum protege me

16:9 a facie impiorum qui me afflixerunt. Inimici mei animam meam circumdederunt ;

16:10 adipem suum concluserunt : os eorum locutum est superbiam.

16:11 Projicientes me nunc circumdederunt me ; oculos suos statuerunt declinare in terram.

16:1 *The prayer of David.* HEAR, O LORD, my justice: attend to my supplication. Give ear unto my prayer, which proceedeth not from deceitful lips.

16:2 Let my judgment come forth from thy countenance: let thy eyes behold the things that are equitable.

16:3 Thou hast proved my heart, and visited it by night, thou hast tried me by fire: and iniquity hath not been found in me.

16:4 That my mouth may not speak the works of men: for the sake of the words of thy lips, I have kept hard ways.

16:5 Perfect thou my goings in thy paths: that my footsteps be not moved.

16:6 I have cried to thee, for thou, O God, hast heard me: O incline thy ear unto me, and hear my words.

16:7 Shew forth thy wonderful mercies; thou who savest them that trust in thee.

16:8 From them that resist thy right hand keep me, as the apple of thy eye. Protect me under the shadow of thy wings.

16:9 From the face of the wicked who have afflicted me. My enemies have surrounded my soul:

16:10 they have shut up their fat: their mouth hath spoken proudly.

16:11 They have cast me forth and now they have surrounded me: they have set their eyes bow-

16:12 Susceperunt me sicut leo paratus ad prædam, et sicut catulus leonis habitans in abditis.

16:13 Exsurge, Domine : præveni eum, et supplanta eum : eripe animam meam ab impio ; frameam tuam

16:14 ab inimicis manus tuæ. Domine, a paucis de terra divide eos in vita eorum ; de absconditis tuis adimpletus est venter eorum. Saturati sunt filiis, et dimiserunt reliquias suas parvulis suis.

16:15 Ego autem in justitia apparebo conspectui tuo ; satiabor cum apparuerit gloria tua.

ing down to the earth.

16:12 They have taken me, as a lion prepared for the prey; and as a young lion dwelling in secret places.

16:13 Arise, O Lord, disappoint him and supplant him; deliver my soul from the wicked one: thy sword

16:14 from the enemies of thy hand. O Lord, divide them from the few of the earth in their life: their belly is filled from thy hidden stores. They are full of children: and they have left to their little ones the rest of their substance.

16:15 But as for me, I will appear before thy sight in justice: I shall be satisfied when thy glory shall appear.

XVII.

17:1 *In finem. Puero Domini David, qui locutus est Domino verba cantici hujus, in die qua eripuit eum Dominus de manu omnium inimicorum ejus, et de manu Saul, et dixit :*

17:2 DILIGAM TE, Domine, fortitudo mea.

17:3 Dominus firmamentum meum, et refugium meum, et liberator meus. Deus meus adjutor meus, et sperabo in eum ; protector meus, et cornu salutis meæ, et susceptor meus.

17:4 Laudans invocabo Dominum, et ab inimicis meis salvus ero.

17:5 Circumdederunt me dolores mortis, et torrentes iniquitatis conturbaverunt me.

17:6 Dolores inferni circumdederunt me ; præoccupaverunt me laquei mortis.

17:7 In tribulatione mea invocavi Dominum, et ad Deum meum clamavi : et exaudivit de templo sancto suo vocem meam ; et clamor meus in conspectu ejus introivit in aures ejus.

17:8 Commota est, et contremuit terra ; fundamenta montium conturbata sunt, et commota sunt : quoniam iratus est eis.

17:9 Ascendit fumus in ira ejus, et ignis a facie ejus exarsit ; carbones succensi sunt ab eo.

17:10 Inclinavit cælos, et descendit, et caligo sub pedibus ejus.

17:11 Et ascendit super cherubim, et volavit ; volavit super pennas ventorum.

17:12 Et posuit tenebras latibulum suum ; in circuitu ejus tabernaculum ejus, tenebrosa aqua in nubibus aëris.

17:13 Præ fulgore in conspectu ejus nubes transierunt ; grando et carbones ignis.

17:14 Et intonuit de cælo Dominus, et Altissimus

17:1 *Unto the end, for David the servant of the Lord, who spoke to the Lord the words of this canticle, in the day that the Lord delivered him from the hands of all his enemies, and from the hand of Saul.*

17:2 I WILL LOVE THEE, O Lord, my strength:

17:3 The Lord is my firmament, my refuge, and my deliverer. My God is my helper, and in him will I put my trust. My protector and the horn of my salvation, and my support.

17:4 Praising I will call upon the Lord: and I shall be saved from my enemies.

17:5 The sorrows of death surrounded me: and the torrents of iniquity troubled me.

17:6 The sorrows of hell encompassed me: and the snares of death prevented me.

17:7 In my affliction I called upon the Lord, and I cried to my God: And he heard my voice from his holy temple: and my cry before him came into his ears.

17:8 The earth shook and trembled: the foundations of the mountains were troubled and were moved, because he was angry with them.

17:9 There went up a smoke in his wrath: and a fire flamed from his face: coals were kindled by it.

17:10 He bowed the heavens, and came down: and darkness was under his feet.

17:11 And he ascended upon the cherubim, and he flew; he flew upon the wings of the winds.

17:12 And he made darkness his covert, his pavilion round about him: dark waters in the clouds of the air.

17:13 At the brightness that was before him the clouds passed, hail and coals of fire.

17:14 And the Lord thundered from heaven, and

dedit vocem suam : grando et carbones ignis.

17:15 Et misit sagittas suas, et dissipavit eos ; fulgura multiplicavit, et conturbavit eos.

17:16 Et apparuerunt fontes aquarum, et revelata sunt fundamenta orbis terrarum, ab increpatione tua, Domine, ab inspiratione spiritus iræ tuæ.

17:17 Misit de summo, et accepit me ; et assumpsit me de aquis multis.

17:18 Eripuit me de inimicis meis fortissimis, et ab his qui oderunt me. Quoniam confortati sunt super me ;

17:19 prævenerunt me in die afflictionis meæ : et factus est Dominus protector meus.

17:20 Et eduxit me in latitudinem ; salvum me fecit, quoniam voluit me,

17:21 et retribuet mihi Dominus secundum justitiam meam, et secundum puritatem manuum mearum retribuet mihi :

17:22 quia custodivi vias Domini, nec impie gessi a Deo meo ;

17:23 quoniam omnia judicia ejus in conspectu meo, et justitias ejus non repuli a me.

17:24 Et ero immaculatus cum eo ; et observabo me ab iniquitate mea.

17:25 Et retribuet mihi Dominus secundum justitiam meam, et secundum puritatem manuum mearum in conspectu oculorum ejus.

17:26 Cum sancto sanctus eris, et cum viro innocente innocens eris,

17:27 et cum electo electus eris, et cum perverso perverteris.

17:28 Quoniam tu populum humilem salvum facies, et oculos superborum humiliabis.

17:29 Quoniam tu illuminas lucernam meam, Domine ; Deus meus, illumina tenebras meas.

17:30 Quoniam in te eripiar a tentatione ; et in Deo meo transgrediar murum.

17:31 Deus meus, impolluta via ejus ; eloquia Domini igne examinata : protector est omnium sperantium in se.

17:32 Quoniam quis deus præter Dominum ? aut quis deus præter Deum nostrum ?

17:33 Deus qui præcinxit me virtute, et posuit immaculatam viam meam ;

17:34 qui perfecit pedes meos tamquam cervorum, et super excelsa statuens me ;

17:35 qui docet manus meas ad prælium. Et posuisti, ut arcum æreum, brachia mea,

the highest gave his voice: hail and coals of fire.

17:15 And he sent forth his arrows, and he scattered them: he multiplied lightnings, and troubled them.

17:16 Then the fountains of waters appeared, and the foundations of the world were discovered: At thy rebuke, O Lord, at the blast of the spirit of thy wrath.

17:17 He sent from on high, and took me: and received me out of many waters.

17:18 He delivered me from my strongest enemies, and from them that hated me: for they were too strong for me.

17:19 They prevented me in the day of my affliction: and the Lord became my protector.

17:20 And he brought me forth into a large place: he saved me, because he was well pleased with me.

17:21 And the Lord will reward me according to my justice; and will repay me according to the cleanness of my hands:

17:22 Because I have kept the ways of the Lord; and have not done wickedly against my God.

17:23 For all his judgments are in my sight: and his justices I have not put away from me.

17:24 And I shall be spotless with him: and shall keep myself from my iniquity.

17:25 And the Lord will reward me according to my justice; and according to the cleanness of my hands before his eyes.

17:26 With the holy, thou wilt be holy; and with the innocent man thou wilt be innocent.

17:27 And with the elect thou wilt be elect: and with the perverse thou wilt be perverted.

17:28 For thou wilt save the humble people; but wilt bring down the eyes of the proud.

17:29 For thou lightest my lamp, O Lord: O my God enlighten my darkness.

17:30 For by thee I shall be delivered from temptation; and through my God I shall go over a wall.

17:31 As for my God, his way is undefiled: the words of the Lord are fire tried: he is the protector of all that trust in him.

17:32 For who is God but the Lord? or who is God but our God?

17:33 God who hath girt me with strength; and made my way blameless.

17:34 Who hath made my feet like the feet of harts: and who setteth me upon high places.

17:35 Who teacheth my hands to war: and thou hast made my arms like a brazen bow.

17:36 et dedisti mihi protectionem salutis tuæ : et dextera tua suscepit me, et disciplina tua correxit me in finem, et disciplina tua ipsa me docebit.

17:37 Dilatasti gressus meos subtus me, et non sunt infirmata vestigia mea.

17:38 Persequar inimicos meos, et comprehendam illos ; et non convertar donec deficiant.

17:39 Confringam illos, nec poterunt stare ; cadent subtus pedes meos.

17:40 Et præcinxisti me virtute ad bellum, et supplantasti insurgentes in me subtus me.

17:41 Et inimicos meos dedisti mihi dorsum, et odientes me disperdidisti.

17:42 Clamaverunt, nec erat qui salvos faceret ; ad Dominum, nec exaudivit eos.

17:43 Et comminuam eos ut pulverem ante faciem venti ; ut lutum platearum delebo eos.

17:44 Eripies me de contradictionibus populi ; constitues me in caput gentium.

17:45 Populus quem non cognovi servivit mihi ; in auditu auris obedivit mihi.

17:46 Filii alieni mentiti sunt mihi, filii alieni inveterati sunt, et claudicaverunt a semitis suis.

17:47 Vivit Dominus, et benedictus Deus meus, et exaltetur Deus salutis meæ.

17:48 Deus qui das vindictas mihi, et subdis populos sub me ; liberator meus de inimicis meis iracundis.

17:49 Et ab insurgentibus in me exaltabis me ; a viro iniquo eripies me.

17:50 Propterea confitebor tibi in nationibus, Domine, et nomini tuo psalmum dicam ;

17:51 magnificans salutes regis ejus, et faciens misericordiam christo suo David, et semini ejus usque in sæculum.

17:36 And thou hast given me the protection of thy salvation: and thy right hand hath held me up: And thy discipline hath corrected me unto the end: and thy discipline, the same shall teach me.

17:37 Thou hast enlarged my steps under me; and my feet are not weakened.

17:38 I will pursue after my enemies, and overtake them: and I will not turn again till they are consumed.

17:39 I will break them, and they shall not be able to stand: they shall fall under my feet.

17:40 And thou hast girded me with strength unto battle; and hast subdued under me them that rose up against me.

17:41 And thou hast made my enemies turn their back upon me, and hast destroyed them that hated me.

17:42 They cried, but there was none to save them, to the Lord: but he heard them not.

17:43 And I shall beat them as small as the dust before the wind; I shall bring them to nought, like the dirt in the streets.

17:44 Thou wilt deliver me from the contradictions of the people: thou wilt make me head of the Gentiles.

17:45 A people, which I knew not, hath served me: at the hearing of the ear they have obeyed me.

17:46 The children that are strangers have lied to me, strange children have faded away, and have halted from their paths.

17:47 The Lord liveth, and blessed be my God, and let the God of my salvation be exalted:

17:48 O God, who avengest me, and subduest the people under me, my deliverer from my enemies.

17:49 And thou wilt lift me up above them that rise up against me: from the unjust man thou wilt deliver me.

17:50 Therefore will I give glory to thee, O Lord, among the nations, and I will sing a psalm to thy name.

17:51 Giving great deliverance to his king, and shewing mercy to David his anointed: and to his seed for ever.

XVIII.

18:1 *In finem. Psalmus David.*

18:2 CÆLI ENARRANT gloriam Dei, et opera manuum ejus annuntiat firmamentum.

18:1 *Unto the end. A psalm for David.*

18:2 THE HEAVENS SHEW FORTH the glory of God, and the firmament declareth the work of his hands.

^{18:3} Dies diei eructat verbum, et nox nocti indicat scientiam.

^{18:4} Non sunt loquelæ, neque sermones, quorum non audiantur voces eorum.

^{18:5} In omnem terram exivit sonus eorum, et in fines orbis terræ verba eorum.

^{18:6} In sole posuit tabernaculum suum ; et ipse tamquam sponsus procedens de thalamo suo. Exsultavit ut gigas ad currendam viam ;

^{18:7} a summo cælo egressio ejus. Et occursus ejus usque ad summum ejus ; nec est qui se abscondat a calore ejus.

^{18:8} Lex Domini immaculata, convertens animas ; testimonium Domini fidele, sapientiam præstans parvulis.

^{18:9} Justitiæ Domini rectæ, lætificantes corda ; præceptum Domini lucidum, illuminans oculos.

^{18:10} Timor Domini sanctus, permanens in sæculum sæculi ; judicia Domini vera, justificata in semetipsa,

^{18:11} desiderabilia super aurum et lapidem pretiosum multum, et dulciora super mel et favum.

^{18:12} Etenim servus tuus custodit ea ; in custodiendis illis retributio multa.

^{18:13} Delicta quis intelligit ? ab occultis meis munda me ;

^{18:14} et ab alienis parce servo tuo. Si mei non fuerint dominati, tunc immaculatus ero, et emundabor a delicto maximo.

^{18:15} Et erunt ut complaceant eloquia oris mei, et meditatio cordis mei in conspectu tuo semper. Domine, adjutor meus, et redemptor meus.

^{18:3} Day to day uttereth speech, and night to night sheweth knowledge.

^{18:4} There are no speeches nor languages, where their voices are not heard.

^{18:5} Their sound hath gone forth into all the earth: and their words unto the ends of the world.

^{18:6} He hath set his tabernacle in the sun: and he, as a bridegroom coming out of his bride chamber, Hath rejoiced as a giant to run the way:

^{18:7} His going out is from the end of heaven, And his circuit even to the end thereof: and there is no one that can hide himself from his heat.

^{18:8} The law of the Lord is unspotted, converting souls: the testimony of the Lord is faithful, giving wisdom to little ones.

^{18:9} The justices of the Lord are right, rejoicing hearts: the commandment of the Lord is lightsome, enlightening the eyes.

^{18:10} The fear of the Lord is holy, enduring for ever and ever: the judgments of the Lord are true, justified in themselves.

^{18:11} More to be desired than gold and many precious stones: and sweeter than honey and the honeycomb.

^{18:12} For thy servant keepeth them, and in keeping them there is a great reward.

^{18:13} Who can understand sins? from my secret ones cleanse me, O Lord:

^{18:14} and from those of others spare thy servant. If they shall have no dominion over me, then shall I be without spot: and I shall be cleansed from the greatest sin.

^{18:15} And the words of my mouth shall be such as may please: and the meditation of my heart always in thy sight. O Lord, my helper, and my redeemer.

XIX.

^{19:1} *In finem. Psalmus David.*

^{19:2} EXAUDIAT TE DOMINUS in die tribulationis ; protegat te nomen Dei Jacob.

^{19:3} Mittat tibi auxilium de sancto, et de Sion tueatur te.

^{19:4} Memor sit omnis sacrificii tui, et holocaustum tuum pingue fiat.

^{19:5} Tribuat tibi secundum cor tuum, et omne consilium tuum confirmet.

^{19:6} Lætabimur in salutari tuo ; et in nomine

^{19:1} *Unto the end. A psalm for David.*

^{19:2} MAY THE LORD HEAR THEE in the day of tribulation: may the name of the God of Jacob protect thee.

^{19:3} May he send thee help from the sanctuary: and defend thee out of Sion.

^{19:4} May he be mindful of all thy sacrifices: and may thy whole burnt offering be made fat.

^{19:5} May he give thee according to thy own heart; and confirm all thy counsels.

^{19:6} We will rejoice in thy salvation; and in the

Dei nostri magnificabimur.

19:7 Impleat Dominus omnes petitiones tuas ; nunc cognovi quoniam salvum fecit Dominus christum suum. Exaudiet illum de cælo sancto suo, in potentatibus salus dexteræ ejus.

19:8 Hi in curribus, et hi in equis ; nos autem in nomine Domini Dei nostri invocabimus.

19:9 Ipsi obligati sunt, et ceciderunt ; nos autem surreximus, et erecti sumus.

19:10 Domine, salvum fac regem, et exaudi nos in die qua invocaverimus te.

name of our God we shall be exalted.

19:7 The Lord fulfil all thy petitions: now have I known that the Lord hath saved his anointed. He will hear him from his holy heaven: the salvation of his right hand is in powers.

19:8 Some trust in chariots, and some in horses: but we will call upon the name of the Lord our God.

19:9 They are bound, and have fallen; but we are risen, and are set upright.

19:10 O Lord, save the king: and hear us in the day that we shall call upon thee.

XX.

20:1 *In finem. Psalmus David.*

20:2 DOMINE, IN VIRTUTE TUA lætabitur rex, et super salutare tuum exsultabit vehementer.

20:3 Desiderium cordis ejus tribuisti ei, et voluntate labiorum ejus non fraudasti eum.

20:4 Quoniam prævenisti eum in benedictionibus dulcedinis ; posuisti in capite ejus coronam de lapide pretioso.

20:5 Vitam petiit a te, et tribuisti ei longitudinem dierum, in sæculum, et in sæculum sæculi.

20:6 Magna est gloria ejus in salutari tuo ; gloriam et magnum decorem impones super eum.

20:7 Quoniam dabis eum in benedictionem in sæculum sæculi ; lætificabis eum in gaudio cum vultu tuo.

20:8 Quoniam rex sperat in Domino, et in misericordia Altissimi non commovebitur.

20:9 Inveniatur manus tua omnibus inimicis tuis ; dextera tua inveniat omnes qui te oderunt.

20:10 Pones eos ut clibanum ignis in tempore vultus tui : Dominus in ira sua conturbabit eos, et devorabit eos ignis.

20:11 Fructum eorum de terra perdes, et semen eorum a filiis hominum,

20:12 quoniam declinaverunt in te mala ; cogitaverunt consilia quæ non potuerunt stabilire.

20:13 Quoniam pones eos dorsum ; in reliquiis tuis præparabis vultum eorum.

20:14 Exaltare, Domine, in virtute tua ; cantabimus et psallemus virtutes tuas.

20:1 *Unto the end. A psalm for David.*

20:2 IN THY STRENGTH, O LORD, the king shall joy; and in thy salvation he shall rejoice exceedingly.

20:3 Thou hast given him his heart's desire: and hast not withholden from him the will of his lips.

20:4 For thou hast prevented him with blessings of sweetness: thou hast set on his head a crown of precious stones.

20:5 He asked life of thee: and thou hast given him length of days for ever and ever.

20:6 His glory is great in thy salvation: glory and great beauty shalt thou lay upon him.

20:7 For thou shalt give him to be a blessing for ever and ever: thou shalt make him joyful in gladness with thy countenance.

20:8 For the king hopeth in the Lord: and through the mercy of the most High he shall not be moved.

20:9 Let thy hand be found by all thy enemies: let thy right hand find out all them that hate thee.

20:10 Thou shalt make them as an oven of fire, in the time of thy anger: the Lord shall trouble them in his wrath, and fire shall devour them.

20:11 Their fruit shalt thou destroy from the earth: and their seed from among the children of men.

20:12 For they have intended evils against thee: they have devised counsels which they have not been able to establish.

20:13 For thou shalt make them turn their back: in thy remnants thou shalt prepare their face.

20:14 Be thou exalted, O Lord, in thy own strength: we will sing and praise thy power.

XXI.

21:1 *In finem, pro susceptione matutina. Psalmus David.*

21:2 DEUS, DEUS MEUS, respice in me : quare me dereliquisti ? longe a salute mea verba delictorum meorum.

21:3 Deus meus, clamabo per diem, et non exaudies ; et nocte, et non ad insipientiam mihi.

21:4 Tu autem in sancto habitas, laus Israël.

21:5 In te speraverunt patres nostri ; speraverunt, et liberasti eos.

21:6 Ad te clamaverunt, et salvi facti sunt ; in te speraverunt, et non sunt confusi.

21:7 Ego autem sum vermis, et non homo ; opprobrium hominum, et abjectio plebis.

21:8 Omnes videntes me deriserunt me ; locuti sunt labiis, et moverunt caput.

21:9 Speravit in Domino, eripiat eum : salvum faciat eum, quoniam vult eum.

21:10 Quoniam tu es qui extraxisti me de ventre, spes mea ab uberibus matris meæ.

21:11 In te projectus sum ex utero ; de ventre matris meæ Deus meus es tu :

21:12 ne discesseris a me, quoniam tribulatio proxima est, quoniam non est qui adjuvet.

21:13 Circumdederunt me vituli multi ; tauri pingues obsederunt me.

21:14 Aperuerunt super me os suum, sicut leo rapiens et rugiens.

21:15 Sicut aqua effusus sum, et dispersa sunt omnia ossa mea : factum est cor meum tamquam cera liquescens in medio ventris mei.

21:16 Aruit tamquam testa virtus mea, et lingua mea adhæsit faucibus meis : et in pulverem mortis deduxisti me.

21:17 Quoniam circumdederunt me canes multi ; concilium malignantium obsedit me. Foderunt manus meas et pedes meos ;

21:18 dinumeraverunt omnia ossa mea. Ipsi vero consideraverunt et inspexerunt me.

21:19 Diviserunt sibi vestimenta mea, et super vestem meam miserunt sortem.

21:20 Tu autem, Domine, ne elongaveris auxilium tuum a me ; ad defensionem meam conspice.

21:21 Erue a framea, Deus, animam meam, et de manu canis unicam meam.

21:1 *Unto the end, for the morning protection, a psalm for David.*

21:2 O GOD MY GOD, look upon me: why hast thou forsaken me? Far from my salvation are the words of my sins.

21:3 O my God, I shall cry by day, and thou wilt not hear: and by night, and it shall not be reputed as folly in me.

21:4 But thou dwellest in the holy place, the praise of Israel.

21:5 In thee have our fathers hoped: they have hoped, and thou hast delivered them.

21:6 They cried to thee, and they were saved: they trusted in thee, and were not confounded.

21:7 But I am a worm, and no man: the reproach of men, and the outcast of the people.

21:8 All they that saw me have laughed me to scorn: they have spoken with the lips, and wagged the head.

21:9 He hoped in the Lord, let him deliver him: let him save him, seeing he delighteth in him.

21:10 For thou art he that hast drawn me out of the womb: my hope from the breasts of my mother.

21:11 I was cast upon thee from the womb. From my mother's womb thou art my God,

21:12 depart not from me. For tribulation is very near: for there is none to help me.

21:13 Many calves have surrounded me: fat bulls have besieged me.

21:14 They have opened their mouths against me, as a lion ravening and roaring.

21:15 I am poured out like water; and all my bones are scattered. My heart is become like wax melting in the midst of my bowels.

21:16 My strength is dried up like a potsherd, and my tongue hath cleaved to my jaws: and thou hast brought me down into the dust of death.

21:17 For many dogs have encompassed me: the council of the malignant hath besieged me. They have dug my hands and feet.

21:18 They have numbered all my bones. And they have looked and stared upon me.

21:19 They parted my garments amongst them; and upon my vesture they cast lots.

21:20 But thou, O Lord, remove not thy help to a distance from me; look towards my defence.

21:21 Deliver, O God, my soul from the sword: my only one from the hand of the dog.

21:22 Salva me ex ore leonis, et a cornibus uni-cornium humilitatem meam.

21:23 Narrabo nomen tuum fratribus meis ; in medio ecclesiæ laudabo te.

21:24 Qui timetis Dominum, laudate eum ; universum semen Jacob, glorificate eum.

21:25 Timeat eum omne semen Israël, quoniam non sprevit, neque despexit deprecationem pauperis, nec avertit faciem suam a me : et cum clamarem ad eum, exaudivit me.

21:26 Apud te laus mea in ecclesia magna ; vota mea reddam in conspectu timentium eum.

21:27 Edent pauperes, et saturabuntur, et laudabunt Dominum qui requirunt eum : vivent corda eorum in sæculum sæculi.

21:28 Reminiscentur et convertentur ad Dominum universi fines terræ ; et adorabunt in conspectu ejus universæ familiæ gentium :

21:29 quoniam Domini est regnum, et ipse dominabitur gentium.

21:30 Manducaverunt et adoraverunt omnes pingues terræ ; in conspectu ejus cadent omnes qui descendunt in terram.

21:31 Et anima mea illi vivet ; et semen meum serviet ipsi.

21:32 Annuntiabitur Domino generatio ventura ; et annuntiabunt cæli justitiam ejus populo qui nascetur, quem fecit Dominus.

21:22 Save me from the lion's mouth; and my lowness from the horns of the unicorns.

21:23 I will declare thy name to my brethren: in the midst of the church will I praise thee.

21:24 Ye that fear the Lord, praise him: all ye the seed of Jacob, glorify him.

21:25 Let all the seed of Israel fear him: because he hath not slighted nor despised the supplication of the poor man. Neither hath he turned away his face from me: and when I cried to him he heard me.

21:26 With thee is my praise in a great church: I will pay my vows in the sight of them that fear him.

21:27 The poor shall eat and shall be filled: and they shall praise the Lord that seek him: their hearts shall live for ever and ever.

21:28 All the ends of the earth shall remember, and shall be converted to the Lord: And all the kindreds of the Gentiles shall adore in his sight.

21:29 For the kingdom is the Lord's; and he shall have dominion over the nations.

21:30 All the fat ones of the earth have eaten and have adored: all they that go down to the earth shall fall before him.

21:31 And to him my soul shall live: and my seed shall serve him.

21:32 There shall be declared to the Lord a generation to come: and the heavens shall shew forth his justice to a people that shall be born, which the Lord hath made.

XXII.

22:1 *Psalmus David.* DOMINUS REGIT ME, et nihil mihi deerit :

22:2 in loco pascuæ, ibi me collocavit. Super aquam refectionis educavit me ;

22:3 animam meam convertit. Deduxit me super semitas justitiæ propter nomen suum.

22:4 Nam etsi ambulavero in medio umbræ mortis, non timebo mala, quoniam tu mecum es. Virga tua, et baculus tuus, ipsa me consolata sunt.

22:5 Parasti in conspectu meo mensam adversus eos qui tribulant me ; impinguasti in oleo caput meum : et calix meus inebrians, quam præclarus est !

22:6 Et misericordia tua subsequetur me omnibus diebus vitæ meæ ; et ut inhabitem in domo Domini in longitudinem dierum.

22:1 *A psalm for David.* THE LORD RULETH ME: and I shall want nothing.

22:2 He hath set me in a place of pasture. He hath brought me up, on the water of refreshment:

22:3 he hath converted my soul. He hath led me on the paths of justice, for his own name's sake.

22:4 For though I should walk in the midst of the shadow of death, I will fear no evils, for thou art with me. Thy rod and thy staff, they have comforted me.

22:5 Thou hast prepared a table before me against them that afflict me. Thou hast anointed my head with oil; and my chalice which inebriateth me, how goodly is it!

22:6 And thy mercy will follow me all the days of my life. And that I may dwell in the house of the Lord unto length of days.

XXIII.

23:1 *Prima sabbati. Psalmus David.* DOMINI EST TERRA, et plenitudo ejus ; orbis terrarum, et universi qui habitant in eo.

23:2 Quia ipse super maria fundavit eum, et super flumina præparavit eum.

23:3 Quis ascendet in montem Domini ? aut quis stabit in loco sancto ejus ?

23:4 Innocens manibus et mundo corde, qui non accepit in vano animam suam, nec juravit in dolo proximo suo :

23:5 hic accipiet benedictionem a Domino, et misericordiam a Deo salutari suo.

23:6 Hæc est generatio quærentium eum, quærentium faciem Dei Jacob.

23:7 Attollite portas, principes, vestras, et elevamini, portæ æternales, et introibit rex gloriæ.

23:8 Quis est iste rex gloriæ ? Dominus fortis et potens, Dominus potens in prælio.

23:9 Attollite portas, principes, vestras, et elevamini, portæ æternales, et introibit rex gloriæ.

23:10 Quis est iste rex gloriæ ? Dominus virtutum ipse est rex gloriæ.

23:1 *On the first day of the week, a psalm for David.* THE EARTH IS THE LORD'S and the fulness thereof: the world, and all they that dwell therein.

23:2 For he hath founded it upon the seas; and hath prepared it upon the rivers.

23:3 Who shall ascend into the mountain of the Lord: or who shall stand in his holy place?

23:4 The innocent in hands, and clean of heart, who hath not taken his soul in vain, nor sworn deceitfully to his neighbour.

23:5 He shall receive a blessing from the Lord, and mercy from God his Saviour.

23:6 This is the generation of them that seek him, of them that seek the face of the God of Jacob.

23:7 Lift up your gates, O ye princes, and be ye lifted up, O eternal gates: and the King of Glory shall enter in.

23:8 Who is this King of Glory? The Lord who is strong and mighty: the Lord mighty in battle.

23:9 Lift up your gates, O ye princes, and be ye lifted up, O eternal gates: and the King of Glory shall enter in.

23:10 Who is this King of Glory? The Lord of hosts, he is the King of Glory.

XXIV.

24:1 *In finem. Psalmus David.* AD TE, DOMINE, levavi animam meam :

24:2 Deus meus, in te confido ; non erubescam.

24:3 Neque irrideant me inimici mei : etenim universi qui sustinent te, non confundentur.

24:4 Confundantur omnes iniqua agentes supervacue. Vias tuas, Domine, demonstra mihi, et semitas tuas edoce me.

24:5 Dirige me in veritate tua, et doce me, quia tu es Deus salvator meus, et te sustinui tota die.

24:6 Reminiscere miserationum tuarum, Domine, et misericordiarum tuarum quæ a sæculo sunt.

24:7 Delicta juventutis meæ, et ignorantias meas, ne memineris. Secundum misericordiam tuam memento mei tu, propter bonitatem tuam, Domine.

24:8 Dulcis et rectus Dominus ; propter hoc legem dabit delinquentibus in via.

24:9 Diriget mansuetos in judicio ; docebit mites

24:1 *Unto the end, a psalm for David.* TO THEE, O LORD, have I lifted up my soul.

24:2 In thee, O my God, I put my trust; let me not be ashamed.

24:3 Neither let my enemies laugh at me: for none of them that wait on thee shall be confounded.

24:4 Let all them be confounded that act unjust things without cause. Shew, O Lord, thy ways to me, and teach me thy paths.

24:5 Direct me in thy truth, and teach me; for thou art God my Saviour; and on thee have I waited all the day long.

24:6 Remember, O Lord, thy bowels of compassion; and thy mercies that are from the beginning of the world.

24:7 The sins of my youth and my ignorances do not remember. According to thy mercy remember thou me: for thy goodness' sake, O Lord.

24:8 The Lord is sweet and righteous: therefore he will give a law to sinners in the way.

24:9 He will guide the mild in judgment: he will

vias suas.

24:10 Universæ viæ Domini, misericordia et veritas, requirentibus testamentum ejus et testimonia ejus.

24:11 Propter nomen tuum, Domine, propitiaberis peccato meo ; multum est enim.

24:12 Quis est homo qui timet Dominum ? legem statuit ei in via quam elegit.

24:13 Anima ejus in bonis demorabitur, et semen ejus hæreditabit terram.

24:14 Firmamentum est Dominus timentibus eum ; et testamentum ipsius ut manifestetur illis.

24:15 Oculi mei semper ad Dominum, quoniam ipse evellet de laqueo pedes meos.

24:16 Respice in me, et miserere mei, quia unicus et pauper sum ego.

24:17 Tribulationes cordis mei multiplicatæ sunt : de necessitatibus meis erue me.

24:18 Vide humilitatem meam et laborem meum, et dimitte universa delicta mea.

24:19 Respice inimicos meos, quoniam multiplicati sunt, et odio iniquo oderunt me.

24:20 Custodi animam meam, et erue me : non erubescam, quoniam speravi in te.

24:21 Innocentes et recti adhæserunt mihi, quia sustinui te.

24:22 Libera, Deus, Israël ex omnibus tribulationibus suis.

teach the meek his ways.

24:10 All the ways of the Lord are mercy and truth, to them that seek after his covenant and his testimonies.

24:11 For thy name's sake, O Lord, thou wilt pardon my sin: for it is great.

24:12 Who is the man that feareth the Lord? He hath appointed him a law in the way he hath chosen.

24:13 His soul shall dwell in good things: and his seed shall inherit the land.

24:14 The Lord is a firmament to them that fear him: and his covenant shall be made manifest to them.

24:15 My eyes are ever towards the Lord: for he shall pluck my feet out of the snare.

24:16 Look thou upon me, and have mercy on me; for I am alone and poor.

24:17 The troubles of my heart are multiplied: deliver me from my necessities.

24:18 See my abjection and my labour; and forgive me all my sins.

24:19 Consider my enemies for they are multiplied, and have hated me with an unjust hatred.

24:20 Keep thou my soul, and deliver me: I shall not be ashamed, for I have hoped in thee.

24:21 The innocent and the upright have adhered to me: because I have waited on thee.

24:22 Deliver Israel, O God, from all his tribulations.

XXV.

25:1 *In finem. Psalmus David.* JUDICA ME, DOMINE, quoniam ego in innocentia mea ingressus sum, et in Domino sperans non infirmabor.

25:2 Proba me, Domine, et tenta me ; ure renes meos et cor meum.

25:3 Quoniam misericordia tua ante oculos meos est, et complacui in veritate tua.

25:4 Non sedi cum concilio vanitatis, et cum iniqua gerentibus non introibo.

25:5 Odivi ecclesiam malignantium, et cum impiis non sedebo.

25:6 Lavabo inter innocentes manus meas, et circumdabo altare tuum, Domine :

25:7 ut audiam vocem laudis, et enarrem universa mirabilia tua.

25:8 Domine, dilexi decorem domus tuæ, et locum habitationis gloriæ tuæ.

25:9 Ne perdas cum impiis, Deus, animam

25:1 *Unto the end, a psalm for David.* JUDGE ME, O LORD, for I have walked in my innocence: and I have put my trust in the Lord, and shall not be weakened.

25:2 Prove me, O Lord, and try me; burn my reins and my heart.

25:3 For thy mercy is before my eyes; and I am well pleased with thy truth.

25:4 I have not sat with the council of vanity: neither will I go in with the doers of unjust things.

25:5 I have hated the assembly of the malignant; and with the wicked I will not sit.

25:6 I will wash my hands among the innocent; and will compass thy altar, O Lord:

25:7 That I may hear the voice of thy praise: and tell of all thy wondrous works.

25:8 I have loved, O Lord, the beauty of thy house; and the place where thy glory dwelleth.

25:9 Take not away my soul, O God, with the

meam, et cum viris sanguinum vitam meam :

25:10 in quorum manibus iniquitates sunt ; dextera eorum repleta est muneribus.

25:11 Ego autem in innocentia mea ingressus sum ; redime me, et miserere mei.

25:12 Pes meus stetit in directo ; in ecclesiis benedicam te, Domine.

wicked: nor my life with bloody men:

25:10 In whose hands are iniquities: their right hand is filled with gifts.

25:11 But as for me, I have walked in my innocence: redeem me, and have mercy on me.

25:12 My foot hath stood in the direct way: in the churches I will bless thee, O Lord.

XXVI.

26:1 *Psalmus David, priusquam liniretur.* DOMINUS ILLUMINATIO MEA et salus mea : quem timebo ? Dominus protector vitæ meæ : a quo trepidabo ?

26:2 Dum appropiant super me nocentes ut edant carnes meas, qui tribulant me inimici mei, ipsi infirmati sunt et ceciderunt.

26:3 Si consistant adversum me castra, non timebit cor meum ; si exsurgat adversum me prælium, in hoc ego sperabo.

26:4 Unam petii a Domino, hanc requiram, ut inhabitem in domo Domini omnibus diebus vitæ meæ ; ut videam voluptatem Domini, et visitem templum ejus.

26:5 Quoniam abscondit me in tabernaculo suo ; in die malorum protexit me in abscondito tabernaculi sui.

26:6 In petra exaltavit me, et nunc exaltavit caput meum super inimicos meos. Circuivi, et immolavi in tabernaculo ejus hostiam vociferationis ; cantabo, et psalmum dicam Domino.

26:7 Exaudi, Domine, vocem meam, qua clamavi ad te ; miserere mei, et exaudi me.

26:8 Tibi dixit cor meum : Exquisivit te facies mea ; faciem tuam, Domine, requiram.

26:9 Ne avertas faciem tuam a me ; ne declines in ira a servo tuo. Adjutor meus esto ; ne derelinquas me, neque despicias me, Deus salutaris meus.

26:10 Quoniam pater meus et mater mea dereliquerunt me ; Dominus autem assumpsit me.

26:11 Legem pone mihi, Domine, in via tua, et dirige me in semitam rectam, propter inimicos meos.

26:12 Ne tradideris me in animas tribulantium me, quoniam insurrexerunt in me testes iniqui, et mentita est iniquitas sibi.

26:13 Credo videre bona Domini in terra viventium.

26:14 Expecta Dominum, viriliter age : et confortetur cor tuum, et sustine Dominum.

26:1 *The psalm of David before he was anointed.* THE LORD IS MY LIGHT and my salvation, whom shall I fear? The Lord is the protector of my life: of whom shall I be afraid?

26:2 Whilst the wicked draw near against me, to eat my flesh. My enemies that trouble me, have themselves been weakened, and have fallen.

26:3 If armies in camp should stand together against me, my heart shall not fear. If a battle should rise up against me, in this will I be confident.

26:4 One thing I have asked of the Lord, this will I seek after; that I may dwell in the house of the Lord all the days of my life. That I may see the delight of the Lord, and may visit his temple.

26:5 For he hath hidden me in his tabernacle; in the day of evils, he hath protected me in the secret place of his tabernacle.

26:6 He hath exalted me upon a rock: and now he hath lifted up my head above my enemies. I have gone round, and have offered up in his tabernacle a sacrifice of jubilation: I will sing, and recite a psalm to the Lord.

26:7 Hear, O Lord, my voice, with which I have cried to thee: have mercy on me and hear me.

26:8 My heart hath said to thee: My face hath sought thee: thy face, O Lord, will I still seek.

26:9 Turn not away thy face from me; decline not in thy wrath from thy servant. Be thou my helper, forsake me not; do not thou despise me, O God my Saviour.

26:10 For my father and my mother have left me: but the Lord hath taken me up.

26:11 Set me, O Lord, a law in thy way, and guide me in the right path, because of my enemies.

26:12 Deliver me not over to the will of them that trouble me; for unjust witnesses have risen up against me; and iniquity hath lied to itself.

26:13 I believe to see the good things of the Lord in the land of the living.

26:14 Expect the Lord, do manfully, and let thy heart take courage, and wait thou for the Lord.

XXVII.

27:1 *Psalmus ipsi David.* AD TE, DOMINE, CLAMA-BO ; Deus meus, ne sileas a me : nequando taceas a me, et assimilabor descendentibus in lacum.

27:2 Exaudi, Domine, vocem deprecationis meæ dum oro ad te ; dum extollo manus meas ad templum sanctum tuum.

27:3 Ne simul trahas me cum peccatoribus, et cum operantibus iniquitatem ne perdas me ; qui loquuntur pacem cum proximo suo, mala autem in cordibus eorum.

27:4 Da illis secundum opera eorum, et secundum nequitiam adinventionum ipsorum. Secundum opera manuum eorum tribue illis ; redde retributionem eorum ipsis.

27:5 Quoniam non intellexerunt opera Domini, et in opera manuum ejus destrues illos, et non ædificabis eos.

27:6 Benedictus Dominus, quoniam exaudivit vocem deprecationis meæ.

27:7 Dominus adjutor meus et protector meus ; in ipso speravit cor meum, et adjutus sum : et refloruit caro mea, et ex voluntate mea confitebor ei.

27:8 Dominus fortitudo plebis suæ, et protector salvationum christi sui est.

27:9 Salvum fac populum tuum, Domine, et benedic hæreditati tuæ ; et rege eos, et extolle illos usque in æternum.

27:1 *A psalm for David himself.* UNTO THEE WILL I CRY, O LORD: O my God, be not thou silent to me: lest if thou be silent to me, I become like them that go down into the pit.

27:2 Hear, O Lord, the voice of my supplication, when I pray to thee; when I lift up my hands to thy holy temple.

27:3 Draw me not away together with the wicked; and with the workers of iniquity destroy me not: Who speak peace with their neighbour, but evils are in their hearts.

27:4 Give them according to their works, and according to the wickedness of their inventions. According to the works of their hands give thou to them: render to them their reward.

27:5 Because they have not understood the works of the Lord, and the operations of his hands: thou shalt destroy them, and shalt not build them up.

27:6 Blessed be the Lord, for he hath heard the voice of my supplication.

27:7 The Lord is my helper and my protector: in him hath my heart confided, and I have been helped. And my flesh hath flourished again, and with my will I will give praise to him.

27:8 The Lord is the strength of his people, and the protector of the salvation of his anointed.

27:9 Save, O Lord, thy people, and bless thy inheritance: and rule them and exalt them for ever.

XXVIII.

28:1 *Psalmus David, in consummatione tabernaculi.* AFFERTE DOMINO, FILII DEI, afferte Domino filios arietum.

28:2 Afferte Domino gloriam et honorem ; afferte Domino gloriam nomini ejus ; adorate Dominum in atrio sancto ejus.

28:3 Vox Domini super aquas ; Deus majestatis intonuit : Dominus super aquas multas.

28:4 Vox Domini in virtute ; vox Domini in magnificentia.

28:5 Vox Domini confringentis cedros, et confringet Dominus cedros Libani :

28:6 et comminuet eas, tamquam vitulum Libani, et dilectus quemadmodum filius unicornium.

28:7 Vox Domini intercidentis flammam ignis ;

28:1 *A psalm for David, at the finishing of the tabernacle.* BRING TO THE LORD, O YE CHILDREN OF GOD: bring to the Lord the offspring of rams.

28:2 Bring to the Lord glory and honour: bring to the Lord glory to his name: adore ye the Lord in his holy court.

28:3 The voice of the Lord is upon the waters; the God of majesty hath thundered, The Lord is upon many waters.

28:4 The voice of the Lord is in power; the voice of the Lord in magnificence.

28:5 The voice of the Lord breaketh the cedars: yea, the Lord shall break the cedars of Libanus.

28:6 And shall reduce them to pieces, as a calf of Libanus, and as the beloved son of unicorns.

28:7 The voice of the Lord divideth the flame of fire:

28:8 vox Domini concutientis desertum : et commovebit Dominus desertum Cades.

28:9 Vox Domini præparantis cervos : et revelabit condensa, et in templo ejus omnes dicent gloriam.

28:10 Dominus diluvium inhabitare facit, et sedebit Dominus rex in æternum.

28:11 Dominus virtutem populo suo dabit ; Dominus benedicet populo suo in pace.

28:8 The voice of the Lord shaketh the desert: and the Lord shall shake the desert of Cades.

28:9 The voice of the Lord prepareth the stags: and he will discover the thick woods: and in his temple all shall speak his glory.

28:10 The Lord maketh the flood to dwell: and the Lord shall sit king for ever.

28:11 The Lord will give strength to his people: the Lord will bless his people with peace.

XXIX.

29:1 *Psalmus cantici, in dedicatione domus David.*

29:2 EXALTABO TE, DOMINE, quoniam suscepisti me, nec delectasti inimicos meos super me.

29:3 Domine Deus meus, clamavi ad te, et sanasti me.

29:4 Domine, eduxisti ab inferno animam meam ; salvasti me a descendentibus in lacum.

29:5 Psallite Domino, sancti ejus ; et confitemini memoriæ sanctitatis ejus.

29:6 Quoniam ira in indignatione ejus, et vita in voluntate ejus : ad vesperum demorabitur fletus, et ad matutinum lætitia.

29:7 Ego autem dixi in abundantia mea : Non movebor in æternum.

29:8 Domine, in voluntate tua præstitisti decori meo virtutem ; avertisti faciem tuam a me, et factus sum conturbatus.

29:9 Ad te, Domine, clamabo, et ad Deum meum deprecabor.

29:10 Quæ utilitas in sanguine meo, dum descendo in corruptionem ? numquid confitebitur tibi pulvis, aut annuntiabit veritatem tuam ?

29:11 Audivit Dominus, et misertus est mei ; Dominus factus est adjutor meus.

29:12 Convertisti planctum meum in gaudium mihi ; conscidisti saccum meum, et circumdedisti me lætitia :

29:13 ut cantet tibi gloria mea, et non compungar. Domine Deus meus, in æternum confitebor tibi.

29:1 A psalm of a canticle, at the dedication of David's house.

29:2 I WILL EXTOL THEE, O LORD, for thou hast upheld me: and hast not made my enemies to rejoice over me.

29:3 O Lord my God, I have cried to thee, and thou hast healed me.

29:4 Thou hast brought forth, O Lord, my soul from hell: thou hast saved me from them that go down into the pit.

29:5 Sing to the Lord, O ye his saints: and give praise to the memory of his holiness.

29:6 For wrath is in his indignation; and life in his good will. In the evening weeping shall have place, and in the morning gladness.

29:7 And in my abundance I said: I shall never be moved.

29:8 O Lord, in thy favour, thou gavest strength to my beauty. Thou turnedst away thy face from me, and I became troubled.

29:9 To thee, O Lord, will I cry: and I will make supplication to my God.

29:10 What profit is there in my blood, whilst I go down to corruption? Shall dust confess to thee, or declare thy truth?

29:11 The Lord hath heard, and hath had mercy on me: the Lord became my helper.

29:12 Thou hast turned for me my mourning into joy: thou hast cut my sackcloth, and hast compassed me with gladness:

29:13 To the end that my glory may sing to thee, and I may not regret: O Lord my God, I will give praise to thee for ever.

XXX.

30:1 *In finem. Psalmus David, pro extasi.*

30:2 IN TE, DOMINE, SPERAVI ; non confundar in æternum : in justitia tua libera me.

30:3 Inclina ad me aurem tuam ; accelera ut eruas me. Esto mihi in Deum protectorem, et

30:1 *Unto the end, a psalm for David, in an ecstasy.*

30:2 IN THEE, O LORD, HAVE I HOPED, let me never be confounded: deliver me in thy justice.

30:3 Bow down thy ear to me: make haste to deliver me. Be thou unto me a God, a protector,

in domum refugii, ut salvum me facias :

30:4 quoniam fortitudo mea et refugium meum es tu ; et propter nomen tuum deduces me et enutries me.

30:5 Educes me de laqueo hoc quem absconderunt mihi, quoniam tu es protector meus.

30:6 In manus tuas commendo spiritum meum ; redemisti me, Domine Deus veritatis.

30:7 Odisti observantes vanitates supervacue ; ego autem in Domino speravi.

30:8 Exsultabo, et lætabor in misericordia tua, quoniam respexisti humilitatem meam ; salvasti de necessitatibus animam meam.

30:9 Nec conclusisti me in manibus inimici : statuisti in loco spatioso pedes meos.

30:10 Miserere mei, Domine, quoniam tribulor ; conturbatus est in ira oculus meus, anima mea, et venter meus.

30:11 Quoniam defecit in dolore vita mea, et anni mei in gemitibus. Infirmata est in paupertate virtus mea, et ossa mea conturbata sunt.

30:12 Super omnes inimicos meos factus sum opprobrium, et vicinis meis valde, et timor notis meis ; qui videbant me foras fugerunt a me.

30:13 Oblivioni datus sum, tamquam mortuus a corde ; factus sum tamquam vas perditum :

30:14 quoniam audivi vituperationem multorum commorantium in circuitu. In eo dum convenirent simul adversum me, accipere animam meam consiliati sunt.

30:15 Ego autem in te speravi, Domine ; dixi : Deus meus es tu ;

30:16 in manibus tuis sortes meæ : eripe me de manu inimicorum meorum, et a persequentibus me.

30:17 Illustra faciem tuam super servum tuum ; salvum me fac in misericordia tua.

30:18 Domine, non confundar, quoniam invocavi te. Erubescant impii, et deducantur in infernum ;

30:19 muta fiant labia dolosa, quæ loquuntur adversus justum iniquitatem, in superbia, et in abusione.

30:20 Quam magna multitudo dulcedinis tuæ, Domine, quam abscondisti timentibus te ; perfecisti eis qui sperant in te in conspectu filiorum hominum !

30:21 Abscondes eos in abscondito faciei tuæ a

and a house of refuge, to save me.

30:4 For thou art my strength and my refuge; and for thy name's sake thou wilt lead me, and nourish me.

30:5 Thou wilt bring me out of this snare, which they have hidden for me: for thou art my protector.

30:6 Into thy hands I commend my spirit: thou hast redeemed me, O Lord, the God of truth.

30:7 Thou hast hated them that regard vanities, to no purpose. But I have hoped in the Lord:

30:8 I will be glad and rejoice in thy mercy. For thou best regarded my humility, thou hast saved my soul out of distresses.

30:9 And thou hast not shut me up in the hands of the enemy: thou hast set my feet in a spacious place.

30:10 Have mercy on me, O Lord, for I am afflicted: my eye is troubled with wrath, my soul, and my belly:

30:11 For my life is wasted with grief: and my years in sighs. My strength is weakened through poverty and my bones are disturbed.

30:12 I am become a reproach among all my enemies, and very much to my neighbours; and a fear to my acquaintance. They that saw me without fled from me.

30:13 I am forgotten as one dead from the heart. I am become as a vessel that is destroyed.

30:14 For I have heard the blame of many that dwell round about. While they assembled together against me, they consulted to take away my life.

30:15 But I have put my trust in thee, O Lord: I said: Thou art my God.

30:16 My lots are in thy hands. Deliver me out of the hands of my enemies; and from them that persecute me.

30:17 Make thy face to shine upon thy servant; save me in thy mercy.

30:18 Let me not be confounded, O Lord, for I have called upon thee. Let the wicked be ashamed, and be brought down to hell.

30:19 Let deceitful lips be made dumb. Which speak iniquity against the just, with pride and abuse.

30:20 O how great is the multitude of thy sweetness, O Lord, which thou hast hidden for them that fear thee! Which thou hast wrought for them that hope in thee, in the sight of the sons of men.

30:21 Thou shalt hide them in the secret of thy

conturbatione hominum ; proteges eos in tabernaculo tuo, a contradictione linguarum.

30:22 Benedictus Dominus, quoniam mirificavit misericordiam suam mihi in civitate munita.

30:23 Ego autem dixi in excessu mentis meæ : Projectus sum a facie oculorum tuorum : ideo exaudisti vocem orationis meæ, dum clamarem ad te.

30:24 Diligite Dominum, omnes sancti ejus, quoniam veritatem requiret Dominus, et retribuet abundanter facientibus superbiam.

30:25 Viriliter agite, et confortetur cor vestrum, omnes qui speratis in Domino.

face, from the disturbance of men. Thou shalt protect them in thy tabernacle from the contradiction of tongues.

30:22 Blessed be the Lord, for he hath shewn his wonderful mercy to me in a fortified city.

30:23 But I said in the excess of my mind: I am cast away from before thy eyes. Therefore thou hast heard the voice of my prayer, when I cried to thee.

30:24 O love the Lord, all ye his saints: for the Lord will require truth, and will repay them abundantly that act proudly.

30:25 Do ye manfully, and let your heart be strengthened, all ye that hope in the Lord.

XXXI.

31:1 *Ipsi David intellectus.* BEATI QUORUM remissæ sunt iniquitates, et quorum tecta sunt peccata.

31:2 Beatus vir cui non imputavit Dominus peccatum, nec est in spiritu ejus dolus.

31:3 Quoniam tacui, inveteraverunt ossa mea, dum clamarem tota die.

31:4 Quoniam die ac nocte gravata est super me manus tua, conversus sum in ærumna mea, dum configitur spina.

31:5 Delictum meum cognitum tibi feci, et injustitiam meam non abscondi. Dixi : Confitebor adversum me injustitiam meam Domino ; et tu remisisti impietatem peccati mei.

31:6 Pro hac orabit ad te omnis sanctus in tempore opportuno. Verumtamen in diluvio aquarum multarum, ad eum non approximabunt.

31:7 Tu es refugium meum a tribulatione quæ circumdedit me ; exsultatio mea, erue me a circumdantibus me.

31:8 Intellectum tibi dabo, et instruam te in via hac qua gradieris ; firmabo super te oculos meos.

31:9 Nolite fieri sicut equus et mulus, quibus non est intellectus. In camo et freno maxillas eorum constringe, qui non approximant ad te.

31:10 Multa flagella peccatoris ; sperantem autem in Domino misericordia circumdabit.

31:11 Lætamini in Domino, et exsultate, justi ; et gloriamini, omnes recti corde.

31:1 *To David himself, understanding.* BLESSED ARE THEY WHOSE iniquities are forgiven, and whose sins are covered.

31:2 Blessed is the man to whom the Lord hath not imputed sin, and in whose spirit there is no guile.

31:3 Because I was silent my bones grew old; whilst I cried out all the day long.

31:4 For day and night thy hand was heavy upon me: I am turned in my anguish, whilst the thorn is fastened.

31:5 I have acknowledged my sin to thee, and my injustice I have not concealed. I said I will confess against myself my injustice to the Lord: and thou hast forgiven the wickedness of my sin.

31:6 For this shall every one that is holy pray to thee in a seasonable time. And yet in a flood of many waters, they shall not come nigh unto him.

31:7 Thou art my refuge from the trouble which hath encompassed me: my joy, deliver me from them that surround me.

31:8 I will give thee understanding, and I will instruct thee in this way, in which thou shalt go: I will fix my eyes upon thee.

31:9 Do not become like the horse and the mule, who have no understanding. With bit and bridle bind fast their jaws, who come not near unto thee.

31:10 Many are the scourges of the sinner, but mercy shall encompass him that hopeth in the Lord.

31:11 Be glad in the Lord, and rejoice, ye just, and glory, all ye right of heart.

XXXII.

32:1 *Psalmus David.* EXSULTATE, JUSTI, IN DOM-
INO ; rectos decet collaudatio.

32:2 Confitemini Domino in cithara ; in psalterio decem chordarum psallite illi.

32:3 Cantate ei canticum novum ; bene psallite
ei in vociferatione.

32:4 Quia rectum est verbum Domini, et omnia
opera ejus in fide.

32:5 Diligit misericordiam et judicium ; misericordia Domini plena est terra.

32:6 Verbo Domini cæli firmati sunt, et spiritu
oris ejus omnis virtus eorum.

32:7 Congregans sicut in utre aquas maris ; ponens in thesauris abyssos.

32:8 Timeat Dominum omnis terra ; ab eo
autem commoveantur omnes inhabitantes
orbem.

32:9 Quoniam ipse dixit, et facta sunt ; ipse
mandavit et creata sunt.

32:10 Dominus dissipat consilia gentium ; reprobat autem cogitationes populorum, et reprobat
consilia principum.

32:11 Consilium autem Domini in æternum manet ; cogitationes cordis ejus in generatione et
generationem.

32:12 Beata gens cujus est Dominus Deus ejus ;
populus quem elegit in hæreditatem sibi.

32:13 De cælo respexit Dominus ; vidit omnes
filios hominum.

32:14 De præparato habitaculo suo respexit super omnes qui habitant terram :

32:15 qui finxit sigillatim corda eorum ; qui intelligit omnia opera eorum.

32:16 Non salvatur rex per multam virtutem, et
gigas non salvabitur in multitudine virtutis
suæ.

32:17 Fallax equus ad salutem ; in abundantia
autem virtutis suæ non salvabitur.

32:18 Ecce oculi Domini super metuentes eum,
et in eis qui sperant super misericordia ejus :

32:19 ut eruat a morte animas eorum, et alat eos
in fame.

32:20 Anima nostra sustinet Dominum, quoniam
adjutor et protector noster est.

32:21 Quia in eo lætabitur cor nostrum, et in
nomine sancto ejus speravimus.

32:1 *A psalm for David.* REJOICE IN THE LORD, O
ye just: praise becometh the upright.

32:2 Give praise to the Lord on the harp; sing to
him with the psaltery, the instrument of ten
strings.

32:3 Sing to him a new canticle, sing well unto
him with a loud noise.

32:4 For the word of the Lord is right, and all his
works are done with faithfulness.

32:5 He loveth mercy and judgment; the earth is
full of the mercy of the Lord.

32:6 By the word of the Lord the heavens were
established; and all the power of them by the
spirit of his mouth:

32:7 Gathering together the waters of the sea, as
in a vessel; laying up the depths in storehouses.

32:8 Let all the earth fear the Lord, and let all
the inhabitants of the world be in awe of him.

32:9 For he spoke and they were made: he commanded and they were created.

32:10 The Lord bringeth to naught the counsels
of nations; and he rejecteth the devices of people, and casteth away the counsels of princes.

32:11 But the counsel of the Lord standeth for
ever: the thoughts of his heart to all generations.

32:12 Blessed is the nation whose God is the
Lord: the people whom he hath chosen for his
inheritance.

32:13 The Lord hath looked from heaven: he hath
beheld all the sons of men.

32:14 From his habitation which he hath prepared, he hath looked upon all that dwell on
the earth.

32:15 He who hath made the hearts of every one
of them: who understandeth all their works.

32:16 The king is not saved by a great army: nor
shall the giant be saved by his own great
strength.

32:17 Vain is the horse for safety: neither shall he
be saved by the abundance of his strength.

32:18 Behold the eyes of the Lord are on them
that fear him: and on them that hope in his
mercy.

32:19 To deliver their souls from death; and feed
them in famine.

32:20 Our soul waiteth for the Lord: for he is
our helper and protector.

32:21 For in him our heart shall rejoice: and in
his holy name we have trusted.

32:22 Fiat misericordia tua, Domine, super nos, quemadmodum speravimus in te.

32:22 Let thy mercy, O Lord, be upon us, as we have hoped in thee.

XXXIII.

33:1 *Davidi, cum immutavit vultum suum coram Achimelech, et dimisit eum, et abiit.*

33:1 *For David, when he changed his countenance before Achimelech, who dismissed him, and he went his way.*

33:2 BENEDICAM DOMINUM in omni tempore ; semper laus ejus in ore meo.

33:2 I WILL BLESS THE LORD at all times, his praise shall be always in my mouth.

33:3 In Domino laudabitur anima mea : audiant mansueti, et lætentur.

33:3 In the Lord shall my soul be praised: let the meek hear and rejoice.

33:4 Magnificate Dominum mecum, et exaltemus nomen ejus in idipsum.

33:4 O magnify the Lord with me; and let us extol his name together.

33:5 Exquisivi Dominum, et exaudivit me ; et ex omnibus tribulationibus meis eripuit me.

33:5 I sought the Lord, and he heard me; and he delivered me from all my troubles.

33:6 Accedite ad eum, et illuminamini ; et facies vestræ non confundentur.

33:6 Come ye to him and be enlightened: and your faces shall not be confounded.

33:7 Iste pauper clamavit, et Dominus exaudivit eum, et de omnibus tribulationibus ejus salvavit eum.

33:7 This poor man cried, and the Lord heard him: and saved him out of all his troubles.

33:8 Immittet angelus Domini in circuitu timentium eum, et eripiet eos.

33:8 The angel of the Lord shall encamp round about them that fear him: and shall deliver them.

33:9 Gustate et videte quoniam suavis est Dominus ; beatus vir qui sperat in eo.

33:9 O taste, and see that the Lord is sweet: blessed is the man that hopeth in him.

33:10 Timete Dominum, omnes sancti ejus, quoniam non est inopia timentibus eum.

33:10 Fear the Lord, all ye his saints: for there is no want to them that fear him.

33:11 Divites eguerunt, et esurierunt ; inquirentes autem Dominum non minuentur omni bono.

33:11 The rich have wanted, and have suffered hunger: but they that seek the Lord shall not be deprived of any good.

33:12 Venite, filii ; audite me : timorem Domini docebo vos.

33:12 Come, children, hearken to me: I will teach you the fear of the Lord.

33:13 Quis est homo qui vult vitam ; diligit dies videre bonos ?

33:13 Who is the man that desireth life: who loveth to see good days?

33:14 Prohibe linguam tuam a malo, et labia tua ne loquantur dolum.

33:14 Keep thy tongue from evil, and thy lips from speaking guile.

33:15 Diverte a malo, et fac bonum ; inquire pacem, et persequere eam.

33:15 Turn away from evil and do good: seek after peace and pursue it.

33:16 Oculi Domini super justos, et aures ejus in preces eorum.

33:16 The eyes of the Lord are upon the just: and his ears unto their prayers.

33:17 Vultus autem Domini super facientes mala, ut perdat de terra memoriam eorum.

33:17 But the countenance of the Lord is against them that do evil things: to cut off the remembrance of them from the earth.

33:18 Clamaverunt justi, et Dominus exaudivit eos ; et ex omnibus tribulationibus eorum liberavit eos.

33:18 The just cried, and the Lord heard them: and delivered them out of all their troubles.

33:19 Juxta est Dominus iis qui tribulato sunt corde, et humiles spiritu salvabit.

33:19 The Lord is nigh unto them that are of a contrite heart: and he will save the humble of spirit.

33:20 Multæ tribulationes justorum ; et de omnibus his liberabit eos Dominus.

33:20 Many are the afflictions of the just; but out of them all will the Lord deliver them.

33:21 Custodit Dominus omnia ossa eorum : un-

33:21 The Lord keepeth all their bones, not one

um ex his non conteretur.

33:22 Mors peccatorum pessima ; et qui oderunt justum delinquent.

33:23 Redimet Dominus animas servorum suorum, et non delinquent omnes qui sperant in eo.

of them shall be broken.

33:22 The death of the wicked is very evil: and they that hate the just shall be guilty.

33:23 The Lord will redeem the souls of his servants: and none of them that trust in him shall offend.

XXXIV.

34:1 *Ipsi David.* JUDICA, DOMINE, nocentes me ; expugna impugnantes me.

34:2 Apprehende arma et scutum, et exsurge in adjutorium mihi.

34:3 Effunde frameam, et conclude adversus eos qui persequuntur me ; dic animæ meæ : Salus tua ego sum.

34:4 Confundantur et revereantur quærentes animam meam ; avertantur retrorsum et confundantur cogitantes mihi mala.

34:5 Fiant tamquam pulvis ante faciem venti, et angelus Domini coarctans eos.

34:6 Fiat via illorum tenebræ et lubricum, et angelus Domini persequens eos.

34:7 Quoniam gratis absconderunt mihi interitum laquei sui ; supervacue exprobraverunt animam meam.

34:8 Veniat illi laqueus quem ignorat, et captio quam abscondit apprehendat eum, et in laqueum cadat in ipsum.

34:9 Anima autem mea exsultabit in Domino, et delectabitur super salutari suo.

34:10 Omnia ossa mea dicent : Domine, quis similis tibi ? eripiens inopem de manu fortiorum ejus ; egenum et pauperem a diripientibus eum.

34:11 Surgentes testes iniqui, quæ ignorabam interrogabant me.

34:12 Retribuebant mihi mala pro bonis, sterilitatem animæ meæ.

34:13 Ego autem, cum mihi molesti essent, induebar cilicio ; humiliabam in jejunio animam meam, et oratio mea in sinu meo convertetur.

34:14 Quasi proximum et quasi fratrem nostrum sic complacebam ; quasi lugens et contristatus sic humiliabar.

34:15 Et adversum me lætati sunt, et convenerunt ; congregata sunt super me flagella, et ignoravi.

34:16 Dissipati sunt, nec compuncti ; tentaverunt me, subsannaverunt me subsannatione ; fren-

34:1 *For David himself.* JUDGE THOU, O Lord, them that wrong me: overthrow them that fight against me.

34:2 Take hold of arms and shield: and rise up to help me.

34:3 Bring out the sword, and shut up the way against them that persecute me: say to my soul: I am thy salvation.

34:4 Let them be confounded and ashamed that seek after my soul. Let them be turned back and be confounded that devise evil against me.

34:5 Let them become as dust before the wind: and let the angel of the Lord straiten them.

34:6 Let their way become dark and slippery; and let the angel of the Lord pursue them.

34:7 For without cause they have hidden their net for me unto destruction: without cause they have upbraided my soul.

34:8 Let the snare which he knoweth not come upon him: and let the net which he hath hidden catch him: and into that very snare let them fall.

34:9 But my soul shall rejoice in the Lord; and shall be delighted in his salvation.

34:10 All my bones shall say: Lord, who is like to thee? Who deliverest the poor from the hand of them that are stronger than he; the needy and the poor from them that strip him.

34:11 Unjust witnesses rising up have asked me things I knew not.

34:12 They repaid me evil for good: to the depriving me of my soul.

34:13 But as for me, when they were troublesome to me, I was clothed with haircloth. I humbled my soul with fasting; and my prayer shall be turned into my bosom.

34:14 As a neighbour and as an own brother, so did I please: as one mourning and sorrowful so was I humbled.

34:15 But they rejoiced against me, and came together: scourges were gathered together upon me, and I knew not.

34:16 They were separated, and repented not: they tempted me, they scoffed at me with

duerunt super me dentibus suis.

34:17 Domine, quando respicies ? Restitue animam meam a malignitate eorum ; a leonibus unicam meam.

34:18 Confitebor tibi in ecclesia magna ; in populo gravi laudabo te.

34:19 Non supergaudeant mihi qui adversantur mihi inique, qui oderunt me gratis, et annuunt oculis.

34:20 Quoniam mihi quidem pacifice loquebantur ; et in iracundia terræ loquentes, dolos cogitabant.

34:21 Et dilataverunt super me os suum ; dixerunt : Euge, euge ! viderunt oculi nostri.

34:22 Vidisti, Domine : ne sileas ; Domine, ne discedas a me.

34:23 Exsurge et intende judicio meo, Deus meus ; et Dominus meus, in causam meam.

34:24 Judica me secundum justitiam tuam, Domine Deus meus, et non supergaudeant mihi.

34:25 Non dicant in cordibus suis : Euge, euge, animæ nostræ ; nec dicant : Devoravimus eum.

34:26 Erubescant et revereantur simul qui gratulantur malis meis ; induantur confusione et reverentia qui magna loquuntur super me.

34:27 Exsultent et lætentur qui volunt justitiam meam ; et dicant semper : Magnificetur Dominus, qui volunt pacem servi ejus.

34:28 Et lingua mea meditabitur justitiam tuam ; tota die laudem tuam.

scorn: they gnashed upon me with their teeth.

34:17 Lord, when wilt thou look upon me? rescue thou soul from their malice: my only one from the lions.

34:18 I will give thanks to thee in a great church; I will praise thee in a strong people.

34:19 Let not them that are my enemies wrongfully rejoice over me: who have hated me without cause, and wink with the eyes.

34:20 For they spoke indeed peaceably to me; and speaking in the anger of the earth they devised guile.

34:21 And they opened their mouth wide against me; they said: Well done, well done, our eyes have seen it.

34:22 Thou hast seen, O Lord, be not thou silent: O Lord, depart not from me.

34:23 Arise, and be attentive to my judgment: to my cause, my God, and my Lord.

34:24 Judge me, O Lord my God according to thy justice, and let them not rejoice over me.

34:25 Let them not say in their hearts: It is well, it is well, to our mind: neither let them say: We have swallowed him up.

34:26 Let them blush: and be ashamed together, who rejoice at my evils. Let them be clothed with confusion and shame, who speak great things against me.

34:27 Let them rejoice and be glad, who are well pleased with my justice, and let them say always: The Lord be magnified, who delights in the peace of his servant.

34:28 And my tongue shall meditate thy justice, thy praise all the day long.

XXXV.

35:1 *In finem. Servo Domini ipsi David.*

35:2 DIXIT INJUSTUS ut delinquat in semetipso : non est timor Dei ante oculos ejus.

35:3 Quoniam dolose egit in conspectu ejus, ut inveniatur iniquitas ejus ad odium.

35:4 Verba oris ejus iniquitas, et dolus ; noluit intelligere ut bene ageret.

35:5 Iniquitatem meditatus est in cubili suo ; astitit omni viæ non bonæ : malitiam autem non odivit.

35:6 Domine, in cælo misericordia tua, et veritas tua usque ad nubes.

35:1 *Unto the end, for the servant of God, David himself.*

35:2 THE UNJUST HATH SAID within himself, that he would sin: there is no fear of God before his eyes.

35:3 For in his sight he hath done deceitfully, that his iniquity may be found unto hatred.

35:4 The words of his mouth are iniquity and guile: he would not understand that he might do well.

35:5 He hath devised iniquity on his bed, he hath set himself on every way that is not good: but evil he hath not hated.

35:6 O Lord, thy mercy is in heaven, and thy truth reacheth, even to the clouds.

35:7 Justitia tua sicut montes Dei ; judicia tua abyssus multa. Homines et jumenta salvabis, Domine,

35:8 quemadmodum multiplicasti misericordiam tuam, Deus. Filii autem hominum in tegmine alarum tuarum sperabunt.

35:9 Inebriabuntur ab ubertate domus tuæ, et torrente voluptatis tuæ potabis eos :

35:10 quoniam apud te est fons vitæ, et in lumine tuo videbimus lumen.

35:11 Prætende misericordiam tuam scientibus te, et justitiam tuam his qui recto sunt corde.

35:12 Non veniat mihi pes superbiæ, et manus peccatoris non moveat me.

35:13 Ibi ceciderunt qui operantur iniquitatem ; expulsi sunt, nec potuerunt stare.

35:7 Thy justice is as the mountains of God, thy judgments are a great deep. Men and beasts thou wilt preserve, O Lord:

35:8 O how hast thou multiplied thy mercy, O God! But the children of men shall put their trust under the covert of thy wings.

35:9 They shall be inebriated with the plenty of thy house; and thou shalt make them drink of the torrent of thy pleasure.

35:10 For with thee is the fountain of life; and in thy light we shall see light.

35:11 Extend thy mercy to them that know thee, and thy justice to them that are right in heart.

35:12 Let not the foot of pride come to me, and let not the hand of the sinner move me.

35:13 There the workers of iniquity are fallen, they are cast out, and could not stand.

XXXVI.

36:1 *Psalmus ipsi David.* NOLI ÆMULARI in malignantibus, neque zelaveris facientes iniquitatem :

36:2 quoniam tamquam fœnum velociter arescent, et quemadmodum olera herbarum cito decident.

36:3 Spera in Domino, et fac bonitatem ; et inhabita terram, et pasceris in divitiis ejus.

36:4 Delectare in Domino, et dabit tibi petitiones cordis tui.

36:5 Revela Domino viam tuam, et spera in eo, et ipse faciet.

36:6 Et educet quasi lumen justitiam tuam, et judicium tuum tamquam meridiem.

36:7 Subditus esto Domino, et ora eum. Noli æmulari in eo qui prosperatur in via sua ; in homine faciente injustitias.

36:8 Desine ab ira, et derelinque furorem ; noli æmulari ut maligneris.

36:9 Quoniam qui malignantur exterminabuntur ; sustinentes autem Dominum, ipsi hæreditabunt terram.

36:10 Et adhuc pusillum, et non erit peccator ; et quæres locum ejus, et non invenies.

36:11 Mansueti autem hæreditabunt terram, et delectabuntur in multitudine pacis.

36:12 Observabit peccator justum, et stridebit super eum dentibus suis.

36:13 Dominus autem irridebit eum, quoniam prospicit quod veniet dies ejus.

36:14 Gladium evaginaverunt peccatores ; inten-

36:1 *A psalm for David himself.* BE NOT EMULOUS of evildoers; nor envy them that work iniquity.

36:2 For they shall shortly wither away as grass, and as the green herbs shall quickly fall.

36:3 Trust in the Lord, and do good, and dwell in the land, and thou shalt be fed with its riches.

36:4 Delight in the Lord, and he will give thee the requests of thy heart.

36:5 Commit thy way to the Lord, and trust in him, and he will do it.

36:6 And he will bring forth thy justice as the light, and thy judgment as the noonday.

36:7 Be subject to the Lord and pray to him. Envy not the man who prospereth in his way; the man who doth unjust things.

36:8 Cease from anger, and leave rage; have no emulation to do evil.

36:9 For the evildoers shall be cut off: but they that wait upon the Lord, shall inherit the land.

36:10 For yet a little while, and the wicked shall not be: and thou shalt seek his place, and shalt not find it.

36:11 But the meek shall inherit the land, and shall delight in abundance of peace.

36:12 The sinner shall watch the just man: and shall gnash upon him with his teeth.

36:13 But the Lord shall laugh at him: for he foreseeth that his day shall come.

36:14 The wicked have drawn out the sword:

derunt arcum suum : ut dejiciant pauperem et inopem, ut trucident rectos corde.

36:15 Gladius eorum intret in corda ipsorum, et arcus eorum confringatur.

36:16 Melius est modicum justo, super divitias peccatorum multas :

36:17 quoniam brachia peccatorum conterentur : confirmat autem justos Dominus.

36:18 Novit Dominus dies immaculatorum, et hæreditas eorum in æternum erit.

36:19 Non confundentur in tempore malo, et in diebus famis saturabuntur :

36:20 quia peccatores peribunt. Inimici vero Domini mox ut honorificati fuerint et exaltati, deficientes quemadmodum fumus deficient.

36:21 Mutuabitur peccator, et non solvet ; justus autem miseretur et tribuet :

36:22 quia benedicentes ei hæreditabunt terram ; maledicentes autem ei disperibunt.

36:23 Apud Dominum gressus hominis dirigentur, et viam ejus volet.

36:24 Cum ceciderit, non collidetur, quia Dominus supponit manum suam.

36:25 Junior fui, etenim senui ; et non vidi justum derelictum, nec semen ejus quærens panem.

36:26 Tota die miseretur et commodat ; et semen illius in benedictione erit.

36:27 Declina a malo, et fac bonum, et inhabita in sæculum sæculi :

36:28 quia Dominus amat judicium, et non derelinquet sanctos suos : in æternum conservabuntur. Injusti punientur, et semen impiorum peribit.

36:29 Justi autem hæreditabunt terram, et inhabitabunt in sæculum sæculi super eam.

36:30 Os justi meditabitur sapientiam, et lingua ejus loquetur judicium.

36:31 Lex Dei ejus in corde ipsius, et non supplantabuntur gressus ejus.

36:32 Considerat peccator justum, et quærit mortificare eum.

36:33 Dominus autem non derelinquet eum in manibus ejus, nec damnabit eum cum judicabitur illi.

36:34 Expecta Dominum, et custodi viam ejus, et exaltabit te ut hæreditate capias terram : cum perierint peccatores, videbis.

36:35 Vidi impium superexaltatum, et elevatum sicut cedros Libani :

they have bent their bow. To cast down the poor and needy, to kill the upright of heart.

36:15 Let their sword enter into their own hearts, and let their bow be broken.

36:16 Better is a little to the just, than the great riches of the wicked.

36:17 For the arms of the wicked shall be broken in pieces; but the Lord strengtheneth the just.

36:18 The Lord knoweth the days of undefiled; and their inheritance shall be for ever.

36:19 They shall not be confounded in the evil time; and in the days of famine they shall be filled:

36:20 because the wicked shall perish. And the enemies of the Lord, presently after they shall be honoured and exalted, shall come to nothing and vanish like smoke.

36:21 The sinner shall borrow, and not pay again; but the just sheweth mercy and shall give.

36:22 For such as bless him shall inherit the land: but such as curse him shall perish.

36:23 With the Lord shall the steps of a man be directed, and he shall like well his way.

36:24 When he shall fall he shall not be bruised, for the Lord putteth his hand under him.

36:25 I have been young, and now am old; and I have not seen the just forsaken, nor his seed seeking bread.

36:26 He sheweth mercy, and lendeth all the day long; and his seed shall be in blessing.

36:27 Decline from evil and do good, and dwell for ever and ever.

36:28 For the Lord loveth judgment, and will not forsake his saints: they shall be preserved for ever. The unjust shall be punished, and the seed of the wicked shall perish.

36:29 But the just shall inherit the land, and shall dwell therein for evermore.

36:30 The mouth of the just shall meditate wisdom: and his tongue shall speak judgment.

36:31 The law of his God is in his heart, and his steps shall not be supplanted.

36:32 The wicked watcheth the just man, and seeketh to put him to death,

36:33 But the Lord will not leave him in his hands; nor condemn him when he shall be judged.

36:34 Expect the Lord and keep his way: and he will exalt thee to inherit the land: when the sinners shall perish thou shalt see.

36:35 I have seen the wicked highly exalted, and lifted up like the cedars of Libanus.

36:36 et transivi, et ecce non erat ; et quæsivi eum, et non est inventus locus ejus.

36:37 Custodi innocentiam, et vide æquitatem, quoniam sunt reliquiæ homini pacifico.

36:38 Injusti autem disperibunt simul ; reliquiæ impiorum interibunt.

36:39 Salus autem justorum a Domino ; et protector eorum in tempore tribulationis.

36:40 Et adjuvabit eos Dominus, et liberabit eos ; et eruet eos a peccatoribus, et salvabit eos, quia speraverunt in eo.

36:36 And I passed by, and lo, he was not: and I sought him and his place was not found.

36:37 Keep innocence, and behold justice: for there are remnants for the peaceable man.

36:38 But the unjust shall be destroyed together: the remnants of the wicked shall perish.

36:39 But the salvation of the just is from the Lord, and he is their protector in the time of trouble.

36:40 And the Lord will help them and deliver them: and he will rescue them from the wicked, and save them, because they have hoped in him.

XXXVII.

37:1 *Psalmus David, in rememorationem de sabbato.*

37:2 DOMINE, NE IN FURORE TUO ARGUAS ME, neque in ira tua corripias me :

37:3 quoniam sagittæ tuæ infixæ sunt mihi, et confirmasti super me manum tuam.

37:4 Non est sanitas in carne mea, a facie iræ tuæ ; non est pax ossibus meis, a facie peccatorum meorum :

37:5 quoniam iniquitates meæ supergressæ sunt caput meum, et sicut onus grave gravatæ sunt super me.

37:6 Putruerunt et corruptæ sunt cicatrices meæ, a facie insipientiæ meæ.

37:7 Miser factus sum et curvatus sum usque in finem ; tota die contristatus ingrediebar.

37:8 Quoniam lumbi mei impleti sunt illusionibus, et non est sanitas in carne mea.

37:9 Afflictus sum, et humiliatus sum nimis ; rugiebam a gemitu cordis mei.

37:10 Domine, ante te omne desiderium meum, et gemitus meus a te non est absconditus.

37:11 Cor meum conturbatum est ; dereliquit me virtus mea, et lumen oculorum meorum, et ipsum non est mecum.

37:12 Amici mei et proximi mei adversum me appropinquaverunt, et steterunt ; et qui juxta me erant, de longe steterunt : et vim faciebant qui quærebant animam meam.

37:13 Et qui inquirebant mala mihi, locuti sunt vanitates, et dolos tota die meditabantur.

37:14 Ego autem, tamquam surdus, non audiebam ; et sicut mutus non aperiens os suum.

37:15 Et factus sum sicut homo non audiens, et non habens in ore suo redargutiones.

37:1 *A psalm for David, for a remembrance of the sabbath.*

37:2 REBUKE ME NOT, O LORD, IN THY INDIGNATION; nor chastise me in thy wrath.

37:3 For thy arrows are fastened in me: and thy hand hath been strong upon me.

37:4 There is no health in my flesh, because of thy wrath: there is no peace for my bones, because of my sins.

37:5 For my iniquities are gone over my head: and as a heavy burden are become heavy upon me.

37:6 My sores are putrified and corrupted, because of my foolishness.

37:7 I am become miserable, and am bowed down even to the end: I walked sorrowful all the day long.

37:8 For my loins are filled with illusions; and there is no health in my flesh.

37:9 I am afflicted and humbled exceedingly: I roared with the groaning of my heart.

37:10 Lord, all my desire is before thee, and my groaning is not hidden from thee.

37:11 My heart is troubled, my strength hath left me, and the light of my eyes itself is not with me.

37:12 My friends and my neighbours have drawn near, and stood against me. And they that were near me stood afar off:

37:13 And they that sought my soul used violence. And they that sought evils to me spoke vain things, and studied deceits all the day long.

37:14 But I, as a deaf man, heard not: and as a dumb man not opening his mouth.

37:15 And I became as a man that heareth not: and that hath no reproofs in his mouth.

37:16 Quoniam in te, Domine, speravi ; tu exaudies me, Domine Deus meus.

37:17 Quia dixi : Nequando supergaudeant mihi inimici mei ; et dum commoventur pedes mei, super me magna locuti sunt.

37:18 Quoniam ego in flagella paratus sum, et dolor meus in conspectu meo semper.

37:19 Quoniam iniquitatem meam annuntiabo, et cogitabo pro peccato meo.

37:20 Inimici autem mei vivunt, et confirmati sunt super me : et multiplicati sunt qui oderunt me inique.

37:21 Qui retribuunt mala pro bonis detrahebant mihi, quoniam sequebar bonitatem.

37:22 Ne derelinquas me, Domine Deus meus ; ne discesseris a me.

37:23 Intende in adjutorium meum, Domine Deus salutis meæ.

37:16 For in thee, O Lord, have I hoped: thou wilt hear me, O Lord my God.

37:17 For I said: Lest at any time my enemies rejoice over me: and whilst my feet are moved, they speak great things against me.

37:18 For I am ready for scourges: and my sorrow is continually before me.

37:19 For I will declare my iniquity: and I will think for my sin.

37:20 But my enemies live, and are stronger that I: and they hate me wrongfully are multiplied.

37:21 They that render evil for good, have detracted me, because I followed goodness.

37:22 Forsake me not, O Lord my God: do not thou depart from me.

37:23 Attend unto my help, O Lord, the God of my salvation.

XXXVIII.

38:1 *In finem, ipsi Idithun. Canticum David.*

38:2 DIXI : CUSTODIAM VIAS MEAS : ut non delinquam in lingua mea. Posui ori meo custodiam, cum consisteret peccator adversum me.

38:3 Obmutui, et humiliatus sum, et silui a bonis ; et dolor meus renovatus est.

38:4 Concaluit cor meum intra me ; et in meditatione mea exardescet ignis.

38:5 Locutus sum in lingua mea : Notum fac mihi, Domine, finem meum, et numerum dierum meorum quis est, ut sciam quid desit mihi.

38:6 Ecce mensurabiles posuisti dies meos, et substantia mea tamquam nihilum ante te. Verumtamen universa vanitas, omnis homo vivens.

38:7 Verumtamen in imagine pertransit homo ; sed et frustra conturbatur : thesaurizat, et ignorat cui congregabit ea.

38:8 Et nunc quæ est exspectatio mea : nonne Dominus ? et substantia mea apud te est.

38:9 Ab omnibus iniquitatibus meis erue me : opprobrium insipienti dedisti me.

38:10 Obmutui, et non aperui os meum, quoniam tu fecisti ;

38:11 amove a me plagas tuas.

38:12 A fortitudine manus tuæ ego defeci in increpationibus : propter iniquitatem corripuisti

38:1 *Unto the end, for Idithun himself, a canticle of David.*

38:2 I SAID: I WILL TAKE HEED TO MY WAYS: that I sin not with my tongue. I have set guard to my mouth, when the sinner stood against me.

38:3 I was dumb, and was humbled, and kept silence from good things: and my sorrow was renewed.

38:4 My heart grew hot within me: and in my meditation a fire shall flame out.

38:5 I spoke with my tongue: O Lord, make me know my end. And what is the number of my days: that I may know what is wanting to me.

38:6 Behold thou hast made my days measurable: and my substance is as nothing before thee. And indeed all things are vanity: every man living.

38:7 Surely man passeth as an image: yea, and he is disquieted in vain. He storeth up: and he knoweth not for whom he shall gather these things.

38:8 And now what is my hope? is it not the Lord? and my substance is with thee.

38:9 Deliver thou me from all my iniquities: thou hast made me a reproach to the fool.

38:10 I was dumb, and I opened not my mouth, because thou hast done it.

38:11 Remove thy scourges from me. The strength of thy hand hath made me faint in rebukes:

38:12 thou hast corrected man for iniquity. And thou hast made his soul to waste away like a

hominem. Et tabescere fecisti sicut araneam animam ejus : verumtamen vane conturbatur omnis homo.

38:13 Exaudi orationem meam, Domine, et deprecationem meam ; auribus percipe lacrimas meas. Ne sileas, quoniam advena ego sum apud te, et peregrinus sicut omnes patres mei.

38:14 Remitte mihi, ut refrigerer priusquam abeam et amplius non ero.

spider: surely in vain is any man disquieted.

38:13 Hear my prayer, O Lord, and my supplication: give ear to my tears. Be not silent: for I am a stranger with thee, and a sojourner as all my fathers were.

38:14 O forgive me, that I may be refreshed, before I go hence, and be no more.

XXXIX.

39:1 *In finem. Psalmus ipsi David.*

39:2 EXPECTANS EXSPECTAVI Dominum, et intendit mihi.

39:3 Et exaudivit preces meas, et eduxit me de lacu miseriæ et de luto fæcis. Et statuit super petram pedes meos, et direxit gressus meos.

39:4 Et immisit in os meum canticum novum, carmen Deo nostro. Videbunt multi, et timebunt, et sperabunt in Domino.

39:5 Beatus vir cujus est nomen Domini spes ejus, et non respexit in vanitates et insanias falsas.

39:6 Multa fecisti tu, Domine Deus meus, mirabilia tua ; et cogitationibus tuis non est qui similis sit tibi. Annuntiavi et locutus sum : multiplicati sunt super numerum.

39:7 Sacrificium et oblationem noluisti ; aures autem perfecisti mihi. Holocaustum et pro peccato non postulasti ;

39:8 tunc dixi : Ecce venio. In capite libri scriptum est de me,

39:9 ut facerem voluntatem tuam. Deus meus, volui, et legem tuam in medio cordis mei.

39:10 Annuntiavi justitiam tuam in ecclesia magna ; ecce labia mea non prohibebo : Domine, tu scisti.

39:11 Justitiam tuam non abscondi in corde meo ; veritatem tuam et salutare tuum dixi ; non abscondi misericordiam tuam et veritatem tuam a concilio multo.

39:12 Tu autem, Domine, ne longe facias miserationes tuas a me ; misericordia tua et veritas tua semper susceperunt me.

39:13 Quoniam circumdederunt me mala quorum non est numerus ; comprehenderunt me iniquitates meæ, et non potui ut viderem. Multiplicatæ sunt super capillos capitis mei, et cor meum dereliquit me.

39:14 Complaceat tibi, Domine, ut eruas me ;

39:1 *Unto the end, a psalm for David himself.*

39:2 WITH EXPECTATION I HAVE WAITED for the Lord, and he was attentive to me.

39:3 And he heard my prayers, and brought me out of the pit of misery and the mire of dregs. And he set my feet upon a rock, and directed my steps.

39:4 And he put a new canticle into my mouth, a song to our God. Many shall see, and shall fear: and they shall hope in the Lord.

39:5 Blessed is the man whose trust is in the name of the Lord; and who hath not had regard to vanities, and lying follies.

39:6 Thou hast multiplied thy wonderful works, O Lord my God: and in thy thoughts there is no one like to thee. I have declared and I have spoken they are multiplied above number.

39:7 Sacrifice and oblation thou didst not desire; but thou hast pierced ears for me. Burnt offering and sin offering thou didst not require:

39:8 then said I, Behold I come. In the head of the book it is written of me

39:9 that I should do thy will: O my God, I have desired it, and thy law in the midst of my heart.

39:10 I have declared thy justice in a great church, lo, I will not restrain my lips: O Lord, thou knowest it.

39:11 I have not hid thy justice within my heart: I have declared thy truth and thy salvation. I have not concealed thy mercy and thy truth from a great council.

39:12 Withhold not thou, O Lord, thy tender mercies from me: thy mercy and thy truth have always upheld me.

39:13 For evils without number have surrounded me; my iniquities have overtaken me, and I was not able to see. They are multiplied above the hairs of my head: and my heart hath forsaken me.

39:14 Be pleased, O Lord, to deliver me, look

Domine, ad adjuvandum me respice.

39:15 Confundantur et revereantur simul, qui quærunt animam meam ut auferant eam ; convertantur retrorsum et revereantur, qui volunt mihi mala.

39:16 Ferant confestim confusionem suam, qui dicunt mihi : Euge, euge !

39:17 Exsultent et lætentur super te omnes quærentes te ; et dicant semper : Magnificetur Dominus, qui diligunt salutare tuum.

39:18 Ego autem mendicus sum et pauper ; Dominus sollicitus est mei. Adjutor meus et protector meus tu es ; Deus meus, ne tardaveris.

down, O Lord, to help me.

39:15 Let them be confounded and ashamed together, that seek after my soul to take it away. Let them be turned backward and be ashamed that desire evils to me.

39:16 Let them immediately bear their confusion, that say to me: 'T is well, 't is well.

39:17 Let all that seek thee rejoice and be glad in thee: and let such as love thy salvation say always: The Lord be magnified.

39:18 But I am a beggar and poor: the Lord is careful for me. Thou art my helper and my protector: O my God, be not slack.

XL.

40:1 *In finem. Psalmus ipsi David.*

40:2 BEATUS QUI INTELLIGIT super egenum et pauperem : in die mala liberabit eum Dominus.

40:3 Dominus conservet eum, et vivificet eum, et beatum faciat eum in terra, et non tradat eum in animam inimicorum ejus.

40:4 Dominus opem ferat illi super lectum doloris ejus ; universum stratum ejus versasti in infirmitate ejus.

40:5 Ego dixi : Domine, miserere mei ; sana animam meam, quia peccavi tibi.

40:6 Inimici mei dixerunt mala mihi : Quando morietur, et peribit nomen ejus ?

40:7 Et si ingrediebatur ut videret, vana loquebatur ; cor ejus congregavit iniquitatem sibi. Egrediebatur foras et loquebatur.

40:8 In idipsum adversum me susurrabant omnes inimici mei ; adversum me cogitabant mala mihi.

40:9 Verbum iniquum constituerunt adversum me : Numquid qui dormit non adjiciet ut resurgat ?

40:10 Etenim homo pacis meæ in quo speravi, qui edebat panes meos, magnificavit super me supplantationem.

40:11 Tu autem, Domine, miserere mei, et resuscita me ; et retribuam eis.

40:12 In hoc cognovi quoniam voluisti me, quoniam non gaudebit inimicus meus super me.

40:13 Me autem propter innocentiam suscepisti ; et confirmasti me in conspectu tuo in æternum.

40:14 Benedictus Dominus Deus Israël a sæculo et usque in sæculum. Fiat, fiat.

40:1 *Unto the end, a psalm for David himself.*

40:2 BLESSED IS HE THAT UNDERSTANDETH concerning the needy and the poor: the Lord will deliver him in the evil day.

40:3 The Lord preserve him and give him life, and make him blessed upon the earth: and deliver him not up to the will of his enemies.

40:4 The Lord help him on his bed of sorrow: thou hast turned all his couch in his sickness.

40:5 I said: O Lord, be thou merciful to me: heal my soul, for I have sinned against thee.

40:6 My enemies have spoken evils against me: when shall he die and his name perish?

40:7 And if he came in to see me, he spoke vain things: his heart gathered together iniquity to itself. He went out and spoke to the same purpose.

40:8 All my enemies whispered together against me: they devised evils to me.

40:9 They determined against me an unjust word: shall he that sleepeth rise again no more?

40:10 For even the man of peace, in whom I trusted, who ate my bread, hath greatly supplanted me.

40:11 But thou, O Lord, have mercy on me, and raise me up again: and I will requite them.

40:12 By this I know, that thou hast had a good will for me: because my enemy shall not rejoice over me.

40:13 But thou hast upheld me by reason of my innocence: and hast established me in thy sight for ever.

40:14 Blessed by the Lord the God of Israel from eternity to eternity. So be it. So be it.

XLI.

41:1 *In finem. Intellectus filiis Core.*

41:2 QUEMADMODUM DESIDERAT CERVUS ad fontes aquarum, ita desiderat anima mea ad te, Deus.

41:3 Sitivit anima mea ad Deum fortem, vivum ; quando veniam, et apparebo ante faciem Dei ?

41:4 Fuerunt mihi lacrimæ meæ panes die ac nocte, dum dicitur mihi quotidie : Ubi est Deus tuus ?

41:5 Hæc recordatus sum, et effudi in me animam meam, quoniam transibo in locum tabernaculi admirabilis, usque ad domum Dei, in voce exsultationis et confessionis, sonus epulantis.

41:6 Quare tristis es, anima mea ? et quare conturbas me ? Spera in Deo, quoniam adhuc confitebor illi, salutare vultus mei,

41:7 et Deus meus. Ad meipsum anima mea conturbata est : propterea memor ero tui de terra Jordanis et Hermoniim a monte modico.

41:8 Abyssus abyssum invocat, in voce cataractarum tuarum ; omnia excelsa tua, et fluctus tui super me transierunt.

41:9 In die mandavit Dominus misericordiam suam, et nocte canticum ejus ; apud me oratio Deo vitæ meæ.

41:10 Dicam Deo : Susceptor meus es ; quare oblitus es mei ? et quare contristatus incedo, dum affligit me inimicus ?

41:11 Dum confringuntur ossa mea, exprobraverunt mihi qui tribulant me inimici mei, dum dicunt mihi per singulos dies : Ubi est Deus tuus ?

41:12 Quare tristis es, anima mea ? et quare conturbas me ? Spera in Deo, quoniam adhuc confitebor illi, salutare vultus mei, et Deus meus.

41:1 *Unto the end, understanding for the sons of Core.*

41:2 AS THE HART PANTETH after the fountains of water; so my soul panteth after thee, O GOD.

41:3 My soul hath thirsted after the strong living God; when shall I come and appear before the face of God?

41:4 My tears have been my bread day and night, whilst it is said to me daily: Where is thy God?

41:5 These things I remembered, and poured out my soul in me: for I shall go over into the place of the wonderful tabernacle, even to the house of God: With the voice of joy and praise; the noise of one feasting.

41:6 Why art thou sad, O my soul? and why dost thou trouble me? Hope in God, for I will still give praise to him: the salvation of my countenance,

41:7 and my God. My soul is troubled within myself: therefore will I remember thee from the land of Jordan and Hermoniim, from the little hill.

41:8 Deep calleth on deep, at the noise of thy flood-gates. All thy heights and thy billows have passed over me.

41:9 In the daytime the Lord hath commanded his mercy; and a canticle to him in the night. With me is prayer to the God of my life.

41:10 I will say to God: Thou art my support. Why hast thou forgotten me? and why go I mourning, whilst my enemy afflicteth me?

41:11 Whilst my bones are broken, my enemies who trouble me have reproached me; Whilst they say to me day be day: Where is thy God?

41:12 Why art thou cast down, O my soul? and why dost thou disquiet me? Hope thou in God, for I will still give praise to him: the salvation of my countenance, and my God.

XLII.

42:1 *Psalmus David.* JUDICA ME, DEUS, et discerne causam meam de gente non sancta : ab homine iniquo et doloso erue me.

42:2 Quia tu es, Deus, fortitudo mea : quare me repulisti ? et quare tristis incedo, dum affligit me inimicus ?

42:3 Emitte lucem tuam et veritatem tuam : ipsa me deduxerunt, et adduxerunt in montem

42:1 *A psalm for David.* JUDGE ME, O GOD, and distinguish my cause from the nation that is not holy: deliver me from the unjust and deceitful man.

42:2 For thou art God my strength: why hast thou cast me off? and why do I go sorrowful whilst the enemy afflicteth me?

42:3 Send forth thy light and thy truth: they have conducted me, and brought me unto thy holy

sanctum tuum, et in tabernacula tua.

⁴²:⁴ Et introibo ad altare Dei, ad Deum qui lætificat juventutem meam. Confitebor tibi in cithara, Deus, Deus meus.

⁴²:⁵ Quare tristis es, anima mea ? et quare conturbas me ? Spera in Deo, quoniam adhuc confitebor illi, salutare vultus mei, et Deus meus.

hill, and into thy tabernacles.

⁴²:⁴ And I will go in to the altar of God: to God who giveth joy to my youth.

⁴²:⁵ To thee, O God my God, I will give praise upon the harp: why art thou sad, O my soul? and why dost thou disquiet me? Hope in God, for I will still give praise to him: the salvation of my countenance, and my God.

XLIII.

⁴³:¹ *In finem. Filiis Core ad intellectum.*

⁴³:² Deus, auribus nostris audivimus, patres nostri annuntiaverunt nobis, opus quod operatus es in diebus eorum, et in diebus antiquis.

⁴³:³ Manus tua gentes disperdidit, et plantasti eos ; afflixisti populos, et expulisti eos.

⁴³:⁴ Nec enim in gladio suo possederunt terram, et brachium eorum non salvavit eos : sed dextera tua et brachium tuum, et illuminatio vultus tui, quoniam complacuisti in eis.

⁴³:⁵ Tu es ipse rex meus et Deus meus, qui mandas salutes Jacob.

⁴³:⁶ In te inimicos nostros ventilabimus cornu, et in nomine tuo spernemus insurgentes in nobis.

⁴³:⁷ Non enim in arcu meo sperabo, et gladius meus non salvabit me :

⁴³:⁸ salvasti enim nos de affligentibus nos, et odientes nos confudisti.

⁴³:⁹ In Deo laudabimur tota die, et in nomine tuo confitebimur in sæculum.

⁴³:¹⁰ Nunc autem repulisti et confudisti nos, et non egredieris, Deus, in virtutibus nostris.

⁴³:¹¹ Avertisti nos retrorsum post inimicos nostros, et qui oderunt nos diripiebant sibi.

⁴³:¹² Dedisti nos tamquam oves escarum, et in gentibus dispersisti nos.

⁴³:¹³ Vendidisti populum tuum sine pretio, et non fuit multitudo in commutationibus eorum.

⁴³:¹⁴ Posuisti nos opprobrium vicinis nostris ; subsannationem et derisum his qui sunt in circuitu nostro.

⁴³:¹⁵ Posuisti nos in similitudinem gentibus ; commotionem capitis in populis.

⁴³:¹ *Unto the end, for the sons of Core, to give understanding.*

⁴³:² We have heard, O God, with our ears: our fathers have declared to us, The work, thou hast wrought in their days, and in the days of old.

⁴³:³ Thy hand destroyed the Gentiles, and thou plantedst them: thou didst afflict the people and cast them out.

⁴³:⁴ For they got not the possession of the land by their own sword: neither did their own arm save them. But thy right hand and thy arm, and the light of thy countenance: because thou wast pleased with them.

⁴³:⁵ Thou art thyself my king and my God, who commandest the saving of Jacob.

⁴³:⁶ Through thee we will push down our enemies with the horn: and through thy name we will despise them that rise up against us.

⁴³:⁷ For I will not trust in my bow: neither shall my sword save me.

⁴³:⁸ But thou hast saved us from them that afflict us: and hast put them to shame that hate us.

⁴³:⁹ In God shall we glory all the day long: and in thy name we will give praise for ever.

⁴³:¹⁰ But now thou hast cast us off, and put us to shame: and thou, O God, wilt not go out with our armies.

⁴³:¹¹ Thou hast made us turn our back to our enemies: and they that hated us plundered for themselves.

⁴³:¹² Thou hast given us up like sheep to be eaten: thou hast scattered us among the nations.

⁴³:¹³ Thou hast sold thy people for no price: and there was no reckoning in the exchange of them.

⁴³:¹⁴ Thou hast made us a reproach to our neighbours, a scoff and derision to them that are round about us.

⁴³:¹⁵ Thou hast made us a byword among the Gentiles: a shaking of the head among the peo-

43:16 Tota die verecundia mea contra me est, et confusio faciei meæ cooperuit me :

43:17 a voce exprobrantis et obloquentis, a facie inimici et persequentis.

43:18 Hæc omnia venerunt super nos ; nec obliti sumus te, et inique non egimus in testamento tuo.

43:19 Et non recessit retro cor nostrum ; et declinasti semitas nostras a via tua :

43:20 quoniam humiliasti nos in loco afflictionis, et cooperuit nos umbra mortis.

43:21 Si obliti sumus nomen Dei nostri, et si expandimus manus nostras ad deum alienum,

43:22 nonne Deus requiret ista ? ipse enim novit abscondita cordis. Quoniam propter te mortificamur tota die ; æstimati sumus sicut oves occisionis.

43:23 Exsurge ; quare obdormis, Domine ? exsurge, et ne repellas in finem.

43:24 Quare faciem tuam avertis ? oblivisceris inopiæ nostræ et tribulationis nostræ ?

43:25 Quoniam humiliata est in pulvere anima nostra ; conglutinatus est in terra venter noster.

43:26 Exsurge, Domine, adjuva nos, et redime nos propter nomen tuum.

ple.

43:16 All the day long my shame is before me: and the confusion of my face hath covered me,

43:17 At the voice of him that reproacheth and detracteth me: at the face of the enemy and persecutor.

43:18 All these things have come upon us, yet we have not forgotten thee: and we have not done wickedly in thy covenant.

43:19 And our heart hath not turned back: neither hast thou turned aside our steps from thy way.

43:20 For thou hast humbled us in the place of affliction: and the shadow of death hath covered us.

43:21 If we have forgotten the name of our God, and if we have spread forth our hands to a strange god:

43:22 Shall not God search out these things: for he knoweth the secrets of the heart. Because for thy sake we are killed all the day long: we are counted as sheep for the slaughter.

43:23 Arise, why sleepest thou, O Lord? arise, and cast us not off to the end.

43:24 Why turnest thou face away? and forgettest our want and our trouble?

43:25 For our soul is humbled down to the dust: our belly cleaveth to the earth.

43:26 Arise, O Lord, help us and redeem us for thy name's sake.

XLIV.

44:1 *In finem, pro iis qui commutabuntur. Filiis Core, ad intellectum. Canticum pro dilecto.*

44:2 ERUCTAVIT COR MEUM verbum bonum : dico ego opera mea regi. Lingua mea calamus scribæ velociter scribentis.

44:3 Speciosus forma præ filiis hominum, diffusa est gratia in labiis tuis : propterea benedixit te Deus in æternum.

44:4 Accingere gladio tuo super femur tuum, potentissime.

44:5 Specie tua et pulchritudine tua intende, prospere procede, et regna, propter veritatem, et mansuetudinem, et justitiam ; et deducet te mirabiliter dextera tua.

44:6 Sagittæ tuæ acutæ : populi sub te cadent, in corda inimicorum regis.

44:7 Sedes tua, Deus, in sæculum sæculi ; virga directionis virga regni tui.

44:1 *Unto the end, for them that shall be changed, for the sons of Core, for understanding. A canticle for the Beloved.*

44:2 MY HEART HATH UTTERED a good word: I speak my works to the king: My tongue is the pen of a scrivener that writeth swiftly.

44:3 Thou art beautiful above the sons of men: grace is poured abroad in thy lips; therefore hath God blessed thee for ever.

44:4 Gird thy sword upon thy thigh, O thou most mighty.

44:5 With thy comeliness and thy beauty set out, proceed prosperously, and reign. Because of truth and meekness and justice: and thy right hand shall conduct thee wonderfully.

44:6 Thy arrows are sharp: under thee shall people fall, into the hearts of the king's enemies.

44:7 Thy throne, O God, is for ever and ever: the sceptre of thy kingdom is a sceptre of up-

44:8 Dilexisti justitiam, et odisti iniquitatem ; propterea unxit te Deus, Deus tuus, oleo lætitiæ, præ consortibus tuis.

44:9 Myrrha, et gutta, et casia a vestimentis tuis, a domibus eburneis ; ex quibus delectaverunt te

44:10 filiæ regum in honore tuo. Astitit regina a dextris tuis in vestitu deaurato, circumdata varietate.

44:11 Audi, filia, et vide, et inclina aurem tuam ; et obliviscere populum tuum, et domum patris tui.

44:12 Et concupiscet rex decorem tuum, quoniam ipse est Dominus Deus tuus, et adorabunt eum.

44:13 Et filiæ Tyri in muneribus vultum tuum deprecabuntur ; omnes divites plebis.

44:14 Omnis gloria ejus filiæ regis ab intus, in fimbriis aureis,

44:15 circumamicta varietatibus. Adducentur regi virgines post eam ; proximæ ejus afferentur tibi.

44:16 Afferentur in lætitia et exsultatione ; adducentur in templum regis.

44:17 Pro patribus tuis nati sunt tibi filii ; constitues eos principes super omnem terram.

44:18 Memores erunt nominis tui in omni generatione et generationem : propterea populi confitebuntur tibi in æternum, et in sæculum sæculi.

rightness.

44:8 Thou hast loved justice, and hated iniquity: therefore God, thy God, hath anointed thee with the oil of gladness above thy fellows.

44:9 Myrrh and stacte and cassia perfume thy garments, from the ivory houses: out of which

44:10 the daughters of kings have delighted thee in thy glory. The queen stood on thy right hand, in gilded clothing; surrounded with variety.

44:11 Hearken, O daughter, and see, and incline thy ear: and forget thy people and thy father's house.

44:12 And the king shall greatly desire thy beauty; for he is the Lord thy God, and him they shall adore.

44:13 And the daughters of Tyre with gifts, yea, all the rich among the people, shall entreat thy countenance.

44:14 All the glory of the king's daughter is within in golden borders,

44:15 clothed round about with varieties. After her shall virgins be brought to the king: her neighbours shall be brought to thee.

44:16 They shall be brought with gladness and rejoicing: they shall be brought into the temple of the king.

44:17 Instead of thy fathers, sons are born to thee: thou shalt make them princes over all the earth.

44:18 They shall remember thy name throughout all generations. Therefore shall people praise thee for ever; yea, for ever and ever.

XLV.

45:1 *In finem, filiis Core, pro arcanis. Psalmus.*

45:2 DEUS NOSTER REFUGIUM et virtus ; adjutor in tribulationibus quæ invenerunt nos nimis.

45:3 Propterea non timebimus dum turbabitur terra, et transferentur montes in cor maris.

45:4 Sonuerunt, et turbatæ sunt aquæ eorum ; conturbati sunt montes in fortitudine ejus.

45:5 Fluminis impetus lætificat civitatem Dei : sanctificavit tabernaculum suum Altissimus.

45:6 Deus in medio ejus, non commovebitur ; adjuvabit eam Deus mane diluculo.

45:7 Conturbatæ sunt gentes, et inclinata sunt

45:1 *Unto the end, for the sons of Core, for the hidden.*

45:2 OUR GOD IS OUR REFUGE and strength: a helper in troubles, which have found us exceedingly.

45:3 Therefore we will not fear, when the earth shall be troubled; and the mountains shall be removed into the heart of the sea.

45:4 Their waters roared and were troubled: the mountains were troubled with his strength.

45:5 The stream of the river maketh the city of God joyful: the most High hath sanctified his own tabernacle.

45:6 God is in the midst thereof, it shall not be moved: God will help it in the morning early.

45:7 Nations were troubled, and kingdoms were

regna : dedit vocem suam, mota est terra.

45:8 Dominus virtutum nobiscum ; susceptor noster Deus Jacob.

45:9 Venite, et videte opera Domini, quæ posuit prodigia super terram,

45:10 auferens bella usque ad finem terræ. Arcum conteret, et confringet arma, et scuta comburet igni.

45:11 Vacate, et videte quoniam ego sum Deus ; exaltabor in gentibus, et exaltabor in terra.

45:12 Dominus virtutum nobiscum ; susceptor noster Deus Jacob.

bowed down: he uttered his voice, the earth trembled.

45:8 The Lord of armies is with us: the God of Jacob is our protector.

45:9 Come and behold ye the works of the Lord: what wonders he hath done upon earth,

45:10 making wars to cease even to the end of the earth. He shall destroy the bow, and break the weapons: and the shield he shall burn in the fire.

45:11 Be still and see that I am God; I will be exalted among the nations, and I will be exalted in the earth.

45:12 The Lord of armies is with us: the God of Jacob is our protector.

XLVI.

46:1 *In finem, pro filiis Core. Psalmus.*

46:2 OMNES GENTES, PLAUDITE MANIBUS ; jubilate Deo in voce exsultationis :

46:3 quoniam Dominus excelsus, terribilis, rex magnus super omnem terram.

46:4 Subjecit populos nobis, et gentes sub pedibus nostris.

46:5 Elegit nobis hæreditatem suam ; speciem Jacob quam dilexit.

46:6 Ascendit Deus in jubilo, et Dominus in voce tubæ.

46:7 Psallite Deo nostro, psallite ; psallite regi nostro, psallite :

46:8 quoniam rex omnis terræ Deus, psallite sapienter.

46:9 Regnabit Deus super gentes ; Deus sedet super sedem sanctam suam.

46:10 Principes populorum congregati sunt cum Deo Abraham, quoniam dii fortes terræ vehementer elevati sunt.

46:1 *Unto the end, for the sons of Core.*

46:2 O CLAP YOUR HANDS, ALL YE NATIONS: shout unto God with the voice of joy,

46:3 For the Lord is high, terrible: a great king over all the earth.

46:4 He hath subdued the people under us; and the nations under our feet.

46:5 He hath chosen for us his inheritance, the beauty of Jacob which he hath loved.

46:6 God is ascended with jubilee, and the Lord with the sound of trumpet.

46:7 Sing praises to our God, sing ye: sing praises to our king, sing ye.

46:8 For God is the king of all the earth: sing ye wisely.

46:9 God shall reign over the nations: God sitteth on his holy throne.

46:10 The princes of the people are gathered together, with the God of Abraham: for the strong gods of the earth are exceedingly exalted.

XLVII.

47:1 *Psalmus cantici. Filiis Core, secunda sabbati.*

47:2 MAGNUS DOMINUS et laudabilis nimis, in civitate Dei nostri, in monte sancto ejus.

47:3 Fundatur exsultatione universæ terræ mons Sion ; latera aquilonis, civitas regis magni.

47:4 Deus in domibus ejus cognoscetur cum suscipiet eam.

47:5 Quoniam ecce reges terræ congregati sunt ; convenerunt in unum.

47:1 *A psalm of a canticle, for the sons of Core, on the second day of the week.*

47:2 GREAT IS THE LORD, and exceedingly to be praised in the city of our God, in his holy mountain.

47:3 With the joy of the whole earth is mount Sion founded, on the sides of the north, the city of the great king.

47:4 In her houses shall God be known, when he shall protect her.

47:5 For behold the kings of the earth assembled themselves: they gathered together.

47:6 Ipsi videntes, sic admirati sunt, conturbati sunt, commoti sunt.

47:7 Tremor apprehendit eos ; ibi dolores ut parturientis :

47:8 in spiritu vehementi conteres naves Tharsis.

47:9 Sicut audivimus, sic vidimus, in civitate Domini virtutum, in civitate Dei nostri : Deus fundavit eam in æternum.

47:10 Suscepimus, Deus, misericordiam tuam in medio templi tui.

47:11 Secundum nomen tuum, Deus, sic et laus tua in fines terræ ; justitia plena est dextera tua.

47:12 Lætetur mons Sion, et exsultent filiæ Judæ, propter judicia tua, Domine.

47:13 Circumdate Sion, et complectimini eam ; narrate in turribus ejus.

47:14 Ponite corda vestra in virtute ejus, et distribuite domos ejus, ut enarretis in progenie altera.

47:15 Quoniam hic est Deus, Deus noster in æternum, et in sæculum sæculi : ipse reget nos in sæcula.

47:6 So they saw, and they wondered, they were troubled, they were moved:

47:7 trembling took hold of them. There were pains as of a woman in labour.

47:8 With a vehement wind thou shalt break in pieces the ships of Tharsis.

47:9 As we have heard, so have we seen, in the city of the Lord of hosts, in the city of our God: God hath founded it for ever.

47:10 We have received thy mercy, O God, in the midst of thy temple.

47:11 According to thy name, O God, so also is thy praise unto the ends of the earth: thy right hand is full of justice.

47:12 Let mount Sion rejoice, and the daughters of Juda be glad; because of thy judgments, O Lord.

47:13 Surround Sion, and encompass her: tell ye in her towers.

47:14 Set your hearts on her strength; and distribute her houses, that ye may relate it in another generation.

47:15 For this is God, our God unto eternity, and for ever and ever: he shall rule us for evermore.

XLVIII.

48:1 *In finem, filiis Core. Psalmus.*

48:2 AUDITE HÆC, omnes gentes ; auribus percipite, omnes qui habitatis orbem :

48:3 quique terrigenæ et filii hominum, simul in unum dives et pauper.

48:4 Os meum loquetur sapientiam, et meditatio cordis mei prudentiam.

48:5 Inclinabo in parabolam aurem meam ; aperiam in psalterio propositionem meam.

48:6 Cur timebo in die mala ? iniquitas calcanei mei circumdabit me.

48:7 Qui confidunt in virtute sua, et in multitudine divitiarum suarum, gloriantur.

48:8 Frater non redimit, redimet homo : non dabit Deo placationem suam.

48:9 et pretium redemptionis animæ suæ. Et laborabit in æternum ;

48:10 et vivet adhuc in finem.

48:11 Non videbit interitum, cum viderit sapientes morientes : simul insipiens et stultus peribunt. Et relinquent alienis divitias suas,

48:12 et sepulchra eorum domus illorum in æternum ; tabernacula eorum in progenie et progenie : vocaverunt nomina sua in terris suis.

48:1 *Unto the end, a psalm for the sons of Core.*

48:2 HEAR THESE THINGS, all ye nations: give ear, all ye inhabitants of the world.

48:3 All you that are earthborn, and you sons of men: both rich and poor together.

48:4 My mouth shall speak wisdom: and the meditation of my heart understanding.

48:5 I will incline my ear to a parable; I will open my proposition on the psaltery.

48:6 Why shall I fear in the evil day? the iniquity of my heel shall encompass me.

48:7 They that trust in their own strength, and glory in the multitude of their riches,

48:8 No brother can redeem, nor shall man redeem: he shall not give to God his ransom,

48:9 Nor the price of the redemption of his soul: and shall labour for ever,

48:10 and shall still live unto the end.

48:11 He shall not see destruction, when he shall see the wise dying: the senseless and the fool shall perish together: And they shall leave their riches to strangers:

48:12 and their sepulchres shall be their houses for ever. Their dwelling places to all generations: they have called their lands by their

48:13 Et homo, cum in honore esset, non intellexit. Comparatus est jumentis insipientibus, et similis factus est illis.

48:14 Hæc via illorum scandalum ipsis ; et postea in ore suo complacebunt.

48:15 Sicut oves in inferno positi sunt : mors depascet eos. Et dominabuntur eorum justi in matutino ; et auxilium eorum veterascet in inferno a gloria eorum.

48:16 Verumtamen Deus redimet animam meam de manu inferi, cum acceperit me.

48:17 Ne timueris cum dives factus fuerit homo, et cum multiplicata fuerit gloria domus ejus :

48:18 quoniam, cum interierit, non sumet omnia, neque descendet cum eo gloria ejus.

48:19 Quia anima ejus in vita ipsius benedicetur ; confitebitur tibi cum benefeceris ei.

48:20 Introibit usque in progenies patrum suorum ; et usque in æternum non videbit lumen.

48:21 Homo, cum in honore esset, non intellexit. Comparatus est jumentis insipientibus, et similis factus est illis.

names.

48:13 And man when he was in honour did not understand; he is compared to senseless beasts, and is become like to them.

48:14 This way of theirs is a stumblingblock to them: and afterwards they shall delight in their mouth.

48:15 They are laid in hell like sheep: death shall feed upon them. And the just shall have dominion over them in the morning; and their help shall decay in hell from their glory.

48:16 But God will redeem my soul from the hand of hell, when he shall receive me.

48:17 Be not thou afraid, when a man shall be made rich, and when the glory of his house shall be increased.

48:18 For when he shall die he shall take nothing away; nor shall his glory descend with him.

48:19 For in his lifetime his soul will be blessed: and he will praise thee when thou shalt do well to him.

48:20 He shall go in to the generations of his fathers: and he shall never see light.

48:21 Man when he was in honour did not understand: he hath been compared to senseless beasts, and made like to them.

XLIX.

49:1 *Psalmus Asaph.* DEUS DEORUM Dominus locutus est, et vocavit terram a solis ortu usque ad occasum.

49:2 Ex Sion species decoris ejus :

49:3 Deus manifeste veniet ; Deus noster, et non silebit. Ignis in conspectu ejus exardescet ; et in circuitu ejus tempestas valida.

49:4 Advocabit cælum desursum, et terram, discernere populum suum.

49:5 Congregate illi sanctos ejus, qui ordinant testamentum ejus super sacrificia.

49:6 Et annuntiabunt cæli justitiam ejus, quoniam Deus judex est.

49:7 Audi, populus meus, et loquar ; Israël, et testificabor tibi : Deus, Deus tuus ego sum.

49:8 Non in sacrificiis tuis arguam te ; holocausta autem tua in conspectu meo sunt semper.

49:9 Non accipiam de domo tua vitulos, neque de gregibus tuis hircos :

49:10 quoniam meæ sunt omnes feræ silvarum, jumenta in montibus, et boves.

49:1 *A psalm for Asaph.* THE GOD OF GODS, the Lord hath spoken: and he hath called the earth. From the rising of the sun, to the going down thereof:

49:2 out of Sion the loveliness of his beauty.

49:3 God shall come manifestly: our God shall come, and shall not keep silence. A fire shall burn before him: and a mighty tempest shall be round about him.

49:4 He shall call heaven from above, and the earth, to judge his people.

49:5 Gather ye together his saints to him: who set his covenant before sacrifices.

49:6 And the heavens shall declare his justice: for God is judge.

49:7 Hear, O my people, and I will speak: O Israel, and I will testify to thee: I am God, thy God.

49:8 I will not reprove thee for thy sacrifices: and thy burnt offerings are always in my sight.

49:9 I will not take calves out of thy house: nor he goats out of thy flocks.

49:10 For all the beasts of the woods are mine: the cattle on the hills, and the oxen.

49:11 Cognovi omnia volatilia cæli, et pulchritudo agri mecum est.

49:12 Si esuriero, non dicam tibi : meus est enim orbis terræ et plenitudo ejus.

49:13 Numquid manducabo carnes taurorum ? aut sanguinem hircorum potabo ?

49:14 Immola Deo sacrificium laudis, et redde Altissimo vota tua.

49:15 Et invoca me in die tribulationis : eruam te, et honorificabis me.

49:16 Peccatori autem dixit Deus : Quare tu enarras justitias meas ? et assumis testamentum meum per os tuum ?

49:17 Tu vero odisti disciplinam, et projecisti sermones meos retrorsum.

49:18 Si videbas furem, currebas cum eo ; et cum adulteris portionem tuam ponebas.

49:19 Os tuum abundavit malitia, et lingua tua concinnabat dolos.

49:20 Sedens adversus fratrem tuum loquebaris, et adversus filium matris tuæ ponebas scandalum.

49:21 Hæc fecisti, et tacui. Existimasti inique quod ero tui similis : arguam te, et statuam contra faciem tuam.

49:22 Intelligite hæc, qui obliviscimini Deum, nequando rapiat, et non sit qui eripiat.

49:23 Sacrificium laudis honorificabit me, et illic iter quo ostendam illi salutare Dei.

49:11 I know all the fowls of the air: and with me is the beauty of the field.

49:12 If I should be hungry, I would not tell thee: for the world is mine, and the fulness thereof.

49:13 Shall I eat the flesh of bullocks? or shall I drink the blood of goats?

49:14 Offer to God the sacrifice of praise: and pay thy vows to the most High.

49:15 And call upon me in the day of trouble: I will deliver thee, and thou shalt glorify me.

49:16 But to the sinner God hath said: Why dost thou declare my justices, and take my covenant in thy mouth ?

49:17 Seeing thou hast hated discipline: and hast cast my words behind thee.

49:18 If thou didst see a thief thou didst run with him: and with adulterers thou hast been a partaker.

49:19 Thy mouth hath abounded with evil, and thy tongue framed deceits.

49:20 Sitting thou didst speak against thy brother, and didst lay a scandal against thy mother's son:

49:21 these things hast thou done, and I was silent. Thou thoughtest unjustly that I should be like to thee: but I will reprove thee, and set before thy face.

49:22 Understand these things, you that forget God; lest he snatch you away, and there be none to deliver you.

49:23 The sacrifice of praise shall glorify me: and there is the way by which I will shew him the salvation of God.

L.

50:1 *In finem. Psalmus David,*

50:2 *cum venit ad eum Nathan propheta, quando intravit ad Bethsabee.*

50:3 MISERERE MEI, Deus, secundum magnam misericordiam tuam ; et secundum multitudinem miserationum tuarum, dele iniquitatem meam.

50:4 Amplius lava me ab iniquitate mea, et a peccato meo munda me.

50:5 Quoniam iniquitatem meam ego cognosco, et peccatum meum contra me est semper.

50:6 Tibi soli peccavi, et malum coram te feci ; ut justificeris in sermonibus tuis, et vincas cum judicaris.

50:7 Ecce enim in iniquitatibus conceptus sum, et in peccatis concepit me mater mea.

50:1 *Unto the end, a psalm of David,*

50:2 *when Nathan the prophet came to him after he had sinned with Bethsabee.*

50:3 HAVE MERCY ON ME, O God, according to thy great mercy. And according to the multitude of thy tender mercies blot out my iniquity.

50:4 Wash me yet more from my iniquity, and cleanse me from my sin.

50:5 For I know my iniquity, and my sin is always before me.

50:6 To thee only have I sinned, and have done evil before thee: that thou mayst be justified in thy words, and mayst overcome when thou art judged.

50:7 For behold I was conceived in iniquities; and in sins did my mother conceive me.

50:8 Ecce enim veritatem dilexisti ; incerta et occulta sapientiæ tuæ manifestasti mihi.

50:9 Asperges me hyssopo, et mundabor ; lavabis me, et super nivem dealbabor.

50:10 Auditui meo dabis gaudium et lætitiam, et exsultabunt ossa humiliata.

50:11 Averte faciem tuam a peccatis meis, et omnes iniquitates meas dele.
50:12 Cor mundum crea in me, Deus, et spiritum rectum innova in visceribus meis.
50:13 Ne projicias me a facie tua, et spiritum sanctum tuum ne auferas a me.
50:14 Redde mihi lætitiam salutaris tui, et spiritu principali confirma me.
50:15 Docebo iniquos vias tuas, et impii ad te convertentur.
50:16 Libera me de sanguinibus, Deus, Deus salutis meæ, et exsultabit lingua mea justitiam tuam.
50:17 Domine, labia mea aperies, et os meum annuntiabit laudem tuam.
50:18 Quoniam si voluisses sacrificium, dedissem utique ; holocaustis non delectaberis.

50:19 Sacrificium Deo spiritus contribulatus ; cor contritum et humiliatum, Deus, non despicies.

50:20 Benigne fac, Domine, in bona voluntate tua Sion, ut ædificentur muri Jerusalem.

50:21 Tunc acceptabis sacrificium justitiæ, oblationes et holocausta ; tunc imponent super altare tuum vitulos.

50:8 For behold thou hast loved truth: the uncertain and hidden things of thy wisdom thou hast made manifest to me.

50:9 Thou shalt sprinkle me with hyssop, and I shall be cleansed: thou shalt wash me, and I shall be made whiter than snow.

50:10 To my hearing thou shalt give joy and gladness: and the bones that have been humbled shall rejoice.

50:11 Turn away thy face from my sins, and blot out all my iniquities.

50:12 Create a clean heart in me, O God: and renew a right spirit within my bowels.

50:13 Cast me not away from thy face; and take not thy holy spirit from me.

50:14 Restore unto me the joy of thy salvation, and strengthen me with a perfect spirit.

50:15 I will teach the unjust thy ways: and the wicked shall be converted to thee.

50:16 Deliver me from blood, O God, thou God of my salvation: and my tongue shall extol thy justice.

50:17 O Lord, thou wilt open my lips: and my mouth shall declare thy praise.

50:18 For if thou hadst desired sacrifice, I would indeed have given it: with burnt offerings thou wilt not be delighted.

50:19 A sacrifice to God is an afflicted spirit: a contrite and humbled heart, O God, thou wilt not despise.

50:20 Deal favourably, O Lord, in thy good will with Sion; that the walls of Jerusalem may be built up.

50:21 Then shalt thou accept the sacrifice of justice, oblations and whole burnt offerings: then shall they lay calves upon thy altar.

LI.

51:1 *In finem. Intellectus David,*
51:2 *cum venit Doëg Idumæus, et nuntiavit Sauli :Venit David in domum Achimelech.*
51:3 QUID GLORIARIS in malitia, qui potens es in iniquitate ?
51:4 Tota die injustitiam cogitavit lingua tua ; sicut novacula acuta fecisti dolum.

51:5 Dilexisti malitiam super benignitatem ; iniquitatem magis quam loqui æquitatem.

51:6 Dilexisti omnia verba præcipitationis ; lingua dolosa.
51:7 Propterea Deus destruet te in finem ;

51:1 *Unto the end, understanding for David,*
51:2 *when Doeg the Edomite came and told Saul: David went to the house of Achimelech.*
51:3 WHY DOST THOU GLORY in malice, thou that art mighty in iniquity?
51:4 All the day long thy tongue hath devised injustice: as a sharp razor, thou hast wrought deceit.

51:5 Thou hast loved malice more than goodness: and iniquity rather than to speak righteousness.

51:6 Thou hast loved all the words of ruin, O deceitful tongue.
51:7 Therefore will God destroy thee for ever:

evellet te, et emigrabit te de tabernaculo tuo, et radicem tuam de terra viventium.

51:8 Videbunt justi, et timebunt ; et super eum ridebunt, et dicent :

51:9 Ecce homo qui non posuit Deum adjutorem suum ; sed speravit in multitudine divitiarum suarum, et prævaluit in vanitate sua.

51:10 Ego autem, sicut oliva fructifera in domo Dei ; speravi in misericordia Dei, in æternum et in sæculum sæculi.

51:11 Confitebor tibi in sæculum, quia fecisti ; et exspectabo nomen tuum, quoniam bonum est in conspectu sanctorum tuorum.

he will pluck thee out, and remove thee from thy dwelling place: and thy root out of the land of the living.

51:8 The just shall see and fear, and shall laugh at him, and say:

51:9 Behold the man that made not God his helper: But trusted in the abundance of his riches: and prevailed in his vanity.

51:10 But I, as a fruitful olive tree in the house of God, have hoped in the mercy of God for ever, yea for ever and ever.

51:11 I will praise thee for ever, because thou hast done it: and I will wait on thy name, for it is good in the sight of thy saints.

LII.

52:1 *In finem, pro Maëleth intelligentiæ David.* DIXIT INSIPIENS in corde suo : Non est Deus.

52:2 Corrupti sunt, et abominabiles facti sunt in iniquitatibus ; non est qui faciat bonum.

52:3 Deus de cælo prospexit super filios hominum, ut videat si est intelligens, aut requirens Deum.

52:4 Omnes declinaverunt ; simul inutiles facti sunt : non est qui faciat bonum, non est usque ad unum.

52:5 Nonne scient omnes qui operantur iniquitatem, qui devorant plebem meam ut cibum panis ?

52:6 Deum non invocaverunt ; illic trepidaverunt timore, ubi non erat timor. Quoniam Deus dissipavit ossa eorum qui hominibus placent : confusi sunt, quoniam Deus sprevit eos.

52:7 Quis dabit ex Sion salutare Israël ? cum converterit Deus captivitatem plebis suæ, exsultabit Jacob, et lætabitur Israël.

52:1 *Unto the end, for Maeleth, understandings to David.* THE FOOL SAID in his heart: There is no God.

52:2 They are corrupted, and become abominable in iniquities: there is none that doth good.

52:3 God looked down from heaven on the children of men: to see if there were any that did understand, or did seek God.

52:4 All have gone aside, they are become unprofitable together, there is none that doth good, no not one.

52:5 Shall not all the workers of iniquity know, who eat up my people as they eat bread?

52:6 They have not called upon God: there have they trembled for fear, where there was no fear. For God hath scattered the bones of them that please men: they have been confounded, because God hath despised them.

52:7 Who will give out of Sion the salvation of Israel? when God shall bring back the captivity of his people, Jacob shall rejoice, and Israel shall be glad.

LIII.

53:1 *In finem, in carminibus. Intellectus David,*
53:2 *cum venissent Ziphæi, et dixissent ad Saul : Nonne David absconditus est apud nos ?*
53:3 DEUS, IN NOMINE TUO SALVUM ME FAC, et in virtute tua judica me.

53:4 Deus, exaudi orationem meam ; auribus percipe verba oris mei.

53:5 Quoniam alieni insurrexerunt adversum me, et fortes quæsierunt animam meam, et non proposuerunt Deum ante conspectum suum.

53:1 *Unto the end, in verses, understanding for David.*
53:2 *When the men of Ziph had come and said to Saul: Is not David hidden with us?*
53:3 SAVE ME, O GOD, BY THY NAME, and judge me in thy strength.

53:4 O God, hear my prayer: give ear to the words of my mouth.

53:5 For strangers have risen up against me; and the mighty have sought after my soul: and they have not set God before their eyes.

53:6 Ecce enim Deus adjuvat me, et Dominus susceptor est animæ meæ.

53:7 Averte mala inimicis meis ; et in veritate tua disperde illos.

53:8 Voluntarie sacrificabo tibi, et confitebor nomini tuo, Domine, quoniam bonum est.

53:9 Quoniam ex omni tribulatione eripuisti me, et super inimicos meos despexit oculus meus.

53:6 For behold God is my helper: and the Lord is the protector of my soul.

53:7 Turn back the evils upon my enemies; and cut them off in thy truth.

53:8 I will freely sacrifice to thee, and will give praise, O God, to thy name: because it is good:

53:9 For thou hast delivered me out of all trouble: and my eye hath looked down upon my enemies.

LIV.

54:1 *In finem, in carminibus. Intellectus David.*

54:2 EXAUDI, DEUS, orationem meam, et ne despexeris deprecationem meam :

54:3 intende mihi, et exaudi me. Contristatus sum in exercitatione mea, et conturbatus sum

54:4 a voce inimici, et a tribulatione peccatoris. Quoniam declinaverunt in me iniquitates, et in ira molesti erant mihi.

54:5 Cor meum conturbatum est in me, et formido mortis cecidit super me.

54:6 Timor et tremor venerunt super me, et contexerunt me tenebræ.

54:7 Et dixi : Quis dabit mihi pennas sicut columbæ, et volabo, et requiescam ?

54:8 Ecce elongavi fugiens, et mansi in solitudine.

54:9 Exspectabam eum qui salvum me fecit a pusillanimitate spiritus, et tempestate.

54:10 Præcipita, Domine ; divide linguas eorum : quoniam vidi iniquitatem et contradictionem in civitate.

54:11 Die ac nocte circumdabit eam super muros ejus iniquitas ; et labor in medio ejus,

54:12 et injustitia : et non defecit de plateis ejus usura et dolus.

54:13 Quoniam si inimicus meus maledixisset mihi, sustinuissem utique. Et si is qui oderat me super me magna locutus fuisset, abscondissem me forsitan ab eo.

54:14 Tu vero homo unanimis, dux meus, et notus meus :

54:15 qui simul mecum dulces capiebas cibos ; in domo Dei ambulavimus cum consensu.

54:16 Veniat mors super illos, et descendant in infernum viventes : quoniam nequitiæ in habitaculis eorum, in medio eorum.

54:17 Ego autem ad Deum clamavi, et Dominus salvabit me.

54:1 *Unto the end, in verses, understanding for David.*

54:2 HEAR, O GOD, my prayer, and despise not my supplication:

54:3 be attentive to me and hear me. I am grieved in my exercise; and am troubled,

54:4 at the voice of the enemy, and at the tribulation of the sinner. For they have cast iniquities upon me: and in wrath they were troublesome to me.

54:5 My heart is troubled within me: and the fear of death is fallen upon me.

54:6 Fear and trembling are come upon me: and darkness hath covered me.

54:7 And I said: Who will give me wings like a dove, and I will fly and be at rest?

54:8 Lo, I have gone far off flying away; and I abode in the wilderness.

54:9 I waited for him that hath saved me from pusillanimity of spirit, and a storm.

54:10 Cast down, O Lord, and divide their tongues; for I have seen iniquity and contradiction in the city.

54:11 Day and night shall iniquity surround it upon its walls: and in the midst thereof are labour,

54:12 and injustice. And usury and deceit have not departed from its streets.

54:13 For if my enemy had reviled me, I would verily have borne with it. And if he that hated me had spoken great things against me, I would perhaps have hidden myself from him.

54:14 But thou a man of one mind, my guide, and my familiar,

54:15 Who didst take sweetmeats together with me: in the house of God we walked with consent.

54:16 Let death come upon them, and let them go down alive into hell. For there is wickedness in their dwellings: in the midst of them.

54:17 But I have cried to God: and the Lord will save me.

54:18 Vespere, et mane, et meridie, narrabo, et annuntiabo ; et exaudiet vocem meam.

54:19 Redimet in pace animam meam ab his qui appropinquant mihi : quoniam inter multos erant mecum.

54:20 Exaudiet Deus, et humiliabit illos, qui est ante sæcula. Non enim est illis commutatio, et non timuerunt Deum.

54:21 Extendit manum suam in retribuendo ; contaminaverunt testamentum ejus :

54:22 divisi sunt ab ira vultus ejus, et appropinquavit cor illius. Molliti sunt sermones ejus super oleum ; et ipsi sunt jacula.

54:23 Jacta super Dominum curam tuam, et ipse te enutriet ; non dabit in æternum fluctuationem justo.

54:24 Tu vero, Deus, deduces eos in puteum interitus. Viri sanguinum et dolosi non dimidiabunt dies suos ; ego autem sperabo in te, Domine.

54:18 Evening and morning, and at noon I will speak and declare: and he shall hear my voice.

54:19 He shall redeem my soul in peace from them that draw near to me: for among many they were with me.

54:20 God shall hear, and the Eternal shall humble them. For there is no change with them, and they have not feared God:

54:21 he hath stretched forth his hand to repay. They have defiled his covenant,

54:22 they are divided by the wrath of his countenance, and his heart hath drawn near. His words are smoother than oil, and the same are darts.

54:23 Cast thy care upon the Lord, and he shall sustain thee: he shall not suffer the just to waver for ever.

54:24 But thou, O God, shalt bring them down into the pit of destruction. Bloody and deceitful men shall not live out half their days; but I will trust in thee, O Lord.

LV.

55:1 *In finem, pro populo qui a sanctis longe factus est. David in tituli inscriptionem, cum tenuerunt eum Allophyli in Geth.*

55:2 MISERERE MEI, Deus, quoniam conculcavit me homo ; tota die impugnans, tribulavit me.

55:3 Conculcaverunt me inimici mei tota die, quoniam multi bellantes adversum me.

55:4 Ab altitudine diei timebo : ego vero in te sperabo.

55:5 In Deo laudabo sermones meos ; in Deo speravi : non timebo quid faciat mihi caro.

55:6 Tota die verba mea execrabantur ; adversum me omnes cogitationes eorum in malum.

55:7 Inhabitabunt, et abscondent ; ipsi calcaneum meum observabunt. Sicut sustinuerunt animam meam,

55:8 pro nihilo salvos facies illos ; in ira populos confringes.

55:9 Deus, vitam meam annuntiavi tibi ; posuisti lacrimas meas in conspectu tuo, sicut et in promissione tua :

55:10 tunc convertentur inimici mei retrorsum. In quacumque die invocavero te, ecce cognovi quoniam Deus meus es.

55:1 *Unto the end, for a people that is removed at a distance from the sanctuary: for David, for an inscription of a title (or pillar) when the Philistines held him in Geth.*

55:2 HAVE MERCY ON ME, O God, for man hath trodden me under foot; all the day long he hath afflicted me fighting against me.

55:3 My enemies have trodden on me all the day long; for they are many that make war against me.

55:4 From the height of the day I shall fear: but I will trust in thee.

55:5 In God I will praise my words, in God I have put my trust: I will not fear what flesh can do against me.

55:6 All the day long they detested my words: all their thoughts were against me unto evil.

55:7 They will dwell and hide themselves: they will watch my heel. As they have waited for my soul,

55:8 for nothing shalt thou save them: in thy anger thou shalt break the people in pieces. O God,

55:9 I have declared to thee my life: thou hast set my tears in thy sight, As also in thy promise.

55:10 Then shall my enemies be turned back. In what day soever I shall call upon thee, behold I know thou art my God.

55:11 In Deo laudabo verbum ; in Domino laudabo sermonem. In Deo speravi : non timebo quid faciat mihi homo.

55:12 In me sunt, Deus, vota tua, quæ reddam, laudationes tibi :

55:13 quoniam eripuisti animam meam de morte, et pedes meos de lapsu, ut placeam coram Deo in lumine viventium.

55:11 In God will I praise the word, in the Lord will I praise his speech. In God have I hoped, I will not fear what man can do to me.

55:12 In me, O God, are vows to thee, which I will pay, praises to thee:

55:13 Because thou hast delivered my soul from death, my feet from falling: that I may please in the sight of God, in the light of the living.

LVI.

56:1 *In finem, ne disperdas. David in tituli inscriptionem, cum fugeret a facie Saul in speluncam.*

56:1 *Unto the end, destroy not, for David, for an inscription of a title, when he fled from Saul into the cave.*

56:2 MISERERE MEI, Deus, miserere mei, quoniam in te confidit anima mea. Et in umbra alarum tuarum sperabo, donec transeat iniquitas.

56:3 Clamabo ad Deum altissimum, Deum qui benefecit mihi.

56:4 Misit de cælo, et liberavit me ; dedit in opprobrium conculcantes me. Misit Deus misericordiam suam et veritatem suam,

56:5 et eripuit animam meam de medio catulorum leonum. Dormivi conturbatus. Filii hominum dentes eorum arma et sagittæ, et lingua eorum gladius acutus.

56:6 Exaltare super cælos, Deus, et in omnem terram gloria tua.

56:7 Laqueum paraverunt pedibus meis, et incurvaverunt animam meam. Foderunt ante faciem meam foveam, et inciderunt in eam.

56:8 Paratum cor meum, Deus, paratum cor meum ; cantabo, et psalmum dicam.

56:9 Exsurge, gloria mea ; exsurge, psalterium et cithara : exsurgam diluculo.

56:10 Confitebor tibi in populis, Domine, et psalmum dicam tibi in gentibus :

56:11 quoniam magnificata est usque ad cælos misericordia tua, et usque ad nubes veritas tua.

56:12 Exaltare super cælos, Deus, et super omnem terram gloria tua.

56:2 HAVE MERCY ON ME, O God, have mercy on me: for my soul trusteth in thee. And in the shadow of thy wings will I hope, until iniquity pass away.

56:3 I will cry to God the most High; to God who hath done good to me.

56:4 He hath sent from heaven and delivered me: he hath made them a reproach that trod upon me. God hath sent his mercy and his truth,

56:5 and he hath delivered my soul from the midst of the young lions. I slept troubled. The sons of men, whose teeth are weapons and arrows, and their tongue a sharp sword.

56:6 Be thou exalted, O God, above the heavens, and thy glory above all the earth.

56:7 They prepared a snare for my feet; and they bowed down my soul. They dug a pit before my face, and they are fallen into it.

56:8 My heart is ready, O God, my heart is ready: I will sing, and rehearse a psalm.

56:9 Arise, O my glory, arise psaltery and harp: I will arise early.

56:10 I will give praise to thee, O Lord, among the people: I will sing a psalm to thee among the nations.

56:11 For thy mercy is magnified even to the heavens: and thy truth unto the clouds.

56:12 Be thou exalted, O God, above the heavens: and thy glory above all the earth.

LVII.

57:1 *In finem, ne disperdas. David in tituli inscriptionem.*

57:1 *Unto the end, destroy not, for David, for an inscription of a title.*

57:2 SI VERE UTIQUE justitiam loquimini, recta judicate, filii hominum.

57:3 Etenim in corde iniquitates operamini ; in terra injustitias manus vestræ concinnant.

57:4 Alienati sunt peccatores a vulva ; erraverunt ab utero : locuti sunt falsa.

57:2 IF IN VERY DEED you speak justice: judge right things, ye sons of men.

57:3 For in your heart you work iniquity: your hands forge injustice in the earth.

57:4 The wicked are alienated from the womb; they have gone astray from the womb: they

57:5 Furor illis secundum similitudinem serpentis, sicut aspidis surdæ et obturantis aures suas,

57:6 quæ non exaudiet vocem incantantium, et venefici incantantis sapienter.

57:7 Deus conteret dentes eorum in ore ipsorum ; molas leonum confringet Dominus.

57:8 Ad nihilum devenient tamquam aqua decurrens ; intendit arcum suum donec infirmentur.

57:9 Sicut cera quæ fluit auferentur ; supercecidit ignis, et non viderunt solem.

57:10 Priusquam intelligerent spinæ vestræ rhamnum, sicut viventes sic in ira absorbet eos.

57:11 Lætabitur justus cum viderit vindictam ; manus suas lavabit in sanguine peccatoris.

57:12 Et dicet homo : Si utique est fructus justo, utique est Deus judicans eos in terra.

57:5 Their madness is according to the likeness of a serpent: like the deaf asp that stoppeth her ears:

57:6 Which will not hear the voice of the charmers; nor of the wizard that charmeth wisely.

57:7 God shall break in pieces their teeth in their mouth: the Lord shall break the grinders of the lions.

57:8 They shall come to nothing, like water running down; he hath bent his bow till they be weakened.

57:9 Like wax that melteth they shall be taken away: fire hath fallen on them, and they shall not see the sun.

57:10 Before your thorns could know the brier; he swalloweth them up, as alive, in his wrath.

57:11 The just shall rejoice when he shall see the revenge: he shall wash his hands in the blood of the sinner.

57:12 And man shall say: If indeed there be fruit to the just: there is indeed a God that judgeth them on the earth.

LVIII.

58:1 *In finem, ne disperdas. David in tituli inscriptionem, quando misit Saul et custodivit domum ejus ut eum interficeret.*
58:2 ERIPE ME DE INIMICIS MEIS, Deus meus, et ab insurgentibus in me libera me.

58:3 Eripe me de operantibus iniquitatem, et de viris sanguinum salva me.
58:4 Quia ecce ceperunt animam meam ; irruerunt in me fortes.
58:5 Neque iniquitas mea, neque peccatum meum, Domine ; sine iniquitate cucurri, et direxi.

58:6 Exsurge in occursum meum, et vide : et tu, Domine Deus virtutum, Deus Israël, intende ad visitandas omnes gentes : non miserearis omnibus qui operantur iniquitatem.
58:7 Convertentur ad vesperam, et famem patientur ut canes : et circuibunt civitatem.

58:8 Ecce loquentur in ore suo, et gladius in labiis eorum : quoniam quis audivit ?

58:9 Et tu, Domine, deridebis eos ; ad nihilum deduces omnes gentes.
58:10 Fortitudinem meam ad te custodiam, quia,

58:1 *Unto the end, destroy not, for David for an inscription of a title, when Saul sent and watched his house to kill him.*
58:2 DELIVER ME FROM MY ENEMIES, O my God; and defend me from them that rise up against me.

58:3 Deliver me from them that work iniquity, and save me from bloody men.
58:4 For behold they have caught my soul: the mighty have rushed in upon me:
58:5 Neither is it my iniquity, nor my sin, O Lord: without iniquity have I run, and directed my steps.

58:6 Rise up thou to meet me, and behold: even thou, O Lord, the God of hosts, the God of Israel. Attend to visit all the nations: have no mercy on all them that work iniquity.
58:7 They shall return at evening, and shall suffer hunger like dogs: and shall go round about the city.

58:8 Behold they shall speak with their mouth, and a sword is in their lips: for who, say they, hath heard us?

58:9 But thou, O Lord, shalt laugh at them: thou shalt bring all the nations to nothing.
58:10 I will keep my strength to thee: for thou

Deus, susceptor meus es :

58:11 Deus meus misericordia ejus præveniet me.

58:12 Deus ostendet mihi super inimicos meos : ne occidas eos, nequando obliviscantur populi mei. Disperge illos in virtute tua, et depone eos, protector meus, Domine :

58:13 delictum oris eorum, sermonem labiorum ipsorum ; et comprehendantur in superbia sua. Et de execratione et mendacio annuntiabuntur

58:14 in consummatione : in ira consummationis, et non erunt. Et scient quia Deus dominabitur Jacob, et finium terræ.

58:15 Convertentur ad vesperam, et famem patientur ut canes : et circuibunt civitatem.

58:16 Ipsi dispergentur ad manducandum ; si vero non fuerint saturati, et murmurabunt.

58:17 Ego autem cantabo fortitudinem tuam, et exsultabo mane misericordiam tuam : quia factus es susceptor meus, et refugium meum in die tribulationis meæ.

58:18 Adjutor meus, tibi psallam, quia Deus susceptor meus es ; Deus meus, misericordia mea.

art my protector:

58:11 my God, his mercy shall prevent me.

58:12 God shall let me see over my enemies: slay them not, lest at any time my people forget. Scatter them by thy power; and bring them down, O Lord, my protector:

58:13 For the sin of their mouth, and the word of their lips: and let them be taken in their pride. And for their cursing and lying they shall be talked of,

58:14 when they are consumed: when they are consumed by thy wrath, and they shall be no more. And they shall know that God will rule Jacob, and all the ends of the earth.

58:15 They shall return at evening and shall suffer hunger like dogs: and shall go round about the city.

58:16 They shall be scattered abroad to eat, and shall murmur if they be not filled.

58:17 But I will sing thy strength: and will extol thy mercy in the morning. For thou art become my support, and my refuge, in the day of my trouble.

58:18 Unto thee, O my helper, will I sing, for thou art God my defence: my God my mercy.

LIX.

59:1 *In finem, pro his qui immutabuntur, in tituli inscriptionem ipsi David, in doctrinam,*

59:2 *cum succendit Mesopotamiam Syriæ et Sobal, et convertit Joab, et percussit Idumæam in valle Salinarum duodecim millia.*

59:3 DEUS, REPULISTI NOS, et destruxisti nos ; iratus es, et misertus es nobis.

59:4 Commovisti terram, et conturbasti eam ; sana contritiones ejus, quia commota est.

59:5 Ostendisti populo tuo dura ; potasti nos vino compunctionis.

59:6 Dedisti metuentibus te significationem, ut fugiant a facie arcus ; ut liberentur dilecti tui.

59:7 Salvum fac dextera tua, et exaudi me.

59:8 Deus locutus est in sancto suo : lætabor, et partibor Sichimam ; et convallem tabernaculorum metibor.

59:9 Meus est Galaad, et meus est Manasses ; et Ephraim fortitudo capitis mei. Juda rex meus ;

59:1 *Unto the end, for them that shall be changed, for the inscription of a title, to David himself, for doctrine,*

59:2 *when he set fire to Mesopotamia of Syria and Sobal; and Joab returned and slew of Edom, in the vale of the saltpits, twelve thousand men.*

59:3 O GOD, THOU HAST CAST US OFF, and hast destroyed us; thou hast been angry, and hast had mercy on us.

59:4 Thou hast moved the earth, and hast troubled it: heal thou the breaches thereof, for it has been moved.

59:5 Thou hast shewn thy people hard things; thou hast made us drink the wine of sorrow.

59:6 Thou hast given a warning to them that fear thee: that they may flee from before the bow: That thy beloved may be delivered.

59:7 Save me with thy right hand, and hear me.

59:8 God hath spoken in his holy place: I will rejoice, and I will divide Sichem; and will mete out the vale of tabernacles.

59:9 Galaad is mine, and Manasses is mine: and Ephraim is the strength of my head. Juda is my

59:10 Moab olla spei meæ. In Idumæam extendam calceamentum meum : mihi alienigenæ subditi sunt.

59:11 Quis deducet me in civitatem munitam ? quis deducet me usque in Idumæam ?

59:12 nonne tu, Deus, qui repulisti nos ? et non egredieris, Deus, in virtutibus nostris ?

59:13 Da nobis auxilium de tribulatione, quia vana salus hominis.

59:14 In Deo faciemus virtutem ; et ipse ad nihilum deducet tribulantes nos.

king:

59:10 Moab is the pot of my hope. Into Edom will I stretch out my shoe: to me the foreigners are made subject.

59:11 Who will bring me into the strong city? who will lead me into Edom?

59:12 Wilt not thou, O God, who hast cast us off? and wilt not thou, O God, go out with our armies?

59:13 Give us help from trouble: for vain is the salvation of man.

59:14 Through God we shall do mightily: and he shall bring to nothing them that afflict us.

LX.

60:1 *In finem. In hymnis David.*

60:2 EXAUDI, DEUS, deprecationem meam ; intende orationi meæ.

60:3 A finibus terræ ad te clamavi, dum anxiaretur cor meum ; in petra exaltasti me. Deduxisti me,

60:4 quia factus es spes mea : turris fortitudinis a facie inimici.

60:5 Inhabitabo in tabernaculo tuo in sæcula ; protegar in velamento alarum tuarum.

60:6 Quoniam tu, Deus meus, exaudisti orationem meam ; dedisti hæreditatem timentibus nomen tuum.

60:7 Dies super dies regis adjicies ; annos ejus usque in diem generationis et generationis.

60:8 Permanet in æternum in conspectu Dei : misericordiam et veritatem ejus quis requiret ?

60:9 Sic psalmum dicam nomini tuo in sæculum sæculi, ut reddam vota mea de die in diem.

60:1 *Unto the end, in hymns, for David.*

60:2 HEAR, O GOD, my supplication: be attentive to my prayer,

60:3 To thee have I cried from the ends of the earth: when my heart was in anguish, thou hast exalted me on a rock. Thou hast conducted me;

60:4 for thou hast been my hope; a tower of strength against the face of the enemy.

60:5 In thy tabernacle I shall dwell for ever: I shall be protected under the covert of thy wings.

60:6 For thou, my God, hast heard my prayer: thou hast given an inheritance to them that fear thy name.

60:7 Thou wilt add days to the days of the king: his years even to generation and generation.

60:8 He abideth for ever in the sight of God: his mercy and truth who shall search ?

60:9 So will I sing a psalm to thy name for ever and ever: that I may pay my vows from day to day.

LXI.

61:1 *In finem, pro Idithun. Psalmus David.*

61:2 NONNE DEO SUBJECTA ERIT ANIMA MEA ? ab ipso enim salutare meum.

61:3 Nam et ipse Deus meus et salutaris meus ; susceptor meus, non movebor amplius.

61:4 Quousque irruitis in hominem ? interficitis universi vos, tamquam parieti inclinato et maceriæ depulsæ.

61:5 Verumtamen pretium meum cogitaverunt repellere ; cucurri in siti : ore suo benedicebant, et corde suo maledicebant.

61:6 Verumtamen Deo subjecta esto, anima mea, quoniam ab ipso patientia mea :

61:1 *Unto the end, for Idithun, a psalm of David.*

61:2 SHALL NOT MY SOUL BE SUBJECT TO GOD? for from him is my salvation.

61:3 For he is my God and my saviour: he is my protector, I shall be moved no more.

61:4 How long do you rush in upon a man? you all kill, as if you were thrusting down a leaning wall, and a tottering fence.

61:5 But they have thought to cast away my price; I ran in thirst: they blessed with their mouth, but cursed with their heart.

61:6 But be thou, O my soul, subject to God: for from him is my patience.

61:7 quia ipse Deus meus et salvator meus, adjutor meus, non emigrabo.

61:8 In Deo salutare meum et gloria mea ; Deus auxilii mei, et spes mea in Deo est.

61:9 Sperate in eo, omnis congregatio populi ; effundite coram illo corda vestra : Deus adjutor noster in æternum.

61:10 Verumtamen vani filii hominum, mendaces filii hominum in stateris, ut decipiant ipsi de vanitate in idipsum.

61:11 Nolite sperare in iniquitate, et rapinas nolite concupiscere ; divitiæ si affluant, nolite cor apponere.

61:12 Semel locutus est Deus ; duo hæc audivi : quia potestas Dei est,

61:13 et tibi, Domine, misericordia : quia tu reddes unicuique juxta opera sua.

61:7 For he is my God and my saviour: he is my helper, I shall not be moved.

61:8 In God is my salvation and my glory: he is the God of my help, and my hope is in God.

61:9 Trust in him, all ye congregation of people: pour out your hearts before him. God is our helper for ever.

61:10 But vain are the sons of men, the sons of men are liars in the balances: that by vanity they may together deceive.

61:11 Trust not in iniquity, and cover not robberies: if riches abound, set not your heart upon them.

61:12 God hath spoken once, these two things have I heard, that power belongeth to God,

61:13 and mercy to thee, O Lord; for thou wilt render to every man according to his works.

LXII.

62:1 *Psalmus David, cum esset in deserto Idumææ.*

62:2 DEUS, DEUS MEUS, ad te de luce vigilo. Sitivit in te anima mea ; quam multipliciter tibi caro mea !

62:3 In terra deserta, et invia, et inaquosa, sic in sancto apparui tibi, ut viderem virtutem tuam et gloriam tuam.

62:4 Quoniam melior est misericordia tua super vitas, labia mea laudabunt te.

62:5 Sic benedicam te in vita mea, et in nomine tuo levabo manus meas.

62:6 Sicut adipe et pinguedine repleatur anima mea, et labiis exsultationis laudabit os meum.

62:7 Si memor fui tui super stratum meum, in matutinis meditabor in te.

62:8 Quia fuisti adjutor meus, et in velamento alarum tuarum exsultabo.

62:9 Adhæsit anima mea post te ; me suscepit dextera tua.

62:10 Ipsi vero in vanum quæsierunt animam meam : introibunt in inferiora terræ ;

62:11 tradentur in manus gladii : partes vulpium erunt.

62:12 Rex vero lætabitur in Deo ; laudabuntur omnes qui jurant in eo : quia obstructum est os loquentium iniqua.

62:1 *A psalm of David when he was in the desert of Edom.*

62:2 O GOD, MY GOD, to thee do I watch at break of day. For thee my soul hath thirsted; for thee my flesh, O how many ways!

62:3 In a desert land, and where there is no way, and no water: so in the sanctuary have I come before thee, to see thy power and thy glory.

62:4 For thy mercy is better than lives: thee my lips shall praise.

62:5 Thus will I bless thee all my life long: and in thy name I will lift up my hands.

62:6 Let my soul be filled as with marrow and fatness: and my mouth shall praise thee with joyful lips.

62:7 If I have remembered thee upon my bed, I will meditate on thee in the morning:

62:8 because thou hast been my helper. And I will rejoice under the covert of thy wings:

62:9 my soul hath stuck close to thee: thy right hand hath received me.

62:10 But they have sought my soul in vain, they shall go into the lower parts of the earth:

62:11 They shall be delivered into the hands of the sword, they shall be the portions of foxes.

62:12 But the king shall rejoice in God, all they shall be praised that swear by him: because the mouth is stopped of them that speak wicked things.

LXIII.

63:1 *In finem. Psalmus David.*

63:2 EXAUDI, DEUS, orationem meam cum

63:1 *Unto the end, a psalm for David.*

63:2 HEAR, O GOD, my prayer, when I make

deprecor ; a timore inimici eripe animam meam.

63:3 Protexisti me a conventu malignantium, a multitudine operantium iniquitatem.

63:4 Quia exacuerunt ut gladium linguas suas ; intenderunt arcum rem amaram,

63:5 ut sagittent in occultis immaculatum.

63:6 Subito sagittabunt eum, et non timebunt ; firmaverunt sibi sermonem nequam. Narraverunt ut absconderent laqueos ; dixerunt : Quis videbit eos ?

63:7 Scrutati sunt iniquitates ; defecerunt scrutantes scrutinio. Accedet homo ad cor altum,

63:8 et exaltabitur Deus. Sagittæ parvulorum factæ sunt plagæ eorum,

63:9 et infirmatæ sunt contra eos linguæ eorum. Conturbati sunt omnes qui videbant eos,

63:10 et timuit omnis homo. Et annuntiaverunt opera Dei, et facta ejus intellexerunt.

63:11 Lætabitur justus in Domino, et sperabit in eo, et laudabuntur omnes recti corde.

supplication to thee: deliver my soul from the fear of the enemy.

63:3 Thou hast protected me from the assembly of the malignant; from the multitude of the workers of iniquity.

63:4 For they have whetted their tongues like a sword; they have bent their bow a bitter thing,

63:5 to shoot in secret the undefiled.

63:6 They will shoot at him on a sudden, and will not fear: they are resolute in wickedness. They have talked of hiding snares; they have said: Who shall see them?

63:7 They have searched after iniquities: they have failed in their search. Man shall come to a deep heart:

63:8 and God shall be exalted. The arrows of children are their wounds:

63:9 and their tongues against them are made weak. All that saw them were troubled;

63:10 and every man was afraid. And they declared the works of God: and understood his doings.

63:11 The just shall rejoice in the Lord, and shall hope in him: and all the upright in heart shall be praised.

LXIV.

64:1 *In finem. Psalmus David, canticum Jeremiæ et Ezechielis populo transmigrationis, cum inciperent exire.*

64:2 TE DECET HYMNUS, DEUS, in Sion, et tibi reddetur votum in Jerusalem.

64:3 Exaudi orationem meam ; ad te omnis caro veniet.

64:4 Verba iniquorum prævaluerunt super nos, et impietatibus nostris tu propitiaberis.

64:5 Beatus quem elegisti et assumpsisti : inhabitabit in atriis tuis. Replebimur in bonis domus tuæ ; sanctum est templum tuum,

64:6 mirabile in æquitate. Exaudi nos, Deus, salutaris noster, spes omnium finium terræ, et in mari longe.

64:7 Præparans montes in virtute tua, accinctus potentia ;

64:8 qui conturbas profundum maris, sonum fluctuum ejus. Turbabuntur gentes,

64:9 et timebunt qui habitant terminos a signis tuis ; exitus matutini et vespere delectabis.

64:1 *To the end, a psalm of David. The canticle of Jeremias and Ezechiel to the people of the captivity, when they began to go out.*

64:2 A HYMN, O GOD, BECOMETH THEE in Sion: and a vow shall be paid to thee in Jerusalem.

64:3 O hear my prayer: all flesh shall come to thee.

64:4 The words of the wicked have prevailed over us: and thou wilt pardon our transgressions.

64:5 Blessed is he whom thou hast chosen and taken to thee: he shall dwell in thy courts. We shall be filled with the good things of thy house; holy is thy temple,

64:6 wonderful in justice. Hear us, O God our saviour, who art the hope of all the ends of the earth, and in the sea afar off.

64:7 Thou who preparest the mountains by thy strength, being girded with power:

64:8 who troublest the depth of the sea, the noise of its waves. The Gentiles shall be troubled,

64:9 and they that dwell in the uttermost borders shall be afraid at thy signs: thou shalt make the outgoings of the morning and of the even-

64:10 Visitasti terram, et inebriasti eam ; multiplicasti locupletare eam. Flumen Dei repletum est aquis ; parasti cibum illorum : quoniam ita est præparatio ejus.

64:11 Rivos ejus inebria ; multiplica genimina ejus : in stillicidiis ejus lætabitur germinans.

64:12 Benedices coronæ anni benignitatis tuæ, et campi tui replebuntur ubertate.

64:13 Pinguescent speciosa deserti, et exsultatione colles accingentur.

64:14 Induti sunt arietes ovium, et valles abundabunt frumento ; clamabunt, etenim hymnum dicent.

LXV.

65:1 In finem. Canticum psalmi resurrectionis. JUBILATE DEO, omnis terra ;

65:2 psalmum dicite nomini ejus ; date gloriam laudi ejus.

65:3 Dicite Deo : Quam terribilia sunt opera tua, Domine ! in multitudine virtutis tuæ mentientur tibi inimici tui.

65:4 Omnis terra adoret te, et psallat tibi ; psalmum dicat nomini tuo.

65:5 Venite, et videte opera Dei : terribilis in consiliis super filios hominum.

65:6 Qui convertit mare in aridam ; in flumine pertransibunt pede : ibi lætabimur in ipso.

65:7 Qui dominatur in virtute sua in æternum ; oculi ejus super gentes respiciunt : qui exasperant non exaltentur in semetipsis.

65:8 Benedicite, gentes, Deum nostrum, et auditam facite vocem laudis ejus :

65:9 qui posuit animam meam ad vitam, et non dedit in commotionem pedes meos.

65:10 Quoniam probasti nos, Deus ; igne nos examinasti, sicut examinatur argentum.

65:11 Induxisti nos in laqueum ; posuisti tribulationes in dorso nostro ;

65:12 imposuisti homines super capita nostra. Transivimus per ignem et aquam, et eduxisti nos in refrigerium.

65:13 Introibo in domum tuam in holocaustis ; reddam tibi vota mea

65:14 quæ distinxerunt labia mea : et locutum

ing to be joyful.

64:10 Thou hast visited the earth, and hast plentifully watered it; thou hast many ways enriched it. The river of God is filled with water, thou hast prepared their food: for so is its preparation.

64:11 Fill up plentifully the streams thereof, multiply its fruits; it shall spring up and rejoice in its showers.

64:12 Thou shalt bless the crown of the year of thy goodness: and thy fields shall be filled with plenty.

64:13 The beautiful places of the wilderness shall grow fat: and the hills shall be girded about with joy,

64:14 The rams of the flock are clothed, and the vales shall abound with corn: they shall shout, yea they shall sing a hymn.

65:1 Unto the end, a canticle of a psalm of the resurrection. SHOUT WITH JOY TO GOD, all the earth,

65:2 sing ye a psalm to his name; give glory to his praise.

65:3 Say unto God, How terrible are thy works, O Lord! in the multitude of thy strength thy enemies shall lie to thee.

65:4 Let all the earth adore thee, and sing to thee: let it sing a psalm to thy name.

65:5 Come and see the works of God; who is terrible in his counsels over the sons of men.

65:6 Who turneth the sea into dry land, in the river they shall pass on foot: there shall we rejoice in him.

65:7 Who by his power ruleth for ever: his eyes behold the nations; let not them that provoke him he exalted in themselves.

65:8 O bless our God, ye Gentiles: and make the voice of his praise to be heard.

65:9 Who hath set my soul to live: and hath not suffered my feet to be moved:

65:10 For thou, O God, hast proved us: thou hast tried us by fire, as silver is tried.

65:11 Thou hast brought us into a net, thou hast laid afflictions on our back:

65:12 thou hast set men over our heads. We have passed through fire and water, and thou hast brought us out into a refreshment.

65:13 I will go into thy house with burnt offerings: I will pay thee my vows,

65:14 which my lips have uttered, And my mouth

est os meum in tribulatione mea.

65:15 Holocausta medullata offeram tibi, cum incenso arietum ; offeram tibi boves cum hircis.

65:16 Venite, audite, et narrabo, omnes qui timetis Deum, quanta fecit animæ meæ.

65:17 Ad ipsum ore meo clamavi, et exaltavi sub lingua mea.

65:18 Iniquitatem si aspexi in corde meo, non exaudiet Dominus.

65:19 Propterea exaudivit Deus, et attendit voci deprecationis meæ.

65:20 Benedictus Deus, qui non amovit orationem meam, et misericordiam suam a me.

hath spoken, when I was in trouble.

65:15 I will offer up to thee holocausts full of marrow, with burnt offerings of rams: I will offer to thee bullocks with goats.

65:16 Come and hear, all ye that fear God, and I will tell you what great things he hath done for my soul.

65:17 I cried to him with my mouth: and I extolled him with my tongue.

65:18 If I have looked at iniquity in my heart, the Lord will not hear me.

65:19 Therefore hath God heard me, and hath attended to the voice of my supplication.

65:20 Blessed be God, who hath not turned away my prayer, nor his mercy from me.

LXVI.

66:1 *In finem, in hymnis. Psalmus cantici David.*

66:2 DEUS MISEREATUR nostri, et benedicat nobis ; illuminet vultum suum super nos, et misereatur nostri :

66:3 ut cognoscamus in terra viam tuam, in omnibus gentibus salutare tuum.

66:4 Confiteantur tibi populi, Deus : confiteantur tibi populi omnes.

66:5 Lætentur et exsultent gentes, quoniam judicas populos in æquitate, et gentes in terra dirigis.

66:6 Confiteantur tibi populi, Deus : confiteantur tibi populi omnes.

66:7 Terra dedit fructum suum : benedicat nos Deus, Deus noster !

66:8 Benedicat nos Deus, et metuant eum omnes fines terræ.

66:1 *Unto the end, in hymns, a psalm of a canticle for David.*

66:2 MAY GOD HAVE MERCY on us, and bless us: may he cause the light of his countenance to shine upon us, and may he have mercy on us.

66:3 That we may know thy way upon earth: thy salvation in all nations.

66:4 Let people confess to thee, O God: let all people give praise to thee.

66:5 Let the nations be glad and rejoice: for thou judgest the people with justice, and directest the nations upon earth.

66:6 Let the people, O God, confess to thee: let all the people give praise to thee:

66:7 the earth hath yielded her fruit. May God, our God bless us,

66:8 may God bless us: and all the ends of the earth fear him.

LXVII.

67:1 *In finem. Psalmus cantici ipsi David.*

67:2 EXSURGAT DEUS, et dissipentur inimici ejus ; et fugiant qui oderunt eum a facie ejus.

67:3 Sicut deficit fumus, deficiant ; sicut fluit cera a facie ignis, sic pereant peccatores a facie Dei.

67:4 Et justi epulentur, et exsultent in conspectu Dei, et delectentur in lætitia.

67:5 Cantate Deo ; psalmum dicite nomini ejus : iter facite ei qui ascendit super occasum. Dominus nomen illi ; exsultate in conspectu ejus. Turbabuntur a facie ejus,

67:1 *Unto the end, a psalm of a canticle for David himself.*

67:2 LET GOD ARISE, and let his enemies be scattered: and let them that hate him flee from before his face.

67:3 As smoke vanisheth, so let them vanish away: as wax melteth before the fire, so let the wicked perish at the presence of God.

67:4 And let the just feast, and rejoice before God: and be delighted with gladness.

67:5 Sing ye to God, sing a psalm to his name, make a way for him who ascendeth upon the west: the Lord is his name. Rejoice ye before him: but the wicked shall be troubled at his presence,

67:6 patris orphanorum, et judicis viduarum ; Deus in loco sancto suo.

67:7 Deus qui inhabitare facit unius moris in domo ; qui educit vinctos in fortitudine, similiter eos qui exasperant, qui habitant in sepulchris.

67:8 Deus, cum egredereris in conspectu populi tui, cum pertransires in deserto,

67:9 terra mota est, etenim cæli distillaverunt, a facie Dei Sinai, a facie Dei Israël.

67:10 Pluviam voluntariam segregabis, Deus, hæreditati tuæ ; et infirmata est, tu vero perfecisti eam.

67:11 Animalia tua habitabunt in ea ; parasti in dulcedine tua pauperi, Deus.

67:12 Dominus dabit verbum evangelizantibus, virtute multa.

67:13 Rex virtutum dilecti, dilecti ; et speciei domus dividere spolia.

67:14 Si dormiatis inter medios cleros, pennæ columbæ deargentatæ, et posteriora dorsi ejus in pallore auri.

67:15 Dum discernit cælestis reges super eam, nive dealbabuntur in Selmon.

67:16 Mons Dei, mons pinguis : mons coagulatus, mons pinguis.

67:17 Ut quid suspicamini, montes coagulatos ? mons in quo beneplacitum est Deo habitare in eo ; etenim Dominus habitabit in finem.

67:18 Currus Dei decem millibus multiplex, millia lætantium ; Dominus in eis in Sina, in sancto.

67:19 Ascendisti in altum, cepisti captivitatem, accepisti dona in hominibus ; etenim non credentes inhabitare Dominum Deum.

67:20 Benedictus Dominus die quotidie : prosperum iter faciet nobis Deus salutarium nostrorum.

67:21 Deus noster, Deus salvos faciendi ; et Domini, Domini exitus mortis.

67:22 Verumtamen Deus confringet capita inimicorum suorum, verticem capilli perambulantium in delictis suis.

67:23 Dixit Dominus : Ex Basan convertam, con-

67:6 who is the father of orphans, and the judge of widows. God in his holy place:

67:7 God who maketh men of one manner to dwell in a house: Who bringeth out them that were bound in strength; in like manner them that provoke, that dwell in sepulchres.

67:8 O God, when thou didst go forth in the sight of thy people, when thou didst pass through the desert:

67:9 The earth was moved, and the heavens dropped at the presence of the God of Sina, at the presence of the God of Israel.

67:10 Thou shalt set aside for thy inheritance a free rain, O God: and it was weakened, but thou hast made it perfect.

67:11 In it shall thy animals dwell; in thy sweetness, O God, thou hast provided for the poor.

67:12 The Lord shall give the word to them that preach good tidings with great power.

67:13 The king of powers is of the beloved, of the beloved; and the beauty of the house shall divide spoils.

67:14 If you sleep among the midst of lots, you shall be as the wings of a dove covered with silver, and the hinder parts of her back with the paleness of gold.

67:15 When he that is in heaven appointeth kings over her, they shall be whited with snow in Selmon.

67:16 The mountain of God is a fat mountain. A curdled mountain, a fat mountain.

67:17 Why suspect, ye curdled mountains? A mountain in which God is well pleased to dwell: for there the Lord shall dwell unto the end.

67:18 The chariot of God is attended by ten thousands; thousands of them that rejoice: the Lord is among them in Sina, in the holy place.

67:19 Thou hast ascended on high, thou hast led captivity captive; thou hast received gifts in men. Yea for those also that do not believe, the dwelling of the Lord God.

67:20 Blessed be the Lord day by day: the God of our salvation will make our journey prosperous to us.

67:21 Our God is the God of salvation: and of the Lord, of the Lord are the issues from death.

67:22 But God shall break the heads of his enemies: the hairy crown of them that walk on in their sins.

67:23 The Lord said: I will turn them from Ba-

vertam in profundum maris :

67:24 ut intingatur pes tuus in sanguine ; lingua canum tuorum ex inimicis, ab ipso.

67:25 Viderunt ingressus tuos, Deus, ingressus Dei mei, regis mei, qui est in sancto.

67:26 Prævenerunt principes conjuncti psallentibus, in medio juvencularum tympanistriarum.

67:27 In ecclesiis benedicite Deo Domino de fontibus Israël.

67:28 Ibi Benjamin adolescentulus, in mentis excessu ; principes Juda, duces eorum ; principes Zabulon, principes Nephthali.

67:29 Manda, Deus, virtuti tuæ ; confirma hoc, Deus, quod operatus es in nobis.

67:30 A templo tuo in Jerusalem, tibi offerent reges munera.

67:31 Increpa feras arundinis ; congregatio taurorum in vaccis populorum : ut excludant eos qui probati sunt argento. Dissipa gentes quæ bella volunt.

67:32 Venient legati ex Ægypto ; Æthiopia præveniet manus ejus Deo.

67:33 Regna terræ, cantate Deo ; psallite Domino ; psallite Deo.

67:34 Qui ascendit super cælum cæli, ad orientem : ecce dabit voci suæ vocem virtutis.

67:35 Date gloriam Deo super Israël ; magnificentia ejus et virtus ejus in nubibus.

67:36 Mirabilis Deus in sanctis suis ; Deus Israël ipse dabit virtutem et fortitudinem plebi suæ. Benedictus Deus !

san, I will turn them into the depth of the sea:

67:24 That thy foot may be dipped in the blood of thy enemies; the tongue of thy dogs be red with the same.

67:25 They have seen thy goings, O God, the goings of my God: of my king who is in his sanctuary.

67:26 Princes went before joined with singers, in the midst of young damsels playing on timbrels.

67:27 In the churches bless ye God the Lord, from the fountains of Israel.

67:28 There is Benjamin a youth, in ecstasy of mind. The princes of Juda are their leaders: the princes of Zabulon, the princes of Nephthali.

67:29 Command thy strength, O God: confirm, O God, what thou hast wrought in us.

67:30 From thy temple in Jerusalem, kings shall offer presents to thee.

67:31 Rebuke the wild beasts of the reeds, the congregation of bulls with the kine of the people; who seek to exclude them who are tried with silver. Scatter thou the nations that delight in wars:

67:32 ambassadors shall come out of Egypt: Ethiopia shall soon stretch out her hands to God.

67:33 Sing to God, ye kingdoms of the earth: sing ye to the Lord: Sing ye to God,

67:34 who mounteth above the heaven of heavens, to the east. Behold he will give to his voice the voice of power:

67:35 give ye glory to God for Israel, his magnificence, and his power is in the clouds.

67:36 God is wonderful in his saints: the God of Israel is he who will give power and strength to his people. Blessed be God.

LXVIII.

68:1 *In finem, pro iis qui commutabuntur. David.*

68:2 SALVUM ME FAC, DEUS, quoniam intraverunt aquæ usque ad animam meam.

68:3 Infixus sum in limo profundi et non est substantia. Veni in altitudinem maris, et tempestas demersit me.

68:4 Laboravi clamans, raucæ factæ sunt fauces meæ ; defecerunt oculi mei, dum spero in Deum meum.

68:5 Multiplicati sunt super capillos capitis mei qui oderunt me gratis. Confortati sunt qui per-

68:1 *Unto the end, for them that shall be changed; for David.*

68:2 SAVE ME, O GOD: for the waters are come in even unto my soul.

68:3 I stick fast in the mire of the deep: and there is no sure standing. I am come into the depth of the sea: and a tempest hath overwhelmed me.

68:4 I have laboured with crying; my jaws are become hoarse: my eyes have failed, whilst I hope in my God.

68:5 They are multiplied above the hairs of my head, who hate me without cause. My enemies

secuti sunt me inimici mei injuste ; quæ non rapui, tunc exsolvebam.

68:6 Deus, tu scis insipientiam meam ; et delicta mea a te non sunt abscondita.

68:7 Non erubescant in me qui exspectant te, Domine, Domine virtutum ; non confundantur super me qui quærunt te, Deus Israël.

68:8 Quoniam propter te sustinui opprobrium ; operuit confusio faciem meam.

68:9 Extraneus factus sum fratribus meis, et peregrinus filiis matris meæ.

68:10 Quoniam zelus domus tuæ comedit me, et opprobria exprobrantium tibi ceciderunt super me.

68:11 Et operui in jejunio animam meam, et factum est in opprobrium mihi.

68:12 Et posui vestimentum meum cilicium ; et factus sum illis in parabolam.

68:13 Adversum me loquebantur qui sedebant in porta, et in me psallebant qui bibebant vinum.

68:14 Ego vero orationem meam ad te, Domine ; tempus beneplaciti, Deus. In multitudine misericordiæ tuæ, exaudi me in veritate salutis tuæ.

68:15 Eripe me de luto, ut non infigar ; libera me ab iis qui oderunt me, et de profundis aquarum.

68:16 Non me demergat tempestas aquæ, neque absorbeat me profundum, neque urgeat super me puteus os suum.

68:17 Exaudi me, Domine, quoniam benigna est misericordia tua ; secundum multitudinem miserationum tuarum respice in me.

68:18 Et ne avertas faciem tuam a puero tuo ; quoniam tribulor, velociter exaudi me.

68:19 Intende animæ meæ, et libera eam ; propter inimicos meos, eripe me.

68:20 Tu scis improperium meum, et confusionem meam, et reverentiam meam ;

68:21 in conspectu tuo sunt omnes qui tribulant me. Improperium exspectavit cor meum et miseriam : et sustinui qui simul contristaretur, et non fuit ; et qui consolaretur, et non inveni.

68:22 Et dederunt in escam meam fel, et in siti mea potaverunt me aceto.

68:23 Fiat mensa eorum coram ipsis in laqueum, et in retributiones, et in scandalum.

68:24 Obscurentur oculi eorum, ne videant, et

are grown strong who have wrongfully persecuted me: then did I pay that which I took not away.

68:6 O God, thou knowest my foolishness; and my offences are not hidden from thee:

68:7 Let not them be ashamed for me, who look for thee, O Lord, the Lord of hosts. Let them not be confounded on my account, who seek thee, O God of Israel.

68:8 Because for thy sake I have borne reproach; shame hath covered my face.

68:9 I am become a stranger to my brethren, and an alien to the sons of my mother.

68:10 For the zeal of thy house hath eaten me up: and the reproaches of them that reproached thee are fallen upon me.

68:11 And I covered my soul in fasting: and it was made a reproach to me.

68:12 And I made haircloth my garment: and I became a byword to them.

68:13 They that sat in the gate spoke against me: and they that drank wine made me their song.

68:14 But as for me, my prayer is to thee, O Lord; for the time of thy good pleasure, O God. In the multitude of thy mercy hear me, in the truth of thy salvation.

68:15 Draw me out of the mire, that I may not stick fast: deliver me from them that hate me, and out of the deep waters.

68:16 Let not the tempest of water drown me, nor the deep swallow me up: and let not the pit shut her mouth upon me.

68:17 Hear me, O Lord, for thy mercy is kind; look upon me according to the multitude of thy tender mercies.

68:18 And turn not away thy face from thy servant: for I am in trouble, hear me speedily.

68:19 Attend to my soul, and deliver it: save me because of my enemies.

68:20 Thou knowest my reproach, and my confusion, and my shame.

68:21 In thy sight are all they that afflict me; my heart hath expected reproach and misery. And I looked for one that would grieve together with me, but there was none: and for one that would comfort me, and I found none.

68:22 And they gave me gall for my food, and in my thirst they gave me vinegar to drink.

68:23 Let their table become as a snare before them, and a recompense, and a stumbling-block.

68:24 Let their eyes be darkened that they see

dorsum eorum semper incurva.

68:25 Effunde super eos iram tuam, et furor iræ tuæ comprehendat eos.

68:26 Fiat habitatio eorum deserta, et in tabernaculis eorum non sit qui inhabitet.

68:27 Quoniam quem tu percussisti persecuti sunt, et super dolorem vulnerum meorum addiderunt.

68:28 Appone iniquitatem super iniquitatem eorum, et non intrent in justitiam tuam.

68:29 Deleantur de libro viventium, et cum justis non scribantur.

68:30 Ego sum pauper et dolens ; salus tua, Deus, suscepit me.

68:31 Laudabo nomen Dei cum cantico, et magnificabo eum in laude :

68:32 et placebit Deo super vitulum novellum, cornua producentem et ungulas.

68:33 Videant pauperes, et lætentur ; quærite Deum, et vivet anima vestra :

68:34 quoniam exaudivit pauperes Dominus, et vinctos suos non despexit.

68:35 Laudent illum cæli et terra ; mare, et omnia reptilia in eis.

68:36 Quoniam Deus salvam faciet Sion, et ædificabuntur civitates Juda, et inhabitabunt ibi, et hæreditate acquirent eam.

68:37 Et semen servorum ejus possidebit eam ; et qui diligunt nomen ejus habitabunt in ea.

not; and their back bend thou down always.

68:25 Pour out thy indignation upon them: and let thy wrathful anger take hold of them.

68:26 Let their habitation be made desolate: and let there be none to dwell in their tabernacles.

68:27 Because they have persecuted him whom thou hast smitten; and they have added to the grief of my wounds.

68:28 Add thou iniquity upon their iniquity: and let them not come into thy justice.

68:29 Let them be blotted out of the book of the living; and with the just let them not be written.

68:30 But I am poor and sorrowful: thy salvation, O God, hath set me up.

68:31 I will praise the name of God with a canticle: and I will magnify him with praise.

68:32 And it shall please God better than a young calf, that bringeth forth horns and hoofs.

68:33 Let the poor see and rejoice: seek ye God, and your soul shall live.

68:34 For the Lord hath heard the poor: and hath not despised his prisoners.

68:35 Let the heavens and the earth praise him; the sea, and every thing that creepeth therein.

68:36 For God will save Sion, and the cities of Juda shall be built up. And they shall dwell there, and acquire it by inheritance.

68:37 And the seed of his servants shall possess it; and they that love his name shall dwell therein.

LXIX.

69:1 *In finem. Psalmus David in rememorationem, quod salvum fecerit eum Dominus.*

69:2 DEUS, IN ADJUTORIUM MEUM INTENDE ; Domine, ad adjuvandum me festina.

69:3 Confundantur, et revereantur, qui quærunt animam meam.

69:4 Avertantur retrorsum, et erubescant, qui volunt mihi mala ; avertantur statim erubescentes qui dicunt mihi : Euge, euge !

69:5 Exsultent et lætentur in te omnes qui quærunt te ; et dicant semper : Magnificetur Dominus, qui diligunt salutare tuum.

69:6 Ego vero egenus et pauper sum ; Deus, adjuva me. Adjutor meus et liberator meus es tu ; Domine, ne moreris.

69:1 *Unto the end, a psalm for David, to bring to remembrance that the Lord saved him.*

69:2 O GOD, COME TO MY ASSISTANCE; O Lord, make haste to help me.

69:3 Let them be confounded and ashamed that seek my soul:

69:4 Let them be turned backward, and blush for shame that desire evils to me: Let them be presently turned away blushing for shame that say to me: 'T is well, 't is well.

69:5 Let all that seek thee rejoice and be glad in thee; and let such as love thy salvation say always: The Lord be magnified.

69:6 But I am needy and poor; O God, help me. Thou art my helper and my deliverer: O Lord, make no delay.

LXX.

70:1 *Psalmus David, filiorum Jonadab, et priorum captivorum.* IN TE, DOMINE, speravi ; non confundar in æternum.

70:2 In justitia tua libera me, et eripe me : inclina ad me aurem tuam, et salva me.

70:3 Esto mihi in Deum protectorem, et in locum munitum, ut salvum me facias : quoniam firmamentum meum et refugium meum es tu.

70:4 Deus meus, eripe me de manu peccatoris, et de manu contra legem agentis, et iniqui :

70:5 quoniam tu es patientia mea, Domine ; Domine, spes mea a juventute mea.

70:6 In te confirmatus sum ex utero ; de ventre matris meæ tu es protector meus ; in te cantatio mea semper.

70:7 Tamquam prodigium factus sum multis ; et tu adjutor fortis.

70:8 Repleatur os meum laude, ut cantem gloriam tuam, tota die magnitudinem tuam.

70:9 Ne projicias me in tempore senectutis ; cum defecerit virtus mea, ne derelinquas me.

70:10 Quia dixerunt inimici mei mihi, et qui custodiebant animam meam consilium fecerunt in unum,

70:11 dicentes : Deus dereliquit eum : persequimini et comprehendite eum, quia non est qui eripiat.

70:12 Deus, ne elongeris a me ; Deus meus, in auxilium meum respice.

70:13 Confundantur et deficiant detrahentes animæ meæ ; operiantur confusione et pudore qui quærunt mala mihi.

70:14 Ego autem semper sperabo, et adjiciam super omnem laudem tuam.

70:15 Os meum annuntiabit justitiam tuam, tota die salutare tuum. Quoniam non cognovi litteraturam,

70:16 introibo in potentias Domini ; Domine, memorabor justitiæ tuæ solius.

70:17 Deus, docuisti me a juventute mea ; et usque nunc pronuntiabo mirabilia tua.

70:18 Et usque in senectam et senium, Deus, ne derelinquas me, donec annuntiem brachium tuum generationi omni quæ ventura est, potentiam tuam,

70:1 *A psalm for David. Of the sons of Jonadab, and the former captives.* IN THEE, O LORD, I have hoped, let me never be put to confusion:

70:2 deliver me in thy justice, and rescue me. Incline thy ear unto me, and save me.

70:3 Be thou unto me a God, a protector, and a place of strength: that thou mayst make me safe. For thou art my firmament and my refuge.

70:4 Deliver me, O my God, out of the hand of the sinner, and out of the hand of the transgressor of the law and of the unjust.

70:5 For thou art my patience, O Lord: my hope, O Lord, from my youth;

70:6 By thee have I been confirmed from the womb: from my mother's womb thou art my protector. Of thee shall I continually sing:

70:7 I am become unto many as a wonder, but thou art a strong helper.

70:8 Let my mouth be filled with praise, that I may sing thy glory; thy greatness all the day long.

70:9 Cast me not off in the time of old age: when my strength shall fail, do not thou forsake me.

70:10 For my enemies have spoken against me; and they that watched my soul have consulted together,

70:11 Saying: God hath forsaken him: pursue and take him, for there is none to deliver him.

70:12 O God, be not thou far from me: O my God, make haste to my help.

70:13 Let them be confounded and come to nothing that detract my soul; let them be covered with confusion and shame that seek my hurt.

70:14 But I will always hope; and will add to all thy praise.

70:15 My mouth shall shew forth thy justice; thy salvation all the day long. Because I have not known learning,

70:16 I will enter into the powers of the Lord: O Lord, I will be mindful of thy justice alone.

70:17 Thou hast taught me, O God, from my youth: and till now I will declare thy wonderful works.

70:18 And unto old age and grey hairs: O God, forsake me not, Until I shew forth thy arm to all the generation that is to come: Thy power,

70:19 et justitiam tuam, Deus, usque in altissima ; quæ fecisti magnalia, Deus : quis similis tibi ?

70:20 Quantas ostendisti mihi tribulationes multas et malas ! et conversus vivificasti me, et de abyssis terræ iterum reduxisti me.

70:21 Multiplicasti magnificentiam tuam ; et conversus consolatus es me.

70:22 Nam et ego confitebor tibi in vasis psalmi veritatem tuam, Deus ; psallam tibi in cithara, sanctus Israël.

70:23 Exsultabunt labia mea cum cantavero tibi ; et anima mea quam redemisti.

70:24 Sed et lingua mea tota die meditabitur justitiam tuam, cum confusi et reveriti fuerint qui quærunt mala mihi.

70:19 and thy justice, O God, even to the highest great things thou hast done: O God, who is like to thee?

70:20 How great troubles hast thou shewn me, many and grievous: and turning thou hast brought me to life, and hast brought me back again from the depths of the earth:

70:21 Thou hast multiplied thy magnificence; and turning to me thou hast comforted me.

70:22 For I will also confess to thee thy truth with the instruments of psaltery: O God, I will sing to thee with the harp, thou holy one of Israel.

70:23 My lips shall greatly rejoice, when I shall sing to thee; and my soul which thou hast redeemed.

70:24 Yea and my tongue shall meditate on thy justice all the day; when they shall be confounded and put to shame that seek evils to me.

LXXI.

71:1 *Psalmus, in Salomonem.*

71:2 DEUS, JUDICIUM TUUM REGI DA, et justitiam tuam filio regis ; judicare populum tuum in justitia, et pauperes tuos in judicio.

71:3 Suscipiant montes pacem populo, et colles justitiam.

71:4 Judicabit pauperes populi, et salvos faciet filios pauperum, et humiliabit calumniatorem.

71:5 Et permanebit cum sole, et ante lunam, in generatione et generationem.

71:6 Descendet sicut pluvia in vellus, et sicut stillicidia stillantia super terram.

71:7 Orietur in diebus ejus justitia, et abundantia pacis, donec auferatur luna.

71:8 Et dominabitur a mari usque ad mare, et a flumine usque ad terminos orbis terrarum.

71:9 Coram illo procident Æthiopes, et inimici ejus terram lingent.

71:10 Reges Tharsis et insulæ munera offerent ; reges Arabum et Saba dona adducent :

71:11 et adorabunt eum omnes reges terræ ; omnes gentes servient ei.

71:12 Quia liberabit pauperem a potente, et pauperem cui non erat adjutor.

71:13 Parcet pauperi et inopi, et animas pauperum salvas faciet.

71:1 *A psalm on Solomon.*

71:2 GIVE TO THE KING THY JUDGMENT, O GOD: and to the king's son thy justice: To judge thy people with justice, and thy poor with judgment.

71:3 Let the mountains receive peace for the people: and the hills justice.

71:4 He shall judge the poor of the people, and he shall save the children of the poor: and he shall humble the oppressor.

71:5 And he shall continue with the sun, and before the moon, throughout all generations.

71:6 He shall come down like rain upon the fleece; and as showers falling gently upon the earth.

71:7 In his days shall justice spring up, and abundance of peace, till the moon be taken away.

71:8 And he shall rule from sea to sea, and from the river unto the ends of the earth.

71:9 Before him the Ethiopians shall fall down: and his enemies shall lick the ground.

71:10 The kings of Tharsis and the islands shall offer presents: the kings of the Arabians and of Saba shall bring gifts:

71:11 And all kings of the earth shall adore him: all nations shall serve him.

71:12 For he shall deliver the poor from the mighty: and the needy that had no helper.

71:13 He shall spare the poor and needy: and he shall save the souls of the poor.

71:14 Ex usuris et iniquitate redimet animas eorum, et honorabile nomen eorum coram illo.

71:15 Et vivet, et dabitur ei de auro Arabiæ ; et adorabunt de ipso semper, tota die benedicent ei.

71:16 Et erit firmamentum in terra in summis montium ; superextolletur super Libanum fructus ejus, et florebunt de civitate sicut fœnum terræ.

71:17 Sit nomen ejus benedictum in sæcula ; ante solem permanet nomen ejus. Et benedicentur in ipso omnes tribus terræ ; omnes gentes magnificabunt eum.

71:18 Benedictus Dominus Deus Israël, qui facit mirabilia solus.

71:19 Et benedictum nomen majestatis ejus in æternum, et replebitur majestate ejus omnis terra. Fiat, fiat.

71:20 Defecerunt laudes David, filii Jesse.

71:14 He shall redeem their souls from usuries and iniquity: and their names shall be honourable in his sight.

71:15 And he shall live, and to him shall be given of the gold of Arabia, for him they shall always adore: they shall bless him all the day.

71:16 And there shall be a firmament on the earth on the tops of mountains, above Libanus shall the fruit thereof be exalted: and they of the city shall flourish like the grass of the earth.

71:17 Let his name be blessed for evermore: his name continueth before the sun. And in him shall all the tribes of the earth be blessed: all nations shall magnify him.

71:18 Blessed be the Lord, the God of Israel, who alone doth wonderful things.

71:19 And blessed be the name of his majesty for ever: and the whole earth shall be filled with his majesty. So be it. So be it.

71:20 The praises of David, the son of Jesse, are ended.

LXXII.

72:1 *Psalmus Asaph.* QUAM BONUS ISRAËL DEUS, his qui recto sunt corde !

72:2 Mei autem pene moti sunt pedes, pene effusi sunt gressus mei :

72:3 quia zelavi super iniquos, pacem peccatorum videns.

72:4 Quia non est respectus morti eorum, et firmamentum in plaga eorum.

72:5 In labore hominum non sunt, et cum hominibus non flagellabuntur.

72:6 Ideo tenuit eos superbia ; operti sunt iniquitate et impietate sua.

72:7 Prodiit quasi ex adipe iniquitas eorum ; transierunt in affectum cordis.

72:8 Cogitaverunt et locuti sunt nequitiam ; iniquitatem in excelso locuti sunt.

72:9 Posuerunt in cælum os suum, et lingua eorum transivit in terra.

72:10 Ideo convertetur populus meus hic, et dies pleni invenientur in eis.

72:11 Et dixerunt : Quomodo scit Deus, et si est scientia in excelso ?

72:12 Ecce ipsi peccatores, et abundantes in sæculo obtinuerunt divitias.

72:13 Et dixi : Ergo sine causa justificavi cor meum, et lavi inter innocentes manus meas,

72:1 *A psalm for Asaph.* HOW GOOD IS GOD TO ISRAEL, to them that are of a right heart!

72:2 But my feet were almost moved; my steps had wellnigh slipped.

72:3 Because I had a zeal on occasion of the wicked, seeing the prosperity of sinners.

72:4 For there is no regard to their death, nor is there strength in their stripes.

72:5 They are not in the labour of men: neither shall they be scourged like other men.

72:6 Therefore pride hath held them fast: they are covered with their iniquity and their wickedness.

72:7 Their iniquity hath come forth, as it were from fatness: they have passed into the affection of the heart.

72:8 They have thought and spoken wickedness: they have spoken iniquity on high.

72:9 They have set their mouth against heaven: and their tongue hath passed through the earth.

72:10 Therefore will my people return here and full days shall be found in them.

72:11 And they said: How doth God know? and is there knowledge in the most High?

72:12 Behold these are sinners; and yet abounding in the world they have obtained riches.

72:13 And I said: Then have I in vain justified my heart, and washed my hands among the inno-

72:14 et fui flagellatus tota die, et castigatio mea in matutinis.

72:15 Si dicebam : Narrabo sic ; ecce nationem filiorum tuorum reprobavi.

72:16 Existimabam ut cognoscerem hoc ; labor est ante me :

72:17 donec intrem in sanctuarium Dei, et intelligam in novissimis eorum.

72:18 Verumtamen propter dolos posuisti eis ; dejecisti eos dum allevarentur.

72:19 Quomodo facti sunt in desolationem ? subito defecerunt : perierunt propter iniquitatem suam.

72:20 Velut somnium surgentium, Domine, in civitate tua imaginem ipsorum ad nihilum rediges.

72:21 Quia inflammatum est cor meum, et renes mei commutati sunt ;

72:22 et ego ad nihilum redactus sum, et nescivi :

72:23 ut jumentum factus sum apud te, et ego semper tecum.

72:24 Tenuisti manum dexteram meam, et in voluntate tua deduxisti me, et cum gloria suscepisti me.

72:25 Quid enim mihi est in cælo ? et a te quid volui super terram ?

72:26 Defecit caro mea et cor meum ; Deus cordis mei, et pars mea, Deus in æternum.

72:27 Quia ecce qui elongant se a te peribunt ; perdidisti omnes qui fornicantur abs te.

72:28 Mihi autem adhærere Deo bonum est ; ponere in Domino Deo spem meam : ut annuntiem omnes prædicationes tuas in portis filiæ Sion.

cent.

72:14 And I have been scourged all the day; and my chastisement hath been in the mornings.

72:15 If I said: I will speak thus; behold I should condemn the generation of thy children.

72:16 I studied that I might know this thing, it is a labour in my sight:

72:17 Until I go into the sanctuary of God, and understand concerning their last ends.

72:18 But indeed for deceits thou hast put it to them: when they were lifted up thou hast cast them down.

72:19 How are they brought to desolation? they have suddenly ceased to be: they have perished by reason of their iniquity.

72:20 As the dream of them that awake, O Lord; so in thy city thou shalt bring their image to nothing.

72:21 For my heart hath been inflamed, and my reins have been changed:

72:22 and I am brought to nothing, and I knew not.

72:23 I am become as a beast before thee: and I am always with thee.

72:24 Thou hast held me by my right hand; and by thy will thou hast conducted me, and with thy glory thou hast received me.

72:25 For what have I in heaven? and besides thee what do I desire upon earth?

72:26 For thee my flesh and my heart hath fainted away: thou art the God of my heart, and the God that is my portion for ever.

72:27 For behold they that go far from thee shall perish: thou hast destroyed all them that are disloyal to thee.

72:28 But it is good for me to adhere to my God, to put my hope in the Lord God: That I may declare all thy praises, in the gates of the daughter of Sion.

LXXIII.

73:1 *Intellectus Asaph.* UT QUID, DEUS, repulisti in finem, iratus est furor tuus super oves pascuæ tuæ ?

73:2 Memor esto congregationis tuæ, quam possedisti ab initio. Redemisti virgam hæreditatis tuæ, mons Sion, in quo habitasti in eo.

73:3 Leva manus tuas in superbias eorum in finem : quanta malignatus est inimicus in sancto !

73:4 Et gloriati sunt qui oderunt te in medio so-

73:1 *Understanding for Asaph.* O GOD, WHY hast thou cast us off unto the end: why is thy wrath enkindled against the sheep of thy pasture?

73:2 Remember thy congregation, which thou hast possessed from the beginning. The sceptre of thy inheritance which thou hast redeemed: mount Sion in which thou hast dwelt.

73:3 Lift up thy hands against their pride unto the end; see what things the enemy hath done wickedly in the sanctuary.

73:4 And they that hate thee have made their

lemnitatis tuæ ; posuerunt signa sua, signa :

73:5 et non cognoverunt sicut in exitu super summum. Quasi in silva lignorum securibus

73:6 exciderunt januas ejus in idipsum ; in securi et ascia dejecerunt eam.

73:7 Incenderunt igni sanctuarium tuum ; in terra polluerunt tabernaculum nominis tui.

73:8 Dixerunt in corde suo cognatio eorum simul : Quiescere faciamus omnes dies festos Dei a terra.

73:9 Signa nostra non vidimus ; jam non est propheta ; et nos non cognoscet amplius.

73:10 Usquequo, Deus, improperabit inimicus ? irritat adversarius nomen tuum in finem ?

73:11 Ut quid avertis manum tuam, et dexteram tuam de medio sinu tuo in finem ?

73:12 Deus autem rex noster ante sæcula : operatus est salutem in medio terræ.

73:13 Tu confirmasti in virtute tua mare ; contribulasti capita draconum in aquis.

73:14 Tu confregisti capita draconis ; dedisti eum escam populis Æthiopum.

73:15 Tu dirupisti fontes et torrentes ; tu siccasti fluvios Ethan.

73:16 Tuus est dies, et tua est nox ; tu fabricatus es auroram et solem.

73:17 Tu fecisti omnes terminos terræ ; æstatem et ver tu plasmasti ea.

73:18 Memor esto hujus : inimicus improperavit Domino, et populus insipiens incitavit nomen tuum.

73:19 Ne tradas bestiis animas confitentes tibi, et animas pauperum tuorum ne obliviscaris in finem.

73:20 Respice in testamentum tuum, quia repleti sunt qui obscurati sunt terræ domibus iniquitatum.

73:21 Ne avertatur humilis factus confusus ; pauper et inops laudabunt nomen tuum.

73:22 Exsurge, Deus, judica causam tuam ; memor esto improperiorum tuorum, eorum quæ ab insipiente sunt tota die.

boasts, in the midst of thy solemnity. They have set up their ensigns for signs,

73:5 and they knew not both in the going out and on the highest top. As with axes in a wood of trees,

73:6 they have cut down at once the gates thereof, with axe and hatchet they have brought it down.

73:7 They have set fire to thy sanctuary: they have defiled the dwelling place of thy name on the earth.

73:8 They said in their heart, the whole kindred of them together: Let us abolish all the festival days of God from the land.

73:9 Our signs we have not seen, there is now no prophet: and he will know us no more.

73:10 How long, O God, shall the enemy reproach: is the adversary to provoke thy name for ever?

73:11 Why dost thou turn away thy hand: and thy right hand out of the midst of thy bosom for ever ?

73:12 But God is our king before ages: he hath wrought salvation in the midst of the earth.

73:13 Thou by thy strength didst make the sea firm: thou didst crush the heads of the dragons in the waters.

73:14 Thou hast broken the heads of the dragon: thou hast given him to be meat for the people of the Ethiopians.

73:15 Thou hast broken up the fountains and the torrents: thou hast dried up the Ethan rivers.

73:16 Thine is the day, and thine is the night: thou hast made the morning light and the sun.

73:17 Thou hast made all the borders of the earth: the summer and the spring were formed by thee.

73:18 Remember this, the enemy hath reproached the Lord: and a foolish people hath provoked thy name.

73:19 Deliver not up to beasts the souls that confess to thee: and forget not to the end the souls of thy poor.

73:20 Have regard to thy covenant: for they that are the obscure of the earth have been filled with dwellings of iniquity.

73:21 Let not the humble be turned away with confusion: the poor and needy shall praise thy name.

73:22 Arise, O God, judge thy own cause: remember thy reproaches with which the foolish man hath reproached thee all the day.

73:23 Ne obliviscaris voces inimicorum tuorum : superbia eorum qui te oderunt ascendit semper.

73:23 Forget not the voices of thy enemies: the pride of them that hate thee ascendeth continually.

LXXIV.

74:1 *In finem, ne corrumpas. Psalmus cantici Asaph.*

74:2 CONFITEBIMUR TIBI, Deus, confitebimur, et invocabimus nomen tuum ; narrabimus mirabilia tua.

74:3 Cum accepero tempus, ego justitias judicabo.

74:4 Liquefacta est terra et omnes qui habitant in ea : ego confirmavi columnas ejus.

74:5 Dixi iniquis : Nolite inique agere : et delinquentibus : Nolite exaltare cornu :

74:6 nolite extollere in altum cornu vestrum ; nolite loqui adversus Deum iniquitatem.

74:7 Quia neque ab oriente, neque ab occidente, neque a desertis montibus :

74:8 quoniam Deus judex est. Hunc humiliat, et hunc exaltat :

74:9 quia calix in manu Domini vini meri, plenus misto. Et inclinavit ex hoc in hoc ; verumtamen fæx ejus non est exinanita : bibent omnes peccatores terræ.

74:10 Ego autem annuntiabo in sæculum ; cantabo Deo Jacob :

74:11 et omnia cornua peccatorum confringam, et exaltabuntur cornua justi.

74:1 *Unto the end, corrupt not, a psalm of a canticle for Asaph.*

74:2 WE WILL PRAISE THEE, O God: we will praise, and we will call upon thy name. We will relate thy wondrous works:

74:3 when I shall take a time, I will judge justices.

74:4 The earth is melted, and all that dwell therein: I have established the pillars thereof.

74:5 I said to the wicked: Do not act wickedly: and to the sinners: Lift not up the horn.

74:6 Lift not up your horn on high: speak not iniquity against God.

74:7 For neither from the east, nor from the west, nor from the desert hills:

74:8 for God is the judge. One he putteth down, and another he lifteth up:

74:9 for in the hand of the Lord there is a cup of strong wine full of mixture. And he hath poured it out from this to that: but the dregs thereof are not emptied: all the sinners of the earth shall drink.

74:10 But I will declare for ever: I will sing to the God of Jacob.

74:11 And I will break all the horns of sinners: but the horns of the just shall be exalted.

LXXV.

75:1 *In finem, in laudibus. Psalmus Asaph, canticum ad Assyrios.*

75:2 NOTUS IN JUDÆA DEUS ; in Israël magnum nomen ejus.

75:3 Et factus est in pace locus ejus, et habitatio ejus in Sion.

75:4 Ibi confregit potentias arcuum, scutum, gladium, et bellum.

75:5 Illuminans tu mirabiliter a montibus æternis ;

75:6 turbati sunt omnes insipientes corde. Dormierunt somnum suum, et nihil invenerunt omnes viri divitiarum in manibus suis.

75:7 Ab increpatione tua, Deus Jacob, dormitaverunt qui ascenderunt equos.

75:8 Tu terribilis es ; et quis resistet tibi ? ex tunc ira tua.

75:9 De cælo auditum fecisti judicium : terra tremuit et quievit

75:1 *Unto the end, in praises, a psalm for Asaph: a canticle to the Assyrians.*

75:2 IN JUDEA GOD IS KNOWN: his name is great in Israel.

75:3 And his place is in peace: and his abode in Sion:

75:4 There hath he broken the powers of bows, the shield, the sword, and the battle.

75:5 Thou enlightenest wonderfully from the everlasting hills.

75:6 All the foolish of heart were troubled. They have slept their sleep; and all the men of riches have found nothing in their hands.

75:7 At thy rebuke, O God of Jacob, they have all slumbered that mounted on horseback.

75:8 Thou art terrible, and who shall resist thee? from that time thy wrath.

75:9 Thou hast caused judgment to be heard from heaven: the earth trembled and was still,

75:10 cum exsurgeret in judicium Deus, ut salvos faceret omnes mansuetos terræ.

75:11 Quoniam cogitatio hominis confitebitur tibi, et reliquiæ cogitationis diem festum agent tibi.

75:12 Vovete et reddite Domino Deo vestro, omnes qui in circuitu ejus affertis munera : terribili,

75:13 et ei qui aufert spiritum principum : terribili apud reges terræ.

75:10 When God arose in judgment, to save all the meek of the earth.

75:11 For the thought of man shall give praise to thee: and the remainders of the thought shall keep holiday to thee.

75:12 Vow ye, and pay to the Lord your God: all you that are round about him bring presents. To him that is terrible,

75:13 even to him who taketh away the spirit of princes: to the terrible with the kings of the earth.

LXXVI.

76:1 *In finem, pro Idithun. Psalmus Asaph.*

76:2 VOCE MEA AD DOMINUM CLAMAVI ; voce mea ad Deum, et intendit mihi.

76:3 In die tribulationis meæ Deum exquisivi ; manibus meis nocte contra eum, et non sum deceptus. Renuit consolari anima mea ;

76:4 memor fui Dei, et delectatus sum, et exercitatus sum, et defecit spiritus meus.

76:5 Anticipaverunt vigilias oculi mei ; turbatus sum, et non sum locutus.

76:6 Cogitavi dies antiquos, et annos æternos in mente habui.

76:7 Et meditatus sum nocte cum corde meo, et exercitabar, et scopebam spiritum meum.

76:8 Numquid in æternum projiciet Deus ? aut non apponet ut complacitior sit adhuc ?

76:9 aut in finem misericordiam suam abscindet, a generatione in generationem ?

76:10 aut obliviscetur misereri Deus ? aut continebit in ira sua misericordias suas ?

76:11 Et dixi : Nunc cœpi ; hæc mutatio dexteræ Excelsi.

76:12 Memor fui operum Domini, quia memor ero ab initio mirabilium tuorum :

76:13 et meditabor in omnibus operibus tuis, et in adinventionibus tuis exercebor.

76:14 Deus, in sancto via tua : quis deus magnus sicut Deus noster ?

76:15 Tu es Deus qui facis mirabilia : notam fecisti in populis virtutem tuam.

76:16 Redemisti in brachio tuo populum tuum, filios Jacob et Joseph.

76:17 Viderunt te aquæ, Deus ; viderunt te aquæ, et timuerunt : et turbatæ sunt abyssi.

76:1 *Unto the end, for Idithun, a psalm of Asaph.*

76:2 I CRIED TO THE LORD with my voice; to God with my voice, and he gave ear to me.

76:3 In the day of my trouble I sought God, with my hands lifted up to him in the night, and I was not deceived. My soul refused to be comforted:

76:4 I remembered God, and was delighted, and was exercised, and my spirit swooned away.

76:5 My eyes prevented the watches: I was troubled, and I spoke not.

76:6 I thought upon the days of old: and I had in my mind the eternal years.

76:7 And I meditated in the night with my own heart: and I was exercised and I swept my spirit.

76:8 Will God then cast off for ever? or will he never be more favourable again?

76:9 Or will he cut off his mercy for ever, from generation to generation?

76:10 Or will God forget to shew mercy? or will he in his anger shut up his mercies?

76:11 And I said, Now have I begun: this is the change of the right hand of the most High.

76:12 I remembered the works of the Lord: for I will be mindful of thy wonders from the beginning.

76:13 And I will meditate on all thy works: and will be employed in thy inventions.

76:14 Thy way, O God, is in the holy place: who is the great God like our God?

76:15 Thou art the God that dost wonders. Thou hast made thy power known among the nations:

76:16 with thy arm thou hast redeemed thy people the children of Jacob and of Joseph.

76:17 The waters saw thee, O God, the waters saw thee: and they were afraid, and the depths were troubled.

76:18 Multitudo sonitus aquarum ; vocem dederunt nubes. Etenim sagittæ tuæ transeunt ;

76:19 vox tonitrui tui in rota. Illuxerunt coruscationes tuæ orbi terræ ; commota est, et contremuit terra.

76:20 In mari via tua, et semitæ tuæ in aquis multis, et vestigia tua non cognoscentur.

76:21 Deduxisti sicut oves populum tuum, in manu Moysi et Aaron.

76:18 Great was the noise of the waters: the clouds sent out a sound. For thy arrows pass:

76:19 the voice of thy thunder in a wheel. Thy lightnings enlightened the world: the earth shook and trembled.

76:20 Thy way is in the sea, and thy paths in many waters: and thy footsteps shall not be known.

76:21 Thou hast conducted thy people like sheep, by the hand of Moses and Aaron

LXXVII.

77:1 *Intellectus Asaph.* ATTENDITE, POPULE MEUS, legem meam ; inclinate aurem vestram in verba oris mei.

77:2 Aperiam in parabolis os meum ; loquar propositiones ab initio.

77:3 Quanta audivimus, et cognovimus ea, et patres nostri narraverunt nobis.

77:4 Non sunt occultata a filiis eorum in generatione altera, narrantes laudes Domini et virtutes ejus, et mirabilia ejus quæ fecit.

77:5 Et suscitavit testimonium in Jacob, et legem posuit in Israël, quanta mandavit patribus nostris nota facere ea filiis suis :

77:6 ut cognoscat generatio altera : filii qui nascentur et exsurgent, et narrabunt filiis suis,

77:7 ut ponant in Deo spem suam, et non obliviscantur operum Dei, et mandata ejus exquirant :

77:8 ne fiant, sicut patres eorum, generatio prava et exasperans ; generatio quæ non direxit cor suum, et non est creditus cum Deo spiritus ejus.

77:9 Filii Ephrem, intendentes et mittentes arcum, conversi sunt in die belli.

77:10 Non custodierunt testamentum Dei, et in lege ejus noluerunt ambulare.

77:11 Et obliti sunt benefactorum ejus, et mirabilium ejus quæ ostendit eis.

77:12 Coram patribus eorum fecit mirabilia in terra Ægypti, in campo Taneos.

77:13 Interrupit mare, et perduxit eos, et statuit aquas quasi in utre :

77:14 et deduxit eos in nube diei, et tota nocte in illuminatione ignis.

77:1 *Understanding for Asaph.* ATTEND, O MY PEOPLE, to my law: incline your ears to the words of my mouth.

77:2 I will open my mouth in parables: I will utter propositions from the beginning.

77:3 How great things have we heard and known, and our fathers have told us.

77:4 They have not been hidden from their children, in another generation. Declaring the praises of the Lord, and his powers, and his wonders which he hath done.

77:5 And he set up a testimony in Jacob: and made a law in Israel. How great things he commanded our fathers, that they should make the same known to their children:

77:6 that another generation might know them. The children that should be born and should rise up, and declare them to their children.

77:7 That they may put their hope in God and may not forget the works of God: and may seek his commandments.

77:8 That they may not become like their fathers, a perverse end exasperating generation. A generation that set not their heart aright: and whose spirit was not faithful to God.

77:9 The sons of Ephraim who bend and shoot with the bow: they have turned back in the day of battle.

77:10 They kept not the covenant of God: and in his law they would not walk.

77:11 And they forgot his benefits, and his wonders that he had shewn them.

77:12 Wonderful things did he do in the sight of their fathers, in the land of Egypt, in the field of Tanis.

77:13 He divided the sea and brought them through: and he made the waters to stand as in a vessel.

77:14 And he conducted them with a cloud by day: and all the night with a light of fire.

77:15 Interrupit petram in eremo, et adaquavit eos velut in abysso multa.

77:16 Et eduxit aquam de petra, et deduxit tamquam flumina aquas.

77:17 Et apposuerunt adhuc peccare ei ; in iram excitaverunt Excelsum in inaquoso.

77:18 Et tentaverunt Deum in cordibus suis, ut peterent escas animabus suis.

77:19 Et male locuti sunt de Deo ; dixerunt : Numquid poterit Deus parare mensam in deserto ?

77:20 quoniam percussit petram, et fluxerunt aquæ, et torrentes inundaverunt. Numquid et panem poterit dare, aut parare mensam populo suo ?

77:21 Ideo audivit Dominus et distulit ; et ignis accensus est in Jacob, et ira ascendit in Israël :

77:22 quia non crediderunt in Deo, nec speraverunt in salutari ejus.

77:23 Et mandavit nubibus desuper, et januas cæli aperuit.

77:24 Et pluit illis manna ad manducandum, et panem cæli dedit eis.

77:25 Panem angelorum manducavit homo ; cibaria misit eis in abundantia.

77:26 Transtulit austrum de cælo, et induxit in virtute sua africum.

77:27 Et pluit super eos sicut pulverem carnes, et sicut arenam maris volatilia pennata.

77:28 Et ceciderunt in medio castrorum eorum, circa tabernacula eorum.

77:29 Et manducaverunt, et saturati sunt nimis, et desiderium eorum attulit eis :

77:30 non sunt fraudati a desiderio suo. Adhuc escæ eorum erant in ore ipsorum,

77:31 et ira Dei ascendit super eos : et occidit pingues eorum, et electos Israël impedivit.

77:32 In omnibus his peccaverunt adhuc, et non crediderunt in mirabilibus ejus.

77:33 Et defecerunt in vanitate dies eorum, et anni eorum cum festinatione.

77:34 Cum occideret eos, quærebant eum et revertebantur, et diluculo veniebant ad eum.

77:35 Et rememorati sunt quia Deus adjutor est eorum, et Deus excelsus redemptor eorum est.

77:15 He struck the rock in the wilderness: and gave them to drink, as out of the great deep.

77:16 He brought forth water out of the rock: and made streams run down as rivers.

77:17 And they added yet more sin against him: they provoked the most High to wrath in the place without water.

77:18 And they tempted God in their hearts, by asking meat for their desires.

77:19 And they spoke ill of God: they said: Can God furnish a table in the wilderness?

77:20 Because he struck the rock, and the waters gushed out, and the streams overflowed. Can he also give bread, or provide a table for his people?

77:21 Therefore the Lord heard, and was angry: and a fire was kindled against Jacob, and wrath came up against Israel.

77:22 Because they believed not in God: and trusted not in his salvation.

77:23 And he had commanded the clouds from above, and had opened the doors of heaven.

77:24 And had rained down manna upon them to eat, and had given them the bread of heaven.

77:25 Man ate the bread of angels: he sent them provisions in abundance.

77:26 He removed the south wind from heaven: and by his power brought in the southwest wind.

77:27 And he rained upon them flesh as dust: and feathered fowls like as the sand of the sea.

77:28 And they fell in the midst of their camp, round about their pavilions.

77:29 So they did eat, and were filled exceedingly, and he gave them their desire:

77:30 They were not defrauded of that which they craved. As yet their meat was in their mouth:

77:31 And the wrath of God came upon them. And he slew the fat ones amongst them, and brought down the chosen men of Israel.

77:32 In all these things they sinned still: and they believed not for his wondrous works.

77:33 And their days were consumed in vanity, and their years in haste.

77:34 When he slew them, then they sought him: and they returned, and came to him early in the morning.

77:35 And they remembered that God was their helper: and the most high God their redeemer.

77:36 Et dilexerunt eum in ore suo, et lingua sua mentiti sunt ei ;

77:37 cor autem eorum non erat rectum cum eo, nec fideles habiti sunt in testamento ejus.

77:38 Ipse autem est misericors, et propitius fiet peccatis eorum, et non disperdet eos. Et abundavit ut averteret iram suam, et non accendit omnem iram suam.

77:39 Et recordatus est quia caro sunt, spiritus vadens et non rediens.

77:40 Quoties exacerbaverunt eum in deserto ; in iram concitaverunt eum in inaquoso ?

77:41 Et conversi sunt, et tentaverunt Deum, et sanctum Israël exacerbaverunt.

77:42 Non sunt recordati manus ejus, die qua redemit eos de manu tribulantis :

77:43 sicut posuit in Ægypto signa sua, et prodigia sua in campo Taneos ;

77:44 et convertit in sanguinem flumina eorum, et imbres eorum, ne biberent.

77:45 Misit in eos cœnomyiam, et comedit eos, et ranam, et disperdidit eos ;

77:46 et dedit ærugini fructus eorum, et labores eorum locustæ ;

77:47 et occidit in grandine vineas eorum, et moros eorum in pruina ;

77:48 et tradidit grandini jumenta eorum, et possessionem eorum igni ;

77:49 misit in eos iram indignationis suæ, indignationem, et iram, et tribulationem, immissiones per angelos malos.

77:50 Viam fecit semitæ iræ suæ : non pepercit a morte animabus eorum, et jumenta eorum in morte conclusit :

77:51 et percussit omne primogenitum in terra Ægypti ; primitias omnis laboris eorum in tabernaculis Cham :

77:52 et abstulit sicut oves populum suum, et perduxit eos tamquam gregem in deserto :

77:53 et deduxit eos in spe, et non timuerunt, et inimicos eorum operuit mare.

77:54 Et induxit eos in montem sanctificationis suæ, montem quem acquisivit dextera ejus ; et ejecit a facie eorum gentes, et sorte divisit eis terram in funiculo distributionis ;

77:55 et habitare fecit in tabernaculis eorum tribus Israël.

77:36 And they loved him with their mouth: and with their tongue they lied unto him:

77:37 But their heart was not right with him: nor were they counted faithful in his covenant.

77:38 But he is merciful, and will forgive their sins: and will not destroy them. And many a time did he turn away his anger: and did not kindle all his wrath.

77:39 And he remembered that they are flesh: a wind that goeth and returneth not.

77:40 How often did they provoke him in the desert: and move him to wrath in the place without water?

77:41 And they turned back and tempted God: and grieved the holy one of Israel.

77:42 They remembered not his hand, in the day that he redeemed them from the hand of him that afflicted them:

77:43 How he wrought his signs in Egypt, and his wonders in the field of Tanis.

77:44 And he turned their rivers into blood, and their showers that they might, not drink.

77:45 He sent amongst them divers sores of flies, which devoured them: and frogs which destroyed them.

77:46 And he gave up their fruits to the blast, and their labours to the locust.

77:47 And he destroyed their vineyards with hail, and their mulberry trees with hoarfrost.

77:48 And he gave up their cattle to the hail, and their stock to the fire.

77:49 And he sent upon them the wrath of his indignation: indignation and wrath and trouble, which he sent by evil angels.

77:50 He made a way for a path to his anger: he spared not their souls from death, and their cattle he shut up in death.

77:51 And he killed all the firstborn in the land of Egypt: the firstfruits of all their labour in the tabernacles of Cham.

77:52 And he took away his own people as sheep: and guided them in the wilderness like a flock.

77:53 And he brought them out in hope, and they feared not: and the sea overwhelmed their enemies.

77:54 And he brought them into the mountain of his sanctuary: the mountain which his right hand had purchased. And he cast out the Gentiles before them: and by lot divided to them their land by a line of distribution.

77:55 And he made the tribes of Israel to dwell in their tabernacles.

77:56 Et tentaverunt, et exacerbaverunt Deum excelsum, et testimonia ejus non custodierunt.

77:57 Et averterunt se, et non servaverunt pactum : quemadmodum patres eorum, conversi sunt in arcum pravum.

77:58 In iram concitaverunt eum in collibus suis, et in sculptilibus suis ad æmulationem eum provocaverunt.

77:59 Audivit Deus, et sprevit, et ad nihilum redegit valde Israël.

77:60 Et repulit tabernaculum Silo, tabernaculum suum, ubi habitavit in hominibus.

77:61 Et tradidit in captivitatem virtutem eorum, et pulchritudinem eorum in manus inimici.

77:62 Et conclusit in gladio populum suum, et hæreditatem suam sprevit.

77:63 Juvenes eorum comedit ignis, et virgines eorum non sunt lamentatæ.

77:64 Sacerdotes eorum in gladio ceciderunt, et viduæ eorum non plorabantur.

77:65 Et excitatus est tamquam dormiens Dominus, tamquam potens crapulatus a vino.

77:66 Et percussit inimicos suos in posteriora ; opprobrium sempiternum dedit illis.

77:67 Et repulit tabernaculum Joseph, et tribum Ephraim non elegit :

77:68 sed elegit tribum Juda, montem Sion, quem dilexit.

77:69 Et ædificavit sicut unicornium sanctificium suum, in terra quam fundavit in sæcula.

77:70 Et elegit David, servum suum, et sustulit eum de gregibus ovium ; de post fœtantes accepit eum :

77:71 pascere Jacob servum suum, et Israël hæreditatem suam.

77:72 Et pavit eos in innocentia cordis sui, et in intellectibus manuum suarum deduxit eos.

77:56 Yet they tempted, and provoked the most high God: and they kept not his testimonies.

77:57 And they turned away, and kept not the covenant: even like their fathers they were turned aside as a crooked bow.

77:58 They provoked him to anger on their hills: and moved him to jealousy with their graven things.

77:59 God heard, and despised them, and he reduced Israel exceedingly as it were to nothing.

77:60 And he put away the tabernacle of Silo, his tabernacle where he dwelt among men.

77:61 And he delivered their strength into captivity: and their beauty into the hands of the enemy.

77:62 And he shut up his people under the sword: and he despised his inheritance.

77:63 Fire consumed their young men: and their maidens were not lamented.

77:64 Their priests fell by the sword: and their widows did not mourn.

77:65 And the Lord was awaked as one out of sleep, and like a mighty man that hath been surfeited with wine.

77:66 And he smote his enemies on the hinder parts: he put them to an everlasting reproach.

77:67 And he rejected the tabernacle of Joseph: and chose not the tribe of Ephraim:

77:68 But he chose the tribe of Juda, mount Sion which he loved.

77:69 And he built his sanctuary as of unicorns, in the land which he founded for ever.

77:70 And he chose his servant David, and took him from the flocks of sheep: he brought him from following the ewes great with young,

77:71 To feed Jacob his servant, and Israel his inheritance.

77:72 And he fed them in the innocence of his heart: and conducted them by the skilfulness of his hands.

LXXVIII.

78:1 *Psalmus Asaph.* DEUS, VENERUNT GENTES in hæreditatem tuam ; polluerunt templum sanctum tuum ; posuerunt Jerusalem in pomorum custodiam.

78:2 Posuerunt morticina servorum tuorum escas volatilibus cæli ; carnes sanctorum tuorum bestiis terræ.

78:3 Effuderunt sanguinem eorum tamquam aquam in circuitu Jerusalem, et non erat qui sepeliret.

78:1 *A psalm for Asaph.* O GOD, THE HEATHENS ARE COME into thy inheritance, they have defiled thy holy temple: they have made Jerusalem as a place to keep fruit.

78:2 They have given the dead bodies of thy servants to be meat for the fowls of the air: the flesh of thy saints for the beasts of the earth.

78:3 They have poured out their blood as water, round about Jerusalem and there was none to bury them.

78:4 Facti sumus opprobrium vicinis nostris ; subsannatio et illusio his qui in circuitu nostro sunt.

78:5 Usquequo, Domine, irasceris in finem ? accendetur velut ignis zelus tuus ?

78:6 Effunde iram tuam in gentes quæ te non noverunt, et in regna quæ nomen tuum non invocaverunt :

78:7 quia comederunt Jacob, et locum ejus desolaverunt.

78:8 Ne memineris iniquitatum nostrarum antiquarum ; cito anticipent nos misericordiæ tuæ, quia pauperes facti sumus nimis.

78:9 Adjuva nos, Deus salutaris noster, et propter gloriam nominis tui, Domine, libera nos : et propitius esto peccatis nostris, propter nomen tuum.

78:10 Ne forte dicant in gentibus : Ubi est Deus eorum ? et innotescat in nationibus coram oculis nostris ultio sanguinis servorum tuorum qui effusus est.

78:11 Introëat in conspectu tuo gemitus compeditorum ; secundum magnitudinem brachii tui posside filios mortificatorum :

78:12 et redde vicinis nostris septuplum in sinu eorum ; improperium ipsorum quod exprobraverunt tibi, Domine.

78:13 Nos autem populus tuus, et oves pascuæ tuæ, confitebimur tibi in sæculum ; in generationem et generationem annuntiabimus laudem tuam.

78:4 We are become a reproach to our neighbours: a scorn and derision to them that are round about us.

78:5 How long, O Lord, wilt thou be angry for ever: shall thy zeal be kindled like a fire?

78:6 Pour out thy wrath upon the nations that have not known thee: and upon the kingdoms that have not called upon thy name.

78:7 Because they have devoured Jacob; and have laid waste his place.

78:8 Remember not our former iniquities: let thy mercies speedily prevent us, for we are become exceeding poor.

78:9 Help us, O God, our saviour: and for the glory of thy name, O Lord, deliver us: and forgive us our sins for thy name's sake:

78:10 Lest they should say among the Gentiles: Where is their God? And let him be made known among the nations before our eyes, By the revenging the blood of thy servants, which hath been shed:

78:11 let the sighing of the prisoners come in before thee. According to the greatness of thy arm, take possession of the children of them that have been put to death.

78:12 And render to our neighbours sevenfold in their bosom: the reproach wherewith they have reproached thee, O Lord.

78:13 But we thy people, and the sheep of thy pasture, will give thanks to thee for ever. We will shew forth thy praise, unto generation and generation.

LXXIX.

79:1 *In finem, pro iis qui commutabuntur. Testimonium Asaph, psalmus.*

79:2 QUI REGIS ISRAËL, INTENDE ; qui deducis velut ovem Joseph. Qui sedes super cherubim, manifestare

79:3 coram Ephraim, Benjamin, et Manasse. Excita potentiam tuam, et veni, ut salvos facias nos.

79:4 Deus, converte nos, et ostende faciem tuam, et salvi erimus.

79:5 Domine Deus virtutum, quousque irasceris super orationem servi tui ?

79:6 cibabis nos pane lacrimarum, et potum dabis nobis in lacrimis in mensura ?

79:7 Posuisti nos in contradictionem vicinis nostris, et inimici nostri subsannaverunt nos.

79:1 *Unto the end, for them that shall be changed, a testimony for Asaph, a psalm.*

79:2 GIVE EAR, O THOU THAT RULEST ISRAEL: thou that leadest Joseph like a sheep. Thou that sittest upon the cherubims, shine forth

79:3 before Ephraim, Benjamin, and Manasses. Stir up thy might, and come to save us.

79:4 Convert us, O God: and shew us thy face, and we shall be saved.

79:5 O Lord God of hosts, how long wilt thou be angry against the prayer of thy servant?

79:6 How long wilt thou feed us with the bread of tears: and give us for our drink tears in measure?

79:7 Thou hast made us to be a contradiction to our neighbours: and our enemies have scoffed

at us.

79:8 Deus virtutum, converte nos, et ostende faciem tuam, et salvi erimus.

79:9 Vineam de Ægypto transtulisti : ejecisti gentes, et plantasti eam.

79:10 Dux itineris fuisti in conspectu ejus ; plantasti radices ejus, et implevit terram.

79:11 Operuit montes umbra ejus, et arbusta ejus cedros Dei.

79:12 Extendit palmites suos usque ad mare, et usque ad flumen propagines ejus.

79:13 Ut quid destruxisti maceriam ejus, et vindemiant eam omnes qui prætergrediuntur viam ?

79:14 Exterminavit eam aper de silva, et singularis ferus depastus est eam.

79:15 Deus virtutum, convertere, respice de cælo, et vide, et visita vineam istam :

79:16 et perfice eam quam plantavit dextera tua, et super filium hominis quem confirmasti tibi.

79:17 Incensa igni et suffossa, ab increpatione vultus tui peribunt.

79:18 Fiat manus tua super virum dexteræ tuæ, et super filium hominis quem confirmasti tibi.

79:19 Et non discedimus a te : vivificabis nos, et nomen tuum invocabimus.

79:20 Domine Deus virtutum, converte nos, et ostende faciem tuam, et salvi erimus.

79:8 O God of hosts, convert us: and shew thy face, and we shall be saved.

79:9 Thou hast brought a vineyard out of Egypt: thou hast cast out the Gentiles and planted it.

79:10 Thou wast the guide of its journey in its sight: thou plantedst the roots thereof, and it filled the land.

79:11 The shadow of it covered the hills: and the branches thereof the cedars of God.

79:12 It stretched forth its branches unto the sea, and its boughs unto the river.

79:13 Why hast thou broken down the hedge thereof, so that all they who pass by the way do pluck it?

79:14 The boar out of the wood hath laid it waste: and a singular wild beast hath devoured it.

79:15 Turn again, O God of hosts, look down from heaven, and see, and visit this vineyard:

79:16 And perfect the same which thy right hand hath planted: and upon the son of man whom thou hast confirmed for thyself.

79:17 Things set on fire and dug down shall perish at the rebuke of thy countenance.

79:18 Let thy hand be upon the man of thy right hand: and upon the son of man whom thou hast confirmed for thyself.

79:19 And we depart not from thee, thou shalt quicken us: and we will call upon thy name.

79:20 O Lord God of hosts, convert us: and shew thy face, and we shall be saved.

LXXX.

80:1 *In finem, pro torcularibus. Psalmus ipsi Asaph.*

80:2 EXSULTATE DEO adjutori nostro ; jubilate Deo Jacob.

80:3 Sumite psalmum, et date tympanum ; psalterium jucundum cum cithara.

80:4 Buccinate in neomenia tuba, in insigni die solemnitatis vestræ :

80:5 quia præceptum in Israël est, et judicium Deo Jacob.

80:6 Testimonium in Joseph posuit illud, cum exiret de terra Ægypti ; linguam quam non noverat, audivit.

80:7 Divertit ab oneribus dorsum ejus ; manus ejus in cophino servierunt.

80:8 In tribulatione invocasti me, et liberavi te. Exaudivi te in abscondito tempestatis ; probavi te apud aquam contradictionis.

80:1 *Unto the end, for the winepresses, a psalm for Asaph himself.*

80:2 REJOICE TO GOD our helper: sing aloud to the God of Jacob.

80:3 Take a psalm, and bring hither the timbrel: the pleasant psaltery with the harp.

80:4 Blow up the trumpet on the new moon, on the noted day of your solemnity.

80:5 For it is a commandment in Israel, and a judgment to the God of Jacob.

80:6 He ordained it for a testimony in Joseph, when he came out of the land of Egypt: he heard a tongue which he knew not.

80:7 He removed his back from the burdens: his hands had served in baskets.

80:8 Thou calledst upon me in affliction, and I delivered thee: I heard thee in the secret place of tempest: I proved thee at the waters of con-

80:9 Audi, populus meus, et contestabor te. Israël, si audieris me,

80:10 non erit in te deus recens, neque adorabis deum alienum.

80:11 Ego enim sum Dominus Deus tuus, qui eduxi te de terra Ægypti. Dilata os tuum, et implebo illud.

80:12 Et non audivit populus meus vocem meam, et Israël non intendit mihi.

80:13 Et dimisi eos secundum desideria cordis eorum ; ibunt in adinventionibus suis.

80:14 Si populus meus audisset me, Israël si in viis meis ambulasset,

80:15 pro nihilo forsitan inimicos eorum humiliassem, et super tribulantes eos misissem manum meam.

80:16 Inimici Domini mentiti sunt ei, et erit tempus eorum in sæcula.

80:17 Et cibavit eos ex adipe frumenti, et de petra melle saturavit eos.

tradiction.

80:9 Hear, O my people, and I will testify to thee: O Israel, if thou wilt hearken to me,

80:10 there shall be no new god in thee: neither shalt thou adore a strange god.

80:11 For I am the Lord thy God, who brought thee out of the land of Egypt: open thy mouth wide, and I will fill it.

80:12 But my people heard not my voice: and Israel hearkened not to me.

80:13 So I let them go according to the desires of their heart: they shall walk in their own inventions.

80:14 If my people had heard me: if Israel had walked in my ways:

80:15 I should soon have humbled their enemies, and laid my hand on them that troubled them.

80:16 The enemies of the Lord have lied to him: and their time shall be for ever.

80:17 And he fed them with the fat of wheat, and filled them with honey out of the rock.

LXXXI.

81:1 *Psalmus Asaph.* DEUS STETIT in synagoga deorum ; in medio autem deos dijudicat.

81:2 Usquequo judicatis iniquitatem, et facies peccatorum sumitis ?

81:3 Judicate egeno et pupillo ; humilem et pauperem justificate.

81:4 Eripite pauperem, et egenum de manu peccatoris liberate.

81:5 Nescierunt, neque intellexerunt ; in tenebris ambulant : movebuntur omnia fundamenta terræ.

81:6 Ego dixi : Dii estis, et filii Excelsi omnes.

81:7 Vos autem sicut homines moriemini, et sicut unus de principibus cadetis.

81:8 Surge, Deus, judica terram, quoniam tu hæreditabis in omnibus gentibus.

81:1 *A psalm for Asaph.* GOD HATH STOOD in the congregation of gods: and being in the midst of them he judgeth gods.

81:2 How long will you judge unjustly: and accept the persons of the wicked?

81:3 Judge for the needy and fatherless: do justice to the humble and the poor.

81:4 Rescue the poor; and deliver the needy out of the hand of the sinner.

81:5 They have not known nor understood: they walk on in darkness: all the foundations of the earth shall be moved.

81:6 I have said: You are gods and all of you the sons of the most High.

81:7 But you like men shall die: and shall fall like one of the princes.

81:8 Arise, O God, judge thou the earth: for thou shalt inherit among all the nations.

LXXXII.

82:1 *Canticum Psalmi Asaph.*

82:2 DEUS, QUIS SIMILIS ERIT tibi ? ne taceas, neque compescaris, Deus :

82:3 quoniam ecce inimici tui sonuerunt, et qui oderunt te extulerunt caput.

82:4 Super populum tuum malignaverunt consilium, et cogitaverunt adversus sanctos tuos.

82:1 *A canticle of a psalm for Asaph.*

82:2 O GOD, WHO SHALL BE LIKE to thee? hold not thy peace, neither be thou still, O God.

82:3 For lo, thy enemies have made a noise: and they that hate thee have lifted up the head.

82:4 They have taken a malicious counsel against thy people, and have consulted against thy saints.

82:5 Dixerunt : Venite, et disperdamus eos de gente, et non memoretur nomen Israël ultra.

82:6 Quoniam cogitaverunt unanimiter ; simul adversum te testamentum disposuerunt :

82:7 tabernacula Idumæorum et Ismahelitæ, Moab et Agareni,

82:8 Gebal, et Ammon, et Amalec ; alienigenæ cum habitantibus Tyrum.

82:9 Etenim Assur venit cum illis : facti sunt in adjutorium filiis Lot.

82:10 Fac illis sicut Madian et Sisaræ, sicut Jabin in torrente Cisson.

82:11 Disperierunt in Endor ; facti sunt ut stercus terræ.

82:12 Pone principes eorum sicut Oreb, et Zeb, et Zebee, et Salmana : omnes principes eorum,

82:13 qui dixerunt : Hæreditate possideamus sanctuarium Dei.

82:14 Deus meus, pone illos ut rotam, et sicut stipulam ante faciem venti.

82:15 Sicut ignis qui comburit silvam, et sicut flamma comburens montes,

82:16 ita persequeris illos in tempestate tua, et in ira tua turbabis eos.

82:17 Imple facies eorum ignominia, et quærent nomen tuum, Domine.

82:18 Erubescant, et conturbentur in sæculum sæculi, et confundantur, et pereant.

82:19 Et cognoscant quia nomen tibi Dominus : tu solus Altissimus in omni terra.

82:5 They have said: Come and let us destroy them, so that they be not a nation: and let the name of Israel be remembered no more.

82:6 For they have contrived with one consent: they have made a covenant together against thee,

82:7 the tabernacles of the Edomites, and the Ismahelites: Moab, and the Agarens,

82:8 Gebal, and Ammon and Amalec: the Philistines, with the inhabitants of Tyre.

82:9 Yea, and the Assyrian also is joined with them: they are come to the aid of the sons of Lot.

82:10 Do to them as thou didst to Madian and to Sisara: as to Jabin at the brook of Cisson.

82:11 Who perished at Endor: and became as dung for the earth.

82:12 Make their princes like Oreb, and Zeb, and Zebee, and Salmana. All their princes,

82:13 who have said: Let us possess the sanctuary of God for an inheritance.

82:14 O my God, make them like a wheel; and as stubble before the wind.

82:15 As fire which burneth the wood: and as a flame burning mountains:

82:16 So shalt thou pursue them with thy tempest: and shalt trouble them in thy wrath.

82:17 Fill their faces with shame; and they shall seek thy name, O Lord.

82:18 Let them be ashamed and troubled for ever and ever: and let them be confounded and perish.

82:19 And let them know that the Lord is thy name: thou alone art the most High over all the earth.

LXXXIII.

83:1 *In finem, pro torcularibus filiis Core. Psalmus.*

83:2 QUAM DILECTA tabernacula tua, Domine virtutum !

83:3 Concupiscit, et deficit anima mea in atria Domini ; cor meum et caro mea exsultaverunt in Deum vivum.

83:4 Etenim passer invenit sibi domum, et turtur nidum sibi, ubi ponat pullos suos : altaria tua, Domine virtutum, rex meus, et Deus meus.

83:5 Beati qui habitant in domo tua, Domine ; in sæcula sæculorum laudabunt te.

83:6 Beatus vir cujus est auxilium abs te : ascensiones in corde suo disposuit,

83:1 *Unto the end, for the winepresses, a psalm for the sons of Core.*

83:2 HOW LOVELY are thy tabernacles, O Lord of hosts!

83:3 my soul longeth and fainteth for the courts of the Lord. My heart and my flesh have rejoiced in the living God.

83:4 For the sparrow hath found herself a house, and the turtle a nest for herself where she may lay her young ones: Thy altars, O Lord of hosts, my king and my God.

83:5 Blessed are they that dwell in thy house, O Lord: they shall praise thee for ever and ever.

83:6 Blessed is the man whose help is from thee: in his heart he hath disposed to ascend by

^{83:7} in valle lacrimarum, in loco quem posuit.

^{83:8} Etenim benedictionem dabit legislator ; ibunt de virtute in virtutem : videbitur Deus deorum in Sion.

^{83:9} Domine Deus virtutum, exaudi orationem meam ; auribus percipe, Deus Jacob.

^{83:10} Protector noster, aspice, Deus, et respice in faciem christi tui.

^{83:11} Quia melior est dies una in atriis tuis super millia ; elegi abjectus esse in domo Dei mei magis quam habitare in tabernaculis peccatorum.

^{83:12} Quia misericordiam et veritatem diligit Deus : gratiam et gloriam dabit Dominus.

^{83:13} Non privabit bonis eos qui ambulant in innocentia : Domine virtutum, beatus homo qui sperat in te.

steps,

^{83:7} in the vale of tears, in the place which he hath set.

^{83:8} For the lawgiver shall give a blessing, they shall go from virtue to virtue: the God of gods shall be seen in Sion.

^{83:9} O Lord God of hosts, hear my prayer: give ear, O God of Jacob.

^{83:10} Behold, O God our protector: and look on the face of thy Christ.

^{83:11} For better is one day in thy courts above thousands. I have chosen to be an abject in the house of my God, rather than to dwell in the tabernacles of sinners.

^{83:12} For God loveth mercy and truth: the Lord will give grace and glory.

^{83:13} He will not deprive of good things them that walk in innocence: O Lord of hosts, blessed is the man that trusteth in thee.

LXXXIV.

^{84:1} *In finem, filiis Core. Psalmus.*

^{84:2} BENEDIXISTI, DOMINE, terram tuam ; avertisti captivitatem Jacob.

^{84:3} Remisisti iniquitatem plebis tuæ ; operuisti omnia peccata eorum.

^{84:4} Mitigasti omnem iram tuam ; avertisti ab ira indignationis tuæ.

^{84:5} Converte nos, Deus salutaris noster, et averte iram tuam a nobis.

^{84:6} Numquid in æternum irasceris nobis ? aut extendes iram tuam a generatione in generationem ?

^{84:7} Deus, tu conversus vivificabis nos, et plebs tua lætabitur in te.

^{84:8} Ostende nobis, Domine, misericordiam tuam, et salutare tuum da nobis.

^{84:9} Audiam quid loquatur in me Dominus Deus, quoniam loquetur pacem in plebem suam, et super sanctos suos, et in eos qui convertuntur ad cor.

^{84:10} Verumtamen prope timentes eum salutare ipsius, ut inhabitet gloria in terra nostra.

^{84:11} Misericordia et veritas obviaverunt sibi ; justitia et pax osculatæ sunt.

^{84:12} Veritas de terra orta est, et justitia de cælo prospexit.

^{84:13} Etenim Dominus dabit benignitatem, et terra nostra dabit fructum suum.

^{84:14} Justitia ante eum ambulabit, et ponet in via gressus suos.

^{84:1} *Unto the end, for the sons of Core, a psalm.*

^{84:2} LORD, THOU HAST BLESSED thy land: thou hast turned away the captivity of Jacob.

^{84:3} Thou hast forgiven the iniquity of thy people: thou hast covered all their sins.

^{84:4} Thou hast mitigated all thy anger: thou hast turned away from the wrath of thy indignation.

^{84:5} Convert us, O God our saviour: and turn off thy anger from us.

^{84:6} Wilt thou be angry with us for ever: or wilt thou extend thy wrath from generation to generation?

^{84:7} Thou wilt turn, O God, and bring us to life: and thy people shall rejoice in thee.

^{84:8} Shew us, O Lord, thy mercy; and grant us thy salvation.

^{84:9} I will hear what the Lord God will speak in me: for he will speak peace unto his people: And unto his saints: and unto them that are converted to the heart.

^{84:10} Surely his salvation is near to them that fear him: that glory may dwell in our land.

^{84:11} Mercy and truth have met each other: justice and peace have kissed.

^{84:12} Truth is sprung out of the earth: and justice hath looked down from heaven.

^{84:13} For the Lord will give goodness: and our earth shall yield her fruit.

^{84:14} Justice shall walk before him: and shall set his steps in the way.

LXXXV.

^{85:1} *Oratio ipsi David.* INCLINA, DOMINE, aurem tuam et exaudi me, quoniam inops et pauper sum ego.

^{85:2} Custodi animam meam, quoniam sanctus sum ; salvum fac servum tuum, Deus meus, sperantem in te.

^{85:3} Miserere mei, Domine, quoniam ad te clamavi tota die ;

^{85:4} lætifica animam servi tui, quoniam ad te, Domine, animam meam levavi.

^{85:5} Quoniam tu, Domine, suavis et mitis, et multæ misericordiæ omnibus invocantibus te.

^{85:6} Auribus percipe, Domine, orationem meam, et intende voci deprecationis meæ.

^{85:7} In die tribulationis meæ clamavi ad te, quia exaudisti me.

^{85:8} Non est similis tui in diis, Domine, et non est secundum opera tua.

^{85:9} Omnes gentes quascumque fecisti venient, et adorabunt coram te, Domine, et glorificabunt nomen tuum.

^{85:10} Quoniam magnus es tu, et faciens mirabilia ; tu es Deus solus.

^{85:11} Deduc me, Domine, in via tua, et ingrediar in veritate tua ; lætetur cor meum, ut timeat nomen tuum.

^{85:12} Confitebor tibi, Domine Deus meus, in toto corde meo, et glorificabo nomen tuum in æternum :

^{85:13} quia misericordia tua magna est super me, et eruisti animam meam ex inferno inferiori.

^{85:14} Deus, iniqui insurrexerunt super me, et synagoga potentium quæsierunt animam meam : et non proposuerunt te in conspectu suo.

^{85:15} Et tu, Domine Deus, miserator et misericors ; patiens, et multæ misericordiæ, et verax.

^{85:16} Respice in me, et miserere mei ; da imperium tuum puero tuo, et salvum fac filium ancillæ tuæ.

^{85:17} Fac mecum signum in bonum, ut videant qui oderunt me, et confundantur : quoniam tu, Domine, adjuvisti me, et consolatus es me.

^{85:1} *A prayer for David himself.* INCLINE THY EAR, O LORD, and hear me: for I am needy and poor.

^{85:2} Preserve my soul, for I am holy: save thy servant, O my God, that trusteth in thee.

^{85:3} Have mercy on me, O Lord, for I have cried to thee all the day.

^{85:4} Give joy to the soul of thy servant, for to thee, O Lord, I have lifted up my soul.

^{85:5} For thou, O Lord, art sweet and mild: and plenteous in mercy to all that call upon thee.

^{85:6} Give ear, O Lord, to my prayer: and attend to the voice of my petition.

^{85:7} I have called upon thee in the day of my trouble: because thou hast heard me.

^{85:8} There is none among the gods like unto thee, O Lord: and there is none according to thy works.

^{85:9} All the nations thou hast made shall come and adore before thee, O Lord: and they shall glorify thy name.

^{85:10} For thou art great and dost wonderful things: thou art God alone.

^{85:11} Conduct me, O Lord, in thy way, and I will walk in thy truth: let my heart rejoice that it may fear thy name.

^{85:12} I will praise thee, O Lord my God: with my whole heart, and I will glorify thy name for ever:

^{85:13} For thy mercy is great towards me: and thou hast delivered my soul out of the lower hell.

^{85:14} O God, the wicked are risen up against me, and the assembly of the mighty have sought my soul: and they have not set thee before their eyes.

^{85:15} And thou, O Lord, art a God of compassion, and merciful, patient, and of much mercy, and true.

^{85:16} O look upon me, and have mercy on me: give thy command to thy servant, and save the son of thy handmaid.

^{85:17} Shew me a token for good: that they who hate me may see, and be confounded, because thou, O Lord, hast helped me and hast comforted me.

LXXXVI.

86:1 *Filiis Core. Psalmus cantici.* FUNDAMENTA ejus in montibus sanctis ;

86:2 diligit Dominus portas Sion super omnia tabernacula Jacob.

86:3 Gloriosa dicta sunt de te, civitas Dei !

86:4 Memor ero Rahab et Babylonis, scientium me ; ecce alienigenæ, et Tyrus, et populus Æthiopum, hi fuerunt illic.

86:5 Numquid Sion dicet : Homo et homo natus est in ea, et ipse fundavit eam Altissimus ?

86:6 Dominus narrabit in scripturis populorum et principum, horum qui fuerunt in ea.

86:7 Sicut lætantium omnium habitatio est in te.

86:1 *For the sons of Core, a psalm of a canticle.* THE FOUNDATIONS thereof are in the holy mountains:

86:2 The Lord loveth the gates of Sion above all the tabernacles of Jacob.

86:3 Glorious things are said of thee, O city of God.

86:4 I will be mindful of Rahab and of Babylon knowing me. Behold the foreigners, and Tyre, and the people of the Ethiopians, these were there.

86:5 Shall not Sion say: This man and that man is born in her? and the Highest himself hath founded her.

86:6 The Lord shall tell in his writings of peoples and of princes, of them that have been in her.

86:7 The dwelling in thee is as it were of all rejoicing.

LXXXVII.

87:1 *Canticum Psalmi, filiis Core, in finem, pro Maheleth ad respondendum. Intellectus Eman Ezrahitæ.*

87:2 DOMINE, DEUS SALUTIS MEÆ, in die clamavi et nocte coram te.

87:3 Intret in conspectu tuo oratio mea, inclina aurem tuam ad precem meam.

87:4 Quia repleta est malis anima mea, et vita mea inferno appropinquavit.

87:5 Æstimatus sum cum descendentibus in lacum, factus sum sicut homo sine adjutorio,

87:6 inter mortuos liber ; sicut vulnerati dormientes in sepulchris, quorum non es memor amplius, et ipsi de manu tua repulsi sunt.

87:7 Posuerunt me in lacu inferiori, in tenebrosis, et in umbra mortis.

87:8 Super me confirmatus est furor tuus, et omnes fluctus tuos induxisti super me.

87:9 Longe fecisti notos meos a me ; posuerunt me abominationem sibi. Traditus sum, et non egrediebar ;

87:10 oculi mei languerunt præ inopia. Clamavi ad te, Domine, tota die ; expandi ad te manus meas.

87:11 Numquid mortuis facies mirabilia ? aut medici suscitabunt, et confitebuntur tibi ?

87:12 Numquid narrabit aliquis in sepulchro misericordiam tuam, et veritatem tuam in perditione ?

87:1 *A canticle of a psalm for the sons of Core: unto the end, for Maheleth, to answer understanding of Eman the Ezrahite.*

87:2 O LORD, THE GOD OF MY SALVATION: I have cried in the day, and in the night before thee.

87:3 Let my prayer come in before thee: incline thy ear to my petition.

87:4 For my soul is filled with evils: and my life hath drawn nigh to hell.

87:5 I am counted among them that go down to the pit: I am become as a man without help,

87:6 free among the dead. Like the slain sleeping in the sepulchres, whom thou rememberest no more: and they are cast off from thy hand.

87:7 They have laid me in the lower pit: in the dark places, and in the shadow of death.

87:8 Thy wrath is strong over me: and all thy waves thou hast brought in upon me.

87:9 Thou hast put away my acquaintance far from me: they have set me an abomination to themselves. I was delivered up, and came not forth:

87:10 my eyes languished through poverty. All the day I cried to thee, O Lord: I stretched out my hands to thee.

87:11 Wilt thou shew wonders to the dead? or shall physicians raise to life, and give praise to thee?

87:12 Shall any one in the sepulchre declare thy mercy: and thy truth in destruction?

87:13 Numquid cognoscentur in tenebris mirabilia tua ? et justitia tua in terra oblivionis ?

87:14 Et ego ad te, Domine, clamavi, et mane oratio mea præveniet te.

87:15 Ut quid, Domine, repellis orationem meam ; avertis faciem tuam a me ?

87:16 Pauper sum ego, et in laboribus a juventute mea ; exaltatus autem, humiliatus sum et conturbatus.

87:17 In me transierunt iræ tuæ, et terrores tui conturbaverunt me :

87:18 circumdederunt me sicut aqua tota die ; circumdederunt me simul.

87:19 Elongasti a me amicum et proximum, et notos meos a miseria.

87:13 Shall thy wonders be known in the dark; and thy justice in the land of forgetfulness?

87:14 But I, O Lord, have cried to thee: and in the morning my prayer shall prevent thee.

87:15 Lord, why castest thou off my prayer: why turnest thou away thy face from me?

87:16 I am poor, and in labours from my youth: and being exalted have been humbled and troubled.

87:17 Thy wrath hath come upon me: and thy terrors have troubled me.

87:18 They have come round about me like water all the day: they have compassed me about together.

87:19 Friend and neighbour thou hast put far from me: and my acquaintance, because of misery.

LXXXVIII.

88:1 *Intellectus Ethan Ezrahitæ.*

88:2 MISERICORDIAS DOMINI in æternum cantabo ; in generationem et generationem annuntiabo veritatem tuam in ore meo.

88:3 Quoniam dixisti : In æternum misericordia ædificabitur in cælis ; præparabitur veritas tua in eis.

88:4 Disposui testamentum electis meis ; juravi David servo meo :

88:5 Usque in æternum præparabo semen tuum, et ædificabo in generationem et generationem sedem tuam.

88:6 Confitebuntur cæli mirabilia tua, Domine ; etenim veritatem tuam in ecclesia sanctorum.

88:7 Quoniam quis in nubibus æquabitur Domino ; similis erit Deo in filiis Dei ?

88:8 Deus, qui glorificatur in consilio sanctorum, magnus et terribilis super omnes qui in circuitu ejus sunt.

88:9 Domine Deus virtutum, quis similis tibi ? potens es, Domine, et veritas tua in circuitu tuo.

88:10 Tu dominaris potestati maris ; motum autem fluctuum ejus tu mitigas.

88:11 Tu humiliasti, sicut vulneratum, superbum ; in brachio virtutis tuæ dispersisti inimicos tuos.

88:12 Tui sunt cæli, et tua est terra : orbem terræ, et plenitudinem ejus tu fundasti ;

88:13 aquilonem et mare tu creasti. Thabor et Hermon in nomine tuo exsultabunt :

88:1 *Of understanding, for Ethan the Ezrahite.*

88:2 THE MERCIES OF THE LORD I will sing for ever. I will shew forth thy truth with my mouth to generation and generation.

88:3 For thou hast said: Mercy shall be built up for ever in the heavens: thy truth shall be prepared in them.

88:4 I have made a covenant with my elect: I have sworn to David my servant:

88:5 Thy seed will I settle for ever. And I will build up thy throne unto generation and generation.

88:6 The heavens shall confess thy wonders, O Lord: and thy truth in the church of the saints.

88:7 For who in the clouds can be compared to the Lord: or who among the sons of God shall be like to God?

88:8 God, who is glorified in the assembly of the saints: great and terrible above all them that are about him.

88:9 O Lord God of hosts, who is like to thee? thou art mighty, O Lord, and thy truth is round about thee.

88:10 Thou rulest the power of the sea: and appeasest the motion of the waves thereof.

88:11 Thou hast humbled the proud one, as one that is slain: with the arm of thy strength thou hast scattered thy enemies.

88:12 Thine are the heavens, and thine is the earth: the world and the fulness thereof thou hast founded:

88:13 the north and the sea thou hast created. Thabor and Hermon shall rejoice in thy name:

88:14 tuum brachium cum potentia. Firmetur manus tua, et exaltetur dextera tua :

88:15 justitia et judicium præparatio sedis tuæ : misericordia et veritas præcedent faciem tuam.

88:16 Beatus populus qui scit jubilationem : Domine, in lumine vultus tui ambulabunt,

88:17 et in nomine tuo exsultabunt tota die, et in justitia tua exaltabuntur.

88:18 Quoniam gloria virtutis eorum tu es, et in beneplacito tuo exaltabitur cornu nostrum.

88:19 Quia Domini est assumptio nostra, et sancti Israël regis nostri.

88:20 Tunc locutus es in visione sanctis tuis, et dixisti : Posui adjutorium in potente, et exaltavi electum de plebe mea.

88:21 Inveni David, servum meum ; oleo sancto meo unxi eum.

88:22 Manus enim mea auxiliabitur ei, et brachium meum confortabit eum.

88:23 Nihil proficiet inimicus in eo, et filius iniquitatis non apponet nocere ei.

88:24 Et concidam a facie ipsius inimicos ejus, et odientes eum in fugam convertam.

88:25 Et veritas mea et misericordia mea cum ipso, et in nomine meo exaltabitur cornu ejus.

88:26 Et ponam in mari manum ejus, et in fluminibus dexteram ejus.

88:27 Ipse invocabit me : Pater meus es tu, Deus meus, et susceptor salutis meæ.

88:28 Et ego primogenitum ponam illum, excelsum præ regibus terræ.

88:29 In æternum servabo illi misericordiam meam, et testamentum meum fidele ipsi.

88:30 Et ponam in sæculum sæculi semen ejus, et thronum ejus sicut dies cæli.

88:31 Si autem dereliquerint filii ejus legem meam, et in judiciis meis non ambulaverint ;

88:32 si justitias meas profanaverint, et mandata mea non custodierint :

88:33 visitabo in virga iniquitates eorum, et in verberibus peccata eorum ;

88:34 misericordiam autem meam non dispergam ab eo, neque nocebo in veritate mea,

88:35 neque profanabo testamentum meum : et quæ procedunt de labiis meis non faciam irrita.

88:14 thy arm is with might. Let thy hand be strengthened, and thy right hand exalted:

88:15 justice and judgment are the preparation of thy throne. Mercy and truth shall go before thy face:

88:16 blessed is the people that knoweth jubilation. They shall walk, O Lord, in the light of thy countenance:

88:17 and in thy name they shall rejoice all the day, and in thy justice they shall be exalted.

88:18 For thou art the glory of their strength: and in thy good pleasure shall our horn be exalted.

88:19 For our protection is of the Lord, and of our king the holy one of Israel.

88:20 Then thou spokest in a vision to thy saints, and saidst: I have laid help upon one that is mighty, and have exalted one chosen out of my people.

88:21 I have found David my servant: with my holy oil I have anointed him.

88:22 For my hand shall help him: and my arm shall strengthen him.

88:23 The enemy shall have no advantage over him: nor the son of iniquity have power to hurt him.

88:24 And I will cut down his enemies before his face; and them that hate him I will put to flight.

88:25 And my truth and my mercy shall be with him: and in my name shall his horn be exalted.

88:26 And I will set his hand in the sea; and his right hand in the rivers.

88:27 He shall cry out to me: Thou art my father: my God, and the support of my salvation.

88:28 And I will make him my firstborn, high above the kings of the earth.

88:29 I will keep my mercy for him for ever: and my covenant faithful to him.

88:30 And I will make his seed to endure for evermore: and his throne as the days of heaven.

88:31 And if his children forsake my law, and walk not in my judgments:

88:32 If they profane my justices: and keep not my commandments:

88:33 I will visit their iniquities with a rod: and their sins with stripes.

88:34 But my mercy I will not take away from him: nor will I suffer my truth to fail.

88:35 Neither will I profane my covenant: and the words that proceed from my mouth I will not make void.

88:36 Semel juravi in sancto meo, si David mentiar :

88:37 semen ejus in æternum manebit. Et thronus ejus sicut sol in conspectu meo,

88:38 et sicut luna perfecta in æternum, et testis in cælo fidelis.

88:39 Tu vero repulisti et despexisti ; distulisti christum tuum.

88:40 Evertisti testamentum servi tui ; profanasti in terra sanctuarium ejus.

88:41 Destruxisti omnes sepes ejus ; posuisti firmamentum ejus formidinem.

88:42 Diripuerunt eum omnes transeuntes viam ; factus est opprobrium vicinis suis.

88:43 Exaltasti dexteram deprimentium eum ; lætificasti omnes inimicos ejus.

88:44 Avertisti adjutorium gladii ejus, et non es auxiliatus ei in bello.

88:45 Destruxisti eum ab emundatione, et sedem ejus in terram collisisti.

88:46 Minorasti dies temporis ejus ; perfudisti eum confusione.

88:47 Usquequo, Domine, avertis in finem ? exardescet sicut ignis ira tua ?

88:48 Memorare quæ mea substantia : numquid enim vane constituisti omnes filios hominum ?

88:49 Quis est homo qui vivet et non videbit mortem ? eruet animam suam de manu inferi ?

88:50 Ubi sunt misericordiæ tuæ antiquæ, Domine, sicut jurasti David in veritate tua ?

88:51 Memor esto, Domine, opprobrii servorum tuorum, quod continui in sinu meo, multarum gentium :

88:52 quod exprobraverunt inimici tui, Domine ; quod exprobraverunt commutationem christi tui.

88:53 Benedictus Dominus in æternum. Fiat, fiat.

88:36 Once have I sworn by my holiness: I will not lie unto David:

88:37 his seed shall endure for ever.

88:38 And his throne as the sun before me: and as the moon perfect for ever, and a faithful witness in heaven.

88:39 But thou hast rejected and despised: thou hast been angry with thy anointed.

88:40 Thou hast overthrown the covenant of thy servant: thou hast profaned his sanctuary on the earth.

88:41 Thou hast broken down all his hedges: thou hast made his strength fear.

88:42 All that pass by the way have robbed him: he is become a reproach to his neighbours.

88:43 Thou hast set up the right hand of them that oppress him: thou hast made all his enemies to rejoice.

88:44 Thou hast turned away the help of his sword; and hast not assisted him in battle.

88:45 Thou hast made his purification to cease: and thou hast cast his throne down to the ground.

88:46 Thou hast shortened the days of his time: thou hast covered him with confusion.

88:47 How long, O Lord, turnest thou away unto the end? shall thy anger burn like fire?

88:48 Remember what my substance is: for hast thou made all the children of men in vain?

88:49 Who is the man that shall live, and not see death: that shall deliver his soul from the hand of hell?

88:50 Lord, where are thy ancient mercies, according to what thou didst swear to David in thy truth?

88:51 Be mindful, O Lord, of the reproach of thy servants (which I have held in my bosom) of many nations:

88:52 Wherewith thy enemies have reproached, O Lord; wherewith they have reproached the change of thy anointed.

88:53 Blessed be the Lord for evermore. So be it. So be it.

LXXXIX.

89:1 *Oratio Moysi, hominis Dei.* DOMINE, REFUGIUM FACTUS ES NOBIS a generatione in generationem.

89:2 Priusquam montes fierent, aut formaretur terra et orbis, a sæculo et usque in sæculum tu es, Deus.

89:1 *A prayer of Moses the man of God.* LORD, THOU HAST BEEN OUR REFUGE from generation to generation.

89:2 Before the mountains were made, or the earth and the world was formed; from eternity and to eternity thou art God.

89:3 Ne avertas hominem in humilitatem : et dixisti : Convertimini, filii hominum.

89:4 Quoniam mille anni ante oculos tuos tamquam dies hesterna quæ præteriit : et custodia in nocte
89:5 quæ pro nihilo habentur, eorum anni erunt.

89:6 Mane sicut herba transeat ; mane floreat, et transeat ; vespere decidat, induret, et arescat.

89:7 Quia deficimus in ira tua, et in furore tuo turbati sumus.
89:8 Posuisti iniquitates nostras in conspectu tuo ; sæculum nostrum in illuminatione vultus tui.
89:9 Quoniam omnes dies nostri defecerunt, et in ira tua defecimus. Anni nostri sicut aranea meditabuntur ;
89:10 dies annorum nostrorum in ipsis septuaginta anni. Si autem in potentatibus octoginta anni, et amplius eorum labor et dolor ; quoniam supervenit mansuetudo, et corripiemur.
89:11 Quis novit potestatem iræ tuæ, et præ timore tuo iram tuam
89:12 dinumerare ? Dexteram tuam sic notam fac, et eruditos corde in sapientia.

89:13 Convertere, Domine ; usquequo ? et deprecabilis esto super servos tuos.
89:14 Repleti sumus mane misericordia tua ; et exsultavimus, et delectati sumus omnibus diebus nostris.
89:15 Lætati sumus pro diebus quibus nos humiliasti ; annis quibus vidimus mala.

89:16 Respice in servos tuos et in opera tua, et dirige filios eorum.
89:17 Et sit splendor Domini Dei nostri super nos, et opera manuum nostrarum dirige super nos, et opus manuum nostrarum dirige.

89:3 Turn not man away to be brought low: and thou hast said: Be converted, O ye sons of men.

89:4 For a thousand years in thy sight are as yesterday, which is past. And as a watch in the night,
89:5 things that are counted nothing, shall their years be.

89:6 In the morning man shall grow up like grass; in the morning he shall flourish and pass away: in the evening he shall fall, grow dry, and wither.
89:7 For in thy wrath we have fainted away: and are troubled in thy indignation.
89:8 Thou hast set our iniquities before thy eyes: our life in the light of thy countenance.

89:9 For all our days are spent; and in thy wrath we have fainted away. Our years shall be considered as a spider:
89:10 the days of our years in them are threescore and ten years. But if in the strong they be fourscore years: and what is more of them is labour and sorrow. For mildness is come upon us: and we shall be corrected.
89:11 Who knoweth the power of thy anger, and for thy fear
89:12 can number thy wrath? So make thy right hand known: and men learned in heart, in wisdom.

89:13 Return, O Lord, how long? and be entreated in favour of thy servants.
89:14 We are filled in the morning with thy mercy: and we have rejoiced, and are delighted all our days.
89:15 We have rejoiced for the days in which thou hast humbled us: for the years in which we have seen evils.

89:16 Look upon thy servants and upon their works: and direct their children.
89:17 And let the brightness of the Lord our God be upon us: and direct thou the works of our hands over us; yea, the work of our hands do thou direct.

XC.

90:1 *Laus cantici David.* QUI HABITAT in adjutorio Altissimi, in protectione Dei cæli commorabitur.

90:2 Dicet Domino : Susceptor meus es tu, et refugium meum ; Deus meus, sperabo in eum.

90:1 *The praise of a canticle for David.* HE THAT DWELLETH in the aid of the most High, shall abide under the protection of the God of Jacob.

90:2 He shall say to the Lord: Thou art my protector, and my refuge: my God, in him will I

90:3 Quoniam ipse liberavit me de laqueo venantium, et a verbo aspero.

90:4 Scapulis suis obumbrabit tibi, et sub pennis ejus sperabis.

90:5 Scuto circumdabit te veritas ejus : non timebis a timore nocturno ;

90:6 a sagitta volante in die, a negotio perambulante in tenebris, ab incursu, et dæmonio meridiano.

90:7 Cadent a latere tuo mille, et decem millia a dextris tuis ; ad te autem non appropinquabit.

90:8 Verumtamen oculis tuis considerabis, et retributionem peccatorum videbis.

90:9 Quoniam tu es, Domine, spes mea ; Altissimum posuisti refugium tuum.

90:10 Non accedet ad te malum, et flagellum non appropinquabit tabernaculo tuo.

90:11 Quoniam angelis suis mandavit de te, ut custodiant te in omnibus viis tuis.

90:12 In manibus portabunt te, ne forte offendas ad lapidem pedem tuum.

90:13 Super aspidem et basiliscum ambulabis, et conculcabis leonem et draconem.

90:14 Quoniam in me speravit, liberabo eum ; protegam eum, quoniam cognovit nomen meum.

90:15 Clamabit ad me, et ego exaudiam eum ; cum ipso sum in tribulatione : eripiam eum, et glorificabo eum.

90:16 Longitudine dierum replebo eum, et ostendam illi salutare meum.

trust.

90:3 For he hath delivered me from the snare of the hunters: and from the sharp word.

90:4 He will overshadow thee with his shoulders: and under his wings thou shalt trust.

90:5 His truth shall compass thee with a shield: thou shalt not be afraid of the terror of the night.

90:6 Of the arrow that flieth in the day, of the business that walketh about in the dark: of invasion, or of the noonday devil.

90:7 A thousand shall fall at thy side, and ten thousand at thy right hand: but it shall not come nigh thee.

90:8 But thou shalt consider with thy eyes: and shalt see the reward of the wicked.

90:9 Because thou, O Lord, art my hope: thou hast made the most High thy refuge.

90:10 There shall no evil come to thee: nor shall the scourge come near thy dwelling.

90:11 For he hath given his angels charge over thee; to keep thee in all thy ways.

90:12 In their hands they shall bear thee up: lest thou dash thy foot against a stone.

90:13 Thou shalt walk upon the asp and the basilisk: and thou shalt trample under foot the lion and the dragon.

90:14 Because he hoped in me I will deliver him: I will protect him because he hath known my name.

90:15 He shall cry to me, and I will hear him: I am with him in tribulation, I will deliver him, and I will glorify him.

90:16 I will fill him with length of days; and I will shew him my salvation.

XCI.

91:1 *Psalmus cantici, in die sabbati.*

91:2 BONUM EST CONFITERI Domino, et psallere nomini tuo, Altissime :

91:3 ad annuntiandum mane misericordiam tuam, et veritatem tuam per noctem,

91:4 in decachordo, psalterio ; cum cantico, in cithara.

91:5 Quia delectasti me, Domine, in factura tua ; et in operibus manuum tuarum exsultabo.

91:6 Quam magnificata sunt opera tua, Domine ! nimis profundæ factæ sunt cogitationes tuæ.

91:7 Vir insipiens non cognoscet, et stultus non intelliget hæc.

91:8 Cum exorti fuerint peccatores sicut

91:1 *A psalm of a canticle on the sabbath day.*

91:2 IT IS GOOD TO GIVE PRAISE to the Lord: and to sing to thy name, O most High.

91:3 To shew forth thy mercy in the morning, and thy truth in the night:

91:4 Upon an instrument of ten strings, upon the psaltery: with a canticle upon the harp.

91:5 For thou hast given me, O Lord, a delight in thy doings: and in the works of thy hands I shall rejoice.

91:6 O Lord, how great are thy works! thy thoughts are exceeding deep.

91:7 The senseless man shall not know: nor will the fool understand these things.

91:8 When the wicked shall spring up as grass:

fœnum, et apparuerint omnes qui operantur iniquitatem, ut intereant in sæculum sæculi : 91:9 tu autem Altissimus in æternum, Domine.

91:10 Quoniam ecce inimici tui, Domine, quoniam ecce inimici tui peribunt ; et dispergentur omnes qui operantur iniquitatem.
91:11 Et exaltabitur sicut unicornis cornu meum, et senectus mea in misericordia uberi.
91:12 Et despexit oculus meus inimicos meos, et in insurgentibus in me malignantibus audiet auris mea.
91:13 Justus ut palma florebit ; sicut cedrus Libani multiplicabitur.
91:14 Plantati in domo Domini, in atriis domus Dei nostri florebunt.

91:15 Adhuc multiplicabuntur in senecta uberi, et bene patientes erunt :
91:16 ut annuntient quoniam rectus Dominus Deus noster, et non est iniquitas in eo.

and all the workers of iniquity shall appear: That they may perish for ever and ever:
91:9 but thou, O Lord, art most high for evermore.

91:10 For behold thy enemies, O Lord, for behold thy enemies shall perish: and all the workers of iniquity shall be scattered.
91:11 But my horn shall be exalted like that of the unicorn: and my old age in plentiful mercy.
91:12 My eye also hath looked down upon my enemies: and my ear shall hear of the downfall of the malignant that rise up against me.
91:13 The just shall flourish like the palm tree: he shall grow up like the cedar of Libanus.
91:14 They that are planted in the house of the Lord shall flourish in the courts of the house of our God.
91:15 They shall still increase in a fruitful old age: and shall be well treated,
91:16 that they may shew, That the Lord our God is righteous, and there is no iniquity in him.

XCII.

92:1 *Laus cantici ipsi David, in die ante sabbatum, quando fundata est terra.* DOMINUS REGNAVIT, decorem indutus est : indutus est Dominus fortitudinem, et præcinxit se. Etenim firmavit orbem terræ, qui non commovebitur.

92:2 Parata sedes tua ex tunc ; a sæculo tu es.

92:3 Elevaverunt flumina, Domine, elevaverunt flumina vocem suam ; elevaverunt flumina fluctus suos,
92:4 a vocibus aquarum multarum. Mirabiles elationes maris ; mirabilis in altis Dominus.

92:5 Testimonia tua credibilia facta sunt nimis ; domum tuam decet sanctitudo, Domine, in longitudinem dierum.

92:1 *Praise in the way of a canticle, for David himself, on the day before the sabbath, when the earth was founded.* THE LORD HATH REIGNED, he is clothed with beauty: the Lord is clothed with strength, and hath girded himself. For he hath established the world which shall not be moved.

92:2 Thy throne is prepared from of old: thou art from everlasting.

92:3 The floods have lifted up, O Lord: the floods have lifted up their voice. The floods have lifted up their waves,
92:4 with the noise of many waters. Wonderful are the surges of the sea: wonderful is the Lord on high.

92:5 Thy testimonies are become exceedingly credible: holiness becometh thy house, O Lord, unto length of days.

XCIII.

93:1 *Psalmus ipsi David, quarta sabbati.* DEUS ULTIONUM DOMINUS ; Deus ultionum libere egit.

93:2 Exaltare, qui judicas terram ; redde retributionem superbis.
93:3 Usquequo peccatores, Domine, usquequo peccatores gloriabuntur ;
93:4 effabuntur et loquentur iniquitatem ; lo-

93:1 *A psalm for David himself on the fourth day of the week.* THE LORD IS THE GOD to whom revenge belongeth: the God of revenge hath acted freely.

93:2 Lift up thyself, thou that judgest the earth: render a reward to the proud.
93:3 How long shall sinners, O Lord: how long shall sinners glory?
93:4 Shall they utter, and speak iniquity: shall all

93:5 Populum tuum, Domine, humiliaverunt, et hæreditatem tuam vexaverunt.

93:6 Viduam et advenam interfecerunt, et pupillos occiderunt.

93:7 Et dixerunt : Non videbit Dominus, nec intelliget Deus Jacob.

93:8 Intelligite, insipientes in populo ; et stulti, aliquando sapite.

93:9 Qui plantavit aurem non audiet ? aut qui finxit oculum non considerat ?

93:10 Qui corripit gentes non arguet, qui docet hominem scientiam ?

93:11 Dominus scit cogitationes hominum, quoniam vanæ sunt.

93:12 Beatus homo quem tu erudieris, Domine, et de lege tua docueris eum :

93:13 ut mitiges ei a diebus malis, donec fodiatur peccatori fovea.

93:14 Quia non repellet Dominus plebem suam, et hæreditatem suam non derelinquet,

93:15 quoadusque justitia convertatur in judicium : et qui juxta illam, omnes qui recto sunt corde.

93:16 Quis consurget mihi adversus malignantes ? aut quis stabit mecum adversus operantes iniquitatem ?

93:17 Nisi quia Dominus adjuvit me, paulominus habitasset in inferno anima mea.

93:18 Si dicebam : Motus est pes meus : misericordia tua, Domine, adjuvabat me.

93:19 Secundum multitudinem dolorum meorum in corde meo, consolationes tuæ lætificaverunt animam meam.

93:20 Numquid adhæret tibi sedes iniquitatis, qui fingis laborem in præcepto ?

93:21 Captabunt in animam justi, et sanguinem innocentem condemnabunt.

93:22 Et factus est mihi Dominus in refugium, et Deus meus in adjutorium spei meæ.

93:23 Et reddet illis iniquitatem ipsorum, et in malitia eorum disperdet eos : disperdet illos Dominus Deus noster.

speak who work injustice?

93:5 Thy people, O Lord, they have brought low: and they have afflicted thy inheritance.

93:6 They have slain the widow and the stranger: and they have murdered the fatherless.

93:7 And they have said: The Lord shall not see: neither shall the God of Jacob understand.

93:8 Understand, ye senseless among the people: and, you fools, be wise at last.

93:9 He that planted the ear, shall he not hear? or he that formed the eye, doth he not consider?

93:10 He that chastiseth nations, shall he not rebuke: he that teacheth man knowledge?

93:11 The Lord knoweth the thoughts of men, that they are vain.

93:12 Blessed is the man whom thou shalt instruct, O Lord: and shalt teach him out of thy law.

93:13 That thou mayst give him rest from the evil days: till a pit be dug for the wicked.

93:14 For the Lord will not cast off his people: neither will he forsake his own inheritance.

93:15 Until justice be turned into judgment: and they that are near it are all the upright in heart.

93:16 Who shall rise up for me against the evildoers? or who shall stand with me against the workers of iniquity?

93:17 Unless the Lord had been my helper, my soul had almost dwelt in hell.

93:18 If I said: My foot is moved: thy mercy, O Lord, assisted me.

93:19 According to the multitude of my sorrows in my heart, thy comforts have given joy to my soul.

93:20 Doth the seat of iniquity stick to thee, who framest labour in commandment?

93:21 They will hunt after the soul of the just, and will condemn innocent blood.

93:22 But the Lord is my refuge: and my God the help of my hope.

93:23 And he will render them their iniquity: and in their malice he will destroy them: the Lord our God will destroy them.

XCIV.

94:1 *Laus cantici ipsi David.* VENITE, EXSULTEMUS DOMINO ; jubilemus Deo salutari nostro ;

94:2 præoccupemus faciem ejus in confessione, et in psalmis jubilemus ei :

94:1 *Praise of a canticle for David himself.* COME LET US PRAISE THE LORD with joy: let us joyfully sing to God our saviour.

94:2 Let us come before his presence with thanksgiving; and make a joyful noise to him

94:3 quoniam Deus magnus Dominus, et rex magnus super omnes deos.

94:4 Quia in manu ejus sunt omnes fines terræ, et altitudines montium ipsius sunt ;

94:5 quoniam ipsius est mare, et ipse fecit illud, et siccam manus ejus formaverunt.

94:6 Venite, adoremus, et procidamus, et ploremus ante Dominum qui fecit nos :

94:7 quia ipse est Dominus Deus noster, et nos populus pascuæ ejus, et oves manus ejus.

94:8 Hodie si vocem ejus audieritis, nolite obdurare corda vestra

94:9 sicut in irritatione, secundum diem tentationis in deserto, ubi tentaverunt me patres vestri : probaverunt me, et viderunt opera mea.

94:10 Quadraginta annis offensus fui generationi illi, et dixi : Semper hi errant corde.

94:11 Et isti non cognoverunt vias meas : ut juravi in ira mea : Si introibunt in requiem meam.

94:3 For the Lord is a great God, and a great King above all gods.

94:4 For in his hand are all the ends of the earth: and the heights of the mountains are his.

94:5 For the sea is his, and he made it: and his hands formed the dry land.

94:6 Come let us adore and fall down: and weep before the Lord that made us.

94:7 For he is the Lord our God: and we are the people of his pasture and the sheep of his hand.

94:8 To day if you shall hear his voice, harden not your hearts:

94:9 As in the provocation, according to the day of temptation in the wilderness: where your fathers tempted me, they proved me, and saw my works.

94:10 Forty years long was I offended with that generation, and I said: These always err in heart.

94:11 And these men have not known my ways: so I swore in my wrath that they shall not enter into my rest.

XCV.

95:1 *Canticum ipsi David, quando domus ædificabatur post captivitatem.* CANTATE DOMINO canticum novum ; cantate Domino omnis terra.

95:2 Cantate Domino, et benedicite nomini ejus ; annuntiate de die in diem salutare ejus.

95:3 Annuntiate inter gentes gloriam ejus ; in omnibus populis mirabilia ejus.

95:4 Quoniam magnus Dominus, et laudabilis nimis : terribilis est super omnes deos.

95:5 Quoniam omnes dii gentium dæmonia ; Dominus autem cælos fecit.

95:6 Confessio et pulchritudo in conspectu ejus ; sanctimonia et magnificentia in sanctificatione ejus.

95:7 Afferte Domino, patriæ gentium, afferte Domino gloriam et honorem ;

95:8 afferte Domino gloriam nomini ejus. Tollite hostias, et introite in atria ejus ;

95:9 adorate Dominum in atrio sancto ejus. Commoveatur a facie ejus universa terra ;

95:10 dicite in gentibus, quia Dominus regnavit. Etenim correxit orbem terræ, qui non commovebitur ; judicabit populos in æquitate.

95:11 Lætentur cæli, et exsultet terra ; commoveatur mare et plenitudo ejus ;

95:1 *A canticle for David himself, when the house was built after the captivity.* SING YE TO THE LORD a new canticle: sing to the Lord, all the earth.

95:2 Sing ye to the Lord and bless his name: shew forth his salvation from day to day.

95:3 Declare his glory among the Gentiles: his wonders among all people.

95:4 For the Lord is great, and exceedingly to be praised: he is to be feared above all gods.

95:5 For all the gods of the Gentiles are devils: but the Lord made the heavens.

95:6 Praise and beauty are before him: holiness and majesty in his sanctuary.

95:7 Bring ye to the Lord, O ye kindreds of the Gentiles, bring ye to the Lord glory and honour:

95:8 bring to the Lord glory unto his name. Bring up sacrifices, and come into his courts:

95:9 adore ye the Lord in his holy court. Let all the earth be moved at his presence.

95:10 Say ye among the Gentiles, the Lord hath reigned. For he hath corrected the world, which shall not be moved: he will judge the people with justice.

95:11 Let the heavens rejoice, and let the earth be glad, let the sea be moved, and the fulness

95:12 gaudebunt campi, et omnia quæ in eis sunt. Tunc exsultabunt omnia ligna silvarum

95:13 a facie Domini, quia venit, quoniam venit judicare terram. Judicabit orbem terræ in æquitate, et populos in veritate sua.

thereof:
95:12 the fields and all things that are in them shall be joyful. Then shall all the trees of the woods rejoice

95:13 before the face of the Lord, because he cometh: because he cometh to judge the earth. He shall judge the world with justice, and the people with his truth.

XCVI.

96:1 *Huic David, quando terra ejus restituta est.* DOMINUS REGNAVIT : exsultet terra ; lætentur insulæ multæ.
96:2 Nubes et caligo in circuitu ejus ; justitia et judicium correctio sedis ejus.

96:3 Ignis ante ipsum præcedet, et inflammabit in circuitu inimicos ejus.
96:4 Illuxerunt fulgura ejus orbi terræ ; vidit, et commota est terra.
96:5 Montes sicut cera fluxerunt a facie Domini ; a facie Domini omnis terra.

96:6 Annuntiaverunt cæli justitiam ejus, et viderunt omnes populi gloriam ejus.
96:7 Confundantur omnes qui adorant sculptilia, et qui gloriantur in simulacris suis. Adorate eum omnes angeli ejus.
96:8 Audivit, et lætata est Sion, et exsultaverunt filiæ Judæ propter judicia tua, Domine.

96:9 Quoniam tu Dominus altissimus super omnem terram ; nimis exaltatus es super omnes deos.
96:10 Qui diligitis Dominum, odite malum : custodit Dominus animas sanctorum suorum ; de manu peccatoris liberabit eos.
96:11 Lux orta est justo, et rectis corde lætitia.

96:12 Lætamini, justi, in Domino, et confitemini memoriæ sanctificationis ejus.

96:1 *For the same David, when his land was restored again to him.* THE LORD HATH REIGNED, let the earth rejoice: let many islands be glad.
96:2 Clouds and darkness are round about him: justice and judgment are the establishment of his throne.
96:3 A fire shall go before him, and shall burn his enemies round about.
96:4 His lightnings have shone forth to the world: the earth saw and trembled.
96:5 The mountains melted like wax, at the presence of the Lord: at the presence of the Lord of all the earth.
96:6 The heavens declared his justice: and all people saw his glory.
96:7 Let them be all confounded that adore graven things, and that glory in their idols. Adore him, all you his angels:
96:8 Sion heard, and was glad. And the daughters of Juda rejoiced, because of thy judgments, O Lord.
96:9 For thou art the most high Lord over all the earth: thou art exalted exceedingly above all gods.
96:10 You that love the Lord, hate evil: the Lord preserveth the souls of his saints, he will deliver them out of the hand of the sinner.
96:11 Light is risen to the just, and joy to the right of heart.
96:12 Rejoice, ye just, in the Lord: and give praise to the remembrance of his holiness.

XCVII.

97:1 *Psalmus ipsi David.* CANTATE DOMINO canticum novum, quia mirabilia fecit. Salvavit sibi dextera ejus, et brachium sanctum ejus.

97:2 Notum fecit Dominus salutare suum ; in conspectu gentium revelavit justitiam suam.

97:3 Recordatus est misericordiæ suæ, et veritatis suæ domui Israël. Viderunt omnes termini

97:1 *A psalm for David himself.* SING YE TO THE LORD a new canticle: because he hath done wonderful things. His right hand hath wrought for him salvation, and his arm is holy.
97:2 The Lord hath made known his salvation: he hath revealed his justice in the sight of the Gentiles.
97:3 He hath remembered his mercy and his truth toward the house of Israel. All the ends of

terræ salutare Dei nostri.

97:4 Jubilate Deo, omnis terra ; cantate, et exsultate, et psallite.

97:5 Psallite Domino in cithara ; in cithara et voce psalmi ;

97:6 in tubis ductilibus, et voce tubæ corneæ. Jubilate in conspectu regis Domini :

97:7 moveatur mare, et plenitudo ejus ; orbis terrarum, et qui habitant in eo.

97:8 Flumina plaudent manu ; simul montes exsultabunt

97:9 a conspectu Domini : quoniam venit judicare terram. Judicabit orbem terrarum in justitia, et populos in æquitate.

the earth have seen the salvation of our God.

97:4 Sing joyfully to God, all the earth; make melody, rejoice and sing.

97:5 Sing praise to the Lord on the harp, on the harp, and with the voice of a psalm:

97:6 with long trumpets, and sound of cornet. Make a joyful noise before the Lord our king:

97:7 let the sea be moved and the fulness thereof: the world and they that dwell therein.

97:8 The rivers shall clap their hands, the mountains shall rejoice together

97:9 at the presence of the Lord: because he cometh to judge the earth. He shall judge the world with justice, and the people with equity.

XCVIII.

98:1 *Psalmus ipsi David.* DOMINUS REGNAVIT : irascantur populi ; qui sedet super cherubim : moveatur terra.

98:2 Dominus in Sion magnus, et excelsus super omnes populos.

98:3 Confiteantur nomini tuo magno, quoniam terribile et sanctum est,

98:4 et honor regis judicium diligit. Tu parasti directiones ; judicium et justitiam in Jacob tu fecisti.

98:5 Exaltate Dominum Deum nostrum, et adorate scabellum pedum ejus, quoniam sanctum est.

98:6 Moyses et Aaron in sacerdotibus ejus, et Samuel inter eos qui invocant nomen ejus : invocabant Dominum, et ipse exaudiebat eos ;

98:7 in columna nubis loquebatur ad eos. Custodiebant testimonia ejus, et præceptum quod dedit illis.

98:8 Domine Deus noster, tu exaudiebas eos ; Deus, tu propitius fuisti eis, et ulciscens in omnes adinventiones eorum.

98:9 Exaltate Dominum Deum nostrum, et adorate in monte sancto ejus, quoniam sanctus Dominus Deus noster.

98:1 *A psalm for David himself.* THE LORD HATH REIGNED, let the people be angry: he that sitteth on the cherubims: let the earth be moved.

98:2 The Lord is great in Sion, and high above all people.

98:3 Let them give praise to thy great name: for it is terrible and holy:

98:4 and the king's honour loveth judgment. Thou hast prepared directions: thou hast done judgment and justice in Jacob.

98:5 Exalt ye the Lord our God, and adore his footstool, for it is holy.

98:6 Moses and Aaron among his priests: and Samuel among them that call upon his name. They called upon the Lord, and he heard them:

98:7 he spoke to them in the pillar of the cloud. They kept his testimonies, and the commandment which he gave them.

98:8 Thou didst hear them, O Lord our God: thou wast a merciful God to them, and taking vengeance on all their inventions.

98:9 Exalt ye the Lord our God, and adore at his holy mountain: for the Lord our God is holy.

XCIX.

99:1 *Psalmus in confessione.*

99:2 JUBILATE DEO, omnis terra ; servite Domino in lætitia. Introite in conspectu ejus in exsultatione.

99:3 Scitote quoniam Dominus ipse est Deus ; ipse fecit nos, et non ipsi nos : populus ejus, et oves pascuæ ejus.

99:4 Introite portas ejus in confessione ; atria

99:1 *A psalm of praise.*

99:2 SING JOYFULLY TO GOD, all the earth: serve ye the Lord with gladness. Come in before his presence with exceeding great joy.

99:3 Know ye that the Lord he is God: he made us, and not we ourselves. We are his people and the sheep of his pasture.

99:4 Go ye into his gates with praise, into his

ejus in hymnis : confitemini illi. Laudate nomen ejus,
99:5 quoniam suavis est Dominus, in æternum
misericordia ejus, et usque in generationem et
generationem veritas ejus.

courts with hymns: and give glory to him.
Praise ye his name:
99:5 for the Lord is sweet, his mercy endureth
for ever, and his truth to generation and generation.

C.

100:1 *Psalmus ipsi David.* MISERICORDIAM ET JU-
DICIUM cantabo tibi, Domine ; psallam,

100:1 *A psalm for David himself.* MERCY AND
JUDGMENT I will sing to thee, O Lord: I will
sing,

100:2 et intelligam in via immaculata : quando
venies ad me ? Perambulabam in innocentia
cordis mei, in medio domus meæ.

100:2 and I will understand in the unspotted way,
when thou shalt come to me. I walked in the
innocence of my heart, in the midst of my
house.

100:3 Non proponebam ante oculos meos rem
injustam ; facientes prævaricationes odivi ; non
adhæsit mihi
100:4 cor pravum ; declinantem a me malignum
non cognoscebam.

100:3 I did not set before my eyes any unjust
thing: I hated the workers of iniquities.
100:4 The perverse heart did not cleave to me:
and the malignant, that turned aside from me, I
would not know.

100:5 Detrahentem secreto proximo suo, hunc
persequebar : superbo oculo, et insatiabili
corde, cum hoc non edebam.

100:5 The man that in private detracted his
neighbour, him did I persecute. With him that
had a proud eye, and an unsatiable heart, I
would not eat.

100:6 Oculi mei ad fideles terræ, ut sedeant mecum ; ambulans in via immaculata, hic mihi
ministrabat.
100:7 Non habitabit in medio domus meæ qui
facit superbiam ; qui loquitur iniqua non
direxit in conspectu oculorum meorum.
100:8 In matutino interficiebam omnes peccatores terræ, ut disperderem de civitate Domini
omnes operantes iniquitatem.

100:6 My eyes were upon the faithful of the
earth, to sit with me: the man that walked in
the perfect way, he served me.
100:7 He that worketh pride shall not dwell in
the midst of my house: he that speaketh unjust
things did not prosper before my eyes.
100:8 In the morning I put to death all the wicked of the land: that I might cut off all the
workers of iniquity from the city of the Lord.

CI.

101:1 *Oratio pauperis, cum anxius fuerit, et in conspectu Domini effuderit precem suam.*
101:2 DOMINE, EXAUDI ORATIONEM MEAM, et
clamor meus ad te veniat.
101:3 Non avertas faciem tuam a me : in
quacumque die tribulor, inclina ad me aurem
tuam ; in quacumque die invocavero te, velociter exaudi me.
101:4 Quia defecerunt sicut fumus dies mei, et
ossa mea sicut cremium aruerunt.
101:5 Percussus sum ut fœnum, et aruit cor meum, quia oblitus sum comedere panem meum.
101:6 A voce gemitus mei adhæsit os meum carni meæ.
101:7 Similis factus sum pellicano solitudinis ;
factus sum sicut nycticorax in domicilio.
101:8 Vigilavi, et factus sum sicut passer solitari-

101:1 *The prayer of the poor man, when he was anx-
ious, and poured out his supplication before the Lord.*
101:2 HEAR, O LORD, MY PRAYER: and let my
cry come to thee.
101:3 Turn not away thy face from me: in the day
when I am in trouble, incline thy ear to me. In
what day soever I shall call upon thee, hear me
speedily.
101:4 For my days are vanished like smoke: and
my bones are grown dry like fuel for the fire.
101:5 I am smitten as grass, and my heart is
withered: because I forgot to eat my bread.
101:6 Through the voice of my groaning, my
bone hath cleaved to my flesh.
101:7 I am become like to a pelican of the wilderness: I am like a night raven in the house.
101:8 I have watched, and am become as a spar-

us in tecto.

101:9 Tota die exprobrabant mihi inimici mei, et qui laudabant me adversum me jurabant :

101:10 quia cinerem tamquam panem manducabam, et potum meum cum fletu miscebam,

101:11 a facie iræ et indignationis tuæ : quia elevans allisisti me.

101:12 Dies mei sicut umbra declinaverunt, et ego sicut fœnum arui.

101:13 Tu autem, Domine, in æternum permanes, et memoriale tuum in generationem et generationem.

101:14 Tu exsurgens misereberis Sion, quia tempus miserendi ejus, quia venit tempus :

101:15 quoniam placuerunt servis tuis lapides ejus, et terræ ejus miserebuntur.

101:16 Et timebunt gentes nomen tuum, Domine, et omnes reges terræ gloriam tuam :

101:17 quia ædificavit Dominus Sion, et videbitur in gloria sua.

101:18 Respexit in orationem humilium et non sprevit precem eorum.

101:19 Scribantur hæc in generatione altera, et populus qui creabitur laudabit Dominum.

101:20 Quia prospexit de excelso sancto suo ; Dominus de cælo in terram aspexit :

101:21 ut audiret gemitus compeditorum ; ut solveret filios interemptorum :

101:22 ut annuntient in Sion nomen Domini, et laudem ejus in Jerusalem :

101:23 in conveniendo populos in unum, et reges, ut serviant Domino.

101:24 Respondit ei in via virtutis suæ : Paucitatem dierum meorum nuntia mihi :

101:25 ne revoces me in dimidio dierum meorum, in generationem et generationem anni tui.

101:26 Initio tu, Domine, terram fundasti, et opera manuum tuarum sunt cæli.

101:27 Ipsi peribunt, tu autem permanes ; et omnes sicut vestimentum veterascent. Et sicut opertorium mutabis eos, et mutabuntur ;

row all alone on the housetop.

101:9 All the day long my enemies reproached me: and they that praised me did swear against me.

101:10 For I did eat ashes like bread, and mingled my drink with weeping.

101:11 Because of thy anger and indignation: for having lifted me up thou hast thrown me down.

101:12 My days have declined like a shadow, and I am withered like grass.

101:13 But thou, O Lord, endurest for ever: and thy memorial to all generations.

101:14 Thou shalt arise and have mercy on Sion: for it is time to have mercy on it, for the time is come.

101:15 For the stones thereof have pleased thy servants: and they shall have pity on the earth thereof.

101:16 And the Gentiles shall fear thy name, O Lord, and all the kings of the earth thy glory.

101:17 For the Lord hath built up Sion: and he shall be seen in his glory.

101:18 He hath had regard to the prayer of the humble: and he hath not despised their petition.

101:19 Let these things be written unto another generation: and the people that shall be created shall praise the Lord:

101:20 Because he hath looked forth from his high sanctuary: from heaven the Lord hath looked upon the earth.

101:21 That he might hear the groans of them that are in fetters: that he might release the children of the slain:

101:22 That they may declare the name of the Lord in Sion: and his praise in Jerusalem;

101:23 When the people assemble together, and kings, to serve the Lord.

101:24 He answered him in the way of his strength: Declare unto me the fewness of my days.

101:25 Call me not away in the midst of my days: thy years are unto generation and generation.

101:26 In the beginning, O Lord, thou foundedst the earth: and the heavens are the works of thy hands.

101:27 They shall perish but thou remainest: and all of them shall grow old like a garment: And as a vesture thou shalt change them, and they

101:28 tu autem idem ipse es, et anni tui non deficient.

101:29 Filii servorum tuorum habitabunt, et semen eorum in sæculum dirigetur.

shall be changed.

101:28 But thou art always the selfsame, and thy years shall not fail.

101:29 The children of thy servants shall continue: and their seed shall be directed for ever.

CII.

102:1 *Ipsi David.* BENEDIC, ANIMA MEA, DOMINO, et omnia quæ intra me sunt nomini sancto ejus.

102:2 Benedic, anima mea, Domino, et noli oblivisci omnes retributiones ejus.

102:3 Qui propitiatur omnibus iniquitatibus tuis ; qui sanat omnes infirmitates tuas :

102:4 qui redimit de interitu vitam tuam ; qui coronat te in misericordia et miserationibus :

102:5 qui replet in bonis desiderium tuum ; renovabitur ut aquilæ juventus tua :

102:6 faciens misericordias Dominus, et judicium omnibus injuriam patientibus.

102:7 Notas fecit vias suas Moysi ; filiis Israël voluntates suas.

102:8 Miserator et misericors Dominus : longanimis, et multum misericors.

102:9 Non in perpetuum irascetur, neque in æternum comminabitur.

102:10 Non secundum peccata nostra fecit nobis, neque secundum iniquitates nostras retribuit nobis.

102:11 Quoniam secundum altitudinem cæli a terra, corroboravit misericordiam suam super timentes se ;

102:12 quantum distat ortus ab occidente, longe fecit a nobis iniquitates nostras.

102:13 Quomodo miseretur pater filiorum, misertus est Dominus timentibus se.

102:14 Quoniam ipse cognovit figmentum nostrum ; recordatus est quoniam pulvis sumus.

102:15 Homo, sicut fœnum dies ejus ; tamquam flos agri, sic efflorebit :

102:16 quoniam spiritus pertransibit in illo, et non subsistet, et non cognoscet amplius locum suum.

102:17 Misericordia autem Domini ab æterno, et usque in æternum super timentes eum. Et justitia illius in filios filiorum,

102:18 his qui servant testamentum ejus, et memores sunt mandatorum ipsius ad faciendum ea.

102:19 Dominus in cælo paravit sedem suam, et

102:1 *For David himself.* BLESS THE LORD, O MY SOUL: and let all that is within me bless his holy name.

102:2 Bless the Lord, O my soul, and never forget all he hath done for thee.

102:3 Who forgiveth all thy iniquities: who healeth all thy diseases.

102:4 Who redeemeth thy life from destruction: who crowneth thee with mercy and compassion.

102:5 Who satisfieth thy desire with good things: thy youth shall be renewed like the eagle's.

102:6 The Lord doth mercies, and judgment for all that suffer wrong.

102:7 He hath made his ways known to Moses: his wills to the children of Israel.

102:8 The Lord is compassionate and merciful: longsuffering and plenteous in mercy.

102:9 He will not always be angry: nor will he threaten for ever.

102:10 He hath not dealt with us according to our sins: nor rewarded us according to our iniquities.

102:11 For according to the height of the heaven above the earth: he hath strengthened his mercy towards them that fear him.

102:12 As far as the east is from the west, so far hath he removed our iniquities from us.

102:13 As a father hath compassion on his children, so hath the Lord compassion on them that fear him:

102:14 for he knoweth our frame. He remembereth that we are dust:

102:15 man's days are as grass, as the flower of the field so shall he flourish.

102:16 For the spirit shall pass in him, and he shall not be: and he shall know his place no more.

102:17 But the mercy of the Lord is from eternity and unto eternity upon them that fear him: And his justice unto children's children,

102:18 to such as keep his covenant, And are mindful of his commandments to do them.

102:19 The Lord hath prepared his throne in

regnum ipsius omnibus dominabitur.

102:20 Benedicite Domino, omnes angeli ejus : potentes virtute, facientes verbum illius, ad audiendam vocem sermonum ejus.

102:21 Benedicite Domino, omnes virtutes ejus ; ministri ejus, qui facitis voluntatem ejus.

102:22 Benedicite Domino, omnia opera ejus : in omni loco dominationis ejus, benedic, anima mea, Domino.

heaven: and his kingdom shall rule over all.

102:20 Bless the Lord, all ye his angels: you that are mighty in strength, and execute his word, hearkening to the voice of his orders.

102:21 Bless the Lord, all ye his hosts: you ministers of his that do his will.

102:22 Bless the Lord, all his works: in every place of his dominion, O my soul, bless thou the Lord.

CIII.

103:1 *Ipsi David.* BENEDIC, ANIMA MEA, DOMINO : Domine Deus meus, magnificatus es vehementer. Confessionem et decorem induisti,

103:2 amictus lumine sicut vestimento. Extendens cælum sicut pellem,

103:3 qui tegis aquis superiora ejus : qui ponis nubem ascensum tuum ; qui ambulas super pennas ventorum :

103:4 qui facis angelos tuos spiritus, et ministros tuos ignem urentem.

103:5 Qui fundasti terram super stabilitatem suam : non inclinabitur in sæculum sæculi.

103:6 Abyssus sicut vestimentum amictus ejus ; super montes stabunt aquæ.

103:7 Ab increpatione tua fugient ; a voce tonitrui tui formidabunt.

103:8 Ascendunt montes, et descendunt campi, in locum quem fundasti eis.

103:9 Terminum posuisti quem non transgredientur, neque convertentur operire terram.

103:10 Qui emittis fontes in convallibus ; inter medium montium pertransibunt aquæ.

103:11 Potabunt omnes bestiæ agri ; expectabunt onagri in siti sua.

103:12 Super ea volucres cæli habitabunt ; de medio petrarum dabunt voces.

103:13 Rigans montes de superioribus suis ; de fructu operum tuorum satiabitur terra :

103:14 producens fœnum jumentis, et herbam servituti hominum, ut educas panem de terra,

103:15 et vinum lætificet cor hominis : ut exhilaret faciem in oleo, et panis cor hominis confirmet.

103:16 Saturabuntur ligna campi, et cedri Libani

103:1 *For David himself.* BLESS THE LORD, O MY SOUL: O Lord my God, thou art exceedingly great. Thou hast put on praise and beauty:

103:2 and art clothed with light as with a garment. Who stretchest out the heaven like a pavilion:

103:3 who coverest the higher rooms thereof with water. Who makest the clouds thy chariot: who walkest upon the wings of the winds.

103:4 Who makest thy angels spirits: and thy ministers a burning fire.

103:5 Who hast founded the earth upon its own bases: it shall not be moved for ever and ever.

103:6 The deep like a garment is its clothing: above the mountains shall the waters stand.

103:7 At thy rebuke they shall flee: at the voice of thy thunder they shall fear.

103:8 The mountains ascend, and the plains descend into the place which thou hast founded for them.

103:9 Thou hast set a bound which they shall not pass over; neither shall they return to cover the earth.

103:10 Thou sendest forth springs in the vales: between the midst of the hills the waters shall pass.

103:11 All the beasts of the field shall drink: the wild asses shall expect in their thirst.

103:12 Over them the birds of the air shall dwell: from the midst of the rocks they shall give forth their voices.

103:13 Thou waterest the hills from thy upper rooms: the earth shall be filled with the fruit of thy works:

103:14 Bringing forth grass for cattle, and herb for the service of men. That thou mayst bring bread out of the earth:

103:15 and that wine may cheer the heart of man. That he may make the face cheerful with oil: and that bread may strengthen man's heart.

103:16 The trees of the field shall be filled, and

quas plantavit :

103:17 illic passeres nidificabunt : herodii domus dux est eorum.

103:18 Montes excelsi cervis ; petra refugium herinaciis.

103:19 Fecit lunam in tempora ; sol cognovit occasum suum.

103:20 Posuisti tenebras, et facta est nox ; in ipsa pertransibunt omnes bestiæ silvæ :

103:21 catuli leonum rugientes ut rapiant, et quærant a Deo escam sibi.

103:22 Ortus est sol, et congregati sunt, et in cubilibus suis collocabuntur.

103:23 Exibit homo ad opus suum, et ad operationem suam usque ad vesperum.

103:24 Quam magnificata sunt opera tua, Domine ! omnia in sapientia fecisti ; impleta est terra possessione tua.

103:25 Hoc mare magnum et spatiosum manibus ; illic reptilia quorum non est numerus : animalia pusilla cum magnis.

103:26 Illic naves pertransibunt ; draco iste quem formasti ad illudendum ei.

103:27 Omnia a te expectant ut des illis escam in tempore.

103:28 Dante te illis, colligent ; aperiente te manum tuam, omnia implebuntur bonitate.

103:29 Avertente autem te faciem, turbabuntur ; auferes spiritum eorum, et deficient, et in pulverem suum revertentur.

103:30 Emittes spiritum tuum, et creabuntur, et renovabis faciem terræ.

103:31 Sit gloria Domini in sæculum ; lætabitur Dominus in operibus suis.

103:32 Qui respicit terram, et facit eam tremere ; qui tangit montes, et fumigant.

103:33 Cantabo Domino in vita mea ; psallam Deo meo quamdiu sum.

103:34 Jucundum sit ei eloquium meum ; ego vero delectabor in Domino.

103:35 Deficiant peccatores a terra, et iniqui, ita ut non sint. Benedic, anima mea, Domino.

the cedars of Libanus which he hath planted:

103:17 there the sparrows shall make their nests. The highest of them is the house of the heron.

103:18 The high hills are a refuge for the harts, the rock for the irchins.

103:19 He hath made the moon for seasons: the sun knoweth his going down.

103:20 Thou hast appointed darkness, and it is night: in it shall all the beasts of the woods go about:

103:21 The young lions roaring after their prey, and seeking their meat from God.

103:22 The sun ariseth, and they are gathered together: and they shall lie down in their dens.

103:23 Man shall go forth to his work, and to his labour until the evening.

103:24 How great are thy works, O Lord? thou hast made all things in wisdom: the earth is filled with thy riches.

103:25 So is this great sea, which stretcheth wide its arms: there are creeping things without number: Creatures little and great.

103:26 There the ships shall go. This sea dragon which thou hast formed to play therein.

103:27 All expect of thee that thou give them food in season.

103:28 What thou givest to them they shall gather up: when thou openest thy hand, they shall all be filled with good.

103:29 But if thou turnest away thy face, they shall be troubled: thou shalt take away their breath, and they shall fail, and shall return to their dust.

103:30 Thou shalt send forth thy spirit, and they shall be created: and thou shalt renew the face of the earth.

103:31 May the glory of the Lord endure for ever: the Lord shall rejoice in his works.

103:32 He looketh upon the earth, and maketh it tremble: he toucheth the mountains, and they smoke.

103:33 I will sing to the Lord as long as I live: I will sing praise to my God while I have my being.

103:34 Let my speech be acceptable to him: but I will take delight in the Lord.

103:35 Let sinners be consumed out of the earth, and the unjust, so that they be no more: O my soul, bless thou the Lord.

CIV.

104:1 *Alleluja.* CONFITEMINI DOMINO, et invocate nomen ejus ; annuntiate inter gentes opera ejus.

104:2 Cantate ei, et psallite ei ; narrate omnia mirabilia ejus.

104:3 Laudamini in nomine sancto ejus ; lætetur cor quærentium Dominum.

104:4 Quærite Dominum, et confirmamini ; quærite faciem ejus semper.

104:5 Mementote mirabilium ejus quæ fecit ; prodigia ejus, et judicia oris ejus :

104:6 semen Abraham servi ejus ; filii Jacob electi ejus.

104:7 Ipse Dominus Deus noster ; in universa terra judicia ejus.

104:8 Memor fuit in sæculum testamenti sui ; verbi quod mandavit in mille generationes :

104:9 quod disposuit ad Abraham, et juramenti sui ad Isaac :

104:10 et statuit illud Jacob in præceptum, et Israël in testamentum æternum,

104:11 dicens : Tibi dabo terram Chanaan, funiculum hæreditatis vestræ :

104:12 cum essent numero brevi, paucissimi, et incolæ ejus.

104:13 Et pertransierunt de gente in gentem, et de regno ad populum alterum.

104:14 Non reliquit hominem nocere eis : et corripuit pro eis reges.

104:15 Nolite tangere christos meos, et in prophetis meis nolite malignari.

104:16 Et vocavit famem super terram, et omne firmamentum panis contrivit.

104:17 Misit ante eos virum : in servum venundatus est, Joseph.

104:18 Humiliaverunt in compedibus pedes ejus ; ferrum pertransiit animam ejus :

104:19 donec veniret verbum ejus. Eloquium Domini inflammavit eum.

104:20 Misit rex, et solvit eum ; princeps populorum, et dimisit eum.

104:21 Constituit eum dominum domus suæ, et principem omnis possessionis suæ :

104:22 ut erudiret principes ejus sicut semetipsum, et senes ejus prudentiam doceret.

104:23 Et intravit Israël in Ægyptum, et Jacob accola fuit in terra Cham.

104:24 Et auxit populum suum vehementer, et firmavit eum super inimicos ejus.

104:1 *Alleluia.* GIVE GLORY TO THE LORD, and call upon his name: declare his deeds among the Gentiles.

104:2 Sing to him, yea sing praises to him: relate all his wondrous works.

104:3 Glory ye in his holy name: let the heart of them rejoice that seek the Lord.

104:4 Seek ye the Lord, and be strengthened: seek his face evermore.

104:5 Remember his marvellous works which he hath done; his wonders, and the judgments of his mouth.

104:6 O ye seed of Abraham his servant; ye sons of Jacob his chosen.

104:7 He is the Lord our God: his judgments are in all the earth.

104:8 He hath remembered his covenant for ever: the word which he commanded to a thousand generations.

104:9 Which he made to Abraham; and his oath to Isaac:

104:10 And he appointed the same to Jacob for a law, and to Israel for an everlasting testament:

104:11 Saying: To thee will I give the land of Chanaan, the lot of your inheritance.

104:12 When they were but a small number: yea very few, and sojourners therein:

104:13 And they passed from nation to nation, and from one kingdom to another people.

104:14 He suffered no man to hurt them: and he reproved kings for their sakes.

104:15 Touch ye not my anointed: and do no evil to my prophets.

104:16 And he called a famine upon the land: and he broke in pieces all the support of bread.

104:17 He sent a man before them: Joseph, who was sold for a slave.

104:18 They humbled his feet in fetters: the iron pierced his soul,

104:19 until his word came. The word of the Lord inflamed him.

104:20 The king sent, and he released him: the ruler of the people, and he set him at liberty.

104:21 He made him master of his house, and ruler of all his possession.

104:22 That he might instruct his princes as himself, and teach his ancients wisdom.

104:23 And Israel went into Egypt: and Jacob was a sojourner in the land of Cham.

104:24 And he increased his people exceedingly: and strengthened them over their enemies,

104:25 Convertit cor eorum, ut odirent populum ejus, et dolum facerent in servos ejus.

104:26 Misit Moysen servum suum ; Aaron quem elegit ipsum.

104:27 Posuit in eis verba signorum suorum, et prodigiorum in terra Cham.

104:28 Misit tenebras, et obscuravit ; et non exacerbavit sermones suos.

104:29 Convertit aquas eorum in sanguinem, et occidit pisces eorum.

104:30 Edidit terra eorum ranas in penetralibus regum ipsorum.

104:31 Dixit, et venit cœnomyia et ciniphes in omnibus finibus eorum.

104:32 Posuit pluvias eorum grandinem : ignem comburentem in terra ipsorum.

104:33 Et percussit vineas eorum, et ficulneas eorum, et contrivit lignum finium eorum.

104:34 Dixit, et venit locusta, et bruchus cujus non erat numerus :

104:35 et comedit omne fœnum in terra eorum, et comedit omnem fructum terræ eorum.

104:36 Et percussit omne primogenitum in terra eorum, primitias omnis laboris eorum.

104:37 Et eduxit eos cum argento et auro, et non erat in tribubus eorum infirmus.

104:38 Lætata est Ægyptus in profectione eorum, quia incubuit timor eorum super eos.

104:39 Expandit nubem in protectionem eorum, et ignem ut luceret eis per noctem.

104:40 Petierunt, et venit coturnix, et pane cæli saturavit eos.

104:41 Dirupit petram, et fluxerunt aquæ : abierunt in sicco flumina.

104:42 Quoniam memor fuit verbi sancti sui, quod habuit ad Abraham puerum suum.

104:43 Et eduxit populum suum in exsultatione, et electos suos in lætitia.

104:44 Et dedit illis regiones gentium, et labores populorum possederunt :

104:45 ut custodiant justificationes ejus, et legem ejus requirant.

104:25 He turned their heart to hate his people: and to deal deceitfully with his servants.

104:26 He sent Moses his servant: Aaron the man whom he had chosen.

104:27 He gave them power to shew his signs, and his wonders in the land of Cham.

104:28 He sent darkness, and made it obscure: and grieved not his words.

104:29 He turned their waters into blood, and destroyed their fish.

104:30 Their land brought forth frogs, in the inner chambers of their kings.

104:31 He spoke, and there came divers sorts of flies and sciniphs in all their coasts.

104:32 He gave them hail for rain, a burning fire in the land.

104:33 And he destroyed their vineyards and their fig trees: and he broke in pieces the trees of their coasts.

104:34 He spoke, and the locust came, and the bruchus, of which there was no number.

104:35 And they devoured all the grass in their land, and consumed all the fruit of their ground.

104:36 And he slew all the firstborn in their land: the firstfruits of all their labour.

104:37 And he brought them out with silver and gold: and there was not among their tribes one that was feeble.

104:38 Egypt was glad when they departed: for the fear of them lay upon them.

104:39 He spread a cloud for their protection, and fire to give them light in the night.

104:40 They asked, and the quail came: and he filled them with the bread of heaven.

104:41 He opened the rock, and waters flowed: rivers ran down in the dry land.

104:42 Because he remembered his holy word, which he had spoken to his servant Abraham.

104:43 And he brought forth his people with joy, and his chosen with gladness.

104:44 And he gave them the lands of the Gentiles: and they possessed the labours of the people:

104:45 That they might observe his justifications, and seek after his law.

CV.

105:1 *Alleluja.* CONFITEMINI DOMINO, quoniam bonus, quoniam in sæculum misericordia ejus.

105:2 Quis loquetur potentias Domini ; auditas faciet omnes laudes ejus ?

105:1 *Alleluia.* GIVE GLORY TO THE LORD, for he is good: for his mercy endureth for ever.

105:2 Who shall declare the powers of the Lord? who shall set forth all his praises?

105:3 Beati qui custodiunt judicium, et faciunt justitiam in omni tempore.

105:4 Memento nostri, Domine, in beneplacito populi tui ; visita nos in salutari tuo :

105:5 ad videndum in bonitate electorum tuorum ; ad lætandum in lætitia gentis tuæ : ut lauderis cum hæreditate tua.

105:6 Peccavimus cum patribus nostris : injuste egimus ; iniquitatem fecimus.

105:7 Patres nostri in Ægypto non intellexerunt mirabilia tua ; non fuerunt memores multitudinis misericordiæ tuæ. Et irritaverunt ascendentes in mare, mare Rubrum ;

105:8 et salvavit eos propter nomen suum, ut notam faceret potentiam suam.

105:9 Et increpuit mare Rubrum et exsiccatum est, et deduxit eos in abyssis sicut in deserto.

105:10 Et salvavit eos de manu odientium, et redemit eos de manu inimici.

105:11 Et operuit aqua tribulantes eos ; unus ex eis non remansit.

105:12 Et crediderunt verbis ejus, et laudaverunt laudem ejus.

105:13 Cito fecerunt ; obliti sunt operum ejus : et non sustinuerunt consilium ejus.

105:14 Et concupierunt concupiscentiam in deserto, et tentaverunt Deum in inaquoso.

105:15 Et dedit eis petitionem ipsorum, et misit saturitatem in animas eorum.

105:16 Et irritaverunt Moysen in castris ; Aaron, sanctum Domini.

105:17 Aperta est terra, et deglutivit Dathan, et operuit super congregationem Abiron.

105:18 Et exarsit ignis in synagoga eorum : flamma combussit peccatores.

105:19 Et fecerunt vitulum in Horeb, et adoraverunt sculptile.

105:20 Et mutaverunt gloriam suam in similitudinem vituli comedentis fœnum.

105:21 Obliti sunt Deum qui salvavit eos ; qui fecit magnalia in Ægypto,

105:22 mirabilia in terra Cham, terribilia in mari Rubro.

105:23 Et dixit ut disperderet eos, si non Moyses, electus ejus, stetisset in confractione in conspectu ejus, ut averteret iram ejus, ne disperderet eos.

105:24 Et pro nihilo habuerunt terram desid-

105:3 Blessed are they that keep judgment, and do justice at all times.

105:4 Remember us, O Lord, in the favour of thy people: visit us with thy salvation.

105:5 That we may see the good of thy chosen, that we may rejoice in the joy of thy nation: that thou mayst be praised with thy inheritance.

105:6 We have sinned with our fathers: we have acted unjustly, we have wrought iniquity.

105:7 Our fathers understood not thy wonders in Egypt: they remembered not the multitude of thy mercies: And they provoked to wrath going up to the sea, even the Red Sea.

105:8 And he saved them for his own name's sake: that he might make his power known.

105:9 And he rebuked the Red Sea, and it was dried up: and he led them through the depths, as in a wilderness.

105:10 And he saved them from the hand of them that hated them: and he redeemed them from the hand of the enemy.

105:11 And the water covered them that afflicted them: there was not one of them left.

105:12 And they believed his words: and they sang his praises.

105:13 They had quickly done, they forgot his works: and they waited not for his counsels.

105:14 And they coveted their desire in the desert: and they tempted God in the place without water.

105:15 And he gave them their request: and sent fulness into their souls.

105:16 And they provoked Moses in the camp, Aaron the holy one of the Lord.

105:17 The earth opened and swallowed up Dathan: and covered the congregation of Abiron.

105:18 And a fire was kindled in their congregation: the flame burned the wicked.

105:19 They made also a calf in Horeb: and they adored the graven thing.

105:20 And they changed their glory into the likeness of a calf that eateth grass.

105:21 They forgot God, who saved them, who had done great things in Egypt,

105:22 wondrous works in the land of Cham: terrible things in the Red Sea.

105:23 And he said that he would destroy them: had not Moses his chosen stood before him in the breach: To turn away his wrath, lest he should destroy them.

105:24 And they set at nought the desirable land.

erabilem ; non crediderunt verbo ejus.

105:25 Et murmuraverunt in tabernaculis suis ; non exaudierunt vocem Domini.

105:26 Et elevavit manum suam super eos ut prosterneret eos in deserto :

105:27 et ut dejiceret semen eorum in nationibus, et dispergeret eos in regionibus.

105:28 Et initiati sunt Beelphegor, et comederunt sacrificia mortuorum.

105:29 Et irritaverunt eum in adinventionibus suis, et multiplicata est in eis ruina.

105:30 Et stetit Phinees, et placavit, et cessavit quassatio.

105:31 Et reputatum est ei in justitiam, in generationem et generationem usque in sempiternum.

105:32 Et irritaverunt eum ad aquas contradictionis, et vexatus est Moyses propter eos :

105:33 quia exacerbaverunt spiritum ejus, et distinxit in labiis suis.

105:34 Non disperdiderunt gentes quas dixit Dominus illis :

105:35 et commisti sunt inter gentes, et didicerunt opera eorum ;

105:36 et servierunt sculptilibus eorum, et factum est illis in scandalum.

105:37 Et immolaverunt filios suos et filias suas dæmoniis.

105:38 Et effuderunt sanguinem innocentem, sanguinem filiorum suorum et filiarum suarum, quas sacrificaverunt sculptilibus Chanaan. Et infecta est terra in sanguinibus,

105:39 et contaminata est in operibus eorum : et fornicati sunt in adinventionibus suis.

105:40 Et iratus est furore Dominus in populum suum, et abominatus est hæreditatem suam.

105:41 Et tradidit eos in manus gentium ; et dominati sunt eorum qui oderunt eos.

105:42 Et tribulaverunt eos inimici eorum, et humiliati sunt sub manibus eorum ;

105:43 sæpe liberavit eos. Ipsi autem exacerbaverunt eum in consilio suo, et humiliati sunt in iniquitatibus suis.

105:44 Et vidit cum tribularentur, et audivit orationem eorum.

105:45 Et memor fuit testamenti sui, et pœnituit eum secundum multitudinem misericordiæ suæ :

105:46 et dedit eos in misericordias, in conspectu

They believed not his word,

105:25 and they murmured in their tents: they hearkened not to the voice of the Lord.

105:26 And he lifted up his hand over them: to overthrow them in the desert;

105:27 And to cast down their seed among the nations, and to scatter them in the countries.

105:28 They also were initiated to Beelphegor: and ate the sacrifices of the dead.

105:29 And they provoked him with their inventions: and destruction was multiplied among them.

105:30 Then Phinees stood up, and pacified him: and the slaughter ceased.

105:31 And it was reputed to him unto justice, to generation and generation for evermore.

105:32 They provoked him also at the waters of contradiction: and Moses was afflicted for their sakes:

105:33 because they exasperated his spirit. And he distinguished with his lips.

105:34 They did not destroy the nations of which the Lord spoke unto them.

105:35 And they were mingled among the heathens, and learned their works:

105:36 and served their idols, and it became a stumblingblock to them.

105:37 And they sacrificed their sons, and their daughters to devils.

105:38 And they shed innocent blood: the blood of their sons and of their daughters which they sacrificed to the idols of Chanaan. And the land was polluted with blood,

105:39 and was defiled with their works: and they went aside after their own inventions.

105:40 And the Lord was exceedingly angry with his people: and he abhorred his inheritance.

105:41 And he delivered them into the hands of the nations: and they that hated them had dominion over them.

105:42 And their enemies afflicted them: and they were humbled under their hands:

105:43 many times did he deliver them. But they provoked him with their counsel: and they were brought low by their iniquities.

105:44 And he saw when they were in tribulation: and he heard their prayer.

105:45 And he was mindful of his covenant: and repented according to the multitude of his mercies.

105:46 And he gave them unto mercies, in the

omnium qui ceperant eos.

105:47 Salvos nos fac, Domine Deus noster, et congrega nos de nationibus : ut confiteamur nomini sancto tuo, et gloriemur in laude tua.

105:48 Benedictus Dominus Deus Israël, a sæculo et usque in sæculum ; et dicet omnis populus : Fiat, fiat.

sight of all those that had made them captives.

105:47 Save us, O Lord, our God: and gather us from among nations: That we may give thanks to thy holy name, and may glory in thy praise.

105:48 Blessed be the Lord the God of Israel, from everlasting to everlasting: and let all the people say: So be it, so be it.

CVI.

106:1 *Alleluja.* CONFITEMINI DOMINO, quoniam bonus, quoniam in sæculum misericordia ejus.

106:2 Dicant qui redempti sunt a Domino, quos redemit de manu inimici, et de regionibus congregavit eos,

106:3 a solis ortu, et occasu, ab aquilone, et mari.

106:4 Erraverunt in solitudine, in inaquoso ; viam civitatis habitaculi non invenerunt.

106:5 Esurientes et sitientes, anima eorum in ipsis defecit.

106:6 Et clamaverunt ad Dominum cum tribularentur, et de necessitatibus eorum eripuit eos ;

106:7 et deduxit eos in viam rectam, ut irent in civitatem habitationis.

106:8 Confiteantur Domino misericordiæ ejus, et mirabilia ejus filiis hominum.

106:9 Quia satiavit animam inanem, et animam esurientem satiavit bonis.

106:10 Sedentes in tenebris et umbra mortis ; vinctos in mendicitate et ferro.

106:11 Quia exacerbaverunt eloquia Dei, et consilium Altissimi irritaverunt.

106:12 Et humiliatum est in laboribus cor eorum ; infirmati sunt, nec fuit qui adjuvaret.

106:13 Et clamaverunt ad Dominum cum tribularentur ; et de necessitatibus eorum liberavit eos.

106:14 Et eduxit eos de tenebris et umbra mortis, et vincula eorum dirupit.

106:15 Confiteantur Domino misericordiæ ejus, et mirabilia ejus filiis hominum.

106:16 Quia contrivit portas æreas, et vectes ferreos confregit.

106:17 Suscepit eos de via iniquitatis eorum ;

106:1 *Alleluia.* GIVE GLORY TO THE LORD, for he is good: for his mercy endureth for ever.

106:2 Let them say so that have been redeemed by the Lord, whom he hath redeemed from the hand of the enemy: and gathered out of the countries.

106:3 From the rising and the setting of the sun, from the north and from the sea.

106:4 They wandered in a wilderness, in a place without water: they found not the way of a city for their habitation.

106:5 They were hungry and thirsty: their soul fainted in them.

106:6 And they cried to the Lord in their tribulation: and he delivered them out of their distresses.

106:7 And he led them into the right way: that they might go to a city of habitation.

106:8 Let the mercies of the Lord give glory to him: and his wonderful works to the children of men.

106:9 For he hath satisfied the empty soul, and hath filled the hungry soul with good things.

106:10 Such as sat in darkness and in the shadow of death: bound in want and in iron.

106:11 Because they had exasperated the words of God: and provoked the counsel of the most High:

106:12 And their heart was humbled with labours: they were weakened, and their was none to help them.

106:13 Then they cried to the Lord in their affliction: and he delivered them out of their distresses.

106:14 And he brought them out of darkness, and the shadow of death; and broke their bonds in sunder.

106:15 Let the mercies of the Lord give glory to him, and his wonderful works to the children of men.

106:16 Because he hath broken gates of brass, and burst iron bars.

106:17 He took them out of the way of their in-

propter injustitias enim suas humiliati sunt.

106:18 Omnem escam abominata est anima eorum, et appropinquaverunt usque ad portas mortis.

106:19 Et clamaverunt ad Dominum cum tribularentur, et de necessitatibus eorum liberavit eos.

106:20 Misit verbum suum, et sanavit eos, et eripuit eos de interitionibus eorum.

106:21 Confiteantur Domino misericordiæ ejus, et mirabilia ejus filiis hominum.

106:22 Et sacrificent sacrificium laudis, et annuntient opera ejus in exsultatione.

106:23 Qui descendunt mare in navibus, facientes operationem in aquis multis :

106:24 ipsi viderunt opera Domini, et mirabilia ejus in profundo.

106:25 Dixit, et stetit spiritus procellæ, et exaltati sunt fluctus ejus.

106:26 Ascendunt usque ad cælos, et descendunt usque ad abyssos ; anima eorum in malis tabescebat.

106:27 Turbati sunt, et moti sunt sicut ebrius, et omnis sapientia eorum devorata est.

106:28 Et clamaverunt ad Dominum cum tribularentur ; et de necessitatibus eorum eduxit eos.

106:29 Et statuit procellam ejus in auram, et siluerunt fluctus ejus.

106:30 Et lætati sunt quia siluerunt ; et deduxit eos in portum voluntatis eorum.

106:31 Confiteantur Domino misericordiæ ejus, et mirabilia ejus filiis hominum.

106:32 Et exaltent eum in ecclesia plebis, et in cathedra seniorum laudent eum.

106:33 Posuit flumina in desertum, et exitus aquarum in sitim ;

106:34 terram fructiferam in salsuginem, a malitia inhabitantium in ea.

106:35 Posuit desertum in stagna aquarum, et terram sine aqua in exitus aquarum.

106:36 Et collocavit illic esurientes, et constituerunt civitatem habitationis :

106:37 et seminaverunt agros et plantaverunt vineas, et fecerunt fructum nativitatis.

106:38 Et benedixit eis, et multiplicati sunt ni-

iquity: for they were brought low for their injustices.

106:18 Their soul abhorred all manner of meat: and they drew nigh even to the gates of death.

106:19 And they cried to the Lord in their affliction: and he delivered them out of their distresses.

106:20 He sent his word, and healed them: and delivered them from their destructions.

106:21 Let the mercies of the Lord give glory to him: and his wonderful works to the children of men.

106:22 And let them sacrifice the sacrifice of praise: and declare his works with joy.

106:23 They that go down to the sea in ships, doing business in the great waters:

106:24 These have seen the works of the Lord, and his wonders in the deep.

106:25 He said the word, and there arose a storm of wind: and the waves thereof were lifted up.

106:26 They mount up to the heavens, and they go down to the depths: their soul pined away with evils.

106:27 They were troubled, and reeled like a drunken man; and all their wisdom was swallowed up.

106:28 And they cried to the Lord in their affliction: and he brought them out of their distresses.

106:29 And he turned the storm into a breeze: and its waves were still.

106:30 And they rejoiced because they were still: and he brought them to the haven which they wished for.

106:31 Let the mercies of the Lord give glory to him, and his wonderful works to the children of men.

106:32 And let them exalt him in the church of the people: and praise him in the chair of the ancients.

106:33 He hath turned rivers into a wilderness: and the sources of water into dry ground:

106:34 A fruitful land into barrenness, for the wickedness of them that dwell therein.

106:35 He hath turned a wilderness into pools of water, and a dry land into water springs.

106:36 And hath placed there the hungry; and they made a city for their habitation.

106:37 And they sowed fields, and planted vineyards: and they yielded fruit of birth.

106:38 And he blessed them, and they were mul-

mis ; et jumenta eorum non minoravit.

tiplied exceedingly: and their cattle he suffered not to decrease.

106:39 Et pauci facti sunt et vexati sunt, a tribulatione malorum et dolore.

106:39 Then they were brought to be few: and they were afflicted through the trouble of evils and sorrow.

106:40 Effusa est contemptio super principes : et errare fecit eos in invio, et non in via.

106:40 Contempt was poured forth upon their princes: and he caused them to wander where there was no passing, and out of the way.

106:41 Et adjuvit pauperem de inopia, et posuit sicut oves familias.

106:41 And he helped the poor out of poverty: and made him families like a flock of sheep.

106:42 Videbunt recti, et lætabuntur ; et omnis iniquitas oppilabit os suum.

106:42 The just shall see, and shall rejoice, and all iniquity shall stop her mouth.

106:43 Quis sapiens, et custodiet hæc, et intelliget misericordias Domini ?

106:43 Who is wise, and will keep these things: and will understand the mercies of the Lord?

CVII.

107:1 *Canticum Psalmi, ipsi David.*

107:1 *A canticle of a psalm for David himself.*

107:2 PARATUM COR MEUM, Deus, paratum cor meum ; cantabo, et psallam in gloria mea.

107:2 MY HEART IS READY, O God, my heart is ready: I will sing, and will give praise, with my glory.

107:3 Exsurge, gloria mea ; exsurge, psalterium et cithara ; exsurgam diluculo.

107:3 Arise, my glory; arise, psaltery and harp: I will arise in the morning early.

107:4 Confitebor tibi in populis, Domine, et psallam tibi in nationibus :

107:4 I will praise thee, O Lord, among the people: and I will sing unto thee among the nations.

107:5 quia magna est super cælos misericordia tua, et usque ad nubes veritas tua.

107:5 For thy mercy is great above the heavens: and thy truth even unto the clouds.

107:6 Exaltare super cælos, Deus, et super omnem terram gloria tua :

107:6 Be thou exalted, O God, above the heavens, and thy glory over all the earth:

107:7 ut liberentur dilecti tui. Salvum fac dextera tua, et exaudi me.

107:7 that thy beloved may be delivered. Save with thy right hand and hear me.

107:8 Deus locutus est in sancto suo : Exsultabo, et dividam Sichimam ; et convallem tabernaculorum dimetiar.

107:8 God hath spoken in his holiness. I will rejoice, and I will divide Sichem and I will mete out the vale of tabernacles.

107:9 Meus est Galaad, et meus est Manasses, et Ephraim susceptio capitis mei. Juda rex meus ;

107:9 Galaad is mine, and Manasses is mine and Ephraim the protection of my head. Juda is my king:

107:10 Moab lebes spei meæ : in Idumæam extendam calceamentum meum ; mihi alienigenæ amici facti sunt.

107:10 Moab the pot of my hope. Over Edom I will stretch out my shoe: the aliens are become my friends.

107:11 Quis deducet me in civitatem munitam ? quis deducet me usque in Idumæam ?

107:11 Who will bring me into the strong city? who will lead me into Edom?

107:12 nonne tu, Deus, qui repulisti nos ? et non exibis, Deus, in virtutibus nostris ?

107:12 Wilt not thou, O God, who hast cast us off? and wilt not thou, O God, go forth with our armies?

107:13 Da nobis auxilium de tribulatione, quia vana salus hominis.

107:13 O grant us help from trouble: for vain is the help of man.

107:14 In Deo faciemus virtutem ; et ipse ad nihilum deducet inimicos nostros.

107:14 Through God we shall do mightily: and he will bring our enemies to nothing.

CVIII.

108:1 *In finem. Psalmus David.*

108:2 DEUS, LAUDEM MEAM NE TACUERIS, quia os peccatoris et os dolosi super me apertum est.

108:3 Locuti sunt adversum me lingua dolosa, et sermonibus odii circumdederunt me : et expugnaverunt me gratis.

108:4 Pro eo ut me diligerent, detrahebant mihi ; ego autem orabam.

108:5 Et posuerunt adversum me mala pro bonis, et odium pro dilectione mea.

108:6 Constitue super eum peccatorem, et diabolus stet a dextris ejus.

108:7 Cum judicatur, exeat condemnatus ; et oratio ejus fiat in peccatum.

108:8 Fiant dies ejus pauci, et episcopatum ejus accipiat alter.

108:9 Fiant filii ejus orphani, et uxor ejus vidua.

108:10 Nutantes transferantur filii ejus et mendicent, et ejiciantur de habitationibus suis.

108:11 Scrutetur fœnerator omnem substantiam ejus, et diripiant alieni labores ejus.

108:12 Non sit illi adjutor, nec sit qui misereatur pupillis ejus.

108:13 Fiant nati ejus in interitum ; in generatione una deleatur nomen ejus.

108:14 In memoriam redeat iniquitas patrum ejus in conspectu Domini, et peccatum matris ejus non deleatur.

108:15 Fiant contra Dominum semper, et dispereat de terra memoria eorum :

108:16 pro eo quod non est recordatus facere misericordiam,

108:17 et persecutus est hominem inopem et mendicum, et compunctum corde, mortificare.

108:18 Et dilexit maledictionem, et veniet ei ; et noluit benedictionem, et elongabitur ab eo. Et induit maledictionem sicut vestimentum ; et intravit sicut aqua in interiora ejus, et sicut oleum in ossibus ejus.

108:19 Fiat ei sicut vestimentum quo operitur, et sicut zona qua semper præcingitur.

108:20 Hoc opus eorum qui detrahunt mihi apud Dominum, et qui loquuntur mala adversus animam meam.

108:1 *Unto the end, a psalm for David.*

108:2 O GOD, BE NOT THOU SILENT IN MY PRAISE: for the mouth of the wicked and the mouth of the deceitful man is opened against me.

108:3 They have spoken against me with deceitful tongues; and they have compassed me about with words of hatred; and have fought against me without cause.

108:4 Instead of making me a return of love, they detracted me: but I gave myself to prayer.

108:5 And they repaid me evil for good: and hatred for my love.

108:6 Set thou the sinner over him: and may the devil stand at his right hand.

108:7 When he is judged, may he go out condemned; and may his prayer be turned to sin.

108:8 May his days be few: and his bishopric let another take.

108:9 May his children be fatherless, and his wife a widow.

108:10 Let his children be carried about vagabonds, and beg; and let them be cast out of their dwellings.

108:11 May the usurer search all his substance: and let strangers plunder his labours.

108:12 May there be none to help him: nor none to pity his fatherless offspring.

108:13 May his posterity be cut off; in one generation may his name be blotted out.

108:14 May the iniquity of his fathers be remembered in the sight of the Lord: and let not the sin of his mother be blotted out.

108:15 May they be before the Lord continually, and let the memory of them perish from the earth:

108:16 because he remembered not to shew mercy,

108:17 But persecuted the poor man and the beggar; and the broken in heart, to put him to death.

108:18 And he loved cursing, and it shall come unto him: and he would not have blessing, and it shall be far from him. And he put on cursing, like a garment: and it went in like water into his entrails, and like oil in his bones.

108:19 May it be unto him like a garment which covereth him; and like a girdle with which he is girded continually.

108:20 This is the work of them who detract me before the Lord; and who speak evils against my soul.

108:21 Et tu, Domine, Domine, fac mecum propter nomen tuum, quia suavis est misericordia tua.

108:22 Libera me, quia egenus et pauper ego sum, et cor meum conturbatum est intra me.

108:23 Sicut umbra cum declinat ablatus sum, et excussus sum sicut locustæ.

108:24 Genua mea infirmata sunt a jejunio, et caro mea immutata est propter oleum.

108:25 Et ego factus sum opprobrium illis ; viderunt me, et moverunt capita sua.

108:26 Adjuva me, Domine Deus meus ; salvum me fac secundum misericordiam tuam.

108:27 Et sciant quia manus tua hæc, et tu, Domine, fecisti eam.

108:28 Maledicent illi, et tu benedices : qui insurgunt in me confundantur ; servus autem tuus lætabitur.

108:29 Induantur qui detrahunt mihi pudore, et operiantur sicut diploide confusione sua.

108:30 Confitebor Domino nimis in ore meo, et in medio multorum laudabo eum :

108:31 quia astitit a dextris pauperis, ut salvam faceret a persequentibus animam meam.

108:21 But thou, O Lord, do with me for thy name's sake: because thy mercy is sweet. Do thou deliver me,

108:22 for I am poor and needy, and my heart is troubled within me.

108:23 I am taken away like the shadow when it declineth: and I am shaken off as locusts.

108:24 My knees are weakened through fasting: and my flesh is changed for oil.

108:25 And I am become a reproach to them: they saw me and they shaked their heads.

108:26 Help me, O Lord my God; save me according to thy mercy.

108:27 And let them know that this is thy hand: and that thou, O Lord, hast done it.

108:28 They will curse and thou will bless: let them that rise up against me be confounded: but thy servant shall rejoice.

108:29 Let them that detract me be clothed with shame: and let them be covered with the their confusion as with a double cloak.

108:30 I will give great thanks to the Lord with my mouth: and in the midst of many I will praise him.

108:31 Because he hath stood at the right hand of the poor, to save my soul from persecutors

CIX.

109:1 *Psalmus David.* DIXIT DOMINUS Domino meo : Sede a dextris meis, donec ponam inimicos tuos scabellum pedum tuorum.

109:2 Virgam virtutis tuæ emittet Dominus ex Sion : dominare in medio inimicorum tuorum.

109:3 Tecum principium in die virtutis tuæ in splendoribus sanctorum : ex utero, ante luciferum, genui te.

109:4 Juravit Dominus, et non pœnitebit eum : Tu es sacerdos in æternum secundum ordinem Melchisedech.

109:5 Dominus a dextris tuis ; confregit in die iræ suæ reges.

109:6 Judicabit in nationibus, implebit ruinas ; conquassabit capita in terra multorum.

109:7 De torrente in via bibet ; propterea exaltabit caput.

109:1 *A psalm for David.* THE LORD SAID to my Lord: Sit thou at my right hand: Until I make thy enemies thy footstool.

109:2 The Lord will send forth the sceptre of thy power out of Sion: rule thou in the midst of thy enemies.

109:3 With thee is the principality in the day of thy strength: in the brightness of the saints: from the womb before the day star I begot thee.

109:4 The Lord hath sworn, and he will not repent: Thou art a priest for ever according to the order of Melchisedech.

109:5 The Lord at thy right hand hath broken kings in the day of his wrath.

109:6 He shall judge among nations, he shall fill ruins: he shall crush the heads in the land of many.

109:7 He shall drink of the torrent in the way: therefore shall he lift up the head.

CX.

110:1 *Alleluja.* CONFITEBOR TIBI, Domine, in toto corde meo, in consilio justorum, et congregatione.

110:2 Magna opera Domini : exquisita in omnes voluntates ejus.

110:3 Confessio et magnificentia opus ejus, et justitia ejus manet in sæculum sæculi.

110:4 Memoriam fecit mirabilium suorum, misericors et miserator Dominus.

110:5 Escam dedit timentibus se ; memor erit in sæculum testamenti sui.

110:6 Virtutem operum suorum annuntiabit populo suo,

110:7 ut det illis hæreditatem gentium. Opera manuum ejus veritas et judicium.

110:8 Fidelia omnia mandata ejus, confirmata in sæculum sæculi, facta in veritate et æquitate.

110:9 Redemptionem misit populo suo ; mandavit in æternum testamentum suum. Sanctum et terribile nomen ejus.

110:10 Initium sapientiæ timor Domini ; intellectus bonus omnibus facientibus eum : laudatio ejus manet in sæculum sæculi.

110:1 *Alleluia.* I WILL PRAISE THEE, O Lord, with my whole heart; in the council of the just: and in the congregation.

110:2 Great are the works of the Lord: sought out according to all his wills

110:3 His work is praise and magnificence: and his justice continueth for ever and ever.

110:4 He hath made a remembrance of his wonderful works, being a merciful and gracious Lord:

110:5 he hath given food to them that fear him. He will be mindful for ever of his covenant:

110:6 he will shew forth to his people the power of his works.

110:7 That he may give them the inheritance of the Gentiles: the works of his hands are truth and judgment.

110:8 All his commandments are faithful: confirmed for ever and ever, made in truth and equity.

110:9 He hath sent redemption to his people: he hath commanded his covenant for ever. Holy and terrible is his name:

110:10 the fear of the Lord is the beginning of wisdom. A good understanding to all that do it: his praise continueth for ever and ever.

CXI.

111:1 *Alleluja, reversionis Aggæi et Zachariæ.* BEATUS VIR qui timet Dominum : in mandatis ejus volet nimis.

111:2 Potens in terra erit semen ejus ; generatio rectorum benedicetur.

111:3 Gloria et divitiæ in domo ejus, et justitia ejus manet in sæculum sæculi.

111:4 Exortum est in tenebris lumen rectis : misericors, et miserator, et justus.

111:5 Jucundus homo qui miseretur et commodat ; disponet sermones suos in judicio :

111:6 quia in æternum non commovebitur.

111:7 In memoria æterna erit justus ; ab auditione mala non timebit. Paratum cor ejus sperare in Domino,

111:8 confirmatum est cor ejus ; non commovebitur donec despiciat inimicos suos.

111:9 Dispersit, dedit pauperibus ; justitia ejus manet in sæculum sæculi : cornu ejus exaltabitur in gloria.

111:1 *Alleluia, of the returning of Aggeus and Zacharias.* BLESSED IS THE MAN that feareth the Lord: he shall delight exceedingly in his commandments.

111:2 His seed shall be mighty upon earth: the generation of the righteous shall be blessed.

111:3 Glory and wealth shall be in his house: and his justice remaineth for ever and ever.

111:4 To the righteous a light is risen up in darkness: he is merciful, and compassionate and just.

111:5 Acceptable is the man that showeth mercy and lendeth: he shall order his words with judgment:

111:6 because he shall not be moved for ever.

111:7 The just shall be in everlasting remembrance: he shall not fear the evil hearing. His heart is ready to hope in the Lord:

111:8 his heart is strengthened, he shall not be moved until he look over his enemies.

111:9 He hath distributed, he hath given to the poor: his justice remaineth for ever and ever: his horn shall be exalted in glory.

111:10 Peccator videbit, et irascetur ; dentibus suis fremet et tabescet : desiderium peccatorum peribit.

111:10 The wicked shall see, and shall be angry, he shall gnash with his teeth and pine away: the desire of the wicked shall perish.

CXII.

112:1 *Alleluja.* LAUDATE, PUERI, DOMINUM ; laudate nomen Domini.

112:2 Sit nomen Domini benedictum ex hoc nunc et usque in sæculum.

112:3 A solis ortu usque ad occasum laudabile nomen Domini.

112:4 Excelsus super omnes gentes Dominus, et super cælos gloria ejus.

112:5 Quis sicut Dominus Deus noster, qui in altis habitat,

112:6 et humilia respicit in cælo et in terra ?

112:7 Suscitans a terra inopem, et de stercore erigens pauperem :

112:8 ut collocet eum cum principibus, cum principibus populi sui.

112:9 Qui habitare facit sterilem in domo, matrem filiorum lætantem.

112:1 *Alleluia.* PRAISE THE LORD, YE CHILDREN: praise ye the name of the Lord.

112:2 Blessed be the name of the Lord, from henceforth now and for ever.

112:3 From the rising of the sun unto the going down of the same, the name of the Lord is worthy of praise.

112:4 The Lord is high above all nations; and his glory above the heavens.

112:5 Who is as the Lord our God, who dwelleth on high:

112:6 and looketh down on the low things in heaven and in earth?

112:7 Raising up the needy from the earth, and lifting up the poor out of the dunghill:

112:8 That he may place him with princes, with the princes of his people.

112:9 Who maketh a barren woman to dwell in a house, the joyful mother of children.

CXIII.

113:1 *Alleluja.* IN EXITU ISRAËL de Ægypto, domus Jacob de populo barbaro,

113:2 facta est Judæa sanctificatio ejus ; Israël potestas ejus.

113:3 Mare vidit, et fugit ; Jordanis conversus est retrorsum.

113:4 Montes exsultaverunt ut arietes, et colles sicut agni ovium.

113:5 Quid est tibi, mare, quod fugisti ? et tu, Jordanis, quia conversus es retrorsum ?

113:6 montes, exsultastis sicut arietes ? et colles, sicut agni ovium ?

113:7 A facie Domini mota est terra, a facie Dei Jacob :

113:8 qui convertit petram in stagna aquarum, et rupem in fontes aquarum.

113:9 Non nobis, Domine, non nobis, sed nomini tuo da gloriam :

113:10 super misericordia tua et veritate tua ; nequando dicant gentes : Ubi est Deus eorum ?

113:11 Deus autem noster in cælo ; omnia quæcumque voluit fecit.

113:12 Simulacra gentium argentum et aurum,

113:1 *Alleluia.* WHEN ISRAEL WENT OUT of Egypt, the house of Jacob from a barbarous people:

113:2 Judea made his sanctuary, Israel his dominion.

113:3 The sea saw and fled: Jordan was turned back.

113:4 The mountains skipped like rams, and the hills like the lambs of the flock.

113:5 What ailed thee, O thou sea, that thou didst flee: and thou, O Jordan, that thou wast turned back?

113:6 Ye mountains, that ye skipped like rams, and ye hills, like lambs of the flock?

113:7 At the presence of the Lord the earth was moved, at the presence of the God of Jacob:

113:8 Who turned the rock into pools of water, and the stony hill into fountains of waters.

113:9 Not to us, O Lord, not to us; but to thy name give glory.

113:10 For thy mercy, and for thy truth's sake: lest the gentiles should say: Where is their God?

113:11 But our God is in heaven: he hath done all things whatsoever he would.

113:12 The idols of the gentiles are silver and

opera manuum hominum.

113:13 Os habent, et non loquentur ; oculos habent, et non videbunt.

113:14 Aures habent, et non audient ; nares habent, et non odorabunt.

113:15 Manus habent, et non palpabunt ; pedes habent, et non ambulabunt ; non clamabunt in gutture suo.

113:16 Similes illis fiant qui faciunt ea, et omnes qui confidunt in eis.

113:17 Domus Israël speravit in Domino ; adjutor eorum et protector eorum est.

113:18 Domus Aaron speravit in Domino ; adjutor eorum et protector eorum est.

113:19 Qui timent Dominum speraverunt in Domino ; adjutor eorum et protector eorum est.

113:20 Dominus memor fuit nostri, et benedixit nobis. Benedixit domui Israël ; benedixit domui Aaron.

113:21 Benedixit omnibus qui timent Dominum, pusillis cum majoribus.

113:22 Adjiciat Dominus super vos, super vos et super filios vestros.

113:23 Benedicti vos a Domino, qui fecit cælum et terram.

113:24 Cælum cæli Domino ; terram autem dedit filiis hominum.

113:25 Non mortui laudabunt te, Domine, neque omnes qui descendunt in infernum :

113:26 sed nos qui vivimus, benedicimus Domino, ex hoc nunc et usque in sæculum.

gold, the works of the hands of men.

113:13 They have mouths and speak not: they have eyes and see not.

113:14 They have ears and hear not: they have noses and smell not.

113:15 They have hands and feel not: they have feet and walk not: neither shall they cry out through their throat.

113:16 Let them that make them become like unto them: and all such as trust in them.

113:17 The house of Israel hath hoped in the Lord: he is their helper and their protector.

113:18 The house of Aaron hath hoped in the Lord: he is their helper and their protector.

113:19 They that fear the Lord hath hoped in the Lord: he is their helper and their protector.

113:20 The Lord hath been mindful of us, and hath blessed us. He hath blessed the house of Israel: he hath blessed the house of Aaron.

113:21 He hath blessed all that fear the Lord, both little and great.

113:22 May the Lord add blessings upon you: upon you, and upon your children.

113:23 Blessed be you of the Lord, who made heaven and earth.

113:24 The heaven of heaven is the Lord's: but the earth he has given to the children of men.

113:25 The dead shall not praise thee, O Lord: nor any of them that go down to hell.

113:26 But we that live bless the Lord: from this time now and for ever.

CXIV.

114:1 *Alleluja.* DILEXI, quoniam exaudiet Dominus vocem orationis meæ.

114:2 Quia inclinavit aurem suam mihi, et in diebus meis invocabo.

114:3 Circumdederunt me dolores mortis ; et pericula inferni invenerunt me. Tribulationem et dolorem inveni,

114:4 et nomen Domini invocavi : o Domine, libera animam meam.

114:5 Misericors Dominus et justus, et Deus noster miseretur.

114:6 Custodiens parvulos Dominus ; humiliatus sum, et liberavit me.

114:7 Convertere, anima mea, in requiem tuam, quia Dominus benefecit tibi :

114:8 quia eripuit animam meam de morte, oculos meos a lacrimis, pedes meos a lapsu.

114:9 Placebo Domino in regione vivorum.

114:1 *Alleluia.* I HAVE LOVED, because the Lord will hear the voice of my prayer.

114:2 Because he hath inclined his ear unto me: and in my days I will call upon him.

114:3 The sorrows of death have compassed me: and the perils of hell have found me. I met with trouble and sorrow:

114:4 and I called upon the name of the Lord. O Lord, deliver my soul.

114:5 The Lord is merciful and just, and our God sheweth mercy.

114:6 The Lord is the keeper of little ones: I was humbled, and he delivered me.

114:7 Turn, O my soul, into thy rest: for the Lord hath been bountiful to thee.

114:8 For he hath delivered my soul from death: my eyes from tears, my feet from falling.

114:9 I will please the Lord in the land of the liv-

ing.

CXV.

115:1 *Alleluja.* CREDIDI, propter quod locutus sum ; ego autem humiliatus sum nimis.

115:2 Ego dixi in excessu meo : Omnis homo mendax.

115:3 Quid retribuam Domino pro omnibus quæ retribuit mihi ?

115:4 Calicem salutaris accipiam, et nomen Domini invocabo.

115:5 Vota mea Domino reddam coram omni populo ejus.

115:6 Pretiosa in conspectu Domini mors sanctorum ejus.

115:7 O Domine, quia ego servus tuus ; ego servus tuus, et filius ancillæ tuæ. Dirupisti vincula mea :

115:8 tibi sacrificabo hostiam laudis, et nomen Domini invocabo.

115:9 Vota mea Domino reddam in conspectu omnis populi ejus ;

115:10 in atriis domus Domini, in medio tui, Jerusalem.

115:1 *Alleluia.* I HAVE BELIEVED, therefore have I spoken; but I have been humbled exceedingly.

115:2 I said in my excess: Every man is a liar.

115:3 What shall I render to the Lord, for all the things he hath rendered unto me?

115:4 I will take the chalice of salvation; and I will call upon the name of the Lord.

115:5 I will pay my vows to the Lord before all his people:

115:6 precious in the sight of the Lord is the death of his saints.

115:7 O Lord, for I am thy servant: I am thy servant, and the son of thy handmaid. Thou hast broken my bonds:

115:8 I will sacrifice to thee the sacrifice of praise, and I will call upon the name of the Lord.

115:9 I will pay my vows to the Lord in the sight of all his people:

115:10 in the courts of the house of the Lord, in the midst of thee, O Jerusalem.

CXVI.

116:1 *Alleluja.* LAUDATE DOMINUM, omnes gentes ; laudate eum, omnes populi.

116:2 Quoniam confirmata est super nos misericordia ejus, et veritas Domini manet in æternum.

116:1 *Alleluia.* O PRAISE THE LORD, all ye nations: praise him, all ye people.

116:2 For his mercy is confirmed upon us: and the truth of the Lord remaineth for ever.

CXVII.

117:1 *Alleluja.* CONFITEMINI DOMINO, quoniam bonus, quoniam in sæculum misericordia ejus.

117:2 Dicat nunc Israël : Quoniam bonus, quoniam in sæculum misericordia ejus.

117:3 Dicat nunc domus Aaron : Quoniam in sæculum misericordia ejus.

117:4 Dicant nunc qui timent Dominum : Quoniam in sæculum misericordia ejus.

117:5 De tribulatione invocavi Dominum, et exaudivit me in latitudine Dominus.

117:6 Dominus mihi adjutor ; non timebo quid faciat mihi homo.

117:7 Dominus mihi adjutor, et ego despiciam inimicos meos.

117:8 Bonum est confidere in Domino, quam confidere in homine.

117:9 Bonum est sperare in Domino, quam sperare in principibus.

117:1 *Alleluia.* GIVE PRAISE TO THE LORD, for he is good: for his mercy endureth for ever.

117:2 Let Israel now say, that he is good: that his mercy endureth for ever.

117:3 Let the house of Aaron now say, that his mercy endureth for ever.

117:4 Let them that fear the Lord now say, that his mercy endureth for ever.

117:5 In my trouble I called upon the Lord: and the Lord heard me, and enlarged me.

117:6 The Lord is my helper: I will not fear what man can do unto me.

117:7 The Lord is my helper: and I will look over my enemies.

117:8 It is good to confide in the Lord, rather than to have confidence in man.

117:9 It is good to trust in the Lord, rather than to trust in princes.

117:10 Omnes gentes circuierunt me, et in nomine Domini, quia ultus sum in eos.

117:11 Circumdantes circumdederunt me, et in nomine Domini, quia ultus sum in eos.

117:12 Circumdederunt me sicut apes, et exarserunt sicut ignis in spinis : et in nomine Domini, quia ultus sum in eos.

117:13 Impulsus eversus sum, ut caderem, et Dominus suscepit me.

117:14 Fortitudo mea et laus mea Dominus, et factus est mihi in salutem.

117:15 Vox exsultationis et salutis in tabernaculis justorum.

117:16 Dextera Domini fecit virtutem ; dextera Domini exaltavit me : dextera Domini fecit virtutem.

117:17 Non moriar, sed vivam, et narrabo opera Domini.

117:18 Castigans castigavit me Dominus, et morti non tradidit me.

117:19 Aperite mihi portas justitiæ : ingressus in eas confitebor Domino.

117:20 Hæc porta Domini : justi intrabunt in eam.

117:21 Confitebor tibi quoniam exaudisti me, et factus es mihi in salutem.

117:22 Lapidem quem reprobaverunt ædificantes, hic factus est in caput anguli.

117:23 A Domino factum est istud, et est mirabile in oculis nostris.

117:24 Hæc est dies quam fecit Dominus ; exsultemus, et lætemur in ea.

117:25 O Domine, salvum me fac ; o Domine, bene prosperare.

117:26 Benedictus qui venit in nomine Domini : benediximus vobis de domo Domini.

117:27 Deus Dominus, et illuxit nobis. Constituite diem solemnem in condensis, usque ad cornu altaris.

117:28 Deus meus es tu, et confitebor tibi ; Deus meus es tu, et exaltabo te. Confitebor tibi quoniam exaudisti me, et factus es mihi in salutem.

117:29 Confitemini Domino, quoniam bonus, quoniam in sæculum misericordia ejus.

117:10 All nations compassed me about; and in the name of the Lord I have been revenged on them.

117:11 Surrounding me they compassed me about: and in the name of the Lord I have been revenged on them.

117:12 They surrounded me like bees, and they burned like fire among thorns: and in the name of the Lord I was revenged on them

117:13 Being pushed I was overturned that I might fall: but the Lord supported me.

117:14 The Lord is my strength and my praise: and he is become my salvation.

117:15 The voice of rejoicing and of salvation is in the tabernacles of the just.

117:16 The right hand of the Lord hath wrought strength: the right hand of the Lord hath exalted me: the right hand of the Lord hath wrought strength.

117:17 I shall not die, but live: and shall declare the works of the Lord.

117:18 The Lord chastising hath chastised me: but he hath not delivered me over to death.

117:19 Open ye to me the gates of justice: I will go into them, and give praise to the Lord.

117:20 This is the gate of the Lord, the just shall enter into it.

117:21 I will give glory to thee because thou hast heard me: and art become my salvation.

117:22 The stone which the builders rejected; the same is become the head of the corner.

117:23 This is the Lord's doing: and it is wonderful in our eyes.

117:24 This is the day which the Lord hath made: let us be glad and rejoice therein.

117:25 O Lord, save me: O Lord, give good success.

117:26 Blessed be he that cometh in the name of the Lord. We have blessed you out of the house of the Lord.

117:27 The Lord is God, and he hath shone upon us. Appoint a solemn day, with shady boughs, even to the horn of the alter.

117:28 Thou art my God, and I will praise thee: thou art my God, and I will exalt thee. I will praise thee, because thou hast heard me, and art become my salvation.

117:29 O praise ye the Lord, for he is good: for his mercy endureth for ever.

CXVIII.

118:1 *Alleluja. ALEPH.* BEATI IMMACULATI in via, qui ambulant in lege Domini.

118:2 Beati qui scrutantur testimonia ejus ; in toto corde exquirunt eum.

118:3 Non enim qui operantur iniquitatem in viis ejus ambulaverunt.

118:4 Tu mandasti mandata tua custodiri nimis.

118:5 Utinam dirigantur viæ meæ ad custodiendas justificationes tuas.

118:6 Tunc non confundar, cum perspexero in omnibus mandatis tuis.

118:7 Confitebor tibi in directione cordis, in eo quod didici judicia justitiæ tuæ.

118:8 Justificationes tuas custodiam ; non me derelinquas usquequaque.

118:9 *Beth.* In quo corrigit adolescentior viam suam ? in custodiendo sermones tuos.

118:10 In toto corde meo exquisivi te ; ne repellas me a mandatis tuis.

118:11 In corde meo abscondi eloquia tua, ut non peccem tibi.

118:12 Benedictus es, Domine ; doce me justificationes tuas.

118:13 In labiis meis pronuntiavi omnia judicia oris tui.

118:14 In via testimoniorum tuorum delectatus sum, sicut in omnibus divitiis.

118:15 In mandatis tuis exercebor, et considerabo vias tuas.

118:16 In justificationibus tuis meditabor : non obliviscar sermones tuos.

118:17 *Ghimel.* Retribue servo tuo, vivifica me, et custodiam sermones tuos.

118:18 Revela oculos meos, et considerabo mirabilia de lege tua.

118:19 Incola ego sum in terra : non abscondas a me mandata tua.

118:20 Concupivit anima mea desiderare justificationes tuas in omni tempore.

118:21 Increpasti superbos ; maledicti qui declinant a mandatis tuis.

118:22 Aufer a me opprobrium et contemptum, quia testimonia tua exquisivi.

118:23 Etenim sederunt principes, et adversum me loquebantur ; servus autem tuus exercebatur in justificationibus tuis.

118:24 Nam et testimonia tua meditatio mea est,

118:1 *Alleluia.* ALEPH. BLESSED ARE THE UNDEFILED in the way, who walk in the law of the Lord.

118:2 Blessed are they who search his testimonies: that seek him with their whole heart.

118:3 For they that work iniquity, have not walked in his ways.

118:4 Thou hast commanded thy commandments to be kept most diligently.

118:5 O! that my ways may be directed to keep thy justifications.

118:6 Then shall I not be confounded, when I shall look into all thy commandments.

118:7 I will praise thee with uprightness of heart, when I shall have learned the judgments of thy justice.

118:8 I will keep thy justifications: O! do not thou utterly forsake me. BETH.

118:9 By what doth a young man correct his way? by observing thy words.

118:10 With my whole heart have I sought after thee: let me not stray from thy commandments.

118:11 Thy words have I hidden in my heart, that I may not sin against thee.

118:12 Blessed art thou, O Lord: teach me thy justifications.

118:13 With my lips I have pronounced all the judgments of thy mouth.

118:14 I have been delighted in the way of thy testimonies, as in all riches.

118:15 I will meditate on thy commandments: and I will consider thy ways.

118:16 I will think of thy justifications: I will not forget thy words. GIMEL.

118:17 Give bountifully to thy servant, enliven me: and I shall keep thy words.

118:18 Open thou my eyes: and I will consider the wondrous things of thy law.

118:19 I am a sojourner on the earth: hide not thy commandments from me.

118:20 My soul hath coveted to long for thy justifications, at all times.

118:21 Thou hast rebuked the proud: they are cursed who decline from thy commandments.

118:22 Remove from me reproach and contempt: because I have sought after thy testimonies.

118:23 For princes sat, and spoke against me: but thy servant was employed in thy justifications.

118:24 For thy testimonies are my meditation:

et consilium meum justificationes tuæ.

118:25 *Daleth.* Adhæsit pavimento anima mea : vivifica me secundum verbum tuum.

118:26 Vias meas enuntiavi, et exaudisti me ; doce me justificationes tuas.

118:27 Viam justificationum tuarum instrue me, et exercebor in mirabilibus tuis.

118:28 Dormitavit anima mea præ tædio : confirma me in verbis tuis.

118:29 Viam iniquitatis amove a me, et de lege tua miserere mei.

118:30 Viam veritatis elegi ; judicia tua non sum oblitus.

118:31 Adhæsi testimoniis tuis, Domine ; noli me confundere.

118:32 Viam mandatorum tuorum cucurri, cum dilatasti cor meum.

118:33 *He.* Legem pone mihi, Domine, viam justificationum tuarum, et exquiram eam semper.

118:34 Da mihi intellectum, et scrutabor legem tuam, et custodiam illam in toto corde meo.

118:35 Deduc me in semitam mandatorum tuorum, quia ipsam volui.

118:36 Inclina cor meum in testimonia tua, et non in avaritiam.

118:37 Averte oculos meos, ne videant vanitatem ; in via tua vivifica me.

118:38 Statue servo tuo eloquium tuum in timore tuo.

118:39 Amputa opprobrium meum quod suspicatus sum, quia judicia tua jucunda.

118:40 Ecce concupivi mandata tua : in æquitate tua vivifica me.

118:41 *Vau.* Et veniat super me misericordia tua, Domine ; salutare tuum secundum eloquium tuum.

118:42 Et respondebo exprobrantibus mihi verbum, quia speravi in sermonibus tuis.

118:43 Et ne auferas de ore meo verbum veritatis usquequaque, quia in judiciis tuis superspravi.

118:44 Et custodiam legem tuam semper, in sæculum et in sæculum sæculi.

118:45 Et ambulabam in latitudine, quia mandata tua exquisivi.

118:46 Et loquebar in testimoniis tuis in conspectu regum, et non confundebar.

118:47 Et meditabar in mandatis tuis, quæ dilexi.

and thy justifications my counsel. DALETH.

118:25 My soul hath cleaved to the pavement: quicken thou me according to thy word.

118:26 I have declared my ways, and thou hast heard me: teach me thy justifications.

118:27 Make me to understand the way of thy justifications: and I shall be exercised in thy wondrous works.

118:28 My soul hath slumbered through heaviness: strengthen thou me in thy words.

118:29 Remove from me the way of iniquity: and out of thy law have mercy on me.

118:30 I have chosen the way of truth: thy judgments I have not forgotten.

118:31 I have stuck to thy testimonies, O Lord: put me not to shame.

118:32 I have run the way of thy commandments, when thou didst enlarge my heart. HE

118:33 Set before me for a law the way of thy justifications, O Lord: and I will always seek after it.

118:34 Give me understanding, and I will search thy law; and I will keep it with my whole heart.

118:35 Lead me into the path of thy commandments; for this same I have desired.

118:36 Incline my heart into thy testimonies and not to covetousness.

118:37 Turn away my eyes that they may not behold vanity: quicken me in thy way.

118:38 Establish thy word to thy servant, in thy fear.

118:39 Turn away my reproach, which I have apprehended: for thy judgments are delightful.

118:40 Behold I have longed after thy precepts: quicken me in thy justice. VAU.

118:41 Let thy mercy also come upon me, O Lord: thy salvation according to thy word.

118:42 So shall I answer them that reproach me in any thing; that I have trusted in thy words.

118:43 And take not thou the word of truth utterly out of my mouth: for in thy words have I hoped exceedingly.

118:44 So shall I always keep thy law, for ever and ever.

118:45 And I walked at large: because I have sought after thy commandments.

118:46 And I spoke of thy testimonies before kings: and I was not ashamed.

118:47 I meditated also on thy commandments, which I loved.

118:48 Et levavi manus meas ad mandata tua, quæ dilexi, et exercebar in justificationibus tuis.

118:49 *Zain.* Memor esto verbi tui servo tuo, in quo mihi spem dedisti.

118:50 Hæc me consolata est in humilitate mea, quia eloquium tuum vivificavit me.

118:51 Superbi inique agebant usquequaque ; a lege autem tua non declinavi.

118:52 Memor fui judiciorum tuorum a sæculo, Domine, et consolatus sum.

118:53 Defectio tenuit me, pro peccatoribus derelinquentibus legem tuam.

118:54 Cantabiles mihi erant justificationes tuæ in loco peregrinationis meæ.

118:55 Memor fui nocte nominis tui, Domine, et custodivi legem tuam.

118:56 Hæc facta est mihi, quia justificationes tuas exquisivi.

118:57 *Heth.* Portio mea, Domine, dixi custodire legem tuam.

118:58 Deprecatus sum faciem tuam in toto corde meo ; miserere mei secundum eloquium tuum.

118:59 Cogitavi vias meas, et converti pedes meos in testimonia tua.

118:60 Paratus sum, et non sum turbatus, ut custodiam mandata tua.

118:61 Funes peccatorum circumplexi sunt me, et legem tuam non sum oblitus.

118:62 Media nocte surgebam ad confitendum tibi, super judicia justificationis tuæ.

118:63 Particeps ego sum omnium timentium te, et custodientium mandata tua.

118:64 Misericordia tua, Domine, plena est terra ; justificationes tuas doce me.

118:65 *Teth.* Bonitatem fecisti cum servo tuo, Domine, secundum verbum tuum.

118:66 Bonitatem, et disciplinam, et scientiam doce me, quia mandatis tuis credidi.

118:67 Priusquam humiliarer ego deliqui : propterea eloquium tuum custodivi.

118:68 Bonus es tu, et in bonitate tua doce me justificationes tuas.

118:69 Multiplicata est super me iniquitas superborum ; ego autem in toto corde meo scrutabor mandata tua.

118:70 Coagulatum est sicut lac cor eorum ; ego vero legem tuam meditatus sum.

118:71 Bonum mihi quia humiliasti me, ut discam justificationes tuas.

118:48 And I lifted up my hands to thy commandments, which I loved: and I was exercised in thy justifications. ZAIN.

118:49 Be thou mindful of thy word to thy servant, in which thou hast given me hope.

118:50 This hath comforted me in my humiliation: because thy word hath enlivened me.

118:51 The proud did iniquitously altogether: but I declined not from thy law.

118:52 I remembered, O Lord, thy judgments of old: and I was comforted.

118:53 A fainting hath taken hold of me, because of the wicked that forsake thy law.

118:54 Thy justifications were the subject of my song, in the place of my pilgrimage.

118:55 In the night I have remembered thy name, O Lord: and have kept thy law.

118:56 This happened to me: because I sought after thy justifications. HETH.

118:57 O Lord, my portion, I have said, I would keep the law.

118:58 I entreated thy face with all my heart: have mercy on me according to thy word.

118:59 I have thought on my ways: and turned my feet unto thy testimonies.

118:60 I am ready, and am not troubled: that I may keep thy commandments.

118:61 The cords of the wicked have encompassed me: but I have not forgotten thy law.

118:62 I rose at midnight to give praise to thee; for the judgments of thy justification.

118:63 I am a partaker with all them that fear thee, and that keep thy commandments.

118:64 The earth, O Lord, is full of thy mercy: teach me thy justifications. TETH.

118:65 Thou hast done well with thy servant, O Lord, according to thy word.

118:66 Teach me goodness and discipline and knowledge; for I have believed thy commandments.

118:67 Before I was humbled I offended; therefore have I kept thy word.

118:68 Thou art good; and in thy goodness teach me thy justifications.

118:69 The iniquity of the proud hath been multiplied over me: but I will seek thy commandments with my whole heart.

118:70 Their heart is curdled like milk: but I have meditated on thy law.

118:71 It is good for me that thou hast humbled me, that I may learn thy justifications.

118:72 Bonum mihi lex oris tui, super millia auri et argenti.

118:73 *Jod.* Manus tuæ fecerunt me, et plasmaverunt me : da mihi intellectum, et discam mandata tua.

118:74 Qui timent te videbunt me et lætabuntur, quia in verba tua supersperavi.

118:75 Cognovi, Domine, quia æquitas judicia tua, et in veritate tua humiliasti me.

118:76 Fiat misericordia tua ut consoletur me, secundum eloquium tuum servo tuo.

118:77 Veniant mihi miserationes tuæ, et vivam, quia lex tua meditatio mea est.

118:78 Confundantur superbi, quia injuste iniquitatem fecerunt in me ; ego autem exercebor in mandatis tuis.

118:79 Convertantur mihi timentes te, et qui noverunt testimonia tua.

118:80 Fiat cor meum immaculatum in justificationibus tuis, ut non confundar.

118:81 *Caph.* Deficit in salutare tuum anima mea, et in verbum tuum supersperavi.

118:82 Defecerunt oculi mei in eloquium tuum, dicentes : Quando consolaberis me ?

118:83 Quia factus sum sicut uter in pruina ; justificationes tuas non sum oblitus.

118:84 Quot sunt dies servi tui ? quando facies de persequentibus me judicium ?

118:85 Narraverunt mihi iniqui fabulationes, sed non ut lex tua.

118:86 Omnia mandata tua veritas : inique persecuti sunt me, adjuva me.

118:87 Paulominus consummaverunt me in terra ; ego autem non dereliqui mandata tua.

118:88 Secundum misericordiam tuam vivifica me, et custodiam testimonia oris tui.

118:89 *Lamed.* In æternum, Domine, verbum tuum permanet in cælo.

118:90 In generationem et generationem veritas tua ; fundasti terram, et permanet.

118:91 Ordinatione tua perseverat dies, quoniam omnia serviunt tibi.

118:92 Nisi quod lex tua meditatio mea est, tunc forte periissem in humilitate mea.

118:93 In æternum non obliviscar justificationes tuas, quia in ipsis vivificasti me.

118:94 Tuus sum ego ; salvum me fac : quoniam justificationes tuas exquisivi.

118:72 The law of thy mouth is good to me, above thousands of gold and silver. JOD.

118:73 Thy hands have made me and formed me: give me understanding, and I will learn thy commandments.

118:74 They that fear thee shall see me, and shall be glad: because I have greatly hoped in thy words.

118:75 I know, O Lord, that thy judgments are equity: and in thy truth thou hast humbled me.

118:76 O! let thy mercy be for my comfort, according to thy word unto thy servant.

118:77 Let thy tender mercies come unto me, and I shall live: for thy law is my meditation.

118:78 Let the proud be ashamed, because they have done unjustly towards me: but I will be employed in thy commandments.

118:79 Let them that fear thee turn to me: and they that know thy testimonies.

118:80 Let my heart be undefiled in thy justifications, that I may not be confounded. CAPH.

118:81 My soul hath fainted after thy salvation: and in thy word I have very much hoped.

118:82 My eyes have failed for thy word, saying: When wilt thou comfort me?

118:83 For I am become like a bottle in the frost: I have not forgotten thy justifications.

118:84 How many are the days of thy servant: when wilt thou execute judgment on them that persecute me?

118:85 The wicked have told me fables: but not as thy law.

118:86 All thy statutes are truth: they have persecuted me unjustly, do thou help me.

118:87 They had almost made an end of me upon earth: but I have not forsaken thy commandments.

118:88 Quicken thou me according to thy mercy: and I shall keep the testimonies of thy mouth. LAMED.

118:89 For ever, O Lord, thy word standeth firm in heaven.

118:90 Thy truth unto all generations: thou hast founded the earth, and it continueth.

118:91 By thy ordinance the day goeth on: for all things serve thee.

118:92 Unless thy law had been my meditation, I had then perhaps perished in my abjection.

118:93 Thy justifications I will never forget: for by them thou hast given me life.

118:94 I am thine, save thou me: for I have sought thy justifications.

118:95 Me exspectaverunt peccatores ut perderent me ; testimonia tua intellexi.

118:96 Omnis consummationis vidi finem, latum mandatum tuum nimis.

118:97 *Mem.* Quomodo dilexi legem tuam, Domine ! tota die meditatio mea est.

118:98 Super inimicos meos prudentem me fecisti mandato tuo, quia in æternum mihi est.

118:99 Super omnes docentes me intellexi, quia testimonia tua meditatio mea est.

118:100 Super senes intellexi, quia mandata tua quæsivi.

118:101 Ab omni via mala prohibui pedes meos, ut custodiam verba tua.

118:102 A judiciis tuis non declinavi, quia tu legem posuisti mihi.

118:103 Quam dulcia faucibus meis eloquia tua ! super mel ori meo.

118:104 A mandatis tuis intellexi ; propterea odivi omnem viam iniquitatis.

118:105 *Nun.* Lucerna pedibus meis verbum tuum, et lumen semitis meis.

118:106 Juravi et statui custodire judicia justitiæ tuæ.

118:107 Humiliatus sum usquequaque, Domine ; vivifica me secundum verbum tuum.

118:108 Voluntaria oris mei beneplacita fac, Domine, et judicia tua doce me.

118:109 Anima mea in manibus meis semper, et legem tuam non sum oblitus.

118:110 Posuerunt peccatores laqueum mihi, et de mandatis tuis non erravi.

118:111 Hæreditate acquisivi testimonia tua in æternum, quia exsultatio cordis mei sunt.

118:112 Inclinavi cor meum ad faciendas justificationes tuas in æternum, propter retributionem.

118:113 *Samech.* Iniquos odio habui, et legem tuam dilexi.

118:114 Adjutor et susceptor meus es tu, et in verbum tuum supersperavi.

118:115 Declinate a me, maligni, et scrutabor mandata Dei mei.

118:116 Suscipe me secundum eloquium tuum, et vivam, et non confundas me ab exspectatione mea.

118:117 Adjuva me, et salvus ero, et meditabor in justificationibus tuis semper.

118:95 The wicked have waited for me to destroy me: but I have understood thy testimonies.

118:96 I have seen an end to all persecution: thy commandment is exceeding broad. MEM.

118:97 O how have I loved thy law, O Lord! it is my meditation all the day.

118:98 Through thy commandment, thou hast made me wiser than my enemies: for it is ever with me.

118:99 I have understood more than all my teachers: because thy testimonies are my meditation.

118:100 I have had understanding above ancients: because I have sought thy commandments.

118:101 I have restrained my feet from every evil way: that I may keep thy words.

118:102 I have not declined from thy judgments, because thou hast set me a law.

118:103 How sweet are thy words to my palate! more than honey to my mouth.

118:104 By thy commandments I have had understanding: therefore have I hated every way of iniquity. NUN.

118:105 Thy word is a lamp to my feet, and a light to my paths.

118:106 I have sworn and am determined to keep the judgments of thy justice.

118:107 I have been humbled, O Lord, exceedingly: quicken thou me according to thy word.

118:108 The free offerings of my mouth make acceptable, O Lord: and teach me thy judgments.

118:109 My soul is continually in my hands: and I have not forgotten thy law.

118:110 Sinners have laid a snare for me: but I have not erred from thy precepts.

118:111 I have purchased thy testimonies for an inheritance for ever: because they are the joy of my heart.

118:112 I have inclined my heart to do thy justifications for ever, for the reward. SAMECH.

118:113 I have hated the unjust: and have loved thy law.

118:114 Thou art my helper and my protector: and in thy word I have greatly hoped.

118:115 Depart from me, ye malignant: and I will search the commandments of my God.

118:116 Uphold me according to thy word, and I shall live: and let me not be confounded in my expectation.

118:117 Help me, and I shall be saved: and I will meditate always on thy justifications.

118:118 Sprevisti omnes discedentes a judiciis tuis, quia injusta cogitatio eorum.

118:119 Prævaricantes reputavi omnes peccatores terræ ; ideo dilexi testimonia tua.

118:120 Confige timore tuo carnes meas ; a judiciis enim tuis timui.

118:121 *Ain.* Feci judicium et justitiam : non tradas me calumniantibus me.

118:122 Suscipe servum tuum in bonum : non calumnientur me superbi.

118:123 Oculi mei defecerunt in salutare tuum, et in eloquium justitiæ tuæ.

118:124 Fac cum servo tuo secundum misericordiam tuam, et justificationes tuas doce me.

118:125 Servus tuus sum ego : da mihi intellectum, ut sciam testimonia tua.

118:126 Tempus faciendi, Domine : dissipaverunt legem tuam.

118:127 Ideo dilexi mandata tua super aurum et topazion.

118:128 Propterea ad omnia mandata tua dirigebar ; omnem viam iniquam odio habui.

118:129 *Phe.* Mirabilia testimonia tua : ideo scrutata est ea anima mea.

118:130 Declaratio sermonum tuorum illuminat, et intellectum dat parvulis.

118:131 Os meum aperui, et attraxi spiritum : quia mandata tua desiderabam.

118:132 Aspice in me, et miserere mei, secundum judicium diligentium nomen tuum.

118:133 Gressus meos dirige secundum eloquium tuum, et non dominetur mei omnis injustitia.

118:134 Redime me a calumniis hominum ut custodiam mandata tua.

118:135 Faciem tuam illumina super servum tuum, et doce me justificationes tuas.

118:136 Exitus aquarum deduxerunt oculi mei, quia non custodierunt legem tuam.

118:137 *Sade.* Justus es, Domine, et rectum judicium tuum.

118:138 Mandasti justitiam testimonia tua, et veritatem tuam nimis.

118:139 Tabescere me fecit zelus meus, quia obliti sunt verba tua inimici mei.

118:140 Ignitum eloquium tuum vehementer, et servus tuus dilexit illud.

118:141 Adolescentulus sum ego et contemptus ; justificationes tuas non sum oblitus.

118:118 Thou hast despised all them that fall off from thy judgments; for their thought is unjust.

118:119 I have accounted all the sinners of the earth prevaricators: therefore have I loved thy testimonies.

118:120 Pierce thou my flesh with thy fear: for I am afraid of thy judgments. AIN.

118:121 I have done judgment and justice: give me not up to them that slander me.

118:122 Uphold thy servant unto good: let not the proud calumniate me.

118:123 My eyes have fainted after thy salvation: and for the word of thy justice.

118:124 Deal with thy servant according to thy mercy: and teach me thy justifications.

118:125 I am thy servant: give me understanding that I may know thy testimonies.

118:126 It is time, O Lord, to do: they have dissipated thy law.

118:127 Therefore have I loved thy commandments above gold and the topaz.

118:128 Therefore was I directed to all thy commandments: I have hated all wicked ways. PHE.

118:129 Thy testimonies are wonderful: therefore my soul hath sought them.

118:130 The declaration of thy words giveth light: and giveth understanding to little ones.

118:131 I opened my mouth and panted: because I longed for thy commandments.

118:132 Look thou upon me, and have mercy on me, according to the judgment of them that love thy name.

118:133 Direct my steps according to thy word: and let no iniquity have dominion over me.

118:134 Redeem me from the calumnies of men: that I may keep thy commandments.

118:135 Make thy face to shine upon thy servant: and teach me thy justifications.

118:136 My eyes have sent forth springs of water: because they have not kept thy law. SADE.

118:137 Thou art just, O Lord: and thy judgment is right.

118:138 Thou hast commanded justice thy testimonies: and thy truth exceedingly.

118:139 My zeal hath made me pine away: because my enemies forgot thy words.

118:140 Thy word is exceedingly refined: and thy servant hath loved it.

118:141 I am very young and despised; but I forget not thy justifications.

118:142 Justitia tua, justitia in æternum, et lex tua veritas.

118:143 Tribulatio et angustia invenerunt me ; mandata tua meditatio mea est.

118:144 Æquitas testimonia tua in æternum : intellectum da mihi, et vivam.

118:145 *Coph.* Clamavi in toto corde meo : exaudi me, Domine ; justificationes tuas requiram.

118:146 Clamavi ad te ; salvum me fac : ut custodiam mandata tua.

118:147 Præveni in maturitate, et clamavi : quia in verba tua supersperavi.

118:148 Prævenerunt oculi mei ad te diluculo, ut meditarer eloquia tua.

118:149 Vocem meam audi secundum misericordiam tuam, Domine, et secundum judicium tuum vivifica me.

118:150 Appropinquaverunt persequentes me iniquitati : a lege autem tua longe facti sunt.

118:151 Prope es tu, Domine, et omnes viæ tuæ veritas.

118:152 Initio cognovi de testimoniis tuis, quia in æternum fundasti ea.

118:153 *Res.* Vide humilitatem meam, et eripe me, quia legem tuam non sum oblitus.

118:154 Judica judicium meum, et redime me : propter eloquium tuum vivifica me.

118:155 Longe a peccatoribus salus, quia justificationes tuas non exquisierunt.

118:156 Misericordiæ tuæ multæ, Domine ; secundum judicium tuum vivifica me.

118:157 Multi qui persequuntur me, et tribulant me ; a testimoniis tuis non declinavi.

118:158 Vidi prævaricantes et tabescebam, quia eloquia tua non custodierunt.

118:159 Vide quoniam mandata tua dilexi, Domine : in misericordia tua vivifica me.

118:160 Principium verborum tuorum veritas ; in æternum omnia judicia justitiæ tuæ.

118:161 *Sin.* Principes persecuti sunt me gratis, et a verbis tuis formidavit cor meum.

118:162 Lætabor ego super eloquia tua, sicut qui invenit spolia multa.

118:163 Iniquitatem odio habui, et abominatus sum, legem autem tuam dilexi.

118:164 Septies in die laudem dixi tibi, super judicia justitiæ tuæ.

118:165 Pax multa diligentibus legem tuam, et

118:142 Thy justice is justice for ever: and thy law is the truth.

118:143 Trouble and anguish have found me: thy commandments are my meditation.

118:144 Thy testimonies are justice for ever: give me understanding, and I shall live. COPH.

118:145 I cried with my whole heart, hear me, O Lord: I will seek thy justifications.

118:146 I cried unto thee, save me: that I may keep thy commandments.

118:147 I prevented the dawning of the day, and cried: because in thy words I very much hoped.

118:148 My eyes to thee have prevented the morning: that I might meditate on thy words.

118:149 Hear thou my voice, O Lord, according to thy mercy: and quicken me according to thy judgment.

118:150 They that persecute me have drawn nigh to iniquity; but they are gone far off from thy law.

118:151 Thou art near, O Lord: and all thy ways are truth.

118:152 I have known from the beginning concerning thy testimonies: that thou hast founded them for ever. RES.

118:153 See my humiliation and deliver me: for I have not forgotten thy law.

118:154 Judge my judgment and redeem me: quicken thou me for thy word's sake.

118:155 Salvation is far from sinners; because they have not sought thy justifications.

118:156 Many, O Lord, are thy mercies: quicken me according to thy judgment.

118:157 Many are they that persecute me, and afflict me; but I have not declined from thy testimonies.

118:158 I beheld the transgressors, and I pined away; because they kept not thy word.

118:159 Behold I have loved thy commandments, O Lord; quicken me thou in thy mercy.

118:160 The beginning of thy words is truth: all the judgments of thy justice are for ever. SIN.

118:161 Princes have persecuted me without cause: and my heart hath been in awe of thy words.

118:162 I will rejoice at thy words, as one that hath found great spoil.

118:163 I have hated and abhorred iniquity; but I have loved thy law.

118:164 Seven times a day I have given praise to thee, for the judgments of thy justice.

118:165 Much peace have they that love thy law,

non est illis scandalum.

118:166 Exspectabam salutare tuum, Domine, et mandata tua dilexi.

118:167 Custodivit anima mea testimonia tua, et dilexit ea vehementer.

118:168 Servavi mandata tua et testimonia tua, quia omnes viæ meæ in conspectu tuo.

118:169 *Tau.* Appropinquet deprecatio mea in conspectu tuo, Domine ; juxta eloquium tuum da mihi intellectum.

118:170 Intret postulatio mea in conspectu tuo ; secundum eloquium tuum eripe me.

118:171 Eructabunt labia mea hymnum, cum docueris me justificationes tuas.

118:172 Pronuntiabit lingua mea eloquium tuum, quia omnia mandata tua æquitas.

118:173 Fiat manus tua ut salvet me, quoniam mandata tua elegi.

118:174 Concupivi salutare tuum, Domine, et lex tua meditatio mea est.

118:175 Vivet anima mea, et laudabit te, et judicia tua adjuvabunt me.

118:176 Erravi sicut ovis quæ periit : quære servum tuum, quia mandata tua non sum oblitus.

CXIX.

119:1 *Canticum graduum.* AD DOMINUM CUM TRIBULARER CLAMAVI, et exaudivit me.

119:2 Domine, libera animam meam a labiis iniquis et a lingua dolosa.

119:3 Quid detur tibi, aut quid apponatur tibi ad linguam dolosam ?

119:4 Sagittæ potentis acutæ, cum carbonibus desolatoriis.

119:5 Heu mihi, quia incolatus meus prolongatus est ! habitavi cum habitantibus Cedar ;

119:6 multum incola fuit anima mea.

119:7 Cum his qui oderunt pacem eram pacificus ; cum loquebar illis, impugnabant me gratis.

CXX.

120:1 *Canticum graduum.* LEVAVI OCULOS MEOS in montes, unde veniet auxilium mihi.

120:2 Auxilium meum a Domino, qui fecit cælum et terram.

120:3 Non det in commotionem pedem tuum, neque dormitet qui custodit te.

and to them there is no stumbling block.

118:166 I looked to thy salvation, O Lord: and I loved thy commandments.

118:167 My soul hath kept thy testimonies: and hath loved them exceedingly.

118:168 I have kept thy commandments and thy testimonies: because all my ways are in thy sight. TAU.

118:169 Let my supplication, O Lord, come near in thy sight: give me understanding according to thy word.

118:170 Let my request come in before thee; deliver thou me according to thy word.

118:171 My lips shall utter a hymn, when thou shalt teach me thy justifications.

118:172 My tongue shall pronounce thy word: because all thy commandments are justice.

118:173 Let thy hand be with me to save me; for I have chosen thy precepts.

118:174 I have longed for thy salvation, O Lord; and thy law is my meditation.

118:175 My soul shall live and shall praise thee: and thy judgments shall help me.

118:176 I have gone astray like a sheep that is lost: seek thy servant, because I have not forgotten thy commandments.

119:1 *A gradual canticle.* IN MY TROUBLE I CRIED TO THE LORD: and he heard me.

119:2 O Lord, deliver my soul from wicked lips, and a deceitful tongue.

119:3 What shall be given to thee, or what shall be added to thee, to a deceitful tongue?

119:4 The sharp arrows of the mighty, with coals that lay waste.

119:5 Woe is me, that my sojourning is prolonged! I have dwelt with the inhabitants of Cedar:

119:6 my soul hath been long a sojourner.

119:7 With them that hated peace I was peaceable: when I spoke to them they fought against me without cause.

120:1 *A gradual canticle.* I HAVE LIFTED UP MY EYES to the mountains, from whence help shall come to me.

120:2 My help is from the Lord, who made heaven and earth.

120:3 May he not suffer thy foot to be moved: neither let him slumber that keepeth thee.

120:4 Ecce non dormitabit neque dormiet qui custodit Israël.

120:5 Dominus custodit te ; Dominus protectio tua super manum dexteram tuam.

120:6 Per diem sol non uret te, neque luna per noctem.

120:7 Dominus custodit te ab omni malo ; custodiat animam tuam Dominus.

120:8 Dominus custodiat introitum tuum et exitum tuum, ex hoc nunc et usque in sæculum.

120:4 Behold he shall neither slumber nor sleep, that keepeth Israel.

120:5 The Lord is thy keeper, the Lord is thy protection upon thy right hand.

120:6 The sun shall not burn thee by day: nor the moon by night.

120:7 The Lord keepeth thee from all evil: may the Lord keep thy soul.

120:8 May the Lord keep thy going in and thy going out; from henceforth now and for ever.

CXXI.

121:1 *Canticum graduum.* LÆTATUS SUM in his quæ dicta sunt mihi : In domum Domini ibimus.

121:2 Stantes erant pedes nostri in atriis tuis, Jerusalem.

121:3 Jerusalem, quæ ædificatur ut civitas, cujus participatio ejus in idipsum.

121:4 Illuc enim ascenderunt tribus, tribus Domini : testimonium Israël, ad confitendum nomini Domini.

121:5 Quia illic sederunt sedes in judicio, sedes super domum David.

121:6 Rogate quæ ad pacem sunt Jerusalem, et abundantia diligentibus te.

121:7 Fiat pax in virtute tua, et abundantia in turribus tuis.

121:8 Propter fratres meos et proximos meos, loquebar pacem de te.

121:9 Propter domum Domini Dei nostri, quæsivi bona tibi.

121:1 *A gradual canticle.* I REJOICED at the things that were said to me: We shall go into the house of the Lord.

121:2 Our feet were standing in thy courts, O Jerusalem.

121:3 Jerusalem, which is built as a city, which is compact together.

121:4 For thither did the tribes go up, the tribes of the Lord: the testimony of Israel, to praise the name of the Lord.

121:5 Because their seats have sat in judgment, seats upon the house of David.

121:6 Pray ye for the things that are for the peace of Jerusalem: and abundance for them that love thee.

121:7 Let peace be in thy strength: and abundance in thy towers.

121:8 For the sake of my brethren, and of my neighbours, I spoke peace of thee.

121:9 Because of the house of the Lord our God, I have sought good things for thee.

CXXII.

122:1 *Canticum graduum.* AD TE LEVAVI OCULOS MEOS, qui habitas in cælis.

122:2 Ecce sicut oculi servorum in manibus dominorum suorum ; sicut oculi ancillæ in manibus dominæ suæ : ita oculi nostri ad Dominum Deum nostrum, donec misereatur nostri.

122:3 Miserere nostri, Domine, miserere nostri, quia multum repleti sumus despectione ;

122:4 quia multum repleta est anima nostra opprobrium abundantibus, et despectio superbis.

122:1 *A gradual canticle.* TO THEE HAVE I LIFTED UP my eyes, who dwellest in heaven.

122:2 Behold as the eyes of the servants are on the hands of their masters, As the eyes of the handmaid are on the hands of her mistress: so are our eyes unto the Lord our God, until he have mercy on us.

122:3 Have mercy on us, O Lord, have mercy on us: for we are greatly filled with contempt.

122:4 For our soul is greatly filled: we are a reproach to the rich, and contempt to the proud.

CXXIII.

123:1 *Canticum graduum.* NISI QUIA DOMINUS erat in nobis, dicat nunc Israël,

123:2 nisi quia Dominus erat in nobis : cum exsurgerent homines in nos,

123:1 *A gradual canticle.* IF IT HAD NOT BEEN THAT THE LORD was with us, let Israel now say:

123:2 If it had not been that the Lord was with us, When men rose up against us,

123:3 forte vivos deglutissent nos ; cum irasceretur furor eorum in nos,

123:4 forsitan aqua absorbuisset nos ;

123:5 torrentem pertransivit anima nostra ; forsitan pertransisset anima nostra aquam intolerabilem.

123:6 Benedictus Dominus, qui non dedit nos in captionem dentibus eorum.

123:7 Anima nostra sicut passer erepta est de laqueo venantium ; laqueus contritus est, et nos liberati sumus.

123:8 Adjutorium nostrum in nomine Domini, qui fecit cælum et terram.

123:3 perhaps they had swallowed us up alive. When their fury was enkindled against us,

123:4 perhaps the waters had swallowed us up.

123:5 Our soul hath passed through a torrent: perhaps our soul had passed through a water insupportable.

123:6 Blessed be the Lord, who hath not given us to be a prey to their teeth.

123:7 Our soul hath been delivered as a sparrow out of the snare of the fowlers. The snare is broken, and we are delivered.

123:8 Our help is in the name of the Lord, who made heaven and earth.

CXXIV.

124:1 *Canticum graduum.* QUI CONFIDUNT IN DOMINO, sicut mons Sion : non commovebitur in æternum, qui habitat

124:2 in Jerusalem. Montes in circuitu ejus ; et Dominus in circuitu populi sui, ex hoc nunc et usque in sæculum.

124:3 Quia non relinquet Dominus virgam peccatorum super sortem justorum : ut non extendant justi ad iniquitatem manus suas,

124:4 benefac, Domine, bonis, et rectis corde.

124:5 Declinantes autem in obligationes, adducet Dominus cum operantibus iniquitatem. Pax super Israël !

124:1 *A gradual canticle.* THEY THAT TRUST IN THE LORD shall be as mount Sion: he shall not be moved for ever that dwelleth

124:2 in Jerusalem. Mountains are round about it: so the Lord is round about his people from henceforth now and for ever.

124:3 For the Lord will not leave the rod of sinners upon the lot of the just: that the just may not stretch forth their hands to iniquity.

124:4 Do good, O Lord, to those that are good, and to the upright of heart.

124:5 But such as turn aside into bonds, the Lord shall lead out with the workers of iniquity: peace upon Israel.

CXXV.

125:1 *Canticum graduum.* IN CONVERTENDO DOMINUS captivitatem Sion, facti sumus sicut consolati.

125:2 Tunc repletum est gaudio os nostrum, et lingua nostra exsultatione. Tunc dicent inter gentes : Magnificavit Dominus facere cum eis.

125:3 Magnificavit Dominus facere nobiscum ; facti sumus lætantes.

125:4 Converte, Domine, captivitatem nostram, sicut torrens in austro.

125:5 Qui seminant in lacrimis, in exsultatione metent.

125:6 Euntes ibant et flebant, mittentes semina sua. Venientes autem venient cum exsultatione, portantes manipulos suos.

125:1 *A gradual canticle.* WHEN THE LORD BROUGHT BACK the captivity of Sion, we became like men comforted.

125:2 Then was our mouth filled with gladness; and our tongue with joy. Then shall they say among the Gentiles: The Lord hath done great things for them.

125:3 The Lord hath done great things for us: we are become joyful.

125:4 Turn again our captivity, O Lord, as a stream in the south.

125:5 They that sow in tears shall reap in joy.

125:6 Going they went and wept, casting their seeds. But coming they shall come with joyfulness, carrying their sheaves.

CXXVI.

126:1 *Canticum graduum Salomonis.* NISI DOMINUS ÆDIFICAVERIT domum, in vanum laboraverunt qui ædificant eam. Nisi Dominus custodierit civitatem, frustra vigilat qui custodit eam.

126:2 Vanum est vobis ante lucem surgere : surgite postquam sederitis, qui manducatis panem doloris. Cum dederit dilectis suis somnum,

126:3 ecce hæreditas Domini, filii ; merces, fructus ventris.

126:4 Sicut sagittæ in manu potentis, ita filii excussorum.

126:5 Beatus vir qui implevit desiderium suum ex ipsis : non confundetur cum loquetur inimicis suis in porta.

126:1 *A gradual canticle of Solomon.* UNLESS THE LORD BUILD the house, they labour in vain that build it. Unless the Lord keep the city, he watcheth in vain that keepeth it.

126:2 It is vain for you to rise before light, rise ye after you have sitten, you that eat the bread of sorrow. When he shall give sleep to his beloved,

126:3 behold the inheritance of the Lord are children: the reward, the fruit of the womb.

126:4 As arrows in the hand of the mighty, so the children of them that have been shaken.

126:5 Blessed is the man that hath filled the desire with them; he shall not be confounded when he shall speak to his enemies in the gate.

CXXVII.

127:1 *Canticum graduum.* BEATI OMNES qui timent Dominum, qui ambulant in viis ejus.

127:2 Labores manuum tuarum quia manducabis : beatus es, et bene tibi erit.

127:3 Uxor tua sicut vitis abundans in lateribus domus tuæ ; filii tui sicut novellæ olivarum in circuitu mensæ tuæ.

127:4 Ecce sic benedicetur homo qui timet Dominum.

127:5 Benedicat tibi Dominus ex Sion, et videas bona Jerusalem omnibus diebus vitæ tuæ.

127:6 Et videas filios filiorum tuorum : pacem super Israël.

127:1 *A gradual canticle.* BLESSED ARE ALL THEY that fear the Lord: that walk in his ways.

127:2 For thou shalt eat the labours of thy hands: blessed art thou, and it shall be well with thee.

127:3 Thy wife as a fruitful vine, on the sides of thy house. Thy children as olive plants, round about thy table.

127:4 Behold, thus shall the man be blessed that feareth the Lord.

127:5 May the Lord bless thee out of Sion: and mayest thou see the good things of Jerusalem all the days of thy life.

127:6 And mayest thou see thy children's children, peace upon Israel.

CXXVIII.

128:1 *Canticum graduum.* SÆPE EXPUGNAVERUNT me a juventute mea, dicat nunc Israël ;

128:2 sæpe expugnaverunt me a juventute mea : etenim non potuerunt mihi.

128:3 Supra dorsum meum fabricaverunt peccatores ; prolongaverunt iniquitatem suam.

128:4 Dominus justus concidit cervices peccatorum.

128:5 Confundantur, et convertantur retrorsum omnes qui oderunt Sion.

128:6 Fiant sicut fœnum tectorum, quod priusquam evellatur exaruit :

128:7 de quo non implevit manum suam qui metit, et sinum suum qui manipulos colligit.

128:8 Et non dixerunt qui præteribant : Benedictio Domini super vos. Benediximus vobis in nomine Domini.

128:1 *A gradual canticle.* OFTEN HAVE THEY FOUGHT against me from my youth, let Israel now say.

128:2 Often have they fought against me from my youth: but they could not prevail over me.

128:3 The wicked have wrought upon my back: they have lengthened their iniquity.

128:4 The Lord who is just will cut the necks of sinners:

128:5 let them all be confounded and turned back that hate Sion.

128:6 Let them be as grass on the tops of houses: which withered before it be plucked up:

128:7 Wherewith the mower filleth not his hand: nor he that gathereth sheaves his bosom.

128:8 And they that have passed by have not said: The blessing of the Lord be upon you: we have blessed you in the name of the Lord.

CXXIX.

129:1 *Canticum graduum.* DE PROFUNDIS clamavi ad te, Domine ;

129:2 Domine, exaudi vocem meam. Fiant aures tuæ intendentes in vocem deprecationis meæ.

129:3 Si iniquitates observaveris, Domine, Domine, quis sustinebit ?

129:4 Quia apud te propitiatio est ; et propter legem tuam sustinui te, Domine. Sustinuit anima mea in verbo ejus :

129:5 speravit anima mea in Domino.

129:6 A custodia matutina usque ad noctem, speret Israël in Domino.

129:7 Quia apud Dominum misericordia, et copiosa apud eum redemptio.

129:8 Et ipse redimet Israël ex omnibus iniquitatibus ejus.

129:1 *A gradual canticle.* OUT OF THE DEPTHS I have cried to thee, O Lord:

129:2 Lord, hear my voice. Let thy ears be attentive to the voice of my supplication.

129:3 If thou, O Lord, wilt mark iniquities: Lord, who shall stand it.

129:4 For with thee there is merciful forgiveness: and by reason of thy law, I have waited for thee, O Lord. My soul hath relied on his word:

129:5 my soul hath hoped in the Lord.

129:6 From the morning watch even until night, let Israel hope in the Lord.

129:7 Because with the Lord there is mercy: and with him plentiful redemption.

129:8 And he shall redeem Israel from all his iniquities.

CXXX.

130:1 *Canticum graduum David.* DOMINE, NON EST EXALTATUM COR MEUM, neque elati sunt oculi mei, neque ambulavi in magnis, neque in mirabilibus super me.

130:2 Si non humiliter sentiebam, sed exaltavi animam meam : sicut ablactatus est super matre sua, ita retributio in anima mea.

130:3 Speret Israël in Domino, ex hoc nunc et usque in sæculum.

130:1 *A gradual canticle of David.* LORD, MY HEART IS NOT EXALTED: nor are my eyes lofty. Neither have I walked in great matters, nor in wonderful things above me.

130:2 If I was not humbly minded, but exalted my soul: As a child that is weaned is towards his mother, so reward in my soul.

130:3 Let Israel hope in the Lord, from henceforth now and for ever.

CXXXI.

131:1 *Canticum graduum.* MEMENTO, DOMINE, DAVID, et omnis mansuetudinis ejus :

131:2 sicut juravit Domino ; votum vovit Deo Jacob :

131:3 Si introiero in tabernaculum domus meæ ; si ascendero in lectum strati mei ;

131:4 si dedero somnum oculis meis, et palpebris meis dormitationem,

131:5 et requiem temporibus meis, donec inveniam locum Domino, tabernaculum Deo Jacob.

131:6 Ecce audivimus eam in Ephrata ; invenimus eam in campis silvæ.

131:7 Introibimus in tabernaculum ejus ; adorabimus in loco ubi steterunt pedes ejus.

131:8 Surge, Domine, in requiem tuam, tu et arca sanctificationis tuæ.

131:9 Sacerdotes tui induantur justitiam, et sancti tui exsultent.

131:10 Propter David servum tuum non avertas faciem christi tui.

131:1 *A gradual canticle.* O LORD, REMEMBER DAVID, and all his meekness.

131:2 How he swore to the Lord, he vowed a vow to the God of Jacob:

131:3 If I shall enter into the tabernacle of my house: if I shall go up into the bed wherein I lie:

131:4 If I shall give sleep to my eyes, or slumber to my eyelids,

131:5 Or rest to my temples: until I find out a place for the Lord, a tabernacle for the God of Jacob.

131:6 Behold we have heard of it in Ephrata: we have found it in the fields of the wood.

131:7 We will go into his tabernacle: We will adore in the place where his feet stood.

131:8 Arise, O Lord, into thy resting place: thou and the ark, which thou hast sanctified.

131:9 Let thy priests be clothed with justice: and let thy saints rejoice.

131:10 For thy servant David's sake, turn not away the face of thy anointed.

131:11 Juravit Dominus David veritatem, et non frustrabitur eam : De fructu ventris tui ponam super sedem tuam.

131:12 Si custodierint filii tui testamentum meum, et testimonia mea hæc quæ docebo eos, et filii eorum usque in sæculum sedebunt super sedem tuam.

131:13 Quoniam elegit Dominus Sion : elegit eam in habitationem sibi.

131:14 Hæc requies mea in sæculum sæculi ; hic habitabo, quoniam elegi eam.

131:15 Viduam ejus benedicens benedicam ; pauperes ejus saturabo panibus.

131:16 Sacerdotes ejus induam salutari, et sancti ejus exsultatione exsultabunt.

131:17 Illuc producam cornu David ; paravi lucernam christo meo.

131:18 Inimicos ejus induam confusione ; super ipsum autem efflorebit sanctificatio mea.

131:11 The Lord hath sworn truth to David, and he will not make it void: of the fruit of thy womb I will set upon thy throne.

131:12 If thy children will keep my covenant, and these my testimonies which I shall teach them: Their children also for evermore shall sit upon thy throne.

131:13 For the Lord hath chosen Sion: he hath chosen it for his dwelling.

131:14 This is my rest for ever and ever: here will I dwell, for I have chosen it.

131:15 Blessing, I will bless her widow: I will satisfy her poor with bread.

131:16 I will clothe her priests with salvation: and her saints shall rejoice with exceeding great joy.

131:17 There will I bring forth a horn to David: I have prepared a lamp for my anointed.

131:18 His enemies I will clothe with confusion: but upon him shall my sanctification flourish.

CXXXII.

132:1 *Canticum graduum David.* ECCE QUAM BONUM et quam jucundum, habitare fratres in unum !

132:2 Sicut unguentum in capite, quod descendit in barbam, barbam Aaron, quod descendit in oram vestimenti ejus ;

132:3 sicut ros Hermon, qui descendit in montem Sion. Quoniam illic mandavit Dominus benedictionem, et vitam usque in sæculum.

132:1 *A gradual canticle of David.* BEHOLD HOW GOOD and how pleasant it is for brethren to dwell in unity.

132:2 Like the precious ointment on the head, that ran down upon the beard, the beard of Aaron, Which ran down to the skirt of his garment:

132:3 as the dew of Hermon, which descendeth upon mount Sion. For there the Lord hath commandeth blessing, and life for evermore.

CXXXIII.

133:1 *Canticum graduum.* ECCE NUNC BENEDICITE DOMINUM, omnes servi Domini : qui statis in domo Domini, in atriis domus Dei nostri.

133:2 In noctibus extollite manus vestras in sancta, et benedicite Dominum.

133:3 Benedicat te Dominus ex Sion, qui fecit cælum et terram.

133:1 *A gradual canticle.* BEHOLD NOW BLESS YE THE LORD, all ye servants of the Lord: Who stand in the house of the Lord, in the courts of the house of our God.

133:2 In the nights lift up your hands to the holy places, and bless ye the Lord.

133:3 May the Lord out of Sion bless thee, he that made heaven and earth.

CXXXIV.

134:1 *Alleluja.* LAUDATE NOMEN DOMINI ; laudate, servi, Dominum :

134:2 qui statis in domo Domini, in atriis domus Dei nostri.

134:3 Laudate Dominum, quia bonus Dominus ; psallite nomini ejus, quoniam suave.

134:4 Quoniam Jacob elegit sibi Dominus ; Israël in possessionem sibi.

134:1 *Alleluia.* PRAISE YE THE NAME OF THE LORD: O you his servants, praise the Lord:

134:2 You that stand in the house of the Lord, in the courts of the house of our God.

134:3 Praise ye the Lord, for the Lord is good: sing ye to his name, for it is sweet.

134:4 For the Lord hath chosen Jacob unto himself: Israel for his own possession.

134:5 Quia ego cognovi quod magnus est Dominus, et Deus noster præ omnibus diis.

134:6 Omnia quæcumque voluit Dominus fecit, in cælo, in terra, in mari et in omnibus abyssis.

134:7 Educens nubes ab extremo terræ, fulgura in pluviam fecit ; qui producit ventos de thesauris suis.

134:8 Qui percussit primogenita Ægypti, ab homine usque ad pecus.

134:9 Et misit signa et prodigia in medio tui, Ægypte : in Pharaonem, et in omnes servos ejus.

134:10 Qui percussit gentes multas, et occidit reges fortes :

134:11 Sehon, regem Amorrhæorum, et Og, regem Basan, et omnia regna Chanaan :

134:12 et dedit terram eorum hæreditatem, hæreditatem Israël populo suo.

134:13 Domine, nomen tuum in æternum ; Domine, memoriale tuum in generationem et generationem.

134:14 Quia judicabit Dominus populum suum, et in servis suis deprecabitur.

134:15 Simulacra gentium argentum et aurum, opera manuum hominum.

134:16 Os habent, et non loquentur ; oculos habent, et non videbunt.

134:17 Aures habent, et non audient ; neque enim est spiritus in ore ipsorum.

134:18 Similes illis fiant qui faciunt ea, et omnes qui confidunt in eis.

134:19 Domus Israël, benedicite Domino ; domus Aaron, benedicite Domino.

134:20 Domus Levi, benedicite Domino ; qui timetis Dominum, benedicite Domino.

134:21 Benedictus Dominus ex Sion, qui habitat in Jerusalem.

134:5 For I have known that the Lord is great, and our God is above all gods.

134:6 Whatsoever the Lord hath pleased he hath done, in heaven, in earth, in the sea, and in all the deeps.

134:7 He bringeth up clouds from the end of the earth: he hath made lightnings for the rain. He bringeth forth winds out of his stores:

134:8 He slew the firstborn of Egypt from man even unto beast.

134:9 He sent forth signs and wonders in the midst of thee, O Egypt: upon Pharao, and upon all his servants.

134:10 He smote many nations, and slew mighty kings:

134:11 Sehon king of the Amorrhites, and Og king of Basan, and all the kingdoms of Chanaan.

134:12 And gave their land for an inheritance, for an inheritance to his people Israel.

134:13 Thy name, O Lord, is for ever: thy memorial, O Lord, unto all generations.

134:14 For the Lord will judge his people, and will be entreated in favour of his servants.

134:15 The idols of the Gentiles are silver and gold, the works of men's hands.

134:16 They have a mouth, but they speak not: they have eyes, but they see not.

134:17 They have ears, but they hear not: neither is there any breath in their mouths.

134:18 Let them that make them be like to them: and every one that trusteth in them.

134:19 Bless the Lord, O house of Israel: bless the Lord, O house of Aaron.

134:20 Bless the Lord, O house of Levi: you that fear the Lord, bless the Lord.

134:21 Blessed be the Lord out of Sion, who dwelleth in Jerusalem.

CXXXV.

135:1 *Alleluja.* CONFITEMINI DOMINO, quoniam bonus, quoniam in æternum misericordia ejus.

135:2 Confitemini Deo deorum, quoniam in æternum misericordia ejus.

135:3 Confitemini Domino dominorum, quoniam in æternum misericordia ejus.

135:4 Qui facit mirabilia magna solus, quoniam in æternum misericordia ejus.

135:5 Qui fecit cælos in intellectu, quoniam in æternum misericordia ejus.

135:6 Qui firmavit terram super aquas, quoniam

135:1 *Alleluia.* PRAISE THE LORD, for he is good: for his mercy endureth for ever.

135:2 Praise ye the God of gods: for his mercy endureth for ever.

135:3 Praise ye the Lord of lords: for his mercy endureth for ever.

135:4 Who alone doth great wonders: for his mercy endureth for ever.

135:5 Who made the heavens in understanding: for his mercy endureth for ever.

135:6 Who established the earth above the wa-

in æternum misericordia ejus.

135:7 Qui fecit luminaria magna, quoniam in æternum misericordia ejus :

135:8 solem in potestatem diei, quoniam in æternum misericordia ejus ;

135:9 lunam et stellas in potestatem noctis, quoniam in æternum misericordia ejus.

135:10 Qui percussit Ægyptum cum primogenitis eorum, quoniam in æternum misericordia ejus.

135:11 Qui eduxit Israël de medio eorum, quoniam in æternum misericordia ejus,

135:12 in manu potenti et brachio excelso, quoniam in æternum misericordia ejus.

135:13 Qui divisit mare Rubrum in divisiones, quoniam in æternum misericordia ejus ;

135:14 et eduxit Israël per medium ejus, quoniam in æternum misericordia ejus ;

135:15 et excussit Pharaonem et virtutem ejus in mari Rubro, quoniam in æternum misericordia ejus.

135:16 Qui traduxit populum suum per desertum, quoniam in æternum misericordia ejus.

135:17 Qui percussit reges magnos, quoniam in æternum misericordia ejus ;

135:18 et occidit reges fortes, quoniam in æternum misericordia ejus :

135:19 Sehon, regem Amorrhæorum, quoniam in æternum misericordia ejus ;

135:20 et Og, regem Basan, quoniam in æternum misericordia ejus :

135:21 et dedit terram eorum hæreditatem, quoniam in æternum misericordia ejus ;

135:22 hæreditatem Israël, servo suo, quoniam in æternum misericordia ejus.

135:23 Quia in humilitate nostra memor fuit nostri, quoniam in æternum misericordia ejus ;

135:24 et redemit nos ab inimicis nostris, quoniam in æternum misericordia ejus.

135:25 Qui dat escam omni carni, quoniam in æternum misericordia ejus.

135:26 Confitemini Deo cæli, quoniam in æternum misericordia ejus. Confitemini Domino dominorum, quoniam in æternum misericordia ejus.

ters: for his mercy endureth for ever.

135:7 Who made the great lights: for his mercy endureth for ever.

135:8 The sun to rule over the day: for his mercy endureth for ever.

135:9 The moon and the stars to rule the night: for his mercy endureth for ever.

135:10 Who smote Egypt with their firstborn: for his mercy endureth for ever.

135:11 Who brought out Israel from among them: for his mercy endureth for ever.

135:12 With a mighty hand and a stretched out arm: for his mercy endureth for ever.

135:13 Who divided the Red Sea into parts: for his mercy endureth for ever.

135:14 And brought out Israel through the midst thereof: for his mercy endureth for ever.

135:15 And overthrew Pharao and his host in the Red Sea: for his mercy endureth for ever.

135:16 Who led his people through the desert: for his mercy endureth for ever.

135:17 Who smote great kings: for his mercy endureth for ever.

135:18 And slew strong kings: for his mercy endureth for ever.

135:19 Sehon king of the Amorrhites: for his mercy endureth for ever.

135:20 And Og king of Basan: for his mercy endureth for ever.

135:21 And he gave their land for an inheritance: for his mercy endureth for ever.

135:22 For an inheritance to his servant Israel: for his mercy endureth for ever.

135:23 For he was mindful of us in our affliction: for his mercy endureth for ever.

135:24 And he redeemed us from our enemies: for his mercy endureth for ever.

135:25 Who giveth food to all flesh: for his mercy endureth for ever.

135:26 Give glory to the God of heaven: for his mercy endureth for ever. Give glory to the Lord of lords: for his mercy endureth for ever.

CXXXVI.

136:1 *Psalmus David, Jeremiæ.* SUPER FLUMINA BABYLONIS illic sedimus et flevimus, cum recordaremur Sion.

136:2 In salicibus in medio ejus suspendimus organa nostra :

136:1 *A psalm of David, for Jeremias.* UPON THE RIVERS OF BABYLON, there we sat and wept: when we remembered Sion:

136:2 On the willows in the midst thereof we hung up our instruments.

136:3 quia illic interrogaverunt nos, qui captivos duxerunt nos, verba cantionum ; et qui abduxerunt nos : Hymnum cantate nobis de canticis Sion.

136:4 Quomodo cantabimus canticum Domini in terra aliena ?

136:5 Si oblitus fuero tui, Jerusalem, oblivioni detur dextera mea.

136:6 Adhæreat lingua mea faucibus meis, si non meminero tui ; si non proposuero Jerusalem in principio lætitiæ meæ.

136:7 Memor esto, Domine, filiorum Edom, in die Jerusalem : qui dicunt : Exinanite, exinanite usque ad fundamentum in ea.

136:8 Filia Babylonis misera ! beatus qui retribuet tibi retributionem tuam quam retribuisti nobis.

136:9 Beatus qui tenebit, et allidet parvulos tuos ad petram.

136:3 For there they that led us into captivity required of us the words of songs. And they that carried us away, said: Sing ye to us a hymn of the songs of Sion.

136:4 How shall we sing the song of the Lord in a strange land?

136:5 If I forget thee, O Jerusalem, let my right hand be forgotten.

136:6 Let my tongue cleave to my jaws, if I do not remember thee: If I make not Jerusalem the beginning of my joy.

136:7 Remember, O Lord, the children of Edom, in the day of Jerusalem: Who say: Rase it, rase it, even to the foundation thereof.

136:8 O daughter of Babylon, miserable: blessed shall he be who shall repay thee thy payment which thou hast paid us.

136:9 Blessed be he that shall take and dash thy little ones against the rock.

CXXXVII.

137:1 *Ipsi David.* CONFITEBOR TIBI, DOMINE, in toto corde meo, quoniam audisti verba oris mei. In conspectu angelorum psallam tibi ;

137:2 adorabo ad templum sanctum tuum, et confitebor nomini tuo : super misericordia tua et veritate tua ; quoniam magnificasti super omne, nomen sanctum tuum.

137:3 In quacumque die invocavero te, exaudi me ; multiplicabis in anima mea virtutem.

137:4 Confiteantur tibi, Domine, omnes reges terræ, quia audierunt omnia verba oris tui.

137:5 Et cantent in viis Domini, quoniam magna est gloria Domini ;

137:6 quoniam excelsus Dominus, et humilia respicit, et alta a longe cognoscit.

137:7 Si ambulavero in medio tribulationis, vivificabis me ; et super iram inimicorum meorum extendisti manum tuam, et salvum me fecit dextera tua.

137:8 Dominus retribuet pro me. Domine, misericordia tua in sæculum ; opera manuum tuarum ne despicias.

137:1 *For David himself.* I WILL PRAISE THEE, O LORD, with my whole heart: for thou hast heard the words of my mouth. I will sing praise to thee in the sight of his angels:

137:2 I will worship towards thy holy temple, and I will give glory to thy name. For thy mercy, and for thy truth: for thou hast magnified thy holy name above all.

137:3 In what day soever I shall call upon thee, hear me: thou shall multiply strength in my soul.

137:4 May all the kings of the earth give glory to thee: for they have heard all the words of thy mouth.

137:5 And let them sing in the ways of the Lord: for great is the glory of the Lord.

137:6 For the Lord is high, and looketh on the low: and the high he knoweth afar off.

137:7 If I shall walk in the midst of tribulation, thou wilt quicken me: and thou hast stretched forth thy hand against the wrath of my enemies: and thy right hand hath saved me.

137:8 The Lord will repay for me: thy mercy, O Lord, endureth for ever: O despise not the work of thy hands.

CXXXVIII.

138:1 *In finem, psalmus David.* DOMINE, PROBASTI ME, et cognovisti me ;

138:2 tu cognovisti sessionem meam et resurrectionem meam.

138:1 *Unto the end, a psalm of David.* LORD, THOU HAST PROVED me, and known me:

138:2 thou hast known my sitting down, and my rising up.

138:3 Intellexisti cogitationes meas de longe ; semitam meam et funiculum meum investigasti :

138:4 et omnes vias meas prævidisti, quia non est sermo in lingua mea.

138:5 Ecce, Domine, tu cognovisti omnia, novissima et antiqua. Tu formasti me, et posuisti super me manum tuam.

138:6 Mirabilis facta est scientia tua ex me ; confortata est, et non potero ad eam.

138:7 Quo ibo a spiritu tuo ? et quo a facie tua fugiam ?

138:8 Si ascendero in cælum, tu illic es ; si descendero in infernum, ades.

138:9 Si sumpsero pennas meas diluculo, et habitavero in extremis maris,

138:10 etenim illuc manus tua deducet me, et tenebit me dextera tua.

138:11 Et dixi : Forsitan tenebræ conculcabunt me ; et nox illuminatio mea in deliciis meis.

138:12 Quia tenebræ non obscurabuntur a te, et nox sicut dies illuminabitur : sicut tenebræ ejus, ita et lumen ejus.

138:13 Quia tu possedisti renes meos ; suscepisti me de utero matris meæ.

138:14 Confitebor tibi, quia terribiliter magnificatus es ; mirabilia opera tua, et anima mea cognoscit nimis.

138:15 Non est occultatum os meum a te, quod fecisti in occulto ; et substantia mea in inferioribus terræ.

138:16 Imperfectum meum viderunt oculi tui, et in libro tuo omnes scribentur. Dies formabuntur, et nemo in eis.

138:17 Mihi autem nimis honorificati sunt amici tui, Deus ; nimis confortatus est principatus eorum.

138:18 Dinumerabo eos, et super arenam multiplicabuntur. Exsurrexi, et adhuc sum tecum.

138:19 Si occideris, Deus, peccatores, viri sanguinum, declinate a me :

138:20 quia dicitis in cogitatione : Accipient in vanitate civitates tuas.

138:21 Nonne qui oderunt te, Domine, oderam, et super inimicos tuos tabescebam ?

138:22 Perfecto odio oderam illos, et inimici facti sunt mihi.

138:23 Proba me, Deus, et scito cor meum ; interroga me, et cognosce semitas meas.

138:24 Et vide si via iniquitatis in me est, et deduc me in via æterna.

138:3 Thou hast understood my thoughts afar off: my path and my line thou hast searched out.

138:4 And thou hast foreseen all my ways: for there is no speech in my tongue.

138:5 Behold, O Lord, thou hast known all things, the last and those of old: thou hast formed me, and hast laid thy hand upon me.

138:6 Thy knowledge is become wonderful to me: it is high, and I cannot reach to it.

138:7 Whither shall I go from thy spirit? or whither shall I flee from thy face?

138:8 If I ascend into heaven, thou art there: if I descend into hell, thou art present.

138:9 If I take my wings early in the morning, and dwell in the uttermost parts of the sea:

138:10 Even there also shall thy hand lead me: and thy right hand shall hold me.

138:11 And I said: Perhaps darkness shall cover me: and night shall be my light in my pleasures.

138:12 But darkness shall not be dark to thee, and night shall be light as day: the darkness thereof, and the light thereof are alike to thee.

138:13 For thou hast possessed my reins: thou hast protected me from my mother's womb.

138:14 I will praise thee, for thou art fearfully magnified: wonderful are thy works, and my soul knoweth right well.

138:15 My bone is not hidden from thee, which thou hast made in secret: and my substance in the lower parts of the earth.

138:16 Thy eyes did see my imperfect being, and in thy book all shall be written: days shall be formed, and no one in them.

138:17 But to me thy friends, O God, are made exceedingly honourable: their principality is exceedingly strengthened.

138:18 I will number them, and they shall be multiplied above the sand: I rose up and am still with thee.

138:19 If thou wilt kill the wicked, O God: ye men of blood, depart from me:

138:20 Because you say in thought: They shall receive thy cities in vain.

138:21 Have I not hated them, O Lord, that hated thee: and pined away because of thy enemies?

138:22 I have hated them with a perfect hatred: and they are become enemies to me.

138:23 Prove me, O God, and know my heart: examine me, and know my paths.

138:24 And see if there be in me the way of iniquity: and lead me in the eternal way.

CXXXIX.

139:1 *In finem. Psalmus David.*

139:2 ERIPE ME, DOMINE, ab homine malo ; a viro iniquo eripe me.

139:3 Qui cogitaverunt iniquitates in corde, tota die constituebant prælia.

139:4 Acuerunt linguas suas sicut serpentis ; venenum aspidum sub labiis eorum.

139:5 Custodi me, Domine, de manu peccatoris, et ab hominibus iniquis eripe me. Qui cogitaverunt supplantare gressus meos :

139:6 absconderunt superbi laqueum mihi. Et funes extenderunt in laqueum ; juxta iter, scandalum posuerunt mihi.

139:7 Dixi Domino : Deus meus es tu ; exaudi, Domine, vocem deprecationis meæ.

139:8 Domine, Domine, virtus salutis meæ, obumbrasti super caput meum in die belli.

139:9 Ne tradas me, Domine, a desiderio meo peccatori : cogitaverunt contra me ; ne derelinquas me, ne forte exaltentur.

139:10 Caput circuitus eorum : labor labiorum ipsorum operiet eos.

139:11 Cadent super eos carbones ; in ignem dejicies eos : in miseriis non subsistent.

139:12 Vir linguosus non dirigetur in terra ; virum injustum mala capient in interitu.

139:13 Cognovi quia faciet Dominus judicium inopis, et vindictam pauperum.

139:14 Verumtamen justi confitebuntur nomini tuo, et habitabunt recti cum vultu tuo.

139:1 *Unto the end, a psalm for David.*

139:2 DELIVER ME, O LORD, from the evil man: rescue me from the unjust man.

139:3 Who have devised iniquities in their hearts: all the day long they designed battles.

139:4 They have sharpened their tongues like a serpent: the venom of asps is under their lips.

139:5 Keep me, O Lord, from the hand of the wicked: and from unjust men deliver me. Who have proposed to supplant my steps.

139:6 the proud have hidden a net for me. And they have stretched out cords for a snare: they have laid for me a stumblingblock by the wayside.

139:7 I said to the Lord: Thou art my God: hear, O Lord, the voice of my supplication.

139:8 O Lord, Lord, the strength of my salvation: thou hast overshadowed my head in the day of battle.

139:9 Give me not up, O Lord, from my desire to the wicked: they have plotted against me; do not thou forsake me, lest they should triumph.

139:10 The head of them compassing me about: the labour of their lips shall overwhelm them.

139:11 Burning coals shall fall upon them; thou wilt cast them down into the fire: in miseries they shall not be able to stand.

139:12 A man full of tongue shall not be established in the earth: evil shall catch the unjust man unto destruction.

139:13 I know that the Lord will do justice to the needy, and will revenge the poor.

139:14 But as for the just, they shall give glory to thy name: and the upright shall dwell with thy countenance.

CXL.

140:1 *Psalmus David.* DOMINE, CLAMAVI AD TE : exaudi me ; intende voci meæ, cum clamavero ad te.

140:2 Dirigatur oratio mea sicut incensum in conspectu tuo ; elevatio manuum mearum sacrificium vespertinum.

140:3 Pone, Domine, custodiam ori meo, et ostium circumstantiæ labiis meis.

140:4 Non declines cor meum in verba malitiæ, ad excusandas excusationes in peccatis ; cum hominibus operantibus iniquitatem, et non communicabo cum electis eorum.

140:5 Corripiet me justus in misericordia, et increpabit me : oleum autem peccatoris non

140:1 *A psalm of David.* I HAVE CRIED TO THEE, O Lord, hear me: hearken to my voice, when I cry to thee.

140:2 Let my prayer be directed as incense in thy sight; the lifting up of my hands, as evening sacrifice.

140:3 Set a watch, O Lord, before my mouth: and a door round about my lips.

140:4 Incline not my heart to evil words; to make excuses in sins. With men that work iniquity: and I will not communicate with the choicest of them.

140:5 The just shall correct me in mercy, and shall reprove me: but let not the oil of the sin-

impinguet caput meum. Quoniam adhuc et oratio mea in beneplacitis eorum :

140:6 absorpti sunt juncti petræ judices eorum. Audient verba mea, quoniam potuerunt.

140:7 Sicut crassitudo terræ erupta est super terram, dissipata sunt ossa nostra secus infernum.

140:8 Quia ad te, Domine, Domine, oculi mei ; in te speravi, non auferas animam meam.

140:9 Custodi me a laqueo quem statuerunt mihi, et a scandalis operantium iniquitatem.

140:10 Cadent in retiaculo ejus peccatores : singulariter sum ego, donec transeam.

ner fatten my head. For my prayer also shall still be against the things with which they are well pleased:

140:6 their judges falling upon the rock have been swallowed up. They shall hear my words, for they have prevailed:

140:7 as when the thickness of the earth is broken up upon the ground: Our bones are scattered by the side of hell.

140:8 But to thee, O Lord, Lord, are my eyes: in thee have I put my trust, take not away my soul.

140:9 Keep me from the snare, which they have laid for me, and from the stumblingblocks of them that work iniquity.

140:10 The wicked shall fall in his net: I am alone until I pass.

CXLI.

141:1 *Intellectus David, cum esset in spelunca, oratio.*

141:2 VOCE MEA AD DOMINUM CLAMAVI, voce mea ad Dominum deprecatus sum.
141:3 Effundo in conspectu ejus orationem meam, et tribulationem meam ante ipsum pronuntio :
141:4 in deficiendo ex me spiritum meum, et tu cognovisti semitas meas. In via hac qua ambulabam absconderunt laqueum mihi.
141:5 Considerabam ad dexteram, et videbam, et non erat qui cognosceret me : periit fuga a me, et non est qui requirat animam meam.
141:6 Clamavi ad te, Domine ; dixi : Tu es spes mea, portio mea in terra viventium.
141:7 Intende ad deprecationem meam, quia humiliatus sum nimis. Libera me a persequentibus me, quia confortati sunt super me.
141:8 Educ de custodia animam meam ad confitendum nomini tuo ; me exspectant justi donec retribuas mihi.

141:1 *Of understanding for David. A prayer when he was in the cave.*

141:2 I CRIED TO THE LORD WITH MY VOICE: with my voice I made supplication to the Lord.
141:3 In his sight I pour out my prayer, and before him I declare my trouble:

141:4 When my spirit failed me, then thou knewest my paths. In this way wherein I walked, they have hidden a snare for me.
141:5 I looked on my right hand, and beheld, and there was no one that would know me. Flight hath failed me: and there is no one that hath regard to my soul.
141:6 I cried to thee, O Lord: I said: Thou art my hope, my portion in the land of the living.
141:7 Attend to my supplication: for I am brought very low. Deliver me from my persecutors; for they are stronger than I.
141:8 Bring my soul out of prison, that I may praise thy name: the just wait for me, until thou reward me.

CXLII.

142:1 *Psalmus David, quando persequebatur eum Absalom filius ejus.* DOMINE, EXAUDI ORATIONEM MEAM ; auribus percipe obsecrationem meam in veritate tua ; exaudi me in tua justitia.
142:2 Et non intres in judicium cum servo tuo, quia non justificabitur in conspectu tuo omnis vivens.
142:3 Quia persecutus est inimicus animam meam ; humiliavit in terra vitam meam ; collo-

142:1 *A psalm of David, when his son Absalom pursued him.* HEAR, O LORD, MY PRAYER: give ear to my supplication in thy truth: hear me in thy justice.
142:2 And enter not into judgment with thy servant: for in thy sight no man living shall be justified.
142:3 For the enemy hath persecuted my soul: he hath brought down my life to the earth. He

cavit me in obscuris, sicut mortuos sæculi.

142:4 Et anxiatus est super me spiritus meus ; in me turbatum est cor meum.

142:5 Memor fui dierum antiquorum ; meditatus sum in omnibus operibus tuis : in factis manuum tuarum meditabar.

142:6 Expandi manus meas ad te ; anima mea sicut terra sine aqua tibi.

142:7 Velociter exaudi me, Domine ; defecit spiritus meus. Non avertas faciem tuam a me, et similis ero descendentibus in lacum.

142:8 Auditam fac mihi mane misericordiam tuam, quia in te speravi. Notam fac mihi viam in qua ambulem, quia ad te levavi animam meam.

142:9 Eripe me de inimicis meis, Domine : ad te confugi.

142:10 Doce me facere voluntatem tuam, quia Deus meus es tu. Spiritus tuus bonus deducet me in terram rectam.

142:11 Propter nomen tuum, Domine, vivificabis me : in æquitate tua, educes de tribulatione animam meam,

142:12 et in misericordia tua disperdes inimicos meos, et perdes omnes qui tribulant animam meam, quoniam ego servus tuus sum.

hath made me to dwell in darkness as those that have been dead of old:

142:4 and my spirit is in anguish within me: my heart within me is troubled.

142:5 I remembered the days of old, I meditated on all thy works: I meditated upon the works of thy hands.

142:6 I stretched forth my hands to thee: my soul is as earth without water unto thee.

142:7 Hear me speedily, O Lord: my spirit hath fainted away. Turn not away thy face from me, lest I be like unto them that go down into the pit.

142:8 Cause me to hear thy mercy in the morning; for in thee have I hoped. Make the way known to me, wherein I should walk: for I have lifted up my soul to thee.

142:9 Deliver me from my enemies, O Lord, to thee have I fled:

142:10 teach me to do thy will, for thou art my God. Thy good spirit shall lead me into the right land:

142:11 for thy name's sake, O Lord, thou wilt quicken me in thy justice. Thou wilt bring my soul out of trouble:

142:12 and in thy mercy thou wilt destroy my enemies. And thou wilt cut off all them that afflict my soul: for I am thy servant.

CXLIII.

143:1 *Psalmus David. Adversus Goliath.* BENEDICTUS DOMINUS Deus meus, qui docet manus meas ad prælium, et digitos meos ad bellum.

143:2 Misericordia mea et refugium meum ; susceptor meus et liberator meus ; protector meus, et in ipso speravi, qui subdit populum meum sub me.

143:3 Domine, quid est homo, quia innotuisti ei ? aut filius hominis, quia reputas eum ?

143:4 Homo vanitati similis factus est ; dies ejus sicut umbra prætereunt.

143:5 Domine, inclina cælos tuos, et descende ; tange montes, et fumigabunt.

143:6 Fulgura coruscationem, et dissipabis eos ; emitte sagittas tuas, et conturbabis eos.

143:7 Emitte manum tuam de alto : eripe me, et libera me de aquis multis, de manu filiorum alienorum :

143:8 quorum os locutum est vanitatem, et dextera eorum dextera iniquitatis.

143:1 *A psalm of David against Goliath.* BLESSED BE THE LORD my God, who teacheth my hands to fight, and my fingers to war.

143:2 My mercy, and my refuge: my support, and my deliverer: My protector, and I have hoped in him: who subdueth my people under me.

143:3 Lord, what is man, that thou art made known to him? or the son of man, that thou makest account of him?

143:4 Man is like to vanity: his days pass away like a shadow.

143:5 Lord, bow down thy heavens and descend: touch the mountains and they shall smoke.

143:6 Send forth lightning, and thou shalt scatter them: shoot out thy arrows, and thou shalt trouble them.

143:7 Put forth thy hand from on high, take me out, and deliver me from many waters: from the hand of strange children:

143:8 Whose mouth hath spoken vanity: and their right hand is the right hand of iniquity.

143:9 Deus, canticum novum cantabo tibi ; in psalterio decachordo psallam tibi.

143:10 Qui das salutem regibus, qui redemisti David servum tuum de gladio maligno,

143:11 eripe me, et erue me de manu filiorum alienorum, quorum os locutum est vanitatem, et dextera eorum dextera iniquitatis.

143:12 Quorum filii sicut novellæ plantationes in juventute sua ; filiæ eorum compositæ, circumornatæ ut similitudo templi.

143:13 Promptuaria eorum plena, eructantia ex hoc in illud ; oves eorum fœtosæ, abundantes in egressibus suis ;

143:14 boves eorum crassæ. Non est ruina maceriæ, neque transitus, neque clamor in plateis eorum.

143:15 Beatum dixerunt populum cui hæc sunt ; beatus populus cujus Dominus Deus ejus.

143:9 To thee, O God, I will sing a new canticle: on the psaltery and an instrument of ten strings I will sing praises to thee.

143:10 Who givest salvation to kings: who hast redeemed thy servant David from the malicious sword:

143:11 Deliver me, And rescue me out of the hand of strange children; whose mouth hath spoken vanity: and their right hand is the right hand of iniquity:

143:12 Whose sons are as new plants in their youth: Their daughters decked out, adorned round about after the similitude of a temple:

143:13 Their storehouses full, flowing out of this into that. Their sheep fruitful in young, abounding in their goings forth:

143:14 their oxen fat. There is no breach of wall, nor passage, nor crying out in their streets.

143:15 They have called the people happy, that hath these things: but happy is that people whose God is the Lord.

CXLIV.

144:1 *Laudatio ipsi David.* EXALTABO TE, Deus meus rex, et benedicam nomini tuo in sæculum, et in sæculum sæculi.

144:2 Per singulos dies benedicam tibi, et laudabo nomen tuum in sæculum, et in sæculum sæculi.

144:3 Magnus Dominus, et laudabilis nimis, et magnitudinis ejus non est finis.

144:4 Generatio et generatio laudabit opera tua, et potentiam tuam pronuntiabunt.

144:5 Magnificentiam gloriæ sanctitatis tuæ loquentur, et mirabilia tua narrabunt.

144:6 Et virtutem terribilium tuorum dicent, et magnitudinem tuam narrabunt.

144:7 Memoriam abundantiæ suavitatis tuæ eructabunt, et justitia tua exsultabunt.

144:8 Miserator et misericors Dominus : patiens, et multum misericors.

144:9 Suavis Dominus universis, et miserationes ejus super omnia opera ejus.

144:10 Confiteantur tibi, Domine, omnia opera tua, et sancti tui benedicant tibi.

144:11 Gloriam regni tui dicent, et potentiam tuam loquentur :

144:12 ut notam faciant filiis hominum potentiam tuam, et gloriam magnificentiæ regni tui.

144:1 *Praise, for David himself.* I WILL EXTOL THEE, O God my king: and I will bless thy name for ever; yea, for ever and ever.

144:2 Every day I will bless thee: and I will praise thy name for ever; yea, for ever and ever.

144:3 Great is the Lord, and greatly to be praised: and of his greatness there is no end.

144:4 Generation and generation shall praise thy works: and they shall declare thy power.

144:5 They shall speak of the magnificence of the glory of thy holiness: and shall tell thy wondrous works.

144:6 And they shall speak of the might of thy terrible acts: and shall declare thy greatness.

144:7 They shall publish the memory of the abundance of thy sweetness: and shall rejoice in thy justice.

144:8 The Lord is gracious and merciful: patient and plenteous in mercy.

144:9 The Lord is sweet to all: and his tender mercies are over all his works.

144:10 Let all thy works, O lord, praise thee: and let thy saints bless thee.

144:11 They shall speak of the glory of thy kingdom: and shall tell of thy power:

144:12 To make thy might known to the sons of men: and the glory of the magnificence of thy

144:13 Regnum tuum regnum omnium sæculorum ; et dominatio tua in omni generatione et generationem. Fidelis Dominus in omnibus verbis suis, et sanctus in omnibus operibus suis.

144:14 Allevat Dominus omnes qui corruunt, et erigit omnes elisos.

144:15 Oculi omnium in te sperant, Domine, et tu das escam illorum in tempore opportuno.

144:16 Aperis tu manum tuam, et imples omne animal benedictione.

144:17 Justus Dominus in omnibus viis suis, et sanctus in omnibus operibus suis.

144:18 Prope est Dominus omnibus invocantibus eum, omnibus invocantibus eum in veritate.

144:19 Voluntatem timentium se faciet, et deprecationem eorum exaudiet, et salvos faciet eos.

144:20 Custodit Dominus omnes diligentes se, et omnes peccatores disperdet.

144:21 Laudationem Domini loquetur os meum ; et benedicat omnis caro nomini sancto ejus in sæculum, et in sæculum sæculi.

kingdom.

144:13 Thy kingdom is a kingdom of all ages: and thy dominion endureth throughout all generations. The Lord is faithful in all his words: and holy in all his works.

144:14 The Lord lifteth up all that fall: and setteth up all that are cast down.

144:15 The eyes of all hope in thee, O Lord: and thou givest them meat in due season.

144:16 Thou openest thy hand, and fillest with blessing every living creature.

144:17 The Lord is just in all his ways: and holy in all his works.

144:18 The Lord is nigh unto all them that call upon him: to all that call upon him in truth.

144:19 He will do the will of them that fear him: and he will hear their prayer, and save them.

144:20 The Lord keepeth all them that love him; but all the wicked he will destroy.

144:21 My mouth shall speak the praise of the Lord: and let all flesh bless thy holy name for ever; yea, for ever and ever.

CXLV.

145:1 *Alleluja, Aggæi et Zachariæ.*

145:2 LAUDA, ANIMA MEA, DOMINUM. Laudabo Dominum in vita mea ; psallam Deo meo quamdiu fuero. Nolite confidere in principibus,

145:3 in filiis hominum, in quibus non est salus.

145:4 Exibit spiritus ejus, et revertetur in terram suam ; in illa die peribunt omnes cogitationes eorum.

145:5 Beatus cujus Deus Jacob adjutor ejus, spes ejus in Domino Deo ipsius :

145:6 qui fecit cælum et terram, mare, et omnia quæ in eis sunt.

145:7 Qui custodit veritatem in sæculum ; facit judicium injuriam patientibus ; dat escam esurientibus. Dominus solvit compeditos ;

145:8 Dominus illuminat cæcos. Dominus erigit elisos ; Dominus diligit justos.

145:9 Dominus custodit advenas, pupillum et viduam suscipiet, et vias peccatorum disperdet.

145:10 Regnabit Dominus in sæcula ; Deus tuus, Sion, in generationem et generationem.

145:1 *Alleluia, of Aggeus and Zacharias.*

145:2 PRAISE THE LORD, O MY SOUL, in my life I will praise the Lord: I will sing to my God as long as I shall be. Put not your trust in princes:

145:3 in the children of men, in whom there is no salvation.

145:4 His spirit shall go forth, and he shall return into his earth: in that day all their thoughts shall perish.

145:5 Blessed is he who hath the God of Jacob for his helper, whose hope is in the Lord his God:

145:6 who made heaven and earth, the sea, and all things that are in them.

145:7 Who keepeth truth for ever: who executeth judgment for them that suffer wrong: who giveth food to the hungry. The Lord looseth them that are fettered:

145:8 the Lord enlighteneth the blind. The Lord lifteth up them that are cast down: the Lord loveth the just.

145:9 The Lord keepeth the strangers, he will support the fatherless and the widow: and the ways of sinners he will destroy.

145:10 The Lord shall reign for ever: thy God, O Sion, unto generation and generation.

CXLVI.

146:1 *Alleluja.* LAUDATE DOMINUM, quoniam bonus est psalmus ; Deo nostro sit jucunda, decoraque laudatio.

146:2 Ædificans Jerusalem Dominus, dispersiones Israëlis congregabit :

146:3 qui sanat contritos corde, et alligat contritiones eorum ;

146:4 qui numerat multitudinem stellarum, et omnibus eis nomina vocat.

146:5 Magnus Dominus noster, et magna virtus ejus, et sapientiæ ejus non est numerus.

146:6 Suscipiens mansuetos Dominus ; humilians autem peccatores usque ad terram.

146:7 Præcinite Domino in confessione ; psallite Deo nostro in cithara.

146:8 Qui operit cælum nubibus, et parat terræ pluviam ; qui producit in montibus fœnum, et herbam servituti hominum ;

146:9 qui dat jumentis escam ipsorum, et pullis corvorum invocantibus eum.

146:10 Non in fortitudine equi voluntatem habebit, nec in tibiis viri beneplacitum erit ei.

146:11 Beneplacitum est Domino super timentes eum, et in eis qui sperant super misericordia ejus.

146:1 *Alleluia.* PRAISE YE THE LORD, because psalm is good: to our God be joyful and comely praise.

146:2 The Lord buildeth up Jerusalem: he will gather together the dispersed of Israel.

146:3 Who healeth the broken of heart, and bindeth up their bruises.

146:4 Who telleth the number of the stars: and calleth them all by their names.

146:5 Great is our Lord, and great is his power: and of his wisdom there is no number.

146:6 The Lord lifteth up the meek, and bringeth the wicked down even to the ground.

146:7 Sing ye to the Lord with praise: sing to our God upon the harp.

146:8 Who covereth the heaven with clouds, and prepareth rain for the earth. Who maketh grass to grow on the mountains, and herbs for the service of men.

146:9 Who giveth to beasts their food: and to the young ravens that call upon him.

146:10 He shall not delight in the strength of the horse: nor take pleasure in the legs of a man.

146:11 The Lord taketh pleasure in them that fear him: and in them that hope in his mercy.

CXLVII.

147:1 *Alleluja.* LAUDA, JERUSALEM, DOMINUM ; lauda Deum tuum, Sion.

147:2 Quoniam confortavit seras portarum tuarum ; benedixit filiis tuis in te.

147:3 Qui posuit fines tuos pacem, et adipe frumenti satiat te.

147:4 Qui emittit eloquium suum terræ : velociter currit sermo ejus.

147:5 Qui dat nivem sicut lanam ; nebulam sicut cinerem spargit.

147:6 Mittit crystallum suam sicut buccellas : ante faciem frigoris ejus quis sustinebit ?

147:7 Emittet verbum suum, et liquefaciet ea ; flabit spiritus ejus, et fluent aquæ.

147:8 Qui annuntiat verbum suum Jacob, justitias et judicia sua Israël.

147:9 Non fecit taliter omni nationi, et judicia sua non manifestavit eis. Alleluja.

147:1 *Alleluia.* PRAISE THE LORD, O JERUSALEM: praise thy God, O Sion.

147:2 Because he hath strengthened the bolts of thy gates, he hath blessed thy children within thee.

147:3 Who hath placed peace in thy borders: and filleth thee with the fat of corn.

147:4 Who sendeth forth his speech to the earth: his word runneth swiftly.

147:5 Who giveth snow like wool: scattereth mists like ashes.

147:6 He sendeth his crystal like morsels: who shall stand before the face of his cold?

147:7 He shall send out his word, and shall melt them: his wind shall blow, and the waters shall run.

147:8 Who declareth his word to Jacob: his justices and his judgments to Israel.

147:9 He hath not done in like manner to every nation: and his judgments he hath not made manifest to them. Alleluia.

CXLVIII.

148:1 *Alleluja.* LAUDATE DOMINUM de cælis ; laudate eum in excelsis.

148:2 Laudate eum, omnes angeli ejus ; laudate eum, omnes virtutes ejus.

148:3 Laudate eum, sol et luna ; laudate eum, omnes stellæ et lumen.

148:4 Laudate eum, cæli cælorum ; et aquæ omnes quæ super cælos sunt,

148:5 laudent nomen Domini. Quia ipse dixit, et facta sunt ; ipse mandavit, et creata sunt.

148:6 Statuit ea in æternum, et in sæculum sæculi ; præceptum posuit, et non præteribit.

148:7 Laudate Dominum de terra, dracones et omnes abyssi ;

148:8 ignis, grando, nix, glacies, spiritus procellarum, quæ faciunt verbum ejus ;

148:9 montes, et omnes colles ; ligna fructifera, et omnes cedri ;

148:10 bestiæ, et universa pecora ; serpentes, et volucres pennatæ ;

148:11 reges terræ et omnes populi ; principes et omnes judices terræ ;

148:12 juvenes et virgines ; senes cum junioribus, laudent nomen Domini :

148:13 quia exaltatum est nomen ejus solius.

148:14 Confessio ejus super cælum et terram ; et exaltavit cornu populi sui. Hymnus omnibus sanctis ejus ; filiis Israël, populo appropinquanti sibi. Alleluja.

148:1 *Alleluia.* PRAISE YE THE LORD from the heavens: praise ye him in the high places.

148:2 Praise ye him, all his angels: praise ye him, all his hosts.

148:3 Praise ye him, O sun and moon: praise him, all ye stars and light.

148:4 Praise him, ye heavens of heavens: and let all the waters that are above the heavens

148:5 praise the name of the Lord. For he spoke, and they were made: he commanded, and they were created.

148:6 He hath established them for ever, and for ages of ages: he hath made a decree, and it shall not pass away.

148:7 Praise the Lord from the earth, ye dragons, and all ye deeps:

148:8 Fire, hail, snow, ice, stormy winds which fulfil his word:

148:9 Mountains and all hills, fruitful trees and all cedars:

148:10 Beasts and all cattle: serpents and feathered fowls:

148:11 Kings of the earth and all people: princes and all judges of the earth:

148:12 Young men and maidens: let the old with the younger, praise the name of the Lord:

148:13 for his name alone is exalted.

148:14 The praise of him is above heaven and earth: and he hath exalted the horn of his people. A hymn to all his saints: to the children of Israel, a people approaching to him. Alleluia.

CXLIX.

149:1 *Alleluja.* CANTATE DOMINO canticum novum ; laus ejus in ecclesia sanctorum.

149:2 Lætetur Israël in eo qui fecit eum, et filii Sion exsultent in rege suo.

149:3 Laudent nomen ejus in choro ; in tympano et psalterio psallant ei.

149:4 Quia beneplacitum est Domino in populo suo, et exaltabit mansuetos in salutem.

149:5 Exsultabunt sancti in gloria ; lætabuntur in cubilibus suis.

149:6 Exaltationes Dei in gutture eorum, et gladii ancipites in manibus eorum :

149:7 ad faciendam vindictam in nationibus, increpationes in populis ;

149:8 ad alligandos reges eorum in compedibus, et nobiles eorum in manicis ferreis ;

149:9 ut faciant in eis judicium conscriptum :

149:1 *Alleluia.* SING YE TO THE LORD a new canticle: let his praise be in the church of the saints.

149:2 Let Israel rejoice in him that made him: and let the children of Sion be joyful in their king.

149:3 Let them praise his name in choir: let them sing to him with the timbrel and the psaltery.

149:4 For the Lord is well pleased with his people: and he will exalt the meek unto salvation.

149:5 The saints shall rejoice in glory: they shall be joyful in their beds.

149:6 The high praises of God shall be in their mouth: and two-edged swords in their hands:

149:7 To execute vengeance upon the nations, chastisements among the people:

149:8 To bind their kings with fetters, and their nobles with manacles of iron.

149:9 To execute upon them the judgment that is

gloria hæc est omnibus sanctis ejus. Alleluja.

written: this glory is to all his saints. Alleluia.

CL.

150:1 *Alleluja.* LAUDATE DOMINUM in sanctis ejus ; laudate eum in firmamento virtutis ejus.

150:2 Laudate eum in virtutibus ejus ; laudate eum secundum multitudinem magnitudinis ejus.

150:3 Laudate eum in sono tubæ ; laudate eum in psalterio et cithara.

150:4 Laudate eum in tympano et choro ; laudate eum in chordis et organo.

150:5 Laudate eum in cymbalis benesonantibus ; laudate eum in cymbalis jubilationis.

150:6 Omnis spiritus laudet Dominum ! Alleluja.

150:1 *Alleluia.* PRAISE YE THE LORD in his holy places: praise ye him in the firmament of his power.

150:2 Praise ye him for his mighty acts: praise ye him according to the multitude of his greatness.

150:3 Praise him with sound of trumpet: praise him with psaltery and harp.

150:4 Praise him with timbrel and choir: praise him with strings and organs.

150:5 Praise him on high sounding cymbals: praise him on cymbals of joy:

150:6 let every spirit praise the Lord. Alleluia.

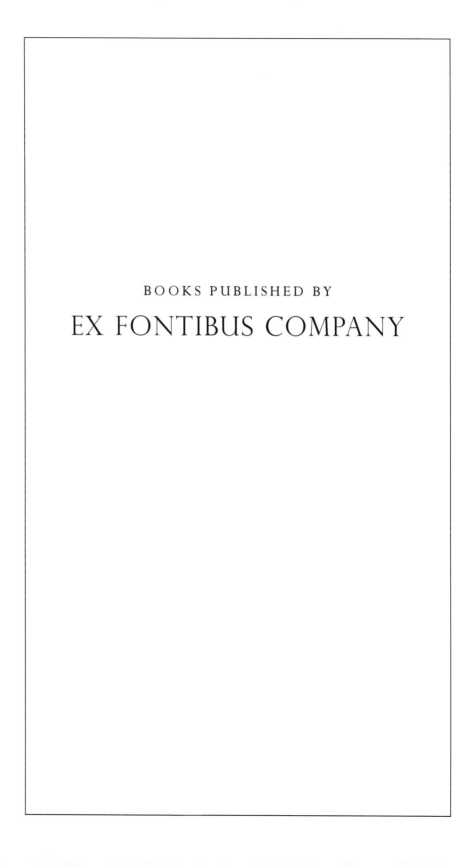

BOOKS PUBLISHED BY

EX FONTIBUS COMPANY

CONTENTS

CATALOGUE LISTING AS OF JUNE 10, 2017

BOOKS PUBLISHED BY

EX FONTIBUS COMPANY

http://www.exfontibus.com
contact@exfontibus.com
http://www.facebook.com/exfont
exfontibuscompany@gmail.com

Our books are sold on our own website, at Amazon.com,
& through other retailers

Get the latest news on our page!

SACRED TEXTS—SCRIPTURE, LITURGICAL TEXTS, AND PRAYER

Biblia Sacra—The Holy Bible in Latin and English [3 vols.]

A beautiful parallel Latin/English edition of the Bible of the medieval Catholic Church, using the Latin of the Clementine Vulgate and the English of Douay-Rheims Challoner Revision. **Vol. 1** includes the Pentateuch (Genesis, Exodus, Leviticus, Numbers, Deuteronomy) and the Historical Books (Joshua, Judges, Ruth, Samuel/Kings, Paralipomenon/Chronicles, Ezra/Nehemiah, Tobit, Judith, Esther). **Vol. 2** contains Job, Psalms, Proverbs, Ecclesiastes, the Song of Songs, Wisdom, Ecclesiasticus (Ben-Sirah), Isaiah, Jeremiah, Lamentations, Baruch, Ezechiel, Daniel, Hosea, Joel, Amos, Obadiah, Jonah, Micah, Nahum, Habakkuk, Zephaniah, Haggai, Zechariah, Malachi, Machabees. **Vol. 3** contains the entirety of the New Testament.

Biblia Sacra—New Testament and Psalms in Latin and English

An elegant smaller volume containing only the New Testament and the Psalms. [This third edition enlarges the formerly-cramped font.]

The Septuagint, with Apocrypha, in English

The Septuagint (LXX), the ancient Greek translation of Jewish sacred writings, is of great importance in the history of both Judaism and Christianity. Translated from Hebrew and other originals in the two centuries before Jesus, the Septuagint

provides important information about the history of biblical text. It captures a moment in time, illuminating for us how Greek-speaking Jews of that time read and interpreted the Hebrew Scriptures that they translated. In its time, it made the Jewish Scriptures accessible to peoples and cultures outside of Judaism through *koine* Greek, the common language of the Mediterranean world. The Septuagint was the Bible of Greek speaking Jews; it was the Bible of the first Christians. It is cited in the New Testament and by the great luminaries of early Christianity. In this edition of the famed translation by Lancelot C. Brenton, many archaisms have been removed and personal pronouns rendered consistent with modern English—yet without sacrificing any of the accuracy, power, or beauty of the original translation.

Kyriale Romanum

Gregorian chant has long transmitted the mystery and majesty of the Catholic liturgical tradition. Newly republished, the Kyriale Romanum of 1961, preserves between its covers an invaluable patrimony of ancient and medieval chants for the Ordinary of the Mass that can be used with both the extraordinary (1962) and the ordinary (post-1970) forms of the Roman Missal. It collects from the Graduale the most frequently-used chant settings throughout the liturgical year, with eighteen mass settings, six credos, and numerous settings for feasts and holy days, including the solemn procession on the feast of Corpus Christi. This beautiful and affordably-priced volume is of great value to all who wish to encounter this venerable musical tradition of the Roman Rite.

The Prayerbook of Ælfwine of Hyde

Decades before the Norman conquest of England in A.D. 1066, a Benedictine monk at Hyde Abbey named assembled a small prayer book from the tradition of early Saxon Christianity. That monk, who later became Abbot of Hyde, passed to his heavenly reward but fifteen years before the influx of Norman culture from France would reshape the prayer and liturgical tradition of English Christianity. The prayers that are preserved in his book bear witness to the zeal and vigor of early English Christianity, with a poetry that stirs the soul over ten centuries since first they were prayed.

THEOLOGY—PATRISTIC AND MEDIEVAL*

ST. IRENÆUS OF LYONS
Against Heresies and Other Writings

The complete text of *Against the Heresies*, with fragments of other writings. Available nowhere else as a standalone volume. Bishop St. Irenaeus of Lyons wrote his *Against Heresies* ca. A.D. 180 to preserve the Christian rule of faith against the Gnostic heresy. To vindicate the Incarnation against the Gnostics, he described and attacked their principal doctrine: the evil origin of the natural world. Affirming the unity of Old and New Testaments, the goodness of the Creator and the created world, and finally the mystery of divinization whereby human beings are elevated into the divine life, the saint produced an outstanding example of early Christian biblical theology. For the early Fathers, doctrines were taught to safeguard the confession of God's saving love revealed through His Incarnation as Jesus Christ. Of such work there is no better example than Irenaeus, disciple of Polycarp, disciple of John the Evangelist.

ORIGEN OF ALEXANDRIA
Against Celsus (Contra Celsum)

This is Origen's great apologetical work, undertaken in answer to the attack on Christianity by the pagan philosopher Celsus. The text that Origen composed to refute Celsus's self-styled Λόγος ἀληθής (*True Discourse*) consists of eight books, and belongs to the latest years of his life. It has always been regarded as the great apologetic work of antiquity; and no one can peruse it without being struck by the multifarious reading, wonderful acuteness, and rare subtlety of mind that it displays. It is a great work that well deserves the notice of the students of Apologetics and of Early Christianity in general.

ST. AMBROSE OF MILAN
Theological and Dogmatic Works (Fathers of the Church vol. 44)

These works present the thought of St. Ambrose, the bishop whose preaching first renewed St. Augustine's interest in Christianity. Included in this volume are several of Ambrose's works on the chief doctrines of the faith: "The Mysteries," "The Holy Spirit," "The Sacrament of the Incarnation of Our Lord," and "The Sacraments," including his famous teaching on the transformation of bread and wine into the Body and Blood of Christ.

---

* Chronological listing.

ST. BASIL OF CÆSAREA

Ascetical Works (Fathers of the Church vol. 9)

Saint Basil the Great writes concerning the spiritual life, the discipline of the passions and growth in illumined love, by which the soul rises to union with God.

Exegetic Homilies (Fathers of the Church vol. 46)

Basil the Great, of Caesarea, here offers homilies on the creation of the cosmos (the Hexameron, or the Six Days), God's providential ordering of the world, and on selected Psalms. A great work of early Christian biblical exegesis and a monument of patristic theology, now available in an attractive and affordable edition.

ST. JOHN CASSIAN

On the Incarnation of the Lord, Against Nestorius

Near the end of his writing career, Cassian the monk was commissioned by an archdeacon—the future Pope Leo the Great—to write a reply to the Christological positions of Nestorius, who saw in Christ two subjects, that of the Word and that of the man Jesus. Cassian's foray into ecclesiastical controversy, a cannonade of arguments from the Scriptures and the early Fathers, offers a blusteringly-effective representation of the general Christological views of East and West. Unsurprisingly, for one such as Cassian who was so concerned with the heights of Christian sanctity, it places special emphasis on the distinction between Christ's divinity and the indwelling of the Word in the saints—for the full divinity of Christ is what indeed makes it possible for *Christ* to be said to dwell within those saints who tread the heights of union with God. What he lacks in the precision of an Athanasius or a Maximus the Confessor, Cassian more than makes up for in the passion of his argumentation.

ST. GREGORY THE GREAT

Dialogues (Fathers of the Church vol. 39)

In the series of dialogues that he patiently holds with his deacon Peter, St. Gregory describes a vision of sacred stability in an unstable world; this stability is to be found in the saint's life, lived in the love of Christ and anchored in the power of God. Through tales of miracles and examples of charity, including a famous dialogue on heaven, hell, purgatory, and the power of the Mass, Gregory illustrates the guiding hand of providence in the life of the saint and in the divine power manifest in that saint's deeds and words. Through these stories he aims to teach his readers to offer themselves on the "altar of the heart" as a living sacrifice of love in union with the sacrifice of Christ on the Cross.

Moralia in Job (Morals on the Book of Job) [3 vols.]

Pope Gregory the Great (r. 590–604) wrote his *Moralia*, or moral homilies on Job, one of his greatest works, before his accession to the See of Peter. Seeking a life of contemplation, Gregory had retired to a house on Rome's Caelian Hill, forming the monastic community of St. Andrew's. Shortly thereafter, however, he was sent obediently but unhappily to Constantinople as papal nuncio (*apocrisarius*) at the court of the Byzantine emperor. There too he gathered a small community to whom he delivered his famed homilies on Job. For Gregory, Job is a figure of Christ, who suffered innocently—not for his sins but for the increase of his merits and the salvation of others by love. These homilies span Christian doctrine, from Creation to final Judgment, from the height of angelic hierarchies to the innermost depths of the human soul. Confident that the Holy Spirit has not idly chosen the words of Scripture, Gregory finds a depth of allegory out of which he draws a brilliant picture of Christ, whose humanity must mark our own and whose Cross is our path to eternal rest. A beautiful meditation on suffering, on the path from fear to love, and on the healing and glorification of the individual soul which, as a member of Christ's body, comes to participate in the life of the holy Trinity. When Gregory was elected bishop of Rome just a few years later, he would continue to draw on and to develop the teaching herein, to guide the spiritual lives of his flock amidst the terror-filled final dissolution of the Western Empire. The teaching of the *Moralia* became a source for the doctors of the middle ages, including Hugh of St. Victor, St. Thomas Aquinas, St. Bonaventure, and many others. Western Christianity today owes an incalculable debt to the homilies that Gregory preached to his small circle of ascetics so many years ago.

ST. JOHN OF DAMASCUS
Writings

St. John Damascene, among the greatest of the Eastern fathers during the patristic age, produced his work *The Fount of Knowledge* as a summary of Christian philosophy and theology. It is one of the most important works of the Greek patristic age. Included are "The Philosophical Chapters," "On Heresies," and the justly-famous "Exact Exposition of the Orthodox Faith"—a veritable *Summa* of the doctrine of the Eastern fathers. Now available in an attractive and affordable edition.

ST. ANSELM OF CANTERBURY
Complete Philosophical and Theological Treatises

We are proud to re-print Jasper Hopkins' philosophically sensitive translations of the complete treatises of Anselm of Canterbury, the "Father of Scholasticism." The present volume contains, in English translation, all of St. Anselm's treatises, as

well as his important Meditation on Human Redemption and four of his didactic letters. Collectively, these constitute his intellectual writings. Included are: *Monologion*; *Proslogion*; *Debate with Gaunilo*; *De Grammatico*; *On Truth* (*De Veritate*); *Freedom of Choice* (*De Libertate Arbitrii*); *The Fall of the Devil* (*De Casu Diaboli*); *Two Letters concerning Roscelin*; *The Incarnation of the Word* (*De Incarnatione Verbi*); *Why God Became a [God-]man* (*Cur Deus Homo*); *Philosophical Fragments*; *A Meditation on Human Redemption* (*Meditatio*); *The Virgin Conception and Original Sin* (*De Conceptu*); *The Procession of the Holy Spirit* (*De Processione*); *Letters on the Sacraments* (*De Sacramentis*); *Foreknowledge, Predestination, Grace, and Free Choice* (*De Concordia*). In an appendix is included a scholarly bibliography of resources on Anselm.

Cur Deus Homo

Available here in an attractive paperback edition, Anselm's famous treatise *Cur Deus Homo* (Why the God-Man?) attempts to show believers that, far from being an unfitting and irrational act, God's incarnation as man was a suitable, even (contingently-speaking) a *necessary* act by which to restore balance to a cosmos afflicted by sin. Anselm's "satisfaction" theory of atonement formalized a tradition with its seeds in the patristic period and set the context for much reflection on the Cross in the Middle Ages and throughout the Reformation period.

Cur Deus Homo and Other Works on Christ [Forthcoming]

This selection focuses on Anselm's treatises, meditations, and prayers that address the Incarnation, the Cross, the Resurrection, and the role of Christ in the spiritual life. Among other works are included his *Epistle on the Incarnation of the Word*, the famous *Cur Deus Homo*, his *Meditation on the Humanity of Christ*, *Meditation on the Passion of Christ*, *Meditation on Human Redemption*, his *On the Dignity and Woe of Humanity's Estate*, and others.

HUGH OF BALMA
On Mystical Theology [Forthcoming]

Translated by Jasper Hopkins.

HUGH OF ST. VICTOR
On the Sacraments of the Christian Faith (De Sacramentis).

Hugh of St. Victor (1096–1141) was a renowned medieval philosopher, theologian, and mystical writer. Because of his great familiarity with the works of St. Augustine, he is sometimes called "the Second Augustine." His work *On the Sacraments of the Christian Faith* (*De Sacramentis Christianae Fidei*), composed about 1134, is his masterpiece as well as his most extensive work. It is a veritable *Summa*, a dogmatic synthesis unrivaled in Hugh's time.

By "sacrament," Hugh means not only grace-giving ceremonial signs and actions but also all "mysteries" of the Scriptures, the natural world, and the Church by which God elevates humankind into His life. Hugh's theology draws on Augustine, Gregory the Great, Anselm, and Abelard; and Hugh was also in contact with Bernard of Clairvaux. In the *De Sacramentis*, Hugh separates all of history into the "work of creation" and the "work of restoration." The work of Creation is the triune God's creative activity, the natures of created things, and the original state and destiny of humanity. Hugh's description of the Six Days of Creation is heavily influenced by Augustine's exegesis of Genesis. Divine Wisdom is the archetypal form of creation. The creation of the world in six days is a "sacrament," that is, a spiritually-illuminating mystery for man to contemplate. God's forming order from chaos to make the world is an instruction that guides human beings to rise in love from their own chaos of ignorance to become creatures of Wisdom and therefore beauty. This kind of mystical-ethical interpretation is typical for Hugh, who finds Wisdom's instruction everywhere in creation and in the Scriptures.

The work of Restoration includes the Incarnation of God the Son "with all its sacraments." Here the word "sacrament" refers to the means of salvation that flow from the Incarnation itself, including what are now called the traditional "seven sacraments." Hugh reflects on the mystery of God's freedom—why the Son came into the world even though this was not strictly necessary. Over all, Hugh's work is both an exegetical treatise and a work of spiritual instruction—an example of the inseparability of doctrinal reflection and spiritual growth as understood by this great twelfth-century theologian.

NICHOLAS OF CUSA
Speculative Theology [Forthcoming]
Translated by Jasper Hopkins.

Early Sermons [Forthcoming]
Translated by Jasper Hopkins.

Didactic Sermons [Forthcoming]
Translated by Jasper Hopkins.

Last Sermons: 1457–1463 [Forthcoming]
Translated by Jasper Hopkins.

10

---

* Alphabetical listing.

whereby the divine image is restored in the soul. This work, which has been out of print for decades, is of interest to any who wish to enhance their understanding of the recent Catholic theological tradition through an acquaintance with this major and often controversial figure.

The One God: A Commentary on the First Part of St. Thomas' Theological Summa

Taking up a commentary on the first part of the *Summa*, Father Garrigou-Lagrange discusses not only the attributes of the one God who revealed Himself to Moses, but treats also of the very basis for this discussion in the first place—the nature of *sacra doctrina* ("holy teaching" or "sacred doctrine") and the pursuit of theology as a "science" (a body of knowledge) that has God Himself for its object and ultimate goal. To comment, therefore, on the first part of the *Summa* is to comment not only on God but also on the theological pursuit to which St. Thomas gave himself—a pursuit that has as its goal the beatific vision of God. In discussing the place of St. Thomas amidst patristic, medieval, and modern theologians, Garrigou-Lagrange argues in behalf both of the sanctifying end of theology and the synthetic genius of St. Thomas who, he says, summed up the preceding tradition and left a deposit of reflection on God that can scarcely be surpassed.

The Trinity and God the Creator: A Commentary on St. Thomas' Theological Summa, I^a, qq. 27-119

Father Garrigou-Lagrange here reflects on the triune God who created the heavens and the earth, and who is the object of that contemplative vision of God to which all human beings are called and which is their ultimate sanctification. In his characteristically-ordered style, Garrigou-Lagrange offers his interpretation of St. Thomas by expounding, explaining, and comparing the teaching of the angelic doctor to that of preceding and subsequent theologians. In particular, Garrigou-Lagrange depicts St. Thomas as fulfilling the foundation laid by St. Augustine: the persons must be treated in distinction but not in separation, for it is only in their mutual relations that they can be known as persons. He also lays special emphasis on the call of all humans to contemplative holiness. The exposition of the Trinity is a beginning of the journey of contemplation by which a man or woman enters the life of God to be reformed according to the likeness of the Trinity in whose image he or she was first created, body and soul.

Beatitude: A Commentary on St. Thomas' Theological Summa, I^a II^æ, qq. 1-54

The central theme of *Beatitude* is the human journey back to God, our Creator. For moral theology is a discipline concerned not merely with the avoidance of sin but also with the cultivation of virtue, with growth in likeness to God. The book has two major parts: First, it considers humankind's ultimate goal: to possess God and to share in His life; secondly, the means by which humans can reach this destination. These means are human acts, those over which a human being has deliberate control. Therefore, this volume covers St. Thomas's treatises on the End of Man, Human Acts, the Passions, and Habit. Or, you may consider it a short commentary on how to live in God's life in this life so as to inherit the vision of him forever in the next. For moral theology is not cold and empty speculation, but a systematic description of what it means to imitate God. There was a time when many moral textbooks leaned heavily on casuistry and laid no systematic doctrinal foundation for their moral discussions and solutions. Such is not the case in this volume. Human acts are the road to humankind's supernatural goal. Any discipline of inquiry must proceed from principles, from causes. As a consequence, moral theology must not be divorced from the study of the passions, habits, grace, virtue, and the gifts of the Holy Spirit. As an introduction for the interested reader, "Beatitude" raises Thomistic moral theology to a new life.

On Faith: A Commentary on St. Thomas' Theological Summa I^a II^ae, qq. 62, 65, 68 and II^a II^ae, qq.1-16

By this commentary, Garrigou-Lagrange wishes to elucidate Thomas Aquinas's teaching on the Theological Virtues--those powers of soul that, infused by the Holy Spirit, enable the soul to respond by knowledge and love to the loving embrace of God Himself. This volume treats especially of the virtue of Faith, whereby God's self-revelation is not simply believed as true, but grasped in its living reality such that one can journey on into the life of God by the power of faith working through love. As a commentary on the *Summa*, this volume is methodical and clear. As a spiritual treatise, it aims to illuminate and to inspire.

Grace: A Commentary on the Summa theologica of St. Thomas, I^a II^æ, qq. 109–114

Father Garrigou-Lagrange synthesizes and develops the teaching of St. Thomas on the deifying life of grace by a creative engagement with the Carmelite theology of St. John of the Cross. He distinguishes the various modes and movements of grace in the spiritual life from conversion to entrance into glory.

Christ the Savior: A Commentary on the Third Part of St. Thomas' Theological Summa

Father Garrigou-Lagrange engages the teaching of St. Thomas on the divine Incarnation by which was wrought the salvation of humankind. Hence he treats the motive of the Incarnation, the hypostatic union, and its effects. He discusses at length such difficult problems as the reconciliation of freedom with absolute impeccability in Christ, the intrinsically infinite value of His merits and satisfaction, His predestination with reference to ours, inasmuch as He is the first of the predestined, and the reconciliation, during the Passion, of the presence of extreme sorrow with supreme happiness experienced by our Lord in the summit of His soul. With reference to the Passion, everything is reduced to the principle of the plenitude of grace. This plenitude, on the one hand, was the cause in the summit of our Lord's soul of the beatific vision and, on the other hand, it was the cause of His most ardent love as priest and victim, so that He willed to be overwhelmed with grief, and die on the cross a most perfect holocaust. In all, Father Garrigou-Lagrange would manifest the unity of Christ inasmuch as He is one personal Being, although He has two really distinct and infinitely different natures. Hence the Person of Christ constitutes the one and only principle of all His theandric operations. At the end of the book is given a compendium on Mariology.

The Love of God and the Cross of Jesus (2 vols.)

Here, Father Garrigou-Lagrange describes the Christian interior life in light of the love of God and the mystery of the Cross. Guided by St. Thomas and of St. John of the Cross, he expounds what lies deepest in the interior life of the Lord Jesus Christ and what consequently must be appropriated most deeply in the life of every Christian who would imitate Him. For it is only by the royal road of the Cross that the Christian soul truly enters into supernatural contemplation of the mysteries of faith and lives lovingly and deeply by them.

ARTHUR F. KRUEGER

Synthesis of Sacrifice according to Saint Augustine: A Study of the Sacramentality of Sacrifice

Sacrifice is, for Augustine, simply that life of love that is both the perfect worship of God and the core of participation in His divine life. Arthur Krueger's is the only book-length study of this central theme of Augustine's theology. Krueger considers the bishop of Hippo on sacrifice and priesthood, both in the abstract and in the concrete sacrifices of the Old and New Testaments. He particularly investigates these themes in their relation to Augustine's notion of sacrament,

which Krueger presents as a "binding and synthesizing concept" at the heart of the great theologian's sacrificial teaching.

JOHN HENRY NEWMAN
Oxford University Sermons

Newman's fifteen sermons on faith and reason, sanctity, and the development of doctrine; preached before the University of Oxford between A.D. 1826 and 1843 by John Henry Newman.

AIDAN NICHOLS, O.P.
Epiphany: A Theological Introduction to Catholicism

Now in its second edition. Renowned Dominican theologian Aidan Nichols presents the Catholic faith as a unique source of illumination for the good, the true, and the beautiful. That faith, he argues, is destined to be, and humbly offered as, light for all peoples. It was as "light" that that the babe Jesus Christ was hailed by the aged prophet Symeon when he was presented in the Jerusalem Temple. The Church, too, has applied the term "epiphany"—shining forth—to his first, pre-verbal contact with the Gentiles, as his mother held him out to the "magi," the representatives of the non-Jewish nations. Thus the title of this book.

The book is a theological "Introduction" because one could hardly encapsulate all the illuminating richness Catholic Christianity can offer. Still, Nichols skillfully weaves into his own work a truly-catholic gathering of other great lights from the tradition.

This is a traditional theology and, as Nichols writes, "a consciously non-liberal theology, but not, I think, an illiberal one, for its subject is the generosity of God in his revealing Word and sanctifying Spirit. . . It is not a neutral work, since it aims to arouse a 'Christian maximalism' and the boldness to seek in Catholicism's theological tradition inspiration for present and future."

This second edition corrects some errors in the original.

EDWARD DENNIS O'CONNOR, C.S.C.
The Dogma of the Immaculate Conception [Forthcoming]

A history of the dogma of the immaculate conception, given in a series of scholarly papers published half a century after the dogma's promulgation. Long out of print but useful to the novice and the specialist alike, this volume takes the long view of Church history and tradition, showing a doctrine's development in action.

MATTHIAS SCHEEBEN
Mariology (complete in one volume)

Writing in the nineteenth century, Matthias Scheeben forged a new creative synthesis of the teaching of the Fathers and of the scholastics. Scheeben's work had a decisive influence on later Catholic theologians such as Hans Urs von Balthasar. His primary theme is the nuptial union of God and the created order through the Incarnation, a marriage of heaven and earth that begins in the conception of Christ in the womb of the virgin Mary. Mary, therefore, is the temple in which God and humankind are reconciled. This and all that flows from it and preceded it by way of preparation is the subject-matter of his work Mariology. He draws together the teaching on the Incarnation, on deification, on the Marian dogmas, sacramental theology, and ecclesiology in a truly beautiful work. Originally published in two volumes, the entire work is gathered here in a single volume for the first time. It has been out of print for decades, now made available once more.

THOMAS G. WEINANDY
Jesus the Christ

Father Thomas G. Weinandy—sometime Oxford tutor and later head of the Secretariat of Doctrine for the United States Conference of Catholic Bishops—opens the fascinating world of Christian theology to all readers. In clear language, he begins in Scripture to draw out the plan of salvation, leading the reader through the development of the Church's grappling with the glorious and paradoxical conviction: That no-one less than God Himself has lived nothing less than a human life. From within the life of the Trinity, to the womb of a young woman, to the Cross upon Calvary, the empty tomb, and the ascension into heaven, Fr. Weinandy unfolds the theological consequences of the Incarnation as the central belief of Christian faith in an understandable Catholic introduction to the theological wisdom of the ages. He hopes that it may be of use to every Christian who wants to understand Jesus and His work of Salvation better.

HISTORY AND CONTROVERSIES

DOM JOHN CHAPMAN
Studies on the Early Papacy

Dom John Chapman, fourth abbot of Downside Abbey, was a renowned scholar of early Christianity. On the question of the papacy in the early Church, he eschews selective apologetics in favor of a reasoned study of textual sources in the context of historical events. At these pivotal moments, he argues, the bishop of Rome both took and was expected to take a prominent and indeed authoritative role. This volume offers much substance to those who wish to take up the question of

papal prerogatives. Chapman argues in favor of the Catholic claims, but does so with such care as a historian that his work has received high approval even from such an eminence as the famed Anglican historian Henry Chadwick who, in his own book on the history of the early Church, saw fit to recommend Chapman's work to readers interested in the question. There have been many successors to Chapman but few, if any, have engaged precisely with the matters that he discusses with such detail and clarity. His book, therefore, remains an important voice in the modern conversation.

EMILY HICKEY
Our Catholic Heritage in English Literature of the First Millennium

(Originally entitled *Our Catholic Heritage in Pre-Conquest English Literature*). Ms. Hickey's reflections sweep us into a magical world of ancient epic, poetry, and allegory--by the verses of Cædmon and Bede; in stories of the Phoenix, the Cross, and King Alfred; in old runes and lost loves--in all of which one again and again discovers that Christ has been the narrative's subject all along. She writes: "This little book makes no claim to be a history of pre-Conquest British Literature. It is an attempt to increase Catholics' interest in this part of the 'inheritance of their fathers.' It is not a formal course, but a sort of talk, as it were, about beautiful things said and sung in old days: things which to have learned to love is to have incurred a great and living debt. I have tried to clothe them in the nearest approach I could find to their original speech, with the humblest acknowledgement that nothing matches that speech itself. If this little book in any way fulfils the wishes of those who have asked me for some thoughts on English Literature, I shall be glad indeed."

LITERATURE—GREAT BOOKS AND GOOD BOOKS

Ex Fontibus Company is proud to present reprints of some difficult-to-find literary texts, such as Alexander Pope's translation of the *Iliad* and the *Odyssey*. However, our offerings are not limited to only the great books. We have also chosen to reprint some that are merely "good" books—yet not for that unworthy of our attention. Indeed, in his book *The Death of Christian Culture*, Dr. John Senior (1923–1999), founder of the once famed Integrated Humanities Program at the University of Kansas, offered a list of 1,0000 "good books" that prepare one to read the "great books." Among the "good" he includes such volumes as the Tarzan novels by Edgar Rice Burroughs:

> Taking all that was best in the Greco-Roman world into itself, Western tradition has given us the thousand good books as preparation for the great ones. . . . For us today, the [useful] cutoff point is World War I, before which cars and the electric light had not yet come to dominate our lives and the experience of nature had not been distorted by speed and the destruction of shadows....[These books are] part of the ordinary cultural matter essential for an English-speaking person to grow in.

Ex Fontibus offers the following—both good books and great—as points of entry into that heritage.

ROBERT HUGH BENSON
Lord of the World

> Interesting it must be to all to whom the deepest convictions of a man's heart are of moment. And in the artistic balance and taste of Father Benson's literary power every reader will find delight.
>
> —*The New York Times*

> Mr. Benson sees the world, . . . generations hence, free at last from all minor quarrels, and ranged against itself in two camps, Humanitarianism for those who believe in no divinity but that of man, Catholicism for those who believe in no divinity but that of God.
>
> —*The London Times*

> "The book as art is beautiful, delicately balanced, deeply inspired, intelligently executed.
>
> —*Putnam's*

One of Pope Francis's favorite novels, Benson's 1907 apocalyptic tale of the Antichrist is one of the first modern dystopias. Humanism has eliminated world conflict but practices a subtle barbarism upon the human mind. Religion is either

suppressed or ignored. The Catholic Church, confined to ghettos, occupies an increasingly perilous position in the public square. The populace turns toward euthanasia as the solution to bodily pain and spiritual crisis. Meanwhile, a mysterious figure of apparent hope, Julian Felsenburgh, rises to become the head of a single world government. The plot follows a priest, Father Percy Franklin, who finds himself caught up in the final and increasingly open struggle between Antichrist and Christ. *Completely re-typeset with Latin phrases translated in footnotes.*

ROBERT HUGH BENSON
The Dawn of All

Benson's alternative to *Lord of the World*, this later novel vividly imagines the final peace of the world in the triumph of Christianity and the re-establishment of the Church at the center of daily life. A mysterious priest who cannot remember his own name, nor even anything of the past, must make his way as a Monsignor in a world undergoing a dramatic transformation in preparation for the return of Christ. The world itself becomes an image of the priest's soul. Benson himself writes: "In a former book, called *Lord of the World*, I attempted to sketch the kind of developments a hundred years hence which, I thought, might reasonably be expected if the present lines of what is called "modern thought" were only prolonged far enough; and I was informed repeatedly that the effect of the book was exceedingly depressing and discouraging to optimistic Christians. In the present book I am attempting — also in parable form — not in the least to withdraw anything that I said in the former, but to follow up the other lines instead, and to sketch — again in parable — the kind of developments about sixty years hence which, I think, may reasonably be expected should the opposite process begin, and ancient thought (which has stood the test of centuries, and is, in a very remarkable manner, being "rediscovered" by persons even more modern than modernists) be prolonged instead." As always, the story is rendered with suitable dramatic tension and—as is characteristic of Benson—a spiritual conflict of individual souls that matches the large-scale conflicts in the wider world. *Completely re-typeset with Latin phrases translated in footnotes.*

CHARLOTTE BRONTË
Jane Eyre

Jane Eyre (originally *Jane Eyre: An Autobiography*) was published in 1847 under the pen name "Currer Bell." The novel follows the emotions and experiences of its title character, including her growth to adulthood and her love for Mr. Rochester, the byronic master of fictitious Thornfield Hall. In its internalization of the action — the focus is on the gradual unfolding of Jane's moral and spiritual sensibility and all the events are colored by a heightened intensity that was

previously the domain of poetry — Jane Eyre revolutionized the art of fiction. Charlotte Brontë has been called the 'first historian of the private consciousness' and the literary ancestor of writers like Joyce and Proust. The novel both reflects and heralds the literary movements of its day, containing elements of social criticism, with a strong sense of morality at its core, an individualistic protagonist, and explorations of class, romantic attraction, religion, and the social position of women.

EDGAR RICE BURROUGHS

The Tarzan Novels, Vol. 1 (Five Novels), Second Edition

The Tarzan novels initiate the young person or the adult into the thrilling and sometimes terrifying world of nature, a world in which one can glimpse something of the eternal Beauty—undimmed even by the savage violence of man and beast. Welcome to the "primeval forest." This omnibus collection presents the first four complete novels of the thrilling adventures of Tarzan of the Apes, along with the collected *Jungle Tales* of Tarzan's early life. Son of an English Lord, raised by the savage apes that killed his father, found again by a civilization that he would never quite come to call his own, he was at home in the primeval forest in which he was reared. Swinging through the treetops, bane of lions, tamer of elephants, terror of cannibals, finder of lost cities, and beloved of the American woman Jane Porter, this knight of the forest, never trained in chivalry, was known to the outside world as John Clayton, Lord Greystoke—but to himself and the denizens of the jungle in which he grew up, he would be forever Tarzan, King of the Apes. Included in this volume: *Tarzan of the Apes*; *The Return of Tarzan*; *The Son of Tarzan*; *The Beasts of Tarzan*; *Jungle Tales of Tarzan*. A new introduction gives the history of Burroughs' novels and addresses certain points that later writers have rightfully questioned. [This second edition enlarges the previously-cramped font, for a more enjoyable reading experience.]

The Tarzan Novels, Vol. 2 (Four Novels), Second Edition

This omnibus collection, second in a series, presents the next four novels of Edgar Rice Burroughs' enthralling Tarzan of the Apes. In *Tarzan the Untamed*, World War I disrupts the peaceful life of Tarzan with his wife Jane on their East African estate. Taking up once more the way of the savage ape-man, Tarzan vows vengeance against the German soldiers that he believes to have murdered his wife. His adventures take him through and across a deadly desert, fighting enemies all the way. In *Tarzan the Terrible*, Tarzan finds himself in the mysterious country of Paul-ul-don, an evolutionary island in the African jungle interior. Here dinosaur descendants and intelligent tailed ape-men live amidst fabulous lost cities. In *Tarzan and the Golden Lion*, our hero rebuilds his life in Africa, only to be

abducted and held prisoner in the lost city of Opar, whose priestess would have him as her mate. Trekking through the legendary Valley of Diamonds, Tarzan finds himself followed by a mysterious man—who is Tarzan's own double! From his stirring descriptions of the jungle itself to his adept conjuring of scenes of action and mystery, Burroughs does not fail to deliver the thrilling narratives that have made Tarzan so very famous. [This second edition enlarges the previously-cramped font, for a more enjoyable reading experience.]

JAMES FENIMORE COOPER
The Complete Leatherstocking Tales (2 volumes)
Cooper's epic historical romances of frontier and Indian life in the early American days created a unique form of American literature. In two volumes five novels are collected, following the order of the stories' internal chronology (rather than historical publication order).
Volume I—*The Deerslayer*; *The Last of the Mohicans*.
Volume II—*The Pathfinder*; *The Pioneers*; *The Prairie*.

HOMER
The Iliad, translated by Alexander Pope

> The thing that best distinguishes this from all other translations of Homer is that it alone equals the original in its ceaseless pour of verbal music. . . . Pope worked miracles in highlighting the play of vowels through his lines. . . . Every word is weighted, with a pressure of mind behind it. This is a poem you can live your way into, over the years, since it yields more at every encounter.
> —"On Reading Pope's Homer," *The New York Times*, 6/1/1997

> Many consider [this translation] the greatest English Iliad, and one of the greatest translations of any work into English. It manages to convey not only the stateliness and grandeur of Homer's lines, but their speed and wit and vividness.
> —Daniel Mendelsohn, "Englishing the Iliad: Grading Four Rival Translations," *The New Yorker* Blog, 11/1/2011

> For Homer to take his place among our classics it must be the case that a rendering could exercise the same spell over the collective ear as English-language poets. You could not memorize Fagles, or Lattimore—or Hobbes, a few phrases apart—while Pope, even at his least Homeric, is memorable. . . . Pope is not superseded.
> —David Ricks, Kings College, London, *Classics Ireland*, vol. 4, 1997

When Alexander Pope's majestic translation of Homer's Iliad appeared between 1715 and 1720, it was acclaimed by Samuel Johnson as "a performance which no

age or nation could hope to equal." Pope himself was only 25 years old. While other translations have since claimed distinction in this or that respect, Pope's translation remains unrivaled in its melodious beauty. This is the Iliad that has formed generations of British and American culture through a beauteous poetics that lends itself to easy recollection. With a clean and crisp text illustrated by the inimitable line drawings of Flaxman, this edition finally gives to audiences a fitting rendering of this monument of English verse which captures uniquely the song of Homer himself.

The Odyssey, translated by Alexander Pope

The tale of Odysseus's return from the war at Troy, seeking Ithaca his home and Penelope his wife. Along the way he encounters the murderous Cyclops, the treacherous Circe, and the nymphs, gods, and goddesses who variously assist and impede his homeward journey. Many are his travails and dramatic his final homecoming wherein he joins battle with Penelope's erstwhile suitors. As with the Iliad, Pope, who had two collaborators on this project, renders Homer into a muscular and euphonious English poetry worthy of reading aloud. This volume is likewise illustrated by Flaxman.

J.-K. HUYSMANS
The Durtal Trilogy

Joris-Karl Huysmans's trilogy of novels charting the religious and life journey of Monsieur Durtal, who once investigated a satanic order in decadent late nineteenth century Paris (*Lá-bas*, "The Depths" or "The Damned"), and now, turning toward God and becoming a Catholic, undertakes a mystical journey of sorts through a monastery (*En Route*; "On the Way"), the cathedral of Chartres (*La Cathédrale*, "The Cathedral"), and finally enters life as a Benedictine oblate (*L'Oblat*, "The Oblate"). This trilogy is intensely autobiographical, following the pattern of Huysmans's own life. Huysmans was an art critic as well as a novelist and thus the exquisitely constructed *Cathedral* has been used by generations of visitors as a guidebook to Chartres Cathedral. This edition offers the flowing translations that brought the original to an English-speaking audience, but with footnoted annotations explaining many of the erudite Huysmans's more obscure references to the artists, saints, and plant-life that populate the unfolding epic of Durtal's journey. Huysmans and his character Durtal are central to French author Michel Houellebecq's best-selling and controversial novel *Submission* (2015).

JOHN HENRY NEWMAN
Callista: A Tale of the Third Century

Callista, a young and beautiful Greek girl, has just arrived with her brother in North African Carthage. Though she is a gifted young woman, she is unhappy with her life. Wooed by a troubled and lovesick young man named Agellius, Callista is drawn into his own struggle between a newfound Christian faith and the traditional pagan beliefs of his mother, a witch. After a terrible plague of locusts, a popular rage breaks out into persecution against the Christians and both Agellius and Callista must face for themselves the question of what indeed is the truth. Written by Newman after his reception into the Catholic Church, this novel of the early Church is surely a bright light in a flourishing nineteenth century genre that produced few classics and many mediocrities. Indeed, Charles Kingsley, whose later attacks prompted Newman's own *Apologia Pro Vita Sua*, had essayed an earlier effort at early Church fiction with the novel *Hypatia*. To Kingley's dismay, Newman's *Callista* had been received as the better work. *Callista* is rich in prose and vivid in its imagining of Christian life in the early Church.